VideoHound's
INDEPENDENT
FILM GUIDE

VideoHound's
INDEPE
FILM
GUIDE

MORE GREAT MOVIE GUIDES FOR SERIOUS FILM FANS

"Its breadth is unsurpassed. ★★★★"—USA TODAY

The Only Guide to Video Originals and Limited Releases

VideoHound's VIDEO PREMIERES

Mike Mayo

VideoHound's Complete Guide to Cult Flicks and Trash Pics

VIDEOHOUND'S® GOLDEN MOVIE RETRIEVER 1998

"The most complete guide of releases on video."
— Boston Herald

The mother of all video guides offers more bite for your buck: reviews and 22,000 movies, with awesome indexing and fun, new categories.

September 1997 • paperback • **ISBN 1-57859-024-8**

VIDEOHOUND'S VIDEO PREMIERES
The Only Guide to Video Originals and Limited Releases

Lots of great movies that never made it to the movie theater are waiting to be discovered at your video store. Find out which are worth watching with reviews of 1,000 action adventures, children's movies, comedies, documentaries and more.

April 1997 • paperback • **ISBN 0-7876-0825-4**

VIDEOHOUND'S COMPLETE GUIDE TO CULT FLICKS AND TRASH PICS

Alternative film fans, your time has come! Find reviews and ratings for 1,000 films by such directors as Ed Wood, Russ Meyer and Roger Corman. Covers Godzilla and Frankenstein, too, and many overlooked gems.

1996 • paperback • **ISBN 0-7876-0616-2**

VISIBLE INK PRESS

Visit us at our website:
www.videohound.com

ALSO AVAILABLE FROM THE HOUND

VideoHound's® Golden Movie Retriever®

VideoHound's Video Premieres:
The Only Guide to Video Originals and Limited Releases

VideoHound's Complete Guide to Cult Flicks and Trash Pics

VideoHound's Vampires on Video

VideoHound's Sci-Fi Experience:
Your Quantum Guide to the Video Universe

VideoHound's Family Video Guide, 2nd Edition

VideoHound's Soundtracks:
Music from the Movies, Broadway, and Television

The VideoHound & All-Movie Guide StarGazer

MusicHound™ Rock: The Essential Album Guide

MusicHound Country: The Essential Album Guide

MusicHound R&B: The Essential Album Guide

MusicHound Blues: The Essential Album Guide

MusicHound Jazz: The Essential Album Guide

NDENT

MONICA SULLIVAN

**Foreword by
Mare Winningham**

Detroit   New York   Toronto   London

VideoHound's®
INDEPENDENT
FILM GUIDE

Copyright   © 1998 by Visible Ink Press

Published by   Visible Ink Press®, a division of Gale Research
835 Penobscot Bldg.
Detroit, MI 48226-4094

Art Director   Mary Krzewinski

Photos   The Kobal Collection

Library of Congress Cataloging-in-Publication Data   Sullivan, Monica, 1950-
Videohound's independent film guide / Monica Sullivan : foreword by Mare Winningham
        p. cm.
    Includes index.
    ISBN 1-57859-018-3 (paper)
    1. Motion pictures—Catalogs. 2. Video recordings—catalogs. 3. Low budget motion pictures—Catalogs.
I. Title
PN1998.S84   1998
016.79143'75—dc21   97-26978
                                                     CIP

ISBN 1-57859-018-3   Printed in the United States of America
All rights reserved

10 9 8 7 6 5 4 3 2 1

A Cunning Canine Production™

CONTENTS

**By Mare
Winningham**

I remember where I was and what I was doing when I heard they wanted me for a part in the minuscule-budgeted 1988 independent feature film *Miracle Mile.* This isn't always the case. Usually I feel circumspective, weighing in my mind the factors of the production (who's responsible for the dang thing), the location (where do I have to move my family), the money (how much will they give me), and the talent (hmmmm), before I can find my way to excitement. But every so often I get the news, hang up the phone, shriek, and begin my happiness dance, the hope and euphoria spreading in my chest.

It happened with *Miracle Mile.* Indie heartthrob Anthony Edwards, who was so good in *Gotcha* and *Heart Like a Wheel,* was already cast in the role of Harry, Everyman on the day the *big one* comes to downtown L.A. I was to play his new-found love, Julie, spending the majority of the movie in a shopping cart, drugged. The script had been profiled in a 1983 article by Stephen Rebello in *American Film* magazine, about the ten best unproduced screenplays, calling it "a rude and flashy piece of comic business by Steve DeJarnatt. The premise: An itinerant trombone player mistakenly intercepts a predawn pay phone call in the L.A. Miracle Mile district. The news isn't good: in precisely 70 minutes, Soviet warheads will nuke the United States into Kingdom Come." Rebello's article followed the movie's beleaguered path from being commissioned by Warner Bros., to writer/director DeJarnatt's refusal to change the fatalistic ending to an it's-only-a-dream finale, to his eventual reclamation and ownership with the hopes of shooting it himself.

Securing a budget of less than $3 million, DeJarnatt had brought his baby near to its start date when I interviewed with him in his office, his cartoons-in-checkered-boxes story board behind him, hearing his plans for our film. Our film. That's how it was to be. I was going to be included in the process of creating this visually stunning love-at-the-end-of-the-world-on-Wilshire-Boulevard movie. The independent film world was a collaborative feat of promise, amid impossible monetary and time constraints that would somehow benefit the movie, in the same way sewing your own clothes can achieve a creation no department store can supply. It inspired the underdog in me.

When I was invited to present an award at the Independent Feature Project West's Independent Spirit Awards, held in a tiny restaurant on La Cienega Blvd. in Los Angeles in 1987, I was by then a certified TV-movie queen. I had starred in over 25 television movies, and my hopes for enjoying the more complex roles offered to my acting peers in independent features were dwindling. The tables at the restaurant held the shining talent of that year's successes: David Lynch and his stellar cast of *Blue Velvet,* Oliver Stone and his winning film *Platoon,* and the emcee was Buck Henry, who introduced one performer/presenter as being the actor from *Deliverance* who was sodomized by a hillbilly. The whole event seemed rebellious and happily low-brow and anti-establishment. Compared to the Academy Awards, which would be televised shortly thereafter, this was the younger, wilder, out-of-control baby brother you always wanted at a party. I couldn't figure out why I'd been invited, but I felt lucky, and hoped it meant I had some indie madness in my future.

In 1990, when Steve and I were nominated for *Miracle Mile,* the venue had changed to the retro Roosevelt Hotel. Martin Scorsese and Jodie Foster were honored, and that same rebel appeal seemed even more provocative, with nominees *sex, lies and videotape* and *Drugstore Cowboy.* I lost, and felt like I won. Everyone in the room had participated in a movie that had been conceived in the peril of penny pinching, and celebrated in the grinning pride of the miraculous. It feels so good to participate in a project budgeted at $3 million, when most studio films refer to their $15 million dollar projects as "the little guys," and the most expensive film ever made cost $200 million, with number two behind it at $145 million. My dad always said frugality can make you happy.

I wouldn't attend another Independent Film Awards ceremony until 1996, when my personal indie ship came in with the release of *Georgia,* by far the best role I had ever been offered in film. Made for around $6 million, written by my friend Barbara Turner (who scripted three TV movies I had been in), directed by the great Ulu Grosbard (filmmaker of indie grandpa *Straight Time*), and starring Jennifer Jason Leigh, an indie-movie crown jewel of an actress (*Miami Blues, Last Exit to Brooklyn*), *Georgia* lifted my acting spirits in every way imaginable. By now the Spirit Award ceremonies were situated in Santa Monica, inside a huge tent on the beach, and televised on cable.

Sam Jackson was master of ceremonies, and he managed to instill the event with irreverence and intelligent celebration. The list of nominees completely overlapped with that year's Academy Award nominations: *Dead Man Walking, Leaving Las Vegas.* I was sad to see the TV cameras, but it figured. Independent films had taken center stage in the world movie market, and 1997, the year of *The English Patient, Sling Blade,* and *Shine,* was around the corner. I lost the Academy Award for Best Supporting Actress to Mira Sorvino for *Mighty Aphrodite,* but I won the Independent Spirit Award. These days, I'm shocked when I have an audition for a studio film, and happily trying to figure out how to support my household of seven on a combination of indie film SAG minimum salary with a cable TV supplement.

I met Monica Sullivan, who wrote the reviews in this guide, when I was publicizing *Wyatt Earp,* a big-budget studio flop that I hope did okay overseas because the director was a sweetie. Monica and I did our radio interview, said goodbye, and were thrown together once again for the publicity of *Georgia.* I believe, at the time, *Georgia* was just beginning its descent into video shelf life, and Monica said she thought it was the best movie of 1996. Her praise for every facet of the film made me leave the interview and head to the phone to call Barbara. Since then, Monica has attended every loud, smoky, dirty bar gig that my band and I have played in the San Francisco area. I sing when I'm not acting, and she writes books when she's not interviewing. I hope you appreciate her reviews (there's an original, raucous, thoughtful mind at work) as much as we both seem to treasure the possibilities of the independent film world.

I t's the shank of the evening and there's more than enough time to watch at least one movie (or maybe two). Do we leaf through the newspaper advertisements or stare at the video listings looking for an "indie"? Of course not. We search for a *good* (or at least entertaining) film. A great cast, an intriguing director and, yes, even hype may help to relieve the fear of the unknown that accompanies every new cinematic experience. What we *don't* do is flock to a movie because it was produced by *whomever.*

Before the collapse of the studio system, pictures produced by MGM, Warner Bros., Fox, RKO, Columbia, Paramount, and Universal had distinctive identities and in-house galaxies of stars. Today, stars go where the deals are and every film has its own look rather than a studio imprint. For the purposes of *VideoHound's Independent Film Guide,* an indie is defined as a film financed and developed outside the studio system. When completed, the indie may wind up with major distribution; that's how fairy tales can come true for directors like Robert Rodriguez, who made 1993's *El Mariachi* on a $7000 budget. Many indie filmmakers spend years arranging financing for a film to be shot in a matter of weeks. They don't necessarily go the independent route because they're waiting for Hollywood to call. The much-revered John Sayles has been making indie gems since 1982 with no inclination to enter an arena in which his carefully crafted projects spin off into dolls, toys, games, and action figures. (Even within that arena, filmmakers seem eager to encourage the perception that a blockbuster movie like 1996's *Independence Day* was a bargain to produce!) But in the world of indies, we won't be discussing film productions that fly every journalist west of the Rockies for a weekend in the desert among the stars (and UFOs). We'll be taking a closer look at that flick charged on a credit card, that great story where the budget will only allow for a technical crew consisting of one sister and one brother-in-law, that life-long dream funded by a lifetime of savings and a credit card or two. Welcome to *VideoHound's Independent Film Guide,* where imagination and tenacity make up for 1,001 power lunches an indie producer can't afford to buy.

The 800 entries that follow represent a fraction of the many independent films that exist primarily because their creators refused to give up on them. They rustled up funds as best they could and made them where they could afford to make them: in Brazil or Kansas or New Jersey. At one point in motion picture history, when the Hollywood studios were responsible for most of what we saw and heard onscreen, independent filmmaking was seen as a desperate career move; if the movie was worthwhile, why wasn't MGM or Warner Bros. or Fox or RKO or Columbia or Paramount or Universal making it? As the independent film has come into its own, we understand why the big studios *couldn't* have made a movie like John Cassavetes' *Shadows* (1960), or Alexander Singer's *A Cold Wind in August* (1961), or Allen and Albert Hughes' *Menace II Society* (1993), and we're grateful to their creators for showing us a grittier, more eloquently real way of looking at life.

Tom DiCillo's *Box of Moonlight,* for example, is a beautifully observed story of how a tightly coiled electrical engineer learns how to appreciate life after a chance meeting with a free spirit known only as The Kid. It's the sort of movie that would have been trampled by too many conflicting approaches at too many studio story conferences. You can almost envision the artistic compromises that would have been made with the script, the cast, even the title. Maybe those compromises would have made the project more "commercial," but 1997's *Box of Moonlight,* DiCillo's superb follow-up to 1995's *Living in Oblivion,* is an enchanting, fully realized film on its own unique terms, and a quintessential indie.

This book was written by yours truly, a movie buff since the age of three when I could easily have spent a whole day watching *Gentlemen Prefer Blondes* with Marilyn Monroe (soon to enter independent production herself with *The Prince and the Showgirl, Some Like It Hot,* and *The Misfits*). Between the ages of 12 and 28, my by-line appeared in the Woodland-Davis Daily *Democrat,* where I wrote about city council meetings and systems analysis lectures (by assignment) and movies and plays (very much by choice, even traveling a grand total of 25,000 miles to see Dame Diana Rigg in four different productions). I took a break to write (and produce) teleplays (*The Subject Doesn't Really Interest Me*—a Northern California Emmy nominee, *What Are You Doing Tonight?*), novels (*The Cat Journals, Slipping through the Jelly Line*), and a children's book (*Joey Bear and Yvette, Private Detectives*), and to co-produce a documentary (*Hollywood Blacklist*). And I never lost my obsession with movies. In 1987, I began delivering film commentary on the radio; I launched *Movie Magazine International* in 1991 and by 1993, both *Movie Magazine* and *Shoestring Radio Theatre* (a radio drama program I started in 1988 and a Golden Reel nominee) were made available to public radio stations across the country via the Public Radio Satellite System.

My obsession dates back, I believe, to the fact that the family television set resided in the parental bedroom. I can't count how many times I missed the last five minutes of a movie when one parent or another turned off the set. AAARGH!!! I played hooky from some family thing at Woodland's State Theatre and was retrieved right in the middle of the best part of *Becket*!!! And, worst of all, when my siblings were fighting over my precious collection of 22 movie magazines in the back seat of the family station wagon, one of the authority figures in the front seat tossed the entire batch in a dumpster and drove away without a backwards glance. (See what happens when you try to control a fledgling movie buff's fanaticism as a child? She grows up to rent six videos a day!)

Flash forward to the early 1980s, when I watched some real obscurities in a screening facility affectionately known as The Dust Bowl. Once I thought I saw a cockroach scamper across a nearby lap, but was corrected with the deathless line that only beetles, slugs, and spiders were indigenous to The Dust Bowl. But I saw *Tomorrow the World* and *So Long at the Fair* there, and many other vintage indies that I've never seen anywhere else. Even though the general perception is that independent filmmaking is a relatively recent phenomenon, free spirits have been making their own movies since 1888 (See *The Missing Reel* by Christopher Rawlence). *VideoHound's Independent Film Guide* reflects that tradition by taking a look at indies made during both the silent and sound eras, including many films that I hope will nudge distributors into expanding their current video lists. I'll also be discussing international indies from something like three dozen countries. (But not, alas, ANY of the films of the late Indian filmmaker Guru Dutt, because, at press time, I was unable to locate even ONE example of his fine work on video. Maybe next time!) Because editorial deadlines and space limitations do exist in the real world, I submit this guide as a point of departure for independent explorers rather than as a comprehensive catalogue; it could easily have been two or three times as long and hopefully, in a future edition, it will be.

About my ratings: they are, naturally, subjective, and I don't expect anyone to agree with all or even most of them. You don't "read" a film by comparing your perceptions to those of some "expert" you don't even know. Many of the films in this book have production values comparable to any studio flick (indie filmmakers really know how to stretch a budget!). Others look cheap beyond belief. I've tried to evaluate each film on its own unique terms. The "4 bones" category, which is about four times longer than the "WOOF!s" list, reflects the fact that I wanted to share as many of my favorite indies as possible. (And even the "WOOF!s" can be great fun, if you're in the mood for them.) The most difficult films to evaluate are the ones where the filmmakers' hearts were clearly in the right place, but they failed to communicate those visions for one reason or another (more often than not, it *isn't* the budget that gets in the way). Each entry includes as much accurate information on the film as could be rustled up, including as many supporting players as I could identify (including those who appear without billing). The comments of the filmmakers saluted in the sidebars are mostly culled from interviews that aired on *Movie Magazine* or from press conferences that I covered during my years as a reporter.

Someone once asked me how could I spend so much of my life doing something that seemed so, well, *passive.* But being a movie buff isn't in the least bit passive to me. A striking fictional film opens up our world in so many pervasive ways, and the more rough edges that are left in the film, the more active our participation in the world becomes. (Was there really a Picnic at Hanging Rock? Would there have been a First, Second, Third, and Fourth Man if the British class structure had been less rigid in the 1930s? How could the tragedy of Matewan have occurred in 20th century America?) If anyone DID ask these questions when the studio system was at its zenith, he (or she) didn't generate enough interest for a studio to consider releasing the answer as a major Hollywood movie, coming-soon-to-a-neighborhood-theatre-near-you. Independent filmmakers, being accountable only to the demands of modest budgets, and their consciences, can and do ask tough questions, quirky questions, questions that may not seem to have any answers at all if you look at the world in strictly blockbuster terms. It is to these renegade filmmakers and their admirers that *VideoHound's Independent Film Guide* is dedicated.

Monica Sullivan
Founding Producer,
Movie Magazine International
http://www.shoestring.org
Email: mmi@shoestring.org

Acknowledgments

Thanks to:

Steve Rubenstein, Jonesy Sullenstein, and Kelly Sullenstein, who worked every bit as hard on this book as I did. Well, maybe not Jonesy and Kelly, but they DID shred reviews and delete files as fast as I could write them.

Michael Ukich, a fine writer and a great friend.

Raymond Formanek, for being Raymond Formanek.

Tom Backos, for picking me up at a bijou and dragging me into radio.

Alvah Bessie, who showed me what true grace means in a harsh world.

Marty and Estela Goldsmith, wonderful artists, friends, and hosts.

Kate Ingram, for being alternative radio's BEST program director.

Leo C. Lee, for believing in *Shoestring Radio Theatre, Movie Magazine,* and me.

Lynn Chadwick and the terrific staff at Western Public Radio.

Randy Parker, for creating our wonderful website (www.shoestring.org), and for being such an impeccable friend and colleague.

Carol Schwartz, for being such an Editor Extraordinaire; Lauri Taylor, for her boundless energy and great voice; and Jeff Hermann, Beth Fhaner, Julia Furtaw, and all the other dynamos at Visible Ink Press.

Mary Krzewinski, artiste, and Marco DiVita, master typesetter.

Andrea Chase, for introducing me to Richard III and Ruan Ling-Yu.

Adam Ling, for being so calm and patient every week.

Dick Prouty, for his enthusiasm and sensayuma.

PLUS: Rob Avila, Timothy Buckwalter, Frank Buske, Larry Carlin, Anita Monga/Castro Theatre, Mark Chase, Heather Clisby, Carol Compton, Chuck & Zoya Csavossy, Martha Daetwyler, Paul Daugherty, Zoe Elton, Cathy & Doug Farmer, Karl Fleischman, Michael Fox, Geoffrey Gallegos, Alanna, Emma, Tess & John Greenham, Mim Herzenstein, Russ Hickman, Carrie Hourihan, Curtis & Heidi Huber, Claude Jarman, Lisa & Bill Collins/Keyhole Mystery Theatre, Karen Larsen, Alex Lau, Tricia Linnane, Nancy Madden, Kara Maurette, Rebeeca Peters/Le Video, Caroline Libresco, Julie Long, Father Harry Mack, Mad Professor Mike Marano, Peggy Martinez, George McRae, Gary Meyer, Auzzie & Laela Mirhashemi, Jennifer Leick/MPI Home Video, Mare Mitchell, Frank Munnich, Mike Neumann, NPR Distribution, John & Annie Osborn, Richard E. Osgood, Damien Pickering, John Quinn, Henry Trentman/Recorded Books, Inc., Bill Banning & Elliott Lavine/Roxie Cinema, Chris Salak, John Sayles, Sylvie Schmid, Sue Braviak/Science Fiction Continuum, Jim Shepard, Emma Sparks, Susan Stanton, Don Stone, Dr. Moira Sullivan, Kathryn Evans/Turner Classic Movies, Craig Valenza, Marisa Vela, Blue Velvet, Clinton Vidal, Miss X, Mary Weems, B.K. Wells, Mare Winningham and her wonderful band, George C. Wolfe and all our wonderful listeners on KUSF, San Francisco, and the Public Radio Satellite System.

Some of the movies in this book are not available on video, and some of them that are may be difficult to find using conventional devices such as the neighborhood video rental chain. Many independent and mail-order video outlets specialize in rare or hard-to-find movies. We have included a small list of such outlets to assist you in your search.

Thomas Video
122 S. Main St.
Clawson, MI 48017
248-280-2833
fax: 248-280-4463

Video Vision
Attn: Chris Hendlin
4603 Bloomington Ave.
Minneapolis, MN 55407
612-728-0000

Video Oyster
145 W. 12th St.
New York, NY 10011
fax: 212-989-3533

Facets Video
1517 W. Fullerton Ave.
Chicago, IL 60614
800-331-6197

A Million and One World-Wide Videos
PO Box 349
Orchard Hill, GA 30266
770-227-7309
800-849-7309
fax: 770-227-0873
fax: 800-849-0873

Movies Unlimted
3015 Darnell Rd.
Philadelphia, PA 19154
800-4-MOVIES

Home Film Festival
PO Box 2032
Scranton, PA 18501
800-258-3456

Alphabetization

Titles are arranged on a word-by-word basis, including articles and prepositions. Leading articles (A, An, The) are ignored in English-language titles; the equivalent foreign articles are not ignored (because so many people—not you, of course—don't recognize them as articles); thus, *The Brothers McMullen* appears in the Bs, but *La Femme Nikita* appears in the Ls. Acronyms appear alphabetically as if regular words; for example, *D.O.A.* is alphabetized as "DOA." Common abbreviations in titles file as if they were spelled out, so *The Island of Dr. Moreau* will be alphabetized as "Island of Doctor Moreau" and *Mr. North* as "Mister North." Movie titles with numbers, such as *8½*, are alphabetized as if the number was spelled out—so this title would appear in the Es as if it were "Eight and a Half."

Sample Review

Each review contains up to 17 tidbits of information, as enumerated below. Please realize that we faked a bit of info in this review for demonstration purposes.

---

① Clerks

② *Clerks* is a promising first film by Kevin Smith about a clerk in a convenience store and a clerk in a video store. It's everything a first film should be: funny, fresh, and original. It was shot in black and white on a budget of $27,000, and its gritty, cinema-verite quality made it seem almost like a slice-of-life documentary rather than the scripted fiction film it really was. Reportedly, preview audiences were so caught up in the lives of the two central characters that they responded negatively when one of them was shown being killed on duty. So the ending was re-shot, a wise choice, because to have turned an 88-minute comedy into an 89-minute tragedy at the last minute wouldn't have worked without some premonitory sequences—which wouldn't have worked, either, because of the scrappy, upbeat tone overall. When Smith made *Mallrats* a year later, the same critics who lionized *Clerks* beyond recognition jumped down hard on the filmmaker's second effort. Smith's *Chasing Amy,* his third picture, is drawing rave reviews. **③** *AKA:* Randal and Dante. 🦴🦴🦴 **④**

⑤ 1994 **⑥** (R) **⑦** 89m/ **⑧** B **⑨** *US* **⑩** Brian O'Halloran, Jeff Anderson, Marilyn Ghigliotti, Lisa Spoonhauer, Jason Mewes; *Cameos:* Kevin Smith; **⑪** *D:* Kevin Smith; **⑫** *W:* Kevin Smith; **⑬** *C:* David Klein; **⑭** *M:* Scott Angley. **⑮** Sundance Film Festival '94: Filmmakers Trophy; Nominations: Independent Spirit Awards '95: Best First Feature, Debut Performance (Anderson), First Screenplay. **⑯** VHS, LV, Closed Caption **⑰** *MAX*

---

1. Title (see also the Alternate Title below, and the "Alternate Titles Index")
2. Description/review
3. Alternate title (we faked it here)
4. One- to four-bone rating (or WOOF!), four bones being the ultimate praise
5. Year released
6. MPAA rating
7. Length in minutes
8. Black and white (B) or Color (C)
9. Country of origin (if other than the U.S.)
10. Cast, including cameos and voiceovers (V)
11. Director(s)
12. Writer(s)
13. Cinematographer(s)
14. Music composer(s)/lyricist(s)
15. Awards, including nominations
16. Format(s), including VHS and Laservideo/disk (LV)
17. Distributor code(s), if available on video (see also "Distributor List" and "Distributor Guide"

A-Ge-Man: Tales of a Golden Geisha

Admirers of Juzo Itami (*The Funeral, Tampopo, A Taxing Woman, A Taxing Woman's Return*) will want to see his 1991 film, *A-Ge-Man: Tales of a Golden Geisha,* featuring a nicely shaded performance by its star Nobuko Miyamoto as Nayoko the geisha. Watching the sympathetic Nayoko do everything in the world for some of the biggest jerks in Japan can be a bit taxing after 108 minutes. At one point, she raises a billion yen for her true love, who promptly starts chasing after a younger women and Nayoko doesn't even sock him! Itami paces the film like a music video and some of the sequences with Toshiyuki Honda's romantic jazz score look like they're headed straight for the Asian video market as is. Although *A-Ge-Man*'s satire is far from subtle, it was still an entertaining and at times quite funny selection at 1991's Mill Valley Film Festival. 🦴🦴🦴

1991 108m/C *JP* Nobuko Miyamoto, Masahiko Tsugawa, Shogo Shimada, Hideji Otaki, Mitsuko; *D:* Juzo Itami; *W:* Juzo Itami; *C:* Zenko Yamazaki; *M:* Toshiyuki Honda. *NYR*

Abandon Ship

I wanted to include *Nightmare Alley* in this book, but there's no way it qualifies as an indie. How 20th Century Fox allowed Tyrone Power to sacrifice his spectacular good looks to play a carnival geek and how Edmund Goulding managed to make a movie that uncompromising under the studio system is one of the great mysteries of Hollywood, circa 1947. So I'm including this Brit flick produced independently by Power a decade later, some twenty months before his sudden death in Madrid after a make-believe sword fight with George Sanders. Power, who came from a long line of actors, desperately wanted to be taken seriously, but legions of female audience members preferred to see him as a sexy swashbuckler. And Power WAS sexy AND hypnotic, no question about it. For the role of Alec Holmes, Power had to look haggard and driven, even as a sultry lifeboat passenger, Edith Middleton (Moira Lister), leered at him for the entire length of the film. As an officer on a mined ocean liner, Holmes is acting captain of a lifeboat designed to hold 14, but crammed with 17 survivors, with an additional 11 people tied to the boat. Since many have sustained critical injuries, dying crew member Frank Kelly (Lloyd Nolan) tells Holmes to abandon those who are too weak to work or all will die. Holmes resists at first, but gradually comes to realize that Kelly is right and starts ordering gravely wounded men and women into the sea. With every trace of Hollywood glamour stripped from his face, Power played Holmes as if his life depended on it—and, in a way, it did, since his critical reputation was so important to him at that point. The supporting cast is outstanding, especially Nolan, Lister, and Mai Zetterling. Director Richard Sale's tight screenplay is supposed to be based on a true story, but heck if I know which one, and I've looked. (Unless maybe, in the 45th anniversary year of the Titanic, the film was trying to make a point about all those half-filled lifeboats?) **AKA:** Seven Waves Away. 🦴🦴🦴🦴

1957 97m/B *GB* Tyrone Power, Mai Zetterling, Lloyd Nolan, Stephen Boyd, Moira Lister, James Hayter, Marie Lohr, Gordon Jackson, Finlay Currie, John Stratton, Victor Maddern, Eddie Byrne, Noel Willman, Ralph Michael, David Langton, Ferdinand "Ferdy" Mayne, Austin Trevor, Moultrie Kelsall, Jill Melford; **D:** Richard Sale; **W:** Richard Sale; **C:** Wilkie Cooper; **M:** Arthur Bliss. **VHS** *COL*

Abel

Abel is a weird little Dutch film written and directed by its star Alex Van Warmerdam, who plays a 31-year-old child still living at home with his parents. The film makes an effort to satirize male vanity and male voyeurism, but when it looks at women, it is content simply to ridicule them. Successful satire requires some level of understanding, an element which is missing in this nonetheless amusing 1987 entry in the Mill Valley Film Festival. 🦴🦴🦴

1987 100m/C *NL* Alex Van Warmerdam, Henri Garcin, Olga Zuiderhoek, Annet Malherbe; **D:** Alex Van Warmerdam; **W:** Alex Van Warmerdam. *NYR*

Absolute Beginners

Julien Temple's underrated *Absolute Beginners* provides an unsettling portrait of London circa 1958. The film has been criticized for its lack of character development and for its last-minute attack on racism, and although these flaws are real, there is much worth seeing and hearing in this flashy study of the emergence of the British teen. Magnetic performances by David Bowie and Sade, amusing bits by Ray Davies and Mandy Rice-Davies, and interesting work by Patsy Kensit and Anita Morris contribute to the striking atmosphere. The impressive photography and great jazz don't hurt, either. We'd like to see this one along with the 1960 Val Guest film *Expresso Bongo,* starring Laurence Harvey and Sir Cliff Richard, which examines the same world from a slightly different perspective. 🦴🦴🦴

1986 (PG) 107m/C *GB* David Bowie, Ray Davies, Mandy Rice-Davies, James Fox, Eddie O'Connell, Patsy Kensit, Anita Morris, Sade Adu, Sandie Shaw; **D:** Julien Temple; **W:** Richard Burridge, Don MacPherson. **VHS, Beta, LV** *NO*

Acting on Impulse

Reviews for *Acting on Impulse* were decidedly mixed, but it's a hoot! Linda Fiorentino IS angry scream queen Susan Gittes, who's had it with her Hollywood "career" and walks off the movie set. She checks into a hotel (as "Dee Dee Slaughter") where a convention for pharmaceutical sales representatives is being held (zzzzzz...), leaving behind her boyfriend (Adam Ant), her P.O.'d director (Paul Bartel), and her murdered producer (Patrick Bachau), whose body is discovered in her trailer. That makes her a suspect, doesn't it? Detective Stubbs (Isaac Hayes) investigates! "Dee Dee" meets Paul Stevens and Cathy Thomas (C. Thomas Howell and Nancy Allen) at the convention, comes on to Paul, gets stalked by a fan, and then there's that suspicion of being a murderer that clings to her like underwear. And, speaking of underwear, there's this side-splitting sight gag about the physical illusion we have of scream queens that Susan/Dee Dee tears away with a single defiant gesture. Fiorentino has the ability to make a truly unpleasant character funny, which makes us like her and want to root for her in spite of ourselves. No comment on Howell, who's out of his league here, but Allen has a good time with her change-of-pace role. And look at the rest of that cast! Cult film freaks will have a feast! Based on a story by Sol Weingarten. 🦴🦴🦴

1993 (R) 94m/C Linda Fiorentino, C. Thomas Howell, Nancy Allen, Adam Ant, Judith Hoag, Patrick Bachau, Isaac Hayes, Paul Bartel, Donny Most, Miles O'Keeffe, Dick Sargent, Charles Lane, Mary Woronov, Zelda Rubinstein, Nicholas Sadler, Peter Lupus, Kim McGuire, Cassandra Peterson, Brinke Stevens, Michael Talbot, Robert Alan Golub, Cliff Dorfman, Craig Shoemaker, Scott Thompson Stevens; **D:** Sam Irvin; **W:** Mark Pittman, Alan Moskowitz; **C:** Dean Lent; **M:** Daniel Licht. **VHS** *ACA*

Actors and Sin

Actors and Sin is HALF of a very good movie, produced independently by Ben Hecht (1893-1964), who adapted two of his short stories for the silver screen. Hecht shared directing chores with cameraman Lee Garmes (1898-1978) and cast Edward G. Robinson (temporarily on the Hollywood grey list) and blacklisted Marsha Hunt in "Actor's Blood." It may have been a supportive professional gesture, but no one remembers the first segment of *Actors and Sin* today. Robinson played Maurice, the distraught father of unhappy Marcia, who killed herself because she failed to make good as an actress. In Hecht's contrived script, Maurice tries to make it seem as if Marcia was murdered so she will achieve the fame

she never received in her lifetime. Fast forward through this segment, unless you just want to watch these stars work together. "Woman of Sin" is also contrived, but it's a funny, clever satire. Eddie Albert is Orlando Higgens, a Hollywood agent who receives a hot new (sexy) script from hot new screenwriter Daisy Marcher. Who IS Miss Marcher? Only Jenny Hecht, the nine-year-old daughter of Ben, who's extremely well directed by her father here. Ben Hecht must have nursed a grudge against obnoxious, precocious Hollywood moppets for 25 years! "Woman of Sin" has bite and snap and a beautifully sustained quality of long-simmering resentment. Hecht's wise to every single trick of devil child Daisy, and daughter Jenny acquits herself admirably in the role. The supporting cast adds to the fun; for a change, we get to SEE, as well as hear, Alan Reed (Fred Flintstone)! 🦴🦴🦴

1952 82m/B Edward G. Robinson, Eddie Albert, Marsha Hunt, Alan Reed, Dan O'Herlihy, Tracey Roberts, Rudolph Anders, Paul Guilfoyle, Alice Key, Douglas Evans, Rick Roman, Jenny Hecht, Jody Gilbert, John Crawford; **D:** Lee Garmes, Ben Hecht; **W:** Ben Hecht; **C:** Lee Garmes; **M:** George Antheil. **VHS, LV** *COL*

The Addiction

Abel Ferrara's *The Addiction* is to *Ms. 45* what Francis Coppola's *The Cotton Club* was to *The Godfather*: a structural re-tread only worshippers at directors' shrines could love. Lili Taylor is excellent as always in the protagonist role, and it's fun to see perennial good girl Annabella Sciorra as a vampire, but Christopher Walken wraps it up as usual in one scene-stealing sequence that makes you wish the rest of the movie had been that good and that funny instead of the pretentious mess it is. It's shot in jokey black and white to minimize the gore. 🦴🦴

1995 (R) 82m/B Lili Taylor, Christopher Walken, Annabella Sciorra, Edie Falco, Paul Calderone, Fredro Star, Kathryn Erbe, Michael Imperioli; **D:** Abel Ferrara; **W:** Nicholas St. John; **M:** Joe Delia. Nomina-

"Is it true that when you were born the doctor turned around and slapped your mother?"
—Mitzi (Hugo Weaving) to Felicia (Guy Pearce) in *The Adventures of Priscilla, Queen of the Desert.*

Felicia, Bernadette, and Mitzi (Guy Pearce, Terence Stamp, Hugo Weaving) in *The Adventures of Priscilla, Queen of the Desert.*

tions: Independent Spirit Awards '96: Best Actress (Taylor), Best Film. **VHS** *PGV*

Adoption

Adoption focuses on a pair of women, one 42, one 17, both of whom are entrapped and want to free themselves. In their struggle to make new beginnings, they lend each other support and friendship, and the script makes it clear that this is not the sort of encouragement men are capable of giving. Sensitively directed and photographed, *Adoption* emerges as a story of strong hope, with realistic performances giving it tenderness and integrity. ***AKA:*** Orkobefogadas. ♫♫♫

1975 89m/B *HU* Kati Berek, Laszlo Szabo, Gyongyver Vigh, Dr. Arpad Perlaky; *D:* Marta Meszaros; *W:* Marta Meszaros, Gyula Hernadi; *C:* Lajos Koltai; *M:* Gyorgy Kovacs. Berlin International Film Festival '75: Golden Berlin Bear. **VHS, Beta** *KIV*

The Adventures of Priscilla, Queen of the Desert

When 1992's *Strictly Ballroom* became an international hit, exhibitors were eager for MORE offbeat Australian movies that would do as well. *The Adventures of Priscilla, Queen of the Desert* fit the bill. Who would ever imagine Terence Stamp, the Oscar-nominated, impossibly gorgeous *Billy Budd* in Sir Peter Ustinov's superb 1962 film of the same name, would EVER play a drag queen named Bernadette? And yet, Stamp, who initially resisted the idea, discovered that Bernadette was a role he was destined to play. The camera is not overly kind to Stamp at 55, yet he invests the role of Bernadette with dignity, elegance, intrigue, and mystery, all the qualities of a great diva. Hugo Weaving and Guy Pearce, too, are terrific as fellow divas Mitzi AKA Tick and Felicia AKA Adam. The three of them hit the road in the title character, an outdated bus. Along the way, Bernadette discovers romance, Tick experiences fatherhood, and Adam learns how not to behave with a gang of red-necked rowdies. The soundtrack is a keeper, with songs galore by Alicia Bridges, Gloria Gaynor, Peaches and Herb, The Village People, Charlene, R. B. Greaves, Lena Horne, Paper Lace, Patti Page, CeCe Peniston, Trudy Richards, White Plains, Vanessa Williams, and Abba. Cast Note: Bill Hunter, who plays a charmer named Bob, and Terence Stamp had previously worked together in the 1985 Stephen Frears film, *The Hit.* 🦴🦴🦴🦴

1994 (R) 102m/C *AU* Terence Stamp, Hugo Weaving, Guy Pearce, Bill Hunter, Sarah Chadwick, Mark Holmes, Julia Cortez; *D:* Stephan Elliott; *W:* Stephan Elliott; *C:* Brian J. Breheny; *M:* Guy Gross. Academy Awards '94: Best Costume Design; Australian Film Institute '94: Best Costume Design; Nominations: Australian Film Institute '94: Best Actor (Stamp), Best Actor (Weaving), Best Cinematography, Best Director (Elliott), Best Film, Best Screenplay; Golden Globe Awards '95: Best Actor—Musical/Comedy (Stamp), Best Film—Musical/Comedy. **VHS, LV** *PGV*

Aelita: Queen of Mars

Okay, so this is no Fritz Lang masterpiece, but for science-fiction buffs, it's a genuinely intriguing curiosity. Made the year that Lenin died and Stalin took over, it looks like the production team had fun with this one, especially the three art directors and the costume designer. Even then, was anyone taking the script all that seriously? For instance, who gets to go to Mars? One inventor (of course), one soldier (why?), and one police informer (that would be Igor Illinski and he is SUCH a ham!). So they get to Mars and guess what they find there? (See alternative title.) That's right, boys, it's

Yet Another Revolution, dang it! (Gee, we thought we applied for this job to get away from all that.) Queen Aelita is something to see, alright. Some stills of the Martian sets and fashions must have slipped over to the U.S. of A. at some point, because our action-packed serials clearly received inspiration from somewhere for those pace-setting styles (I wonder if Ed Bernds and Zsa Zsa Gabor got a good look at Aelita before they made *Queen of Outer Space*). *Aelita* isn't camp yet, not really, but naive perhaps, and a little giddy. Based on Alexei Tolstoy's play. *AKA:* Aelita: The Revolt of the Robots. 🦴🦴🦴

1924 113m/B *RU* Yulia Solntseva, Nikolai Batalov, Igor Illinski, Nikolai Tseretelli, Vera Orlova, Pavel Poi, Konstantin Eggert, Yuri Zavadski, Valentina Kuindzi, N. Tretyakova; *D:* Yakov Protazanov; *W:* Fedor Ozep, Aleksey Fajko; *C:* Yuri Zhelyabuzhsky, Emil Schoenemann. **VHS, LV** *KIV, FCT, SNC*

The African Queen

John Huston cooperatively made films under the studio system between the ages of 35 and 45: five for Warner Bros., one for Columbia, and two for MGM. After chafing at the bit for a full decade, he wanted to make movies his way and without interference. (Huston's *The Red Badge of Courage* ended the 27-year reign of MGM's Louis B. Mayer, who lost a production dispute with Dore Schary in 1951.) Huston couldn't get much further away from Hollywood than the Belgian Congo, where he traveled with stars Humphrey Bogart, Katharine Hepburn, and with Mrs. Bogart, Lauren Bacall. *The African Queen,* Huston's first film in Technicolor, set the standard for the hard-drinking, tough-living man's man who winds up opening his heart to an uptight missionary spinster. Their mutual goals and their gradually evolving love for each other transforms them both. Robert Morley, Peter Bull, Theodore Bikel, and Walter Gotell also appear in small but key roles in this British-financed independent feature, the

"Well, I ain't sorry no more, you crazy, psalm-singing, skinny old maid."
—Charlie Allnut (Humphrey Bogart) to Rose Sayer (Katharine Hepburn) in *The African Queen.*

The Hound Salutes:
TERENCE STAMP
The Adventures of Priscilla,
Queen of the Desert

Bernadette [his character] is a transsexual. Hugo Weaving and Guy Pearce play drag queens, so they're guys who dress up, but Bernadette is one of those creatures who knew from very early on in life, since she was three or four years old, that she was a woman in a man's body. It was a mistake that she's spent her life trying to rectify. In the beginning of the movie, Bernadette's lover has died and she's very depressed, and Tick, this choreographer friend of hers says, 'Come with me. I'm doing this gig. Let's go to Alice Springs. See the outback. It'll take you out of yourself.' So Bernadette goes and unbeknownst to her, he's invited this other friend along, this glamorous but incredibly tedious young drag queen called Adam. It's a musical comedy, and there are these wonderful show numbers that they do, and it's about the adventures that these urban creatures have in this unknown terrain. They've never been outside the city and they're suddenly faced with the beauties and the ravages of life in the outback. I thought that Bernadette looked like Lauren Bacall myself. There is a lot of sadness in her life. To be a transsexual facing that part of your life where a straight woman would be appreciating her grandchildren isn't really available to Bernadette. She's lonely and she's losing her looks, so there is an integral sadness about her, but like many minorities, she's tough and she's putting a brave face on it. I just thought in order to be honest and real, the core of her being had to be in a moment of great soul-searching. It was an arduous shoot, it was always fun, but it was extremely hard work: you finish a 15-hour day, you have five or six hours of sleep, you jump in the car and you drive for nine hours to do a sunset shoot. It was a heavy-duty movie, and of course it was $2 million, so it was on a wing and a prayer. It wasn't like we had huge Winnebagos and limousines and great transportation. We shot and drove and drove and shot. It was all taxing in the heat of the outback, which was often 112-115 degrees. Hopefully, I would never have to do drag again; false nails are not something to become a habit....

"I love making films. I think that making films is the most fun thing I can think of to do. I'd love to make the sort of films that Cary Grant made and Alfred Hitchcock made. I'd love to visit beautiful cities and do good work, and I'm hoping that people will understand that *Priscilla* is a comedy and that I could do comedy. I would like those roles to be open to me. I'd like to make good, fun movies. I made a film with Ken Russell in Israel immediately after *Priscilla*.

"[On Making the "Toby Dammit" segment of 1968's *Spirits of the Dead*]: Federico Fellini's working style was very simple in the way that great intelligence always manifests itself. Fellini must have understood very early on that what an artist most wants is to be loved by his director. Now that sounds very simple, but it's something that very few directors understand. Fellini understood that and he loved you. The price is you had to love him, but that was very easy, because he was incredibly lovable, so you would meet him, you would fall in love with him and then he would love you. And then, you would do anything for him. And what he really did was create that loving space around you, he would welcome any suggestion from anyone on the set, he would say, 'The film is bigger than you. You never know.' I said, 'What is it about directing if I ever want to direct a film? How is it?' He said, 'Terence, I am like a midwife. This film is finished, it's complete, but it's in another dimension. This job as director is bringing it into this dimension and the unveiling can come from anyone, because this film is not judgmental, it can come from the prop man, it can come from you, it can come from anyone, so I always keep a little corner open.' And that was from a great man. It's the lesser men who are not open to suggestions because it's their vision and their vision is superior. Fellini was the opposite of that."

The films of Oscar nominee TERENCE STAMP include: *Billy Budd, The Collector, Far from the Madding Crowd, Blue, Iron Cowboy, Teorema, Divine Nymph, Superman 1-2 The Thief of Baghdad, Meetings with Remarkable Men, Together? Vatican Conspiracy, Insanity, The Hit, Alamut Ambush, Cold War Killers, Deadly Recruits, Legal Eagles, Link, The Sicilian, Wall Street, Alien Nation, Young Guns, Genuine Risk,* **and** *The Real McCoy.*

After Dark, My Sweet

first of five in a row Huston made outside of Hollywood. There's no question that *African Queen* would have been a much different movie (less real and less exciting) if it had been shot on a studio back lot. It gave Bogie his one and only Oscar, and created a whole new image for Hepburn, one that she maintained for over 45 years. Based on the novel by C.S. Forester. 🦴🦴🦴🦴

1951 105m/C *GB* Humphrey Bogart, Katharine Hepburn, Robert Morley, Theodore Bikel, Peter Bull, Walter Gotell, Peter Swanwick, Richard Marner; **D:** John Huston; **W:** John Huston, James Agee; **C:** Jack Cardiff. Academy Awards '51: Best Actor (Bogart); Nominations: Academy Awards '51: Best Actress (Hepburn), Best Director (Huston), Best Screenplay. **VHS, Beta, LV** *FOX, FCT, TLF*

Jim Thompson's tightly written novels grab you by the throat and never let go until you finish reading them, usually about an hour later. We wish we could say the same thing about James Foley's movie version of *After Dark, My Sweet*. But alas no, and definitely no. This is a clear case of aficionados being so in love with the original source material that they attempt a meticulous (i.e. laborious) translation to the big screen. The results will please neither film noir buffs nor contemporary thriller fans. Foley's previous credits include two Madonna videos ("Live to Tell" and "Papa Don't Preach") and the excruciating feature *Who's That Girl?*, also starring Madonna. For a guy who cut his teeth on fast-paced videos, Foley seems determined to prove that he also has a forte for sluggish direction, and prove it he does for nearly two hours. Jason Patric portrays a character distractingly named Kevin Collins, for reasons best known to Foley. In Thompson's 1955 novel, the protagonist's name was Bill Collins, so why change the name to that of one of the most famous missing children in America, especially in a film about kidnapping? He meets up with a widow named Fay and her cohort named Uncle Bud, who soon draw him into a not-terribly-well-organized kidnapping scheme. Most of the film looks like a series of acting school exercises, none of which makes the slender plot any more compelling. Foley fails to build any appreciable momentum, even at points that ordinarily lend themselves to SOME tension. Jason Patric is far from fascinating as Collins, Rachel Ward is somewhat less than beguiling as Fay, and Bruce Dern is way over the top as Uncle Bud. The only interesting performance is delivered by Corey Carrier as Jack, a bratty kid mistakenly targeted as the kidnapping victim. Unfortunately, he's only onscreen for a minute or two. For those who care, there is one love scene: you see quite a lot of Patric's derriere, hardly anything at all of Ward. If you've ever seen Stanley Kubrick's *Paths of Glory* or *The Killing,* both with Jim Thompson screenplays, we doubt that you'll agree with Bruce Dern that "Thompson would have been proud of what we did with his material." For a better interpretation of Thompson material, rent Burt Kennedy's *The Killer Inside Me* with Stacy Keach instead of *After Dark, My Sweet!* 🦴

1990 (R) 114m/C Jason Patric, Rachel Ward, Bruce Dern, George Dickerson, James Cotton, Corey Carrier, Rocky Giordani; **D:** James Foley; **W:** Robert Redlin, James Foley; **M:** Maurice Jarre. **VHS, LV, Closed Caption** *LIV*

After Hours

Actor Griffin Dunne reportedly abstained from sex while making *After Hours* because director Martin Scorsese wanted to maintain the tension of his character throughout a long Soho night filled with weird experiences and strange prowlers-who-only-come-out-when-it's-dark. Dunne plays a Manhattan computer guy with no money who's confronted first by Rosanna Arquette, Linda Fiorentino, and Teri Garr, then, in rapid succession by Verna Bloom, Cheech and Chong, John Heard, Dick Miller, Catherine O'Hara, Will Patton, Bronson Pinchot, Rockets Redglare, and Scorsese himself in a nightclub sequence (the list goes on and on). Dunne, who went on to direct his father Dominick as a restaurant critic putting a cockroach-infested fork in his mouth no less than ten times in 1997's *Addicted to Love,* told *US* magazine's Amy Taubin that *Hours* and *Love* are first cousins. (Except that *Love* is, in his words, "corny and old-fashioned." Either that or what was the ultimate Catholic nightmare in 1985 has evolved into aw-shucks romanticism in 1997.) P.S. WHY did it take movie goers so many years (and over fifteen flicks!) to appreciate Linda Fiorentino? 🦴🦴🦴

1985 (R) 97m/C Griffin Dunne, Rosanna Arquette, John Heard, Teri Garr, Catherine O'Hara, Verna Bloom, Linda Fiorentino, Dick Miller, Bronson Pinchot, Will Patton, Rockets Redglare; **Cameos:** Richard "Cheech" Marin, Thomas Chong, Martin Scorsese; **D:** Martin Scorsese; **C:** Michael Ballhaus; **M:** Howard Shore. Cannes Film Festival '86: Best Director (Scorsese); Independent Spirit Awards '86: Best Director (Scorsese), Best Film. **VHS, Beta, LV, Closed Caption** *WAR*

Alambrista!

The best scripted film of 1978's San Francisco International Film Festival may well have been Robert M. Young's *Alambrista!,* a compassionate study of the Mexican immigrants who entered the U.S. illegally in the late 1970s in search of better employment. Focusing on one unmarried father named Roberto (touchingly played by Domingo Ambriz), Young reveals the frightening, nomadic, and altogether unfree lives the Mexican farmworkers must lead in order to send money home to their families. *Alambrista!* has a strong documentary quality: Young's training was in that filmmaking tradition. He shows how Roberto goes from farm to farm, harvesting fruits and vegetables, and how he lives briefly with a Stockton waitress (stunningly played by Linda Gillin, who also made a couple of chiller-thrillers). For the most part, Roberto's new life is horrible: lonely and exhausting, and filled with the terror of discovery by immigration authorities. *Alambrista!* evokes memories of *The Grapes of Wrath,* and the picture deserves much wider distribution than it received on the now-defunct *Visions* series via PBS. A must on video, not only for Young's superb storytelling, but also because it gives a chance to see the early work of Oscar nominees Ned Beatty and Edward James Olmos, as well as the late Trinidad Silva (*Crackers, Colors, The Night Before*). 🦴🦴🦴🦴

1977 110m/C Domingo Ambriz, Trinidad Silva, Linda Gillin, Ned Beatty, Julius W. Harris, Paul Berrones, Edward James Olmos, Stephen Walker, Blake Ritson; **D:** Robert M. Young; **W:** Robert M. Young. *NYR*

Alice

Alice has been identified by the folks at Roxie Releasing as "militant surrealism."

It was one of the San Francisco International Film Festival's rare treats in the spring of 1988, and although it is certainly an unusual adaptation of the Lewis Carroll Wonderland classic, it is not as obsessive and scary as many grownups might have you believe. When we saw it one Palm Sunday with a crowd of Berkeley youngsters, they appeared to relish Alice's adventures as much as we did. None seemed overly disturbed by the imagery, but every child is unique, so do preview this one before you organize a kindergarten birthday party with *Alice* as the centerpiece. ♫♫♫

1988 84m/C *GB* Kristina Kohoutova; **D:** Jan Svankmajer. **VHS** *ICA, TPV*

Allonsanfan

Allonsanfan stars the wonderful Marcello Mastroianni as a grudging revolutionary, circa 1816. This early Taviani film is somewhat uneven compared to their later efforts, but Mastroianni, as usual, makes it all worthwhile. The most meaningful moments occur when the Tavianis permit some honest emotion to creep into the story. The brilliant cinematography is by Giuseppe Ruzzolini. ♫♫♪

1973 115m/C *IT* Marcello Mastroianni, Laura Betti, Renato de Carmine, Lea Massari, Mimsy Farmer, Claudio Cassinelli, Bruno Cirino; **D:** Paolo Taviani, Vittorio Taviani; **W:** Paolo Taviani, Vittorio Taviani; **C:** Giuseppe Ruzzolini; **M:** Ennio Morricone. **VHS, Beta** *FCT, WBF*

The Amazing Mr. X

When film lovers conjure up memories of strong women in the 1940s, they may recall Joan Crawford with her thick lipstick and huge shoulder pads, but our favorite unsung actress of that era is Lynn Bari. Bari was a cool brunette with a deep hypnotic voice who glided through seventy films for 20th Century Fox between 1934-56. In the early days of her career, she would pass in and out of the plot so fast that her appearances would only register with her most meticulous admirers. By the time she hit her stride, her film career was nearly over. Fans who appreciated her fresh and easy banter as the mystery writer with Randolph Scott in *Home Sweet Homicide* or as a murder suspect with George Raft in *Nocturne* would not have many more Lynn Bari movies to enjoy before she moved on to television and the stage. *The Amazing Mr. X/The Spiritualist* was Bari's last important film as a central character. Carole Landis had originally been cast as a woman haunted by the "ghost" of her husband, but the beautiful Landis was haunted by a life beyond her control, and killed herself a few weeks before shooting was due to begin. Bari, benefiting enormously from the breathtaking camera work of the great John Alton, gave the role a depth and understanding that the essentially comic Landis would not have been able to supply. Whether drifting along a dark beach in flowing white evening gowns or registering a wry awareness of her fiance's romantic limitations, Bari gracefully sustained the delicate balance between world weariness and genuine vulnerability. Also in the cast were the ubiquitous Richard Carlson as her earnest but awkward love interest, the gently appealing Cathy O'Donnell, and Turhan Bey, delivering a surprisingly textured performance in the title role. Because *The Amazing Mr. X/The Spiritualist* lapsed into the public domain and is so often televised in murky prints that fail to do justice to Alton's cinematography, it has yet to acquire the reputation that it deserves. If actualized, rumors of a 35mm. video may help to redress that injustice. Afterwards, you can try to find a rental copy of *Nocturne,* then join the throng of Lynn Bari aficionados who are mystified by why such an intriguing presence continues to remain an unknown quantity today. **AKA:** The Spiritualist. ♫♫♫

1948 79m/B Turhan Bey, Lynn Bari, Cathy O'Donnell, Richard Carlson, Donald Curtis, Virginia Gregg; **D:** Bernard Vorhaus; **C:** John Alton. **VHS, Beta** *NOS, SNC, RXM*

The Ambulance

The presence of Eric Roberts in a movie like Larry Cohen's *The Ambulance* shows how his career has changed from the heady days when he was an Oscar contender. *The Ambulance* has all the trappings of an old-fashioned mystery: Roberts plays a cartoonist who falls for a mystery woman (Janine Turner) on the street. Before she passes out and is taken away in an ambulance, she slips him the vital clue that she's a diabetic. Yep, it turns out that mad doctor Eric Braeden is abducting all the diabetics he can and selling them for medical research. Larry Cohen clearly doesn't want you to think about that premise too long, and energetic Roberts won't LET you in any case. Still, *The Ambulance* has a great femme cop (Megan Gallagher), an even better nutty cop (James Earl Jones), and the Oscar-winning, scene-stealing Red Buttons as a wily old reporter who tries to help our poor driven hero. *Return of the Killer Tomatoes! The Lift, The Refrigerator,* and now *The Ambulance*. What's next? 🦴🦴🦴

1990 (R) 95m/C Eric Roberts, James Earl Jones, Megan Gallagher, Richard Bright, Janine Turner, Eric (Hans Gudegast) Braeden, Red Buttons, Laurene Landon, Jill Gatsby, Nicholas Chinlund; **D:** Larry Cohen; **W:** Larry Cohen. **VHS, LV, Closed Caption** COL, EPC

American Boyfriends

Canadian writer/director Sandy Wilson came up with this sequel to her 1985 hit, *My American Cousin*. Although Wilson tends to rely too heavily on 1965 media caca, there is no denying the considerable charm of Margaret Langrick as Sandy Wilcox and the immense charisma of John Wildman, seen all too briefly in a reprise of his role as Butch Walker. 🦴🦴🦴

1989 (PG-13) 90m/C CA Margaret Langrick, John Wildman, Jason Blicker, Lisa Repo Martell; **D:** Sandy Wilson; **W:** Sandy Wilson. **VHS, Beta, LV** LIV

American Heart

Take a good look at Jeff Bridges' performance as Jack in *American Heart* and then ask yourself what this three-time Oscar nominee has to DO to win an Academy Award. Bridges deservedly received recognition as Best Actor at the Independent Spirit Awards for his lived-in performance as an ex-convict, filled with despair and forced by circumstances to care for his adolescent son, Nick (superbly played by Edward Furlong). Nick has an aching need for his father's love and approval, but Jack has been so beaten by life that at first he can only grudgingly tolerate his son's presence. Directed by Martin (*Streetwise*) Bell, who thoroughly understands the difficult subject matter, *American Heart* resists sentimental short cuts and simplistic resolutions to dig all the way down to the core of this wrenching situation, and there's nary a false note in Peter Silverman's gritty, hard-hitting script. Bridges co-produced this little-seen American masterpiece, which represents an unequivocal high point in his long career. 🦴🦴🦴🦴

1992 (R) 114m/C Jeff Bridges, Edward Furlong, Lucinda Jenney, Tracey Kapisky, Don Harvey, Margaret Welsh; **D:** Martin Bell; **W:** Peter Silverman; **M:** James Newton Howard. Independent Spirit Awards '94: Best Actor (Bridges); Nominations: Independent Spirit Awards '94: Best Cinematography, Best First Feature, Best Supporting Actor (Furlong), Best Supporting Actress (Jenney). **VHS, LV** LIV, BTV

American Matchmaker

American Matchmaker is an archival treasure filmed in Yiddish by legendary cult director Edgar Ulmer in 1940. You may remember its star, Leo Fuchs (1911-94), as a character actor in 1990's *Avalon*. But nearly 60 years ago, the Polish emigre cut a dashing figure in the title role of a confirmed-bachelor-turned-Manhattan-matchmaker. Ulmer's escapist comedy is lighter than air; you'd never know from the subject

matter that this gentle satire was released the year after the Nazi invasion of Poland. *AKA:* Amerikaner Shadkhn. 🦴🦴🦴

1940 87m/B Leo Fuchs, Judith Abarbanel, Rosetta Bialis, Yudel Dubinsky, Abe Lax; *D:* Edgar G. Ulmer. **VHS** *ERG*

American Strays

The big name cast may lure you, but you'll be chafing at the bit within the first few seconds of Michael Covert's *American Strays*. If Luke Perry wanted to terminate his status as a heartthrob, this lousy movie would do the trick, if any of his fan club members ever bother to rent *American Strays*. And what is Oscar nominee Jennifer Tilly doing here, slumming? With bad luck, this one might be played endlessly on cable television, dissolving the luster of each and every participant. Disjointed and dumb. **WOOF!**

1996 (R) 97m/C Carol Kane, Jennifer Tilly, Eric Roberts, John Savage, Luke Perry, Joe Viterelli, James Russo, Vonte Sweet, Sam Jones, Brion James, Toni Kalem, Melora Walters; *D:* Michael Covert; *W:* Michael Covert; *C:* Sead Mutarevic; *M:* John Graham. **VHS** *APX*

...And God Spoke

Soupy Sales as Moses, Eve Plumb as Mrs. Noah, Lou Ferrigno as Cain; yeah, those are the first actors you think about when casting a Biblical epic, right? *...And God Spoke* is a mockumentary on the making of the nonexistent movie of the same name. It focuses on the trials and tribulations of two independent producers (Clive Walton and Marvin Handleman, played by

Michael Riley and Stephen Rappaport) as they attempt to film the best-selling book of all time. The team, best known for *Alpha Deatha De Kappa, Dial S for Sex,* and *Nude Ninjas,* now go after a target audience of four billion Bible readers. Clearly, Clive and Marvin are not among that group; they're unsure whether there were eight or ten disciples, and their vision of the loaves and fishes sequence (later scrapped for budgetary reasons) includes Pepperidge Farm goldfish crackers standing in for the fishes. Later, when they get into deeper financial scrapes, Marvin agrees that Moses will include a product placement pitch, delivering 20th century soft drinks as well as Commandments to the stock footage multitude from the 19th century. And of course, despite scathing reviews, *...And God Spoke* is a huge $42 million hit, attracting long lines of devoted groupies who wear Biblical gear to repeat screenings. As good-natured satire, *...And God Spoke* falls somewhere in between *The Making of Bikini School III* and *This Is Spinal Tap.* The performances are energetic and clever; it's fun to see Sales, Jan Brady, and the incredible Hulk again, and all in the same movie (and it's blessedly short). If the entire film had been in the same vein as the auditions for casting agent Charlie Rose, or the power clash between Marvin and the A.D. in a staff meeting, *...And God Spoke* would have been a non-stop side-splitter. As is, it's still a painless way to spend 82 minutes. 🦴🦴

1994 (R) 82m/C Michael Riley, Stephen Rappaport, Soupy Sales, Lou Ferrigno, Eve Plumb, Andy Dick, R.C. Bates, Fred Kaz, Daniel Tisman; **D:** Arthur Borman; **W:** Gregory S. Malins, Michael Curtis. **VHS** *WEA*

And the Band Played On

In spite of all the hands that have clearly fiddled with *And the Band Played On,* it is still as good a film as we are likely to get anytime soon about the early years of the AIDS epidemic. And if millions decide to

watch it only to see dozens of big stars acting their hearts out in cameos, they may still learn more about AIDS than they have from the guarded sound bites that represent their major source of information to date. What will the inhabitants of this planet in the 25th century think of how we handled these plague years after watching a movie like *And the Band Played On*? Historically, deadly plagues have always revealed the dark side of human nature as this one does; plague victims are either shunned or rushed to their graves by the ignorance of both their communities and their doctors. Throughout much of the 20th century, we've clung to the touching notion that science could solve our every problem, forgetting that the great influenza plague of 1918 claimed twice as many lives as World War I. Because the progress of that virus was so swift and so deadly, its victims left behind very little documentation. But the AIDS epidemic has been with us for the better part of two decades with no respite in sight at press time. There is certainly no happy ending from the guy on the white horse, the former Center for Disease Control researcher Don Francis, earnestly played by Matthew Modine. Except for his dedication to his work, we know nothing about him. In fact, we learn nothing about the cipher-like doctors who fight the government bureaucracy as they struggle to identify and treat the virus; Glenne Headly and Lily Tomlin are among them. Ronald Reagan and Jerry Falwell play themselves courtesy of old video tapes, and Robert Gallo, another bad guy fixated on winning the Nobel Prize, is well played by Alan Alda. When the film does try to show the private life of someone like the late gay activist Bill Kraus, it gets it wrong, by dredging up the old movie bio cliche of the discontented lover who's jealous of all that political activism. In trying to reach middle America, the film is scrupulous about not depicting anyone who appears to be TOO gay. It reinforces the point that straight people and hemophiliacs could

The Hound Salutes:
REBECCA MILLER
Writer/director, *Angela*

Actually, I did see the auditions of 1,200 little girls for the parts of Angela and Ellie. They weren't all auditions. Many of them were meetings where we taped girls answering a few questions, mostly having to do with their spiritual lives, the things that they thought about with regards to whether or not they thought there were angels, whether or not there was a devil, what it looked like, whether there was a God, et cetera. Some kids don't think about those things, and some kids have a very complex system, sometimes a secret system that they carry around with them, and so that was part of it, although, of course, looks were part of it also, and, ultimately, the ability to act. We started with their inner lives.

"I never thought about what it was like to be the daughter of Marilyn Monroe because I wrote the part of May before Anna Thomson walked through the door, looking a lot like she does in the movie. She had that hair, she had that face, she had that body, she pretty much dressed like that. I embraced the coincidence and saw the rightness of it in many ways.

"It's important that viewers sense the religious ambiguity in the film because I have ambiguous feelings about religion. I've always been instinctively someone who had a kind of faith which I've either been trying to get rid of desperately or trying to find a place for. MY first questions as a person, as a very young child, were basically religious questions, about whether there was a devil, whether there was a God, whether there was a Hell. The film warns against trying to find all the answers. I think that that's always something difficult with spiritual matters. In other words, with certainty: this is the way that's right and there is no other way. Angela's trying so hard by following the signs. She lives following the signs. Everything is a sign for something else and she's trying to develop a religious code. In so doing, Angela endangers herself, terribly. I'm in great favor of embracing the mystery of spirituality and of life, and don't deny that in any way, but I have an inherent mistrust of canon and of organized religion.

"With characters like The Sleepwalker and Lucifer, The Fallen Angel, I like to push the parameters of the absurd and still stay within a believable framework in terms of character and story, partly because I can tell my story more effectively that way and put more emphasis on certain aspects with elements of the absurd. Also, that's always been my orientation. I've always had a penchant for surrealism, for the language of dreams."

contract the virus or that babies might be born with AIDS and THAT'S when government leaders began to focus on the spread of the disease, by then out of control. But as the first widely distributed major film to deal with the politics of AIDS, it is successful in attracting our attention, concern, and hopefully, effective international demands for a timely cure. *And the Band Played On,* by the late journalist Randy Shilts, originally aired on the Home Box Office cable network and was also released theatrically in Europe. ♫♫♫

1993 (PG-13) 140m/C Matthew Modine, Alan Alda, Ian McKellen, Lily Tomlin, Glenne Headly, Richard Masur, Saul Rubinek, Charles Martin Smith, Patrick Bauchau, Nathalie Baye, Christian Clemenson; *Cameos:* Richard Gere, David Clennon, Phil Collins, Alex Courtney, David Dukes, David Marshall Grant, Ronald Guttman, Anjelica Huston, Ken Jenkins, Richard Jenkins, Tcheky Karyo, Swoosie Kurtz, Jack Laufer, Steve Martin, Dakin Matthews, Peter McRobbie, Lawrence Monoson, B.D. Wong, Donal Logue, Jeffrey Nordling, Stephen Spinella; *D:* Roger Spottiswoode; *W:* Arnold Schulman; *C:* Paul Elliott; *M:* Carter Burwell. **VHS, LV, Closed Caption** *HBO*

An Angel at My Table

Jane Campion's *An Angel at My Table* began life as a three-part series on New Zealand television, which (dare we say this?) is the best way to see this 157-minute movie. After all, it is based on three different autobiographical novels by Janet Frame, *To the Island, An Angel at My Table,* and *The Envoy from Mirror City.* Kerry Fox plays Frame, who was misdiagnosed as a schizophrenic and spent eight years in a mental institution receiving electroshock therapy before the error was corrected. Extremely well acted and directed, *An Angel at My Table* is nonetheless very heavy going all at once—especially first thing in the morning, which is when most reviewers see new movies. This explains (if not excuses) all the bad tempers and bad manners one is likely to observe at press screenings. *An Angel at My Table* won many awards all over the world, but then so did *Breaking the Waves* and any number of worthy candidates which are long, depressing, and make you feel like a heel for wanting to watch *Sullivan's Travels* instead. ♫♫♪

1989 (R) 157m/C *NZ* Kerry Fox, Alexia Keogh, Karen Fergusson, Iris Churn, K.J. Wilson, Martyn Sanderson; *D:* Jane Campion; *W:* Laura Jones; *C:* Stuart Dryburgh. Chicago Film Critics Awards '91: Best Foreign Film; Independent Spirit Awards '92: Best Foreign Film. **VHS** *COL, NLC*

Angela

This strange movie about two little girls growing up with a depressed mother (who somewhat resembles Marilyn Monroe) was written and directed by Rebecca Miller, the daughter of Arthur Miller. It's a moderately interesting (but slooow and rather heavy going) examination of a childhood dominated by a fear of the Devil. Miranda Stuart Rhyne and Charlotte Blythe are good as the kids, Angela, ten, and Ellie, six, and Anna Thomson is eerily evocative as their mother. Cinematographer Ellen Kuras won a Filmmakers Trophy at 1995's Sundance Film Festival. ♫♫♪

1994 105m/C Miranda Stuart Rhyne, Charlotte Blythe, Anna Thomson, John Ventimiglia, Vincent Gallo; *D:* Rebecca Miller; *W:* Rebecca Miller; *C:* Ellen Kuras; *M:* Michael Rohatyn. Sundance Film Festival '95: Best Cinematography, Filmmakers Trophy. **VHS** *NYR*

Angels and Insects

We know that something's off from the very beginning of *Angels and Insects;* Paul Brown's surreal costumes are a dead giveaway. In spite of or, perhaps, because of them, William Adamson (Mark Rylance) determines to marry Eugenia (Patsy Kensit). Eugenia is lovely, but vague. There's something wrong with the marriage from the start, and William isn't even close to solving the riddle when one day he receives a message to return home early and realizes, in an empirical flash, exactly why Eugenia has distanced herself from him for so long. Then Kristin Scott Thomas

"Whom can I tell that I should not destroy in the telling?"

—William Adamson (Mark Rylance) holds a secret in *Angels and Insects.*

SALLY KIRKLAND
Anna

The big surprise when the Academy Award nominations for 1987's Best Actress were announced in early 1988 was first-time nominee Sally Kirkland, then 43. Kirkland had been making film appearances in small roles (*Cinderella Liberty, The Way We Were, The Sting, Bite the Bullet, Love Letters*) for the better part of two decades. With the title role in *Anna*, Kirkland found herself among a distinguished group of nominees that included Glenn Close, future winners Cher and Holly Hunter, and two-time winner Meryl Streep. Although Kirkland won several other awards that year, including the Golden Globe, none of the roles that followed had the depth or range of *Anna*. Kirkland went on to make a quality made-for-cable movie (1990's *Heat Wave*), to play small roles (as in 1991's *JFK*), and to work in offbeat comedies (1989's *Cold Feet* and 1993's *Cheatin' Hearts*). Another "part where (she) can really show the work to its glory" may still be in Sally Kirkland's future.

How did I become involved with the project of *Anna*? Well, my manager brought me the script and said they were looking for an actress in New York who could be believably Polish, and they said 'star name only,' and I'd like to think that in the industry I'm a star. Maybe by the time this film gets around America and Ohio, I will be, too. But anyway, the thing I knew I had going for me is that I'm really good with dialects and I teach them. And so I quickly learned Polish dialect, and then switched it to Czech so now Anna talks like this, you know: I come from Prague, 1968. I learned that and then I tested three times over a period of two months, put on ten pounds, let myself go to pot, so to speak, for the part, and I hope that people who know me versus the characterization will appreciate the craft of acting because clearly, you can see me now. I am not her, except in spirit, and that's the marvel of Lee Strasberg's method acting which I've been involved with for 20 years, and which I teach at the Actors Studio. And so all those wonderful actors that I know you all admire, Bobby De Niro, Al Pacino, Dustin Hoffman, Paul Newman, Jane Fonda, Geri Page, et cetera, I've been working out with them since the '60s, and finally I got a part where I can really show the work to its glory, and so does that answer your question?"

(made up to look severe and efficient, but secretly lusting for William all this time) makes HER move. Writer/director Philip Haas and co-scripter Belinda Haas succeed in drawing us into a weird and disturbing climate. (I'm trying to come up with a picture that revolves around insects where the central characters were quite normal, but I'm drawing a blank here.) Based on A.S. Byatt's novella *Morpho Eugenia.* 𝄢𝄢𝄢

1995 (R) 116m/C *GB* Mark Rylance, Patsy Kensit, Kristin Scott Thomas, Jeremy Kemp, Douglas Henshall, Chris Larkin, Annette Badland, Anna Massey, Saskia Wickham; *D:* Philip Haas; *W:* Belinda Haas, Philip Haas; *C:* Bernard Zitzermann; *M:* Alexander Balanescu. Nominations: Academy Awards '96: Best Costume Design. **VHS** *HMK*

Anna

Anna is a showcase for Sally Kirkland, who tears into the role of a neglected Czechoslovakian actress with all the passion of a neglected American actress who has no time to waste reserving her energy. Kirkland gets down and dirty with this part, and she has the artistic courage to sacrifice her own good looks in order to create a more believable portrait of Anna, who has both good and bad days. Life does things to people, and Kirkland doesn't hesitate to show the extremes. In some close-ups, as when a beloved old teacher brings her to tears, she resembles a small child fearful of being swallowed by the world's promises and its lies. In others, as when Anna realizes that her protegee has borrowed her life story and claimed it as her own, her rage is limitless and we share the agony of the older woman who has no resources left on which to draw, not even memory. "Oscar nomination" is written all over Sally Kirkland's star performance, and yet she is a real ensemble player, too, for her sequences with model Paulina Porizkova and Robert Fields would be nowhere near as moving without a powerful interplay between the characters. Yurek Bogayevicz directs with a sensitive understanding of the realities of the acting profession, and

Agnieszka Holland's screenplay offers a sharp perspective on the generational conflicts between women. The film has been compared to both *All About Eve* and *Sunset Boulevard,* but it differs from both in significant respects. The expatriate theme, as well as the intense examination of trust lost and trust found, contribute to make *Anna* a fresh entry in the catalogue of show business sagas. 𝄢𝄢𝄢𝄢

1987 (PG-13) 101m/C Sally Kirkland, Paulina Porizkova, Robert Fields, Stefan Schnabel, Larry Pine, Ruth Maleczech; *D:* Yurek Bogayevicz; *W:* Yurek Bogayevicz, Agnieszka Holland; *C:* Bobby Bukowski; *M:* Greg Hawkes. Golden Globe Awards '88: Best Actress—Drama (Kirkland); Independent Spirit Awards '88: Best Actress (Kirkland); Los Angeles Film Critics Association Awards '87: Best Actress (Kirkland); Nominations: Academy Awards '87: Best Actress (Kirkland). **VHS, Beta, LV, Closed Caption** *VES, LIV*

Anne of Green Gables

There were two prior movies of Lucy Maud Montgomery's (1874-1942) classic novel, but Kevin Sullivan's version starring Megan Follows is far and away the best. In 1911, William Desmond Taylor (1877-1922) directed Mary Miles Minter (1902-84) in a Paramount film scripted by Frances Marion (1886-1973). Minter was beautiful, but not much of an actress, and her association with Taylor seems to have led directly to his murder in 1922 and to her speedy retirement in 1923. Moreover, beloved Prince Edward Island received short shrift both from Taylor and from George Nicholls, Jr., who made the 1934 talking picture starring Dawn O'Day (1918-93), re-named Anne Shirley for the title character. Shirley was a delightful Anne, but for readers who wanted to see every single incident they had read about in the 1908 book, a 79-minute film couldn't provide the detail craved by Anne-atics. And so it took 77 years for Kevin Sullivan and Joe Weisenfeld to come up with the perfect adaptation, and the perfect Anne, Marilla (Colleen Dewhurst), and Matthew (Richard Farns-

MARLEEN GORRIS
Antonia's Line

I wish *Antonia's Line* were autobiographical, but it isn't at all. Even though my maternal grandmother was quite a strong character, she didn't look at all like Antonia. She was a very small, thin, bird-like woman who always dressed in black. She became a widow quite early on and raised four children, so she MUST have been quite a strong woman, but Antonia isn't really based on anyone in particular; she really is a figment of my imagination.

"Of course, as a child, you see things, and you don't realize you see them. In every village in those days, in the '50s, you had a village idiot. You don't see them around anymore, so that is where the idea of the village idiot comes from. For most of the other characters, I'm not really aware of having known them when I was young. The whole idea of the Mad Madonna, who is a Catholic, and the Protestant, who obviously is a Protestant, probably stems from the idea that in the Catholic village where I grew up, you had no Protestant people walking around. In those days, things like that mattered. They don't matter anymore, at least not in Holland, but that's probably what gave me the idea of having a sad woman baying at the moon; she couldn't marry the love of her life because of different religious dogmas.

"I hope that things are opening up for women over 40, but I doubt it. It would be nice if actresses over 40 got better parts than they did, but Utopia's a long way off, I'm afraid."

worth). 1985 audiences treasured this 197-minute labor of love, turning it into an instant classic. I don't care how jaded you think you are, this irresistible red-haired motor mouth from another time (that would be Anne) will melt your cold, cold heart. Exquisitely filmed on Prince Edward Island by Rene Ohashi. Followed by an equally fine 1987 sequel (*Anne of Avonlea*) and a long-running series in the '90s, *Avonlea* (an Emmy winner as outstanding children's program). 🦴🦴🦴🦴

1985 197m/C *CA* Megan Follows, Colleen Dewhurst, Richard Farnsworth, Patricia Hamilton, Schuyler Grant, Jonathan Crombie, Marilyn Lightstone, Charmion King, Rosemary Radcliffe, Jackie Burroughs, Robert Collins, Joachim Hansen, Cedric Smith, Paul Brown, Miranda de Pencier, Jennifer Inch, Wendy Lyon, Christiane Krueger, Trish Nettleton, Morgan Chapman; *D:* Kevin Sullivan; *W:* Kevin Sullivan, Joe Weisenfeld; *C:* Rene Ohashi; *M:* Hagood Hardy. **VHS, Beta, LV, Closed Caption** *KUI, TOU, IGP*

Another Country

One of the saddest things about 1987's *Less Than Zero* (besides watching the way-too-believable performance of real-life substance abuser Robert Downey, Jr.), is realizing that the director of that abysmal flick,

Marek Kanievska, had helmed one of my favorite films of 1984. How could the man who made *Another Country,* one of the most sensitive films EVER about homosexuality, appear to give homophobia equal screen time just three years later? Rupert Everett plays Guy Bennett, who's meant to be real-life spy Guy Burgess (1911-63). Journalist Betsy Brantley comes to interview him at his flat in Russia and discovers that the aging traitor is somewhat of a broken-hearted Anglophile. What happened? Guy talks about his schooldays when he befriended a Marxist named Tommy Judd (newcomer Colin Firth at his most luscious) and kvetched about Mummy Imogen (Anna Massey), and fell in love with Harcourt (angelic Cary Elwes before he began to pump iron). Guy wants to be accepted by his schoolmates, but the homosexual activity they enjoy in private and condemn in public is intrinsic to his nature. As his infatuation with Harcourt deepens, Guy becomes increasingly vulnerable to the forces that lead to his break from Great Britain's social structure. Once the break occurs, he accepts his lot as a permanent outsider with resignation, no longer feeling any loyalty to the country of his birth, only a wistful yearning for its trappings. A good companion piece to *Another Country* is Alan Bennett's *An Englishman Abroad,* directed by John Schlesinger in 1983 and based on star Coral Browne's (1913-91) real-life encounter with Guy Burgess (Alan Bates). Reportedly, American audiences have a rough time making sense of the Burgess-Maclean-Philby triumvirate or comprehending subsequent revelations about the Queen's de-knighted art historian Anthony Blunt (1907-83). Everett's poignant portrayal really ought to speak for itself, but if not, John Costello's *The Mask of Treachery* (Collins, 1988) is crammed with over 760 pages worth of information on the subject. EXTRA NOTE: As a teenager, the ninth Earl Spencer appeared in several sequences here, one where he sings his sister Princess Diana's favorite hymn, "I

Vow to Thee My Country," and another sequence where he bares his backside in a community shower. 🎞🎞🎞🎞

1984 90m/C *GB* Rupert Everett, Colin Firth, Michael Jenn, Robert Addie, Anna Massey, Betsy Brantley, Rupert Wainwright, Cary Elwes, Arthur Howard, Tristan Oliver, Frederick Alexander, Adrian Ross-Magenty, Geoffrey Bateman, Philip Dupuy, Jeffrey Wickham, Gideon Boulting, Ivor Howard, Charles Spencer; *D:* Marek Kanievska; *W:* Julian Mitchell; *C:* Peter Biziou; *M:* Michael Storey. Nominations: Cannes Film Festival '84: Best Film. **VHS, Beta, LV**

Antonia's Line

This is the most accessible film by Marleen Gorris, whose previous efforts include 1983's *A Question of Silence* and 1985's *Broken Mirrors.* It's a family saga revolving around matriarch Antonia (Willeke Van Ammelrooy) and her large clan. The male characters are mainly utilitarian necessities here, but that's a step up from the murder victim/serial killer roles they've been assigned in other Gorris pictures. Gorris' 1995 Oscar winner blends humor with feminist insights and is beautifully photographed by Willy Stassen. (In Dutch with English subtitles.) 🎞🎞🎞

1995 (R) 102m/C *NL* Willeke Van Ammelrooy, Els Dottermans, Veerle Van Overloop, Thyrza Ravesteijn, Jan Decleir, Mil Seghers, Jan Steen, Marina De Graaf; *D:* Marleen Gorris; *W:* Marleen Gorris; *C:* Willy Stassen; *M:* Ilona Seckaz. Academy Awards '95: Best Foreign Language Film; Nominations: British Academy Awards '96: Best Foreign Language Film. **VHS** *BMG*

The Applegates

The Applegates is the story of a colony of misguided Amazonian arthropods who believe that their only chance for survival depends on their exterminating the human race. They send a family of four bugs to Ohio. Their mission: to impersonate a nuclear family of humans named

The Hound Salutes:
JENNIFER MONTGOMERY
Art for Teachers of Children

JENNIFER MONTGOMERY photographed and directed her own screenplay, *Art for Teachers of Children*. For this autobiographical study of a 14-year-old's seduction at boarding school by the married advisor at her dormitory, Montgomery cast 22-year-old Caitlin Grace McDonnell as her adolescent self, and Duncan Hannah, 40, as her former lover. The film takes a neutral position regarding the long-term effects of the affair on a schoolgirl that young, but the audience response at film festivals has been filled with controversy. Although Montgomery said that she wanted to work through her rage at the experience, there is little rage in the character we see onscreen, or in the cool, low-key script.

A lot of my films have been about the powerlessness of parents to control what happens to their kids. There's a lot of pathos in that. There was a split between my parents' beliefs as good civil libertarians and their gut need to protect me. I think they did a balancing act. They were both Bohemian lefties and they didn't want to interfere, but I think there's a lot of sadness behind that. The most therapeutic participation in the film is my own mother's playing of herself."

Dick, Jane, Sally, and Johnny, and then blow up a nuclear power plant. Ed Begley, Jr., Stockard Channing, Camile Cooper, and Bobby Jacoby star as the statistically average Applegate family, with Dabney Coleman as the leader of their colony, Aunt Bea. Director Michael (*Heathers, The Truth About Cats and Dogs*) Lehmann's script never does explain how the bugs transform themselves into humans. His satire focuses on how the bugs are twisted by American society. Dick has an affair with his secretary, Jane becomes a chargeaholic, Sally gets pregnant, and Johnny gets hooked on drugs. Whenever any humans threaten to expose them, the bugs-in-disguise turn them into hostages. What makes the movie work is the twisted characterizations of the family. Ed Begley,

Jr., is just right as Dick. He may know the definition of "normal," but he has no idea how he's supposed to act under the circumstances. Future Oscar nominee Stockard Channing, one of America's most underappreciated actresses, is a delight as Jane, her growing mania for possessions dissolving her carefully maintained facade. The kids are good, too. Cami Cooper's role requires her to shift from innocence to evil and back again in the blink of eye and she conveys both with enormous skill. As her little brother, Bobby Jacoby is heartbreakingly innocent before some drug-dealing twins get their clutches on them. Lehmann's satire gets really broad as the family members start lying to each other right and left; *The Applegates* may not appeal to you if you demand good taste from a movie. Its humor can be brutal, but on some weird level, we prefer Lehmann's good-natured, what-the-hell attack on Middle America here to Tim Burton's mean-spirited vision of suburbia in *Edward Scissorhands*. **AKA:** Meet the Applegates. 🦴🦴▽

1989 (R) 90m/C Ed Begley Jr., Stockard Channing, Dabney Coleman, Cami Cooper, Bobby Jacoby, Glenn Shadix, Susan Barnes, Adam Biesk, Savannah Smith Boucher; **D:** Michael Lehmann; **W:** Michael Lehmann, Redbeard Simmons. **VHS, Beta, LV, Closed Caption** *MED, FOX, VTR*

Art for Teachers of Children

We've listened to DOZENS of after-the-fact stories from teenage girls seduced by adult males and from adult males who seduced teenage girls. The girls always seem to affect a cynical tone about experiences that clearly turned their lives upside down. The men are more flip; it was no big deal, she wanted it, she was screwed up anyway, yackety-yack. So Jennifer Montgomery's *Art for Teachers of Children*, documenting a sexual relationship between a 14-year-old student and her 28-year-old married school counselor, is a major button pusher from frame one. Montgomery's black-and-white feature film debut is atrociously acted (with a 22-year-old woman and 40-year-old guy in the leading roles) and stubbornly resists expressing ANY point of view. "There's nothing worse than boring men who make bad art," Montgomery's real-life mother (and no actress) intones on the soundtrack. See, Montgomery, then 33, wanted to make her fact-based movie about art, but why choose this particular topic if she didn't want to make some sort of comment about men who lust after children and the children who love them? It's haunting, though, in the same way those flat narratives about being a sexual plaything tug at your heart when they're recited by women who are old-at-18. 🦴🦴

1995 82m/B Caitlin Grace McDonnell, Duncan Hannah, Coles Burroughs, Bryan Keane; **D:** Jennifer Montgomery; **W:** Jennifer Montgomery; **C:** Jennifer Montgomery. **VHS** *ZGI*

Ashes and Diamonds

If you want to watch Zbigniew Cybulski (1927-67) when he helped to put Polish films on the international movie map, don't miss *Ashes and Diamonds*. For marketing purposes, American publicists referred to Cybulski as the Polish James Dean, an overconvenient but apt comparison. Cybulski wore tinted prescription glasses throughout *Ashes and Diamonds* because of vision problems, but they also increased his mysterious allure. In the film, set on the last day of the war, his character must kill a man he doesn't want to kill and probably doesn't have to kill. He resists the job, but fate in the form of a poorly timed order is against him. *Ashes and Diamonds* says more about the postwar world of 1958 than it does of wartime life in 1945, especially when it contrasts Cybulski's destiny with his haphazard and rather naive pursuit of a young barmaid. In real life, Cybulski lived fast and died young while trying to board a train. His death increased his legendary status and several of his films (1954's *A Generation*, 1960's *Innocent Sorcerers*, 1965's *The Saragossa Manuscript*) are still shown constantly in art houses all over the world. It is perhaps besides the point that, for all his tremendous presence and seemingly careless appeal, Cybulski often overacted like mad. As is evident here, he seldom approached his roles in a disciplined way or gave careful shadings to the characters he portrayed. But TRY tearing your eyes away from Andrzej Wajda's *Ashes and Diamonds* for a single second when Cybulski is onscreen. **AKA:** Popiol i Diament. 🦴🦴🦴🦴

1958 105m/B PL Zbigniew Cybulski, Eva Krzyzewska, Adam Pawlikowski, Bogumil Kobiela, Waclaw

Zastrzezynski; **D:** Andrzej Wajda. Venice Film Festival '59: International Critics Award. **VHS, Beta, LV** ING, MRV, NLC

Attica

Cinda Firestone made this documentary with her folk's money (the Firestone Tire and Rubber Company). Her honest study of the Attica uprising benefits from outstanding research. Firestone produced, directed, and edited (with Tucker Ashworth) Attica herself, and her frank interviews with Attica's inmates are shrewdly spliced next to contrasting statements by Attica's officials. ♪♪♪

1974 80m/C D: Cinda Firestone; **C:** Roland Barnes, Jay Lamarch, Mary Lampson, Jesse Goodman, Carol Stein, Kevin Keating. NYR

Aventurera

For a film buff, discovering a movie like Aventurera is better than finding buried treasure. Before we saw it, we'd never heard of its star, Ninon Sevilla, and now we can't wait to see some of her other movies (like 1949's Senora Tentacion and 1956's Yambao) even without subtitles and cut up with commercials on Spanish-language television channels. The pace of this 1949 Mexican film noir is breathtaking. In the first few minutes of the movie, we meet Sevilla as an innocent young girl named Elena whose mother runs off with another man. After her broken-hearted father commits suicide, Elena must find work, but every job she takes results in unwanted pawing. Finally, an old acquaintance named Lucio takes her to a nightclub, plies her with champagne, and promises to help her become a well paid secretary. Instead, Elena finds herself working for the ruthless Rosaura, owner of a Juarez brothel. Elena not only has to sing and dance for the nightclub patrons, but share her bed with them as well! As the plot thickens, we learn that Rosaura is leading a double life in Guadalajara, that Elena is a fast learner of most of life's bitter truths, and that even a knife-wielding hunchbacked thug named El Rengo is not all that he seems to be. The eight production numbers are on the same level as those in a low-budget Columbia musical of the '40s, but Sevilla's over-the-top sensuality makes them sparkle. And when she isn't singing and dancing, her skill at projecting rage and resentment helps the 101-minute running time whiz by. Many of Sevilla's best scenes are with Andrea Palma, who plays Rosaura. Both women have a million reasons to hate each other, and Sevilla and Palma give their convoluted characters a surprising degree of dramatic realism in their highly charged sequences together. None of the male actors (except for Miguel Incian as El Rengo) are in the same league as Sevilla or Palma, but at least none of them looks or sounds like Glenn Ford, the bane of bargain basement California noir. How many more gems like Aventurera are shelved in the vaults of other countries, waiting to be brought to life again on the movie screens of today? For starters, at least give us more Ninon Sevilla films, especially those with tantalizing titles like Victims of Sin and Sensuality. San Francisco's legendary Castro Movie Palace deserves credit for bringing Aventurera to contemporary audiences—we had no idea what a cinematic treat we've been missing all these years. ♪♪♪♪

1949 101m/B MX Ninon Sevilla, Andrea Palma, Miguel Incian. NYR

An Average Little Man

An Average Little Man is two films in one, really: half wildly funny, the other half gratuitously violent. Alberto Sordi, Shelley Winters, and Vincenzo Crocitti deliver superb performances as an excited family preparing for the son's (Crocitti) first examinations for employment. Their lives are normal enough until something goes hideously wrong, and the family crumbles for reasons that have nothing to do with them. The point here seems to be that life, as silly, dull, ordinary, petty, wonderful, or rewarding as it is, can be disrupted. And when it IS, the people who are left behind can never return to what they were before. When deep love and happiness end for Sordi's character, he replaces them with other feelings equally intense, that draw him into an entirely different life. Over 30 audience members missed this important point altogether when they walked out of a screening at 1977's San Francisco International Film Festival, perhaps feeling that Monicelli illustrated his viewpoint with excessive bloodletting. Based on the book by Vincenzo Cerami. *AKA:* Un Borghese Piccolo Piccolo; Gran Bollito; A Very Little Man. 🦴🦴🦴

1977 120m/C *IT* Alberto Sordi, Shelley Winters, Vincenzo Crocitti, Romolo Valli, Renzo Carboni; *D:* Mario Monicelli; *W:* Mario Monicelli, Sergio Amidei; *M:* Giancarlo Chiaramello. *NYR*

Back Street Jane

First-time feature director Ronnie Cramer may indeed have made "excellent" rock videos for his Denver band, Alarming Trends, but *Back Street Jane* is a real snoozer. The characters, all of whom are mired in the drug scene, are dull and dumb. Maybe you have to have 99 joints on the wall to get into this one. Cramer's camera work is somewhat better than his directing, which is only slightly better than his script. **WOOF!**

1989 m/B Monica McFarland, Marlene Shapiro, Sheila Ivy Traister; *D:* Ronnie Cramer; *W:* Ronnie Cramer; *C:* Ronnie Cramer. **VHS**

Backbeat

Backbeat begins with stylish titles that capture the pace and feel of the early '60s and then cuts to an absolutely perfect girl singer in a club, circa 1960: cute, dressed to the nines in a bright yellow dress and demure hair bow, and singing drekky music slightly off-key. One thing to leads to another, and the two young male protag-

onists are fighting in an alley with a gang of thugs much bigger than they are. One of them sustains severe head injuries, and his ultimate fate is left in no doubt. And somehow, in spite of all that, there's still no sense of *Here Comes Beethoven* or the lavish costume ball before the Battle of Waterloo, a real tribute to *Backbeat*'s director Iain Softley. Even though we know how the story of the Beatles will end (indeed, books exist which account for nearly every day of the group's entire career), Softley wisely chooses NOT to be comprehensive. Instead, he tells a short and simple story of how the friendship between Stuart Sutcliffe (Stephen Dorff) and John Lennon (Ian Hart) evolved as the group paid their dues in a string of grimy nightclubs in Hamburg and Liverpool. The other Beatles appear in recognizable sketch form: ambitious Paul McCartney (Gary Bakewell), dweeby George Harrison (Chris O'Neill), laconic Pete Best (Scot Williams), and even Ringo Starr, who didn't become a Beatle until 1962, is represented in a brief cameo. And then there's Astrid Kirchherr (Sheryl Lee), whose "je ne sais effin' quoi" bewitches Sutcliffe into making a decision he needed to make anyway. Never much of a musician, Sutcliffe left the band to devote more time to his art. His best friend grumbles and grumbles and grumbles about his departure (after all, with whom else can he share an evening with a couple of girls on adjoining bunk beds?) but eventually adjusts. And then, because of Act One, Scene One, the movie is over, except for the overfamiliar epilogue crawl. Still, Softley approaches potentially intimidating material in a fresh and vibrant way. Luckily for today's audiences, he is not a reverent worshipper at a well tread shrine; he is a fine, evocative storyteller. With the help of charismatic performances from Dorff, Hart, and Lee, *Backbeat* succeeds in conveying the frantic fun that was crammed into the eight days a week of another time. 🦴🦴🦴

1994 (R) 100m/C *GB* Stephen Dorff, Sheryl Lee, Ian Hart, Gary Bakewell, Chris O'Neill, Scot Williams,

Kai Wiesinger, Jennifer Ehle; *D:* Iain Softley; *W:* Michael Thomas, Stephen Ward, Iain Softley; *M:* Don Was. **VHS, LV, Closed Caption** *PGV*

Bad Lieutenant

This is a guy movie with heavy doses of Catholic gobbledy-gook. Harvey Keitel is the Bad Lieutenant, and his award-winning performance will keep you watching despite the scumminess of his character. In one sequence, he stops a couple of young girls in a car and won't let them go unless they'll let him masturbate while he ogles them—yuchhh.... "What a lech!" I overheard one male viewer yell as he laughed affectionately. Some guys worship every frame of this film and re-play the final sequence over and over again on video. Whatever turns 'em on, I guess, but

for this viewer, once was way too much. The script was co-written by Abel Ferrara and 1981's *Ms. 45* herself, Zoe Tamerlaine, now Zoe Lund. 🦴🦴

1992 (NC-17) 98m/C Harvey Keitel, Brian McElroy, Frankie Acciario, Peggy Gormley, Stella Keitel, Victor Argo, Paul Calderone, Leonard Thomas, Frankie Thorn; *D:* Abel Ferrara; *W:* Zoe Tamerlaine Lund, Abel Ferrara; *M:* Joe Delia. Independent Spirit Awards '93: Best Actor (Keitel). **VHS, LV, Closed Caption** *LIV, FCT*

The Balance

The Balance focuses on a strong, compassionate wife and career woman in her early 30s, who puts marriage, work, and self on the line for reasons that are not entirely clear to her. Maja Komorowska's performance is magnetic and warm, completely involving us in her story. The score has all the force of any of the actors here, strengthening the impact of the simplest of sequences. ♪♪♪

1975 99m/C Maja Komorowska, Piotr Fronczewski, Marek Piwowski; **D:** Krzysztof Zanussi; **W:** Krzysztof Zanussi; **C:** Slawomir Idziak; **M:** Wojciech Kilar. *NYR*

The Balcony

Joseph Strick's *The Balcony* gave Lee Grant a chance to sink her teeth into a meaty character role twelve years after her movie career was put on hold because of the Hollywood blacklist. Grant and the always over-the-top Shelley Winters portray 1963-style lesbians in Madame Irma's House of Illusion brothel. Jean Genet's plot is played out against a revolutionary backdrop and Peter Falk and Leonard Nimoy are two of Madame Irma's customers. Note: Nimoy also co-starred with Paul Mazursky and Michael Forest in Jean Genet's *Deathwatch,* the 1967 directing debut of the late Vic Morrow (1932-82). ♪♪♪

1963 87m/B Peter Falk, Shelley Winters, Lee Grant, Kent Smith, Peter Brocco, Ruby Dee, Jeff Corey, Leonard Nimoy, Joyce Jameson; **D:** Joseph Strick. Nominations: Academy Awards '63: Best Black and White Cinematography. **VHS, Beta, LV** *MFV*

The Ballad of Little Jo

Suzy Amis delivers an outstanding performance as a woman passing as a man, based on a real life character of the Old West. As unwed mother Josephine Monaghan, she is rejected by her rich family and heads west. She quickly discovers how difficult life is for a woman alone, and invents a new identity for herself as a male loner named Little Jo (who rather resembles Eric Stoltz). Ornery men quit hassling her and hopeful mothers in the nearby town think that Little Jo might make a great catch for their daughters, but Little Jo wisely tends to business and remains a loner. That is, until Little Jo becomes attracted to the hired hand (wonderfully played by David Chung), who quickly recognizes her true identity. Their subsequent relationship eases the underlying loneliness Little Jo would otherwise feel, but the endless masquerade does exact an enormous internal toll, which Amis reveals with subtle skill. Engrossing from start to finish, the film made me want to see writer/director Maggie Greenwald's other pictures, which include 1988's *Home Remedy* and the 1989 film noir, *The Kill Off.* As for Suzy Amis, her splendid work in a starring role here definitely made me wonder why her considerable talents were so squandered a year later in a nothing part in 1994's *Blown Away.* ♪♪♪

1993 (R) 110m/C Suzy Amis, Bo Hopkins, Ian McKellen, Carrie Snodgress, David Chung, Rene Auberjonois, Heather Graham, Anthony Heald, Sam Robards, Ruth Maleczech; **D:** Maggie Greenwald; **W:** Maggie Greenwald; **M:** David Mansfield. Nominations: Independent Spirit Awards '94: Best Actress (Amis). **VHS, Closed Caption** *COL*

The Ballad of the Sad Cafe

Quick: you're casting a movie set in a Depression-era mill town in the South and you need someone to play Miss Amelia, a love-starved local recluse. Who's the first person on your short list? Outstanding actress that she is, Vanessa Redgrave does not spring immediately to mind. Did anyone try to contact, say, Sissy Spacek or Shelley Duvall? This screen adaptation of Carson McCullers' *The Ballad of the Sad Cafe* shows how three miscast Oscar winners can flounder under the guidance of an inexperienced, first-time director. British character actor Simon Callow has been seen to good effect in the Merchant Ivory films *Room with a View* and *Maurice* as well as *The Good Father,* but he's out of his depth with such an ambitious first project. The first few minutes offer a good clue as to what will be wrong with the rest of the film. There are several vignettes of varying length which are supposed to show something about the characters in this town, only they don't. Unfortunately, none of the vignettes build on each other and

b

WHIT STILLMAN
Barcelona

You really noticed it [Anti-Americanism] back then [the film is set in the early '80s in Spain]. It was before Spain had decided to join NATO. There was a big debate about Spain joining NATO. There was a lot of resentment of the United States and American foreign policy. And then kind of a personal, somewhat snobbish, looking down at Americans and American habits. It was a bit contradictory because at the same time there was an embracing of a lot of American popular culture and movies in a way that they're not even embraced here.... Sharon Stone is sort of a national goddess and serious, political columnists and commentators on the left devote columns to Sharon Stone, and then they sort of lambaste our vulgar popular culture, and I think that they sort of haven't put things properly in perspective.

"Ted Boynton [Taylor Nichols, as one of the two American main characters] has gotten into sales through no fault of his own, but he's trying to make a career out of it. His cousin comes to visit. His cousin is Fred [Christopher Eigeman, as the other American main character] who comes from San Francisco and is a Navy Lieutenant J.G., but he's not a typical Navy guy at all. He's more of a cynical, glib PR guy. He's the advance man for the sixth fleet and a real pain in the neck for his cousin.... I had to cut a lot of the intellectual talk because you can have too much of it, and I could only have stuff that related in some way to their character or the plot.

"[The code the Spanish women lived by] was something similar to a feeling in the United States in the '70s. In this case it was more profound and more widespread and it lasted longer. I think it was that feeling when the sexual stereotypes of the past had been overthrown, and the sexual roles about who was going to choose a sexual partner was changed. Barcelona was the most progressive advanced city in Spain, and women from Barcelona were famous in Spain as being women who were in control of their lives and their sexual lives. There was this feeling that they would decide who they slept with and they'd sleep with either nobody or anybody, and that sex was something to be enjoyed. It was definitely pre-venereal disease sensibility, pre-AIDS sensibility. It was kind of a wild feeling from an American point of view. It was so different from the feeling in the United States in the early '80s when everything sort of slipped back into old forms, old roles, and people had sort of been a little bit burned by some of the stuff that had been going on in the '70s and were withdrawing and getting back into a calmer, quieter, more monogamous life."

WHIT STILLMAN also wrote and directed 1990's *Metropolitan.*

there's nothing particularly riveting about any of the images that Callow selects. After nearly an hour, the story begins with the arrival of Miss Amelia's husband, portrayed by Keith Carradine, and the last half of the film sets us up for their final confrontation, a fist fight in which neither pulls a single punch. It's probably the least exciting fist fight we've ever seen on film, although Callow certainly tries hard to make it seem as if it OUGHT to be. There are, for example, countless close-ups of the spectators wringing their handkerchiefs. We've never seen a screen fight in which both fighters lead with their chins so much. Redgrave and Carradine successfully aim for each other's teeth throughout the entire fight, and fail to lose a single tooth. Stylistic decision or bad choreography? Redgrave and Carradine ignite no onscreen sparks alone or together. At one point, Redgrave and Cork Hubbert go to see a movie in a neighboring town. The newsreels are crammed with F.D.R., but the unlikely feature attraction is a 1929 Hoover-era flop with Norma Talmadge and Gilbert Roland, *New York Nights.* Of all the cast, Hubbert fares the best with Callow's over-the-top direction, but everyone, even Redgrave and the extras, is somewhat guilty of overacting. The worst offender is Rod Steiger, in a small part as a preacher who invests his relatively brief screen time with enough subtext for twenty five roles. It's hard to tell whether Callow was intimidated by his star-studded cast, the material, the period, or the locale, but nothing about *The Ballad of the Sad Cafe* seems real. It's more like a travelogue you might be forced to sit through in Quaintness 101. Callow will be more fondly remembered for the lovable character who stuck his finger down his throat in a folk-style wedding service during 1994's *Four Weddings and a Funeral.* ♫♫

1991 (PG-13) 100m/C *GB* Vanessa Redgrave, Keith Carradine, Cork Hubbert, Rod Steiger, Austin Pendleton, Beth Dixon, Lanny Flaherty, Mert Hatfield, Earl Hindman, Anne Pitoniak; *D:* Simon Callow; *W:* Michael Hirst; *C:* Walter Lassally; *M:* Richard Robbins. **VHS, LV, Closed Caption** *COL*

Barcelona

It's good to see Christopher Eigeman (as Fred) in a movie again, four years after *Metropolitan.* Taylor Nichols is in it, too, as his cousin Ted. I once traveled to Paris with a couple of brothers from Spain and the rivalry between them crowded out any other social possibilities for the trip. Like them, Fred and Ted's rivalry never lets up for an instant, but since they're in a movie and they are Eigeman and Taylor, it's a treat to listen to them bicker about sex and politics, politics and sex. (I might not want to travel with them, though.) Fred is beautifully unaware what a jerk he is, while Ted does have a nagging awareness that he IS a twit. Fred's first words to Ted in a Barcelona hospital are priceless. All this, and Mira Sorvino, too! Another winner for writer/director Whit Stillman. ♫♫♫

1994 (PG-13) 102m/C Taylor Nichols, Christopher Eigeman, Tushka Bergen, Mira Sorvino, Pep Munne, Francis Creighton, Thomas Gibson, Jack Gilpin, Nuria Badia, Hellena Schmied; *D:* Whit Stillman; *W:* Whit Stillman; *M:* Tom Judson, Mark Suozzo. Independent Spirit Awards '95: Best Cinematography. **VHS, LV** *NLC, TTC, IME*

Barefoot Gen

Animation often has the curious effect of lulling us into a false sense of security. We expect that the appealing images onscreen will amuse and entertain us, but not make us think too deeply or cry. The 1955 British version of George Orwell's *Animal Farm* changed our perceptions of what an animated film could be. 1983's *Barefoot Gen* offers a devastating contrast to live action films like MGM's *Above and Beyond,* which idealized the bombers of Hiroshima by casting cinematic icon Robert Taylor as the pilot. Artist Keiji Nakazawa was six years old when his home was destroyed by the bombing of Hiroshima on August 6, 1945. Miraculously, he survived, and 28 years later he published *Barefoot Gen,* based on his own experiences on that fateful day. Nakazawa hoped one day to develop the cartoon into

**Jeffrey Wright
expresses himself
in *Basquiat*.**

a feature-length film, and at 48 he finally achieved his dream. *Barefoot Gen* is the powerful result. The film starts out by giving us a bit of background on World War II, then shifts to the antics of two little boys. We know what an impact the war has made on their lives; they fight over a potato before reluctantly sharing it with their mother who is expecting another baby. Because of their enormous vitality, the irrepressible children take center stage and the war seems like a distant backdrop. The impact of the bombing, however, is enormous and immediate. Familiar characters are reduced to skeletons within seconds. The collapse of Gen's world is shown in a wrenching sequence when he must decide to save himself and his expectant mother rather than die with the rest of his family. Except for the sudden loss of his hair, Gen appears to have

emerged unscathed from the bombing, but the tragic aftereffects of the Hiroshima bombing are everywhere. A soldier, not realizing what has happened to him, dies in a daze right in front of Gen. Gen's frail mother gives birth to an adorable little girl, but cannot feed her. Another woman who has lost her child tries to kill the infant, but then bursts into tears and offers to nurse the baby for her. Gen forages for food, finally stumbling on an unaffected cache of rice. An orphan appears on the scene, the exact double of Gen's doomed brother. He is instantly adopted into the family and the film's lighthearted vitality returns, but with a difference. To earn money to buy milk for the baby, the children accept a disagreeable job: taking care of a former artist whose family has rejected him now that he is disabled. Simply by being children, the little boys ignite his flagging spirits and his will to live and work, but there are no Pollyanna endings in *Barefoot Gen*. Gen's resilience is the theme of this deeply disturbing movie, and it is highly recommended for both adults and older children (over age 12). 🦴🦴🦴🦴

1983 90m/C *JP* **D:** Mamoru Shinzaki; **W:** Keiji Nakazawa; **M:** Kentaro Hada. *NYR*

Basquiat

Jean Michel Basquiat is not exactly a household name today, although he has all the ingredients for legendary status: early fame, early death, umpteen mentions in Andy Warhol's diary, etc. He was an artist who slept on the streets, but believed he was fresh as a daisy (although Warhol's diaries say otherwise). At his scruffiest, he romances waitress Gina Cardinale (Claire Forlani); their moments together are the least interesting in the film. There are other rewards in Julian Schnabel's onscreen study of his fellow artist, though. David Bowie, who had the benefit of the most personal contact with Warhol, is the third actor to play him since 1991. (Crispin Glover and Jared Harris preceded him in *The Doors* and *I Shot Andy Warhol*.) Although the physical resemblance isn't particularly striking, Bowie is otherwise persuasive as Basquiat's patron and friend. The fickle cruelty of the New York art world is rendered with economic precision in a vivid restaurant sequence. Moreover, the evolution of Basquiat's longtime friendship with Benny Dalmau (colorfully played by Benicio Del Toro) reveals how Basquiat is changed as the opinion of his new acquaintances comes to mean more to him than he may care to admit. Familiar folks from other indie flicks (Dennis Hopper as a shrewd art buyer, Gary Oldman as artist Albert Milo, plus Willem Dafoe, Parker Posey, Elina Lowensohn, Paul Bartel, and Courtney Love) help to enhance *Basquiat*'s sense of time and place. Christopher Walken has his usual one sequence as a nut (an interviewer this time), and Tatum O'Neal, then 32, drifts in and out of focus in a bit as a stereotypical (mindless, rich) customer. At the core, Jeffrey Wright plays Basquiat as gifted, sweet, and hell-bent on accumulating an impressive resume before the ultimate fix. *Basquiat* boasts an excellent soundtrack. (Recommended for further research: Mary Woronov's terrific 1995 book, *Swimming Underground*, which spares no one in Andy Warhol's set, least of all herself.) **AKA:** Build a Fort Set It on Fire. 🦴🦴🦴

1996 (R) 108m/C Jeffrey Wright, David Bowie, Dennis Hopper, Gary Oldman, Christopher Walken, Michael Wincott, Benicio Del Toro, Parker Posey, Elina Lowensohn, Courtney Love, Claire Forlani, Willem Dafoe, Paul Bartel, Tatum O'Neal, Chuck Pfeiffer; **D:** Julian Schnabel; **W:** Julian Schnabel; **C:** Ron Fortunato; **M:** John Cale. Independent Spirit Awards '97: Best Supporting Actor (Del Toro); Nominations: Independent Spirit Awards '97: Debut Performance (Wright). **VHS, LV, Closed Caption** *MAX*

Bastard out of Carolina

This exceptional first film by director Anjelica Huston was first intended for broadcast on Turner Network Television, which would have aired it with commercials. It was actually a blessing that it first aired on the Showtime Network without interruption ten days before Christmas. (Showtime had originally planned to make the film until director Allison Anders resigned, then it wound up at TNT with Huston and the rest is history.) There is no tasteful way to show the horror of child abuse on film without running into the *Rashomon* syndrome: did that nice-looking stepfather actually rape his wife's daughter? Did the little girl provoke him? Seduce him? Lie? Then it becomes a mystery and takes the point of view away from the child. Twelve-year-old Jena Malone is remarkable as "Bone" Boatwright, whose performance was partly inspired by her conversations with a close friend who experienced child abuse. With her sad little face and frail physical presence, Malone would break

"When I speak nobody believes me, but when I write it down everybody knows it to be true."

—Michael Wincott as Rene Ricard in *Basquiat*.

anyone's heart, but her ability to communicate how she internalizes her wretched life is her greatest strength as an actress here. Top-billed Jennifer Jason Leigh is less satisfactory as her mother, Anney. Leigh tends to work from the outside in; sometimes it works spectacularly well, sometimes it doesn't. By playing Anney in a perpetual daze, she's outclassed here by fellow cast members Grace Zabriskie, Diana Scarwid, Christina Ricci, and best of all, Glenne Headley. Fortunately, Leigh's straight-line, untextured interpretation doesn't compromise the film, since the toughest acting assignment belongs to Ron Eldard as Glen Waddell. Eldard had previously done an expert job playing a loose cannon with surface appeal named Shep opposite Julianna Margulies' Carol Hathaway on *E.R.* His violent impulses come from a different place as the repellent Glen, and you can see why he would attract outsiders while carrying on his own private war of nerves with Bone. He's diseased, but frighteningly sane, and his eroticism is clearly detached from the target of his abuse. The sequences revealing Glen's abuse of Bone are so clear and so real that you'll want to jump into the narrative and tear her away from him, which may be the whole point of *Bastard out of Carolina*. It isn't exposure of child abuse that destroys families, but the abuse itself, a distinction that hasn't always been made entirely clear in previous movies that focus on this crime against children. Huston's directorial debut is a bold, brave film with no easy answers, but with plenty of haunting questions about the never ending nightmares that represent childhood for far too many children on this planet. Based on the best-selling novel by Dorothy Allison. 𝄞𝄞𝄞𝄞

1996 (R) 97m/C Jennifer Jason Leigh, Jena Malone, Ron Eldard, Glenne Headly, Lyle Lovett, Dermot Mulroney, Christina Ricci, Michael Rooker, Diana Scarwid, Susan Traylor, Grace Zabriskie; *D:* Anjelica Huston; *W:* Anne Meredith; *C:* Anthony B. Richmond; *M:* Van Dyke Parks. Nominations: Independent Spirit Awards '97: Debut Performance (Malone). **VHS** *BMG*

The Battle of the Sexes

The Catbird Seat is treasured by James Thurber fans for taking the sort of teeth-gnashing experience everyone dreads and discovering an ingenious way out of it. Mr. Martin (Peter Sellers) is a quiet Edinburgh accountant for Mr. Macpherson's (Robert Morley) textile company. He wishes to be left alone and he certainly leaves everyone else alone. That is, until Angela Barrows (Constance Cummings) arrives on the job. Mrs. Barrows (there's no polite way to say this) is an...American efficiency expert. She has the effect on shy Mr. Martin of a new piece of chalk S-C-R-E-E-C-H-I-N-G against a chalk board. She's loud. She has her own, very definite agenda. She lives in her own world. Regrettably, that world happens to be Mr. Martin's world, too, and he was here first! Mr. Martin is very unhappy. But then he realizes there is a solution in sight: he decides there's nothing for it but to murder Mrs. Barrows. What happens next is the stuff of which classic British comedies are made. Director Charles Crichton skillfully escalates the war of nerves between Mrs. Barrows and old Mr. Martin (Cummings was 49 and Sellers was 34, but he'd specialized in playing elderly characters for years). The character actors are first rate: Ernest Thesiger is Mr. Macpherson, Senior (right!) and Michael Goodliffe is charmingly dry as a detective. 𝄞𝄞𝄞

1960 88m/B *GB* Peter Sellers, Robert Morley, Constance Cummings, Jameson Clark, Ernest Thesiger, Donald Pleasence, Moultrie Kelsall, Alex Mackenzie, Roddy McMillan, Michael Goodliffe, Norman MacOwen, William Mervyn; *D:* Charles Crichton; *W:* Monja Danischewsky; *C:* Freddie Francis; *M:* Stanley Black. **VHS, Beta** *MRV*

Beat the Devil

This was Bogie's and Huston's sixth and final film together. Huston and Capote intended it to be an Italian-style satire of

The Maltese Falcon, but audiences of the '50s failed to appreciate it on that level. Television viewers and revival house devotees finally got the joke. It's a kick to watch and so different from the studio films Bogie and Huston made in the '40s. NO ONE receives a flattering gaze from cinematographer Oswald Morris, and Jennifer Jones is not treated like a delicate china doll or an unearthly creature as she is in most of her other pictures. Robert Morley (who was in *The African Queen* with Bogie) is Petersen, a part clearly designed for Sydney Greenstreet, and Peter Lorre, in his fifth and final movie with Bogie, appears as O'Hara! At one point, Bogie, Jones, Gina Lollobrigida, Morley, Lorre, Edward Underdown, and Ivor Barnard are hauled into the police station and only released when Bogie promises the officer that he will arrange for him to meet his idol, Rita Hayworth! Great fun. Based on the novel by James Helvick. 🦴🦴🦴

1953 89m/C Humphrey Bogart, Gina Lollobrigida, Peter Lorre, Robert Morley, Jennifer Jones, Edward Underdown, Ivor Barnard, Bernard Lee, Marco Tulli; ***D:*** John Huston; ***W:*** John Huston, Truman Capote; ***C:*** Oswald Morris. **VHS, Beta, LV, Closed Caption** *MRV, NOS, COL*

Beauty and the Beast

For many people, Jean Cocteau's 1946 version of *Beauty and the Beast* is the loveliest film ever made and one of the few that we wish we could go back in time to see again for the very first time. (The only American film of that era with even a fraction of its sense of imagination, wonder, and style is Val Lewton's 1944 classic *Curse of the Cat People,* most notably the sequences in the enchanted garden when Simone Simon as an ethereal ghost romps with Ann Carter as a lonely little girl.) *Beauty and the Beast* is a classic fairy tale about loneliness and love. Beauty (Josette Day) is a hard-working girl with simple tastes and very few dreams. She agrees to stay with the Beast mainly to save her father's life

after he steals a rose from the Beast's garden to bring home to her. But the Beast (Jean Marais) is gentle and honest with her and she begins to care about him. The Academy of Motion Picture Arts and Sciences was napping in 1946 when Cocteau's exquisite *Le Belle et le Bete* was released. *Beauty and the Beast* seldom fails to wrap its spell around those who still believe in fairy tales and Jean Cocteau believed in them with a passion all his life. Although he is faithful to a child's eye view of fairy tales, his film is filled with surreal visions and sly humor for adult appreciation. ***AKA:*** La Belle et le Bete. 🦴🦴🦴🦴

1946 90m/B *FR* Jean Marais, Josette Day, Marcel Andre, Mila Parely, Nane Germon, Michel Auclair, Georges Auric; ***D:*** Jean Cocteau. **VHS, Beta, LV** *HMV, MLB, CRC*

Bedazzled

Nowadays, when we discuss the Seven Deadly Sins, we don't kid around, but in the Swinging '60s, Peter Cook and Dudley Moore got away with it in this side-splitting Faustian comedy, co-scripted by its stars. Cook (1937-95) is The Devil, George Spiggot; Moore, then 32, is Stanley Moon, Wimpy's short order cook. Stanley is desperately in love with Wimpy's counter girl, Margaret Spencer (Eleanor Bron, 33), and George offers him seven wishes in exchange for his soul. In his pursuit of Margaret, Stanley squanders them, but he does get a rather good understanding of the Devil and the chance to meet all Seven Deadly Sins. Raquel Welch, 27, is Lillian Lust. (And yes, that IS Dame Edna Everage's alter ego as Envy!) The pleasure of watching Cook and Moore work together was shared by Brits and Americans alike for the better part of two decades. Some of the funniest sight gags and most incisive dialogue in *Bedazzled* represent the best of their work in British television. Cook and Moore also won two Tonys and a Grammy together (plus two other Grammy nominations) for their bright, satirical work as a team. At 43, Moore emigrated to Hol-

MILCHO MANCHEVSKY

Before the Rain

The film sort of came out of my trip back to Macedonia. I live in New York and I spend most of my time in New York. I went back to Macedonia for the first time in a long period. Just being back sort of pushed me to write something very personal for myself, and coming from the inside. Also, going back at the time when the civil war in the Balkans was just beginning, while it was still brewing and before there was any real violence, I got this sensation of a great expectation, of something in the air, of this pressure like just before it's going to rain, when you feel pressure inside your mouth, when it's just going to open up and go loose.

"There was both enormous potential and difficulties [with the fact that the Macedonian villages hadn't changed in hundreds of years]. The potential being the look of the villages because we tried to recreate this ancient archaic look. Because part of what we were trying to say in the film was that this kind of behavior, and this kind of reaction to thy neighbor goes back hundreds of years. At first, actually, as people start watching the film there's a lot of them who think it's a period piece the first five or ten minutes of the film. We very consciously wanted to achieve that. The difficulties, however, were that most of these places were very difficult to access. Usually, the better the place looks the more

lywood and quickly established himself as an Oscar-nominated movie star. Except for a 16-month comedy series in the early '80s (that lasted eight times longer than TWO of Moore's comedy series in the '90s), Cook remained in England. He drank, put on weight (he once joked about playing Fat King Farouk), accepted cameo roles, and died too young of an intestinal hemorrhage. Until another bright, satirical team, Stephen Fry and Hugh Laurie, arrived on the scene, Peter Cook and Dudley Moore were regarded by many comedy buffs as two of Britain's wittiest treasures. (Other Cook-Moore films: *The Wrong Box* and *Those Daring Young Men in Their Jaun-*

ty *Jalopies*. Skip Paul Morissey's *The Hound of the Baskervilles!*) 🦴🦴🦴🦴

1968 (PG) 107m/C *GB* Dudley Moore, Peter Cook, Eleanor Bron, Michael Bates, Raquel Welch, Bernard Spear, Parnell McGarry, Howard Goorney, Daniele Noel, Barry Humphries, Robert Russell, Lockwood West, Robin Hawdon, Evelyn Moore, Charles Lloyd Pack; *D:* Stanley Donen; *W:* Dudley Moore, Peter Cook; *C:* Austin Dempster; *M:* Dudley Moore. **VHS, Beta, LV** *FOX*

Before the Rain

Aleksandar (Rade Serbedzija) left Macedonia to live and work in London as a photog-

difficult to access it is. For a couple of them, we had to build little stretches of roads so that we could bring the equipment and the people there. I would very much want to thank everyone who let us work in their houses, who just opened their doors and let us shoot there and let us trample all over their vegetables. They were very, very warm and very open to us, and accepted us in the various villages, because we kept moving so it wasn't just one or two places. We were constantly on the move. The film captures pretty much every corner of Macedonia, even though it makes it look like only two places.

"The expectation and the buildup are such that people get more involved in waiting for the violence to happen. It's fairly realistic in that it doesn't just happen to someone out there, and it just doesn't happen to a Stallone foe, but it happens to people that we know. And I think this is the key, I think we get to care about these people. We spend a long time with them, and once we accept them as our friends, when something happens to them, it's as if it's happening to friends in real life. So we get much more affected, we do care much more about them. I've seen people cry at screenings, and it really surprised me as I never expected that to happen. I think it's this association, this caring about the characters, that makes the violence in this film seem more violent. But even if the film itself were more violent, I wouldn't mind it because it's still nothing compared to the real violence taking place in a few places in the world as we speak, so I'm not embarrassed to show it. I don't think we should ignore what is going on at this moment."

rapher many years ago. He returns to his former homeland as a war correspondent and is saddened by what his country has become. He is witness to an execution in Bosnia shortly before he goes back to see what has become of his old village. War is everywhere, ignited by racial hatred. Milcho Manchevski divides the narrative into three chapters: "Words," which shows how a monk named Kiril (Gregoire Colin of 1993's *Pas Tres Catholique*) is affected by Zamira (Labina Mitevska) when she seeks shelter in a monastery; "Faces," which focuses on Aleksandar's intimate relationship with Anne (Katrin Cartlidge), a photographic editor who is expecting a baby;

and "Pictures," revealing a country under siege. **AKA:** Po Dezju. 🦴🦴🦴

1994 120m/C *GB FR MA* Rade Serbedzija, Katrin Cartlidge, Gregoire Colin, Labina Mitevska; **D:** Milcho Manchevski; **W:** Milcho Manchevski; **C:** Manuel Teran; **M:** Anastasia. Independent Spirit Awards '96: Best Foreign Film; Venice Film Festival '94: Golden Lion; Nominations: Academy Awards '94: Best Foreign Language Film. **VHS** *PGV*

The Belles of St. Trinian's

If there's anything more inviting than the prospect of the great Alastair Sim in a comedy, it would be TWO Alastair Sims, one of them in drag as Miss Fitton, Headmistress of St. Trinian's School for Young Ladies, the other as her brother, Clarence. The story is inspired by the cartoons of Ronald Searle, first published in *Punch* magazine. The Belles, to put it mildly, are bloody terrors—frightening schoolmistresses, local merchants, and even the police. The plot is a born-again screwball comedy, with Joyce Grenfell, Hermione Baddeley, Beryl Reid, Guy Middleton, and Richard Wattis getting mixed up in some of the funniest situations. Sidney James and Joan Sims would later work together in the long-running series of *Carry On* comedies. There were four *St. Trinian's* comedies in all: 1957's *Blue Murder at St. Trinian's,* 1960's *The Pure Hell of St. Trinian's,* and 1966's *The Great St. Trinian's Train Robbery.* George Cole was in all of them as Flash Harry, but he (and we) would miss Sim, who bowed out after handing over the reins to Terry Thomas in *Blue Murder.* (Cecil Parker and Frankie Howard received top billing in the last two entries.) 🦴🦴🦴

1953 86m/B *GB* Alastair Sim, Joyce Grenfell, Hermione Baddeley, George Cole, Eric Pohlmann, Renee Houston, Beryl Reid, Balbina, Jill Braidwood, Annabelle Covey, Betty Ann Davies, Diana Day, Jack Doyle, Irene Handl, Arthur Howard, Sidney James, Lloyd Lamble, Jean Langston, Belinda Lee, Vivian Martin, Andree Melly, Mary Merrall, Guy Middleton, Joan Sims, Jerry Verno, Richard Wattis; **D:** Frank Launder; **W:** Frank Launder, Sidney Gilliat, Val Valentine; **C:** Stanley Pavey; **M:** Malcolm Arnold, Malcolm Arnold. **VHS, Beta** *REP*

Bellissima

Luchino Visconti's *Bellissima* focuses on a marginal fixture at Cinecitta studios: the ubiquitous stage mother. Anna Magnani wants stardom for her little girl and a better life for her small brood. In America, the stage mother is rarely shown as anything other than a selfish, conniving bitch who mercilessly exploits her offspring: the 1955 performance of Jo Van Fleet as Lillian Roth's mother in Daniel Mann's *I'll Cry Tomorrow* is a good example. But in Italy, with a director willing to examine the economic conditions that ignited stage mothers, stardom for children is shown as an escape from poverty for entire families. Magnani's deep emotional understanding of her character lets her get away with sequences which few other actresses could inject with sympathy. *Bellissima* is marred by a moralistic and unbelievable conclusion that Visconti reportedly fought hard to resist. Like all of Magnani's films, however, *Bellissima* demands compulsive attention because of the riveting presence of its star. 🦴🦴🦴

1951 130m/B *IT* Anna Magnani, Walter Chiari, Alessandro Blasetti, Tina Apicella, Gastone Renzelli; **D:** Luchino Visconti; **W:** Luchino Visconti, Cesare Zavattini, Francesco Rosi, Suso Cecchi D'Amico. **VHS** *CIG, APD*

Bellman and True

Bellman and True, a British thriller produced by George Harrison, is a bare-bones crime saga about computers, blood, and money, with a no-star cast and senseless characters. At one point, one crook tells another not to try to be Michael Caine, but in fact, Caine or Bob Hoskins or Peter O'Toole might be just what the doctor ordered to punch up this movie. We say "might be," because a magnetic star would still have to contend with novelist Desmond Lowden's script, which he wrote with director Richard Loncraine. What's supposed to be unusual about this story is that its central character, invisibly played by Bernard Hill, presumably cares about his young stepson, Kieran O'Brien. However, he's constantly endangering the kid's life and exposing him to vicious gangsters. There's a woman in the plot, Frances Tomelty, but she makes even less sense than the men. (Footnote: Bernard Hill played John Lennon in the 1974 Willy Russell musical, *John, Paul, George, Ringo...and Bert* opposite Trevor Eve as Paul McCartney, Phillip Joseph as George Harrison, and Antony Sher as Ringo Starr.) 🦴🦴

1988 (R) 112m/C *GB* Bernard Hill, Kieran O'Brien, Richard Hope, Frances Tomelty, Derek Newark, John Kavanagh, Ken Bones; *D:* Richard Loncraine; *W:* Richard Loncraine, Desmond Lowden; *M:* Colin Towns. **VHS, Beta** *MGM, CAN, VES*

The Belly of an Architect

Many of the press corps laughed hysterically at Peter Greenaway's *The Belly of an Architect,* starring Brian Dennehy and Chloe Webb. They laughed at things like Dennehy plunging headfirst onto the roof of a car at the same time as wife Webb's baby was being born. Obviously, Greenaway's work is fraught with humor that you have to be on the same wave length to appreciate. The title, by the way, is literal. You will see more extreme close-ups of Dennehy's bulging stomach than you can possibly imagine. As counterpoint, much of the two-hour film was shot with the principal action in extreme long shots, which makes this film a nightmare to watch on television or video. When Dennehy goes berserk at an outdoor restaurant, for example, Greenaway focuses on two female extras. When Dennehy is spying on Webb's fling with a rotter named Caspasian Speckler, we can barely see either one of them. The plot is your standard older-man-is-dying-while-his-pretty-young-wife-has-an-affair-with-an-Italian, but it kept several film critics in stitches, anyway. Confession 1: We missed every single in-joke. Question 1: Why are figs funny? Confession 2: We do not know who Etienne-Louis Boullee is. Question 2: What is so side-splitting about the name Stourley Kracklite? This movie plus Fred Zinneman's similarly themed *Five Days One Summer,* plus Mary Lambert's one-of-a-kind *Siesta,* is yet another addition to our growing list of triple bills from hell. Trivia note: France's Lambert Wilson plays just about the same part in both the Zinneman film and in *The Belly of an Architect.* **WOOF!**

1991 (R) 119m/C *GB IT* Brian Dennehy, Chloe Webb, Lambert Wilson; *D:* Peter Greenaway; *W:* Peter Greenaway. **VHS, LV** *NO*

The Best Way

Claude Miller worked with Francois Truffaut on eight movies before he made the shift from assistant to director. Unlike Truffaut, Miller's view of life is harsh and blunt. Marc, the major character in *The Best Way,* is discovered romping alone in woman's clothing by Philippe, a fellow boy's camp director. The two begin a brutal, uneasy relationship, with Marc (Patrick Bouchitey) consistently cast as underdog. Philippe (Patrick Dewaere) taunts Marc, belittles him, tosses him in the water, even hits him, and still Marc comes back for more. At the end, an unusual resolution occurs between the two, and Miller stages it with tense excitement. By this time, he has drawn us into Marc's humiliation so completely that we are nearly as involved in his pain as he is. Sadly, both Dewaere and Christine Pascal ended their thriving careers by committing suicide, Dewaere at 35 in 1982 and Pascal at 42 in 1996. *AKA:* The Best Way to Walk; La Meilleure Facon de Marcher. 🦴🦴🦴

1976 85m/C *FR* Patrick Dewaere, Patrick Bouchitey, Christine Pascal, Claude Pieplu; *D:* Claude Miller; *W:* Luc Beraud, Claude Miller; *C:* Bruno Nuytten; *M:* Alain Jomy. **VHS, Beta** *FCT*

Betrayed

The films of Costa-Gavras are often complicated, controversial, and disturbing. *Betrayed* is all three. When we see a man onscreen who appears to be a dutiful son, a kind father, and a considerate lover, we draw certain conclusions about his character. So, unfortunately, does federal agent Debra Winger, who is assigned to investigate the allegedly homicidal white supremacist character portrayed by Tom Berenger. The film's approach requires considerable courage to sustain, and its harsh observations about some aspects of this country put some of its original audiences on the defensive. It may remind others of Alfred Hitchcock's 1946 classic

Notorious, in which Ingrid Bergman sleeps with Nazi Claude Rains and reports to her lover, American agent Cary Grant, who punishes her with his obvious resentment and disapproval of the sexual work he requires her to do. *Notorious* was fairly kinky for its era, but with *Betrayed,* Costa-Gavras is concerned with far more fundamental issues. The rootless, parentless Winger finds herself falling in love with Berenger and disconnecting from her agency contact John Heard. If she loves her target, he can't be a neo-Nazi, can he? He even hates the Nazi uniform and those who wear it. Her job becomes uglier to her, and more duplicitous. Winger perfectly captures the numbness of a human being who must deny her own feelings in order to survive. Berenger, too, gives his impossible role so much understanding that it's hard to imagine almost any other contemporary actor in the role. Their gritty scenes together are stripped of glamour, which lends their tortured love considerable credibility. Also outstanding are John Mahoney, one of the finest character actors alive today, as a decent man who rationalizes the evil he does, and a beautiful seven-year-old child named Maria Valdez as Berenger's ingratiating daughter. Screenwriter Joe Eszterhas succeeds in showing how complicated personal ethics become once you start caring about someone. People outside gnarled relationships might wonder how anyone could give a damn about a homophobic, racist murderer, particularly a sane one. Costa-Gavras suggests some uncomfortable answers; it's well worth checking out *Betrayed* to discover them. 🎬🎬🎬

1988 (R) 112m/C Tom Berenger, Debra Winger, John Mahoney, John Heard, Albert Hall, Jeffrey DeMunn; **D:** Constantin Costa-Gavras; **W:** Joe Eszterhas; **C:** Patrick Blossier. **VHS, Beta, LV, Closed Caption** *MGM*

Beware of Pity

Stefan Zweig was an idealistic Austrian writer whose dreams of a united Europe were shattered by World War II. In 1942, he fled with his wife to Brazil where both committed suicide. Zweig left behind an impressive body of work, including several biographies, a novel called *Beware of Pity,* and many short stories, including "The Royal Game" and "Letter from an Unknown Woman," filmed by Max Ophuls for Universal in 1948. Maurice Elvey directed *Beware of Pity* in 1946 as a vehicle for two German expatriate stars, Lilli Palmer and the formally cool Albert Lieven, then 40. Although Palmer was then 35, her onscreen specialty between 1935 and 1986 was playing bewitching leading ladies and she is altogether compelling as the rich and youthful Baroness Edith. An extended ballroom sequence reveals her immediate infatuation with Lieven's aloof Lieutenant Anton Marek. Unfortunately, the large-eyed beauty has been crippled by an accident, rendering her an unsuitable dance partner, not to mention an ineligible bride, at least in HIS eyes. Her crush evolves into a lifelong obsession, and Marek's distaste for her is barely concealed by patronizing segues and ultra-polite humor. The more she reveals her love for him, the more he shuns her, until she is forced to recognize how far apart their feelings are. The best acting in the film is delivered by Dame Gladys Cooper, then 58, who began her movie career at 25 and was something of a real-life pin-up girl during World War I. There's not a shred of self-pity in her immaculate performance as the blind wife of the Baroness' doctor, who tries hard to change destiny. We can never figure out whether *Beware of Pity* is some sort of a tribute to a self-contained careerist or if the conscience-ridden Zweig was trying to show the enormous damage emotional clods wreak on their love-starved victims. Either way, *Beware of Pity* is a beautifully filmed tale of romantic longing with expert playing by the two leads. It is also a wistful reminder of the irreplaceable pre-Sarajevo days that inevitably evoke fairy tales through their sheer visual loveliness. But the emotional

b

37

INDEPENDENT FILM GUIDE

Opposite page: **Dennis Quaid and Ellen Barkin in *The Big Easy.***

rot has sunk in already; there's never-ending isolation and suffering for the victimized Baroness and a pointless series of military pursuits for the walled-off Lieutenant. ♪♪♪

1946 129m/B Lilli Palmer, Albert Lieven, Cedric Hardwicke, Gladys Cooper, Ernest Thesiger, Freda Jackson, Linden Travers, Ralph Truman, Peter Cotes, Jenny Laird, Emrys Jones, Gerhard Kempinski, John Salew, Kenneth Warrington; *D:* Maurice Elvey; *W:* W.P. Lipscomb, Elizabeth Barron, Margaret Steen. **VHS** *HMK*

The Big Easy

Although purists might deny that today's color film noir efforts approach the excellence of the crisp black-and-white noir visions of another time, *The Big Easy* by Daniel Petrie, Jr., certainly comes close. One of the best things about the film is its realistic depiction of sex between two people who don't know each other very well. Only in the movies are such pairings flawless, and *The Big Easy* shows some of the timing and pacing problems which are more true to real life. Then, the script keeps the mismatched couple at odds with each other for most of the film, and with gifted actors like Dennis Quaid and Ellen Barkin, the resulting undercurrents in emotion between the pair are more erotic than a dozen bedroom scenes would be. The New Orleans atmosphere and music add spice to this tale of a cop and a lawyer investigating police corruption in the New South, and the supporting cast members, with the exception of one wimp of a villain, are extremely well chosen. A bit by perennial film noir heavy Marc Lawrence adds to the fun. ♪♪♪

1987 (R) 101m/C Dennis Quaid, Ellen Barkin, Ned Beatty, John Goodman, Ebbe Roe Smith, Charles

Ludlam, Lisa Jane Persky, Tom O'Brien, Grace Zabriskie, Marc Lawrence; *D:* Jim McBride; *W:* Dan Petrie Jr.; *C:* Alfonso Beato; *M:* Brad Fiedel. Independent Spirit Awards '88: Best Actor (Quaid). **VHS, Beta, LV, Closed Caption** *HBO, FCT*

Big Night

This excellent film is to struggling owners of small Italian restaurants what *Strictly Ballroom* is to Open Amateurs dancing on Federation steps at the Pan Pacific Grand Prix championships. *Big Night* takes a look at Primo and Secondo Pilaggi, two Italian brothers living and working in 1950s New Jersey: Primo (Tony Shalhoub), a genius chef who can't promote, and Secondo (Stanley Tucci), a genius promoter who can't begin to approach his brother's skill in the kitchen. Each needs the other and each resents the other. They continue to do what they do best, and decide to splurge on a Big Night in honor of Louis Prima (1911-78). Primo cooks the meal of a lifetime, and Secondo hustles the potential backers of a lifetime. The cards in the brothers' pricey gamble are stacked against them, and Secondo knows it. Ian Holm gives another vintage performance as a sleazy business competitor, and Campbell Scott (who also co-directed), Isabella Rossellini, and Minnie Driver are also seen to good advantage. This is the perfect dinner and a video movie, although you're going to wish you could eat some of Primo's creations. The last sequence in the film is deservedly memorable because it is simultaneously complex and simple (like Primo's masterpieces) and, even more extraordinary, it was shot all in one take. *Big Night* is a triumph for writer/director Tucci, who clearly learned a great deal about the art of filmmaking during the seven years he played character parts in the Hollywood fluff machine. 🎬🎬🎬🎬

1995 (R) 109m/C Tony Shalhoub, Stanley Tucci, Ian Holm, Minnie Driver, Campbell Scott, Isabella Rossellini, Mark Anthony, Allison Janney; *D:* Stanley Tucci, Campbell Scott; *W:* Stanley Tucci, Joseph Tropiano; *C:* Ken Kelsch. Independent Spirit Awards '97: Best Supporting Actor (Tucci); National Society of Film Critics Awards '96: Best Supporting Actor

(Shalhoub); Sundance Film Festival '96: Best Screenplay; Nominations: Independent Spirit Awards '97: Best First Feature, Best First Feature (Shalhoub, Tucci). **VHS, LV, Closed Caption** *COL*

Black Beauty

Filmmakers have tried many times, with variable results, to transfer Anna Sewell's classic children's book *Black Beauty* to the screen. First published in 1877, when many regarded horses as mere vehicles for their convenience, Sewell's novel was a shocking consciousness raiser. Written for the audience who would be most vulnerable to its grim message, *Black Beauty* was so effective that no child could ever forget it. It's hard to imagine any young reader who could grow up without caring about the welfare of the horses who played such a crucial role in late 19th and early 20th century transportation. Unsurprisingly, the sheer brutality of the subject matter frightened movie producers. Films made in 1946 and 1971 softened the harshness of Black Beauty's plight by padding storylines with romantic triangles and cute kids. Caroline Thompson's faithful adaptation may have finally got it right. Beautifully filmed, many portions of the book survive intact: Black Beauty's idyllic infancy and adolescence, his subsequent sale to aristocratic owners who abuse him in the name of fashion, his hard life working for a poor but kindly cab driver, his unbearable existence pulling a cart, and finally his fairy tale reunion with the grown-up stable boy who cares for him in his retirement. Along the way, we see man's inhumanity to animals in many ways: ignorance, indifference, neglect, and drunkenness, as well as a near-fatal stable fire and the systematic destruction of a spirited horse named Ginger. For very small children, all this may be too strong a dose of reality. (Several cried and had to leave the screening of *Black Beauty* that we attended.) Director Thompson still deserves high marks for her sincere effort to capture the sadness, cruelty, and small joys of life in another time. (Cast Note:

b

"Bite your teeth into the ass of life."
—Pascal (Ian Holm) imparts an assertive bit of advice in *Big Night*.

INDEPENDENT FILM GUIDE

The Hound Salutes:
STANLEY TUCCI
Big Night

First I wanted to write a film. You read a lot of bad scripts and you read some good ones, and you think 'I wonder if I can do this.' So I started a long time ago, eight years ago or something, writing. Then I asked my cousin to join me, and he did. We wrote on and off until we started to take ourselves seriously, and then said, 'Let's really do this.' And we came up with the script, and by that point I knew I wanted to direct it but I wanted a co-director. Campbell Scott read the script and loved it so we went from there. It has to do with having made a lot of movies. As an actor you want to create the whole after a certain point, and a lot of actors feel this way.

"We decided that the '50s was the best time [to set the film] because it was the time when mass production was really starting to happen. When everything in America was becoming bigger and bigger and quicker and more superficial in a way. Things were less made by hand. It seemed to be the best time to place these old world men in that new world.

"The film is about commerce versus art and what choice do you make and what compromises you make as an artist, or don't make.

"I like the scene [where Stanley Tucci is cooking eggs and there is no dialogue] not because it is me cooking eggs, but I like the scene as a whole. It was very specific in the way we shot the scene. I really wanted to take the time and allow someone to do something in real time. You don't get a chance to see that on film. And I think that if you know and care about the characters enough you can take that time. I think we've proven that you can do that. I'm very happy it worked.... People are afraid of silence, especially in film. If there's nothing going on you have to put in music or sound effects. Something. And I just felt you don't have to do that. Sometimes. It really depends on what it is. Sometimes you need it and sometimes you don't.

"The humor is not put in to soften the blow or anything. The humor is an integral part of the film because it is an integral part of the characters' lives. And I think that if any of us take ourselves too seriously then our work isn't good. To me, any good work of art has humor in it."

Eleanor Bron and Peter Cook co-starred in *Bedazzled*. Bron went on to play mean Miss Minchin in 1995's *A Little Princess*. Sadly, this was Cook's swan song. Only 57, he died in 1995.) 🦴🦴🦴

1994 (G) 88m/C Andrew Knott, Sean Bean, David Thewlis, Jim Carter, Alun Armstrong, Eleanor Bron, Peter Cook, Peter Davison, John McEnery, Nicholas Jones; **D:** Caroline Thompson; **W:** Caroline Thompson. **VHS, LV, Closed Caption** *WAR*

Black Joy

Black Joy focuses on life in Brixton, a Jamaican neighborhood in London. Funny, well acted, and poetically written, the film lives up to its title and offers an appealing glimpse at the life of Trevor Thomas as Benjamin Jones, a new arrival from Guyana. He promptly becomes involved with the girlfriend of a gangster; repercussions follow! This was the first dramatic feature made by black artists to be released in Great Britain, where it originally ran 109 minutes. Based on Jamal Ali's play *Dark Days and Light Nights*. Simmons later directed 1990's *Little Sweetheart*. 🦴🦴🦴

1977 97m/C *GB* Norman Beaten, Trevor Thomas, Dawn Hope, Floella Benjamin, Oscar James, Paul Medford, Shango Baku, Azad Ali, Charles Pemberton, Vivian Stanshall, Kevin O'Shea; **D:** Anthony Simmons; **W:** Anthony Simmons, Jamal Ali; **C:** Phil Meheux; **M:** Lou Reizner. *NYR*

Black Litter

Widely praised for its frighteningly accurate view of the fascist mentality, *Black Litter,* for this viewer, anyway, fell into the Operation-Was-a-Success-but-the-Patient-Died file. Its brutal conclusion draws too heavily on Woman-As-Symbol gimmickry, which takes the edge off the 80-something minutes worth of satire that leads up to it. Nothing short of controversial and extremely well acted, *Black Litter* won Manuel Gutierrez Aragon the Director's Prize at the Berlin Film Festival. **AKA:** Camada Negra. 🦴🦴▽

1977 84m/C *SP* Jose Alonso, Angela Molina, Maria Luisa Ponte, Joaquin Hinojosa, Emilio Fornet; **D:** Manuel Gutierrez Aragon; **W:** Manuel Gutierrez Aragon, Jose Luis Borau; **C:** Magi Torruella; **M:** Jose Nieto. *NYR*

Black Moon

Black Moon is pure mumble-jumble, with gorgeous cinematography by Sven Nykvist and pretty faces belonging to Sir Rex Harrison's granddaughter Cathryn, Joe Dallesandro, and Alexandra Stewart to charm us into thinking that what we're watching can't be all that bad. But it is. It starts in a rather interesting way, with scary and seductive imagery. But then the lushness folds up on itself as if to protect us from the insight that no one really knows what the heck they're doing here. Vaguely reminiscent of *Last Year at Marienbad, Black Moon* is a colorful grab bag of garbled, pretentious goofiness. (Louis Malle's previous hits were *Murmur of the Heart* and *Lacombe, Lucien.* He would next make *Pretty Baby* and *Atlantic City.*) **WOOF!**

1975 100m/C *FR* Cathryn Harrison, Joe Dallesandro, Alexandra Stewart, Therese Giehse; **D:** Louis Malle; **W:** Louis Malle, Joyce Bunuel, Ghislain Uhry; **C:** Sven Nykvist. *NYR*

Black Narcissus

In 1960, director Michael Powell enraged British audiences with *Peeping Tom,* a sympathetic look at a psychotic killer and the kinky upbringing that contributed to his adult illness. The fact that Alfred Hitchcock's *Psycho* was wildly successful that same year didn't matter. Contemporary critics resented such an in-depth view of the dark side of human nature from a staid and genteel filmmaker like Powell. If they'd really looked at Powell's earlier films with Emeric Pressburger, they might not have been so shocked. For all its elegant beauty, 1947's *Black Narcissus* might be the most subversive movie ever made about nuns. Based on a Rumer Godden novel about five nursing sisters who are sent to the Himalayas to convert an abandoned palace into a school and hospital, the resulting

they find that the people distract them from their vocations. Moreover, Sisters Clodagh and Ruth wind up competing for the attention of the preoccupied Mr. Dean. The scene in which the lonely Sister Ruth finally descends into madness is accomplished with a bit of music, a tube of lipstick, and superb direction, yet the effect is as shocking as if she'd stripped to her knickers. *Black Narcissus,* like *Peeping Tom,* is available on home video and is well worth a reappraisal or fresh discovery. ♫♫♫♫

1947 101m/C *GB* Deborah Kerr, David Farrar, Sabu, Jean Simmons, Kathleen Byron, Flora Robson, Esmond Knight, Jenny Laird, Judith Furse, May Hallitt, Nancy Roberts; *D:* Michael Powell, Emeric Pressburger; *C:* Jack Cardiff. Academy Awards '47: Best Art Direction/Set Decoration (Color), Best Color Cinematography; New York Film Critics Awards '47: Best Actress (Kerr). **VHS, Beta, LV** *MLB*

Blackmail

An archival print of the silent version of *Blackmail* still exists and, as good as the early talkie is, the silent version is an altogether better film, with a fluid style and a minimum of intertitles. Joan Barry (later to star in *Rich and Strange* for Hitchcock) read Anny Ondra's dialogue just offscreen and Harvey Braban plays the talking inspector. (Sam Livesey had played the silent inspector.) The talkie grafts dialogue sequences onto long stretches of silent footage. But if you compare *Blackmail* with *Atlantic,* another 1929 British talkie, Hitchcock's skill with the new technique is clearly in evidence. Look at the breakfast sequence where the repetition of the word "knife" not only grates on the conscience of a guilty young girl, but on our nerves as well. In *Atlantic*, however, the Titanic could have sunk many times over in the pauses between the following words: "Sir... I... have... something... to... tell... you... something... I... feel... you... should... know.... The... ship... has... one... hour... to... live." Movies, even the ones that talk, MOVE, and Hitchcock knew that better than any British director during the transition to sound. Oh, and you can't miss

Kanchi and Sister Clodagh (Jean Simmons and Deborah Kerr) in *Black Narcissus.*

film focuses on the personality changes of women in isolation. The catalyst for their change is provided by Mr. Dean, the dashingly virile estate agent portrayed by David Farrar. He reminds Deborah Kerr's Sister Clodagh of her sensual girlhood in Ireland, but he represents something far more intense for bitter Sister Ruth, played to the hilt by Kathleen Byron. In the safety of their own country surrounded by other nuns, the women might have been spared the unrelieved temptations provided by nostalgia, lust, and envy. Powell and Pressburger show how their inability to cope with those temptations is due more to their reluctance to face themselves than to any lack of religious conviction. Although they are sent to the Himalayas to help the people there,

Hitchcock's cameo here: he's reading a newspaper on a subway while being bothered by a little boy. 🦴🦴🦴

1929 86m/B *GB* Anny Ondra, John Longden, Sara Allgood, Charles Paton, Cyril Ritchard, Donald Calthrop, Charles Paton, Hannah Jones, Percy Parsons, Johnny Butt, Harvey Braban, Phyllis Monkman; *Cameos:* Alfred Hitchcock; *D:* Alfred Hitchcock; *W:* Alfred Hitchcock, Charles Bennett, Benn W. Levy, Garnett Weston. **VHS, Beta, LV** *REP, MRV, NOS*

Blessing

It's an unhappy time down on the Wisconsin dairy farm in this tale of family life. Embittered patriarch Jack (Guy Griffis) can barely make a go of it, and takes his frustrations out by beating his cows and climbing to the top of the silo. Despairing wife Arlene (Carlin Glynn) enters newspaper lotteries and collects religious statues while daughter Randi (Melora Griffis) keeps delaying leaving the farm because of a nagging sense of responsibility. Claustrophobic atmosphere. Writer/director Paul Zehrer was nominated for 1995's Independent Spirit Award for his first screenplay. 🦴🦴

1994 94m/C Guy Griffis, Carlin Glynn, Melora Griffis, Gareth Williams, Clovis Siemon; *D:* Paul Zehrer; *W:* Paul Zehrer; *C:* Stephen Kazmierski; *M:* Joseph S. DeBeasi. Nominations: Independent Spirit Awards '95: First Screenplay. **VHS** *LEO*

Blithe Spirit

Condomine (Sir Rex Harrison) lives in the country with second wife Ruth (Constance Cummings), but the spirit of his delectable first wife Elvira (Kay Hammond) turns up to make mischief. Madame Arcati (Dame Margaret Rutherford) tries to return Elvira to the spirit world where she belongs, but Elvira has other ideas. As you might expect from director David Lean and that cast, this tale by Coward is deliciously well paced and played and the film even won an Oscar for special effects, which were state of the art by 1945 standards. If Rutherford had done nothing else in her career, she would reign in immortality as THE Madame Arcati. Instead, she's also THE Miss Letitia Prism, THE Duchess of Brighton, THE Miss Jane Marple, et cetera. (For the record, THIS Kay Hammond is NOT the Kay Hammond who played Mary Todd in D.W. Griffith's *Abraham Lincoln* 15 years earlier. Why do you think so many actors have three names today? Film historians have been trying to unravel the filmographies of same-named actors, like the Misses Hammond, for far too long.) 🦴🦴🦴🦴

1945 96m/C *GB* Rex Harrison, Constance Cummings, Kay Hammond, Margaret Rutherford, Hugh Wakefield, Joyce Carey, Jacqueline Clarke; *D:* David Lean; *C:* Ronald Neame; *M:* Richard Addinsell. Academy Awards '46: Best Special Effects. **VHS** *MLB*

Blood Simple

Blood Simple put the Coen Brothers on the map and deservedly so. M. Emmet Walsh is the slimiest private investigator you can possibly imagine, or he wouldn't have accepted an assignment to murder the lover (John Getz) of Dan Hedaya's wife, newcomer Frances McDormand. When this flick first came out, movie buffs said it was the *Citizen Kane* of film noir, and it did re-invent much of what we'd expected to see and hear in film noir. Terrific performances, dazzling camera work, a passionate understanding of the genre, and a gleeful propensity to knock its viewers right out of their seats made *Blood Simple* a revolutionary picture in many ways. Unlike the 1981 neo noir *Body Heat*, *Blood Simple* is not an homage, but a fiercely original work in every way. Dead men may wear yellow, but real detectives don't! 🦴🦴🦴🦴

1985 (R) 96m/C John Getz, M. Emmet Walsh, Dan Hedaya, Frances McDormand, Samm-Art Williams; *D:* Joel Coen; *W:* Joel Coen, Ethan Coen; *C:* Barry Sonnenfeld; *M:* Carter Burwell. Independent Spirit Awards '86: Best Actor (Walsh), Best Director (Coen); Sundance Film Festival '85: Grand Jury Prize. **VHS, Beta, LV, Closed Caption** *USH*

Blue Country

Jean-Charles Tacchella, who gifted the world with 1976's *Cousin, Cousine,* serves up a new treat with 1977's *Blue Country.* A sparkling cast, headed by

b

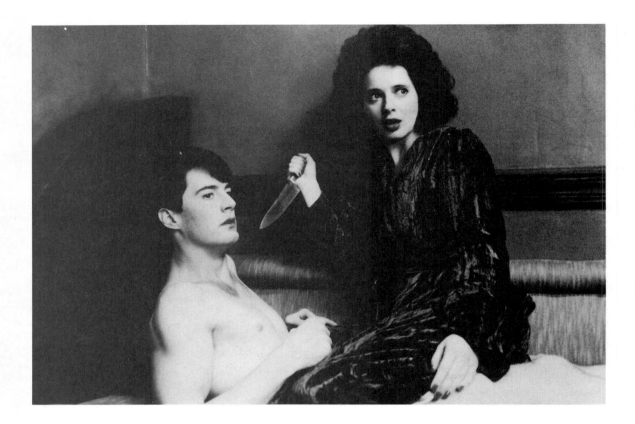

Brigitte Fossey and Jacques Serres, enlivens this very funny romp in the French countryside, with Tacchella's artfully shaded screenplay lending a bit of poignance to their stories. **AKA:** Le Pays Bleu. 🦴🦴🦴

1977 (PG) 104m/C *FR* Brigitte Fossey, Jacques Serres, Ginette Garcin, Armand Meffre, Ginette Mathieu, Roger Crouzet; **D:** Jean-Charles Tacchella; **W:** Jean-Charles Tacchella; **C:** Edmond Sechan; **M:** Gerard Anfosso. **VHS, Beta** *COL*

The Blue Kite

This Chinese nominee for 1995's Independent Spirit Award's Best Foreign Language Film appeared to be unavailable for reappraisal at San Francisco video outlets, although it can be purchased through Kino on Video. Fifteen years of political and cultural upheaval in China is shown through the eyes of young troublemaker Tietou, who certainly earns his nickname of "Iron-head" after his 1954 birth. Soon his father is sent to a labor reform camp and his mother remarries—only to be faced with more struggles as the years go by. The kite is Tietou's cherished toy, and it keeps getting lost or destroyed but is always being rebuilt, offering one token of hope. In Chinese with English subtitles. 🦴🦴🦴

1993 138m/C *CH* Lu Liping, Zhang Wenyao, Pu Quanxin; **D:** Tian Zhuangzhuang; **W:** Xiao Mao. Nominations: Independent Spirit Awards '95: Best Foreign Language Film. **VHS** *KIV*

Blue Velvet

I don't know who ever came up with the idea that the suburbs are a great place to raise kids; they're absolutely terrifying! I spent 15 of the worst years of my life in the Sacramento Valley (first Davis, then Woodland) before making my escape on a

Greyhound bus on Friday, August 31, at 5:30 a.m. David Lynch understands the true horror of suburbia. It looks okay, but underneath, there's all sorts of weird stuff going on. Kyle MacLachlan (as Jeffrey Beaumont, who finds an ear), Isabella Rossellini (as Dorothy), Dean Stockwell, AND Dennis Hopper (as Frank Booth) all in the same movie! What more could any Grand Guignol devotee ask for? Laura Dern is his sweet, innocent girlfriend. Hope Lange, Brad Dourif, Priscilla Pointer, and Lynch regular Jack (*Eraserhead*) Nance (who was murdered in real life after a fight in a doughnut shop in 1997) round out the cast. A deeply disturbing movie with superb cinematography by Frederick Elmes, and a great evocative score by Angelo Badalamenti, who went on to compose Lynch's *Wild at Heart* (also starring Dern) and the classic *Twin Peaks* theme. *Blue Velvet* revitalized the careers of Stockwell and Hopper (although not, alas, the underrated Lange), and if it encouraged pigeons NOT to move into suburban nightmares like Lumberton, so much the better, dang it! 🦴🦴🦴🦴

1986 (R) 121m/C Brad Dourif, Kyle MacLachlan, Isabella Rossellini, Dennis Hopper, Laura Dern, Hope Lange, Jack Nance, Dean Stockwell, George Dickerson, Priscilla Pointer; **D:** David Lynch; **W:** David Lynch; **C:** Frederick Elmes; **M:** Angelo Badalamenti. Independent Spirit Awards '87: Best Actress (Rossellini); Los Angeles Film Critics Association Awards '86: Best Director (Lynch), Best Supporting Actor (Hopper); Montreal World Film Festival '86: Best Supporting Actor (Hopper); National Society of Film Critics Awards '86: Best Cinematography, Best Director (Lynch), Best Film, Best Supporting Actor (Hopper); Nominations: Academy Awards '86: Best Director (Lynch). **VHS, Beta, LV, Closed Caption** WAR

Bodies, Rest & Motion

...We used to live in a town where the main extracurricular activity was having, talking about, or cleaning up after sex; no wonder the leading cause of death was cracking up on the county road that led into town. Our driving ambition between ages ten and eighteen was to leave town,

but if we'd been 28 at the time, it would have taken us all of eight minutes to get out. Welcome to 94 minutes of *Bodies, Rest & Motion,* which began life as a play by Roger Hedden. We're trying to imagine if we would have enjoyed it more watching actual people drift across a stage at fifty-odd bucks a performance. We don't think so, although the occasional quirky line might have benefited more from the give-and-take that exists between performers and their audiences in a live setting. Here is the minimalist plot: Nick (Tim Roth) and Beth (Bridget Fonda) plan to move from Enfield to Butte, only Nick runs out on Beth so she has a one night stand with Sid the house painter (Eric Stoltz) and then runs out on him. At movie's end, Nick is outraged that Beth ran out on him after he ran out on her and Sid is wandering along a highway, looking for Beth. Window dressing is provided by Phoebe Cates as Beth's best friend, Carol, who is also Nick's ex-lover. And that, action lovers, is it, except for a heavenly choir that accompanies this riveting narrative at far-from-heavenly moments. Michael Steinberg's film apparently is trying to wring extra mileage out of the 1991 success of *Slacker*—only Richard Linklater's satire was fresher and funnier and he didn't force us to stick with the same set of banal characters for the length of HIS movie. The guy in back of us laughed most of the way through *Bodies, Rest & Motion*; we wonder what he does for kicks when he's alone. 🦴

1993 (R) 94m/C Phoebe Cates, Bridget Fonda, Tim Roth, Eric Stoltz, Scott Frederick, Scott Johnson, Alicia Witt, Rich Wheeler, Peter Fonda; **D:** Michael Steinberg; **W:** Roger Hedden; **M:** Michael Convertino. **VHS, LV, Closed Caption** NLC, BTV

Boss' Son

This early Bobby Roth film is an autobiographical account of why he isn't taking over his father's job as boss of a carpet mill. Despite the extremely personal primary source material, Roth manages to achieve just enough emotional distance, to the great advantage of his film. Working on a tiny budget of $500,000, Roth assembled an impressive cast of veterans, all of whom outshine Asher Brauner as the protagonist. As young Bobby, Brauner is too cold and detached for us to care about his inner conflicts regarding his own class and that of his co-workers. The balance problems aren't fatal, but they do weaken a potentially dynamite study of the American class system. Roth's compassionate script and direction, plus Henry G. Sanders' poignant performance, make this a memorable, if incompletely realized, effort. Roth's future movies include 1984's *Heartbreakers* and 1992's *Keeper of the City,* both starring Peter Coyote. 🦴🦴🦴

1978 97m/C Rita Moreno, James Darren, Asher Brauner, Rudy Solari, Henry Sanders, Richie Havens, Piper Laurie, Elena Verdugo; **D:** Bobby Roth; **W:** Bobby Roth; **C:** Alfonso Beato. **VHS, Beta** *VES, LIV*

Bound

This sizzling neo-noir was just as much fun for me to watch as many classic entries of the 1940s and the '50s. Jennifer Tilly is femme fatale Violet stuck with a schmuck named Caesar (Joe Pantoliano). When a butch ex-convict named Corky (Gina Gershon) enters her life, it's love and lust at first sight. Many bodies later, the Wachowski Brothers use all the best ingredients to bring their film to a satisfying conclusion. As Violet, Tilly has the half-finished look of the women in the Superman cartoons made by the Fleischer Bros. in the early 1940s, while Gershon's Corky evokes countless noir heroes who've almost given up on life until they meet the right woman and come up with the perfect heist plan that no one else can understand, much less carry out. That's all there is to the narrative structure, but it's well acted and well scripted with some fresh twists in the imagery department. 🦴🦴🦴🦴

1996 (R) 107m/C Gina Gershon, Jennifer Tilly, Joe Pantoliano, John P. Ryan, Barry Kivel, Christopher Meloni, Peter Spellos, Richard Sarafian, Mary Mara, Susie Bright, Ivan Kane, Kevin M. Richardson, Gene Borkan; **D:** Andy Wachowski, Larry Wachowski; **W:** Andy Wachowski, Larry Wachowski; **C:** Bill Pope; **M:**

Don Davis. Nominations: Independent Spirit Awards '97: Best Cinematography; MTV Movie Awards '97: Best Kiss (Jennifer Tilly/Gina Gershon). **VHS, LV, Closed Caption** *REP*

A Boy and His Dog

Harlan Ellison has been outraging people through most of his career as a professional writer. He admits frankly that much of this is hype. Contemporary writers have to be strong personalities to get booked on the chat shows that will promote their work. Ellison considers *A Boy and His Dog* to be one of the best science-fiction novellas he's ever written, and director L.Q. Jones' screen adaptation became an instant cult film when it was first released in 1975. We have yet to meet a woman who wasn't offended by it or a man who wasn't amused by it. Halfway through a 1975 press screening of *A Boy and His Dog,* we walked out, seriously intending not to return. A nice man in the lobby stopped us, reassured us that the last half of the movie was much better than the first, and told us that we'd feel a lot better if we went back. We did not feel a lot better. In fact, we felt simply horrible when director/screenwriter L.Q. Jones and actor/producer Alvy Moore appeared out of nowhere directly after the film, and proceeded to say how great they were and how awful many of the critics in attendance were for not liking their movie. *A Boy and His Dog* features fine performances by Susanne Benton as A Girl and an even better one by Tiger the Dog, who previously starred in *The Brady Bunch.* It also offers incredible sex, violence at its most vicious, and a theme that is embarrassing in its treatment, if thoughtful in its content. Oh, yeah, the plot. It's set in the future, it shows how a telepathic Boy (Don Johnson, then 25) and his Dog survive despite all those people out there. It's also supposed to be funny. *A Boy and His Dog* is still igniting controversy on home video over two decades after its theatrical release. Cutting-edge satire or yet another cinematic cheap shot at women? It's your call. **WOOF!**

1975 (R) 87m/C Don Johnson, Susanne Benton, Jason Robards Jr., Charles McGraw, Alvy Moore; **D:** L.Q. Jones; **W:** L.Q. Jones; **V:** Tim McIntire. **VHS, Beta, LV** *FRF, MED, MRV*

The Boy from Mercury

Martin Duffy's *The Boy from Mercury* looks like it was shot in saturated Technicolor from the 1940s, but it's actually a brand-new movie from Ireland, starring Rita Tushingham, Tom Courtenay, and a young charmer named James Hickey as Harry, a fatherless child who's convinced he's a creature from another planet. (All those weekly Flash Gordon serials fuel his imagination.) Tushingham and Courtenay are more animated here than they've been in quite some time, and Hickey is altogether winning as the little would-be alien. 𝄞𝄞𝄞

1996 99m/C *IR* James Hickey, Rita Tushingham, Tom Courtenay, Hugh O'Conner; **D:** Martin Duffy; **W:** Martin Duffy; **C:** Seamus Deasy; **M:** Stephen McKeon. *NYR*

Boy Next Door

The BBC has always been fascinated by pop iconography, and *Boy Next Door* might easily qualify to be a segment on A&E's *Biography* series. This portrait of Boy George is chockful of clips and wistful ruminations about what went wrong and when and why. Boy George's story ends on a bright note with a career upswing and an apparent recovery from drug addition. (As of 1997, he's a weekly columnist for the *Express,* a British tabloid.) 𝄞𝄞𝄞

1993 50m/C *GB* **D:** Mark Kidel. *NYR*

The Boys of St. Vincent

The Boys of St. Vincent is a hard-hitting Canadian drama set in a Newfoundland orphanage for boys run by the Catholic Brothers. But Brother Lavin, the orphanage's well respected director, has a secret life with the children under his care. He uses them as sexual outlets and, if they reject his advances or his authority, he beats them until they require medical attention. The three-hour-plus plot revolves around Kevin, one of Brother Lavin's special boys, who runs away rather than submit to him. What happens next is the subject of a 15-year cover-up. Were children at the orphanage actually abused by the Brothers? Should the police have intervened more forcefully? Why did the Catholic authorities simply transfer the guilty Brothers rather than make them face criminal charges? The long-term effects of sexual abuse are finally being faced by international courts after decades of ignoring children's complaints against so-called pillars of the community, a theme which is strongly reinforced in *The Boys of St. Vincent.* The kids have no rights. They are harassed and intimidated by their abusers. Well meaning social workers, detectives, friends, and family members are ineffectual. The drama also deals with the cyclical nature of child abuse, that the abused grow up to abuse others as well. One of the more likable of Kevin's fellow victims grows up to be a drug addict and a street hustler, and during his court appearance it is revealed that as a teenager he abused little boys half his age. We watch his horrifying and tragic descent from freckle-faced charmer to a broken man of 25 who would rather die than face himself. The script suggests that Brother Lavin, too, was abused as a child, but since we only see him as a menacing adult, filled with rage and self-pity, he has no claim whatever on our sympathy. Henry Czerny made the most of his 1993 role as Brother Lavin, subsequently attracting the attention of

Don Siegel [1912-91] was a fine director and a friend of mine, and Walter Wanger [1894-1968], who produced *Riot in Cell Block 11* [Allied Artists, 1954], had shot a guy in the back seat of a car because he was in there with his wife. The only reason I mention that is because we shot *Riot* in Folsom Prison, and since Wanger had committed a felony, as producer he couldn't get into Folsom Prison himself without permission, see? But I was the most unlikely guy to be a hard-nosed criminal in Folsom Prison. As a matter of fact, when that thing opened, I took all my friends down there and they had a scene at the very beginning where they open up a door with a big 'X' on it. These are the most hardened criminals at Folsom Prison, and you have to be a two-time loser to get in there, and when they opened the door and I was standing there with a butch hair cut and a tooth pick in my mouth, all of the people I brought in the audience fell out of their seats, see? And of course, no one else knew what they were laughing about....

"I got into producing in 1962 with a guy I knew, L.B. Jones. We were partners and we decided we might as well create something for ourselves, because during the hiatus period there really wasn't anything going on six months of the year, so we made a picture called *The Devil's Bedroom* [Allied Artists, 1963]. Now *The Devil's Bedroom* by 1990s' standards would be G-rated. It didn't have anything in it except the title. We went down to Texas and shot it for $22,000, and it got on the screen. As a matter of fact, back in the '60s a funny guy came up one day and he said he saw it in a burlesque house. I said, 'A burlesque house?' He said, 'I paid $5 to see it.' Now $5 to see a movie in those days was large. I said, 'I'd love to go see that because there's nothing in it. There's no sex, there's no violence....' It must have been the title: *The Devil's Bedroom.* People came to see *The Devil's Bedroom* and there wasn't any. The way we got that title was we had a bunch of guys searching through the woods with torches and someone said, 'Did you look over by the devil's bedroom?' That was the only thing we connected the title with in the picture. That was how we sold it. People came to see *The Devil's Bedroom* and there was no devil's bedroom. I always wanted to sit in the back and watch these guys go, 'What in the heck was that? I paid $5 to see this?' It wasn't a bad movie, but for $22,000, what's it going to be?....

"*A Boy and His Dog* really is either loved or hated. Harlan Ellison wrote the novella and he won an award. We won an award on the picture, too, from all the fans around the United States and the world. That was an exciting movie. It was low-budget, we shot it out near Barstow, and it was one of Don Johnson's first big efforts [after *Zachariah* and *Harrad Experiment*] and we were lucky to get Jason Robards because he was just coming off that big accident he had, and he was a pro to work in a low-budget picture like that, after all the starring vehicles he'd been in [Robards won Academy Awards for his next two films, *All the President's Men* and *Julia*.]. We're quite proud of that effort. That's become a science-fiction classic....

"There are two sorts of producers: independent producers and one of those guys in the majors who sits on his tuchus and gets all sorts of large money for making large decisions about business. The independent producer has to try to get the money, help with the casting, help with getting the director and the crew, go out in the field, find the locations, the whole thing. Independent producers are 'hands-on' types. They're really involved. It starts out with the script approval. Once you say 'roll 'em,' as much as you've been prepared, holes appear in front of you all the time. It's things that you didn't anticipate and there's no place to call. You don't go to a telephone and call up the office: You're it. You get together with the other people involved and say, 'Hey guys, what are we going to do?' That's the neat part about it, though. It's really fun to do it that way."

ALVY MOORE'S films include: *Susan Slept Here, The Wild One, Annapolis Story, Designing Woman, The Perfect Furlough, The Wackiest Ship in the Army, For Love or Money, Three Nuts in Search of a Bolt, The Gnome-Mobile, Witchmaker, The Brotherhood of Satan, Herbie Rides Again, The Specialist, Smokey and the Hotwire Gang, Cotton Candy, Ms. 45, Scream, They're Playing with Fire, Here Come the Littles,* and *Intruder.* Moore also appeared as Hank Kimball on *Green Acres* from 1965-71.

Grana; **D:** John N. Smith; **W:** Sam Grana, John N. Smith, Des Walsh; **C:** Pierre Letarte; **M:** Neil Smolar. Nominations: Independent Spirit Awards '95: Best Foreign Language Film. **VHS** *NYF*

Emily Watson in *Breaking the Waves*.

Breaking the Waves

This extremely long film (17 minutes longer than *Secrets and Lies,* which felt like forever) is not suitable for everyone on Planet Earth, like, for example, ME. I suspect that it impressed the Grand Jury at the Cannes Film Festival because of its power and its sincerity, and because of Emily Watson's tremendously hard work as Bess. Obviously I can't speak for The Deity, with whom Bess has so MANY conversations, but I suspect that God is a lot more forgiving of us (and, consequently, BESS) than we are of ourselves or each other. Bess' course of action is entirely clear to her, but her masochism is a mystery to me for the entire length of the narrative. Why should she punish herself by sleeping with other men because her husband is in an accident? To demonstrate that religious fervor is irrational? Or pointless? One senses the Victorian sensibility of an Emily Bronte (*Wuthering Heights*) or a William Somerset Maugham (*Christmas Holiday*) lurking about this sad story set in the 1970s. For someone who grew up listening skeptically to old nun's tales of little boys pocketing the Communion wafer, thereby drowning the whole Congregation in the Blood of Christ, Bess' self-torture clearly made a heckuva lot more sense to the filmmakers than it did to me. The ending made me feel like I'd just walked in front of a Mack truck. According to the May 7, 1997, *Express,* Helena Bonham Carter withdrew from the role of Bess, explaining that she "loved the part, but had an allergic reaction to the idea of this girl, whose husband is a paraplegic, who goes and prostitutes herself in the belief that it will make him better." If *Breaking the Waves* is your favorite movie—and it was for two viewers who recommended it to me without reservations—

more than one Hollywood producer. (Follow-up projects included the indies *Northern Extremes* and *When Night Is Falling,* plus blockbusters like *Clear and Present Danger* and *Mission: Impossible.*) The timing of 1995's limited theatrical release of *The Boys of St. Vincent* was ironic, since Newt Gingrich seemed to feel that more orphanages were just what we needed at that point in his career as Speaker of the House. Viewers of *The Boys of St. Vincent* can weigh the pros and cons on THAT issue for themselves! ♫♫♫♫

1993 186m/C *CA* Henry Czerny, Johnny Morina, Sebastian Spence, Brian Dodd, David Hewlett, Jonathan Lewis, Jeremy Keefe, Phillip Dinn, Brian Dooley, Greg Thomey, Michael Wade, Lise Roy, Timothy Webber, Kristine Demers, Ashley Billard, Sam

great, but I've lost my early tenacity for sitting through films-as-agony except by accident!!! 🦴🦴🦴

1995 (R) 152m/C *DK FR* Emily Watson, Stellan Skarsgard, Katrin Cartlidge, Adrian Rawlins, Jean-Marc Barr, Sandra Voe, Udo Kier, Mikkel Gaup; *D:* Lars von Trier; *W:* Lars von Trier; *C:* Robby Muller; *M:* Joachim Holbek. Cannes Film Festival '96: Grand Jury Prize; Cesar Awards '97: Best Foreign Film; New York Film Critics Awards '96: Best Actress (Watson), Best Cinematography, Best Director (von Trier); National Society of Film Critics Awards '96: Best Actress (Watson), Best Cinematography, Best Director (von Trier), Best Film; Nominations: Academy Awards '96: Best Actress (Watson); British Academy Awards '96: Best Actress (Watson); Golden Globe Awards '97: Best Actress—Drama (Watson), Best Film—Drama; Independent Spirit Awards '97: Best Foreign Film. **VHS, Closed Caption** *EVE*

Breathless

Iowa-born Jean Seberg was only 17 years old when director Otto Preminger chose her to play the title role in *Saint Joan.* It was a spectacular way to launch a career and her subsequent failure in the film was equally spectacular; *Saint Joan* was chosen as the worst movie of the century by the Harvard Lampoon. Preminger gave her another chance with *Bonjour Tristesse,* but Deborah Kerr attracted most of the critical attention for that Francoise Sagan adaptation. Seberg's career could have ended right there had she not been cast in Jean-Luc Godard's *Breathless.* All the things about Seberg that had seemed so out of place in splashy American movies were just right in this fast-paced New Wave film from the year 1959. Suddenly, her skin-deep qualities seemed mysterious, part of a larger phenomenon, and the less emotional understanding she brought to her interpretation of an essentially thoughtless young waif, the better. Or so it seemed at the time when *Breathless* was first released. In fact, when Seberg stares blankly into the camera after her lover calls her a little bitch and says, "A little what? I don't understand," it is her very lack of expression that haunts us today. *Breathless* is perhaps the most enjoyable of Godard's films (it didn't hurt that Fran-

cois Truffaut collaborated on the script) and it turned Jean-Paul Belmondo, then 26, into an overnight star. Seberg's career received a much-needed boost and she made dozens of international films over the next 18 years. Seberg's naivete was genuine: she took her life in 1979 after being hounded by the F.B.I. for her involvement with the Black Panthers. She once admitted that she had neither the will nor the way to cope with Hollywood pressures and added, "I don't think any healthy, well balanced person would want to become an actress." She projected youth, health, and a superficial version of happiness in *Breathless* which may well leave today's audiences out of breath. *AKA:* A Bout de Souffle. 🦴🦴🦴🦴

1959 90m/B *FR* Jean-Paul Belmondo, Jean Seberg, Daniel Boulanger, Jean-Pierre Melville, Liliane Robin; *D:* Jean-Luc Godard; *W:* Jean-Luc Godard. Berlin International Film Festival '60: Best Director (Godard). **VHS, Beta** *NOS, MRV, CVC*

Bride to Be

Bride to Be is quite unintentionally funny. It's yet another Son-Wants-His-Dad's-Girl yarn, only this time, the kid's going to be a priest. (What about his immortal soul?) Peter Day does an unmemorable acting job as the son. Sarah Miles is so quiet in the title role that at first it does seem that she can neither hear nor speak (nope, the screenwriter just didn't give her any words to say!) and Sir Stanley Baker looks thoroughly embarrassed here as the father. *AKA:* Pepita Jiminez. 🦴

1975 115m/C *SP* Sarah Miles, Stanley Baker, Peter Day, Eduardo Bea, Vicente Soler, Jose Maria Caffarell, Maria Vico; *D:* Rafael Morena Alba; *C:* Jose Luis Alcaine; *M:* Stelvio Cipriano. *NYR*

Brief Encounter

Early in his long career, Sir David Lean made several small, beautifully observed films about love, about death, about how people survive, and about how things end.

The Hound Salutes:
EMILY WATSON
Best Actress Oscar nominee,
Breaking the Waves

Bess [her character] is one of those people who has no skin somehow. She loves Jan to the point of extremity. She's very, very giving. She has a childish open heart and is completely guiless, so she's regarded as a simpleton by the people in the community where she lives, which is a repressive, religious community.... Writer/director Lars von Trier is very well known in Scandinavia and maybe on the continent of Europe. In Britain, people don't know him that well; they're quite insular in their tastes. His working process has really transformed itself over the progress of his career. If you see a film like 1992's *Zentropa,* which is very very formal, every picture is beautifully designed, it's about ideas and mood and expression, and then you watch 1995's *The Kingdom,* which has been described as 'E.R. on acid', really. It's the most extraordinary piece of work. It's a farce, it's a hospital soap drama, it's a ghost story, it's a thriller, it's everything. It's really strange. And with that, he began to change his process of working. He had a reputation of being quite difficult for actors; his prime objective was to get the picture right and the acting was secondary to that, but on *The Kingdom,* he began to change that. When you watch *The Kingdom,* what holds the story together is the contact between the actors, and he's broken a lot of the rules of filmmaking. He's crossing the line all the time with jump cuts and really strange editing and really strange shots. It's all hand-held cameras and very wacky. But what connects you is the contact between the actors and that process continued with *Breaking the Waves.* We shot whole sequences in real time. What was at the center of the film is the emotional story, and that's incredibly liberating for the actors, because it's like being in a kind of improvisation all the time. The camera was hand held throughout and the cameraman didn't watch rehearsals, so he never really knew what we were going to do, so it was like, well, do you know when they do exploratory operations and they send a little peephole into you and they look around? That's what the camera was like: this ranging beast in the room with you, trying to watch what was going on."

Lars von Trier's first film is 1984's *The Element of Crime.*

Our favorite David Lean film is *Brief Encounter,* which we can watch over and over again and never grow tired of it. The story is deceptively simple and we discover it in bits and pieces. We see a woman and a man talking quietly in a railway tea shop. Another woman joins them, chattering animatedly until the man leaves ever so quietly. The first woman nearly faints, but is soon en route home with her chattering companion. As far as real time goes after that, the woman sits quietly at home with her well meaning husband and her own memories until the end of the film. But her memories, as Lean makes abundantly clear, have shattered her life and it is only her enormous capacity for traditional routines that saves her from death and despair. We learn why that ordinary little incident in the railway tea shop was the most heartrending time of her life. Lean and screenwriter Sir Noel Coward chose just what to show with great care and the only choice that appears out of place, ironically, inspired Billy Wilder to make *The Apartment* in 1960. Because his canvas was so small in *Brief Encounter,* Lean embellished it further with sound: a haunting narration, a sweeping Rachmaninoff-based score, plus a batch of typically British catch phrases. The crisp acting by the supporting cast, and especially by its stars Celia Johnson and Trevor Howard, rooted *Brief Encounter* in a definite time and place and rinsed away excessive sentiment. Yet despite its very Englishness, *Brief Encounter* does not date. It doesn't matter how the world has changed. These people in these circumstances made these choices, and even today, we might well imagine people making the very same choices all over again. ♫♫♫♫

1946 86m/B *GB* Celia Johnson, Trevor Howard, Stanley Holloway, Cyril Raymond, Joyce Carey, Everley Gregg, Margaret Barton, Dennis Harkin, Valentine Dyall, Marjorie Mars, Irene Handl; *D:* David Lean; *W:* Noel Coward; *C:* Robert Krasker. National Board of Review Awards '46: 10 Best Films of the Year; New York Film Critics Awards '46: Best Actress (Johnson); Nominations: Academy Awards '46: Best Actress (Johnson), Best Director (Lean), Best Screenplay. **VHS, Beta** *PAR, HMV*

A Brief History of Time

Theoretical physicist Stephen Hawking was given two years to live when he contracted Lou Gehrig's disease in the early 1960s, but, over three decades later, he shows no indications OR inclinations of fulfilling that prophecy. As always, Errol Morris does a remarkable job of communicating an interesting subject on his own unique terms. Even if you barely squeaked by with a "C" in physics, *A Brief History of Time* supplies many lucid and compelling visualizations of Hawking's theories. One quibble is that Morris does not identify the many speakers in the film until the final credits. This wouldn't even work in a book, much less a movie! We figure out who Hawking's mother and sister are, but the comments of his many scientific colleagues have less of a context, since non-scientists don't know who they are (until after it's over) or what any of them have done, ever, unless they look it up. Yes, the movie is about Hawking, but who the heck ARE all these guys who talk about him at length? The final shot is both poignant and eloquent: Hawking's wheelchair, labeled "STEPHEN," is shown against a starry sky. Left out of the film is the fact that Hawking was then in the process of divorcing his long-time wife Jane, unseen except in early candids, but much-discussed on camera. He married his long-time nurse Elaine Mason in September, 1994. Hawking, who has not been able to speak since 1985, said his wedding vows through a voice synthesizer created by his bride's ex-husband. ♫♫♫

1992 (G) 85m/C Stephen Hawking; *D:* Errol Morris; *W:* Stephen Hawking; *C:* John Bailey; *M:* Philip Glass. Sundance Film Festival '92: Filmmakers Trophy. **VHS, Beta, Closed Caption** *PAR, BTV, WSH*

Brilliant Lies

Richard Franklin's *Brilliant Lies* is talky and stage-bound, feeling much longer than its 93-minute running time. Susy

Conner (*Strictly Ballroom*'s Gia Carides) is a definite target of Gary Fitzgerald's (Anthony LaPaglia) sexual harassment, or is she? She asks sister Katie (Gia's real-life sister, Zoe) to back up her version of events, but Katie recalls that some of the events Susy describes actually happened to them both as children abused by their father, Brian (Ray Barrett). The script buys into most of the commonly accepted myths about harassment allegations: that mercenary women lie, that child molesters grow old and can be let off the hook for the sake of family harmony, that no one is truly innocent so everyone is somewhat guilty, and a lot of other rubbish that a good cast can't redeem. (Cast Note: Gia Carides and Anthony LaPaglia are real-life husband and wife.) 🦴🦴

1996 93m/C *AU* Gia Carides, Anthony LaPaglia, Zoe Carides, Ray Barrett, Michael Veitch, Neil Melville, Catherine Wilkin, Grant Tilly; *D:* Richard Franklin; *W:* Richard Franklin, Peter Fitzpatrick; *C:* Geoff Burton; *M:* Nevida Tyson-Chew. Nominations: Australian Film Institute '95: Best Actress (Carides), Best Supporting Actor (Barrett), Best Supporting Actress (Carides). **VHS**

Brother's Keeper

In both *Brother's Keeper* and *Paradise Lost: The Child Murders of Robin Hood Hills,* the filmmakers take a look at a murder case in which community members have pretty much made up their minds about the innocence or guilt of the accused. There is also a heavily charged side issue in each case to cloud the evidence: in *Keeper,* it's incest; in *Paradise,* it's Satanism. I've heard audience members for both films insist that it's SO obvious what REALLY happened. (To them, maybe, but not to me!) Joe Berlinger and Bruce Sinofsky succeed in building reasonable doubts, which is all any investigative reporters can hope to do. There is one gory bloodletting sequence that has nothing to do with the rest of the story, but it emphasizes the pervasive atmosphere that the people in *Brother's Keeper* belong

in another time and place, not in the New York countryside of the early 1990s. 🦴🦴🦴

1992 104m/C *D:* Joe Berlinger, Bruce Sinofsky. National Board of Review Awards '92: Best Feature Documentary; New York Film Critics Awards '92: Best Feature Documentary; Sundance Film Festival '92: Audience Award. **VHS, LV** *FXL, BTV*

The Brothers McMullen

This overpraised indie about three Irish Catholic brothers in Long Island, New York, is a guaranteed button pusher for Irish Catholic women, which is why I originally disqualified myself from reviewing it. (Hey, is anyone out there laboring under the delusion that movie reviewers are objective ROBOTS? Dream on, baby!) Ed Burns' next movie, *She's the One,* was widely panned, but the fact is they're both practically the same AVERAGE movie. Shortly before the release of the very funny date movie, *The Truth About Cats and Dogs,* Janeane Garafalo did stand-up at San Francisco's Punch Line and UNrecommended this one as a date movie. It is mortally depressing to think of guys as adolescents from the obstetrics ward to the funeral parlor, but *The Brothers McMullen* reinforces this largely accepted (and often true) myth about Irish Catholic men. That's why Irish Catholic women (often) hesitate before marrying them. Jack is married to a perfectly nice woman and has an affair with an irresponsible hedonist (or so Burns' script suggests) who IS responsible for two things: Jack's lapse from (1) his religious faith, and (2) his marital vows. Barry wants to be a writer and his perfectly nice girlfriend will interfere with that (or so Burns' script suggests), so quite a lot of screen time is devoted to that. Patrick is engaged to marry a Jewish-American princess, whose father would set him up for life, but he's seriously interested in a (lapsed Catholic) woman who wants to hit the road with him if he'll pay for half of the new car. Oh, and did you know that it's easy to be a Good

Catholic if you marry your one True Love? Got an extra 98 minutes for burning issues like these? How about 193 minutes for a mediocre double feature that also includes *She's the One?* (Newcomer Maxine Bahns is charming in each flick.) 🎬🎬

1994 (R) 98m/C Edward Burns, Jack Mulcahy, Mike McGlone, Connie Britton, Shari Albert, Elizabeth P. McKay, Maxine Bahns, Jennifer Jostyn, Catharine Bolt, Peter Johansen; **D:** Edward Burns; **W:** Edward Burns; **M:** Seamus Egan. Independent Spirit Awards '96: Best First Feature; Sundance Film Festival '95: Grand Jury Prize. **VHS, Closed Caption** *FXV*

Bullets over Broadway

This valentine to Broadway is a full notch above Tay Garnett's *Main Street to Broadway,* a star-studded fest that crammed the best theatrical troupers of that era (including wonderful Tallulah Bankhead) into a slight story about a first-time playwright (newcomer Tom Morton, whom no one got a chance to remember before he was forgotten). *Bullets'* story line involving fledgling writer David Shayne (John Cusack) basically functions as an immobile jungle gym around which colorful characters do cartwheels with intriguing subplots. Best of all are gangster Chazz Palminteri and his boss' no-talent girlfriend Jennifer Tilly, who both want to break into show business in the worst way. (Now why couldn't they have been cast in 1993's *Born Yesterday?*) The atmosphere and period details are simultaneously faithful and satirical. Every stock company has an idol whom the other members tolerate, but the audiences worship (that would be chain-eating Jim Broadbent here). Dianne Wiest, if not in Bankhead's league, won an Oscar as the stage diva who's on 24 hours a day, and Rob Reiner, Mary-Louise Parker, and Joe Viterelli add to the background flavor. You won't mind a bit that Cusack, at the center of this infectious whirlwind of energy, fades into the wallpaper most of the time. 🎬🎬🎬🎬

1994 (R) 106m/C Dianne Wiest, John Cusack, Jennifer Tilly, Rob Reiner, Chazz Palminteri, Tracey Ullman, Mary-Louise Parker, Joe Viterelli, Jack Warden, Jim Broadbent, Harvey Fierstein, Annie-Joe Edwards; **D:** Woody Allen; **W:** Woody Allen, Douglas McGrath; **C:** Carlo DiPalma. Academy Awards '94: Best Supporting Actress (Wiest); Chicago Film Critics Awards '94: Best Supporting Actress (Wiest); Golden Globe Awards '95: Best Supporting Actress (Wiest); Independent Spirit Awards '95: Best Supporting Actor (Palminteri), Best Supporting Actress (Wiest); Los Angeles Film Critics Association Awards '94: Best Supporting Actress (Wiest); New York Film Critics Awards '94: Best Supporting Actress (Wiest); National Society of Film Critics Awards '94: Best Supporting Actress (Wiest); Screen Actors Guild Award '94: Best Supporting Actress (Wiest); Nominations: Academy Awards '94: Best Art Direction/Set Decoration, Best Costume Design, Best Director (Allen), Best Original Screenplay, Best Supporting Actor (Palminteri), Best Supporting Actress (Tilly); British Academy Awards '95: Best Original Screenplay; Independent Spirit Awards '95: Best Film, Best Screenplay. **VHS, LV, Closed Caption** *MAX*

Burnt by the Sun

Burnt by the Sun deservedly won an Oscar for Best Foreign Language Film of 1994. It captures a heartbreakingly lovely summer day in the country. Bolshevik hero Serguei Kotov is madly in love with his wife and small daughter and their life together is joyful and serene. The arrival of his wife's former lover Dimitri appears to be no more than a catch-up-on-the-past visit at first. But gradually, Serguei realizes that he is about to give his family the ultimate gift: a treasured memory and the secure knowledge of his love for them. Director Nikita Mikhalkov skillfully weaves the light-hearted ambiance of a happy family with vaguely disturbing sexual games, far more disquieting political undercurrents, and finally, sheer horror. The unclouded sweetness of the relationship between Serguei and his little girl is beautifully conveyed by Mikhalkov and his real-life daughter Nadia. **AKA:** Outomlionnye Solntsem. 🎬🎬🎬🎬

1994 (R) 134m/C *RU FR* Nikita Mikhalkov, Ingeborga Dapkounaite, Oleg Menshikov, Nadia Mikhalkov, Andre Oumansky, Viatcheslav Tikhonov, Svetlana Krioutchkova, Vladimir Ilyine; **D:** Nikita Mikhalkov; **W:** Nikita Mikhalkov, Rustam Ibragimbekov; **M:** Eduard Artemyev. Academy Awards '94: Best Foreign Language Film; Cannes Film Festival '94: Grand Jury

There were a couple of things I wanted to do. First, I had never seen a film about the Irish-American or the Irish-Catholic experience. I had seen plenty of films about Italian Americans, Jewish Americans, African Americans, but really, there had been nothing to my knowledge about an Irish-American family. So that's one thing I wanted to do. The other thing I wanted to do was take a look at Catholicism and sexuality and how that upbringing affects men and women in their 20s and 30s and how they're dealing with it. The third thing I wanted to do was take a look at brothers and how brothers communicate and how they confide in one another and the way that they talk about things they won't say to their best friends and their girlfriends and their wives. That was something I wanted to look at.

"With Patrick, especially, there were a lot of things I wanted to say about Catholicism, so I exaggerated Patrick a little bit, because I wanted to have fun with it, I didn't want to get preachy, I didn't want to beat the audience over the head. Personally, I haven't gone through what Patrick's gone through in a long time. I don't practice anymore, but a lot of his experiences are things I've heard, growing up. I don't hear too much anymore from guys my age, but certainly when we were growing up, those were real issues.

"The father who dies at the beginning of the film is this alcoholic abusive guy. With the brothers, I wanted to show how each brother has reacted differently to living in that man's house. Barry's reaction...I think that's where his fear of commitment comes from. I think he probably recognizes a little bit of his father in him and he's kind of terrified. Maybe he doesn't want to do to some woman what his father did to their mother. Patrick clings to religion. Jack tries to go in the opposite direction of his dad, trying to be the best husband he can possibly be.

"I was working full time at *Entertainment Tonight* as a production assistant in New York, basically driving the van, fetching coffee, things like that. I had written seven screenplays prior to that. I thought that would be the way to get my foot in the door in Hollywood. That wasn't happening. All I was getting was rejection letter after rejection letter. Finally, my father said to me, 'If you want to be a filmmaker, go out and make a film.' A number of other films had come out in years before, such as Nick Gomez's *Laws of*

Gravity, Whit Stillman's *Metropolitan*—guys who had gone out with $30,000 and made these smaller, shoestring-budgeted films, so I thought, 'That's what I'm going to do.' I wrote a screenplay I knew I could shoot inexpensively; that's why I set it in the house I grew up in—I knew that was a location I wouldn't have to pay for. That's why I cast myself in the film. That was one less headache to worry about. I knew I could guarantee that I would show up everyday. And I asked my dad then for a little start-up money and we shot the film over eight months; we shot on weekends, the actors worked for deferred pay, the crew, the lights, the camera, even the editing facilities, we were able to defer all those costs and even about a quarter of the way into the film, when we ran out of our $25,000 start-up money, the lab in New York— DuArt Film Labs—even deferred the rest of the cost of processing, so that was really hundreds of thousands of dollars they deferred. So that's how I was able to do it. I asked for a lot of favors and I had a lot of support.

"I was working full-time, so when I'd get out of work at six or seven, we'd go to the editing facilities and we'd work till about five in the morning. This one particular day, we were editing till about five and I have to be at work at eight o'clock that morning, because we're going to do an interview with Jodie Foster at her hotel room. So we set up the lights, we get set for the interview, they're doing it out in the living room area of the hotel room, and the rest of us go into the bedroom where the monitors are set up and we're going to watch the interview. I made the mistake of sitting and eventually laying down on the bed and falling asleep during the interview. Apparently, I was snoring so loud that the microphones picked it up and they had to stop the interview and wake me up and her people were very upset, but apparently, she thinks it's pretty funny.

"You hear about all these horror stories after Sundance: 'Package a deal, Babe,' and all that stuff, and it really does happen. If a script had a character and his name began with Mc, O, or Fitz, I got it, and it ranged from everything like, 'We want you to direct this project,' or 'Would you be willing to write a screenplay about this?' or even 'How do you feel about acting in this piece?' But before Sundance, I knew what I wanted to do. I wanted to write and direct my own films. If I was going to act, I was going to act in those films. So when these offers came to me, I knew that I wasn't interested in anything like that. What I wanted to do was make sure that as soon as possible, I could be on the set of a film, making another one of my films."

Prize; Nominations: Australian Film Institute '96: Best Foreign Film; British Academy Awards '95: Best Foreign Film. **VHS, LV** *COL*

Business as Usual

Economic sanctions may be the only thing that sexual bullies understand. This is the point that a gutsy young working class film-maker, Lezli-Ann Barrett, makes with her first movie, *Business as Usual.* Glenda Jackson plays the "manageress" of a Liverpool boutique to whom model Cathy Tyson appeals for help against the unwelcome advances of Mr. Barry, the area manager. None too thrilled to be caught in the middle, Jackson's character nonetheless complains to Barry, who promptly fires her without written notice. When she

later asks for the reason for her dismissal in writing, Barry, who has already hired her replacement, has her removed from the store by the police. Her husband, a former embattled union leader, has lost his spirit and fears that she will lose hers by fighting back. However, her father and son, both labor organizers, are full of fight and urge her to enlist the help of her union. One of the interesting elements in *Business as Usual* is that the film shows how union leaders are sometimes willing to make harsh compromises with management in order to relieve tense labor struggles. By showing Jackson's husband (wonderfully played by John Thaw) as a defeated, weary, intensely proud man whose finest combats are behind him, Barrett's script also shows what an exhausting thing it is to fight on behalf of other workers. And the film certainly does not glamourize the long hours of picketing, the police harassment, and the media trivialization of sexual harassment issues. Barrett's screenplay is also interesting for her sensitive depiction of Tyson's boyfriend, well played by poet Craig Charles, Tyson's real-life husband. In the movies, targets of harassment are often aligned with some drippy character who first blames the victim and then withdraws emotional support. Tyson perfectly captures the pain and confusion of the harassment target and her scenes alone with Charles are tender and believable. The source of all this agony, Mr. Barry, is hardly a villain, just an average, run-of-the-mill jerk, who thinks that downgrading women is funny. As portrayed by Eamon Boland, he is not particularly bright and rather frightened of both men and women. All that is beside the point, of course, when he tries to halt a woman's career simply because she sees through his games. Production values on *Business as Usual* are deliberately gritty, a far cry from the glossy films in which Jackson usually stars. When Barrett got nowhere trying to submit her scripts to Jackson through an agent, she went to see her in a play and personally asked her to read the script. Even with Jackson's acceptance, it took years for Barrett to raise the money and attract the connections that, luckily for viewers, made *Business as Usual* possible. Note: In real life, Jackson won a Labor seat in Parliament in 1992. 🦴🦴🦴

1988 (PG) 89m/C Glenda Jackson, Cathy Tyson, John Thaw, Craig Charles, Eamon Boland; *D:* Lezli-Ann Barrett; *W:* Lezli-Ann Barrett. **VHS, Beta, Closed Caption** *WAR*

Butley

It's hard to imagine a story in which a man loses both his wife and his best friend in the same day could possibly be slow-paced. But it IS, and only Alan Bates' powerhouse performance in the title role keeps Simon Gray's attenuated structure from falling apart. If Jimmy Porter, the angry young man of the late John

Osborne's *Look Back in Anger* had made it past the 1950s and gone on to be a university professor, he might have become just such a man as Butley. True, Butley does not have Jimmy Porter's savagery; he has replaced that with a humorous attitude that is both appealing and aggravating. He has become A Difficult Bloke to Understand. He's too pathetic to be truly comic, and too lacking in irony to be truly tragic. Nor does he have the richness of character that might at least make him a tragicomic figure. He stumbles through life, anyway, annoying the hell out of everyone in such a charming way that it is hard for anyone to leave him. But leave him they do, and this is what *Butley* is all about. There's not much else here: one dull office setting, people walking in and out. We meet these people only briefly, and we see them chiefly through Butley's eyes. We also hear far too many discussions of characters we only catch a glimpse of, or worse, never meet at all. Through it all, Bates injects passion into every one of his lines. Butley may be sloppy, lazy, and frustrated, but he is also filled with an intellectual vitality, and Bates makes the struggles of this man, lugging around both a liquor bottle and his long-unfinished book about T.S. Eliot in his briefcase, wholly worth two hours of our concern and attention. The late Jessica Tandy (1909-94) plays Edna Shaft, the only other role of any length. (*Butley* won the Evening Standard award as Best Play and was a 1973 Tony nominee for Best Play. Bates won the Tony for Best Dramatic Actor. *Butley* was released theatrically overseas in 1976.) An American Film Theatre production. 🦴🦴🦴

1974 127m/C *GB CA* Alan Bates, Jessica Tandy, Richard O'Callaghan, Susan Engel, Michael Byrne, Georgina Hale, Simon Rouse, John Savident, Oliver Maguire, Susan Wooldridge; *D:* Harold Pinter; *W:* Simon Gray; *C:* Gerry Fisher. **VHS** *NO*

Butterfly Kiss

The May 1996 issue of *Films in Review* arrived three months late, as usual. It fea-

tured pages and pages about the so-called Golden Age of Hollywood, attenuated reviews of movies that have been out for ages, and a color cover shot of Dian Hanson. (Who?) But this quaint little publication also seemed to contain a few words of warning for folks like, well, us. It appears that contributor Rocco Simonelli is steamed about audience members with the NOIVE not to like Michael Winterbottom's *Butterfly Kiss,* starring Amanda Plummer and Saskia Reeves. Says Rocco: "It's viewers such as yourselves who are the true cause of Hollywood's decline in recent years, its pervasive unwillingness to take chances. The next time you're bitching about the tedium and lack of imagination embodied by most Hollywood fare, remember it was YOU who wielded the knife." Gee, Rocco, we thought that was Amanda Plummer! As far as we can recall, we sent all our knives to the cleaners before we saw *Butterfly Kiss.* Even if it didn't have Michael Winterbottom's mitts all over it, you wouldn't have to tell us it was a guy who came up with yet another psycho lesbian movie. What is so daring and innovative about *Basic Instinct* or *Single White Female*? Lesbian looney-tunes have been around at least as long as the early days of the silent flickers. Loving women equals killing people, especially men, and usually after sex. It goes with this particular stretch of cinematic territory. Casting Amanda Plummer as the homicidal Eunice is rather stacking the deck, because she can be every bit as much of a ham as her dad Christopher. The only surprise here is Saskia Reeves as Eunice's submissive lover Miriam. Reeves photographs entirely differently in color than she does in black and white. Through most of the film, Miriam drags herself through life like a wimpy Sigourney Weaver, but in black and white, she reveals flashes of wit, humor, and irony in the best tradition of Dame Maggie Smith. This despite Winterbottom's edict for Reeves to make Miriam flat and boring. And what do lesbians do in the daytime besides get rid of the bodies they carved up the night before? After a 1996 screening at San Francisco's Lesbian and Gay Film Festival, *Butterfly Kiss* had a brief commercial run at nationwide Landmark Theatres, then made a fast flight to video. **WOOF!**

1994 85m/C *GB* Amanda Plummer, Saskia Reeves, Paul Brown, Des McAleer, Ricky Tomlinson; *D:* Michael Winterbottom; *W:* Frank Cottrell Boyce; *C:* Seamus McGarvey; *M:* John Harle. **VHS** *TRI*

Cabeza de Vaca

We're always leery of movies with the proviso "Patient viewers will be rewarded." That usually means that we will feel bored and guilty for 90-120 minutes, wondering what in the world is happening onscreen that is so blazingly wonderful. *Cabeza de Vaca* has received some nice notices from *Daily Variety,* the *Village Voice,* the *L.A. Times,* and *Time* magazine, but we felt like we wandered into Ethnography 101 by mistake. There is no character you can care about one way or the other with the exception of a short guy with no arms who yells a lot. The action takes place in the early 16th century and revolves around a Spanish explorer who lives among the Indians for eight years. There is more blood than dialogue in the movie, a bit of magic here and there, and the obligatory bare chest whenever a rare female drifts into focus. Thinking that the film might appeal more to men than to women, we asked for another opinion from a male viewer, but *Cabeza de Vaca* left him equally cold. The film on video may very well succeed in attracting a receptive audience who will appreciate this epic, which has been described as a Mexican *Dances with Wolves.* 🦴🦴

1990 (R) 111m/C *MX SP* Juan Diego, Daniel Gimenez Cacho, Roberto Sosa, Carlos Castanon, Gerardo Villarreal, Roberto Cobo, Jose Flores, Ramon Barragan; *D:* Nicolas Echevarria; *W:* Guillermo Sheridan, Nicolas Echevarria; *M:* Mario Lavista. **VHS** *NHO, FCT*

Caddie

Based on the true story of an anonymous woman who raised her two children alone after her husband ran off with her best friend, *Caddie* makes a hopeful statement for strong, resilient women who don't spend their lives waiting for a romantic prince to sweep them off their feet, but make the best of circumstances, even when they're dreary. Unable to find any other job but a bar maid, Caddie works energetically for her kids and herself. Director Donald Crombie suggests that the world is filled with Caddies, worthy of more dignity and respect than they've ever received. At one point, Peter, Caddie's true love from Greece (ably played by Takis Emmanuel), tells her that she isn't like all the other women who work in bars. Her snappy retort is filled with rage at the stereotype. Helen Morse is wonderful as Caddie, persuasively revealing the woman who can tackle everything, even the Great Depression, on her own terms. A guy at the screening I attended mentioned that Caddie's poverty seemed too beautiful to be real, but I beg to differ. Early in the film, it is revealed that Caddie would transform the most sordid surroundings into a decent place for herself and her family. There ARE women like Caddie in the world and, luckily for us, screenwriter Joan Long wrote about one of them for all the world to see. 🦴🦴🦴

1976 107m/C *AU* Helen Morse, Jack Thompson, Takis Emmanuel, Jacki Weaver; *D:* Donald Crombie; *W:* Joan Long; *C:* Peter James; *M:* Patrick Flynn. **VHS, Beta** *HBO*

Cafe Nica: Portraits from Nicaragua

John Knoop's 45-minute documentary *Cafe Nica* is too short to do justice to its subjects, the Nicaraguan people affected by war. The film lacks a strong point of view as well as the depth that would lend meaning to all those fleeting talking heads. 🦴🦴

1987 45m/C *D:* John Knoop; *C:* John Knoop. **VHS** *NO*

Camille Claudel

The life of Camille Claudel offers several good answers to the age-old question (probably asked by a man!): "Why are there no great woman artists?" For one thing, many make the mistake of sleeping with great male artists! For another, artistic cliques, standards, and histories are dominated by men. When we first tried to look up Camille Claudel, only recognized as a major sculptor since 1984, her name, predictably, was missing from the encyclopedia, although her brother Paul and her lover Auguste Rodin both received extensive entries. Luckily, her biography by Reine-Marie Paris is available in paperback, extensively illustrated with photographs of Camille's finest sculptures. Camille Claudel is also the focus of the fine French film starring Isabelle Adjani in the title role and Gerard Depardieu as Auguste Rodin. Marilyn Goldin's eloquent screenplay shows how difficult it was for Camille to establish herself as an artist in the late 19th and early 20th century. Like a benevolent despot, Rodin offered Camille a position in his studio, but he sealed himself off to her once their affair was over and he could no longer accept her unique, deeply threatening visions as an artist. According to her biographer, there is some evidence in the Rodin Museum to support Camille's belief that her consignment to artistic obscurity was the work of Rodin. In any event, Camille never recovered from Rodin's rejection and by 1913, her family committed her to an asylum, where she spent the last 30 years of her life before her death at the age of 78. She never sculpted again, although she wrote many lucid letters to her much-loved brother Paul, who was responsible for her confinement. Isabelle Adjani plays Camille to the hilt, perfectly capturing her clashing needs for love and work. Depardieu's Rodin is more of an enigma, but then so are most men who profess to love two women in different ways. Laurent Grevill

C

**INDEPENDENT
FILM GUIDE**

plays Paul Claudel as a self-righteous drip, but Alain Cuny steals every scene he's in as Camille's father, the only man who seems to love and understand her exactly as she is. Note: a photograph of the real Camille Claudel at age twenty reveals intelligence, pride, strength, and beauty. All are assets for a woman and an artist but, as Bruno Nuytten's disturbing film shows, they are sometimes fatal for a student and a mistress. (In French with English subtitles.) ♪♪♪♪

1989 (R) 149m/C *FR* Isabelle Adjani, Gerard Depardieu, Laurent Grevill, Alain Cuny, Madeleine Robinson, Katrine Boorman; *D:* Bruno Nuytten; *W:* Bruno Nuytten, Marilyn Goldin; *M:* Gabriel Yared. Cesar Awards '89: Best Actress (Adjani), Best Art Direction/Set Decoration, Best Cinematography, Best Costume Design, Best Film; Nominations: Academy Awards '89: Best Actress (Adjani), Best Foreign Language Film. **VHS, Beta, LV** *ORI, IME*

Cannibal Women in the Avocado Jungle of Death

Cannibal Women in the Avocado Jungle of Death was our favorite of all the movies we rented in the month of March, 1990. It features a change of pace role for Shannon Tweed, who was then featured on the Playboy Channel in *Barbi, Shannon and Candy,* a tribute to three former Playmates. In THIS movie, she plays a feminist anthropology professor. Our favorite character in the movie is Bunny, her worst student, who thinks that she's the best one in the class. Bunny, played by Karen (*Return of the Killer Tomatoes*) Mistal, is always talking about her sexual fantasies. The two of them have to go into the jungles of San Bernadino to find another feminist professor, Adrienne Barbeau. They enlist the aid of a fairly useless male guide (played by Bill Maher) with whom Bunny promptly falls in love. You see, Bunny would like to be a feminist, but she never

CAN remember which side she's on. Also, she can't quite abandon her sexual fantasies of being wrapped up in red licorice and...love it! Great fun at a video party with plenty of free-spirited friends. ♪♪♪

1989 (PG-13) 90m/C Shannon Tweed, Adrienne Barbeau, Karen Mistal, Barry Primus, Bill Maher; *D:* J.F. Lawton; *W:* J.F. Lawton. **VHS, Beta, LV, Closed Caption** *PAR*

Careful

Careful is receiving the sort of ecstatic (and strategically placed) reviews that assure it a place in cult movie circles for many years to come. On the basis of its unique visual style alone, it is well worth a look, but whether *Careful* succeeds in luring you into its spell may depend on your ability to accept the artistic choices of its director, Guy Maddin. *Careful* is a movie we found easy to admire but hard to love, and we tried. Its striking use of colors, its playful nod to scratchy soundtracks, intertitles, and other outdated film conventions, its sincere attempt to reveal how repression ignites overwhelming passion; all provide clear evidence of the quirky and original talent of its director. But ultimately, Guy Maddin's limited abilities as a storyteller are not equal to his ambitious visions. His characters are more like puppets than flesh-and-blood people. If they make a sound when they are sexually aroused, they may be buried by an avalanche, a theoretically intriguing dilemma, but less than riveting to observe even when accompanied by a bag of visual tricks. None of the folks in this movie affect us quite as deeply as when they are in repose and no emotion or language gets in the way. Maddin's use of formal speech patterns is deliberate. The script was translated from English into Icelandic and then back again. Intellectuals may worship this approach, but we found it as draining as all the overproduced set pieces in Sergei Eisenstein's *Ivan the Terrible,* another so-called classic that's difficult to be moved by, however great it is to watch.

Recommended for viewing after *Careful:* the great Gosia Dobrowolska, rather underused here, in John Dingwall's Australian classic *Phobia,* which wrings more emotion out of two characters on a single set than Maddin does in this kaleidoscopic romp in a Canadian grain elevator. 🦴🦴

1994 100m/C Kyle McCulloch, Gosia Dobrowolska, Jackie Burroughs, Sarah Neville, Brent Neale, Paul Cox, Victor Cowie, Michael O'Sullivan, Vince Rimmer, Katya Gardner; **D:** Guy Maddin; **W:** Guy Maddin, George Toles; **M:** John McCulloch. **VHS** *KIV*

Carmen Miranda: Bananas Is My Business

Carmen Miranda. The name alone conjures up memories of Technicolor Fox musicals of the '40s at their zenith. Carmen Miranda was a bundle of energy and mischief, and the first Brazilian entertainer to become an international superstar. She was also to solidify the Latina standard for the silver screen. As Rita Moreno, who won an Academy Award six years after Miranda's death, observed wryly, "We had to be peppy. But I wanted to be an actress." After *West Side Story,* the versatile Moreno made no movies for years. But if Carmen Miranda ever chafed at being a high-priced specialty act, she never seemed to show it, at least not onscreen. *Carmen Miranda: Bananas Is My Business,* Helena Solberg's documentary of her legendary career, is mainly valuable for its rare film clips, dating back to the '30s. But the subtext, that Miranda was "Our Carmen," namely Brazil's own, tends to grate after awhile. Once Miranda left Brazil for first Broadway, then Hollywood, she returned just three times in sixteen years, once to be treated with indifference by upper crust Brazilian audiences, once to recover from exhaustion, and finally for her funeral. It was because little Helena's parents wouldn't let her join the million people lining the streets for the services that she became obsessed with Carmen Miranda's complicated relationship with her homeland. But the evidence she chooses to illustrate her theories is largely supplied by subjective voiceovers and a few interviews with wistful friends, family, colleagues, and employees. Nowhere is it made clear that Miranda wanted any other life than the one she had. True, she died young, on the very night that a television performance left her breathless. (The actual clip is shown in slow motion.) But dying young doesn't necessarily mean living unhappily, and the unsupported gossip that Solberg includes only reveal her own iconographic obsession, not the real Carmen Miranda. If you want to know the real Carmen Miranda, rent one of her many festive movies on video: *Down Argentine Way, Weekend in Havana,* and *Springtime in the Rockies* are three of her best Fox vehicles; *A Date with Judy* and *Nancy Goes to Rio* are two examples of her years at MGM; *Doll Face* and *Lucky Stiff,* which are minor showcases of her work, are fun to watch today; *Copacabana* co-starring Groucho Marx has been colorized recently to fairly good advantage; and, best of all, *The Gang's All Here* is a constant cable attraction. (That's the Busby Berkeley confection in which Carmen Miranda immortalized *The Lady with the Tutti Frutti Hat* for posterity.) It's sad that Carmen Miranda probably loved Brazil far more than Brazil ever loved her back. Her legacy of 14 musicals ensures that she will be remembered far longer than the native audiences who scorned her for her success. 🦴🦴🦴

1995 92m/C D: Helena Solberg; **W:** Helena Solberg. **VHS** *FXL*

Carnival of Souls

For many years, *Carnival of Souls* was our idea of a genuinely scary movie, far more frightening than *Frankenstein* or *Dracula.* In fact, if we watched *Carnival of Souls* while we were babysitting, we wanted to

Candace Hilligoss watches the *Carnival of Souls.*

wake up all the kids so they could protect us from its terrors. *Carnival of Souls* was the only feature ever made by Herk Harvey, who was stiffed by distributors in 1962 and never made a dime on the film's original release. The film became a late-night television staple and gradually acquired a loyal audience. Harvey eventually bought back the movie rights and 1989 audiences were finally able to see his original uncut version in a 35 mm. print. Paradoxically, Harvey's film succeeds because and in spite of its tiny budget. The amateur performances and script banalities demand considerable viewer patience. With more generous funding, though, the film might have strayed from the once-in-a-lifetime cast and claustrophobic settings which make it so distinctive. We know we're not in Hollywood anymore from the very beginning. The flat Kansas landscapes and

untrained faces have little connection with the cultural symbols that saturate most of the big studio films of 1962. We're light years away from the Warner Bros. and Paramount studios that are processing *The Music Man* and Elvis Presley musicals. A pretty girl appears to be the victim of a drowning accident, only she picks herself up and travels to another town where she is hired as a church organist and moves into a boarding house. As portrayed by Candace Hilligoss, the girl is extremely sensitive to her surroundings yet somehow disconnected from them. A slimy fellow boarder tries to pick her up. She vacillates between fending him off and encouraging his attention. She shops for clothes in a local department store until she realizes that no one can see her or hear her. She practices on the church organ until she discovers that she has no control over what she plays. She tries to get out of town only to be confronted with one obstacle after another. A psychiatrist and a priest offer empty reassurances. A Carnival of Souls beckons her to accept her true fate. *Frankenstein* and *Dracula* provide us with plenty of cheap thrills, but we are unlikely to bump into either of them in real life. All of us WILL come face to face with our own mortality and *Carnival of Souls* reminds us that, no matter how much we resist, the outcome is inevitable. 🦴🦴🦴

1962 80m/B Candace Hilligoss, Sidney Berger, Frances Feist, Stan Levitt, Art Ellison, Harold (Herk) Harvey; **D:** Harold (Herk) Harvey. **VHS, Beta, LV** *MRV, SNC, NOS*

Carrington

People who say that a woman is ahead of her time are usually men. Since so little is expected of them, women often follow paths which make more sense to them as individuals than to anyone else, including many of their male biographers. Dora Carrington was an early 20th century eccentric and a wonderful painter. She fell in love with the witty, sickly, and broke gay writer Lytton Strachey. Although she didn't fully realize it until he was on his deathbed, Strachey fell in love with her, too. They lived together for many years, meeting their sexual needs with other partners, but arranging their entire lives so they could be together. Writer/director Christopher Hampton goes into considerable detail about the financial arrangements the two have to make to live together, and we're afraid we lost track of the count and the amount during one of Carrington's many affairs. But Jonathan Pryce and Emma Thompson are just dear as the unlikely couple who wrote their own rules in the idyllic English countryside. What do they see in each other? It's only obvious. He is honest, charming, and fun, she is loyal, loving, and unique. Except for Strachey, Carrington is accountable to no one but herself, certainly not to a spouse or

her many lovers. But she's as strung on Strachey as a woman can be. Strachey's light, dry, satirical books are still in print, including his biography of Queen Victoria which is considered to be his masterpiece. For his time, Strachey's biographical approach was revolutionary; no previous writer had succeeded in revealing an icon like Victoria in such deeply human terms. Jonathan Pryce does a beautiful job showing just why Lytton Strachey captivated his generation, and Emma Thompson is an ideal foil as his much-loved companion who is quirky to everyone but herself. Art critics (who rarely ever wrote about her before this movie) complain that we don't get to see enough of Carrington's work in the film, but we don't get to read any of Strachey's work here either. This is above all a sensitively rendered love story, and Hampton and cast deserve high marks for making *Carrington* so vital and real to contemporary audiences. 🦴🦴🦴🦴

1995 (R) 120m/C *FR GB* Emma Thompson, Jonathan Pryce, Steven Waddington, Sam West, Rufus Sewell, Penelope Wilton, Jeremy Northam, Peter Blythe, Janet McTeer, Alex Kingston, Sebastian Harcombe, Richard Clifford; **D:** Christopher Hampton; **W:** Christopher Hampton; **C:** Denis Lenoir; **M:** Michael Nyman. Cannes Film Festival '95: Special Jury Prize, Best Actor (Pryce); National Board of Review Awards '95: Best Actress (Thompson); Nominations: British Academy Awards '95: Best Actor (Pryce), Best Film. **VHS, LV** *PGV*

Cat and Mouse

Cat and Mouse is a straightforward murder mystery, graced by the presence of gorgeous Michele Morgan. The wry performance by Serge Reggiani as a single-minded detective is perfection itself. Claude Lelouch can't resist adding an obligatory (if excellent) car chase sequence. Great fun! 🦴🦴🦴◗

1978 (PG) 107m/C *FR* Michele Morgan, Serge Reggiani, Jean-Pierre Aumont, Philippe Labro, Philippe Leotard, Valerie Lagrange, Michel Perelon, Christine Laurent; **D:** Claude Lelouch; **W:** Claude Lelouch; **C:** Andre Perlstein; **M:** Francis Lai. **VHS, Beta** *COL*

HERK HARVEY
On when he first became aware that *Carnival of Souls* had become a cult classic

Actually, that's kind of surprising in the sense that we weren't really aware that it was. But, once in a while, either John Clifford, the writer, or I would get a letter from somebody, especially from New York or California, that they had seen it and knew that it had been made in Lawrence [Kansas] and just wanted to know more about the film because they had never heard of it. This kind of thing. And then we started seeing articles in magazines and this sort of thing saying the cult film *Carnival of Souls* was being shown, and so we thought, well gee, how about that. It's becoming a cult film.

"I think that there are images in the film that are lasting. I think the location, I think the character of Candace Hilligoss, I think there are several things in it that are sort of lasting images, and I think some of the people saw it at younger ages, and were impressed by it. And then as they got older maybe some of them talked about it and said 'Have you seen this?' and maybe the fact that it wasn't available, actually, made it more of a cult thing because somebody could say, I've seen it and you haven't, and it could be that's one of the things that promoted it, I don't know."

Caught

Caught is about Nick (Arie Verveen), a youthful drifter, who gets caught up in the lives of a middle-aged couple, Betty and Joe (Maria Conchita Alonso and Edward James Olmos), who own a Mom-and-Pop fish store in Jersey City. When Betty and Joe's adult son Danny (Steve Schub), now a married parent, comes home, he is angered by the fact that his place in his parent's lives seems to have been usurped by Nick. Alonso and Robert Young regular Olmos attracted good notices for their performances as Betty and Joe, and *Caught* also received attention for the "sexual steaminess" of some erotic sequences between Betty and Nick. Based on the novel *Into It* by screenwriter Edward Pomerantz. 🦴🦴

1996 (R) 109m/C Edward James Olmos, Maria Conchita Alonso, Arie Verveen, Steven Schub, Bitty Schram, Shawn Elliot; **D:** Robert M. Young; **W:** Edward Pomerantz; **C:** Michael Barrow; **M:** Chris Botti. Nominations: Independent Spirit Awards '97: Best Actress (Alonso), Best Director (Young), Debut Performance (Verveen). **VHS, LV, Closed Caption** COL

Celia: Child of Terror

Australian writer/director Ann Turner offers one of the few honest depictions of the dark side of childhood, as seen by a nine-year-old girl growing up in the 1950s. Rebecca Smart is remarkable as the little girl who turns to voodoo magic in an effort to cope with unfair grownups, unyielding politicians, and cruel playmates. The character of Celia has been compared by some critics to Rhoda Penmark in *The Bad Seed,* but the comparison isn't especially apt. Under less stressful conditions, Celia might have resorted to less drastic remedies to solve her very real problems. But, as the film makes clear, friends and grown-ups who might have provided solid sympathetic support are torn away from her for reasons her family fails to make clear to her. The only things that really belong to her are her rabbit Murgatroyd and her violent fantasies, and both serve as catalytic agents for her ultimate corruption. (It isn't giving away too much if we advise you not to get too attached to Murgatroyd.) *Celia* may be an exaggeration of reality, but not by much, and *Celia* was by far the best of 1990's Women in Film festival entries. 🦴🦴🦴

1990 110m/C *AU* Rebecca Smart, Nicholas Eadie, Victoria Longley, Mary-Anne Fahey; *D:* Ann Turner; *W:* Ann Turner. **VHS, Beta** *NO*

Cemetery Man

Michele Soavi's *Cemetery Man* played at selected Landmark Theatres in the spring of 1996 to generally grumpy reviews, but for goofball entertainment, we thought it was a kick to watch. It was certainly a helluva lot more fun than Paul Schrader's *My Dinner with Androids,* I mean, *The Comfort of Strangers,* which came and went in 1991. Rupert Everett stars again as a bit of an idiot, but at least he isn't bored in this one. He's Francisco Dellamorte, a grave keeper with a problem: the dead keep returning to life and he has to shoot them in the head to get rid of them once and for all. One day, an old geezer kicks off and his beautiful widow arrives on the scene to pay her respects. As soon as she says, "I love my husband," she and Dellamorte are frolicking on his gravestone. The husband returns as a zombie and proceeds to bite her to death. Or at least that's Dellamorte's first impression. Too late, he finds out that she was only frightened and, because of his usual approach with zombies, he's lost her forever, or at least until she returns as another character, and another. (Anna Falchi is the well endowed object of his desire.) The plot takes increasingly strange turns as motorcyclists collide with Boy Scouts in a school bus and Dellamorte starts shooting the living as well as the dead. There's a rich, haunting look to the film that may remind you of the Mario Bava horror classics of the 1960s, or of the 1980s films of Dario Argento. It's no accident; Argento is Soavi's cinematic mentor. Three of the big gripes about this film are (1) It seems to go around in circles, (2) It steals sequences from other movies, and (3) The frequent bloodletting is comedic to the point of absurdity. True enough, and that may be why *Cemetery Man* collected dust in an Italian studio vault for two years. But Rupert Everett is always an arresting presence, and if you're in the mood for this sort of senseless foolishness (as we obviously were), you may giggle your way into insensibility. Attention die-hard movie buffs: if character actor Mickey Knox looks familiar to you, he should! Once upon a time, he worked with Bogart, Cagney, and Lancaster in such film noir treats of 1949 as *Knock on Any Door, White Heat,* and *I Walk Alone.* **AKA:** Dellamorte Delamore; Of Death, Of Love. 🦴🦴🦴

1995 (R) 100m/C *IT* Rupert Everett, Anna Falchi, Francois Hadji-Lazaro; *D:* Michele (Michael) Soavi; *W:* Gianni Romoli; *C:* Mauro Marchetti; *M:* Manuel De Sica. **VHS, Closed Caption** *FOX*

Center Stage

In spite of the fact that portions of *Center Stage* were shown out of sequence at the Berlin Film Festival, Maggie Cheung still won a much-deserved Best Actress Award for her breathtaking performance as Ruan Ling-Yu. *Variety's* review was just a tad chilly, although its critic neglected to mention the mixed-up reels at the screening in his report, tsk-tsk. He did describe the "inadequate" translation, which is exactly what occurred when I first saw it. Imagine, if you will, two Ruan Ling-Yu fans shaking a fellow viewer who could only read the Cantonese subtitles when many sequences (including the climax!) of an edited copy of the film were entirely in Mandarin. Luckily, Tai Seng Video has come up with the full (154 minute) version with English subtitles so Western audiences can savor Maggie Cheung's exquisite work here to full advantage. Ruan Ling-Yu was China's leading actress in 1935 when she committed suicide, leaving behind a note, "Gossip is a dreadful thing." Her offscreen life was difficult and complex, but on film Ruan Ling-Yu was wonderfully perceptive and deeply lucid. Cheung, with her own unique style and presence, succeeds in unlayering the mystery behind this legendary star. In one heartbreaking sequence, Cheung as Ling-Yu has already made her decision to die, but she moves with elegant grace among the members of her profession, responding with warm affection to the well wishers who are already celebrating her introduction to talking pictures (Chinese films were silent until 1935). Director Stanley Kwan recreates the look and feel of the '30s and includes footage of the real Ruan Ling-Yu in *The Peach Blossom Weeps Tears of Blood, The Goddess,* and *New Women.* Black-and-white interviews with aging contemporaries of the late actress are also included, as well as discussions with Cheung about her own approach to the material. Even die-hard movie buffs may never have heard of Ruan Ling-Yu; *Center Stage* is an excellent introduction to her life and work, and Cheung's riveting star turn is not to be missed! ***AKA:*** The Actress; Ruan Ling-Yu; The New China Woman. 🦴🦴🦴

1991 154m/C *HK* Maggie Cheung, Tony Leung, Shin Hong, Carina Lau, Lawrence Ng, Waise Lee, Cheung Chung, Siu Sheung, Yip Sang; ***D:*** Stanley Kwan; ***W:*** Yau Tai On-Ping; ***C:*** Poon Hang-Seng. **VHS** *TAI*

Century

Century is everything *The Age of Innocence* wanted to be and wasn't: an atmospheric re-creation of the mood and feeling of a vanished time. Martin Scorsese tried to accomplish this with an extravagant budget and extended close-ups of lavish meals. But money and food, however useful in real life, shouldn't have the burden of stealing scenes from the actors. With a much smaller budget, writer/director Stephen Poliakoff has kept the focus where it belongs in *Century,* on the superb cast who interpret his excellent screenplay. As we approach the 21st century, we find ourselves evaluating the last few years of the 20th. Which of our customs and traditions will survive and endure, which will be hermetically sealed in this era and rendered obsolete by the year 2001? The progressive doctor, played with languid charm by Charles Dance, is a man who appears far ahead of the late 19th century, but, in fact, his influence is forever trapped within it because of a fatal flaw. The young medical student earnestly played by Clive Owen is inspired by Dance's character, but ultimately disillusioned by him. His immigrant father, wonderfully played by the late Sir Robert Stephens (1931-95), wants to give a spectacular welcome to the new age in his adopted country, even though his neighbors in the British countryside avoid and distrust him because of his Eastern European background. And the shimmering Miranda Richardson, as one of the women employed in Dance's medical institute, is determined to make a free-spirited life for herself, regardless of the obstacles. The conflict between Dance and Owen is at the heart of the film: Dance hires women (and one black man) to work at his institute and treats them with respect. He gives his students valuable training and the chance to learn on the job. He even encourages Owen's independent medical research, as long as he and everyone else recognizes who's in charge. But Dance has his own murky agenda, carefully concealed from the wealthy benefactress who backs the institute (the great Joan Hickson, seen all too briefly in two marvelous sequences with Owen). After the frustrated Owen discovers what Dance is really up to, he enlists Richardson's help and graduates from devoted admirer to fierce adversary. The battle is only partly successful; the fledgling medical pioneer loses valuable research opportunities by taking on the system that once nurtured him. And that, in a way, is the point of *Century*; however much we rage against the inequities in our own time, it will always have the edge on us. Poliakoff and cast drive home this concept with fresh and startling meaning. 🎞🎞🎞🎞

1994 (R) 112m/C *GB* Clive Owen, Charles Dance, Miranda Richardson, Robert Stephens, Joan Hickson, Lena Headey, Neil Stuke; *D:* Stephen Poliakoff; *W:* Stephen Poliakoff; *C:* Witold Stok; *M:* Michael Gibbs. **VHS** *PGV*

Chain of Desire

Remember Max Ophuls' classic 1950 film *La Ronde,* based on Arthur Schnitzler's play? The one in which just about everyone in an all-star cast (Anton Walbrook, Serge Reggiani, Simone Simon, Simone Signoret, Daniel Gelin, Danielle Darrieux, Fernand Gravet, Odette Joyeux, Jean-Louis Barrault, Isa Miranda, Gerard Philipe) had affairs with each other? So did Roger Vadim, who remade it, not very well, in 1964. So did Temistocles Lopez, who remade it in 1993. The "advantage" this time is that the Production Code of 1934-69 need be considered no longer when making a movie about pointless sex. Alma D'Angeli (Linda Fiorentino) and Jesus (Elias Koteas) are the first sexual adventurers. There are 14 lust-driven Manhattanites in this movie. In place of the sophisticated, dry humor of Ophuls, we get Lopez' message for the '90s, delivered in an understated way—but if you have a pulse, it will still hit you with a thud. 🎞🎞

1993 107m/C Linda Fiorentino, Elias Koteas, Malcolm McDowell, Grace Zabriskie, Tim Guinee, Assumpta Serna, Patrick Bauchau, Seymour Cassel, Kevin Conroy, Angel Aviles, Holly Marie Combs, Jamie Harold, Dewey Weber, Suzanne Douglas; *D:* Temistocles Lopez; *W:* Temistocles Lopez; *C:* Nancy Schreiber; *M:* Nathan Birnbaum. Nominations: Independent Spirit Awards '94: Best Cinematography. **VHS, Beta, LV** *PSM*

Chameleon Street

I wonder if the real William Douglas Street ever saw 1960's *The Great Impostor,* in which Tony Curtis as Ferdinand Waldo Demara, Jr., teaches school without a credential, impersonates a novice in a Trappist monastery, works as a prison warden's deputy, and performs a successful operation as a Canadian naval lieutenant without a medical degree. At any rate, Street (Wendell B. Harris) wanted a more interesting way of life than to work for a burglar alarm company in Detroit. Street, too, performs surgery AND impersonates a *Time* reporter AND pretends to be an exchange student from Africa AND speaks French AND practices law. *Chameleon Street* isn't particularly well acted or well directed but it is fun and there's a great costume ball sequence. 🎞🎞🎞

1989 (R) 95m/C Wendell B. Harris Jr., Angela Leslie, Amina Fakir, Paula McGee, Mano Breckenridge, David Kiley, Anthony Ennis; *Cameos:* Coleman A. Young; *D:* Wendell B. Harris Jr.; *W:* Wendell B. Harris Jr.; *C:* Daniel S. Noga; *M:* Peter S. Moore. Sundance Film Festival '90: Grand Jury Prize. **VHS, LV** *ACA, FCT*

Champion

Ring Lardner's bitter short story about the lionization of a loser who bullied his way to the top of the fight game was transformed into a larger-than-life portrait of an antihero by the soon-to-be-blacklisted screenwriter Carl Foreman. Many of the illustrations that made the original yarn so cynical are included in the film, but the approach changed completely. Midge Kelly is a jerk because he is a jerk, according to Lardner. As portrayed by the likable Kirk Douglas, Midge Kelly is an ambitious young hustler who is jerked around by the circumstances of his limited life and who makes errors in judgment that propel him straight through his spectacular rise and inevitable fall.

Therefore, even though Midge Kelly is shown beating up his crippled brother and abandoning his wife on their wedding day, neglecting his mother, pursuing and dumping a married woman, and using yet a third woman for his own gain, Kirk Douglas invests his pathetic character with such an unconscious, driven quality that we cannot help identifying with his struggle. He manipulates everyone in sight, yet when he says "I'm not going to be a 'hey, you' all my life. I'm going to make something of myself," it is not hard to sympathize with his desire to improve his wretched existence. Midge Kelly's going to be champion even if it kills him. When we watch his agonized scrambling for recognition and see his broken body and battered face, we understand his brother's refusal to condemn him and not for the hard-boiled reasons supplied by Lardner. This is what winning at any cost does to some people, says Foreman. Midge Kelly's victims, who learned to swallow their losses, are in far better shape than he is. He may be achieving immortality, but they are learning how to live. ♫♫♫

1949 99m/B Kirk Douglas, Arthur Kennedy, Marilyn Maxwell, Ruth Roman, Lola Albright, Paul Stewart; **D:** Mark Robson; **W:** Carl Foreman; **C:** Franz Planer; **M:** Dimitri Tiomkin. Academy Awards '49: Best Film Editing (Harry Gerstad); Nominations: Academy Awards '49: Best Actor (Douglas), Best Black and White Cinematography (Planer), Best Screenplay (Foreman), Best Supporting Actor (Kennedy), Best Original Score (Tiomkin). **VHS, Closed Caption** REP

Chan Is Missing

Chan Is Missing is the first movie I saw in a theatre that I remember trying to press the pause button so I could rewind the film to see a favorite sequence twice (I got my first VCR in May, 1982). Obviously, I couldn't do it, but the impulse was there. It's about a couple of taxi drivers in San Francisco who hunt for Chan after he vanishes with their five grand meant to pay for a taxi license. The great black-and-white footage of Chinatown captures the look,

pace, and feel of the neighborhood in the early '80s, and Wayne Wang gets performances out of his then-unknown cast. *Chan Is Missing* launched Wayne Wang's successful career as a director and also gave us a chance to see future director Peter Wang (*A Great Wall, Laserman*) as Henry the Cook. Lauren Chew (Amy) was in *Dim Sum,* Wayne Wang's next picture, and Marc Hayashi (Steve) co-starred with Peter Wang in *Laserman.* ♫♫♫

1982 80m/B Wood Moy, Marc Hayashi, Laureen Chew, Judy Mihei, Peter Wang, Presco Tabios, Frankie Allarcon, Virginia Cerenio, Roy Chan, George Woo, Emily Yamasaki, Ellen Yeung; **D:** Wayne Wang; **W:** Wayne Wang, Terrel Seltzer, Isaac Cronin; **C:** Michael G. Chin; **M:** Robert Kikuchi-Yngojo. **VHS** NYF

Chaplin

With Sir Richard Attenborough at the helm, *Chaplin* promised to be yet another overblown movie biography, and that it certainly is. However, it is largely redeemed by the truth that its gifted cast succeed in conveying onscreen. The centerpiece of the movie is Robert Downey, Jr., who is nothing short of superb in the title role. Moira Kelly also delivers absolutely beguiling performances as Chaplin's first and last loves, Hetty Kelly and Oona O'Neill. There is a lovely early sequence with Downey and Kelly that effectively captures Chaplin's romantic spirit struggling to express itself against the backdrop of a frosty London night. Many of *Chaplin*'s finest moments deal with unfamiliar material like this encounter, and Chaplin's studio days are lovingly recreated with some nice color work that takes on the patina of hand-painted tintypes. Where Attenborough and screenwriters William Boyd, Bryan Forbes, and William Goldman seem to fight their own film is by establishing, but ineffectively reinforcing, a through-line from a not particularly memorable meeting between Chaplin and a young J. Edgar Hoover to Chaplin's permanent exile from America over 30 years later. Kevin Dunn's portrayal of Hoover, of course, is your standard vindictive voyeur that's been floating around on movie screens since 1972. Moreover, Chaplin's legendary contemporaries like Mabel Normand and Mary Pickford are dismissed as overrated bitches when they were every bit as wonderful in their own way as Chaplin was. You'd also think, to look at Paul Rhys' sincere interpretation of Syd Chaplin, that he functioned strictly as his brother's agent. In fact, he was a wonderfully talented comedian in his own right, and his 1925 production of *Charley's Aunt* is the best and funniest of all the movie versions of the Brandon Thomas classic. Admittedly, you'd expect a movie about Chaplin, based on his autobiography, to focus mainly on the title character. But when you see stars like Kevin Kline in a particularly sensitive turn as Douglas Fairbanks and Dan Aykroyd as Mack Sennett (God, where is his ego, to show his ENTIRE naked stomach in one shot?), and the enchanting Penelope Ann Miller as Edna Purviance and Diane Lane capturing a great deal of Paulette Goddard's vivacity, you can't help thinking that it was THIS crowd that represented Chaplin's world. Why couldn't we have seen more of them, instead of sporadic set pieces illustrating J. Edgar Hoover's detached paranoia? That the filmmakers attempted more than they could fully explore may have been somewhat of an error in judgment, but with all *Chaplin*'s flaws, there is still so much of value in this movie that it is definitely worth careful appraisal on video. 🦴🦴🦴

1992 (PG-13) 135m/C *GB* Robert Downey Jr., Dan Aykroyd, Geraldine Chaplin, Kevin Dunn, Anthony Hopkins, Milla Jovovich, Moira Kelly, Kevin Kline, Diane Lane, Penelope Ann Miller, Paul Rhys, John Thaw, Marisa Tomei, Nancy Travis, James Woods, David Duchovny, Deborah Maria Moore, Bill Paterson, John Standing, Robert Stephens, Peter Crook; *D:* Richard Attenborough; *W:* Bryan Forbes, William Boyd, William Goldman; *C:* Sven Nykvist; *M:* John Barry. British Academy Awards '92: Best Actor (Downey); Nominations: Academy Awards '92: Best Actor (Downey), Best Art Direction/Set Decoration, Best Original Score. **VHS, LV, Closed Caption** *LIV, MOV, FCT*

Charley's Aunt

Sydney Chaplin (1885-1965) is the whole show in this delightful silent comedy. Charlie's handsome older brother is a charmer as Babbs (AKA Lord Fancourt Babberly), and he's even better as the sweet little old lady who's supposed to be "Charley's Aunt from Brazil, where the nuts came from." The REAL Donna Lucia D'Alvabarez is fetching Eulalie Jensen (1885-1952). Babbs is in love with Ela (Ethel Shannon, 1898-1951), Jack Chesney's (David James) in love with Kitty Verdun (Priscilla Bonner, 1899-1996), and Charley Whykeham's (Jimmy Harrison, 1908-77) in love with Amy (Mary Akin) but he's having a bit of a problem with her grumpy Uncle Stephen. When Babbs turns up at St. Olde's College in Oxford University as Donna Lucia, Uncle Stephen (James E. Page, 1870-1930), and Jack's father Sir Francis (Phillips Smalley, 1865-1939), compete for "her" attention. Meanwhile, Brassett the butler (Lucien Littlefield, 1895-1960) does his best to look befuddled. Littlefield lost his hair while still quite young, so he spent most of his long career playing much older men. I used to wonder about the enormous eyes of silent movie stars; was it just make-up or was it some sort of lighting effect? Then I saw Priscilla Bonner up close in San Francisco's Sheraton Palace Hotel in 1984. She looked very much like Kitty Verdun and her lovely large eyes were absolutely real. An early talkie version of *Charley's Aunt* was made in 1930 and it creaks in comparison with this lively farce. Based on Brandon Thomas' 1892 play, which is so fresh and so funny that it will probably make people laugh in the 21st century. 🦴🦴🦴🦴

1925 75m/B Sydney Chaplin, Ethel Shannon, Lucien Littlefield, Alec B. Francis, Mary Akin, Priscilla Bonner, Jimmy Harrison, David James, Eulalie Jensen, James E. Page, Phillips Smalley; *D:* Scott Sidney; *W:* F. McGrew Willis, Joe Farnham; *C:* Gus Peterson, Paul Garnett. **VHS, Beta** *GPV, FCT*

JOEY LAUREN ADAMS

Chasing Amy

Kevin Smith is such an amazing writer; you really don't even want to come close to touching his stuff or giving him some sort of advice on what to do with his material. He wrote the first draft and that's pretty much what we shot. There were some times when I would say, 'I wouldn't say it like that,' and he would say, 'Yes, you say it like that everyday,' because he's very good at hearing people's inflections and we'd have little arguments about that, but as far as Alyssa's dialogue, no. I think it might have been harder for Ben Affleck as Holden, because he agreed with the Holden character and he thought he should be really upset, and he has every right to be upset, and the whole point of the movie is he doesn't have a right to be upset that she had sex with two guys at once in high school. It was interesting watching it with an audience in Berlin, because I think they're a little more sophisticated and they were like, 'And so? She had sex with two guys at once? Next!'"

JOEY LAUREN ADAMS' films include *Dazed and Confused, The Program, S.F.W., Sleep with Me, Mallrats, Bio-Dome,* and *Michael.*

Chasing Amy

After the award-winning *Clerks* and the critically panned *Mallrats,* writer/director Kevin Smith worked hard on his third film. The result, *Chasing Amy,* is his best effort to date. It certainly contains a beautifully written, star-making role for Joey Lauren Adams as its central character Alyssa, and two carefully observed male characters (Holden and Banky, played by Ben Affleck and Jason Lee) with more than enough shadings and textures to fill several features. Childhood friends Holden and Banky collaborate on a cult comic. Alyssa arrives on the scene, and Holden falls head over heels in love with her. There are only three problems: first, Alyssa is looking for a best friend, not a lover. Second, watch the movie!! Third, watch the movie!!! Smith's script is charged with honest intensity and the performances by Adams, Affleck, and Lee are excellent. In the end credits, Smith apologizes to the critics who hated *Mallrats.* He won't have to apologize to anyone for *Chasing Amy* except to those who want to know what will happen to Alyssa, Holden, and Banky after the final reel. We sort of know, anyway, in the same bittersweet way we know about all the different scrawls on all the different candids in long-unopened high school yearbooks. 🦴🦴🦴

1997 (R) 105m/C Ben Affleck, Joey Lauren Adams, Jason Lee, Dwight Ewell, Jason Mewes, Kevin Smith; *D:* Kevin Smith; *W:* Kevin Smith; *C:* David Klein; *M:* David Pirner. **VHS** *NYR*

Children of Paradise

Children of Paradise/Les Enfants du Paradis was made in France over a two-year period between 1943 and 1945 during a time when the Nazis had overtaken the country. The Nazis demanded severe restrictions not only on the content of French films, but also on their length. Director Marcel Carne and screenwriter Jacques Prevert envisioned a lavish historical epic that was twice the length of an average feature, but told the Nazis that they were actually making two movies, secretly hoping, of course, that the war would be over long before their masterpiece was released. Moreover, Jewish composer Joseph Kosma and Jewish designer Alexandre Trauner were in danger at all times of being captured by the Nazis. Because she fell in love with a German officer, Arletty (1898-1992), the beautiful actress who played the leading role of Garance, was at one point imprisoned and sentenced to death. (She received a stay of execution and survived.) None of the incredible tensions that the cast and crew must have endured can be seen in the resulting three-plus hour film, released after the Allied liberation. Despite its length, this lyrical saga of love and longing moves like lightning. Because *Children of Paradise* showed the vanished world of the mid-19th century (magnificently photographed by Roger Hubert) and focused largely on a central female character, it has been favorably compared with *Gone with the Wind*. But for all its boisterous theatrical backdrops and passionate emotional undercurrents, *Paradise* is a far more subtle film. Jean-Louis Barrault (1910-94) plays Baptiste, a famous mime, who yearns for the elusive Garance as she moves from one man to another. She agrees to spend the night with this hopeless romantic with the words, "Love is so very simple." Baptiste turns her down and by the time the two get a second chance, love has become irretrievably complicated for them both. Arletty and Barrault have never been better and the supporting cast (which includes Pierre Brasseur, Maria Casares, Albert Remy, Leon Larive, Marcel Herrand, Pierre Renoir, Jeanne Marken, and Gaston Modot) deliver vivid performances in carefully chosen roles. (Arletty and Barrault later made appearances in 1962's *The Longest Day*.) **AKA:** Les Enfants du Paradise. 🦴🦴🦴🦴

1945 188m/B *FR* Jean-Louis Barrault, Arletty, Pierre Brasseur, Maria Casares, Albert Remy, Leon Larive, Marcel Herrand, Pierre Renoir, Jeanne Marken, Gaston Modot; **D:** Marcel Carne; **W:** Jacques Prevert; **C:** Roger Hubert; **M:** Maurice Thiriet, Joseph Kosma. **VHS, LV** *HMV, CRC, FCT*

Children of the Damned

In the fall of 1963, Anton Leader tried to duplicate the success of the original *Village of the Damned* with *Children of the Damned*. Ian Hendry and Alan Badel (both wearing obvious rugs) run around town trying to figure out what an international batch of alien-spawned children have in mind. Barbara Ferris is on hand to translate because NONE of those whiz kiddies can act. To make a story like this work, you really have to go for the audiences' visceral connection with the material. Long military strategy sequences and endless philosophizing just don't cut it. The lack of a deeply impassioned protagonist (which, yeah, even snide George Sanders could be when he halfway tried, as he did in *Village*) ultimately scuttled whatever dreams the producers may have had for ten more damned children sequels. 🦴🦴

1963 90m/B *GB* Ian Hendry, Alan Badel, Barbara Ferris, Alfred Burke, Sheila Allen, Clive Powell, Frank Summerscales, Mahdu Mathen, Gerald Delsol, Roberta Rex, Franchesca Lee, Harold Goldblatt, Ralph Michael, Martin Miller, Lee Yoke-Moon; **D:** Anton Leader; **W:** John Briley. **VHS, LV** *MGM*

INDEPENDENT FILM GUIDE

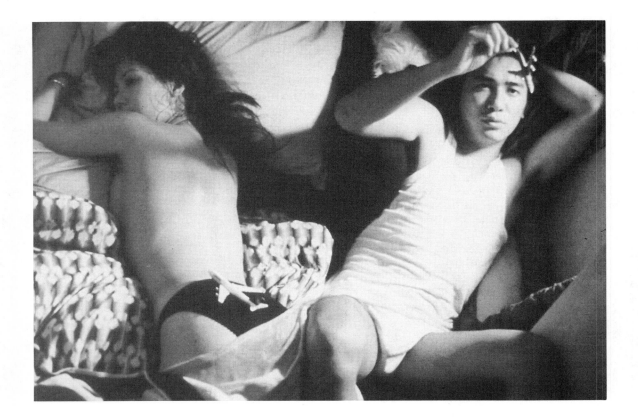

The Children of Theatre Street

The Children of Theatre Street marked (H.S.H. Princess) Grace Kelly of Monaco's (1928-82) return to the big screen after a two-decade absence. She narrated this circumspect examination of the Leningrad Academy, a Russian ballet school. The Soviet Union withdrew its endorsement of the film after its release because the names of three dancers who defected (including Rudolf Nureyev, 1938-93) were mentioned. Unfortunately, director Robert Dornhelm showed all the tedium of the ballet dancers in training, with very little of the excitement. 𝄞𝄞

1977 92m/C *RU* Angelina Armeiskaya, Alec Timoushin, Lena Voronzova, Michaela Cerna, Galina Messenzeva, Konstantin Zaklinsky; **D:** Robert Dornhelm; **W:** Beth Gutcheon; **C:** Karl Kofler. Nominations: Academy Awards '77: Best Feature Documentary. **VHS, Beta** *MVD, PBC, KUL*

The Chocolate War

The Chocolate War gets off to an irritating start. Writer/director Keith Gordon crams its first few minutes with stylistic flourishes that serve to confuse rather than intrigue, especially since this flashy approach is soon abandoned in favor of a straightforward narrative. Then it wrings more dramatic mileage out of the annual school candy sale than you would ever have thought possible. We are introduced to Brother Leon, a nutcase if ever there was one, who has his eyes on the head-mastership of St. Trinity School for Boys. We also meet the conscienceless Archie, who leads the school's secret society, the Vigils. And then there is Jerry, who initially seeks their acceptance but winds up disillusioned and dispirited by what he learns about both. Former actor Keith Gordon has assembled rather an offbeat cast: the great John Glover is over the top as always as weird Brother Leon, Ilan Mitchell-Smith seems a bit vague as Jerry, but Wally Ward is right on target as the sociopathic Archie. Adam Baldwin is still in high school eight years after *My Bodyguard,* and the film's only comic relief is furnished by the reliable Bud Cort as Brother Jacques. Based on Robert Cormier's novel, *The Chocolate War* has nothing good to say about self-serving systems or about those who protect them; the film deserves credit for exploring some universal truths in the worthiest of settings, an all-male Catholic school. 🦴🦴🦴

1988 **(R) 95m/C** John Glover, Jenny Wright, Wally Ward, Bud Cort, Ilan Mitchell-Smith, Adam Baldwin; *D:* Keith Gordon; *W:* Keith Gordon. **VHS, Beta, LV, Closed Caption** *MCG*

A Chorus of Disapproval

If you enjoyed Jeremy Iron's performance in Barbet Schroeder's vastly overrated *Reversal of Fortune,* or even if you didn't, you might enjoy seeing him in *A Chorus of Disapproval,* directed by Michael Winner. Winner began his career in 1957 by directing *This Is Belgium.* Strapped for funds, he shot much of the travelogue in the British suburban town of East Grinstead. He achieved fame and fortune with the American-made *Death Wish* movies, but his early work on films like *The Jokers* and *I'll Never Forget What's 'is Name* reveal a remarkable feeling for sharp satire that he seldom exploits. Winner was a good choice to direct Sir Alan Ayckbourn's *A Chorus of Disapproval,* a charming satire about the antics of an amateur suburban theatrical troupe.

Like many other Ayckbourn works, including *The Norman Conquests,* the satire is in-house. The characters may not behave in irreproachable ways, but they are not condemned for their shortcomings; they are simply shown as the intensely human lot they are. Jeremy Irons is ideally cast as a widowed twit who auditions for the company led by Sir Anthony Hopkins. Hopkins is an insensitive boor, but he is completely devoted to the company and takes the newcomer under his wing. Faster than you can say, "What is there to do in this little town?," we learn that the chief indoor sport is extramarital affairs. There is a swinging couple played by the seductive Jenny Seagrove and a rather puffy Gareth Hunt, who invite Irons and a friend over for fun and games, but Irons is so dense that he brings a sweet little dowager who spends the evening sleeping through a television documentary. There is Hopkins' wife (Prunella Scales), who falls head over heels for the shy young stranger. Meanwhile, Alexandra Pigg and Patsy Kensit fight for the reluctant approval of a grungy kid in the troupe. For one of Britain's most prolific playwrights, Ayckbourn leads a somewhat insulated life. At one point in his career, he maintained that he wrote everything for a suburban repertory theatre, not for West End showcases, television, or the movies, and his work still remains untouched by urban sophistication. As a writer, his chief fascination remains suburbia, a world he observes with affection and wit. Along the way, we see pettiness and treachery, but we also see continuity and strength. Some of Britain's finest actors are in the cast of *A Chorus of Disapproval* (Sylvia Syms, Lionel Jeffries, Barbara Ferris, Richard Briers) and Winner's surprisingly low-key approach here is ideal for this sort of delicate material. 🦴🦴🦴

1989 **(PG) 105m/C** *GB* Jeremy Irons, Anthony Hopkins, Jenny Seagrove, Lionel Jeffries, Patsy Kensit, Gareth Hunt, Prunella Scales, Sylvia Syms, Richard Briers, Barbara Ferris, Alexandra Pigg; *D:* Michael Winner; *W:* Michael Winner, Alan Ayckbourn; *M:* John Du Prez. **VHS, Beta** *NO*

Chungking Express

The girlfriend of Cop 223 (Takeshi Kaneshiro) has just left him, and while he drowns his sorrows in a pineapple binge, he tries to see if any of his old girlfriends will go out with him. Then he meets a tough blonde drug dealer (superstar Bridget Lin)! The girlfriend (Valerie Chow) of Cop 663 (Superstar Tony Leung) has just left him, and while he's at a fast-food restaurant called the Midnight Express, counter girl Faye Wang makes it very clear that she wants him. So clear, in fact, that she completely obsesses on him, rather like the hero-worshipping kids in 1964's *The World of Henry Orient.* How many times can you listen to "California Dreamin'" without screamin'? (Wang's character plays the 1966 hit every chance she gets.) Terrific acting and direction plus stylish cinematography and editing made *Chungking Express* the premiere Rolling Thunder selection from Wong Kar-Wei aficionado Quentin Tarantino. 🎵🎵🎵

1995 (PG-13) 102m/C *HK* Bridget Lin, Takeshi Kaneshiro, Tony Leung, Faye Wang, Valerie Chow, Piggy Chan; *D:* Wong Kar-Wai; *W:* Wong Kar-Wai; *C:* Christopher Doyle, Lau Wai-Keung; *M:* Frankie Chan, Roel A. Garcia. Nominations: Independent Spirit Awards '97: Best Foreign Film. **VHS, LV, Closed Caption** *MAX*

Cinema Europe

If you ever saw the 1979 Thames television series *Hollywood: The Pioneers,* you already know what meticulous documentarians Kevin Brownlow and David Gill are. Still available on home video, the series revealed the silent movie era, not as creaky, dusty subject matter suitable mainly for museum browsing, but as the vital, hypnotic period for art and entertainment that it really was. Well, Brownlow and Gill have produced a new BBC series that only the lucky subscribers to Turner Classic Movies were able to see in early July of 1996. Their *Cinema Europe* series is a sure bet for home video, so keep your eyes open for it at your favorite neighborhood outlet. *Cinema Europe* bypasses American movies entirely and focuses only on films that were made in Europe. We first discover where it all began and learn that European filmmaking techniques predated cinematic innovations long assumed to originate in America. Subsequent entries, such as *Art's Promised Land, The Unchained Cinema,* and *The Music of Light* show how lovely and lyrical silent films could be at their best: in Sweden, in Russia, in Germany, in France. The toning and tinting of silent pictures created and sustained moods and atmospheres we still can't take for granted in 1997 when we see them at their pristine best. There were even sound experiments as long ago as 1906, but the movies stayed silent through the late 1920s. For most of this study of European cinema, Brownlow and Gill seem affectionate and awestruck by the artistic and technical wizardry of the early masters. And then they take a sharply critical look at the British film industry in a segment titled *Opportunity Lost.* Why couldn't England make films and develop stars as well as their European neighbors did? We see a 1913 version of *Hamlet* and note that the cameraman can't even keep up with the star! Actress/screenwriter Joan Morgan is unknown here, but her acting career began in 1914 at age nine and continued through 1938 in 37 films, as she explains in a lively series of anecdotes brimming with memories. British cinema didn't really come alive until Sir Alfred Hitchcock, and he, as Kenneth Branagh's narration firmly reminds us, was far more influenced by German expressionism than by any homegrown celluloid endeavors. By the time we arrive, all too soon, at *End of an Era,* we're convinced: in leaving the silent era, we lost something precious, magical, and, all too often, irretrievable. You can still rent a few remaining silent treasures on video, but you may have to hunt for them or try one of the mail order houses that still stocks them. In the meanwhile, *Cinema Europe* is a must for any true buff of the silent era. ✐✐✐✐

1996 360m/C D: David Gill, Kevin Brownlow; **W:** David Gill, Kevin Brownlow; **C:** David Gill, Kevin Brownlow; **M:** Carl Davis, Philip Appleby. *NYR*

Cinema Paradiso

Cinema Paradiso, Italy's winner in the 1989 Oscar competition, is half of a great movie. Its simple premise is that motion pictures have a profound effect on all our lives. For the first hour, this theme is charmingly illustrated by the evolving friendship between Alfredo, the movie projectionist in a small village and Toto, a little boy who adores him. Toto also adores flammable nitrate film, the projection booth, and everything in sight in the "Cinema Paradiso." Seen through Toto's eyes, a movie theatre is an enchanted palace and we do not wonder why he idolizes Alfredo, despite the older man's insistence that only an imbecile would be a projectionist. (The film gets much of its strength from Philippe Noiret and Salvatore Cascio's beautiful performances as Alfredo and Toto.) The second hour looks and feels like a different movie: Toto saves Alfredo's life when the theatre is destroyed by fire and later takes over his job as projectionist. Every male fantasy appears to be carved in stone in the second half: the elusive girl who is seduced by relentless pursuit and then lost by circumstances, the young man who is forbidden to look fondly on his humble beginnings lest he be sidetracked from success by nostalgia, even the peculiar conviction that shunning loved ones is a necessary part of adult life. Just when it looks as if writer/director Giuseppe Tornatore has forgotten why he made the film, he floods the screen with fragments from Toto's magical childhood at the "Cinema Paradiso," all the love scenes that were censored by the village priest. It's pure mush, but it's irresistible mush. Most audiences will leave remembering the winning truths of Part One and forgetting the laborious falseness of Part Two. The last sequence succeeds in making *Cinema Paradiso* seem to be a much better film than it really is. ***AKA:*** Nuovo Cinema Paradiso. ✐✐✐

1988 123m/C *IT* Philippe Noiret, Jacques Perrin, Salvatore Cascio, Marco Leonardi, Agnes Nano, Leopoldo Trieste; **D:** Giuseppe Tornatore; **W:** Giuseppe Tornatore; **M:** Ennio Morricone. Academy Awards '89: Best Foreign Language Film; British Academy Awards '90: Best Actor (Noiret), Best Foreign Film, Best Original Screenplay, Best Supporting Actor (Cascio); Cannes Film Festival '89: Grand Jury Prize; Golden Globe Awards '90: Best Foreign Film. **VHS, LV, 8mm** *HBO, APD*

Citizen Ruth

This superb satire takes NO prisoners in a razor-sharp examination of both sides of the abortion issue. Laura Dern is terrific as Ruth, a glue-sniffing, pregnant, unfit mother of four who is busted for fetus endangerment, and then learns that the judge will go easy on her if there's no fetus to endanger. Faster than you can count up to 400 bucks, Kurtwood Smith and Mary Kay Place as Norm and Gail Stoney are paying Ruth's bail, and taking her home to stay in their immaculate Christian home. What's the catch? Ruth has to HAVE Baby Tanya, of course, because it will send a powerful message to America from all those nice right-to-life folks. Ruth hears the word "message," panics, and hunts for the nearest tube of glue. Her next trial and tribulation is with the nice folks who believe in a woman's-right-to-her-own-body. They take Ruth home to stay with them, too. What's the catch? Ruth has to exercise her freedom to choose an abortion, of course, because it will send a powerful message to America from all those nice folks who believe in THAT freedom, of course. Ruth hears the word "message," panics again, and indulges in more substances! But there IS one non-partisan message in which Ruth has faith, and it is this delicious concept that wipes out every argument either side can contrive. The well

Randal and Dante (Jeff Anderson and Brian O'Halloran) take a short break from their jobs in *Clerks.*

chosen supporting cast (Swoosie Kurtz, Kelly Preston, M.C. Gainey, Kenneth Mars, Alicia Witt, Tippi Hedren as Super Feminist Jessica Weiss, and even Diane Ladd as Ruth's mom) adds to the surreal quality of Ruth's dilemma and her wildly skewed alternatives. And check out the adolescent boy who's the constant attendant of Blaine Gibbons, the right-to-life spokesman played by Burt Reynolds. He's a subtle symbol of hypocrisy at the top of the power chain, reinforced by Norm Stoney's lustful leering at Ruth while playing the good Christian husband and father to the hilt. If even one whiff of politically correct banana oil makes you RETCH, *Citizen Ruth* is YOUR movie! ***AKA:*** Precious; Meet Ruth Stoops. ♫♫♫♫

1996 (R) 104m/C Laura Dern, Swoosie Kurtz, Mary Kay Place, Kurtwood Smith, Kelly Preston, Burt Reynolds, M.C. Gainey, Kenneth Mars, Kathleen Noone, David Graf, Tippi Hedren, Alicia Witt, Diane Ladd; ***D:*** Alexander Payne; ***W:*** Alexander Payne, Jim Taylor; ***C:*** James Glennon; ***M:*** Rolfe Kent. Montreal World Film Festival '95: Best Actress (Dern). **VHS, LV, Closed Caption** *TOU*

City of Hope

Again, no one asked me, but *City of Hope* is a much worthier contender for Picture of the Year than *Silence of the Lambs.* John Sayles' rich portrait of the complexity of urban life offers sharp, revealing performances from Vincent Spano as Nick, Joe Morton as Councilman Wynn, and Tony LoBianco as Nick's father Joe. Sayles exposes the "any means necessary" approach to deal-making in the city, even when it leads to tragedy. He also shows the inevitable malaise and despair that accompany such cold ruthlessness. Nick doesn't care and wants out; Wynn does care, but his reform efforts are blocked at every turn; and Joe loves his son, but establishes an impossible blueprint for his life. All the actors in the large cast are outstanding, including Sayles as a sleazebag named Carl. *City of Hope,* a far more cohesive film than *Lone Star,* is long overdue for a major reassessment. ♫♫♫♫

1991 (R) 132m/C Vincent Spano, Tony LoBianco, Joe Morton, Todd Graff, David Strathairn, Anthony John Denison, Barbara Williams, Angela Bassett, Gloria Foster, Lawrence Tierney, John Sayles, Maggie Renzi, Kevin Tighe, Chris Cooper, Jace Alexander, Frankie Faison, Tom Wright, Michael Mantell, Josh Mostel, Joe Grifasi, Louis Zorich, Gina Gershon, Rose Gregorio, Bill Raymond, Maeve Kinkead, Ray Aranha; *D:* John Sayles; *W:* John Sayles; *C:* Robert Richardson; *M:* Mason Daring. Independent Spirit Awards '92: Best Supporting Actor (Strathairn). **VHS, LV, 8mm, Closed Caption** COL

The City of Lost Children

I'm one of the viewers who said, "Huh?" after watching this movie. Then I heard a much-televised promotion in which a critic described it as "eye candy." It isn't for children, but it focuses on them, so I guess it's for grownups who are on the edge of their seats at the notion of an inventor stealing kid's dreams because he can't have any. Best for those who like this sort of thing. *AKA:* La Cite des Enfants Perdus. ♫♫

1995 (R) 114m/C *FR* Ron Perlman, Daniel Emilfork, Joseph Lucien, Judith Vittet, Dominique Pinon, Jean Claude Dreyfus, Odile Mallet, Genevieve Brunet, Mireille Mosse; *D:* Jean-Marie Jeunet, Marc Caro; *W:* Jean-Marie Jeunet, Marc Caro, Gilles Adrien; *C:* Darius Khondji; *M:* Angelo Badalamenti; *V:* Jean-Louis Trintignant. Cesar Awards '96: Best Art Direction/Set Decoration; Nominations: Cesar Awards '96: Best Cinematography, Best Costume Design, Best Score; Independent Spirit Awards '96: Best Foreign Language Film. **VHS, LV, Closed Caption** COL

Clean, Shaven

Schizophrenic Peter Winter (Peter Greene in a stunning performance) is searching bleak

Miscou Island, off the New Brunswick coast, for his young daughter, whom his mother put up for adoption after Peter was institutionalized and his wife died. Peter's being tailed by Detective McNally (Robert Albert), who suspects him of a child's murder, and his tenuous hold on reality slowly disintegrates into torment and self-mutilation. Debut for director/writer Lodge Kerrigan. Greene can also be seen in *Laws of Gravity, Judgment Night,* and *The Mask.* Jennifer MacDonald is in *Headless Body in Topless Bar.* ♫♫

1993 80m/C Peter Greene, Robert Albert, Jennifer MacDonald, Megan Owen, Molly Castelloe; *D:* Lodge Kerrigan; *W:* Lodge Kerrigan; *C:* Teodoro Maniaci; *M:* Hahn Rowe. Nominations: Independent Spirit Awards '95: Best First Feature. **VHS** ORI

Clerks

Clerks is a promising first film by Kevin Smith about a clerk in a convenience store and a clerk in a video store. It's everything a first film should be: funny, fresh, and original. It was shot in black and white on a budget of $27,000, and its gritty, cinema-verite quality made it seem almost like a slice-of-life documentary rather than the scripted fiction film it really was. Reportedly, preview audiences were so caught up in the lives of the two central characters that they responded negatively when one of them was shown being killed on duty. So the ending was re-shot, a wise choice, because to have turned an 88-minute comedy into an 89-minute tragedy at the last minute wouldn't have worked without some premonitory sequences—which wouldn't have worked, either, because of the scrappy, upbeat tone overall. When Smith made *Mallrats* a year later, the same critics who lionized *Clerks* beyond recognition jumped down hard on the filmmaker's second effort. Smith's *Chasing Amy,* his third picture, is drawing rave reviews. ♫♫♫

1994 (R) 89m/B Brian O'Halloran, Jeff Anderson, Marilyn Ghigliotti, Lisa Spoonhauer, Jason Mewes; *Cameos:* Kevin Smith; *D:* Kevin Smith; *W:* Kevin Smith; *M:* Scott Angley. Sundance Film Festival '94: Filmmakers Trophy; Nominations: Independent Spir-

"I'm not even supposed to be here today!"

—Convenience store clerk Dante Hicks (Brian O'Halloran), having an incredibly bizarre day at work, recites this line repeatedly in *Clerks.*

Valerie Hobson and
Laurence Olivier as
Kay Hammond and
Tony McVane in
Clouds over Europe.

it Awards '95: Best First Feature, Debut Performance (Anderson), First Screenplay. **VHS, LV, Closed Caption** *MAX*

Closet Land

Four audience members walked out of the advance screening of *Closet Land,* a heavy-handed and overly stylized film about the psychological torture of a female political prisoner. *Closet Land* is a "safe" propaganda film produced by Ron Howard with the blessing of Amnesty International. Who is going to be FOR the torture of a pretty young woman in a flowing white dress? Both actress Madeleine Stowe and the dress go through the entire 90-minute film looking absolutely terrific. Stowe is the captive of the plumby voiced Alan Rickman,

who wears a suit and tie most of the time and has just a hint of five o' clock shadow by film's end. So much for harsh realism. And where will we be watching this movie? In comfortable living rooms a few steps away from gleaming kitchens and light years away from the unnamed countries where torture occurs. Since few of us are likely to voluntarily place ourselves in danger in abusive faraway countries, the most we can do is give a few bucks to Amnesty International. But you can do that after watching television's short public service announcements from Glenn Close and Robin Willlams. So let's look at *Closet Land* as a film. The images reinforce the help-lessness of women. The soundtrack reinforces the eroticism traditionally associated with the helplessness of women. And the rhetoric is foolhardy. It is the duty of a political prisoner to escape, not to engage in the lost cause of educating one's captors. This prisoner uses precisely the same techniques for escape that she did as a child, reinforcing the false notion that women learn nothing about self-protection between infancy and adulthood. There is even a moment when *Closet Land* appears to be veering in the kinky direction of Liliana Cavani's *The Night Porter,* but then Stowe makes a sacrificial speech. A much better, more realistic movie about this subject is Poland's long-banned *Interrogation,* also available on home video. But 1982's *Interrogation* is a film about survival, not martyr-dom, and Krystyna Janda is not a pretty pin-up like Madeline Stowe. Janda's prison is a gritty, grimy place, not a polished, stage-bound chamber, and no one in *Interrogation* has cinematic credentials on the order of *Stakeout* or *Die Hard.* First-time writer/director Radha Bharadwaj is a talented, well meaning artist who convinces only the faith-ful and the safe. Ultimately, her *Closet Land* is the politically correct equivalent of *Triumph of the Will.* **WOOF!**

1990 (R) 95m/C Madeleine Stowe, Alan Rickman; *D:* Radha Bharadwaj; *W:* Radha Bharadwaj; *M:* Richard Einhorn. **VHS, Beta, LV, Closed Caption** *FXV, VTR*

Closing Numbers

Strong performances and mature story lines distinguished many of 1994's entries at the 18th Annual International Lesbian and Gay Film Festival. The highlight of Stephen Whittaker's *Closing Numbers* is a bravura performance by the much underrated Jane Asher, who hasn't had this meaty a role since she made *Deep End* with Jerzy Skolimowski in 1970. Asher plays a happily married wife and mother without a clue that her husband is bisexual until she confronts the man with whom he's been having an affair. THEY'VE been having safe sex, the lover tells her, but SHE is at risk because of unprotected one-night stands in her husband's past. She reacts with rage at first, then numbly continues with the routine of her life, with a few differences. She has an HIV test and is introduced by the lover to working with one of his AIDS patients. All the while, her husband remains in deep denial, and their son is extremely hostile to his parent's much-changed relationship. Asher's beautifully drawn study of a woman in limbo is unforgettable. 🎞🎞🎞

1993 95m/C *GB* Jane Asher, Tim Woodward, Patrick Pearson, Nigel Charnock; **D:** Stephen Whittaker. *NYR*

Clouds over Europe

Tim Whelan's *Clouds over Europe/Q Planes,* released less than six months before World War II, shows how much Great Britain had changed in the eighteen months since 1937's *Non-Stop New York.* There is a not-so-subtle grim edge to this playful treatment of pre-war espionage. *Clouds over Europe* made a great impression on 16-year-old movie fan Patrick Mac-Nee, who stored away his impressions of Ralph Richardson's wry secret service agent for future reference. (MacNee's memory was to prove handy when he played John Steed in *The Avengers* televi-

sion series.) Valerie Hobson, icily portrayed in 1989's *Scandal,* was a warm and lively presence in British films for over twenty years and she does a fine job here as a persistent journalist. Laurence Olivier costars as a dashing test pilot in *Clouds over Europe.* **AKA:** Q Planes. 🎞🎞🎞

1939 82m/B Laurence Olivier, Valerie Hobson, Ralph Richardson, George Curzon, George Merritt, Gus McNaughton, David Tree, Sandra Storme, Hay Petrie, Frank Fox, Gordon McLeod, John Longden, Reginald Purdell, John Laurie, Pat Aherne; **D:** Tim Whelan; **W:** Ian Dalrymple; **C:** Harry Stradling. **VHS, Beta, LV**

Coffee with Lemon

Award-winning actress Tatyana Vasilyeva stars in Leonid Gorovets' *Coffee with Lemon.* Great Russian actor Valery Ostrovsy (Alexander Abdulov) goes to Israel with his wife (Vasilyeva) and son, hoping for a better life. He winds up out of work because he can't speak Hebrew. Then he finds out he's won an award for his performance in a film he made before leaving Russia. This Israeli entry suggests that talent only appears to transcend the perennial challenge of a Jewish identity, and its downbeat conclusions indicate that, drawn to its most illogical extremes, belief in such an apparition leads to tragic consequences. By some startling coincidence, Alexander Proshkin's *To See Paris and Die,* made in Russia in 1993 and also starring Vasilyeva, had pretty much the same theme. 🎞🎞

1994 94m/C *IS* Alexander Abdulov, Tatyana Vasilyeva; **D:** Leonid Gorovets. *NYR*

Cold Feet

Someone must have had cold feet about making *Cold Feet* because Thomas McGuane's screenplay sat on the shelf for nearly 13 years. This starring vehicle for Oscar-nominee Sally Kirkland is supposed to be a comedy. The press kit even let reviewers know what the funny parts are and why; if you don't laugh, well, heck, maybe you just don't have a sense of humor. The film is 94 minutes long and Kirkland has a different costume change for every scene. She dives into the part with such enthusiasm that it almost doesn't matter that her role makes no sense at all. Her co-stars Keith Carradine and Tom Waits are supposed to be endearing in a peculiar sort of way. Carradine's irresponsible cowboy ditches fiancee Kirkland with Waits, a psychotic killer who's even played as a folk hero. (Waits shoots a doctor in cold blood and then overacts for the rest of the movie while Kirkland nibbles on Cheez Whiz and crackers.) Small details are ignored: if you cut a horse open to stuff him with emeralds, you always have to sew him back up again if you want him to live, except in this movie. Also, even though Waits slices Carradine's ear and Carradine did, after all, watch him shoot that doctor, Carradine still lets his much-loved nine-year-old daughter play with Waits without supervision. We thought that was really strange. We only laughed at one thing: a movie marquee features *Chicks with Zip Guns* as the main attraction and *Rancho Deluxe* as the second feature. It's an in-joke but at least we got this one. Thomas McGuane wrote *Rancho Deluxe* back in 1975 and its star Jeff Bridges has an unbilled bit in *Cold Feet* as a bartender. Another in-joke is the presence of Kirkland's real-life old flame Rip Torn as an all-purpose sheriff and minister at her onscreen wedding. If you agree with McGuane that Montana in and of itself is hilarious, then *Cold Feet* just may be your movie. 🦴🦴

1989 (R) 94m/C Keith Carradine, Tom Waits, Sally Kirkland, Rip Torn, Kathleen York, Bill Pullman, Vincent Schiavelli, Jeff Bridges; **D:** Robert Dornhelm; **W:** Thomas McGuane, Jim Harrison; **C:** Bryan Duggan; **M:** Tom Bahler. **VHS, Beta, LV** *LIV*

A Cold Wind in August

Lola Albright is a meltingly lovely blonde from Akron, Ohio, who will probably best be remembered for her role as a nightclub singer in television's *Peter Gunn* series. Although she created a vivid impression in 36 movies between 1948 and 1977, Albright received just one starring role onscreen, in 1961's *A Cold Wind in August,* based on the Burton Wohl novel. Albright plays a forty-week-a-year stripper who cherishes the twelve weeks she can try to lead a more conventional life in a New York apartment building. Among her own age group (36), she is hard and brittle, determined to distance herself from the fantasies of men who want her to fill their needs, not her own. On a sultry summer day, the 17-year-old son of the building supervisor arrives at her doorstep, ready to fix her air conditioner. Around this awkward, intimidated kid, her tough shell dissolves, and she finally allows herself to feel something. The kid is nicely played by Scott Marlowe, who had been playing troubled teens for over five years by this point, so the extreme difference in their ages had to be spelled out in the acting and by Alexander Singer's skillful direction, rather than the script. In fact, there is one sequence in a park where this supposedly mismatched couple draw stares that don't make sense since Albright looks so young and Marlowe is so obviously not a teenager. The moments when the film really works are when Albright brilliantly reveals her loss of self over a love that means everything in the world to her, yet is clearly, by its very nature, ephemeral. The rare quality of this film lies in its sympathetic understanding of the acting women have to do to survive, and in its depiction of the strong disapproval men feel when women stop acting. Strong supporting performances are delivered by two great character actors: Joe De Santis, as the kid's compassionate father, and another *Peter Gunn* alumnus, Herschel Bernardi, as a friend who stoically endures a friendship with Albright's character, suffering all the while from his unrequited love for her. *A Cold Wind in August* is a hard film to find today, not yet released on home video, and surfacing only very occasionally on television late at night. But when you consider the example of *Butterfield 8,* a slick and phony piece of splashy Metro drek that won Elizabeth Taylor the 1960 Oscar, the virtues of a small, independent gem like *A Cold Wind in August* sparkle in comparison. (Condemned by the Legion of Decency during its original release.) 🦴🦴🦴

1961 80m/B Lola Albright, Scott Marlowe, Herschel Bernardi, Joe De Santis; **D:** Alexander Singer. *NYR*

Coldblooded

The way that critics pounced on *Coldblooded,* we thought its filmmakers were trying to produce a snuff film or plagiarize *Pulp Fiction* or both. That's until we actually sat down and watched this low-key satire. Clearly, its original audiences didn't appreciate first-time director M. Wallace Wolodarsky's sense of humor at all, but we did. Jason Priestley is Cosmo Reif, the bookie of a mobster named Gordon (played by Robert Loggia). When Gordon needs a new hit man, he thinks first of Cosmo, even though he doesn't have any experience. That's all right; Steve, the other hit man, will train him. Peter Riegert, one of the great character actors of his generation, is so memorable as Steve that he steals every scene he's in, even when Wolodarsky didn't write them to favor him. Steve hates his job; he drinks alone and cries alone, then wakes up with a hangover and goes to work. Cosmo doesn't much like the job, either, but finds that he's surprisingly good at it. Instead of crying and drinking, he joins a health club and falls for Jasmine, the lovely yoga teacher, played by the lovely ingenue Kimberly Williams. Up to this point, Cosmo has only been able to retain the attention of Honey the Hooker (Janeane Garofalo). But now he has visions of a better life with Jasmine, but without Gordon, his henchman John, or even Steve. Only one hitch: Jasmine doesn't like the idea of living with a hit man; but then, neither does Cosmo. *Coldblooded* is played so broadly, it's hard

to imagine that anyone thought it was a documentary or a justification of the need for hit men anymore than Jonathan Swift's modest proposal of the 18th century actually called for the children of the poor to be eaten by the rich. Who could believe that anyone who looked like Jason Priestley would lead such a dull, drab life? Or that a charmer like Peter Riegert couldn't talk his way out of any assignment? Or that Kimberly Williams would consider a hit man to be her nicest boyfriend? Hey, it's only a movie, but it made US laugh! 🦴🦴🦴🦴

1994 (R) 92m/C Jason Priestley, Peter Riegert, Kimberly Williams, Robert Loggia, Janeane Garofalo, Josh Charles, David Anthony Higgens, Doris Grau; **Cameos:** Talia Balsam, Michael J. Fox; **D:** M. Wallace Wolodarsky; **W:** M. Wallace Wolodarsky; **C:** Robert Yeoman; **M:** Steve Bartek. **VHS** *PGV*

Color Adjustment

When we look at early images of television, an atmosphere of false innocence saturates everything we see. We don't think of the real-life Donna Reed, infuriated by relentless male visions of what the perfect wife and mother should be, we don't think of the real-life Robert Young and his offscreen struggles with alcoholism, we don't think of the real-life Nelson family, nearly torn apart by custody battles; we prefer to think of serene communities like Mayfield where Wally and the Beaver are always twelve and nine years old and Ward and June Cleaver are always there for their little boys. But as false as white images on television are, at least they exist. In the early 1950s, as *Color Adjustment,* Marlon Riggs' absorbing 1991 film shows, you could stop counting shows about black Americans after *Beulah* and *Amos 'n' Andy.* Both series were originally created and played by middle-aged white guys for radio. (Yes, *Beulah,* too. Marlin Hurt and Bob Corley were the voices of *Beulah* the maid long before Ethel Waters and Louise Beavers took the role on television.) The N.A.A.C.P. fought hard to get the racial stereotypes of *Amos 'n' Andy* off the air and finally succeeded in 1953, although the show persisted in reruns through 1966. After that, there were only sporadic efforts to acknowledge black artists on television. Nat "King" Cole was given a shot at his own weekly variety show, but the series failed to attract a sponsor after its first season. Bill Cosby's role as Alexander Scott on *I Spy* provided a breakthrough of sorts, but the doors opened very slowly and only for the most non-threatening images of black Americans, like the nurse *Julia,* interpreted by Diahann Carroll. (*Room 222,* clearly inspired by the huge international success of *To Sir with Love,* gave slightly more realistic roles as teachers to the late Lloyd Haynes and to Denise Nicholas.) But it was Norman Lear's *All in the Family,* with two of its enormously popular spin-offs, *Good Times* and *The Jeffersons,* that finally convinced network executives that shows about black Americans could be ratings leaders. Even so, black images popularized by television in the 1990s are often just as unrealistic as their 1950s predecessors were. Television projects with a conscience like *East Side, West Side, Roots, Frank's Place,* and *The Cosby Show* are examined in the context of what is actually happening in the lives of television viewers and contrasted with thoughtful observations by the late James Baldwin, Diahann Carroll, Esther Rolle, Tim Reid, and others. As always, the late Marlon Riggs offers welcome counterpoint at a time when we are all challenging what we see and hear in the media. If you can find it, you won't want to miss *Color Adjustment.* 🦴🦴🦴🦴

1991 88m/C D: Marlon Riggs; **W:** Marlon Riggs; **C:** Rick Butler; **M:** Mary Watkins. **VHS** *CAL*

Color of a Brisk and Leaping Day

While living in L.A. at the end of WWII, Chinese-American John Lee (Peter Alexander) learns that the Yosemite Valley Railroad is being scrapped and becomes determined to save it, in part as an homage to his grandfather who emigrated to work as a railroad laborer. A romantic train fanatic himself, Lee arranges financing from wealthy businessman Pinchot (John Diehl) but must make the railroad pay within a year—unlikely, as the automobile rapidly takes over as preferred transportation. Well captures a 1940s atmosphere, but pacing and dialogue are uneven. Director/writer Christopher Munch is best known for *The Hours and Times.* 🦴🦴

1995 87m/B Peter Alexander, Jeri Arredondo, Henry Gibson, Michael Stipe, John Diehl, David Chung, Diana Larkin, Bok Yun Chon; **D:** Christopher Munch; **W:** Christopher Munch; **C:** Rob Sweeney. Sundance Film Festival '96: Best Cinematography; Nominations: Independent Spirit Awards '97: Best Cinematography. **VHS** *NYR*

Combination Platter

Combination Platter was made by Tony Chan when he was only 23 years old. It gives us a light-hearted, sharply observed look at the immigration experience, as seen from the perspective of Robert (Jeff Lau) who comes to New York from Hong Kong without a green card. Robert's helpful friend Andy (Kenneth Lu) introduces him to women, even though Robert is shocked by the idea that he can become a citizen by marrying an American. His first job is as a waiter in a Chinese restaurant and this is where he learns about life in America. Chan and Edwin Baker won a much-deserved award for Best Screenplay at 1993's Sundance Film Festival. 🦴🦴🦴

1993 84m/C Jeff Lau, Colleen O'Brien, Lester Chan, Thomas S. Hsiung, David Chung, Colin Mitchell, Kenneth Lu, Eleonara Khilberg, James DuMont; **D:** Tony Chan; **W:** Tony Chan, Edwin Baker; **C:** Yoshifumi Hosoya; **M:** Brian Tibbs. Sundance Film Festival '93: Best Screenplay; Nominations: Independent Spirit Awards '94: Best First Feature, Best Screenplay, Best Supporting Actor (Chung). **VHS** *AVI*

The Comfort of Strangers

1961's *Last Year at Marienbad* has gone begging for the perfect film to round out a double bill suitable for residents of Limbo and/or Purgatory. Now at last there IS one! *The Comfort of Strangers,* the latest from everybody's favorite divinity school dropout: Grand Rapids, Michigan's own Paul Schrader. Let's hear it! Or to be more precise, let's hear whaaat? How about some hot dialogue from the one and only Harold Pinter, Schrader's accomplice in this cinematic minefield. HE: "Why is there no other word for thigh?" SHE: "It's a perfectly good word, what's wrong with it?" HE: "Yes, but..." Then HE goes on to list a dreary and depressing series of anatomical euphemisms and bemoans the fate of the humble word "thigh." This riveting sequence says a lot about the rest of the film. Natasha Richardson plays a young British mother of two who leaves them at home to travel to Venice with her even-more British lover Rupert Everett. The match is not made in heaven and it is clear that they are beginning to bore each other. There are only a zillion restaurants in Venice, but one night they can't find one and who should crawl out of the nearest dark alley but a slimy stranger in a white suit? (Christopher Walken, of course, typecast this time with in all-purpose Italian-Bavarian accent!) They follow the stranger down some dark alleys to a crummy bar he assures them is really good, but turns out to be HIS bar, where no food is available. They chew on breadsticks, swallow wine, and listen to stories from this character, who amazingly, is even more boring than they are. The next morning, the couple wakes up in the street where SHE gets sick. The next day, they try to avoid the stranger, but he drags them to his house, anyway. His "Canadian" wife is Helen Mirren, who watches them while they sleep and then tells them about it. Before they all have dinner that night, Walken punches Everett in the stomach for no good reason.

The couple resumes their stupefyingly dull holiday until they see Mirren waving to them from her window. Not wishing to be rude, they pop in to say hello. Walken invites Everett to follow him down more dark alleys, Mirren prepares a drink for Natasha Richardson, and two people walk out of the movie theatre, one of them hissing, "Oh, the English!" Three guys in front of us are in stitches, WE are in stitches, and at least one stuffed shirt is disgusted with all of us for not accepting this beautiful work of art with appropriate reverence. Our reaction probably counts as two venial sins, at least. We went home and enjoyed watching *Goldfinger* AND *Arsenic and Old Lace,* which just may count as FOUR mortal sins, oh dear. *My Dinner with Androids,* whoops, sooo sorry, we did mean *The Comfort of Strangers* is available for your consideration on home video. **WOOF!**

1991 (R) 102m/C Christopher Walken, Natasha Richardson, Rupert Everett, Helen Mirren; **D:** Paul Schrader; **W:** Harold Pinter; **C:** Dante Spinotti; **M:** Angelo Badalamenti. **VHS, Beta, Closed Caption** *PAR, FCT*

Confessions of a Window Cleaner

Robin Askwith looks as though someone once gave his face a severe punching. He stars as the "romantic" hero of four London-based comedies, in which he discovers new professions and different sets of women on the job. It's difficult to believe that Askwith could attract such frenzy from his female patrons, but he does have a certain awkward appeal. In spite of the relentless schoolboy-level humor, the film manages to garner some honest laughter, particularly in the family sequences co-starring Anthony Booth and Sheila White as Sidney and Rosie Noggett, and Bill Maynard and Dandy Nichols as Mr. and Mrs. Lea. Followed by *Confessions of a Pop Performer* (1975), *Confessions of a Driving Instructor,* and *Confessions from a Holiday Camp*

(1977), all starring Robin Askwith as Timothy Lea and based on Lea's novels. 🦴🦴🦴

1974 m/C *GB* Robin Askwith, Anthony Booth, Sheila White, Bill Maynard, Dandy Nichols; **D:** Val Guest. *NYR*

The Conformist

A chill sets in every time we see the gutless "Conformist" in Bernardo Bertolucci's classic adaptation of Alberto Moravia's 1951 novel. And then, a few years go by, and we're swept up in the film's spell all over again as if we were watching it for the first time. We suspect that the film would have been unbearable to watch if any other artist than Bertolucci had been at the helm or any actor other than Jean-Louis Trintignant had been cast in the title role. Trintignant is the thinking man's wimp: as he is swept along by events and circumstances in Fascist Italy, his face maps out all the untaken roads and unmade choices. But if there is a heart and soul to the film it is possessed by the cool lesbian played by Dominique Sanda. *The Conformist,* the film that launched Bertolucci's international career, cost just 3/4 of a million dollars to make, but Sanda's mere presence makes the film look and feel far more expensive. From her seduction on a polished table to her doomed flight from assassins, Sanda is the perfect sacrificial symbol of that era, a fact not lost on Vittorio De Sica, who went on to cast her in the Oscar-winning *Garden of the Finzi Continis.* Although Trintignant's internal angst and his aimless domestic life with Stefania Sandrelli (whom Sanda's character tries to lure both on and off the dance floor) receive most of the screen time, it is Sanda's haunting presence that lingers in the memory. Note: a new restored print of *The Conformist* surfaced in 1994, including the five-minute "Dance of the Blind" sequence shorn by Paramount from the original 1971 release. **AKA:** Il Conformist. 🦴🦴🦴🦴

1971 (R) 108m/C *IT FR GE* Jean-Louis Trintignant, Stefania Sandrelli, Dominique Sanda, Pierre Clementi, Gastone Moschin, Pasquale Fortunato; **D:** Bernardo Bertolucci; **W:** Bernardo Bertolucci; **C:** Vittorio Storaro; **M:** Georges Delerue. National Board of Review Awards '71: 5 Best Foreign Films of the Year; National Society of Film Critics Awards '71: Best Cinematography (Storaro), Best Director (Bertolucci); Nominations: Academy Awards '71: Best Adapted Screenplay. **VHS, Beta, LV** *PAR, APD*

Coup de Torchon

Jim Thompson was an Oklahoma-born paperback writer who wrote riveting tales about superficially boring people with humdrum routines and hellish interior lives. Thompson wrote two screenplays for Stanley Kubrick, and four of his novels have inspired both American and French filmmakers. In 1982, Bertrand Tavernier made *Coup de Torchon/Clean Slate,* switching Thompson's *Pop.1280* locale to Equatorial Africa, circa 1938. The film won an Oscar nomination, but to me, it was as jarring as watching Agatha Christie's Saint Mary Mead transformed into Beverly Hills with story line intact. Philippe Noiret is a lumbering, cuddly teddy bear of a man, totally incapable of projecting the dark side of his homicidal character. I knew the film was losing me when I asked myself, "Why does he kill?" and my only answer was, "Well, it's in the script." Stephane Audran and Isabelle Huppert contribute to the unreal proceedings and the whole thing is splashed with an overpowering jazz score by Philippe Sarde. The bizarre film has its aficionados, but the fact that the gruesome plot is played for laughs may strike some as obscene. Decide for yourself! **AKA:** Clean Slate. 🦴🦴🦴

1981 128m/C *FR* Philippe Noiret, Isabelle Huppert, Guy Marchand, Stephane Audran, Eddy Mitchell, Jean-Pierre Marielle, Irene Skobline; **D:** Bertrand Tavernier; **W:** Bertrand Tavernier; **M:** Philippe Sarde. Nominations: Academy Awards '81: Best Foreign Language Film. **VHS** *HMV*

Cousin, Cousine

One of the most delicious releases of 1976 was Jean-Charles Tacchella's *Cousin, Cousine*. This tender French offering is a gentle, lyrical story about two distant cousins who meet at various family gatherings and how they gradually fall in love. Marie-Christine Barrault and Victor Lanoux play the lovers with delightful subtlety. They are wonderfully supported by a cast that includes Guy Marchand and Marie-France Pisier as their spouses. There is also a rambunctiously real group of child actors. Director/screenwriter Tacchella suggests that it is the people who invest themselves fully in life who have the privilege of savoring love at its most profound. *Cousin, Cousine* is that rare film that gets remarkable mileage out of harmony. 🦴🦴🦴🦴

1976 (R) 95m/C *FR* Marie-Christine Barrault, Marie-France Pisier, Victor Lanoux, Guy Marchand, Ginette Garcin, Sybil Maas; **D:** Jean-Charles Tacchella; **W:** Jean-Charles Tacchella; **M:** Gerard Anfosso. Cesar Awards '76: Best Supporting Actress (Pisier); National Board of Review Awards '76: 5 Best Foreign Films of the Year; Nominations: Academy Awards '76: Best Actress (Barrault), Best Foreign Language Film, Best Original Screenplay. **VHS, Beta, LV** *TPV, IME, FOX*

Crash

No question about it, *Crash* is one strange flick. Only in the movies do we ever see couples with the same sexual intentions glance at each other for less than ONE second and find themselves in lustful embrace the very NEXT microsecond. In *Crash,* no one asks anyone, "Voulez-vous couchez avec moi ce soir?" or "Why don't we do it in the City Dump?" Everyone just KNOWS. It's a mystery, originally spun by J. G. Ballard in his 1973 novel. James Spader, who's played the full spectrum of sexual nuts onscreen, is married to Catherine (Deborah Unger). He gets in an accident with Helen (Holly Hunter) and her husband. The husband dies, James and Helen are injured, and both are soon "exploring their sexuality" at re-enact-

ments of James Dean's and Jayne Mansfield's fatal crashes, at a greatest-hits video screening of car crashes, and best of all, in actual cars where actual people have died. My late friend Alvah might have said that a flick like *Crash* is symbolic of a disintegrating society. Well, we all bring our own baggage to a movie like this, so I asked my friend Raymond, "How and why are they getting off on all this stuff? Are they really as happy as they look?" Raymond said that they were experiencing pleasure, but not fulfillment, which is rather a difficult concept for a former convent school girl to unravel. *Crash* does take us into its own world in a way that David Lynch's *Lost Highway* (because of the intermittent boredom factor) does not. Unger (who appeared in 1993's *Hotel Room* along with Mariska Hargitay, a survivor of the Mansfield crash) has an intriguing aura and Rosanna Arquette, complete with leg brace, really looks as if she was BORN to be in *Crash*. This is the sort of movie that works for its NC-17 rating. No one but Cronenberg would touch a project like *Crash;* fortunately, he did. *Crash* may be weird, twisted, and sick, but it's always dispassionate, thoughtful, and riveting. 🦴🦴🦴

1995 (NC-17) 98m/C *CA* James Spader, Holly Hunter, Elias Koteas, Deborah Unger, Rosanna Arquette, Peter MacNeill; **D:** David Cronenberg; **W:** David Cronenberg; **C:** Peter Suschitzsky; **M:** Howard Shore. Cannes Film Festival '96: Special Jury Prize; Genie Awards '96: Best Adapted Screenplay, Best Cinematography, Best Director (Cronenberg), Best Film Editing; Nominations: Genie Awards '96: Best Film, Best Sound. **VHS, LV** *NLC, CRC*

Creepers

One of the best Dario Argento titles available on home video (if you're lucky enough to run across the uncut 109-minute original INSTEAD of the chopped-up 82-minute version) is the 1985 horror classic *Creepers*. It stars Jennifer Connelly, then 15, whose youthful beauty was strikingly comparable with that of the young Elizabeth Taylor, and who was certainly a much better actress than Taylor at the same age. As in many early Taylor films, Connelly's character gets along better with animals (particularly insects) than with people. Connelly is stuck in a crummy girls' school where she is susceptible to sleepwalking, especially when she hears about all the terrible things that are happening to the young girls in the area. The grisly violence in this film is SO overstated that it's doubtful that even the most squeamish viewer could take it TOO seriously. The over-the-top performances by Daria Nicolodi and the great Donald Pleasence emphasize the fact that IT'S ONLY A MOVIE, folks. Anyway, we KNOW that Dario Argento couldn't be such a churl as to let anything happen to Jennifer Connelly, who looks cool and elegant even when she's sticking her finger down her throat. He must be a nice man to provide such excellent acting opportunities for all those bees and maggots, not to mention one scene-stealing monkey! If you can't find Dario Argento movies at the local Bijou, the following titles are well worth the search: 1970's *The Bird with the Crystal Plumage* starring Tony Musante, 1971's *Cat o'Nine Tails* with the late James Franciscus and a great Ennio Morricone score, 1975's *Deep Red* starring David Hemmings, 1988's *Terror at the Opera* with the late Ian Charleson, 1982's *Unsane* starring Tony Franciosa, 1990's *Two Evil Eyes* with Harvey Keitel in an adaptation of Poe's *The Black Cat* and, of course, *Creepers,* the perfect movie to watch when you're all alone without a telephone on a dark and spooky night. **AKA:** Phenomena. 🦴🦴🦴

1985 (R) 82m/C *IT* Jennifer Connelly, Donald Pleasence, Daria Nicolodi, Elenora Giorgi, Dalia di Lazzaro, Patrick Bauchau, Fiore Argento; **D:** Dario Argento; **W:** Franco Ferrini, Dario Argento; **M:** Simon Boswell. **VHS, Beta** *MED*

Crime of Passion

Ah, the joys of 1957, when men were men and women twiddled their thumbs. Kathy Ferguson (Barbara Stanwyck) begins this movie with an exciting job as a columnist for a San Francisco newspaper. She even plays a key role in clearing up a murder case. She's en route to Manhattan on a fast-paced career track, when she makes a quick stop in Los Angeles to meet Detective Lieutenant Bill Doyle of the L.A.P.D. (Sterling Hayden) for dinner. One thing leads to another, and before you can say, "Darn my socks for me, Darling," she is MRS. Bill Doyle, trapped in a suburb, with no outlet for her tremendous energy. She's bored with her life and she hates Bill's friends on the force AND their wives, so she takes up a new hobby: promoting Bill's career. This means sleeping with his boss, Inspector Tony Pope (Raymond Burr), and alienating him from other detectives who might get the job she wants Bill to have. (See what happens when a gal leaves a great job to do nothing?) Even though Kathy Ferguson Doyle is basically a screw up, Stanwyck invests the role with eloquence and angst. The dull life that her character rails about IS everything that she says it is. The obvious choice over 40 years later isn't even mentioned as an option: go back to the work you love and if Bill doesn't like it, TOUGH! This seems eminently more sensible than: sleep with Bill's boss, but don't tell Bill, and make sure you do something to get caught, so Bill will feel like a sap, anyway. Yeah, there's a lot of rage against women in *Crime of Passion,* but you can't stop watching it because of Stanwyck and Burr. (Hayden's thankless part must have grated on him after starring in *The Asphalt Jungle* for John Huston and *The Killing* for Stanley Kubrick.) And yes, that IS Stuart Whitman in a bit as a lab technician, four years away from his 1961 Academy Award nomination for *The Mark.* 🦴🦴🦴

1957 85m/B Barbara Stanwyck, Sterling Hayden, Raymond Burr, Fay Wray, Royal Dano, Virginia Grey, Dennis Cross, Robert Griffin, Jay Adler, Malcolm Atterbury, S. John Launer, Brad Trumbull, Skipper McNally, Jean Howell, Peg La Centra, Nancy Reynolds, Marjorie Owens, Robert Quarry, Joe Conley, Stuart Whitman; **D:** Gerd Oswald; **W:** Jo Eisinger;

C: Joseph LaShelle; *M:* Paul Dunlap. **VHS, Closed Caption** MGM, FCT

Criminal Law

Criminal Law opens with a sequence in which attorney Gary Oldman is shown defending a wholesome-looking killer portrayed by Kevin Bacon. Oldman destroys an eyewitness account because she was wrong about when she last purchased diapers. If she was wrong about the diapers, Oldman contends, why couldn't she wrong about identifying the murderer? Sure, says the jury, and Bacon is a free man. At this point, the film could have gone anywhere, and that's the main problem with *Criminal Law*. It goes EVERYWHERE. At first, Mark Kasden's script appears to be commenting on a legal system that frees Bacon to kill again and again, with Oldman as his reluctant collaborator. But then, perhaps encouraged by the ongoing Wade vs. Roe controversy, Kasdan tries to show how having an abortionist for a mother unhinges Bacon. The images of the smoking and flaming victims are too grisly for us to feel sorry for this demented killer. So the script introduces a strong female character (Karen Young) who goes to bed with Oldman for reasons best known to Kasdan. Then she beats up Bacon before she vanishes from the plot. A dying professor is dragged in to make Oldman cry at the astonishing news that law and justice are different. When all else fails, Officer Joe Don Baker patiently explains that "Crazy killers are crazy," resulting in unintentional audience laughter and a bullet in the stomach. Bacon and Oldman beat each other up, sort of, in an empty courtroom. Bacon cries some more. It's a stretch for him as an actor. Oldman, too. And Martin Campbell's direction of this suspenseless thriller is "stylish." The producers say so. They aren't concerned about the reviews. *Criminal Law* was originally hyped by manipulative commercials in which nameless people were shown walking out of a theatre and saying how great the film and the actors are. Who were these people and why were they there? Why should anyone trust them? Most of THEM probably couldn't remember the last time THEY bought diapers! 🎞🎞

1989 (R) 113m/C Kevin Bacon, Gary Oldman, Karen Young, Joe Don Baker, Tess Harper; *D:* Martin Campbell; *W:* Mark Kasden; *M:* Jerry Goldsmith. **VHS, Beta, LV** HBO, WAR

The Crossing Guard

Sean Penn comes of age as a mature screenwriter and director with this beautifully rendered study of forgiveness. Jack Nicholson and Anjelica Huston play the divorced parents of a little girl killed by hit-and-run drunk driver David Morse, who has just completed his term in prison for manslaughter. Huston is re-married to a patient, decent guy and has come to terms with her grief over her lost child, but the embittered Nicholson has not and cannot. All he can think of when Morse is released is that now he can finally kill him. He pays a visit to him, gun in hand, but it doesn't go off, and Morse asks him to reconsider his decision for a few days. Morse is genuinely regretful for his crime, and still feels enormous guilt as he remembers his victim's last words. Nicholson continues to stew in his own anguish and self-imposed isolation until his long-numbed conscience awakens him from a nightmare. In his terror, he calls his ex-wife for help, and then Huston and Nicholson share a sequence charged with gut-grinding emotional honesty. What follows for Nicholson is uglier than any nightmare, as he is finally forced to confront the potential killer within himself. Nicholson, Huston, and Morse are all outstanding. An interesting touch for film noir buffs is that classy chanteuse Hadda Brooks, who appeared in Nicholas Ray's *In a Lonely Place* in 1950 (in which Humphrey Bogart battled with HIS private demons), is also in *The Crossing Guard,* looking as elegant as ever. 🎞🎞🎞🎞

**INDEPENDENT
FILM GUIDE**

1994 (R) 111m/C Jack Nicholson, Anjelica Huston, David Morse, Robin Wright, Robbie Robertson, Piper Laurie, Richard Bradford, John Savage, Priscilla Barnes, Kari Wuhrer, Jennifer Leigh Warren, Richard Sarafian, Jeff Morris, Joe Viterelli, Eileen Ryan, Ryo Ishibashi, Michael Ryan, Nicky Blair, Gene Kirkwood, Jason Kristofer, Hadda Brooks; **D:** Sean Penn; **W:** Sean Penn; **C:** Vilmos Zsigmond; **M:** Jack Nitzsche. Nominations: Golden Globe Awards '96: Best Supporting Actress (Huston); Independent Spirit Awards '96: Best Supporting Actor (Morse); Screen Actors Guild Award '95: Best Supporting Actress (Huston). **VHS, LV, Closed Caption** *TOU*

Crumb

Watching *Crumb* made me think about *Grey Gardens,* the 1975 documentary the Maysles brothers filmed about the odd mother and daughter who were related to Jacqueline Bouvier Kennedy. There are so many odd mothers and daughters on the planet; were those two chosen only because they were so closely related to the First Lady? Watching *Crumb* also made me think about *Gates of Heaven,* the 1978 documentary Errol Morris did about a pet cemetery and the two brothers who maintained it. As the camera focused on these cooperative subjects, it made them look rather foolish and rather odd. The Crumb family is also rather odd, but would we be so interested in these previously anonymous people if underground comic artist Robert Crumb weren't related to them? It's one thing to watch a movie about troubled make-believe people and feel relieved that we don't have to live their lives, but to watch *Crumb* and feel relieved that we aren't Max and Charles Crumb makes me wonder: how many families could be so closely scrutinized and emerge with any dignity whatsoever? Unfortunately, fame is the bench mark of success in America. If you don't achieve it (or don't want it), why does that invalidate your life when a documentary filmmaker comes to pay a call about a legendary sibling? (Two Crumb sisters refused to be a part of this film.) Every life has its patches of depression, imperfection, and inactivity. Many lives are conducted in seclusion.

Many fathers are "sadistic bull(ies)." And it's unimaginable that there's a teenage boy alive who DOESN'T indulge in sexual fantasies. As a documentary, *Crumb* won wide acclaim for its director, Terry Zwigoff, who worked six years on the project. I wouldn't LET anyone into my life for six years who only wanted to examine it, good and bad, with a camera and then distribute the edited results all over the world. Would you? Are Robert Crumb and his family still speaking to Terry Zwigoff? If not, is that still okay because strangers enjoyed this film so much in neighborhood theatres? Were so-called primitive tribes that far off when they believed that a camera would steal their souls? I give it four bones for the cognoscenti, but for myself, no comment. 🦴🦴🦴🦴

1994 (R) 119m/C D: Terry Zwigoff. National Society of Film Critics Awards '95: Best Feature Documentary; Sundance Film Festival '95: Best Cinematography, Grand Jury Prize. **VHS, LV, Closed Caption** *COL*

Crush

There's something deeply satisfying about seeing a real menace onscreen. No explanations, no excuses—she's bad because she's bad and that's that! Marcia Gay Harden, who played sultry Ava Gardner in *Sinatra* and soft-hearted Shelby Goddard in *The Spitfire Grill* IS Lane, a genuine Wicked Woman of the Silver Screen. Don't be her friend, don't go to bed with her, and don't, whatever you do, get in a car with her if she's behind the wheel. That's what Christina (Donough Rees) the literary critic does (it figures), and she's left for dead (uh-oh) when Lane crashes the car. Lane goes to the home of novelist Colin (William Zappa) and immediately seduces him, then goes to work on daughter Angela (Caitlin Bossley), who's still a teenager. No, this isn't a Shannon Tweed movie, although it does sound like one, doesn't it? The difference lies in Harden's brilliant, what-the-hell interpretation as Lane. I don't how she worked out her character but she's so damn funny, I was cracking up through

Opposite page: **Robert Crumb in** *Crumb.*

most of the movie. Writer/director Alison Maclean has an eye and ear for this sort of satire, and she chose the right actors for the right jobs. 🦴🦴🦴

1993 97m/C *NZ* Marcia Gay Harden, Donough Rees, William Zappa, Caitlin Bossley; **D:** Alison Maclean; **W:** Alison Maclean, Anne Kennedy. **VHS** *FXL, ORI*

The Crying Game

Amaze your friends! Ask them who was the first singer to make "The Crying Game" a number Five Brit Hit for 12 weeks. They will say, "Boy George, of course," and you will say, "No, Dave Berry on August 6, 1964," and since the entire U.S. of A. was pre-occupied with The Beatles' first national tour in August, 1964, they will say, "Who?" Since, on college campuses, a generation seems to last about four years or so, it's possible that someone born in the '80s might not know the secret of *The Crying Game.* If you've already seen 1994's *Naked Gun 33 1/3: The Final Insult,* fergeddit, it's too late, but if you really have just arrived on Planet Earth from Planet Mars, *The Crying Game* is Neil Jordan's Oscar-winning story of Fergus (Stephen Rea), a member of the I.R.A., who becomes friends with Jody, a captive British soldier (Forest Whitaker), and who later looks up Jody's lover, Dil (Jaye Davidson). That's as far as I'm going with this, in case you WERE born in the '80s OR emigrated from Mars and didn't have to watch that *Naked Gun* movie on the flight to Earth. Acting by everyone (including Miranda Richardson as Jude, another I.R.A. member) is first rate. Like many classic movies, *The Crying Game* is so well made and so much a part of film lore that it's hard to remember that it really has only been part of our cinematic consciousness since 1992. 🦴🦴🦴🦴

1992 (R) 112m/C *IR* Stephen Rea, Jaye Davidson, Miranda Richardson, Forest Whitaker, Adrian Dunbar, Jim Broadbent, Ralph Brown, Breffini McKenna, Joe Savino, Birdie Sweeney, Andre Bernard; **D:** Neil Jordan; **W:** Neil Jordan; **C:** Ian Wilson; **M:** Anne Dudley. Academy Awards '92: Best Original Screenplay; Australian Film Institute '93: Best Foreign Film; Chicago Film Critics Awards '92: Best Foreign Film; Independent Spirit Awards '93: Best Foreign Film; Los Angeles Film Critics Association Awards '92: Best Foreign Film; New York Film Critics Awards '92: Best Screenplay, Best Supporting Actress (Richardson); National Society of Film Critics Awards '92: Best Actor (Rea); Writers Guild of America '92: Best Original Screenplay; Nominations: Academy Awards '92: Best Actor (Rea), Best Director (Jordan), Best Film Editing, Best Picture, Best Supporting Actor (Davidson). **VHS, LV, Closed Caption** *LIV, MOV, BTV*

Curse of the Starving Class

Subtlety is in short supply in Sam Shepard's *Curse of the Starving Class,* a first effort by director J. Michael McClary. James Woods overacts like he never heard the expression "Less is More" and his co-stars Kathy Bates, Randy Quaid, Louis Gossett, Jr., and a maggot-ridden lamb all seem to follow his lead. I can imagine few movie experiences more painful than to watch this movie on a double bill with *Silent Tongue,* another Sam Shepard turkey. Would it have been any better if Bruce Beresford had directed as well as adapted the script? Maybe, but we'd still be stuck with the brother taking a leak on his sister's 4-H project, for reasons best known to Shepard. **WOOF!**

1994 (R) 102m/C James Woods, Kathy Bates, Henry Thomas, Kristin Fiorella, Randy Quaid, Louis Gossett Jr.; **D:** Michael McClary; **W:** Bruce Beresford; **C:** Dick Quinlan. **VHS, LV, Closed Caption** *THV*

Cutter's Way

Cutter's Way by Ivan Passer was quickly identified as new age film noir by the few people who actually saw it during its original 1981 run. It is not, however, the comfortable sort of film noir which makes it easy for you to go willingly wherever the hero wants to take you. *Cutter's Way* is an intensely uncomfortable film to watch and there are no heroes anywhere in sight, just

three ragged people who stumble on a brutal murder. In 1981, John Heard had the talent and drive to become one of the major actors of his generation. He didn't quite make it, but at least he got the chance to sink his teeth into the meaty role of Cutter, a crippled vet who hates the world for many good reasons. The perennially underrated Jeff Bridges slid into the role of Cutter's best friend Bone with his usual skill, and Lisa Eichhorn portrayed Cutter's bitter wife (and Bone's occasional bed partner). Their amateur murder investigation is conducted with rage and with plenty of mistakes made along the way. *Cutter's Way* was a pioneering noir effort of the '80s, not as atmospheric as the enormously successful *Body Heat,* also released in 1981, nor as likable as 1987's *The Big Heat.* Passer's film was an interesting study of three seedy low lifes mustering the conviction to clash with a corrupt and powerful killer in sunny Santa Barbara. *AKA:* Cutter and Bone. 🦴🦴🦴

1981 (R) 105m/C Jeff Bridges, John Heard, Lisa Eichhorn, Ann Dusenberry, Stephen Elliott, Nina Van Pallandt, George Dickerson; *D:* Ivan Passer; *C:* Jordan Cronenweth; *M:* Jack Nitzsche. Edgar Allan Poe Awards '81: Best Screenplay. **VHS, Beta, LV** *MGM*

Daddy Nostalgia

Dirk Bogarde and Jane Birkin in a film by Bertrand Tavernier? Sounds pretty good, doesn't it? Regretfully, *Daddy Nostalgia,* which sounds terrific on paper, is slow as molasses to watch. Tavernier's own father was dying as the film was being made, but the director chose to approach the subject of mortality at an oblique angle and the results are false and boring. Birkin's character is filled with adolescent concerns and behavior, a bit weird to watch in a woman of 45. And sorry, we just can't accept a screen personality as strong as Bogarde as he mopes around a French villa, waiting to die. He may have been able to pull it off in *Death in Venice,* but Tavernier isn't Visconti and screenwriter

Colo Tavernier O'Hagan isn't Thomas Mann. The threadbare premise of the film is that Birkin's character was neglected as a child and she still yearns for Daddy's approval 40 years later. Bogarde is an insensitive, unappealing lout who can't talk with either his French wife (Odette Laure) or his very British daughter. Birkin has agreed to visit for a pre-determined amount of time, and when the time is up, she leaves. The last act occurs off camera, so nothing much happens for 105 minutes except that you get a chance to see how Bogarde looks and sounds these days (great, on both counts). Too bad his first theatrical feature since 1978 is such a sluggish vehicle. Bogarde deserves a much better swan song than *Daddy Nostalgia. AKA:* These Foolish Things. 🦴🦴

1990 105m/C *FR* Dirk Bogarde, Jane Birkin, Odette Laure; *D:* Bertrand Tavernier; *W:* Colo Tavernier O'Hagan; *M:* Antoine Duhamel. **VHS** *FCT*

Dance with a Stranger

Dance with a Stranger made Miranda Richardson a star and ignited the career of director Mike Newell. Released midway through the Thatcher years (1979-91), the film was typical of its era in that it cast a harsh gaze on the early 1950s, while clearly reveling in their ambiance. Ruth Ellis is the tough-as-nails (translation: walking wounded) manageress of a bar. From the instant that race car driver David Blakely (kinky Rupert Everett) orders a gin and tonic, Ellis (Richardson) is hooked, although she does her best to feign indifference. In fact, at many points during their two-year (1953-55) affair, either Ellis or Blakely was heartily fed up with the other, although never at the same time. Ellis recognizes that they are out of each other's league and although Blakely denies it, he knows it, too. Complicating the situation is Ruth's sad-eyed little boy Andy (Matthew Carroll, in a heart-wringing performance), and Desmond Cussen (Ian Holm, in an on-target piece of work), who's

passion, and hardly a candidate for the death penalty. Although 50,000 signatures were finally collected on one petition protesting her execution, Ellis was hanged with unseemly haste, less than 95 days after Blakely's death, and nowhere near enough time to launch an effective campaign to save her life, especially during the most crucial early days of the newspaper strike. 𝄞𝄞𝄞𝄞

1985 (R) 101m/C *GB* Miranda Richardson, Rupert Everett, Ian Holm, Joanne Whalley, Matthew Carroll, Tom Chadbon, Jane Bertish, David Trughton, Paul Mooney, Stratford Johns, Susan Kyd, Leslie Manville, Sallie-Anne Field, Martin Murphy, Michael Jenn, Daniel Massey; *D:* Mike Newell; *W:* Shelagh Delaney; *C:* Peter Hannan; *M:* Richard Hartley. Cannes Film Festival '85: Best Film. **VHS, Beta, LV, Closed Caption** *VES, LIV*

Dangerous Liaisons

Underwhelmed by 1988's *Dangerous Liaisons* with Glenn Close and John Malkovich? Then check out Roger Vadim's 1960 version of the 1782 novel by Choderlos de Laclos. Jeanne Moreau and the late Gerard Philipe star in this sexual tug of war between a ruthless husband and wife who get a bang out of tormenting their respective victims. Her target is an unsophisticated young man played by Jean-Louis Trintignant, his victim is a happily married (right!) bride portrayed by the director's wife, Annette Stroyberg. Moreau and Philipe are such cool customers that their roles make much more sense than they did with Close and Malkovich. The evil, beat atmosphere is enhanced by Thelonius Monk's timeless jazz score. *AKA:* Les Liaisons Dangereuses; Dangerous Love Affairs. 𝄞𝄞𝄞

1960 111m/B *FR IT* Gerard Philipe, Jeanne Moreau, Jeanne Valeri, Annette Vadim, Simone Renant, Jean-Louis Trintignant, Nikolas Vogel; *D:* Roger Vadim; *W:* Roger Vadim; *M:* Thelonious Monk. **VHS, LV** *INT, APD, TPV*

Dark Habits.

obsessed with Ellis all the time, not just sporadically like Blakely. That cast of characters is just about all that anyone could ask for in a mad love story—only this story is true, brilliantly adapted by Shelagh (*A Taste of Honey*) Delaney, who was all of 16 when Cussen drove the love-crazed Ellis to the scene of the crime where she gunned down Blakely on Easter Sunday, 1955. Joanne Whalley is a bar girl named Christine. Historical Note: What *Dance with a Stranger* doesn't tell us is that Ellis (1926-55, and the last woman hanged in Great Britain) killed Blakely (1929-55) just before a newspaper strike. If the presses had been rolling at full speed, would Ellis' life have been spared? In France, the killing was widely regarded as a crime of

Dark Habits

Director Pedro Almodovar simmered in Madrid for a full decade while doing extra film jobs, making Super 8 movies and working for the telephone company. He made eleven movies between 1980 and 1995, of which 1986's *Matador* is the fifth and 1984's *Dark Habits* is the third. *Dark Habits* is the work of a still maturing artist. Sexual obsession is one thing, but Catholicism is a far more primal target for satire. The film gets free mileage out of nuns on acid, nuns shooting up, and nuns sniffing cocaine, plus the lesbian mother superior who must finance all these activities, not to mention their pet tiger's food expenses. Underneath all these absurdities, the story line is straightforward, as are most of Almodovar's plots. *Dark Habits* is one long joke, not too far removed from the playground fantasies of parochial schoolchildren, but it is basically a warm-up for the far more ambitious projects Almodovar was yet to make. His fourth and sixth films, 1985's *What Have I Done to Deserve This?* and 1986's *Law of Desire,* both starred the legendary Carmen Maura. **AKA:** Entre Tinieblas. 🎬🎬🎬

1984 116m/C *SP* Carmen Maura, Christina Pascual, Julieta Serrano, Marisa Paredes; **D:** Pedro Almodovar; **W:** Pedro Almodovar. **VHS, Beta, LV** *CCN, TPV*

Das Boot

A two and a half hour war movie set in a German submarine? Eh! So I passed on *Das Boot* in 1981. Then I read that it was being re-released in 1997 in a three and a half hour version, and I even heard GUYS grumbling about it at that length. But my friend Michael had seen the earlier version and he said it was great, so we went to the Bridge Theatre one Saturday night in the spring. I braced myself for the worst, namely, the same thing that happened when I went to see *Platoon* in 1986 or *Secrets and Lies* in 1997: Film as Agony. But *Das Boot* had me in its spell for every second of its 210-minute running time.

Wolfgang Petersen, who definitely knows how to helm a thriller (*In the Line of Fire, Outbreak*), makes the day-to-day tasks aboard the submarine seem significant and vital. Because of the way it was shot, you almost feel as if you're a part of the crew, which must have been a much more shocking realization to American audiences in 1981. The men aboard the sub are doing a job; no one spouts Nazi propaganda. In fact, during one surreal sequence off the sub, when they are honored at a way-too-lavish buffet by beautifully dressed National Socialists, the captain (Juergen Prochnow) doesn't even respond when he's on the receiving end of the "Heil Hitler" salute. The German crew members are not cartoons, which is all we ever saw before *Das Boot.* And yet, even though we wince every time we hear a depth charge or watch the crew repair a potentially fatal leak, the film makes no attempt to whitewash or glorify the German military effort. In the final sequence, Peterson shows the futility of war as graphically as Lewis Milestone did over half a century earlier in *All Quiet on the Western Front.* If the longer version of *Das Boot* winds up in video stores, try breaking it up with an intermission. It's an excruciatingly intense experience. **AKA:** The Boat. 🎬🎬🎬🎬

1981 (R) 210m/C *GE* Juergen Prochnow, Herbert Gronemeyer, Klaus Wennemann, Hubertus Bengsch, Martin Semmelrogge, Bernd Tauber, Erwin Leder, Martin May, Heinz Honig, U. A. Ochsen, Claude-Oliver Rudolph, Jan Fedder, Ralph Richer, Joachim Bernhard, Oliver Stritzel, Konrad Becker, Lutz Schnell, Martin Hemme; **D:** Wolfgang Petersen; **W:** Wolfgang Petersen; **C:** Jost Vacano; **M:** Klaus Doldinger. Nominations: Academy Awards '82: Best Adapted Screenplay, Best Cinematography, Best Director (Petersen), Best Film Editing, Best Sound. **VHS, Beta, LV** *COL, APD, GLV*

Daughters, Daughters

Sexist horsefeathers this, but I had yet another argument (with a guy) who went ballistic when I said so. When will I ever learn? HIS P.O.V.: "It's okay to zero in on a

I wanted to tell an old tale, but in a very different way, just like a poet will take everyday, mundane events and issues, but will phrase it so that it seems fresh and new, something that you'll always remember. You'll remember a phrase or a line of poetry that you really like. I wanted to do a very cinematic film. I wanted to do an historical drama in a way that had never been done before, in a way that would stick in the minds and the imaginations of the American people. In this particular story, I relied very heavily on striking images that haunt, enchant, and take the viewers off into a Zen-like experience, and let them start thinking about their own extended family.... I think we've all seen enough depictions of rape on television and in theatres. The important thing was not to focus on the rape of one of the characters, but on the result of the rape and how this woman had to deal with her day-to-day experience after the fact. Rape was something that occurred so regularly. There are so many African Americans who are in families where one child was not even the product of a white land owner because that was way, way back, but of just a white person, and I wanted to take a look at how the family dealt with that. It is something that's very real in the black community. There was a lot of race mixing.... There were tremendous problems [making the film]. There was Hurricane Hugo and we had to evacuate the islands. There were blood-sucking gnats and mosquitoes, there were windstorms, there was rain.... Everyone really enjoyed being on the island. It's a fascinating place. It looks almost prehistoric. There's such a variety of terrain. There's sea, there are very high sand dunes, there's a dense forest....

"I didn't know the characters that I wrote about in the film: I've read about them, I've heard about them, and most of them are composite characters, based upon events and issues of the time. For me, the character of Yellow Mary represents the loss of the black woman's self-esteem during Reconstruction because of her life as a prostitute and how she became a prostitute after having worked with a family where the male of the family was sexually abusing her. All of this is implied, it's never said, but many women understand it."

man's obsessive struggle to father a son after eight daughters, because it's a comedy from Israel." MY P.O.V.: "Director Moshe Mizrahi is condescending towards ALL his characters, male and female. Shai K. Ophir, who plays the father, is a competent actor, but the screenplay he writes with Mizrahi debases everyone. No one laughs WITH the characters because they're too crudely drawn and no one laughs AT them because they're not funny enough to carry the contrived premise." So there. 🦴

1974 88m/C IS Shai K. Ophir, Zaharira Harifai, Yoseph Shiloah, Michal Bat-Adam; **D:** Moshe Mizrahi; **W:** Moshe Mizrahi, Shai K. Ophir; **C:** Adam Greenberg; **M:** Alex Cagan. *NYR*

Daughters of the Dust

At 113 minutes, *Daughters of the Dust* deserved a context for its narrative. Instead, we get beautiful cinematography, and a very leisurely paced look at the lives of five women before they leave their island to emigrate to the Georgia coast. They can act, but Julie Dash's storytelling skills are decidedly embryonic. Set in 1902. 🦴🦴

1991 113m/C Cora Lee Day, Barbara O, Alva Rogers, Kaycee Moore, Cheryl Lynn Bruce, Adisa Anderson, Eartha D. Robinson, Bahni Turpin, Tommy Hicks, Malik Farrakhan, Cornell (Kofi) Royal, Vertamae Crosvenor, Umar Abdurrahman, Sherry Jackson, Rev. Ervin Green; **D:** Julie Dash; **W:** Julie Dash; **C:** A. Jafa Fielder; **M:** John Barnes. Sundance Film Festival '91: Best Cinematography. **VHS** *KIV, FCT, PMS*

Day for My Love

Day for My Love features the most adorable four-year-old child (Sylva Kamenicka). She dies very early in the story, but her laughing presence infects the entire movie. Marta Vancurova and Vlastimil Harapes star as the young couple who must cope with the loss of their young child, and build a new life for themselves while making peace with their past. Very well scripted by Marketa Zinnerova and a bit too artily shot by Jiri Machane, *Day for My Love* is enhanced by Juraj Herz's strong direction, as well as the excellent acting throughout. 🦴🦴🦴

1977 91m/C CZ Marta Vancurova, Vlastimil Harapes, Sylva Kamenicka, Dana Medricka, Jirinaova Sejbalova; **D:** Juraj Herz; **W:** Marketa Zinnerova; **C:** Jiri Machane; **M:** Petr Hapka. *NYR*

The Daytrippers

Produced by Steven Soderbergh, Greg Mottola's *The Daytrippers* follows a family as they try to patch up the ailing marriage of the older daughter, Eliza (Hope Davis). Is husband Louis (Stanley Tucci) having an affair or what? *The Daytrippers* is more concerned with the "or what" than the affair. What adult daughter would let herself be dragged around by Mom and Dad (Anne Meara and Pat McNamara), sister Jo (Parker Posey), and would-be brother-in-law Carl (Liev Schreiber)? Somehow, Mottola makes the characters and situations seem funny and real and it doesn't hurt one bit that Marcia Gay Harden and co-producer Campbell Scott are also in the cast. 🦴🦴🦴

1996 m/C Hope Davis, Stanley Tucci, Parker Posey, Liev Schreiber, Pat McNamara, Anne Meara, Campbell Scott, Marcia Gay Harden, Andy Brown; **D:** Greg Mottola; **W:** Greg Mottola; **C:** John Inwood.

The Dead

Nothing would have kept us away from John Huston's swan song, *The Dead,* but we suspect that the overall sentimental response to the film is based more on a lifelong admiration for Huston's work than to the film itself. We have a hunch that some audience members find all these Irish bores quaint or precious, but we did NOT. James Joyce's 1914 story is a pleasure to read for the loveliness of its language, but *The Dead* was harder for us to sit through in a theatre. We would cheer-

"Just room for one inside, sir!"

—After narrowly cheating death, Hugh Grainger (Antony Baird) receives this oddly tempting offer from a passing hearse in *Dead of Night.*

fully pay to avoid the dull family get-together shown on film, or to listen to an elderly woman sing off-key, and she does over and over again. Maybe we would have to be 81 years old to find the experience, as Huston did, "funny and dear and terribly sad," or to find the film itself "a soul-shaking experience," but we tend to doubt it. Huston includes one beautiful exterior shot at night that evokes the frailty of time in a way that the rest of the film does not. ♪♪

1987 (PG) 82m/C *GB* Anjelica Huston, Donal McCann, Marie Kean, Donal Donnelly, Dan O'Herlihy, Helen Carroll, Frank Patterson; *D:* John Huston; *C:* Fred Murphy; *M:* Alex North. Independent Spirit Awards '88: Best Director (Huston), Best Supporting Actress (Huston); National Board of Review Awards '87: 10 Best Films of the Year; National Society of Film Critics Awards '87: Best Film; Nominations: Academy Awards '87: Best Adapted Screenplay, Best Costume Design. **VHS, Beta, LV, Closed Caption** *LIV, VES, TVC*

Dead Calm

Nicole Kidman and Sam Neill are a cute couple, but I wouldn't get in a car with her or on a boat with either one of them. Five minutes into *Dead Calm,* her baby is hurled through a windshield. There is actually no reason for this sequence except to establish why Kidman and Neill go on a sea cruise alone to recover. It also prepares you for the violence this accident-prone couple will experience throughout the rest of the film. When a psycho (screechingly overacted by Billy Zane) rows over to their boat from his own doomed vessel, Neill doesn't believe their visitor's tall tale of botulism and death from contaminated salmon. Neill rows to the vessel to investigate, leaving Kidman and their pet dog alone with the psycho. (Warning: don't get too attached to that mutt.) You see, Neill has 25 years experience at sea, but you'll have to take his word for it. For a small craft skipper, he is constantly endangering his boat, his crew, and himself. He spends what seems like half the movie trying to save himself from drowning by breaking down a vessel door he had no reason to go

through at all. Meanwhile, Kidman and that psycho just never can seem to get along. He beats her up, rapes her, kicks down doors, and destroys her radio. She drugs his lemonade, shoots him with an arrow, ties him up, and tries to throw him overboard. Australian director Phillip Noyce, also responsible for the 1986 dud *Echoes of Paradise,* telegraphs each move by all three well in advance. Try to imagine the dumbest thing any of them can do and sure enough, there it is, right onscreen. Was the Charles Williams novel this much of a mess? Tantalizing Back Story: one of Orson Welles' many unfinished films was an earlier version of *Dead Calm* entitled *Dead Reckoning,* starring Jeanne Moreau and himself in the Kidman/Neill roles and Laurence Harvey as the psycho. Financing and/or Harvey's early death scuttled the project, although footage from this incomplete work survives. ♪♪ ▽

1989 (R) 97m/C *AU* Sam Neill, Billy Zane, Nicole Kidman, Rod Mullinar; *D:* Phillip Noyce; *W:* Terry Hayes; *C:* Dean Semler; *M:* Graeme Revell. **VHS, Beta, LV, 8mm, Closed Caption** *WAR, FCT*

Dead Man

I fidgeted all the way through Jim Jarmusch's *Dead Man.* This is one of those long-winded black-and-white Westerns that makes you want to bag the screening and spend the time necking instead. Johnny Depp plays the title role with excruciating fidelity, and Robert Mitchum plays a cameo role, but that's about it. There's a line at the beginning that pretty much says it all, unless you need empirical evidence of just how soporific Depp can be. ♪♪

1995 (R) 121m/B Johnny Depp, Gary Farmer, Lance Henriksen, Michael Wincott, Mili Avital, Crispin Glover, Gabriel Byrne, Iggy Pop, Billy Bob Thornton, Jared Harris, Jimmie Ray Weeks, Mark Bringleson, John Hurt, Alfred Molina, Robert Mitchum; *D:* Jim Jarmusch; *W:* Jim Jarmusch; *C:* Robby Muller; *M:* Neil Young. New York Film Critics Awards '96: Best Cinematography; National Society of Film Critics Awards '96: Best Cinematography; Nominations: Independent Spirit Awards '97: Best Cinematography, Best

Film, Best Screenplay, Best Supporting Actor (Farmer). **VHS, LV, Closed Caption** *TOU*

Dead Man Walking

Susan Sarandon is Sister Helen Prejean, death row inmate Matthew Poncelet's (Sean Penn) last chance at spiritual salvation. Poncelet murdered two young people in cold blood and is numb to the horror of his crime. Seeing Sister Helen is better than nothing, so he asks her to keep visiting him at Angola prison in New Orleans where he waits to die. On an early visit, he tries to hit on her, but she slaps him down with a sarcastic verbal retort and continues with the serious work of saving his soul. Although Sister Helen is opposed to the death penalty, Oscar nominee Tim Robbins' superb film shows both sides with careful, non-judgmental attention. The victims' parents are in agony, Poncelet has a shattering change of heart due to Sister Helen's steady influence, and there is a vivid sequence showing his emotion-charged encounter with his family at the prison. Penn won an Oscar nomination as Matthew Poncelet and, after a career filled with outstanding performances, Sarandon won her first Academy Award for her unforgettable portrait of Sister Helen Prejean. Scott Wilson (Chaplain Farley) starred as Dick Hickock in 1967's *In Cold Blood.* ♫♫♫♫

1995 (R) 122m/C Susan Sarandon, Sean Penn, Robert Prosky, Raymond J. Barry, R. Lee Ermey, Celia Weston, Lois Smith, Scott Wilson, Roberta Maxwell, Margo Martindale, Barton Heyman, Larry Pine; **D:** Tim Robbins; **W:** Tim Robbins; **C:** Roger Deakins; **M:** David Robbins. Academy Awards '95: Best Actress (Sarandon); Independent Spirit Awards '96: Best Actor (Penn); Screen Actors Guild Award '95: Best Actress (Sarandon); Nominations: Academy Awards '95: Best Actor (Penn), Best Director (Robbins), Best Song ("Dead Man Walking"); Australian Film Institute '96: Best Foreign Film; Golden Globe Awards '96: Best Actor—Drama (Penn), Best Actress—Drama (Sarandon), Best Screenplay; Independent Spirit Awards '96: Best Supporting Actress (Weston); MTV Movie Awards '96: Best Female Performance (Sarandon); Screen Actors Guild Award '95: Best Actor (Penn). **VHS, LV, DVD** *PGV*

Dead of Night

For those who believe that Hell may mean repeating your earthly mistakes over and over again with one agonizing moment of realization every time that THIS is to be your fate for the rest of eternity, *Dead of Night* is one very scary flick, best seen with lots of friends who won't leave you alone afterwards. Mervyn Johns plays an architect who wakes up after a nightmare and then goes to a farmhouse where he has an appointment. He thinks he's seen it before! The guests then tell scary stories to each other. A race car driver tells the story of his dream about a hearse driver who has room for one more. When he later hears a bus driver say the same thing, he refuses to get on and watches in horror as the bus crashes right afterward. Then a young girl (Sally Ann Howes) tells about a Christmas party where she runs into a little boy named Francis, the brother of Constance Kent, who was accused of his murder in 1860. This Alberto Cavalcanti entry is followed by John Baines' "The Haunted Mirror" (directed by Robert Hamer), in which a young wife watches as her new husband is nearly driven mad by an antique mirror that takes over his personality. Basil Radford and Naunton Wayne then provide comedy relief in H.G. Wells' "The Inexperienced Ghost" (directed by Charles Crichton), about two golfers who both want the same girl. It's a trifle, but a welcome one. The tension would have been nearly unbearable if we'd gone straight from the "The Haunted Mirror" into Cavalcanti's justly famous "Ventriloquist's Dummy" (starring Michael Redgrave) and then back to the chilling story of the nightmare-ridden architect. *Dead of Night* has a cumulative effect. It lulls us with sly humor, then makes the hair stand up on the back of our necks with sheer terror. The linking story and the hearse driver dream are based on the E.F. Benson stories "Room in the Tower" and "The Bus Conductor" and are both directed by Basil

Dearden. Ealing forever, and not only for comedies! 𝄞𝄞𝄞𝄞

1945 102m/B *GB* Michael Redgrave, Sally Ann Howes, Basil Radford, Naunton Wayne, Mervyn Johns, Roland Culver, Googie Withers, Frederick Valk, Antony Baird, Judy Kelly, Miles Malleson, Ralph Michael, Mary Merrall, Renee Gadd, Michael Allan, Robert Wyndham, Esme Percy, Peggy Bryan, Hartley Power, Elizabeth Welch, Magda Kun, Carry Marsh; *D:* Alberto Cavalcanti, Charles Crichton, Basil Dearden, Robert Hamer; *W:* T.E.B. Clarke, John Baines, Angus MacPhail; *C:* Jack Parker, H. Julius; *M:* Georges Auric. **VHS, Beta** *REP, RXM, CNG*

Dealers

If you like to watch Rebecca DeMornay and Paul McGann work, you can see them in *Dealers,* an incomprehensible drama about London high finance. For much of the film's running time, we had no idea what was going on or why. DeMornay and McGann work themselves into a frenzy to achieve a goal that neither seems to care about. After reading the press kit, which clarifies stuff that screenwriter Andrew Maclear should have explained onscreen, we didn't care, either. That's a fatal flaw for a 92-minute movie. Colin Bucksey's crisp direction and the attractive leads would be more effective in a better film. Also worth noting is Derrick O'Connor, who does wonders with a sparsely written character role. **WOOF!**

1989 (R) 92m/C *GB* Rebecca DeMornay, Paul McGann, Derrick O'Connor; *D:* Colin Bucksey; *W:* Andrew Maclear. **VHS, Beta, LV** *ACA, IME*

Dear Michael

The excellent Italian picture *Dear Michael* explores the wanderings of Mara, a gypsy-ish mother (Mariangela Melato) and her baby. Mara has an idea who the father is, and spends her time moving in and out of the homes of his friends and relatives. Melato, so effective in the Lina Wertmuller films *Seduction of Mimi, Love and Anarchy, Swept Away,* and *Summer Night...,* wrings enormous sympathy out of her role here. Her ability to add new dimensions to her sometimes unbearable characters are

truly imaginative. Whether she's breaking up with a lover who cannot stand her, scolding an impatient cab driver, or enduring a boring social evening with a group of "intellectuals," Melato provides *Dear Michael* with its funniest and most human moments. Director Mario Monicelli and screenwriters Suso Cecchi D'Amico and Tonino Guerra skillfully blend Mara's story into that of her former lover's family. With the addition of superb, understated performances by the late Delphine Seyrig, Aurore Clement, and particularly Fabio Carpi as one of Mara's befuddled lovers, *Dear Michael* is among the most memorable films of 1976. Melato's other films on video include: *By the Blood of Others, To Forget Venice, So Fine,* and *Dancers.* **AKA:** *Caro Michele.* 𝄞𝄞𝄞

1976 108m/C *IT* Mariangela Melato, Delphine Seyrig, Aurore Clement, Lou Castel, Marcella Michelangeli, Fabio Carpi; *D:* Mario Monicelli; *W:* Suso Cecchi D'Amico, Tonino Guerra; *C:* Tonino Delli Colli; *M:* Nino Rota. *NYR*

Dear Victor

At first, *Dear Victor* gives every indication that it's going to be a comedy, then a savage plot twist occurs: Film Festivalitis? Yes, that strange and sometimes frightening condition that afflicts directors who don't want to make a choice about the direction of their narratives, so the choice is made FOR them by tuned-out audiences! The compensatory surprise here is Alida Valli, who's simply wonderful and very funny as a singer who COULD have been an opera star. **AKA:** *Ce Cher Victor.* 𝄞𝄞𝄞

1975 102m/C *FR* Bernard Blier, Jacques Dufilho, Alida Valli, Alice Reichen, Jacqueline Doyen, Philippe Castelli, Jacques Rispal; *D:* Robin Davis; *W:* Robin Davis, Robin Laurent; *C:* Yves Lafaye; *M:* Bernard Gerard. *NYR*

Death and the Maiden

Roman Polanski sets up a gripping dilemma here and then dribbles it. Why do we have to forgive the unforgivable? Why do we have to live and let live when we've been victimized by a person who clearly didn't care whether or not we lived or died? Three fine actors (Ben Kingsley, Sigourney Weaver, Stuart Wilson) grapple with this situation for 103 minutes until the credits roll. In a number of ways, it rather reminds me of 1986's *Extremities,* where we are reminded over and over again that a reprehensible character deserves for the woman he raped to treat him like a human being. Can't someone, ANYONE else do that little thing? Polanski succeeds in making us feel as trapped as his characters, but the muddled, well intentioned narrative thread tends to be unplayable at times, especially by Weaver, who has the hardest job here. Based on the play by Ariel Dorfman. 🦴🦴🤍

1994 (R) 103m/C Sigourney Weaver, Ben Kingsley, Stuart Wilson; *D:* Roman Polanski; *W:* Rafael Yglesias, Ariel Dorfman; *C:* Tonino Delli Colli; *M:* Wojciech Kilar. Nominations: Independent Spirit Awards '95: Best Director (Polanski). **VHS, LV, Closed Caption** *TTC, NLC, IME*

The Deceivers

The Deceivers appears to have everything going for it: a handsome hero (Pierce Brosnan), fine support from excellent character actors Shashi Kapoor and Saeed Jaffrey, fascinating Indian locations, and a plot that promises mystery, suspense, and danger. It bogs down in murky character development, a fatal lack of conviction about who the villains are, and an obvious series of false discussions that drag the plot down at every turn. ("I can't do it." "Yes, you can." "No, I can't." "You must." and so forth until we cut to the next scene with Brosnan doing what he couldn't with no effort at all.) Based on a true story, *The Deceivers* are also known as Thugees, a weird, murderous cult that thrived in India, circa 1825. We tend to be suspicious of internal problems that can only be sorted out by British outsiders or by Shirley Temple; after all, Great Britain had

and has its share of weird murderers and nobody ever suggests that Rajahs be imported to clear up those problems. That said, the film is further burdened by Brosnan's bewildered performance. When the Irish actor appeared in *The Long Good Friday* with Bob Hoskins, he delivered a crisp, menacing performance, quite free of any tendency to sweeten his character. After four years of playing a heroic television detective, Brosnan seems more interested in stardom (with substance, of course!) than in acting. It's hard to figure out what he's trying to do with his character, a problem we don't have with co-stars Kapoor and Jaffrey. Also in the cast are David Robb, who specializes in playing husbands of icons of the '60s (Hayley Mills) and the '80s (Diana, Princess of Wales). Keith Michell, considerably puffier than in his lean days onstage in the '70s when he played Peter Abelard in the nude, is virtually unrecognizable here. *The Deceivers* is produced by Ismail Merchant, taking a busman's holiday from his meticulous production team of Ruth Prawer Jhabvala and James Ivory. With a script straight out of Screenwriting I by Michael Hirst (from John Masters' novel) and clumsy schoolboy direction by Nicholas Meyer, Merchant seems to be taking a crash course in the *Classics Illustrated* school of filmmaking. 🦴🦴

1988 (PG-13) 112m/C *IN GB* Pierce Brosnan, Saeed Jaffrey, Shashi Kapoor, Keith Michell, David Robb; *D:* Nicholas Meyer; *W:* Michael Hirst; *C:* Walter Lassally. **VHS, Beta, LV, Closed Caption** *WAR*

Deep End

Jane Asher is a fine actress whose well publicized social life offscreen has eclipsed virtually everything she's ever done onscreen. In the case of the rarely shown *Deep End,* it's a shame, because her performance here is outstanding. John Moulder-Brown is 15-year-old Michael, who gets a job as a Men's Attendant at London's Newford public bathhouse. He falls hard for Women's Attendant Susan

(Asher), who's about eight years older. She's having a not particularly satisfying relationship with an older man and is touched, at least at first, by Michael's crush on her. But as time wears on, she can no longer juggle all the disparate elements of her life, and Michael is devastated by her growing disinterest in his devotion to her. Inevitably, something has to give, and it does in a way that startles this mismatched pair as much as it does us. *Deep End* is a shockingly overlooked study of adolescent obsession at its most extreme, meticulously scripted and directed and remarkably acted by the two leads. Don't miss it! 🦴🦴🦴🦴

1970 88m/C *GB GE* Jane Asher, John Moulder-Brown, Diana Dors, Karl Michael Vogler, Christopher Sandord; *D:* Jerzy Skolimowski; *W:* Jerzy Skolimowski, Jerry Gruza, Bloeslav Sulik; *C:* Charly Steinberger; *M:* Cat Stevens. **VHS** *NO*

A Delicate Balance

The credits for *A Delicate Balance* sound so tantalizing, it's sad that the film itself is such a drag to watch. Six years earlier on Broadway, the original play by Edward Albee had won the Pulitzer Prize, and actress Marian Seldes won a Tony for her performance. (Co-stars Hume Cronyn and Rosemary Murphy were also nominated, and the venerable Jessica Tandy was in it, too.) Maybe it was one of those unfilmable plays, or maybe its stars were too high profile to be persuasive in roles they weren't exactly born to play, or maybe it simply wasn't Tony Richardson's cup of tea. Luis Bunel's, maybe? Edward Albee and Eugene O'Neill were the only American playwrights represented in 13 American Film Theatre productions of the early 1970s. *A Delicate Balance* was released theatrically overseas in 1976. The only noteworthy thing about this movie was meeting Celeste Holm at a San Francisco matinee screening in the theatre lobby. She asked me if I accepted the premise of the film (No!) and if I wanted an autograph, would I give her a quarter for UNICEF? (Yes!) 🦴🦴

1973 134m/C *GB CA* Katharine Hepburn, Paul Scofield, Lee Remick, Kate Reid, Joseph Cotten, Betsy Blair; *D:* Tony Richardson; *W:* Edward Albee; *C:* David Watkin. **VHS** *NO*

Delusion

Delusion is an accurate title for a movie that is deliberately reminiscent of many other noir films. Those films, which include Edgar Ulmer's *Detour* and Alfred Hitchcock's *Vertigo,* deliver a lot more than *Delusion* ever does. It starts out well: a schnook named George (Jim Metzler) steals nearly $250,000 to save his ailing company, then drives his Volvo into the desert with the loot. Faster than you can say *Psycho,* George runs into a fruitcake named Chevy (Kyle Secour) with a weak stomach and a girlfriend named Patti. Patti is sporadically crafty, especially when craftiness will advance the plot. But George is always a schnook and Chevy is always a fruitcake and 100 minutes of these two tend to make Patti's cipher-like personality seem more complex than it really is. Jerry Orbach is seen in a brief appearance. So is Jennifer Rubin's bare chest. And so is a moderately intriguing plot twist that Patti and the audience know about, but not George or Chevy. Don't be misled, though: writer/director Carl Colpaert takes that title very seriously. Everything in his picture is a tease, from the spectacular golden landscapes, to the deceptively provocative emotional subtext, to the emptiness of the treasure that lies within everyone's reach and no one's grasp. *Delusion* is a film about hard-core losers living by rules that don't work. There is not even a minimal effort to supply the characters with depth; you already know much more about them than you'll ever want to know. *Delusion*'s very emptiness may guarantee it an audience. But for anyone who really loves film noir, Colpaert's decision to tie up the plot with Lee Hazelwood's *These Boots Are Made for*

Opposite page: **Tom Neal and Ann Savage in** *Detour.*

The Hound Salutes:

MARTIN GOLDSMITH

His name was Martin Goldsmith. He carried a pen. He had been writing for nearly 65 years.

I started writing when I was 15. I left school when I was 15. I dropped out of high school—never finished high school—and I hit the road. This was during the depths of the Depression and I rode freights and all sorts of things like that, banged around the country, and then I thought I'd try to write a little bit about some of the things that happened to me."

In 1938, at the age of 24, he wrote his first novel, *Detour,* **forming the basis for the 1946 Edgar Ulmer film noir of the same name which many consider to be the best "B" movie ever made. In** *Detour,* **the late Tom Neal and Ann Savage star as Al and Vera, a doomed couple who meet on the road and spend all their time together trying to destroy each other. At one point, Al resisted Vera's efforts to persuade him to impersonate a dead heir to a fortune. Seven years later, in 1952, Martin Goldsmith won an Academy Award nomination for the original story of** *The Narrow Margin,* **a classic film noir directed by Richard Fleischer.**

"We had our tricks. One way is that if there was something that was censorable, that we knew would create an argument, we would, on the page before it, put something absolutely horrendous, that we knew they would get terribly upset about, and which was far worse then anything we had put on the page following...and then they would let us put the next page through very easily. And that's how we got things through."

In *The Narrow Margin,* **the late Charles McGraw plays a tough cop assigned to protect a gun moll portrayed by Marie Windsor. Their hostile relationship is played out in claustrophobic train compartments. By 1964, the film noir genre was in decline on the big screen, but on television, Rod Serling explored many of the same dramatic concerns in** *The Twilight Zone.* **Martin Goldsmith wrote a teleplay entitled "What's in the Box?" for the series, which gave William Demarest and Joan Blondell some meaty roles as a two-timing cabdriver and his combative wife. Towards the end of his life, there was a resurgence of interest in Martin Goldsmith's** *Detour,* **and production companies sued each other for the rights to remake the movie. One producer, Wade Williams, cast Tom Neal, Jr., in his father's most famous role. Since both his novel and the film slipped into the public domain many years ago, Martin Goldsmith remained comfortably distant from all this, although** *Detour's* **dark story remained as disturbing to its creator (1914-94) as it continues to be to contemporary audiences.**

"I can't believe I was that bad at the age of 24; there are some things in there that absolutely horrify me."

Walking reveals *Delusion*'s threadbare ingredients: something old, nothing new, something borrowed, nothing blue. 🦴🦴

1991 (R) 100m/C Jim Metzler, Jennifer Rubin, Kyle Secor, Robert Costanzo, Tracey Walter, Jerry Orbach; *D:* Carl Colpaert; *W:* Carl Colpaert, Kurt Voss; *M:* Barry Adamson. **VHS, LV** *COL*

Destiny Turns on the Radio

Quentin Tarantino as Johnny Destiny. Right. And the Emperor was really wearing clothes. But Mr. T is an Oscar winner. He's the 1990's Big Thing. Why not be a movie star and an influential screenwriter and a hot director, too? Tarantino was promoted more in the television spots than the so-called stars, Dylan McDermott, Nancy Travis, James LeGros, and James Belushi, as if his Midas touch could rub off on first-time screenwriters Robert Ramsey and Matthew Stone and on fledgling director Jack Baran. It can't, of course. The script is the stuff of formulaic hacks, and Baran's idea of great direction is to tell McDermott he's in an action flick, THEN tell Travis she's in a romantic comedy, THEN tell LeGros his character is brain dead, and THEN tell Belushi and his henchmen that their characters require constant reassurances about their virility; they even scratch their crotches in synch. All of this was developed at The Sundance Institute, so some critics have been charitable about this maiden effort. But it's a mess. Travis is a nightclub singer whose voice is dubbed by a singer who's ever so slightly off-key, so the Hoagy Carmichael classic "Baltimore Oriole" is ruined, ditto "That Old Black Magic." (You can hear Louis Prima and Keely Smith sing it right on the soundtrack.) A restrained Bobcat Goldthwaite plays an undercover cop who spends most of the movie tied to a vibrating bed with an apple taped in his mouth. A real knee slapper, no? Tarantino has set the world on fire as a screenwriter and director, but he is not of strong enough presence to dazzle anyone as Johnny Destiny. And for critics to be kind to *Destiny Turns on the Radio* sets Baran, Ramsay, and Stone up for their second effort to be (surprise) received far worse than their dreadful debut, since it lacks the je ne sais quoi of *Destiny*. It's a curiosity piece alright, but it's lucky that night prowling movie cats usually have eight or nine lives to spare. **WOOF!**

1995 (R) 101m/C Dylan McDermott, Nancy Travis, James LeGros, Quentin Tarantino, Allen (Goorwitz) Garfield, James Belushi, Tracey Walter, Bob(cat) Goldthwait; *D:* Jack Baran; *W:* Robert Ramsey, Matthew Stone; *C:* James L. Carter; *M:* Steven Soles. **VHS, Closed Caption** *HBO*

Detour

Detour is THE grunge classic of all time. In most cases, when you watch a poverty row film, you find yourself wishing that they had just a bit more time or money to do things properly: if only the wallpaper in the hero's apartment and the police station weren't identical; if only the same three extras weren't in the background in every single sequence. But *Detour,* shot on a next-to-nothing budget in less than a week, is perfect just the way it is. The main reason, of course, is that the brilliant director, Edgar G. Ulmer, who rarely got a chance at an "A" movie, was at the helm. No one could wring more from a poverty row effort than Ulmer, as he demonstrated in his superior work on films like *Bluebeard* and *Strange Illusion.* Superstar John Garfield might have seemed like an ideal choice for the role of the protagonist in *Detour,* but in fact, Tom Neal WAS Al Roberts. Neal kicked around Hollywood from the late '30s through the early '50s, launching his career at the prestigious MGM studios, but he descended swiftly to grade-Z programmers, in part because of his unsavory offscreen behavior. (He later wound up in prison for killing one of his wives.) If ever a camera recorded the face of a loser, Tom Neal was the quintessential loser. He was 31 in 1945, the year *Detour* was shot, and while superficially attractive, he seemed drenched in world-weariness and defeatism. Ann Savage, then a

24-year-old starlet, sacrificed her good looks to play the role of Vera, a femme fatale with a vengeance. No other young actress of her era ever made herself so unlovely for the sake of a role: no make-up, ragged hair, a wardrobe from Hell. If you catch a dolled-up version of Savage in any of her glossy Columbia films, you'll find it hard to believe you're looking at the same person. In the course of little over an hour, Al and Vera meet, join forces, and destroy each other on the road, spitting dialogue at each other that you're unlikely to hear in any other '40s movie. Among the lighter-than-air films of that time, *Detour* stands alone as a grim chunk of realism and it's still every bit as hard-hitting in the '90s. 🦴🦴🦴🦴

1946 67m/B Tom Neal, Ann Savage, Claudia Drake, Edmund MacDonald, Tim Ryan, Esther Howard; *D:* Edgar G. Ulmer; *W:* Martin Goldsmith; *M:* Erdody. **VHS, Beta, LV** *BAR, MRV, SNC*

The Devil Is a Woman

Maybe it was movies like *The Devil Is a Woman* that eventually lured Glenda Jackson off the sound stages and into Parliament. She dons spiked belts here in her role as a weird mother superior who keeps the residents of her convent under her thumb. The script is your basic, silly, half-baked attack on the Catholic hierarchy; not a bad target, perhaps, but if you're going to satirize an institution, at least deal with it on its own terms. Unconvincing and ridiculous beyond belief, *Devil* doesn't even come close. *AKA:* Il Sorriso del Grande Tentatore. **WOOF!**

1975 185m/C *GB IT* Glenda Jackson, Claudio Cassinelli, Lisa Harrow, Adolfo Celi, Arnoldo Foa, Rolf Tasna, Dulio Del Prete, Gabriele Lavia, Francesco Rabal; *D:* Damiano Damiani; *W:* Damiano Damiani, Fabrizio Onofri, Audrey Nohra; *C:* Mario Vulpiani; *M:* Ennio Morricone. *NYR*

Diamonds in the Snow

In the city of Bendzin, Poland, three small children among thousands were being torn away from their families during the Nazi occupation. The little girls grew up to participate in the making of *Diamonds in the Snow.* The award-winning documentary is directed by Mira Reym Binford, who recalls her own experiences and interviews two others among the twelve surviving children of the town, Ada Raviv and Shulamit Levin. In Dr. Binford's case, her life was protected by another refugee who nonetheless beat her up. As an adult, she searches for his own children and learns that after the war they were no better treated than she was, a discovery which helps to heal much of her early pain and confusion. 🦴🦴🦴

1994 59m/C D: Mira Reym Binford. **VHS** *CIG*

Diary of a Hitman

Sherilyn Fenn may not have the marquee value of Kim Basinger—yet—but just wait. The smashingly talented alumnus of *Twin Peaks* can act rings around most other actresses of her generation as she demonstrates in Roy London's 1992 film noir sleeper, *Diary of a Hitman,* starring Forest Whitaker. Whitaker plays a hired gun who is paid by Lewis Smith to execute his wife (Fenn) and their baby. Whitaker's character has already begun to agonize over his profession, but he is unprepared for Fenn's sheer vivacity. He hesitates, and that hesitation forms the basis for Kenneth Pressman's narrative (based on his play, *Insider's Price*). Fenn gives extraordinary dimension to the role of the would-be victim. First, she can't wait for her husband to come home; then, as she realizes that Whitaker has come to kill her baby and herself on her husband's orders, she fights like a tiger to survive. One by one, she tries every resource at her disposal, always tapping into her internal strengths as an actress, never employing the easy external tricks that might have created a flashy, but far less real, character. Whitaker, too, is quite moving as the conscience-stricken assassin. With a brilliant series of emotional mood swings, he captures both the extreme danger and the capacity for deep feeling that are central to the life-and-death conflict in *Diary of a Hitman.* Michel Columbier's fine jazz score enhances Roy London's striking visual style, and the supporting cast members (James Belushi, Seymour Cassel, Lois Chiles, and a nearly unrecognizable Sharon Stone) are exceptionally good; they are usually the stars in other films. The killer with a heart of gold is the stuff of pure theatre, nearly a cliche. Thanks to the expert work of Forest Whitaker and Sherilyn Fenn, the complex relationship between killer and victim also serves to reveal the existential angst lurking beneath all our meaningless rituals. 🦴🦴🦴

1991 (R) 90m/C Forest Whitaker, James Belushi, Sherilyn Fenn, Sharon Stone, Seymour Cassel, Lewis Smith, Lois Chiles, John Bedford-Lloyd; **D:** Roy London; **W:** Kenneth Pressman; **M:** Michel Colombier. **VHS, LV, Closed Caption** *COL*

Different for Girls

Richard Spence's *Different for Girls* is a love story with a twist. It's the tale of Kim Foyle and Paul Prentice (well played by Steven Mackintosh and Rupert Graves), who develop a romance under unusual circumstances. It seems that once upon a time Prentice was friends with a classmate named Karl at a Catholic school for boys. The boy Karl evolved into the girl Kim after a sex change operation and the mutual attraction between Kim and Prentice needs some sort of reassuring context since they both consider themselves to be straight. Got that? The film is nothing earth-shattering, but it is well made, pleasant, and straightforward. 🦴🦴🦴

1996 (R) 92m/C *GB* Rupert Graves, Steven Mackintosh, Miriam Margolyes, Saskia Reeves, Neil Dudgeon, Charlotte Coleman; **D:** Richard Spence; **W:**

Tony Merchant; **C:** Sean Van Hales; **M:** Stephen Warbeck. Montreal World Film Festival '95: Best Film. **VHS** *NYR*

Dinner for Adele

This charming film from Czechoslovakia, a surprise hit at international film festivals, is inspired by the Nick Carter detective stories that enjoyed a vogue at the turn of the 20th century. *Dinner for Adele/Adele Hasn't Had Her Supper Yet* is about a man-eating plant, some early flying machines, a mad scientist, a sane scientist, a delightful strudel of a girl who makes terrific strawberry dumplings, a fat detective and, last but not least, the famous slender detective Nick Carter whose motto is "Always prepared!" How do they all fit together? Hopefully, a shrewd American distributor will acquire the video rights, so more viewers will have the fun of discovering Adele all over again. (Adele is the animated plant. The wonderfully capable Czech actor Michal Docolomansky plays Nick Carter.) **AKA:** Adele Hasn't Had Her Supper Yet. 🦴🦴🦴🦴

1978 100m/C *CZ* Michal Docolomansky, Rudolf Hrusinsky, Milos Kopecky, Nada Konvalinkova, Ladislav Pesek; **D:** Oldrich Lipsky. *NYR*

Dirty Dancing

I used to love Jennifer Grey when she had her own nose on her face in the 1980s; it was cute, it gave her character, and it suited her. Now, I don't always recognize her face on the video boxes and she's indistinguishable from so many other ingenues of the 1990s. For the long summer of 1987, Grey and co-star Patrick Swayze epitomized romance as they danced together all night long. It's set in another place (the Catskills) and time (1963), when teenagers still spent summers with their parents at resort hotels in the country. More accurately, *Dirty Dancing* is 1963 grafted onto 1987, because the music and the dance styles are from the later era. But female audiences identified with Grey's character,

"Nobody puts Baby in a corner!"

—Johnny (Patrick Swayze) stands by his girl in *Dirty Dancing.*

INDEPENDENT FILM GUIDE

Baby and Johnny
(Jennifer Grey and
Patrick Swayze)
practice a new step
in *Dirty Dancing*.

and empathized with her discovery of the universal truths about that age in that rarefied atmosphere. *Dirty Dancing* isn't a perfect movie, but it's a very pleasant way to spend 97 minutes. Emile Ardolino also directed 1992's *Sister Act*. ♫♫♫

1987 (PG-13) 97m/C Patrick Swayze, Jennifer Grey, Cynthia Rhodes, Jerry Orbach, Jack Weston, Jane Brucker, Kelly Bishop, Lonny Price, Charles "Honi" Coles, Bruce Morrow; **D:** Emile Ardolino; **W:** Eleanor Bergstein; **M:** John Morris. Academy Awards '87: Best Song ("(I've Had) the Time of My Life"); Golden Globe Awards '88: Best Song ("(I've Had) the Time of My Life"); Independent Spirit Awards '88: Best First Feature. **VHS, Beta, LV, Closed Caption, DVD** *LIV, VES*

Dites-Lui Que Je L'Aime

Dites-Lui Que Je L'Aime is a disappointing second film by Claude Miller, who made

such a promising debut with 1976's *The Best Way*. *Dites-Lui...* seems to have been crafted by a self-indulgent film student. Based on a Patricia Highsmith novel, the plot revolves around a completely unsympathetic accountant (listlessly played by Gerard Depardieu), who pursues former girlfriend Dominique Laffin, now a married mother. Meanwhile, gorgeous masochist Miou-Miou pursues Depardieu, and a married drip subsequently pursues Miou-Miou. For 107 minutes, all the characters throw each other around and yell a lot. The best moment occurs when Gerard Depardieu kicks in a television set while Paul Anka is singing, which gives you some idea how droll the rest of this flick is. **AKA:** This Sweet Sickness; Tell Her I Love Her. ♫♫

1977 107m/C *FR* Gerard Depardieu, Miou-Miou, Dominique Laffin, Claude Pieplu, Christian Clavier, Jacques Denis, Josiane Balasko, Veronique Silver,

Jacqueline Jeanne, Michel Such; **D:** Claude Miller; **W:** Claude Miller, Luc Beraud. **VHS** *WAC, FCT*

D.O.A.

Independent producer Harry M. Popkin made several interesting films in the late 1940s and early 1950s, most with an emphasis on location shooting. *D.O.A.* is extremely effective in this respect because when Edmond O'Brien as Frank Bigelow runs through the streets of San Francisco and Los Angeles, the actual neighborhoods give his story a realistic touch that no lighting tricks or rear screen projections could match. Bigelow is a C.P.A. in the small town of Banning. He wants to have fun in San Francisco, alone, without Pamela Britton along as his girlfriend Paula Gibson. Oddly, his first few hours in the city have a comedic feel, which makes his subsequent predicament all the more terrifying. He goes to a jazz bar at Fisherman's Wharf, meets a cute girl named Jeanie (Virginia Lee), takes one small sip of the wrong drink and his fate is sealed, permanently, although he doesn't know it yet. By the time he gets around to seeking medical attention, it's too late—he's already dying of radiation poisoning. The rest of the movie follows Bigelow as he tries to trace who did this to him and why. I don't know of any other film noir where the victim is able to investigate his own murder in advance (except for the remakes of this one), although Ephraim Katz's *Film Encyclopedia* lists a 1931 German movie by Robert Siodmak, *Looking for His Murderer/Der Mann der Seinen Morder Sucht.* (Anyone know if that movie still survives?) The application of radioactive poison as an instrument of death was an example of the postwar paranoia that would reach its zenith in Robert Aldrich's 1955 indie, *Kiss Me Deadly.* Future Oscar winner O'Brien is excellent, and *D.O.A.* is undoubtedly director Rudolph Mate's finest work. This was the debut film for Beverly Garland as Miss Campbell and also for Neville Brand as Chester. Brand had the interesting talent of projecting charisma AND ugliness in the same shot. A great screen villain was born! WARNING: Oscar-winning cameraman Ernest Laszlo (1905-84) did NOT work his fingers to the bone on this film noir to have someone colorize his efforts! Please buy/rent *D.O.A.* in black and white! 🦴🦴🦴

1949 83m/B Edmond O'Brien, Pamela Britton, Luther Adler, Neville Brand, Beverly Garland, Lynne Baggett, William Ching, Henry Hart, Laurette Luez, Virginia Lee, Jess Kirkland, Cay Forrester, Michael Ross; **D:** Rudolph Mate; **W:** Russel Rouse, Clarence Green; **C:** Ernest Laszlo; **M:** Dimitri Tiomkin. **VHS, Beta** *SNC, NOS, VYY*

The Dog Who Loved Trains

This early film by Goran (*Someone Else's America*) Paskalyevic tells the story of Mika, an escaped prisoner (Svetlana Bojakvic), and the two men who "help" her. One is a cowboy stuntman who once doubled for Kirk Douglas (Bata Zivojinovic). The other is a slightly mentally disabled young man (beautifully played by Irfan Mensur) who is searching for his childhood dog. For Mika, there seems to be no escape, only a never-ending series of geographical transitions. The gripping direction throughout retains our interest in Mika's flight. 🦴🦴🦴

1978 ?m/C YU Svetlana Bojakvic, Bata Zivojinovic, Irfan Mensur; **D:** Goran Paskalyevic. *NYR*

Don's Party

All director Bruce Beresford does with David Williamson's stage play *Don's Party* is show that when people drink too much they become obnoxious. They tell each other What They Really Think and flirt with each other's spouses. In the morning, of course, all their sharp insights dissolve into hangovers. Harmless, but silly. Beresford went on to a distinguished career as an international director. Williamson worked again with Beresford and wrote screenplays for Peter Weir and other directors. 🦴🦴

GREGG ARAKI
Underground
Guerrilla Filmmaker

My films are the films I want to make, a reaction to the tripe and the pablum fed by the international media; the things that I want to see, we don't normally see. My personality tends to be on the rebellious side, and the University of Southern California (where I went to film school) is sort of a fascist school. It has very clear-cut, formulaic ideas of what film is and what film should be. My aesthetic and ideas of film evolved from that, by reacting against that. I had a very rough time there. A lot of the faculty didn't like me very much; there were teachers who threatened to flunk me and wanted to kick me out of the school, so in a way it was like a Hollywood testing ground because U.S.C.'s very much like Hollywood. My films and my attitude were not going over very well with the faculty there, and I figured it was pretty much the same in mainstream Hollywood. I've sort of become infamous for saying if someone gave me $100,000, I'd make TEN films instead of making one big film."

Critically acclaimed, award-winning writer/director/producer/cinematographer/editor GREGG ARAKI'S films include *Three Bewildered People in the Night* (budget: $5,000), *The Long Weekend (o' despair), The Living End* (budget: $23,000), *Totally F***d Up, Nowhere,* and *The Doom Generation.* (It has been estimated that with the amount of money that Francis Ford Coppola spent on *The Godfather, Part 3,* Araki could have made 10,000 feature-length films.)

1976 90m/C *AU* Pat Bishop, Graham Kennedy, Candy Raymond, Veronica Lang, John Hargreaves, Ray Barrett, Claire Binney, Graeme Blundell, Jeanie Drynan; **D:** Bruce Beresford; **W:** David Williamson; **C:** Donald McAlpine. Australian Film Institute '77: Best Actress (Bishop). **VHS, Beta** *FCT*

The Doom Generation

"A Heterosexual Movie by Gregg Araki"? How about a re-tread of 1987's *Three Bewildered People in the Night,* also by Araki? Rose McGowan gives a vivid performance as Amy Blue, but the theme here, that figurative and literal lost puppies deserve whatever they get, is illustrated in nauseating detail, rather like a low-budget homage to *Natural Born Killers,* released the previous year. One particularly gory sequence also recalls 1995's *Dead Presidents,* although the brutal imagery made more sense in the context of the Hughes brothers film. How many ways can you show a menage a trois in which the object of the film is to get the guys alone together? Ditch the impediment? (Although in this case you'd be losing the best actor in the film.) Araki's first flick was lionized beyond recognition at 1988's Lesbian and

Gay Film Festival. By the time 1989's fest rolled around, the critics were back to normal with mixed reactions to *The Long Weekend (o' despair)*. *The Living End, Totally F***ed Up, The Doom Generation,* and *Nowhere* followed. Look for *The Love Boat*'s Lauren ("Cruise Director Julie McCoy") Tewes and *The Brady Bunch*'s Christopher ("Peter") Knight as television news anchors. ♪

1995 (R) 84m/C Rose McGowan, James Duval, Johnathon Schaech; *Cameos:* Parker Posey, Lauren Tewes, Christopher Knight, Margaret Cho, Skinny Puppy; *D:* Gregg Araki; *W:* Gregg Araki; *C:* Jim Fealy. Nominations: Independent Spirit Awards '96: Debut Performance (McGowan). **VHS** *THV*

A Dream of Passion

Jules Dassin's contemporary vision of the Medea myth was dissolved by critics, who thought that Melina Mercouri overacted and the update itself was just plain silly. It isn't great, but it isn't the wretched mess they insisted it was upon release. *A Dream of Passion* actually serves up some pretty good acting by Mercouri, Ellen Burstyn, and Andreas Voutsinas (best known for being Christopher Hewett's partner in 1968's *The Producers*). Mercouri plays an actress playing Medea, Burstyn plays a tormented religious fanatic whose real-life actions parallel that of the tragic Medea. They share some nerve-shattering sequences and there are also some mesmerizing moments when Mercouri's character speaks directly to the camera. Eighteen years after taking the world by storm with her Oscar-nominated performance in Dassin's *Never on Sunday, A Dream of Passion* was very nearly the end of the line for Mercouri (1923-94), at least onscreen. By 1978, she was a major player in Greek politics. Burstyn, of course, went on to make many more films as one of America's leading actresses. ♪♪♪

1978 (R) 105m/C *GR SI* Ellen Burstyn, Melina Mercouri, Andreas Voutsinas; *D:* Jules Dassin; *W:* Jules Dassin. **VHS, Beta** *NLC*

Dreamchild

When Gavin Millar's *Dreamchild* was released in 1985, its star Coral Browne (1913-91) seemed a sure bet for an Oscar nomination. The film won favorable attention on the art house circuit for its unusual approach to the true-life story of Alice Hargreaves, who inspired Charles Dodgson to write *Alice in Wonderland*. As written by Dennis Potter, *Dreamchild* is a film of great imagination and style, enhanced by Ian Holm's touching performance as Charles Dodgson and by Coral Browne's commanding presence as 80-year-old Alice. ♪♪♪

1985 (PG) 94m/C *GB* Coral Browne, Ian Holm, Peter Gallagher, Jane Asher, Nicola Cowper, Amelia Shankley, Caris Corfman, Shane Rimmer, James Wilby; *D:* Gavin Millar; *W:* Dennis Potter; *C:* Billy Williams; *M:* Max Harris, Stanley Myers. **VHS, Beta** *MGM*

Drugstore Cowboy

Before there was *Trainspotting* and Ewan McGregor, there was *Drugstore Cowboy* and Matt Dillon. He's excellent here as a junkie trying to escape the drug scene, circa 1971. Delicately lovely teenager Heather Graham (the real-life daughter of an FBI agent, she later starred as Annie Blackburne on *Twin Peaks*) is the sacrificial lamb of the group, and the impetus for Matt's driving ambition to turn his life around. His girlfriend, well played by Kelly Lynch, finds it harder to leave the scene. Max Perlich played a similar role in 1991's *Rush*. William S. Burroughs, then 75, also makes an appearance. This scrupulously detailed study of drugstore thieves and junkies seems to deglamorize their lives without any intrusive commentary, but I've heard more than one former drug abuser say that this movie makes them homesick for the good old days, B.C. (Before Crack!). ♪♪♪♪

1989 (R) 100m/C Matt Dillon, Kelly Lynch, James Remar, James LeGros, Heather Graham, William S. Burroughs, Beah Richards, Grace Zabriskie, Max Perlich; *D:* Gus Van Sant; *W:* Gus Van Sant, Daniel Yost; *M:* Elliot Goldenthal. Independent Spirit Awards '90:

"**People use drugs to relieve the pressures of their everyday life—like having to tie their shoes.**"

—Bob (Matt Dillon) tries to explain his addiction to a wide variety of drugs to a social worker in *Drugstore Cowboy*.

Best Actor (Dillon), Best Cinematography, Best Screenplay, Best Supporting Actor (Perlich); Los Angeles Film Critics Association Awards '89: Best Screenplay; New York Film Critics Awards '89: Best Screenplay; National Society of Film Critics Awards '89: Best Director (Van Sant), Best Film, Best Screenplay. **VHS, Beta, LV** *LIV, FCT*

East and West

East and West is an Austrian re-discovery from the year 1924 starring Molly Picon. Picon, then 26, was something of a Yiddish "It" girl, just as rambunctious as Clara Bow, although far more wholesome, of course. Still, she does eat up a storm on the Day of Atonement and clearly loves to dance with the boys. Unlike the fragile Miss Bow, Molly Picon was built to last; she was still making movies until eight years before her death in 1992 at the age of 94. *East and West* is a fine showcase for Picon's boundless energy and charm. 🦴🦴🦴

1924 85m/B *AU* Molly Picon, Jacob Kalish, Sidney Goldin; **D:** Ivan Abramson, Sidney Goldin. **VHS** *NCJ*

Easy Rider

In his 1995 autobiography *Endless Highway,* David Carradine writes that *Easy Rider* was financed by Peter Fonda's Diner's Club card. Eventually, of course, it was picked up by Columbia, made everyone a fortune and gave Jack Nicholson the first of his many Oscar nominations. The turning point was the Cannes Film Festival, where this $375,000 road movie, partly shot in 16mm., won the First Film prize for director Dennis Hopper. (Although, as Vincent Canby sniffed in opposite full-page ads in the *New York Times,* "there was only one other picture competing in that category." Let HIM try making an indie someday!) Then other honors began flooding in: Hopper received a special award from the National Society of Film Critics, which also named Jack Nicholson best supporting actor. The New York Film Critics Circle gave supporting actor recognition to Nicholson. Columbia poured money into *Easy Rider*'s advertising campaign and the film became a blockbuster, winding up among the studio's top four moneymakers of the decade. But if Columbia executives had monkeyed around with *Easy Rider* from its inception, it would have emerged as a very different film. As a first-time viewer, I found the Oscar-nominated screenplay to be extremely uneven, but every guy I ever saw it with thought it was perfect. The mood of the film is bleak and depressing. (There are few things youthful international audiences appreciate more than a sharply critical view of the Land of Opportunity.) Lost in their drug haze, Wyatt (Fonda) and Billy (Hopper) are a deeply boring team, but most of the guys I knew in 1969 worshipped the both of them. The movie didn't kick into gear for me until Nicholson, as George Hanson, arrives on the scene. He is such a free spirit, far freer than either Wyatt or Billy, and his sheer pleasure at the prospect of a free life is a joy to see. I wouldn't follow Wyatt or Billy anywhere, but George is such a bright, sweet clueless soul that you can't help falling in love with him. You WANT his life to have a happy ending and when he isn't around, the bleakness and depression engulf the screen once more. *Easy Rider* also paints an unbelievably ugly portrait of the South. Even New Orleans, as seen by the perpetually stoned Wyatt and Billy, looks creepy and sinister. Many of the younger audiences in the San Francisco Bay Area thought that *Easy Rider*'s depiction of the South was as accurate as a documentary (it isn't) and were afraid to travel there, just because of this movie (THEIR loss)! The rock soundtrack is a great time capsule of its era. 🎵🎵🎵

1969 (R) 94m/C Peter Fonda, Dennis Hopper, Jack Nicholson, Karen Black, Toni Basil, Robert Walker Jr., Luana Anders, Luke Askew, Toni Basil, Warren Finnerty, Mac Mashorian, Antonio Mendoza, Sabrina Scharf, Phil Spector; **D:** Dennis Hopper; **W:** Terry Southern, Peter Fonda, Dennis Hopper; **C:** Laszlo Kovacs. Cannes Film Festival '69: Best First Feature (Hopper); New York Film Critics Awards '69: Best Supporting Actor (Nicholson); National Society of Film Critics Awards '69: Best Supporting Actor (Nicholson); Nominations: Academy Awards '69: Best Story & Screenplay, Best Supporting Actor (Nicholson); Cannes Film Festival '69: Best Film. **VHS, Beta, LV, 8mm** *COL, CCB*

Eat a Bowl of Tea

After the 1987 bomb *Slamdance,* director Wayne Wang returns to the low-key, personal style of filmmaking which won critical praise for his earlier movies, *Chan Is Missing* and *Dim Sum. Eat a Bowl of Tea* focuses on the family pressures that nearly destroy the marriage of a young Chinese couple, circa 1949. We first thought that the husband was suffering from a problem that was far more easily correctable than impotence, but it's so rare for any film to focus serious attention on the sexual difficulties within marriage, that Wang's sensitive entry deserves high marks for making the effort. *Eat a Bowl of Tea* is beautifully atmospheric, with lush period detail and sympathetic performances by Cora Miao and Russell Wong as the confused partners. 🎵🎵🎵

1989 (PG-13) 102m/C Cora Miao, Russell Wong, Lau Siu Ming, Eric Tsiang Chi Wai, Victor Wong, Jessica Harper, Lee Sau Kee; **D:** Wayne Wang; **W:** Judith Rascoe; **M:** Mark Adler. **VHS, Beta, LV, Closed Caption** *COL*

Eat Drink Man Woman

This mouth-watering film by Ang Lee shows a great chef (Sihung Lung as Chu) at work making superb meals every Sunday for his three daughters (a teacher, an executive, and a clerk at Wendy's). Since he IS their father, he is filled with opinions about

**Old Wen (Jui Wang)
samples one of
Chef Chu's (Sihung
Lung) culinary
creations in *Eat
Drink Man Woman.***

what his grown children (who still live with him) should do with their lives. Lung, Ah-Leh Gua, and Winston Chao also starred in Ang Lee's *The Wedding Banquet* the previous year. An absolutely scrumptious date movie, but eat FIRST! ♫♫♫♫

1994 (R) 123m/C *TW* Sihung Lung, Kuei-Mei Yang, Yu-Wen Wang, Chien-Lien Wu, Sylvia Chang, Winston Chao, Ah-Leh Gua, Lester Chen; **D:** Ang Lee; **W:** Ang Lee, James Schamus, Hui-Ling Wang; **C:** Jong Lin; **M:** Mader. National Board of Review Awards '94: Best Foreign Film; Nominations: Academy Awards '94: Best Foreign Language Film; Golden Globe Awards '95: Best Foreign Film; Independent Spirit Awards '95: Best Actor (Lung), Best Actress (Wu), Best Cinematography, Best Director (Lee), Best Film, Best Screenplay. **VHS, LV** *HMK*

Eat the Rich

Eat the Rich, a British comedy featuring cameo appearances by Paul and Linda McCartney, is about restaurants, blood,

and money. It stars Lanah Pellay, a whining London drag queen whose number one hit, *Pistol in My Pocket,* can be heard on the movie's soundtrack. When Lanah, as Alex the waiter, is fired from a posh eatery, s/he forms a gang and vows revenge. So, yes, you can take that title literally. In addition to the McCartneys, Angie Bowie, Sandie Shaw, Koo Stark, and Miranda Richardson pop up in small parts. Peter Richardson (any relation?) wrote and directed *Eat the Rich,* which we had the bad luck to see before breakfast. *Eat the Rich* is no great shakes, but may attract what is tactfully known as a cult audience. **WOOF!**

1987 (R) 89m/C *GB* Nosher Powell, Lanah Pellay, Fiona Richmond, Ronald Allen, Sandra Dorne, Angie Bowie, Sandie Shaw; **Cameos:** Paul McCartney, Linda McCartney, Bill Wyman, Koo Stark, Miranda Richardson; **D:** Peter Richardson; **W:** Peter Richardson. **VHS, Beta** *COL*

Eating Raoul

I really love Paul and Mary Bland. I don't know that I'd want to live next door to them, but they're so nice and so much in love and so happy, sort of like Gomez and Morticia Addams. Their dream is to open a restaurant, and, as luck would have it, this real creep tries to attack Mary and when Paul kills him by mistake, they realize that the creep has money and it's THEIRS, THEIRS, THEIRS!!! But they can't just leave the creep lying there dead like that, it's unhygenic or something. Paul and Mary figure it out, along with a sure-fire scheme to make even more MONEY! MONEY! MONEY! Is this a great country or what? Paul Bartel and Mary Woronov, who co-directed, have terrific chemistry together, and take a look at that supporting cast! Endless repeat value on this one. (Robert Beltran went on to play First Officer Chakotay on *Star Trek: Voyager*.) ♪♪♪♪

1982 (R) 83m/C Mary Woronov, Paul Bartel, Robert Beltran, Buck Henry, Ed Begley Jr., Edie McClurg, John Paragon, Richard Blackburn, Hamilton Camp, Bill Curtis, Susan Saiger; **D:** Mary Woronov, Paul Bartel; **W:** Paul Bartel, Richard Blackburn. **VHS, Beta** *FOX*

Echoes of Paradise

Philip Noyce's *Echoes of Paradise/Shadows of the Peacock* treats the age-old theme of the married woman with young children who has a fling with a promiscuous young man who is totally wrong for her, who realizes it 90 long minutes later, and who returns to her family with an experience she appears to have placed well behind her. It fails to answer the question of the '80s (and '90s): if yesterday's filmmakers could treat international crises like two World Wars and the Great Depression within months of their respective beginnings, why don't many of today's filmmakers wake up to the fact that the '80s (and the '90s) are the Plague Years? A woman who hops into bed with an obvious gigolo or male prostitute isn't looking

for mere adventure or heightened identity anymore. She's risking a long, painful death for herself and agony for her family who watch her die. If condoms are too threatening to deal with on film, then filmmakers can always set the film in another period when casual sex was less deadly. Even if Noyce HAD done that, though, this movie would still be an uninvolving snoozer, with little but the scenery to recommend it. *AKA:* Shadows of the Peacock. **WOOF!**

1986 (R) 90m/C *AU* Wendy Hughes, John Lone, Rod Mullinar, Peta Toppano, Steve Jacobs, Gillian Jones; **D:** Phillip Noyce. **VHS, Beta, LV** *ACA*

Eddie and the Cruisers

The coming attractions trailer for *Eddie and the Cruisers* was so awful that I almost didn't see it theatrically. Apparently, there were quite a few other people who felt the same way because *Eddie and the Cruisers* didn't attract much attention until it hit the video stores. Then it became so famous that the soundtrack became a hot item, and a 1989 sequel was filmed in Canada with Michael Pare and Matthew Laurance (but none of the other original participants). Anyway, you either like this movie or you don't. Ellen Barkin (as reporter Maggie Foley) doesn't. She is quoted as saying, "(It's) the only movie I've made that really upsets me. I hate it. And now it's out on video, so it never dies. People come up to me and say, 'You were great in (it).' And I say, 'Sorry, that wasn't me.'" She says all those mean things about THIS movie and not one squawk about Mary Lambert's *Siesta*??? Aaargh.... I enjoy *Eddie and the Cruisers*. Barkin IS great in it. Pare was then at a fairly confident point in his career when you could actually see how Eddie Wilson could become the focal point of a cult. Tom Berenger as outsider Frank Ridgeway gives the viewers someone with whom to identify during Eddie and the Cruisers' many in-house fights. And Joe Pantoliano

"Excuse me, the baby panda, is it fried in honey?"

—A customer at Bastard's inquires about the exotic menu in *Eat the Rich*.

MARY WORONOV

on making her first movie
The Chelsea Girls for Andy Warhol

For a first movie, *The Chelsea Girls* was kind of great because you could say whatever you liked. I never got that chance again. You could do whatever you liked. Warhol just sort of pointed the camera and then he ran the film until the film ran out, and that was the end of the movie. The people around it, I mean I thought they were just great. They were, like, very, very dramatic and very high, too. I never got to make movies like that again. That was the problem, I really liked it.

"[Andy Warhol] did not do anything. He was extremely shy. He was so shy he didn't even like to read. He didn't like to answer the phone or do anything like that. When I first knew him he wasn't walking around with a tape recorder, but after a awhile he would just depend on a tape recorder so he wouldn't have to talk to anybody. He would just go, 'Oh, oh, that's nice. Would you speak here?' And you'd talk to this tape recorder instead of him and he liked that. He didn't make anybody do anything. I would say that he was a vacuum. When people came, like for instance, when he did a movie, nobody really did the movie until he got there, so he was definitely a force. But, when he came on the set then everybody would start acting for him and he was just like a negative vacuum. He would suck up the energy, and these people would start trying to get a reaction out of him and it was never there, and they would end up doing whatever they wanted or doing things that they didn't want. But it was mostly because he did not tell them anything. They had to fill it in. You know, like when someone doesn't talk after a while you begin to talk for them and fill in what they're supposed to say and to read meaning into their words. Nobody could sort of understand it, he was just this kind of blankness."

MARY WORONOV can be seen in *Eating Raoul* **(also directed),** *Silent Night, Bloody Night, Cover Girl Models, Death Race 2000, Hollywood Boulevard, Hollywood Man, Jackson County Jail, Sugar Cookies, The Movie House Massacre, Rock 'n' Roll High School, Angel of H.E.A.T., Night of the Comet, The Princess Who Never Laughed, Challenge of a Lifetime, Hellhole, Chopping Mall, Nomads, Terrorvision, Black Widow, Kemek, Let It Ride, Scenes from the Class Struggle in Beverly Hills, Club Fed, Mortuary Academy, Motorama, Rock 'n' Roll High School Forever, Warlock,* **and** *Good Girls Don't Die.* **In 1995, Journey Editions published her book** *Swimming Underground, My Years with the Warhol Factory.*

is especially good as Doc, the group-manager-turned-dee-jay. Another probable factor in the film's popularity is the fact that, a dozen years after Jim Morrison's death, there were many fans who wished he were still around to create music; the script here plays around with that wish fulfillment fantasy quite a bit. You could do a lot worse on a rainy night than to rent this well acted little film from 1983. 🎵🎵 🎵

1983 (PG) 90m/C Tom Berenger, Michael Pare, Ellen Barkin, Joe Pantoliano, Matthew Laurance, Helen Schneider, David Wilson, Michael "Tunes" Antunes, Joe Cates, John Stockwell, Barry Sand, Howard Johnson, Robin Karfo, Rufus Harley, Bruce Brown, Louis D'Esposito, Michael Toland, Bob Garrett, Joanne Collins; **D:** Martin Davidson; **W:** Martin Davidson, Arlene Davidson; **C:** Fred Murphy; **M:** John Cafferty. **VHS, Beta, LV, 8mm, Closed Caption** MVD, NLC

Eddie and the Cruisers 2: Eddie Lives!

Eddie and the Cruisers was far from a masterpiece, but it boasted an intriguing mystery, a satisfying structure, and a fine cast which included Tom Berenger, Ellen Barkin, Joe Pantoliano, and Helen Schneider, none of whom returned for *Eddie Lives!* The ineptly promoted 1983 film also earned the reputation of being better than it was because it attracted a huge audience when it was released on video. Some of the excruciating dialogue wasn't quite so painful on the small screen, and the excellent soundtrack performed by John Cafferty and the Beaver Brown Band sold in the millions. The sequel reveals that Eddie Wilson as portrayed by Michael Pare was to the first film what Tweety Bird was to the Sylvester the Cat cartoons. (Try imagining Tweety without Sylvester and you realize how dependent this non-character is on the much more interesting personality whose life revolves around him.) For those who care, Michael Pare is back as Eddie and a Canadian Geena Davis lookalike named Marina Orsini's got him.

Eddie, also known as Joe West, is just as obnoxious as ever, but he meets an equally obnoxious young rocker who tries to lure him back into show business. Eddie drags his heels at first (they have to pad the running time somehow), but he is soon back to his old self, ordering everyone around just like in the old days. Meanwhile, greedy promoters (is that redundant?) are trying to cash in on Eddie's old records and tapes, encouraging Eddie sightings and lookalike contests. The only mystery in *Eddie Lives!* is whether transferring it to video will shrink its enormous flaws. Jean-Claude Lord's direction varies between mediocre and so-bad-I-can't-believe-I'm-watching-this, the acting is mostly wretched (three of the members of Eddie's new band cannot act at all so they just sit there when they're not playing, how exciting), and the script is strictly from hunger. The better cast members include Bernie Coulson and Anthony Sherwood plus Matthew Laurence from the original cast, who's already talking about *Eddie 3.* Larry King, Bo Diddley, Martha Quinn, and Merrill Shindler play themselves. You could probably pick up the album somewhere for the price of a movie ticket and spare yourself 106 minutes of squirming through the resuscitation of a jerk who still looks 29 long after he took that dive off the pier in 1964. **WOOF!**

1989 (PG-13) 106m/C CA Michael Pare, Marina Orsini, Matthew Laurance, Bernie Coulson, Anthony Sherwood; **Cameos:** Larry King, Bo Diddley, Martha Quinn, Merrill Shindler; **D:** Jean-Claude Lord; **W:** Charles Zev Cohen; **M:** Leon Aronson. **VHS, Beta, LV** CCB, IME

8½

Federico Fellini's *8 1/2* was one of the loveliest films of 1963 and it's every bit as exquisite today. The dream cast is headlined by Marcello Mastroianni, Claudia Cardinale, Anouk Aimee, and Barbara Steele. All this plus Nino Rota's haunting score and the brilliant cinematography of Gianni Di Venanzo combined to make *8 1/2* one of the most widely admired and

117

relentlessly imitated movies of its era. Many tried, but none quite captured the overwhelming sense of love and longing the great Fellini gave to this unsparingly honest examination of a successful director on the verge of a nervous breakdown. Cast Notes: Madeleine LeBeau played Yvonne in *Casablanca* twenty years earlier; Mark Herron was Judy Garland's fourth husband from 1965 to 1967. **AKA:** Otto E Mezzo; Federico Fellini's 8 1/2. 🦴🦴🦴🦴

1963 135m/B *IT* Marcello Mastroianni, Claudia Cardinale, Anouk Aimee, Sandra Milo, Barbara Steele, Rossella Falk, Eddra Gale, Mark Herron, Madeleine LeBeau, Caterina Boratto; **D:** Federico Fellini; **W:** Tullio Pinelli, Ennio Flaiano, Brunello Rondi, Federico Fellini; **C:** Gianni Di Venanzo; **M:** Nino Rota. Academy Awards '63: Best Costume Design (B & W), Best Foreign Language Film; National Board of Review Awards '63: 5 Best Foreign Films of the Year; New York Film Critics Awards '63: Best Foreign Film; Nominations: Academy Awards '63: Best Art Direction/Set Decoration (B & W), Best Director (Fellini), Best Story & Screenplay. **VHS, Beta, LV** *VES, MRV, MPI*

Eight Men Out

If there is any financial protection at all for ballplayers today, it is probably because, over 75 years later, we are still haunted by the 1919 World Series scandal which inspired John Sayles to write and direct *Eight Men Out*. The film reveals how vulnerable the underpaid Chicago White Sox were to self-serving operators like Arnold Rothstein, Bill Burns, and Abe Attell. The team's grievances against club owner Charles Comiskey were real, but their decision to profit by throwing the series was a sickening one. The games in which the players listlessly go through the motions are as painful to watch as they must have been for the original players to experience. Sayles also shows, on at least one occasion, the threat of physical violence, when a thug threatens to kill a team player's wife if he doesn't comply with the fix. *Eight Men Out* succeeds in making its point that good people can and do go wrong under certain circumstances and it also fills

today's audiences with sadness that eight gifted players lost their careers and their reputations when they allowed themselves to be manipulated by opportunistic gamblers. For a movie with so many stellar names in the cast, there is a real ensemble feel to the production which greatly enhances its message. John Cusack, Charlie Sheen, and D.B. Sweeney deliver three of the eight extremely effective performances by the team, and John Mahoney does another solid character turn as their coach. Michael Lerner and Christopher Lloyd are appropriately slimy as Rothstein and Burns, and the late John Anderson (1922-92) steals a magnificent scene as the new baseball commissioner. Robert Richardson's cinematography helps to capture the atmosphere of the era, particularly in the film's striking conclusion. With Sayles at the helm (and in a cameo as Ring Lardner), *Eight Men Out* is highly recommended even if you don't particularly care for baseball. 🦴🦴🦴

1988 (PG) 121m/C John Cusack, D.B. Sweeney, Perry Lang, Jace Alexander, Bill Irwin, Clifton James, Michael Rooker, Michael Lerner, Christopher Lloyd, Studs Terkel, David Strathairn, Charlie Sheen, Kevin Tighe, John Mahoney, John Sayles, Gordon Clapp, Richard Edson, James Reed, Don Harvey, John Anderson, Maggie Renzi; **Cameo:** John Sayles; **D:** John Sayles; **W:** John Sayles; **C:** Robert Richardson; **M:** Mason Daring. **VHS, Beta, LV, Closed Caption** *ORI, FCT*

El Mariachi

Robert Rodriguez kept it simple for his first film and, as a result, plunged head first into the movie business with a splash at age 24. All El Mariachi (Carlos Gallardo) wants is a chance to sing. All drug dealer Azul (Reinol Martinez) wants is a chance to avenge himself on Moco (Peter Marquardt), his former partner. Unhappily, El Mariachi and Azul are identically dressed in black and each carry a guitar case, but Azul's case...does NOT carry a guitar! Consuelo Gomez is sexy Domino, who thinks El Mariachi is cute, but the bloodthirsty Moco thinks Domino is cute, so that's a problem. In 1995, Rodriguez directed *Des-*

Opposite page: **Carlos Gallardo, Mariachi, in** *El Mariachi.*

perado, his own expensive 106-minute remake of this violent, funny little film, but it's the $7,000 81-minute original version that everyone will remember. Filmed in Acuna, Mexico. ♫♫♫

1993 (R) 81m/C MX Carlos Gallardo, Consuelo Gomez, Peter Marquardt, Jaime de Hoyos, Reinol Martinez, Ramiro Gomez; **D:** Robert Rodriguez; **W:** Robert Rodriguez, Carlos Gallardo; **C:** Robert Rodriguez. Independent Spirit Awards '94: Best First Feature; Sundance Film Festival '93: Audience Award; Nominations: Independent Spirit Awards '94: Best Director (Rodriguez). **VHS, Beta, LV, 8mm** COL, FCT, BTV

Emmanuelle

In 1975, *Emmanuelle* was the most popular movie in France. It was called "a sexual Vogue" by someone or other and also an "'X' you can take your wife to." If adult audiences required THAT much assurance, they needed more help than mere publicity hacks could provide! The ultimate comment on the film? *Emmanuelle* stinks, then and now. It is the story of an innocent young girl (Sylvia Kristel) who joins her husband (Daniel Sarky) in Bangkok. Just how innocent any girl can be who seduces two men on the flight to Bangkok is left to our imaginations. But no matter. All the wives in Bangkok are bored; there is nothing for them to do. This is the stuff that old X-rated films are made of. Emmanuelle befriends a young archeologist (Marika Greene, who'd once worked with Bresson). The tension mounts; maybe Emmanuelle will get a job, too? Maybe then she won't be so bored! But no. She has a disillusioning fling with the archeologist, and then searches for "fulfillment" with a 67-year-old "expert" named Mario (played by Alain Cuny, a Shakespearean actor who'd worked with Carne, Malle, Fellini, Bunuel, and Rosi and now with JUST JAECKIN on THIS?!). The film gets very cerebral after that. "What's eroticism to you?" Mario asks Emmanuelle. Well, Emmanuelle is not sure. She thinks maybe it's the "cult of sensual joy," or something like that. Wrong, says Mario. It's really the "rejection of the subterfuge to lucidity." Well, I'm certainly glad Mario cleared THAT up, or I'd never have known. Mario also tells her that "to arrive at the unknown, you must leave reason behind." (Translate that: rape can set you free.) Then, director Jaeckin decides that what his X-rated French masterpiece really needs is symbolism. See, there's this chicken at the beginning of the film that gets his head cut off. Are you following? Later on, Emmanuelle smears on enough mascara to initiate a world-wide Maybelline shortage, and—SURPRISE!—dons feathers. She hates uptight people now. She's ready to compete with Ziggy Stardust anytime. The film is only 92 minutes long, but you could have fooled me. If it weren't for Richard Suzuki's impressive cinematography, I wouldn't have one good thing to say about this movie. If you're looking for a film that puts women in their place and that gives new meaning to words like dull and annoying, by all means, indulge in *Emmanuelle*'s endless psychological inanities. **WOOF!**

1974 92m/C FR Sylvia Kristel, Alain Cuny, Marika Green, Daniel Sarky; **D:** Just Jaeckin; **C:** Richard Suzuki; **M:** Pierre Bachelet. **VHS, Beta** COL

Emma's Shadow

"The Poor Little Rich Girl" is among the most familiar images on the silver screen. Mary Pickford first played her in a strange little film from 1917. Her only escape from her emotionally deprived life is through an accidental drug overdose! In 1936, Shirley Temple preferred the company of radio troupers Alice Faye and Jack Haley to benign neglect from Michael Whalen, her tycoon father. (The Depression twist in this one was the threatening presence of a sex maniac down the hall.) In 1982, Bridgette Anderson orchestrated her own kidnapping in *Savannah Smiles*. The 1988 Danish film *Emma's Shadow* explores many of these tried and true situations, but with a fresh, strong approach that helped it to become a prize winner at the Cannes Film Festival. Emma, beautifully played by Line Kruse, is the 11-year-old child of a wealthy couple who barely notice she's alive. She runs away and literally bumps into a sewer worker whom she adopts as her best friend on sight. Although he is an ex-convict and far from the brightest man in the world, Emma nonetheless adores him and starts cooking up a successful scheme to wring money out of her folks. She spends the money on an elaborate meal at a deluxe hotel, to be shared by her new friend and two little boys in the neighborhood. The boys pile into a bubble bath and Emma gazes worshipfully at her friend as he drinks himself silly. The in-joke here is that Emma's friend is played by Borje Ahlstedt, so good in *Fanny and Alexander,* who launched his career 25 years ago in the *I Am Curious, Yellow and Blue* films. Writer/director Soeren Kragh-Jacobsen treads a very fine line here, so that you're always aware of the underlying sensuality, but are relieved that it STAYS underlying. As in most films of this type, the child is the focal point throughout and Line Kruse delivers a wonderfully shaded performance as Emma. She is fiercely protective of Ahlstedt's character, seeing through his rough, bumbling exterior into the kind, decent, and considerate soul who is able to give her far more than her high-rolling but uncomprehending parents. Despite its award-winning status and excellent reviews, *Emma's Shadow* has yet to acquire the reputation it deserves in this country, but it's been given a new life on video. See it before a Hollywood studio turns it into a yucky American transplant. ***AKA:*** Skyggen Af Emma. 🦴🦴🦴🦴

1988 93m/C *DK* Bjorje Ahistedt, Line Kruse; *D:* Soeren Kragh-Jacobsen; *W:* Soeren Kragh-Jacobsen. **VHS** *ORI, FCT, FXL*

Enchanted April

In the 1980s, Mike Newell was best known for his work on tough, gritty projects like *Blood Feud, Dance with a Stranger,* and *The Good Father. Enchanted April,* a delicate comedy of manners and wishful thinking at best, seemed an odd choice for this hard-hitting director. Based on a novel by Elizabeth von Arnim (who was the Countess Russell in real life), *Enchanted April* was a resounding flop when Harry Beaumont first filmed it for RKO studios in 1935. Ann Harding portrayed a middle-aged Shirley Temple who brought joy into every life she touched, with the notable exception of the audience. In 66 interminable minutes, Harding was able to lure back her straying husband, Frank Morgan, bring two young lovers together, patch up the marriage of Kay Alexander and Reginald Owen, AND warm the heart of a gruff old lady played by Jessie Ralph. Unsurprisingly, Ralph and Owen stole every sequence they were in, and, equally unsurprisingly, *Enchanted April* brought Ann Harding's reign as grande dame of the RKO lot to a grinding halt. The new version of *Enchanted April* is a VAST improvement over the original, which is not to say that it will succeed in bringing joy into every life it touches. The Ann Harding role this time around is played by comedienne Josie Lawrence, who at least is able to bring a down-to-earth foundation to the endless whimsicality of her character. Miranda Richardson seems more uncomfortable in a repressed role, although she does her best with it. In the role of the aristocratic beauty who was originally played by the serenely lovely Jane Baxter, Polly Walker tries hard as Lady Caroline Dester, but she looks and sounds like a contemporary punk, nothing at all like a 1922 deb chafing at the bit. The male parts are much less crucial, but Michael Kitchen comes off best as Mr. Briggs, a shell-shocked vet turned landlord, who can barely distinguish between one discontented tenant and another. Briggs is interesting as a representative of the dwindling romantic choices open to British women of the early 1920s. Many of their generation's most dazzling charmers had been blown to bits in World

KRISTIN SCOTT THOMAS AND ANTHONY MINGHELLA

The English Patient

Kristin Scott Thomas: "The role I played in *The Pompatus of Love* just intrigued and enchanted me. It was a sweet little script [by actor Jon Cryer]. It's a question of when you discover something like that, up until now, anyway, had I wanted to take part in this little adventure that they're going on, whether it's a great big adventure like Brian DePalma's *Mission Impossible* or *The Pompatus of Love* or *The Confessional,* which is a Canadian film that I made with Robert Lepage, which was an extraordinary experience. I'd heard all about Robert Lepage, he's very famous in London for his *Needles and Opium* and for his production of *A Midsummer Night's Dream.* I'd heard all about him, I'd read these incredible reviews about him and then suddenly he's in Paris and he wants to meet ME, which is great! So I meet this man, he's a complete genius and he says, 'Will you be in my film? This is the story.' So I say, 'Yes!' Eventually, he gave me the script: I couldn't make head nor tail of the script. I didn't know what it was! It was a tiny little part, but I really wanted to work with Lepage, I loved the idea of going off and doing this mysterious thing. I really didn't know what I was doing, but I would do it anyway. And it's things like that that are why I do the diverse things that I do. It's a question of wanting to dive in and join in. It's like party time....

"I made a conscious decision not to manipulate the audience's emotions in *The English Patient.* The first time I saw the film, I thought, 'Maybe I should have tried to get more sympathy for the character. Maybe I should have tried to milk it a bit.' But now I see the film and I'm thinking, 'No, because then I would have fallen into that trap of crocodile tears: Oh-she's-going-to-cry-she's-going-to-cry-she's-going-to-cry!' And then the audience cries. I hate going to a film, because I'm a great crier when I go to films: I'm very easily triggered. There are certain buttons you just push and I think it's the same. You can go to a weepie and you just know everyone's sitting there snuffling. No one's really quite sure why they're doing it and you feel cheated at the end: 'Damn! I was MADE to cry. I did NOT want to cry.' You feel tricked and I hate that, and I prefer the emotion that you get from a punch in the belly.... When I first slap Ralph Fiennes as The Count, the slap is a sort of 'Pull yourself together! Wake up! Realize what's happening! And how DARE you string me along and dump me? And how DARE you put me in the situation that I'm in now?' It's a multi-featured slap. In the book, certainly, they have a very, very physically vigorous relationship, full of thumping and scratching and biting and there's one moment that I love that I wish we could have had in the film: There's a fork that goes into his back. What were they doing? And he has to pass it off as a bite from a fox or a scorpion."

Oscar nominee KRISTIN SCOTT THOMAS' films include *Under the Cherry Moon, A Handful of Dust, The Tenth Man, The Endless Game, Framed, Spymaker, Bitter Moon, The Bachelor, Weep No More My Lady, Four Weddings and a Funeral, An Unforgettable Summer, Angels and Insects, Gulliver's Travels,* **and** *Richard III.*

Anthony Minghella: "A screenplay is like an architectural document to me and that's how I tried to view it. It's not a beautiful object in the way that a book is beautiful. The prose in a book has to be its own evocation of ideas and people and places. A screenplay's much more like the drains are going to go here, this is where the electricity is, the windows have to be this big and they have to be reinforced. It's much more of a campaign plan, and its structural organization was what most intrigued me, because I also had the blessing of knowing that all I needed to do was to do that and then I could realize it myself later. I tried to find a way of giving myself the structural support in order to find a new sort of lyricism, which was some correlative of the lyricism of the book. It's a film about maps. This was my map. Did I find that simple? The answer is resoundingly no. Not only that, but people thought I was pretty stupid to attempt it because it's a book which is so complicated, so fragmented, and so resistant to narrative and so beautiful. Stupid or otherwise, I had such a dream of what the film could be like. Also, I kept telling myself, 'Look, forget about the difficulties! Think what you could end up with! You could end up with a film which has love, war, sex, damage, death, intrigue, mystery, puzzles, arguments.' It's such a big package that I tried to keep that in my sight so I could get there and make an event which was as rewarding as films which have pleased me as an audience member. I wanted to make a film that would delight me."

Oscar winner ANTHONY MINGHELLA wrote and directed 1991's *Truly, Madly, Deeply,* **and he also directed 1993's** *Mr. Wonderful.*

War I and the men who were left, like Briggs, were irreversibly changed. *Enchanted April* may mean less to California audiences than to British viewers, used to the cold rain and a relentless parade of twits. For four women (including the scene-stealing Joan Plowright) to flower in the very villa where von Arnim wrote her novel clearly might have meant something to 1922 readers, but it meant nothing at all to 1935 moviegoers and will probably be regarded as a mere historical curiosity today. One can only hope that the works of von Arnim will not be run into the ground by filmmakers like every syllable of E. M. Forster has been over the last decade. P.S. If you're truly enthralled by von Arnim, 1944's *Mr. Skeffington* with Bette Davis and Claude Rains (all 146 minutes of it!) is also available on video. 🦴🦴🦴

1992 (PG) 93m/C *GB* Miranda Richardson, Joan Plowright, Josie Lawrence, Polly Walker, Alfred Molina, Jim Broadbent, Michael Kitchen, Adriana Fachetti; **D:** Mike Newell; **W:** Peter Barnes; **M:** Richard Rodney Bennett. Golden Globe Awards '93: Best Actress—Musical/Comedy (Richardson), Best Supporting Actress (Plowright); Nominations: Academy Awards '92: Best Adapted Screenplay, Best Costume Design, Best Supporting Actress (Plowright). **VHS, Beta, LV, Closed Caption** *PAR, MOV, WAR*

The English Patient

Once, a long time ago, I was a member of the National Academy of Television Arts and Sciences. After a few bewildering industry functions, I let my membership lapse. So I'm not even marginally qualified to vote with the members of the Academy for Best Picture of the Year. But if I COULD have voted in 1996, I would have, for *Fargo*! More than enough people are worshipping *The English Patient* that I don't need to join them. It's the sort of big, circuitous movie that always wins Best Picture. Okay, so it's an indie, but it's an indie that looks, sounds, and feels like *Gandhi*, except for Juliette Binoche and Naveen Andrews as Hana and Kip. This is not to knock Ralph Fiennes and Kristin

Scott Thomas, who are very good, just the picture's naggingly pompous undertones AND overtones. Fiennes' character (Hungary's own Count Almasy) falls hard for Katherine, AKA Mrs. Geoffrey Clifton (Scott Thomas). Since boring old Geoffrey is played by Colin Firth, he's practically asking for his wife to be whisked away by a handsome count. The climax of this film may be terribly romantic in a gloppy sort of way, but it's all so avoidable that you can't blame destiny for this one. Oh well, people in love WILL do anything, won't they? Like lose their minds. And their wits. And their humility. And their sense of logic...and proportion. There was this skirmish going on at the time, World War II, I believe it was called? Am I supposed to quiver with anticipation every time Katherine and the Count exchange a guilty glance? Because I don't. Best Pictures of the Year don't really do it for me, anyway (I've concurred with precisely five choices in the entire history of the Academy). I can (almost) stand the very best ones every ten or twenty years. As for the rest, once is enough, thanks. In order for a movie to be acceptable to the Academy membership, it can't be quirky or cutting edge, it has to say something positive about the human spirit, which must be Binoche's and Andrews' function here. To be honest, Hana and Kip are worth a heckuva lot more attention than the central characters, mainly because they ARE played by Binoche and Andrews. Oh, and the costumes here are nearly as ghastly as the ones in *Secrets and Lies*. 🦴🦴🦴

1996 (R) 162m/C Ralph Fiennes, Kristin Scott Thomas, Juliette Binoche, Willem Dafoe, Naveen Andrews, Colin Firth, Julian Wadham, Juergen Prochnow, Kevin Whately, Clive Merrison, Nino Castelnuovo; **D:** Anthony Minghella; **W:** Anthony Minghella; **C:** John Seale; **M:** Gabriel Yared. Academy Awards '96: Best Art Direction/Set Decoration, Best Cinematography, Best Costume Design, Best Director (Minghella), Best Film Editing, Best Picture, Best Sound, Best Supporting Actress (Binoche), Original Dramatic/Comedy Score; Directors Guild of America Awards '96: Best Director (Minghella); Golden Globe Awards '97: Best Film—Drama, Best Original Score; Los Angeles Film Critics Association Awards '96: Best Cinematography; National Board of Review Awards '96: Best Supporting Actress

(Binoche), Best Supporting Actress (Scott Thomas); Broadcast Film Critics Association Awards '96: Best Director (Minghella), Best Screenplay; Nominations: Academy Awards '96: Best Actor (Fiennes), Best Actress (Scott Thomas), Best Adapted Screenplay, Best Sound Effects Editing; British Academy Awards '96: Best Actor (Fiennes), Best Actress (Scott Thomas), Best Adapted Screenplay, Best Director (Minghella), Best Film, Best Supporting Actress (Binoche); Golden Globe Awards '97: Best Actor—Drama (Fiennes), Best Actress—Drama (Scott Thomas), Best Director (Minghella), Best Screenplay, Best Supporting Actress (Binoche); Screen Actors Guild Award '96: Best Actor (Fiennes), Best Actress (Scott Thomas), Best Supporting Actress (Binoche), Cast; Writers Guild of America '96: Best Adapted Screenplay. **VHS** *MAX*

The Englishman Who Went Up a Hill But Came Down a Mountain

The Englishman Who Went Up a Hill But Came Down a Mountain is a direct descendant of the classic Ealing comedies circa 1949. A quaint, decidedly regional British situation is gently but persistently satirized for the entire film. In this case, we are looking at a small village in Wales, where a visual quote about the chief recreational activity (i.e. making babies) is affectionately reminiscent of the opening shot of *Whisky Galore*. The point of the story—that World War I has so devastated the young male population of Ffynnon Garw that the village needs a symbol like the first mountain in Wales to bolster its identity—is lighter than air. (For that matter, so was the premise of *Whisky Galore*.) Writer/ director Christopher Monger embroiders this delicate tale, derived from his grandfather's bedtime stories, with loving detail. Hugh Grant is Reginald, the English twit who comes to survey Ffynnon Garw's so-called mountain and winds up falling in love with the place. As usual, the devilishly attractive Grant stutters and mumbles his way

through the plot as if he'd never been out on a date. But this time at least, there's a plausible reason for his social jitters. Tara Fitzgerald, Grant's restless bride in *Sirens,* is bewitching here as Betty of Cardiff, who persuades Reginald and his drunk surveying partner George Garrad (ever so drily played by Ian McNeice) to stick around the village a bit longer. The lynchpin of the community is Colm Meaney as bartender Morgan the Goat, who's responsible for so many ginger-haired babies born during the war years. And then there is Ian Hart as a shell-shocked war veteran named Johnny (not Lennon for a change), and Kenneth Griffith, then 74, who began his career playing small roles in Will Hay comedies at Ealing while barely out of his teens. In recent years, he's often cast as venerable clerics (he had previously worked with Grant in *Four Weddings and a Funeral*) and he makes a nice foil here as Morgan's fire and brimstone nemesis. *The Englishman Who Went Up a Hill But Came Down a Mountain* hasn't a smidgin of breathtaking suspense, but it's lovely to look at and its gentle humor wins this delightful entry the status of one of 1995's most charming sleepers. 🦴🦴🦴

1995 (PG) 96m/C *GB* Hugh Grant, Tara Fitzgerald, Colm Meaney, Ian McNeice, Ian Hart, Kenneth Griffith; *D:* Christopher Monger; *W:* Christopher Monger; *C:* Vernon Layton; *M:* Stephen Endelman. **VHS, LV, Closed Caption** *TOU*

Enid Is Sleeping

When we first saw *About Last Night* in 1986, we were enormously impressed by the quirky talent of a young actress named Elizabeth Perkins. In 1988, she made *Big* and *Sweet Hearts Dance,* both so saturated by cutesy concepts that she tended to get lost in the proceedings. Then there was 1986's *From the Hip,* 1993's *Indian Summer,* and 1995's *Moonlight and Valentino* in which she was even MORE lost, PLUS 1991's *He Said, She Said,* more cutesy conceptual crap. Just when it seemed like

Perkins was stuck in a conventional leading lady rut, she made a little-heralded black comedy with Judge Reinhold, 1990's *Enid Is Sleeping.* Since it came along not long after 1989's *Weekend at Bernie's* and may have seemed to share the same concept, *Enid* might easily have died an unfair death, except for one thing. Perkins and director Maurice Phillips rescued the badly edited film from the ailing studio that ordered the cuts and assembled the film as THEY wanted it to be shown. The delightful results have been retitled *Over Her Dead Body.* Maureen Mueller IS Enid, the sister from Hell. June (Perkins) is her little sister who has been having an affair with Enid's husband (Reinhold), a cop in a sleepy Southwestern town. Enid surprises them in bed, one thing leads to another, and the rest of the movie shows how June tries to get rid of Enid. The hilarious script gets astonishing mileage out of the dumbest cast of characters you can possibly imagine. Reinhold's character continues his daily routine with his partner Jeffrey Jones, who watches too many movies along the lines of *Beverly Hills Cop.* When he's actually confronted with violence, he's filled with panic and nausea. Rhea Perlman is their ditzy dispatcher. Meanwhile, Perkins brilliantly runs the full gamut of emotional distress as she tries to deal with Enid and every lowlife in the Southwest, including Michael J. Pollard. We've seldom laughed at a video as much as we did with *Over Her Dead Body,* and although most outlets won't have 128 copies of this sleeper, it's well worth searching for, anyway. Perkins went on to break hearts in 1991's *The Doctor* and to pick up (hopefully) fat paychecks for *The Flintstones* and *Miracle on 34th Street* in 1994. What, and give up show business? Make your own movie, Elizabeth! If you can work wonders rescuing *Enid,* you can work miracles with an indie that's yours from opening to closing credits! **AKA:** Over Her Dead Body. 🦴🦴🦴🦴

1990 (R) 105m/C Elizabeth Perkins, Judge Reinhold, Rhea Perlman, Maureen Mueller, Jeffrey Jones, Michael J. Pollard; **D:** Maurice Phillips; **W:** Maurice Phillips; **C:** Alfonso Beato. **VHS** *VES, LIV*

The Entertainer

The Entertainer is the 1960 film in which Laurence Olivier, then 53, bid farewell to the romantic roles of his youth. Olivier surrounded himself with the angry young men of that era: director Tony Richardson, writer John Osborne, and unknown actors Albert Finney and Alan Bates. The bitter film represents a complete departure from his previous work. It also ended his twenty-year marriage to actress Vivien Leigh: Joan Plowright, the young actress who played his daughter, would become Lady Olivier within the year. *The Entertainer* is saturated with yearnings for a life which only seems desirable to outsiders. Olivier plays a seedy music hall artiste who lusts after beauty contest winner Shirley Anne Field. Meanwhile, he pretends not to know his own family, refusing to face his reflection in their eyes. It is a harsh portrait, unclouded by the sentiment which flaws his work in the 1952 film *Carrie.* Olivier won an Oscar nomination for *The Entertainer,* revitalizing his career as a strong character actor. 🦴🦴🦴🦴

1960 97m/B *GB* Laurence Olivier, Brenda de Banzie, Roger Livesey, Joan Plowright, Daniel Massey, Alan Bates, Shirley Anne Field, Albert Finney, Thora Hird; **D:** Tony Richardson; **W:** Nigel Kneale, John Osborne; **C:** Oswald Morris; **M:** John Addison. Nominations: Academy Awards '60: Best Actor (Olivier). **VHS** *FCT, TPV*

Equinox

Someday, some Alan Rudolph devotee will come up with a book about why he or she IS one, and I have a hunch I will be no more enlightened than I am now. *Equinox* is well acted but sluggish hooey about twins Henry and Freddie (Matthew Modine in a dual role) who both inherit a fortune. An even more frustrating movie to watch than *Trouble in Mind,* if that's possible. 🦴🦴

1993 (R) 110m/C Matthew Modine, Lara Flynn Boyle, Lori Singer, Marisa Tomei, Fred Ward, M. Emmet Walsh, Tyra Ferrell, Tate Donovan, Kevin J. O'Connor, Gailard Sartain; **D:** Alan Rudolph; **W:** Alan

Rudolph; **C:** Elliot Davis. Nominations: Independent Spirit Awards '94: Best Actor (Modine), Best Cinematography, Best Film, Best Supporting Actress (Boyle). **VHS, LV, Closed Caption** COL, FCT

Evergreen

Once upon a time, going to talking pictures in America meant that we only saw American movies. 1933's *The Private Life of Henry VIII* changed all that. Not only did this very British film win its star, Charles Laughton, the Academy Award for best actor, but it also proved that audiences were receptive to pictures made outside of Hollywood. Unfortunately, musical comedies don't always travel well across the Atlantic, so, with one exception, British musicals didn't make a real splash in America until the Beatles made *A Hard Day's Night* in 1964. The one exception was the work of Jessie Matthews, and her greatest triumph was 1934's *Evergreen*. *Evergreen* co-stars Jessie Matthews' husband at the time, Sonnie Hale (1902-59) in a comic role, and they made several films together as a team throughout the decade. Barry MacKay, best remembered as Scrooge's nephew in MGM's *A Christmas Carol*, also plays opposite Matthews. Betty Balfour (1903-79), a big star in British silent comedies, plays the second lead, and the caddish blackmailer is played by an American-born character actor named Hartley Power (1894-1966). Everyone in the production is young, between 27 and 40, and they all breathe life into what is basically a pretty implausible tale. That may be why *Evergreen*, along with its many English cultural references, never made it to Broadway. Jessie Matthews always looks so cheerful onscreen it's hard to believe that she was a woman on the verge of a nervous breakdown all through *Evergreen*. Only the careful handling of director Victor Saville (1897-1979) kept the production rolling along at a rapid clip. (Saville had a long career in both countries, eventually producing 1955's *Kiss Me Deadly*.) Matthews' personal problems and wrenching memories about the making of *Evergreen* did lead to a breakdown when it was shown at a retrospective in her honor many years later. None of her private unhappiness shows up on film, however. Matthews' graceful dancing and bright personality plus a lovely Rodgers and Hart score made *Evergreen* a smash hit. In her later years, Jessie Matthews wrote her autobiography, *Over My Shoulder*, and played a supporting role in *Edward and Mrs. Simpson* as Wallis' aunt. She was still working the year of her death at age 74 in 1981. ♫♫♫

1934 91m/B *GB* Jessie Matthews, Sonnie Hale, Betty Balfour, Barry Mackay, Ivor McLaren, Hartley Power, Patrick Ludlow, Marjorie Gaffney; **D:** Victor Saville; **W:** Emlyn Williams; **M:** Richard Rodgers, Harry Woods, Lorenz Hart, Harry Woods. **VHS, Beta, LV** *VYY, HMV, THV*

Every Man for Himself & God Against All

In 1828, a most unusual young man turned up in Nuremberg. For the next five years, he was a source of wonder and, perhaps, fear to the intelligentsia. Who was he? Where had he come from? Why had he been deprived of a normal existence his entire life? Was he descended from royalty? His murder in 1833 only intensified the riddle. Artists and scholars continue to study Kaspar Hauser to the present day. Possibly the most heartfelt view of the subject was provided by Werner Herzog's 1975 masterpiece, *Every Man for Himself & God Against All/The Mystery of Kaspar Hauser*. Under Herzog's brilliant direction, Bruno S attempts and succeeds at the impossible: stripping his entire personality of each and every trace of socialization. His Kaspar is like a baby who grows from infancy to adulthood without learning a thing. His social vulnerability is the quality that attracts small children who laboriously teach him how to speak, one word at a time; nursery rhymes, as one boy explains patiently to a little girl, are too difficult for him to learn. Kaspar is later exploited as a freak attraction, but he escapes and goes on to lead a life of what appears to be non-stop education in sheltered circumstances. His questions are strong, clear, and child-like, but because he is a man, they are interpreted as a threat. Or so Herzog suggests. The tenderness and compassion with which Kaspar is initially received evolves into suspicion and violence. Just when the whole world appears to be opening up for Kaspar, he is the object of two murderous attacks, the second eventually proving fatal. His efforts at socialization end and he reverts to the infant's heartrending gestures for someone, anyone, to stop the pain. When Bruno S is onscreen, it's impossible to tear your eyes away from his one-of-a-kind performance, but Herzog wisely gives a spare but eloquent context for *Every Man for Himself & God Against All/The Mystery of Kaspar Hauser.* An anatomical dissection of Kaspar Hauser is quickly carried out, revealing nothing but our eagerness to search for answers, even when they're wrong. In contrast, Herzog shows us the landscapes that surround his story, recreating the lush color experiments of photographers of the mid-19th century. Herzog's anachronistic images and Bruno S' newly reborn eyes make more sense of the mystery than all the state-of-the-art scientific bumbling of 1833 or 1998. **AKA:** The Mystery of Kaspar Hauser; Jeder Fur Sich Und Gott Gegen Alle; The Enigma of Kaspar Hauser. ♫♫♫♫

1975 110m/C *GE* Bruno S, Brigitte Mira, Walter Laderigast, Hans Musaus, Willy Semmelrogge, Michael Kroecher, Henry van Lyck; **D:** Werner Herzog; **W:** Werner Herzog; **M:** Albinoni Pachelbel, Orlando Di Lasso. Nominations: Cannes Film Festival '75: Best Film. **VHS, Beta** *NYF, APD, GLV*

Everything Ready, Nothing Works

This early Lina Wertmuller film is a fast, occasionally funny yarn about how some young Sicilian men and women make a start in Northern Italy (Milan, to be specific), even though they have no money and are constantly being victimized. There is one semi-rape sequence. The victim loves it. Wertmuller shows the moment, then lets it go without comment. She would explore sexual politics in much greater depth in 1975's *Swept Away....* ♫ ♫

1974 107m/C *IT* Luigi Diberti, Lina Polito, Nine Bignamini, Sara Rapisarda, Guiliana Calandra, Isa Danieli; **D:** Lina Wertmuller; **W:** Lina Wertmuller; **C:** Giuseppe Rotunno; **M:** Piero Piccioni. *NYR*

Exotica

Before he was *Nowhere Man,* Bruce Greenwood was Francis the tax inspector in Atom Egoyan's *Exotica.* Francis is a nightly customer at the Exotica strip club, mainly because Christina (Mia Kirschner) works there. Francis' interest in Christina disturbs Eric (Elias Koteas), the club deejay who used to go with her. But obsession always finds a way to feed itself. There are many subterranean currents in *Exotica* and Egoyan gives us tantalizing glimpses of all of them. The club, a world in itself, taps into the fantasies of all who drift into it, yet there's a ubiquitous sense of unease that all is not well in that world. A fine cast, a hypnotic script, and lush art direction contribute to make *Exotica* an eerie experience with plenty of repeat value. ♫♫♫

1994 (R) 104m/C *CA* Mia Kirshner, Elias Koteas, Bruce Greenwood, Don McKellar, Victor Garber, Arsinee Khanjian, Sarah Polley, Calvin Green, David Hemblen; **D:** Atom Egoyan; **W:** Atom Egoyan; **C:** Paul Sarossy; **M:** Mychael Danna. Genie Awards '94: Best Art Direction/Set Decoration, Best Cinematography, Best Costume Design, Best Director (Egoyan), Best Film, Best Screenplay, Best Supporting Actor (McKellar), Best Original Score; Toronto-City Award '94: Best Canadian Feature Film; Nominations: Genie Awards '94: Best Actor (Greenwood), Best Actor (Koteas); Independent Spirit Awards '96: Best Foreign Film. **VHS, LV, Closed Caption** *MAX*

Eye of
the Needle

It's an old story: an attractive woman is married to a man who hasn't touched her in years. She preserves the conventions of the relationship, anyway, at least until the first devil-may-care stranger arrives on the scene. Well, okay, so far it's an old story. But in 1981's *Eye of the Needle,* based on the Ken Follett WW2 suspense thriller, we see a rare example of a strong screen heroine whose power isn't drained by her libido. Kate Nelligan lives fitfully on an island with her husband (who's crippled emotionally as well as physically). When sad-eyed Donald Sutherland turns up, they're in bed together the first night they meet. Sutherland's well drawn character has a dark secret: he's a vicious killer and Nazi spy determined to snafu the D-Day invasion. By the time he winds up on Nelligan's island, he's single-handedly racked up a distressingly high body count and her husband is next on the list. The violence is complemented by a lavish Miklos Rozsa score, as are the romantic sequences, so his transformation from conscienceless assassin to love-struck interloper is surreal. We're used to seeing the GOOD guy be accompanied by such a passionate soundtrack. The moment when Nelligan's character, who has had long years of practice concealing her emotions, realizes who Sutherland is, is subtle but extremely intense. Without a wasted word or gesture, she launches a strategy of attack. It has nothing to do with anything she has ever been before—she simply operates on pure emotions and sheer nerve to defend herself and her small child. It's unusual to watch a woman steel herself to be as ruthless as her male adversary, disregarding the deep pain she clearly feels in the process. Director Richard Marquand effectively captures the timeless existential conflict between Nelligan's and Sutherland's characters while still sustaining the mood and pace of a wartime thriller. 🦴🦴🦴

1981 (R) 112m/C Donald Sutherland, Kate Nelligan, Ian Bannen, Christopher Cazenove, Philip Brown, Stephen MacKenna, Faith Brook, Colin Rix, Alex McCrindle, John Bennett, Sam Kydd, Rik Mayall, Bill Fraser; *D:* Richard Marquand; *W:* Stanley Mann; *M:* Miklos Rozsa. **VHS, Beta** *MGM, FOX*

The Fable of
the Beautiful
Pigeon
Fancier

Ruy Guerra's attractive trifle about a vain and selfish dandy focuses on his obsession for a lovely young matron. It's hard to care much about the dandy since his obsession is so detached and it's harder still to care about the matron since she functions more as a symbol than as a real character. Based on the Gabriel Garcia Marquez novel, *Love in the Time of Cholera.* Garcia Marquez's *Letters from the Park* (also made in 1988) is much better. In Spanish with English subtitles. ***AKA:*** Fabula de la Bella Palomera. 🦴🦴

1988 73m/C *SP* Ney Latorraca, Claudia Ohana, Tonia Carrero, Dina Stat, Chico Diaz; *D:* Ruy Guerra. **VHS, LV** *FXL, FCT*

Face to Face

Face to Face is an unrelieved downer, but a brilliant one. Liv Ullman plays Jenny, a psychiatrist with a dull, mean family, who tries to kill herself. She is saved by a fellow doctor (Erland Josephson) with problems of his own: his young male lover just left him for a wealthy female patron. Jenny's world is SO unpleasant: her grandmother leaves her alone when she is ill, her husband flies back from America for ONE day after her suicide attempt, her daughter reproaches her with the information that her mother never really liked her anyway, Josephson leaves for Jamaica the day after her life-and-death crisis, Jenny is robbed and nearly raped when she tries to help a young patient...surprisingly, her suicide attempt has nothing to do with any of

**INDEPENDENT
FILM GUIDE**

these situations. She is seeking, rather, the rare ability to FEEL things, truly and deeply. Her voyage through a terrible crisis forces her to test and tap this ability in a way she's never done before. Ingmar Bergman is at his most personal and self revealing here, and Sven Nykvist draws us into Jenny's electrifying world with harsh-tender close-ups. The picture ends on a sad, but hopeful note; its final image of two elderly people caressing one another was quite complete without Jenny's commentary: "Love embraces everything, even death." **AKA:** Ansikte mot Ansikte. ♪♪♪

1976 136m/C *SW* Liv Ullmann, Erland Josephson, Gunnar Bjornstrand, Aino Taube-Henrikson, Sven Lindberg, Kary Sylway, Sif Ruud; **D:** Ingmar Bergman; **W:** Ingmar Bergman; **C:** Sven Nykvist. Golden Globe Awards '77: Best Foreign Film; Los Angeles Film Critics Association Awards '76: Best Actress (Ullmann), Best Foreign Film; National Board of Review Awards '76: Best Actress (Ullmann); New York Film Critics Awards '76: Best Actress (Ullmann); Nominations: Academy Awards '76: Best Actress (Ullmann), Best Director (Bergman). **VHS** *PAR*

The Fallen Idol

Baines and Julie (Ralph Richardson and Michele Morgan) are having an affair, and mean Mrs. Baines (Sonia Dresdel) doesn't like it. Meanwhile, Felipe (Bobby Henrey, then 9) is bored and lonely (no parents in sight), so he hangs out with his hero Baines and with Julie, and steers clear of Mrs. Baines. Then Felipe believes that he's witnessed the murder of Mrs. Baines by none other than Baines! This interesting study of adult behavior through a child's eyes is based on Graham Greene's *The Basement Room*; Greene also collaborated on the screenplay. The camera sticks with Felipe. We see what he sees and even when he's wrong, we still root for things to go well for him. Henrey made just one other movie, 1951's *The Wonder Kid* with Oskar Werner and Sebastian Cabot. **AKA:** The Lost Illusion. 🦴🦴🦴🦴

1949 92m/B *GB* Ralph Richardson, Bobby Henrey, Michele Morgan, Sonia Dresdel, Jack Hawkins, Bernard Lee, Denis O'Dea, Dora Bryan, Walter Fitzgerald, Karel Stepanek, Geoffrey Keen, James Hayter, Dandy Nichols, George Woodbridge, John Ruddock, Joan Young, Gerard Heinz; **D:** Carol Reed; **W:** Graham Greene, Lesley Storm, William Templeton; **C:** Georges Perinal. British Academy Awards '48: Best Film; National Board of Review Awards '49: 10 Best Films of the Year, Best Actor (Richardson); New York Film Critics Awards '49: Best Director (Reed); Nominations: Academy Awards '49: Best Director (Reed), Best Screenplay. **VHS, Beta, LV** NOS, MRV, PSM

False Weights

False Weights lumbers along for 145 minutes. We are stuck with an unsympathetic village official most of the time, with occasional relief supplied by subplots mashed into the major narrative. Jerzy Lipmann's cinematography is stunning, but this vague film doesn't work as a character study, so it certainly doesn't succeed as a social statement. Bernhard Wicki's previous efforts, 1959's *The Bridge* and 1965's *Morituri*, were better received in the U.S., winning a total of three Oscar nominations between them (he also wrote the screenplay for 1962's *The Longest Day*). 🦴

1974 145m/C *GE* Helmut Qualtinger, Agnes Fink, Bata Zivoijnovic, Evelyne Opela, Kurt Sowinetz, Istvan Iglody; **D:** Bernhard Wicki; **W:** Fritz Hochwalder; **C:** Jerzy Lipmann; **M:** George Grutz. NYR

Fargo

Fargo was 1996's sentimental favorite, according to longtime admirers of the Coen brothers' amazing body of work. From 1985's *Blood Simple* to 1987's *Raising Arizona,* from 1990's *Miller's Crossing* to 1991's *Barton Fink,* the Coen brothers have thrust their black comedies

into the American consciousness in bold and inventive ways. The good-hearted police chief Marge Gunderson (Frances McDormand) is exactly what we NEVER see in a crime saga. She's pregnant, she has morning sickness, she's hasn't a duplicitous bone in her body, and yet she matter-of-factly gets to work SOLVING things, and then goes home to cuddle with her husband. The kidnap scheme dreamed up by Jerry Lundegaard (William H. Macy) is as screwed-up in the blueprint stage as it is in reality. The greedy kidnappers he hires are deadly serious, but bloody inept. Everything is played out against the snowy landscape of Minnesota, and even Harve Presnell (star of the '60s musicals *The Unsinkable Molly Brown* and *Paint Your Wagon*) puts in an appearance as the kidnap victim's father. Of all the top domestic indie releases of 1996, only Billy Bob Thornton's creation of Karl Childers in *Sling Blade* came anywhere near triggering the widespread adoption of catch phrases that *Fargo*'s Police Chief Marge Gunderson did. *Fargo* may be based an actual events from 1987, but the Coen brothers have clearly taken the inspiration for their screenplay from bits and pieces of several crimes of the Midwest. You may want to see this one twice. 🦴🦴🦴🦴

1996 (R) 97m/C William H. Macy, Frances McDormand, Steve Buscemi, Peter Stormare, Harve Presnell, Steve Reevis, John Carroll Lynch, Kristin Rudrud, Steve Park; **Cameos:** Jose Feliciano; **D:** Joel Coen; **W:** Ethan Coen, Joel Coen; **C:** Roger Deakins; **M:** Carter Burwell. Academy Awards '96: Best Actress (McDormand), Best Original Screenplay; Australian Film Institute '95: Best Foreign Film; Cannes Film Festival '96: Best Director (Coen); Independent Spirit Awards '97: Best Actor (Macy), Best Actress (McDormand), Best Cinematography, Best Director (Coen), Best Film, Best Screenplay; National Board of Review Awards '96: Best Actress (McDormand), Best Director (Coen); New York Film Critics Awards '96: Best Film; Screen Actors Guild Award '96: Best Actress (McDormand); Writers Guild of America '96: Best Original Screenplay; Broadcast Film Critics Association Awards '96: Best Actress (McDormand), Best Film; Nominations: Academy Awards '96: Best Cinematography, Best Director (Coen), Best Film Editing, Best Picture, Best Supporting Actor (Macy); British Academy Awards '96: Best Actress (McDormand), Best Director (Coen), Best Film, Best Original

Screenplay; Cesar Awards '97: Best Foreign Film; Directors Guild of America Awards '96: Best Director (Coen); Golden Globe Awards '97: Best Actress—Musical/Comedy (McDormand), Best Director (Coen), Best Film—Musical/Comedy, Best Screenplay; MTV Movie Awards '97: Best On-Screen Duo (Peter Stormare/Steve Buscemi); Screen Actors Guild Award '96: Best Supporting Actor (Macy). **VHS, LV, Closed Caption, DVD** *PGV*

The Favor, the Watch, and the Very Big Fish

The Favor, the Watch, and the Very Big Fish might have been a screwball comedy for the early 1990s, if anyone had drifted into movie theatres to see it. It stars three endearing actors, Bob Hoskins, Jeff Goldblum, and Natasha Richardson, as three strangers who drift into an intriguing romantic triangle. Along the way, writer/director Ben Lewin (who based his film on the Marcel Ayme short story, "Rue Saint-Sulpice") pokes gentle fun at voiceover artists for pornographic films, the folks who manufacture religious art objects, and star-crossed lovers. Hoskins plays Louis Aubinard, an innocent (and virginal) French photographer who is looking for the ideal Jesus to pose for a series of devotional illustrations. After an idyllic chance meeting with a voiceover artist named Sybil (Richardson), he manages to connect with a former piano player played by Goldblum, who is still suffering after the death of his long-dead mother and also from the loss of the idyllic love of his life, a one-time waitress named Sybil. Yes, it's the same Sybil. For the rest of the movie, Sybil searches for each man so she can explain why she appears to have jilted him, the piano player suffers agonies because he suspects that his photographer friend Louis loves Sybil, and Louis stolidly remains a loyal friend to his new model while hoping against hope that he will one day be reunited with Sybil. The fun is watching the three leads at work. At one point, Hoskins exclaims with a perfectly straight face, "I'm not a great actor!," a line ONLY a great actor could safely deliver. As in his previous British films, *The Tall Guy* and *Mister Frost,* Goldblum chews the scenery in another bizarre role that only he could render plausible. The much-underrated Natasha Richardson is delightful as Sybil and a great supporting cast (Angela Pleasence, Jean-Pierre Cassel, and Michel Blanc as Louis' martinet employer) make *The Favor, the Watch, and the Very Big Fish* a pleasure to watch. (If you're easily offended by borderline satire, you can always watch Bing Crosby on video as Father O'Malley!) 🦴🦴🦴

1992 (R) 89m/C *GB FR* Bob Hoskins, Jeff Goldblum, Natasha Richardson, Michel Blanc, Jacques Villeret, Angela Pleasence, Jean-Pierre Cassel, Bruce Altman; **D:** Ben Lewin; **W:** Ben Lewin; **M:** Vladimir Cosma. **VHS, LV, Closed Caption** *THV, FCT*

Fear

Fear begins promisingly and even features a low-budget earthquake sequence. Tomislav Pinter's cinematography is immaculate, the acting is impressive throughout, and the sets and costumes certainly convey the decadent atmosphere Matjaz Klopcic tries to explore here. The main problems with this attractive film are Klopcic's uncompelling screenplay and listless direction. Unfortunately, when film festival novices see a boring mess like this one, they often think it's THEIR fault, and that if they went to more movies or even flew to Yugoslavia, they would GET it. FERgeddit! If you think it's a thumping bore, it probably is. **AKA:** Strah. 🦴🦴

1975 105m/C *YU* Ljuba Tadic, Milena Zupancic, Anton Petje, Milena Dravic; **D:** Matjaz Klopcic; **W:** Matjaz Klopcic; **C:** Tomislav Pinter. *NYR*

A Feast at Midnight

The posters for *A Feast at Midnight* are evocative of the heady days when Christopher Lee reigned supreme at Hammer Studios: "A 500-year-old school. A prehistoric form master...And a 10-year old chef." The 10-year-old chef is Freddie Findlay, who is introduced as Magnus with this film. Lee is Major Longfellow (AKA Raptor), his mean Latin professor. And the 500-year-old school? The production company paid a visit to a boarding school in England, inquiring if they could use the school as an elaborate set for a five-week shooting schedule during the spring holidays. The producers then cast the students in the picture, and *A Feast at Midnight* was ready for the front burner. The premise is that Magnus is miserable at boarding school; he's no good at sports and the other boys bully him. Magnus IS good at one thing: creating elaborate desserts in the kitchen for a secret eating club called the Scoffers. The lighter-than-air story is enacted with great sweetness by the kids, and yes, this one WILL make you hungry. It's a charmer. (And it's a treat to see Christopher Lee in a movie, even if he isn't playing a vampire!) 🦴🦴🦴

1995 185m/C *AU* Christopher Lee, Robert Hardy, Edward Fox, Freddie Findlay, Lisa Faulkner, Sam West; *D:* Justin Hardy; *W:* Justin Hardy, Yoshi Nishio; *C:* Tim Maurice-Jones; *M:* David A. Hughes, John Murphy. *NYR*

Federal Hill

Ralph (Nicholas Turturro), Nicky (Anthony DeSando), Frank (Michael Raynor), Bobby (Jason Andrews), and Joey (Robert Turano) are long-time Italian buddies in Providence, Rhode Island, and they still meet at Joey's every week to play cards. Ralph (a thief) and Nicky (a drug dealer) are best friends. When Nicky sells some coke to Wendy (Libby Langdon) for a party, he shows up for it with Ralph. Ralph gets nowhere at the party, but Nicky winds up in a thing with Wendy and he decides to leave his pals for her. Ralph says that Wendy's just using Nicky for a fling, then loser Bobby gets in trouble and Ralph gets in trouble for helping Bobby. It all gets tied up in melodramatic fashion, but while it lasts, it's never dull, it's some-

times funny and it's always well acted in great black and white. Which makes more sense/cents? To light a film for black and white, but shoot it in color, finish it, then release it theatrically in black and white for film noir purists and in both versions for the home video market OR to spend a small fortune colorizing a 1994 film? Michael Corrente colorized *Federal Hill*. I know why there are two versions: there are actually people (including my one-time upstairs neighbor) who refuse to look at any movie that's not in color. But to *colorize* your brand new movie? The mind boggles. 🦴🦴🦴

1994 (R) 100m/B Anthony De Sando, Nicholas Turturro, Libby Langdon, Michael Raynor, Jason Andrews, Frank Vincent, Robert Turano, Michael Corrente; *D:* Michael Corrente; *W:* Michael Corrente; *C:* Richard Crudo; *M:* Bob Held, David Bravo. Nominations: Independent Spirit Awards '95: Best Supporting Actor (Turturro). **VHS, LV, Closed Caption** *THV*

Feed

With 27 days to go in the 1992 presidential campaign, Kevin Rafferty and James Ridgeway's *Feed* could not have been released at a better time. Here are the candidates as they would rather you had NEVER seen them, getting ready to go on television and trying to create a Presidential impression. Only Jerry Brown just can't seem to cover that dang bald spot of his, no matter how much he combs forward what's left of his hair. He wanted his campaign to seem effortlessly low-key, but he whines, whines, whines when a female aide can't straighten his tie just right. And HE can't do it, either. Bob Kerrey, sucking soda through a straw, just can't seem to erase the image of a choir boy, as a television moderator observes, supposedly off the record, but preserved forever on film. The late Paul Tsongas made the mistake of being photographed in swimming trunks, not even trying to suck in his stomach, and he also made a wild guess at the 1992 cost of a gallon of milk: $1.79! Ross Perot tells interminable dull jokes, always looking as if he's ready for an alien from

outer space to give him advice. Bill Clinton doesn't seem to have any off-guard moments. He can always think of something to say, no matter how many times he's drilled about Gennifer Flowers. (Flowers makes an appearance, too, enthusing about Clinton's soft lips.) And George Bush can, does, and will sit in front of a television camera for long, long moments on end, rarely saying a word to break the ice. People click off to candidates for the most inconsequential of reasons: one voter rejected Tsongas because he wore a pocket protector. A Democratic candidate makes the mistake of trying to shake the hands of two Republican voters and is sternly admonished by one woman: "A lady always presents her hand first." All the footage comes from the 1992 New Hampshire primary when the candidates apparently felt that most of what they said and did would be unseen by the rest of the country. Seeing the candidates like this, unvarnished and totally dependent on the folks from the media who surround them is far more absorbing than watching them blather prepared speeches for hours on end. Even if it IS dated, *Feed* is fascinating and well worth a video search. ♫♫♫

1992 76m/C D: Kevin Rafferty, James Ridgeway. **VHS** *CCP, BTV, FRF*

The Feldmann Case

The Feldmann Case represents the outstanding debut of director Bente Erichsen, who wrote her screenplay after reading the novel *Echo from Scream Pond,* based on a true World War II story about the Norwegian underground. There is a striking contrast between the official findings of the case and the director's own ethical viewpoint. The interpretative clash adds to the suspense: we know what happened to the rich Jewish couple who tried to escape the Nazis, what we don't know is why, and this is Erichsen's main concern. A well acted, extremely gutsy film, *The Feldmann Case*

is not yet available on video, although it should be! ♫♫♫♫

1987 89m/C *NO* Finn Kvalen, Sverre Anker Ousdal, Bjorn Sundquist, Ingerid Vardung; **D:** Bente Erichson; **W:** Bente Erichson. *NYR*

Female Trouble

Female Trouble is John Waters' favorite movie. It's all about the fictitious adventures of Dawn Davenport from her life as a suburban brat to her electrifying destiny. Divine gives another superstar performance in this underground classic, made for $25,000 in 1974. ♫♫

1974 (R) 95m/C Divine, David Lochary, Mary Vivian Pearce, Mink Stole, Edith Massey, Danny Mills, Cookie Mueller, Susan Walsh; **D:** John Waters; **W:** John Waters. **VHS, Beta** *NO*

Fire Maidens from Outer Space

I got yelled at for enjoying this movie and grilled afterwards: "Wouldn't you rather watch a GOOD movie than a BAD one?" Not necessarily! *Fire Maidens from Outer Space,* which looks like it was shot in someone's back yard, revolves around the efforts of five astronauts to save the Fire Maidens of Jupiter's thirteenth moon from this whatchamacallit in wrinkled long underwear! Anthony Dexter, whose career hit the automatic skids after starring in 1951's *Valentino,* is Astronaut Luther Blair. Susan Shaw, one of Britain's most promising starlets of the late 1940s and early 1950s, is Hestia. Paul Carpenter, Harry Fowler, and Sydney Tafler are Astronauts Larson, Sydney Stanhope, and Dr. Higgins. Some of these actors deleted this movie from their resumes. I don't know a thing about any of the other actors. I stopped watching movies with the person who yelled at me, but I haven't stopped watching this movie. There really IS something exhilarating about (a) stupefying

Opposite page: **Aunt Ida (Edith Massey) shows off her figure in *Female Trouble.***

Ben Stiller, Patricia
Arquette, and Tea
Leoni in *Flirting
with Disaster*.

cheapness, (b) technical incompetence, (c) artistic nadirs, (d) all of the above. **WOOF!**

1956 80m/B *GB* Anthony Dexter, Susan Shaw, Paul Carpenter, Harry Fowler, Jacqueline Curtiss, Sydney Tafler, Maya Koumani, Jan Holden, Kim Parker, Rodney Diak, Owen Berry; *D:* Cy Roth; *W:* Cy Roth. **VHS** *CNM, MLB*

First Communion

Rene Feret's *First Communion* is a portrait of a family over a 100-year span; it has much the same effect as the spinning pages of a huge scrapbook filled with the faces of people who may mean a great deal to each other, but not to a stranger who casually picks up the scrapbook. Since Feret tells us that it isn't important who married whom over the years or who

died, it's exactly like watching a bunch of someone else's home movies. The ballad that's supposed to hold everything together is insipid, but Jean-Francois Robin's cinematography is exquisite, and the main redeeming virtue of this immature first film. *AKA:* La Communion Solonnelle. 🦴🦴

1977 185m/C *FR* Claude-Emile Rosen, Claude Bouchery, Vincent Pinel, Yveline Ailhaud, Patrick Fierry, Jany Gastaldi, Marcel Dalio, Philippe Leotard, Rene Feret; *D:* Rene Feret; *W:* Rene Feret; *C:* Jean-Francois Robin; *M:* Sergio Ortego. *NYR*

Five Corners

If you're looking for a pattern in the career of Oscar-winning screenwriter John Patrick Shanley, try to figure out what *Moonstruck, Five Corners, The January Man, Joe Versus the Volcano* (which he also directed), *Alive, We're Back! A Dinosaur's Story,* and *Congo* have in common. That isn't a trick question, because heck if WE know, either. Shanley is capable of writing sequences of both heartfelt realism and mind-boggling mediocrity (contrast the first and second halves of *Joe*). Most of the story line of *Five Corners,* which played at the Mill Valley Film Festival in the fall of 1987, is strong and clear. At one point in this story about teens in 1964, though, violence occurs without warning, and the sequence is like "a stun gun to your brain," as Angela Chase, a teen from a later era, might say. Are these completely gratuitous moments really necessary? What do they give the narrative that it doesn't already have? Don't they, in fact, take away from the other 90 minutes that have already established the psychosis behind the violence? It is this lack of balance that would topple other Shanley screenplays. On the plus side, the acting by Jodie Foster (who won an Independent Spirit Award), Tim Robbins, and John Turturro is excellent, and so is James Newton Howard's score. 🦴🦴⅃

1988 (R) 92m/C Jodie Foster, John Turturro, Todd Graff, Tim Robbins, Elizabeth Berridge, Rose Gregorio, Gregory Rozakis, Rodney Harvey, John Seitz; **D:** Tony Bill; **W:** John Patrick Shanley; **C:** Fred Murphy; **M:** James Newton Howard. Independent Spirit Awards '89: Best Actress (Foster). **VHS, Beta** *MGM*

Flirting with Disaster

There's something about Ben Stiller in a movie that just makes me go AAARGH. He shows up in *Reality Bites*: AARGH. He shows up in this one: AARGH. He may be a terrific guy offscreen, but onscreen he reeks of Yuppieville. Maybe he should grow a beard. Get a growl in his voice. Anything to give him an edge. David O. Russell's movie has so many edges, you might think that one of them would rub off on Ben Stiller. But noooooo.... Luckily, *Flirting with Disaster* has a large cast. There's Patricia Arquette, who looks as young here as she looked old in *Lost Highway*. Josh Brolin (NOT Ben Stiller) licks her armpit. Amazing.

There's Tea Leoni as a shrink. Sure. There's Alan Alda and Lily Tomlin as a hippie dippie couple; now, there's a concept. There's George Segal and Mary Tyler Moore, who are SO uptight you could market the both of them as slingshots. Russell talked Moore into a few underwear sequences. No comment. In spite of the overall weirdness, everyone acts as if everything is normal; Moore flosses her teeth and asks Segal, "Where's your sense of romance?" It's funny! 🦴🦴🦴

1995 (R) 92m/C Ben Stiller, Patricia Arquette, Tea Leoni, Alan Alda, Mary Tyler Moore, George Segal, Lily Tomlin, Josh Brolin, Richard Jenkins, Celia Weston, Glenn Fitzgerald, Beth Ostrosky, Cynthia Lamontagne, David Patrick Kelly, John Ford Noonan, Charles Oberly; **D:** David O. Russell; **W:** David O. Russell; **C:** Eric Alan Edwards; **M:** Stephen Endelman. Nominations: Independent Spirit Awards '97: Best Director (Russell), Best Screenplay, Best Supporting Actor (Jenkins), Best Supporting Actress (Tomlin). **VHS, LV, Closed Caption** *TOU*

Fly by Night

Slapdash, skin-deep look at a couple of rappers who team up with a third (authentic rapper Darryl Mitchell as Rich's cousin Kayam) to achieve fame. When they do, they hate it. Do Steve Gomer and Todd Graff know what makes their characters (Jeffrey Sams as Rich, Ron Brice as I) tick? If they do, it isn't onscreen. There's an exciting score, though. 🦴🦴

1993 (PG-13) 93m/C Jeffrey D. Sams, Ron Brice, Darryl (Chill) Mitchell, Todd Graff, Leo Burmester, Soulfood Jed, Lawrence Gilliard, Omar Carter, Maura Tierney, Yul Vazquez, M.C. Lyte, Christopher-Michael Gerrard, Ebony Jo-Ann; **D:** Steve Gomer; **W:** Todd Graff; **C:** Larry Banks; **M:** Kris Parker, Sidney Mills, Dwayne Sumal. Sundance Film Festival '93: Filmmakers Trophy. **VHS, Closed Caption** *COL*

For a Lost Soldier

For a Lost Soldier was San Jose's opening night selection at the Gay and Lesbian Film Festival in 1993. It arrived with an impressive award from a festival in Turin. A grown-up choreographer (Jeroen Krabbe) reminisces about those good old World War II days when he was a boy of 12 or so and had a fling with a grown-up soldier. Their fairly explicit romps in bed are shown as warm and cozy, and we never see what happens to the child between the end of their affair and his well established adult life. (It may have been in the original Dutch book, but it isn't onscreen.) Other short films at the festival that year were much more honest; several focused on how their protagonists are completely bewildered by conflicting emotions about sex and tormented by a fear of being abandoned as a result of the choices they make. For grown-ups to convince themselves that very young children recover quickly from intense emotional experiences may be convenient for them, but the reality for the kids is much different. The unreal romantic lushness of *For a Lost Soldier,* therefore, makes it an ideal advert and/or propaganda for the North American Man/Boy Love Association. 🦴

1993 92m/C *NL* Marten Smit, Andrew Kelley, Jeroen Krabbe, Feark Smink, Elsje de Wijn, Derk-Jan Kroon; *D:* Roeland Kerbosch; *W:* Roeland Kerbosch; *M:* Joop Stokkermans. **VHS** *FXL, ORI*

For Queen and Country

For Queen and Country is bogged down with good intentions and by characters who function as symbols rather than as people. The thrust of the film is that Great Britain does not care about the lower classes, and if the country makes use of a poor man in wartime, he can expect a life of hopelessness when he returns home. Denzel Washington is so good in the central character of Reuben that he grabs our attention and sympathy in spite of the rigid symbolism of his role. Also good are Dorian Healy as Fish, a friend crippled by his tour of duty, and Amanda Redman as Stacey, a woman who is interested in Reuben until she recognizes his evolving need for violent solutions. The rest of the cast, including veteran character actor George Baker, are given

no chance to do much more than advance the plot. I have the same reservations about director Martin Stellman's turgid screenplay for 1987's *Defense of the Realm.* By wanting to make a predetermined point with as few words as possible, he reduces most of the characters to delivery people. In *For Queen and Country,* nearly all of the first 90 minutes of the plot are absorbed with establishing the unjust poverty suffered by Reuben and Fish, something a writer without such a rigid agenda could have shown in a fraction of the time. In fact, a single moment reveals that if the British bureaucracy had been a bit less unyielding, Reuben and Stacey might have been able to make a go of it. But Stellman chooses to show the moment as anticlimactic, then wraps it all up with violence and deja vu and says what? That because the British government is unfair to disconnected veterans that they might as well pack it in the day they get their discharge papers? That's what Stellman's persistent images indicate. There are suggestions of other resolutions, but that would have disturbed the conclusion's contrived symmetry. There are quite a few things wrong with *For Queen and Country* but Denzel Washington isn't one of them, and the film is worth seeing for his commanding performance alone. 🦴🦴▽

1988 (R) 105m/C *GB* Denzel Washington, Dorian Healy, Amanda Redman, Sean Chapman, Bruce Payne, Geff Francis, George Baker; *D:* Martin Stellman; *W:* Martin Stellman; *M:* Michael Kamen. **VHS** *NYR*

Forbidden Choices

Yeh, if I made a fictional indie with a moniker like *The Beans of Egypt, Maine,* I'd consider giving it a catchier title, too. It sounds like a National Geographic documentary instead of the soap opera that it is. Actually, that IS the title of Carolyn Chute's novel and it IS about the Bean family who live in Egypt, Maine. The head of the Bean family of nine is Reuben (Rutger Hauer?!$#%), but he's in jail, so Roberta (Kelly Lynch) is raising them on her own. Earlene Pomerleau (Martha Plimpton, the film's chief virtue) thinks the Beans are neat, especially Beal (Patrick McGaw). Well, what else does she have in her life but a tyrannical, Bible-thumping Daddy (Richard Sanders)? Anyway, that new title refers to Beal and zzzzzz.... **AKA:** The Beans of Egypt, Maine. 🦴🦴

1994 (R) 109m/C Martha Plimpton, Kelly Lynch, Rutger Hauer, Patrick McGaw, Richard Sanders; **D:** Jennifer Warren; **W:** Bill Phillips; **C:** Stevan Larner; **M:** Peter Manning Rob. Nominations: Independent Spirit Awards '95: Best Cinematography, Best Supporting Actress (Lynch). **VHS, LV, Closed Caption** *WEA*

Forbidden Games

Francois Boyer wrote the screenplay for *Les Jeux Interdits* in 1946, but World War II was over and no one wanted to see another war movie. So he turned it into a novel and producer Robert Dorfman WAS interested in making a movie of a successful book. An entirely new screenplay was drafted by Jean Aurenche and Pierre Bost with director Rene Clement (1913-96), who decided to film the story on a farm that was actually poor, as indicated in the script. He began a search for the two children who were to star in the picture. Brigitte Fossey, who was heartrending as the orphaned Paulette, was only five years old. Georges Poujouly, who would play Michel, was just eleven. The narrative sticks with the kids to show the horrors of war. Michel protects Paulette from the sadness and loneliness of her situation by coming up with a game to bury dead animals they find in the countryside and placing crosses (stolen from the church cemetery) on top of their homemade graves. The game comforts them both, although the adults are none too pleased by the sacrilegious aspect of the rituals. Under pressure, Michel says he will give up the crosses if the grownups promise they won't take Paulette away. They agree, and

Michel learns, much too young, about the ugliness of betrayal. Paulette's fate, to wander among a crowd of other refugees, is devastating. She cries for "Michel!" over and over again. The "Forbidden Games," along with the kind little boy who nurtured her, are lost to her. Forever? We don't know about Paulette and Michel, but in real life, Fossey went on to a successful acting career when she grew up. In one of her most intriguing pictures, 1984's *The Future of Emily* (co-starring Ivan Desny and Hildegarde Knef), she played an actress reflecting on her career since childhood. At one point, she discusses a role she played at five, sighing, "it was my best performance." (Fossey's other films include *The Wanderer, Honor Among Thieves, Going Places, Blue Country, The Man Who Loved Women, Quintet, Chanel Solitaire, La Boum, Enigma,* and *The Last Butterfly.*) Poujouly also found work—as a supporting actor in other French films, including 1958's *Frantic.* And Jacques Marin, who plays Georges, continued to appear as a character actor in international films for many years. The initial reaction to Clement's film was mixed. Although *Forbidden Games* won many awards in Italy, Britain, and America, including an Oscar, the French were horrified by the way their post-war society appeared to the rest of the world. But *Forbidden Games* remains the best known and most treasured French film of its time. (Clement's other films include *The Walls of Malapaga, Gervaise, The Day and the Hour, Joy House, Is Paris Burning?, Rider on the Rain,* and *And Hope to Die*). **AKA:** Les Jeux Interdits. 🦴🦴🦴🦴

1952 90m/B *FR* Brigitte Fossey, Georges Poujouly, Amedee, Louis Herbert, Suzanne Courtal, Jacques Marin, Laurence Badie, Andre Wasley, Louis Sainteve; **D:** Rene Clement; **W:** Rene Clement, Jean Aurenche, Pierre Bost, Francois Boyer; **M:** Narciso Yepes. Academy Awards '52: Best Foreign Language Film; British Academy Awards '53: Best Film; National Board of Review Awards '52: 5 Best Foreign Films of the Year; New York Film Critics Awards '52: Best Foreign Film; Venice Film Festival '52: Best Film; Nominations: Academy Awards '54: Best Story. **VHS, Beta, LV** *NOS, APD, NLC*

INDEPENDENT FILM GUIDE

Forgotten Silver

Peter Jackson's *Forgotten Silver* may be an eyelash too clever for its own good. It looks like a documentary of a forgotten New Zealand filmmaking pioneer named Colin McKenzie, but it's essentially a reconstruction of silent movie history if an obscure bloke, rather than D.W. Griffith, had been responsible for early cinematic innovations. (If you've ever seen *The Missing Reel*, a film by Christopher Rawlence about an authentic forgotten filmmaking pioneer, you're aware that stranger things have been known to happen.) Still, *Forgotten Silver* is obviously an affectionate look at a vanished era, and Jackson, Sam Neill, Leonard Maltin, et al obviously had a ball making it. ♫♫♪

1996 53m/C *NZ* Sam Neill, Leonard Maltin, Harvey Weinstein, John O'Shea, Hannah McKenzie, Lindsay Shelton, Johnny Morris, Marguerite Hurst, Costa Botes; ***D:*** Peter Jackson; ***W:*** Peter Jackson. *NYR*

The 400 Blows

Antoine Doinel (Jean-Pierre Leaud) is one troubled 12-year-old kid. His mother (Claire Maurier) wanted to have an abortion when she learned she was expecting him and Antoine knows it. She is unfaithful to his father (Albert Remy) and both are indifferent to Antoine. He skips school, steals, and lies about the cause of his behavior by saying that his mother is dead. He is sent to an institution but escapes, and the shot of Antoine on the beach is one of the most indelible images of childhood ever. Jean-Pierre Leaud seems so real as Antoine, it's

hard to believe he's acting. But he is, and Truffaut took infinite care to see that his young discovery hit just the right notes in his first movie. Partly based on Truffaut's own life, *The 400 Blows* gave us a view of childhood that we'd never before seen in such realistic detail. A groundbreaking picture in every way, it was and still is an enormously influential film on more than two generation of filmmakers. *AKA:* Les Quatre Cents Coups. ♫♫♫♫

1959 97m/B *FR* Francois Truffaut, Jean-Pierre Leaud, Claire Maurier, Albert Remy, Guy Decomble, Georges Flament, Patrick Auffay, Jeanne Moreau, Jean-Claude Brialy, Jacques Demy, Robert Beauvais; *D:* Francois Truffaut; *W:* Francois Truffaut, Marcel Moussey; *C:* Henri Descae; *M:* Jean Constantin. Cannes Film Festival '59: Best Director (Truffaut); New York Film Critics Awards '59: Best Foreign Film; Nominations: Academy Awards '59: Best Story & Screenplay. **VHS, Beta, LV** *HMV, MRV, APD*

Four Weddings and a Funeral

Like 1992's *Strictly Ballroom, Four Weddings and a Funeral* is the sort of delicious confection that actually improves with repeat viewings. It's the story of a dashing bachelor named Charles (Hugh Grant) who goes to wedding after wedding, screwing up left and right (he loses vital wedding paraphernalia LIKE THE RING, has a severe case of foot-in-mouth disease, is forever at the wrong place at the wrong time, et cetera), until he finally comes to terms with how he can slip into the whole system with the least pain and effort. *Four Weddings* was a hit in England and an even bigger hit in America. The reasons for this transatlantic phenomenon are obvious: there are many flattering references to American cultural symbols; American songs galore on the soundtrack; and, of course, Gaffney, South Carolina's own Andie MacDowell as Carrie, the object of Charles' desire. This satire of love and death, moreover, is warm and affectionate. Lovely touches abound, like Simon

Callow sticking his finger down his throat at a gloppy folk song during one ceremony, the picture-perfect casting-against-type of politically radical Corin Redgrave as an aristocrat, the bride who kisses total strangers and tells them how much she loves them to the accompaniment of the groom's assessment of her alcoholic intake, bridesmaid Lydia (Sophie Thompson) who doesn't want to scrape the bottom of the barrel with Bernard but engages in some lusty wedding-bound necking with him anyway, Charles' endearing roommate Scarlett (Charlotte Coleman) who dreams of meeting Rhett at one of these functions, and Charles' sharply observed friend (Kristin Scott Thomas), who calls his ex-girlfriend Duckface and who is, of course, madly in love with Charles. And these represent a very small fraction of our favorite sequences. (Two words more: Rowan Atkinson!) *Four Weddings and a Funeral* is a keeper, to savor during those hours when the world seems dreary and depressing and you really need a movie filled with laughter and wit. ♫♫♫♫

1994 (R) 118m/C *GB* Hugh Grant, Andie MacDowell, Simon Callow, Kristin Scott Thomas, James Fleet, John Hannah, Charlotte Coleman, David Bower, Corin Redgrave, Rowan Atkinson, Rosalie Crutchley, Kenneth Griffith, Jeremy Kemp, Sophie Thompson; *D:* Mike Newell; *W:* Richard Curtis; *C:* Michael Coulter; *M:* Richard Rodney Bennett. Australian Film Institute '94: Best Foreign Film; British Academy Awards '94: Best Actor (Grant), Best Director (Newell), Best Film, Best Supporting Actress (Scott Thomas); Chicago Film Critics Awards '94: Most Promising Actor (Grant); Golden Globe Awards '95: Best Actor—Musical/Comedy (Grant); Writers Guild of America '94: Best Original Screenplay; Nominations: Academy Awards '94: Best Original Screenplay, Best Picture; Directors Guild of America Awards '94: Best Director (Newell); Golden Globe Awards '95: Best Actress—Musical/Comedy (MacDowell), Best Film—Musical/Comedy, Best Screenplay; MTV Movie Awards '95: Breakthrough Performance (Grant). **VHS, LV, DVD** *PGV*

France, Incorporated

Alain Corneau's *France, Incorporated* offers a shattering sci-fi speculation on

HUGH GRANT
Four Weddings and a Funeral

Comedy is really where I belong. My first five years as an actor were all in comedy in the theatre. And then when I went into films, it just happened to be rather a serious film, 1987's *Maurice,* that I first did and I know what film people are like: they see me in one thing and they think that's my slot, and so I got an awful lot of other serious parts after that, but I kept saying, 'Give me comedy!' And then my breakthrough came when I did 1992's *Bitter Moon,* this Roman Polanski film where I get quite a lot of laughs in that, and finally English producers saw that I could do that.... Working with Roman Polanski is unusual, that's for sure. On an English film set, I roll up early in the morning, and I'm given a nice cup of tea and a doughnut, and with Roman Polanski's film, I turned up at lunchtime because he won't work in the morning, he's too hung over from the night before. I had a long lunch and a few glasses of wine, and then I gradually drifted through makeup, and then I might be offered some drugs, and then there's his wife [Emmanuelle Seigner] who's making up with one of the make-up girls, and it's that sort of stuff.... To be honest, making *Four Weddings and a Funeral* was a nightmare. We had not nearly enough time, in the way of small-budget films, and not a lot of extras. It was nuts. One particular time when we were in a hotel and I was having a sex scene with Andie

INDEPENDENT FILM GUIDE

what life would be like in the year 2222 if hard drugs were legalized. The versatile Canadian actress Allyn Ann McLerie (*Words and Music, Phantom of the Rue Morgue, The Reivers, They Shoot Horses, Don't They?, Cinderella Liberty, All the President's Men*) is well cast as a tough-minded businesswoman who attempts to commercialize heroin as aggressively as cigarettes were marketed in the 1950s. There is nothing pretty about the sex and violence in this X-rated fantasy. The interesting premise occasionally lapses into facile slickness, though. 🦴🦴🦴

1974 100m/C *FR* Michel Bouquet, Allyn Ann McLerie, Roland Dubillard, Joel Barcellos, Michel Vitold, Ann Zacarias, Francis Blanche, Daniel Ceccaldi, Gerard Desarthe; **D:** Alain Corneau; **W:** Alain Corneau, Jean-Claude Carriere; **C:** Pierre William Glenn; **M:** Clifton Chenier. *NYR*

Frankenhooker

At the beginning of *Frankenhooker,* we see the extremely pretty Elizabeth, whom boyfriend Jeffrey Franken thinks is too fat. On the other hand, Jeffrey looks and is just plain weird. He wants Elizabeth to be perfect and when she meets her demise in a freak garden accident, he makes careful plans to reassemble her. And so yet another *Frankenstein* variation is born. This one is pretty good, probably because it doesn't pretend to be anything other than what it

MacDowell, we overran so horribly that there was a real-life bridal couple who were coming into that particular room, and we only got out with about three seconds to spare before they actually would have found us in bed.... We rehearsed for a week or so. I was pretty intimidated to begin with, because she's a huge star and she's ridiculously attractive, but I found out she was human. After about a week, I caught her dribbling while she was drinking a cup of tea....

"I am living with someone, but I am a bit terrified of marriage. I've said before, I wouldn't mind marriage if it was on a grand scale, a Von Trapp sort of marriage in *The Sound of Music* with a big castle and nice Julie Andrews as my wife, but I'd like the children before she started dressing them in curtains, I'd like them still in sailor suits coming downstairs, and I could blow a whistle and they'd just bugger off again because I can't be dealing with mess with children, all that sort of business of squalling on the floor with those hideous toys that they have now. I hate those colors. They're so offensive. Why can't they use those nice, muted earth colors?.... I don't want to talk about it, but I was deprived...I have very few toys myself."

HUGH GRANT'S films include 1985's *Jenny's War*, 1988's *The Dawning, The Lair of the White Worm,* and *White Mischief*; 1990's *Impromptu*; 1991's *The Big Man: Crossing the Line*; 1993's *Night Train to Venice* and *The Remains of the Day*; 1994's *The Englishman Who Went Up a Hill But Came Down a Mountain, An Awfully Big Adventure, Restoration,* and *Sirens* ; 1995's *Nine Months* and *Sense and Sensibility*; and 1996's *Extreme Measures.*

is, a low-budget black comedy for the midnight matinee crowd. James Lorinz and Patty Mullen have a good time in the leading roles and cult favorites Shirley Stoler and Louise Lasser pop up in supporting roles. There are plenty of body parts in the picture, but they're so obviously clunky and fake that we can't imagine anyone being seriously frightened by them. *Frankenhooker* is the first movie we've seen that makes jokes about crack; a good companion piece would be the equally bizarre *Mystery of the Leaping Fish* made in 1916 by D.W. Griffith and Tod Browning with Douglas Fairbanks as Coke Ennyday. At the sold-out premiere screening we attended at San Francisco's Roxie Cinema, the audience

was already having conversations with the characters onscreen, a sure sign that *Frankenhooker* will be around for some time to come. 🦴🦴🦴

1990 (R) 90m/C James Lorinz, Patty Mullen, Charlotte J. Helmkamp, Louise Lasser, Shirley Stoler; *D:* Frank Henenlotter. **VHS, LV, Closed Caption** *SGE, FCT*

Frankenstein Unbound

There have been close to 100 movies made about Dr. Frankenstein and his monster, so why not yet another variation on the legend from the one and only Roger

Corman, directing his first film in decades? This is the third film in four years to make use of the Byron-Godwin-Shelley triangle (*Gothic* and *Haunted Summer* were the others) but they're mainly in this picture as atmospheric window dressing. John Hurt plays who else but an American scientist from the future who has created a machine that is raising havoc with time and space. He is not as conscience-stricken as he could be and when he winds up in early 19th century Switzerland, he heads straight for the nearest tavern. He asks if he can share a table with who else but Raul Julia's Dr. Frankenstein? (Do you ever wonder why time travelers never seem to run into ordinary blokes?) Hurt is staggered by the quick realization that Dr. Frankenstein is not a very nice man and resolves to Do Something About It. He meets Mary Godwin (Bridget Fonda) at a witchcraft trial for a little girl accused of a murder committed by Dr. Frankenstein's monster. When Mary expresses sympathy for the child, he follows his literary idol to the Swiss retreat she shares with Byron and Shelley. "You're not English, are you?" a prissy Byron (Jason Patric) inquires after hearing John Hurt's thick British accent. "No," Hurt answers heartily. "I'm Dr. Joe from America!" Bridget Fonda, fetchingly costumed as Mary Godwin, is unable to help save the world from Frankenstein, because she hasn't even written the book yet! Her presence in the film is explained when Dr. Joe goes to bed with her. And that's all we ever see of Mary Godwin. Dr. Frankenstein continues to be not very nice and we finally see his monster. His make-up is overdone, his dialogue is overwritten, and Roger Corman gets to stage all sorts of violence he could never get away with at American International Pictures. He still cuts corners in inimitable Roger Corman fashion, though. *Frankenstein Unbound* was backed by investors from Italy where the movie was shot on location. But Swiss and Italian vegetation are quite different: to the best of our knowledge, there aren't

any palm trees in the Swiss Alps are there? The conclusion looks like it was shot in the property department for every science-fiction movie made in Italy since 1979. There are some nice touches: our favorite character was Dr. Joe's talking car, which has the capacity to run off copies of entire books. The look of the film is extremely lush, but the editing is sloppy, as if Corman started out to make a pretty good movie and then someone from outside the project slapped it together. *Frankenstein Unbound* was basically dumped by its eventual distributor, 20th Century Fox, but in spite of this cavalier treatment, it may attract a cult viewing audience. *AKA:* Roger Corman's Frankenstein Unbound. 🦴🦴

1990 (R) 86m/C John Hurt, Raul Julia, Bridget Fonda, Jason Patric, Michael Hutchence, Catherine Rabett, Nick Brimble, Catherine Corman, Mickey Knox; *D:* Roger Corman; *W:* Roger Corman, F.X. Feeney; *M:* Carl Davis; *V:* Terri Treas. **VHS, Beta, LV, Closed Caption** *FOX*

Frankie Starlight

Frankie Starlight was among our favorites at 1995's crop of films at the San Francisco International Film Festival. The stars on the record are Anne Parrillaud, Matt Dillon, and Gabriel Byrne, but the real stars are Alan Pentony and Corban Walker, who play the title character as a child and as an adult. The film shows what led up to Walker writing a novel about his tragic mother (Parrillaud) and her lovers (Byrne and Dillon), as well as the repercussions after his book is published. Also in the cast is young Georgina Cates, who created such a vivid impression in Mike Newell's *An Awfully Big Adventure* earlier in 1995. Michael Lindsay-Hogg directs this beautifully filmed tale by Chet Raymo and Ronan O'Leary. 🦴🦴🦴

1995 (R) 100m/C *IR* Corban Walker, Alan Pentony, Gabriel Byrne, Anne Parrillaud, Matt Dillon, Georgina Cates, Darbnia Molloy, Niall Toibin, Rudi Davies; *D:* Michael Lindsay-Hogg; *W:* Chet Raymo, Ronan O'Leary; *C:* Paul Laufer; *M:* Elmer Bernstein. **VHS, LV, Closed Caption** *NLC*

Freeway

To us, THIS is the golden age of the movies. To be sure, Hollywood studios are still the same cumbersome, second-guessing, bandwagon-climbing monstrosities they've always been. But in the bad old days, actors who wanted to try something different in the low-budget independent arena found themselves in professional coventry for the duration. Some of their careers never recovered from the industry impression that they were on the skids. Today, careers get jump starts, actors receive Academy recognition, and hot new directors generally do their best work away from the meddling mitts of major studio flunkies. Reese Witherspoon, for example, has played peaches-and-cream roles for the last five years: for MGM in *Man in the Moon,* for Disney in *A Far Off Place,* for Polygram in *S.F.W.* Who better to cast as the ultimate Little Red Riding Hood in Matthew Bright's abrasively funny and ferociously smart *Freeway.* As Vanessa Lutz, Witherspoon digs into the DNA of every disadvantaged kid who ever got shafted by society and comes up with a scary portrait of exactly what makes her tick...AND explode. Vanessa's history includes shoplifting, prostitution, arson, and violence, but she remains unjaded and achingly vulnerable. She is, in fact, the ideal target for the Big Bad Wolf (Keifer Sutherland as Bob Wolverton), a misleadingly sympathetic pillar of society who works with kids and lives in a nice house with his pretty wife, Brooke Shields (giving her career a much-needed jump start after three years of cinematic inactivity). Shields doesn't know about her hubby's secret stash of porno magazines or the fact that HE is THE I-5 serial killer, preying on defenseless hookers. Vanessa has any number of remarkable dimensions to her character, but 'defenseless' is not among them. On her way to Granny's trailer, she accepts a Spanish gun from a doomed boyfriend, so when Bob moves in for the kill, Vanessa is ready. But the movie doesn't end there, Big Bad Bob Wolverton being one of those invincible types who just doesn't know how to lie down dead after being riddled in the head and back with bullets. Bright still has a great deal to say about how society has a firm grip on deceptively obvious formulas that are far more easily assimilated than the truth. Sutherland has a blast-and-a-half as the Wolf, but if they gave Oscars for the most outstanding hitchhiker since Ann Savage snagged Tom Neal in 1945's *Detour,* Witherspoon would win for *Freeway* with NO serious competition. Don't miss this once-in-a-lifetime performance! 🦴🦴🦴🦴

1995 (R) 102m/C Reese Witherspoon, Kiefer Sutherland, Brooke Shields, Wolfgang Bodison, Dan Hedaya, Amanda Plummer, Bokeem Woodbine, Brittany Murphy; **D:** Matthew Bright; **W:** Matthew Bright; **C:** John Thomas; **M:** Danny Elfman. **VHS, Closed Caption** *REP*

French Provincial

A BORING movie starring Jeanne Moreau and Marie-France Pisier? Sad, but true. Moreau starts out as a laundress and winds up as the president of a factory. Marrying well helped, but very little else is explained in this deliberately enigmatic film spanning the years 1900-75. After this far from gripping start, Andre Techine went on to a career as a world-class filmmaker, directing *The Bronte Sisters, Rendezvous, Scene of the Crime,* and *Wild Reeds.* **AKA:** Souvenirs d'en France. 🦴

1975 95m/C *FR* Jeanne Moreau, Michel Auclair, Marie-France Pisier, Orane Demazis, Claude Mann, Julien Guiomar, Michele Moretti, Aram Stephane; **D:** Andre Techine; **W:** Andre Techine, Marilyn Goldin; **C:** Bruno Nuytten; **M:** Philippe Sarde. *NYR*

Fresh

Twelve-year-old "Fresh" (Sean Nelson) is a New York drug runner, working for heroin dealer Esteban (Giancarlo Esposito) while living with his Aunt Frances (Cheryl Freeman) and his many female cousins. He isn't supposed to see his down-and-out dad Sam (Samuel L. Jackson), but does so anyway, and learns how to play speed chess with him. Chess, the ultimate war game, gives Fresh a strategy for survival when he becomes an eyewitness to two murders committed by a terrifying crack dealer named Jake (Jean LaMarre). Boaz Yakin gives us a bleak view of childhood and brings out outstanding performances from veterans Esposito and Jackson, and also from young Nelson and LaMarre. And the well developed chess angle provides *Fresh* with a fascinating, if cynical resolution. 🦴🦴🦴

1994 (R) 114m/C *FR* Samuel L. Jackson, Giancarlo Esposito, Sean Nelson, N'Bushe Wright, Ron Brice, Jean LaMarre, Luis Lantigua, Yul Vazquez, Cheryl Freeman; *D:* Boaz Yakin; *W:* Boaz Yakin; *C:* Adam Holender. Independent Spirit Awards '95: Debut Performance (Nelson); Sundance Film Festival '94: Special Jury Prize, Filmmakers Trophy; Nominations: Independent Spirit Awards '95: Best Supporting Actor (Esposito). **VHS, Beta, LV, Closed Caption** *MAX*

Fright

This is THE babysitter movie to watch when you're alone with a baby whose parents have gone out for dinner and your boyfriend wants to keep you company and you suspect that the baby's mother might have a homicidal ex-husband lurking about the house. This is Amanda's (Susan George) dilemma, and what she faces when nice Dr. and Mrs. Helen Cordell (John Gregson and Honor Blackman) leave her to mind baby Tara for the evening wouldn't even BEGIN to happen to any member of the Baby-Sitters Club. Saturated with blood and violence, *Fright* offers George a strong part as the resourceful Amanda, and also gives Ian Bannen plenty of chances to chew up the scenery. Baby Tara (the director's child) is cute. *AKA:* Night Legs. 🦴🦴▿

1971 (PG) 84m/C *GB* Susan George, Honor Blackman, Ian Bannen, John Gregson, George Cole, Dennis Waterman, Tara Collinson, Maurice Kaufman, Michael Brennan, Roger Lloyd Pack; *D:* Peter Collinson; *W:* Tutor Gates; *C:* Ian Wilson; *M:* Harry Robinson. **VHS** *REP, MOV*

From Hollywood to Deadwood

An interesting blend of humor and the private eye genre can be found in Rex Pickett's *From Hollywood to Deadwood*. Pickett's clever script helped to bolster the wonderful rapport between the two leads, played by San Francisco Bay Area actors Scott Paulin and Jim Haynie. They play two private eyes in search of Lana Dark, a mysterious actress who fled in the middle of her latest movie. Haynie and Paulin bring a likeable, self-effacing quality to their scuzzy roles, but Barbara Schock can't act worth beans in the film's pivotal role. Still, this is a pretty good little film. 🦴🦴

1989 (R) 90m/C Scott Paulin, Jim Haynie, Barbara Schock; *D:* Rex Pickett; *W:* Rex Pickett. **VHS, Beta, LV, Closed Caption** *MED, FCT, IME*

From the Journals of Jean Seberg

Jean Seberg was a pretty blonde from Iowa who was voted "most likely to succeed" when she graduated from high school in 1956. The following year, she was the first teenager to play *Saint Joan* onscreen. She received enormous publicity prior to the film's release, but both Seberg and director Otto Preminger were raked over the coals by critics and audiences alike. (The Harvard Lampoon cited *Saint Joan* as the worst film of the century 1857-1957 and complained that Seberg was "soporific as a saint and insipid as a sinner.") After a start like that, there was nowhere to go but up, or back to Iowa. Seberg chose to make another film with Preminger, *Bonjour Tristesse*. If that movie had been her first, the career of Jean Seberg might have been quite different. As it was, her good work in her second movie still supplied her with a shot at international stardom in the heady early days of the French New Wave. Jean-Luc Godard's

Breathless, written by Francois Truffaut and co-starring Jean-Paul Belmondo, gave Seberg her most fondly remembered role. As an American teen selling the N.Y. *Herald Tribune* on the streets of Paris, she was vivid and affecting, and her ultra-short haircut and off-the-rack wardrobe launched a new look for young girls of the late '50s to emulate. Jean Seberg appeared to be here to stay, but like her sophisticated facade, the public illusion was more persuasive than her private reality. Despite fine performances in dozens of underrated domestic and French movies, Seberg's life and career may well have been doomed from the moment she left her Midwestern home in Marshalltown. In *From the Journals of Jean Seberg,* Mark Rappaport's fictitious approach to her life, a former babysitting charge who grew up around the corner from Seberg tells the story of a sensitive small town girl driven to professional and personal despair. Mary Beth Hurt, then 47, plays the Jean Seberg who might have been, had she overcome the tragedy of her life with Rappaport's blessed sense of irony. The film traces the work of such contemporaries as Jane Fonda and Vanessa Redgrave who achieved greater fame and recognition than Seberg and were better protected emotionally during their days of political activism. The fragile Seberg tried to kill herself annually on the anniversary of her baby daughter's death, after being hounded by the FBI who leaked false rumors that the premature infant had been fathered by a Black Panther. In *From the Journals of Jean Seberg,* Rappaport (who also assembled 1992's *Rock Hudson's Home Movies*) tells an immensely sad story with effective detail and compassionate honesty. ♫♫♫

1995 97m/C Mary Beth Hurt; *D:* Mark Rappaport; *W:* Mark Rappaport; *C:* Mark Daniels. **VHS** *WBF, PPI*

From the Pole to the Equator

Even if avant-garde film isn't your favorite type of movie, we highly recommend what Yervant Gianikian and Angela Ricci Lucchi have done with *From the Pole to the Equator.* These two filmmakers from Milan assembled their film from 35mm. nitrate originals shot in 1910 by early Italian cinematographer Luca Comerio. Comerio traveled with an adventuring baron named Franchetti and captured some extraordinary footage of faraway lands, as well as early films of land and air vehicles. The old movies are in variable condition and are reprinted and hand-tinted by Gianikian and Ricci Lucchi, who add an effective score by California musicians Keith Ullrich and Charles Anderson. We couldn't take our eyes off the screen for the full 96 minutes when we saw it in 1987 at the Pacific Film Archive, and we predict that *From the Pole to the Equator* may have the same effect on those who discover it on a video shelf. ♫♫♫

1987 96m/C *IT GB* **D:** Yervant Gianikian, Angela Ricci Lucchi; **M:** Keith Ullrich, Charles Anderson. *NYR*

Fun

The past and the future are in color in *Fun,* the present is in grim black and white. The protagonists are two very young girls who share confidences and cuddle after spending the most fun day they'll ever have together. What's their idea of fun? Going to malls, hanging out, playing games, ringing doorbells, and yelling at the occupants. Oh, and brutally stabbing to death a sweet little old lady who is kind to them. Why? Counselor Leslie Hope and journalist William R. Moses attempt to find out during the course of this very disturbing character study, based on James Bosley's play. Renee Humphrey and Alicia Witt are remarkable as two troubled teens who manipulate their adult interrogators and resist every effort from those who want to help them understand their crime. Plenty of nightmares here! ♫♫♫

1994 95m/C Alicia Witt, Renee Humphrey, Leslie Hope, William R. Moses, Ania Suli; *D:* Rafael Zelinski; *W:* James Bosley; *C:* Jens Sturup; *M:* Marc Tschantz. Nominations: Independent Spirit Awards '95: Debut Performance (Witt), First Screenplay. **VHS**

"[*Funnybones*] is the third and last of my hometown stories. The first was a little film called *Treacle,* and *Hear My Song* was the second. Although I set *Hear My Song* loosely in a world called Liverpool, it's a Blackpool story. *Funnybones* is set mostly in Blackpool, which, for those who don't know, is about half way up the left hand side, and it's a seaside resort that I was brought up in. It was a place that in the '50s and '60s was a mecca for comedians and everybody played Blackpool. Actually, Jerry Lewis and Dean Martin played Blackpool. Frank Sinatra, Sammy Davis, Jr., Bob Hope, Marlene Dietrich, they all played Blackpool. In fact, if you came to Britain and you were going to do London plus one stop, it invariably was Blackpool. So, on the one hand it's my tribute to my home town and to a certain kind of comedian. 'Funnybones' is a way of describing a certain kind of comedian. You either have or you don't have 'funnybones.' The 'funnybones' comedian is funny. He doesn't tell funny, he is funny. Funny to look at, a funny persona. The 'non-funnybones' comedian tells funny. He would walk on stage with a newspaper and read something topical and get a laugh. Of course he would. But the 'funnybones' comedian, if he walked on stage with that newspaper, he would probably use it to hit someone. You come from a different place.

"What the film is really about, by which I mean what keeps me going while making it (at dawn as you drive to location thinking 'What the hell am I doing this film for, it's killing me?) is really portrayed by the two half-brothers in the film. One played by Oliver Platt and the other played by Lee Evans. They are two totally different types. One is American and the other is English. But far beyond that, Oliver Platt is playing a character who is a comedian with the daunting prospect of trying to be a comedian with Jerry Lewis for his father (he's an icon of comedy), and failing miserably. He bombs horrendously in Las Vegas and then makes a trip to Blackpool, where he spent the first six years of his life, and it's a quest for the perfect comedy material of the physical kind, of the visual slapstick. And also to find out for him why they were taken away very mysteriously when he was six. Why, as he puts it, the sun stopped shining when he was six years old.

"He finds that he has an illegitimate half brother, Jack [Lee Evans]. Now these two half brothers represent, for me, an opposite, a polarity that I think exists in all of us and certainly in me which is on the one hand you have the character of Tommy, played by Oliver Platt, who is educated and moneyed and privileged and analytical and able to exploit and very neurotic. On the other hand you have Jack, who is poor and destitute, without education, and instinctive and dangerous to the point where he actually killed a guy whilst getting his biggest laugh. He's called 'Mad Jack' but it's just that he has a simple mind. In other words, if you hit someone hard and the audience laughs and you hit him harder and the audience laughs more, where do you actually stop? So, it's dangerous to put someone like Jack in that situation. By the end of the film there's a situation where having seen this comedian kill once, you suspect that's what's going to happen again. Because to put him in that situation and feed him so much approval from the audience who are loving him that much, it's too dangerous a thing to do. So those two differences, the personal manager if you like [he says pointing to his head], versus the wild beast [he says pointing to somewhere around the solar plexus] is what I think exists in all of us. The manager and the person who likes to play are endlessly being reconciled in all of us, I think.

"I started writing it [*Funnybones*] seven and a half years ago. Basically, I wrote very freely. I decided to be driven by feelings first. I mean, I like films that provoke feelings first then thought in that order. I think that's a basic criteria for me. I remember I had two little signs on the wall. One was 'Quality Control,' which was out there for the last screenplay as well, which means things like no gag on a whim. There are big laughs in the movie but the audience is usually laughing at something that is there for another reason as well. It's my style, I suppose. The other sign on the wall was 'Think French,' by which I simply meant to myself that I should be very happy to live in an abstract world so the film is more like a dream, I think, than a story. I like films that are tales, not stories, that create a world that actually doesn't really exist. I think people want to go to the cinema to see a world that doesn't exist, although they hope would exist or even that they fear, if they want to be terrified which is fine. So it was very hard. It's multi-stranded in its plotting and it does all pull together at the very end of the film. It's like a kind of modern Dickens, isn't it? It's actually the Dickensian Muppet show."

'95: Debut Performance (Witt), First Screenplay. **VHS** *GRE*

The Funeral

Johnny Tempio (Vincent Gallo) has been murdered, and as Ray (Christopher Walken) and Chez (Christopher Penn) recall their brother's short life at his funeral, they are obsessed with avenging his death. Whodunit? Gangster Gaspare Spoglia (Benicio Del Toro)? Ray's and Chez' wives (Annabella Sciorra and Isabella Rossellini) don't care. They are in love with their husbands and don't want them to die. "When I'm dead, I'm gonna roast in Hell. I believe that," Walken as Ray says as only he can, then he adds fatalistically, "The trick is to get used to it." What the Tempio brothers choose to get used to may not be what viewers want to get used to, but *The Funeral*, set in the '30s and scripted by Nicholas (*King of New York*) St. John (instead of Abel Ferrara himself) is at least a full notch above the mindless symbolic whack-off of *Bad Lieutenant*, with sterling performances by all.

1996 (R) 96m/C Christopher Walken, Benicio Del Toro, Vincent Gallo, Christopher Penn, Isabella Rossellini, Annabella Sciorra, John Ventimiglia, Paul Hipp, Gretchen Mol; *D:* Abel Ferrara; *W:* Nicholas St. John; *C:* Ken Kelsch; *M:* Joe Delia. Nominations: Independent Spirit Awards '97: Best Actor (Penn), Best Cinematography, Best Director (Ferrara), Best Film, Best Screenplay. **VHS** *HMK*

Funny Bones

For us, the jewel of 1995's San Francisco International Film Festival was Peter Chelsom's *Funny Bones*, about which the less said the better. *Funny Bones* really must be seen to be believed and appreciated.

This very black comedy stars young American character actor Oliver Platt and young Britcom newcomer Lee Evans. The film's extremely dark undercurrents aren't just plot driven—they give *Funny Bones* its emotional core. Shot at the legendary comedy factory of Ealing Studios, on location in Las Vegas, and in Blackpool, *Funny Bones* is the ideal blend of Golden Age tradition and Chelsom's cutting edge humor. What are Jerry Lewis, Ruta Lee, Oliver Reed, Leslie Caron, and Harold Nicholas all doing in the same movie? The enormous risks taken in *Funny Bones* wouldn't be nearly as breathtaking without their combined 231 years of razor-sharp timing and onscreen charisma. 🦴🦴🦴

1994 (R) 128m/C Oliver Platt, Lee Evans, Leslie Caron, Jerry Lewis, Oliver Reed, Ian McNeice, Ruta Lee, Richard Griffith, George Carl, Freddie Davies; *D:* Peter Chelsom; *W:* Peter Chelsom, Peter Flannery; *C:* Eduardo Berra; *M:* John Altman. **VHS, LV, Closed Caption** *TOU*

Gal Young 'Un

Winner of the Grand Jury Prize at the Sundance Film Festival in 1981, *Gal Young 'Un* is set during the Prohibition era, in which a rich, middle-aged woman living on her property in the Florida backwoods finds herself courted by a much younger man. She discovers she is being used to help him set up a moonshining business. Unsentimental story of a strong woman, based on a Marjorie Kinnan Rawlings story. Director Victor Nunez won his second Grand Jury Prize at the Sundance Film Festival in 1993 for *Ruby in Paradise,* starring 1994's Independent Spirit Award winning actress Ashley Judd. 🦴🦴🦴

1979 105m/C Dana Preu, David Peck, J. Smith; *D:* Victor Nunez. Sundance Film Festival '81: Grand Jury Prize. **VHS, Beta** *ACA, ICA*

Galileo

A fine supporting cast somewhat compensates for the casting of over-the-top Topol as Galileo. Otherwise, another American Film Theatre production with nothing special to recommend it. (*Galileo* was released theatrically overseas in 1976.) 🦴🦴🦴

1973 145m/C *GB CA* Chaim Topol, Edward Fox, Michael Lonsdale, Richard O'Callaghan, Tom Conti, Mary Larkin, Judy Parfitt, John McEnery, Patrick Magee, Michael Gough, Colin Blakely, Clive Revill, Georgia Brown, Tim Woodward, John Gielgud, Margaret Leighton, Henry Woolf, Ronald Radd, Madeleine Smith; *D:* Joseph Losey; *W:* Joseph Losey, Bertolt Brecht, Barbara Bray; *C:* Michael Reed; *M:* Hanns Eisler. **VHS** *NYR*

The Garden

This is the Melanie Griffith movie very few American audiences have ever seen. At a 1977 press conference during the San Francisco International Film Festival, several catty reviewers asked why SHE had been cast. One of its creators later told me, "Everyone seems to be making fun of us for casting Melanie Griffith in the movie. But she was the best American actress who would take her clothes off that we could get!" Well, the future Oscar nominee IS pretty awful as an ersatz angel. But the real star of the film is Jerusalem, which has never been lovelier, especially with Valery Galperin behind the camera. Victor Nord's interpretation of Yoseff Avissar's whimsical script is deft and there are some good performances here, most notably by Shai K. Ophir and Tuvio Tavi. 🦴🦴

1977 93m/C *IS* Shai K. Ophir, Melanie Griffith, Tuvio Tavi, Tsachi Noi, Shoshanah Duer, Seadia Damar; *D:* Victor Nord; *W:* Yosef Avissar; *C:* Valery Galperin; *M:* Noah Shariff. *NYR*

Gas Food Lodging

This Allison Anders film takes its time showing the lives of waitress Nora (Brooke Adams) and her daughters Trudi (Ione Skye) and Shade (Fairuza Balk). The best thing about the movie is Balk's award-winning performance as a teenager confused by the haphazard life she shares with her

"I would say life is pretty pointless, wouldn't you, without the movies?"

—Johnny Tempio (Vincent Gallo), a gangster with ideas, in *The Funeral.*

151

INDEPENDENT FILM GUIDE

mother and sister. James Brolin makes a classy, lived-in appearance as Shade's dad, John. Aside from that, things seem to lumber along almost as slowly in this one as they would in 1993's *Ruby in Paradise* by Victor Nunez (except *Ruby* is 15 minutes longer). Skye and Donovan Leitch are real-life siblings. Shot on location in Deming, New Mexico. 🦴🦴

1992 (R) 100m/C Brooke Adams, Ione Skye, Fairuza Balk, James Brolin, Rob Knepper, Donovan Leitch, David Lansbury, Jacob Vargas, Chris Mulkey, Tiffany Anders; *D:* Allison Anders; *W:* Allison Anders; *C:* Dean Lent; *M:* J. Mascis, Barry Adamson. Independent Spirit Awards '93: Best Actress (Balk). **VHS, LV, Closed Caption** *COL*

Gaslight

People who pine for the good old days when Hollywood studios had a stranglehold on the worldwide film industry might appreciate how good old MGM made an international hit out of 1944's *Gaslight*. *Gaslight* was originally made in England four years earlier with Diana Wynyard and Anton Walbrook. Since neither Wynyard nor Walbrook were MGM stars, what's a rich powerful studio to do? Bingo! Buy up all the prints, suppress them, and make a big, expensive movie with REAL stars, like Ingrid Bergman and Charles Boyer. We're not knocking Bergman and Boyer. Two of Bergman's Swedish hits had already been re-made in Hollywood: *Intermezzo* with Bergman herself and *A Woman's Face* with Joan Crawford. But this original version, with far more subtle direction and performances, is actually far more terrifying than the best that Hollywood could buy! Only menacing teenager Angela Lansbury, as Hollywood's Nancy, is WAY superior to the original Nancy, Cathleen Cordell. Interestingly, Lansbury's mother, Moyna MacGill, has a small role in the first movie. You can still dig the re-make and deplore MGM's strategy in (nearly) destroying every trace of the existence of this film. *AKA:* Angel Street. 🦴🦴🦴

1940 88m/C *GB* Anton Walbrook, Diana Wynyard, Frank Pettingell, Cathleen Cordell, Robert Newton,

Jimmy Hanley, Minnie Rayner, Mary Hinton, Marie Wright, Jack Barty, Moyna MacGill, Darmora Ballet; *D:* Thorold Dickinson; *W:* A.H. Rawlinson, Bridget Boland; *C:* Bernard Knowles; *M:* Richard Addinsell. **VHS** *FCT*

Genevieve

Genevieve is the perfect movie to watch when you're in the world's worst mood; it will cheer you up in no time. John Gregson and Kenneth More are two antique car buffs obsessed with winning the annual Brighten-to-London run. Dinah Sheridan and Kay Kendall are along for the ride. That's all there is to it, but with that cast and the gifted Henry Cornelius at the helm, *Genevieve* is fondly remembered as the brightest British comedy of the year. Not too many people remember Kay Kendall today, but with her break-through film *Genevieve,* she emerged as the funniest comedienne to hit the silver screen since Carole Lombard. Kendall played a trumpet-playing model with a huge dog named Suzy who's stuck for the weekend with the canine-loathing More. All four leads were charming in the film, but the extremely droll Kendall was the real surprise. William Rose's screenplay and Larry Adler's harmonica score (both Oscar nominees) added to the infectious fun, and the well chosen supporting cast included one-time Sherlock Holmes star Arthur Wontner (1875-1960) and the delightful Joyce Grenfell. Not to mention that splendid title character in three-strip Technicolor! 🦴🦴🦴🦴

1953 86m/C *GB* John Gregson, Dinah Sheridan, Kenneth More, Kay Kendall, Geoffrey Keen, Reginald Beckwith, Arthur Wontner, Joyce Grenfell, Leslie Mitchell, Michael Medwin, Michael Balfour, Edie Martin, Harold Siddons; *D:* Henry Cornelius; *W:* William Rose; *M:* Larry Adler. British Academy Awards '53: Best Film; Golden Globe Awards '55: Best Foreign Film; Nominations: Academy Awards '54: Best Story & Screenplay, Best Original Score. **VHS, Beta** *LCA*

Georgia

Addison DeWitt is alive and well and residing in the offices of *Time* magazine. His name these days is Richard Corliss, but his critical approach is the same, and one of his 1995 critiques is even semi-cobbled from *All About Eve.* Luckily, Richard Corliss was ineligible for 1995's Academy Awards. Unluckily he seemed to believe that he was on some sort of a mission from God to keep Jennifer Jason Leigh from winning an Oscar for her remarkable performance in *Georgia.* Leigh, claimed Corliss, is too "small" to deserve the critical raves she's received ever since *Georgia* was screened at Cannes in the spring of 1995. Such praise was like a "migraine" to Corliss and he insisted that "this racket must cease." Because he said so, of course. Because Leigh is good enough for cable but not for Oscar. Because she's so "very, very bad." Any poor dear who thinks otherwise must be delusional or at least "mistaken" about what constitutes good acting. *Georgia,* an outstanding independent release, was not made for the Addison DeWitts of this planet. Jennifer Jason Leigh is nothing short of electrifying as Sadie Flood, a down-and-out, not particularly talented singer who drinks and drugs up a storm while draining everyone who comes near her. Her far more gifted sister Georgia (beautifully played by Oscar-nominee Mare Winningham) wisely protects herself from Sadie's whirlwind existence, but at a price. Georgia is so self-contained that her life is blessed with every trapping of success but joy. When the sisters are together, their collective loneliness fills up the screen. Films that have attempted to show the lives of musicians at their grittiest always seem to miss several beats when it comes to conveying emotional honesty. Other writers and directors have tried to capture the Sadies and Georgias of the world, but never with such depth and passion. That's why Barbara Turner's skillfully constructed screenplay and Ulu Grosbard's scrupulous direction give the two stars such crucial support. Each and every character in *Georgia* brings a unique voice that supplies strong counterpoint to the hermetically sealed alliance between the sisters. Particularly fine performances are contributed here by Ted Levine and Max Perlich as the men in their lives. And Leigh and Winningham will tear the heart out of any innocent audience member who still has a pulse. Whichever way you look at it (unless you happen to be a latter-day Addison De HALF Witt!), *Georgia* is a tremendous achievement. We've already seen it six times (and counting!). ♪♪♪♪

1995 (R) 117m/C Jennifer Jason Leigh, Mare Winningham, Ted Levine, Max Perlich, John Doe, John C. Reilly, Jimmy Witherspoon; *D:* Ulu Grosbard; *W:* Barbara Turner; *C:* Jan Kiesser. Independent Spirit Awards '96: Best Supporting Actress (Winningham); Montreal World Film Festival '95: Best Actress (Leigh), Best Film; New York Film Critics Awards '95: Best Actress (Leigh); Nominations: Academy Awards '95: Best Supporting Actress (Winningham); Independent Spirit Awards '96: Best Actress (Leigh), Best Director (Grosbard), Best Supporting Actor (Perlich); Screen Actors Guild Award '95: Best Supporting Actress (Winningham). **VHS, LV, Closed Caption** *TOU*

The Ghost Goes West

Robert Donat plays a dual role here as Murdoch and Donald Ghourie. Eugene Pallette is Joe Martin, who wants to buy a Scottish castle and take it home with him to Florida. Jean Parker is Joe's pretty daughter, Peggy. The only thing is the ghost has to stay with the castle, so when Joe and Peggy leave with their new purchase, the ghost goes with them. With Robert Sherwood and Geoffrey Kerr as screenwriters and the great Rene Clair at the helm, *The Ghost Goes West* promised to be very special, and it was. The fine supporting cast adds to the fun and you haven't lived 'til you've seen Eugene Pallette in a kilt! ♪♪♪

1936 90m/B *GB* Robert Donat, Jean Parker, Eugene Pallette, Elsa Lanchester, Ralph Bunker, Patricia Hilliard, Everley Gregg, Mortan Selten, Chili Bouchier, Mark Daly, Herbert Lomas, Elliot Mason, Jack Lambert, Hay Petrie; *D:* Rene Clair; *W:* Robert Sherwood, Geoffrey Kerr; *C:* Harold Rosson. **VHS, Beta** *HBO*

MARE WINNINGHAM
Georgia

Well, the film is called *Georgia,* but not because it focuses on her so much. It really is the story of Sadie, whom Jennifer Jason Leigh plays, and she is—well, Jennifer calls her a failed singer, but I could fight her on that. But anyway, she is someone who has a drug and alcohol problem and is in the shadow of her older, successful sister. She wants desperately to be her sister, so hence the title *Georgia.* And she's hungrily pursuing her sister for validation, for love, and for, I guess, a hundred hungry reasons that only Sadie could personify. And Georgia lives outside of the city, outside of Seattle where they grew up. She lives in the farmhouse that they grew up in, and she has a band, a husband and two children, and a seemingly idyllic life. She's an extremely private person. She needs to be alone. She's the most solitary character I've ever seen portrayed or written about, and there's a part of her that's just unavailable to anyone which she is trying to be true to, to the world, and especially to her sister who cannot live with that. She wants her sister's availability and it's not possible, so Sadie's chasing, Georgia's running, and there are problems whenever they're in the same place at the same time.

"I never saw [Georgia] as guarded so much as private, with the difference being that with the one you're trying to avoid something, and with the other you're trying to let people know this is who you are, and this is what you require. Barbara Turner [the screenwriter and Jennifer Jason Leigh's mother] used to tell me that Georgia just was not of this world. She was someone who was doing time here, and I think her songwriting and her singing are the passionate aspects of her life. The relationship [between Georgia and Sadie] is so complicated because there is something that Sadie has that Georgia will never have: a vigor and a pursuit of life's celebrations, and that I'm sure leads to her problems with alcohol and drugs. But I think Georgia's feeling that that kind of desperation and that kind of hunger, if you're not trying to be someone else, can be very interesting and magnetic. In Sadie's case, I think Georgia feels like she's just on a downward spiral, and she's on a road that's hopeless because she'll never be able to give herself. She's always pursuing someone else, it's someone else's voice she's imitating. It's someone else's words that she's copying and saying, and so trying to pass off that kind of desperation as a voice, as a singing voice, doesn't fly with Georgia. The structure of the piece is so brave because the screenwriter sets you up from the beginning behind Sadie. You immediately—even with all the self-destructive behavior—you gotta love her. She's just such a whirlwind of hope and promise and indestructibility while being self destructive. And you just get so behind that character, and the writer chooses to make Georgia sort of peripheral in a way that is unavailable. But yet through the course of the film, so much of what you're hearing about Georgia is Sadie's projection. As you actually sort of come to know Georgia; of course, it takes much longer to know what sort of pain she's dealing with: the pain of having a person that you love but have absolutely nothing in common with. And also the fact that you don't like the self destructive choices that Sadie's making, and so Georgia's effort to be honest in front of Sadie does make Georgia quite sad, I think, and very, very lonely. Although Georgia's solitary by choice, it's still a very lonely existence.

"The reason you don't see Georgia smile is because you don't see Georgia away from Sadie in the film, and that's another choice. Every time that you see Georgia, Sadie's lurking and/or grabbing, and it is such a struggle for Georgia to remain true to herself with this person there. You don't ever see Sadie sober or straight until the end when she's in rehab. It's a shock to see her straight, and you see the release of the love that Georgia feels. Georgia has a genuine familial smile in the hospital room when she (in all her honesty) has a sort of meaningless exchange with Sadie in which she informs her sister (through Sadie's drug rehabilitation fog) that Sadie's confusing the details of her life like an old person who's trying to put memories together and it's all overlapping. Georgia's sort of informing Sadie, 'No, you don't have the details right,' and for some reason it ends up in this very touching bond exchange between the two of them where they just end up laughing. It's something only siblings could experience, and it just has to do with the ridiculousness of the moment."

MARE WINNINGHAM'S films include *Special Olympics, One Trick Pony, The Thorn Birds, Threshold, Single Bars, Single Women, St. Elmo's Fire, Nobody's Fool, A Winner Never Quits, Made in Heaven, Shy People, God Bless the Child, Miracle Mile, Turner and Hooch, Eye on the Sparrow, Fatal Exposure, Hard Promises, Intruders, Better Off Dead, The War, Wyatt Earp, Letter to My Killer,* and *The Boys Next Door.*

Girl Gang

This stunning film, which appears to violate every single item in the then-current production code, was considered lost for over 40 years. Joanne Arnold is a tall, voluptuous brunette who'll do anything for a fix, and Timothy (*Glen or Glenda?*) Farrell is the sleaziest dope dealer you'll ever see. *Girl Gang* reveals, in graphic detail, exactly how to shoot heroin PLUS how to remove a bullet from a college girl on a kitchen table (she doesn't make it). To join the local dope club, girls must have sex with five guys whether the girls (OR the guys) want to or not; it's a RULE! The acting and everything else about this shocking expose/searing indictment/lousy movie (take your pick) is dreadful, but you may not be able to keep from staring at it, like bugs under a rock. Expected to be available on video soon for Farrell's many loyal fans. **WOOF!**

1954 60m/B Joanne Arnold, Timothy Farrell; **D:** Robert Derteno. *NYR*

Girlfriends

Nobody asked us, but we always thought that Melanie Mayron was among the most appealing actresses of her generation in the days when she created delightful characters like Ginger, Marsha, and Susan in enjoyable flicks like *Harry and Tonto, Car Wash,* and *Girlfriends.* She was healthy, self-possessed, and reassuring, with no actressy mannerisms or ticks. Even though Mayron, then 26, was cast as a young photographer opposite some formidable actors in *Girlfriends* (Bob Balaban, Christopher Guest, Kathryn Walker, Eli Wallach, Amy Wright, Kristopher Tabori,

and the late Viveca Lindfors, Mike Kellin, and Kenneth McMillan), she walked off with the movie. But Warner Bros. in 1978 wasn't Warner Bros. in 1938. There were no Melanie Mayron projects in the works. Instead, there were a long series of prestigious character roles. By 1987, a lean, resculpted Mayron emerged as Melissa Steadman on *thirtysomething* (ABC, 1987-91). She was playing a photographer again, and she won her first Emmy, but she looked sad-eyed and high-strung, perfect for the series, but rather less so for those who remember her natural joie de vivre as Susan Weinblatt. (A hint of that playful quality could be seen when she played a cop named Crystal in 1990's *My Blue Heaven*.) *Girlfriends* was made in the very early days of the A.F.I. grant program, designed to encourage women to make their own films. The $10,000 seed money got the project off and rolling, but did not lead to a directing career for Claudia Weill. (Her two follow-up films included 1980's sprightly, but little seen *It's My Turn* and 1988's *Once a Hero*.) Screenwriter Vicki Polon re-surfaced as a co-scripter on 1993's *Mr. Wonderful*. 🦴🦴🦴

1978 (PG) 87m/C Melanie Mayron, Anita Skinner, Eli Wallach, Christopher Guest, Amy Wright, Viveca Lindfors, Bob Balaban, Kathryn Walker, Kristopher Tabori, Mike Kellin, Kenneth McMillan; **D:** Claudia Weill; **W:** Vicki Polon. Sundance Film Festival '78: Grand Jury Prize. **VHS, Beta** *WAR, FRF*

Girls in Chains

Hey, everybody, it's guilty pleasure time, and for tonight's snack, we are not featuring that bizarre (male) hot dog that leaps into a (female?) bun, but ta-dah!: *Fashion Victims of 1943,* also known as *Girls in Chains.* Talk about having to see a movie to believe how cheap it can really be. Director Edgar G. Ulmer must have been out to set some sort of a record with this one. Arline Judge, real-life veteran of seven well publicized divorces, stars as MISS Helen Martin, who is trying to overhaul the women's prison system. She is handicapped in her sincere reformation efforts by the fact that her brother-in-law is none other than the notorious gangster, Johnny Moon. (In case we have trouble remembering his name, composer Erdody helpfully grafts Louis Lambert's "When Johnny Comes Marching Home" onto his "original" score, again and AGAIN.) And, then of course, there are life-and-death decisions to be made about what hat Helen should wear while breaking into an office to lift incriminating files. Helen chooses a creation with a far-reaching white net accentuated by what look like circles of white felt. Although her choice does not seem to have set off any hat purchase shock-waves among other fashion victims of 1943, Helen likes it enough to wear it in ANOTHER sequence. (And yes, the shifty night watchman does notice her wearing that thing.) When Helen goes to nightclubs (with chandeliers, a juke box, armchairs, and a bartender who is always wiping the same glass), she likes to wear pace-setting print dresses with airplanes on them and styles her hair as if a lawnmower ran through the middle of it. The reason she goes to nightclubs is to be interrupted by an incoherent old drunk who leaks vital, but unintelligible, information. The bad guys decide that this blabbermouth needs to be taught a lesson, so they pick him up at midnight and toss him into some stock footage of Hoover Dam at high noon. He does not die or even stop talking, only winds up in traction at a hospital. The good guys corner the bad guys in a hallway cluttered with 19 or 20 chairs and then there's a nice expressionistic climax on a moonlit rooftop. By the way, the title characters, led by Barbara Pepper, do not wear chains, but most have higher heels than usual for prisoners in Cell Block Z. According to Edger G. Ulmer, this movie made a FORTUNE, which just goes to prove that we do not know how to recognize the unappreciated genius and stylish symbolism that were poured into *Girls in Chains.* 🦴🦴🦴

1943 72m/B Arline Judge, Roger Clark, Robin Raymond, Barbara Pepper, Dorothy Burgess, Clancy

ROSE TROCHE AND GUINEVERE TURNER

Go Fish

Guinevere Turner: "We wrote them [Guinevere Turner as Max and V.S. Brodie as Ely] very much wanting to make very different people from each other, a very unlikely pair. They're both parodies, I think, caricatures, in a way of what I would call a combination of lesbian stereotype and folklore. Max is essentially the gung-ho baby dyke and Ely is essentially shy."

Rose Troche: "Now that I think about it more, I think they present more kinds of subtle personality changes, especially in the movie. I think both characters change to a point where it's very feasible they come together. Max shows her vulnerability early on as well as her very obnoxious nature. I think they are a little bit more complicated than being so stereotypical because they're not, actually, because Ely has that kind of transformation."

Rose Troche: "[In exploring their relationship] we wanted to explore different kinds of geeks."

Guinevere Turner: "We wanted them to be sort of vulnerable, goofy characters."

Rose Troche: "Like they both ARE in their own way. I mean everybody thinks Max is really hip but it's the case with anybody who overdoes their hipness to cover up a vulnerability. Whereas Ely takes a very direct approach to covering up her vulnerability, which is to be completely exposed and kind of not deal with people that much. So they're really not, to me, they're not that different. They're not that different at all. They're kind of dorky.... I think people think that we're trying to make Max hip when we're trying to make her dorky hip. Like she's all doing that home girl thing and

---

Cooper, Sid Melton, Betty Blythe, Peggy Stewart, Francis Ford; **D:** Edgar G. Ulmer; **W:** Albert Beich; **C:** Ira Morgan; **M:** Erdody. **VHS, Beta** *NOS, SNC, DVT*

Girls Town

Nikki (Aunjanue Ellis), one of a group of four friends, kills herself after being raped. Patti (Lili Taylor), Emma (Anna Grace), and Angela (Bruklin Harris) try to come to terms with their loss and mostly wind up acting out (vandalizing the rapist's car, snapping at each other, et cetera).

Although the actors have given themselves sharp dialogue to say, the sequences don't build on each other to increase the narrative's impact. Intriguing directions for character development are suggested and then abandoned. Good acting helps. 🦴🦴

1995 (R) 90m/C Lili Taylor, Anna Grace, Bruklin Harris, Aunjanue Ellis, Guillermo Diaz, John Ventimiglia; **D:** Denise Casano; **W:** Denise Casano, Jim McKay, Lili Taylor, Anna Grace, Bruklin Harris, Aunjanue Ellis; **C:** Russell Fine. Sundance Film Festival '96: Filmmakers Trophy; Nominations: Independent Spirit Awards '97: Best Supporting Actress (Taylor). **VHS** *HMK*

she's white. She's not really doing that in a gross way at all...she's taking on these fashions. She's supposed to be kind of young and kind of dumb, and even that discussion when they come back from the theatre where she just says 'Like, I think we can't just have dissension in the ranks, you know.' It's just like such a basic, almost militant line like thinking about things. She's flailing around, you know, a bit. I think she is looking for a personality to latch on to and kind of wants to be this, kind of politicized dyke and doesn't know what to do with it."

Rose Troche: "I think [the film is getting so much attention] because it is a lesbian film. I don't think that if this were a heterosexual film with the same subject matter it would be getting this much attention. This whole wondering if it is going to be crossover or not, that would be OK, but that's not so much the concern or the genesis of the project, even."

Guinevere Turner: "On the other hand, I think one of the main reasons that the Samuel Goldwyn Company bought it is because they thought it had the potential to be a crossover film, and also because they know that the lesbian audience will flock, as they have to other lesbian films."

Rose Troche: "I feel like I want to be respected as a filmmaker, and in order to be respected as a filmmaker it becomes very difficult to push aside the label of 'lesbian' because people see you as that first and then they completely kind of, they almost kind of write you off on that level. I mean I put a lot of work into *Go Fish*. I kind of want to be respected for that: for a certain amount of ingenuity in terms of making something out of nothing. So it is problematic. It is a very problematic thing, because I can't separate that from all the identities: I am a lesbian. I am a woman. I am Puerto Rican. It's all these things that are my identity. It's like what surfaces and in this case it's a film. It's my first film, so I want to be a filmmaker."

Go Fish

Go Fish is a bit too self-consciously arty for its own good. We hope that the rules and regulations for P.C. lesbians are meant as satire, not as a code of conduct. It looks as though *Go Fish* were a fun movie to make, but it is less fun to listen to the copious self-analysis that accompanies each move that Max (Guinevere Turner) makes towards Ely (V.S. Brodie). *Maedchen in Uniform* and *These Three* are better acted, *Fried Green Tomatoes* and *The Incredibly True Adventure of Two Girls in Love* are livelier, *Nadja* and *French Twist* are funnier, *Daughters of Darkness* and *Bound* have better stories AND.... Okay, we confess, it was those damn toenails! Watching someone you barely know do any of the following on Date One (paring toenails, belching after chug-a-lugging beer, or asking you to slide egg albumen down each other's throats a la *Tampopo*) is not our idea of Nirvana. So happy that Max and Ely found each other! ♪♪♪

1994 (R) 87m/B Guinevere Turner, V.S. Brodie, T. Wendy McMillan, Anastasia Sharp, Migdalia Melendez; **D:** Rose Troche; **W:** Guinevere Turner, Rose Troche; **C:** Ann T. Rossetti; **M:** Brendan Dolan, Jennifer Sharpe. Nominations: Independent Spirit Awards '95: Best Supporting Actress (Brodie). **VHS** *HMK, FCT*

Golden Gate

Okay, everybody, let's play movie producer! Here's the story: first, we need Matt Dillon in the lead, because at the age of 30, he can convincingly age from 22 to 38 without ever changing his suit or hair. Dillon starts out as eager beaver FBI agent Kevin Walker, who just wants to get laid and make a name for himself in the Bureau. So he tells this girl he wants to lay (Teri Polo as Cynthia) that justice means more to him than the law, and he deliberately frames a Chinese laundry worker for being part of a Communist conspiracy. Cynthia walks out on fledgling agent Walker. The Chinese laundry worker spends the years 1952 through 1962 in prison, during which time his motherless little girl grows up to be Joan Chen, 33, as Marilyn Song. Ordered by the FBI to continue surveillance on her newly released father, Walker stalks him into an early grave, courtesy of a suicide leap from the Golden Gate Bridge. Then, because Walker wants to lay Song, he tells her nice things about her father that he claims he learned as a public defender. They make out next to the Golden Gate Bridge where the proud agent can't help bragging about the original news coverage of her father's conviction. Sure enough, Song finds the original front page picture of Walker framing her father and splits. Six years later, Agent Walker is ordered by the FBI to begin surveillance on Song, now an instructor at the University of California at Berkeley. Since Walker framed her father for being part of a Communist conspiracy, why not frame Song too, complete with the help of a University official? But this creep we've been stuck with for 95 minutes, who's never shown even a sliver of a conscience, suddenly has a change of heart in the final reel. So: there will be a karmic finale for FBI Agent Kevin Walker at the Golden Gate Bridge and a happy ending for Marilyn Song, so she can narrate the movie. PLUS: they can even say these lines to each other, to be excerpted in the coming attractions trailer and ALL the posters: "Some loves are impossible." "But they are loves just the same." What do you think? Great, huh? And producer Michael Brandman did think that David Henry Hwang's idea was great, just great: "When a playwright as uniquely talented as David has an idea he wants to pursue, I am smart enough simply to say yes." So now you know. The spirit of self-styled movie mogul Howard Hughes, who ran RKO into the ground with Red Menace flicks like *I Married a Communist,* is alive and well in 1994. We can't all be movie producers, but at least we can say some movies are stinkers. But they are made just the same. **WOOF!**

1993 (R) 95m/C Matt Dillon, Joan Chen, Bruno Kirby, Teri Polo, Tzi Ma, Stan Egi, Peter Murnik, Jack Shearer, George Giudall; **D:** John Madden; **W:** David Henry Hwang; **C:** Bobby Bukowski; **M:** Elliot Goldenthal. **VHS, LV, Closed Caption** *TOU*

A Good Man in Africa

A Good Man in Africa is an odd hybrid of a film. For much of its running time, you may find yourself giggling at the sheer silliness of the situations its protagonist gets himself into, but the heart of the film seems to have been given short shrift. What's more, the whole thing ends on a flat, abrupt, and entirely unsatisfying note. The cast is as uneven as William Boyd's script. Colin Friels at 40 is a bit long in the tooth to be playing junior diplomat Morgan Leafy, a character whose approach to life is essentially adolescent: any 15-year-old kid of your acquaintance is likely to be more street savvy. (Friels' natural comedic gifts help somewhat.) John Lithgow, only nine years older than

Friels, rather overdoes the aging British diplomat yearning for a knighthood and a cushy berth. By trying to get every detail just right, Lithgow loses the essence of his character. (Watch the fine actress playing the small role of a visiting Duchess to see how an understated Brit ought to be played.) Sadder still is Dame Diana Rigg as Lithgow's frustrated wife, badly photographed, unflatteringly garbed, with god-awful dialogue to deliver. At one point, her character dashes into the night with Leafy, dodging bullets, racing through fields, ducking under fences. The brief interlude is evocative of the heady days when Mrs. Emma Peel was the classiest female sleuth on the planet, but it all ends with a thud when Rigg is given more wretched lines to say and then dismissed with Leafy's voiceover. Louis Gossett, Jr., and Joanne Whalley are two halves of a match made in heaven: he's a crooked political leader, she supplies sexual favors in exchange for favors in the real world. And then there is the incorruptible title character, Dr. Alex Murray, played to cool perfection by Sean Connery. Like Rigg, Connery is given a chance to recreate a moment from another time: playing a golf game that isn't really a golf game. His opponent may not be in the same league as Auric Goldfinger, but in his own blundering way, Leafy is more of a threat. The two meet again and again, with Connery savoring all of the film's best lines and stealing every scene. Check out his last moment in the film; only Barbara Stanwyck has ever managed to achieve anything like it with such riveting subtlety. It's such a great moment, in fact, that you wonder why anyone would dare to tack on the inadequate sequence that follows it. Reportedly, *A Good Man in Africa* was re-edited after an earlier version mystified audiences, so we can expect Bruce Beresford to come up with the inevitable "director's cut." 🎷🎷

1994 (R) 95m/C Colin Friels, Sean Connery, Louis Gossett Jr., John Lithgow, Joanne Whalley, Diana Rigg; **D:** Bruce Beresford; **W:** William Boyd; **C:** Andrzej Bartkowiak. **VHS** *USH*

The Good Soldier

Since this is the only filmed version of Ford Madox Ford's classic novel, it deserves a video release. Originally made for Granada television, it was nominated for an international Emmy and featured on-target performances by the late Jeremy Brett in the title role, the late Susan Fleetwood as his long-suffering wife Leonora Ashburnham, and Robin Ellis and Vickery Turner as dense John and despicable Florence Dowell. The novel was light years ahead of its time in tone and structure, and director Kevin Billington took extraordinary pains to preserve both its dark humor and its bitter irony. Acting throughout is first rate, and Elizabeth Garvie is especially affecting as Nancy Rufford. John Ratzenberger, then a British resident, makes a surprise cameo appearance, not long before his tenure on *Cheers.* Lushly filmed on location at Bad Nauheim, Marburg, and Wiesbaden, as well as Holker Hall, Cambria; Croxteth Hall, Liverpool; Stanway House, Gloucestershire; and Chetham's Library, Manchester. 🎷🎷🎷

1981 113m/C *GB* Robin Ellis, Vickery Turner, Jeremy Brett, Susan Fleetwood, Elizabeth Garvie, Pauline Moran, John Ratzenberger, Geoffrey Chater, Roger Hammond, John Grillo, Alan Downer, Waldemar Ruhl, Kenneth Midwood, William Merrow; **D:** Kevin Billington. *NYR*

The Good Wife

Once upon a time, there was a type of movie called a woman's picture, AKA a four-handkerchief weeper. These films were invariably written and directed by men, the plots usually involved the heroine having to choose between security and sex, and there were always strong undercurrents of moral disapproval, even when they were charged with considerable sympathy. Today the woman's picture has been inherited by a new breed of director, no longer restrained by an obsolete production code. In 1986, Ken Cameron made *The Good Wife* with Rachel Ward, Bryan Brown, and Sam Neill, working from an original screenplay by Peter Kenna. If the film is remembered at all today, it is largely because of the excellent performances by the three leading players, but it is also of interest for its mid-1980s perspective on the downward spiral of sexual addiction. Ward is the title character, living in rural Australia with her husband and his younger brother. The kindest way to describe the bedside manner of the two men is erotically challenged. Their brawls with each other last far longer than their encounters with Ward's character. Although she gets nothing that could remotely be described as a kick from either brother, she remains a dutiful companion to them both until the dapper stranger played by Neill arrives on the scene. When he makes a humiliating and perfunctory pass at her, she rebuffs him instinctively, even though it is clear that she is interested in him. He starts his new job at a local bar and she returns to her familiar work routines, but with a difference. When it is clear that the stylish bartender is an unabashed philanderer, she begins to stalk him. He has moved on to fresh prey, but her obsession has become impersonal and all-encompassing; she applies lipstick, buys a new dress, and hangs out at the bar, drinking brandy after brandy just so she can stare at him and give him endless opportunities to reject her in front of the entire town. She leaves her home and moves into a room across the street so she can watch him seduce another man's wife, hoping for some signal that will make sense of her self-inflicted torture. Screenwriter Kenna has a good grasp of the psychological make-up of his characters and their eloquent self-awareness is well accompanied by Cameron Allan's persistent neurotic score. Ward and the men eventually work themselves into the sort of frenzy for which there can be no satisfactory conclusion. For most of *The Good Wife*'s running time of 97 min-

utes, however, director Cameron does manage to reveal a bit of the mystery behind his title character's longing to feel something, anything, in her own lifetime, even if it's unrelieved despair from a cold-blooded stranger. *AKA:* The Umbrella Woman. ♫♫♫

1986 (R) 97m/C *AU* Rachel Ward, Bryan Brown, Sam Neill, Steven Vidler, Bruce Barry, Jennifer Claire; *D:* Ken Cameron; *W:* Peter Kenna; *M:* Cameron Allan. **VHS, Beta, LV** *BAR, IME*

Grace of My Heart

I spent a dozen hours of my life in 1996 watching *The Beatles Anthology.* I don't know how much more thorough an in-house project could have been. It had every scrap of footage, with massive commentary by the group, their producer, their press officer, and their tour manager. Yet I found myself recalling, with increasing fondness, the devastating and very funny 70-minute satire *All You Need Is Cash,* made by Eric Idle and Neil Innes in 1978. Irreverent fiction sometimes does it better than the most scrupulously produced documentary. Allison Anders' *Grace of My Heart* pays tribute to the female songwriters of the '60s who slogged their youth away in tiny offices creating words and music for big stars to turn into hits. The two factors we most enjoyed about the film just as easily turn others off. Illeana Douglas, to us, is one of the great undiscovered treasures in movies today. In films like *Cape Fear, Grief, Search and Destroy,* and *To Die For,* Douglas has consistently turned in performances evocative of 1940s "B" queens, but with a daffy, vulnerable twist all her own. Illeana Douglas aficionados won't be able to get enough of her in *Grace of My Heart,* but if she ain't your type, this movie won't be either, since she's in virtually every sequence. And if you're sick to death of the 1960s, see something else! Unfortunately, we attended a screening with a group of bickering critics who had trouble with the star, the subject, or both,

AND they were disappointed by the song-writer's romantic choices. They also complained because the soundtrack was dubbed by vocalists. Hey, we're talking Allison Anders here, not some megabuck studio with a demographic survey team. Anders' script and direction are terrific, filled with realistic observations and deft touches missing in male-oriented rock films like the otherwise excellent *Stardust.* John Turturro is exceptional as the no-nonsense producer, Bridget Fonda contributes a nice bit as a gay teen idol (her dad Peter was cut out of the film as Guru Dave, although his voice remains on the soundtrack), and Matt Dillon as a destructive genius sounds eerily like Dennis Hopper. *Grace of My Heart* is a charmingly gritty look at a grittily charming character. Regardless of what you may read about this one in print, give *Grace of My Heart* a chance. Recommended for further research on video: *Girl Groups,* crammed with colorful if not always accurate recollections as well as vintage clips of some terrific performances of that era. ✐✐✐

1996 (R) 116m/C Illeana Douglas, John Turturro, Matt Dillon, Eric Stoltz, Bruce Davison, Patsy Kensit, Bridget Fonda, Jennifer Leigh Warren, Chris Isaak; ***D:*** Allison Anders; ***W:*** Allison Anders; ***C:*** Jean-Yves Escoffier; ***M:*** Larry Klein; ***V:*** Peter Fonda. **VHS, LV, Closed Caption** *USH*

Grand Isle

The opening night selection for 1991's On Screen: A Celebration of Women in Film Festival was *Grand Isle,* based on Kate Chopin's 1899 novel *The Awakening.* It's the story of a young mother married to a jerk who pines for another jerk who teaches her how to swim but who actually sleeps with a third jerk. She attempts art work in the nude, burns all her paintings, and drowns herself after her swimming teacher walks out on her twice. *The Awakening,* along with *Mill on the Floss* and *Wuthering Heights,* is required reading in feminist literature classes, especially if you subscribe to the theory that a woman's entire range of choices at the

turn of the century consisted of three jerks or death. But heck, even Queen Victoria's granddaughter (Princess Marie Louise, 1872-1956) obtained a divorce in 1900, with grandma's blessing and consent and if she didn't walk into the sea afterwards, the times couldn't have been all that repressive! The ideal director for this sort of delicate material would have been someone like Joan Micklin Silver, who has enormous skill at capturing the look, feel, and sensibility of other eras (*Hester Street, Bernice Bobs Her Hair*) without ever caricaturizing them. But instead, actress/producer Kelly McGillis chose Mary (*Siesta, Pet Sematary 1-2*) Lambert whose visions are invariably hermetically sealed and pretentious. If you can accept the fact that any of the shadowy guys in this story are capable of repressing a strapping creature like McGillis, you may like *Grand Isle,* which wound up on T.N.T. a year after its premiere. (Actually, the underused Glenne Headly, who also appears in the film, would have been a far better casting choice in the lead.) ✐✐

1991 94m/C Kelly McGillis, Adrian Pasdar, Julian Sands, Jon DeVries, Glenne Headly, Anthony De Sando, Ellen Burstyn; ***D:*** Mary Lambert; ***W:*** Hesper Anderson. **VHS, LV, Closed Caption** *TTC*

Great Expectations

For Sir David Lean's 1946 film of Charles Dickens' *Great Expectations,* John Mills and Valerie Hobson were cast as Pip and Estella, and a one-time advertising copywriter named Alec Guinness, then 32, was cast in the pivotal role of Herbert Pocket. It was the first of seven films Guinness would make with Lean over the next 38 years. *Great Expectations* and Lean received Best Picture and Best Director Oscar nominations, and the film won two Academy Awards for Guy Green's cinematography and Wilfred Shingleton's art direction. It is perhaps the best of the Dickensian movies, and it certainly etched some indelible impressions on its audi-

ences: Martita Hunt's Miss Havisham chained to her memories and her dreams of revenge, Jean Simmons' haughty young Estella at the start of a gradual slide into near-madness, and the eerie opening graveyard scene between the boy Pip (Anthony Wager) and the convict Magwitch (Finlay Currie). The mid-Victorian era is captured with precision, as well as the brooding sadness that flavors much of the original novel. 🦴🦴🦴🦴

1946 118m/B *GB* John Mills, Valerie Hobson, Anthony Wager, Alec Guinness, Finlay Currie, Jean Simmons, Bernard Miles, Francis L. Sullivan, Martita Hunt, Freda Jackson, Torin Thatcher, Hay Petrie, Eileen Erskine, George "Gabby" Hayes, Everley Gregg, O.B. Clarence; *D:* David Lean; *W:* David Lean, Ronald Neame; *C:* Guy Green. Academy Awards '47: Best Art Direction/Set Decoration (B & W), Best Black and White Cinematography; National Board of Review Awards '47: 10 Best Films of the Year; Nominations: Academy Awards '47: Best Director (Lean), Best Picture, Best Screenplay. **VHS, Beta, LV** *PAR, LCA, HMV*

Grief

Mark (Craig Chester) is a writer on the syndicated daytime TV show *The Love Judge*. Still numb from his lover's death from AIDS the previous year, Mark begins to take an interest in fellow writer Bill (Alexis Arquette), while writer Paula (Lucy Gutteridge) desires to become the show's new producer and secretary Leslie (Illeana Douglas) wants to take her place as the new writer. Present producer Jo (Jackie Beat) tries to keep her office family in line while sorting out her personal life. Writer/director Richard Glatzer wrote *Divorce Court* scripts for five years, so you might think that his own screenplay would have a bit more bite. It does, but only during Illeana Douglas' sequences. 🦴🦴

1994 86m/C Craig Chester, Alexis Arquette, Lucy Gutteridge, Illeana Douglas, Jackie Beat, Carlton

Wilborn; **D:** Richard Glatzer; **W:** Richard Glatzer. **VHS** *ACA, SHV*

The Grifters

Jim Thompson's tightly written novels grab you by the throat and never let go until you finish reading them. *The Grifters* supplies movie audiences with an equivalent cinematic wallop. Ironically, it took a British director, Stephen Frears, to do full justice to Thompson, and *The Grifters* is arguably the finest film noir to emerge in recent years. *The Grifters* examines con artists in extreme close-up. For most of the narrative, Frears uses a straightforward matter-of-fact approach to tell a fairly bizarre, always chilling tale. In *The Grifters,* Anjelica Huston plays the sort of mother seldom seen on screen. As Lilly, her life has been one con after another, with no respite in sight. She is not devoid of feelings, she has simply learned that feelings are easily expendable in her line of work. Throughout the film, we see how other con artists retire after brutal experiences, which merely sideline Lilly for a moment or two. In contrast, her son Roy (John Cusack) doesn't have the stomach to be a con artist. His timing is off. His recovery time is slow. Worst of all, Roy lacks Lilly's sharp knack for reading people, especially a fellow grifter named Myra (Annette Bening). Cusack does his best job to date here and the usually elegant Bening is so grimy as Myra that she is able to achieve the effects of aromarama without the help of scratch and sniff cards. Veteran character actors Pat Hingle and Henry Jones also contribute to the film's pungent atmosphere. But it is Anjelica Huston's film all the way. Remember the final sequence in *Double Indemnity* when Barbara Stanwyck lies to Fred MacMurray for the umpteenth time and nearly gets away with it? Screen moments like this defy dissection and analysis, and Anjelica Huston has so many of them in *The Grifters*: the way she can take in stride a cigarette being ground onto her palm; the way she can work scams on everyone, even her own kid, without batting an eye. There was one point in the film when we thought she was going to bite the dust for sure and all we could think was, "We don't care what sort of a monster she is. If she dies, this movie is over!" And then there is the film's startling conclusion, which will knock you for a loop even if you've read the book. In 1969 at age 17, Anjelica was regarded as one of the world's worst actresses when she made her movie debut in *A Walk with Love and Death,* directed by father John. Over the years, she has emerged as a wise and charismatic presence onscreen and her delicious portrayal in *Prizzi's Honor* was clearly just a warm-up for the work we will hopefully see her do in the future. In the meanwhile, Anjelica Huston's work in *The Grifters* simply has to rank among the all-time great noir performances ever. ✧✧✧✧

1990 (R) 114m/C Anjelica Huston, John Cusack, Annette Bening, Pat Hingle, J.T. Walsh, Charles Napier, Henry Jones, Gaillard Sartain; **D:** Stephen Frears; **W:** Donald E. Westlake; **M:** Elmer Bernstein. Independent Spirit Awards '91: Best Actress (Huston), Best Film; Los Angeles Film Critics Association Awards '90: Best Actress (Huston); National Society of Film Critics Awards '90: Best Actress (Huston), Best Supporting Actress (Bening); Nominations: Academy Awards '90: Best Actress (Huston), Best Adapted Screenplay, Best Director (Frears), Best Supporting Actress (Bening). **VHS, Beta, LV, Closed Caption** *USH, HBO, FCT*

Grim Prairie Tales

Grim Prairie Tales is director/screenwriter Wayne Coe's first movie and his heart, if not his maturity as an artist, is definitely in the right place. Brad Dourif plays the sort of innocent who would have provided fodder for a monster in a different sort of movie. As it is, James Earl Jones comes barreling into his camp with a dead body in tow. Although Jones is armed with a full arsenal of death-dealing weapons, he proposes instead that he and Brad tell each other stories next to the campfire all night long. Only in the movies! The stories have the raw and unfinished feel of promising

"He's so crooked he could eat soup with a corkscrew."

——Myra (Annette Bening) about her old partner Cole (J.T. Walsh) in *The Grifters.*

165

INDEPENDENT FILM GUIDE

"We go
together
...like
guns and
ammuni-
tion."

—Annie Starr
(Peggy Cummins)
sweettalks her
beau, Bart Tare
(John Dall), in
Gun Crazy.

first drafts, but who knows what tales emerged from 19th century travelers when they didn't have pesky movie reviewers to evaluate their yarns? Coe's artistic, political, and sexual sensibilities belong strictly in the 20th century, however. For one sequence, he even thought it would be neat if the character had an animated nightmare. Not only is the animation poor, but the context is all wrong. Occasionally, Coe stumbles onto chilling home truths. His tale of a good family man who also happens to be a lyncher is well told from the perspective of the man's horrified daughter and deeply troubled wife. We also liked the dark little story about a misplaced act of chivalry resulting in an unexplained but definitely weird sexual encounter. Except for Dourif and Jones and the little girl who plays the lyncher's daughter, the casting could have been better, although Marc McClure, William Atherton, and Lisa Eichhorn fare the best. 🦴🦴

1989 (R) 90m/C Brad Dourif, James Earl Jones, Marc McClure, William Atherton, Scott Paulin, Lisa Eichhorn; **D:** Wayne Coe; **W:** Wayne Coe; **C:** Janusz Kaminski. **VHS, LV** *ACA, FCT*

Gun Crazy

Peggy Cummins IS Annie Laurie Starr in this film noir classic! Three years after her ignominious firing from Otto Preminger's *Forever Amber* (reportedly because she looked like a little girl playing dress-up in period costumes), Cummins showed that she could be every bit as sexy as her replacement, Linda Darnell, in a blonde wig. In this beautifully directed saga by Joseph H. Lewis, Starr is a sideshow attraction in a carnival, sleeping with her yucky boss Packett (Berry Kroeger), and impressing small town crowds with her shooting expertise. Then Bart Tare (John Dall) walks by with a couple of his friends. Bart's had an interesting history with guns. As a child (Russ Tamblyn), he was obsessed with them—not with killing, just with guns, and was sent to reform school by Judge Willougby (Morris Carnovsky).

Bart quickly impresses Annie with HIS shooting expertise, and they fall into instant lust, sort of a menage a trois, really—Annie, Bart, and guns. Packett hires Bart for the act and he tours with the carnival, until he and Annie get married. Then a jealous Packett fires them both, and they lose their legitimate arena for expressing their passion with guns. It isn't really poverty that leads them to the next step, but Annie's desire to use a gun again. Bart resists her suggestion that they become bank robbers and tries to leave, but the bond between them is too strong and their fate is sealed. There is a wonderful sequence as they approach the bank, shot from the back seat of the car, with all-natural lighting. It just looks so real, and the acting by Cummins and Dall is so artless that for a moment we forget we're watching a movie with actors—it's like we intruded on an actual hold-up. If *Gun Crazy* were re-released today, it would bat most neo noir entries out of the ball park. Independently produced by the King brothers, Frank and Maurice, who also made 1945's *Dillinger. Gun Crazy* is based on the *Saturday Evening Post* story by MacKinlay Kantor. Millard Kaufman fronted for blacklisted screenwriter Dalton Trumbo, who was the most prolific of the Hollywood Ten: he won Oscars for *Roman Holiday* (using a front) and *The Brave One* (with a pseudonym) while still on the blacklist. Lewis' other excellent noir films include *My Name Is Julia Ross, So Dark the Night, Undercover Man, A Lady Without Passport,* and *The Big Combo.* **AKA:** Deadly Is the Female. 🦴🦴🦴🦴

1949 87m/B Peggy Cummins, John Dall, Berry Kroeger, Morris Carnovsky, Anabel Shaw, Nedrick Young, Trevor Bardette, Russ Tamblyn, Harry Lewis, Mickey Little, Paul Frison, Dave Bair, Stanley Prager, Virginia Farmer, Anne O'Neal, Frances Irwin, Don Beddoe, Robert Osterloh, Shimen Ruskin, Harry Hayden; **D:** Joseph H. Lewis; **W:** Dalton Trumbo; **C:** Russell Harlan; **M:** Victor Young. **VHS** *FOX, FCT*

Guncrazy

Drew Barrymore and James LeGros star in *Guncrazy,* a film that both exploits Barrymore's checkered off-screen image and protects her status as a 17-year-old minor. The result is a weak, if violent, story which backs away from every sexual issue it raises. Barrymore doesn't really have sufficient depth as an actress yet to play a junior league Bonnie Parker, although Ione Skye, another badly neglected member of the cast, could have tackled the leading role with ease and honors. Skip this one and rent Joseph H. Lewis' classic 1949 film noir *Gun Crazy* instead. 🦴

1992 (R) 97m/C Drew Barrymore, James LeGros, Billy Drago, Rodney Harvey, Ione Skye, Joe Dallesandro, Michael Ironside; **D:** Tamra Davis; **W:** Matthew Bright. **VHS, Beta, LV, Closed Caption** *ACA, PMS*

Hackers

In the beginning, hackers were, well, sort of geeky. They could be supporting characters in the movies, the experts that the cool heroes went to see when they needed help. But they rarely left their computer terminals. Iain (*Backbeat*) Softley's movie, *Hackers,* is the latest cinematic effort to lionize hackers and turn them into the cool heroes. The protagonist hacker is state-of-the-art cute. His female nemesis (and eventual girlfriend) wears brown eyeshadow and black lipstick. Virtually all of their fellow hackers are whizzes on skateboards, a phenomenon that rarely occurs in real life. And as for the computer graphics, there's no such thing as a dull or undecorated screen. None of that "Do you really want to do this?" crap, just bold, colorful images, seamlessly edited into the dazzling, fast-paced lives that hackers lead. (And if you swallow the premise, we can make you a sensational deal on the Golden Gate Bridge.) The bad guys are Fisher Stevens (overacting as usual) and Lorraine Bracco (totally wasted). The main hacker's mother is Alberta Watson, who also played the incestuous mom in *Spanking the Monkey.* (In some sequences, she appears to be wearing the same bathrobe, an inside joke?) All the hackers seem to have "hot new star" stamped on their foreheads. They talk about megabytes and RAM as if they were discussing their favorite sexual positions. (True to hacker mythology, though, there isn't any real sex, only fantasies.) Everyone's an eyelash too old to be a pin-up in teen magazines Like *All Stars* or *Tiger Beat.* And the "hackers of the world unite" anthem is just dumb. The producers hope that the pulsing soundtrack, the fashions, and the erotically charged atmosphere will lure kiddies into theatres/video outlets in droves. (Jonny Lee Miller made a better career move by playing third lead in *Trainspotting* than by starring in this one.) 🦴🦴

1995 (PG-13) 105m/C Jonny Lee Miller, Angelina Jolie, Fisher Stevens, Lorraine Bracco, Jesse Bradford, Wendell Pierce, Alberta Watson, Laurence Mason, Renoly Santiago, Matthew Lillard, Penn Jillette; **D:** Iain Softley; **W:** Rafael Moreu; **C:** Andrzej Sekula; **M:** Simon Boswell. **VHS, LV, Closed Caption** *MGM*

Hand in Hand

This touching story of the friendship between a Roman Catholic boy (Philip Needs as Michael O'Malley) and a Jewish girl (Loretta Parry as Rachel Mathias) could easily have been heavy handed with the wrong director. Philip Leacock, who guided the very young Vincent Winter and Jon Whiteley to Academy Awards in 1953's *The Little Kidnappers,* was clearly the right guy for the job. Michael and Rachel get along just fine until he is teased about the friendship by his schoolmates, who tell him that Jesus Christ was killed by the Jewish people. Rachel is happily preparing an after school feast for him when he repeats what his friends told him. "We never killed anyone!" she cries and runs off. But the kids miss each other, and eventually run away together to speak to the Queen. They don't get to meet her, but they do have a chat with Lady Caroline (Sybil Thorndike) at one of the Queen's homes, and eventually, their respective parents enlist Father Timothy and a Cantor to help the kids with their dilemma. The best thing about *Hand in Hand* is the won-

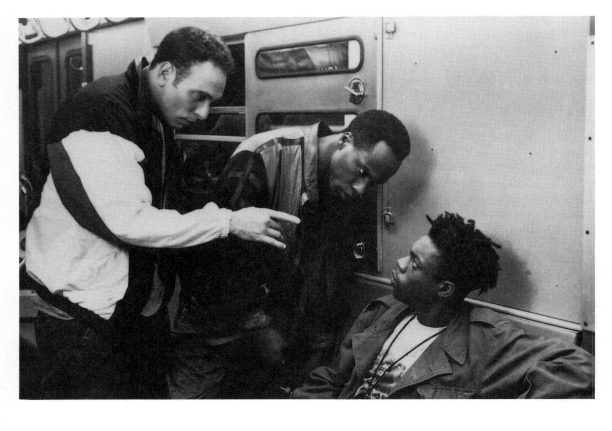

derful rapport between Needs and Parry. Their friendship is understated and most believable. (Parry was later signed by Walt Disney to appear in 1963's *The Horse Without a Head,* co-starring Vincent Winter.) ♫♫♫

1960 78m/B *GB* John Gregson, Sybil Thorndike, Finlay Currie, Loretta Parry, Philip Needs, Miriam Karlin, Derek Sydney, Kathleen Byron; *D:* Philip Leacock; *W:* Leopold Atlas, Diana Morgan, Sidney Harmon. *NYR*

A Handful of Dust

Many feel the reason for the transatlantic success of *Dynasty* and *Brideshead Revisited* is that nothing delights Britishers and Americans more than watching their overseas cousins commit upper-class suicide. It makes sense, especially when you realize that hours and hours devoted to pover-ty-stricken characters in unphotogenic surroundings seldom pack the same visual wallop. Nope, if we're going to watch people run themselves into the ground, let's also have the startling insight that all those palaces and spectacular estates can't possibly save them from themselves. As *Brideshead Revisited* showed, Evelyn Waugh was passionately in love with the exclusive aristocratic world he satirized in so many of his books. *A Handful of Dust,* based on Waugh's 1934 novel, provides more of the same rich and foolish twits, gorgeous and amoral wives, foolish pastimes that destroy the family heir, and the usual obligatory splendor as a backdrop. James Wilby, 30, plays Lord Tony Last whose bride, Lady Brenda (Kristin Scott Thomas, 28), develops a sudden craving to take an economics class, and we all know what THAT means. Faster than you can say "satin sheets," Brenda is shown rolling in bed with a brainless, disloyal rotter named (of course) Beaver. The affair (of course) rocks the very foundations of what a proper upper-class marriage should be, but Brenda doesn't have to pay too high a price for her bad manners. For reasons that make very little sense, though, poor Tony winds up stuck in a Brazilian jungle, forced to read Dickens novels to a loonie played by Sir Alec Guinness. It takes about two hours to plow through this well acted London Weekend Television production, directed by Charles Sturridge, who also helmed *Brideshead Revisited.* There's one funny sequence when Lord Tony, eager to give the undeserving Lady Brenda grounds for divorce, dutifully trots off to a seaside hotel to stage his adultery with a woman who can't find anyone to take care of her little girl. Private detective John Junkin, irritated when all he sees is Lord Tony babysitting the kid on the pier and in the hotel dining room, patiently explains that, no, this isn't the way the game is played. The rest of the story is supposed to be hilarious too, and for those who believe that the rich are inherently cursed, it probably is, so if you enjoy this sort of fare, *A Handful of Dust* just may be your movie! 🦴🦴🦴

1988 (PG) 114m/C *GB* James Wilby, Kristin Scott Thomas, Rupert Graves, Alec Guinness, Anjelica Huston, Judi Dench, Cathryn Harrison, Pip Torrens, John Junkin; ***D:*** Charles Sturridge; ***W:*** Charles Sturridge, Tim Sullivan, Derek Granger; ***M:*** George Fenton. British Academy Awards '88: Best Supporting Actress (Dench); Nominations: Academy Awards '88: Best Costume Design. **VHS, Beta** *COL, TVC*

The Hands of Orlac

When *The Hands of Orlac* was first shown in Vienna, grown women fainted and their male companions complained to the theatre manager. The manager asked Conrad Veidt if he would say something to the crowd to circumvent a riot. Reportedly, Veidt so moved the audience that, not only did he receive an ovation, but the movie went on to enjoy spectacular success (and

with good reason). Is this silent movie better than 1935's *Mad Love* starring Peter Lorre and 1960's *The Hands of Orlac* with Mel Ferrer? Unquestionably! Veidt (1893-1943) was one of the most expressive actors of the silent screen. Moviegoers who know him only as *Caligari*'s Cesare the somnambulist or as Jaffar in *The Thief of Bagdad* or as *Casablanca*'s Major Strasser don't really know Conrad Veidt. As pianist Paul Orlac, he believes that his hands (crushed in an accident) have been replaced with those of a murderer. He believes the murderer to be the sinister-looking gent played by Fritz Kortner (1892-1970), and so do we. Orlac feels that he can no longer touch his wife (Alexandra Sorina) or play ever again. Actually, screenwriter Ludwig Nerz and director Robert Wiene (1881-1938) are playing fast AND clever with us, but as long as the illusion lasts, we are nearly as caught up in Orlac's torture as he is (and I'm not talking about a dream sequence here). In the best of all possible worlds, *The Hands of Orlac* would be released on video with the Clubfoot Orchestra's outstanding score, first performed at San Francisco's Castro Theatre in early 1997. (Based on the novel by Maurice Renard.) 🦴🦴🦴🦴

1925 92m/B *AT* Conrad Veidt, Fritz Kortner, Carmen Cartellieri, Paul Adkonas, Alexandra Sorina; ***D:*** Robert Wiene; ***W:*** Ludwig Nerz. **VHS** *LSV*

Hangin' with the Homeboys

Because *Hangin' with the Home Boys* starred a cast of talented unknowns and New Line Cinema did not heavily promote it, the film needed (and deserved) favorable word-of-mouth reviews to do well at the box office. It's exactly the TYPE of movie we ordinarily detest: four guys hang out together one night every week, preferring their own company to anyone else's, and of course ragging on every female that crosses their path. That said, *Hangin' with the Home Boys* is a delight to watch mainly because of writer/director Joseph B. Vasquez' superb understanding of what makes his characters tick. Moreover, the women in the story, although they are seen one-dimensionally by the four guys, are drawn with considerable depth. Willie (Doug E. Doug) is so convinced that his poverty is rooted in the fact he is black that he spends the entire evening sponging off his buddies. Tom (Mario Joyner) wants to be a great actor like William Shatner, even hustling agents as he peddles magazines over the telephone to survive. Johnny (John Leguizamo) works for a supermarket, has fantasies about women, and is terrified to apply for a scholarship that will free him from his safe, spare existence. The most obnoxious of the four is Fernando (Nestor Serrano) who lives off women and wants to be known as Vinny so people will think he's Italian instead of Puerto Rican. Kimberly Russell, Mary B. Ward, Christine Claravall, and Rosemarie Jackson are seen briefly but vividly as the women in their lives, and Reggie Montgomery has a sparkling cameo as a street person named Pasta. Because its executive producer Janet Grillo insisted that film companies take on the project or leave it exactly as is, Vasquez' film is strikingly free of all the telltale evidence that accompanies development process tampering. When 19 or 20 executives start monkeying around with someone's baby, the results are inevitably slick and riddled with cliches. (The difference between the very real confusion young men feel around women and Hollywood's exploitation of that confusion to justify onscreen female bashing is overwhelming.) Although Vaquez clearly likes Willie, Tom, Vinny, and Johnny, their rough edges have not been smoothed away to make them more conventionally appealing. *Hangin' with the Home Boys* is highly recommended as a compassionate, extremely funny film about an authentic time in the past of its creator. (Vasquez' other films include *The Bronx War* and *Street Hitz.*) 🎵🎵🎵

1991 (R) 89m/C Mario Joyner, Doug E. Doug, John Leguizamo, Nestor Serrano, Kimberly Russell, Mary B. Ward, Christine Claravall, Rosemark Jackson, Reggie Montgomery; **D:** Joseph B. Vasquez; **W:** Joseph B. Vasquez. Sundance Film Festival '91: Best Screenplay. **VHS, LV, Closed Caption** *NLC, FCT*

A Hard Day's Night

Yes, *A Hard Day's Night* was a Brit indie, made quickly to cash in on the Beatle's surge in popularity after their February 1964 appearance on *The Ed Sullivan Show.* Producer Walter Shenson hoped that Beatlemania would last at least through June, when the movie was due to hit theatres. The selection of Richard Lester as director was by no means a guarantee that the movie would be a blockbuster. He had, after all, helmed *It's Trad, Dad,* a little-known 1962 Helen Shapiro musical, remembered today only by die-hard film buffs. Also known as *Ring-A-Ding Rhythm,* this 73-minute film was packed with then-household names like Chubby Checker, John Leyton, Gary (US) Bonds, and the late Gene Vincent and Del Shannon. It was also filled with Lester's then-innovative cinematic techniques, but it went nowhere fast, as did many Brit flicks of that era, like 1963's *Summer Holiday* and *It's All Happening* with, respectively, Sir Cliff Richard and Tommy Steele. Alright, the Beatles could sing, but could they act? Alun Owen prepared his Oscar-nominated screenplay with the assumption that they could not, and then, when the rushes revealed that at least three of the Beatles were surprisingly relaxed on camera (the dashing Sir Paul McCartney was not among them), Owen quickly came up with more dialogue for them. An American tour that coincided with the film's U.S. release helped to make it one of 1964's most profitable releases. The international audiences of 1964 were clearly hungry for a lightning-paced, tongue-in-cheek glimpse of life in the fast lane, and *A Hard Day's Night* supplied it. We wanted to believe that being a Beatle was fun and zany, just like in this movie; it was a shock to discover in *Let It Be,* a mere six years later, how far the sparkling Beatle image was removed from a much-grittier reality. As fiction, *A Hard Day's Night* holds up. This is how we would like for the life of the Beatles to be, so this is what we want to remember. (Self-effacing Ringo Starr, the last to join the group, was, by virtue of being the best actor in the bunch, the quintessential Beatle; he went on to make the most films as an actor, and is, with shifting members of his All-Starr band, the only former Beatle to tour with any regularity into the 1990s.) 🦴🦴🦴🦴

1964 90m/B *GB* John Lennon, Paul McCartney, George Harrison, Ringo Starr, Wilfrid Brambell, Norman Rossington, John Junkin, Victor Spinetti, Anna Quayle, Deryck Guyler, Richard Vernon, Lionel Blair, Eddie Malin, Robin Ray, Alison Seebohm, David Saxon; *D:* Richard Lester; *W:* Alun Owen. Nominations: Academy Awards '64: Best Story & Screenplay (Owen), Best Original Score. **VHS, Beta, LV, CD-I** *MVD, MPI, CRC*

Hard Traveling

Alvah Bessie (1904-85) wrote *Bread and a Stone* in 1941 and then watched his promising career as an Oscar-nominated screenwriter turn to ashes when he was interrogated by the House Un-American Activities Committee as a member of the Hollywood Ten. He went to jail for contempt of Congress and continued to write, although not in Hollywood. (He did adapt his novel *The Symbol* for Columbia's 1974 Connie Stevens vehicle, *The Sex Symbol.*) Before his death in 1985, Bessie got to see the completed version of *Hard Traveling* that was adapted and directed by his son Dan. This well intentioned effort is a movie out of its time. The life-and-death Depression issues that made *Bread and a Stone* so gripping to read apparently meant less to audiences in the Reaganomics era. J.E. Freeman, Ellen Geer, Barry Corbin, James Gammon, and Jim Haynie are all fine character actors,

but none of them has the sort of onscreen charisma that makes us care vitally about every breath s/he takes. Even the extras in a courtroom sequence are too representative of the mid-'80s in look and manner for us to get lost in the story and transport ourselves to the times of hard traveling. I tried turning off the color and watching this in black and white once and it helped somewhat, but not entirely. While at Warner Bros., Alvah Bessie tried to persuade Bette Davis to use her influence so that the studio would buy the book. Davis seemed interested until she asked if the downbeat ending could be changed, and he told her that he wanted the ending to remain intact. That was that. In the 1940s, they didn't buy the book for the screen, and in the 1980s, they didn't have the look for the screen. 🦴🦴🦴

1985 (PG) 99m/C J.E. Freeman, Ellen Geer, Barry Corbin, James Gammon, Jim Haynie; *D:* Dan Bessie; *W:* Dan Bessie. **VHS, Beta** *VTR, NWV*

Hawks

In 1969, Timothy Dalton outraged everyone with the statement that he intended to be an even better actor than Laurence Olivier. *Hawks* is the first time we've been able to agree that Dalton might finally be on the way to achieving that goal. Anthony Edwards and Dalton play two dying patients who escape from a British hospital and steal an ambulance. They flee to the Netherlands for a holiday where they plan to spend their dying days in an Amsterdam whore house. Instead, they meet two English girls in pursuit of a Dutch character who made one of them pregnant. A fine screenplay by Roy Clarke makes *Hawks* a surprising delight and Robert Ellis Miller's steady, sure direction keeps the whole thing in balance. Anthony Edwards is excellent as the American football player sidelined by illness, but Dalton's performance is a true star turn, packed with charisma, tenderness, vitality, anguish, and humor. It's by far the best thing he's done onscreen. Janet McTeer is wonderful

"You think slow, Nick. You move fast, but you think slow."

—Al Molin (Norman Lloyd) chides his partner in crime Nick Robey (John Garfield) in *He Ran All the Way.*

as the awkward unwed mother who towers over and captivates Dalton, and Sheila Hancock is very good as her best friend. Because it's really about life with no-holds-barred, *Hawks* is one of the very few films about death that we actually enjoyed and would be willing to see again. 🦴🦴🦴

1989 (R) 105m/C *GB* Anthony Edwards, Timothy Dalton, Janet McTeer, Jill Bennett, Sheila Hancock, Connie Booth, Camille Coduri; **D:** Robert Ellis Miller; **W:** Roy Clarke. **VHS, Beta, LV, 8mm, Closed Caption** *PAR*

He Ran All the Way

A 19-year-old guy asked me who John Garfield was the other day and I nearly died! There must be at least 15 of the movies he made between 1938 and 1948 on the shelves of most neighborhood video outlets. Unfortunately, *Nobody Lives Forever, The Breaking Point,* and his swan song, *He Ran All the Way,* are not among them. Garfield, who began his career with the Group Theatre, was like a breath of fresh air when he first arrived in Hollywood. He wasn't a completely bad guy, but he hated fuss and pretense. He hated to be manipulated, too, but that didn't stop men and women alike from trying to use him for their own purposes. When he fell, he fell hard, and his naked face revealed every conflicting emotion that ran across it. In *He Ran All the Way,* Garfield plays a thief named Nick who becomes involved in a robbery with Al (Norman Lloyd). Al is wounded in the attempt and Nick shoots a guard, then flees to the neighborhood swimming pool. He meets a girl (Shelley Winters as Peggy Dobbs) and follows her home. At first, her parents (Wallace Ford and Selena Royle) and little brother (Bobby Hyatt) welcome Nick into their home, even leaving him alone with Peggy while they catch a movie. But Al's fears escalate when the family returns home. His guilty conscience convinces him that they've heard about the robbery, and he takes them hostage. When he learns that he killed the guard in the robbery, he feverishly makes plans to run away

with Peggy. This independent production was the only job Garfield could get in the last year of his life. Berry and Butler were under investigation by the House Committee on Un-American Activities and Garfield's turn was next. He was due to appear before the Committee and, during the grueling wait, he died of a heart attack, aggravated by emotional strain and sleep deprivation. The fear that Garfield projects in his final performance onscreen had never been this intense before; he looks like he's gnawing a part of himself away in order to escape. Winters, then 29, is believable as the girl who's torn between her family and a desperate man for the first time in her life. No one knows what sort of a career or life Garfield might have had if he'd lived, but during his too-brief time in Hollywood, he gave the working class a recognizable face and voice with which to identify, and gave each role a no-nonsense approach, almost as if he weren't acting at all. Other noir films starring Garfield include *The Postman Always Rings Twice, Body and Soul,* and *Force of Evil.* Based on the novel by Sam Ross. 🦴🦴🦴

1951 77m/B John Garfield, Shelley Winters, Wallace Ford, Selena Royle, Bobby Hyatt, Gladys George, Norman Lloyd, Jimmy Ames; **D:** John Berry; **W:** Guy Endore, Hugo Butler; **C:** James Wong Howe; **M:** Franz Waxman. *NYR*

Hear My Song

The career of actress Shirley Anne Field says a great deal about the motion picture industry in Britain. The beautiful and talented Field began playing small roles in the mid-'50s while still a teenager. Within a few years, she was attracting attention in international hits like *The Entertainer* with Laurence Olivier and *Saturday Night and Sunday Morning* with Albert Finney. She seemed to be all over the place in the early 1960s, but with the waning of the British vogue in films, her career faded by the end of the decade. With 1985's *My Beautiful Laundrette,* Field reemerged as a stunning character actress of enormous skill and she went on to play vivid supporting roles in *Shag, Setting It Right,* and *The Rachel Papers.* Field is not the centerpiece of Peter Chelsom's *Hear My Song,* but her appearance in this charming film about the resurrection of real-life Irish tenor Josef Locke was certainly an inspired casting decision. *Hear My Song* revolves around the efforts of young concert promoter Micky O'Neill (played by screenwriter Adrian Dunbar) who is trying to make a mint by presenting a return engagement of the great Locke. He hires a look-a-like (William Hootkins) who has done fairly well with small-time gigs by trading on his resemblance to Locke. But when the fake Locke makes a pass at one Cathleen Doyle (played with conviction by Field) who was, as a former Miss Dairy Goodness of 1958, in love with the real Locke, the jig is up. Since Doyle is the mother of Micky's girlfriend and both women are furious with him, he has no choice but to comb the countryside looking for Locke. When he finally locates him, there's another stumbling block: Locke is a tax fugitive and has no interest in making a comeback that will attract as much attention from the police (including David McCallum!) as from a nostalgic audience. For those who enjoy watching vintage Ealing comedies on the Late Show, *Hear My Song* compares favorably with many of the best efforts from that enchanted studio. Ned Beatty does a delicious job as Locke, even if he was born in Kentucky! Although *Hear My Song* is certainly not a film for cynics, it offers an affectionate and funny view of some engaging characters and, of course, a terrific role for Shirley Anne Field. Peter Chelsom's film is well worth a look on video. 🦴🦴🦴🦴

1991 (R) 104m/C *GB* Ned Beatty, Adrian Dunbar, Shirley Anne Field, Tara Fitzgerald, William Hootkins, David McCallum; *D:* Peter Chelsom; *W:* Peter Chelsom; *M:* John Altman. **VHS, Beta, Closed Caption** PAR

Heartland

Conchata Ferrell is quite wonderful as a widow in her 30s who accepts a position as Rip Torn's housekeeper in Wyoming in the year 1910. Torn is rather a Gloomy Gus, but the two of them get used to each other over the course of the film. The unconventional casting added to the realism of Richard Pearce's film, as did the fact that the screenplay was based on the journals of a real-life pioneer woman, Elinore Randall Stewart. If you love Torn on *The Larry Sanders Show,* here's a chance to see him in a very different part. 🦴🦴🦴

1981 (PG) 95m/C Conchata Ferrell, Rip Torn, Barry Primus, Lilia Skala, Megan Folson; *D:* Richard Pearce. Sundance Film Festival '81: Grand Jury Prize. **VHS, Beta** *NO*

Heat and Dust

In the summer of 1963, there were few 22-year-old actresses on the planet with more charisma than Julie Christie when she popped up as Liz, luring Tom Courtenay's *Billy Liar.* Sparkling with health and joie de vivre, Christie starred in a dozen major films over a 15-year span, then was offscreen for nearly five years, an eternity for an actress in her 40s. *Heat and Dust* was the vehicle she selected for her return. She was still lovely, delightful, and charming as a researcher named Anne, but the script was stacked in favor of a NEW 22-year-old actress who was playing her Great Aunt Olivia: Greta Scacchi. The contemporary investigations of the free-spirited Anne simply didn't carry the narrative weight of her rambunctious ancestor of the 1920s. Olivia is an eager young bride when she first comes to India to join her husband, Douglas Rivers (Christopher Cazenove), a civil servant. Both Olivia and Anne are caught up in the spell of India, but neither is ever fully accepted there. Olivia has an affair with Nawab (Shashi Kapoor), a local ruler, and Anne, too, has a brief romance with a young man. But their restless, rebellious personalities keep them isolated and alone, at odds with the country they both love, and never quite fitting in anywhere. *Heat and Dust*

INDEPENDENT FILM GUIDE

Peter Chelsom is going to be one of the big directors. He's extremely talented and knows exactly what he wants. Thank goodness he wanted me for the part of this former beauty queen, because Cathleen Doyle could have been written for me. Peter's just great; he's a name to watch. He did a documentary before this, I don't want this to sound like a eulogy or just tributing Peter for the sake of it, but he's worth it. He's such a good director, he's so clever, but he's learned his business backwards. He's in his mid-30s, and he's been doing commercials, and before that he was an actor [in *A Woman of Substance* and *Sorrel and Son*], so he knows the business very well. And those beautiful scenes in the movie were all shot by a women, Sue Gibson, the cinematographer, and it's her first motion picture, too.

"[*Hear My Song*] started when Peter Chelsom was driving home from shooting one of his commercials about four years ago, and somebody gave him a tape of Josef Locke's voice. He heard the voice and the story came to him. Then he went to meet Josef Locke and said, 'I want to write a story about your life,' and Josef Locke was rather reluctant and a bit of a recluse. Peter persisted and persisted and persisted, then he went on working and he was friends with Adrian Dunbar. Peter wrote the story, then they wrote the screenplay together, then they pursued Joe, who could be very tricky and a bit surly, and finally they got the rights, and then they started trying to make the film. Then they had to find the backing and Channel Four helped them and Limelight. They had a struggle, but they did it. And here we are today.

"I didn't compare [*Hear My Song*] to the Ealing films when I was making it because it's so immediate and so now, but when I see it, I can see it's both then and now. I just had a feeling of joy doing it. A lot of filming is arduous and tedious. *Hear My Song* wasn't. And one thing about having a small budget: it makes you put everything onto the screen. There was no wasted energy, no wasted temperament. Ned Beatty [as Josef Locke] was a delight to work with, and so was Adrian Dunbar [as Micky O'Neill] and Tara Fitzgerald [as Nancy Doyle] and everybody. [NOTE: David McCallum, Illya Kuryakin from MGM's *Man from U.N.C.L.E.* series, plays a police chief!] We worked very hard and we had SUCH fun.

"Harold Berens, who played Benny Rose, the Cockney conductor...was an old variety performer first, then when that dried up, he went into radio where he was famous for his catch phrases all through the war, then he had a career as a nightclub entertainer, and now he's come back in films, and you know what the sweetest story is? Harold was sitting on the stairs on the last day of filming, and I said, 'Harold, you look very sad.' And he said, 'I'm very sad, Girl.' And I said, 'Why are you sad, Harold?' 'Oh, I love this job,' he said. 'Do you think I'm going to make films from now on? Have I got another career?' I said, 'I'm sure you have, Harold. How old are you today?' He said, '84.' 'Well,' I said, 'You're 84 years young!' So let's hope he has a GREAT career!"

NOTE: Harold Berens (1903-95) began his film career in 1943's *Candlelight in Algeria* with James Mason. He went on to make 1947's *Dual Alibi* with Herbert Lom, 1949's *Third Time Lucky* (as a waiter) with Glynis Johns, 1950's *Up for the Cup* (as an auctioneer), *A Kid for Two Farthings* with Diana Dors, and *The Secret* with Andre Morell (both 1955), 1956's *Not So Dusty* (as a driver), 1960's *Bluebeard's Ten Honeymoons* (as a jeweler) with George Sanders, *A Weekend with Lulu* (as a cardseller) with Shirley Eaten, and *What a Whopper!* with Adam Faith (both 1961), *The Painted Smile* with Liz Fraser, *Behave Yourself* with Dennis Price and *Live Now—Pay Later* with Ian Hendry (all 1962), 1969's *The Magic Christian* (as a waiter) with Ringo Starr, 1972's *Straight on Till Morning* with Rita Tushingham, and 1982's *Trail of the Pink Panther* (as a clerk) with David Niven, plus five other films and even an *Avengers* episode.

"I'd like to be financially stable, which sounds odd, doesn't it, but I only do these gems of movies every four years or so, but I'd like to go putting on the screen women who are real. They can be beautiful at any age. I think that men have been allowed to be heroes for all their ages, and I hope that I'm beginning to be able to do that with women. They don't have to be 23. When I started, they said to me, 'Well, you've got good bone structure, but make the most of it, because at 25, it's all over. You've got two extra years.' Pathetic...and I believed them! And now I want to put on the screen women who are real, and it seems to be working because I've had a lot of feedback from my own sex, saying how much they like these characters that I'm creating, so that's good, isn't it?"

SHIRLEY ANNE FIELD can be seen in *Beat Girl, The Entertainer, War Lover, Peeping Tom, House of the Living Dead, My Beautiful Laundrette, Two By Forsyth, Getting It Right, The Rachel Papers,* and *Shag: The Movie.*

launched Scacchi's international career and over the next decade she played more than 15 major roles that took full advantage of her stunning looks before she settled into secondary character parts by the time she was 34 (!). The intriguing script for this beautifully made Merchant/Ivory production is based on the novel by Ruth Prawer Jhabvala. ♪♪♪♪

1982 (R) 130m/C *GB* Julie Christie, Greta Scacchi, Shashi Kapoor, Christopher Cazenove, Nickolas Grace, Julian Glover, Susan Fleetwood, Patrick Godfrey, Jennifer Kendal, Madhur Jaffrey, Barry Foster, Amanda Walker, Sudha Chopra, Sajid Khan, Zakir Hussain, Ratna Pathak, Charles McCaughan, Parveen Paul; *D:* James Ivory; *W:* Ruth Prawer Jhabvala, Saeed Jaffrey, Harish Khare; *C:* Walter Lassally; *M:* Richard Robbins. British Academy Awards '83: Best Adapted Screenplay; Nominations: Cannes Film Festival '83: Best Film. **VHS, Beta** *USH*

Heat and Sunlight

This boring improvisational exercise won the Grand Jury Prize at the Sundance Film Festival in 1988. Thanks to a clever advertising campaign ("BANNED BY DISTRIBUTORS!" which does sound a whole lot better than "REJECTED BY DISTRIBUTORS!" doesn't it?), Rob Nilsson was able to attract a few more audience members into the few theatres that agreed to carry it. To cut costs, Nilsson transferred 1/2-inch Betacam video to 35mm film. It's about jealousy and sex, sex and jealousy, zzzzz.... Nilsson's previous credits include *Northern Lights, Signal 7,* and *On the Edge.* **WOOF!**

1987 98m/B Rob Nilsson, Consuelo Faust, Bill Bailey, Don Bajema, Ernie Fosselius; *D:* Rob Nilsson; *W:* Rob Nilsson; *M:* Mark Adler. Sundance Film Festival '88: Grand Jury Prize. **VHS, Beta, LV** *CVC*

Heathers

Three years before *Heathers,* Wynona Ryder only had eyes for Corey Haim as *Lucas.* THIS film turned Ryder and Christian Slater into full-fledged teen stars, although Slater's Jack Nicholson imitation wore thin for this viewer by his second line of dia-

logue. Ryder is wonderful, though, running the full gamut of teen angst, first as the virtual slave of the three nastiest Heathers in high school, then as the can't-live-with-him/can't-live-without-him accomplice of Slater, who determines to rid the world of Heathers once and for all. Shannen Doherty is one of the Heathers, reportedly catching the attention of Tori ("Donna Martin") Spelling, who urged father Aaron to consider casting her as Brenda Walsh on *Beverly Hills 90210.* Screenwriter Daniel Waters and director Michael Lehmann reunited for the ill-fated *Hudson Hawk.* Otherwise, Lehmann directed quirky comedies (*The Applegates, Airheads,* and the very funny *Truth About Cats and Dogs*) and Waters wrote scripts for films like *The Adventures of Ford Fairlane, Batman,* and *Demolition Man.* But *Heathers* remains the most prominent achievement on both their resumes; with its bracing satirical edge and a fearless disregard for good taste, *Heathers* is unlike any teen flick seen before or since. ♪♪♪♫

1989 (R) 102m/C Winona Ryder, Christian Slater, Kim Walker, Shannen Doherty, Lisanne Falk, Penelope Milford, Glenn Shadix, Lance Fenton, Patrick Laborteaux; *D:* Michael Lehmann; *W:* Daniel Waters; *M:* David Newman. Edgar Allan Poe Awards '89: Best Screenplay; Independent Spirit Awards '90: Best First Feature. **VHS, Beta, LV, Closed Caption** *VTR, NWV, FCT*

Heavenly Creatures

Peter Jackson's remarkable film tells the true crime story of Pauline Parker, 16, and Juliet Hulme, 15, two schoolgirls who beat Pauline's mother to death with bricks wrapped in stockings after visiting a tea shop with her in Canterbury, New Zealand. The motive: Pauline and Juliet were about to be separated and they believed that the murder would keep them together forever. For some reason, they chose the parent with the least amount of power: Juliet's parents were the chief proponents of the move. At their 1954 trial in Christchurch, they were sentenced to be detained "until Her Majesty's pleasure be made known."

Parker was 20 and Hulme was 19 when they were released in 1958, but they had been forbidden contact with each other since their arrest. *The Express* (a British tabloid) finally found Parker after a diligent search, but the identity of Hulme was revealed directly after *Heavenly Creatures'* release. As mystery writer Anne Perry, she had established an international following. Perry did say, that as a result of a serious illness, she had been prescribed mind-altering drugs that might have unduly influenced her actions at the time of the murder. Jackson takes the girls back in time a couple of years before the trial, when Parker was 14 and Hulme was 13. They get caught up in a wild fantasy life, not too dissimilar from the teenaged protagonists of 1964's *The World of Henry Orient.* And it does look like quite a lot of fun, until it gets out of hand. Because of their extreme youth, it's hard to say whether the two girls were actually lesbians as their parents feared or were just great friends play acting anything and everything in sight. When Hulme becomes ill and must go to hospital for her health, their association becomes obsessive. Could this murder have been prevented? Jackson mostly concerns himself with the friends and their interior world, which he renders in a very appealing, non-judgmental way. Melanie Lynskey looks just like old news photos of Pauline, and Kate Winslet became a first-time Oscar nominee in 1995 for *Sense and Sensibility.* 🦴🦴🦴🦴

1994 (R) 110m/C *NZ* Melanie Lynskey, Kate Winslet, Sarah Pierse, Diana Kent, Clive Merrison, Simon O'Connor; *D:* Peter Jackson; *W:* Peter Jackson, Frances Walsh; *C:* Alun Bollinger. Nominations: Academy Awards '94: Best Original Screenplay; Australian Film Institute '95: Best Foreign Film. **VHS, LV, Closed Caption** *TOU*

Heavy

One hundred and nineteen minutes is a long time to spend at a pizzeria where you'd normally get a meal to go because you don't want to eat it THERE. But since James Mangold put a lot of thought into this one, here's the story. Victor (Pruitt Tay-lor Vince) is fat, shy, and lives with his mother, Dolly. Dolly (Shelley Winters) is ailing, in her early 70s, and also fat. Dolores (Deborah Harry) is a waitress in her late 40s. She's been around the block more than once but never looked twice at Vince. Leo (Joe Grifasi) is a regular in his 50s. Joining this exciting group is, yes, LIV TYLER as Callie, the new 17-year-old waitress! Her boyfriend is a mechanic named Jeff (Evan Dando of the Lemonheads) and Victor is more than twice Callie's age, but he's inspired to start a weight loss program, anyway. It took a long time for this subtle, well acted, slow movie to find a distributor. Tyler, naturally, received most of the attention. Her track record to date has been just fair, though: *Silent Fall, Empire Records, Inventing the Abbotts,* and her breakthrough film, *Stealing Beauty.* 🦴🦴🦴

1994 (R) 104m/C Pruitt Taylor Vince, Shelley Winters, Liv Tyler, Deborah Harry, Evan Dando, Joe Grifasi; *D:* James Mangold; *W:* James Mangold; *C:* Michael Barrow; *M:* Thurston Moore. Sundance Film Festival '95: Special Jury Prize. **VHS, Closed Caption** *COL*

Heavy Petting

Heavy Petting is a dry hump of a movie, with all the assets and liabilities of early sex: the promotional teaser might be a turn-on, but the experience itself is something of a let-down. Obie Benz's shapeless movie is strongly reminiscent of Philippe Mora's *Brother, Can You Spare a Dime,* a 1975 documentary that attempted to reveal the 1930s with period newsreels and movie clips but without a narrative thrust. Working without a script, Benz cross-edited old educational films and movie clips together, showing the results every so often to his friends to see if he had a movie yet. He worked hard for seven years and his friends and many audiences may well love *Heavy Petting.* We found ourselves losing interest after half an hour, though, and the last 45 minutes were somewhat less than enthralling. Benz

"You are not fat, you are not. Honey, you're husky, you're... you're well built, you're macho!"

——Dolly (Shelley Winters) tries in vain to inspire her son Victor (Pruitt Taylor Vince) in *Heavy.*

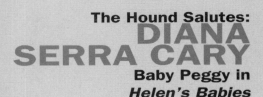
The most interesting change [in child stardom from the '20s to the '80s] I've noticed is that children in the old days, even on the stage, were confronted with tragedy. For example, during the Depression, Shirley Temple films always dealt with the child solving the problem, not being a part of the problem, and this was considered, that's what kids are for, and what they're capable of, heroines and heroes, even though they're children. Now you find that the television child star tends to be the kid next door, and has to be either funny or sheltered from all kinds of reality. They're not expected to cope with big deals, big problems.

"In Victorian America, there were not many options open to women, if they were alone. If they had children, their husband was dead or had left them, they could take in laundry, they could cook, they could take in boarders, or they could put their children on the stage. Putting the child on the stage was sometimes a very big gamble. You didn't always get much money back. So it was economic necessity, yes, to put the child on the stage because many mothers didn't want to have to sink to complete prostitution.

"To me, I always got into the feeling of the historical thing, if there was a period about it, I was fascinated with the period. I remember after my childhood career was over and I returned to films and talkies after the '30s, I enjoyed when they'd do things like *The Great Waltz* which was a story of the Strauss family, and I'd love these things where we'd

asked a dozen men and eleven women to describe their early attitudes about sex. Not all of their commentary is particularly enlightening or perceptive, but Ann Magnuson is funny at least, and the late Abbie Hoffman looks like the jolliest and least likely candidate for suicide ever. We don't even want to think about the last time William Burroughs and Allen Ginsberg, 75 and 63 when the movie first came out in 1989, indulged in heavy petting and neither looks like he wants to be in the movie. Also, were the 1950s the sole province of white teens? Sidney Poitier only shows up once in a *Blackboard Jungle*

clip. This tired celebration of over-obvious cultural symbols obviously wasn't our movie, but if you think it might be yours, video is the best way to see it. 🦴🦴

1989 75m/C David Byrne, Josh Mostel, Sandra Bernhard, Allen Ginsberg, Ann Magnuson, Spalding Gray, Laurie Anderson, John Oates, Abbie Hoffman, Jacki Ochs; *D:* Obie Benz. **VHS, Beta, LV** *ACA*

Helen's Babies

We have yet to see this movie, but not for lack of trying. When we heard that a print

do real period costumes and dancing and waltzing and other types of things like that. I remember on the set when I was a teenager, we did *Ah! Wilderness,* and the other girls, as soon as the cameras would quit, would pick up their skirts and cross their legs and smoke cigarettes, and I was so caught up in the period, I couldn't do that. I used to stay all day in that period.

"I wanted to be a writer since I was eight years old. It was something I could do in great privacy and being a child star, when I went out to a restaurant to eat, people used to stare in the glass windows and look in, so you have no privacy. I started about eight years old writing novels back stage when I was in vaudeville. My novels were ten pages long, and I remember I was very upset when some young writer wrote her first book at 16 and I said, 'I've got to do mine before I'm 12.'

"There is one film that they found in which I starred, *Helen's Babies,* which featured myself, Edward Everett Horton, and a young girl who was a newcomer named Clara Bow. A gentlemen who's writing a life of Clara Bow [NOTE: David Stenn, with family and studio cooperation, edited by Jacqueline Kennedy Onassis at Doubleday] researched that film and found that it was available in Russia, and he has gotten the film. There is interest behind the Iron Curtain, in [the former] Yugoslavia, and other countries. They did not have the practice of returning the film when they had used it as in this country they did, and so what happened is when they sent the film back to our studios, the producers burned it for the $2.50 worth of silver nitrate. Those that went to the Iron Curtain are still there."

DIANA SERRA CARY'S autobiography *Whatever Happened to Baby Peggy?* was published by St. Martin's Press in October 1996.

had surfaced in a Moscow archive, we sent letter after letter, trying to track it down. We tried asking a film archive if there was any way it could be shown there. No dice! But we WILL see this movie some day. *Helen's Babies* first surfaced as a very funny children's book by John Habberton, focusing on the trials and tribulations of a Victorian bachelor (circa 1875) who, due to circumstances beyond his control, must temporarily care for his sister's two small children. In the book, Toddie and Budge were little boys, but for the independent film production, the story was redesigned as a vehicle for child star Baby Peggy and co-star Jean Carpenter. Surviving stills suggest that the time frame may have been updated by 40 years, as well. Director William A. Seiter (1892-1964) went on to direct the Shirley Temple classics *Dimples, Stowaway,* and *Susannah of the Mounties.* Cinematographer William Daniels (1895-1970) shot such MGM classics as *Anna Christie, Cat on a Hot Tin Roof,* and *How the West Was Won,* and won the Oscar for *The Naked City.* Edward Everett Horton (1886-1976), one of the drollest character actors ever, played Uncle Harry, and lovely Clara Bow (1905-65) appeared as his romantic inter-

est, Alice Mayton. Baby Peggy grew up to be writer Diana Serra Cary, author of such carefully researched and beautifully written books as *The Hollywood Posse, Hollywood's Children,* and *Whatever Happened to Baby Peggy? Helen's Babies* may or may not be a comedy classic, but with that cast and that crew, we hope that Grapevine Video or some other kind distributor will put us out of our misery and let us see this one soon!

1925 m/B Baby Peggy, Jean Carpenter, Clara Bow, Edward Everett Horton, Claire Adams, Richard Tucker, George Reed, Mattie Peters; *D:* William A. Seiter; *W:* Hope Loring, Louis Leighton; *C:* William H. Daniels. *NYR*

Hester Street

When *Hester Street* was first released, major stardom was predicted for its star Carol Kane and a glorious future as a world-class director awaited Joan Micklin Silver...I'll be back after I beat up a few pillows to spare everyone the institutional sexism rant.... This beautiful film knocked everyone sideways in the mid-'70s. Carol Kane's look was so right for this period film, like she'd just stepped out of a daguerrotype. As it turns out, Kane's look is right for every time. She can be a flapper, a babysitter, a hippie, a mom...but she's been typed, somehow, as a wild child, so we see her in many marginal roles in many marginal films where she steals everything in her scattered sequences that isn't nailed down and then drifts out of the plot. Like a lovely wraith, we can't forget her. Micklin, who went on to make several more fine films (but not enough for this longtime admirer), carefully observes the dilemma faced by every immigrant who comes to America. As a nation of immigrants, do we reject the values of the country we left behind and embrace our adopted country on its own terms, or do we try preserve our unique identity and share it with those who come after it? Steven Keats, who plays Kane's husband, has already made his choice. By pursuing the flirtatious Dorrie Kavanaugh,

he rejects both his bride and her Old World customs. (Sadly, both Keats and Kavanaugh died relatively young in real life. He committed suicide in 1994 at the age of 49 and she died at 38 in 1983, after switching from acting to a career as an opera singer.) ♫♫♫

1975 92m/B Carol Kane, Doris Roberts, Steven Keats, Mel Howard, Dorrie Kavanaugh, Stephen Strimpell; *D:* Joan Micklin Silver; *M:* William Bolcom. Nominations: Academy Awards '75: Best Actress (Kane). **VHS, Beta** *FRF, VES*

Hidden Children

Oral histories about the Holocaust are offered by John Walker's *Hidden Children,* a 1994 Canadian documentary. Walker's visits with six Jewish survivors of World War II supply a painful reminder of what it is like for small children to be torn away from their families and adjust to new names and completely different lives. ♫♫♡

1994 52m/C *CA D:* John Walker. *NYR*

The Hidden Room

Naunton Wayne turns detective in this war of nerves between Dr. Clive Riordan (Robert Newton) and his lovely wife's American lover, Bill Kronin (Phil Brown). Clive wants to dissolve Bill in an acid bath, but he wants to choose just the right moment when he's under the least suspicion. Meanwhile, Clive's lovely wife Storm (lovely Sally Gray) wants to know what the heck is going on, although she never considers the acid bath. The only ones who keep their cool here are Wayne as kindly Supt. Finsbury and (though it ain't easy) Bill, who has A Plan. Everyone's good in what feels like a Victorian melodrama updated to post-war London. Wonder if Levinson and Link watched this Brit noir while germinating Lt. Columbo? *AKA:* Obsession. ♫♫♫

1949 98m/B *GB* Robert Newton, Sally Gray, Naunton Wayne, Phil Brown, Olga Lindo, Russell Waters, James Harcourt, Allan Jeayes, Stanley Baker; *D:*

Edward Dmytryk; **W:** Alec Coppel; **M:** Nino Rota. **VHS, Beta** *NOS, SNC, RXM*

High Heels

Pedro Almodovar's early films had so many outrageous trappings that it was easy for many to overlook the fact that his scripts have always been fairly conventional. His concerns as a storyteller are pretty basic: who did what, who loves whom, how do we get from here to there? It is because of Almodovar's genius for exploring the raw emotions that ignite many gnarled relationships that his simple plot lines seem to take on a surreal quality. His ninth film, *High Heels,* received some lukewarm reviews, undoubtedly because it is stripped of some of the wilder elements that first put Almodovar on the map. But for those who take *High Heels* on its own terms, there are genuine rewards in this overlooked 1991 release. *High Heels* examines the troubled relationship between a television anchor woman (Victoria Abril) and her much more famous mother (Marisa Paredes). The two are in not-so-subtle competition with each other, but they are also very much in need of each other's love. They share the same name (Rebecca) and they also share the same lover (Feodor Atkine), whom the daughter is unlucky enough to marry. The daughter is also best friends with a drag queen who impersonates her mother onstage. The drag queen has several other identities in the film and serves as something of a catalyst for the relationship between the two women. Miguel Bose also appears as a not-so-mysterious judge who investigates the murder of the younger Rebecca's husband. Since the identity of the killer is never in doubt, Almodovar focuses steadily on how the murder affects the relationships of the characters. In that respect, Almodovar does his usual clinical yet passionate job. If you want the same movie from the director every time, rent one of your old favorites on video. If you want to see what Pedro Almodovar was up to in 1991, *High Heels* is an absorbing, well crafted film that's definitely worth a look. **AKA:** Tacones Lejanos. ♫♫♫

1991 (R) 113m/C SP Victoria Abril, Marisa Paredes, Miguel Bose, Feodor Atkine, Bibi Andersen, Rocio Munoz; **D:** Pedro Almodovar; **W:** Pedro Almodovar; **M:** Ryuichi Sakamoto. Cesar Awards '93: Best Foreign Film. **VHS, Beta, Closed Caption** *PAR*

High Season

Admirers of Jacqueline Bisset will be pleased at the fact that the actress has finally been cast in a well-above-average movie, *High Season.* This fine comedy is the first feature directed by writer Clare Peploe, who works with husband Bernardo Bertolucci. It's about survival on a Greek island, which is not the same as survival on Skid Row. The scenery is gorgeous enough to make anyone forget about finances. Bisset plays a broke photographer who wants to sell a vase she received from her old friend Sebastian Shaw. The buyer is Sir Robert Stephens (1931-95), who definitely has been around the block a few times since he played Sherlock Holmes in 1970. Stephens wants art historian Shaw to claim that the vase is fake. Shaw doesn't mind, especially since the vase is not exactly what it seems to be. But then, neither is Shaw. And neither is the obnoxious English tourist couple who hang around Bisset's house. *High Season* gets its laughs from what we know about the characters and their relationships with each other. The humor is mostly English, although Irene Papas and Paris Tselios have some good scenes as the Greek mother and son who have to cope with all these weird people. And this group is definitely daffy, in a careless, uncontrived way. At one point, Bisset yells at her artist husband (James Fox) for being too lazy to patch up their relationship problems. Meanwhile, his bed partner casually gets dressed and makes her exit, scarcely noticed by either of them. The film is filled with "hold on now, this is really serious" sequences which are punctured by a reality that refuses to recognize the finality of any single moment. After all, when was the last time you saw a woman plunge into passionate sex with a strange fellow simply because he fixed the flushing mechanism on her toilet? ♫♫♫

1988 (R) 95m/C *GB* Jacqueline Bisset, James Fox, Irene Papas, Sebastian Shaw, Kenneth Branagh, Robert Stephens, Leslie Manville, Paris Tselios; *D:* Clare Peploe; *W:* Clare Peploe, Mark Peploe; *C:* Chris Menges; *M:* Jason Osborn. **VHS, Beta, LV, 8mm** *FCT, NLC*

His Picture in the Papers

Movie lore has it that Anita Loos sold a script to D.W. Griffith for the Biograph film *The New York Hat* (starring Mary Pickford and Lionel Barrymore) while she was still a teenager. Since Loos was just four foot eleven, it wouldn't have been that hard to convince Mr. Griffith that she was only 19 in 1912, unless he'd picked up a copy of San Francisco's *Sunday Call* on February 16, 1902, when Loos, then at the Denham School on Bush Street, wrote, "What I Hope to Be When I Grow Up: Having not fully made up my mind as to what I shall become when I am a woman, the answer to that question will be difficult for me to give. So far in my life, my ambitions have inclined toward being a ship architect. The idea of taking up this profession was given to me by Longfellow's poem 'The Building of the Ship,' which we had as literature work in the seventh grade. My choice for being a ship architect rather than the architect of a house or other buildings is because the city is overrun with the latter, while there are comparatively few people who draw the plans of ships. I think also that the occupation which I so far have intended to take up is a quiet and refined business for a woman. If I had any talent at all in drawing or painting, I would like to be an artist, but as the only drawing I can do is mechanical, the occupation of an architect suits me. I will not think too seriously over this subject as I am only 12 years old." Okay, so Loos was 23, not 19

when she first broke into films, but it was a close call for movie fans. We might never have HEARD of *Gentlemen Prefer Blondes* or Lorelei Lee had her creator toiled instead on blueprints for ships instead of scripts for the silver screen! Loos wrote well over 150 screenplays between 1912 and 1942, including several for Douglas Fairbanks. *His Picture in the Papers* ran 68 minutes and focused on Peter Prindle, who does all sorts of wild stunts (driving his car over a cliff, boxing with a pro, diving from a ship and swimming all the way to shore, jumping from trains), just to get his picture in the papers. Without Loos' sparkling titles, the film might have been shorn down to two reels; luckily the critics screened it before the editor started splicing away and the movie, Fairbanks, and Loos ALL got their pictures in the papers! It was a happy teaming of a supremely confident star and a very clever screenwriter and it set the standard for all future Fairbanks vehicles (he went on to star in 45 from 1915 to 1934). ♫♫♫

1916 68m/B Douglas Fairbanks Sr., Clarence Handysides, Rene Boucicault, Jean Temple, Charles Butler, Homer Hunt, Loretta Blake, Helena Rupport; *D:* John Emerson; *W:* John Emerson, Anita Loos. **VHS, Beta, 8mm** *NOS, VYY, GPV*

Hollywood on Trial

Hollywood on Trial is the story behind *The Front*. It doesn't make for pleasant watching or listening, yet it is certainly a long-overdue account. In October 1947, Alvah Bessie, Herbert Biberman, Lester Cole, Edward Dmytryk, Ring Lardner, Jr., John Howard Lawson, Albert Maltz, Samuel Ornitz, Adrian Scott, and Dalton Trumbo were among the top writers and directors in Hollywood. One month later, no one in Hollywood would hire them. All went to prison. Dmytryk later removed himself from the blacklist by testifying against former Communists. Trumbo (1905-76), was able to remove himself from the blacklist when

Otto Preminger (1906-86) hired him to write the screenplay for *Exodus*. (He had won two pseudonymous Academy Awards for 1953's *Roman Holiday* and 1956's *The Brave One*.) Lardner's blacklist lasted 17 years, until he wrote *The Cincinnati Kid*. By 1978, he would win his second Academy Award for *M.A.S.H.* (the first was for 1942's *Woman of the Year*). For others, like Bessie and Cole (both 1904-85), Biberman (1900-71), Lawson (1894-1977), Ornitz, and Scott (1912-73), death would come before they were hired to work on another Hollywood film. Only Maltz (1908-85) was credited with *Two Mules for Sister Sarah* in 1970. Hollywood is filled with hard-luck yarns, yet the history of Hollywood has rarely been adequately developed. With *Hollywood on Trial,* it finally was, due to the efforts of producer James C. Gutman, director David Helpern, Jr., and screenwriter Arnie Reisman. The story they have to tell about Hollywood is far from flattering, but it deserves telling and re-telling. As a 100-minute documentary, *Hollywood on Trial* barely scratches the surface, yet, even in 1976, Helpern suggested that this may be due to the many people who were and are still reluctant to discuss the period during which the House Committee on UnAmerican Activities had free reign over the lives and destinies of many American citizens. 🦴🦴🦴🦴

1976 100m/C Lester Cole, Gary Cooper, Howard da Silva, Edward Dmytryk, Ring Lardner Jr., Albert Maltz, Zero Mostel, Otto Preminger, Ronald Reagan, Gale Sondergaard, Dalton Trumbo, Alvah Bessie; *D:* David Helpern; *W:* Arnie Reisman; *C:* Barry Abrams. **VHS, Beta, LV** *MPI*

Homage

They don't give Academy Awards to little gems like *Homage,* but if they did, Blythe Danner would most assuredly deserve one. Danner, who's been quietly working her magic in indies and quality television specials over the last 25 years, steals great blocks of screen time away from co-stars Sheryl Lee, Frank Whaley, Bruce Davison, and the breathtaking landscapes of New Mexico. A low-key study of fanatical celebrity worship at its most deadly, *Homage* draws its greatest strength from the complexity of its three central characters. Blythe Danner is Elizabeth, a great teacher and a far-from-ideal mother, who lives alone on her ranch. When she's in need of a handyman, leave it to Frank Whaley as Archie to fulfill her every wish. Archie is the most dangerous sort of psycho, brilliant, charming, and deceptively vulnerable. When Elizabeth's troubled, alcoholic, semi-famous daughter Lucy comes home for a visit, Archie shifts into stalking gear. Lucy (played to the hilt by Sheryl Lee) slips easily into the "go away closer" routines that work for her in Tinseltown. She teases Archie by walking braless around the house, by drinking and flirting, and by letting him hold her hand a moment or two before wrenching it away. Archie, it seems, has a screenplay for his idol, but she doesn't like it. In two fairly graphic sequences, he masturbates to her naked image on a video monitor and while reading about her sex life in a purloined journal. To his credit, Frank Whaley doesn't pull any punches in this extremely difficult role. He could have sweetened his character with eroticism, with genuine poignance, or with an eyelash flicker of sanity, but he does none of the above. Whaley's Archie is always playing the angles to the bitter end. Mother and daughter have a brief moment of redemption by allowing each other to see their very worst sides before they accept the bond of trust each has always dreamed about. None of Archie's pitiless manipulations can rob them of that. And Danner's Elizabeth, finally, triumphs over her flawed impulses and deliberate misunderstandings to emerge from her exile into life. Writer Mark Medoff and director Ross Kagen Marks take Hollywood's ultimate violent cliche and turn it inside out in *Homage,* a little-known wonder that merits a better fate. 🦴🦴🦴

1995 (R) 100m/C Frank Whaley, Blythe Danner, Sheryl Lee, Bruce Davison, Danny Nucci; *D:* Ross

Kagen Marks; **W:** Mark Medoff; **C:** Tom Richmond;
M: W.G. Snuffy Walden. **VHS** *AVI*

The Homecoming

Vivien Merchant (1929-82) was a wonderful actress who left behind far too few examples of her brilliant work on film. She met her future husband, Harold Pinter, in repertory and they were married in 1956. A full decade later, Merchant, then 37, first attracted the attention of international audiences as Lily, opposite Michael Caine's *Alfie.* Merchant was seen the following year as Rosalind in the Joseph Losey film *Accident,* scripted by Pinter. More prominently, she starred on Broadway as Ruth in *The Homecoming.* Her co-stars Paul Rogers and Ian Holm as Max and Lenny, playwright Pinter, and director Peter Hall all received Tony awards at the first televised ceremony, and Merchant received a nomination. When *The Homecoming* was produced by American Film Theatre six years later, most of the creative personnel who made the play a success were signed on for the movie (including Terence Rigby as Joey, but excluding John Normington as Sam and Michael Craig as Teddy, who were replaced by Cyril Cusack and Michael Jayston), a decision that should have been made for some of the other compromised A.F.T. productions. You can't take your eyes off Merchant when she's onscreen, and her delivery of Pinter's dialogue here makes us wish that they had preserved more of their work together onscreen. Merchant's Broadway triumph in *The Homecoming* was one of the high points of her much too brief career. By 1980, Pinter had left her for

Lady Antonia Fraser, and Merchant spent the next two years drinking herself to death. Her obituary notices made sad reading for those who had seen her as Mrs. Pugh in *Under Milkwood,* as the delightful Mrs. Oxford preparing inedible gourmet meals and offering sensible advice to Alec McCowen's straightforward Inspector Oxford in *Frenzy,* and as Queen Maria Theresa in the Richard Chamberlain swashbuckler *The Man in the Iron Mask,* directed by Mike Newell. Hers was a rare and delicate talent and it's sad to think of the delicious Merchant performances we've missed over the last two decades. (*The Homecoming* was released theatrically overseas in 1976.) 🎭🎭🎭

1973 114m/C *GB CA* Cyril Cusack, Ian Holm, Michael Jayston, Vivien Merchant, Terence Rigby, Paul Rogers; *D:* Peter Hall; *W:* Harold Pinter; *C:* David Watkin; *M:* Thelonious Monk. *NO*

Hoop Dreams

Hoop Dreams is nearly three hours long, but the men and women who made it spent nearly five years on it, accumulating an average of an hour's worth of footage every week. It focuses on William Gates and Arthur Agee, two black Chicago teenagers, and their heartrending efforts to become professional basketball players. When you think of the obstacles that must have occurred during a project of this scope, you wonder how Gates and Agee were able to stand such close observation for such an extended length of time. You also wonder about the filmmakers; when setbacks occurred (and there were plenty), did anyone consider scrapping this picture? The intimacy of 1973's *An American Family* was almost too extreme; to see a marriage break up in front of cameras both parties knew were there became the topic of a national debate. Did we really need to watch such intensely personal moments on television? *Hoop Dreams* is even more unsparing of the privacy of its subjects; one of the boys (and we) see his own father buying drugs to support his crack

habit. There are other family difficulties and financial problems and injuries and corrective surgery and a hold-up and more. No kid should have to grow up with this much stress, and yet half a million high school kids hope to be among the 25 who are drafted annually to become professional basketball players. *Hoop Dreams* tells the true story of two kids who tried to buck those tremendous odds and how their lives changed as a result. 🎭🎭🎭🎭

1994 (PG-13) 169m/C Arthur Agee, William Gates; *D:* Steve James; *C:* Peter Gilbert. Chicago Film Critics Awards '94: Best Film; Los Angeles Film Critics Association Awards '94: Best Feature Documentary; MTV Movie Awards '95: Best New Filmmaker Award (James); National Board of Review Awards '94: Best Feature Documentary; New York Film Critics Awards '94: Best Feature Documentary; National Society of Film Critics Awards '94: Best Feature Documentary; Sundance Film Festival '94: Audience Award; Nominations: Academy Awards '94: Best Film Editing. **VHS, LV** *NLC*

Hot Millions

This very funny sleeper came and went in the summer of 1968. Within six months Maggie Smith would become an international star, but no one knew that yet. Those who did see *Hot Millions* in theatres or who catch it now on cable television can see what stage buffs knew very early on: that Maggie Smith is among the funniest comediennes of her generation. She certainly has plenty of chances to show her flair for comedy here as Patty, a hopeless muddler who screws up one job after another. She is befriended by Marcus Pendleton (Peter Ustinov), who gets her a job where he works, but she muffs that, too. Fellow office worker Gnatpole (Bob Newhart) has an eye on Patty, too, but she only has eyes for the kindly Marcus and they get married. Marcus has big plans involving computers, none of which are legal, and Klemper (Karl Malden) is on his trail. But Patty has a few big (and extremely clever, considering her employment history) plans of her own, all of which she keeps to herself. Robert Morley and Cesar Romero are on hand for the fun, and Usti-

**INDEPENDENT
FILM GUIDE**

dent in the lives of John Lennon and Brian Epstein while they were on a Barcelona holiday. It has attracted rave reviews all over the world and the look of the film is exactly right for the period. But since both Lennon and Epstein are long dead, why make THIS movie, rather than any other, about their long professional association? Well, if the film had been about a well dressed fictional man of the world and his young, gifted, and fictional client, would *The Hours and Times* have attracted the attention it has? No, it would not. Ethical considerations aside, incomplete forward passes generally occupy a minute, not an hour, of screen time. Very well acted by David Angus as Brian and by Ian Hart as John, though. (Hart played the role a second time in 1994's more elaborate *Backbeat*.) ♫♫♫

1992 60m/B David Angus, Ian Hart, Stephanie Pack, Robin McDonald, Sergio Moreno, Unity Grimwood; *D:* Christopher Munch; *W:* Christopher Munch. Sundance Film Festival '92: Special Jury Prize. **VHS** *FXL, BTV*

A House in the Hills

Chances are that you missed *A House in the Hills* on the big screen. We're still trying to figure out whether or not we would have liked it if we'd seen it in a theatre instead of on video. Like many contemporary thrillers, it deals with the menace of everyday phenomena in 20th century life. In *A House in the Hills,* the very appealing Helen Slater is a waitress by day and an actress in her dreams. She accepts a position as a house-sitter for strangers and, sure enough, it's the job from hell. There was a murder next door, the somewhat hostile lady of the house tells her. (Does Slater quit? Of course not!) The man of the house is weird, too; as soon as they meet, he compares the petals of his precious roses to female genitalia. (WHY doesn't she quit? I DON'T KNOW!) Anyway, they split and Helen immediately starts rummaging through closets and trying on

Ian Hart and David Angus as Beatle John Lennon and manager Brian Epstein in *The Hours and Times*.

nov co-wrote the screenplay. Well worth a hunt and/or setting the alarm for Red Eye Theatre. ♫♫♫

1968 106m/C *GB* Peter Ustinov, Maggie Smith, Karl Malden, Bob Newhart, Robert Morley, Cesar Romero, Melinda May, Ann Lancaster, Margaret Courtenay, Lynda Baron, Billy Milton, Peter Jones, Raymond Huntley, Kynaston Reeves; *D:* Eric Till; *W:* Ira Wallach, Peter Ustinov. **VHS, Closed Caption** *MGM*

The Hours and Times

Die-hard Beatles fans may quibble with the historical accuracy of Christopher Munch's 1992 movie, but *The Hours and Times* is in fact inspired by an authentic 1963 inci-

clothes when burglar Michael Madsen shows up. But they Fall in Love for the weekend, so that's okay. Nope, the guy you got to watch out for is the lumpy next door neighbor, Jeffrey Tambor, who looks like he should be playing the sort of roles that the late Richard Deacon used to get, but whose career has taken a much odder turn. *A House in the Hills* succeeds in spite of its predictable self; Slater is brave and resourceful, especially when she's swinging shovels, and Madsen has the sort of lived-in charm that has made him an always pleasant discovery on the video shelf. 🦴🦴🎗

1993 (R) 91m/C Helen Slater, Michael Madsen, Jeffrey Tambor, James Laurenson, Elyssa Davalos, Toni Barry; **D:** Ken Wiederhorn; **W:** Ken Wiederhorn; **C:** Josep Civit; **M:** Richard Einhorn. **VHS, LV, Closed Caption** *LIV*

House of Cards

Rule Number One for today's screenwriters is "Write lean." You'd think that a 109-minute movie like *House of Cards* would be long enough to say just about everything it had to say about the efforts of a mother and a psychiatrist to help a troubled child recover from the trauma of her father's sudden death. But let's say they cut—oh—11 minutes from that lean screenplay, minutes when they might have explained why a presumably caring mother barely notices when her daughter Sally clicks off to the outside world. Minutes when they might have explained why Mom continues to appear cavalier as her little girl's deep distress becomes more and more obvious. Or minutes when they might have explained why Mom could expose Sally to a high architectural structure when the kid has nearly fallen to her death twice. All these missing minutes turn what could have been a consistently absorbing story into one that grinds to a halt every so often as you ask yourself, "Why the heck did they do that?" Screenwriter Michael Lessac was the director on this one, so the film's flaws and

virtues can fairly be attributed to his vision or lack of same. The Mom in *House of Cards* was originally supposed to he a Dad, but when Kathleen Turner heard that Lessac wanted William Hurt for the lead, she said, "Hey, what about me?" and the role was hers. Would it have made more sense if a FATHER was the clueless parent? Maybe, because we expect mothers to be the caretakers. Since Turner's character, very definitely, is established as the parent responsible for raising Sally, her laissez faire behavior makes us question both her inclinations and her ability to help her kid. Dr. Tommy Lee Jones is brought into the plot to strike a few subterranean sexual sparks with Mom (they never ignite) and to drag Sally into a clinical setting where autistic and other troubled kids remain in their own irretrievable inner worlds. Mom resists this approach and tries another, with the aid of a recently ubiquitous cinematic tool: virtual reality. The device is mostly hooey, but works at the level of science fiction. In fact, the entire movie plays well enough, in fits and starts, to make you realize that a few more drafts would have turned *House of Cards* into the thoughtful, lovely film it deserved to be. 🦴🦴

1992 (PG-13) 109m/C Kathleen Turner, Asha Menina, Tommy Lee Jones, Shiloh Strong, Esther Rolle, Park Overall, Michael Horse, Anne Pitoniak; **D:** Michael Lessac; **W:** Michael Lessac. **VHS, LV, Closed Caption** *LIV, BTV, FCT*

House of Games

Writer David Mamet made his directorial debut with *House of Games* starring his then-wife Lindsay Crouse. The sequences with Crouse in action as a psychiatrist really do not work, but once she starts investigating the world of con artists, the plot really starts to hum. Screenwriter Mamet seems more interested in the psychiatrist's dark side than he is in her professional veneer. Crouse is ideally cast opposite Joe Mantegna as the weirdly paired couple who need each other like a

coffin needs nails. Both are cool customers who know how to turn on the heat when it serves their purposes. There's rarely been a film with such a perfect middle and such unsatisfactory opening and closing scenes. Still, from the moment Crouse enters the House of Games until she leaves Charlie's Tavern for the last time, you may find yourself as hypnotized by sleaze as she is. 🎞🎞🎞

1987 (R) 102m/C Joe Mantegna, Lindsay Crouse, Lilia Skala, J.T. Walsh, Meshach Taylor, Ricky Jay, Mike Nussbaum, Willo Hausman; **D:** David Mamet; **W:** David Mamet; **C:** Juan Ruiz-Anchia; **M:** Alaric Jans. **VHS, Beta, LV** *HBO, FCT*

The House of the Spirits

Readers with warm memories of Isabel Allende's classic 1982 novel, *La Casa de los Espiritus,* are well advised to treasure them and skip Miramax's ILL-advised screen translation with an award-winning international cast. From the moment you see the horrifyingly miscast Jeremy Irons trying to look like a poor suitor from Chile, you KNOW that every second of this 138-minute mess is going to be a DOOZY! I may be the only person who saw *Reversal of Fortune* who was convinced that Irons won the 1990 Oscar as Claus Von Bulow by neglecting to blow his nose before he said his lines, and he's even worse here: "Hey, everybody, I'm not really from the Isle of Wight, check out the wig, check out the make-up, and check out the weird voice; alright, so it wouldn't fool anyone in Chile, but you'll never guess how I did it!" I can guess, though, and it's grisly to listen to his phlegm-ridden delivery for two hours and eighteen minutes. Next on the miscast list is Glenn Close as Jeremy

Irons' sister. Maybe it's the fact that the film spans fifty years and she never ages or even changes her clothes. Close is hung up on her sister-in-law Clara, played by Meryl Streep, who is the only member of the cast who escapes looking downright silly. Vanessa Redgrave is seen briefly as Streep's mother, and the narration is supplied by the very American Winona Ryder as the daughter of Irons and Streep. It IS within the realm of possibility that even this cast might have been credible with a different script and a different director, but the script and direction here are both supplied by Bille August. Rarely has such impressive source material wound up in the hands of someone so totally out of touch with it. Where Allende's book is non-judgmental and compassionate, August's interpretation is laughable. How else can one explain a sequence in which Irons rapes Sarita Choudhury, that is followed immediately by Ryder's off-camera line, "My father earned everything he got by his own work?" Jeremy Irons and Meryl Streep age on-camera, except that Streep's hands are as smooth as a baby's on her deathbed. Maria Conchita Alonso is supposed to be Irons' contemporary, but the older he gets, the younger she looks; C'MON, NO ONE NOTICED THIS IN CONTINUITY? Or was this stifled by the fact that August won an Oscar so he HAD to know what he was doing? August telegraphs every relationship shift, every plot development, every chuckle, every impending tragedy—did I mention that this thing was 138 minutes long? Cast Note: Besides Armin Mueller-Stahl, Antonio Banderas, Miriam Colon, Vincent Gallo, Jan Niklas, Teri Polo et al, the beautiful little girl who plays Clara as a child is Meryl Streep's real-life ten-year-old daughter, Mary Willa Gummer, billed here as Jane Gray. **WOOF!**

1993 (R) 109m/C Meryl Streep, Jeremy Irons, Glenn Close, Winona Ryder, Antonio Banderas, Armin Mueller-Stahl, Vanessa Redgrave, Sarita Choudhury, Maria Conchita Alonso, Vincent Gallo, Miriam Colon, Jan Niklas, Teri Polo, Jane Gray; **D:** Bille August; **W:** Bille August; **M:** Hans Zimmer. **VHS, LV, Closed Caption** *LIV*

The House on Carroll Street

The House on Carroll Street is an old-fashioned political thriller directed by Peter Yates, who began his career directing television episodes of *Danger Man* and *The Saint*. There is very little gore in the film and much more emphasis on the tension created by soft sounds, shadows, and atmosphere. Yates' approach actually suits the material quite well, giving the film the look and feel of the 1951 era in which it was set. Viewers who did not live through the McCarthy era might not understand the terror faced by ordinary people with decent political convictions who were absolutely dominated and, sometimes, driven out of their professions, by the hysteria ignited by Senator Joseph McCarthy. His fictional equivalent here, played to the hilt by Mandy Patinkin, may seem the most unsubtle of villains to those who never knew McCarthy, but at the height of his powers, between 1950 and 1954, even those who saw through him couldn't stop him. Screenwriter Walter Bernstein was blacklisted in 1948 after working on one Burt Lancaster film noir, and he didn't work in Hollywood for another eleven years. His script captures the fear of that illogical time, and he has written nicely shaded roles for the principals. Kelly McGillis is an interesting heroine, capturing the gutsiness shared by many who lost their jobs through blacklisting. Remember Kent Smith in the '40s *Cat People* movies on the late show? Jeff Daniels may be his closest cinematic equivalent today, slightly stupid, sorta sweet, and the perfect leading man for a stunning female star. Jessica Tandy has a good bit as McGillis' new employer after she is fired from her magazine job. The whole thing is well edited and photographed, with a romantic score by Georges Delerue. The plot, for all its realistic background details, is pure fiction. In real-life, McGillis would have cooled her heels for a decade working at poverty-level jobs, but Bernstein gives her an exciting

INDEPENDENT FILM GUIDE

Reid)-Make-It-to-the-Party-Even-Though-His-Dad-Grounded-Him? *House Party* was so popular that two sequels followed in the next four years, but neither matched the spontaneity of Reginald Hudlin's original film. 🦴🦴🦴

1990 (R) 100m/C Christopher Reid, Christopher Martin, Martin Lawrence, Tisha Campbell, Paul Anthony, A.J. Johnson, Robin Harris; *D:* Reginald Hudlin; *W:* Reginald Hudlin; *M:* Marcus Miller. Sundance Film Festival '90: Best Cinematography. **VHS, Beta, LV** *NLC, FCT*

Household Saints

I can see why *Household Saints* intrigued non-Catholic audiences, but for me, it fell into the "Oh, Those Crazy Catholics!" file. Actually, it reminded me of the morbid stories the nuns used to tell us in Catholic school, which we were almost positive Never Happened. We heard the grisliest one from our second grade teacher and I have to admit we egged her on. Two nurses put an amputated arm in the bed of a third nurse, just to play a trick on her. When they check in on her later, she is completely mad and sucking the fingers of the amputated arm. What a nice story for seven-year-old kids.... Lili Taylor nails it as Teresa, who thinks she sees Jesus (Sebastien Roche) in her apartment and wants to be a saint when she dies. Creepy. The rest of the cast is quite good, especially Vincent D'Onofrio as Joseph Santangelo, but director Nancy Savoca's *True Love* and *Dogfight* are better. Based on a novel by Francine Prose. 🦴🦴🦴

1993 (R) 124m/C Tracey Ullman, Vincent D'Onofrio, Lili Taylor, Judith Malina, Michael Rispoli, Victor Argo, Michael Imperioli, Rachael Bella, Illeana Douglas, Joe Grifasi, Sebastien Roche; *D:* Nancy Savoca; *W:* Nancy Savoca, Richard Guay; *C:* Bobby Bukowski; *M:* Stephen Endelman. Independent Spirit Awards '94: Best Supporting Actress (Taylor); Nominations: Independent Spirit Awards '94: Best Actor (D'Onofrio), Best Screenplay. **VHS, Closed Caption** *COL*

Julia (Rachel Ward) and Dennis Bagley (Richard E. Grant) in *How to Get Ahead in Advertising.*

mystery to solve and a government agent as an ally. For those who want more low-down on the Communist witch hunt years, watch *The Front. The House on Carroll Street* makes fine use of its 111-minute running time in an intriguing blend of politics and suspense. 🦴🦴🦴

1988 (PG) 111m/C Kelly McGillis, Jeff Daniels, Mandy Patinkin, Jessica Tandy; *D:* Peter Yates; *W:* Walter Bernstein; *C:* Michael Ballhaus; *M:* Georges Delerue. **VHS, Beta, LV, Closed Caption** *HBO*

House Party

Any comedy about a party without grownups is my idea of a fun flick. *House Party* features a likeable cast, great dance numbers, and suspense, as in Will-Kid-(Christopher

How to Get Ahead in Advertising

Once upon a time, Bruce Robinson was an actor. He played Benvolio in *Romeo and Juliet* and co-starred with Isabelle Adjani in *The Story of Adele H....* Many years later, he won an Oscar nomination for writing *The Killing Fields* and in 1987 he directed his first movie, *Withnail and I,* starring Richard E. Grant. That film, like *How to Get Ahead in Advertising,* was produced by George Harrison. If his scripts are any indication, Robinson's eclectic life has served him well. The intensity of his dialogue suggests years of angry simmering and he wastes no time now getting straight to the point: advertising is the root of all evil. The less said about how Robinson develops this theme, the better, since we nearly took a pass on the film when we heard the plot. As Robinson showed with his debut feature, though, he knows exactly where and how he's going, most of the time. *How to Get Ahead* would make an insane double bill with a similarly themed Cary Grant comedy from 1948, *Mr. Blandings Builds his Dream House.* The frustration of both ad men elicits hilarity, but where Mr. Blandings is lulled into security with Myrna Loy's Mrs. Blandings in post-war Connecticut, Richard E. Grant's character is so consumed by his profession that even the compassionate Rachel Ward is unable to retrieve him. Robinson's script is a raging polemic by film's end, which is a visual drag especially since the force of his argument has already been conveyed so well by the ad man's internal struggle for his own soul. Still, the sharpness of Robinson's language as well as Richard E. Grant's dazzling transformation make *How to Get Ahead in Advertising* one of the most original and bracing British comedies of the late 1980s. ♪♪♪

1989 (R) 95m/C *GB* Richard E. Grant, Rachel Ward, Susan Wooldridge, Mick Ford, Richard Wilson, John Shrapnel, Jacqueline Tong; *D:* Bruce Robinson; *W:* Bruce Robinson; *M:* David Dundas, Rick Wentworth. **VHS, Beta, LV** *VTR, CRC*

Hu-Man

Hu-Man may call itself a "visual feast," but it's SOOO boring. It wastes the talents of Terence Stamp and Jeanne Moreau; director Jerome Lapperrousaz gives them little to do but say about 15 lines of dialogue in his 93-minute screenplay. It's an Orpheus re-tread. Stamp's an actor from the future who's decided to be the first time traveler. His ex-mistress Moreau wants him to be on her television show before he begins his travels. *Hu-Man* seems little more than a massive stage for a mysterious concept, the exact nature of which is never revealed. **WOOF!**

1976 93m/C *FR* Terence Stamp, Jeanne Moreau, Agnes Stevenin, Frederik Van Pallandt; *D:* Jerome Lapperrousaz; *W:* A. Ruellan, G. Lapperrousaz; *C:* Jimmy Glasberg. *NYR*

The Hungarians

Zoltan Fabri tries to make *The Hungarians* a more substantial film than it really is. He focuses on some migrant farm workers who go to Germany, partly for the money and partly to avoid fighting in World War II. The weak script seems to make the statement that everyone picks on the Hungarians and it's a shame, really, because they're such nice people. Unfortunately, neither the dramatic situations nor any of the characters are developed very well. The best thing about this movie is Gyorgy Illes' fine cinematography. ♪♪

1978 m/C *HU* Andras Ambrus, Noemi Apor, Jozsef Bihari; *D:* Zoltan Fabri; *C:* Gyorgy Illes. *NYR*

I Am Cuba

Agitprop Russian-Cuban co-production illustrates different aspects of the Cuban revolution from the toppling of Batista's decadent Havana to idealistic soldiers and student revolutionaries. Lots of oratory and deliberate artificiality combined with cinematographer Sergei Urusevsky's stunning high-contrast photography. A 1996 Independent Spirit Award nominee for Best Foreign Film. 🐾🐾

1964 141m/B *CU RU* Luz Maria Collazo, Jose Gallardo, Sergio Corrieri, Jean Bouise, Raul Garcia, Celia Rodriguez; *D:* Mikhail Kalatozov; *W:* Yevgeny Yevtushenko, Enrique Pineda Barnet; *C:* Sergei Urusevsky; *M:* Carlos Farinas. Nominations: Independent Spirit Awards '96: Best Foreign Language Film. **VHS** *MIL, FCT*

I Have Killed

It wasn't easy sustaining a career as a Japanese matinee idol, yet Sessue Hayakawa (1889-1973) was able to avoid the stereotypical roles that most Asian actors of his generation had to play. Even when he was assigned to a part in which the racism was taken for granted, Hayakawa invested the role with such strong sensuality that the racist message was subverted through sheer charisma. Take 1915's *The Cheat*: the unstated text is that Fannie Ward's branding by Hayakawa is A Fate Worse Than Death. But clearly there were many female audience members who were attracted to Hayakawa and they turned out in droves to make him one of the top stars in 1915. Four years later, Hayakawa starred in *The Tong Man,* torn between his love (for Helen Jerome Eddy) and duty. In spite of his obvious box office appeal, especially to women, jobs in Hollywood were not as plentiful as they might have been and Hayakawa signed on to make *I Have Killed* in France. Once again, he is torn; the wife (Huguette Duflos) of a close friend with a bad heart is being blackmailed by a slime and Hayakawa comes gallantly to her rescue. Maybe a little TOO gallantly, for even in France, he couldn't cruise off into the sunset with her, only alone. To stack the deck even more, her child gets along famously with Hayakawa. Isn't it amazing, what a great husband and father he might have been, if only...? (Things were different, of course!) In 1931, Hayakawa as

Scotland Yard investigator Ah Kee starred opposite Anna May Wong as Ling Moy in *Daughter of the Dragon,* with Swedish character actor Warner Oland as Fu Manchu. Hayakawa picked up a whole new generation of fans when he became a character actor himself in such films as *Tokyo Joe, Three Came Home, The Bridge on the River Kwai* (for which he won an Oscar nomination), *The Geisha Boy, Green Mansions, Hell to Eternity,* and Walt Disney's *The Swiss Family Robinson. I Have Killed* is vintage Hayakawa; his underplaying wipes out everyone else's histrionics and you'll be seeing his eyes in your dreams long after the movie's over. 🐾🐾🐾

1924 90m/B *FR* Sessue Hayakawa, Huguette Duflos, Max Maxudian, Maurice Sigrist, Pierre Daltour, Denise Legeay, Jules De Spoly, Andre Volbert; *D:* Roger Lion; *W:* Roger Lion; *C:* Maurice Defassiaux. *NYR*

I Like It Like That

I Like It Like That is not an indie, but deserves inclusion here as the first feature written and directed by a black woman (Darnell Martin) for a major studio (Hail Columbia!) in Hollywood. There are only two well known stars in it, Griffin Dunne as Stephen Price, a recording industry executive, and Rita Moreno as Rosario Linares, a nagging mother-in-law. The best performances in the movie are given by little-known actors, mainly Lauren Velez as the female protagonist, Lisette Linares. Lisette and her yucky husband, Chino (Jon Seda), have three kids (Tomas Melly as Li'l Chino, Desiree Casado as Minnie, and Isaiah Garcia as Pee Wee). Chino is busted for stealing a stereo and Lisette has to get a job FAST. Price hires her as his assistant, but soon the neighborhood is gossiping that Lisette only got the job because she's having sex with him. When Chino is out of jail and hears the false gossip, he has sex with neighborhood girl Magdalena Soto (Lisa Vidal). By this point, you may wonder why Lisette doesn't leave Chino. (I sure the hell would!) Life, this film suggests, doesn't work that way. Although Martin's sympathy is clearly with Lisette, she has a humorous take on the problems faced by the rest of the Linares clan, including Lisette's transsexual brother, Alexis (Jesse Borrego). But the humor renders tolerable stuff that really shouldn't be, not for Lisette, and certainly not for her kids. Nonetheless, it's a promising cinematic start for Martin and for Velez. 🦴🦴🦴

1994 (R) 106m/C Lauren Velez, Jon Seda, Lisa Vidal, Jesse Borrego, Griffin Dunne, Rita Moreno, Tomas Melly, Desiree Casado, Isaiah Garcia; **D:** Darnell Martin; **W:** Darnell Martin; **C:** Alexander Grusynski; **M:** Sergio George. Nominations: Independent Spirit Awards '95: Best Actor (Seda), Best Actress (Velez), Best Cinematography, Best First Feature. **VHS, LV, Closed Caption** COL

I Married a Witch

One of the coolest movie stars between 1941 and 1947 was...Veronica Lake (1919-73) AND *I Married a Witch* is one of her coolest movies. Along with her father, Daniel (Cecil Kellaway, 1893-1973), she is burned at the stake during the Puritan era. For their part in this nefarious deed, the male descendants of the Wooley family are doomed forever to be the most miserable married men on Earth. Cut to the early 1940s: Wallace Wooley (Fredric March, 1897-1975) is about to be married to Estelle Masterson (Susan Hayward, 1917-75), a real shrew. Not if Jennifer (Lake) can help it! Wooley also wants to be Governor with the support of his future father-in-law, J.R. (Robert Warwick, 1878-1964). He "rescues" Jennifer from a fire (well, she IS a witch!), and she proceeds to bewitch him, as only she can. Estelle and J.R. don't like it one bit. Tough. Jennifer and Daniel make mischief in Wooley's life, until she falls in love with him and loses her magic powers. (There's a lesson here!) French director Rene (*The Ghost Goes West*) Clair (1898-1981) keeps things moving at a merry clip, and Robert Benchley (1889-1945) is a delight as always as Dr. Dudley White. His Algonquin Round Table crony Marc Connelly

(1890-1980) contributed to the splendid adaptation of Thorne Smith's *The Passionate Witch*. Look for exquisite five-year-old Ann Carter as Jennifer's daughter, soon to receive rave reviews as Amy for Val Lewton's *The Curse of the Cat People* and as Beatrice for Mark Hellinger's *The Two Mrs. Carrolls*. P.S. Ten years after what turned out to be the highlight of her career, Lake accepted a television assignment on an episode of *Tales of Tomorrow* entitled "Flight Overdue." Her glorious blonde mane had been hacked away in favor of a butch cut suitable for an aviatrix. The primitive video lighting was harsh on a young woman of 32, and so were the ghastly costumes. But the saddest thing about the show is the script. Lake speaks forcefully of her right to live her life as she chooses and, after her Amelia Earhart-style disappearance, Walter Brooke as her icky husband says, "I'm glad she's gone and at last I'm free." This horrifying bit of sexual propaganda from the spring of 1952 nearly broke my heart. 🦴🦴🦴🦴

1942 77m/B Veronica Lake, Fredric March, Susan Hayward, Robert Benchley, Cecil Kellaway, Elizabeth Patterson, Robert Warwick, Eily Malyon, Mary Field, Nora Cecil, Emory Parnell, Helen St. Rayer, Aldrich Bowker, Emma Dunn, Harry Tyler, Ralph Peters, Ann Carter; **D:** Rene Clair; **W:** Robert Pirosh, Marc Connelly; **C:** Ted Tetzlaff; **M:** Roy Webb. Nominations: Academy Awards '42: Best Original Score. **VHS, Beta, LV** MLB, WAR

I Met a Murderer

James Mason was years away from achieving international stardom when he made *I Met a Murderer* in 1939 with Roy Kellino as director and cinematographer and his future wife Pamela Kellino as co-star. All three produced the low-budget film and the two stars collaborated on adapting Mrs. Kellino's short story for the screen. This excellent early showcase for James Mason focuses on a fugitive who wanders around the country with a writer; the film benefits from the on-location filming. Its sympathetic depiction of a man who shoots his wife (Sylvia Coleridge) only after she shoots his

Lili Taylor as Valerie Solanas in *I Shot Andy Warhol*.

dog provided the film with a noir atmosphere that was unusual for British movies of that era. ♫♫♫

1939 79m/B James Mason, Pamela Kellino, Sylvia Coleridge, William Devlin, Esma Cannon, James Harcourt; **D:** Roy Kellino; **C:** Roy Kellino. **VHS** *SNC, NOS, DVT*

I Shot Andy Warhol

Valerie Solanas is not a historical figure for whom one automatically feels a great deal of sympathy. Until I saw Lili Taylor's take on her, I always thought she was a precursor of would-be assassins like Squeaky Fromme or Sara Jane Moore. If you compare her story with the one told in

Basquiat, you wonder why she would even want to solicit Warhol's approval, every card in his deck was so stacked against her. But she did want his approval, and her mental health steadily declined as a result. There is one rather sad sequence in which Solanas carefully chooses just the right outfit to meet a would-be publisher. She is so excited by what she hopes will be her big break and she tries so hard to create a dignified impression. Most of the time, though, she lugs around deep hostility towards everyone, while hoping that her work will win acceptance in spite of her behavior. As in every film that revolves around Andy Warhol (played here by Jared Harris), there are the usual eccentric roles that actors wanting to give their careers a jump start would do anything to play. Stephen Dorff is Candy Darling, a Warhol superstar who died at 26 in 1974. Jamie Harrold is Jackie Curtis, a Warhol superstar who died at 38 in 1985. Michael Imperioli is Ondine, a Warhol superstar who died at 51 in 1989. On the other hand, Reginald Rodgers, Miriam Cyr, and Tahnee Welch are living legends Paul Morrisey, Ultra Violet, and Viva. The filmmakers try hard to show that Solanas wanted to do more with her life than shoot Andy Warhol, but as she antagonizes every single one of her supporters, her manifesto shrinks in importance compared to the one act of violence that got her in the history books. Now—the big news for 1998 is that Lili Taylor and Melissa Etheridge will be starring in dueling versions of *The Janis Joplin Story.* One can only hope that Etheridge's acting is a notch above Madonna's or k.d. lang's, but bets are on that Taylor will give her usual tremendous performance as the definitive Janis. ♫♫♫

1996 (R) 100m/C Lili Taylor, Jared Harris, Stephen Dorff, Martha Plimpton, Donovan Leitch, Tahnee Welch, Michael Imperioli, Lothaire Bluteau, Anna Thompson, Peter Friedman, Jill Hennessey, Craig Chester, James Lyons, Reginald Rodgers, Jamie Harrold, Edoardo Ballerini, Lynn Cohen, Miriam Cyr, Isabel Gillies, Eric Mabius; **D:** Mary Harron; **W:** Mary Harron, Daniel Minahan; **C:** Ellen Kuras; **M:** John Cale. Nominations: Independent Spirit Awards '97: Best First Feature. **VHS** *HMK*

194

INDEPENDENT FILM GUIDE

I Wasn't Made for These Times

The Beach Boys dominated international music charts between 1962 and 1969 as living proof that the California sun, the Pacific ocean, and non-stop "Good Vibrations" could keep five Hawthorne surfer boys frozen in time as teenagers forever. Dennis Wilson's 1983 drowning and Brian Wilson's 1991 autobiography *Wouldn't It Be Nice* revealed that, long before their rise and fall and resurrection, life was far from happy-go-lucky for the group. *I Wasn't Made for These Times,* a 70-minute documentary by filmmaker Don Was, takes a look at Brian Wilson today, with brief appearances by mother Audree, brother Carl, daughters Carnie and Wendy, and even ex-wife Marilyn. Dr. Eugene Landy, the controversial therapist whom Brian Wilson credited with saving his life, is nowhere in evidence, although Wilson refers to him somewhat dismissively just once. Despite the decision to make the film in timeless black and white, Was' film is not even remotely nostalgic, nor is there any attempt to examine the Beach Boys' career in scholarly fashion. This appears to be how Brian Wilson wants to be seen and remembered at the age of 52, clearly ravaged by his youthful excesses, but still eager for audience acceptance and attention as a solo artist. ♫♫♫

1994 70m/B Brian Wilson, Carnie Wilson, Wendy Wilson; *D:* Don Was. *NYR*

The Iceman Cometh

The idea for the American Film Theatre was laudable: the very best American plays, interpreted by the very best American actors, and helmed by the very best American directors. Season tickets would be sold in advance to subscribers who presumably cared about the preservation of American theatrical classics on film...whoa, let me stop right there. It sounds rather elitist, doesn't it? And PAY for eight movies all at once? (Well, okay, there WAS a special rate for students.) The ordering information said that only subscribers would ever be able to see these movies, which seems to be true, because *The Iceman Cometh,* the personal favorite of its director John Frankenheimer, didn't appear to turn up anywhere after its original screenings in 1973. Two-thirds of its cast members are now deceased and it did provide Frederic March, Robert Ryan, and Martyn Green with fitting swan songs to their long careers. There are many memorable moments in this ensemble piece, but it also gave this audience member my one and only movie hangover. It's 17 minutes LONGER than *Gone with the Wind,* and it all takes place in one bar where the mostly male patrons discuss their need for illusions. For example, Harry Hope (March) can't leave the bar—he'll get run over by a car if he does. Some reviewers in 1973 felt that Jason Robards, as the greatest actor of his generation to interpret Eugene O'Neill, should have played Hickey instead of Lee Marvin. Oscar-winner Marvin wound up being okay instead of great in the role, which compromises the film's value to scholars AND audiences, then and now. The acting by everyone else (especially by March, Ryan, and Jeff Bridges, with two Oscars and seven nominations between them) is remarkable, but it's still very heavy going and undoubtedly benefits writers of O'Neill theses the most. ♫♫▽

1973 239m/C Lee Marvin, Fredric March, Robert Ryan, Jeff Bridges, Martyn Green, George Voskovec, Moses Gunn, Tom Pedi, Evans Evans, Bradford Dillman, Sorrell Booke, John McLiam; *D:* John Frankenheimer; *C:* Ralph Woolsey. *NO*

If. . .

I was so desperate to see a movie one winter in Venice that I watched a revival screening of *If...,* dubbed in German and with Italian subtitles (neither of which I can understand or read). It was still every bit as subversive as I remember, and a bracing antidote to so many schoolboy sagas, where the status quo is rigidly maintained at any cost. Malcolm McDowell is pretty scary here as Mick Travers, but nowhere near as scary as he would become as Alex De Large in 1972's *A Clockwork Orange*. (It would be several YEARS before I could look at a McDowell picture again after that.) *If...* is a product of its time in that all paths lead to the revolution, but no paths lead from it. Mick and his mates succeed in bringing down the headmaster, but what then? Outside of this movie, there was Labour Leader Harold Wilson (1916-95, who DIDN'T go to public school), Conservative Edward Heath, Wilson again, Labour Leader James Callaghan, Conservatives Margaret Thatcher and John Major, and Labour Leader Tony Blair. But Conservatives and Labour Leaders alike try to woo the opposite party these days, and the most moderate Conservatives may well be more liberal than Tony Blair; not exactly the stuff of which anarchists and revolutions are made. Still, the energy and intensity of the revolt in *If...* is what sticks in your memory, not the middle-aged character actor that Malcolm McDowell has become. Based on John Howlett's *Crusaders*. 🎬🎬🎬🎬

1969 (R) 111m/C *GB* Malcolm McDowell, David Wood, Christine Noonan, Richard Warwick, Robert Swann, Arthur Lowe, Mona Washbourne, Graham Crowden, Hugh Thomas, Guy Rose, Peter Jeffrey, Geoffrey Chater, Mary MacLeod, Anthony Nicholls, Ben Aris, Charles Lloyd Pack, Rupert Webster, Brian Pettifer, Sean Bury, Michael Cadman; **D:** Lindsay Anderson; **W:** David Sherwin; **C:** Miroslav Ondricek; **M:** Marc Wilkinson. Cannes Film Festival '69: Best Film. **VHS, Beta, LV** *PAR*

If I Had It to Do Over Again

Who's going to believe that Anouk Aimee, attractive as ever at 44, would fall for the 14-year-old son of her best friend, especially with the shady past her character has had? Moreover, Catherine Deneuve (at 33, but looking much younger) is absolutely unbelievable as a woman who's been in prison for 16 years. Expository sequences are omitted and all the characters are unevenly developed in Lelouch's flimsily constructed screenplay here. Needless to say, though, Aimee and Deneuve make *If I Had It to Do Over Again* a most pleasant film to watch. **AKA:** Second Chance; Si C'Etait a Refaire. 🎬🎬½

1976 94m/C *FR* Anouk Aimee, Catherine Deneuve, Charles Denner, Francis Huster; **D:** Claude Lelouch; **W:** Claude Lelouch; **C:** Jacques Lefrancois. *NYR*

Impact

Ella Raines (1921-88) was a cool, green-eyed brunette (with auburn highlights) who twice made the cover of *Life* magazine when she starred in two '40s noir films for Universal, *Phantom Lady* and *Criss Cross*. Two years before her 1943 film debut, a stove exploded in her face, fortunately resulting in just temporary damage to her hair and eyebrows. (The experience later added to the realism of her performance when she played a woman whose face had been scarred in *The Second Face*.) Raines' career started out strong and she always gave good performances, but her films declined in quality and importance during her five-year contract. 1949's *Impact* was made independently in San Francisco, making fine use of both the city itself and the surrounding Bay area, including Sausalito and Larkspur. With better distribution, it might have picked up the reputation it deserves, for rarely has a film noir been as expertly convoluted as this one has. It has everything! Infidelity, attempted murder, accidental death, amnesia, false imprisonment, exciting courtroom sequences, missing evidence, a missing witness...what more could anyone ask for at three in the morning? Ella Raines plays a resourceful garage mechanic who stops at nothing to free the man she loves (Brian Donlevy). The excellent cast also features Charles Coburn as a tenacious inspector, lovely Helen Walker as the wife from hell, Anna May Wong as the loyal employee who holds they key to the mystery, and Mae Marsh as Raines' mom. Only a few of Raines' films are available on video (including some episodes of her 1954 television series, *Janet Dean, Registered Nurse*). Luckily, *Impact* is among them. 🦴🦴🦴

1949 83m/B Brian Donlevy, Ella Raines, Charles Coburn, Helen Walker, Anna May Wong, Philip Ahn, Art Baker, Tony Barrett, Harry Cheshire, Lucius Cooke, Sheilah Graham, Tom Greenway, Hans Herbert, Linda Johnson, Joe Kirk, Clarence Kolb, Mary Landa, Mae Marsh; **D:** Arthur Lubin; **W:** Dorothy Reid, Jay Dratler; **C:** Ernest Laszlo; **M:** Michel Michelet. **VHS, Beta** *NOS, MRV, DVT*

Impromptu

It's holiday time in the 1830s and the Duke and Duchess d'Antan (Anton Rodgers, Emma Thompson) have invited a glittering array of guests to their mansion: Frederic Chopin (1810-49, Hugh Grant), Franz Liszt (1811-86, Julian Sands), Marie d'Agoult (Bernadette Peters), and Eugene Delacroix (1798-1863, Ralph Brown). Who should crash the house party but George Sand (1804-76, Judy Davis)? This dynamo winds up with the crush to end all crushes on Chopin, whom Grant plays as a twit (duh!). Also on hand is Sand's current lover Felicien Mallefille (Georges Corraface) and future (?) lover Alfred de Musset (Mandy Patinkin), but so what? It's a delight to see these venerable artists so young and high-spirited here and having such a rattling good time in the romantic department, with passionate minglings galore. Another view of Sand's romance with Chopin is 1975's *Notorious Woman* with Rosemary Harris and George Chakiris (and Jeremy Irons as Liszt). 🦴🦴🦴🦴

1990 (PG-13) 108m/C Judy Davis, Hugh Grant, Mandy Patinkin, Bernadette Peters, Julian Sands, Ralph Brown, Georges Corraface, Anton Rodgers, Emma Thompson, Anna Massey, John Savident, Elizabeth Spriggs; **D:** James Lapine; **W:** Sarah Kernochan; **C:** Bruno de Keyzer. Independent Spirit Awards '92: Best Actress (Davis). **VHS, LV** *TVC, MOV*

In a Wild Moment

In a Wild Moment is Claude Berri's view of a March-September affair. This light and enjoyable comedy benefits from a terrific cast and Berri's above-average screenplay. Middle-aged male movie critics at that time were staggered that teenage girls and middle-aged males HAD affairs. When *In a Wild Moment* was remade in 1984 as Stanley Donen's *Blame It on Rio* (with a terrific cast including Michael Caine, Michelle Johnson, Joseph Bologna, Demi Moore, and Valerie Harper) middle-aged male movie critics at THAT time were staggered that teenage girls and middle-aged males HAD affairs. La plus ca change, la plus ca meme.... 🦴🦴🦴

1978 m/C *FR* Jean-Pierre Marielle, Agnes Soral, Victor Lanoux, Christine Dejoux, Martine Sarcey; **D:** Claude Berri; **W:** Claude Berri. *NYR*

In Celebration

Three successful brothers return to the old homestead for their parents' 40th wedding celebration. With that cast and that director, audiences expected more from *In Celebration* than this walled-in, slightly above average American Film Theatre production. (*In Celebration* was released theatrically overseas in 1976.) Based on a play by David Storey. 🦴🦴▽

1975 (PG) 131m/C *GB CA* Alan Bates, James Bolam, Brian Cox, Constance Chapman, Gabrielle Daye, Bill Owen; **D:** Lindsay Anderson; **C:** Dick Bush. **VHS** *NO*

In the Name of the Father

If U.S. audiences have a difficult time understanding the paternalistic relationship between Northern Ireland and Great Britain, *In the Name of the Father* reveals the deadlock in sharp relief. While huge land masses like Australia and Canada are successfully and peacefully breaking away from the British Empire, tiny Northern Ireland remains painfully tied to a government determined to keep it under control. That control is a key issue in Jim Sheridan's 1993 film, based on Gerry Conlon's autobiography *Proved Innocent.* As a very young and rebellious man, Conlon (beautifully played by Daniel Day-Lewis here) was constantly getting in minor skirmishes with the law. None were particularly serious, but all contributed to making him vulnerable to the far more serious charge of blowing up two pubs as a terrorist. Conlon and his equally devil-may-care friend Paul Hill (portrayed by John Lynch) are innocent, but they are hounded around the clock without legal representation by British authorities, determined to secure speedy convictions. Finally, while they are both half-mad from sleep deprivation and relentless interrogations, they make false confessions, and squirm through their subsequent trial. ("We were bored out of our minds," Day-Lewis as Conlon intones on the soundtrack.) The grim results: not only were both innocent men imprisoned, but their friends and families as well, including Conlon's father, Guiseppe (Pete Postlethwaite, in an Oscar-nominated performance). It is in prison that Conlon gradually becomes politicized by meeting one of the terrorists who was actually responsible for the bombings. He also learns to love and respect his father, a frail but overwhelmingly decent man who retains his deep faith despite the hardships of prison life. Enter Emma Thompson, just right as Gareth Peirce, the Conlons' new attorney who works tirelessly for their release. She is able to prove what the British authorities knew all along, that not only were the Conlons and their associates entirely innocent, but that crucial evidence was suppressed, and all were kept in prison many years after the real terrorists revealed their identities. Strong stuff and still a sore point among many officials of the British crown, so don't expect *In the Name of the Father* to be the honored film at the next Royal Command Performance. Director Sheridan packs an incredible amount of information into his 127-minute film, spanning the mid-'70s through the early '90s. His powerful economy with images is demonstrated from the very first sequence when the horror of the first bombing takes place in mid-gesture, as it would in real life. By keeping the evolving relationship of father and son in strong focus and by making sure that all the period details are dead on center, Sheridan says more about the tortured Irish-British bond than dozens of other films on the subject. ♫♫♫♫

1993 (R) 127m/C *GB IR* Daniel Day-Lewis, Pete Postlethwaite, Emma Thompson, John Lynch, Corin Redgrave, Beatie Edney, John Benfield, Paterson Joseph, Marie Jones, Gerard McSorley, Frank Harper, Mark Sheppard, Don Baker, Britta Smith, Aidan Grennell, Daniel Massey, Bosco Hogan, Daniel Massey; **D:** Jim Sheridan; **W:** Jim Sheridan, Terry George; **C:** Peter Biziou; **M:** Trevor Jones, Bono, Sinead O'Connor. Berlin International Film Festival '94: Golden Berlin Bear; Nominations: Academy Awards '93: Best Actor (Day-Lewis), Best Adapted Screenplay, Best Director (Sheridan), Best Film Editing, Best Picture, Best Supporting Actor (Postlethwaite), Best Supporting Actress (Thompson); British Academy Awards '93: Best Actor (Day-Lewis), Best Adapted Screenplay; Golden Globe Awards '94: Best Actor—Drama (Day-Lewis), Best Film—Drama, Best Song ("(You Made Me the) Thief of Your Heart"), Best Supporting Actress (Thompson). **VHS, LV, Closed Caption** *USH*

In the Soup

Adolpho Rollo (Steve Buscemi) wants to be a filmmaker in the worst way. Scam maestro Joe (Seymore Cassel) says HE'LL be the producer! For the next 93 minutes, Joe shows Adolpho how to con his way through life and into feature film production. Buscemi and Cassel are great together, and Cassel's splashy role recalls his glory days of 1971 when he co-starred opposite Gena Rowlands in *Minnie and Moskowitz* for John Cassavetes. Jennifer Beals (who is married to director Alexandre Rockwell) is charming as Angelica, the object of Adolpho's affection. Many indie legends also contribute to the fun in assorted cameos. For the record, *In the*

Soup was not colorized by computer. It was filmed on color stock and released in black and white. For those who can only watch a color movie, *In the Soup* is available on video in color. Happily, it's also available on video in scrumptious black and white. 🦴🦴▽

1992 (R) 93m/B Steve Buscemi, Seymour Cassel, Jennifer Beals, Will Patton, Pat Moya, Stanley Tucci, Sully Boyar, Rockets Redglare, Elizabeth Bracco, Ruth Maleczech, Debi Mazar, Steven Randazzo, Francesco Messina; *Cameos:* Jim Jarmusch, Carol Kane; *D:* Alexandre Rockwell; *W:* Tim Kissell, Alexandre Rockwell; *C:* Phil Parmet; *M:* Mader. Sundance Film Festival '92: Grand Jury Prize. **VHS, LV, Closed Caption** *ACA*

In the Spirit

In the Spirit's inept promotion campaign must have killed it at the box office. It probably didn't help that Peter Falk, who is terrific in the first half of the film, vanishes mysteriously and never comes back. He is so good that you wish he would return for a line or two at film's end, but no! Jeannie Berlin, playing the world's most boring hooker, wrote an often-hilarious script for her mother Elaine May and Marlo Thomas, who work surprisingly well together under Sandra Seacat's brisk direction. May only needs to raise an eyebrow or lower her voice to get a laugh, thus supplying the perfect counterpoint for Thomas' kinetic energy. Melanie Griffith and Olympia Dukakis have cameo roles in this nicely paced crime caper, which does a delicious job of satirizing Had-I-But-Known mysteries and phony New Ageism. 🦴🦴▽

1990 (R) 94m/C Elaine May, Marlo Thomas, Jeannie Berlin, Peter Falk, Melanie Griffith, Olympia Dukakis, Chad Burton, Thurn Hoffman, Michael Emil, Christopher Durang, Laurie Jones; *D:* Sandra Seacat; *W:* Jeannie Berlin, Laurie Jones; *M:* Patrick Williams. **VHS, Beta** *ACA*

The Incident

The first ten minutes of Larry Peerce's *The Incident* draw us into the grim world of two sadistic jerks played by 31-year-old Tony Musante and 27-year-old Martin Sheen in their film debuts. Then we meet a series of couples who are about to board a New York subway. Diana Van der Vlis wants to take a taxi but her husband (Ed McMahon, in a surprisingly effective performance) grumbles about the expense and insists on a less expensive route home. A couple in their 60s (Thelma Ritter and Jack Gilford) bicker all the way to the station. Ruby Dee tries to calm down her angry husband, Black activist Brock Peters. Robert Fields makes an attempt to pick up Gary Merrill, who seems interested at first, then terrified at the implications. Mike Kellin is convinced that his wife Jan Sterling had been making passes at everyone at a cocktail party. A young couple, Victor Arnold and 23-year-old Donna Mills, make out before boarding the subway car. And local soldier Bob Bannard introduces an Oklahoma soldier with a broken arm (brilliantly played by 25-year-old Beau Bridges) to New York City night life. Director Peerce had made his remarkable directing debut in 1964 with the award-winning interracial love story *One Potato, Two Potato,* also beautifully filmed in black and white. Peerce's early, more personal works placed extremely complex characters against sharply critiqued contemporary American landscapes and *The Incident* is no exception. Once everyone is settled on the subway for the ride home, Musante and Sheen proceed to terrorize everyone on the train. They seize on the passengers' most obvious fears (sexuality, race, age) and strip away every illusion of pride or courage in all but one person. *The Incident* has few flattering observations to make about this group of strangers on the subway. It's hardly an advertisement for public transportation, and there are no feel-good remedies for the internal and actual violence ignited by Musante's and Sheen's characters. *The Incident* reveals the urban despair and dissolving community ties of the late '60s as few films of that era did. Musante and Sheen played archetypical punks; we had seen their like before and would see them again. But *The*

ALEXANDRE ROCKWELL AND JENNIFER BEALS

In the Soup

Alexandre Rockwell: "I wrote the script for *In the Soup,* and the beautiful and magnificent Seymour Cassel came to stay with us for a couple of weeks before we started rehearsals, and he's like Joe, the guy in the movie: he's full of life. I try to go to sleep at night, I wake up and he's lying in bed next to me, tapping me on the shoulder, saying, 'Let's play!' That's Seymour Cassel: he's a life force."

Jennifer Beals: "It's a lot of fun to act with him, too. I never knew what was going to happen. I never had any idea. It makes it easier."

Alexandre Rockwell (singing): "Am I blue?.... It's to the cast's credit that they really didn't improvise much. Really good actors look like they're improvising. Basically, it's like sports, like when Michael Jordan goes to the hoop—it looks like he's doing some incredibly improvised move, but the guy's done one million lay-ups to make it look like that. Seymour [Cassel], Jennifer [Beals], and Steve [Buscemi] are really great. However, they're comfortable and there's a difference between being comfortable and improvising material. In rehearsals, I try anything. So what happens is that it's the last draft of the script, we bang it around, and we try different things, and that's when they add things, and that's when they try different things. They're very comfortable with the script, and they don't feel they're being forced to do something that's unnatural for them. I wanted to get that *Zorba the Greek* quality to the film. It's about the education of Adolpho Rollo, an innocent guy with another guy who's full of life and you never know exactly where Joe the con artist guy stands, but he has a big heart."

Jennifer Beals: "I recommend working with your husband if you really love each other. I wouldn't recommend it if you had a superficial marriage of convenience, because it would be all over."

Alexandre Rockwell: "So she doesn't fully recommend it. She's not fully behind it. I'm trying to get her to trust me after seven years."

Jennifer Beals: "After saying, 'Put your salary back in the movie!' Steve Buscemi and I put our salaries back in the movie, because we're absolutely committed to this project. But I would say definitely, because, hopefully, there's no one you can trust more."

Alexandre Rockwell: "The best compliment to Jennifer was that when we were mixing the film at the end in the sound studio, the sound mixer turned to me after ten days of work and said, 'Which part did Jennifer Beals play?' And I said, 'That's the woman, Angelica, one of the main characters.' He turned red because he knows I'm married to Jennifer and he said, 'Oh my God, I didn't know that was her, because it's such a different part for her.' Jennifer plays a Dominican woman with a very strong accent. Jennifer's very beautiful in this movie as Angelica, and I don't think she's ever been that way before...and it's a black-and-white movie, so it's got a different look to it, too. I wanted to get a film that broke down rules. I'm not interested in the conformity of filmmaking. I wanted to surprise myself and have same fun making it. I went back to films like Jean Vigo's *Zero for Conduct* and John Cassavetes' *Shadows* and Jean-Luc Godard's *Breathless* and *Band of Outsiders*...."

Jennifer Beals: "And *The Honeymooners*. I LOVE *The Honeymooners!*"

Alexandre Rockwell: "I love *The Honeymooners!* I love The Three Stooges! Mix that up with Godard and that's what you get: knucklehead-with-highbrow. We call it Knuckle Highbrow!"

Jennifer Beals: "Knucklebrow!"

Alexandre Rockwell: "And she's not a funny person."

Jennifer Beals: "No, I'm not. Absolutely no sense of humor whatsoever."

Alexandre Rockwell: "Don't cross her: She's from the south side of Chicago."

Jennifer Beals: "I didn't play it as if I was in a big broad comedy. I try to play the situation for what it is. It's like Jessica Lange in *Tootsie*. She isn't playing comedy, but it's funny because of the situation. There are times in the middle of a scene in *In the Soup* when I just wanted to laugh so hard. Working with Stanley Tucci, who plays Gregoire, there are times he's so funny, it was all I could do not to laugh."

Alexandre Rockwell: "I think really good comedy comes from reality. The most jokes are told in wartime trenches, but that only comes out of struggle and humanity. Charlie Chaplin knew that real humor comes out of real struggle. This film is human; if I fail on a human level, then I'm fine failing, I don't mind doing that. *In the Soup* is not a movie of high art. It's a movie about people."

ALEXANDRE ROCKWELL'S films include *Sons* and *Four Rooms*. JENNIFER BEALS' films include *Flashdance, Cinderella, The Bride, The Gamble, Split Decisions, Vampire's Kiss, Club Extinction, Blood and Concrete: A Love Story, Indecency, Day of Atonement, Terror Stalks the Class Reunion, Dead on Sight, Mrs. Parker and the Vicious Circle, Caro Diario, Devil in a Blue Dress,* and *Four Rooms*.

Incident showed something far more disturbing. No one was going to make our private worlds all better again with homilies and heroism. Private solutions might be found to combat the evils in the night, but the social order and harmony would not be restored by them. *The Incident* is a timeless and eerie look into the world of the future made as the once-mighty Hollywood studios of the past were collapsing. Writer Nicholas E. Baehr adapted his screenplay for *The Incident* from his 1963 teleplay "Ride with Terror" that aired on NBC's *Dupont Show of the Month.* Gene Hackman, then 33, and Tony Musante, then 22, starred. 🦴🦴🦴

1967 99m/B Martin Sheen, Tony Musante, Beau Bridges, Ruby Dee, Jack Gilford, Thelma Ritter, Brock Peters, Ed McMahon, Gary Merrill, Donna Mills, Jan Sterling, Mike Kellin, Bob Bannard, Diana Van Der Vlis, Victor Arnold, Robert Fields; *D:* Larry Peerce; *W:* Charles Fox, Nicholas E. Baehr; *M:* Charles Fox. **VHS, Beta, LV** *FOX*

The Innocents

The Innocents lingers in your mind long after you see it. We are used to being on Deborah Kerr's side whenever she's cast in a film, but HERE, well, she's high-strung and obsessive as Miss Giddens, the new governess. Is it because her little charges Miles and Flora are playing with lascivious ghosts or is it because she's in love with their Uncle (Michael Redgrave), and hasn't had much of an outlet in her sheltered life for lascivious fantasies of any description? Why was little Miles expelled from school? Why does she kiss little Miles on the mouth like a lover? (Or is HE kissing HER on the mouth like a lover?) Why does little Miles talk like the ghost of a man named Quint (Peter Wyngarde)? Why does Miss Giddens see the ghost of Miss Jessel (Clytie Jessop) at the lake? Why doesn't the housekeeper Mrs. Grose (Megs Jenkins) know ANYTHING? The children get weirder and weirder, and Miss Gidden gets more and more paranoid about the ghosts, and although we SEE ghosts, we see them through the increasingly unreliable eyes of the governess. And as for the precocious behavior of the children, isn't it a childhood obligation to drive any new authority figure out of her mind? Director Jack Clayton meticulously recreates the Victorian world, and his superb cameraman Freddie Francis employs filmmaking techniques popularized during the silent era, e.g. extended dissolves. The unusual look of the film unsettles us as viewers, and we go back and forth between our sympathy for Miss Giddens and our increasing fears that she's doing more harm to her charges than any ghost ever could. Compounding the conflict is the fact that Martin Stephens (Miles) had already played the devil child of George Sanders and Barbara Shelley in Wolf Rilla's *Village of the Damned* the previous year. Plus! Newcomer Pamela Franklin (Flora) had the spookiest look in her wide eyes. Those eyes would help to make her a horror film staple for the next 15 years. *The Innocents* has great repeat value. Depending on your mood, it becomes an entirely different story each time you see it. (Megs Jenkins played Mrs. Grose again in a 1974 color telefeature starring Lynn Redgrave.) 🦴🦴🦴

1961 85m/B GB Deborah Kerr, Michael Redgrave, Pamela Franklin, Martin Stephens, Peter Wyngarde, Megs Jenkins, Clytie Jessop, Isla Cameron, Eric Woodburn; *D:* Jack Clayton; *W:* Truman Capote, William Archibald, John Mortimer; *C:* Freddie Francis; *M:* Georges Auric. **VHS, Closed Caption** *FXV*

Inside Monkey Zetterland

Surprise: Monkey Zetterland (Steve Antin) is the son of a Jewish smother mother (Katherine Helmond as Grace). I can't imagine Helmond being married to Bo Hopkins (who plays Monkey's rarely seen father, Mike), but she is, and her other kids are hairdresser Brent (Tate Donovan), and Grace (Patricia Arquette), who just broke up with pregnant Cindy (Sofia Coppola). But wait, there's more, namely Monkey's friends: Sandra Bernhard as Imogene, who never shuts up; Debi Mazar as his Mean Girlfriend Daphne; and political terrorists Sophie and Sasha. (I can't imagine Martha Plimpton being married to Rupert Everett, either, but she is.) Hey guys, let's get together and make a movie. Okay!...About what? How wacky we all are, of course. Okay...And then what? Well, isn't that enough? If it is, this is your movie. ♫♫

1993 (R) 92m/C Steve Antin, Patricia Arquette, Sandra Bernhard, Sofia Coppola, Tate Donovan, Katherine Helmond, Bo Hopkins, Debi Mazar, Martha Plimpton, Rupert Everett, Ricki Lake, Lance Loud, Francis Bay, Luca Bercovici; **D:** Jefery Levy; **W:** John Boskovich, Steve Antin; **C:** Christopher Taylor; **M:** Rick Cox, Jeff Elmassian. Nominations: Independent Spirit Awards '94: Best Supporting Actor (Donovan). **VHS, LV** *PSM*

Interlude

The interesting thing about *Interlude,* released within a couple of months of the Summer of Love, was that it showed a couple being passionate, rather than casual, about love; it made at least as persuasive a case for romance in 1967 as *When Tomorrow Comes* (with Irene Dunne and Charles Boyer) had in 1939 or the first *Interlude* (with June Allyson and Rosanno Brazzi) had in 1957. Stefan Zeiter (Oskar Werner) is a 45-year-old world-class conductor (and married) and Sally (Barbara Ferris) is a 27-year-old dolly bird journalist (and single). Her assignment is to interview him, and she makes mistakes right and left and her flakiness enchants him. Until Stefan's gorgeous and gracious wife Antonia arrives on the scene (Virginia Maskell, and yes, that IS Patrick McGoohan's co-star in "The Arrival," the first episode of *The Prisoner* series), Stefan and Sally are obsessed with each other. The supporting cast includes Alan Webb (1906-82) as Andrew, and Nora Swinburne, 65, as Mary (in the penultimate role of a career that began in 1920). Also in the

cast are Donald Sutherland, then 33, as Lawrence, and John Cleese, 28, in his very first role as a television public relations man. All the elements of the future Basil Fawlty are in place: the nervous energy, the twittiness, the fathomless desire to impress everyone in sight, and that odd blend of ingratiating abrasiveness that only Cleese can convey with a shift of expression or tone. Werner was a 1965 Oscar nominee for his exquisitely tortured performance as a dying doctor in love with a doomed passenger (fellow nominee Simone Signoret) in *Ship of Fools* and few could convey erotic anguish as well as he. Ferris, too, hits all the right notes as Sally. She had been Dinah, the Dave Clark Five's leading lady in 1965's *Catch Us If You Can/Having a Wild Weekend,* John Boorman's first film. *Interlude* accurately reflects the discrepancy between the devil-may-care atmosphere of its era and the timeless ache of the human heart for a life filled with some meaning. Timi ("Hurt") Yuro sings the title song. ♫♫♫

1967 113m/C *GB* Oskar Werner, Barbara Ferris, Virginia Maskell, John Cleese, Bernard Kay, Robert Lang, Geraldine Sherman, Donald Sutherland, Nora Swinburne, Alan Webb; **D:** Kevin Billington; **W:** Hugh Leonard, Lee Langley. *NYR*

The Interrogation

As always, 1990's Mill Valley Film Festival was jam-packed with the sort of movies which help to make it our favorite of all the festivals we go to each year. One Polish entry you won't want to miss is *The Interrogation.* Krystyna Janda plays Tonia, a nightclub performer and good-time girl who's taken in for questioning by the security police and winds up with a grueling five-year prison rap. She is drunk when she's first brought into custody and even the next day, she does not understand how serious her plight is. She willingly reveals that she went to bed with a guy that the police are looking for, but so what, what's the big deal? Gradually, she

I'd known him [director Charles Crichton] since 1969. Believe it or not, we nearly made a movie together that year, and the producer sold it to another producer after I'd worked on it with Charlie for some time and discovered just how good he really was, and this other producer wouldn't use Charlie so we all walked away from the project including Marty Feldman, and I said to Charlie, 'Someday...,' and then I got into the Python years and the *Fawlty Towers* years and then about ten years later Charlie started directing films for my management and sales training film company and we worked together on about ten different films. These were only films of about 30 minutes in length. [They also worked together in 1988's *A Fish Called Wanda.*]

"There is very, very little difference [between British and American humor]. And I know that will surprise people...I think that the reason that we sometimes don't laugh at each other's humor is almost invariably because we don't understand the reference or the cultural meaning of the joke. For example, a lot of English humor is lost on the Americans because you don't understand this strange class system we have and how a lot of English humor is about somebody trying to get out of the working class into the middle class. But once the understanding is there, once an American understands what the joke is or once an Englishman understands what the joke is, then you find, I think, that the sense of

learns more about her position, her true friends, and the complexity of her relationship with one of her guards. A film with none of the easily identifiable prison stereotypes, *The Interrogation* is brilliantly written, directed, and acted. It was finally released after an eight-year ban (1982-90). **AKA:** Przesluchanie. 🦴🦴🦴

1982 118m/C *PL* Krystyna Janda, Janusz Gajos, Adam Ferency, Agnieszka Holland, Anna Romantowska; **D:** Richard Bugajski. **VHS** *KIV, FCT*

Iphigenia

At the risk of sounding facile, Agamemnon emerges as a real clod in Michael Cacoy-

annis' *Iphigenia*. Your sympathy will be with Clytemnestra (Irene Papas) and Iphigenia (Tatiana Papamoskou, then 12) all the way, as they are the real heroes in this vigorously rendered re-telling of Euripides' tragedy. Yorgos Arvanitis' camera work injects excitement into the longish narrative. But how could Agamemnon (Costa Kazakos) even THINK of sacrificing such an adorable daughter as Tatiana's Iphigenia? 🦴🦴🦴

1977 130m/C *GR* Irene Papas, Costa Kazakos, Tatiana Papamoskou, Costas Carras, Christos Tsangas, Panos Michalopoulas; **D:** Michael Cacoyannis; **W:** Michael Cacoyannis; **C:** Yorgos Arvanitis; **M:** Mikis Theodorakis. Nominations: Academy Awards

humor is very, very similar, with one slight, what can I say, variation, and that is that I think Americans love one-liners. They love the wisecrack, the gag. The English are happy to laugh at a silly situation and don't, to quite the same extent as the Americans, need a gag to trigger the laugh, and I think that that is a genuine difference. But otherwise, I don't think that there's any difference except in the spelling.

"I was at Cambridge, being a good, dutiful, and extremely boring legal student. I studied law for three years there and I discovered that there was a club there, I think it's like the Hasty Pudding at Harvard and all the other places, where we gathered in a little club room—we actually owned the lease of this club—and it had a little stage down one end and you used to be able to go in and get a cheap lunch, and twice a term we would do a show lasting two-and-a-half, three hours, at which everyone in the club would get up and perform material. And it was a wonderful experience because everyone else in the club— i.e., in the audience—was going to get up later and do their bit, so the audience was essentially friendly which I think is very important when you're learning comedy, and that's why I think stand-up comedians have such a rough time starting in clubs a lot of the time. And that led on to my doing a show at the end of my third year at Cambridge in the local professional theatre. As a result, somebody from the BBC offered me a job in radio, which remains to this day my favorite medium....

"It's not only that I don't much like writing by committee. It is, in fact, impossible. Anybody who's ever sat with three other people trying to write something knows that one of the four is always in disagreement. It's one of the rules...of human behavior. If you have three people together, if you're lucky, and the wind's blowing in the right direction, you can sometimes get them to agree. Two is the ideal number."

'77: Best Foreign Language Film; Cannes Film Festival '77: Best Film. **VHS, Beta** COL, FHS

The Island of Dr. Moreau

The Hawaiian island antics in the lightweight *A Very Brady Sequel* are far more cerebral than anything we saw in the 1996 remake of *The Island of Dr. Moreau*, directed by John Frankenheimer. Although Burt Lancaster and Michael York did their best in 1977 to recreate the terror of H.G.Wells' 1896 novel, nothing since 1933 has come along to surpass or even equal the chills in

Island of Lost Souls starring Charles Laughton and Bela Lugosi. The stars this time are Marlon Brando as Dr. Moreau (who gets a laugh every time he tries on a new costume designed by Norma Moriceau, complete with hair styling by Vera Mitchell and chalky makeup by Philip Rhodes) and Val Kilmer as Dr. Montgomery (who gets a laugh when he tries to imitate Brando, complete with a Norma Moriceau creation of his very own and the obligatory chalky makeup by John Elliott and Leonard Engleman). Both actors dabble with British accents, Brando all the time and Kilmer when he's aping Brando. With David Thewlis in the film as castaway Edward Douglas, why did they

even bother? Fetching Fairuza Balk is on hand as Aissa, the most successful of Moreau's experiments in gene splicing. (She's unhappy with her looks, though: "I want to look like you!" she wails on Brando's shoulder, supplying the narrative with yet another laugh.) Moreau is a Nobel Prize Winner chafing in the island heat, Montgomery is a brilliant neurosurgeon gone to seed on drugs, but they're both such dim bulbs that you wonder how either of them managed to pass Surgery 101. A crash course in Systems Analysis might have helped, too. As it is, when Moreau's experiments turn on their master, he tries to soothe them with a few bars of Gershwin's *Rhapsody in Blue* on the piano. Most of the principals are out of the picture 20 minutes before it's over, although Ron Perlman does get to wave to David Thewlis and spout something philosophical before the credits. Buy the book. Rent the earlier videos. This Moreau is for Brando and Kilmer completists only. **WOOF!**

1996 (PG-13) 91m/C Marlon Brando, Val Kilmer, David Thewlis, Fairuza Balk, Marco Hofschneider, Temuera Morrison, Ron Perlman; **D:** John Frankenheimer. Nominations: Golden Raspberry Awards '96: Best Director (Frankenheimer), Worst Picture, Worst Supporting Actor (Kilmer, Brando), Worst Screenplay. **VHS, LV, Closed Caption** *NLC*

It Takes Two

My Chauffeur wasn't seen by too many people when it was released to theatres in 1986, but it introduced us to the films of director David Beaird, who seems attracted to conventional comedy plots, although he approaches them in a decidedly offbeat way. *It Takes Two,* for example, tells the old story of the kid who suffers from pre-wedding jitters and who pours all his anxieties into symbolic escape, in this case, an expensive Italian car and its braless saleswoman. There's an insistent theme that marriage will be the end of the line for him as a free spirit and that afterwards his life will be an endless series of concessions to his wife and sacrifices to society. Although that theme isn't really explored in depth, it's always there, eroding whatever joy the kid allows himself to feel. His final surrender to convention is bathed in cuteness, but there's an underlying thud because he never has stood up for himself and his luck in finding others to help him obviously won't last forever. Except for the protagonist, most of the film's characters lack dimension and Beaird permits pointless racist "jokes" to gum up the uneven script. The cast of *It Takes Two,* especially Anthony Geary in a colorful featured role, is capable and the slight film does have some interesting moments. 🎵🎵

1988 (PG-13) 79m/C George Newbern, Leslie Hope, Kimberly Foster, Barry Corbin, Anthony Geary; ***D:*** David Beaird; ***M:*** Carter Burwell. **VHS, Beta, Closed Caption** *MGM*

It's All True

"On my desk in a script of the film was a long steel needle. It had been driven entirely through the script and to the needle was attached a length of red wool. This was the mark of the voodoo...." Yep, that was Orson Welles describing one of the many disasters that made the 1942 film *It's All True* impossible to complete in his own lifetime. If Welles were alive today, according to his daughter Beatrice, "He would never restore one of his old films. He would say, 'Hey, give me the money and I'll make a movie NOW!'" In the absence of the unrealized Orson Welles projects we will never get to see, his *It's All True* collaborators rescued the original raw footage and then edited a tantalizing 22-minute segment into a full-length documentary about the making of the entire film. The "Four Men on a Raft" segment reveals the truth about what Welles and his crew were able to accomplish on this ill-fated South American film. It also supplies compelling evidence that Welles' reputation was destroyed, not by artistic extravagance or undisciplined work habits, but by studio executives who needed an excuse to get rid of him. Both Welles and Walt Disney were recruited by the ambitious Nelson Rockefeller to promote Pan American relations during separate trips to South America in the early days of World War II. Disney, who was one of RKO's greatest assets and also politically sympathetic to Rockefeller, delivered two crowd-pleasing entertainments, *Saludos Amigos* and *Three Caballeros.* Welles was a maverick, no friend of Rockefeller, and his splashy film debut, *Citizen Kane,* had attracted critical raves, but was essentially a money-loser for RKO. (It lost $160,000 in its original release.) But Welles was only 26, eager for a new challenge and politically naive, and he accepted studio assurances that he would be able to edit *The Magnificent Ambersons* in South America. Disney, then 40 and the survivor of many setbacks in his 22-year career, knew how to play the studio game. Welles didn't. The loss was ours, since Welles did know how to make movies. *It's All True* would never have been a travelogue blockbuster in the Disney style and RKO knew it. But the "Four Men on a Raft" segment is a beautifully made story of discovery, loss, resourcefulness, and courage, considerably enhanced by contemporary sound technicians. Welles wrung such exceptional performances out of a non-professional cast that it's easy to understand why he tried so long and so hard to finish *It's All True.* Unlike *The Epic that Never Was,* about the making of Josef von Sternberg's *I, Claudius,* enough remains of *It's All True* to make the restoration of Welles' "Legendary Lost Classic" survive on its own merits. Any filmmaker worth his or her salt would die to make a movie as good as this one, and unfortunately Welles is no longer here to say that he could have told us that long ago. Recommended: 1995's *Orson Welles: The One-Man Band.* 🎵🎵🎵🎵

Cho) is on hand, as well as his inconsolable mother (Lee Grant), uncomfortable father (George Segal), and even Roddy McDowall as a by-the-book gay Catholic in his late 60s who tells all and sundry that suicide is illegal, and a mortal sin, to boot. The weekend-long party continues anyway, and a star-studded guest list (Marlee Matlin, Bronson Pinchot, Bruce Davison, Devon Gummersall, Paul Regina, Olivia Newton-John, Christopher Atkins, Dennis Christopher, Ron Glass) pay their last farewells to Nick, who's determined to check out in his own way, in his own time. Written and directed by Randal Kleiser, *It's My Party,* along with 1990's superior (and shorter) *Longtime Companion* by Norman Rene, will be a time capsule for the AIDS era, when young people all over the world watched the long, lingering deaths of the best and brightest of their own generation. Before they lose each other forever, and Nick and Brandon discover what made them fall in love to begin with, audiences are advised to have an entire box of Kleenex within reach. (Try not to watch this one alone at night or on a double bill with *Dark Victory*.) ♫♫♡

1995 (R) 120m/C Eric Roberts, Gregory Harrison, Marlee Matlin, Lee Grant, George Segal, Bronson Pinchot, Bruce Davison, Devon Gummersall, Roddy McDowall, Margaret Cho, Paul Regina, Olivia Newton-John, Christopher Atkins, Dennis Christopher, Ron Glass; *D:* Randal Kleiser; *W:* Randal Kleiser; *C:* Bernd Heinl; *M:* Basil Poledouris. **VHS, LV, Closed Caption** *MGM*

1993 (G) 85m/C D: Richard Wilson, Bill Krohn, Myron Meise, Orson Welles; *W:* Richard Wilson, Bill Krohn, Myron Meise; *M:* Jorge Arriagada. **VHS, LV** *PAR*

It's My Party

Yes, there are parties like the one in this movie; we know folks with enough stamina to handle that much grief. Eric Roberts plays Nick Stark, a young man dying of AIDS, who decides to throw a party "celebrating" his own suicide. His former lover Brandon Theis (Gregory Harrison) turns up, much to the resentment of Nick's other friends who feel that Brandon abandoned Nick when he needed him most. Nick's supportive best friend (Margaret

Jack's Back

Jack's Back is a well made "B" film, with surprisingly little violence for a tale about a latter day Jack the Ripper. James Spader, who paid his dues playing one-dimensional villains in a succession of teen flicks, is quite good in a dual role as twins caught up in the case. *Salvador's* Cynthia Gibb plays an interesting, resourceful heroine in this promising effort by writer/director Rowdy Herrington. Chris Mulkey, a likable actor in 1988's abysmal *Patti Rocks,* is seventh-billed as a police detective and he gives considerable texture to the small role. The script takes the time to provide a context for each character and every plot twist, which makes it stand out from other films of the genre. An understated, low-key entry like *Jack's Back* had difficulty attracting an audience during its brief theatrical run, but it's a pleasure to see Spader and Gibb show what they can do with some decent material at this stage of their careers. Note: Herrington's future efforts would include *Road House, Gladiator,* and *Striking Distance* ♬♬♬

1987 (R) 97m/C James Spader, Cynthia Gibb, Rod Loomis, Rex Ryon, Robert Picardo, Jim Haynie, Chris Mulkey, Danitza Kingsley; **D:** Rowdy Herrington; **W:** Rowdy Herrington. **VHS, Beta, LV, Closed Caption** *PAR*

Jacques Brel Is Alive and Well and Living in Paris

Jacques Brel Is Alive and Well and Living in Paris features dozens of deeply moving song-stories about love, death, loneliness, bullfighting, old age, war, and bittersweet romance. "Carousel" perhaps best illustrates Brel's style. The tune begins cheerfully, with a sense of magic. We hear of cotton candy. The lovely, gay mood of the song shifts. The rhythm speeds up. The carousel is no longer pleasant but dizzy. It becomes a metaphor for life, a mad whirl from which there is no escape. The song ends in terror. The theme of beautiful, bright things turning ugly and frightening is developed in other song-stories; in "The Bulls," there is cheering at the beginning. Gradually, the glories of past wars are lauded, along with the matador. Finally, he cries, "Saigon!" No cheers this time. The score for the original cast show album is a classic; it was awarded a Grammy nomination in 1968. In an intimate, cabaret-style setting, song-stories like "If You Go Away," "The Middle Class,"

"Marieke," "Funeral Tango," and "Brussels" can be seen and heard to best advantage. But not even the participation of Jacques Brel himself could recapture a delightful evening in the theatre on film. This American Film Theatre Production is an unimaginative transfer, and viewers of the future may well wonder why the work of Jacques Brel was loved so much by the audiences of his own time. ♬♬

1975 98m/C *FR* Elly Stone, Mort Shuman, Joe Masiell, Jacques Brel; **D:** Denis Heroux. *NYR*

Jane Eyre

When we want to see *Jane Eyre,* we can buy the 1934 version from Sinister Cinema or we can rent the 1944 all-star classic from Fox Video or we can watch the 1970 telefeature that turns up every so often on double-digit UHF channels or we can plow through all six hours of the 1983 PBS miniseries. Clearly, there is no shortage of Jane Eyres and Edward Rochesters in this century. Does this 1847 saga by Charlotte Bronte have anything new to say to the audiences of 1996? Director Franco Zeffirelli clearly thinks so, and his latest movie is a fairly faithful adaptation marred by serious miscasting. William Hurt may look like the subject of an early daguerreotype, but the instant he opens his mouth, we get to hear a Mr. Rochester who owes more to Elmer Fudd than Orson Welles. His interpretation throws the film off balance; aside from a self-conscious scowl, he seems entirely disinterested in Jane or Thornfield or anything. Charlotte Gainsbourg's Jane speaks with a constant lisp, which may not be as detectable in her many French film assignments, but it clearly eliminates the possibility of Jane's extended narrations. (The charismatic Amanda Root has a small role as Miss Temple; why couldn't SHE have played Jane opposite someone like Gabriel Byrne?) Elle Macpherson's Blanche Ingram is reduced to a walk-on bit, ditto Maria Schneider as Rochester's mad first wife. Joan Plowright is wonderful as Mrs. Hud-

Jane Eyre (Charlotte Gainsbourg) and Rochester (William Hurt) in *Jane Eyre.*

son and Billie Whitelaw has a few splendid, but all-too-brief sequences as Grace Poole. This *Jane Eyre* sounds like it will be better than it looks until you're watching it and then it looks better than it sounds. Do we care a fig for THESE repressed lovers? Not this time; bring back Orson Welles and Joan Fontaine and Hillary Brooke! ♫♫

1996 (PG) 116m/C William Hurt, Anna Paquin, Charlotte Gainsbourg, Joan Plowright, Elle Macpherson, Geraldine Chaplin, Fiona Shaw, John Wood, Amanda Root, Maria Schneider, Josephine Serre, Billie Whitelaw; **D:** Franco Zeffirelli; **W:** Franco Zeffirelli, Hugh Whitemore; **C:** David Watkin; **M:** Alessio Vlad, Claudio Capponi. **VHS, LV, Closed Caption** *TOU*

John and Julie

Whatever became of Colin Gibson and Lesley Dudley? They were the two adorable stars of *John and Julie,* who go all the way to London to see the coronation of Queen Elizabeth II. (Actual footage of the Queen and her family waving from the balcony at Buckingham Palace appears in the film.) Needless to say, there's an uproar when their families learn out about it. Peter Sellers has a funny early role as befuddled Police Constable Diamond who tries to help them find their six-year-old children and Wilfrid Hyde-White is his usual impeccable, congenial self as Sir James. Richard Dimbleby, whose son Jonathan would grow up to write about the failed marriage of H.R.H. Prince Charles, repeats his famed commentary on the Coronation. ♫♫♫

1955 82m/C *GB* Moira Lister, Noelle Middleton, Constance Cummings, Wilfrid Hyde-White, Sidney James, Joseph Tomelty, Colin Gibson, Lesley Dudley, Megs Jenkins, Patric Doonan, Peter Sellers, John Stuart, Vincent Ball, Colin Gordon, Peter Jones, Katie Johnson, Cyril Smith, Andrew Cruikshank, Winifred

Shotter, Richard Dimbleby, Wynfold Vaughn Thomas; **D:** William Fairchild; **W:** William Fairchild. **VHS** *NYR*

Jonah Who Will Be 25 in the Year 2000

Alain Tanner's *Jonah Who Will Be 25 in the Year 2000* was among the best of the entries at 1976's San Francisco International Film Festival. Tanner tries to convey depth in superficial terms, but with imagination, humor, and insight. The results are awesome. The stories of eight people connected to one another by the political events of 1968, swirl in and around each other. Tanner's sure, sensitive touch blends and balances his study into a solidly constructed film, despite its lack of a conventional plot. The sequences involving an inventive high school teacher and his class convey Tanner's deep wonder at the world, as well as his hope for a future that values the opinions of young and old alike. **AKA:** Jonas—Qui Aura 25 Ans en l'An 2000. 𝄫𝄫𝄫

1976 110m/C *SI* Jean-Luc Bideau, Myriam Meziere, Miou-Miou, Jacques Denis, Rufus, Dominique Labourier, Roger Jendly, Miriam Boyer, Raymond Bussieres, Jonah; **D:** Alain Tanner; **W:** Alain Tanner; **C:** Renato Berta; **M:** Jean-Marie Senia. National Society of Film Critics Awards '76: Best Screenplay. **VHS** *NYF*

Joyless Street

When Greta Garbo came to Hollywood with director Mauritz Stiller, she was streamlined, plucked, garbed, and coiffured to MGM perfection, whether or not it suited the role she was playing. This was not the case in G.W. Pabst's *Joyless Street,* where Garbo looked exactly like what she was supposed to be: a gauche and rather awkward young woman, still living at home with her father Josef (Jaro Furth) and little sister Rosa (Loni Nest). Greta gets a job, but soon finds herself fighting off the advances of her employer. Under such circumstances, she begins to consider prostitution at the urging of Frau Griefer (Valeska Gert). Much of the narrative focuses on the character played by Asta Nielsen (1883-1972), then seven films away from her 1932 swan song after a career that began in 1910. Fed up with unemployment, she HAS become a prostitute, but becomes dangerously obsessed with one of her clients, who eventually discards her. Meanwhile, hefty butcher Josef Geiringer (Werner Krauss) refuses to serve the long line of hungry people who wait in vain for a scrap of meat to bring home to their families. ("I have meat," he taunts them, "But not for you!") Audiences of the late 1920s (the film didn't reach America until 1927 when Garbo was already an international star) found Pabst's vision of post-war Vienna to be too decadent and too grim. Over the years, the picture has acquired a reputation among Pabst admirers who consider *Joyless Street* to be one of his finest films. It certainly shows why Vienna would be so vulnerable to a German takeover the following decade. Ground down by World War I, Vienna was no longer the glittering capitol it had been in the 19th century. It had become a city of contrasts: newly rich men and women courtesy of the black market versus poverty-stricken families devastated by the war. Pabst lays bare that contrast by cutting from bold images of booze-soaked nightclubs to close-ups of starving people in doorways, shivering in the cold night air. We may have been on a collision course with a worldwide Depression, but no one wanted to face it in a movie theatre yet. Edited by Anatol Litvak and based on a novel by Hugo Battauer. **AKA:** Street of Sorrow; Die Freudlose Gasse. 𝄫𝄫𝄫𝄫

1925 96m/B *GE* Greta Garbo, Werner Krauss, Asta Nielson, Jaro Furth, Loni Nest, Max Kohlhase, Silva Torf, Karl Ettlinger, Ilka Gruning, Agnes Esterhazy, Alexander Musky, Valeska Gert; **D:** G.W. Pabst; **W:** Willi Haas; **C:** Guido Seeber, Curt Oertel, Walter Robert Lach. **VHS, Beta, LV** *VYY, MRV, FST*

**INDEPENDENT
FILM GUIDE**

less. Ju Dou and her lover make no attempt to hide their affair in front of him, although they conceal the affair from the villagers on penalty of death. The triangle becomes progressively more and more tortured and, without giving too much of the plot away, it's no wonder that Tianbai, Ju Dou's baby, evolves into rather a strange child. Director Zhang Yimou's interpretation of Liu Heng's novel-based screenplay is masterful; it was his wonderfully cinematic decision to transplant the story into a dye factory. The colorful dye factory serves the function of a fifth character and is symbolic of everything the lovers have to gain and lose. Beautifully acted and photographed, *Ju Dou* lingers in the mind, both for its compelling narrative and its deeply disturbing emotional landscape. Although the film is set entirely in the '20s, the hopelessness of Ju Dou's situation persisted in China of the '90s, where women could still be bought and sold for as little as $400. ♫♫♫♫

1990 (PG-13) 98m/C CH Gong Li, Li Bao-Tian, Li Wei, Zhang Yi, Zheng Jian; *D:* Zhang Yimou; *C:* Gu Changwei. Nominations: Academy Awards '90: Best Foreign Language Film. **VHS, LV** *LIV, BTV*

Julia and Julia

Here's a word of advice to filmmakers who plan to shave production costs by shooting your major motion pictures in the new, improved high-definition video process: DON'T! If Oscar-nominated cinematographer Giuseppe Rotunno couldn't pull it off in *Julia and Julia,* you won't be able to either at this stage of the game. The process looks okay, better then a kinescope, anyway, if every single one of your actors doesn't move a muscle. Once you yell "action," though, there's no such thing as a fluid motion onscreen, and if you're working with pigeons as extras, forget it. You may as well substitute Dramamine for Jujubes because you'll need it after 96 minutes. The closest equivalent to the high-definition video experience is the stretch printing process used by film

Daniel (Sting) and Julia (Kathleen Turner) in *Julia and Julia.*

Ju Dou

Ju Dou was the first Chinese film to be nominated for an Academy Award. The Chinese government fought the nomination for the film, which had effectively been banned in its own country. *Ju Dou* is sharply critical of the traditional rural customs that prevailed in the 1920s. Ju Dou, the title character, is purchased as the third wife of Jinshan, an abusive old man who beats her when she fails to produce an heir. The young woman enters into an affair with Tianqing, her husband's nephew, but they must pretend that their baby is the son of Ju Dou's husband. The husband is soon the victim of an accident, which paralyzes him and leaves him help-

INDEPENDENT FILM GUIDE

preservationists when they restore silent films. The headache you get from watching that process is almost worth it when you're screening a rare treasure from 1903. But even if you weren't bombarded by *Julia and Julia*'s excruciating aesthetic problems, you still would be stuck with director Peter Del Monte's loco script. *Julia and Julia* is about a woman (Kathleen Turner) on her honeymoon with her husband (Irish actor Gabriel Byrne, with an all-purpose Spanish-Italian accent) whose car explodes after she's made her narrow escape. Widowed, she leads a solitary life as a travel agent in Trieste, Italy, until she drives through a tunnel one night and enters a time warp. Maybe her husband Paolo wasn't killed. Maybe she's really been married to him all those years, and maybe they even have a little boy named Marco (Alexander Van Wyk, who spends more time in bed than most of the grownups do). Wouldn't that be nice? But wait. There's a snag. What is Julia going to do about her lover Daniel, deftly played by Sting? In a mysterious shift back to her former life, Julia sells Sting a ticket to Dubrovnik. A flight to Dubrovnik would write him out of the script too easily, though. What's a poor traveler in a time warp to do? Have no fear, "Life is wonderful," as a blissful Julia informs us before film's end. **WOOF!**

1987 (R) 98m/C Kathleen Turner, Sting, Gabriel Byrne, Gabriele Ferzetti, Angela Goodwin, Alexander Van Wyk; *D:* Peter Del Monte; *W:* Peter Del Monte; *C:* Giuseppe Rotunno; *M:* Maurice Jarre. **VHS, Beta, LV, Closed Caption** *FOX*

Just Another Girl on the I.R.T.

Seventeen-year-old Chantel (Ariyan Johnson) dreams about zapping through high school and going on to medical school. Then she meets Tyrone (Kevin Thigpen), has sex with him, fritters away the abortion money he gives her, and her options

and dreams scatter like commuters on the I.R.T. Leslie Harris makes a promising directorial debut, newcomer Johnson's portrait of a tough Brooklyn teen is energetic and convincing, and Thigpen is also memorable as sexy Tyrone. A raw, bleak look at a mouthy character who thwarts her own best interests at every turn. 🦴🦴

1993 (R) 96m/C Ariyan Johnson, Kevin Thigpen, Ebony Jerido, Jerard Washington, Chequita Jackson, William Badget; *D:* Leslie Harris; *W:* Leslie Harris; *C:* Richard Conners. Sundance Film Festival '93: Special Jury Prize; Nominations: Independent Spirit Awards '94: Best Actress (Johnson). **VHS, LV** *LIV, FCT*

Just Like a Woman

If *Just Like a Woman* had originated in Hollywood story conferences, it would have emerged as a broad farce crammed with puns and sight gags and stripped of any real insight. But, just like in 1987's *Personal Services,* wonderful Julie Walters is our sympathetic tour guide into another world. Based on Monica Jay's book, *Geraldine,* Christopher Monger's film takes a look at Gerald Tilson (Adrian Pasdar), drawn to transvestism since childhood. He keeps this part of his life private (although one does wonder how he manages with a wife and two children). The wife discovers Geraldine's wardrobe, thinks it belongs to another woman, and files for divorce. Gerald acquiescently agrees to end his marriage, convinced that his wife would never believe, much less understand, the truth. He rents a room in Monica's (Julie Walters) house and, warmed by her kind and jolly nature, falls in love with her and confides in her for the first time in his life. The truth, which is complex and not undemanding of considerable adjustment, winds up setting them both free. Nick Evans' script is quite good and Walters and Pasdar are terrific together. 🦴🦴🦴

1995 (R) 102m/C *GB* Adrian Pasdar, Julie Walters, Paul Freeman, Susan Wooldridge, Gordon Kennedy, Ian Redford, Shelley Thompson; *D:* Christopher Monger; *W:* Nick Evans; *C:* Alan Hume; *M:* Michael Storey. **VHS** *HMK*

Just Like in the Movies

Just Like in the Movies is a likable independent feature from the directing/screenwriting team of Bram Towbin and Mark Halliday. It also provides an extremely fine role for Jay O. Sanders as Ryan Legrand, private eye. The film is hardly a recruiting movie for those with dreams of exciting and dangerous undercover assignments. Legrand's job strictly involves following husbands and wives who suspect infidelity; a more sordid job is hard to imagine. Legrand is also a definite creep, the world's worst date, and embarrassingly awkward on divorced dad days with his son as well. Somehow, the film invests its protagonist with a few appealing qualities; maybe it has something to do with the fact that he tries so hard and everyone else in the film despises him so thoroughly. Perennial celluloid sidekick Alan Ruck once again plays Legrand's droll sidekick: "Just Like in the Movies!" 🦴🦴🦴

1990 98m/C Jay O. Sanders, Alan Ruck, Katherine Borowitz, Michael Jeter, Alex Vincent; *D:* Bram Towbin, Mark Halliday; *W:* Bram Towbin, Mark Halliday; *C:* Peter Fernberger; *M:* John Hill. *NYR*

Kafka

This is not the film the cognoscenti were expecting from Steven Soderbergh after *sex, lies and videotape,* so they raked it and him over the coals. I thought it was pretty interesting and definitely the work of a free spirit. It's set in 1919 Prague and Kafka (1883-1924, Jeremy Irons) is leading a pretty drab life, clerking by day, scribbling by night. He gets mixed up in a strange tale of terror, culminating in a trip to the Castle of Dr. Murnau (Ian Holm as the villain of the piece). It's all in creepy black and white, except for the castle segment that is in color. And look at that mouth-watering cast (Joel Grey, Jeroen Krabbe, Armin Mueller-Stahl, Alec Guinness)! What do you want from a second movie: "more sex, more lies and more videotape?" Get over it! 🦴🦴🦴

1991 (PG-13) 100m/C Jeremy Irons, Theresa Russell, Joel Grey, Ian Holm, Jeroen Krabbe, Armin Mueller-Stahl, Alec Guinness, Brian Glover, Robert Flemyng, Keith Allen, Simon McBurney; *D:* Steven Soderbergh; *W:* Lem Dobbs; *C:* Walt Lloyd; *M:* Cliff Martinez. Independent Spirit Awards '92: Best Cinematography. **VHS, Beta, LV, Closed Caption** *PAR, PMS*

Kalifornia

The flat voiceover narration gives us the road map for *Kalifornia*. A writer (David Duchovny) and his photographer girlfriend (Michelle Forbes) are en route to California, doing a word-and-picture tour of the locales of famous American murders along the way. To share expenses, they accept, sight unseen, the companionship of serial killer Brad Pitt and his deliberately oblivious girlfriend, Juliette Lewis. At first glance, Forbes observes that Pitt and Lewis are dumb, and Lewis decides that Duchovny and Forbes are strange. The two men, however, form an inexplicable bond, so all four hit the road. The writer (shades of silly Geraldine Chaplin searching for symbolism with her tape recorder in *Nashville* here) feels that by visiting murder sites and recording his observations, he will understand how and why people kill. And, of course, all the time, Pitt is wiping people out in men's restrooms and service stations; it takes the others half the movie to get a firm grasp of the obvious. Screenwriter Tim Metcalfe finds this situation amusing; the old educated-hicks-want-to-experience-real-life-but-fall-to-pieces-when-they-do formula. The film works best when the focus is on Juliette Lewis, clearly one of the best actresses of her generation and absolutely fearless about exposing the truth of her characters, without a flicker of self-protective reserve. Like all great actors, she works from the inside out; director Dominic Sena gives her props and bits of business to work with, but she works equally well with the force of her naked emotions. We might split a gut if anyone else summed up a serial killer with an inadequate description like "mean," but Lewis breaks your heart with the sequence. There ain't a question in your mind that while she's raging at Pitt, she means it. Unfortunately, none of the rest of the cast is in Lewis' league. Forbes is a good actress; she might very well wrap up another movie, but not 1994's *Swimming with Sharks,* for reasons beyond her control. In *Kalifornia,* she is an excellent foil for Lewis, and the two women share some of the film's best moments. The sequences with Pitt and Duchovny work less well. Both actors work from the outside in, and the impact of their performances is nowhere near as intense as the basic narrative would have you believe. *Kalifornia* is mostly an absorbing film and it looks great. The film would have done even better if it had taken its emotional cue from the unforced honesty of Juliette Lewis, instead of trying to wring existential mileage out of the unanswerable questions posed by its dippy protagonist. 🦴🦴⋎

1993 (R) 117m/C Brad Pitt, Juliette Lewis, David Duchovny, Michelle Forbes, Sierra Pecheur, Lois Hall, Gregory Mars Martin; *D:* Dominic Sena; *W:* Tim Metcalfe; *C:* Bojan Bazelli; *M:* Carter Burwell. **VHS, LV, Closed Caption** *PGV, BTV*

Kama Sutra: A Tale of Love

For reasons that are beyond us, *Kama Sutra* received a critical roasting. It's a Tale of Love—well, 16th century sexual politics, really—through the eyes of women who are trained from childhood to please men. Sarita Choudhury is Princess Tara, fated to marry a king, Raj Singh (*The English Patient*'s Naveen Andrews). But Tara is cruel to her maid Maya (Indira Varma), who seduces the king before the wedding night in revenge, and is exiled from her village by Tara. Needless to say, the union of the princess and the king begins badly and goes downhill from there.

Maya lands on her feet, though, and soon attracts the professional attention of Jai, a handsome sculptor (Ramon Tikaram). When Jai learns that he can't focus on his work and the lovely Maya, too, she embarks on a crash course in Kama Sutra, winding up as Raj Singh's favorite palace courtesan. Mira Nair focuses on how the women of the 16th century develop the only power they are permitted to wield and how the men in their lives, more often than not, would rather die than deal with that power on its own terms. Filmed in spectacular Technicolor, *Kama Sutra* is a feast for the eyes and Indira Varma makes an appealing first impression. *Kama Sutra: A Tale of Love* works wonderfully well on the level of an adult fairy tale. It doesn't even try to be a 16th century documentary. If Nathaniel Hawthorne could speculate about 17th century colonial America in 1850's *The Scarlet Letter,* what's the big deal about Mira Nair creating a compelling fantasy about the women of another time? For a bunch of middle-aged male movie critics who got all hot and bothered about *Kama Sutra*'s "historical accuracy," it seemed to be a VERY big deal. Hey, guys, if that's all you want, read a history book! 🦴🦴🦴

1996 117m/C *IN* Indira Varma, Sarita Choudhury, Ramon Tikaram, Naveen Andrews, Devi Rekha; *D:* Mira Nair; *W:* Mira Nair, Helena Kriel; *C:* Declan Quinn; *M:* Mychael Danna. **VHS** *THV*

Kansas City

Robert Altman and Jennifer Jason Leigh are like the little girl with the curl in the middle of her forehead; when they are good, they are very, very good, but when they are bad, they are horrid. For *Kansas City,* both are at their worst: Altman rambling and out of control, Leigh meticulously creating a role from all the non-essential externals and losing the heart and soul of her character in the process. The threadbare plot, set in 1934, has Leigh kidnapping Miranda Richardson, as the strung-out wife of a presidential advisor, so that

**Harry Belafonte is
Seldom Seen in
*Kansas City.***

her husband will be forced to influence crooked nightclub owner Harry Belafonte into freeing the larcenous love of Leigh's life. (Who else but Dermot Mulroney, who only gets to talk in one sequence? And Michael Murphy is all-but-invisible as the FDR crony.) Leigh's idol is supposed to be Jean Harlow, but she seems to have obsessed on early Warner Bros. talkies starring Glenda Farrell and Joan Blondell without learning a thing about the secret of their appeal. Watching Leigh's face twist into actressy mannerisms and listening to her fake her way through gun-moll slang is, to put it kindly, excruciating. Blessedly, Richardson is on hand as the so-called victim. Richardson's subterranean mysteries offer welcome counterpoint to Altman's banal script and Leigh's tedious contortions. We were stunned to see the gushing praise that Jack Kroll gave this mess in *Newsweek*; the entire review

could be splashed verbatim on *Kansas City* advertisements. But 1996 was the summer of serious fawning for deeply flawed films, like *Lone Star,* that might be politely dismissed in a season less saturated with computer wizardry. There has to be more to a movie than that it NOT have special effects. Altman thinks he's found it in the Hey Hey nightclub sequences where Ron Carter, Craig Handy, Joshua Redman, and James Carter are meant to evoke jazz legends like Coleman Hawkins and Lester Young. However, the structure here is basically Leigh talking out of the side of her mouth, cut to jazz, back to Leigh, back to more jazz, and so on with little connecting detail. Altman even admits that the screenplay was knitted together from two separate yarns. When Altman is at the peak of his form, as in *M.A.S.H.* and *Nashville,* no one can tell a story with more brilliance or greater preci-

sion. But *Kansas City*—sadly—is way down there at the bottom, along with *Popeye* and *Pret-A-Porter*.

1995 (R) 110m/C Jennifer Jason Leigh, Miranda Richardson, Harry Belafonte, Michael Murphy, Dermot Mulroney, Steve Buscemi, Brooke Smith, Jane Adams; *D:* Robert Altman; *W:* Frank Barhydt, Robert Altman; *C:* Oliver Stapleton; *M:* Hal Willner. New York Film Critics Awards '96: Best Supporting Actor (Belafonte). **VHS, LV, Closed Caption** *NLC*

Kids

A very grim look at the lives of depressingly young children. Telly (Leo Fitzpatrick) is terminally incapable of zipping it up. He will succumb to AIDS eventually but he doesn't know it yet. However, Jennie (Chloe Sevigny), who's tested HIV positive, DOES know it. She was among a long line of virgins who had sex for the first time with Telly. Telly seduces a very young blonde (Sarah Henderson) at the start of *Kids,* and picks up Darcy (Yakira Peguero) by picture's end. The tragic irony is Telly probably enjoys bragging about his virginal conquests to his friend Gasper (Justin Pierce) even more than he digs the sex. *Kids* shows a parentless world where a gang of homophobic, racist kids drift through the streets of Manhattan, and where children of ten turn on and/or drink themselves into a stupor. Harmony Korine was just 19 when she wrote *Kids,* and Larry Clark was over 50 when he directed it.

1995 90m/C Leo Fitzpatrick, Justin Pierce, Chloe Sevigny, Rosario Dawson, Sarah Henderson, Harold Hunter, Yakira Peguero, Joseph Knafelmacher; *D:* Larry Clark; *W:* Harmony Korine; *C:* Eric Alan Edwards; *M:* Louis Barlow. Independent Spirit Awards '96: Debut Performance (Pierce); Nominations: Independent Spirit Awards '96: Best First Feature, Best Supporting Actress (Sevigny). **VHS, LV, Closed Caption** *THV*

Kika

Pedro Almodovar thrived in the post-Franco era, directing a series of nine films that challenged our ideas of how sexuality, violence, comedy, and tragedy could be conveyed onscreen. His tenth film, premiering at 1994's San Francisco International Film Festival, reveals evidence of an unmistakable, and we hope, temporary decline. Almodovar's best films have always dealt with his own concerns and his own culture. In *Kika,* he drew his inspiration from the media feeding frenzy that surrounded the William Kennedy Smith rape trial. How humiliating, perhaps more humiliating than the rape itself, Almodovar observed, that the alleged victim's underwear was shown on U.S. television. And, although tabloid television has invaded Spain as well, his source material is essentially external. His understanding of the lives of the people who are affected by tabloid television is not terribly profound; in *Kika,* for the first time, Almodovar fails to get inside the skin of his characters. The title role is well played by Veronica Forque as a distaff version of Candide, but her relentless cheerfulness makes no sense, especially in a rape sequence. She may be uncomfortable, but for the most part, she takes the act for granted. To her, the true villain is not her rapist, but Andrea Scarface (Victoria Abril), who obtains footage of the rape and televises it. In the entire 115-minute film, Kika only expresses outraged sensibilities for an instant, and the moment passes very quickly. All of the stock Almodovar ingredients are in place: the dry wit in moments of high drama, the sheer speed of Almodovar's story telling style, even the zany fringe characters who would add ironic contrast to a more compelling central premise. With his latest strained effort at grabbing the attention of international audiences, Almodovar strays further and further from his greatest artistic gift: the ability to see all the way down to the darkness of the human soul with clarity and compassion. *Kika* is only a tourist's eye view of serial killings, voyeurism, and the contemporary media. Rent *Matador* or *Law of Desire* on home video instead and look forward to better things from Almodovar on the big screen in the future.

1994 115m/C *SP* Veronica Forque, Peter Coyote, Victoria Abril, Alex Casanovas, Rossy de Palma; *D:* Pedro Almodovar; *W:* Pedro Almodovar. **VHS** *THV*

Kill Me Again

She is a "greedy, two-faced bitch." He is a member in good standing of the Dumb Dicks of America. As played by Joanne Whalley and Val Kilmer, they are a match made in a casting director's heaven. We first saw *Kill Me Again* at San Francisco's Geneva Drive-in on a double bill with the Judd Nelson movie *Relentless,* a film which makes *Kill Me Again* look like *The Maltese Falcon.* Actually, *Kill Me Again* brings to mind quite a few noir classics, including *Double Indemnity* and *Out of the Past.* When Whalley takes it off and turns it on, you want to believe every single one of her lies. The film is saturated with sleaze and violence, and it's never boring (which is more than we can say for *Relentless*). Michael Madsen plays a great old-fashioned psycho and writer/director John Dahl makes interesting use of fire, water, and the rest of the limited resources in this tightly budgeted yarn. If you don't expect *Murder My Sweet,* you'll have fun. 🦴🦴🦴

1989 (R) 93m/C Val Kilmer, Joanne Whalley, Michael Madsen, Jonathan Gries, Bibi Besch; *D:* John Dahl; *W:* John Dahl, David Warfield. **VHS, Beta, Closed Caption** *MGM*

Killer Inside Me

Ever since the Creative Arts Book Company in Berkeley began re-printing Jim Thompson's novels in its Black Lizard series, we've been trying to track down the movies that were inspired by his books, and it hasn't been easy. 1979's *Serie Noire* based on *A Hell of a Woman,* for example, was made in France by Alain Corneau, and if it's shown up on cable or at a video outlet or on the revival circuit, we must have been out of town. Burt Kennedy's *The Killer Inside Me* was released by Warner Bros. in 1976, and even though it features an all-star cast (Stacy Keach, Susan Tyrell, Tisha Sterling, Don Stroud, Julie Adams, and the late character actors Keenan Wynn, Charles

McGraw, John Dehner, Royal Dano, and John Carradine), this one is hard to see, although well worth waiting for. Berkeley alumnus Keach gives a crisp, controlled performance as the sheriff whose violent core is obscured by his nice guy facade. The film perfectly captures the Thompson atmosphere of frightening undercurrents of emotion, which are set in motion by seemingly innocuous sights, sounds, and gestures. The only irritating sequences in *Killer* (although perhaps they were meant to be irritating) are the colossally dull relationship spats between Keach and Sterling. Keach's moments with Stroud and Carradine are played with very dark, very weird humor. Along with *Serie Noire, The Killer Inside Me* tops our wish list of film noir double bills we'd most like to see on the big screen. 🦴🦴🦴

1976 (R) 99m/C Stacy Keach, Susan Tyrrell, Tisha Sterling, Keenan Wynn, John Dehner, John Carradine, Don Stroud, Charles McGraw, Julie Adams, Royal Dano; *D:* Burt Kennedy; *W:* Robert Chandlee. **VHS, Beta** *WAR, OM*

The Killing of a Chinese Bookie

How does a single act of violence, executed on a grand scale, fit into the fabric of people's lives, why does it happen, and what sort of person commits such an act? These are some of the questions explored in John Cassavetes' 1976 film, *The Killing of a Chinese Bookie.* The main source of Cosmo Vitelli's validation is his strip club, the "Crazy Horse West." When faced with the loss of his club, Vitelli realizes that the value of his life can not be regained with the same slow measures he used to build it. After incurring an enormous gambling debt, he freely chooses to pay back his losses by killing a man he never met. Cassavetes tells his story in a deliberate, leisurely style, carefully selecting his cast so that each moment rings true. Ben Gazzara makes every one of Vitelli's moves

INDEPENDENT FILM GUIDE

Opposite page: **Stacy Keach in** *The Killer Inside Me.*

The Hound Salutes:
JOHN CASSAVETES

John Cassavetes could have taken the money and run. Many actors of his generation did. Or he could have proved himself as a director with an independent feature, and then found himself a secure berth as a seamless commercial filmmaker. Cassavetes, who died February 3, 1989, at the age of 59, didn't want to do any of that. He wanted to make movies in his own idiosyncratic way. What's more, he gambled his money and reputation to show his artistic visions to average moviegoers, the ones who would never go near an art house theatre. When he lost his patience with distributors who didn't know how to promote his offbeat projects, he would peddle them himself, enlisting the help of his wife, actress Gena Rowlands, and his lifelong friends Peter Falk and Ben Gazzara.

A typical Cassavetes film is embarrassing to watch. People who don't like to confront themselves often cite Cassavetes as their least favorite filmmaker. Even for those who are willing to take an emotional risk, sitting through a movie like 1974's *A Woman Under the Influence* can be pure agony. The first time I saw the picture, which won his wife an Academy Award nomination for Best Actress, I found myself cringing at its brutal honesty. While Cassavetes stripped away the cinematic gauze that might have protected moviegoers from painful truths in *Faces* and *Husbands,* his sincerity provided consoling counterpoint in *Minnie and Moscowitz* and *Gloria.* As a writer, he always seemed in the grip of violent emotions about durable experiences: love, marriage, friendships, and family. Accepting the pain of reality somehow lessens its sting, and it is not unusual to find flashes of humor in the grimmest of sequences. Cassavetes also explored relationships between men and women in minute detail, and the roles he developed for Gena Rowlands, Lynn Carlin, Joan Blondell, and others were among the most complex and full blooded of the last three decades.

The intense, angry young actor of the '50s evolved into an intense, angry writer/director by 1960. Time eventually worked its usual mischief on his health, but it never mellowed him. At his best and at his worst, he never reminds us of anyone but John Cassavetes, a man who shared what he had to say with originality and without compromise.

seem as if he were contemplating their expense to him. Virginia Carrington, a real-life waitress at the Hamburger Hamlet discovered by Cassavetes in 1973, delivers another excellent performance. Murder in this film is simply a price tag, a disturbing concept, but one that Cassavetes reveals with brilliant distinction. 🦴🦴🦴

1976 (R) 109m/C Ben Gazzara, Jean-Pierre Cassel, Zizi Johari, Soto Joe Hugh, Robert Phillips, Timothy Carey, Morgan Woodward, Virginia Carrington; **D:** John Cassavetes; **W:** John Cassavetes; **C:** Frederick Elmes. **VHS, Beta, Closed Caption** *TOU, FCT*

Kind Hearts and Coronets

Kind Hearts and Coronets is a cynical comedy about money, beautifully narrated by Dennis Price as Louis Mazzini, who would do anything to get it. He murders one member of the d'Ascoyne family after another, all played by Sir Alec Guinness. Unfortunately, Louis is tried for a crime he didn't do, killing the boring husband of his long-time sweetheart, Sibella (Joan Greenwood). He records his homicidal activities in his prison cell and hopes for a pardon. Another Ealing masterpiece, and a sure-fire antidote for run-of-the-mill blues. Lovely Valerie Hobson is Edith, the one d'Ascoyne Louis longs to marry. Based on the Roy Horniman novel *Israel Rank.* 🦴🦴🦴🦴

1949 104m/B *GB* Alec Guinness, Dennis Price, Valerie Hobson, Joan Greenwood, Audrey Fildes, Miles Malleson, Clive Morton, Cecil Ramage, John Penrose, Hugh Griffith, John Salew, Eric Messiter, Anne Valery, Arthur Lowe, Jeremy Spenser; **D:** Robert Hamer; **W:** Robert Hamer, John Dighton; **C:** Douglas Slocombe; **M:** Ernest Irving. National Board of Review Awards '50: 5 Best Foreign Films of the Year. **VHS, Beta, LV** *REP, FCT, HMV*

Kiss Me Deadly

Robert Aldrich's *Kiss Me Deadly* succeeds in creating such a grimy atmosphere that you want to take a bath after seeing it. When Ralph Meeker as Mickey Spillane's Mike Hammer leaves a room, tough guys say, "Open a window." Yet Hammer is the HERO in this violent 1955 blend of hard-boiled detective yarn, atomic bomb paranoia, plus all the corny poetic ramblings Spillane liberally injects into the plot. Except for Cloris Leachman, most of the babes in the film sank from sight after making the picture. Meeker, too, an excellent actor, never again received such a flashy part, although he continued to deliver solid performances in character roles through the 1970s. The physical ordinariness of the stars fits in perfectly with the anonymity most of us are reduced to when dealing with our radioactive fears. Serving as counterpoint for the rough, scary stuff with which Hammer must deal, A. I. Bezzerides' script for *Kiss Me Deadly* is bitingly funny, and Aldrich's never-subtle directing style is well suited to Mickey Spillane's volcanic world. 🦴🦴🦴🦴

1955 105m/B Ralph Meeker, Albert Dekker, Paul Stewart, Wesley Addy, Cloris Leachman, Strother Martin, Marjorie Bennett, Jack Elam, Maxine Cooper, Gaby Rodgers, Nick Dennis, Jack Lambert, Percy Helton; **D:** Robert Aldrich; **W:** A. I. Bezzerides; **C:** Ernest Laszlo. **VHS, Beta, LV, Closed Caption** *MGM, FCT*

Kiss of the Spider Woman

Molina (William Hurt) and Valentin (Raul Julia) are cellmates in a South American prison. Only his fantasies of Grade-Z Hollywood flicks keep Molina going over the long haul. At first revolutionary Valentin disdains the gay Molina, but gradually, the Spider Woman (smoldering Sonia Braga) becomes absolutely real to them both. Hurt won an Oscar and Julia (1940-94) was equally deserving of a nomination as well. He was a thoughtful, charismatic actor of incredible range and, as I think of all the meaty roles he could have made his own well into the next century, I miss him terribly. Based on a novel by Manuel Puig and dynamically directed by Hector Babenco. 🦴🦴🦴

INDEPENDENT FILM GUIDE

1920s and 1930s were able to build new lives in Mexico. Crammed with seldom-seen archival footage, Goldberg's documentary reveals the process of starting over with a nuts and bolts approach; all the interviewees are wonderfully eloquent and candid about their experiences. 🦴🦴🦴

1994 93m/C *MX* **D:** Daniel Goldberg. *NYR*

The Krays

We were glutted with gangster movies in the fall of 1990, a fact of life certain to affect the reception of a film like *The Krays* starring Gary and Martin Kemp of Spandau Ballet fame. The Kray Twins owned a succession of nightclubs in the '60s. They made it their business to be seen and photographed with the right people, some of whom ironically appear in this film. Portions of a 1963 British film called *Sparrows Can't Sing* were filmed at one of their clubs and the Krays mingled with the cast at the opening night party. But, as Ronald Kray's character aptly points out in this film, "Glamour is fear." London's East End certainly had abundant reasons to fear the Krays. When they weren't hanging out with Judy Garland and other international celebrities, the Krays were brutal homicidal thugs. They thought nothing of sustaining their empire through murder and did so on several occasions, some of which are horrifyingly reenacted in their movie biography. In contrast, the rest of their lives were painfully ordinary. Both were devoted to their mother, Violet, who obligingly served them tea and biscuits as they plotted their assorted gangland strategies. Ronald's private life was filled with a succession of attractive young boys while Reginald doggedly pursued a young woman named Frances Shea (renamed Dawson in the film). It is the film's perspective on Frances that sets *The Krays* apart from most other gangster films. Frances descended into madness and suicidal despair after she married Reginald Kray. Her freedom of mobility began and ended with their relationship, and no mate-

Luis Molina (William Hurt) is consoled by Valentin (Raul Julia) in *Kiss of the Spider Woman.*

1985 (R) 119m/C *BR* William Hurt, Raul Julia, Sonia Braga, Jose Lewgoy, Milton Goncalves, Nuno Leal Maia, Denise Dumont; **D:** Hector Babenco; **W:** Leonard Schrader; **M:** John Neschling, Wally Badarou. Academy Awards '85: Best Actor (Hurt); British Academy Awards '85: Best Actor (Hurt); Cannes Film Festival '85: Best Actor (Hurt); Independent Spirit Awards '86: Best Foreign Film; Los Angeles Film Critics Association Awards '85: Best Actor (Hurt); National Board of Review Awards '85: Best Actor (Hurt), Best Actor (Julia); Nominations: Academy Awards '85: Best Adapted Screenplay, Best Director (Babenco), Best Picture. **VHS, Beta, LV, 8mm, Closed Caption** *COL, BTV, NLC*

A Kiss to this Land

Daniel Goldberg's *A Kiss to this Land* shows how Jewish immigrants of the

rial benefits could compensate for the terror she experienced when her life was no longer her own. The cliche, that women are attracted to and blinded by money and power, is shattered by Philip Ridley's sharply observed account of Frances Kray. Billie Whitelaw does a superb turn as Violet Kray and the Kemp brothers are quite good as the twins. Show business veteran Jimmy Jewel (1909-93) has fun with a grandfather role and even gets a chance to perform "Balling the Jack." Kate Hardie does a touchingly sensitive job as Frances, and Tom Bell is slimily venal as always as a vicious but gutless hood. Victor Spinetti and Barbara Ferris, one-time show business acquaintances of the twins, have one good sequence as Frances' parents. Peter Medak, who was an assistant director on *Sparrows Can't Sing,* knew the Kray twins in the heady early '60s, long before their criminal careers crashed to a halt. (Ronald died at 61 in 1995). Because of Medak's exceptional feeling for the period and for his subjects, *The Krays* may be the sort of film that will linger in your mind weeks and months after you've seen it. ✂✂✂✂

1990 (R) 119m/C *GB* Gary Kemp, Martin Kemp, Billie Whitelaw, Steven Berkoff, Susan Fleetwood, Charlotte Cornwell, Avis Bunnage, Kate Hardie, Alfred Lynch, Tom Bell, Steven Berkoff, Victor Spinetti, Barbara Ferris, Julia Migenes-Johnson, John McEnery, Sadie Frost, Norman Rossington, Murray Melvin; *D:* Peter Medak; *W:* Philip Ridley; *M:* Michael Kamen. **VHS, LV, 8mm, Closed Caption** *COL, FCT*

La Femme Nikita

For the record, Anne Parillaud IS *La Femme Nikita* in a well made, solidly constructed French thriller that also features the legendary Jeanne Moreau. So leave it to Hollywood to co-opt, distort, and screw up a huge international hit. Question: what is the difference between the 1990 indie *La Femme Nikita* and the 1993 Warner Bros. release *Point of No Return*? Answer: *Point of No Return* is in English. I'm trying to imagine the extent of director John Bad-

ham's professional pride, although I suppose at his shameless level it must be easy to face himself in the mirror since he was paid a whopping salary for plagiarizing Luc Besson's directing style. I'm not kidding; *Point of No Return* not only has the same directorial slant and dialogue PLUS near-identical reconstruction of all the original sequences, but it ALSO has the same damn camera angles on many of the shots. After all the time that John Ritter and the late Michael Landon spent shoving the "Where there's a will, there's an A" philosophy down everyone's throats, you'd think there'd be a better way to spend zillions of dollars than redoing French movies because Americans can't read subtitles. The whole point of the re-make seems to be that if a dame puts on a little lipstick and fluffs up her hair, she has most of what she needs as the ideal professional assassin. But of course, all those cosmetics also supply her with a conscience, so U.S. audiences are treated to dilemmas on the order of "Oh gee whiz, should I shoot that guy or go to bed with my boyfriend?" Apparently 1993 audiences were expected to respond in droves to that burning ethical quandary, because Warner Bros. wanted *Point of No Return* to be an even huger international hit than the superior French flick. Bridget Fonda, Gabriel Byrne, Dermot Mulroney, Miguel Ferrer, and Anne Bancroft round out the cast of Badham's overproduced photocopy. There are SOME differences between *La Femme Nikita* and the remake. You see, Nikita and her boyfriend went to Venice on holiday, while Fonda and Mulroney went to New Orleans and the fist-fights and gunshots sounded real in the original, while Hollywood SFX cranked them up to drown out nuclear explosions and Fonda listened to Nina Simone and Nikita didn't and...on Monday, January 13, 1997, *La Femme Nikita* (with 26-year-old Australian Peta Wilson making her television debut) became a weekly series on the U.S.A. cable network. On the small screen, in a fundamental corruption of Luc

Gary Kemp and Martin Kemp as the stylish, sadistic Kray brothers, and Billie Whitelaw as their mother, in *The Krays*.

Besson's enigmatic character, Nikita was not a killer, but a wronged woman, and an innocent! ♫♫♫

1991 (R) 117m/C *FR* Anne Parillaud, Jean-Hugues Anglade, Tcheky Karyo, Jeanne Moreau, Jean Reno, Jean Bouise; *D:* Luc Besson; *W:* Luc Besson; *C:* Thierry Arbogast; *M:* Eric Serra. Cesar Awards '91: Best Actress (Parillaud). **VHS** *THV, FCT, BTV*

Lacombe, Lucien

In this 1974 film by Louis Malle, we are presented with an unlikely object of audience sympathy. Lucien (Pierre Blaise) smashes little birds with slingshots, finks on the village schoolmaster who's a member of the French resistance, and forces himself on his Jewish girlfriend immediately after her father has been picked up by the Nazis. Through it all, newcomer Blaise gives an accurate performance as the

detached, dispassionate, even dumb farm-boy-turned-German cop, except when he repeatedly narrows his eyes just like the bad guys in old Hollywood movies. It's a tricky topic for a 130-minute picture, especially one as leisurely paced as this one. Malle de-emphasizes Lucien's every action. Even when Lucien helps his girl and her granny flee from the Nazis, Malle gives him a plausible motivation: the arresting officer has just ripped off Lucien's stolen watch. Naturally, Lucien has a characteristic plan to get it back, and, only incidentally, get his friends off the hook. Because of Lucien's predictability, there are few genuine surprises in the film, but one of the best plot strands shows the relationship Lucien develops with his tailor (Holger Lowenadler) and his daughter (Aurore Clement). Grudgingly, and for individual reasons, the three learn to accept or, at least, get used to one another as human beings, despite considerable underlying tension. Lucien has the choice of turning them in or not, the girl can use Lucien to get her to Spain and, sadly, the tailor comes to realize that his family's safety depends entirely on his daughter's acceptance of Lucien's attentions. Clement does a graceful, touching job as the girl, and Lowenadler's portrait of the tailor is a perfect blend of restrained anger and opportunistic dignity. Stunningly photographed by Tonino Delli Colli, *Lacombe, Lucien* is an absorbing movie on many levels. (Cast Note: Pierre Blaise died at 24, the year after *Lacombe, Lucien* was released; Aurore Clement later starred in 1983's *Paris, Texas* for Wim Wenders.) 🦴🦴🦴

1974 130m/C *FR* Pierre Blaise, Aurore Clement, Holger Lowenadler, Therese Giehse; *D:* Louis Malle; *W:* Louis Malle, Patrick Modiano; *C:* Tonino Delli Colli; *M:* Django Reinhardt, Andre Claveau. *NYR*

The Lady Confesses

Yes, Hugh Beaumont did have an acting career long before he became Ward Cleaver, but you can't see him in a movie in a revival theatre without hearing a near-deafening buzz: "Oh-my-God! That's-Beaver's-father!" *The Lady Confesses* is fun because Beaumont's wholesome appeal has a sinister twist here. And Mary Beth Hughes IS front and center all the way through, trying to solve the mystery. You may remember Edmund MacDonald and Claudia Drake from the cast of *Detour.* Cheap-cheap-cheap, but never dull. 🦴🦴

1945 66m/B Mary Beth Hughes, Hugh Beaumont, Edmund MacDonald, Claudia Drake, Emmett Vogan, Barbara Slater, Edward Howard, Dewey Robinson, Carol Andrews; *D:* Sam Newfield; *W:* Helen Martin, Irwin H. Franklyn; *M:* Lee Zahler. **VHS** *NOS, SNC*

The Lady in White

Writer/director Frank LaLoggia clearly spent a great deal of time and care to make his film exactly the way he wanted it: *Lady in White* is a lovely, gentle film that really understands childhood terrors on their own terms. Lukas Haas, whose large brown eyes were so memorable in 1986's *Witness,* plays ten-year old writer Frank Scarlatti. Frankie's vivid imagination scares his classmates when he reads *The Beast that Destroyed London* to them on Halloween Day, 1962. Two of them, Donald and Louie, decide to scare Frankie by locking him in the school cloakroom overnight. While there, Frankie has intense nightmares about his dead mother and wakes up to watch the re-enactment of the 1951 murder of Melissa, a beautiful little red-haired ghost, by her invisible slayer. She asks for Frankie's help, but then he is nearly strangled by the same child-killer who murdered Melissa. Frankie is shown astrally projecting, and, in a beautifully photographed sequence, agreeing to help Melissa. When LaLoggia sticks with Frankie, he never makes a false step. There are suggestions that he may not have had faith in his basic material. He wants to make a social statement about civil rights, too. He also strains to pump comedy and nostalgia into the proceedings by making buffoons of Frankie's elderly grandparents and by oversweetening some of the family scenes. None of these strategies is particularly effective or necessary. Frankie's nightmares, his meetings with Melissa, his search for her mother, and his discovery of the killer are quite chilling enough for any horror movie. Instead of padding the plot with extranea, time could either have been shaved or better spent exploring the personality of the killer, since his identity is no surprise. Eerie use is made of the 1933 Bing Crosby hit, "Did You Ever See a Dream Walking?," but if that were the killer's favorite song, Frankie would have known who he was right away, not after 92 minutes. The acting by Lukas Haas as Frankie, Jason Presson as his brother Gene, Joelle Jacob as the haunting Melissa, and by Len Cariou, Alex Rocco, and Katherine Helmond as the grown-ups is sensitive and convincing. Laloggia and his cousin raised the production money from four thousand investors in upstate New York where this film was made. The results? Even though *Lady in White* only has a PG-13 rating, it is the first horror movie in ages that genuinely frightened us. ✒✒✒

1988 (PG-13) 92m/C Lukas Haas, Len Cariou, Alex Rocco, Katherine Helmond, Jason Presson, Renata Vanni, Angelo Bertolini, Jared Rushton, Joelle Jacob; *D:* Frank Laloggia; *W:* Frank Laloggia; *C:* Russell Carpenter; *M:* Frank Laloggia. **VHS, Beta, LV, Closed Caption** NO

The Lady Vanishes

The Lady Vanishes was Alfred Hitchcock's ticket to Hollywood. When we got a Eurailpass in 1975 and took Amtrak cross-country in 1977, we were disappointed that we didn't meet any cool passengers like Iris Henderson (Margaret Lockwood) or Gilbert Redman (Michael Redgrave) or Charters and Caldicott (Basil Radford and Naunton Wayne) or a high-heeled nun (Catherine Lacey) or Miss Froy (May Whitty). *The Lady Vanishes* revealed how a variety of personalities react to international conflict. The pacifist played by Cecil Parker is portrayed as a pompous fool, a not-so-subtle indication of the British mood 12 months before the invasion of Poland. As for production values, Hitchcock didn't even try to conceal the fact that he was saving shillings by using a miniature train for exteriors. (A life-long penny pincher, Hitchcock continued to use painted sets and rear-screen projection throughout his long career.) Nor was he unduly concerned by the fact that a frail old lady with a tune in her head was the ONLY one who could save the day. As it turned out, international audiences didn't mind, either. They loved the wit, style, and speed of *The Lady Vanishes*, and especially the veddy British Charters and Caldicott (Radford and Wayne made ten films as a team throughout the 1940s). The lovely and talented Margaret Lock-

wood received an invitation to Hollywood, but, after playing third fiddle to Shirley Temple and Randolph Scott in 1939's *Susannah of the Mounties*, she made a fast trip back; Lockwood became Great Britain's most popular female star. Americans wanted every British import to be as great as *The Lady Vanishes*. That wasn't possible, of course, so the Hitchcock family had to come to us. Hitchcock's cameo occurs in a London train station. Kathleen Tremaine plays Miss Froy's impostor. Googie Withers (who isn't on the train) was in 1996's *Shine* along with Redgrave's daughter, Lynn. ✒✒✒✒

1938 99m/B *GB* Margaret Lockwood, Paul Lukas, Michael Redgrave, May Whitty, Googie Withers, Basil Radford, Naunton Wayne, Cecil Parker, Linden Travers, Catherine Lacey; *Cameos:* Alfred Hitchcock; *D:* Alfred Hitchcock; *W:* Sidney Gilliat, Frank Launder; *M:* Louis Levy. New York Film Critics Awards '38: Best Director (Hitchcock). **VHS, Beta, LV** SNC, NOS, MED

Ladybird, Ladybird

Poor Cow is a British flick that I've always wanted to see, but have never been able to find. It starred the late Carol White (1941-91) as Joy in the title role, and Terence Stamp, 28, as Dave. Adapted (from Neil Dunn's novel) and directed by Kenneth Loach, 31, this 1967 drama explored the life of a woman who moved in with her incarcerated husband's best friend. The sympathetic concern that Loach showed for the poor cow of the late 1960s is now focused on single mother of four-going-on-five, Maggie Conlan (Crissy Rock in a fact-based character). The not-so-hidden-agenda of the film is to show how the Social Service System in Great Britain harms rather than helps the people it seeks to benefit (this was also D.W. Griffith's message to the world in 1916's *Intolerance*). Maggie has had an ugly history. The victim of childhood abuse from her Dad, she grew up to be the victim of a horrific beating from a lover. Just as things seem to be looking up for Maggie (she meets Vladimir

Vega as nice Jorge Arellano from Paraguay in a bar), she gets pregnant again. Social Services people take her baby away and Immigration Services people try to kick Jorge out of the country. It all looks pretty hopeless, and then we learn what happened to the real Maggie. Because of the violence and despair of the narrative, the film sometimes seems as if it'll go on forever, even though it's only 102 minutes. Loach guides Rock through a difficult, award-winning performance, and the performances by the other cast members, especially Chilean actor Vega, are vividly rendered. 🦴🦴🦴

1993 (R) 102m/C *GB* Crissy Rock, Vladimir Vega, Ray Winstone, Sandie Lavelle, Mauricio Venegas, Clare Perkins, Jason Stracey, Luke Brown, Lily Farrell; *D:* Ken Loach; *W:* Rona Munro; *C:* Barry Ackroyd; *M:* George Fenton. Berlin International Film Festival '94: Best Actress (Rock); Nominations: Independent Spirit Awards '95: Best Foreign Language Film. **VHS** *HMK*

The Ladykillers

Katie Johnson was WAY down on the cast list of most of the movies that she made, but in *The Ladykillers,* she was the star, and high time, too. She's absolutely terrific as Mrs. Wilberforce, a sweet little old lady who outwits a bunch of crooks who plan to murder her. Alec Guinness, looking his all-time seediest, was "Professor" Marcus, the leader of the gang, Cecil Parker WAS the "Major," Herbert Lom was Louis, chubby Peter Sellers was Harry, and Danny Green was One-Round, who adores Mrs. Wilberforce on sight. They all pretend to be members of a string quintet so they can hole up in her place while figuring out what to do with the loot from a bank heist. The contrast between darling Mrs. Wilberforce and these thugs is hilarious, particularly as they try to fit into her genteel world with catastrophic results. Ealing at its all-time zenith! *AKA:* The Lady Killers. 🦴🦴🦴🦴

1955 87m/C *GB* Alec Guinness, Cecil Parker, Katie Johnson, Herbert Lom, Peter Sellers, Danny Green, Jack Warner, Kenneth Connor, Edie Martin, Jack Melford; *D:* Alexander MacKendrick; *W:* William Rose; *C:* Otto Heller; *M:* Tristram Cary. British Academy Awards '55: Best Actress (Johnson), Best Screenplay. **VHS, Beta** *REP, FCT, HMV*

Lair of the White Worm

Ken Russell's *Lair of the White Warm* just may be the only film you'll ever see in which an archeologist in kilts wards off a vampire cop by playing the bagpipes. It also functions as a cautionary tale to Boy Scouts who may be tempted to accept a lift from a ravishing lady vampire in a Jaguar. And, like Hillaire Belloc, Victorian author of such Cautionary Verses as *Jim, Who Ran Away from His Nurse, and Was Eaten by a Lion* and *Matilda, Who Told Lies, and Was Burned to Death,* Russell adapted a little-known Bram Stoker work with tongue in cheek and both eyes and ears receptive to humor. There are more groan jokes about sex in the script than there is sex, and there are, of course, the obligatory British digs at Class, the Police, and Hospitals. Fetching Amanda Donohoe portrays evil vampire Lady Sylvia Marsh who kidnaps first the Trent parents and then their innkeeper daughters, Eve and Mary (Catherine Oxenberg and Sammi Davis). Will Lord James (Hugh Grant) and Angus Flint (Peter Capaldi) reach the girls in time? We can at least rest assured that, along the way, Russell will use every item in his usual bag of tricks. The acting from all four leads is funny and sincere, and Oxenberg, traditionally cast as princesses-in-waiting, is quite good as a working class damsel-in-distress. Too silly to be scary and an eyelash too smug to be entirely clever, *Lair of the White Worm* will nonetheless please horror fans too young to remember the early serials to which Russell owes his greatest debt. 🦴🦴🦴

1988 (R) 93m/C *GB* Amanda Donohoe, Sammi Davis, Catherine Oxenberg, Hugh Grant, Peter Capaldi, Stratford Johns, Paul Brooke, Christopher Gable; *D:* Ken Russell; *W:* Ken Russell; *M:* Stanislas Syrewicz. **VHS, Beta, LV** *VES, LIV, TPV*

Lamerica

Gino (Enrico Lo Verso) and Fiore (Michele Placido) are Italian partners who dream up what they believe is a sure-fire scheme to make some money in Albania, now that its Communist system is out of power. They're not allowed to run a company because they're not Albanians, so they hustle an old man (Carmelo Di Mazzarelli as Spiro) to be the figurehead of a bogus shoe factory. Spiro is a long-time political prisoner, so he has no desire to remain in Albania an instant longer than necessary after his release, and he makes a quick escape to Italy with Gino in hot pursuit. The apolitical Gino, who only wants to make a quick buck with Fiore, is forced to learn more about political survival than he had planned when he finally catches up with Spiro. This film by Gianni Amelio (*Open Doors, Stolen Children*) won an Academy Award nomination as 1995's Best Foreign-Language Film, as well as an Independent Spirit Award. ♫♫♫

1995 120m/C *IT* Enrico Lo Verso, Michele Placido, Carmelo Di Mazzarelli, Piro Milkani; **D:** Gianni Amelio; **W:** Gianni Amelio, Andrea Porporati, Alessandro Sermoneta; **C:** Luca Bigazzi; **M:** Franco Piersanti. Nominations: Independent Spirit Awards '97: Best Foreign Film. **VHS** *NYR*

L'Amour en Herbe

L'Amour En Herbe is wonderfully written and directed by Roger Andrieux. Andrieux coaxes terrific performances out of an inexperienced cast, including Pascal Meynier and Guilhaine Dubos as Marc and Martine, a 16-year-old boy and 17-year-old girl who fall in love. The simple love story emphasizes the more complicated background against which it develops: are love-struck children the only ones who never make concessions to life? In one disturbing sequence, Andrieux focuses on a personal/professional conflict faced by Marc's adored older brother (Bruno Raffaelli). The choice he makes stuns and disillusions Marc, a reality that changes forever the lives of the innocent young lovers. Andrieux next directed 1980's *La Petite Sirene/The Little Mermaid*. **AKA:** Budding Love; Tender Love. ♫♫♫

1977 100m/C *FR* Pascal Meynier, Guilhaine Dubos, Michel Galabru, Francoise Prevost, Alix Mahieux; **D:** Roger Andrieux; **W:** Roger Andrieux, Jean-Marie Benard; **C:** Ramon Suarez; **M:** Maxime Le Forestier. **VHS** *FCT*

Lancelot of the Lake

Lancelot of the Lake was a smash hit at the Cannes Film Festival. We wonder why. It's such a bloody, boring picture with little to recommend it besides Pasqualino De Santos' immaculate cinematography (unless you get some sort of a kick out of frozen acting styles and blood flowing out of helmets at a rapid clip). Robert Bresson's re-working of the Camelot mythology includes the search for the Holy Grail (hmmm...was 1975's funnier but equally bloody *Monty Python and the Holy Grail* a SATIRE of this movie?), Lancelot's romance with Guinivere, and the ill-fated joust that brought an end to the legendary Round Table. **AKA:** Lancelot Du Lac; The Grail; Le Graal. ♫

1974 85m/C *FR* Luc Simon, Laura Duke Condominas, Vladimir Antolek-Oresek, Humbert Balsan, Patrick Bernard, Arthur De Montalembert; **D:** Robert Bresson; **W:** Robert Bresson; **C:** Pasquale De Santos; **M:** Philippe Sarde. **VHS** *NYF*

The Land that Time Forgot

The Land that Time Forgot is inspired by one of Edgar Rice Burroughs' non-Tarzan books. Starring the late Doug McClure

Opposite page: **Lady Sylvia Marsh (Amanda Donohoe) in Ken Russell's** ***The Lair of the White Worm.***

Linda Fiorentino in
The Last Seduction.

(1935-95) as Bowen Tyler, it deals with the age-old story of a crew of men (plus Susan Penhaligon as a character named Lisa Clayton thrown in for good measure) who accidentally stumble on a mysterious territory, jam-packed with cave men and prehistoric beasts. It's basically a pretty good flick, but the dinosaurs, ship models, and special effects ALL look fake. And why does someone always have to be carried away by that prehistoric predecessor of the vaudevillian hook, the pterodactyl? John McEnery gives dignity to his role as the German Captain Van Schoenvorts and Bobby Parr looks less ridiculous than most actors who wind up playing cavemen named Ahm. 🦴🦴🦴

1975 (PG) 90m/C *GB* Doug McClure, John McEnery, Susan Penhaligon, Keith Barren, Anthony Ainley,

Godfrey James, Bobby Parr, Declan Mulholland, Colin Farrell, Ben Howard, Roy Holder, Andrew McCulloch, Ron Pember, Steve James; *D:* Kevin Connor; *W:* James Cawthorn, Michael Moorcock; *C:* Alan Hume; *M:* Douglas Gamley. **VHS, Beta** *LIV, VES*

The Last Days of the Last Tsar

There was no time to grieve for the last of the Romanovs after Nicholas II, Alexandra, and their five children were massacred at Ekaterinburg in 1918. The Soviet Union, then in its infancy, did not permit such a threatening luxury. Yet the sense of loss must have been intense to endure through nearly 75 years of repression. When the collapse of the Soviet Union made it safe to express such emotions, the Russian people recalled the Romanovs with affection and nostalgia. Director Anatoli Ivanov captures the sadness of the final rituals of the doomed Romanovs in his 1992 film, *The Last Days of the Last Tsar*. Ivanov blends archival footage with some of the most skillful re-enactments we've ever seen. In many cases, the look and tempo of the new footage so precisely matches the original films that it is only the fact that we know certain events would never have been recorded for posterity that allows us to tell the difference between them. 1971's *Nicholas and Alexandra* gave us the chocolate box version of the Tsar's demise. Ivanov's deeply poetic account is a far more eloquent and illuminating examination of the Romanov tragedy and its aftermath. 🦴🦴🦴

1992 m/C *D:* Anatoli Ivanov. **VHS** *CYR*

Last Exit to Brooklyn

Welcome to Hell, circa 1952. The Korean War is still going on, as we can see from the young men who depart from the nearby Navy yards. Closer to home, a factory strike has been going on for six months,

230

INDEPENDENT FILM GUIDE

with no end in sight. Harry Black (Stephen Lang) has been stealing from the strike funds so that he can have an extramarital affair with his gay lover (Alexis Arquette as Georgette). Fired by his boss Boyce (Jerry Orbach), Harry's dumped by the lover, makes a pass at a kid, and is nearly beaten to death by a street gang for same. Meanwhile, Jennifer Jason Leigh, with her usual courage for taking huge artistic risks, is Tralala, a hooker who entices tricks with fat wallets into the clutches of the violent gang. But Tralala is picked up by one soldier who falls in love with her and, hoping that his wallet will belong exclusively to her, she plays his girlfriend for a few days, receiving nothing but a "My Darling Tralala" letter for her efforts. She invites a bar full of rough trade to have sex with her; at this point, the book and the movie part company, although both are so horrific you'll wind up feeling like you've been hit by a truck. Leigh, light years away from the wholesome waitress she played in 1982's *Fast Times at Ridgemont High,* is absolutely riveting as the lost Tralala. *Last Exit to Brooklyn* is tough, grim material, filmed on location by a West German film company. Director Uli Edel's other credits include *Christiane F., Body of Evidence,* and *Tyson,* and screenwriter Desmond Nakano went on to write *American Me* and *White Man's Burden.* Based on the 1964 novel by Hubert Selby, Jr., who appears briefly as the driver of a car. 🦴🦴🦴

1990 (R) 102m/C Jennifer Jason Leigh, Burt Young, Stephen Lang, Ricki Lake, Jerry Orbach, Maia Danzinger, Stephen Baldwin, Peter Dobson, Jason Andrews, James Lorinz, Sam Rockwell, Camille Saviola, Cameron Johann, John Costelloe, Christopher Murney, Alexis Arquette; **D:** Uli Edel; **W:** Desmond Nakano; **C:** Stefan Czapsky, Stefan Czapsky; **M:** Mark Knopfler. New York Film Critics Awards '89: Best Supporting Actress (Leigh). **VHS, LV** *COL, FCT*

The Last Seduction

Suzy Amis in *Blown Away.* Anne Archer in *Patriot Games* AND *Clear and Present Danger.* Linda Hamilton in *Silent Fall.* What do all these actresses have in common? Wimpo women's parts! They're there for hugging and kissing. They wait while the HERO fights in all sorts of dangerous situations. They may even be brain surgeons! But so what? They have NO meaningful moments onscreen. And then there's Linda Fiorentino as Bridget Gregory in John Dahl's *The Last Seduction.* Now there's our kind of screen queen. Her husband (Bill Pullman?!) hits her and she runs off with their heist money. Love it! Then she runs away and has sex with this small town guy played by Peter Berg. He wants to get to know her better, she doesn't. Not unless he plays her games her way. And she plays rough. Not since *Double Indemnity*'s Phyllis Dietrichson have we seen such a remorseless manipulator. Steve Barancik's screenplay goes from strength to strength; every time you start to wonder what Bridget could possibly do after a string of dastardly deeds, she pulls off a nasty string of encores with ease. Bridget MOSTLY lays her cards upon the table. She may not let the guys in on all the details, but at least the outlines of every single one of her traps are visible to the naked eye. Linda Fiorentino is the only actress we know who's able to elicit sympathy even when we spend most of a movie convinced she's a cold-blooded killer, as in 1993's *Acting on Impulse.* But that was just a warm-up for her expert work in *The Last Seduction.* After watching movie after movie in which the good guys blow away 292 people, we can't see why 1994 audiences would have a problem with a small-scale, if full-blown villainess. And we hope Fiorentino decides to stay mean; anyone can pour coffee and whine about the hero's job, but NO ONE ever gave scenes with a plate of cookies or a can of mace such a sinister edge! 🦴🦴🦴🦴

1994 (R) 110m/C Linda Fiorentino, Peter Berg, J.T. Walsh, Bill Nunn, Bill Pullman; **D:** John Dahl; **W:** Steve Barancik; **M:** Joseph Vitarelli. Independent Spirit Awards '95: Best Actress (Fiorentino); New York Film Critics Awards '94: Best Actress (Fiorentino). **VHS, LV, Closed Caption** *PGV*

"Some People Have a Dark Side, She Had Nothing Else."

—The tag line from *The Last Seduction.*

INDEPENDENT FILM GUIDE

I was sent *The Last Seduction* from a studio. I read the script and thought, 'They'll never make this movie, and I don't want to spend a year of my life rewriting and developing this.' No, I really didn't take it very seriously. Then, after I'd finished *Red Rock West,* my agent sent me this script [again] and I said, 'They really want to make this script like it is?' And he said, 'Yeah, that's what they're saying. They don't want to spend a lot of money on it, but they want to make it like it is.' So I said, 'Great, I'd love to talk to them.' I just thought it was the funniest, weirdest thing I'd read in quite some time and that's what they wanted to do, so it was a perfect match.

"The leading character, Bridget Gregory, is fairly unsympathetic; she's relentless, she's driving her way non-stop through the story, and she gets to the end having committed several hideous acts and gets away. This is very unusual for a Hollywood film to have this sort of story. Usually, the good guys win and the bad guys go away, so it posed an interesting moral dilemma to me and I felt challenged by that. I was surprised that a script like this would come across where you could have so much fun with black comedic elements of the script and where the sex is very humorous. I never found it to be exactly sexy, but the people who were making it felt they were making a small, inexpensive, sexy thriller. And we said, 'Fine, we're making a small, sexy thriller.' All of us who were making the film were very aware of what we were doing, including Linda Fiorentino, Bill Pullman, and Peter Berg. The only advice we got from the people who were funding the movie was, 'Make sure there's a lot of nudity.' And thus, the movie: I see Bridget Gregory as the pivotal character, rather than the protagonist. We're introduced to her and we believe that she's the protagonist, especially when she's slapped by her husband Clay. We're immediately put in her camp by thinking, 'This is a weird relationship between these two

Last Summer

Last Summer focuses on a beautifully photographed but threatening shift of circumstances: a family facing relocation. Christo Christov's style has undeniable conviction. Sometimes, he splashes his intense visions all over the screen, flecked with sharp images of passion and brutality. The elements can destroy people (as when a cow kicks an old man to death), but they can also save them (as when another man finds shelter on a river raft). *Last Summer* was a departure for Christov, who has achieved greater fame as an artist of spectacular creations. 🐾🐾

people and there's some sort of abuse,' so we're willing to give Bridget Gregory the benefit of the doubt, to say she's innocent of the wrongdoings, and we're on her side immediately. Then we meet Mike Swayle, Peter Berg's character in the movie, and we think, 'Okay, here's the pivotal character.' I think what happens is that during the course of the story, Bridget slides out of the protagonist role and into the pivotal character, and Mike starts to take over the role of the protagonist. In either case, why can't Clay and Mike see through Bridget? My only answer to that is love's very strange. People do very strange things with each other in abusive relationships for so long that I think there's a sort of need and longing that Bridget's fulfilling for Mike.

"Peter Berg's successful at portraying Mike as a gullible, lost guy who, when Bridget walks into the bar, he sees someone who'll resurrect his manhood. And here she comes. Mike falls for Bridget, but he allows that to happen. It's a very difficult role to play, and I think he does it very well. It was exciting casting the picture because one of the things about doing an inexpensive movie is that people leave you alone and let you do what you want. This was a $2 1/2 million film—and Hollywood can go through that in two weeks— so there weren't a lot of expectations and pressure. They didn't feel the need to line it with well known stars, because they didn't have the money to do that.

"It was exciting for us to find people who were terrific for the parts, who understood the script, and who were willing to go along with us and have some fun making this film. Basically, it gave us a lot of creative freedom, and the atmosphere on the set was that no one was making a lot of money but we were all having fun with this really nasty character and this delightful script that Steve Barancik created. I try to tell interesting stories, and I find that the audience is as smart and many times smarter than I am. There's a dangerous mistake that many people make: they feel that audiences aren't as sophisticated as they are. They look down at and condescend to the public. I find that to be a grievous error. I've tried to make interesting, fun, intelligent stories (including *Kill Me Again*) that I feel audiences will respond to. Why I've gotten so lost in the shuffle between Hollywood and the public, I don't know."

1974 90m/C *BU* Grigor Vachkov, Bogdan Spasov, Lili Metodieva, Dimiter Ikonomov, Vesko Zehirev; *D:* Christo Christov; *W:* Yordan Radichov; *C:* Tsevetan Chobanski. *NYR*

Law of Desire

In Pedro Almodovar's *Law of Desire,* the great Carmen Maura invests her role as transsexual actress Tina Quintero with such extremes of fire and ice, both beautifully controlled, that you can watch nothing else when she is onscreen. The plot structure, which caves in at key points, is quite similar to Clint Eastwood's 1971 thriller, *Play Misty for Me.* However, Almodovar's sexual and political concerns extend far beyond showing obsession and possession between two young men in Spain's gay community against the backdrop of a dazzling theatrical atmosphere (an earlier collaboration by Almodovar and Maura was 1985's *What Have I Done to Deserve This?*). **AKA:** La Ley del Deseo. 🦴🦴🦴🦴

1986 100m/C *SP* Carmen Maura, Eusebio Poncela, Antonio Banderas, Bibi Andersson, Miguel Molina, Manuela Valasco, Nacho Martinez; **D:** Pedro Almodovar; **W:** Pedro Almodovar. **VHS, Beta, LV** *CCN, TPV*

Le Grand Chemin

France's *Le Grand Chemin/The Grand Highway* shows how the visit of a shy little boy throws the lives of a group of villagers into high relief. In revealing his all-too-human characters, writer/director Jean-Loup Hubert says something about the good and bad that is in all of us and how we must accept both in order to grow up. The acting, especially by youngsters Antoine Hubert and Vanessa Guedj, is fresh and truthful and the Britanny village, circa 1959, is beautifully photographed. **AKA:** The Grand Highway. 🦴🦴🦴

1987 107m/C *FR* Anemone, Richard Bohringer, Antoine Hubert, Vanessa Guedj, Christine Pascal, Raoul Billerey, Pascale Roberts; **D:** Jean-Loup Hubert; **W:** Jean-Loup Hubert; **M:** Georges Granier. Cesar Awards '88: Best Actor (Bohringer), Best Actress (Anemone). **VHS, Beta, LV** *FCT, IME, PBS*

Le Sexe des Etoiles

Les Sexe des Etoiles is a film without a neat wrap-up. Marianne Mercier plays a young girl who longs for the love of her transsexual father, played by Denis Merrier. After her parent's bitter split, she tries to draw him back into her lonely life (leading to moments like the one in which he is being cruised at a diner and she walks in with a cheery, "Hi, Dad!"). When she is forced to make a choice, she acknowledges for the first time the very real difference between her real "Dad" and the idol-ized father of her fantasies. Director Paule Baillargeon played the curator in Patricia Rozema's *I've Heard the Mermaids Singing.* **AKA:** The Sex of the Stars. 🦴🦴🦴

1993 100m/C *CA* Marianne-Coquelicot Mercier, Denis Mercier, Tobie Pelletier, Sylvie Drapeau; **D:** Paule Baillargeon; **W:** Monique Proulx. Genie Awards '93: Best Sound. **VHS** *ICA*

Leather Boys

Before he moved to America in 1966, Sidney J. Furie (*The Ipcress File*) was considered a remarkable director and 1963's *The Leather Boys* represents some of his finest work. This thoughtful film is an interesting study of latent homosexuality clashing against the more conventional life envisioned by Rita Tushingham as a young bride named Dot. Dot is in love with a biker named Reggie (Colin Campbell) who, prior to his marriage, spent most of his time hanging out with his best friend Pete (Dudley Sutton). Domestic life quickly takes its toll on Dot and Reggie as he turns more and more to Pete to relieve the crushingly familiar routine of adult life. Dot, too, finds herself forced into playing an increasingly unattractive role in Reggie's life, basically because she doesn't know what else to do. As their relationship founders, Dot suspects that Reggie and Pete may have more in common than their passion for motorcycles. It's all very understated and bittersweet, in common with many "kitchen sink" Brit flicks of the late '50s and early '60s. Yet the superb performances and Furie's gritty approach to Gillian Freeman's sensitive screenplay give *The Leather Boys* a unique quality that resonates far beyond the obvious title and inevitable conclusion. 🦴🦴🦴

1963 103m/C *GB* Rita Tushingham, Dudley Sutton, Gladys Henson, Colin Campbell, Avice Landon, Lockwood West, Betty Marsden, Johnny Briggs, Geoffrey Dunn, Dandy Nichols; **D:** Sidney J. Furie; **W:** Gillian Freeman. **VHS, Beta** *NO*

Leaving Las Vegas

As Miss Jean Brodie would say, "For those who like that sort of thing, that is the sort of thing they like." Before we'd re-evaluate this downer, we'd do the following, and all on the same day: (1) take care of that root canal, (2) squirm through a tetanus shot, and (3) look up that kid from fourth grade who used to pull up his eyelids to show us what was underneath. Note: Nicolas Cage and Elisabeth Shue are the healthiest, most athletic-looking dissolutes we've seen to date. (Check out their shoulder blades.) ♫

1995 (R) 120m/C Nicolas Cage, Elisabeth Shue, Julian Sands, Laurie Metcalf, David Brisbin, Richard Lewis, Valeria Golino, Steven Weber; **D:** Mike Figgis; **W:** Mike Figgis; **C:** Declan Quinn; **M:** Mike Figgis. Academy Awards '95: Best Actor (Cage); Golden Globe Awards '96: Best Actor—Drama (Cage); Independent Spirit Awards '96: Best Actress (Shue), Best Cinematography, Best Director (Figgis), Best Film; Los Angeles Film Critics Association Awards '95: Best Actor (Cage), Best Actress (Shue), Best Director (Figgis), Best Film; National Board of Review Awards '95: Best Actor (Cage); New York Film Critics Awards '95: Best Actor (Cage), Best Film; National Society of Film Critics Awards '95: Best Actor (Cage), Best Actress (Shue), Best Director (Figgis); Screen Actors Guild Award '95: Best Actor (Cage); Nominations: Academy Awards '95: Best Actress (Shue), Best Adapted Screenplay, Best Director (Figgis); British Academy Awards '95: Best Actor (Cage), Best Actress (Shue), Best Adapted Screenplay; Directors Guild of America Awards '95: Best Director (Figgis); Golden Globe Awards '96: Best Actress—Drama (Shue), Best Director (Figgis), Best Film—Drama; Independent Spirit Awards '96: Best Actor (Cage), Best Screenplay; Screen Actors Guild Award '95: Best Actress (Shue); Writers Guild of America '95: Best Adapted Screenplay. **VHS, LV, Closed Caption** *MGM*

Legacy

The print was not a good one. At first, the movie seemed slow when it wasn't offensive and offensive when it wasn't slow. Yet gradually, this study of the crack-up of a frustrated woman of 40 proved to be a moving and affecting experience. *Legacy* was all the more remarkable in that it was virtually a four-person operation, made on

an $18,000 budget and filmed in eight days. Not only did Karen Arthur and company finish the project with flair, they even reported that filmmaking under such severe limitations was altogether worthwhile and that other would-be filmmakers should go and do likewise. After making *Legacy*, Arthur went on to work fairly steadily, directing movies for television. ♫♫♫

1975 90m/C Joan Hotchkis, Sean Allan, George McDaniel, Dixie Lee; **D:** Karen Arthur; **W:** Joan Hotchkis; **C:** John Bailey; **M:** John Kellaway. **VHS, Beta** *DCL*

Legacy of the Hollywood Blacklist

Legacy of the Hollywood Blacklist, Judy Chaikin's concise, well edited documentary, focuses on the widows and children of the men who were blacklisted half a century ago, all of whom are still coping with the pain of the past. For those interested in seeing the work of some of the blacklisted artists who had to go underground, *Salt of the Earth,* a deeply moving 1954 film of a Chicano mine workers strike, is highly recommended. ♫♫♫

1987 60m/C D: Judy Chaikin; **W:** Judy Chaikin, Eve Goldberg; **C:** Rick Rosenthal, Cathy Zheutlin, Kristin Glover; **M:** Michael Andreas. **VHS, Beta** *NO*

Let Him Have It

Without wallowing in nostalgia, Peter Medak attempts to understand the world in which he grew up with an admirably low-key directing style. Medak's view of post-war Britain is far from flattering, and it may be hard for Americans to understand the toll that extended rationing placed on Brits until 1954 for food and 1957 for petrol. The 1950s were not a good time for Britain, and the country lost a great deal in international prestige as the decade wore on and its inflexible leaders continued to make one error in judgment after another.

Chet Baker and friend in the documentary Let's Get Lost.

al causes at 61), if segregated from a society which no longer believed in the death penalty at the time of their crimes. The wrongful executions of Timothy Evans, Ruth Ellis, and Derek Bentley (this film's protagonist, who never killed anyone) reflected the values of an era that has long since passed, but it would be false to show that era without revealing why those values were once important. Medak clearly extends measured sympathy for people who acted out against what they saw as a dreary and changeless way of life. If only for the splendid acting, both *The Krays* and *Let Him Have It* are well worth seeing, and it is Medak's thoughtful voice as a filmmaker that gives even sharper poignance to his well-crafted studies of how Britain grudgingly entered the 20th century, well over fifty years too late. At press time, Iris Bentley continued her 45-year fight for her brother Derek's posthumous pardon—a pardon for a murder he never committed. Also recommended for Britain's shifting position on the death penalty: 1971's *10 Rillington Place,* 1985's *Dance with a Stranger.* 🦴🦴🦴🦴

1991 (R) 115m/C *GB* Christopher Eccleston, Paul Reynolds, Tom Bell, Eileen Atkins, Clare Holman, Michael Elphick, Mark McGann, Tom Courtenay, Ronald Fraser, Michael Gough, Murray Melvin, Clive Revill, Norman Rossington, James Villiers; *D:* Peter Medak. **VHS, LV** *NLC*

Let's Get Lost

Let's Get Lost was nominated for an Oscar and *The Thin Blue Line* wasn't. As callous as it sounds, that may be because at least the Academy members knew who the late Chet Baker was, unlike Randall Dale Allan. Twenty minutes into Bruce Weber's sluggish study of a jazz artist in decline, our question was not "What's going to happen next?" but "Do we have to watch all this?," a fatal response to a documentary that will drag on for over two long hours. Will it keep you on the edge of your seat to observe that a man of 57

Let Him Have It tries to recreate some of the feeling of that era by showing the tattered rituals as the strong sources of comfort they represented to a country of bewildered men, women, and children. Medak also casts striking images from the 'kitchen sink' school of filmmaking like Tom Courtenay, who has never been better, as an agonized father, and the scene-stealing Murray Melvin as a school master who demands the hidden arsenal of guns that his students have brought to class, and the usually unsympathetic James Villiers as a compassionate but ineffectual barrister. *The Krays,* filmed by Medak in 1990, is a film about vicious criminals who were still alive and well (at least through 1995, when Ronnie died of natur-

with a history of drug and alcohol abuse does not look 24 years old? It seems to come as news to Bruce Weber: "Do you know how much it hurts me to see you looking like this?" he asks the star of his film. "Well, Bruce," Baker drawls, "I AM 57 years old." Weber started out as a fashion photographer and it's obvious from the images he chooses: See Chet looking great. See Chet looking like hell. He even "casts" young Chet Baker looka-likes in his "documentary": See what Chet would look like if...; who cares but Weber? And the rest of his documentary choices play like raw filler for the tabloids. We hear from no less than one mother, three children, one ex-wife, and three past and present girlfriends, all of whom bicker about their relationship with Chet Baker. Weber to Baker's mother: "Did he disappoint you as a son?" Vera Baker doesn't want to answer but is too polite to tell the man with the camera to buzz off. "Yes," she says finally. "But don't let's go into that." If Vera Baker won't come across with the dirt, Weber asks Baker himself about the time he was beat up and lost his teeth. Then he cuts to a girlfriend. ("Chet lied about the way that happened.") When an ex-wife tells Weber that Baker's girlfriend is evil and then asks him to cut something out, he leaves everything in, including her request. Unsurprisingly, the Baker family could no longer stand Weber by the time of the film's release. What happens in *Let's Get Lost* is that we learn more about Bruce Weber than Chet Baker. Thirty to forty minutes could be edited from this picture with no harm done, but we'd still be stuck with Weber's vision of Chet Baker as well as his one-of-a-kind insight that a great trumpet player could be a real creep. If you want to know the trumpet player, listen to Baker's Complete Pacific Jazz Live Recordings from 1953-1957 and skip *Let's Get Lost.* 🎵🎵

1988 125m/B Chet Baker; *D:* Bruce Weber. Nominations: Academy Awards '88: Best Feature Documentary. **VHS** *MVD, COL*

Letters from the Park

Letters from the Park is about two shy young people who hire a clerk for the purpose of a romance by mail. The clerk falls in love with the romance and pours all his energies into the correspondence. The graceful narrative is enhanced with delicate humor and charming performances by the three leads. *Letters from the Park,* Tomas Gutierrez Alea's beautifully directed tale about love and longing, was co-scripted by its original author, Gabriel Garcia Marquez. 🎵🎵🎵

1988 85m/C *CU* Victor Laplace, Ivonne Lopez, Miguel Paneque; *D:* Tomas Gutierrez Alea; *W:* Gabriel Garcia Marquez, Tomas Gutierrez Alea. **VHS** *FXL, FCT, APD*

Licensed to Kill

Filmmaker Arthur Dong was the victim of a hate crime in the 1970s. Since his assailants were all juveniles, their criminal records were sealed. Long after coming to terms with the attack, Dong wanted to understand how and why hate crimes continue to occur, from the perspective of seven murderers of gay men. Donald Aldrich, the only one of the seven on death row, murdered a 23-year-old male victim the month he turned 29. Prior to that, Aldrich had been looking for gay men he could hurt and rob. Corey Burley, sentenced to life in prison for the murder of a 29-year-old male victim, smiles broadly and talks like a stand-up comic. Without a voice track, you might think this engaging young man (he was only 21 at the time of the murder) was describing his thriving career. Sad-eyed William Cross was raped by a family friend as a child and was sentenced to 25 years in prison for killing a 51-year-old fellow resident of a Chicago hotel. Then 28, he had never recovered from the rape and didn't recall that he had stabbed his victim seven times. Raymond Childs, who also received a sentence of

Twenty years ago I was attacked by gay bashers. And ever since that night I always wondered why these things happened. I mean it hasn't only happened to me. It's been happening to a lot of people. I'm an Asian-American man and I'm certainly out as an Asian-American man, you can't hide that fact, but I've never been attacked as one. Not that it doesn't happen, but I personally haven't been. It has just been an obsession for me to cover this topic in some way on film. And it's led me to the making of this film.

"My approach to the men in the film is from a very honest point of view. I wanted to be very straightforward with them in terms of telling them what I wanted to do with this film. From the beginning I told them I was looking for men who had been convicted of killing homosexuals and interviewing them on camera for a documentary on their lives and what led up to the crimes. I approached them as a filmmaker, very much from a journalist's point of view. And that I was here to report what I find. There was a report put out by the National Coalition of Anti-Violence Programs. It's a national organization of 23 chapters. Every year they put out a report that compiles the statistics of anti-gay and -lesbian hate crimes. One year they had a summary of murders that happened within the past few years and there was a list of over 200 of them. From that list I picked out about 40 names, 40 cases, and wrote to them and told them what I was wanting to do. Fifteen of them actually responded and said, 'Yeah, I'll be a part of this.' I went to visit actually ten of them and six of them ended up being in the film, and I used another additional interview that was taped by the police in the confession session.

"My whole experience in the interviewing process, actually being there with the men, was guided by my quest to speak to these men as human beings. To be in a room with them as a fellow human being. Because there's no denying that they were. They're human beings, they're not monsters. We may call them monsters figuratively speaking or demons, but they're one of us. We can't deny that. They're one of our species. That whole philosophy guided me through the whole process of making this film."

25 years, was also 28 when he stabbed a well known lawyer 27 times. Sgt. Kenneth French was 22 when he killed a woman and three men while shooting up a family restaurant. French, who had just consumed a fifth of whiskey during a screening of Clint Eastwood's *The Unforgiven* (with its saloon massacre finale), was angered by President Clinton's position about gays in the military. Personable and articulate Jay Johnson, who is gay himself, came from the proverbial good family and once wanted to enter politics. When he learned that he was HIV-positive at 23, he decided to achieve fame as a serial killer instead. He was sentenced to two life terms after killing two men, including a Minnesota state senator. And Jeffrey Swinford, the least remorseful of a generally remorseless group and the first due for release, was 22 when he murdered a young male acquaintance. He was sentenced to twenty years, but may be paroled much earlier than that. All seven killed because of their hatred of gays. *Licensed to Kill* is a difficult picture to watch because Dong humanizes his victims by giving them a chance to tell their stories without a debate. Police video footage of an actual confession, news clips, and films of crime scenes are also included. Arthur Dong's film tells us ugly truths about America and its mass perception of gays that tend to reinforce individual acts of violence. We may not want to face these truths, but clearly Dong's searing study is long overdue. ♫♫♫

1997 80m/C D: Arthur Dong; **W:** Arthur Dong; **C:** Robert Shepard; **M:** Miriam Cutler. Sundance Film Festival '97: Best Director (Dong), Filmmakers Trophy (Dong). *NYR*

Life Is Cheap...But Toilet Paper Is Expensive

Wayne Wang appears to be an artist struggling for his own voice in his fifth effort, *Life Is Cheap...But Toilet Paper Is Expensive.* Like Pedro Almodovar, director of *Tie Me Up...Tie Me Down,* Wang is using an inferior product to battle a censorship issue. It's hard to render much enthusiasm for a movie when its denouement consists of a wisecrack delivered while the protagonist is eating a pile of manure. Earlier in the film, Wang shows a man on a toilet, complete with sound effects. There is also an eight-minute long chase with no real resolution and with the chasee often chasing the chaser. Accident or design? Hard to tell, since Wang, in a six-item statement then released to the press, admitted that he went with a crew to Hong Kong "with no particular perspective or commercial interest in mind." Wang combines documentary footage of ducks being slaughtered for market with a next-to-nothing plot involving the delivery of a suitcase filled with junk. The cast consists of actors with variable abilities. Executive producer John K. Chan impersonates an anthropologist, but not as well as Bonnie Ngai portrays his unwilling bride. Mr. and Mrs. Kai-Bong Chau, complete with the punk coats and car which attracted the attention of Robin Leach and *Lifestyles of the Rich and Famous,* appear as themselves. Character actor Victor Wong is great as always, but why is he in this movie? Well, Wayne Wang "wanted to take a critical and sardonic look at...contemporary Hong Kong society," so he assembled a screenplay with his director of photography, Amir M. Mokri (who shoots better than he writes). The resulting 89 minutes gave him "a better understanding of the world" although bewildered audiences may have some trouble with that. *Life Is Cheap* did not receive a rating when it was released theatrically, so the director identified it as an "A" picture: for Adults. Wang insists that the project is neither the "technical drill" IT appears to be nor the "business venture" HE appears to be trying to hype with a ratings issue. Wayne's GOOD films include *Chan Is Missing, Dim Sum: A Little Bit of Heart, Eat a Bowl of Tea,* and *The*

Joy Luck Club. As for this butt-wiper wannabe, is it cutting edge art or is it pretentious trash? You decide!!! **WOOF!**

1990 89m/C Victor Wong, John K. Chan, Bonnie Ngai, Kai-Bong Chau; **D:** Wayne Wang; **W:** Wayne Wang, Amir M. Mokri; **C:** Amir M. Mokri. *NYR*

Lightning Jack

Watching *Lightning Jack* is like spending an hour and a half with a well meaning but boring uncle who thinks he's cute and clever and funny and demands every conceivable chance to prove all three. At a social gathering, you'd be sitting there with a smile chained to your face, waiting for someone, anyone, to change his needle. But no one has that excuse at the neighborhood bijou, which made the $5.5 million dollars *Lightning Jack* raked in at the box office in its opening week rather a mystery. It's the story of an Australian outlaw and his mute sidekick, played by Paul Hogan and 1996 Oscar winner Cuba Gooding, Jr. Their interaction with outsiders is minimal, which means audiences get to sit through one sequence after another in which Lightning Jack explains to his partner what a cool mate he is. Either you have a taste for this sort of thing or you don't. If you don't, you can look at the scenery or wait for the few short moments when Beverly D'Angelo and/or Roger Daltrey are onscreen or play "Who Is That?" with the old-time character actors in the cast (including Pat Hingle, Ben Chapman, and L.Q. Jones). Cuba Gooding, Jr., does his best in a role that, as written by 1986 Oscar nominee Hogan, plumbs the depth of bad taste. Hogan also produced *Lightning Jack* by charming the socks off 5,860 private Australian investors. Next time, they'll probably demand *Crocodile Dundee III AND IV* and insist that he film them in the outback. Now if someone could just convince Paul Hogan that guys over 55 don't HAVE to be so dang cute...in the meanwhile, there's always pre-sold works-for-hire like 1996's *Flipper*. **WOOF!**

1994 (PG-13) 93m/C Paul Hogan, Cuba Gooding Jr., Beverly D'Angelo, Kamala Dawson, Pat Hingle, Richard Riehle, Frank McRae, Roger Daltrey, L.Q. Jones, Max Cullen; **D:** Simon Wincer; **W:** Paul Hogan; **C:** David Eggby; **M:** Bruce Rowland. **VHS, LV** *HBO*

Like Water for Chocolate

Like Water for Chocolate is one of Mexico's biggest hits and it did equally well here, thanks to an excellent cast, lush cinematography, and its frank exploration of sexual tensions within the family. That said, the film is not be to everyone's taste and it certainly wasn't ours, dealing as it does with every imaginable stomach disorder for many of its 126 minutes. *AKA:* Como Agua para Chocolate. 🎜🎜

1993 (R) 105m/C *MX* Lumi Cavazos, Marco Leonardi, Regina Torne, Mario Ivan Martinez, Ada Carrasco, Yareli Arizmendi, Caludette Maille, Pilar Aranda; **D:** Alfonso Arau; **W:** Laura Esquivel; **C:** Steven Bernsein; **M:** Leo Brower. Nominations: British Academy Awards '93: Best Foreign Language Film; Independent Spirit Awards '94: Best Foreign Film. **VHS, LV** *TOU*

The Linguini Incident

Despite lackluster returns at the box office, *The Linguini Incident* is notable for several reasons. It is the first Rosanna Arquette movie we can recall in which she wears clothes in every single scene. It is also the first romantic comedy for David ("Oh well, there's always Bowie: HE'LL play a Martian") Bowie. *The Linguini Incident* is also an hilarious spoof of Manhattan trendsetters, best exemplified by Eszter Balint, an appealing fresh talent who plays Vivian, a gun-toting underwear designer. Arquette has never been funnier or more charming as Lucy, who works nights as a waitress and auditions for radical feminist touring troupes during the day. Lucy's goal is to fill the footsteps of escape artist Harry Houdini so she can feed her collecting habit: buying Houdini memorabilia. (The late, great Viveca Lindfors has a couple of nice sequences as a memorabilia dealer named Miracle who just happens to have Mrs. Houdini's wedding ring in stock for a mere five grand.) Bowie is Monte, a new bartender at the restaurant Dali, where Lucy also works. He hits on one waitress after another, hoping to marry one of them, ostensibly to earn his green card. His mysterious involvement with Dante and Cecil, the restaurant Dali's fey owners (played by Andre Gregory and Buck Henry) isn't explained until well into the plot, but he and Lucy manage to connect in a quirky sort of way. The screenplay was written by first-time director Richard Shepard in collaboration with Oakland writer Tamar Brott, who based much of *The Linguini Incident* script on her early experiences as a New York waitress. It would be easy for a film like this to have a brittle, cynical feel, but largely because of the affection Shepard and Brott feel for each and every character, they have done a good job reinventing all the conventions they satirize and/or romanticize. Many of the restaurant details are just right, from the good-cop/bad-cop style of the Dali's owners to the enormous contrast between the lush dining room and the far from glamorous kitchen the patrons never get to see. Marlee Matlin (in her first theatrical feature since 1987's ill-fated *Walker*) has a delightful character bit as the cashier at the Dali; and Julian Lennon, Iman, and even the 1940s Warner Bros. starlet Andrea King make brief appearances as dinner patrons. A photograph of the charismatic Houdini appears, too, but anyone who has had the bad luck to see Harry in 1921's *The Man from Beyond* knows that the even more charismatic David Bowie, with one blue eye, one brown eye, and a mouthful of crooked teeth, can act rings around this dreamy icon from another time. 🎬🎬🎬

1992 (R) 99m/C Rosanna Arquette, David Bowie, Eszter Balint, Andre Gregory, Buck Henry, Viveca Lindfors, Marlee Matlin, Lewis Arquette, Andrea King; *Cameos:* Julian Lennon, Iman; *D:* Richard Shepard; *W:* Tamar Brott, Richard Shepard; *M:* Thomas Newman. **VHS, LV, Closed Caption** *IME*

Lisa

Lisa is the first film we rented just because we liked the clip they were playing in the video store. (We don't recall seeing ANY other advertisements for this movie, which is a 1990 variation on 1965's *I Saw What You Did* theme). Karen Clark's screenplay clearly has some firsthand understanding of what it's like to he an isolated 14-year-old girl. Lisa and her best friend start out by playing casual games with the telephone. Lisa's friend, complete with obnoxious kid brother and idealized parents who let her go out on dates, soon loses interest in the games. Lisa, the daughter of an overly protective single working mother, continues playing a dangerous telephone game with a serial killer. While he stalks his victims, she stalks him with considerable skill but without a clue as to the real implications of the game. Television actresses Staci Keanan and Cheryl Ladd are convincing as Lisa and her mother and the conclusion, without a male rescuer in sight, provides a satisfying payoff to this overlooked theatrical release. 🎬🎬🎬

1990 (PG-13) 95m/C Staci Keanan, Cheryl Ladd, D.W. Moffett, Tanya Fenmore, Jeffrey Tambor, Julie Cobb; *D:* Gary Sherman; *W:* Karen Clark. **VHS, Closed Caption** *FOX*

Lisztomania

Lisztomania is a movie to avoid, with a score by Rick Wakeman that would horrify Liszt. The conceit here is that Franz Liszt (Roger Daltrey) was the first pop star. If you can handle that, you won't have any trouble seeing Ringo Starr as the Pope, either. Director Ken Russell is way out of control with this tasteless schlock. He would next tackle the life of Rudolph Valentino. **WOOF!**

1975 (R) 106m/C *GB* Roger Daltrey, Sara Kestelman, Paul Nicholas, Fiona Lewis, Ringo Starr, Veronica Quilligan, Nell Campbell, John Justin, Andrew Reilly, Anulka Dziubinska, Rick Wakeman, Rikki Howard, Felicity Devonshire, Aubrey Morris, Kenneth Colley, Ken Parry, Otto Diamont, Murray Melvin, Andrew

Faulds, Oliver Reed; **D:** Ken Russell; **W:** Ken Russell; **C:** Peter Suschitzsky; **M:** Rick Wakeman. **VHS, Beta, LV** *WAR*

Little Dorrit, Film 1: Nobody's Fault

The Charles Dickens the 20th century prefers to remember is the man who wrote about the Ghosts of Christmas Past, Present, and Future. Dickens also wrote about the boys David and Oliver who evolved, at least on film, into nostalgic symbols of wretched childhoods whose lives were sweetened by sudden charity. Yet Dickens was also a severe critic of a 19th century society that lionized apparent success and imprisoned economic failures. *Little Dorrit* was originally published as a monthly serial between 1855 and 1857, and it might be easier on contemporary admirers to see Christine Edzard's splendid film in one- or two-hour portions. However, seeing all six hours in one day will allow you to indulge yourself in the full cumulative power of the narrative as well as the sheer beauty of Edzard's skillful interpretation. Also, the parallel structures of parts one and two, both with subtle but definite variations in points of view, provide treats best appreciated in single day viewings. You won't find any of the things which are usually so wrong with today's movies about the past in *Little Dorrit*; no garish lighting, no bright lipsticks, no synthetic fabrics. What you will find is a vivid, unsentimental look at London from another time. Forty years after he played Herbert Pocket in David Lean's *Great Expectations,* Alec Guinness is magnificent as William Dorrit, whose poverty is only made bearable by constant self-deception. It's a complex, fascinating role, and Guinness makes the most of it. Another stunning character, played by Miriam Margolyes, offers a detailed por-

trait of Flora, a coquette who never grew up but instead grew out (and out and out). She is reminiscent of Dora, the delicate child bride of *David Copperfield* and for good reason. Both Dora and Flora are based on Maria Beadnell, with whom Dickens fell in love as a young man. In real life, she didn't die as a beautiful girl, but married another man and became, in her own words, "fat, old, and ugly." We see Flora fluttering about and are saddened, as Dickens must have been, by the realization that such a surfeit of charm is only bearable in the very young. Also worth watching are the sharp exchanges between the late Joan Greenwood as Mrs. Clennam and Max Wall as her wily steward Flintwich, plus the bitchy competition between Amelda Brown as Fanny Dorrit and Eleanor Bron as a banker's snobbish wife. 🦴🦴🦴

1988 369m/C *GB* Alec Guinness, Derek Jacobi, Cyril Cusack, Sarah Pickering, Joan Greenwood, Max Wall, Amelda Brown, Daniel Chatto, Miriam Margolyes, Bill Fraser, Roshan Seth, Michael Elphick, Eleanor Bron, Patricia Hayes, Robert Morley, Sophie Ward; **D:** Christine Edzard; **W:** Christine Edzard; **C:** Bruno de Keyzer; **M:** Giuseppe Verdi. Los Angeles Film Critics Association Awards '88: Best Film, Best Supporting Actor (Guinness); Nominations: Academy Awards '88: Best Adapted Screenplay, Best Supporting Actor (Guinness). **VHS, Beta, LV, Closed Caption** *WAR, SIG, TVC*

Little Dorrit, Film 2: Little Dorrit's Story

Nineteenth century London was not quite as rosy as it appears in contemporary storybooks. Typhoid ran rampant among rich and poor alike, debtor's prisons were a fact of life, and work was often synonymous with unrelieved drudgery. And then there was something called a government bureaucracy that first engulfed and finally drained those who tried to grapple with it. In *Little Dorrit,* named 1988's picture of the year by the National Board of Review, director Christine Edzard is scrupulously faithful to Charles Dickens' critical view of the period. Both *Nobody's Fault* (AKA *Poverty*), focusing on Derek Jacobi as Arthur Clennam, and *Little Dorrit's Story* (AKA *Riches*), told from Amy Dorrit's perspective, are compulsively watchable, the cinematic equivalent of a book you can't put down. What Clennam lacks in drive and imagination, he makes up for in kindness and decency. Clennam wanders through a world of far more colorful characters than himself, but as portrayed by the innately charismatic Jacobi, his low-key demeanor constantly seems on the edge of some sort of private revolution. Interestingly, it is Amy Dorrit, even more low-key than himself, who provides the catalytic change. When Clennam looks at Little Dorrit, played by 20-year-old newcomer Sarah Pickering, she appears more delicate than glass, but Amy actually proves to be a diamond in the rough. Little Dorrit certainly doesn't see herself as frail while she resourcefully makes her own way in the world. Producers for this Dickensian epic are Richard Goodwin and John Brabourne (the late Lord Mountbatten's son-in-law), who showed us another glimpse of an eroding Empire with *A Passage to India*. It's actually possible to catch the entire epic of *Nobody's Fault* and *Little Dorrit's Story* in one day. Allow an hour for dinner and you may find that you'll spend the most memorable day of the season in another time and place, courtesy of your VCR. Despite its length, *Little Dorrit* is well worth making a special point to see. Christine Edzard and company have certainly provided me with six hours that I'll never forget. ♫♫♫

1988 369m/C *GB* Alec Guinness, Derek Jacobi, Cyril Cusack, Sarah Pickering, Joan Greenwood, Max Wall, Amelda Brown, Daniel Chatto, Miriam Margolyes, Bill Fraser, Roshan Seth, Michael Elphick, Patricia Hayes, Robert Morley, Sophie Ward, Eleanor Bron; *D:* Christine Edzard; *W:* Christine Edzard; *C:* Bruno de Keyzer; *M:* Giuseppe Verdi. Los Angeles Film Critics Association Awards '88: Best Film, Best Supporting Actor (Guinness). **VHS, Beta, LV, Closed Caption** *WAR, SIG, TVC*

The Little Kidnappers

Watch Charlton Heston's 1996 Canadian re-make if you must, but the original movie is far superior. Duncan MacRae didn't have to impersonate a stern Scottish Grandaddy, he lived and breathed the role of Jim MacKenzie. Anyway, the focus rightfully belongs on the kids: Jon Whiteley, eight, and Vincent Winter, six, deservedly won Oscars as Harry and Davy, who really want a dog, but when Grandaddy says no, they start doting on a "babby" of their very own. Director Philip Leacock showed such sensitivity and skill on the film that a bright future was predicted for him. He made a few more good films with kids (*Escapade, The Spanish Gardener* with Whiteley, *Hand in Hand*), but after 1960, his career veered towards telefeatures, none of them particularly distinguished. Whiteley appeared in a few more films, including *Moonfleet* with Stewart Granger. Winter appeared in *The Dark Avenger* with Errol Flynn, *Time Lock* with Sean Connery, *Gorgo* with Bill Travers, and a string of Disney films: *Greyfriars Bobby, Almost Angels, The Horse Without a Head,* and *The Three Lives of Thomasina.* Bring back special Oscars for best juvenile actors, so they don't have to compete with adult stars! *AKA:* The Kidnappers. ♫♫♫♫

1953 95m/B *GB* Duncan MacRae, Adrienne Corri, Jon Whiteley, Vincent Winter, Jean Anderson, Theodore Bikel, Francis De Wolff, James Sutherland, John Rae, Jack Stewart, Jameson Clark, Howard Connell; *D:* Philip Leacock; *W:* Neil Paterson. *NYR*

Little Nemo: Adventures in Slumberland

Little Nemo: Adventures in Slumberland has quite a few things going for it. Ray Bradbury created the concept for Chris Columbus' screenplay and the animation

effectively blends a fluid Disney-style animation with the charm of the original artwork by Winsor McCay. The thing that didn't work for us was the overpowering soundtrack. It was distracting to hear vocalists (including Melissa Manchester) blasting numbers reminiscent of Broadway show tunes when we were trying to focus on the story. The plot revolves around Little Nemo's vivid dreams, especially his valiant efforts to free the residents of Slumberland from the terrifying control of Nightmareland. Mickey Rooney is the voice of Flip the Frog, a character more mischievous than evil, even though he is responsible for most of the disasters that threaten the good guys. Rene Auberjonois plays Professor Genius, who is not much of a help to Nemo (Gabriel Damon) and his pet squirrel Icarus in a crisis. The whole thing is directed by Disney veteran William T. Hurtz. *Nemo* may be overcute for adult

audiences, lacking the sly wit which makes the best of children's animation absorbing to adult viewers. (This is something that Disney himself would have made sure was the object of extensive research and development before the cameras ever rolled.) But, except for those songs and a dull teach-the-kiddies-a-lesson-in-responsible-values sub-theme, it's a painless way to pass 85 minutes and it even succeeded in giving us a nightmare or two when we got home. 🦴🦴⚥

1992 (G) 85m/C D: William T. Hurtz, Masami Hata; **W:** Chris Columbus, Richard Outten; **M:** Tom Chase, Steve Rucker; **V:** Gabriel Damon, Mickey Rooney, Rene Auberjonois, Daniel Mann, Laura Mooney, Bernard Erhard, William E. Martin. **VHS, LV** *HMD*

Little Odessa

After 1992's *Reservoir Dogs,* Tim Roth could have played a killer in his sleep. As hitman Joshua Shapira, he goes back to Brighton Beach (where he grew up) to kill his next target. The situation of a killer being sheltered within an American family was previously explored in 1943's *Shadow of a Doubt,* but in that film, the Merry Widow Killer returns to a bright, glistening home in Santa Rosa, California, filled with a mostly happy, mostly loving family whose sole problem seems to be an occasional twitch of small town boredom. In *Little Odessa,* Joshua faces father Arkady (Maximilian Schell) who hates his guts, mother Irina (Vanessa Redgrave) who is close to death, and kid brother Reuben (Edward Furlong) who loves him, in spite of the fact that he knows Joshua is rotten all the way down to the bone. For his first film, James Gray, 24, has written and directed a dark, unrelieved downer. 𝄞𝄞𝄽

1994 (R) 98m/C Tim Roth, Edward Furlong, Moira Kelly, Vanessa Redgrave, Maximilian Schell, Paul Guilfoyle, Natasha Andreichenko, David Vadim, Mina Bern, Boris McGiver, Mohammed Ghaffari, Michael Khumrov, Dmitry Preyers, David Ross, Ron Brice, Jace Kent, Marianna Lead, Gene Ruffini; *D:* James Gray; *W:* James Gray; *C:* Tom Richmond; *M:* Dana Sano. Nominations: Independent Spirit Awards '96: Best Actor (Roth), Best Cinematography, Best First Feature, Best Supporting Actress (Redgrave). **VHS, LV, Closed Caption** *LIV*

The Little Prince

The Little Prince was a major disappointment in 1974, and still is, for those who would like to see a decent adaptation of Antoine De Saint-Exupery's (1900-44) delicate little book. Every time the orchestra begins to play another awful song in the terrible score, you'll shudder with embarrassment. Director Stanley Donen seems to have the unerring knack of making his cast look ridiculous here. Occasionally, he permits the book's wise, gentle themes to slip into the film, but most of the time, he's far more concerned with how big and expensive he can make everything look. I have never heard one kid ask to see this one on video, but, for the record: Richard

Kiley is the Pilot, Steven Warner is the title character, the late Bob Fosse has his moments as the Snake, Gene Wilder steals a few more moments as the Fox, Joss Ackland is the King, Clive Revill is the Businessman, Victor Spinetti is the Historian, Graham Crowden is the General, and Donna McKechnie is Rose. Avoid this cinematic massacre and read the 1943 book instead. 𝄞𝄞

1974 (G) 88m/C *GB* Richard Kiley, Bob Fosse, Steven Warner, Gene Wilder, Joss Ackland, Clive Revill, Victor Spinetti, Graham Crowden, Donna McKechnie; *D:* Stanley Donen; *W:* Alan Jay Lerner; *C:* Christopher Challis; *M:* Frederick Loewe, Alan Jay Lerner. Golden Globe Awards '75: Best Score; Nominations: Academy Awards '74: Best Song ("Little Prince"), Best Original Score. **VHS, Beta, LV** *PAR*

A Little Princess

The Little Princess is the most frequently televised of all the Shirley Temple vehicles made by 20th Century Fox between 1934 and 1940, and with good reason. Someone forgot to renew the film's 1939 copyright and it lapsed into the public domain in 1967. It is among the best of Temple's childhood movies with a strong storyline, great supporting cast, and the obligatory dream sequence which ensured that the Ideal Toy Corporation would market yet another Shirley doll in lavish princess costume. But the one element of the picture that strayed from Francis Hodgson Burnett's 1888 novel *Sara Crewe,* was an unrealistic insistence that Sara's search for her father, reported dead in action, be given a fairy tale ending. The 1995 version of *A Little Princess* retains the fairy tale ending with a slightly more plausible twist. Even those who are sated by the Temple version will be pleasantly surprised by director Alfonso Cuaron's update. The setting has been transferred to America and the period moved up a bit in time to the First World War. Liesel Matthews, the new Sara, neither sings nor dances, but she does tell magical stories about India (beautifully interpreted by Cuaron). Eleanor

Bron, also seen in 1994's *Black Beauty,* adopts an American accent to play mean schoolmistress Miss Amelia Minchin, although the script here suggests a reason for her relentless nastiness. Adorable Vanessa Lee Chester plays Sara's friend Becky this time (Chester would play *Harriet the Spy*'s best friend the following year) and all the other kids are well cast and appealingly believable. Sara's sunny personality and some colorful sight gags take the edge off grim plot turns. All in all, *A Little Princess* still has something to say to the kids who were born over a century after its creation. And think about this, parents: no singing, no dancing, and no Queen Victoria! 🦴🦴🦴🦴

1995 (G) 97m/C Liesl Matthews, Eleanor Bron, Liam Cunningham, Rusty Schwimmer, Arthur Malet, Vanessa Lee Chester, Errol Sitahal, Heather DeLoach, Taylor Fry; **D:** Alfonso Cuaron; **W:** Richard LaGravenese, Elizabeth Chandler; **C:** Emmanuel Lubezki; **M:** Patrick Doyle. Nominations: Academy Awards '95: Best Art Direction/Set Decoration, Best Cinematography. **VHS, LV, Closed Caption** *WAR*

Living in Oblivion

Tom DiCillo's *Living in Oblivion* began life as *Scene 6, Take 1* (manically well acted by Steve Buscemi as director Nick Reve), all about the technical nightmares that occur on a low-budget film where the six-day old milk is the most experienced member of the crew. The 17-minute segment, shown at the San Francisco International Film Festival, wound up as the first sequence in the finished film. The second sequence, interestingly, is about an egotistical, not very bright star (James LeGros as Chad Palomino), who tries to manipulate the shoot and everyone on the set to his own advantage. Watch this on a double bill with 1992's *Johnny Suede* and connect the dots: Brad Pitt starred in that first directorial effort by DiCillo, along with Catherine Keener, who's also in *Oblivion* as Chad's co-star Nicole. The third segment involves Nicole, a dwarf, and Nick's mother. *Oblivion* is a very funny flick about

what it's like to make an indie, with great work by Dermot Mulroney as the cinematographer with an eye patch, and by Rica Martens as a motherly looking actress delivering sharp asides re: the mise-en-scene between takes. Rent it and laugh till you cry. 🦴🦴🦴

1994 (R) 92m/C Steve Buscemi, Catherine Keener, James LeGros, Dermot Mulroney, Danielle von Zerneck, Robert Wightman, Rica Martens, Hilary Gilford, Peter Dinklage, Kevin Corrigan, Matthew Grace, Michael Griffiths, Ryna Bowker, Francesca DiMauro; **D:** Tom DiCillo; **W:** Tom DiCillo; **C:** Frank Prinzi; **M:** Jim Farmer. Sundance Film Festival '95: Best Screenplay; Nominations: Independent Spirit Awards '96: Best Film, Best Screenplay, Best Supporting Actor (LeGros). **VHS, LV, Closed Caption** *COL*

Lolita

I first read Vladimir Nabokov's classic novel *Lolita* late at night with a flashlight when I was way too young for it, 12. At that age, the idea of any middle-aged man slobbering all over a kid was the ultimate gross-out, although I must confess that I couldn't put down the book all night long. The idea of returning to the original source material has always made me squeamish, but Stanley Kubrick's 1962 screen adaptation has been a kick to watch over and over again. In spite of some rather unfair reviews at the time of the film's original release, James Mason IS Humbert Humbert, the ideal incarnation of elegant sleaze. In real life, Mason was a fairly down-to-earth guy, but only a few of his directors, like Kubrick and *Georgy Girl*'s Silvia Narizzano, captured his authentic self-deprecating charm. You rarely think of sensuous, brooding Mason discussing junky American cultural symbols with crushing familiarity, but as Humbert Humbert, he is obsessed not only with a seductive child but also with the cheap trappings that surround her. To get the kid, he even pursues her mother, portrayed, with her usual egoless desire for the truth, by Shelley Winters, then just 40. Winters, who had not then acquired the padding that sustained the illusion that she was many years older than she really was, nevertheless stuffs herself into a series of outfits that are several sizes too small. Even better, she is absolutely merciless at exposing the intense sexual competition at the heart of many mother-daughter relationships. The sequences in which Winters' character tries to entice Humbert wearing low-cut leopard pajamas while Lolita ignites his ardor with a sullen request for a mayonnaise-ridden sandwich are both painful and hilarious to watch. For many original audience members, Peter Sellers as Claire Quilty wrapped up the picture, and the role gave the inventive Sellers a chance to lose himself in many memorable roles-within-the-role. The movie was shot in England, providing a comfortable distance between Kubrick and the native land he lampoons so relentlessly for two and a half hours. Kubrick lets none of his fantasizing characters off the hook, not the lust-driven Humbert, not the treacherous Lolita and her unlucky Mama, and certainly not the devilish Quilty. A 1996 movie of *Lolita* with Jeremy Irons and Dominique Swain is reportedly on the shelf; see the Kubrick version first for his unforgettable vision of America as an endless succession of highways and hotel rooms. They all may promise incredible sex, but they actually lead to a far more credible nowhere. 🦴🦴🦴🦴

1962 152m/B *GB* James Mason, Shelley Winters, Peter Sellers, Sue Lyon, Gary Cockrell, Jerry Stovin, Diana Decker, Lois Maxwell, Cec Linder, Bill Greene, Shirley Douglas, Marianne Stone, Marion Mathie, James Dyrenforth, C. Denier Warren, Terence Kilburn, John Harrison; **D:** Stanley Kubrick; **C:** Oswald Morris; **M:** Nelson Riddle. Nominations: Academy Awards '62: Best Adapted Screenplay. **VHS, Beta, LV** *MGM, CRC*

London Kills Me

Hanif Kureishi has written some fine screenplays for director Stephen Frears, but left to his own devices, the best he can come up with is *London Kills Me,* a shapeless film about the down-and-out residents of Ladbroke Grove. Beware of movies where the synopsis and the auteur's explanation of why he had to make the movie fill up six pages of the press kit! If it ain't on the screen, fergeddit! The plot (such as it is) revolves around a street person named Clint who resolves to find a pair of shoes so he can get a job as a waiter. This 105-minute odyssey takes place among a low-life crowd from which Clint is trying to escape. Unless aristocratic cheekbones make you go weak in the knees, no one emerges as a character you can care about one way or the other. Most of the film's few laughs were for a pudgy bit player who's obsessed by Elvis Presley and when a bit player overshadows the so-called leading characters, you KNOW the script is in trouble. There's also a character who swallows prescription drugs by the handful and ingests harder drugs in an assortment of grisly ways, but I can't tell you much else about her. Jon Pertwee's son Sean plays a tiny role as a gullible German tourist along with Pippa Hinchley, who starred in a *Fergie and Andrew* movie in the fall of 1992. Roshan Seth is wasted in an ill-defined, peripheral role, and poor Gordon (*My Beautiful Laundrette*) Warnecke is seen briefly as a sort of a henchman. *London Kills Me*? No, but this movie did, all 105 minutes of it. 🦴

1991 (R) 105m/C *GB* Justin Chadwick, Steven Mackintosh, Emer McCourt, Roshan Seth, Fiona Shaw, Brad Dourif, Gordon Warnecke, Sean Pertwee, Pippa Hinchley; **D:** Hanif Kureishi; **W:** Hanif Kureishi. **VHS, LV, Closed Caption** *LIV, PMS*

Lone Star

John Sayles is perhaps the most thoughtful and individualistic of today's independent filmmakers. He could easily cross over to make a mass audience action flick, but he never has and very likely never will, knock wood. His 1996 project, *Lone Star,* is an ambitious movie about a lot of different stuff, but the dots aren't always connected. The script has a first draft feel that suggests those dots could easily have been connected with a few more revisions. Our feeling is that the actors were ready when the script wasn't, and Sayles figured that he could compensate for the uneven screenplay with careful direction, which just kills us when we think about other meticulously crafted Sayles classics like *City of Hope* and *Passion Fish*. The fact that a full-page director's statement PLUS a diagram (to explain the ten major characters) were actually included in the press kit says a lot. The fact that we have to watch the whole dang 137-minute movie to discover something that's been collecting dust in the sheriff's ex-wife's garage for-like-ever (?!) says even more. Considering its denouement, *Lone Star* might be a more compelling yarn if it were a comedy or a satire instead of a star-crossed romance grafted onto a murder mystery. Chris Cooper does a nice, understated job as Sheriff Sam Deeds, and Elizabeth Pena is a strong presence as Pilar, his lost love, but they're playing with a sucker deck in a no-nonsense style; both are way too smart for us to believe that THEY believe their material. Kris Kristofferson is mean Sheriff Charley Wade from the 1950s and Matthew McConaughey plays Buddy Deeds, his enigmatic replacement. Both are seen in sketchy flashbacks, remembered by marginal older characters who are then played by younger actors who don't exactly look or sound like them. (Who would, after forty years? It really does get awfully confusing.) When we find out who killed Wade, does it matter? When we see the generational ripples created by his slaying, do they matter? And then Sayles comes up with a weird ending that only a daft critter from another planet would find acceptable; what can we say except, "Did they run out of blue pencils on location?" and "Weren't there any b.s. detectors on the payroll?" Sayles' idea, to say something about how history affects the present, isn't terrible, but how he says it in *Lone Star* is sort of a mess. You may wind up talking to yourself after watching *Lone Star*: "WHY in tarnation did he wrap

it up like that? Was he bitten by a rattlesnake or what?" Who knows? Perhaps because Sayles is practically worshipped by his admirers, his *Lone Star* screenplay was nominated for an Oscar, which says more about the state of the art in 1996 than it does about the best efforts of this always intriguing artist. ♫♫

1995 (R) 137m/C Chris Cooper, Matthew McConaughey, Kris Kristofferson, Elizabeth Pena, Joe Morton, Ron Canada, Clifton James, Miriam Colon, Frances McDormand; *D:* John Sayles; *W:* John Sayles; *C:* Stuart Dryburgh; *M:* Mason Daring. Independent Spirit Awards '97: Best Supporting Actress (Pena); Nominations: Academy Awards '96: Best Writing; British Academy Awards '96: Best Original Screenplay; Golden Globe Awards '97: Best Screenplay; Independent Spirit Awards '97: Best Actor (Cooper), Best Film, Best Screenplay; Writers Guild of America '96: Best Original Screenplay. **VHS, LV, Closed Caption** COL

The Lonely Passion of Judith Hearne

It took 33 years and producer George Harrison to bring Brian Moore's classic novel, *The Lonely Passion of Judith Hearne,* to the screen. But it was well worth the long wait. Thanks, George! This is the Catholic critique to end all Catholic critiques, and now that we've seen Dame Maggie Smith as Judy and Bob Hoskins as Jim, we can't imagine any other actors who could have played them half as well. Marie Kean and Ian McNeice are perfect too as Judy's unbelievably seedy landlady and her repellent son. Under Jack Clayton's careful direction, Judy is not good and Jim is not bad. Peter Nelson's masterful screenplay scrutinizes many crises of conscience that Catholics still struggle to understand on a daily basis. For those who may feel that John Huston's *The Dead* is essentially a mausoleum piece, check out how Clayton and Nelson capture a living, breathing chunk of the seductive Irish Catholic culture. It may not always make sense and, yes, it is often a very lonely life, yet *The Lonely Passion of Judith*

Hearne succeeds in showing how powerful its grip really is. 🦴🦴🦴

1987 (R) 116m/C *GB* Maggie Smith, Bob Hoskins, Wendy Hiller, Marie Kean, Ian McNeice, Alan Devlin, Rudi Davies, Prunella Scales; **D:** Jack Clayton; **W:** Peter Nelson; **M:** Georges Delerue. British Academy Awards '88: Best Actress (Smith). **VHS** *CAN*

The Long Good Friday

The Mirror Crack'd (set in The Coronation Year 1953) and *The Long Good Friday* (set in The Wedding of the Century Year 1981) were both released the same month that Prince Charles and Lady Diana announced their engagement to the world. We can't think of two films that better revealed the dissolution of Things Past and the destiny of Things to Come. *The Long Good Friday* focused on Brit gangster Harold Shand (Bob Hoskins), who despaired at the erosion of the Great Britain that once was, at the same time he was scrambling to make a deal with the American Mafia, represented by a tough guy named Charlie (Eddie Constantine, 1917-93). But wait. IRA bombings are destroying Harold's life-long dream. What's a patriotic thug to do? *The Long Good Friday* is doom-laden from Reel One to its final incredible sequence featuring some of the best acting (by Hoskins) you'll ever see. At an earlier point in the story, Hoskins must slaughter a trusted colleague in spectacularly bloody fashion, AND, at the same time reveal the anguish he feels for killing a friend. No one else in 1980 could quite touch Hoskins as an actor, which makes his later work in fluff like *Sweet Liberty, Hook,* and *Super Mario Bros.* a source of anguish for this long-time admirer. Helen Mirren co-stars as Victoria, George Coulouris (1903-89) makes one of his last film appearances, and Pierce Brosnan has one of his first small roles in this classic Brit film noir (Pierce Brosnan also plays a small role in *The Mirror Crack'd,* but THAT, like Charles and Diana, is another story). Produced by George Harrison's Handmade Films. 🦴🦴🦴🦴

1980 109m/C *GB* Bob Hoskins, Helen Mirren, Dave King, Bryan Marshall, George Coulouris, Pierce Brosnan, Derek Thompson, Eddie Constantine, Brian Hall, Stephen Davies, P. H. Moriarty, Paul Freeman, Charles Cork, Paul Barber, Patti Love, Ruby Head, Dexter Fletcher, Roy Alon; **D:** John MacKenzie; **W:** Barrie Keefe; **C:** Phil Meheux; **M:** Francis Monkman. Edgar Allan Poe Awards '82: Best Screenplay. **VHS, Beta** *VTR*

Longtime Companion

Longtime Companion shows how a happy, creative, close-knit group of friends are decimated by the AIDS virus throughout the '80s. First to go is John (Dermot Mulroney), then David's lover, Sean (Mark Lamos), a television writer. Bruce Davison deservedly won an Oscar nomination as David for an achingly restrained performance reflecting the real-life role that lovers continue to play all over the world. *Longtime Companion* transcends the terminal illness genre because of its funny, perceptive, timely script and because of its strong cast, including Campbell Scott as Willy, Stephan Caffrey as Fuzzy, and the luminous Mary-Louise Parker as Fuzzy's sister Liza. The most wrenching moment occurs on the beach where everyone enjoyed the sand, the sun, and the surf in the early '80s. We revisit it at decade's end with the sad knowledge that nearly everyone has died since then. There is a heartbreaking fantasy where the ghosts of the characters we have come to know and love are laughing on the beach again, while Blondie sings, "The tide is high and I'm moving on...." 🦴🦴🦴🦴

1990 (R) 100m/C Stephen Caffrey, Patrick Cassidy, Brian Cousins, Bruce Davison, John Dossett, Mark Lamos, Dermot Mulroney, Mary-Louise Parker, Michael Schoeffling, Campbell Scott, Robert Joy, Brad O'Hara; **D:** Norman Rene; **W:** Craig Lucas; **C:** Tony Jennelli. Golden Globe Awards '91: Best Supporting Actor (Davison); Independent Spirit Awards '91: Best Supporting Actor (Davison); New York Film Critics Awards '90: Best Supporting Actor (Davison); National Society of Film Critics Awards '90: Best Supporting Actor (Davison); Sundance Film Festival '90: Audience Award; Nominations: Academy Awards '90: Best Supporting Actor (Davison). **VHS** *THV, FCT, BTV*

Lost Highway

Lost Highway takes its time getting started; nearly a third of the running time creeps by before anything remotely approaching a narrative thrust turns up. Fred and Renee Madison (Bill Pullman and Patricia Arquette) keep finding videotapes on their doorstep. Then, blink-and-you'll-miss-it, Fred is in a death row jail cell, awaiting his execution via the electric chair for Renee's murder. (There IS no electric chair in California, where this story appears to be set, but so what?) Somehow, Fred changes places with Pete Dayton (Balthazar Getty). Since Pete isn't Fred, he is sent home to Mom and Dad (Pete's dad is none other than Gary Busey). Pete continues going out with the girl down the block (Natasha Gregson Wagner) and working as a garage mechanic for

his boss Arnie (Richard Pryor). One of the clients at the garage is Mr. Eddy (Robert Loggia), who has a bad-news/half-his-age girlfriend. (Surprise! Patricia Arquette IS Alice Wakefield, only now she resembles a washed-out version of the late blonde starlet Joyce Jameson.) Faster than you can say "Mr.-Eddy-will-kill-us-if-he-ever-finds-out," Pete and Alice are looking for trouble and finding it. Among the other characters who pop up is a weird Mystery Man with an ominous aura (Robert Blake). And so this movie goes: on and on until it's over. Like Lynch's *Twin Peaks* series, *Lost Highway* is flecked with interesting touches amidst long stretches of total boredom. Yeah, this looks, sounds, and feels like a rough draft, but David Lynch fans won't mind. 🎞🎞

1996 (R) 135m/C Bill Pullman, Patricia Arquette, Balthazar Getty, Robert Loggia, Robert (Bobby)

Blake, Gary Busey, Jack Nance, Richard Pryor, Natasha Gregson Wagner, Lisa Boyle, Michael Massee, Jack Kehler, Henry Rollins, Gene Ross, Scott Coffey; *D:* David Lynch; *W:* David Lynch, Barry Gifford; *C:* Peter Deming; *M:* Angelo Badalamenti. **VHS** *PGV*

Lost in the Stars

This is one of the few American Film Theatre productions I wouldn't mind seeing again. Brock Peters and a strong supporting cast benefited from on-location filming in Jamaica and the West Indies under the direction of Daniel Mann. 🎜🎜🎜

1974 114m/C Brock Peters, Melba Moore, Raymond St. Jacques, Clifton Davis, Paula Kelly; *D:* Daniel Mann; *W:* Maxwell Anderson; *M:* Kurt Weill. *NYR*

Love and a .45

After 1994's *Natural Born Killers* exploited the illusion that violence is sexy, follow-up clones were inevitable. Case in point: *Love and a .45,* directed by C.M. Talkington. Or maybe no one directed this thing. Maybe C.M. just pointed cameras at the actors and told them to ham it up. And they do; every single one of them, without exception, overacts his or her little heart out. The leader of the pack in this department is Rory Cochrane, so good as the stoned Slater in *Dazed and Confused* when he was directed by Richard Linklater. As Billy the Psycho here, he never shouts when he can scream and never screams when he can blow someone's head off. We assume we're supposed to root for the idiotic runaway lovers Watty and Starlene Watts, who are played by Gil Bellows and Renee Zellweger. After all, they never would have gotten into trouble if it weren't for Billy the Psycho, it's all HIS fault. But Watty and Starlene are, for all their wildly overplayed mugging on camera, a deeply boring couple. Her parents are two over-the-hill hippies played by Ann Wedgeworth and Peter Fonda. Starlene's dad tore his throat out

while under the influence of something or other in the 1960s, so he has to communicate with a voice box. The cameo is humiliating enough for *Easy Rider*'s Peter Fonda, but it's downright painful to see the excellent, underrated character actress Ann Wedgeworth in such a throwaway role. Well, you can always listen to Jesus and Mary Chain, Meat Puppets, Butthole Surfers, Kim Deal, and Johnny Cash on the soundtrack and wonder why the onscreen zeroes get to be media stars and how many more movie clones will ask the same damn thing over and over again. **WOOF!**

1994 (R) 101m/C Gil Bellows, Renee Zellweger, Rory Cochrane, Ann Wedgeworth, Peter Fonda, Jeffrey Combs, Jace Alexander; *D:* C.M. Talkington; *W:* C.M. Talkington; *M:* Tom Verlaine. Nominations: Independent Spirit Awards '95: Debut Performance (Zellweger). **VHS, LV, Closed Caption** *THV*

Love and Duty

At the time of her suicide at 25, Ruan Ling-Yu was China's leading actress and the sudsy *Love and Duty* shows why. As Yang Naifan, Ling-Yu ages from a sheltered school girl to a chic matron to a runaway lover to an old-before-her-time seamstress, raising her illegitimate daughter without the support of her long-dead lover. Ling-Yu worked from the inside out, so her evolution is persuasively achieved with very little make-up. (Only her front tooth is blacked out as the seamstress, something no Western star of comparable magnitude would ever dare to do!) With a minimalist, deeply moving acting style, Ling-Yu skillfully interprets Yang Naifan's many transformations, and, interestingly, her inner turmoil is revealed in a series of fantasies that show the intense psychological pressures that crush her spirit at every turn. *Love and Duty* gives us a fascinating glimpse at a China that appears both ultra-modern and saturated with tradition. Our sympathy for Yang Naifan's lover is lost when he insists that she abandon her small children, our interest in her absent-minded husband increases as we see what a tender and considerate father he is to their son and daughter. But Ruan Ling-Yu's greatest gift as an actress was her ability to dig into the soul of a character so that her many fans could set aside whatever troubling questions they may have had about WHY someone like Yang Naifan made such incomprehensible life choices. We don't DARE drag our eyes away from her face for a single second, because Ruan Ling-Yu solves mysteries of the heart with such subtle expressions and simple gestures. The greatest mystery of all, of course, is why, until quite recently, a jewel like Ruan Ling-Yu was known only to the audiences of her own time and country. She died just as the Chinese film industry was launching sound films, leaving behind a note, "Gossip is a dreadful thing." Among her few extant films are 1931's *The Peach Blossom Weeps Tears of Blood* plus *The Goddess* and *New Women,* both filmed in 1934. *AKA:* Lian'ai Yu Yiwu. ♫♫♫

1931 152m/B *CH* Ruan Ling-Yu, Jin Yan, Chen Yanyan, Li Yi; *D:* Bu Wancang; *W:* Zhu Shilin; *C:* Huang Shaofen. *NYR*

Love and Human Remains

Canada's *Love and Human Remains* supplies a quirky look at the romantic rituals of two roommates; he's gay and she's straight, sort of. They both want to meet a nice guy but they're afraid, and why not? There's a serial killer on the loose. She succumbs to a one-night stand with a romantic lesbian at her gym and then falls for a bartender before she discovers he's married. He waits tables at age 30, and tries to be responsible by side-stepping a fling with a 17-year-old bus boy who had a crush on him when he was a television child star. Meanwhile, his psychic friend senses danger from the serial killer, who continues to terrorize the women of Montreal. With a well chosen cast of unknowns

and brisk direction from Denys Arcand, Brad Fraser's script is on target more often than not, with humor and affection to spare for each and every character (except, of course, the serial killer, who remains a marginal figure throughout). ♫♫♫

1993 (R) 100m/C *CA* Thomas Gibson, Ruth Marshall, Cameron Bancroft, Mia Kirshner, Joanne Vannicola, Matthew Ferguson, Rick Roberts; *D:* Denys Arcand; *W:* Brad Fraser; *C:* Paul Sarossy. Genie Awards '94: Best Adapted Screenplay. **VHS, LV** *COL*

Love Jones

A contemporary Chicago nightclub, the Sanctuary, is the gathering spot for middle-class black urbanites looking for romance. Would-be writer/poet Darius (Larenz Tate) spouts provocative verse to beautiful photographer Nina (Nia Long), who's not too happy with men at the moment (she's just been dumped). But they make a connection, with both protesting a little too much that's it just a "sex thing." Funny what happens when love clearly enters the picture. Theodore Witcher's directorial debut features fine lead performances. ♫♫♫

1996 (R) 105m/C Larenz Tate, Nia Long, Isaiah Washington, Lisa Nicole Carson, Khalil Kain, Bill Bellamy, Leonard Roberts, Bernardette L. Clarke; *D:* Theodore Witcher; *W:* Theodore Witcher; *C:* Ernest Holzman; *M:* Darryl Jones. Sundance Film Festival '97: Audience Award. **VHS** *NYR*

Love Unto Waste

Stanley Kwan's *Love Unto Waste* is a flashy existential film about love and friendship in Hong Kong of the 1980s. The strong performances by its young cast (Tony Leung would later make a strong impression in Kwan's *Centre Stage/The Actress,* released in 1992) should have won this exceptional import wider U.S. distribution than it initially received. ♫♫♫

1986 97m/C *HK* Tony Leung, Chow Yun-Fat, Irene Wan, Elaine Jin, Tsai Chin; *D:* Stanley Kwan; *W:* Lai Kit, Chiu Tai An-Ping. **VHS** *FCT*

The Luckiest Man in the World

Who could resist a movie premise like this one? A rich jerk named Sam is ten minutes late for a plane that crashes on take-off with no survivors. At the airport, the victims' heartbroken relatives scream at Sam: "Why you?" In the men's room, Sam ponders his escape from certain death and determines to be kinder to the people in his life. The only problem is, they're all used to Sam being a jerk and won't accept him any other way. Pulitzer Prize-winning playwright Frank D. Gilroy directs his own screenplay for *The Luckiest Man in the World,* a wise and funny satire revolving around one creep's response to the randomnesss of fate. Philip Bosco is ideally cast as Sam, bringing a sharp comic bite to his unbearable character. The rest of the cast is populated with little-known but well chosen New York actors and the production values are rock-bottom adequate. Gilroy's dialogue is so good and the direction is so on target that I can't help feeling that the whole point of *The Luckiest Man in the World* might have been buried under an expensive Hollywood budget and a distracting stellar line-up. 🦴🦴🦴

1989 82m/C Philip Bosco, Doris Belack, Joanne Camp, Matthew Gottlieb, Arthur French, Stan Lachow; **D:** Frank D. Gilroy; **W:** Frank D. Gilroy. *NYR*

Lucky Jim

"Oh, Lucky Jim, how I envy him..." Well, who wouldn't, when he's played by the delightful Ian Carmichael, long before he inherited the role of Lord Peter Wimsey? The thing is, university lecturer Jim Dixon is far from lucky, although he'd certainly like to be. This wonderfully played, deftly directed vintage Britcom is a good one to rent when you're home sick with a head cold; it will have you laughing your way to health in no time. Cast Notes: Canadian actress Sharon Acker, then 22, makes her debut here; she would later star in three short-lived U.S. television series of the 1970s, including the ill-fated *Perry Mason* show in which she—ahem—TRIED to inherit Barbara Hale's role as Della Street. Kenneth Griffith turned up in 1994's *Four Weddings and a Funeral* and John Welsh (1905-85) was dear old Merriman in *The Duchess of Duke Street.* 🦴🦴🦴

1958 91m/B *GB* Ian Carmichael, Terry-Thomas, Hugh Griffith, Sharon Acker, Jean Anderson, Maureen Connell, Clive Morton, John Welsh, Reginald Beckwith, Kenneth Griffith, Jeremy Hawk, Harry Fowler; **D:** John Boulting; **W:** Jeffrey Dell, Patrick Campbell; **M:** John Addison. **VHS, Beta** *NO*

Lullaby

At first, *Lullaby* offers a child's-eye view of sheer loveliness unclouded by foreboding. But then the little girl is kidnapped and not returned to her family for so long that she recognizes nothing of her former life. The sequences where her mother tries everything to wring a memory from her lost daughter are truly heart wrenching. The beautiful surroundings mean nothing to her without her child's love, a point made with conviction by director Nana Janelidze. **AKA:** Ivnana. 🦴🦴🦴

1994 70m/C Nata Murvanidze, Nine Abuladze, Maya Bagrationi; **D:** Nan Janelidze; **W:** Nino Natroshvili; **C:** Georgi Beridze; **M:** Jansug Kakhidze, Vakhtang Kakhidze. *NYR*

Lumiere

Jeanne Moreau assembled an impressive cast (including Keith Carradine, who has very little to do here) and technical crew, but the result is a carefully wrought film in every respect except one: Moreau, clearly wanting to reveal the strong ties that bind women together, gets sidetracked by, and overwhelmed with, the superficial ways in which her characters express their concern for one another. She never takes her characters one step further. In one sequence, a lady invites her male seducer to join her for a tryst. She has, in fact, dumped two other men so that she may be alone with this guy, and never at any point does she suggest to her pursuer that she wants anything from him other than casual sex. When he follows through on her invitation, she wriggles away from him, and Moreau's direction implies criticism that he would even begin to construe such an idea. Moreau casually sprinkles this sort of skin-deep critique throughout her script. Only one female character in *Lumiere* is fully dimensional, and that seems to be due more to the skill of Lucia Bose, than to the insubstantial part Moreau wrote for her. Francois Simon and Francis Huster are quite moving as two men whom Moreau discards in her onscreen role as Sarah. The four women Moreau attempts to capture with such complexity emerge as selfish drips, and not very interesting selfish drips at that. 🎬🎬

1976 (R) 101m/C *FR* Jeanne Moreau, Lucia Bose, Francine Racette, Caroline Cartier, Keith Carradine, Francois Simon, Francis Huster, Bruno Ganz, Rene Feret, Niels Arestrup, Jerome Lapperrousaz; *D:* Jeanne Moreau; *W:* Jeanne Moreau; *C:* Ricardo Aronvich; *M:* Astor Piazzolla. **VHS, Beta**

Luther

An earnest but dull look at Martin Luther (Stacy Keach), as seen by John Osborne. It don't mean a thing if it ain't got that swing. (*Luther* was released theatrically overseas in 1976.) An American Film Theatre Production. 🎬🎬

1974 (G) 112m/C Stacy Keach, Patrick Magee, Hugh Griffith, Robert Stephens, Alan Badel, Julian Clover, Judi Dench, Leonard Rossiter, Maurice Denham, Peter Cellier, Thomas Heathcote, Malcolm Stoddard, Bruce Carstairs; *D:* Guy Green; *W:* Edward Anhalt, John Osborne; *C:* Frederick A. (Freddie) Young; *M:* John Addison. **VHS** *NO*

M

M made Peter Lorre (1904-64) immortal and rightly so; by humanizing a monstrous killer, he changed forever how we would perceive such characters. There really was a child murderer; his name was Peter Kurten (1883-1931), and he had not yet been executed at the time of *M*'s release. Unlike the tormented Hans Becker played by Lorre, Kurten felt no remorse for his many crimes, only a clinical fascination with them afterwards. Otto Wernicke (1893-

1965) gives a superb performance as Inspector Lohmann, who tracks down Becker. Fritz Lang, who had spent considerable time at Berlin Alexanderplatz closely observing the police in action, used his in-depth knowledge of their methods to add to the realism of the narrative. There actually were criminal characters among the thugs who judge Becker for his crimes, one of whom asked Lang to speed up the shooting as the police were expected in an hour. Gustav Grundgens (1899-1963), who played Schranker, the underworld chief, was the real-life model for the central character of Klaus Mann's *Mephisto*. Mann (1906-49), who was Grundgens' brother-in-law, killed himself because he couldn't publish *Mephisto*. Grundgens, whose career flourished during the Third Reich, was unable to achieve real professional acceptance after the war, and he, too, killed himself. *M* seems like a different movie every time you see it. There is the horror of knowing what victim Elsie Beekman is too young to realize, and then there is deep empathy for her mother. Even so, there is intense compassion for her murderer. You cannot hate him, because of Lang's and Thea von Harbou's exceptionally written address to the underworld, and because of the deep complexity of Lorre's interpretation of a man who kills because he must. Peter Lorre explained his approach to his most famous role by saying, "My only concern was to understand WHY. I did understand." Unsurprisingly, *M* is Fritz Lang's own favorite of all his films. 🎬🎬🎬🎬

1931 99m/B *GE* Peter Lorre, Ellen Widmann, Inge Landgut, Gustav Grundgens, Otto Wernicke, Ernest Stahl-Nachbaur, Franz Stein, Theodore Loos, Fritz Gnass, Fritz Odemar, Paul Kemp, Theo Lingen, Georg John, Karl Platen, Rosa Valetti, Hertha von Walther, Rudolf Blumner; *D:* Fritz Lang; *W:* Fritz Lang, Thea von Harbou; *C:* Fritz Arno Wagner, Gustav Rathje; *M:* Edvard Grieg. National Board of Review Awards '33: 10 Best Films of the Year. **VHS, Beta, LV, 8mm** *SNC, NOS, HHT*

Mac

John Turturro's film about three Italian brothers was far more effective with this viewer than Edward Burns' movie about *The Brothers McMullen*. Perhaps this is because the inspiration (Turturro's late father) feels more real. Turturro gets inside the bickering and the fighting to show the genuine love and strong bonds beneath the surface in the Vitelli family. He plays the title role, also known as Niccolo; Michael Badalucco and Carl Capotorto are his younger siblings Vico and Bruno; Katherine Borowitz (Mrs. John Turturro) is Mac's wife, Alice; and Ellen Barkin is Oona, a '50s-style kook. The wonderful acting by all more than compensates for the fact that the low budget clearly didn't cover authentic period details. In a family saga like this one, the authentic expression of feelings is clearly far more vital. 🎜🎜🎜

1993 (R) 118m/C John Turturro, Carl Capotorto, Michael Badalucco, Katherine Borowitz, John Amos, Olek Krupa, Ellen Barkin, Joe Paparone, Nicholas Turturro, Dennis Farina, Steven Randazzo; **D:** John Turturro; **W:** Brandon Cole, John Turturro; **C:** Ron Fortunato; **M:** Richard Termini, Vin Tese. Nominations: Independent Spirit Awards '94: Best Director (Turturro), Best First Feature. **VHS, LV, Closed Caption** *COL, FCT*

Madeleine

Madeleine Smith was a Victorian murderess...or was she? Director David Lean wanted audiences of the 1950s to have a question in their minds after seeing his film. Apparently, Madeleine (played by Lean's wife, Ann Todd) had a lusty relationship with Emile L'Angelier (Ivan Desny). Her father (Leslie Banks) wanted her to marry a man named Minnoch (Norman Wooland) who was more suited to her station in life. Scenting either hush money or a lucrative alliance, L'Angelier threatened to show Madeleine's letters to Mr. Smith. Not long after, Madeleine entered a chemist's shop, purchased a bottle of arsenic from a Mr. Murdoch (Ivor Barnard), and soon L'Angelier was writhing in agony from a fatal dose of arsenic. Who done it? We won't be able to tell from the Scottish court transcripts; Madeleine's guilt was "not proven." Madeleine herself never discussed her guilt

or innocence after she was dismissed by the court. It's an unsolved mystery, and, nearly 150 years after the fact, it's liable to remain one forever. With so many unyielding participants, Lean reveals how everyone's strict code of behavior led directly to murder. For all Lean's meticulous attention to every historical detail, the film's one flaw was inevitable. These are the most passionless of people; indeed, if there had been one spark of genuine passion, Lean might be making a film about a legendary elopement or a shocking rebellion, instead of a cool, conscienceless disposal of a human impediment to a rigid way of life. Recommended for further research: Mary S. Hartman's superb 1977 Pocket Book, *Victorian Murderesses* (including Miss Smith)! **AKA:** The Strange Case of Madeleine. 🎜🎜🎜

1950 114m/B Ann Todd, Leslie Banks, Ivan Desny, Norman Wooland, Barbara Everest, Susan Stranks, Patricia Raine, Elizabeth Sellars, Edward Chapman, Jean Cadell, Eugene Deckers, Amy Veness, John Laurie, Henry Edwards, Ivor Barnard, Barry Jones, David Morne, Andre Morell, Douglas Barr; **D:** David Lean; **W:** Nicholas Phipps, Stanley Haynes; **C:** Guy Green; **M:** William Alwyn. **VHS, Beta** *LCA*

The Madness of King George

When *Edward and Mrs. Simpson* first hit international television screens in 1978, the actor playing Walter Monckton, a bespectacled advisor to the King, nearly stole the entire show. Nigel Hawthorne continued to play supporting roles in films and on television, but onstage, he was recognized as the star his enormous talent ought to have made him on big and small screens alike. Finally, Hawthorne has been given the chance to show movie fans just what theatrical audiences have been raving about. In *The Madness of King George,* Hawthorne achieves the impossible; who other than Prince Charles has ever extended a shred of sympathy to George III? But Hawthorne succeeds in making us care about the mad monarch of

**His Majesty King
George (Nigel
Hawthorne) in
*The Madness of
King George.***

ing (Amanda Donohoe) have other ambitions, AND crafty approaches for achieving them. Bennett nails down all the political intrigues with wit and humor and with a sharp understanding of who the real players are. Being on the wrong side at an inconvenient time can lead to royal banishment even faster than outright treachery. You may need to make deals with the traitors, but it's easier to sacrifice a friend who's too intimately familiar with regal fallibility. One of Hawthorne's best moments as the recovering King comes in a garden sequence when he tries to show a courtier how much better he is by reading from Shakespeare. Alas, after picture's end, the King finally did lose his mind, and George IV's regency and reign considerably eroded the prestige and influence of the monarchy until his niece Victoria acceded to the throne, but that's another story. (Oscar nominee Hawthorne's other films on video include *S*P*Y*S, Holocaust, A Tale of Two Cities, The Hunchback of Notre Dame, A Woman Called Golda, Firefox, Pope John Paul II, Jenny's War, Tartuffe, Demolition Man,* and *Richard III.* Mirren, of course, can be seen in dozens of films on video dating all the way back to 1968's *A Midsummer Night's Dream.*) 🎭🎭🎭🎭

1788. At best, His Majesty was, by many accounts, not a bad sort and well meaning, but was easily led by self-serving advisors much brighter than he was. For most of Alan Bennett's retelling of George's nervous breakdown, we do not see him at his best, but wracked with a disease later suspected to be porphyria, then diagnosed as madness by the king's advisors. After assorted barbaric attempts to treat his illness, the King is referred to a Doctor Willis (splendidly played by Ian Holm), who proposes a radical cure. Meanwhile, his dissipated and profligate son (Rupert Everett is ideally cast as the future King George IV) schemes to wrest power away from his daft father so that he may be appointed Regent. The loyal Queen Charlotte (Oscar nominee Helen Mirren) and her lady-in-wait-

1994 (R) 110m/C *GB* Nigel Hawthorne, Helen Mirren, Ian Holm, Rupert Everett, Amanda Donohoe, Rupert Graves, Julian Wadham, John Wood, Julian Rhind-Tutt; *D:* Nicholas Hytner; *W:* Alan Bennett; *M:* George Fenton. Academy Awards '94: Best Art Direction/Set Decoration; British Academy Awards '95: Best Actor (Hawthorne); Cannes Film Festival '95: Best Actress (Mirren); Nominations: Academy Awards '94: Best Actor (Hawthorne), Best Adapted Screenplay, Best Supporting Actress (Mirren); British Academy Awards '95: Best Actress (Mirren), Best Adapted Screenplay, Best Cinematography, Best Director (Hytner), Best Film, Best Supporting Actor (Holm), Best Score. **VHS, LV, Closed Caption** *HMK*

The Maids

In spite of the cast, *The Maids* is one of the least imaginative productions in the American Film Theatre series, and that's saying something. Skip this film version of Jean Genet's play and see 1994's *Sister My Sis-*

ter instead. It isn't perfect, but it won't bore you like this one will. *The Maids* was released theatrically overseas in 1976. ♪

1975 95m/C *GB CA* Glenda Jackson, Susannah York, Vivien Merchant, Mark Burns; **D:** Christopher Miles; **W:** Christopher Miles, Robert Enders; **C:** Douglas Slocombe; **M:** Laurie Johnson. **VHS** *NO*

The Making of "A Hard Day's Night"

The Making of "A Hard Day's Night" unravels one mystery we've been trying to solve for-absotively-ever: if Phil Collins, then 14, made his film debut in it, where the heck WAS he? Collins himself answers the question and shows us a crowd shot in which only his family could recognize him screaming along with all the other teenaged extras. This new documentary, produced by and featuring Walter Shenson, who made the original film, reveals other little-known facts about the world's most famous rock musical: Ringo's choice of reading material in the movie was *Anatomy of a Murder*; John WASN'T in the fondly remembered field sequence; and the title song over the credits was, literally, written overnight, after the rest of the movie was already completed. Also included is the "You Can't Do That" number, shaved from the final release, as well as an informal trailer the Beatles shot to promote the picture. The surprise for producer Walter Shenson and director Richard Lester was that the Beatles were such naturals in their very first movie. Alun Owen's Oscar-nominated screenplay was deliberately composed of very short bits of dialogue so that none of its four stars would have to say or do anything that would expose their lack of training as actors. Surprise, surprise; under the expert guidance of Lester, they turned out to be so engaging onscreen that Owen wrote extra sequences to highlight George Harrison and Ringo Starr. Moreover, at least a dozen of John Lennon's ad-libs remained in the finished movie. (Charitably unmentioned is the fact that one of Sir Paul McCartney's solo moments wound up on the cutting room floor due to his self-conscious performance.) The years have been kind to actor Victor Spinetti, who recalls his work in the film with obvious pride and pleasure. Clearly, *A Hard Day's Night,* made thousands of miles away from executive busy mitts in Hollywood, was a happy experience for its fortunate creators. *The Making of "A Hard Day's Night"* is an affectionate look back at the musical classic helmed by the man MTV has long identified as its father. The great Richard Lester accepts the compliment, but characteristically, insists on a blood test. ♪♪♪♪

1994 60m/C Phil Collins, The Beatles, Victor Spinetti, Alun Owen; **D:** Richard Lester. **VHS** *MPI*

Mallrats

Clerks wasn't a smash hit or anything, but the black-and-white debut film did well enough in art houses for Gramercy Pictures to lure its young writer/director into making a color movie about *Mallrats.* After watching the rushes, did Kevin Smith wonder for an instant about giving all the credit to Alan Smithee? We may never know the answer to that one, but it would have been a kinder gesture to his promising career if he had. Although this dreadful film was supposedly written after *Clerks,* it feels like the first draft of something that was written in high school, stashed in a closet, and forgotten until Hollywood started panting for a follow-up project. You want a funny mall movie, rent *Fast Times at Ridgemont High.* You want excruciating jokes, lousy acting, lame sight gags, and a plotline that should have been tossed in a dumpster at the very first story conference, *Mallrats* is the scum de la scum, BENEATH the pile of ultra-bad teen movies, in fact. Anyway, Shannen Doherty was pushing 25 at the time, way too old to be lusting after a guy (execrable newcomer Jason Lee) who sticks his fist up his butt and then shakes hands with his best

I don't like to answer off the top of my head, but I will, anyway. You must know everything beforehand for a political film. You have to work according to a definite plan, with no surprises. Most of my films grow as they are made. I admire *Z* and *State of Siege,* but I couldn't have made them. I have no courage or spirit to make a movie with everything already decided. Political films, as opposed to propaganda movies, must be against something. I make movies in favor of love, children, books, people in the cinema. I can't make movies about ridiculous, stupid, or unpleasant people."

friend's future father-in-law for a laugh. Are you beginning to get the level of the agony factor here? Marvel Comics veteran Stan Lee appears as himself. Game show maestro Art James and Priscilla Barnes (in a particularly humiliating cameo) are also in this piece of crap. Even if there's nothing else on the video shelf, don't talk yourself into seeing *Mallrats* even if someone else is paying. (Smith apologized to the critics who hated *Mallrats* in the end credits of his much better follow-up film, 1997's *Chasing Amy,* and Jason Lee's acting had even improved by then, too.) **WOOF!**

1995 (R) 95m/C Shannen Doherty, Jeremy London, Jason Lee, Claire Forlani, Michael Rooker, Priscilla Barnes, Renee Humphrey, Ben Affleck, Joey Adams, Jason Mewes, Brian O'Halloran, David Brinkley, Kevin Smith; *Cameos:* Stan Lee; *D:* Kevin Smith; *W:* Kevin Smith; *C:* David Klein; *M:* Ira Newborn. **VHS, LV, Closed Caption** *USH*

The Man in the Glass Booth

The Man in the Glass Booth is unique among the 13 American Film Theatre productions because its star, Maximilian

Schell, won an Academy Award nomination for Best Actor in the title role, the only participant to be so honored. Aside from that, we're looking at another stagey filmed play, a common failing among all but one of these movies (that would be Lord Laurence Olivier's *Three Sisters,* made in 1970). Actor/playwright Robert Shaw was so angered by this interpretation of his play that he demanded his name be removed from the film credits. Donald Pleasence had originated the Broadway role (somewhat modeled after Adolf Eichmann) under Harold Pinter's direction. 🦴🦴🐾

1975 (PG) 117m/C Maximilian Schell, Lois Nettleton, Luther Adler, Lawrence Pressman, Henry Brown, Richard Rasof; *D:* Arthur Hiller; *W:* Edward Anhalt; *C:* Sam Leavitt. Nominations: Academy Awards '75: Best Actor (Schell). **VHS** *NO*

The Man Who Knew Too Much

The 1956 re-make of *The Man Who Knew Too Much* is big and expensive and it has "Que Sera, Sera," but the little kid in it drives me nuts, and I hate it when Jimmy Stewart gives Doris Day a sedative before he tells her about the kidnapping and she doesn't even return his volley with a left hook, she just goes into hysterics. Everything I detest about the 1950s is tossed into this one: bad clothes, bad dialogue, and bad manners. But the 1934 version is an altogether different story. Nova Pilbeam is a genuinely appealing kid and we do worry about her welfare in the hands of a slime like Peter Lorre. And Leslie Banks and Edna Best are a witty and sophisticated couple with individual interests and a lightly bantering style well suited to their free and easy marriage. We don't want anything to hurt their family and we're with them all the way as they draw on their own ingenious resources to save their daughter. The sheer speed of the narrative makes this sparkling ORIGINAL Hitchcock classic the one to look for on the video shelf. Bigger isn't always better and the story doesn't need another 45 minutes of singing and yakking, anyway. 🦴🦴🦴

1934 75m/B *GB* Leslie Banks, Edna Best, Peter Lorre, Nova Pilbeam, Pierre Fresnay, Frank Vosper, Hugh Wakefield, Cicely Oates, D. A. Clarke-Smith, George Curzon, Henry Oscar, Wilfrid Hyde-White; *D:* Alfred Hitchcock; *W:* Emlyn Williams, Charles Bennett, A.H. Rawlinson, Edwin Greenwood, D. B. Wyndham-Lewis. **VHS, Beta** *SNC, MRV, NOS*

The Man Who Loved Women

Love can be both sweet and fatal, the late Francois Truffaut (1932-84) says in his 1977 film, *The Man Who Loved Women*. Charles Denner plays a man who sneers at Don Juans, but behaves just like them. He's so obsessed with romance that he gets hit by a car and falls out of a hospital bed just because he wants to get a better look at all the pretty girls there are in the world. Chasing women delights him and dooms him, and he has his choice of the prettiest woman in France, including Brigitte Fossey and Leslie Caron. At one point, Truffaut starts to say, yes, lasting love IS important, repetitive trysts ARE

meaningless, but he drops these ideas very quickly by cutting to yet another brief affair lovingly photographed by Nestor Almendros. Whatever Truffaut wants to say about love here, he has said it better many times before. Despite its provocative subject matter and Truffaut's expert handling of same, *The Man Who Loved Women* remains essentially a fluff piece. *AKA:* L'Homme Qui Aimait les Femmes. 🦴🦴🦴

1977 119m/C *FR* Charles Denner, Brigitte Fossey, Leslie Caron, Nelly Borgeaud, Genevieve Fontanel, Nathalie Baye, Sabine Glaser; *D:* Francois Truffaut; *W:* Francois Truffaut, Suzanne Schiffman, Michel Fermaud; *C:* Nestor Almendros; *M:* Maurice Jaubert. National Board of Review Awards '77: 5 Best Foreign Films of the Year. **VHS, Beta, LV, Closed Caption** *MGM, BTV*

The Man with the Movie Camera

Dziga Vertov's *The Man with the Movie Camera* was made nearly 70 years ago, but it might well put many of today's avant-garde efforts to self-conscious shame. It is pure cinema, by a director madly in love with the medium, and like any delirious lover, he tries to capture life at a breathless pace. Vertov's fast-paced 66-minute movie is filled with fun and wit. *AKA:* Chelovek S Kinooapparatom. 🦴🦴🦴🦴

1923 66m/B *RU D:* Dziga Vertov; *W:* Dziga Vertov; *C:* Mikhail Kaufman. **VHS** *NYR*

The Manchurian Candidate

Among the best movies released in 1988 was a 26-year-old film noir directed by John Frankenheimer. *The Manchurian Candidate* boasts a beautifully constructed script by Frankenheimer and George Axelrod, a terrific cast headed by Frank Sinatra, Laurence Harvey, and Angela Lansbury, and a dark

premonitory vision that reveals all the horrors of the late '60s in embryo. Those who would like to remember 1962 as an innocent year can look elsewhere for nostalgia. *The Manchurian Candidate* is grim, gripping entertainment. Filmed within five years of Senator Joe McCarthy's death, the movie makes use of the paranoid Cold War era, and also reveals the slickness of the characters who marketed our national fears. Angela Lansbury was only 37 when she played 34-year-old Laurence Harvey's villainous mother, but she gets away with it and steals every scene she's in. Lithuanian-born Harvey never was convincing in American roles, although he certainly played enough of them, yet he is otherwise sympathetic and restrained in the pivotal role. Frank Sinatra could be a fine actor when he wanted to be, and he plays with cool, crisp authority here. Not many people remember an attractive, talented starlet named Leslie Parrish, but she is shown to good advantage opposite Harvey. One bit of miscasting is Puerto Rican Henry Silva as a Korean, an especially odd choice in a picture which also features Khigh Deigh. There's also a weak love interest bit for Janet Leigh opposite Sinatra. *The Manchurian Candidate* was made in the midst of the Kennedy years and yet it's atypical of films of that era in that it's genuinely noir and genuinely prophetic. It runs rings around most of today's thrillers. 🦴🦴🦴🦴

1962 126m/B Frank Sinatra, Laurence Harvey, Angela Lansbury, Janet Leigh, James Gregory, Leslie Parrish, John McGiver, Henry Silva, Khigh Deigh; *D:* John Frankenheimer; *W:* George Axelrod, John Frankenheimer; *C:* Lionel Lindon; *M:* David Amram. Golden Globe Awards '63: Best Supporting Actress (Lansbury); National Board of Review Awards '62: Best Supporting Actress (Lansbury); Nominations: Academy Awards '62: Best Film Editing, Best Supporting Actress (Lansbury). **VHS, Beta, LV, Closed Caption** *MGM*

Manny & Lo

Amanda/Manny, 11 (Scarlett Johansson), and Laurel/Lo, 16 (Aleksa Palladino), are sisters, but they were adopted by different parents. They run away together, but Lo finds out she's expecting a baby, so they kidnap Elaine (Mary Kay Place), who works in a baby store. What's Elaine's story? They don't know, but Lo knows she needs help, so Manny, Lo, and Elaine are off to the woods until the baby comes. This offbeat first feature written and directed by Lisa Krueger is filled with warmth, charm, and good acting by the kids. And wonderful Mary Kay Place is an absolute treasure as Elaine. 🦴🦴🦴

1996 (R) 90m/C Mary Kay Place, Scarlett Johansson, Aleksa Palladino, Paul Guilfoyle, Glenn Fitzgerald, Cameron Boyd, Novella Nelson, Angie Phillips; *D:* Lisa Krueger; *W:* Lisa Krueger; *C:* Tom Krueger; *M:* John Lurie. Nominations: Independent Spirit Awards '97: Best Actress (Johansson), Best First Feature, Best Supporting Actress (Place). **VHS, LV, Closed Caption** *COL*

The Mark

The recidivism rate for child molesters is so high that no one in his or her right mind would want to place a child in the unsupervised care of a known pedophile. That said, *The Mark* plans a unique form of violence on the viewer. Stuart Whitman gives the finest performance of his career as convicted child molester Jim Fuller. Fuller has served his time in prison, and has also received intensive therapy from Dr. McNally (Rod Steiger). He wants to become a useful member of society, but his past has shattered him, drained his confidence, and turned him into a haunted, hesitant man, terrified of nearly every emotional impulse. (God, what a part this must have been for Whitman to play!) He meets Ruth Leighton (Maria Schell) at his new job and they become friends. Ruth, a single mother with a young daughter named Janie (Amanda Black), is aware that Fuller has experienced deep unhappiness, but so has she, and she knows nothing about his conviction for child molestation. Janie, starved for a father figure in her life, adores Fuller, but he distances himself from her need for affection. Meanwhile, his friendship with her mother evolves into a romance. Well, you

Opposite page: **Frank Sinatra and Laurence Harvey in** *The Manchurian Candidate.*

LISA KRUEGER AND MARY KAY PLACE
Manny & Lo

Lisa Krueger: "One afternoon, I was listening to the radio and they were talking about Chrissie Hynde of The Pretenders and how she was taking time off from this hard-core rock 'n' roll career to raise her children, and I thought that was such an odd contrast, and I guess I was fascinated with what that's all about, especially since I don't have kids."

Mary Kay Place: [on playing women who want babies in *The Big Chill* and *Manny & Lo*]: "I think there's some baby energy that keeps coming again and again in my life and what does this mean? I don't know, but it is interesting, isn't it?.... [On *My So-Called Life*]: I was a big fan of that series and I was thrilled to play Camille, a small but recurring part on it. It was beautifully written by Winnie Holzman and she really nailed that coming-of-age experience in a way that I don't think we've ever seen before. And then she had Claire Danes as Angela Chase, who was able to execute the scripts so brilliantly, and Scott Winant, who directed the series."

Lisa Krueger: "I have to credit Mary Kay Place with teaching me the importance of a really detailed, strong, voluminous, multi-dimensional story for each character. You don't ever have to say a word about that history in the movie for the audience to feel it somehow. Certainly, they'd feel its absence, if I didn't actually do my homework as a writer. Mary Kay Place did her homework as an actress when she came up to the Sundance Filmmaker's Lab and worked with me on a few scenes. At that moment, I realized that was part of my job as the writer/director. This being my first time out, I didn't realize that. But we sure had a great time working out the background of her character Elaine together: We melded together our two visions of Elaine's past."

Mary Kay Place: "Elaine was a hard role to play, but in the best possible way. It was a juicy role and it was so exciting to do all of the work. As I kept uncovering layers of Elaine, I kept finding more things to uncover. It just kept multiplying."

Lisa Krueger: "It sounds so disgustingly corny, but I really had one of those proverbial peak experiences at the Sundance Filmmaker's Lab. I realized somehow that there was a way in which filmmaking could mirror life and could be a strong and powerful way to be alive. I feel that was what the Lab was about. It's about how to be generous with people that you're working with in a way that hopefully carries over into your life and for me it did."

MARY KAY PLACE can be seen in *New York, New York, Starting Over, Private Benjamin, Modern Problems, The Big Chill, Waltz Across Texas, For Love or Money, Explorers, The History of White People in America, Smooth Talk, The Girl Who Spelled Freedom, A New Life, Portrait of a White Marriage, Bright Angel, Crazy from the Heart, Captain Ron,* and *Samantha. Manny & Lo* is LISA KRUEGER's directorial debut.

can see where all this is leading: it's only a matter of time before Fuller's past and present collide, and they do, thanks to an investigative reporter. The underlying theme is that since Jim Fuller has been "cured," Society should give him another chance to lead a normal life. This was a kindly perspective for 1961, but it's also gobbledy-gook. The viewpoint here is that if Ruth is really in love with him, she must trust him alone with her daughter because he's "cured." They can all be a normal family and Fuller can forget his past. Well, it's only a movie, and the filmmakers meant well, but that may explain why you don't see *The Mark* too often on television. Maria Schell and Rod Steiger are ideally cast as Ruth and Dr. McNally, and Stuart Whitman's moving performance as Jim Fuller cannot be faulted (he won an Oscar nomination for it, but lost to Maximilian Schell). Based on a novel by Charles Israel. 🦴🦴🦴🦴

1961 127m/B *GB* Stuart Whitman, Maria Schell, Rod Steiger, Brenda de Banzie, Maurice Denham, Donald Wolfit, Paul Rogers, Donald Houston, Amanda Black, Russell Napier, Marie Devereux; *D:* Guy Green; *W:* Sidney Buchman, Raymond Stross; *M:* Richard Rodney Bennett. Nominations: Academy Awards '61: Best Actor (Whitman). **VHS, Beta** *NO*

The Marquise of O

Eric Rohmer's *The Marquise of O* is based on a 17th century book by Heinrich von Kleist and very much evokes the paintings of that time; every sequence of this beautifully photographed story would be suitable for framing. Rohmer paces his tale in a leisurely, deliberate manner; it is extraordinary that he injects passion and down-to-earth fun in such a staid subject. He is able to achieve this partly by his scrupulous attention to period details of the early 1800s, and mainly by the ease with which he renders his heroine's strength. 🦴🦴🦴

1976 102m/C *FR GE* Edith Clever, Bruno Ganz, Peter Luhr, Edda Seipel, Otto Sander, Ruth Drexel; *D:* Eric Rohmer; *W:* Eric Rohmer; *C:* Nestor Almendros. *NYR*

The Marriage

The Marriage may just be the most vicious movie ever made regarding that particular institution, yet Arnaldo Jabor's ability to scrape close to the very core of human feelings is not only dazzling, it's right on the money. The neurotic, tempestuous music of Astor Piazzola emphasizes to perfection the feverish emotions in Jabor's film. Jabor's flamboyant style, given full rein in *The Marriage,* is never gratuitous, being well balanced by the presence of leading man Paulo Porto. Porto seems perpetually bewildered by his own responses to events as much as he does by the wild circumstances which tend to surround him. Jabor also directed 1973's *All Nudity Will Be Punished,* a dark love story. Less successful was Jabor's 1981 film, *I Love You,* with Sonia Braga. **AKA:** O Casamento. 🦴🦴🦴

1976 113m/C *GB* Adriana Prieto, Paulo Porto, Camila Amado, Nelson Dantas, Erico Vidal, Fregolente, Maria Rubia; *D:* Arnaldo Jabor; *W:* Arnaldo Jabor; *C:* Dib Lufti; *M:* Astor Piazzolla. *NYR*

Martha and I

Martha and I was warmly received at the San Francisco International Film Festival in 1991 but after its distributor went bankrupt, it sat on the shelf for three years until this beautifully made German entry acquired a new distributor. Based on the childhood experiences of Czech director Jiri Weiss, the film stars Michel Piccoli and Marianne Saegebrecht in two exceptional performances as a Jewish doctor and German cook who confound their families by marrying and living happily ever after together, or at least until the imminent Nazi invasion of Czechoslovakia. Longtime admirers of Weiss, Piccoli, and Saegebrecht won't want to miss this one. 🦴🦴🦴

1991 107m/C *GE* Marianne Saegebrecht, Michel Piccoli, Vaclov Chalupa, Ondrej Vetchy; *D:* Jiri Weiss; *W:* Jiri Weiss; *C:* Viktor Ruzicka; *M:* Jiri Stivin. **VHS** *NYR*

INDEPENDENT FILM GUIDE

Union organizer Joe
Kenehan (Chris
Cooper) arrives in
Matewan.

Matador

Matador begins with its male lead masturbating to splatter videos. Then the female lead stabs a sexual partner as she climaxes. The rest of the movie shows how these two perfectly matched people meet and prepare for their mutual idea of the ultimate orgasm: simultaneous death. Writer/director Pedro Almodovar doesn't regard all this as aberrant or tragic, nor does he pass any moral judgments on his characters. Things like this happen all the time, his film says, and the main ones who get hurt are those who can't believe that there are people who freely choose to play it this way. The guy has another girlfriend, for example, with relentless faith that her love can save him from what he wants most. It can't, of course, but she tortures herself as he happily dashes off to screw his Doppelganger. Then there's the guy's student, who faints at the sight of blood, but who shares a strange psychic connection with his teacher, which forces him to claim guilt for the other's crimes. Almodovar, a post-Franco director with a vengeance, has clearly freed himself from the self-censorship that was inevitable for Spain's filmmakers during the repressive fascist regime. He has a way of plunging all the way to the bottom of the worst nightmares and examining each and every aspect in a way that is both clinical and passionate. His exhaustive explorations, far from destroying the enchantment of obsession, confront fatal charms on their own terms and render them plausible and even erotic. It is because he is so unsparing in his pursuit of truth that he can reveal the darkest human behavior and not be offensive, as a lesser artist surely would be with some of the huge risks Almodovar takes in *Matador*. 🦴🦴🦴🦴

1986 90m/C *SP* Assumpta Serna, Antonio Banderas, Nacho Martinez, Eva Cobo, Carmen Maura, Julieta Serrano, Chus Lampreave; *D:* Pedro Almodovar; *W:* Pedro Almodovar, Jesus Ferrere; *M:* Bernardo Bonazzi. **VHS, Beta, LV** *CCN, TPV*

Matewan

Matewan is the sort of picture that illustrates why independent film production is so necessary. John Sayles wrote the screenplay in the '70s, but no Hollywood studio was remotely interested in making a movie about a real-life massacre in which a dozen coal miners were murdered in West Virginia during the '20s. Sayles made it anyway, and it is among the most powerful works of his memorable career. Ah, Hollywood studios; how could any hotshot iceberg turn down a script with lines like these: "You want to be treated like men? You want to be treated fair? Well, ya ain't men to the coal company, you're equipment. They'll use you till you wear out or break down or you're buried under a slate fall, and then they'll get a new one, and they don't care what color it is or where it comes from." Chris Cooper is labor organizer Joe Kenehan, who tries to form a union in Mingo County, West Virginia. The threatened coal company then hired the Baldwin Felts detective agency to evict the coal miners from their homes. The agency had previously carried out an illegal 1914 eviction order in Colorado where gunmen murdered 20 people, including a dozen women and children who were burned alive. The eviction order was just as illegal in Mingo County, and Police Chief Sid Hatfield (David Straithairn) and the coal miners knew it. Hatfield became a hero to the coal miners by killing agency gunmen Al Felts (Frank Hoyt Taylor), but it didn't stop the massacre. Moreover, Hatfield himself was murdered (with his wife watching) by agency gunman C.E. Lively (Bob Gunton) within 15 months of the Matewan massacre. This harsh, brutal historical incident was little remembered by anyone outside the UMWA until Sayles and his brilliant cast and crew made this film.

A movie like *Matewan* should be as important to motion-picture history and our understanding of U.S. history as *The Grapes of Wrath*. Perhaps, over time, it will be. 🎞🎞🎞🎞

1987 (PG-13) 130m/C Chris Cooper, James Earl Jones, Mary McDonnell, William Oldham, Kevin Tighe, David Strathairn, Jace Alexander, Gordon Clapp, Mason Daring, Joe Grifasi, Bob Gunton, Jo Henderson, Jason Jenkins, Ken Jenkins, Nancy Mette, Josh Mostel, Michael B. Preston, Maggie Renzi, Frank Hoyt Taylor, Tom Wright; *Cameos:* John Sayles; *D:* John Sayles; *W:* John Sayles; *C:* Haskell Wexler; *M:* Mason Daring. Independent Spirit Awards '88: Best Cinematography; Nominations: Academy Awards '87: Best Cinematography. **VHS, Beta, LV, Closed Caption** *ORI, WAR*

Maurice

Maurice continues Berkeley-born director James Ivory's exploration of the English upper crust's high-class worries. Based on E.M. Forster's novel, the 139-minute film would not be hurt if it were half an hour shorter. It should come as no shock that there is a class structure in England and that schoolboys run off at the mouth, but it is tedious to watch long sequences convincing us of these kindergarten truths. The film works best when it shows the loneliness of the closet homosexual at the turn of the century. In a world which celebrates heterosexuality, the loneliness can only be relieved by an expression of sexuality, but even for the privileged in Great Britain, the consequences once included imprisonment. We see how two young men face their sexuality, one burying it in convention, the other acquiring strength by accepting himself as he is. It takes enormous reserves of courage to see through fear and disarm it. Very few can risk the social disapproval such an effort requires, which lends a rosy cast to the idealistic conclusion. The usual Ivory production values prevail, including gorgeous sets and costumes. *Maurice* is blessed with a top-notch cast, including then ubiquitous Denholm Elliott and Ben Kingsley as an oddly accented American hypnotist who has the film's

"Stone Mountain doesn't move one piece of coal unless it's a union man who moves it."

—Union organizer Joe Kenehan (Chris Cooper) makes this brave statement as scab mine workers defect and join the strike in *Matewan.*

INDEPENDENT FILM GUIDE

Tyrin Turner and Julian Roy Doster in Menace II Society.

out of situations that do not ordinarily lend themselves to comedy. ♫♫♫

1987 98m/C *GE* Rainer Grenkowitz, Nadja Engelbrecht, Alexander Hauff, Thomas Bestvater; **D:** Peter Timm; **W:** Peter Timm; **C:** Karl Eichhamer. *NYR*

Men in Love

Men in Love is reportedly the first feature film to be shot on BETA-SP and digitally mastered on D1-component before being transferred to 35mm. Producer/actor Scott Catamas believes that his $350,000 movie looks like it was shot on a budget of $2 million. A cast of inexperienced, mostly nonprofessional actors do their best with a sentimental and self-conscious story about safe sex in the era of AIDS. Long shots and action sequences instantly reveal the picture's video origins, despite Fawn Yacker's expert camera work. *Men in Love,* directed by Marc Huestis, rates an 'A' for its intentions but barely squeaks by with a 'C' for the results. ♫♫

1990 93m/C Doug Self, Joe Tolbe, Emerald Starr, Kutira Decosterd, Scott Catamas; **D:** Marc Huestis; **C:** Fawn Yacker. **VHS** *WBF, FCT*

Menace II Society

In the first few minutes of *Menace II Society,* a teenaged boy named Caine (Tyrin Turner) watches as O-Dog (Larenz Tate) guns down a Korean couple who run a shop in Watts, California. Unlike O-Dog, Caine Lawson wants to leave this way of life, but he can't see a way out. Fellow gang member Sharif (Vonte Sweet) is the son of a teacher, Mr. Butler (Charles S. Dutton), who lets Caine know that education is one way out. Another gang member, Stacy (Ryan Williams), receives a college scholarship to play football in Kansas, and he asks Caine to go with him. And Caine's girlfriend, Ronnie (Jada Pinkett), tries to persuade Caine to move to Atlanta with her. Despite these possibilities, Caine has been worn down by a life filled with guns and drugs, violence and death. Unsurpris-

best line, "England has always been disinclined to accept human nature." ♫♫♫

1987 (R) 139m/C *GB* James Wilby, Hugh Grant, Rupert Graves, Mark Tandy, Ben Kingsley, Denholm Elliott, Simon Callow, Judy Parfitt, Helena Bonham Carter, Billie Whitelaw, Phoebe Nicholls, Barry Foster; **D:** James Ivory; **W:** James Ivory, Kit Hesketh-Harvey; **M:** Richard Robbins. Nominations: Academy Awards '87: Best Costume Design. **VHS, Beta, LV, Closed Caption** *ORI, IME, WAR*

Meier

Meier is an enjoyable West German entry written and directed by Peter Timm. Its working class hero, played with considerable charm by Rainer Grenkowitz, tries to have the best of both worlds, East and West. The film gets considerable mileage

ingly, he's fatalistic about his life, if he ever has a chance to HAVE a future. The Hughes brothers, who are twins, were only 21 when they made their directorial debut. Both *Menace II Society* and their equally compelling follow-up film, 1995's *Dead Presidents* starring Tate, are filled with disturbing images of realistic bloodletting and the raging, urban sound of raw language. The core of their films, a deep understanding of each and every character, more than justifies their take-no-prisoners approach to filmmaking. We really NEED directors with such penetrating insights into contemporary society. ♫♫♫

1993 (R) 104m/C Tyrin Turner, Larenz Tate, Samuel L. Jackson, Glenn Plummer, Julian Roy Doster, Bill Duke, Charles S. Dutton, Jada Pinkett, Vonte Sweet, Ryan Williams; *D:* Allen Hughes, Albert Hughes; *W:* Tyger Williams; *C:* Lisa Rinzler. Independent Spirit Awards '94: Best Cinematography; MTV Movie Awards '94: Best Film; Nominations: Independent Spirit Awards '94: Best Actor (Turner), Best First Feature. **VHS, LV, Closed Caption** *COL, NLC, IME*

Metamorphosis

Metamorphosis offers a striking visualization of the Franz Kafka story, set in Prague, circa 1900. In this first filmed version of the story, we finally SEE Gregor Samsa being turned into a bug, much to the revulsion of his family. A U.S. version released 15 years later didn't fly. *AKA:* Forvandlingen. ♫♫♪

1975 90m/C *SW* Ernst Gunther, Gunn Wallgren, Peter Schildt, Inga-Lili Carlsson, Per Oscarsson; *D:* Ivo Dvorak; *W:* Ivo Dvorak, Lars Forssell; *C:* Jiri Tirl. *NYR*

The Method

The Method is clearly a well intentioned effort by Joseph Destein and 13 other men who worked on the film with him. It's the old story about the middle-aged woman who leaves home and family to find herself by taking acting lessons and by playing hookers on film. The filmmakers try to solve plot problems by picking up the slack with undeveloped sub-plots involving minor characters. Remember the pompous white teachers in the Black Actors School sketch in Robert Townsend's *Hollywood Shuffle*? *The Method*'s pompous white male teachers show women how to be women, but their lessons, like this film, present a false vision lacking any real depth or understanding. Taylor Gilbert had previously appeared in *Torment* and *Alone in the T-Shirt Zone.* Rob Nilsson's writing and directing credits include *Northern Lights, Signal 7, On the Edge,* and *Heat and Sunlight.* ♫♫

1987 100m/C Melanie Dreisbach, Kathryn Knotts, Deborah Swisher, Taylor Gilbert, Anthony Cistaro, Richard Arnold, Rob Reece, Jack Rikess, Robert Elross, Jean Shelton; *D:* Joseph Destein; *W:* Rob Nilsson, Joseph Destein, Joel Adelman; *C:* Stephen Lighthill; *M:* Ray Obiedo. *NYR*

Metropolis

Metropolis was set 74 years in the future in the year 2000. Fritz Lang "detested it after it was finished"; he wanted it to include elements of magic and the occult, ghosts and ghouls, instead of the notion that "human beings were nothing but part of a machine." Lang credits Thea von Harbou with the original concept ("She had foresight and was right"), but the execution was all his ("I was wrong"). But Lang's view of the film is not shared by those who have seen the film over the years. The effect of all that photogenic machinery on an audience is visceral in the extreme. Even contemporary science-fiction flicks would benefit from the lavish art direction of Lang's epic. The amazing Brigitte Helm, only 21, plays both kindly Maria and the evil robot. The electricity between the robot and the 30,000 extras pre-dates every political rally/revival meeting/rock concert we can possibly imagine! And the fact that all those thousands would willingly follow the robot to their doom gives *Metropolis* an eerily premonitory quality, considering so many things that were to come between 1927 and the year 2000. *Metropolis* provides a timeless view of an ever-timely theme. (NOTE: The

ALLEN HUGHES
Menace II Society

We [he and brother Albert Hughes] were interested in doing films, little home movies like *Scarface, Part II,* around the age of eleven, because we had a video camera our mother gave us. I went to film school and we had to do three short films as projects, two Super 8mm. and one 16mm. The director of CB 4 told us where to distribute the tapes. Then we went to a couple of record companies and one of them was Hollywood Basic, who had a rap group in Oakland, California, called Raw Fusion, and ever since then we've been working in music videos and then *Menace II Society* came about like that. I was shooting a drive-by sequence and we used a real sawed-off shotgun, which is a felony. When I was shooting it, I was thinking to myself, 'If someone sees this from the house, just this section of the car, they'll think it's a real drive-by.' And while I was thinking that, I saw about five cop cars swoop around the corner. They all pulled against the wall and checked all my equipment, and they just wouldn't believe it was a film. They thought we were covering up by using film equipment for an actual crime. They asked us whose shotgun it was and all that stuff. No one admitted whose it was or they'd go to jail. No one was admitting it: 'It's not mine,' 'It's not mine'....

"I don't think Caine [Tyrin Turner] fully understands what he's coming up against in *Menace II Society.* He's just so used to it from his whole childhood. It's like life to him. Life is death to him. He doesn't know any other way. There's no means of getting out. That's the way he lives. He doesn't even think about it. There's a naivete to him. There's a couple of guys like O-Dog [Larenz Tate] in South Central. I think everyone knows one of those people from down there, one crazy guy who's totally wigged out. He's been totally abused

---

original score by the Clubfoot Orchestra, performed at San Francisco's Castro theatre, is far superior to the score composed by Giorgio Moroder.) ♪♪♪♪

1926 115m/B *GE* Brigitte Helm, Alfred Abel, Gustav Froehlich, Rudolf Klein-Rogge, Fritz Rasp, Heinrich George, Theodore Loos, Erwin Biswanger, Olaf Storm, Hans Leo Reich, Heinrich Gotho; *D:* Fritz Lang; *W:* Fritz Lang, Thea von Harbou; *C:* Karl Fre-

und, Gunther Rittau, Eugene Schufftan; *M:* Gottfried Huppertz. **VHS, Beta, LV** *SNC, NOS, MRV*

Metropolitan

Christopher Eigeman looks and sounds like he's out of another time, like you'd find him at one of Jay Gatsby's garden parties immaculately tailored, supplying Scott AND

since he was little and he turns into an abuser. That's the take we took on that character: he's America's Nightmare.

"We shot *Menace II Society* in Watts. It went well. We had no problems; we hired people from the neighborhood as extras and we hired the gang members as our security, and they kept everything in line with no problem at all. They loved having us down there. We had a problem from the white cops who didn't want us to go in certain areas: 'Don't go in that neighborhood,' 'Don't go in that neighborhood.' That was the only problem. They were just trying to tell us not to shoot down there....

"We both call 'Cut' whenever it's time to call 'Cut', but I take care of the visuals and the camera department and the lighting, and my brother Albert will take care of the actors and the performances.... Sometimes we argue for a while and usually it gets resolved. If it has to do with acting, my brother Albert usually gets the last say-so, and if it has to do with me behind the camera, the technical side, I have the last say-so on it, so we can argue our point and get mad at each other, but the bottom line is that each one of us has a final say-so in those arenas....

"I was in too much of a daze at first to be nervous when we started shooting. Everything came so quick. My brother Albert was a little intimidated at first, directing Bill Duke, because Bill Duke's a big guy and just meeting him is intimidating. But after a while, those guys put us at ease and just hung around us and started rubbing our shoulders, 'Take your time,' and everything like that, and they were cool so we got everything we had to do done. Our target audience is black, because that's where we make our money for the film, but we made it for the people who don't live this lifestyle, who don't understand how criminals get to be criminals in the black community. They always see the evening news about how someone got shot in the forehead and laid out on the ground. It seems so savage and it is, but we have to understand what went on behind those crimes and how the person who did that crime evolves into that character; what he talked about before that crime and what he talked about afterwards, and that's what we tried to do."

Zelda Fitzgerald with literary inspiration for dozens of short stories. He was in Whit Stillman's first two pictures and Noah Baumbach's debut film, but I only see him in Pacific Bell commercials these days. Even though he's great in them, I'd rather see him at the movies. Edward Clements as Tom Townsend runs into a group of young socialites who need an extra male. Even though he's out of their league, he joins them and, through guarded responses, wins their acceptance. Eigeman as Nick shows Tom the ropes and he's in. The lives of the socialites really do seem as if they belong to an earlier era, but Stillman's dialogue is so bright and witty (especially as delivered by Eigeman) that most of the 98 minutes whizzes by, until Nick drops out

of the plot. I had to wait four years to see Eigeman again, co-starring with Taylor Nichols in Stillman's *Barcelona.* What's the matter with movie producers these days, anyway? Don't they recognize a star when they see one? ♫♫♫

1990 (PG-13) 98m/C Carolyn Farina, Edward Clements, Taylor Nichols, Christopher Eigeman, Allison Rutledge-Parisi, Dylan Hundley, Isabel Gillies, Bryan Leder, Will Kempe, Elizabeth Thompson; **D:** Whit Stillman; **W:** Whit Stillman; **M:** Mark Suozzo. Independent Spirit Awards '91: Best First Feature; New York Film Critics Awards '90: Best Director (Stillman); Nominations: Academy Awards '90: Best Original Screenplay. **VHS, LV** COL, FCT

Miami Blues

How often have you watched a movie and wondered: "How in the world were they able to get this project past the story board?" In the case of *Miami Blues,* we have a pretty good hunch which sequences attracted Jonathan Demme to produce it, but that doesn't necessarily mean that YOU have to blow your entertainment allowance on it. *Miami Blues* is your basic home movie with a budget. Although the direction by Roger Corman alumnus George (*Private Duty Nurses, Hot Rod*) Armitage is described (by the press kit) as "precise," he pretty much lets stars Alec Baldwin and Jennifer Jason Leigh overact their little hearts out. The characters they play are generic psycho and generic ditz, complete with accompanying stock mannerisms. This permits executive producer Fred Ward to steal the film with his usual roguish charm and easy underplaying. The plot (Will Sgt. Ward catch the insane Baldwin?) is so predictable that the minor shocks in the movie are supplied by its very occasional gross-outs. Shirley Stoler and Charles Napier are on hand for the hard core film buffs. And in the "So-that's-how-they-get-away-with-it"   department,

writer/director George Armitage pulled into the first convenience store he could find while scouting for movie locations. He went up to the owner and said, "I'm with a film company and we'd like to drive a truck through your front door." The store owner, who'd already been held up several times, said "yes" without batting an eye. Believe it or don't! (After *Miami Blues,* Armitage went on to co-script 1996's *The Late Shift,* a Golden Globe winner for actress Kathy Bates.) 𝄞𝄞

1990 (R) 97m/C Fred Ward, Alec Baldwin, Jennifer Jason Leigh, Nora Dunn, Charles Napier, Jose Perez, Paul Gleason, Obba Babatunde, Martine Beswick, Shirley Stoler; **D:** George Armitage; **W:** George Armitage; **M:** Gary Chang. New York Film Critics Awards '90: Best Supporting Actress (Leigh). **VHS, Beta, LV, Closed Caption** *ORI, IME*

Michael Collins

Galway-born actor George Brent used to be a dispatch rider for Michael Collins. He escaped Ireland with a price on his head and eventually wound up in Hollywood at the Warner Bros. studio. Had the future of Ireland not been his preeminent concern, Michael Collins could have torn up the silver screen. Check out the newsreels of the early 1920s; Collins appears onscreen and you can't look at anything else. His skin, like that of many great stars, photographs so vividly you feel you can reach out and feel it, and his style, gestures, and charisma would be timeless in any era. Michael Collins had more important things on his mind than newsreel cameramen, namely an Irish Republic free of British control. Neil Jordan scrupulously charts the IRA's campaign of that time and, despite his finest efforts to create a movie that is both historically accurate and dramatically gripping, *Michael Collins* came under heavy attack from international political scholars who charged that considerable liberties had been taken with the truth. Well, you can plow through history books or you can see this film, starring the well chosen Liam Nee-

son. For the record, Harry Boland (Aidan Quinn) and Collins did indeed fight together, but not in the Easter Uprising of 1916. Boland was killed in a hotel room instead of a sewer. Informer Ned Broy (Stephen Rea) was not executed by the British; he is a composite of two other fighters who WERE tortured and killed by the British. Collins did not actually see the hanging of Tom Cullen (Stuart Graham), although hangings of Irish rebels did, in fact, occur. Joe O'Reilly (Ian Hart) was not with Collins when he was assassinated. And no, Kitty Kiernan (Julia Roberts) and Collins didn't meet like THAT. So now you know. It is difficult to show a pure political power struggle onscreen without some fidgety nitpickers asking when we get to hear some humor or see some sex. Despite all this, Jordan's epic is a masterful one and will likely find a more receptive audience on video than it did in theatrical release. And the tension between Collins and future Irish Prime Minister Eamon De Valera (1882-1975, played here by Alan Rickman) is revealed with chilling economy. If he had lived, Collins probably would not have joined George Brent in Hollywood at the Warner Bros. studio, but current affairs in the Irish Republic might be very different today. (Cast Note: Neeson and Roberts previously co-starred in 1988's *Satisfaction.*) 𝄞𝄞𝄞𝄞

1996 (R) 117m/C Liam Neeson, Aidan Quinn, Alan Rickman, Stephen Rea, Julia Roberts, Ian Hart, Sean McGinley, Gerard McSorley, Stuart Graham, Brendan Gleeson, Charles Dance, Jonathan Rhys Myers; **D:** Neil Jordan; **W:** Neil Jordan; **C:** Chris Menges; **M:** Elliot Goldenthal. Los Angeles Film Critics Association Awards '96: Best Cinematography; Venice Film Festival '96: Golden Lion, Best Actor (Neeson); Nominations: Academy Awards '96: Best Cinematography, Original Dramatic/Comedy Score; British Academy Awards '96: Best Supporting Actor (Rickman); Golden Globe Awards '97: Best Actor—Drama (Neeson), Best Score. **VHS, DVD** *WAR*

Mina Tannenbaum

At first, *Mina Tannenbaum* evokes memories of the 1991 British comedy, *Antonia*

271

and *Jane,* although director Martine Dugowson's incisive reflections on a 25-year friendship are in no way softened by humor. Instead, we see two young women sustained and strengthened by the friendship each wishes she had, rather than what's actually there. Mina, the more sensitive and artistic of the two, yearns for a friend that would listen to her for hours as she describes a deep crush. Mortally bored and mostly deceptive with Mina, Ethel is far more adaptable and willing to settle for what she can get. The friendship limps along for many years, always meaning more to Mina than to Ethel, until the inevitable break. *Mina Tannenbaum* is a real button pusher; maybe you'd better see it with anyone EXCEPT an old friend in shaky standing! ♫♫♫

1993 128m/C *FR* Romane Bohringer, Elsa Zylberstein, Nils Tavernier, Florence Thomassin, Jean-Philippe Ecoffey, Stephane Slima; *D:* Martine Dugowson; *W:* Martine Dugowson; *C:* Dominique Chapuis. **VHS** *NYF*

The Miracle

A storm of controversy erupted when Roberto Rossellini's *The Miracle* was released with *The Human Voice* in 1948 as a two-part film, *L'Amore.* Cardinal Spellman in New York was particularly outraged at this tale of a simple woman who sleeps with a bum (portrayed by screenwriter Federico Fellini) under the impression that he is Saint Joseph. The next item on her agenda is giving birth to Jesus Christ, a plan that is greeted with derision by the people of her village. Blasphemous or not, *The Miracle* and *The Human Voice* gave Anna Magnani a superb showcase, and she made the most of it. She began her career in small parts like the maid she played in *Deadline,* a 1934 Vittorio De Sica comedy. Magnani's enormous talent might well have been consigned to servant roles for the rest of her life on film had it not been for Rossellini's and her own willingness to give the movies a realism they had never had before. **AKA:** Ways of Love. ♫♫♫

1948 43m/B *IT* Anna Magnani, Federico Fellini; *D:* Roberto Rossellini; *W:* Federico Fellini. **VHS, Beta** *NOS, FCT, APD*

Miracle Mile

When *Miracle Mile* was first released, some reviewers commented on the improbability of a ringing pay telephone alerting protagonist Harry (Anthony Edwards) to a nuclear nightmare. But how did we learn about Chernobyl in 1986, anyway? And doesn't Death sometimes (in 1997, actually) arrive in the form of two drops of dimethyl-mercury that leak through latex gloves? *Miracle Mile* begins as a sweet, romantic story about Harry and Julie (Mare Winningham), with no premonitory warning shots. And then Harry picks up the telephone and hears a terrified voice describing the ultimate nuclear war, due globally within the hour. You have 60 minutes to live: what would you do? Harry goes looking for Julie. Along the way, Harry sees people doing what they normally do: hanging out in an all-night diner, working out in a health club. Julie has taken Valium to help her sleep and Harry doesn't tell her at first about the inevitable. He tells her estranged folks, though (wonderfully played by John Agar and Lou Hancock) and the two resolve many year's worth of conflicts in an instant and drive off into the night together. What Harry decides to do with his last hour doesn't exactly appear to be shared by Julie, especially since she doesn't know what the heck is going on at first. The soundtrack by Tangerine Dream is strikingly similar to their score for 1983's *Risky Business,* only here the persistent theme leads, literally, Nowhere, instead of to a Party. Steve DeJarnatt evokes the escalating tension of 1950's *D.O.A.* for 1988, in a way that the actual remake of *D.O.A.,* also filmed in 1988, does not. Existentially well acted by Edwards and Winningham. O-lan Jones can also be seen in *Shelf Life,* directed by Paul Bartel in 1994. ♫♫♫

1989 (R) 87m/C Anthony Edwards, Mare Winningham, John Agar, Denise Crosby, Lou Hancock, Mykel

T. Williamson, Kelly Jo Minter, Kurt Fuller, Robert DoQui, Danny De La Paz, O-lan Jones, Alan Rosenberg, Claude Earl Jones; **D:** Steve DeJarnatt; **W:** Steve DeJarnatt; **C:** Theo van de Sande; **M:** Tangerine Dream. Nominations: Independent Spirit Awards '90: Best Screenplay (DeJarnatt), Best Supporting Actress (Winningham). **VHS, Beta, LV, Closed Caption** *HBO*

The Missing Reel

The history of the motion picture industry has always been shrouded in mystery. Take the very first filmmaker, for example. In November of 1888, Louis Aime Augustin Le Prince patented his camera, and some of the films he made in October of that year still survive. One shows the Yorkshire garden of his British father-in-law, the other records traffic crossing Leeds Bridge. The following year, Le Prince used perforated film for the first time. Why don't we remember Le Prince as well as we do Thomas Edison today? On September 16, 1890, Le Prince planned to demonstrate a brand new movie projector for the Secretary of the Paris Opera. He was last seen carrying the projector and his films as he boarded a Paris-bound train at Dijon. The inventor, his equipment, and all of his films vanished without a trace, and Le Prince became a mere footnote in film history, barely acknowledged throughout the first century of the cinema. Then writer Christopher Rawlence became intrigued by the unsolved mystery and also by the role Le Prince had played in the evolution of film. His research made both a compelling 321-page book, published by Atheneum, as well as a fine feature-length documentary. Rawlence speaks with members of the Le Prince family, reconstructs events from Le Prince's life, and does some solid investigative work to show what led up to the disappearance and why. Great viewing for neophytes AND scholars! ✐✐✐✐

1990 90m/C John Hart-Dyke, Mona Bruce, Steve Shill, Alison Skilbeck, William Whymper, George Malpas, Vincent Marzello, Ron Berglas, Billy Le Prince

Huettel; **D:** Christopher Rawlence; **W:** Christopher Rawlence; **C:** Chris Morphet; **M:** Francis Shaw. *NYR*

Mrs. Parker and the Vicious Circle

Dorothy Parker (1893-1967) left behind a few recordings of her voice, which Jennifer Jason Leigh listened to over and over again, trying to get every inflection just right. Audiences either loved or hated Leigh's voice as Parker; it was the centerpiece of her interpretation. Let's see—if Parker only made a few recordings, she could not have been very comfortable making them, and her personality might well have been...lost in the process? Uhm...maybe, but she WAS nominated for a Grammy in 1961 for the *World of Dorothy Parker* album she recorded for the Verve label. Voice aside, Leigh plays Parker as a chronically unhappy woman, obsessed with Robert Benchley (1889-1945) when her real-life obsession appears to have been with her husband and *Star Is Born* collaborator Alan Campbell (they were both nominated for Oscars for their screenplay and Parker was a nominee again in 1947 for *Smash Up*). It's unlikely that if the real Parker had been half as miserable as Leigh's Parker, she would have been drinking lunch with the guys everyday at the Algonquin Round Table. Then and now, guys may prefer lunch with wine, but seldom with a whiner. Campbell Scott was much praised for his performance as Benchley, and he would be bloody marvelous if he were playing anyone BUT Benchley. As anyone who is addicted to Benchley's short films knows, no one could look at Benchley without smiling, and no one could read his books or listen to him at the movies without laughing (check out 1928's original *Sex Life of a Polyp!* OR *How to Sleep*, a 1935 Oscar winner!). Scott plays Benchley as sensitive, concerned, lean, and humorless. In trying to include every one of the

Algonquin wits, Rudolph does justice to no one, really. Everyone passes into the frame for a second before s/he's gone. And there's still identity fudging. Some of the female characters are composites, probably for legal reasons. At least Rudolph waited until Helen Hayes (1900-93) died before painting her husband Charles MacArthur (1895-1963) as a faithless jerk. As a fiction flick, this one ain't half bad, but I'd rather watch Sally Kellerman and John Lithgow in Parker's *The Big Blonde* or Robert Benchley delivering his own dialogue in Hitchcock's *Foreign Correspondent*. **AKA:** Mrs. Parker and the Round Table. 🦴🦴 ♥

1994 (R) 124m/C Jennifer Jason Leigh, Matthew Broderick, Andrew McCarthy, Campbell Scott, Jennifer Beals, Tom McGowan, Nick Cassavetes, Sam Robards, Rebecca Miller, Wallace Shawn, Martha Plimpton, Gwyneth Paltrow, Peter Gallagher, Lili Taylor; **D:** Alan Rudolph; **W:** Rudolph Coburn, Randy Sue Coburn; **C:** Jan Kiesser; **M:** Mark Isham. Chicago Film Critics Awards '94: Best Actress (Leigh); National Society of Film Critics Awards '94: Best Actress (Leigh); Nominations: Golden Globe Awards '95: Best Actress—Drama (Leigh); Independent Spirit Awards '95: Best Actor (Scott), Best Actress (Leigh), Best Director (Rudolph), Best Film, Best Screenplay. **VHS, LV, Closed Caption** NLC, IME

Mr. North

Mr. North is a 1988 movie that, except for the color and the sound, is virtually indistinguishable from any Cinderella yarn of 1928. Ah, for the good old days when integration meant marriage between the immigrant Irish and the third generation Irish, when amusing the rich provided the poor with access to their privileged world, and when every young dreamer enjoyed a fairytale ending. Set in Newport, Rhode Island, in 1926, the plot revolves around Theophilus North (Anthony Edwards, then 26), who yearns to be a free man and begins his quest by reading to the rich. He makes friends with Robert Mitchum (too young at 71 in a role intended for the late John Huston) by supplying him with candy and diapers, panaceas for incontinence. He makes friends with lovely Virginia Madsen and unrecognizable Mary Stuart Masterson by reassuring one of her worth with a kiss on the mouth and curing the other of her migraine with a tap on the forehead. Theophilus makes enemies, too: Tammy Grimes doesn't like the uppity young man and neither does Dr. David Warner, who's losing patients to this amateur quack. But, with a little help from Harry Dean Stanton and Lauren Bacall, Mr. North wins the day and control of Mitchum's money, dancing off into the night with Anjelica Huston. Madsen's character is happy: she winds up married to the grandson of an Irish mogul, played by (who else?) Joe Kennedy's grandson, Christopher Lawford. Everyone is happy except for the characters played by Grimes and Warner and the audience members who swallow this confection, yearning for satire as a mild antidote. Adapted by John Huston from Thornton Wilder's old-fashioned 1973 novel, *Mr. North* was directed by Danny Huston without a trace of irony. The clothes and the locations are beautiful, the cast is fun to look at, but *Mr. North* is little more than a foggy memory of an era that seems to exist only in the neverneverland of yellowing rotogravures. 🦴🦴

1988 (PG) 90m/C Anthony Edwards, Robert Mitchum, Lauren Bacall, Harry Dean Stanton, Anjelica Huston, Mary Stuart Masterson, Virginia Madsen, Tammy Grimes, David Warner, Hunter Carson, Christopher Durang, Mark Metcalf, Katharine Houghton, Christopher Lawford; **D:** Danny Huston; **W:** John Huston, Janet Roach, James Costigan; **M:** David McHugh. **VHS, Beta, LV, Closed Caption** NO

A Modern Affair

A Modern Affair is a first directorial effort by Vern Oakley, working with a script by Paul Zimmerman. The plot is your basic telefeature about the female executive who goes to a sperm bank to have a baby and then wants to know who the father is. This one could be sold to the Lifetime channel as is, but it has a nice performance by the criminally underrated Lisa Eichhorn and not a bad co-star in Stanley

Tucci, previously seen stealing Bridget Fonda's Macadamia nuts in *It Could Happen to You.* **AKA:** Mr. 247. 🎬🎬

1994 (R) 91m/C Lisa Eichhorn, Stanley Tucci, Caroline Aaron, Tammy Grimes, Robert Joy, Wesley Addy, Cynthia Martells, Mary Jo Salerno; **D:** Vern Oakley; **W:** Paul Zimmerman; **C:** Rex Nicholson; **M:** Jan Hammer. **VHS, Closed Caption** COL

Mommy

What you notice first about *Mommy* is how good an actress Patty McCormack was and still is. Since McCormack never relied on the tricks of most kiddie stars (baby talk, cuteness, innocence, OR sweetness), she didn't miss them when she moved into adult roles. As the title character, McCormack projects skin-deep politeness, but we all know what's underneath her mask: a sociopathic murderer! This time, it's her daughter (Rachel Lemieux) who's at her wit's end, trying first to protect Mommy from herself and eventually, to protect herself from Mommy! *Mommy* appears to have been shot on high-definition video (the sequel will be on film, rather than tape), but lit for film. One has to admire the ingenuity of Max Allan Collins: his script is great, his directing style pushes all the right buttons, and he's assembled an astonishingly fine cast, considering the fact that he probably had to stretch every dollar into doing the job of five. 🎬🎬🎬

1995 89m/C Patty McCormack, Majel Barrett, Jason Miller, Brinke Stevens, Rachel Lemieux, Mickey Spillane, Michael Cornelison, Sarah Jane Miller; **D:** Max Allan Collins; **W:** Max Allan Collins; **C:** Phillip W. Dingeldein; **M:** Richard Lowry. **VHS** MNC

Mona Lisa

Bob Hoskins gets out of prison and asks slimy gangster Michael Caine for a job. He winds up driving around an expensive call girl (Cathy Tyson). Hoskins keeps a pretty tight lid on his loneliness and desperation, but by caring about his nightly charge, he's in over his head. Neil Jordan would later re-work and satirize some of the themes

here in 1992's *The Crying Game,* but *Mona Lisa* is emotion at its most raw; Hoskins works without a net as only he can. Tyson delivers a lovely performance in her first film. Sadly, for those who admire her work here, she's made few pictures since: Wes Craven's *The Serpent and the Rainbow,* Lezli-Ann Barrett's *Business As Usual,* a small role in Nigel Finch's *The Lost Language of Cranes,* and another brief appearance in Antonia Bird's *Priest.* One nice touch puts Jordan leagues in front of noir pretenders who allow bloodletting and machismo to speak for them because they have nothing to say, really. A rabbit enters the frame at one point in the story. In any other neo noir flick of the '80s or '90s, that rabbit would have a life expectancy of five or ten minutes, max. But the rabbit survives everything. You don't have to worry about that rabbit. Keep watching. The rabbit isn't a Player; there's no reason to rub him out. Not everyone in Hoskins' world gets off that lightly and as he prepares to stand up to Caine and his henchmen, you hope that this time, things will work out for him. The odds are against him (remember that lonely ride at the conclusion of *The Long Good Friday?*), but he's going to go down fighting till the bitter end. 🎬🎬🎬🎬

1986 (R) 104m/C *GB* Bob Hoskins, Cathy Tyson, Michael Caine, Clarke Peters, Kate Hardie, Robbie Coltrane, Zoe Nathenson, Sammi Davis, Rod Bedall, Joe Brown, Pauline Melville; **D:** Neil Jordan; **W:** David Leland, Neil Jordan; **M:** Michael Kamen. British Academy Awards '86: Best Actor (Hoskins); Cannes Film Festival '86: Best Actor (Hoskins); Golden Globe Awards '87: Best Actor—Drama (Hoskins); Los Angeles Film Critics Association Awards '86: Best Actor (Hoskins), Best Supporting Actress (Tyson); New York Film Critics Awards '86: Best Actor (Hoskins); National Society of Film Critics Awards '86: Best Actor (Hoskins); Nominations: Academy Awards '86: Best Actor (Hoskins). **VHS, Beta, LV** VTR

Money Madness

Here's Hugh Beaumont in another "B" movie for *Leave It to Beaver* fans who just HAVE to see Ward Cleaver acting like a

The Hound Salutes:
PATTY MCCORMACK
Mommy

Did you sneak downstairs when everyone was asleep and watch *The Bad Seed* in spite of your parents' warning? For many little girls who grew up in the '50s, Rhoda Penmark was even more scary than Frankenstein or Dracula.... Rhoda, who killed three people by the time she was eight years old, could easily be that pretty little blue-eyed blonde who sat across the classroom. The thing that was so unthinkable four decades ago, that any mother's precious baby could possibly murder for material gain, is less of a shocker now, and so we are extended the luxury of laughing at the same Rhoda who used to give us nightmares. Actress PATTY McCORMACK, who personified curdled perfection as adorably evil little Rhoda, was an Academy Award nominee at the age of ten for her spine-tingling performance in 1956's *The Bad Seed*. She went on to make 1958's *All Mine to Give* and 1960's *The Adventures of Huckleberry Finn,* and returned to films as an adult to make 1984's *Invitation to Hell* and 1988's *Saturday the 14th Strikes Back.* 1995's *Mommy* was the brainchild of Iowa mystery writer Max Allan Collins, who drew on the legend of Rhoda Penmark to create a character in which Mommy is the psycho and her little girl is the seemingly ineffectual voice of sanity. *Mommy* attracted the sort of cast (and reviews) many filmmakers with much higher budgets might envy. Majel Barrett, Jason Miller, Brinke Stevens, Mickey Spillane, and Iowa Film Festival award winner Rachel Lemieux as the child all gave Patty McCormack solid support. At press time, a 1997 sequel, made on an even smaller budget, was in the works.

Max Allan Collins is the one who started this whole thing. The whole film was financed in the town of Muscatine, Iowa. It's amazing. They really got behind this movie. Hopefully, people will rent it and they'll be paid nicely for it. They invested their own money in this because Max is an Iowa person who stayed in Muscatine, even though he had success elsewhere. For *Mommy 2,* Rachel Lemieux and Brinke Stevens are back, and A Minor Consideration Founder Paul Petersen plays a writer named Paul. Gary [*WKRP*] Sandy lives in Kentucky, and I knew him from long ago, so he drove up to be in it, too, and [character actor] Arlen Dean Snyder was in it because he happened to be teaching in Iowa. You think this must be meant to be because these people were available. We made *Mommy* for so little money. If anyone wants to make a really low-budget movie, contact Max Allan Collins. I don't know how he does it, but he does it."

real rat once in a while. He's a fiend in this one as "Steve Clark" (it's an alias). In one sequence, he asks Julie (Frances Rafferty) to turn up the radio so the neighbors won't be disturbed while he rubs out someone who rubs him the wrong way. And watch what he does to Julie's Aunt Cora (Cecil Weston); is this where Eddie Haskell learned his exclusive tips on supercilious courtesy? Meanwhile, Donald (Harlan Warde) waits patiently for Julie to come to her senses and notice HIM once in a while. An ultra cut-rate exploration of amour fou. Don't look at the wallpaper and set decorations too closely! 🦴🦴

1947 ?m/C Hugh Beaumont, Frances Rafferty, Harlan Warde, Cecil Weston, Ida Moore, Danny Morton, Joel Friedkin, Lane Chandler; *D:* Peter Stewart, Sam Newfield; *W:* Al Martin; *C:* Jack Greenhalgh. **VHS** *SNC*

Morgan!

From his breakthrough appearance in the 1966 Karel Reisz classic *Morgan: A Suitable Case for Treatment* right on up to the present day, David Warner has specialized in playing strange dudes, each role progressively weirder than the one that preceded it. His body of work provides a feast for fans of offbeat cult films, although we can think of no other actor of his stature who is such a shy enigma offscreen. *Morgan!* is a stylish study of an nutty anarchist who does everything in his power to regain his delectable ex-wife's affections, including kidnapping her, trying to blow up her future mother-in-law, and harassing her current lover on the job. Clips from *King Kong* and old Tarzan movies reinforce Morgan's ultimate fantasy: to carry off the very sophisticated, very urban Vanessa Redgrave into the jungle where they can be free of society's restraints. Since Morgan's unsympathetic rival Sir Robert Stephens (1931-95) deserves no better fate than to be shoved face first into a wedding cake, Morgan grabs our interest and sympathy from the very first reel. *Morgan!* was a dream role for a young, little-known actor and Warner made the most of

it. One of Warner's unique qualities as an actor is to drag the viewer into an assortment of twisted minds, by projecting intense vulnerability and contrasting it with cool, crisp control. Follow-up roles included fat parts in prestige films that were little seen outside of his native Britain and, more typically, a long line of villains and psychos. Watching vintage David Warner performances, you may wonder why such a nutcase is allowed to move undisturbed through civilized society. Warner is definitely not the guy you'd want to meet in a dark alley, and audiences can never quite trust him in ordinarily trustworthy professions. David Warner's name on a cast list generally means that you can have fun watching him, if no one else, for even after nearly 35 years onscreen, he's always a fascinating, unpredictable presence. *AKA:* Morgan: A Suitable Case for Treatment; A Suitable Case for Treatment. 🦴🦴🦴🦴

1966 93m/B *GB* Vanessa Redgrave, David Warner, Robert Stephens, Irene Handl, Bernard Bresslaw, Arthur Mullard, Newton Blick, Nan Munro, Graham Crowden, John Rae, Peter Collingwood, Edward Fox; *D:* Karel Reisz; *W:* David Mercer. British Academy Awards '66: Best Screenplay; Cannes Film Festival '66: Best Actress (Redgrave); Nominations: Academy Awards '66: Best Actress (Redgrave), Best Costume Design (B & W). **VHS, Beta, LV** *NO*

Morgan's Cake

San Francisco Bay area filmmaker Rick Schmidt is the author of *Feature Filmmaking at Used Car Prices* and he isn't kidding about that title. The press kit for *Morgan's Cake* begins with a list of virtually every dollar that was spent on the movie, as well as informative tips on how he was able to make the best use of his time and money. Roughly, production expenses cost $3,700, salaries added up to $2,900, and post-production at Palmer and Monaco film labs totaled $8,400. Three investors contributed to the movie's $15,000 budget. The 87-minute feature took nine days to shoot and the plucky Schmidt wrote, directed, filmed, edited, and produced it all by

277

INDEPENDENT FILM GUIDE

himself. The results are occasionally touching and amusing but always lacking the creative energy and original insights that characterize the best rock bottom efforts. Morgan Schmidt-Feng, the director's son, is a cute kid, but both his story and his personality wear thin after 20 minutes. Ultimately, reading about the making of *Morgan's Cake* is much more interesting than watching the movie itself. Schmidt, who had made four films by 1990, admitted at the time that he hadn't found his voice as a director yet and we wouldn't care to argue with him. You can see *Morgan's Cake* if you can find it (it doesn't appear to be available on video) or buy *Feature Filmmaking at Used Car Prices* at used bookstores and make your own movie! 🦴🦴

1988 87m/B Morgan Schmidt-Feng, Willie Boy Walker, Rachel Pond, M. Louise Stanley, Aaron Leon Kenin, Eliot Kenin, John Claudio; *D:* Rick Schmidt; *W:* Rick Schmidt; *C:* Rick Schmidt, Kathleen Beller; *M:* Gary Thorp. *NYR*

Mother Kusters Goes to Heaven

This successful West German effort by Rainer Werner Fassbinder focuses on the title character, played by Brigitte Mira. Mother Kusters is a woman who finds herself drawn into politics after her husband's suicide; she acquires our sympathy slowly, but relentlessly. At first, she appears to be a woman unfairly hanging on to her grown children and her memories. Gradually, however, her awareness of the world grows with her knowledge of herself. Her speech before the members of a political group who exploit her husband's story for their own purposes provides the film with its most moving moments. Fassbinder and Mira brilliantly show us Mother Kusters' growth with sensitive compassion for both her position and her predicament. A bonus is the presence of Karl Boehm, better known for his work in *Unnatural, The Wonderful World of the Brothers Grimm,* and

Peeping Tom. Boehm also worked with Fassbinder on *Fox and His Friends.* *AKA:* Mutter Kusters Fahrt Zum Himmel. 🦴🦴🦴

1976 108m/C *GE* Brigitte Mira, Ingrid Caven, Armin Meier, Irm Hermann, Gottfried John, Margit Carstensen, Karl-Heinz Boehm; *D:* Rainer Werner Fassbinder; *W:* Rainer Werner Fassbinder; *C:* Michael Ballhaus. **VHS** *NYF*

Mother's Boys

Mother's Boys, deemed to be unworthy of an advance press screening and therefore destined for automatic box office failure, is, in fact, not a bad little film. It stars Jamie Lee Curtis as Jude, a deeply disturbed woman who's already abandoned her family twice and is now back for a third stab at re-engaging their affections. Her husband, Peter Gallagher, has finally adjusted to her departure and is trying to build a new life with Joanne Whalley, the assistant principal at the school attended by his three little boys. But 12-year-old Kes, the oldest son (extraordinarily well played by Luke Edwards), still yearns for the mother he adored as a small child. He acts out, sulks, and withdraws from the new life his father and brothers seem all too eager to lead. Kes is a sitting duck for the expert game player who knows how to manipulate his emotions better than anyone: Jude. We haven't seen much of Jamie Lee Curtis in the movie villain department, and she makes the most of her star turn here. She's smart, sexy, and cunning, but there's clearly something vital missing at the core of her personality. We don't know why she split for three years and neither does she. She invents reasons for her behavior that only SEEM to make sense; dig a little deeper and they're gobbledygook. Her mother, the wonderful Vanessa Redgrave, gives us a clue dating back to Jude's childhood, and considering all the grief Jude puts her kids through, it's more than evident that she's re-enacting painful rituals from her past. With enough well acted Sturm und Drang for several movies,

Mother's Boys plays quite well with an audience, including the one in your living room on a lazy Sunday afternoon. 🎬🎬🎬 **1994 (R) 96m/C** Jamie Lee Curtis, Peter Gallagher, Joanne Whalley, Luke Edwards, Vanessa Redgrave, Colin Ward, Joss Ackland, Paul Guilfoyle, John C. McGinley, J.E. Freeman, Ken Lerner, Lorraine Toussaint, Joey Zimmerman, Jill Freedman; **D:** Yves Simoneau; **W:** Richard Hawley, Barry Schneider; **C:** Elliot Davis; **M:** George S. Clinton. **VHS, LV, Closed Caption** MAX, TOU

Motorama

Motorama is a shapeless travelogue about a ten-year-old boy whose big dream is to collect all eight letters in the title so that he can compete for $500 million in a national contest. It turns out that the contest is full of hot air and so is the movie, in spite of all its stellar cameos (Shelley Berman, Martha Quinn, Michael J. Pollard, Drew Barrymore, etc.). The chief problem with *Motorama* is that its small protagonist doesn't get a chance to do much more than function as a mouthpiece for some half-baked observations about society by the so-called grownups who wrote and directed this mess. 🎬 **1991 (R) 89m/C** Jordan Christopher Michael, Martha Quinn, Flea, Michael J. Pollard, Meat Loaf, Drew Barrymore, Garrett Morris, Robin Duke, Sandy Baron, Mary Woronov, Susan Tyrrell, John Laughlin, John Diehl, Robert Picardo, Jack Nance, Vince Edwards, Dick Miller, Allyce Beasley, Shelley Berman; **D:** Barry Shils; **W:** Joe Minion; **M:** Andy Summers. **VHS** COL, BTV

Moulin Rouge

This is the movie that started me on a lifelong love affair with Henri De Toulouse-Lautrec (1864-1901), and once again, it was John Huston who ignited the affair, just as he had with Sam Spade and *The Maltese Falcon* on his very first assignment as a young director. *Moulin Rouge* was a nominee the year that Cecil B. De Mille's *The Greatest Show on Earth* won the Academy Award for Best Picture of 1952, even though Huston's recreation of

the Paris art scene of the 1890s is a far superior film. Jose Ferrer was also nominated for the physically painful role of the aristocratic Toulouse-Lautrec, who captured the gaiety of Montmartre night life, while moving through life with a sad, resigned dignity. Huston got a wonderful performance out of Colette Marchand, playing Marie Charlet, the young model who tormented Toulouse-Lautrec more out of personal desperation than any real malice. However, Toulouse-Lautrec's friendship with Myriamme Hayem (Suzanne Flon) seems to owe more to Pierre la Mure's novel than it does to reality. Certainly, some of the other colorful characters here played far more authentic roles in the artist's life. There really was a La Goulue (Katherine Kath), of course; her real name was Louise Weber (1870-1929), and Toulouse-Lautrec's posters of the dancer will long outlive them both. Jane Avril (1868-1943) survived a difficult childhood to become one of the great entertainers of her day. Zsa Zsa Gabor delivers one of her better performances as the charming dancer immortalized in Toulouse-Lautrec's posters. Toulouse-Lautrec's friend Maurice Joyant (1864-1930, played by Lee Montague) wrote one of the first biographies of the artist. Like Toulouse-Lautrec, Huston was well born, and both artists shared a deep passion for the truth plus a strong determination to establish their own reputations quite separate and apart from the circumstances of their birth. Both succeeded, although Toulouse-Lautrec undoubtedly paid the higher price. Huston lovingly recreates the Moulin Rouge in all its garish splendor, paying meticulous attention to the Technicolor process, trying to get every detail just right. (*Moulin Rouge* did win the Oscar for art direction and set decoration that year.) It's a sad, exquisite film of an irretrievably vanished era that still has the power to lure us into its spell, if only in our dreams. 🎬🎬🎬🎬

1952 119m/C Jose Ferrer, Zsa Zsa Gabor, Christopher Lee, Peter Cushing, Colette Marchand, Katherine Kath, Michael Balfour, Eric Pohlmann, Suzanne

Flon, Claude Nollier, Muriel Smith, Mary Clare, Walter Crisham, Harold Kasket, Jim Gerald, George Lannes, Lee Montague, Maureen Swanson, Tutte Lemkow, Jill Bennett, Theodore Bikel; **D:** John Huston; **W:** John Huston, Anthony Veiller; **C:** Oswald Morris. Academy Awards '52: Best Art Direction/Set Decoration (Color), Best Costume Design (Color); National Board of Review Awards '53: 5 Best Foreign Films of the Year; Nominations: Academy Awards '52: Best Actor (Ferrer), Best Director (Huston), Best Film Editing, Best Picture, Best Supporting Actress (Marchand). **VHS, Beta, LV** *MGM*

Mountains of the Moon

Mountains of the Moon, like many movies about explorers, raises an inevitable question: how would these sagas emerge if they had been told from the point of view of the natives rather than the outsiders who invaded their homelands? British explorers of the past were a stubborn lot, determined to impose inappropriate values and customs on uncharted territories even when it when meant the loss of lives and limbs. To his credit, director Bob Rafelson takes scrupulous care not to romanticize the conflicts and adventures of Richard Burton and John Speke, who sought a passage to the Nile in 1857. Rafelson's honest depiction of the physical hardships endured during the expedition is painfully real, especially during several intense and quite explicit sequences. Patrick Bergin and Iain Glen pull out all the stops as Burton and Speke and Richard E. Grant delivers another riveting performance as an Iago-like character who tries to drive them apart. Fiona Shaw creates a strong impression as Isabel Burton and Bernard Hill has a splendid cameo as Dr. Livingstone. We're still waiting for that movie from the natives' point of view, but in the meanwhile, *Mountains of the Moon* offers a masterful behind-the-scenes account of the dark and dazzling lives of 19th century explorers. Put Rafelson's epic on a triple bill with *Scott of the Antarctic* and *Burke and Wills* and you may wonder how Great Britain ever won a reputation as an empire builder. 🦴🦴🦴🦴

1990 m/C Patrick Bergin, Iain Glen, Richard E. Grant, Fiona Shaw, John Savident, James Villiers, Adrian Rawlins, Peter Vaughan, Delroy Lindo, Bernard Hill; **D:** Bob Rafelson; **W:** Bob Rafelson, William Harrison; **C:** Roger Deakins; **M:** Michael Small. **VHS, LV** *NYR*

Much Ado about Nothing

Kenneth Branagh wanted to breathe life into the works of William Shakespeare, and that he definitely has. This rambunctious romantic comedy is filled with fun and high spirits, not to mention four glittering American stars. Well, if Branagh had filled EVERY role with moonlighting actors from *Masterpiece Theatre,* you'd be looking at a movie that was at Cannes on April 15th and on PBS by April 22nd! Branagh and Emma Thompson are the battling Benedick and Beatrice and Robert Sean Leonard and Kate Beckinsale are the young lovers Claudio and Hero. Add Michael Keaton as Dogberry, Keanu Reeves as Don John, Denzel Washington as Don Pedro and then we can play! All this and the sunny scenery of Tuscany, too! 🦴🦴🦴

1993 (PG-13) 110m/C *GB* Kenneth Branagh, Emma Thompson, Robert Sean Leonard, Kate Beckinsale, Denzel Washington, Keanu Reeves, Michael Keaton, Brian Blessed, Phyllida Law, Imelda Staunton, Gerard Horan, Jimmy Yuill, Richard Clifford, Ben Elton, Richard Briers; **D:** Kenneth Branagh; **W:** Kenneth Branagh; **C:** Roger Lanser; **M:** Patrick Doyle. Nominations: Golden Globe Awards '94: Best Film—Musical/Comedy; Independent Spirit Awards '94: Best Actress (Thompson), Best Film. **VHS, LV, Closed Caption** *COL*

Murder on the Orient Express

Until *Murder on the Orient Express* was released, big screen adaptations of the works of Dame Agatha Christie (1890-1976) were few and far between. And then came this sumptuous production with a cast headed by 11 Oscar winners and/or nominees. Set in 1930, the plot focuses on a group of highly suspicious-looking passengers aboard the Orient Express (from the classy, gum-chewing Lauren Bacall to the nervous, newly married young Count played by Michael York). The real fun of this leisurely whodunit is guessing which screen legend will next appear. Albert Finney's makeup as Hercule Poirot was such a shock to 1974 audiences that it undoubtedly contributed to the Oscar nomination he won for his interpretation. One of the wittiest wisecracks belongs to Sir John Gielgud, perfecting his persona as a butler seven years before he won an Oscar for it in *Arthur.* Occasionally, it all gets to be a bit much; the late Ingrid Bergman won her third Oscar as a neurotic missionary, but who could believe her for one second in that role? Sidney Lumet's direction and Geoffrey Unsworth's cinematography add to the overall elegance, and mysterious, creepily shot flashbacks are used to focus on details relevant to the crime-solving. Followed by another adaptation of a Poirot novel by Christie, 1978's *Death on the Nile,* with Sir Peter Ustinov assuming the role of the Belgian detective. 🦴🦴🦴

1974 (PG) 128m/C *GB* Albert Finney, Martin Balsam, Ingrid Bergman, Lauren Bacall, Sean Connery, Richard Widmark, Anthony Perkins, John Gielgud, Jacqueline Bisset, Jean-Pierre Cassel, Wendy Hiller, Rachel Roberts, Vanessa Redgrave, Michael York, Colin Blakely, George Coulouris, Denis Quilley, Vernon Dobtcheff, Jeremy Lloyd; **D:** Sidney Lumet; **W:** Paul Dehn; **C:** Geoffrey Unsworth; **M:** Richard Rodney Bennett. Academy Awards '74: Best Supporting Actress (Bergman); British Academy Awards '74: Best Supporting Actor (Gielgud), Best Supporting Actress (Bergman); National Board of Review Awards '74: 10 Best Films of the Year; Nominations: Academy Awards '74: Best Actor (Finney), Best Adapted Screenplay, Best Cinematography, Best Costume Design, Best Original Score. **VHS, Beta, LV** *PAR, BTV*

Muriel's Wedding

An unusual friendship is explored in the Australian entry by P. J. Hogan, *Muriel's Wedding.* Muriel (Toni Collette) is a chunky young woman who dreams of a lavish wedding and warm acceptance from a clique who reject her at every opportunity. Muriel is also a compulsive liar and a thief who thinks nothing of feeding her unrealistic dreams with a string of deceptions. While on holiday, she meets the hedonistic, chain-smoking Rhonda (newcomer Rachel Griffiths), who thinks nothing of blasting the exclusive clique with the truth, and who clearly adores Muriel on sight. Of course, Truth wins the day in this extremely uneven film; key sequences appear to have wound up on the cutting room floor, diminishing the overall dramatic impact, and even fine acting by Collette can't make Muriel a truly riveting central character. The scene stealer in this one is the luminous Griffiths; we found ourselves wishing that the movie had revolved around Rhonda instead of Muriel, and missed her every second she was off-screen. International filmmakers, take note! 🦴🦴🦴

1994 (R) 105m/C *AU* Toni Collette, Bill Hunter, Rachel Griffiths, Jeanie Drynan, Gennie Nevinson Brice, Matt Day, Sophie Lee, Rosalind Hammond, Belinda Jarrett, Daniel Lapaine; **D:** P.J. Hogan; **W:** P.J. Hogan; **M:** Peter Best. Australian Film Institute '94: Best Actress (Collette), Best Film, Best Sound, Best Supporting Actress (Griffiths); Nominations: Australian Film Institute '94: Best Director (Hogan), Best Screenplay, Best Supporting Actor (Hunter), Best Supporting Actress (Drynan); British Academy Awards '95: Best Original Screenplay; Golden Globe Awards '96: Best Actress—Musical/Comedy (Collette); Writers Guild of America '95: Best Original Screenplay. **VHS, LV, Closed Caption** *MAX*

Murmur of the Heart

You can make a comedy about any subject, but getting audiences to watch it is a whole other problem. In 1971, Louis Malle wrote and directed *Murmur of the Heart,* about a young boy with a heart condition who winds up in bed with his ravishing mother. The French Movie Commission wanted to ban the film, but later decided to restrict attendance to adult audiences. Those who actually saw the movie in France and America

loved it, but *Murmur* was then, and remains today, a classic seen by very few people. Only an artist like the late Louis Malle could attempt such a tricky project, much less get away with it. The director wisely decides to stick with the kid and we see his life through his eyes. Because of his delicate condition, he is an outsider. Because his mother is an Italian married to a Frenchman, her status is also that of an outsider. When they go off to the country together for his health, their shared isolation forces him to see her as a person rather than as only his mother. His charming Mama (wonderfully played by Lea Massari) is pretty much of a mystery, but it's obvious that she's a good soul and so is her son. Nothing very tragic is going to come of anything that happens between these two. The director knows exactly when enough is enough, throughout the entire narrative. There isn't an image, a gesture, or a line that's even

mildly gratuitous. The first time you see *Murmur,* you may watch the proceedings wondering when the director is going to stumble. He never does. The second time you see it, it'll be obvious that all Malle's skill went into developing his likable characters and their unusual situation. The comic outcome, improbable in real life, works beautifully as a film fantasy. 🦴🦴🦴🦴

1971 (R) 118m/C *FR* Benoit Ferreux, Daniel Gelin, Lea Massari, Corinne Kersten, Jacqueline Chauveau, Marc Wincourt, Michael Lonsdale; *D:* Louis Malle; *W:* Louis Malle. Nominations: Academy Awards '72: Best Story & Screenplay; Cannes Film Festival '71: Best Film. **VHS, Beta, LV** *ORI*

Mushrooms

Alan Madden's *Mushrooms* shows how two dotty best friends cover up the accidental death of their lodger. They absolutely HAVE to do that with a cop in the house as their other lodger. The cop's in love with one of them, but that won't help them unless they can cook up a sure-fire scheme...that's it! How could it fail to work? This dark comedy from Australia is a gem. 🎵🎵🎵

1995 93m/C *AU* Julia Blake, Simon Chilvers, Lynette Curran, Christina Andersson; **D:** Alan Madden; **W:** Alan Madden; **C:** Louis Irving; **M:** Paul Grabowsky. *NYR*

My Beautiful Laundrette

My Beautiful Laundrette was a landmark film for Daniel Day-Lewis, Stephen Frears, and Hanif Kureishi, but not alas, for the appealing Gordon Warnecke, who plays Omar, the central character. (He would make an appearance, along with Fergie impersonator Pippa Hinchley, in Kureishi's *London Kills Me* six years later.) Omar remodels a seedy laundry with his friend Johnny (Day-Lewis) and they turn it into a stylish money-maker. The stunner for international audiences of 1985 was that Frears revealed the expression of Omar's and Johnny's sexuality in such unstressed fashion. And because it is unstressed, its impact on gay cinema was enormous. Prior to *Laundrette,* a gay relationship in a movie was either A Joke or A Big Deal. In *Laundrette,* it was neither. It was simply a part of the story. Kureishi's screenplay pays far more attention to how and where Pakistani workers fit into the conservative British economy that endured from 1979-97. (By stunning coincidence, it was a time when the Royal Family acted out the most, perhaps functioning as distracting national jesters for Mrs. Thatcher and Mr. Major?) Also included is a demonstration of how magic effects the affair of Omar's married uncle and his lady friend Rachel (Shirley Anne Field), who sighs, "Your wife is a very clever woman." A rich, meticulously rendered film with a marvelous cast. Cast note: Day-Lewis, the son of Poet-Laureate Cecil Day-Lewis and actress Jill Balcon, made his film debut at age 14 in *Sunday Bloody Sunday.* He married writer/director Rebecca (1994's *Angela*) Miller after appearing in the 1996 film of playwright Arthur Miller's *The Crucible.* 🎵🎵🎵🎵

1985 (R) 93m/C *GB* Gordon Warnecke, Daniel Day-Lewis, Saeed Jaffrey, Roshan Seth, Shirley Anne Field, Derrick Branche, Rita Wolf, Souad Faress, Richard Graham, Dudley Thomas, Garry Cooper, Charu Bala Choksi, Neil Cunningham, Walter Donohue, Stephen Marcus, Badi Uzzaman; **D:** Stephen Frears; **W:** Hanif Kureishi; **C:** Oliver Stapleton; **M:** Ludus Tonalis, Stanley Myers. National Board of Review Awards '86: Best Supporting Actor (Day-Lewis); New York Film Critics Awards '86: Best Screenplay, Best Supporting Actor (Day-Lewis); National Society of Film Critics Awards '86: Best Screenplay; Nominations: Academy Awards '86: Best Original Screenplay. **VHS, Beta, LV, Closed Caption** *ORI, WAR*

My Family

I first became of aware of filmmakers Anna Thomas and Gregory Nava in 1981 when I saw Thomas' *The Haunting of M,* a Scottish ghost story starring Shelagh Gilbey as Marianna and Nina Pitt as her sister. I haven't been able to get the film out of my head, although sadly, I've never been able to find it on cable or video. The idea then was that Thomas and Nava would alternate as writers and directors. The following year, they both wrote *End of August,* which IS on video, but not in my neck of the woods. I'd like to see it if only to compare it with 1992's *Grand Isle,* since they're both based on Kate Chopin's *The Awakening. El Norte* was their breakthrough film (which Nava directed), then came (yuck) *A Time of Destiny* (which Nava directed) and THEN came *My Family* (which Nava directed). My question is: when am I going to see a movie helmed by Anna Thomas, reflecting HER experiences and HER interests? Yes, she's been a screenwriter on all of the above movies, but *The Haunting of M* had a look and feel quite different from any of the projects she's worked on since. *My Family* is a good, well acted, multi-generational saga, but the emphasis is on the patriarchal, rather than the matriarchal line of the Sanchez family. First we see Jose (Jacob Vargas, Eduardo

Lopez Rojas), then we see Jose's son Chucho (Esai Morales), then we see Jose's younger son Jimmy (Jonathan Hernandez, Jimmy Smits), then we see yet another son, Memo (Enrique Castillo), and so on.... Their trials and tribulations dominate the 126-minute running time. AND it's narrated by a writer named Paco (Edward James Olmos). Who are the women in this story? There's Jose's wife Maria (Jennifer Lopez, Jenny Gago), who has six kids. There's daughter Irene (Maria Canals, Lupe Ontiveros), who gets married and runs a restaurant, and daughter Toni (Constance Marie), who becomes a nun and a political activist. There's Jimmy's wife Isabel (Edpidio Carillo) who has his son. But the only moments of any real drama in their lives occur when Maria and baby Chucho survive the river rapids on a raft, and when Toni protects Isabel from the death squads of El Salvador. Otherwise, whether the Sanchez boys are good or bad, the story line remains focused on THEM and the melodramatic twists and turns of THEIR lives. In that respect, *My Family* is evocative of the long-running radio soap opera *One Man's Family,* which ran for 27 years. (PLEASE direct another movie, Ms. Thomas!) *AKA:* Mi Familia. ♫♫♪

1994 (R) 126m/C Jimmy Smits, Esai Morales, Eduardo Lopez Rojas, Jenny Gago, Elpidia Carrillo, Lupe Ontiveros, Jacob Vargas, Jennifer Lopez, Scott Bakula, Edward James Olmos, Michael De Lorenzo, Maria Canals, Leon Singer, Jonathan Hernandez, Constance Marie, Enrique Castillo, Mary Steenburgen; **D:** Gregory Nava; **W:** Gregory Nava, Anna Thomas; **C:** Edward Lachman; **M:** Pepe Avila, Mark McKenzie. Nominations: Academy Awards '95: Best Makeup; Independent Spirit Awards '96: Best Actor (Smits), Best Supporting Actress (Lopez). **VHS, LV, Closed Caption** *NLC, TTC*

My Left Foot

Daniel Day-Lewis was a sure bet for an Academy Award from the instant audiences first saw him as Christy Brown. *My Left Foot,* a splendid film written and directed by Jim Sheridan, is based on the book by Brown, who refused to let a major obstacle like cerebral palsy prevent him from achiev-

ing recognition as an artist and a writer. The key to Brown's success, the film makes clear, is largely due to the efforts of his loving, no-nonsense Irish mother, briskly played by Oscar winner Brenda Fricker. Brown grew up in a large, rambunctious family who included him in every group activity. The Browns are dirt poor, headed by a boozy and often harsh father (subtly played by the late Ray McAnally). Nonetheless, Brown receives constant encouragement and plenty of love until finally he finds a way to communicate with his left foot. Later, he receives speech lessons and artistic encouragement from Dr. Eileen Cole (sympathetically portrayed by Fiona Shaw) who helps to organize his first one-man show. Later, he initiates a wholehearted romantic pursuit of his attractive nurse Mary (Ruth McCabe, in a devilish performance). The whole story, which might have been pure goo in the hands of a sentimental director, is presented with matter-of-fact vigor by Day-Lewis and director Sheridan. Many of the best and funniest lines in this delightful movie are unquotable and you'll want to discover them for yourselves, anyway. ♫♫♫♫

1989 (R) 103m/C *IR* Daniel Day-Lewis, Brenda Fricker, Ray McAnally, Cyril Cusack, Fiona Shaw, Hugh O'Conor, Adrian Dunbar, Ruth McCabe, Alison Whelan; **D:** Jim Sheridan; **W:** Shane Connaughton, Jim Sheridan; **M:** Elmer Bernstein. Academy Awards '89: Best Actor (Day-Lewis), Best Supporting Actress (Fricker); British Academy Awards '89: Best Actor (Day-Lewis), Best Supporting Actor (McAnally); Independent Spirit Awards '90: Best Foreign Film; Los Angeles Film Critics Association Awards '89: Best Actor (Day-Lewis), Best Supporting Actress (Fricker); Montreal World Film Festival '89: Best Actor (Day-Lewis); New York Film Critics Awards '89: Best Actor (Day-Lewis), Best Film; National Society of Film Critics Awards '89: Best Actor (Day-Lewis); Nominations: Academy Awards '89: Best Adapted Screenplay, Best Director (Sheridan), Best Picture. **VHS, Beta, LV, Closed Caption** *HBO, BTV, HMV*

My Life As a Dog

This sweet little film is about a boy of 12 (Anton Glanzelius) who is sent to stay with relatives during his mother's illness. It's set in 1950s Sweden and is filled with colorful village characters and an irresistible tomboy with whom he tumbles into as much puppy love as he can handle at that age. The unexpected success of *My Life As a Dog* stunned exhibitors and woke up U.S. producers; Lasse Hallstrom was welcomed to Hollywood to make *Once Around, What's Eating Gilbert Grape?*, and *Something to Talk About*. **AKA:** Mitt Liv Som Hund. 🦴🦴🦴🦴

1985 101m/C *SW* Anton Glanzelius, Tomas Van Bromssen, Anki Liden, Melinda Kinnaman, Kicki Rundgren, Ing-mari Carlsson; *D:* Lasse Hallstrom. Golden Globe Awards '88: Best Foreign Film; Independent Spirit Awards '88: Best Foreign Film; New York Film Critics Awards '87: Best Foreign Film; Nominations: Academy Awards '87: Best Adapted Screenplay, Best Director (Hallstrom). **VHS, Beta, LV** *PAR, HMV*

My Own Private Idaho

Zzzzzz...Of course, I didn't know at the time that I was watching self-destruction in action, I thought I was just watching a couple of actors delivering dialogue that was written for them by the director. Even if I had known what was going to happen in front of the Viper Club in the wee hours of Halloween, 1993, my reaction to *My Own Private Idaho* would still be zzzzzz.... There's a very long, very boring gay version of Shakespeare's *Henry IV* here that you have to fidget through or leave. Major critics raved about the performance of River Phoenix, then 21, as a narcoleptic gay hustler, but any of his performances from 1985's *Explorers* through 1991's *Dogfight* are better. Reportedly, his serious involvement with drugs began with this picture and in two of his last three films his performances were way out of control. In any event, both Keanu Reeves and River Phoenix had the burden of bringing Gus Van Sant's screenplay to life, and it couldn't have been easy. This will remain a cult film no matter what anyone says about it, like James Dean's auto safety spot with Gig Young and Tyrone

Power's public service message about preventing heart disease. 🦴🦴

1991 (R) 105m/C River Phoenix, Keanu Reeves, James Russo, William Richert, Rodney Harvey, Michael Parker, Flea, Chiara Caselli, Udo Kier, Grace Zabriskie, Tom Troupe; *D:* Gus Van Sant; *W:* Gus Van Sant; *C:* John Campbell, Eric Alan Edwards. Independent Spirit Awards '92: Best Actor (Phoenix), Best Screenplay; National Society of Film Critics Awards '91: Best Actor (Phoenix). **VHS, LV, Closed Caption** *COL, NLC*

Mystery of the Last Tsar

This watchable but sketchy film arrives on the heels of two superior documentaries, *Last of the Tsars* and *The Last Days of the Last Tsar*; it incorporates footage from *Days* that reconstructs the slaughter of the Romanov family at Ekaterinburg. The screenwriter is Peter Kurth, author of the well written but now debunked *Anastasia: The Riddle of Anna Anderson*. Kurth got caught up in the long-running fantasy that the child of a Polish factory worker was actually the youngest daughter of Nicholas and Alexandra. (His book, which may now be filed under the F for Fiction section of your neighborhood library, was the basis for NBC's 1986 fairy tale, *Anastasia: The Mystery of Anna* starring Amy Irving as the would-be Grand Duchess and Olivia De Havilland as Marie, Claire Bloom as Alexandra, Omar Sharif as Nicholas, Rex Harrison as Cyril, and Christian Bale as Alexei.) It's a legend that refuses to die, especially since the remains of Anastasia and Alexei have yet to be found. However, since *The Mystery of the Last Tsar* identifies itself as a documentary, one might wish that facts AND speculations were not given equal (and confusing) weight. But then, even the surviving Romanovs cannot agree about who the "real" successor to Nicholas II is or is not. The most engaging moments are supplied by family members who bicker about what "roles" they should play in contemporary Russia and who are most "qualified" to play those roles. Playwright Edvard Radzinsky describes the

INDEPENDENT FILM GUIDE

death scene as if he were hyping a lavish theatrical production. Historian Robert Massie and forensic pathologist Dr. William H. Maples offer more reflective and sober commentary, but there's no getting around the fact that this is a bit of a re-hash, designed for casual viewers with only the mildest interest in the subject matter. On a more compelling note, an animated version of *Anastasia* was scheduled for imminent release at press time, with accompanying doll and other assorted tie-in merchandise especially for little would-be grand duchesses everywhere. ♫♫♡

1997 77m/C D: Victoria Lewis; **W:** Peter Kurth; **C:** Michael Anderson, Chris Li; **M:** Caleb Sampson, John Kusiak. *NYR*

Mystic Pizza

This charming story about three teenage girls growing up in Mystic, Connecticut,

won its director a Best First Film prize at 1989's Independent Spirit Awards. With that sort of encouragement, better movies were expected of director Donald Petrie than *Opportunity Knocks, The Favor, Grumpy Old Men,* and *Richie Rich.* But back in Mystic, the characters played by Annabeth Gish, Julia Roberts, and Lili Taylor are protected in a time capsule as best friends forever. There are wonderful performances, too, from Vincent D'Onofrio as Taylor's boyfriend, William R. Moses as the quintessential married man who's playing both ends against the middle (and who's Such A Nice Guy to Gish's naive babysitter), and from the great character actress Conchata Ferrell. The perceptive script by Amy Holden Jones (who went on to write *Beethoven, Indecency, The Getaway,* and *Indecent Proposal*—hmm...do we see a trend here when fine indie artists go to Hollywood?) nails down the restless atmosphere of young women itching to leave the over-familiar surroundings in which they grew up, but filled with nostalgia for the associations that made their childhood bearable. ♫♫♫

1988 (R) 101m/C Annabeth Gish, Julia Roberts, Lili Taylor, Vincent D'Onofrio, William R. Moses, Adam Storke, Conchata Ferrell, Joanna Merlin; **D:** Donald Petrie; **W:** Amy Holden Jones, Perry Howze, Alfred Uhry; **M:** David McHugh. Independent Spirit Awards '89: Best First Feature. **VHS, Beta, LV, Closed Caption** *VTR*

Nadja

Abel Ferrara's *The Addiction* flops because he wanted to make a movie about vampires that wasn't a vampire movie. Doncha just hate filmmakers who consider that genre to be beneath them? (Hey, anyone who makes a frozen turkey like *Fear City* has no right to sneer at time-honored bloodsuckers.) Michael Almereyda's *Nadja* is another story. *Nadja* is fun! Let's face it, any movie that was partly shot in Pixelvision with a Fisher Price toy camera AND casts Professor Peter Fonda as Dr. Van Helsing (in the venerable tradition of Edward van Sloan) has got to be a kick. When a drained Lucy (Galaxy Craze) explains that she ate a bag of M & M's except for the yellow ones and Fonda vigorously intones to his nephew, "Let's face it, Jim, she's a zombie!," it can't help being a kick and a half. The title character (played by Elina Lowensohn) looks sorta like Gale Sondergaard, Gloria Holden, and Frida Kahlo all rolled into one. Her twin brother Edgar (Jared Harris) is one of those nice vampires who only wants to get married to his nurse Cassandra (Suzy Amis) and live happily ever after. Clearly made on the cheap, *Nadja* is nonetheless impressively atmospheric and saucily respectful to vampires. ♫♫♫

1995 (R) 92m/B Elina Lowensohn, Suzy Amis, Galaxy Craze, Martin Donovan, Peter Fonda, Karl Geary, Jared Harris; **Cameos:** David Lynch; **D:** Michael Almereyda; **W:** Michael Almereyda; **C:** Jim Denault; **M:** Simon Fisher Turner. Nominations: Independent Spirit Awards '96: Best Actress (Lowensohn), Best Cinematography, Best Director (Almereyda). **VHS** *HMK*

Naked

For Mike Leigh fans, *Naked* is a Must-See Movie. For yours truly, it is 131 minutes of talking, only 11 minutes less than *Secrets and Lies*. It's the story of a man named Johnny (David Thewlis) who talk-talk-talks his way through the flick and eventually is beaten up. See *Secrets and Lies* review for the reason why I am the Last Person on Earth to be writing one syllable about ANY Mike Leigh movie (although Thewlis is no less an actor here than he is in *Black Beauty, Restoration, The Island of Dr. Moreau*, etc.). **AKA:** Mike Leigh's Naked. ♫♫℣

1993 (R) 131m/C *GB* David Thewlis, Lesley Sharp, Katrin Cartlidge, Greg Cruttwell, Claire Skinner, Peter Wight, Ewen Bremmer, Susan Vidler, Deborah MacLaren, Gina McKee; **D:** Mike Leigh; **W:** Mike Leigh; **C:** Dick Pope; **M:** Andrew Dickson. Cannes Film Festival '93: Best Actor (Thewlis), Best Director (Leigh); New York Film Critics Awards '93: Best Actor (Thewlis); National Society of Film Critics Awards '93: Best Actor (Thewlis); Nominations: British Academy Awards '93: Best Film; Independent Spirit Awards '94: Best Foreign Film. **VHS, LV** *COL, IME*

The Nasty Girl

The Nasty Girl is an irreverent film about a serious (and true) subject: how one Bavarian town reacted when a young girl tried to investigate its history during the Third Reich. Lena Stolze is an enchanting presence as Sonja, a much-loved and much-honored young scholar who is vilified when she starts digging into her home town's past. Initially, she believes her community to be filled with citizens who resisted National Socialism, but her research indicates otherwise. The people who seem to be most concerned by her investigation are her parent's generation, her husband, and teenagers. All of them are too young to be much threatened by old scandals, but threatened they definitely are, and Sonja is the recipient of bureaucratic harassment, family pressures, and anonymous persecution. Director Michael Verhoeven adds many unsettling touches, some which

The Hound Salutes:
MICHAEL ALMEREYDA AND PETER FONDA
Nadja

Michael Almereyda: "I wanted to make a horror movie. I started with that, and I was rummaging around, and the appealing thing about vampires is that they're the most modern and human monsters of all the myths and legends in horror movies that seemed the most appealing, and the most accessible to me. So, it wasn't much of a leap to try to take that story and put it in New York and try and re-imagine it in those terms."

Peter Fonda: "With Michael Almereyda's direction, the way the script was and the way I prepared the [Van Helsing] role I didn't play it funny. I played it as straight as I could. As a matter of fact, I would take it more and more down as we'd go through a different take. I'd try and flatten everything out—the whole idea was not to be acting. So there's some moments when I had to come up and be a little manic, and it's startling and funny when I do the stuff with the glasses and things like that. But the rest of it, I'm not acting at all, I'm just doing this straight character, and the most normal thing in life is to stake these creatures. That's what I am up to, and that's all I have ever done. The weird part is that I would not normally be called upon to do this role. Given the band of actors who have played this role, more people would think of me as riding a motorcycle and smoking a joint and that's the end of the conversation.... I didn't think about it while I was doing it as funny. Every time we'd finish I would be cracking up because it was so off the wall. The dialogue is wonderful; Michael Almereyda writes great dialogue and great characters. All you have to do is play it. It's a dream for an actor."

MICHAEL ALMEREYDA also wrote and directed 1989's *Twister.* His screenplays include 1988's *Cherry 2000* and 1994's *Search and Destroy.*

PETER FONDA received the best reviews of his career for his performance in 1997's *Ulee's Gold,* directed by Victor Nunez. Other Peter Fonda films: *Tammy and the Doctor, Lilith, The Wild Angels, The Trip, Spirits of the Dead, Easy Rider, Hired Hand, The Last Movie, Dirty Mary Crazy Larry, Killer Force, Race with the Devil, Fighting Mad, Futureworld, 92 in the Shade, Outlaw Blues, High Ballin', Wanda Nevada, The Hostage Tower, Cannonball Run, Spasms, Split Image, Jungle Heat, Certain Fury, Hawken's Breed, Mercenary Fighters, Fatal Mission, The Rose Garden, South Beach, Deadfall, Love and a .45, Molly and Gina,* and *Escape from L.A.*

work, some which don't. The backgrounds for many of the sequences are black-and-white stills from the wartime period or color footage of the town itself, presumably to remind us of the emotional landscapes Sonja is revealing. Sonja's childhood, of course, is shot in crisp black and white until she falls in love and her world is seen in vivid colors. (Filmmakers tend to see the past in black and white even though Technicolor has been around since 1917!) Lena Stolze plays Sonja from the years 1976 to 1990 when she ages from the oldest-looking 12 year old in the world to an extremely young-looking woman in her middle 20s. In fact, Sonja's chief adversary is supposed to have been a clergyman in 1936, when the actor playing the role looks like HE night have been all of 12 years old! Because of Verhoeven's excellent intentions, terrific pacing, and quirky viewpoint, the film can be forgiven for a confusing time line and narrative lapses. The enormously appealing personality of Stolze is what you'll remember most about *The Nasty Girl,* especially in Sonja's scenery-chewing finale. 🦴🦴🦴

1990 (PG-13) 93m/C *GE* Lena Stolze, Monika Baumgartner, Michael Gahr; *D:* Michael Verhoeven; *W:* Michael Verhoeven. British Academy Awards '91: Best Foreign Film; New York Film Critics Awards '90: Best Foreign Film; Nominations: Academy Awards '90: Best Foreign Language Film. **VHS** *HBO*

Never Take Candy from a Stranger

This low-key little film was released without fanfare and has no reputation whatever, but it offers an intelligent look at child molestation, especially for its era. Janina Faye and Frances Green play Jean and Lucille, two nine-year-old girls who dance naked for Mr. Olderberry after he promises to give them candy. When Jean tells her mother (Gwen Watford) about it that night, her father (Patrick Allen) tries to resolve the matter with the old man's son (Bill Nagy). But then Jean has a nightmare and her father reports

the incident to Captain Hammond (Bud Knapp), who refuses to do anything because, even though the old man is a chronic offender, he IS the town founder. The captain even suggests that the family might be happier elsewhere. The movie reveals that resolving such matters in court is of little avail, at least in 1960. Lucille's parents spirit her out of town for the duration, so Jean is all alone on the stand. Jean's parents finally agree that they WOULD be happier elsewhere and decide to move. But first, Jean goes over to Lucille's house to say goodbye and the two little girls stroll over to Moon Lake. The chilling conclusion leaves the viewer in no doubt whatever about the severity of child molestation. The fact that the molester is played by the venerable Felix Aylmer (1889-1979), who usually plays judges and other benign authority figures, drives home the point that the molester MUST be dealt with directly, not tolerated, regardless of his community standing. This is still strong stuff now; in the Eisenhower era, *Never Take Candy from a Stranger* didn't have a chance. I've yet to meet anyone who's ever seen it, even though it IS on video. Freddie Francis, who won the Oscar that year for *Sons and Lovers* and who would photograph *The Innocents* the following year, does a superb job here, especially in the gripping Moon Lake sequence. Faye, Watford, and Allen are very good as Jean and her parents, and Aylmer is downright spooky! Based on Roger Caris' play, *The Pony Cart.* 🦴🦴🦴

1960 81m/B *GB* Gwen Watford, Patrick Allen, Felix Aylmer, Niall MacGinnis, Alison Leggatt, Bill Nagy, MacDonald Parke, Michael Gwynn, Bud Knapp, Janina Faye, Frances Green, James Dyrenforth, Estelle Brody, Robert Arden, Vera Cook; *D:* Cyril Frankel; *W:* John Hunter; *C:* Freddie Francis; *M:* Elizabeth Luytens. **VHS** *NYR*

New Jersey Drive

Another depressing movie about a youth gang. This group steals cars. Although praised for its realism, the film depicts all

INDEPENDENT FILM GUIDE

Nico Icon

While watching Susanne Ofteringer's *Nico Icon*, we kept asking ourselves, "Why the heck did she make a documentary about THIS thumping bore of a mannequin whose chief distinction was looking good in designer originals and whose toneless singing voice appealed mainly to audiences who must have been as strung out on heroin as she was?!" If you're going to make a movie about a one-time junkie, why not an interesting and outrageous one like Marianne Faithfull, who could and can act and sing rings around Nico, and is still alive!? Hmmm...maybe that's it. Maybe the fact that Nico DIED after falling off a bicycle in the south of France made the storyline simple: "Beautiful Selfish Model Sleeps with Famous Men (Alain Delon, Jim Morrison, Jackson Browne) and Goes to Hell, But Not Before She Shares Her Legacy with Her Son by Turning Him on to Heroin." Four of the voices in Jean Stein's biography of Edie Sedgwick are also in *Nico Icon* (Danny Fields, Paul Morrisey, Billy Name, Viva). Does that mean we can expect more unriveting movies on all the other non-luminaries in Andy Warhol's Factory? Hope not! At least this story of a woman who loved no one (and vice versa) is short. And the archival footage may be of some interest if you happen to be a '60s clipaholic. Yeah, if we get to vote on a movie about a '60s icon, please make a great one about super diva Marianne Faithfull and let Rosanna Arquette be the star! Faithfull's live concerts (with songs from Noel Coward, Harry Nilsson, and Kurt Weill) are something to see, hear, and treasure well into the 21st century! 🎵🎵

1995 (R) 75m/C *GE* **D:** Susanne Ofteringer; **W:** Susanne Ofteringer. **VHS** *NYR*

the cops as (white, male) villains and all the car thieves as unrepentant criminals, so there's no one you can really root for. The acting is good (Gabriel Casseus received a nomination for his debut performance as Midget at the Sundance Film Festival), but the pervasive mood is one of total despair, unrelieved by any remedy except LEAVING. Spike Lee served as executive producer. 🎵🎵

1995 (R) 98m/C Sharron Corley, Gabriel Casseus, Saul Stein, Andre Moore, Donald A. Faison, Conrad Meertin Jr., Deven Eggleston, Gwen McGee, Koran C. Thomas, Samantha Brown, Christine Baranski, Robert Jason Jackson, Roscoe Orman, Dwight Errington Myers, Gary DeWitt Marshall; **D:** Nick Gomez; **W:** Nick Gomez, Michel Marriott; **C:** Adam Kimmel; **M:** Wendy Blackstone. Nominations: Independent Spirit Awards '96: Debut Performance (Casseus). **VHS, LV, Closed Caption** *USH*

Night on Earth

Jim Jarmusch shows five different taxi drivers and their passengers in Los Angeles, New York, Paris, Rome, and Helsinki, all on the same night on Earth. Winona Ryder as Corky the cabbie and Gena Rowlands as Victoria Snelling the Los Angeles casting agent work extremely well together in their segment, as do Giancarlo Esposito as YoYo the Brooklyn cabbie and Armin Mueller-Stahl as his East German passenger, Helmut. Highly recommended for Jarmusch fans, pretty good for everyone else. 🦴🦴▽

1991 (R) 125m/C Winona Ryder, Gena Rowlands, Giancarlo Esposito, Armin Mueller-Stahl, Rosie Perez, Beatrice Dalle, Roberto Benigni, Paolo Bonacelli, Matti Pellonpaa, Kari Vaananen, Sakari Kuosmanen, Tomi Salmela, Lisanne Falk, Isaach de Bankole, Alan Randolph Scott, Anthony Portillo, Richard Boes, Pascal Nzonzi, Emile Abossolo-M'Bo; **D:** Jim Jarmusch; **W:** Jim Jarmusch; **C:** Frederick Elmes; **M:** Tom Waits, Kathleen Brennan. Independent Spirit Awards '93: Best Cinematography. **VHS, LV** NLC, FAF

Night Tide

If the '60s had been the '40s and Curtis Harrington had had his way, he would have become a film director in the dark, brooding style of his idol, Val Lewton. With the explosion of color film in the mid-'60s, that didn't quite happen, and Harrington did the best he could with television movies like *How Awful About Allan, The Cat Creature,* and *Killer Bees,* plus the occasional offbeat theatrical feature. But in 1963, he was permitted one chance to make a black-and-white classic: *Night Tide.* Clearly inspired by *The Cat People,* this haunting love story stars an impossibly young-looking Dennis Hopper as a naive sailor who falls in love with a mysterious mermaid at a seaside carnival. Hopper not only looks like a baby here, he's so painfully vulnerable, it's hard to believe that he could play a grungy, lived-in *Easy Rider* within six years of this film. The late Luana Anders, another future cast member of *Easy Rider,* is the nice normal girl who supplies chilling commentary on Hopper's dark-eyed seductress Linda Lawson. While Harrington is deeply sympathetic to the dilemma faced by his central characters, he effectively contrasts their romance with graphic nightmare fantasies.

Night Tide is THE perfect film to watch on a dark and stormy night. 🦴🦴🦴

1963 84m/B Dennis Hopper, Gavin Muir, Luana Anders, Marjorie Eaton, Tom Dillon; **D:** Curtis Harrington. **VHS** SNC, FRG, TPV

A Night to Remember

Eva Hart (1905-96) thought that of all the movies made about the Titanic, *A Night to Remember* came the closest to capturing those last few hours aboard the "unsinkable" ship, and Miss Hart ought to know; as a seven-year-old child, she was saved from drowning by her no-nonsense mother, Esther, but her father Benjamin went down with the ship. The large cast is upstaged by the White Star liner, but there are some unforgettable moments here by some very fine actors. Michael Goodliffe (1914-76) as Titanic designer Thomas Andrews gives a performance of such agonized restraint that it's almost impossible to believe that he's acting. Courteous and gracious nearly to the end, only a flicker of his dark eyes betrays the horror that he takes such pains to conceal. George Rose (1920-88) as Charles Joghlin does absolutely everything wrong, yet he is said to have survived his many hours paddling in the Atlantic because the massive quantities of alcohol he consumed served as a sort of anti-freeze. (Remember that if you're ever on the world's "safest" cruise.) Honor Blackman was still an English rose at this stage of her career (no leather on A-deck), but acquits herself admirably as a first class passenger who must confront the reality of instant widowhood. Kenneth More (1914-82) was at the height of his popularity, so who better to play Herbert Lightoller, who enforced the policy of "women and children first" and then managed to swim to safety? If there were villains of the piece besides arrogance, carelessness, and neglect, Bruce Ismay (played as "The Chairman" by Frank Lawton, 1904-69), who urged that the Titanic beat some sort of speed record through

The Earl of Warwick (Cedric Hardwicke) and Lady Jane Grey (Nova Pilbeam) in *Nine Days a Queen.*

The Earl of Warwick
(Cedric Hardwicke)
and Lady Jane Grey
(Nova Pilbeam) in
Nine Days a Queen.

the icy waters, Phillips (Kenneth Griffith), who ignored ice warning after ice warning all day Sunday, and Captain Lord (Laurence Naismith, 1908-92), who went to bed early while the Titanic sent repeated distress signals less than ten miles away, top the list of the usual suspects. *A Night to Remember,* with its contracting perspectives of useless opulence and imminent mortality, makes April 15, 1912, seem like yesterday, not over 85 years in the past. ♪♪♪♪

1958 119m/B Kenneth More, David McCallum, Anthony Bushell, Honor Blackman, Michael Goodliffe, George Rose, Laurence Naismith, Frank Lawton, Alec McCowen, Jill Dixon, John Cairney, Joseph Tomelty, Jack Watling, Richard Clarke, Ralph Michael, Kenneth Griffith; *D:* Roy Ward Baker; *W:* Eric Ambler; *C:* Geoffrey Unsworth. Golden Globe Awards '59: Best Foreign Film; National Board of Review Awards '58: 5 Best Foreign Films of the Year. **VHS, Beta, LV** *PAR, HMV*

Night Train to Munich

The essence of the very British *Night Train to Munich* is captured in the comic performances of Basil Radford and Naunton Wayne, reprising their roles in *The Lady Vanishes* as Charters and Caldicott. Working with a tight script by Frank Launder and Sidney Gilliat, Sir Carol Reed skillfully reveals how ordinary people react to war. Faced with an international crisis, Charters tries to call Berlin to retrieve the golf clubs he loaned to a friend. Charters and Caldicott then find themselves caught up in a world of spies, which they resist at first. It is not until they are insulted by a Gestapo officer that the realities of war penetrate their consciousness and they make an effort to help their old school chum, played by Sir Rex Harrison. Radford and Wayne were to brighten ten British films together during their dozen years as a team, satirizing the old school boys who never grew up. Obsessed with cricket and other sports, touchingly convinced that everyone in the world knows that British is best, innately decent, terrified of women and forthright action, Charters and Caldicott were enormously appealing representatives of a type that vanished when the British empire shriveled. Oh, yes, there IS an all-star cast in this one, headed by Margaret Lockwood and Paul Henreid, plus plenty of political tension AND sexual tension, but to character actor devotees, Charters and Caldicott are practically the whole story. You can see Radford and Wayne at their best in this fast-paced 1940 thriller. Recommended for further viewing: 1945's *Dead of Night,* 1946's *A Girl in a Million,* and 1949's *Passport to Pimlico.* **AKA:** Night Train; Gestapo. 🦴🦴🦴🦴

1940 93m/B *GB* Margaret Lockwood, Rex Harrison, Paul Henreid, Basil Radford, Naunton Wayne, James Harcourt, Felix Aylmer, Roland Culver, Raymond Huntley, Austin Trevor, Keneth Kent, C.V. France, Frederick Valk, Morland Graham, Wally Patch, Irene Handl, Albert Lieven, David Horne; **D:** Carol Reed; **W:** Frank Launder, Sidney Gilliat. **VHS, Beta** *KIV, DVT, HEG*

Nina Takes a Lover

There's a very old joke that bartenders still tell sometimes about the real identities of their weekend clientele. If by some extraordinary chance you haven't heard the joke, *Nina Takes a Lover* may seem like a fresh take on the ancient concept of the wife having a fling while her husband is out of town. The title character tries to explain to a nosy journalist that "It's more complicated than that." But it isn't—it's exactly that and no more, except for the always beautiful San Francisco locations (with Oakland doubling for its neighboring city in a few sequences). One might wonder about the direction of Laura San Giacomo's career which was sizzling hot at the time she made *sex, lies and videotape,* but lost steam fast in a succession of supporting roles in films that took a dive or showcased other players. From being "devastatingly erotic" at age 27 in her breakthrough film to looking like a little girl playing dress-up (at age 30!) in *Under Suspicion,* San Giacomo's cinematic identity seems distressingly out of focus. (In fact, she had signed on for episodic television by 1997.) As Nina, she delivers the sort of low-key performance suitable for a telly feature of the week, entirely in keeping with both the spirit and the execution of writer/director Alan Jacobs' first feature. Brit Paul Rhys is an agreeable presence as the enigmatic photographer who pursues her and beyond that, what can we say? If it's a new joke to you and you enjoy the scenery, *Nina Takes a Lover* may be just the video ticket for a wistful spring evening. 🦴🦴

1994 (R) 100m/C Laura San Giacomo, Paul Rhys, Michael O'Keefe, Cristi Conaway, Fisher Stevens; **D:** Alan Jacobs; **W:** Alan Jacobs; **C:** Phil Parmet; **M:** Todd Boekelheide. **VHS, LV, Closed Caption** *COL*

Nine Days a Queen

Here's irony for you: in the year of three kings (Edward VIII plus Georges V and VI), British producer Sir Michael Balcon (Daniel Day-Lewis' grandfather, by the way) assembled this lavish production set in 1553, ALSO the year of three monarchs (Edward VI, Lady Jane Grey, and Mary I). Did Sir Michael (and the Americans) know something four months into the uncrowned king's reign that loyal monarchists did not? Probably. If Lord Beaverbrook (1879-1964) of the *Daily Express and Evening Standard* knew, Balcon MUST have known. Enough of 20th century gossip! Let's get back to historical...gossip...of the 16th century. *Nine Days a Queen* boasts touching performances by Nova Pilbeam as Lady Jane Grey (1537-54), and by Desmond Tester as the frail Edward VI (1537-53). Before his death of tuberculosis at 15, Edward was persuaded

by the Earl of Warwick (Sir Cedric Hard-wicke) to change the order of succession in Lady Jane's favor. Jane, also 15, was too young and naive to present any serious challenge to the ascendancy of Mary I (1516-58), played by Gwen Francon-Davies. Jane's father was a much greater threat, so both were beheaded, along with Jane's young husband, Lord Guilford Dudley (Sir John Mills). It's a very sad tale, well and economically told; it's a good 64 minutes shorter than the sumptuous 1985 re-make starring Helena Bonham Carter. Miles Malleson, who plays Lady Jane's father, co-scripted with director Robert Stevenson. *AKA:* Lady Jane Grey; Tudor Rose. ♫♫♫

1936 80m/B *GB* John Mills, Cedric Hardwicke, Nova Pilbeam, Sybil Thorndike, Leslie Perrins, Felix Aylmer, Miles Malleson, Frank Cellier, Desmond Tester, Gwen Francon-Davies, Martita Hunt, John Laurie, Roy Emerton, John Turnbull, J.H. Roberts; *D:* Robert Stevenson; *W:* Robert Stevenson, Miles Malleson. **VHS, Beta** *HHT, DVT*

Nine Months

Marta Meszaros is a fine writer and director who makes a number of important universal statements in *Nine Months.* Widely praised for her award-winning 1975 movie, *The Adoption,* Meszaros has a sharp eye for the details that determine the direction of her character's lives. Why does her strong, brave, self-reliant heroine (Lili Minori) fall for the violent tactics of the foreman who wants to marry her? She resists him up to the point when he breaks into her room and tears her clothing, then she undresses him tenderly and feeds him from a bowl filled with bread and vegetables. Meszaros shows us how a woman can break out of a trap in which she finds herself, but not why she would choose such a fascist dork to begin with. Minori is plain and pudgy, yet she seems quite lovely as she struggles to maintain her work, her studies, her child, and her dignity. Jan Nowicki plays the role of the stubborn fiancee to the hilt, his piercing blue eyes expressing his feelings better than reams of dialogue. And Janos Kende's exceptional cinematography makes the drab factories, laboratories, and train stations in and around Budapest seem almost beautiful. ♫♫♫

1977 93m/C *HU* Lili Monori, Jan Nowicki, Dzsoko Roszics; *D:* Marta Meszaros; *W:* Marta Meszaros, Gyula Hernadi, Ildiko Korodi; *C:* Janos Kende; *M:* Gyorgy Kovacs. *NYR*

1984

To make a movie like *1984* IN 1984, as Michael Radford did, is to make a quaint period piece by default. It's bleak, it's interesting, but the whole raison d'etre for the film (to scare us out of our wits at what COULD happen!) is missing. When the novel was written in 1948, fears about the future had many people wondering if any of us would survive until 1984. Seven years later, in an edgy, Cold War-ridden world, Orwell's dark visions were still quite persuasive to 1950s audiences. A film noir atmosphere pervades the original film by Michael Anderson in 1956, enhanced by the casting of American noir icons like Edmond O'Brien as Winston Smith and Jan Sterling as Julia. Smith's great fear of rats is successfully exploited in the creepy Orwellian universe presided over by Michael Redgrave as O'Connor. Julia, too, is confronted with her greatest fear, and each betrays the other and their mutual dreams of love. They know that Big Brother is always watching. And WE know there are always more rats in the dark, the better to give us nightmares, My Dears...no 1980s special effects can compete with our terrorized imaginations...definitely worth a re-issue on video! ♫♫♫♫

1956 90m/B *GB* Edmond O'Brien, Jan Sterling, Michael Redgrave, David Kossoff, Mervyn Johns, Donald Pleasence, Carol Wolveridge, Ernest Clark, Ronan O'Casey, Kenneth Griffith; *D:* Michael Anderson Sr.; *W:* William Templeton, Ralph Gilbert Bettinson; *C:* N. Peter Rathvon. *NYR*

Nobody's Fool

Love hurts, and Cassie (Rosanna Arquette) is finding out just how much it hurts as *Nobody's Fool* begins. She hates her job as a waitress in a bar (except for her friend Pat, nicely played by Mare Winningham), she hates being dumped by her boyfriend Billy (Jim Youngs) when she told him she was pregnant, she hates that she had to give the baby up for adoption, and she hates the fact that she's tried so many times to kill herself without success. She's making yet another unsuccessful suicide bid in the opening sequence, and it's clear from her energy, humor, and vitality that she doesn't really want to die. Then an engaging technician named Riley (Eric Roberts) comes to town with a touring theatrical troupe. Cassie starts to perk up a bit, but the part of her that feels good feeling bad still casts longing glances in Billy's direction. Evelyn Purcell does a fine job showing how disconnected a girl like Cassie can feel in a small town like Buckeye. Ironically, *Nobody's Fool* was released on the same day as ex-husband Jonathan Demme's *Something Wild*. It's a lovely, much underappreciated film, and Rosanna Arquette and Eric Roberts are delightful as Cassie and Riley. 🦴🦴🦴

1986 (PG-13) 107m/C Rosanna Arquette, Eric Roberts, Mare Winningham, Louise Fletcher, Jim Youngs, Gwen Welles, Stephen Tobolowsky, Charlie Barnett, Lewis Arquette; **D:** Evelyn Purcell; **W:** Beth Henley; **C:** Misha Susov; **M:** James Newton Howard. **VHS, Beta, LV, Closed Caption** ORI, WAR

Non-Stop New York

Non-Stop New York was directed by Robert Stevenson, who went on to direct many of Walt Disney's greatest hits. Its star, Anna Lee (Mrs. Stevenson), wasn't much of an actress in 1937 and her onscreen teaming with John Loder produced no sparks. Also in the cast as a musical prodigy is 18-year-old Desmond Tester, heartily disliked by so many male audience members that you might mistake him for the villain of the film. The real star of *Non-Stop New York* is an incredible airliner which zips across the Atlantic, in spite of the fact that it is weighed down by massive staterooms and a convenient observation deck for passengers. The plane is, in fact, more like a luxury ocean liner, but by the time that contraption is up in the air, Stevenson has guided the characters into so many preposterous situations with such giddy results, that you won't mind going along for a far-from-real ride. 🦴🦴🦴

1937 71m/B Anna Lee, John Loder, Francis L. Sullivan, Frank Cellier, Desmond Tester, Athene Seyler, William Dewhurst, Drusilla Wills, Jerry Verno, James Pirrie, Ellen Pollock, Arthur Goullet, James Carew, Alf Goddard, Danny Green; **D:** Robert Stevenson; **W:** Curt Siodmak, Roland Pertwee, Derek Twist, J.O.C. Orton, E.V.H. Emmett. **VHS** NOS, SNC

Nosferatu

Why do we love *Nosferatu*, F. W. Murnau's German classic from the year 1922? Let us TRY to count the ways: When we see the captain's records for the doomed ship, the Demeter, we always get a shiver at this chilling indication of the blood-sucking horrors yet to come. And when the horrible-looking vampire played by Max Schreck gazes at the bleeding hand of Jonathan Harker, he leers, "Blood! Your precious blood!" as only Schreck can. And THIS *Nosferatu* is PURE evil; there's no feeling sorry for his character as we sometimes do for the charming Draculas later played by Bela Lugosi, Christopher Lee, and Louis Jourdan. The film itself, even by 1922 standards, is clearly drawn larger than life, especially when compared with the subtlety of such other F. W. Murnau classics as *The Last Laugh* and *Sunrise*. Alexander Granach, who would one day star in *Ninotchka* with Greta Garbo, portrays Renfield as a caricature. The rest of the cast, including hordes of rats plus Gustav Von Wangenheim and Greta Schroder as the Harkers, are also in over-the-top gear. The overacting suits this particular *Symphony*

of Horrors, which Murnau himself revamped for sound in 1930, the year before his death on a California highway. **AKA:** Nosferatu, Eine Symphonie des Grauens; Nosferatu, A Symphony of Terror; Nosferatu, A Symphony of Horror; Nosferatu, The Vampire. 🦴🦴🦴

1922 63m/B *GE* Max Schreck, Alexander Granach, Gustav von Wagenheim, Greta Schroeder; **D:** F.W. Murnau. **VHS, Beta, LV** *GPV, MRV, NOS*

Not Fourteen Again

Gillian Armstrong's *Not Fourteen Again* is rather a distaff version of Michael Apted's acclaimed *7-14-21-28-35 Up* series of documentaries. So far, the director has filmed her three subjects at 14, 18, 26, and 33. With a spritely soundtrack, she shows the evolving lives of Carrie, Josie, and Diana, all of whom raised girls of their own, whom Armstrong films as well. One of the women faces the eternal dilemma: should she continue a rewarding career or have a baby? We get an answer the next time Armstrong returns to film her. She's happy that she had the baby, happy in general, but she's BORED. How can you be happy AND bored? We suspect that you'd have to film every second of someone's life, and even then, you might blink and miss that answer. 🦴🦴🦴

1996 110m/C D: Gillian Armstrong; **C:** Steve Arnold; **M:** Peter Dasent. *NYR*

Not of this Earth

Remember *Not of this Earth,* the 1957 Roger Corman movie about an alien vampire? Well, the movie you tried to forget is also the movie Jim Wynorski was born to re-make. Following in Beverly Garland's footsteps is Traci Lords, reportedly writing a cautionary book about her experiences making adult films in real life. In the movie, she plays a nurse and Arthur Roberts inherits the role which shot the late Paul Birch to obscurity. Dick Miller is not re-cast in the new movie, but Lenny Juliano, a young actor with a flair for comedy, has some good sequences as the alien's chauffeur. The acting of the nurse's cop-boyfriend is nothing to write home about, but luckily he has little to do. *Not of this Earth* would be fun to watch with other "great" horror films like *Cat Women of the Moon* starring Marie Windsor and the late Sonny Tufts. **WOOF!**

1988 (R) 92m/C Traci Lords, Arthur Roberts, Lenny Juliano, Rebecca Perle, Ace Mask, Roger Lodge; **D:** Jim Wynorski; **W:** Jim Wynorski, R.J. Robertson. **VHS, Beta** *MGM*

Number One

At 42 minutes, *Number One* just barely qualifies as a feature film, but Dyan Cannon packs quite a number of astute observations about kids and sex into the brief running time. One sequence, in which a little boy is chastised at the dinner table, is almost unbearable to watch. As writer/director/composer, Cannon shows more understanding and compassion for her characters than she did with any of the acting roles she tackled between 1970 and 1977. Working with a nominal budget, Cannon (and cameraman Fred Elmes) elicited strong performances from a cast of young children and she received an Oscar nomination for her first directorial effort. 🦴🦴🦴

1976 42m/B Nan Martin, Allen (Goorwitz) Garfield, Gary Lockwood; **D:** Dyan Cannon; **W:** Dyan Cannon; **C:** Frederick Elmes; **M:** Dyan Cannon. *NYR*

Nuns on the Run

Nuns on the Run with Eric Idle and Robbie Coltrane is pretty funny, although any movie with that title and those stars deserves to be VERY funny. One reason it isn't is because *Nuns on the Run* is set up almost exactly the same way as the great Billy Wilder's *Some Like It Hot.* In that movie, Tony Curtis and Jack Lemmon play two characters who hide out from gangsters by pretending to be members of an all-girls band. In *Nuns on the Run,* Idle and Coltrane play two characters who hide out from gangsters by pretending to be nuns in a convent. There's even a dizzy blonde (Camille Coduri) who has the same plot functions as Marilyn Monroe did in *Some Like It Hot.* She even walks into things when she isn't wearing her glasses, just like Monroe did in *How to Marry a Millionaire.* The comedies that make us laugh the loudest are the ones which make us laugh when we don't expect to laugh. But when we know the plot, no matter how silly Eric and Robbie look in nun's clothes, no gag can be that much of a surprise. Janet Suzman is as good as she can be in the skimpy supporting role that director Jonathan Lynn wrote for her, but it IS odd to see Eric Idle hand scenes to other cast members on a platter. He is so low-key in *Nuns on the Run* that Robbie Coltrane gets most of the laughs. Still, watching these two impersonate Sister Euphemia of the Five Hounds and Sister Inviolata of the Immaculate Conception is good for a few giggles, especially if you ever went to Catholic school. And Coltrane dancing in a nun's outfit is definitely a sight to see. 🗡🗡🗡

1990 (PG-13) 95m/C Eric Idle, Robbie Coltrane, Janet Suzman, Camille Coduri, Robert Patterson, Tom Hickey, Doris Hare, Lila Kaye; *D:* Jonathan Lynn; *W:* Jonathan Lynn. **VHS, Beta, LV** FOX

The Obsessed

If you're merely looking for a whodunit, *Obsessed* will disappoint you. There's no suspense in it. What I think is funny about this movie is the way that Gregory Black (David Farrar) and Elizabeth the housekeeper (Geraldine Fitzgerald) are always yelling at each other when they're not having sex. At least I THINK they have sex; maybe they yell each other to sleep in bed, too. Anyway, it's 1890 and Gregory's wife Edwina is dead. The unthinkable starts to occur to the lovers. Maybe she/he done her in?! A kindly inspector (Roland Culver) snoops around, asking the maid (Jean Cadell as Ellen) to answer his questions about poison and such, and Gregory and Elizabeth have to account for themselves, too, of course. But even THIS doesn't stop them from fighting with each other! Farrar and Fitzgerald give this one everything they've got, poor dears, since Maurice Elvey doesn't seem to give anyone much help. Culver is wonderful, as always. Based on a play by William Dinner and William Morum. *AKA:* The Late Edwina Black. 🗡🗡🗡

1951 77m/B *GB* David Farrar, Geraldine Fitzgerald, Roland Culver, Jean Cadell, Mary Merrall, Harcourt Williams, Charles Heslop, Ronald Adam, Sydney Monkton; *D:* Maurice Elvey; *W:* Charles Frank, David Evans. **VHS, LV** SNC, NOS, MOV

The Odessa File

This untidy, overlong potboiler didn't do much for Jon Voight's career; in fact, except for 1976's *End of the Game,* he vanished from the big screen until his Oscar-winning performance in 1978's *Coming Home.* Frederick Forsyth wrote the best-selling novel (about a 1963 Nazi conspiracy based in Hamburg) that inspired it and Ronald (*The Poseidon Adventure*) Neame directs with his usual melodramatic style. Every cliche you can possibly imagine is recycled in this "thriller." There is the obligatory sequence when the heroine whines to the hero, "I may not be here when you get back," before he sets off for Adventures Unknown. On the other hand, there is the obligatory sequence when the villain asks the hero if he can smoke and— Voila!—the cigarette and his gun just happen to be in the same drawer. And, as the piece de resistance, there is the obligatory sequence when some crazy Nazi screams about ruling the world. The best thing about *The Odessa File* is Maria Schell's cameo appearance. In five vivid moments, Schell reveals more about the tragic consequences of war than the lumbering 128 minutes that surround her all-too-brief appearance. (If you have a problem accepting Schell, 48, as the mother of Jon Voight, 36, though, you're not alone!) 🦴🦴

1974 (PG) 128m/C *GB GE* Jon Voight, Mary Tamm, Maximilian Schell, Maria Schell, Derek Jacobi, Peter Jeffrey, Klaus Lowitsch, Kurt Meisel, Hannes Meesember, Garfield Morgan, Shmuel Rodensku, Ernst Schroder, Noel Willman, Hans Canineberg, Towje Kleiner, Gunnar Moiler; **D:** Ronald Neame; **W:** Kenneth Ross, George Markstein; **C:** Oswald Morris; **M:** Andrew Lloyd Webber. **VHS, Beta, LV, Closed Caption** *GKK*

Old Enough

Slow-moving coming-of-age comedy on the rich kid-poor kid friendship theme. Director Marisa Silver's directing debut won the 1984 Sundance Grand Jury Prize; she went on to make *Permanent Record, Vital Signs, He Said, She Said,* and *Indecency.* 🦴🦴

1984 (PG) 91m/C Sarah Boyd, Rainbow Harvest, Neill Barry, Danny Aiello, Susan Kingsley, Roxanne Hart, Alyssa Milano, Fran Brill, Anne Pitoniak; **D:** Marisa Silver; **W:** Marisa Silver; **C:** Michael Ballhaus. Sundance Film Festival '84: Grand Jury Prize. **VHS, Beta** *MED*

Oleanna

Let me preface this by mentioning that *House of Games, Things Change,* and *Homicide* are among my favorite movies of 1987-91. And then there's...*Oleanna.* When I was in my first year at UCD, I was stuck with a professor who couldn't stand being a professor. I couldn't stand him. He wrote nice things on my papers and he spoke well of me to others, but whenever we were in the same room, he was whiny and belligerent, and finally I went to his office to ask him what I had to do to pass his class without having to see him anymore. Without looking up from his desk, he said, "Three papers. Any subject. I don't care." And that ended it. (It also meant I wound up getting my degree and credential by NEVER going to any class if writing papers were the option instead of showing up.) I thought about this profes-

sor when I saw a professor named John in David Mamet's *Oleanna.* How do these guys get tenure? They're so clueless about their effect on others and teaching is all about the effect that someone who knows has on a student who doesn't know. John is a windbag, in love with the sound of his own voice. His student Carol (let me put this charitably) is unfinished and easily led. She doesn't know her own mind yet and she simmers through harangues she doesn't want to hear when she COULD (a) speak up for herself or (b) split. When these two get together, *Oleanna* becomes a LOOONG (90 minutes) polemical rant. William H. Macy, a fine actor, and Debra Eisenstadt do what they can with their unplayable, slogan-driven parts. Somehow, Mamet's heart does not seem to be in *Oleanna* since there's nothing in the text to show that he cares about either character. For a writer who cares vitally about every character in *House of Games, Things Change,* and *Homicide,* this is sad. **WOOF!**

1994 90m/C William H. Macy, Debra Eisenstadt; **D:** David Mamet; **W:** David Mamet; **C:** Andrzej Sekula; **M:** Rebecca Pidgeon. Nominations: Independent Spirit Awards '95: Best Actor (Macy). **VHS, LV, Closed Caption** *HMK*

Oliver Twist

Filmgoers today mainly remember Jackie Coogan for two roles: 1921's *The Kid* with Charlie Chaplin and 1964's Uncle Fester on *The Addams Family* television series. Coogan, however, made many movies as a child and even more as an adult character actor. Until its rediscovery some years back, one of his earliest and best silent files was long feared lost. Coogan was barely eight when *Oliver Twist* was released, a bit young for the part that is usually played by boys of nine or ten, but his small size makes his character even more lovable. Lon Chaney's makeup as Fagin is somewhat overwhelming and he has so few close-ups (most of those seem reserved for his young co-star!) that although he looks the part, his performance does not have quite the same impact as later Fagins of the sound era. However, George Siegmann is truly frightening as the vicious Bill Sykes and Gladys Brockwell creates a vivid impression as the terrified Nancy. The film was adapted and directed in workman-like style by Glasgow-born Frank Lloyd. This thrifty but thoroughly respectable version of the Charles Dickens classic was independently produced by Sol Lesser, who went on to make a dozen *Tarzan* pictures. Like many other silent features, *Oliver Twist* was preserved not in Hollywood but in Czechoslovakia, where it was finally located in the late 1970s. Blackhawk Films then restored the film with the help of Lesser and Coogan, who reconstructed its missing intertitles. This *Oliver* is well worth seeing, not only for comparison purposes with the later British classics by David Lean, Carol Reed, and Clive Donner, but also for the wonderfully appealing work of Jackie Coogan whose brimming eyes would melt the heart of ANY curmudgeon in frozen storage. 🦴🦴🦴

1922 77m/B Jackie Coogan, Lon Chaney Sr., Gladys Brockwell, George Siegmann, Esther Ralston; **D:** Frank Lloyd. **VHS, Beta** *NOS, CCB, KIV*

On Approval

This rare jewel of a film gives us a chance to see Tony-winning Beatrice Lillie (1895-1989) at her sparkling best. How does she manage to play a character who's simultaneously insufferable AND endearing? As rich Maria Wislack in *On Approval,* Lillie is a social brute who doesn't know she's a social brute. There's no individual malice behind her verbal barbs; her meanness towards everyone is only exceeded by her unconsciousness of same. Watching Lillie in action is rather like studying the effect of a laser beam; her sharp yet subtle humor is achieved by focused intensity on a person, place, or thing. She sticks to the point, sincerely believing she can do no wrong, ever. Meanwhile, she's surrounded by chaos, the direct result of virtually everything she says and does. Lil-

lie didn't think much of Hollywood, yet she tried to become a star there four times for four different studios. In 1926, she made *Exit Sailing* opposite Jack Pickford. It's extremely funny to watch today, but apparently MGM executives felt otherwise. In 1929, she appeared in the Warner Bros. musical, *Show of Shows*; the following year, she starred as Lady Diana in the Fox musical *Are You There?* (widely appreciated at a recent revival screening); and in 1938 she made the Paramount musical *Doctor Rhythm* opposite Bing Crosby. Except for a cameo bit as a revivalist in 1956's *Around the World in 80 Days* and a sixth-billed role as Mrs. Meers in the 1967 Universal musical *Thoroughly Modern Millie, On Approval* is Lillie's only film on video. Luckily it's also the best. Producer/director/ screenwriter/star Clive Brook (1887-1974) re-vamped the 1926 play by Sir Frederick Lonsdale (1881-1954) by setting it in the Edwardian era, adding a tongue-in-cheek prologue and a zany dream sequence. His dream cast included himself as the always-broke George, Duke of Bristol; Roland Culver (1900-84) as the equally broke Richard Halton; and Googie Withers, then 27, as millionairess Helen Hale. Along with Lillie's Maria, they agree to spend time alone together in a Scottish castle..."On Approval." The Herculean efforts involved in making this one-of-a-kind cinematic treat must have exhausted Brook; he retired after a successful career spanning 25 years, re-emerging onscreen just once for Universal's *The List of Adrian Messenger* in 1963. Culver continued making films right up through Michael Palin's *The Missionary* in 1983. Withers appeared most recently in the 1996 Australian release, *Shine.* A 1980s version of *On Approval,* set in the 1920s, aired on *Masterpiece Theatre* starring the late Jeremy Brett in a rare comic role as George, Penelope Keith as Maria, Benjamin Whitrow as Richard, and Lindsay Duncan as Helen. 🦴🦴🦴🦴

1944 80m/B *GB* Clive Brook, Beatrice Lillie, Googie Withers, Roland Culver, O.B. Clarence, Lawrence

**Bill Paxton in
One False Move.**

downer, as it drains the humor and energy out of the 100 minutes that went before it. Perhaps Brassard, who also scripted, didn't know how to wrap up this rich slice of life. (Great shot: the hash slinger shoves every object she can get her hands on into her restaurant's Soup Du Jour, then storms out, resigning in full glory to every diner in the joint.) 🦴🦴🦴

1974 100m/C *CA* Denise Filatrault, Michele Rossignol, Frederique Colin, Sophie Clement, Andre Montmorency, Jean Archambault, Gilles Renaud, Manda Parent, Claude Gai, Rita Fontaine, Beatrice Picard, Amulette Garneau, Denis Drouin; ***D:*** Andre Brassard; ***W:*** Andre Brassard, Michel Tremblay; ***C:*** Attila Dory. *NYR*

One False Move

One False Move represents a promising directing debut for Carl Franklin and a chance to see some fine actors at work, notably Cynda Williams and Bill Paxton. The film begins with an extended and quite graphic bloodletting sequence, but nothing else in the narrative, not even the climax is anywhere that explicit. Paxton plays Sheriff Dale "Hurricane" Dixon, seemingly an eager beaver small-town hick who tags along after a couple of big city cops until he realizes that the execution-style drug murders they are investigating hit very close to home. Five years earlier, he and Lila Walker (Williams), a young black teenage shoplifter, had a baby son before she left town. Dixon later married and started a family of his own, who know nothing about his relationship with Lila or his little boy. Lila changes her name to Fantasia and winds up on drugs in Los Angeles with two bad dudes named Ray and Pluto. Unfortunately, Ray is played by the screenwriter Billy Bob Thornton who writes much better than he acts, and Pluto, although effectively played by Michael Beach, is only identified by his 150 I.Q. and his fondness for knives. (If he'd switched roles with Beach, would Billy Bob have written a better part for Pluto?

Hanray, Elliot Mason, Hay Petrie, Marjorie Munks, Molly Munks; ***D:*** Clive Brook; ***W:*** Terence Young, Clive Brook. **VHS, Beta** *KIV, MRV, HHT*

Once Upon a Time in the East

Canadian theatrical director Andre Brassard's little-known movie debut was one of the most enjoyable entries at 1974's San Francisco International Film Festival. Transvestites, an alcoholic, a hash slinger, a down-and-out singer, a troubled pregnant girl, and others share their lives and make the best of what they can get from their respective situations. The ending is a

Maybe, but nothing would have helped his acting!) This casting decision hurts because Fantasia is supposed to be dominated by the homicidal Ray and she looks as if she could eat him for breakfast. Cynda Williams does a beautiful job with the material she is given, although she is too glowingly healthy and alert to make a completely convincing strung-out junkie. *One False Move* suffers from a storyline that zaps all over the place with secondary characters and then drags for long stretches, especially when Billy Bob as Ray has to spend much time onscreen. It works best when it focuses on the relationship between Lila and the Sheriff, especially as they wait out a long night attempting to trap Ray and Pluto. Since Billy Bob Thorton's writing and acting skills improved enormously by the time he directed 1996's *Sling Blade, One False Move* is well worth a look on video for an early portrait of the artist as a young man. 🦴🦴🦴

1991 (R) 105m/C Bill Paxton, Cynda Williams, Michael Beach, Jim Metzler, Earl Billings, Billy Bob Thornton, Natalie Canderday, Robert Ginnaven, Robert Anthony Bell, Kevin Hunter; *D:* Carl Franklin; *W:* Billy Bob Thornton, Tom Epperson; *C:* James L. Carter. Independent Spirit Awards '93: Best Director (Franklin); MTV Movie Awards '93: Best New Filmmaker Award (Franklin). **VHS, LV, Closed Caption** *COL, FCT*

100 Days after Childhood

This beautifully photographed tribute to youthful romance in a summer camp is lovely to look at. It's episodic; each segment shows different teenagers learning to meet life's challenges by working within their limitations. Wonder what all those cute kids are up to these days? *AKA:* Sto Dnei rossle Detstwa. 🦴🦴

1975 93m/C *RU* Boris Tokarev, Tatiana Drubich, Irina Malysheva, Nina Menschikova, Serge Shakurov; *D:* Sergei Solovjov; *W:* Sergei Solovjov, Alexander Alexandrov; *C:* Leonid Kalaschnikov; *M:* Isaak Schvarts. *NYR*

101 Nights

Agnes Varda pays tribute to the centenary of the cinema with *101 Nights*. Monsieur Cinema is played by Michel Piccoli, only 70, as a 100-year-old movie fan confined to a wheelchair. The film is packed with international stars at their most charming (Belmondo, Delon, Deneuve, De Niro, Depardieu, Mastroianni), and its slender premise is bolstered by Varda's sheer love of movie lore, past and present. 🦴🦴🦴

1995 125m/C *FR GB* Michel Piccoli, Marcello Mastroianni, Henri Garcin, Julie Gayet, Mathieu Demy, Emmanuel Salinger; *D:* Agnes Varda; *W:* Agnes Varda; *C:* Eric Gautier. *NYR*

One Night Stand

Do you ever wonder what might happen if an international critic decided to make a movie? Okay, we all know whatever became of Francois Truffaut. Pierre Rissient was a likable critic/film publicist who secured a screening for his first feature film at the San Francisco International Film Festival. Rissient might have done himself some good by consulting a script doctor first. The screenplay is ludicrous. *One Night Stand* should have been run out of Hong Kong, where it was filmed, during PRE-production. Degrading to women, and even more degrading to the leading actor who degrades them (the late Richard Jordan has this thankless role), the movie drew extended hisses and numerous boos from unappreciative audience members. **WOOF!**

1976 102m/C *HK FR* Richard Jordan, Ting Pei, Tien Ni, Mei Fang, Tsang Kong, Ken Wayne, Marie Daems; *D:* Pierre Rissient; *W:* Pierre Rissient, Kenneth White; *C:* Alain Derobe. *NYR*

One Sings, the Other Doesn't

One Sings, the Other Doesn't is a so-so look at a pair of feminists who stay in

Tilda Swinton and
Billy Zane star as
Orlando and
Shelmerdine in
Orlando.

roles once played by women, she's indicating a reactionary trend every bit as disagreeable as the one it's replacing. At least in THIS screenplay, Varda is persistent, but fairly cagey about ideologies, at the expense of a more substantial story. Her other films include *Cleo from 5 to 7, Le Bonheur, Vagabond, Le Petit Amour,* and *Jacquot. AKA:* L'Une Chante L'Autre Pas. ♫♫♪

1977 105m/C *FR BE* Valerie Mairesse, Therese Liotard, Robert Dadies, Ali Affi, Jean-Pierre Pellegrin, Francois Wertheimer; **D:** Agnes Varda; **W:** Agnes Varda; **C:** Charlie Van Damme; **M:** Francois Wertheimer. **VHS, Beta** *COL*

The Only One

The Only One provides a compassionate look at a marital break-up, seen from the husband's point of view. Nikolai and Tanya are an attractive, deeply in love, dream-filled couple, who divorce and go their separate ways after a misunderstanding. Still, there is a bond between them that their different directions cannot dissolve. Josef Heifetz treats this familiar situation with deep understanding and sharply rendered knowledge of the forces that link the lovers to each other. The performances by the three leading players here are well worth seeing. ♫♫♫

1976 95m/C *RU* Elena Proklova, Valery Zolothuhin, Ludmila Gladunko, Vladimir Vyssozki; **D:** Josef Heifetz; **W:** Josef Heifetz, Pavel Nilin; **C:** Heinrich Marandzhjan; **M:** Nadeshda Simonian. *NYR*

Open Season

Sometimes films play at festivals and are never seen again, unless the filmmaker makes a deal with a cable network or a video distributor. *Open Season* poses the rather esoteric question: what would happen if all the television shows we THOUGHT had low ratings (like the ones on PBS) suddenly were declared THE top-rated shows? Bet you've really stayed awake nights worrying about that one, huh? Well, in Robert Wuhl's 1995 film, it's a mistake, but the whole country thinks

touch over a 15-year period. Apple, the singer (Valerie Mairesse), repeats the same dumb lyrics over and over: "I am woman, I'm me," as her quiet friend Suzanne (Therese Liotard) works at a family planning clinic to support her two fatherless children. Charlie Van Damme photographs the story attractively and the two leads give strong performances. Yet Agnes Varda's screenplay is, at least sporadically, inane. At one point, she has Apple offer her Iranian husband a deal. He can leave her and take their baby if he gives her another child, thus relegating him to the role of a functional accessory in her existence. In every previous sequence, their love had seemed real enough. If Varda is suggesting that men assume the shadowy

it's reality and our entire society changes as a result. I guess you might call this a high-concept flick. The best thing about this movie is Maggie Han, who plays Wuhl's wife. Otherwise, good actors like Taylor and Shaver are wasted as nitwit television executives. Wuhl later played one of the nitwit movie executives in Mario Puzo's *The Last Don* for CBS. 🦴🦴

1995 (R) 97m/C Robert Wuhl, Rod Taylor, Gailard Sartain, Maggie Han, Joe Piscopo, Helen Shaver, Dina Merrill, Saul Rubinek, Steven C. White, Timothy Arrington, Barry Flatman, Tom Selleck, Alan Thicke, Jimmie Walker; **D:** Robert Wuhl; **W:** Robert Wuhl; **C:** Stephen Lighthill; **M:** Marvin Hamlisch. **VHS, Closed Caption** *REP*

The Orders

The Orders is directed with thought and care by Michel Brault, who also did the screenplay. It's about the unjust suspension of civil liberties in Quebec during 1970. Told entirely from the viewpoint of the victims, *The Orders* stars many of the people who were actually arrested, although they take on different roles. Acting by the nonprofessionals, though low-key, is heartbreakingly affecting. If it could happen to them in Quebec, it could happen to anyone, anywhere. What would you do if the police came in the middle of the morning and took you away to jail, forcing you to leave your children and never once explained why? Brault shows us what THEY did, making us angry, making us think. *The Orders* deservedly won the Director's Prize at the Cannes Film Festival. **AKA:** Les Ordres. 🦴🦴🦴🦴

1975 107m/C *CA* Helene Louiselle, Jean Lapointe, Guy Provost, Claude Gauthier, Louise Forestier; **D:** Michel Brault; **W:** Michel Brault; **C:** Michel Brault, Francois Protat; **M:** Phillipe Gagnon. *NYR*

Orlando

This unique adaptation of Virginia Woolf's 1928 novel is about the title character (Tilda Swinton), who lives for 400 years. Orlando starts out as a man and, "in the fullness of time," becomes a woman. The conceit allows us to see how women are treated over the centuries, courtesy of Orlando's extraordinary perspective. There are many treats in store for Woolf fans, the marvelous casting of Quentin Crisp as old Queen Elizabeth I, for one, and the appearance of *Lovejoy*'s Dudley Sutton as King James I, for another. It was partly filmed on location in St. Petersburg and Uzbekistan. And writer/director Sally Potter, who must be a whirlwind of energy, even wrote some of the songs. (And it's a refreshing 93 minutes long!) 🦴🦴🦴

1992 (PG-13) 93m/C *GB RU FR NL* Tilda Swinton, Charlotte Valandrey, Billy Zane, Lothaire Bluteau, John Wood, Quentin Crisp, Heathcote Williams, Dudley Sutton, Thom Hoffman, Peter Eyre, Jimmy Somerville; **D:** Sally Potter; **W:** Sally Potter; **C:** Alexei Rodionov; **M:** Bob Last. Nominations: Academy Awards '93: Best Art Direction/Set Decoration, Best Costume Design; Independent Spirit Awards '94: Best Foreign Film. **VHS, LV, Closed Caption** *COL*

Orphans

Nikolay Goubenko made an extraordinary U.S. debut as a director with *The Orphans*, partly based on his own childhood experiences after World War II. The picture introduced little A. Tscherstvov, the best child actor at the San Francisco International Film Festival since six-year-old Ana Torrent appeared in 1973's *Spirit of the Beehive*. Young Tscherstvov grabs our attention so completely that dialogue is nearly unnecessary, though he does quite well with Goubenko's sensitive screenplay. His expressive blue eyes lend poignance to every sequence of this tale about a group of war orphans who attend school in 1945 Russia. Goubenko, too, is effective as a teacher who is unable to cope with the needs of the children in his care. Beautifully photographed, *The Orphans* also features strong supporting performances by Y. Boudraitis and E. Bourkov. 🦴🦴🦴

1977 97m/C *RU* Nikolai Gubenko, Y. Boudraitis, A. Tcherstvov, A. Kaliaguine, E. Bourkov, J. Bolotova, R. Bikov, E. Evstigneev; **D:** Nikolai Gubenko; **C:** Alexander Kniajinsky. **VHS, Beta** *FCT*

"Same person. No difference at all... just a different sex."
—Tilda Swinton as the androgynous Orlando in *Orlando*.

INDEPENDENT FILM GUIDE

Ossessione

Four years before Tay Garnett made MGM's *The Postman Always Rings Twice,* James M. Cain's grim tale of adultery starring Lana Turner and John Garfield, Luchino Visconti directed Clara Calamai and Massimo Girotti in 1942's *Ossessione.* The film ran into censorship difficulties in fascist Italy and copyright problems everywhere else. A key element in the Visconti version is the erosion of Calamai's desirability as she becomes more vulnerable to Girotti. John Garfield can not free himself from his fix on Lana Turner, even though he tries with Audrey Totter. Although Girotti doesn't shrink from engulfing Calamai, he is terrified by her reciprocal attentions. The same woman he once wanted fills him with fear and revulsion, and it is painful to watch as her eroticism begins to disgust him. *Ossessione* is a more uncomfortable film than 1946's glossy *Postman,* but Visconti spells out some unpleasant truths about the differing effects of passion on men and women. 🦴🦴🦴🦴

1942 135m/B *IT* Massimo Girotti, Clara Calamai, Juan deLanda, Elio Marcuzzo; **D:** Luchino Visconti. **VHS, Beta** *FCT, TPV*

Our Daily Bread

1934's *Our Daily Bread* was King Vidor's most direct statement to date on how he perceived the American dream. Never again would he be as self-revealing about his personal solutions to the grim realities of life. He cast Karen Morley, a sensitive and deeply political actress, in the role of Mary Sims, a young woman grappling with poverty. For the co-starring role of Mary's husband John, Vidor chose Tom Keene, a limited but sincere actor who rather resembled Vidor himself. In an unsuccessful concession to box office realities, Vidor assigned the bad girl role of Sally to Barbara Pepper. (She liked to listen to jazz and we all know what THAT means.) The cast was rounded out by fine character actors John Qualen as an influential farmworker named Chris and Addison Richards as Louie, a taciturn but memorable convict. The script, written by Vidor with his then-wife Elizabeth Hill, is the dewy-eyed rural equivalent of any Warner Bros. or Fox musical starring Ruby Keeler or Shirley Temple. To lick the Depression, Mr. and Mrs. Sims take over a beat-up farm. When they realize they can not handle the place alone, they enlist the services of other down-and-out Depression victims. Individually, they are nothing, but working shoulder-to-shoulder, everyone digs in together to make the farm a growing cooperative concern. (Shades of *42nd Street* and *Stand Up and Cheer*!) And then sex arrives in the person of a bleached blonde to threaten Mr. Sims as well as everyone else's efforts. After watching the films Vidor made between 1925 and 1959, one might become convinced that the director regarded sex as the root of all evil. A Good Woman like Mrs. Sims treats her manchild with maternal affection and functions as a reliable emotional pillow. Men realize their true potential with the support of such Good Women, but they also chomp at the bit and run off to play with Tramps whenever they appear. It's always the Tramp's fault (naturally) and a Good Woman invariably takes her disloyal manchild back. In Vidor's earlier works, his other artistic statements provide a welcome relief from such tiresome Sunday school lessons. When *Our Daily Bread* emerged as a box office flop, Vidor was faced with a difficult decision. He could make his artistic statements about the power of the common man more accessible to mass audiences or he could switch to commercial melodramas. He made the latter choice, and it's sometimes hard to believe that the same man who directed *Our Daily Bread*'s final inspiring irrigation sequence would also be responsible for the sudsy *Stella Dallas* three years later. **AKA:** Miracle of Life. 🦴🦴🦴🦴

1934 80m/B Karen Morley, Tom Keene, John Qualen, Barbara Pepper, Addison Richards; *D:* King Vidor; *W:* Elizabeth Hill, King Vidor. **VHS, Beta, LV** *NOS, BAR, VYY*

Padre Padrone

Padre Padrone is a very hard film that makes no compromises with its bleak story, which is based on the true experiences of Gavino Ledda, who wrote the book that inspired Paulo and Vittorio Taviani's screenplay. The Tavianis also directed this low-budget study of a young shepherd and the bitter relationship he endures with his cruel father, who shapes, but does not define his life. The son's adult solution to make his life his own is extraordinary, yet utterly convincing. **AKA:** Father Master; My Father, My Master. 🦴🦴🦴

1977 113m/C *IT* Omero Antonutti, Saverio Marconi, Marcella Michelangeli, Fabrizio Forte; *D:* Paolo Taviani, Vittorio Taviani; *W:* Paolo Taviani, Vittorio Taviani; *C:* Mario Masini; *M:* Egisto Macchi. Cannes Film Festival '77: Best Film. **VHS, Beta** *COL*

Pandora's Box

Pandora's Box stars the late great Louise Brooks as Lulu and Francis Lederer (still alive well into his 90s, nearly 70 years after he co-starred opposite Brooks) as Alva Schon. In 1925's *Joyless Street,* G.W. Pabst revealed a Germany of harsh extremes: decadent jazz clubs near food lines where people wait hours at a time for a piece of butcher's meat. Innocent Lulu lives in the ugly world of 1928, but she cannot understand how she unwittingly contributes to that world. She loves guys of all sizes, shapes, and ages, except that sometimes they get mad at her and turn on her and then she gets into a whale of a lot of trouble. Like Dr. Ludwig Schon, who starts acting like he's too good for her once he gets engaged to another woman. And when he shows up with the other woman at Lulu's revue on opening night, what girl wouldn't get mad and refuse to go on with the show until she'd gotten even? And then, after she'd worked the angles so that Dr. Schon had to marry her, it wasn't her fault if he got mad at her for flirting with a Countess or for fooling around with her old pals before her wedding night. The world believes that Lulu is a femme fatale, dragging every man down to her level, but Lulu is her own greatest victim, representing much too much to much too many. Like every great director, Pabst exploited the actor's feelings towards each other to their onscreen advantage. He seduced a striking lesbian performance out of Alice Roberts as the Countess; he used Brooks' attraction to Gustav Diesl as Jack the Ripper to inject poignance into their brief but vivid moments together. And Fritz Kortner's real-life dislike of Brooks was ideal for Dr. Schon's obsessive hatred of Lulu. In her beautifully written reminiscences of working with Pabst, Brooks frankly admits that she never thought of herself as much of an actress. But her flickering image remains powerful today. And *Pandora's Box* yields a legion of treasures for first-time viewers and for long-time admirers who've memorized every frame of Pabst's masterpiece. *AKA:* Die Buechse Der Pandora. 🦴🦴🦴🦴

1928 110m/B *GE* Louise Brooks, Fritz Kortner, Francis Lederer, Carl Goetz, Alice Roberts, Gustav Diesl; *D:* G.W. Pabst; *W:* G.W. Pabst. **VHS, Beta** *GPV, MRV, VDM*

Paradise Lost: The Child Murders at Robin Hood Hills

Paradise Lost: The Child Murders At Robin Hood Hills is a deeply sobering film experience. Joe Berlinger and Bruce Sinofsky (*Brother's Keeper*) had astonishing access to the Arkansas case, from the discovery of the children's bodies to client-lawyer discussions, from the tearful anguish of the victim's families to chilling rationalizations by the convicted killers. Some segments are eerily myopic as when the West Memphis townspeople are advised not to talk to the media while Berlinger and Sinofsky record the whole thing on video. (Weren't THEY part of the media?) Later, Berlinger and Sinofsky even supply the court with crucial evidence obtained directly from a witness. The grisly details and straightforward presentation contribute to the feeling that you're watching a docu-DRAMA, not the matter-of-fact documentary that it is. 🦴🦴🦴

1995 150m/C *D:* Joe Berlinger, Bruce Sinofsky; *C:* Robert Richman. **VHS, Closed Caption** *CAF, HBO*

Paradise Place

Paradise Place sounds like it ought to be better than it is. After all, Ingmar Bergman produced it and Gunnel Lindblom, a leading actress in many of his movies, directed it. It features fine performances by Birgitta Valberg and Sif Ruud as a pair of old friends, and by Agneta Ekmanner, an exceptionally pretty child who plays Valberg's granddaughter. And the Swedish countryside couldn't be lovelier. Yet Lindblom tries so hard to make her thematic points that she sacrifices a sense of drama (as the grownups drone on about how society has corrupted their children, one of their own kids is quietly going mad, to their complete indifference). Much of her story takes the form of chatty philosophizing, and by the time action crawls into the final reel, the audience is lost in zzz's and/or a coffee break. *AKA:* Summer Place; Paradistorg. 🦴🦴

1977 112m/C *SW* Birgitta Valberg, Sif Ruud, Margaretha Bystrom, Agneta Ekmanner, Inga Landgre, Solveig Ternstrom, Dagny Lind, Goran Stangertz, Holger Lowenadler; *D:* Gunnel Lindblom; *W:* Gunnel

Lindblom, Ulla Isaakson; **C:** Tony Forsberg; **M:** George Riedel. *NYR*

Paris, France

We wonder whether *Paris, France* would seem better if we'd seen it as a silent movie. As it was, we kept wondering how in the world its small cast was able to talk so much during their complicated physical routines without hyperventilating or passing out or something. It's a long movie, too, 111 minutes worth of blathering and gymnastics, during which the characters rant and rave about John Lennon, sexual etiquette, and each other. Halfway through all this, we found ourselves reflecting on how the producers of Shannon Tweed movies are able do this sort of thing in a much more entertaining way. Whatever her profession (sexual therapist, anthropologist, chat show host) Shannon Tweed is always self-possessed, with an unerring knack for knowing what to do, whom to do it with, and when. She's strong and interesting and her crisply delivered dialogue is reserved for the moments she needs it most. Back to *Paris, France*: Leslie Hope, who bears a slight resemblance to Debra Winger, is never allowed to shut up for an instant. For those of you who are looking for a plot, this is it: Hope is married to a publisher who thinks he's going to die in three days. Meanwhile, she has an affair with the poet who's living with her husband's business partner. Harsh words are exchanged about everyone's techniques, obsessions, and manners until the credits roll. All you'll see of Paris is the Eiffel Tower, but you can't have everything in an NC-17 movie. Now, in *Cannibal Women in the Avocado Jungle of Death* (only 90 minutes and PG-13) you get Shannon Tweed as a feminist professor AND Karen Mistal as her worst student, Bunny, who never can decide whether being wrapped up in red licorice is anti-feminist or not, PLUS Adrienne Barbeau, and ALL in the jungles of San Bernardino! It's what we call a Guilty Pleasure, as opposed to a Film-As-Pain entry like *Paris, France*. **WOOF!**

1994 (NC-17) 111m/C *CA* Leslie Hope, Peter Outerbridge, Victor Ertmanis, Raoul Trujillo, Dan Lett; **D:** Gerard Ciccoritti; **W:** Tom Walmsley; **M:** John McCarthy. **VHS** *APX*

Paris Is Burning

Why is a documentary about vogueing at New York drag balls called *Paris Is Burning*? Heck if I know, but Jennie Livingston's documentary is a valuable record of its era, filmed at the Paris Ballroom in the Bronx between 1985-89. The contestants, mostly black or Hispanic gay males, get to be stars for as long as they're in costume. Except for the postscript, it's funny and nonjudgmental and at 71 minutes in length, it won't wear out its welcome. 🦴🦴🦴

1991 (R) 71m/C Dorian Corey, Pepper Labeija, Venus Xtravaganza, Octavia St. Laurant, Willi Ninja, Anji Xtravaganza, Freddie Pendavis, Junior Labeija; **D:** Jennie Livingston. National Society of Film Critics Awards '91: Best Feature Documentary; Sundance Film Festival '91: Grand Jury Prize. **VHS** *ACA, FCT*

Party Girl

The onscreen presence of Parker Posey is among the bright spots of moviegoing in the 1990s. Posey poured gallons of energy into many indie flicks of the decade; *Party Girl* was her chance to break out of background roles into genuine leading status. The success of the *Party Girl* movie led to a very short-lived television series starring Christine ("Marcia") Taylor of *The Brady Bunch* films. So whatever her critics may say about Parker Posey, she gave Daisy von Scherler Mayer's debut film a stylish edge that definitely lingers in the mind. As Mary, Posey is broke and headed nowhere fast when her godmother (played by Sasha von Scherler, the director's mum) reluctantly gives her a chance in a library job. Mary learns the Dewey Decimal System as if her life depended on it. Ditzy characters, sharp dialogue, and the eccen-

INDEPENDENT FILM GUIDE

Parker Posey parties in *Party Girl*.

tric party scene all contribute to the lively ambiance, but it's Parker Posey's high-voltage performance that makes filing books and picking up Mustafa the falafel vendor (Omar Townsend) seem vital. Very good repeat value on this one. 🦴🦴🦴

1994 (R) 94m/C Parker Posey, Omar Townsend, Anthony De Sando, Guillermo Diaz, Sasha von Scherler, Liev Schreiber; **D:** Daisy von Scherler Mayer; **W:** Harry Birckmayer, Daisy von Scherler Mayer; **C:** Michael Slovis; **M:** Anton Sanko. **VHS, LV, Closed Caption** COL

Pas Tres Catholique

Tonie Marshall's *Pas Tres Catholique* is an intriguing study of a private detective, thoughtfully played by Anemone. The mysteries she has to resolve mostly have to do with her own life, and especially the young son who is a stranger to her (Gregoire Colin is an attractive presence as teenaged Baptiste). What the film lacks in genuine narrative drive is more than compensated for by Anemone's remarkably shaded performance. **AKA:** Something Fishy. 🦴🦴🦴

1993 100m/B *FR* Anemone, Christine Boisson, Michel Didym, Gregoire Colin, Denis Podalydes, Roland Bertin, Bernard Verley, Michel Roux; **Cameos:** Micheline Presle; **D:** Tonie Marshall; **W:** Tonie Marshall; **C:** Dominique Chapuis. Nominations: Cesar Awards '95: Best Actress (Anemone).

Pass the Ammo

Pass the Ammo, another recent effort by David Beaird, is a televangelism spoof starring Tim Curry and Annie Potts as a pair of preachers who are kidnapped on camera by a gang that includes Linda Kozlowski, a disgruntled victim of their media pitching. The effectiveness of the satire is variable and some of the screenwriter's ideas may have looked better on paper than they do onscreen. Curry is believably charismatic, Potts is quite fetching as his glamorous wife, Anthony Geary is wonderful as their subversive engineer, and the sheer force of their personalities plus the *Pass the Ammo*'s obvious critique of the Bakker empire may propel the whole thing along with sympathetic viewers. 𝄢𝄢𝄢

1988 (R) 93m/C Bill Paxton, Tim Curry, Linda Kozlowski, Annie Potts, Anthony Geary, Dennis Burkley, Glenn Withrow, Richard Paul; *D:* David Beaird; *W:* Neil Cohen, Joel Cohen; *M:* Carter Burwell. **VHS, Beta, LV** *LIV*

Passion Fish

Passion Fish is an example of what John Sayles can do without a net, the net being all the stuff people think they want to see in a movie. It's like falling in love with someone who isn't your type. If you care about someone, what the heck does your so-called type matter? May-Alice used to be a soap opera star on television, but while on the way to a leg waxing in Manhattan, she was in an accident with a cab and the lower half of her body became paralyzed. So May-Alice becomes a Louisiana recluse, chain-drinking and chain-watching the telly until Nurse Chantelle arrives on the scene. Chantelle tosses the liquor, determined to make good on this job so that she can prove she's worthy of her daughter's custody. (There's drug addiction in Chantelle's past.) May-Alice starts getting interested in old flame Rennie (David Strathairn) again, and Chantelle has a glint in her eye for Sugar LeDoux (Vondie Curtis-Hall). The fact that these guys have 15 kids between them is academic, considering the rarefied life that May-Alice (Mary McDonnell) and Chantelle (Alfre Woodard) are leading. Both deliver exceptional performances, and Sayles' gentle, easy-going script and direction open a viewer's heart just as the onscreen characters are trying to open theirs. 𝄢𝄢𝄢

1992 (R) 136m/C Mary McDonnell, Alfre Woodard, David Strathairn, Vondie Curtis-Hall, Nora Dunn, Sheila Kelley, Angela Bassett, Mary Portser, Maggie Renzi, Leo Burmester, Shauntisa Willis, John Henry, Michael Laskin; *D:* John Sayles; *W:* John Sayles; *C:* Roger Deakins; *M:* Mason Daring. Independent Spirit Awards '93: Best Supporting Actress (Woodard); Nominations: Academy Awards '92: Best Actress (McDonnell), Best Original Screenplay. **VHS, LV, Closed Caption** *COL, MOV, BTV*

Passionate Thief

It is New Year's Eve in Rome and the 52-year-old movie extra played by Anna Magnani is filled with hope for the night. She longs for romance, adventure, and excitement and finds all three, though not in the way she had anticipated. She runs into a drunk middle-aged American businessman played by Fred Clark. She keeps running into another Cinecitta bit actor portrayed by Toto, then 62. And finally she meets Ben Gazzara, then 30, the title character of *The Passionate Thief*, directed by Mario Monicelli. In this 1960 film, Monicelli captures all the tension that traditionally accompanies New Year's Eve, a night when we think of our progress as human beings, our ability to attract and sustain love, and our own mortality. To stave off such cosmic musings, there are parties and celebrations and endless glasses of champagne. Magnani's character is forever in pursuit of The Ultimate Party, but there are obstacles wherever she turns. She is late for a bash with co-workers, who leave the rendezvous point without her. She spends much precious time alone on public transportation after being ditched by Gazzara and Toto. She is spared the knowledge that the hot-fingered Gazzara, her romantic target for the night, has no interest in her and only wants to pick up some stolen loot, with Toto as a reluctant accomplice. With Magnani in the role, the adolescent longings of this small-time actress are quite contagious. She believes in love, in the future, and in herself. She is not jaded by life's many setbacks, although she certainly has

The Hound Salutes:
JOHN SAYLES
Passion Fish

I don't think in terms of career moves. I don't think people follow what I do that closely to say, 'Oh, we're tired of *Matewan, Eight Men Out,* and *City of Hope,* we want something else.' But I do think the main difference was that I had just done three movies in a row where almost all the plot was put forward by men. Knowing as many underemployed actresses as I do, and having had the basic idea for *Passion Fish* for a long time, it seemed like this would be a good time to make a movie that's more about women....

"One of the things about *City of Hope* is that even though it was a movie with about fifteen leads, I wanted a feeling like if the camera had just kept following any one of those characters, you could have had a whole movie about that person, and that's very much how I asked the actors to prepare for it: 'You're not an extra in this movie, you're not a small character, this movie is about YOU, even though the camera may not follow you when you take a left and the camera goes right'.... One of the most important things for us as independent filmmakers is control over the final cut and control over the casting. No matter what you write, if you cast the wrong actors, and they may be very good actors, but they may not be right for the roles or you may not want to re-write behavior for a person who's 20 years old. If you cast an actor who's 40 years old, it may not seem cute and innocent, it may seem pathological. So you have to be very, very careful to control your casting. I had

plenty of reasons. She is willing to pay for her mistaken dreams and she seems invulnerable to despair. Magnani's and Toto's tour-de-force performances contribute to make *The Passionate Thief* a very funny, immensely touching story. *AKA:* Risate de Gioia; Joyous Laughter. 🦴🦴🦴

1960 100m/C *IT* Anna Magnani, Ben Gazzara, Fred Clark, Toto, Edy Vessel; *D:* Mario Monicelli. **VHS, Beta** *NLC*

Pastime

A bittersweet baseball elegy set in the minor leagues in 1957. A boyish 41-year-old pitcher can't face his impending retirement and pals around with the team's pariah, a 17-year-old black rookie. Splendidly written and acted, it's a melancholy treat whether you're a fan of the game or not, and safe for family attendance. Shot at Chicago's Comiskey Park (now leveled). Note major league cameos. *AKA:* One Cup of Coffee. 🦴🦴🦴

1991 (PG) 94m/C William Russ, Scott Plank, Glenn Plummer, Noble Willingham, Jeffrey Tambor, Deirdre O'Connell, Ricky Paull Goldin; *Cameos:* Ernie Banks, Harmon Killebrew, Duke Snider, Bob Feller, Bill Mazeroski, Don Newcombe; *D:* Robin B. Armstrong; *W:* Robin B. Armstrong. Sundance Film Festival '91: Audience Award. **VHS, LV** *COL*

worked with Mary McDonnell in *Matewan* [she played Elma Radnor, the boarding house owner], and I had worked with Alfre Woodard indirectly in 1986. I'd written a movie for television called *Unnatural Causes* about Agent Orange [John Ritter, Woodard, Patti LaBelle, John Vargas, Gwen E. Davis, and Sayles as Lloyd, directed by Lamont Johnson with music by Charles Fox], and she had played Maude DeVictor, the lead in that. So we had met before and exchanged 'Oh-I'd-love-to-work-with-you-again.' If it were a diving competition, *Passion Fish* would be a degree of difficulty of ten. I really needed actors who could play subtext at the same time as they were doing something else. They both play people who are hiding a lot and holding a lot back. So you need actors who can do that and do it in the very difficult situation of a movie where you don't get to do it in order....

"In the first week, we did all of the movie starts with May-Alice going through rehabilitation, which she doesn't want any part of and is resisting, so that Mary McDonnell got to do the most intense physical work and the most intense emotional work when she's alone, all in one lump. And then the next week, we started with Alfre Woodard as Chantelle, but the vagaries of filmmaking and the amount of money and time we had meant that we had to jump around out of sequence. And there, a lot of what you do is sit with the actors and say, 'Okay, this is the scene that just happened. We may or may not have shot it yet. This is the scene that's about to happen, we may or may not have shot it yet. This is what just happened in your life that may or may not even be onscreen, so this is the mood you're in: Go to it!'.... I think that being an actor myself does help me as a director."

JOHN SAYLES' films as a writer/director include: *Return of the Secaucus 7, Baby It's You, Lianna, The Brother from Another Planet, The Secret of Roan Inish,* and *Lone Star.*

Peeping Tom

Peeping Tom was made in 1960, the same year as Alfred Hitchcock's *Psycho,* but Powell's film was much kinkier and demanded far more from its audiences than the wildly successful *Psycho* did. It is not hard to sympathize with the shy, soft-spoken innkeeper played by Anthony Perkins and to wonder if maybe he and Janet Leigh will have a romance, but you want to warn innocent Anna Massey to stay away from the obsessed photographer portrayed by Karl Boehm. *Peeping Tom* was panned upon release by critics who had apparently thought Michael Powell was the maker of staid and genteel films. They must have gone out for popcorn when Kathleen Byron's insane nun applied her lipstick in *Black Narcissus,* for Powell had slipped in a hint of the dark side of human nature in many of his films. He doesn't pull any punches in *Peeping Tom,* and the film emerges as one of the most fascinating character studies of a killer ever put on film. That's Powell, by the way, in the old home movies showing the photographer's father. 🦴🦴🦴🦴

1960 88m/C Karl-Heinz Boehm, Moira Shearer, Anna Massey, Maxine Audley, Esmond Knight, Shirley

INDEPENDENT FILM GUIDE

Anne Field, Brenda Bruce, Pamela Green, Jack Watson, Nigel Davenport, Susan Travers, Veronica Hurst, Martin Miller; *Cameos:* Michael Powell; *D:* Michael Powell. **VHS, Beta, LV** *HMV, AOV*

Permanent Record

In *Permanent Record,* Marisa Silver's excellent film on teen suicide, Alan Boyce is so appealing as a troubled young composer that his death is genuinely horrifying; we never stop thinking about him or missing him for the rest of the movie. His best friend is wonderfully played by Keanu Reeves, so good in 1987's *River's Edge.* The well written script neither glamorizes suicide nor betrays the believability of its characters. Although the suicide in the film appears inevitable, the resulting trauma could have resulted in a chain reaction, which wasn't helped by the moralistic approach of heavy authority figures and was only circumvented by other adults who were able to identify and cope with the kids' grief. ♫♫♫

1988 (PG-13) 92m/C Alan Boyce, Keanu Reeves, Michelle Meyrink, Jennifer Rubin, Pamela Gidley, Michael Elgart, Richard Bradford, Barry Corbin, Kathy Baker, Dakin Matthews; *D:* Marisa Silver; *W:* Jarre Fees, Alice Liddle, Larry Ketron; *C:* Frederick Elmes; *M:* Joe Strummer. **VHS, Beta, LV, Closed Caption** *PAR*

Persuasion

Admirers of Jane Austen won't want to miss *Persuasion,* starring Amanda Root as a selfless Austen heroine swayed from the course of true love by family considerations. This delicately played study of English country life circa 1814 features a spirited performance by Root and a fine supporting cast: Corin Redgrave and Sophie Thompson from *Four Weddings and a Funeral,* Phoebe Nicholls from *Brideshead Revisited,* and the late Susan Fleetwood from *Heat and Dust.* ♫♫♫

1995 (PG) 104m/C *GB* Amanda Root, Ciaran Hinds, Susan Fleetwood, Corin Redgrave, Fiona Shaw, John Woodvine, Phoebe Nicholls, Sam West, Sophie Thompson, Judy Cornwell, Felicity Dean, Simon Rus-

sell Beale, Victoria Hamilton, Emma Roberts; *D:* Roger Mitchell; *W:* Nick Dear, Jeremy Sams; *C:* John Daly. **VHS, LV, Closed Caption** *COL*

Phantom of Liberty

Even at 74, Luis Bunuel (1900-83) could still romp with his audiences with an appreciation of playfulness at its deepest and purest levels, jesting here, poking there. *The Phantom of Liberty* is a delicious film: warm, humorous, and delightful. Stories of pornography, violence, death, Catholicism, and convention all wind into each other, and each and every subject is ribbed to bits by film's end. (Only Bunuel could direct a dinner sequence as wild as the one you'll see in this film!) Bunuel's next film, 1977's *That Obscure Object of Desire,* was his swan song. *AKA:* Le Fantome de la Liberte; The Specter of Freedom. ♫♫♫♫

1974 104m/C *FR* Adrianna Asti, Jean-Claude Brialy, Michel Piccoli, Adolfo Celi, Monica Vitti, Milena Vukotic, Michel Lonsdale, Claude Pieplu, Julien Bertheau, Paul Frankeur, Paul Leperson, Bernard Verley; *D:* Luis Bunuel; *W:* Luis Bunuel, Jean-Claude Carriere; *C:* Edmond Richard. National Board of Review Awards '74: 5 Best Foreign Films of the Year. **VHS, Beta, LV** *XVC, APD*

Phobia

Phobia, John Dingwall's riveting movie from Australia, is a good bet for inclusion in a list of the ten best first films ever made. The film stars Polish actress Gosia Dobrowolska as Renate Simmons, whose naked face reveals her progressive recognition of the depth of her agoraphobia. This paralyzing fear of open spaces thwarts her efforts to heal herself at every turn. Renate's husband and "phobic companion" is played by Sean Scully, whose multi-layered performance as Bob won him an Australian Academy Award nomination. Scully starred in the Walt Disney classics *The Prince and the Pauper, Almost Angels,* and *The Scarecrow of Romney Marsh* between 1962 and 1964 and also in 1981's *Sara*

INDEPENDENT FILM GUIDE

Opposite page: **Anna Massey in *Peeping Tom.***

Dane. Scully has surpassed his early promise and now, with his preternatural knack for zooming in on the heart of sexual frustration, he has the potential to become one of the leading actors of his generation. (Grown-ups may not have been aware of the underlying sexual tension in Scully's juvenile work, but pre-teen girls certainly were!) Dingwall's *Phobia* script is a dizzying blend of terror and comedy, of love and loathing, of compassion and scrutiny. To suggest both the brighter days and the gradual disintegration of this tortured couple, the director uses the effective device of old home videotapes, Bob's obsessive preoccupation. Dingwall also makes marvelous use of his own suburban home in Newport, New South Wales, although one hopes that the place is more fun for him to live in than this searing film suggests. ♫♫♫♫

1988 85m/C Sean Scully, Gosia Dobrowolska; *D:* John Dingwall; *W:* John Dingwall. *PAR*

The Piano

The Piano is a long, brooding story about sexual politics circa 1850. Oscar winners Holly Hunter and Anna Paquin play Ada and Flora McGrath, who leave Scotland in order to settle in New Zealand with Ada's new husband, Stewart, whom neither of them has ever seen. After a rough voyage, they are confronted with the stark loneliness of their new home and the loss of Ada's most treasured belonging, her piano; Stewart (Sam Neill) won't carry it to his house. He gives what is not his to give to George Baines (Harvey Keitel), another settler. Ada pines for her piano and George pines for her; they soon make an arrangement where she can buy it back from him with escalating erotic favors. Mother and daughter, who have always been close, find themselves at opposite ends of Stewart's power struggle. All Flora can see is that Stewart appears to be doing his best and they are, after all, living with him. Ada, who is mute, cannot explain the complexities of her situation to her daughter, who is too young to know how she is placing her mother in grave danger. Nothing is simple in Jane Campion's artfully woven screenplay (also an Oscar winner), which evolves in increasingly strange and disturbing ways. The strong imagery here is the stuff that nightmares are made of, especially the final shot. Hunter turned up later in David Cronenberg's *Crash* as a crash survivor strung out on crash-related sex; Paquin next played young *Jane Eyre* for Franco Zeffirelli and then made kiddie matinee movies in Hollywood. ♫♫♫

1993 (R) 120m/C *AU* Holly Hunter, Harvey Keitel, Sam Neill, Anna Paquin, Kerry Walker, Genevieve Lemon; *D:* Jane Campion; *W:* Jane Campion; *C:* Stuart Dryburgh; *M:* Michael Nyman. Academy Awards '93: Best Actress (Hunter), Best Original Screenplay, Best Supporting Actress (Paquin); Australian Film Institute '93: Best Actor (Keitel), Best Actress (Hunter), Best Cinematography, Best Costume Design, Best Director (Campion), Best Film, Best Film Editing, Best Screenplay, Best Sound, Best Original Score; British Academy Awards '93: Best Actress (Hunter); Cannes Film Festival '93: Best Actress (Hunter), Best Film; Golden Globe Awards '94: Best Actress—Drama (Hunter); Independent Spirit Awards '94: Best Foreign Film; Los Angeles Film Critics Association Awards '93: Best Actress (Hunter), Best Cinematography, Best Director (Campion), Best Screenplay, Best Supporting Actress (Paquin); National Board of Review Awards '93: Best Actress (Hunter); New York Film Critics Awards '93: Best Actress (Hunter), Best Director (Campion), Best Screenplay; National Society of Film Critics Awards '93: Best Actress (Hunter), Best Screenplay; Writers Guild of America '93: Best Original Screenplay; Nominations: Academy Awards '93: Best Cinematography, Best Costume Design, Best Director (Campion), Best Film Editing, Best Picture; British Academy Awards '94: Best Director (Campion), Best Film, Best Original Screenplay, Best Original Score; Directors Guild of America '93: Best Director (Campion); Golden Globe Awards '94: Best Director (Campion), Best Film—Drama, Best Screenplay, Best Supporting Actress (Paquin), Best Original Score. **VHS, LV, Closed Caption** *LIV*

Picnic at Hanging Rock

1975's *Picnic at Hanging Rock,* Peter Weir's exquisitely lensed Australian film, is something of a cautionary tale about the conflict between nature and civilization. Three girls and their teacher persist in imposing themselves on a threatening landscape about which they know nothing except its age. They fail, and the one girl who does return can't remember why. Even before they leave the picnic, their attachments to the others are loose, and they are riddled with a sense of their own mortality. Unlike most contemporary treatments of the past which thrust current sensibilities on an earlier time, Weir's international classic reveals Valentine's Day 1900 on its own terms, with the exception of one new twist on the old chestnut of separated twins. The sweet-voiced Helen Morse perfectly illustrates the interior strength and surface gentleness that survived best in that era. The faces, especially the hauntingly lovely Anne Lambert, are straight out of an old photograph album and the dialogue betrays no ironic premonitions of how the new century will disrupt the Victorian world. Based on a novel by Joan Lindsay, who never revealed whether her chiller was inspired by a true story—or not! ♫♫♫♫

1975 (PG) 110m/C *AU* Margaret Nelson, Rachel Roberts, Dominic Guard, Helen Morse, Jacki Weaver, Vivean Gray, Anne Lambert; *D:* Peter Weir; *C:* John Seale; *M:* Bruce Smeaton. **VHS, Beta** *VES, OM*

Picture Bride

It is 1918. Seventeen-year-old Riyo arrives in Hawaii from Yokohama. She is marrying Matsuji (Akira Takayama) and they only know each other through the exchange of photographs. When she learns that Matsuji sent her a 25-year-old picture, she feels tricked and will not let him sleep with her. She has no money to go home, but determines to do so as soon as she earns the $300 return fare by working on a sugar plantation at 65 cents a day. If only Riyo had gone on to show the gumption that she proved she already had when she first arrived in Hawaii, *Picture Bride* would he a much more gripping film. Instead, we get

"And at the same moment my father was struck dead my mother was struck dumb. She never spoke another word."

—Flora McGrath's (Anna Paquin) narration sets up the story in *The Piano.*

INDEPENDENT FILM GUIDE

female bonding, tragedy, submission, and acquiescence. We don't know what Riyo feels and the emotional territory that Kayo Hatta covers here is awfully familiar. Better films about the immigrant experience include 1979's *Gaijin* by Tiruka Yamasaki and 1991's *1000 Pieces of Gold* by Nancy Kelly. Toshiro Mifune makes a cameo appearance as a benshi (narrator) of a silent movie. 🎬🎬

1994 (PG-13) 95m/C *JP* Yoko Sugi, Youki Kudoh, Akira Takayama, Tamlyn Tomita, Cary-Hiroyuki Tagawa; *Cameos:* Toshiro Mifune; *D:* Kayo Hatta; *W:* Kayo Hatta, Mari Hatta, Diane Mark; *C:* Claudio Rocha; *M:* Cliff Eidelman. Sundance Film Festival '95: Audience Award; Nominations: Independent Spirit Awards '96: Best First Feature. **VHS, LV, Closed Caption** *TOU*

Pink String and Sealing Wax

Googie Withers came within an eyelash of giving Britain's top female star (Margaret Lockwood, with whom she'd appeared in 1938's *The Lady Vanishes*) a run for her money at the box office. This examination of a Victorian murderess (set in Brighton, circa 1880) is a fine vehicle for Withers, who clearly knows the secret that any great screen villain knows, namely that her character can do no wrong. Gordon Jackson is the youth who is seduced into her plans for homicide and Mervyn Johns does an excellent job as a father who nearly loses his family because of his rigid views on right and wrong. John Carol is as much of a dirty rat as you'll ever see in this sort of melodrama, and Mary Merrall, Jean Ireland, and Sally Ann Howes are appealing as the mother and daughters who learn how to manipulate an impossible family situation to their advantage. The minor characters are effective too, especially Catherine Lacey as Miss Porter, a tipsy but genteel barfly. The title refers to a catch phrase of the era and has nothing to do with the story. Based on the play by Roland Pertwee. 🎬🎬🎬

1945 89m/B *GB* Mervyn Johns, Mary Merrall, Gordon Jackson, Googie Withers, Sally Ann Howes, Catherine Lacey, Garry Marsh, Frederick Piper, Don Stannard, Valentine Dyall; *D:* Robert Hamer; *W:* Robert Hamer. **VHS, Beta** *SNC*

Pitfall

Pitfall is the second of three noir films Andre de Toth directed between 1944 and 1954. Only four years after *Murder My Sweet,* Dick Powell isn't Philip Marlowe anymore, he's insurance agent John Forbes, Sue's (Jane Wyatt) husband and Tommy's (Jimmy Hunt) father. Forbes once nurtured an adolescent fantasy that his life would be more interesting and more rewarding, but now the years of domestic rituals and insurance claims stretch ahead of him in all their yawning dullness. Forbes and a private investigator named Mack MacDonald (Raymond Burr) are trying to recover goods purchased with robbery loot. They meet model Mona Stevens (Lizabeth Scott), the robber's girlfriend, retrieve the goods, and the credits roll. Whoa, rewind! Well, what do you THINK happens? Frustrated agent and frustrated detective meet gorgeous blonde Mona, they all become pals (Sue and Tommy, too), and the credits roll. NOPE, this is Noirville. If John and Mona have an affair, all hell will break loose and it does. Remember: Mack is frustrated, too. Mona has a boyfriend in jail (Byron Barr as Bill Smiley). Sue doesn't know about Mona, which means she'll HAVE to know about Mona, and life will never be the same. The moral? Don't choke on your adolescent fantasies! We're practically in the 1950s, boys and girls, domestic rituals and insurance claims are GOOD for you, sex with the cool blonde who hates the detective who wants to have sex with the cool blonde instead of you is BAD for you. Again: Wife and work: GOOD. Affair with Mona: BAD. De Toth shows how the crushing weight of the familiar would drive a guy like John Forbes to go wild. He also shows that the familiar is equally crushing to Sue Forbes, and only her faith in a faithless partner makes it any more bearable for her. And de Toth gets a really sick and twisted performance out of Burr, who's aces as Mack! Look for de Toth's *Dark Waters* and *Crime Wave,* also on video. Based on the novel by Jay Dratler. 🦴🦴🦴

1948 85m/B Dick Powell, Jane Wyatt, Lizabeth Scott, Raymond Burr, John Litel, Byron Barr, Ann Doran, Jimmy Hunt, Selmer Jackson, Margaret Wells, Dick Wassel; *D:* Andre de Toth; *W:* Karl Kamb; *C:* Harry Wild; *M:* Louis Forbes. **VHS, LV** *REP, FCT*

Pixote

Both 1981's *Pixote* by Hector Babenco and 1984's *Streetwise* by Martin Bell offer a harsh portrait of the lives led by street children. Both *Streetwise* and *Pixote* (a horrifying fictional saga of a ten-year-old murderer) raise disturbing questions for which neither film provides answers. Bell and Babenco attracted considerable reputations for their honesty in showing the toll of street hustling on the very young. The children are clearly no better off, and in the case of *Pixote*'s young star, the doors to acting which were opened by his appearance in an international hit were quickly slammed. Young Fernando Ramos Da Silva eventually returned to the street life he shared with three million children in Sao Paulo. He was killed in a shootout with the police early in 1987. 🦴🦴🦴🦴

1981 127m/C *BR* Fernando Ramos Da Silva, Marilia Pera, Jorge Juliao, Gilberto Moura, Jose Nilson dos Santos, Edilson Lino; *D:* Hector Babenco; *W:* Hector Babenco; *M:* John Neschling. Los Angeles Film Critics Association Awards '81: Best Foreign Film; New York Film Critics Awards '81: Best Foreign Film; National Society of Film Critics Awards '81: Best Actress (Pera). **VHS, Beta** *COL*

Plan 9 from Outer Space

It's hard to put a WOOF!! by this movie, because I enjoy it so much. I have this six-hour tape that includes the following: (1) *Queen of Outer Space,* (2) *Attack of the 50 Ft. Woman,* (3) this movie, and (4) *Bait.* Put this tape in the VCR at midnight and

Voila! Auf Wiedershen, Insomnia! Tor Johnson couldn't do dialogue, Vampira wouldn't do dialogue, and Mona McKinnon shouldn't do dialogue, EVER! Ask Gregory Walcott about this movie and he'll tell you about co-starring with Claudette Colbert in 1955! Ask Conrad Brooks about this movie and he'll tell you everyone got paid! Tom Keene (who looks absolutely shell-shocked as Col. Edwards) starred in 1934's *Our Daily Bread* under the direction of King Vidor! Joanna Lee won a 1974 Emmy as a writer! I have a hunch that many contemporary young directors are oddly inspired by Ed Wood and his films. (Wood also wrote and/or directed *Jail Bait, Female, Revenge of the Dead, Hellborn, Glen or Glenda?,* and *Bride of the Monster.*) They can't all be the greatest director of all time and they know it. That inner voice that nags even the greatest artists into feeling that the projects into which they've poured all their energies, may turn out to be nothing after all, is far more prevalent than, say, crushing self-confidence. It's hard to resist an optimistic soul like Ed Wood who tried his very hardest and who did, in fact, entertain people, if not in the way he'd always dreamed of doing. *AKA:* Grave Robbers from Outer Space. **WOOF!**

1956 78m/B Bela Lugosi, Tor Johnson, Lyle Talbot, Vampira, Gregory Walcott, Tom Keene, Dudley Manlove, Mona McKinnon, Duke Moore, Joanna Lee, Bunny Breckinridge, Criswell, Carl Anthony, Paul Marco, Norma McCarty, David DeMering, Bill Ash, Conrad Brooks, Edward D. Wood Jr.; *D:* Edward D. Wood Jr.; *W:* Edward D. Wood Jr.; *C:* William C. Thompson. **VHS, Beta, LV** *NOS, SNC, MED*

Platoon

I saw plenty of movies between 1978 and 1985, but never the Best Picture of the Year, by choice. As I listened to people drone on and on about their favorite sequences from these films, I really didn't think I was missing anything and still don't. My own favorites were movies I watched over and over again and still do, stuff like *Dinner for Adele, Escape from*

The Hound Salutes:
GREGORY WALCOTT
Plan 9 from Outer Space

Actor GREGORY WALCOTT co-starred with Claudette Colbert in 1956's *Texas Lady* and made films with Tony Curtis (1961's *The Outsider*) and Lee Marvin (1972's *Prime Cut*). In 1994, he appeared in Tim Burton's *Ed Wood* as a potential backer. Walcott achieved immortality as Jeff Trent in 1957, when *Plan 9 from Outer Space* was on the bottom half of a double bill with *Time Lock,* featuring a Scottish newcomer named Sean Connery.

'll probably go to my grave NOT remembered for the movies that I did with Steven Spielberg [1974's *The Sugarland Express*] and Clint Eastwood [1972's *Joe Kidd* and *The Eiger Sanction*] and John Ford [1955's *Mister Roberts*] and Martin Ritt and Howard Hawks, but they'll remember me for that stupid *Plan 9 from Outer Space.* It drives me nuts, but I've learned to laugh about it. It was probably my most unexciting acting performance in my life. The thing was shot in four days and I walked on the set at two in the afternoon for the last scene I had to do. I said to Ed Wood, 'Where is the interior of the cockpit?' He said, 'Well, they're constructing it.' I kept waiting for them to bring it out until two carpenters walked on the set with two masonite boards. They bent them into an arch and fastened them to the floor and dragged in some pieces from the flying saucer, put in a shower curtain, and THAT was the cockpit. I was baffled. The old cameraman, who was quite good, shook his head in dismay and lit the set so that everything was out of focus except our noses. Ed Wood, who looked a little like Errol Flynn, was a charming schemer. You couldn't trust him, but you couldn't help but admire him because when he started a project, he wanted to finish it. He'd go to all kinds of extremes to get people to put money in it. I thought *Plan 9* would die out in the woods somewhere and I dodged it for years, but I kept getting calls and letters from magazines and newspapers in England and Germany and Japan, so I finally decided that it's not going to go away, so I might as well have fun with it."

Alcatraz, Somewhere in Time, True Confessions, Fast Times at Ridgemont High, Heat and Dust, Another Country, and *Dance with a Stranger.* Now that I've established my qualifications as a bit of a Philistine, I have to say that what burns in my memory about *Platoon* is that goofball moment from one of the *Naked Gun* pictures when a deliriously happy Leslie Nielsen and Priscilla Presley come bounding out of the movie theatre where *Platoon* is playing as Herman's Hermits sing "Something Tells Me I'm into Something Good." I was dragged to see *Platoon* by a guy who predicted that it would be the Best Picture of the Year. All I knew was that I'd already seen the Best Picture of the Year and that was *Salvador*! But you can resign yourself to anything, even a 113-minute war movie with no female characters in it. Based on the true experiences of its filmmaker, *Platoon* is graphic and well acted, especially by Willem Dafoe. It launched a wave of other Vietnam war movies which I didn't see. Once you've been scared to bits by *On the Beach* and *Fail-Safe,* what's the point? I give it four bones for the cognoscenti, and two bones for fans of Leslie Nielsen and/or James Woods, for an average of 🦴🦴🦴

1986 (R) 113m/C Charlie Sheen, Willem Dafoe, Tom Berenger, Francesco Quinn, Forest Whitaker, John C. McGinley, Kevin Dillon, Richard Edson, Reggie Johnson, Keith David, Johnny Depp; **D:** Oliver Stone; **W:** Oliver Stone; **C:** Robert Richardson; **M:** Georges Delerue. Academy Awards '86: Best Director (Stone), Best Film Editing, Best Picture, Best Sound; British Academy Awards '87: Best Director (Stone); Directors Guild of America Awards '86: Best Director (Stone); Golden Globe Awards '87: Best Director (Stone), Best Film—Drama, Best Supporting Actor (Berenger); Independent Spirit Awards '87: Best Cinematography, Best Director (Stone), Best Film, Best Screenplay; National Board of Review Awards '86: 10 Best Films of the Year; Nominations: Academy Awards '86: Best Cinematography, Best Original Screenplay, Best Supporting Actor (Berenger, Dafoe). **VHS, Beta, LV, Closed Caption** *LIV, BTV*

The Player

The Player did for Robert Altman's career at the age of 67 what *Prizzi's Honor* had done for John Huston's career seven years earlier at the age of 79: it turned him into a hot young director all over again. This savage satire of Hollywood, informed by a myriad of details that could only be assembled via thorough scrutiny over the long haul, is every bit as brilliant a depiction of Hollywood in the '90s as *Sunset Boulevard* was of Hollywood in the '50s. The less said about this masterwork the better, because a large share of the fun comes from not knowing who or what's going to pop up next. If it's a textbook scenario, Heaven help Hollywood in the 21st century. The first shot is a jaw dropper, ditto Tim Robbins' and Vincent D'Onofrio's

performances as the symbol and sacrificial lamb of the industry. And, if you really want to blow your mind, watch *The Player* on a double bill with 1957's *The Delinquents,* Altman's very first movie! 🦴🦴🦴🦴

1992 (R) 123m/C Tim Robbins, Greta Scacchi, Fred Ward, Whoopi Goldberg, Peter Gallagher, Brion James, Cynthia Stevenson, Vincent D'Onofrio, Dean Stockwell, Richard E. Grant, Dina Merrill, Sydney Pollack, Lyle Lovett, Randall Batinkoff, Gina Gershon; **Cameos:** Michael Tolkin, Louise Fletcher, Dennis Franz, Malcolm McDowell, Ray Walston, Rene Auberjonois, David Alan Grier, Jayne Meadows, Michael Bowen, Steve James, Brian Tochi, Burt Reynolds, Cher, Nick Nolte, Jack Lemmon, Lily Tomlin, Marlee Matlin, Julia Roberts, Bruce Willis, Anjelica Huston, Elliott Gould, Sally Kellerman, Steve Allen, Richard Anderson, Harry Belafonte, Shari Belafonte, Karen Black, Gary Busey, Robert Carradine, James Coburn, Cathy Lee Crosby, John Cusack, Brad Davis, Peter Falk, Teri Garr, Leeza Gibbons, Scott Glenn, Jeff Goldblum, Joel Grey, Buck Henry, Kathy Ireland, Sally Kirkland, Andie MacDowell, Martin Mull, Mimi Rogers, Jill St. John, Susan Sarandon, Rod Steiger, Joan Tewkesbury, Robert Wagner; **D:** Robert Altman; **W:** Michael Tolkin; **C:** Jean Lepine; **M:** Thomas Newman. British Academy Awards '92: Best Adapted Screenplay; Cannes Film Festival '92: Best Actor (Robbins), Best Director (Altman); Chicago Film Critics Awards '93: Best Director (Altman); Golden Globe Awards '93: Best Actor—Musical/Comedy (Robbins), Best Film—Musical/Comedy; Independent Spirit Awards '93: Best Film; New York Film Critics Awards '92: Best Cinematography, Best Director (Altman), Best Film; Writers Guild of America '92: Best Adapted Screenplay; Nominations: Academy Awards '92: Best Adapted Screenplay, Best Director (Altman), Best Film Editing. **VHS, LV, Closed Caption, DVD** *NLC, CRC, MOV*

Poison

A film in three segments, inspired by three Jean Genet stories: "Hero," a comedy set in Suburbia, shows how a seven-year-old boy's Mom, teacher, and friends try to explain why he killed Dad. In "Horror," another comedy, a mad scientist drinks this sex-drive fluid and looks and acts like a homicidal monster afterwards. "Homo," not a comedy, shows the mutual seduction of a couple of French prisoners. There's masturbation, anal intercourse, sadomasochism, plus a sequence where a bunch of guys spit into a kid's mouth. Not for all tastes, including mine. 1995's *Safe*

"Can we talk about something other than Hollywood for a change? We're educated people."

—Griffin Mill's (Tim Robbins) comment is met with dead silence, then raucous laughter, in *The Player.*

319

INDEPENDENT FILM GUIDE

**Tim Robbins plays
ruthless studio
executive Griffin
Mill in *The Player.***

by director Todd Haynes is better. I give *Poison* three bones for the hipsters, but for me, just 🦴

1991 (R) 85m/C Edith Meeks, Larry Maxwell, Susan Norman, Scott Renderer, James Lyons, Millie White, Buck Smith, Anne Giotta, Al Quagliata, Michelle Sullivan, John R. Lombardi, Tony Pemberton, Andrew Harpending; *D:* Todd Haynes; *W:* Todd Haynes; *C:* Maryse Alberti; *M:* James Bennett. Sundance Film Festival '91: Grand Jury Prize. **VHS** *FXL*

Popcorn

As horror movies go, *Popcorn* is about what you'd expect from a story that takes place at the fictitious Oceanview campus of the University of California but is filmed entirely on location in Jamaica. With the money the seven producers saved hiring non-union crews, they were able to cast Ray Walston in a take-a-leak-and-you'll-miss-him cameo PLUS Tony Roberts for a badly played feature role as a professor. In

the film-as-pain division, *Popcorn* is more fun than a root canal, but not half as enjoyable as renting an old American International video (or even *Cannibal Women in the Avocado Jungle of Death!*). The least painful segments of the film are the recreations of old horror movies from the '50s and '60s. There are no 3-D movies called *The Mosquito,* no *Attack of the Electrified Man* complete with wired theatre seats, no aromatic stinkers entitled *The Stench.* But someone associated with *Popcorn* obviously has fond memories of the gimmickry that helped to sell similar films in the past and there is genuine enthusiasm in these all-too-brief sequences. Unfortunately, the actual narrative of *Popcorn* has something to do with the legend of a terrible homicidal filmmaker, history repeating itself, characters trusting the wrong people, et cetera. Jill Schoelen, who turned in a fairly decent performance in *The Stepfather,* squeaks her way through *Popcorn* with negligible help from director Mark Herrier. Also wasted is Dee Wallace Stone, who presumably got to spend some time soaking up the Jamaican sun during the long stretches of the film when she is nowhere in sight. *Popcorn* might actually have been a much better movie if it had more of a visceral connection with the genre. After watching *Andy Hardy from Carvel meets Freddy from Elm Street in the Bahamas,* you may be groaning but not from fright. 🦴🦴

1989 (R) 93m/C Jill Schoelen, Tom Villard, Dee Wallace Stone, Derek Rydell, Elliott Hurst, Kelly Jo Minter, Malcolm Danare, Ray Walston, Tony Roberts; **D:** Mark Herrier; **W:** Alan Ormsby. **VHS, LV, 8mm** *COL*

The Postman

The Postman wrapped on June 3, 1994. Its star, Massimo Troisi, long overdue for a heart transplant, was killed by a heart attack within 24 hours. When he died, very few American audiences knew who Troisi was, but within a year, the whole world had fallen in love with Mario, the self-effacing title character in Michael Radford's *The Postman/Il Postino.* When exiled Chilean poet Pablo Neruda (1904-73, wonderfully portrayed by Phillipe Noiret) comes to stay on Isla Negra in 1952, Mario volunteers to be his postman. They become friends, and Mario asks Neruda if he will help him win Beatrice, the object of his desire (played by the absolutely gorgeous Maria Grazia Cucinotta). Troisi's beautifully sustained performance received a posthumous Academy Award nomination, and heartfelt tears from millions of moviegoers who were moved both by Mario and by the 41-year-old actor who sacrificed his life to play the role. Troisi can also be seen in 1983's *Hotel Colonial,* co-starring Robert Duvall, John Savage, and Rachel Ward. Just don't expect as perfectly realized a film as *The Postman/Il Postino.* **AKA:** Il Postino. 🦴🦴🦴🦴

1994 (PG) 115m/C *IT* Massimo Troisi, Philippe Noiret, Maria Grazia Cucinotta, Linda Moretti, Renato Scarpa, Anna Buonaiuto, Mariana Rigillo; **D:** Michael Radford; **W:** Massimo Troisi, Michael Radford, Furio Scarpelli, Anna Pavignano, Giacomo Scarpelli; **C:** Franco Di Giacomo; **M:** Luis Bacalov. Academy Awards '95: Original Dramatic/Comedy Score; British Academy Awards '95: Best Director (Radford), Best Foreign Film, Best Score; Broadcast Film Critics Association Awards '95: Best Foreign Language Film; Nominations: Academy Awards '95: Best Actor (Troisi), Best Adapted Screenplay, Best Director (Radford), Best Picture; British Academy Awards '95: Best Actor (Troisi), Best Adapted Screenplay; Cesar Awards '97: Best Foreign Film; Directors Guild of America Awards '95: Best Director (Radford); Screen Actors Guild Award '95: Best Actor (Troisi). **VHS** *TOU*

Powwow Highway

Gary Farmer is Philbert Bono, a Cheyenne Indian en route to New Mexico, who gives a ride to his activist friend Buddy Red Bow (A. Martinez). Their eye-opening travels give them and us a grim picture of Native American reservations, where living conditions and employment opportunities are poor. Under such day-to-day hardships, it becomes nearly impossible to maintain a sense of pride in past accomplishments and customs. Based on David Seals' novel. The large, mostly Native American cast includes Graham Greene as a Viet Nam veteran. 🦴🦴🦴

1989 (R) 105m/C Gary Farmer, A. Martinez, Amanda Wyss, Rene Handren-Seals, Graham Greene; **D:** Joanelle Romero, Jonathan Wacks; **W:** Janet Heaney, Jean Stawarz; **C:** Toyomichi Kurita; **M:** Barry Goldberg. Sundance Film Festival '89: Filmmakers Trophy. **VHS, Beta** *FCT*

Priest

For reasons which escape us, the 1994 movie *Priest* made the hierarchy of the Catholic Church far more nervous than 1993's *The Boys of St. Vincent,* a superior telefeature eventually broadcast in prime time on the Arts and Entertainment network. There were NO effective role models on that disturbing study of sexual abuse and its subsequent cover-up by Catholic brothers in a Canadian orphanage for young boys. No clergy member in *Priest* remotely approaches the evil villainy of St.

The Hound Salutes:
ROBERT ALTMAN
The Player

As I started recruiting people [for the film's cameos], I simply called them up. I gave them all the same pitch in 25 words or less. I said, 'I'm making a film about a studio executive who murders a writer and gets away with it.' And there's a laugh on the other end of the phone and I say 'It's got a happy ending.' And they say, 'Count me in. I'll do it'…. I think it's like signing a petition. I think that they agreed to this, and they were not the least bit self-serving in it. No one asked to read the script. None of them said, 'Can I bring my makeup man?' None of them asked 'What am I wearing? Who's the cameraman?' Nothing. They just said 'Where do I show up?'…I suppose some people turned me down, and I would not have been surprised if everybody had turned me down, nor would I have held it against anybody because if I were in that situation I don't think I would have done it…I lost several people because of schedules.

"We couldn't find an ending for this film that worked. They were all cheats. Every ending was a cop out and we said 'What isn't a cop out?' Well, the truth of the matter is, this is just a movie. This is a movie and we're trying to make a movie that's going to sell. So why not, we've got this perfect device here, turn around and say: Yeah, this guy's a writer…. It's like the ending of M.A.S.H. 'The movie you're about to see is the movie you have just seen.' I had all the sex, the nudity, the suspense. All that stuff is in my movie. Because it's an essay, you know. Which is not going to send people rushing down to the theatre to buy tickets, to see an essay. But that's really what it is. It's a discussion on this subject. And I use bad movies and bad movie techniques to make my point.

"If everybody in the world goes to see *The Player,* it ain't going to make the same money that *Star Wars* made because you're not going to see any 15- or 16-year-old people in this movie. They'll sit there and get bored, they won't get it, it's no fun for them. So by making the film, I've lost the vast majority of the audience but, so what. I mean this picture's made a profit already so why should anybody be upset about that."

The films of Oscar-nominee ROBERT ALTMAN include *Countdown, That Cold Day in the Park, Brewster McCloud, M.A.S.H., McCabe and Mrs. Miller, The Long Goodbye, Thieves Like Us, Nashville, Buffalo Bill and the Indians, A Wedding, Quintet, Popeye, Come Back to the Five and Dime, Jimmy Dean, Jimmy Dean, Streamers, Secret Honor, Beyond Therapy, Fool for Love, Dumb Waiter, O.C. and Stiggs, The Room, Aria, The Caine Mutiny Court Martial, Tanner '88, Vincent and Theo, Short Cuts,* **and** *Ready to Wear.*

Vincent's Brother Lavin, chillingly played by Henry Czerny. Antonia Bird's 1994 film reveals the ongoing moral dilemma faced by many Catholic priests today and suggests that the Church remains stubbornly out of touch with the tormented souls it professes to care for. Father Greg (Linus Roache) is a young Catholic priest determined to play by the book. "Sin is sin," he snaps at Father Matthew (Tom Wilkinson) when he discovers that the latter is sleeping with Maria the housekeeper (Cathy Tyson). But both Father Matthew and Maria are unrepentant about their living situation and tell Father Greg to mind his own business. For Father Greg, that includes a secret life in gay bars where he picks up Graham (Robert Carlyle). It also includes his self-doubts about the secrecy of the confessional when Lisa, a 14-year-old parishioner tells him about her incestuous relationship with her father. (Here's a tip for kids watching the film who are lucky enough to find a sympathetic priest who'll listen to their complaints about parental sex and/or violence; if you tell them outside of the confessional, great priests— and they do exist—can do something to help.) Father Greg feels powerless about his lover, especially when Graham shows up in Church on Sunday for Communion, and about Lisa, especially when her sociopathic father threatens him. Filmmakers before Bird (including Alfred Hitchcock with *I Confess* and Mike Hodges with *A Prayer for the Dying*) have had difficulty explaining the secrecy of the confessional to general audiences. But Father Greg, for all of Roache's fine acting, would be a dim bulb about his life choices even if he weren't a priest. E.g., if you want to have a private sex life AND be a dogmatic theologian, don't have sex on a public beach. It all gets very melodramatic after that, and *Priest,* unlike *The Boys of St. Vincent,* never quite escapes its television origins. But it asks some searching questions, many at least as agonizing as those raised by Peter, the Church's first Pope, on a grim Good Friday almost two thousand years ago. (Cast Note: At press time, Tom Wilkinson, who gets all the best, most compassionate, and sanest lines as Father Matthew in *Priest,* had been cast as the irate Marquess of Queensbury opposite Stephen Fry as Oscar and Jude Law as Lord Alfred "Bosie" Douglas in the forthcoming film *Wilde.*) 🦴🦴

1994 (R) 98m/C *GB* Linus Roache, Tom Wilkinson, Cathy Tyson, Robert Carlyle, James Ellis, John Bennett, Rio Fanning, Jimmy Coleman, Lesley Sharp, Robert Pugh, Christine Tremarco; *D:* Antonia Bird; *W:* Jimmy McGovern; *C:* Fred Tammes; *M:* Andy Roberts. Nominations: Australian Film Institute '95: Best Foreign Film. **VHS** *TOU*

The Prime of Miss Jean Brodie

The Prime of Miss Jean Brodie was my favorite movie of 1969. For a kid raised on the often baffling rules of Holy Rosary Convent School in Woodland, California, Jean Brodie seemed to me to be the coolest teacher in the universe. Charismatic, idiosyncratic, fearless, and funny, Jean Brodie (Dame Maggie Smith, then 34) was worshipped by her students, adored by her very married lover Teddy Lloyd (Sir Robert Stephens, then 37 and Smith's real-life husband), and cordially hated by Headmistress Miss Mackay (Dame Celia Johnson, then 60). I can't count how many times I watched the movie and then tried to fill in the blanks of the original novel by Muriel Spark. Spark freely admitted that she only found her true voice as a writer after she converted to Catholicism. Now what did THAT mean? Spark's satire of the sexually obsessed Catholic art teacher played by Sir Robert could not have been more biting. Teddy Lloyd was a breeder whose "unfortunate affiliation with the Church of Rome" (Jean Brodie's words) led him to sire masses of kids with Mrs. Lloyd while not-so-secretly lusting after the radiant Jean Brodie. And when she wearied of the dance, she actually selected a succes-

p

323

INDEPENDENT FILM GUIDE

**Linus Roache
in *Priest*.**

sor from among her young students to replace her in his bed. Lloyd and one of Brodie's OTHER students (the dependable and much-overlooked Sandy, played by Pamela Franklin, then 18) had other ideas, however, a reality that would present *The Prime of Miss Jean Brodie* with its gravest threat. The critics of 1969 raved about the powerful acting of Dame Maggie (who deservedly won her first Oscar that year). They sighed wistfully about the dozens of years that separated Dame Celia's superb work here from her affecting performance as Laura in *Brief Encounter.* And Pamela Franklin, who had first captivated international audiences as Flora in 1961's *The Innocents,* seemed on the verge of major stardom. (Franklin nearly turned down the role because she didn't want to play another schoolgirl, but was persuaded otherwise and tore into the role of Sandy, who evolves from worshipful naivete into

resentful treachery.) Sir Robert, too, added genuine poignance to the deceptively lightweight predicament of the mediocre painter with delusions of superiority. And Gordon Jackson, then 48, who would later achieve his greatest fame on *Upstairs, Downstairs* as Hudson, the quintessential butler, is just right as music teacher Gordon Lowther, yearning to marry Jean Brodie and settling for a semi-discreet affair. Jay Presson Allen's powerful screenplay and Ronald Neame's meticulous direction made the political and sexual concerns of 1930's Edinburgh seem immediate and timeless. (Sadly for her admirers, Franklin made just five more films, and only 1973's *The Legend of Hell House* is worth staying up late to see. Jane Carr as Mary MacGregor, the least likely to succeed among Jean Brodie's set, went on to star opposite Judd Hirsch in NBC's *Dear John* from 1988 to 1992.) ♫♫♫♫

1969 (PG) 116m/C *GB* Maggie Smith, Pamela Franklin, Robert Stephens, Celia Johnson, Gordon Jackson, Jane Carr; *D:* Ronald Neame; *W:* Jay Presson Allen; *C:* Ted Moore. Academy Awards '69: Best Actress (Smith); British Academy Awards '69: Best Actress (Smith), Best Supporting Actress (Johnson); Golden Globe Awards '70: Best Song ("Jean"); National Board of Review Awards '69: Best Supporting Actress (Franklin); Nominations: Academy Awards '69: Best Song ("Jean"); Cannes Film Festival '69: Best Film. **VHS, Closed Caption** *TCF, BTV*

Princess and the Goblin

Our niece Emma, then two years old, had severe reservations about 1994's *Thumbelina,* so we weren't quite sure how she would react to *The Princess and the Goblin.* Who knows what will or won't frighten very small children? This time around, Emma wasn't even mildly alarmed, not by dark caverns or subterranean creatures or a ghost in the castle tower. The three-year-old boy in the row behind us, though, screamed bloody murder at a huge close-up of one of the goblins. *The Princess and the Goblin* is based on George MacDonald's fairy tale from the year 1872. It revolves around the Princess Irene and her efforts to save the kingdom from an evil scheme hatched by the Froglip, the Goblins' leader. Irene is helped by the spirit of her magical grandmother, by her faithful cat Turnip, and by her young friend Curdle. Most of the grownups are fairly ineffectual; they're forever riding off somewhere or falling asleep or simply not paying attention. So it's the kids to the rescue for most of the narrative's 82 minutes. The artwork is nicely done and the voice artists (including Claire Bloom as Irene's grandmother and Joss Ackland as the King) are well chosen. Yet there seems to be a remote quality at the core of this movie as if the filmmakers felt they were skating on thin ice and were trying maybe a bit too hard to keep MacDonald's delicate allegory in balance: scary but not too horrifying, instructive but not too preachy, light-hearted but don't forget that Irene has to confront her

own fears in order to allay those of everyone else. Well, *The Princess and the Goblin* is a brave effort and Turnip the cat is a charming distraction, at least. If it does well, MacDonald also wrote *Irene and Curdle* in 1882, supplying ample source material for a sequel. 🦴🦴

1992 (PG) 82m/C *V:* Joss Ackland, Claire Bloom, William Hootkins; *D:* Jozsef Gemes. **VHS** *DOV, HMD*

The Private Life of Henry VIII

International audiences (and especially Hollywood industry types) started paying attention to British films after they saw *The Private Life of Henry VIII.* Charles Laughton and Elsa Lanchester were welcomed to California with outstretched arms, and so were Binnie Barnes, Merle Oberon, and Wendy Barrie. Laughton created such an indelible impression as Henry VIII that every actor who portrays the much-married monarch has had to cope with the everlasting influence of his Oscar-winning interpretation. The film focuses on the subject of most concern to 1933 audiences: not politics, not religion, but WIVES, the last five of them, anyway. The most prominent one here is Binnie Barnes as Catherine Howard. Elsa Lanchester is the funniest as Anne of Cleves, since she is trying her darndest to look ghastly, because Henry isn't her type and she doesn't want to lose her head. We only get a quick look at lovely Merle Oberon as Anne Boleyn before she DOES lose her head, but Wendy Barrie is a zestier Jane Seymour than most of the pale young things who have to die giving birth to King Edward VI. Robert Donat is so attractive and kind as Thomas Culpepper and SO necessary since Laughton's Henry is such an oaf. The sixth wife? That would be Everley Gregg as Catherine Parr, a good woman, and consequently of no interest to this lively narrative! 🦴🦴🦴🦴

1933 97m/B *GB* Charles Laughton, Binnie Barnes, Elsa Lanchester, Robert Donat, Merle Oberon, Miles

Mander, Wendy Barrie, John Loder, Lady Tree, Franklin Dyall, Claud Allister, William Austin, Gibb McLaughlin, Sam Livesey, Lawrence Hanray, Everley Gregg, Judy Kelly, John Turnbull, Frederick Culley, Hay Petrie, Wally Patch; *D:* Alexander Korda; *W:* Arthur Wimperis, Lajos Biro; *C:* Georges Perinal. Academy Awards '33: Best Actor (Laughton); Nominations: Academy Awards '33: Best Picture. **VHS, Beta, LV** *HBO, NOS, PSM*

The Private Life of Sherlock Holmes

Peter O'Toole and Peter Sellers as Sherlock Holmes and Doctor Watson? It sounded great to director Billy Wilder in the early '60s, too. Unfortunately, the working relationship between the three never made it to the starting gate. Wilder apparently felt that O'Toole's demands were in the prima donna league and he made the mistake of calling Sellers an "unprofessional rat fink." Harsh words far a man who'd already had one heart attack during a Wilder movie. (Sellers was replaced by Ray Walston on 1964's *Kiss Me Stupid.*) So *The Private Life of Sherlock Holmes* was released in 1970 starring stage actors Robert Stephens and Colin Blakely in the leads (who come very close to playing Holmes and Watson as a well adjusted gay couple, especially Holmes, who looks like he's wearing mascara, rouge, and lipstick). Although both were extremely good actors, the resulting film was still far from the masterpiece Wilder hoped it would become. The main problem, according to Wilder, is that United Artists insisted that nearly an hour be trimmed from its three hour running time. Edited to 125 minutes, all the flashbacks to Holmes' earlier life (actually Wilder's own past) are eliminated, including crucial sequences that contain Wilder's main reasons for making the picture. Even though we learn more about Wilder's sexual humor than we do about the great detective, *The Private Life of Sherlock Holmes* is a lavish contribution to the canon with an intriguing script and genuine affection for the late Victorian era (circa 1887). 🎬🎬🎬🎬

1970 (PG-13) 125m/C *GB* Robert Stephens, Colin Blakely, Genevieve Page, Irene Handl, Stanley Holloway, Christopher Lee, Clive Revill, Catherine Lacey, Tamara Toumanova, Mollie Maureen, Michael Balfour; *D:* Billy Wilder; *W:* Billy Wilder, I.A.L. Diamond; *M:* Miklos Rozsa. **VHS, LV** *FOX*

Professor Mamlock

Professor Mamlock would be a remarkable film no matter when it was made. The fact that it was a Soviet attack on National Socialism so threatened American audiences that it was originally banned in several states. Nazi characters are shown as ordinary human beings, still capable of shifting allegiance, as one sympathetic female character does. The film's thrust is softened by the position that Jews must rely on help from outsiders rather than themselves, but it does show why Professor Mamlock's apoliticism helped to make him an easy target. *Professor Mamlock* is not available on video, although it should be! Not to be confused with the 1961 East German re-make with the same title, which was written and directed by Konrad Wolfe. 🎬🎬🎬

1938 100m/B *RU* S. Mezhinski, Y. Kochurov, M. Timofeyev, E. Nikitina, Otto Zhakov, V. Chesnokov, B. Svetlov, N. Shaternikova; *D:* Adolph Minkin, Herbert Rappaport; *W:* Adolph Minkin, Herbert Rappaport; *C:* G. Filatov. *NYR*

The Profiteer

For reasons that escape us, *The Profiteer* played just twice at the Cannes Film Festival before it was banned in Italy. The film is successful on many levels: as comedy, as satire, as a portrait of the opportunist as a young man. The scenes from a funeral and a procession at Lourdes are both apt and hilarious. Giancarlo Marinangeli makes a devilish debut as a mean little man who befriends the title character. Sergio Nasca's remarkably impressive first film builds to a surprising, highly dramatic finish. Of the cast, only Al Cliver, Janet Agren, and Leopoldo Trieste are familiar to video buffs. Cliver and Agren haven't made any other unbad movies as far as we know, but character actor Trieste has worked with Fellini, Germi, Campanile, Petri, Bellochio, Rossi, Coppola, and Tornatore. 🦴🦴🦴

1974 97m/C *IT* Al Cliver, Janet Agren, Leopoldo Trieste; **C:** Giuseppe Aquari. *NYR*

Project A: Part 2

Jackie Chan came to America in 1987 as the honored guest of the San Francisco International Film Festival. At that time, despite the failure of 1985's *The Protector,* co-starring Danny Aiello, he was eager to be as big a star in the U.S. as he was in Hong Kong. It was not until 1996's *Rumble in the Bronx* that he finally broke into the American consciousness with a splash, and by then he was the biggest movie star in the world everywhere BUT in the U.S. In *Project A: Part 2,* stunts look like a snap, but don't try them at home! As he meticulously explained to the international press corp assembled at the festival, even Chan is vulnerable to an aching back, sore ankles, and a skull fracture. This action-packed spectacle is fast and funny, featuring an irresistible performance by Chan as Dragon Ma, an honest Hong Kong cop, circa 1900. There IS a *Project A: Part 1,* starring Samo Hung, but *Project A: Part 2* is a self-contained story, and extremely entertaining for international audiences on its own unique terms. 🦴🦴🦴

1987 101m/C *CH* Jackie Chan, Maggie Cheung, Carina Lau, David Lam; **D:** Jackie Chan; **W:** Edward Tang, Jackie Chan. **VHS** *FCT*

Public Access

Bryan Singer's *The Usual Suspects* won two Academy Awards (Best Screenplay and Best Supporting Actor) in 1995. *Public*

Access is not in the same league, but it's an interesting first effort by a filmmaker who clearly learned a great deal from the experience. Whiley Pritcher (Ron Marquette) arrives in the small town of Brewster, and launches a public access call-in show with the theme: "What's wrong with Brewster?" A question more to the point might be: "What's wrong with Whiley Pritcher?" but we never hear the answer to that one (maybe he's an underachieving relative of Keyser Soze!). Pritcher becomes as much of a celebrity as one can be in a backwater community like Brewster, and then...oh, watch it for yourself! Christopher McQuarrie collaborated with Michael Feit Dougan and Singer on the script (when he worked alone on *Suspects,* he won an Oscar). A promising start to what we hope will be long and increasingly fascinating careers for both Singer and McQuarrie. 🦴🦴🦴

1993 (R) 90m/C Ron Marquette, Dina Brooks, Burt Williams, Charles Kavanaugh, Larry Maxwell, Brandon Boyce; **D:** Bryan Singer; **W:** Bryan Singer, Christopher McQuarrie, Michael Feit Dougan; **C:** Bruce Douglas Johnson; **M:** John Ottman. Sundance Film Festival '93: Grand Jury Prize. **VHS** *TRI*

Pulp Fiction

Pulp Fiction is a dizzying ride through the violent Los Angeles that exists in the mind of its creator, Quentin Tarantino. It is a world of lethal small-time and not particularly brilliant thugs who exhaustively discuss the differences between American and French-style McDonald's as they kill time before a hit. It is a world where the time-worn cliche of Mr. Big's sexy wife being taken for a date by his henchman is turned inside out with terrifying and hilarious results. It is a world where even the awesome Mr. Big finds himself in a situation where no one knows that he is Mr. Big and none of his faithfully honored rules apply. Although the whole point of the film is to pay twisted tribute to the conventions of film noir, the 154-minute script might have become a silly and long-winded mess if anyone but Tarantino had been at the

JACKIE CHAN
Project A: Part 2

I started in the movie business since when I was young, when I was seven years old I was a child actor, but also at the same time I was trained in a martial arts school like an opera. So I was a child actor, became a stunt man, stunt director, director, producer, actor, everything now.

"Even now, I would stay here, this is like a dream. I don't know why I suddenly came back to America. A long time ago...I tried to get into the American market, but it was difficult. I totally failed. Very disappointed, I just packed my luggage, everything, and went back to Asia. And suddenly, American New Line company, they buy my movie, release it in North America in 2000 theatres. I don't believe it. Why? I do know I have a lot of following all those years, but not like in Asia. In Asia, me, it's like E.T. Everybody knows, from a three year old child to an eighty year old man. Everybody knows me. But in America I know there's a lot of fan club members, a lot of friends. But I think I'm not like E. T. but I'm trying to, I'm coming now. I try.

"Right now I'm very nervous and happy. Happy that I am coming back to try again. Nervous, I am scared to fail again. If I fail again, it would really, really, really destroy me. The whole confidence really. But no matter what, I try."

JACKIE CHAN'S films include *The World of Suzie Wong, The Big Brawl, Young Tiger, Eagle's Shadow, Half a Loaf of Kung Fu, Jackie Chan's Police Force, New Fist of Fury, Protector, The Armour of God, Project A: Parts 1 and 2, Dragons Forever, The Deadliest Art,* **and** *Police Story 3: Super Cop.*

helm. Nowhere is this more clear than in one of the funniest segments in which Mr. Big's problem-solver (crisply played by Harvey Keitel) must step in to resolve a situation caused by a clueless hit man (John Travolta). As genuine pulp fiction, this essentially banal yarn might barely have passed muster on the printed page. But onscreen, under Tarantino's sure guiding hand (the director also plays a central role in this segment), it's a priceless demonstration of gangland hygiene; the seg-

ment's humor and wit are driven by the sheer banality of the situation. Moreover, it leads directly into the brilliant wrap-up of the circular narrative. The film opens and closes in a ubiquitous L.A. diner with Pumpkin and Honey Bunny (Tim Roth and Amanda Plummer), but we don't know what the pair have to do with the rest of the story until film's end. The powerhouse ensemble cast includes folks who are normally above-the-title stars in any other movie: Bruce Willis and Maria de

Medeiros, Eric Stoltz and Rosanna Arquette, Samuel L. Jackson, Christopher Walken, and Frank Whaley. John Travolta may not be the obvious choice as Vincent Vega, the world's dumbest hit man, but he acquits himself admirably in the role he describes as his sixth comeback. He even gets a chance to be a heroin-ridden twist contestant in a surrealistic nightclub. His dancing partner is Uma Thurman as Mia, AKA Mrs. Marsellus Wallace (this film's Mr. Big). Thurman is provocative and appealing as the seductive former starlet who imbibes $5 milkshakes and lines of coke with equal conviction. And check out the incredible retro-style club with James Dean, Buddy Holly, Marilyn Monroe, and Mamie Van Doren as the waiters and waitresses and real 1950s convertibles as the booths! *Pulp Fiction* deservedly won the best picture prize at 1994's Cannes Film Festival. The film shows what those who grumbled about *True Romance,* scripted but not directed by Tarantino, subliminally realized: that his films need his vision as well as his ear. Luckily for audiences, *Pulp Fiction* is vintage Tarantino from breathless start to breathtaking finish. 🦴🦴🦴🦴

1994 (R) 154m/C John Travolta, Samuel L. Jackson, Uma Thurman, Harvey Keitel, Tim Roth, Amanda Plummer, Maria De Medeiros, Ving Rhames, Eric Stoltz, Rosanna Arquette, Christopher Walken, Bruce Willis, Frank Whaley, Steve Buscemi, Quentin Tarantino; **D:** Quentin Tarantino; **W:** Roger Roberts Avary, Quentin Tarantino; **C:** Andrzej Sekula. Academy Awards '94: Best Original Screenplay; British Academy Awards '94: Best Original Screenplay, Best Supporting Actor (Jackson); Cannes Film Festival '94: Best Film; Chicago Film Critics Awards '94: Best Director (Tarantino), Best Screenplay; Golden Globe Awards '95: Best Screenplay; Independent Spirit Awards '95: Best Actor (Jackson), Best Director (Tarantino), Best Film, Best Screenplay; Los Angeles Film Critics Association Awards '94: Best Actor (Travolta), Best Director (Tarantino), Best Film, Best Screenplay; MTV Movie Awards '95: Best Film, Best Dance Sequence (John Travolta/Uma Thurman); National Board of Review Awards '94: Best Director (Tarantino), Best Film; New York Film Critics Awards '94: Best Director (Tarantino), Best Screenplay; National Society of Film Critics Awards '94: Best Director (Tarantino), Best Film, Best Screenplay; Nominations: Academy Awards '94: Best Actor (Travolta), Best Director (Tarantino), Best Film Editing, Best Original Screenplay, Best Picture, Best Support-

ing Actor (Jackson), Best Supporting Actress (Thurman); Australian Film Institute '95: Best Foreign Film; Directors Guild of America Awards '94: Best Director (Tarantino); Golden Globe Awards '95: Best Actor—Drama (Travolta), Best Director (Tarantino), Best Film—Drama, Best Supporting Actor (Jackson), Best Supporting Actress (Thurman); Independent Spirit Awards '95: Best Supporting Actor (Stoltz); MTV Movie Awards '95: Best Male Performance (Travolta), Best Female Performance (Thurman), Best On-Screen Duo (John Travolta/Samuel L. Jackson), Best Song ("Girl, You'll Be A Woman Soon"); Screen Actors Guild Award '94: Best Actor (Travolta). **VHS, LV, Closed Caption** *MAX*

Pygmalion

You need an iron bottom to sit through all 170 minutes of *My Fair Lady,* notwithstanding Rex Harrison, Stanley Holloway, Wilfrid Hyde-White, Theodore Bikel, Mona Washbourne, Jeremy Brett, Robert Coote, Dame Gladys Cooper, Lerner and Loewe's score, Cecil Beaton's costumes, et cetera, et cetera, et cetera. But the original *Pygmalion* starring Leslie Howard, Wendy Hiller, Wilfrid Lawson, and Marie Lohr clocks in at a brisk 96 minutes WITH Shaw's blessing (he won an Oscar for collaborating on the screenplay). With his consent, a prologue and 14 additional sequences were included to make the story more like a movie and less like a play. Hiller was Shaw's personal choice as Eliza Doolittle. He would have preferred, however, to see Charles Laughton as Professor Henry Higgins, insisting that *Pygmalion* was NOT a love story and that Leslie Howard was hopelessly wrong (!) for the part. However, Shaw agreed to let the film close with a hint that Eliza will remain with Higgins, since he did have a shrewd understanding of Howard's enormous popularity at the box office. The original *Pygmalion* is crisp and cool, the perfect blueprint for the hit Broadway musical of 1956 (*My Fair Lady* was based on this movie, not Shaw's 1913 play). Leslie Howard and Anthony Asquith co-directed with skill and assurance, in spite of the fact that producer Gabriel Pascal was breathing down their necks throughout filming. Moreover, lead-

"She's so deliciously low, so horribly dirty...I shall make a duchess of this draggletailed guttersnipe."

—Professor Henry Higgins (Leslie Howard) speaking of Eliza Doolittle (Wendy Hiller) in *Pygmalion.*

ing lady Hiller had a real-life toothache during the ballroom sequence (especially written for the movie, at Asquith's insistence), which could not have been easy on a 26-year-old newcomer in a Schiaparelli gown with only one prior screen credit. None of the production woes show up in the shimmering finished product; *Pygmalion* was Britain's top money maker of the year, Howard went on to make an even bigger money maker in Hollywood (*Gone with the Wind*) and Hiller next starred in another Shaw adaptation, *Major Barbara.* Here's a trivia question for die-hard buffs. Q: Who was the cinematographer for both *Pygmalion* and *My Fair Lady*? A: Harry Stradling, Oscar winner for *The Picture of Dorian Gray* and *My Fair Lady.* 🎜🎜🎜🎜

1938 96m/B *GB* Leslie Howard, Wendy Hiller, Wilfred Lawson, Marie Lohr, Scott Sunderland, David Tree, Everley Gregg, Leueen McGrath, Jean Cadell, Eileen Beldon, Frank Atkinson, O.B. Clarence, Esme Percy, Violet Vanbrugh, Iris Hoey, Viola Tree, Irene Browne, Kate Cutler, Cathleen Nesbitt, Cecil Trouncer, Stephen Murray, Wally Patch, H.F. Maltby; *D:* Anthony Asquith, Leslie Howard; *W:* W.P. Lipscomb, Anatole de Grunwald, Cecil Lewis, Ian Dalyrymple, George Bernard Shaw; *C:* Harry Stradling. Academy Awards '38: Best Adapted Screenplay; Venice Film Festival '38: Best Actor (Howard); Nominations: Academy Awards '38: Best Actor (Howard), Best Actress (Hiller), Best Picture. **VHS, Beta, LV** *MON, NOS, COL*

Queen Kelly

Queen Kelly is one of the great might-have-beens in movie history. Directed by the great Erich von Stroheim and starring the legendary Gloria Swanson, fresh from her Oscar-nominated triumph as *Sadie Thompson, Queen Kelly* promised to be yet another mouth-watering excursion into the world of the rich and decadent. It was.

But Swanson, who was then in the midst of an affair with its married producer, Joseph Kennedy, was convinced that von Stroheim's sexy epic would be censored by Will Hays. About a third of the film had been made when Swanson walked off the set without warning to tattle on von Stroheim to Kennedy and *Queen Kelly* ended production that very day. She made an effort to release a truncated version of the film in the early '30s and even included a segment in 1950s *Sunset Boulevard,* in which von Stroheim made an ironic appearance as her butler. What remains of *Queen Kelly* is tantalizing: it draws on all our fantasies of one night of romance between a star-struck schoolgirl and the handsome prince. Von Stroheim is entirely sympathetic to the plight of young Patricia Kelly and makes her situation even more poignant by supplying her with an unforgettable nemesis. Seena Owen is mesmerizing as the possessive Queen who wants to have the wild prince Wolfram all to herself, whether or not he loves her. In one breathtaking sequence, after the Queen has caught the two of them in bed together, she banishes her rival from the palace, whipping her unmercifully as amused male courtiers laugh at the spectacle. This is the sort of sequence that might be unplayable, or at the very least diminished, in a sound film, but von Stroheim stages the primal conflict between the two women in such a lavish operatic style that it's almost impossible not to get caught up in the underlying emotions. With such a remarkable start, what's missing from the film may be even sadder than all those missing reels of *Greed.* At least we can read *McTeague,* the Frank Norris novel on which *Greed* was based. But *Queen Kelly* is a pure von Stroheim screen original from start to finish and his interpretation of the African brothel where the disgraced Kelly is forced to live in exile is filled with a sexual candor rarely seen on the screen before or since. Granted, von Stroheim's vision of the brothel is over the top, but the surviving footage still offers fascinating and unique insights into the sexual politics that informed his every film. Even in its incomplete form, *Queen Kelly* is still something to see; don't miss it! 🎞️🎞️🎞️🎞️

1929 113m/B Gloria Swanson, Walter Byron, Seena Owen, Tully Marshall, Madame Sul Te Wan; **D:** Erich von Stroheim. **VHS, Beta, LV, 8mm** *NOS, KIV, VYY*

Queens Logic

Screenwriter-turned-actor Tony Spiridakis asks us to believe that the inhabitants of Queens are more real than anyone else and that no one in the neighborhood is full of crap. That, believe it or don't, is the payoff for *Queens Logic,* about five lifelong buddies who are still the most important people in each other's lives. This may very well represent new territory for its young writer, but the material will be awfully familiar to any cable subscriber with a VCR. Federico Fellini examined five Adriatic buddies in the 1953 classic, *I Vitelloni* and George Lucas explored many similar rite-of-passage themes in 1973's *American Graffiti.* More recently, Nancy Savoca directed 1989's no-star but fun-to-watch *True Love,* an unpretentious little film that showed rather than explained pre-wedding jitters in the Bronx. Most of the characters in this 1991 re-tread by Spiridakis have little to do and are very sketchily drawn. Ken Olin is a frustrated artist who doesn't know what he wants. Kevin Bacon is a frustrated Hollywood actor (you can tell by the pink sunglasses) who hates phonies. Tony Spiridakis is a frustrated Manhattan actor (you can tell by the terrible Brando imitation) who wants a woman who will howl at the moon. And John Malkovich is a frustrated but choosy gay man (he says so often enough) who prefers his straight childhood friends to anyone he might pick up in a bar. Tom Waits has a cameo as a Queens weirdo and Jamie Lee Curtis has a cameo as a rich weirdo. Spiridakis is a not-terribly original writer who has a sporadically good ear for dialogue and is also the least colorful onscreen presence in

Rose (Laura Dern) and Buddy (Lukas Haas) in *Rambling Rose*.

the film. Luckily for audiences, Joe Mantegna is the star of *Queens Logic*. No matter how many cliched situations Mantegna is stuck in, he packs them all with an intense vitality that's hard to resist. Chloe Webb also works wonders with the thankless role of a long-suffering hairdresser who waits patiently for her much-adored fiancee to grow up. And deep-voiced Linda (*The Last Seduction*) Fiorentino creates a vivid impression as a young mother of two who clearly has had it waiting for her childlike husband. The action takes place on the weekend of Chloe Webb's wedding to Ken Olin. Will they get married and remain true to Queens or not? (Hint: "I Fooled Around and Fell in Love" is on the soundtrack.) *Queens Logic* is directed by Steven Rash, who began his career making *The Buddy Holly Story* and *Can't Buy Me Love* and later went on to direct Pauly Shore in

Son-in-Law and Whoopi Goldberg in *Eddie* (Spiridakis went on to write the poorly received *If Lucy Fell*.) 🎬🎬

1991 (R) 116m/C John Malkovich, Kevin Bacon, Jamie Lee Curtis, Linda Fiorentino, Joe Mantegna, Ken Olin, Tom Waits, Chloe Webb, Ed Marinaro, Kelly Bishop, Tony Spiridakis; *D:* Steve Rash; *W:* Tony Spiridakis; *M:* Joe Jackson. **VHS, LV, Closed Caption** *LIV*

The Railway Children

If you're looking for a movie on video with a little more respect for its subject than, say, 1991's *Hook* has for Peter Pan, 1970's *The Railway Children* is a fine example. Director Lionel Jeffries wisely tackles this much-loved children's book on its own terms. The story opens when the police arrive to take Father Charles Waterbury into custody straight after a holiday performance of *Peter Pan.* We know right away that this Father is a decent, free-spirited man. His three children clearly adore him and he yells louder than anyone to save Tinkerbell's life. But he spends Christmas night and most of the film in prison (unfairly, it turns out), while his wife quietly works for his release. (Mother is beautifully played by Dinah Sheridan with the sly humor that helped to make *Genevieve* such a gem in the early '50s.) The three children include Jenny Agutter, who at 18 was an eyelash too mature for her role as Bobbie, but she's wonderful anyway in a delicately shaded performance. Along with her younger siblings Phyllis and Peter, she is given no real information about their predicament as the family leaves the city and struggles to survive in the Yorkshire countryside. Mother writes magazine stories and her offspring make new friends by hanging about a nearby railway line. By not minding their own business they are able to combat their loneliness and isolation, and they develop a great deal of empathy for others in the process. Ultimately they are able to free themselves from their greatly reduced circumstances. Making *The Railway Children* demanded tremendous discipline on Jeffries' part. He could easily have torn the whole thing by mucking about with material for which he clearly had enormous affection to spare. Jeffries chose to honor the sheer simplicity of *The Railway Children,* and let the story tell itself. *The Railway Children* was filmed in Technicolor by one of the world's finest cinematographers, Arthur Ibbetson. Intricate attention was paid to period detail, not only with the sets and the costumes, but also with the atmosphere and the attitudes of 1905. When grownups return to the world of childhood, we really need to tread lightly, for we remember good and bad alike without real precision. *The Railway Children* offers a gentle, understated view of another time that may be even more appealing today than it was to the first-time readers of E. Nesbit's Edwardian classic. 🦴🦴🦴🦴

1970 104m/C *GB* Jenny Agutter, William Mervyn, Bernard Cribbins, Dinah Sheridan, Iain Cuthbertson, Sally Thomsett, Peter Bromilow, Ann Lancaster, Gary Warren, Gordon Whiting, David Lodge; *D:* Lionel Jeffries. **VHS, Beta** *NO*

Rambling Rose

Martha Coolidge is among the best working directors in America today, and she should have received an Oscar nomination for *Rambling Rose.* One of the drags of the pre-Oscar media buzz is seeing a bunch of guys sitting around a table yakking about how fine directors like Coolidge aren't "ready" to be an Oscar nominee because it's Demme's "turn" this year (or Levinson's or Stone's) or anyone's but a smashingly talented, perceptive female director like Coolidge. Laura Dern and Diane Ladd WERE nominees for this extraordinary film that takes a sensitive look at Rose, a randy teenaged nanny who is threatened with a hysterectomy because a couple of men (Robert Duvall and the doctor played by Kevin Conway) are threatened by her sexuality. A sequence where Ladd's character stands up for Rose's right to be free of these judgmental meddlers is a highlight. Another is a very delicately handled sequence in which Rose's 13-year-old charge (Lukas Haas) learns more about what makes his nanny happy than he really has the right to know. Screenwriter Calder (*The Strange One*) Willingham adapted his own autobiographical novel. Filmed in Wilmington, North Carolina. 🦴🦴🦴

1991 (R) 115m/C Laura Dern, Diane Ladd, Robert Duvall, Lukas Haas, John Heard, Kevin Conway, Robert John Burke, Lisa Jakub, Evan Lockwood; *D:* Martha Coolidge; *W:* Calder Willingham; *M:* Elmer Bernstein. Independent Spirit Awards '92: Best Director (Coolidge), Best Film, Best Supporting Actress (Ladd); National Board of Review Awards '91: 10 Best Films of the Year; Nominations: Academy Awards '91: Best Actress (Dern), Best Supporting Actress (Ladd). **VHS, LV** *LIV*

Reasons of State

This film about a hypocritical Latin American dictator was co-produced in Mexico, Cuba, and France. Despite a skimpy budget of $2 million, Chilean director Miguel Littin has made a film of epic dimensions, shooting in all three countries and employing a huge cast. Unhappily, *Reasons of State* suffers from sluggish pacing and a 145-minute run time. Too many cooks, perhaps? ♫ ♡

1978 145m/C *MX FR CU* Katy Jurado; **D:** Miguel Littin. *NYR*

Reckless

The Christmas season terrifies us more than anything that could possibly go bump in the night. The only reason we saw *Reckless* at THAT time of year was because, with Craig Lucas as the screenwriter and Mia Farrow as the star, we were reasonably sure that it would supply a strange and skewed take on the holidays. And it does. Mia Farrow is a blissful housewife with a wonderful life except for one thing: her husband has taken a contract out on her life. Guilt-stricken, he confesses the whole thing to his wife and urges her to jump out the window before the hired killer turns up. Farrow wanders around in the snow until she hitches a ride from Scott Glenn, who takes her home to his crippled wife, Mary-Louise Parker. Parker also pretends to be a deaf-mute so that Glenn will stay with her (no, we didn't get it either!), and the sweet couple adopt Farrow and make her feel right at home. So, Farrow creates a new life for herself at the nonprofit organization where Glenn gets her a job and all is well until the next Christmas.... Poor Mia Farrow. Talk about the Perils of Pauline; this sweet, gentle lady has to put up with everything! She's great in the role, retaining the doll-like sense of innocent wonder that kept audiences rooting for her in *Rosemary's Baby* and *The Purple Rose of Cairo*. Scott Glenn, too, does a nice job in a rather whacked-out role (for him). And Stephen Dorff makes a brief but affecting appearance as Farrow's long-lost son. *Reckless* travels its own weird one-of-a-kind route with the prolific Lucas as tour guide. It isn't exactly a foolproof antidote for the cheery warmth we're supposed to be feeling the last six weeks of the year, but *Reckless* beats being anesthetized by the 10,000th broadcast of *It's a Wonderful Life*. ♫♫♡

1995 (PG-13) 91m/C Mia Farrow, Scott Glenn, Mary-Louise Parker, Tony Goldwyn, Stephen Dorff, Eileen Brennan, Giancarlo Esposito, Deborah Rush; **D:** Norman Rene; **W:** Craig Lucas; **C:** Frederick Elmes; **M:** Stephen Endelman. **VHS, LV, Closed Caption** *HMK*

The Red House

Independent producer Sol Lesser was pleased when *The Red House* played to packed houses, but whether that was due to the tremendous performances by Edward G. Robinson and Judith Anderson or to the passionate make-out sequences between gorgeous Tibby (Julie London, 21) and strapping Teller (Rory Calhoun, 29), the box office receipts don't say. *The Red House* is an unusual film noir, because it takes place in a rural, rather than an urban setting. Robinson is Pete Morgan, a disabled farmer with a secret, plus a phobia about anyone going near The Red House on his property. Lon McCallister is Nath Storm, Pete's hired hand and the so-called love interest in the story. He's sort of a nerd, actually, pining over the always occupied Tibby, and only acquiescing to the gentle affection of Allene Roberts as Meg Morgan. But Pete's secret and his phobia don't go away—they fester and elicit attention in spite of his resistance. Moreover, the horrors of his own past creep up on him. In an urban setting, there would be plenty of distractions, but here, there are constant reminders of what happened in The Red House, and Miklos Rosza's score going into hysterics everytime Pete even

THINKS about The Red House....Yes, it IS very melodramatic, but Robinson gives the role everything he's got. Everyone in the cast is good with the exception of McCallister, who looks like a cheerful soul, even though he can barely act at all. Also that year, Delmer Daves went subjective with Humphrey Bogart, Lauren Bacall, and his own adaptation of David Goodis' urban noir novel, *Dark Passage*. *The Red House* is based on the novel by George Agnew Chamberlain. ♫♫♫

1947 100m/B Edward G. Robinson, Lon McCallister, Judith Anderson, Allene Roberts, Rory Calhoun, Ona Munson, Julie London, Harry Shannon, Arthur Space, Walter Sande, Pat Flaherty; **D:** Delmer Daves; **W:** Delmer Daves; **C:** Bert Glennon; **M:** Miklos Rozsa. **VHS, Beta** *CNG, NOS, SNC*

The Red Poster

The Red Poster tells the story of 23 members of the French Underground who were killed by the Nazis in 1944. Director/writer Frank Cassenti shifts uneasily back and forth between cinematic and theatrical styles as if he is grasping for the best structure to support the meaning of the narrative. Cassenti was once Constantin Costa-Gavras' assistant, but seems to have no other credits of note. **AKA:** L'Affiche Rouge. ♫♫

1976 90m/C *FR* Roger Ibanez, Pierre Clementi, Laszlo Szabo, Anicee Alvina; **D:** Frank Cassenti; **W:** Rene Richen, Frank Cassenti; **C:** Philippe Rousselot; **M:** Cuarteto Cedron. *NYR*

Red Rock West

Red Rock West went nowhere until San Francisco's Roxie Cinema picked it up for an extended run. (1990's *Kill Me Again*, another good film noir by John Dahl, only played in the San Francisco Bay area at the Geneva Drive-In.) With an appreciative audience, its sharp script and on-target performances became obvious. Nicolas Cage IS Mike, who tries to get out of Red Rock

West, Wyoming, but no dice. Wayne (who else but J.T. Walsh?) wants to kill his wife Suzanne (Lara Flynn Boyle), and mistakes Mike for the hired killer (who else but Dennis Hopper as Lyle?). Oh, and Suzanne has some ideas of her own; soon Mike is in Noir-ville up to his eyeballs. Invite some friends over for this one! ♫♫♫

1993 (R) 98m/C Nicolas Cage, Dennis Hopper, Lara Flynn Boyle, J.T. Walsh, Timothy Carhart, Dan Shor, Dwight Yoakam, Bobby Joe McFadden, Craig Reay, Vance Johnson, Robert Apel, Dale Gibson, Ted Parks, Babs Bram, Robert Guajardo, Sarah Sullivan; **D:** John Dahl; **W:** John Dahl, Rick Dahl; **C:** Marc Reshovsky; **M:** William Olvis. Nominations: Independent Spirit Awards '95: Best Director (Dahl), Best Screenplay. **VHS, LV, Closed Caption** *COL*

The Refrigerator

A crowd pleaser at 1991's Mill Valley Film Festival is *The Refrigerator,* a movie that will strike terror into the hearts of anyone who's ever walked into a kitchen. Julia (*The Unbelievable Truth*) McNeal plays Eileen, a young actress married to Steve (David *Amateur* Simonds), the biggest jerk in Manhattan. They move into a dump on the Lower East Side, expecting to fix it up, but the apartment soon possesses them both, day and night. The worst culprit is the refrigerator from Hell, an unlikely but photogenic fiend. Nicholas A.E. Jacobs' low-budget film is laced with horror and humor and benefits from a strong cast, including some devastating performances from the inanimate actors. ♫♫♪

1991 86m/C David Simonds, Julia McNeal, Angel Caban, Nena Segal, Jaime Rojo, Michelle DeCosta; **D:** Nicholas A.E. Jacobs; **W:** Nicholas A.E. Jacobs. **VHS** *NO*

The Remains of the Day

Upstairs Downstairs and *The Duchess of Duke Street* became television classics for a variety of reasons. Each was a sharply observed examination of an irretrievable time with a very definite bias: that the

Miss Kenton (Emma Thompson) gets close to Mr. Stevens (Anthony Hopkins) in *The Remains of the Day.*

mired in empty household rituals that he is unable to attract or accept love from those who are only too willing to give it to him. The Merchant Ivory team has supplied the usual candy box trappings to this character study. In trying to have it BOTH ways (oh, wasn't it great AND awful in the 1930s!), Stevens emerges as a pathetic joke and the centerpiece of the most boring prestige film of 1993. Since at least a dozen people walked out of the screening that we attended and we cast several impatient glances at our wrist watches over the course of 135 minutes, it's only fair to mention that not one real thing happens to Stevens in the whole movie. What? Aren't there a lot of big stars in *The Remains of the Day* like Oscar winners Sir Anthony Hopkins and Emma Thompson, plus James Fox, Christopher Reeve, Peter Vaughan, Hugh Grant, Michael Lonsdale, and Tim Pigott-Smith? Sure, but even the greatest actors need SOME directorial guidance. Even the most indulgent audiences need a payoff. How riveted are we going to get by a man who spends an entire film on the verge of feeling a single honest emotion? How much will we root for a woman who gets so caught up in the drab routines of this dweeb that she regards their working life together as the happiest time in her life? And how enthralled will we be by the fact that every major event over a twenty year span happens OFF camera? On the edge of our seats?...NOT!!! And then, four years after *The Remains of the Day* won a stupefying quantity of awards, we saw Christopher Guest's hilarious *Waiting for Guffman,* and now, go figure, WE WANT OUR *REMAINS OF THE DAY* LUNCHBOXES! 🦴🦴

1993 (PG) 135m/C *GB* Anthony Hopkins, Emma Thompson, James Fox, Christopher Reeve, Peter Vaughan, Hugh Grant, Michael Lonsdale, Tim Pigott-Smith; *D:* James Ivory; *W:* Ruth Prawer Jhabvala; *C:* Tony Pierce-Roberts; *M:* Richard Robbins. British Academy Awards '93: Best Actor (Hopkins); Los Angeles Film Critics Association Awards '93: Best Actor (Hopkins); National Board of Review Awards '93: Best Actor (Hopkins); Nominations: Academy Awards '93: Best Actor (Hopkins), Best Actress (Thompson), Best Adapted Screenplay, Best Art

working classes learned to adjust to a changing world in a way that the aristocracy could not. This perspective, along with appealing characters, nostalgic detail, and beautifully crafted scripts, charmed audiences all over the world. Each series had a reliable male staff member who took every aspect of his work very seriously, but who was always an object of affection and respect. We would trust our lives with Hudson (Gordon Jackson) or Starr (John Cater). At times, the quiet dignity of these men took on heroic, larger than life dimensions. Kazuo Ishiguro's slender novel, *The Remains of the Day,* had a different perspective on Stevens, the faithful family retainer of one Lord Darlington. She saw him as an essentially tragic figure, so

Direction/Set Decoration, Best Costume Design, Best Director (Ivory), Best Original Screenplay, Best Picture; British Academy Awards '94: Best Actress (Thompson), Best Adapted Screenplay, Best Director (Ivory), Best Film; Directors Guild of America Awards '93: Best Director (Ivory); Golden Globe Awards '94: Best Actor—Drama (Hopkins), Best Actress—Drama (Thompson), Best Director (Ivory), Best Film—Drama, Best Screenplay. **VHS, LV, 8mm, Closed Caption** COL

Reno's Kids: 87 Days Plus 11

Reno's Kids: 87 Days Plus 11 is the first documentary feature by actress Whitney (Dorothy Baxter on NBC's *Hazel*, 1961-65) Blake. The director is justifiably proud of her film, which shows a semester in the life of Daly City teacher Reno Taini and his life-toughened students, who learn how to confront the system head-on and win. Blake has selected some extraordinary footage of the class at work and at play, a technique which serves the film's purpose far better than the traditional talking-heads format. 🦴🦴🦴

1987 99m/C D: Whitney Blake; **C:** Frances Reid. NYR

Repulsion

Most films about madness glamorize the subject or shift the point of view to a sane observer. Roman Polanski's 1965 British film *Repulsion* provides a rare screen examination of insanity from the perspective of the person who is going mad. Twenty-one-year-old Catherine Deneuve portrays Carol Ledoux, a quiet manicurist who loses her grip on the most fundamental aspects of her routine life. Bridget, a sympathetic colleague (played by Helen Fraser), tries to cure her blues with a Charlie Chaplin imitation, but Carol is beyond help. When her much-older sister (Yvonne Furneaux, then 37) takes a holiday with her lover (Ian Hendry), she leaves Carol all alone. Sexual repression is the most obvious symptom of her mental anguish, but left to her own

devices, Carol plummets into an irreversible nightmare. Deneuve's glacial face and expressive eyes serve her well here; her lovely mask conceals the festering psychosis within and an ordinary flat becomes her prison as she grows progressively more ill. Her landlord (Patrick Wymark) can't read her, a well-meaning suitor (John Fraser) can't read her, and household objects take on a deeply sinister quality. This one will make you want to sleep with the lights on for a MONTH. 🦴🦴🦴🦴

1965 105m/B *GB* Catherine Deneuve, Yvonne Furneaux, Ian Hendry, John Fraser, Patrick Wymark, James Villiers, Renee Houston, Helen Fraser, Mike Pratt; **D:** Roman Polanski; **W:** Roman Polanski, Gerard Brach, David Stone. **VHS, Beta, LV** VDM, VCN, MRV

Reservoir Dogs

While recognizing that American cinema in the 1990s would not be what it is today without Quentin Tarantino and acknowledging his originality and talent AND being forever grateful that he cast Lawrence Tierney in such a terrific role here as Joe Cabot, *Reservoir Dogs* is not the sort of flick I can watch over and over again. Many guys of my acquaintance can and do—I can't and don't. I have also been asked why I didn't think the bloody torture scenes in the warehouse were funny. How can I answer a question like that? Because I didn't. Except for Cabot's son, Nice Guy Eddie (Christopher Penn), most of the characters are named after colors: White (Harvey Keitel), Orange (Tim Roth), Pink (Steve Buscemi), Blonde (Michael Madsen), Brown (Tarantino), and Blue (Eddie Bunker). The extremely well acted plot revolves around a diamond heist gone wrong. *Variety's* Todd McCarthy said it best when the picture was first shown at the Sundance Film Festival: "(*Reservoir Dogs*) is about nothing other than a bunch of macho guys and how big their guns are." I give it four bones for the guys, but for me, just 🦴🦴🦴

Catherine Deneuve in *Repulsion*.

1992 (R) 100m/C Harvey Keitel, Tim Roth, Michael Madsen, Steve Buscemi, Christopher Penn, Lawrence Tierney, Kirk Baltz, Quentin Tarantino, Eddie Bunker, Randy Brooks; *D:* Quentin Tarantino; *W:* Quentin Tarantino; *C:* Andrzej Sekula. Independent Spirit Awards '93: Best Supporting Actor (Buscemi). **VHS, LV, Closed Caption, DVD** *LIV, BTV*

The Return of Tommy Tricker

Tommy, his sister, and their friends work their magic to free Charles Meriweather from the Bluenose sailing ship stamp he's been imprisoned in for 60 years. But when they try to bring Charlie back, they rescue his younger sister Molly instead. But Molly suddenly begins aging and it's up to Tommy to figure out how to save her (and still rescue Charlie). 🎞🎞🎞

1994 100m/C CA Michael Stevens, Joshawa Mathers, Heather Goodsell, Paul Nocholls, Andrew Bauer-Gador, Adele Gray; *D:* Michael Rubbo; *W:* Michael Rubbo; *C:* Thomas Vamos. **VHS** *HMD*

Rhinoceros

Zero Mostel won the 1961 Tony for *Rhinoceros*—so who better to recreate his original Broadway role on film? And who better to turn Eugene Ionesco's play into a fun, wacky movie than Tom O'Horgan, the original director of *Hair*? Reunite Mostel with Gene Wilder, his Oscar-nominated co-star for *The Producers*, add Oscar nominee Karen Black and Tony nominee Joe Silver to the ensemble, and voila! Who says theatre on film has to be dull? It was inept misfires like this one that contributed to the demise of the American Film Theatre. Why subscribe to lousily executed movies like *Rhinoceros* when real Gene Wilder movies were playing down the block—*Blazing Saddles* and *Young Frankenstein,* not to mention other 1974 gems like *Chinatown, The Conversation,* and *Day for Night*? **WOOF!**

1974 101m/C *GB CA* Zero Mostel, Gene Wilder, Karen Black, Robert Weil, Joe Silver, Marilyn Chris; *D:* Tom O'Horgan. *NO*

Rhythm Thief

Simon (Jason Andrews) bootlegs dubs of New York's underground bands to sustain his grungy life. Musicians in the bands hate his guts. His one-time girl friend Marty (Eddie Daniels) turns up and disrupts his low-life existence with the information that she and Simon's mother were in a mental institution together. Simon spends some time with Marty in Far Rockaway, but then he returns to New York to bootleg once again. Good acting and writing shine through this rock bottom indie, which deserves wider distribution at video outlets. 🦴🦴

1994 88m/B Jason Andrews, Eddie Daniels, Kimberly Flynn, Kevin Corrigan, Sean Haggerty, Mark Alfred, Paul Rodriguez, Cynthia Sley; *D:* Matthew Harrison; *W:* Matthew Harrison, Christopher Grimm; *C:* Howard Krupa; *M:* Danny Brenner. Sundance Film Festival '95: Special Jury Prize; Nominations: Independent Spirit Awards '96: Debut Performance (Andrews). **VHS** *NYR*

Rich and Strange

Rich and Strange is an early Hitchcock film that's widely available, but rarely discussed. It's a comedy and just what the title says it is. Joan Barry (1902-89) had previously dubbed the voice for Anny Ondra in 1929's *Blackmail.* She has very little onscreen chemistry with actor Henry Kendall (1892-1967), who was reportedly gay. Except for *The Lodger, Blackmail,* and *Murder,* Hitchcock's pre-1934 films are a mixed bag; he had yet to be typed as a master of the macabre. As in the 1941 screwball comedy *Mr. and Mrs. Smith,* Hitchcock added darkly humorous touches here and there to *Rich and Strange* that carry his unique signature. If you don't demand that your spine be tingled by this one, you'll have fun with it. *AKA:* East of Shanghai. 🦴🦴🦴

1932 92m/B *GB* Henry Kendall, Joan Barry, Betty Amann, Percy Marmont, Elsie Randolph; *D:* Alfred Hitchcock; *W:* Alfred Hitchcock, Alma Reville. **VHS, LV** *REP, SNC, MLB*

Ricochets

Ricochets evolved from an Israeli army training film into the theatrical release it became. It transcends its modest start, but simplifies the conflict between Israel and Lebanon by examining the problems of one small fighting unit. Still, since it never claims to show anything other than war from the Israeli soldier's point of view, the amount of military criticism in this effort is surprising, considering its origins. *AKA:* Shtei Etzbaot Mi'Tzidon. 🦴🦴🦴

1987 91m/C *IS* Roni Pinovich, Shaul Mizrahi, Dudu Ben-Ze'ev, Alon Aboutboul; *D:* Eli Cohen; *W:* Eli Cohen, Baruch Nevo, Zvi Kretzner; *C:* Yechiel Ne'eman; *M:* Benny Nagari. *NYR*

Rita, Sue & Bob Too

There is probably no subject that both men and woman lie about as much as sex, but moments into *Rita, Sue & Bob Too* it seems that the filmmakers are out to set some sort of a record for sexual dishonesty. Just for starters, we are asked to accept that the line "Can either of you put a rubber johnny on?" would trigger unbridled lust in two 16-year-old babysitters when their 40-year-old employer drives them home at his wife's suggestion. Since he has a track record with babysitters, it's hard to believe that any 27-year-old woman would set herself up like that, as well as the two girls, but the incredulity continues. Although Rita and Sue are both virgins, they experience no pain whatever from their first sexual experience. Sex with each takes one minute flat, he's ready to roll

without a break, and both girls share a simultaneous climax with Bob. If viewers have gotten this far, then they may have no problem accepting the fact that Bob's attractive wife is frigid due to her hatred of French kisses, and sterilization, not because she's married to a faithless jerk who lies to her, then blames her for his problems. The script was written by a talented teenager named Andrea Dunbar (1961-). She writes of Northern England in an observant, uninterpretive style: "If it's put there on a plate, he's going to take it. He wouldn't be much of a man if he didn't" is the sort of sexual propaganda that her female characters can and do swallow. Other instructive lyrics: "We're having a gang bang. It's the thing to do. We'd like to give you one." The women in the film are punished not only for having sex, but also for being sexual fantasies. *Rita, Sue & Bob Too* hardens prejudices rather than challenges them: a cute boy from Pakistan, whom Sue sees for a while, is shown as violent, manipulative, and mercenary. He is written out of the plot when a white neighbor telephones the police the minute he enters his neighborhood. Although teens Rita and Sue are obviously played by women in their 20s, the cast of unknowns is talented, the Bradford scenery is attractive, and there is a gritty quality to director Alan Clarke's (1935-90) vision of the drabness of these characters' lives. **WOOF!**

1987 (R) 94m/C *GB* Michelle Holmes, George Costigan, Siobhan Finneran, Lesley Sharp, Willie Ross, Patti Nicholls, Kulvinder Ghir; **D:** Alan Clarke; **W:** Andrea Dunbar; **M:** Michael Kamen. **VHS, Beta, LV** *ORI, WAR*

River of Grass

No-budget noirish crime/romance set in the swampy, low-rent Florida area between Miami and the Everglades. Uncaring and frankly dumb housewife/mom Cozy (Lisa Bowman) hooks up with the boozing Lee Ray (Larry Fessenden) and the dim duo take an illegal dip in a private pool. Cozy manages to fire off Lee's gun and thinks she hit a man who suddenly appeared. Not bothering to find out if this is true, they decide to hole up in a motel until they can figure out what to do. You won't really care but director Kelly Reichardt does have a way with visuals, so things aren't a total loss. 🎵🎵

1994 80m/C Lisa Bowman, Larry Fessenden, Dick Russell; **D:** Kelly Reichardt; **W:** Jesse Hartman, Kelly Reichardt; **C:** Jim Denault. Nominations: Independent Spirit Awards '96: Best First Feature, Debut Performance (Bowman). **VHS** *NYR*

River's Edge

River's Edge was one of the most disturbing movies of 1987. Tim Hunter's study of how a high school gang reacts to the murder of one of their friends showed a conscience-free group, easily led by the always stoned Crispin Glover. The only one with any feeling for the dead girl seems to be Keanu Reeves, who went on to deliver impressive performances in *Permanent Record* and *Dangerous Liaisons.* Dennis Hopper, who co-stars as a lunatic (again), also appeared in 1955's *Rebel Without a Cause,* directed by Nicholas Ray. The original ad for *Rebel* could describe both films: "Teenage terror torn from today's headlines!" 🎵🎵🎵

1987 (R) 99m/C Keanu Reeves, Crispin Glover, Daniel Roebuck, Joshua Miller, Dennis Hopper, Ione Skye, Roxana Zal, Tom Bower, Constance Forslund, Leo Rossi, Jim Metzler; **D:** Tim Hunter; **W:** Neal Jimenez; **C:** Frederick Elmes; **M:** Jurgen Knieper. Independent Spirit Awards '88: Best Film, Best Screenplay; Sundance Film Festival '87: Special Jury Prize. **VHS, Beta, LV, 8mm, Closed Caption** *NLC*

Road Games

Steven Spielberg first attracted critical attention in 1971 when he directed a television movie called *Duel* starring Dennis Weaver. It's a suspenseful little saga about a battle to the death between a

Opposite page: **Joan Barry and Henry Kendall as Emily and Fred Hill in Hitchcock's** *Rich and Strange.*

his partner, a dog whom he thinks is a wild dingo. It's a dream part for an actor, and Keach makes the most of it. Curtis has less to do, but her comparatively few onscreen moments show why she was later able to steal *A Fish Called Wanda* and *Fierce Creatures.* The plot hinges around a daft killer whom everyone thinks is Keach, so he has to prove his innocence by finding the real madman. There's an interesting exploration of Keach's own assumptions about women which trip him up, as well as them. *Road Games* on video is an ingratiating 100-minute ride. If you check out *The Killer inside Me* at the same time, you may wonder why Stacy Keach isn't approached more often with roles that are worthy of his considerable talent. Franklin later went on to direct *Psycho 2, Cloak and Dagger, FX 2,* and *Sorrento Beach.* 🦴🦴🦴

1981 (PG) 100m/C *AU* Stacy Keach, Jamie Lee Curtis; *D:* Richard Franklin. **VHS, Beta** *COL, NLC*

Roads to the South

Yves Montand, Laurent Malet, and Miou-Miou dignify a watery script about a political father and son who clash in the aftermath of Franco's death. As with 1968's *Secret Ceremony,* the director (1909-84) seems awfully detached from both the story and the characters. When Montand came to the San Francisco International Film Festival to "plug" the film, he kvetched about Joseph Losey's direction, Jorge Semprun's screenplay, and Michel Legrand's blasting score. Montand said that Bobby Roth's *The Boss' Son* was a far superior movie, then returned home to immerse himself in French politics until his death in 1991 at age 70. 🦴🦴

1978 100m/C *FR* Laurent Malet, Yves Montand, Miou-Miou; *D:* Joseph Losey; *W:* Jorge Semprun; *M:* Michel Legrand. **VHS, LV** *CVC, IME, FCT*

compact car and a truck, but there's very little character development, so *Duel* doesn't have much in the way of repeat value. A similar film with a lesser reputation emerged in Australia a decade later and the best thing about *Road Games* is the richness of its characters, which are played to perfection by American actors Stacy Keach and Jamie Lee Curtis. The director, Richard Franklin, like Brian De Palma, is an avid fan of Alfred Hitchcock. Unlike De Palma, Franklin's sense of humor is suggestive, rather than graphic, and more in tune with what Hitchcock himself might enjoy. Keach's character insists that "just because (he) rides a truck, it doesn't make (him) a truck driver." Keach talks to himself a lot, or rather he talks to

Robert et Robert

Robert et Robert is Claude Lelouch's valentine to the so-called losers of the world, and it would be difficult to find a more heartfelt salute. Based largely on the history of actor Jacques Villeret, who plays a real-life character based on himself, *Robert et Robert* shows the warm and funny friendship shared by a pair of bachelors seeking wives through a computer dating service. They never do find lasting ceremonial bliss, but both blossom from knowing each other. Lelouch clearly cares about his characters and he translates that caring to audiences with great sweetness and a lovely visual style. (Villeret and Charles Denner are perfect as the two Roberts, and Jacques Lefrancois' photography is excellent.) 🦴🦴🦴

1978 105m/C *FR* Charles Denner, Jacques Villeret, Jean-Claude Brialy, Macha Meril, Germaine Montero, Regine; **D:** Claude Lelouch; **W:** Claude Lelouch; **C:** Jacques Lefrancois. Cesar Awards '79: Best Supporting Actor (Villeret). **VHS, Beta** *COL*

Rock Hudson's Home Movies

Unless it's spoofing old educational short subjects, *Mystery Science Theater 3000* drives me nuts. I don't care if that guy and the robots want to yak through *Dating Do's and Don'ts,* but I want to HEAR Beverly Garland and Marie Windsor, not THEM, okay? I don't think I'd mind watching movies with Mark Rappaport, though. He does his homework, he knows how to read a film, and he's funny. How many people can sit through a marathon of Rock Hudson movies, anyway? But this 63-minute study, drily narrated by Eric Farr, shows the films in the context of the time in which they were made. Even at kiddie matinees, I used to wonder why Rock Hudson's he-man status was the joke of so many films, like he was such a hunk that he couldn't possibly be a mama's boy or pregnant or even an indoor guy!!! In film after film, these same themes would sneak up again and again, until 1966's *Seconds,* still one of the scariest movies I've ever seen. But as Rappaport's illuminating commentary reveals, *Seconds,* too, was more of the same, only in a threatening rather than comedic vein. The clips are well chosen and Rappaport's thoughtful, witty analysis is interesting to hear, whether or not you agree with all of it. Rappaport would go on to examine the career of another ill-fated star in *From the Journals of Jean Seberg* (narrated by Mary Beth Hurt). At press time, an exploration of Howard Hughes was in the planning stages. 🦴🦴🦴

1992 63m/C Eric Farr; **D:** Mark Rappaport; **W:** Mark Rappaport. **VHS** *WBF, PPI*

Rockers

Rockers, helmed with assurance by Theodoros Bafaloukos, is a fascinating first film, both for its lively reggae music, and for its intriguing variation on the Robin Hood theme. Leroy Wallace makes an engaging appearance as a broke drummer named Horsemouth, who takes on a batch of rich crooks, with some help from his friends. *Rockers* is subtitled, rendering comprehensible the deeply accented English spoken in Jamaica. The soundtrack album is now a collector's item. 🦴🦴🦴

1980 100m/C *JM* Jacob Miller; **M:** Bunny Wailer, Burning Spear, Gregory Isaacs. **VHS** *MVD*

The Rolling Stones Rock and Roll Circus

Well, It just goes to show that artists can be their own worst critics. This film remained unreleased until 1996 because the Rolling Stones were concerned that they had been upstaged by the Who. In fact, *Rock and Roll Circus* was a great

Rockers.

nia, that ended the decade with a harsh aftertaste. *Rock and Roll Circus* is such a great rediscovery, it makes us wonder: how many more filmed records of vintage concerts are collecting dust in vaults? 🎵🎵🎵

1968 65m/C *GB* Rolling Stones, Marianne Faithfull, John Lennon, Yoko Ono, Eric Clapton, Taj Mahal; *D:* Michael Lindsay-Hogg. **VHS, LV** *PGV*

Room at the Top

Laurence Harvey (1928-73) is such a snide cad. He could have been the new George Sanders, except he didn't outlive him by very long. As Joe Lampton, he is an opportunistic slime, heartlessly seducing a rich man's daughter to advance himself. The woman Joe really wants is Alice (Simone Signoret, 1921-85), unhappily married to a twit named George Aisgill (Allan Cuthbertson, 1920-88). Why Alice wants a transparent hustler like Joe is a mystery, but want him she does and she is devastated when he leaves her to marry well. Joe is beaten brutally before the so-called "happy ending," actually a grim resignation to a much grimmer fate, since his bride Susan (Heather Sears, 1935-94) knows that they can never be happy. There was a follow-up film in 1965: Joe Lampton, his in-laws, and George Aisgill are all back in *Life at the Top,* but Jean Simmons has replaced Heather Sears and Honor Blackman plays Joe's new sexual diversion when he isn't playing local politics. The stakes had been reduced, because Lampton had already sold his soul and his humanity in the first film. By 1973's *Man at the Top,* Kenneth Haigh was Joe Lampton, dealing with unfamiliar characters in another game altogether. What made *Room at the Top* so special was the moral tension between Joe and Alice as each sees a different sort of life reflected in the other's eyes. When Simone Signoret won the Best Actress Oscar, it would be 37 years before another French actress (Juliette Binoche for *The English Patient*) would

show then and would be a great show today with no qualifications. It's fun to watch John Lennon at his goofiest, to hear *Sympathy for the Devil* with the original Stones line-up, and to experience so many of the very best rock acts of 1968. To watch this film on a triple bill with David Maysle's *Gimme Shelter* and Lindsay-Hogg's *Let It Be* would be a wistful reminder of how much the world had...and lost...in a chillingly brief passage of time. *Rock and Roll Circus* was filmed in December 1968, the Beatles' last concert on a rooftop was filmed the following month, Brian Jones drowned on July 3, 1969, and by December 1969, the Stones (with new member Mick Taylor) were the centerpiece of the deadly concert at Altamont, Califor-

bring home the Academy Award. Based on the novel by John Braine. 🦴🦴🦴🦴

1959 118m/B *GB* Laurence Harvey, Simone Signoret, Heather Sears, Hermione Baddeley, Avril Ungar, Donald Wolfit, Wendy Craig, Allan Cuthbertson, Ian Hendry, Donald Houston, Raymond Huntley, Miriam Karlin, Wilfred Lawson, Richard Pasco, Mary Peach, Prunella Scales, Beatrice Varley, John Westbrook; **D:** Jack Clayton; **W:** Neil Paterson; **C:** Freddie Francis; **M:** Mario Nascimbene. Academy Awards '59: Best Actress (Signoret), Best Adapted Screenplay; British Academy Awards '58: Best Actress (Signoret), Best Film; Cannes Film Festival '59: Best Actress (Signoret); Nominations: Academy Awards '59: Best Actor (Harvey), Best Director (Clayton), Best Picture, Best Supporting Actress (Baddeley). **VHS** *NO*

A Room with a View

Here's the deal: Helena Bonham Carter is in love with Julian Sands, but she settles for Daniel Day-Lewis (who isn't cute like he was in *My Beautiful Laundrette,* but rather resembles a gopher). What on Earth is that unhappy love-sick girl going to do? This is the central story of E.M. Forster's *A Room with a View,* along with the usual meticulous examination of Edwardian England that is de rigeur for all three of the Merchant-Ivory films based on the works of E.M. Forster. (The others are *Maurice* and *Howard's End.*) Bonham Carter and Sands are the quintessential romantic couple, circa 1908, and Venice has never been so photogenic. An Oscar winner for its screenplay, art direction, and costumes, *A Room with a View* also received nominations for Best Picture, for director James Ivory, and for Denholm Elliott and Maggie Smith (Smith is a hoot as always as Carter's aunt). Two other Forster adaptations are David Lean's *A Passage to India* and Charles Sturridge's *Where Angels Fear to Tread.* 🦴🦴🦴🦴

1986 117m/C *GB* Helena Bonham Carter, Julian Sands, Denholm Elliott, Maggie Smith, Judi Dench, Simon Callow, Daniel Day-Lewis, Rupert Graves, Rosemary Leach; **D:** James Ivory; **W:** Ruth Prawer Jhabvala; **C:** Tony Pierce-Roberts. Academy Awards '86: Best Adapted Screenplay, Best Art Direction/Set Decoration, Best Costume Design;

British Academy Awards '86: Best Actress (Smith), Best Film, Best Supporting Actress (Dench); Golden Globe Awards '87: Best Supporting Actress (Smith); Independent Spirit Awards '87: Best Foreign Film; National Board of Review Awards '86: 10 Best Films of the Year, Best Supporting Actor (Day-Lewis); New York Film Critics Awards '86: Best Cinematography, Best Supporting Actor (Day-Lewis); Writers Guild of America '86: Best Adapted Screenplay; Nominations: Academy Awards '86: Best Cinematography, Best Director (Ivory), Best Picture, Best Supporting Actor (Elliott), Best Supporting Actress (Smith). **VHS, Beta, LV, Closed Caption** *FOX, HMV*

The Rosary Murders

The Rosary Murders does an admirable job of tackling one of film's most unyielding subjects. It is extremely difficult for non-Catholics and Catholics alike to understand the vow of silence taken by Catholic confessors when human lives are at stake. Perhaps only another priest can identify with the agony faced by Father Donald Sutherland when he hears the confession and learns the identity of a murderer who has every intention of murdering again. Unlike many recent crime sagas, the film makes its victims real and it does not sweeten the character of the killer by showing him as a nice guy flawed with sexual and psychological quirks. It does fall prey to the movie cliche of the pretty woman who falls for the priest, and it also drags in the bombastic Detroit pastor with a mind lock on arbitrary problem solving, which clouds his understanding of church law. As portrayed by Charles Durning, this egomaniac is to Catholic priests what Shelley Winters is to Jewish mothers. The stereotype does exist, but in a film that strains away from the obvious in so many other ways, its inclusion is both unimaginative and regrettable. The acting is otherwise quite good, Elmore Leonard's complex script based on William Kienzle's novel is directed with subtlety by Fred Walton, and the details that give the film its density are very well chosen. 🦴🦴🦴

1987 (R) 105m/C Donald Sutherland, Charles Durning, Belinda Bauer, Josef Sommer, James Murtaugh,

John Danelle, Addison Powell, Kathleen Tolan; *D:* Fred Walton; *W:* Fred Walton, Elmore Leonard. **VHS, Beta, LV, Closed Caption** *VTR*

Rouge

Stanley Kwan's *Rouge* is an extremely interesting ghost story about a lovely wraith who returns to Hong Kong in the 1980s searching for her lover, with whom she had made a suicide pact over half a century before. The fine acting by Anita Mui as the ghost and by Alex Man and Emily Chu as the young couple who try to help her, plus Bill Wong's excellent camera work helped to make *Rouge* an award winner in Taiwan. Anita Mui was Kwan's first choice to play the late legendary actress Ruan Ling-Yu in 1992's *Centre Stage/The Actress* (she was replaced by Maggie Cheung). *AKA:* Yanzhi Kou. ♫♫♫

1987 99m/C *HK* Anita Mui, Leslie Cheung, Alex Man, Emily Chu; *D:* Stanley Kwan; *W:* Lei Bik Wah, Chiu Tai An-Ping; *C:* Bill Wong; *M:* Michael Lai. **VHS** *FCT*

Ruby in Paradise

At the risk of sounding cranky...forget it, I don't care...*Ruby in Paradise* DOES make me cranky! Ashley Judd is a wonderful actress, and I hope she wins an Academy Award some spring night in the not-too-distant future, but watching *Ruby in Paradise* is like watching (1) grass grow, (2) paint dry, (3) writers write, AND (4) pigeons sleep ALL AT THE SAME TIME! Put some meat on the bones of this script! Give Ruby something to DO into which she can really sink her teeth! Never mind, there are too many folks who love *Ruby in Paradise* exactly the way it is to adjust its sluggish pace at this point. Now I've seen what Judd can do with a juicy role, like Pam Anderson in *Normal Life* and Norma Jean in *Norma Jean and Marilyn,* watching her wander through a plotless flick like this one simply isn't MY idea of Paradise. 🦴🦴

1993 (R) 115m/C Ashley Judd, Todd Field, Bentley Mitchum, Allison Dean, Dorothy Lyman, Betsy Dowds; **D:** Victor Nunez; **W:** Victor Nunez; **C:** Alex Vlacos; **M:** Charles Engstrom. Independent Spirit Awards '94: Best Actress (Judd); Sundance Film Festival '93: Grand Jury Prize; Nominations: Independent Spirit Awards '94: Best Cinematography, Best Director (Nunez), Best Film, Best Screenplay, Best Supporting Actor (Field). **VHS, LV, Closed Caption** REP

Sabotage

Remember when Hitchcock played a cameo in *Blackmail* as a subway passenger being bothered by a little boy? In *Sabotage,* he created considerable suspense by showing a young boy as he dawdled through the city streets while carrying a bomb timed to explode. By creating tension through rapid cross-cutting and then relieving it with horror, Hitchcock tried to do something that was quite a few decades ahead of its time. The audiences of his own time were horrified and outraged and he decided never to do THAT again. Only he did, many times—he just played with the audience's sense of morality; it was perfectly alright, he found, to relieve tension with horror if the character was a mean lesbian (Dame Judith Anderson in *Rebecca*), a treacherous spy (Edmund Gwenn or Herbert Marshall in *Foreign Correspondent* or Norman Lloyd in *Saboteur*), a Merry Widow killer (Joseph Cotten in *Shadow of a Doubt*), a hired poseur (Kim Novak in *Vertigo*), a thief (Janet Leigh in *Psycho*), or a barmaid (Anna Massey) just dumb enough to trust Barry Foster. Only make sure that Doris Day sings "Que Sera, Sera" until her kid is rescued! *Sabotage* has a good performance by Sylvia Sidney, who resolves to Do Something about the boy's death, plus the usual menacing turn by Oscar Homol-

ka, and the usual masculine turn by the powerfully built John Loder. As for Desmond Tester, who played the unlucky Steve, *Sabotage* was the fourth of nine films he made between 1935 and 1939. His next character as a child prodigy was so obnoxious that the future cast and crew of 1937's *Non-Stop New York* (including John Loder) might have reacted with cynicism if he'd taken a flying leap into the stratosphere without benefit of parachute. **AKA:** Woman Alone. 🦴🦴🦴

1936 81m/B Oscar Homolka, Sylvia Sidney, John Loder, Desmond Tester, Joyce Barbour, Matthew Boulton, S. J. Warmington, William Dewhurst, Austin Trevor, Torin Thatcher, Aubrey Mather, Peter Bull, Charles Hawtrey, Martita Hunt, Hal Walters, Frederick Piper; **D:** Alfred Hitchcock; **W:** Charles Bennett, Ian Hay, Alma Reville, E.V.H. Emmett, Helen Simpson. **VHS, Beta, LV, 8mm** SNC, NOS, HHT

Safe

Safe is an unforgettable viewing experience in a theatre. I don't know that I'd want to see it on the small screen, though. Writer/director Todd Haynes makes no concession to his film's eventual release on video. Protagonist Carol is frequently shown in extreme long shots, the better to emphasize how engulfed she is by the threatening environment. This perspective works wonderfully well as Carol's health is drained away from her and she seeks increasingly radical solutions over the course of two hours. Do try to see *Safe* in a theatre so you can catch Julianne Moore's outstanding performance (AND her paranoia) without binoculars! 🦴🦴🦴

1995 (R) 119m/C Julianne Moore, Peter Friedman, Xander Berkeley, Susan Norman, James LeGros, Mary Carver, Kate McGregor Stewart, Jessica Harper, Brandon Cruz; **D:** Todd Haynes; **W:** Todd Haynes; **C:** Alex Nepomniaschy; **M:** Ed Tomney. Nominations: Independent Spirit Awards '96: Best Actress (Moore), Best Director (Haynes), Best Film, Best Screenplay. **VHS, LV, Closed Caption** COL

Salmonberries

k.d. lang wants to be an actor in the worst way. And she's succeeding...in the worst way. Anyone catch her on ABC's historic *Ellen* episode April 30, 1997? Okay, so that was a bit. But she had entire sequences in Mario Puzo's *The Last Don* on May 13-14, 1997, yelling about art as Daryl Hannah's movie director. (CBS claimed an national audience of 30 million for this small-screen *Godfather.*) lang's reactions reminded me of someone. Could it possibly be Madonna in the 1987 bow-wow, *Who's That Girl?* Yes, and it also reminded me of k.d. lang in the little-seen Percy Adlon film *Salmonberries.* Adlon, who'd enjoyed considerable success with *Celeste, The Last Five Days, Sugar Baby, Bagdad Cafe, Rosalie Goes Shopping,* and *Younger and Younger,* could NOT attract a U.S. distributor for *Salmonberries!* Finally, San Francisco's Roxie Cinema agreed to screen it in early 1994. Co-starring Rosel Zech (so good as *Veronika Voss* for Fass-binder in 1982) and Chuck Connors (per-haps hoping that this flick would do for his career what *Bagdad Cafe* had done for Jack Palance), *Salmonberries* is listed as a 1989 credit in at least one Chuck Con-nors filmography. The Berlin Wall had already been opened by that time, a reality that dates the story since Zech had tried to escape Berlin with her lover, who was killed in the attempt. Somehow, Zech car-ries on and winds up in Alaska with lang as her lover. It is odd to watch a fine actor like Zech play sequences with someone who can barely act at all; not exactly fasci-nating, but...weird. lang sings the same song over and over again on the sound-track. Connors (1921-92) has very little to do. I wonder if they actually had to go to Alaska to shoot this thing. Anyway, lang's agent has undoubtedly been instructed to look for other parts to diversify lang's career. Think of the possibilities.... 𝄢

1991 (R) 94m/C *GE CA* Rosel Zech, k.d. lang, Chuck Connors; *D:* Percy Adlon; *W:* Percy Adlon, Felix Adlon. **VHS** *FCT*

Salut Victor!

Salut Victor! was a wonderfully appealing opening night entry at 1989's San Francis-co's Lesbian and Gay Film Festival. The plot revolves around two elderly men in a rather posh health care facility. Both are gay, but Philippe Lanctot (Jean-Louis Roux) is restrained and a bit of a prude, while Victor Laprade (Jacques Godin) is a flam-boyant hedonist. Although the two men could not be less alike, they become friends and Philippe realizes that he is enjoying life for the first time in many years. A visit to Philippe's club/restaurant becomes an exciting adventure with the rambunctious Victor as company, and their plans to take a balloon ride together are as much fun as the ride itself would have been. Very well acted and directed. *AKA:* Bye Bye Victor. 𝄢𝄢𝄢

1989 84m/C Jean-Louis Roux, Jacques Godin; *D:* Anne Claire Poirier; *W:* Marthe Blackburn; *C:* Michel Brault; *M:* Joel Vincent Bienvenue. **VHS** *NFB, FRA*

Salvador

If for no other reason than the hilarious sequence where James Woods as Richard Boyle pays his first visit to the confession-al in 32 years, *Salvador* would be ingrained in my consciousness forever. But *Salvador,* co-written by Boyle and based on his own experiences as a photojournalist in El Salvador, gets underneath my skin for its entire 123-minute running time. Boyle is unsparing of his own flaws, and Woods may have missed out on an Oscar because he didn't try to weaken its sear-ing honesty in any way. James Belushi is also very good as Doctor Rock, and if you want your heart tugged all the way down to your toes, check out Cynthia Gibb's perfor-mance as Cathy Moore. Woods as Boyle develops a conscience in spite of himself in this gritty account of life in El Salvador in 1980-81. 𝄢𝄢𝄢𝄢

1986 (R) 123m/C James Woods, James Belushi, John Savage, Michael Murphy, Elpidia Carrillo, Cyn-thia Gibb, Tony Plana, Colby Chester, Will MacMillan, Jose Carlos Ruiz, Jorge Luke, Juan Fernandez, Valerie Wildman; *D:* Oliver Stone; *W:* Oliver Stone, Richard Boyle; *C:* Robert Richardson; *M:* Georges Delerue. Independent Spirit Awards '87: Best Actor (Woods); Nominations: Academy Awards '86: Best

Actor (Woods), Best Original Screenplay. **VHS, Beta, LV, Closed Caption** *LIV, IME, VES*

Sammy & Rosie Get Laid

Stephen Frears' *Sammy & Rosie Get Laid* is every bit as unsettling to viewers as its title was to theatrical exhibitors. This is a densely plotted story about a London couple whose unconventional life is changed when the husband's father arrives on the scene from Pakistan. The father, played by Indian star Shashi Kapoor, is responsible for atrocities back home, but he is unprepared for the war zone he finds in London, following the real-life killing of a black woman by a policeman. American viewers, sated with the London they usually see whenever the Princess of Wales changes hairstyles, will also find screenwriter Hanif Kureishi's visions of riot-torn streets disturbing. The world of the Queen and her Prime Ministers is one that can be entered only by the most privileged of blacks and Pakistanis, or by the children who offer them flowers. The rest live in a world where violence is always near and where sex is an acceptable escape. *Sammy & Rosie* is so complex it would benefit from repeated viewings, but the performances by Kapoor, Claire Bloom, and newcomers Ayub Khan Din and Frances Barber are as clear as a bell. 🦴🦴🦴

1987 97m/C *GB* Shashi Kapoor, Frances Barber, Claire Bloom, Ayub Khan Din, Roland Gift, Wendy Gazelle, Meera Syal; **D:** Stephen Frears; **W:** Hanif Kureishi; **M:** Stanley Myers. **VHS, Beta, LV** *ORI, WAR*

Saraband for Dead Lovers

Forget H.R.H. Charles, The Prince of Wales, and return to the days when H.R.H. Prince George-Louis of Hanover was so mean to his wife Sophie-Dorothea that he divorced her twenty years before he ever became H.M. King George I and imprisoned her in the castle of Ahlden for the last 32 years of her life. She was forbidden to see her children after the divorce, and her ex-husband hated the future King George II just because he looked like his mother. Strong stuff, and who better to play George-Louis and Sophie-Dorothea than Peter Bull (1912-84, and one of Britain's best heavies from 1934 on) and Joan Greenwood (1921-87, and one of Britain's most regal leading ladies from 1940 on)? *Saraband for Dead Lovers* was released a couple of months before Prince Charles' birth in 1948, and like it or don't, he owes his very existence to the sad and lonely woman so rarely mentioned in the history books. As a vivacious teen, Sophie-Dorothea didn't want to marry a cold fish like George-Louis, and she frequently asked her father if a divorce were ever possible. After 11 years of this so-called marriage, she fell in love with Count Philip Koenigsmark of Sweden (who better than eminently attractive Stewart Granger, 1913-93?). The lovers planned to run away together, and then...in agreement with many scholars, *Saraband* speculates on what happened next. *Saraband* is an intelligent historical romance, with colorful court schemers (Dame Flora Robson is outstanding as Countess Platen) and well mounted spectacle. And Greenwood and Granger strike considerable sparks as the dead lovers from another time. Over three centuries later, when will the descendants of the Hanoverians ever learn? 🦴🦴▽

1948 96m/C *GB* Stewart Granger, Joan Greenwood, Francoise Rosay, Flora Robson, Frederick Valk, Peter Bull, Anthony Quayle, Megs Jenkins, Michael Gough, David Horne, Miles Malleson, Allan Jeayes, Guy Rolfe; **D:** Basil Dearden; **W:** John Dighton, Alexander MacKendrick. **VHS** *TIM*

Scandal

Even more so than the Americans, the British seem particularly vulnerable to sex scandals. Sex is essential for producing heirs, but the preservation of appearances often seems to be far more essential. Not that it matters, but the Profumo scandal of

1963 has always seemed like much ado about nothing. It certainly didn't deserve to lead to suicide, betrayal, exile, social ostracism, and political disgrace. The centerpiece of the scandal was an artistic, name-dropping osteopath named Dr. Stephen Ward, sensitively portrayed in *Scandal* by John Hurt. Ward liked to surround himself with "good time girls" (prostitutes is too strong a word) and never seemed to get laid himself. The best that Ward could hope for was to increase his sphere of influence by encouraging the liaisons of his protegees with potential dukes and lords. One big mystery in the scandal is why Christine Keeler was worth (as she claims) even a five-night stand when Mrs. Profumo was the beautiful and elegant Valerie Hobson. Hobson, star of such classics as *Bride of Frankenstein, Great Expectations,* and *Kind Hearts and Coronets,* had given up a long and suc-

cessful film career to marry Profumo in 1954, and she remained loyal to him before, during, and after the scandal. One hot Saturday night on July 8, 1961, the couple attended a party at the Cliveden estate of Lord and Lady Astor where they met Ward, Keeler, and Eugene "Honey Bear" Ivanov, a Soviet attache. *Scandal* fudges on certain details. A wife would have to be brain dead not to see the sexual games between Profumo and Keeler as they are shown in the film. In real life, Keeler's friend Mandy Rice-Davies named Valerie Hobson's former co-star, Douglas Fairbanks, Jr., as one of her lovers. His name is changed to David Fairfax, Jr., in the film. The actual son-in-law of Fairbanks, Richard Morant, appears in *Scandal* as a playboy. Britt Ekland, described by her former husband, the late Peter Sellers, as "a professional girl friend and an amateur actress" is sixth-billed as a party hostess at an orgy. *Scandal* is mostly Hurt's film, although Joanne Whalley is quite good as Christine. As Mandy Rice-Davies, Bridget Fonda extends her family's onscreen charisma to the third generation. Sir Ian McKellen isn't given much to say or do with the role of Profumo. The film solicits intense sympathy for Keeler and Ward and largely succeeds, thanks to Hurt and Whalley. Director Michael Caton-Jones films the first half of the picture rather like a comedy. All the childish games appear to be great fun, which they probably were while they lasted. Even in 1963, the notion of a War Minister sharing military secrets with a five-night stand must have seemed fantastic to anyone but a Big Mouth with a vivid imagination like Stephen Ward. But there's no compassionate grown up around to protect these adult youngsters from hurting themselves, and hurt themselves they did, until revisionist filmmakers romanticized them for 1989 audiences. 🦴🦴🦴🦴

1989 (R) 105m/C *GB* John Hurt, Joanne Whalley, Ian McKellen, Bridget Fonda, Jeroen Krabbe, Britt Ekland, Roland Gift, Daniel Massey, Leslie Phillips, Richard Morant; *D:* Michael Caton-Jones; *W:* Michael Thomas; *M:* Carl Davis. **VHS, Beta, LV** *HBO*

The Scarlet Pimpernel

The Scarlet Pimpernel must have been Margaret Truman's favorite film while her father Harry was President; she arranged for it to be screened no less than 16 times, according to *Guinness' Movie Facts and Feats.* This picture has absolutely everything. Leslie Howard is exactly what a stylish dandy AND a shrewd renegade should be. Even with all the swashbuckling, Howard as Sir Percival Blakeney comes up with some astonishingly subtle moments, like when he must conceal that he's madly in love with his wife (gorgeous Merle Oberon), whom he believes to be a traitor. Raymond Massey is rather a one-note Chauvelin, though. If you want to see how the part can be played to perfection,

see the 1982 version with Ian McKellen in which lust, jealousy, rage, and revenge are brilliantly conveyed with the simplest of gestures and with slight, vivid shifts of expression. *The Scarlet Pimpernel* consolidated the enormous impact producer Alexander Korda had made on American audiences with 1933's *The Private Life of Henry VIII,* starring the Oscar-winning Charles Laughton. In many ways, this is a richer, more complex yarn, but the Motion Picture Academy members, still reeling from the previous year, only nominated domestic productions in 1934. 🦴🦴🦴🦴

1934 95m/B *GB* Leslie Howard, Joan Gardner, Merle Oberon, Raymond Massey, Anthony Bushell, Nigel Bruce, Bramwell Fletcher, Walter Rilla, O.B. Clarence, Ernest Milton, Edmund Breon, Melville Cooper, Gibb McLaughlin, Morland Graham, Allan Jeayes; *D:* Harold Young; *W:* Robert Sherwood, Arthur Wimperis, Lajos Biro. **VHS, Beta** *CNG, NOS, PSM*

Scenes from a Marriage

The runaway hit of 1974's San Francisco International Film Festival was this searing entry by Ingmar Bergman, originally made for Swedish television. In spite of its length (168 minutes, cut down from 360 minutes), Bergman uses every second, exploring the hardest of truths about the relationship between two people. Sven Nykvist's flawless camera work doesn't let us leave Liv Ullman and Erland Josephson for very long and everything else blends beautifully in this masterful film. Ullman's gem of a performance will haunt you for years. 🦴🦴🦴🦴

1973 (PG) 168m/C *SW* Liv Ullmann, Erland Josephson, Bibi Andersson, Jan Malmsjo, Anita Wall; *D:* Ingmar Bergman; *W:* Ingmar Bergman; *C:* Sven Nykvist. Golden Globe Awards '75: Best Foreign Film; National Board of Review Awards '74: 5 Best Foreign Films of the Year; New York Film Critics Awards '74: Best Actress (Ullmann), Best Screenplay; National Society of Film Critics Awards '74: Best Actress (Ullmann), Best Film, Best Screenplay, Best Supporting Actress (Andersson). **VHS, Beta** *HMV*

"I'm not getting to the truth of our relationship....I don't think there exists one truth."

—Johan (Erland Josephson) gets brutally honest in *Scenes from a Marriage.*

Scenes from the Class Struggle in Beverly Hills

Viewers who see Paul Bartel's *Scenes from the Class Struggle in Beverly Hills* will either love it or hate it. We hated it, even though it wasn't worth hating. There's a mean-spirited streak to this self-styled "restoration comedy," something which might seem hilarious to Bartel and his aficionados. And for all Bartel's efforts to outrage, stale situations are recycled, old stereotypes are revived, and talented actors are wasted. Jacqueline Bisset's performance, for example, seems like an audition for a *Dynasty* revival, since Joan Collins's character has presumably been killed off with a back flip off a balcony. Sample dialogue, Bisset to servant: "You're not supposed to think, you're supposed to wrap brussel sprouts in bacon." Robert Beltran and real-life AIDS victim Ray Sharkey make a bet that whoever goes to bed with his employer first, wins. Sharkey's prize is anal intercourse with Beltran and no condoms in sight. Beltran rides off with Mary Woronov; this is happily ever after? A bad writer played by Ed Begley, Jr., arrives with bride Arnetia Walker, who's mistaken for a servant at first because she's black. She has anal intercourse with one of the men, and fools around with a leukemia-ridden teen. Et cetera. There's also a young girl (real-life murder victim Rebecca Schaeffer) who winds up traipsing off with the diet doctor played by Paul Bartel, who looks something like 3 1/2 times her age, a dog named Bojangles (don't get too attached to him...), a fat ghost played by Paul Mazursky, a womanizing gynecologist played by Wallace Shawn, and a Mexican maid played by Edith Diaz. Sexual chemistry between any two of these characters chosen at random is ZERO. There is one funny bit in which a porn video is recreated, complete with bad acting and fractured pronunciations. But the humor in the sequence is stifled by the fact that we have to watch it with the dying (and masturbating) kid. Another false note is struck when Bartel shows a journalist running away in horror after listening to the frank language of Bisset and her friends at the breakfast table. Oh, please...journalists are more likely to react in horror to the size of their paychecks. It would take far more than rude behavior at breakfast to shock them, much less horrify them. Watching *Scenes from the Class Struggle in Beverly Hills* is like being a four a.m. straggler at a very dull party. Check out 1982's much funnier *Eating Raoul* with Bartel, Woronov, and Beltran instead. **WOOF!**

1989 (R) 103m/C Jacqueline Bisset, Ray Sharkey, Mary Woronov, Robert Beltran, Ed Begley Jr., Wallace Shawn, Paul Bartel, Paul Mazursky, Arnetia Walker, Rebecca Schaeffer, Edith Diaz; *Cameos:* Little Richard; *D:* Paul Bartel; *W:* Bruce Wagner; *M:* Stanley Myers. **VHS, Beta, LV** *NO*

Search and Destroy

Once again, I'm giving a movie an extra half bone for the presence of Illeana Douglas, because she's such a scene-stealing treat to watch. (And that's no mean feat in a flick that co-stars Dennis Hopper, Christopher Walken, and John Turturro.) Until 1996's *Grace of My Heart* was released, I combed the video shelves for ANY movie with Douglas in it: 1991's *Cape Fear,* 1993's *Alive* and *Household Saints,* 1994's *Grief,* 1995's *To Die For,* and this flick by David Salle, which might have been even wilder if Michael (*Twister, Nadja*) Almereyda had directed his own screenplay. Someone, PUH-LEEZE make the terrific Illeana Douglas a name above the title STAR!!! 🦴🦴🦴

1994 (R) 91m/C Griffin Dunne, Dennis Hopper, Rosanna Arquette, Christopher Walken, John Turturro, Illeana Douglas, Ethan Hawke; *Cameos:* Martin Scorsese; *D:* David Salle; *W:* Michael Almereyda; *C:* Michael Spiller, Bobby Bukowski; *M:* Elmer Bernstein. **VHS, LV, Closed Caption** *HMK*

Seclusion Near a Forest

Seclusion is about a family and their efforts to obtain a summer cottage. It is also the story of how people adjust to their own needs for territory and how they reconcile themselves to other people's morality. At first, the family waits for their old landlord to go away or die so they can have the place to themselves. Later, they grow to depend on his strength and common sense. Josef Kemr is wonderful as the old man and Jiri Menzel (*Closely Watched Trains*) explores the gentle themes here with humor and insight. **AKA:** Na Samote u Lesa. 🦴🦴🦴

1976 92m/C *CZ* Zdenek Sverak, Jan Triska; **D:** Jiri Menzel; **W:** Zdenek Sverak; **C:** Jaromir Sofr; **M:** Jiri Sust. *NYR*

The Second Awakening of Christa Klages

This West German film is essentially a simplistic fairy tale, but so well acted, scripted, and directed that its many implausibilities can be forgiven. Tina Engel, in the title role, commits a "political" robbery with a pair of male cohorts when her kindergarten becomes strapped for funds. The rest of the film shows how she deals with the consequences of her crime. Her colleagues refuse to accept the money and a female witness pursues her, in this feminist variation on *Les Miserables*. Engel, a plain and chunky yet attractive actress, is excellent as Christa, her performance enhanced by a superb supporting cast, including the entrancing Peter Schneider in a romantic role. Margarete von Trotta does a forceful job directing her own script (co-written with Luisa Francia). Franz Rath's expert camera work and Klaus Doldinger's effective score add to the suspense. **AKA:** Das Zweite Erwachen der Christa Klages. 🦴🦴🦴

1978 90m/C *GE* Tina Engel, Peter Schneider; **D:** Margarethe von Trotta; **W:** Margarethe von Trotta, Luisa Francia; **C:** Franz Rath; **M:** Klaus Doldinger. *NYR*

Second Coming of Suzanne

When we saw *Second Coming* (with its creator in attendance), it was a total embarrassment, wasting its talented cast, and deserving of every BOO it got. If you don't mind being exploited by self-indulgent, chest-beating harangues against exploitation, enjoy! Inspired by the Leonard Cohen song and made in the San Francisco Bay area, the film's executive producer was Michael's proud father, Gene Barry. 🦴

1980 90m/C Sondra Locke, Richard Dreyfuss, Gene Barry, Paul Sand, Jared Martin; **D:** Michael Barry; **W:** Michael Barry; **C:** Isidore Mankofsky. **VHS, Beta** *GEM*

The Secret of Roan Inish

Based on Rosalie K. Fry's novel, *Secret of the Ron Mor Skerry*, *The Secret of Roan Inish* is a charming and gentle fable, featuring a delightful performance by newcomer Jeni Courtney as ten-year-old Fiona. Fiona is enchanted by her grandfather's stories about her baby brother, Jamie, who once drifted out to sea, and about the lovely Selkie Seal/Lady, who once came on land to live with Fiona's family. Mason Daring's atmospheric score adds to the mood and tone of the piece, which represents a point of departure for writer/director John Sayles. Set in County Donegal, it's the perfect movie for St. Patrick's Day or anytime you feel like being wrapped in the spell of another time and place. 🦴🦴🦴

1994 (PG) 102m/C Jeni Courtney, Michael Lally, Eileen Colgan, John Lynch, Richard Sheridan, Susan Lynch, Cillian Byrne; **D:** John Sayles; **W:** John Sayles; **C:** Haskell Wexler; **M:** Mason Daring. Nominations:

S

Independent Spirit Awards '96: Best Director (Sayles), Best Film, Best Screenplay. **VHS, LV, Closed Caption** *COL*

Secrets and Lies

Mike Leigh became the darling of international film festivals and archives in 1986. We dutifully attempted to watch a selection of the Leigh oeuvres at that time. 1976's *Nuts in May* was nothing special, but okay; at least we could make out the dialogue in that one. Then, in rapid succession, we found ourselves chain-drinking endless cups of tea and coffee after walking out on a string of Leigh flicks: 1980's *Grown Ups,* 1982's *Home Sweet Home,* 1983's *Meantime,* 1984's *Four Days in July.* The thick dialects were impossible for us to decipher without benefit of subtitles. With *Secrets and Lies,* Mike Leigh became a world-class, Oscar-nominated film director. And we still had trouble plowing through the dialects, at least during a LOOONG series of introductory sequences (some extraneous) that set the plot in motion. We like the late character actress Irene Handl (1900-87) just fine, but if she were the central character in any of the movies in which we saw her, we'd reach for the mute button. THIS is our dilemma with the Oscar-nominated Brenda Blethyn, a fine actress, with a face that wells up with enough raw emotion to ignite a dozen soap operas, and a (cultivated) screechy voice like Handl's that is painful to listen to during the course of two hours and 22 minutes. Blethyn as Cynthia lives out her dreary life with her sullen daughter Roxanne (Claire Rushbrook). Cynthia sees less of her brother Maurice (Timothy Spall) than she would like because she can't stand his wife Monica (Phyllis Logan) and vice-a versa. Into this cozy group, a sophisticated optometrist (renamed Hortense by her adopted parents) comes looking for Cynthia, her birth mother. Marianne Jean-Baptiste is quite wonderful as the well read, soft-spoken young woman who is determined to get to know her mother after the deaths of the parents who raised her. There's a wrap-up which is, for all the surface grit, deeply false and way too pat. In real-life families, the revelation of secrets and the exposure of lies don't get resolved in a few moments of hugs and tears. They invariably lead to violent brawls and long years of silence between emerging family factions. Even though it's a pseudo-depiction of life rather than an honest one, *Secrets and Lies* IS the breakthrough film for which Leigh will be best remembered. The clothes, as always in a Leigh film, are ghastly. 🎞🎞🎞

1995 (R) 142m/C *GB* Brenda Blethyn, Marianne Jean-Baptiste, Timothy Spall, Claire Rushbrook, Phyllis Logan, Lee Ross, Ron Cook, Leslie Manville, Irene Handl; *Cameos:* Alison Steadman; *D:* Mike Leigh; *W:* Mike Leigh; *C:* Dick Pope; *M:* Andrew Dickson. Cannes Film Festival '96: Best Actress (Blethyn), Best Film; Golden Globe Awards '97: Best Actress (Blethyn); Independent Spirit Awards '97: Best Foreign Film; Los Angeles Film Critics Association Awards '96: Best Actress (Blethyn), Best Director (Leigh), Best Film; Nominations: Academy Awards '96: Best Actress (Blethyn), Best Director (Leigh), Best Picture, Best Supporting Actress (Jean-Baptiste), Best Writing; British Academy Awards '96: Best Actor (Spall), Best Actress (Blethyn), Best Director (Leigh), Best Film, Best Original Screenplay, Best Supporting Actress (Jean-Baptiste); Cesar Awards '97: Best Foreign Film; Directors Guild of America Awards '96: Best Director (Leigh); Golden Globe Awards '97: Best Film—Drama, Best Supporting Actress (Jean-Baptiste); Screen Actors Guild Award '96: Best Actress (Blethyn); Writers Guild of America '96: Best Original Screenplay. **VHS** *FXV*

Separate Tables

British playwright Terrence Rattigan specialized in intricately crafted dramas about ordinary men and women whose interior worlds were shattered when they were forced to face themselves truthfully for the first time. Unsurprisingly, many of his plays, like *The Winslow Boy* and *The Browning Version* became splendid film vehicles for Britain's finest actors and actresses. When *Separate Tables* was first performed onstage as two one-act plays,

Margaret Leighton and Eric Portman played different leading characters for each act, gimmickry that probably would not have worked in a movie. Independent producers Burt Lancaster, Harold Hecht, and James Hill hired Laurence Olivier and Vivien Leigh to play an estranged couple, and cast David Niven and Deborah Kerr against type as a phony war hero and the mousy spinster who adores him from afar. Lancaster and Olivier soon realized that they would not be able to work together and both Olivier and Leigh withdrew from the project. Lancaster decided to play the part that Olivier had vacated and Delbert Mann stepped in as director. Rita Hayworth, then engaged to marry co-producer James Hill, was quickly signed to play the estranged wife. These (mis)casting decisions resulted in half of a great movie, and even the half that isn't great is redeemed by the Oscar-winning performance of Wendy Hiller as Lancaster's discarded mistress. The more interesting half revolves around the self-styled Major Pollock, who faces social castigation after misbehaving in a movie theatre. The *West Hampshire Weekly News* details the facts of the case as well as his military career, and the first reaction of his fellow residents at the Beauregard Hotel is to throw him out. David Niven, usually smooth, elegant, and charming, shed all of these mannerisms to create a new character, filled with uncertainty and doubt. It was far and away the most challenging role of Niven's long career, and he won an Oscar for the part, considerably helped by Deborah Kerr's touching performance as his disillusioned admirer. Gladys Cooper once again played a domineering mama to the hilt, and other recognizable British types were sharply observed by Cathleen Nesbitt, Sir Felix Aylmer, and May Hallatt. Rattigan firmly believed that "British is best" and that even his country's greatest flaws could be compensated for by individual acts of kindness and decency. There may have been a great deal of wishful thinking in Rattigan's world view, but it's hard not

to get caught up in the plight of poor Major Pollock and the lonely souls who surround him. 𝄞𝄞𝄞

1958 98m/B Burt Lancaster, David Niven, Rita Hayworth, Deborah Kerr, Wendy Hiller, Rod Taylor, Gladys Cooper, Felix Aylmer, Cathleen Nesbitt, Rod Taylor, Audrey Dalton, May Hallatt, Priscilla Morgan, Hilda Plowright; **D:** Delbert Mann; **W:** John Gay; **C:** Charles B(ryant) Lang; **M:** David Raksin. Academy Awards '58: Best Actor (Niven), Best Supporting Actress (Hiller); Golden Globe Awards '59: Best Actor—Drama (Niven); National Board of Review Awards '58: 10 Best Films of the Year; New York Film Critics Awards '58: Best Actor (Niven); Nominations: Academy Awards '58: Best Actress (Kerr), Best Adapted Screenplay, Best Black and White Cinematography, Best Picture, Best Original Score. **VHS, Beta** *MGM, FOX, FCT*

Serial Mom

There comes a time in every femme fatale's movie life when she looks at the scripts she's being offered and realizes, "Hey, no one's offering me parts where I get to say lines like, 'I never forget a face once I've sat on it.' I'd better start thinking about my next career move." In the case of Kathleen Turner, then 39, 1994's *Serial Mom* was it. When she made her screen debut in *Body Heat* in 1981, John Waters was just beginning to think in terms of conventional casting; Divine alone might not have lured mallrats into multiplexes to see *Polyester,* but DIVINE AND TAB HUNTER?! Times change and now even Sam Waterston, who ordinarily plays candidates for canonization, is on hand as a latter-day Carl Betz to Turner's twisted Donna Reed. Also in *Serial Mom* are Ricki Lake and Matthew Lillard as the kids, Misty and Chip; Mink Stole, Patty Hearst, and Mary Jo Catlett as the Serial Mom's nemeses; L7 as the house band; and even Traci Lords, Joan Rivers, and Suzanne Somers in cameo roles. For the most part, *Serial Mom* is a sick and cynical film about the sick and cynical homage mass murderers receive in our society. But, since Waters admittedly reads the books and sees the films about assorted lunatics who inspired this film, he makes

no effort to supply an antidote to the media's obsession with them. Instead, his perspective flips back and forth between the ultra-correct Serial Mom AND her poor victims who have the bad taste to watch Chesty Morgan videos under the blankets or to sing along with lousy Hollywood musicals while eating meat. When Serial Mom isn't stalking prey, she's shown in a flattering, if extreme light. After all, garbage men, uh, sanitation engineers adore her. With a few exceptions (the Chesty Morgan fanatic and Patty Hearst as Juror #8, who commits the blunder of wearing white shoes after Labor Day), the nicest thing you can say about Serial Mom's targets is that, uh, sanitation engineers DON'T adore them. And that too dovetails into society's worship of living psychos as magazine pin-ups. Very rarely does the media focus on naming, much less characterizing, the ghosts they leave behind. *Serial Mom,* in Waters' own demented way, is a film of deep moral intensity, with a solemn respect for homespun values. Just rent Alfred Hitchcock's *Shadow of a Doubt* afterwards for an in-your-face clue to its satirical roots. (Cast Note: Turner next joined the ensemble cast of 1995's *Moonlight and Valentine,* Waterston went on to make John Duigan's *The Journey of August King,* Lake re-made the 1950 Barbara Stanwyck film noir *No Man of Her Own* as 1996's *Mrs. Winterbourne,* and Lillard signed on for the 1995 Iain Softley flick, *Hackers.*) ♫♫♫

1994 (R) 93m/C Kathleen Turner, Ricki Lake, Sam Waterston, Matthew Lillard, Mink Stole, Traci Lords; *Cameos:* Suzanne Somers, Joan Rivers, Patty Hearst; *D:* John Waters; *W:* John Waters; *M:* Basil Poledouris. **VHS, LV, Closed Caption** *HBO*

Servant and Mistress

Bruno Gantillon focuses on a sado-masochistic relationship between a house-keeper-turned-heiress and a diplomat-turned-butler. *Servant and Mistress* is a seamlessly constructed film; not a word or

a gesture between the two leads is wasted. With careful direction and a tasteful screenplay, this strong story of cruelty and humiliation is woven into another, more subtle romantic theme. It's a tricky balance, and Gantillon and cast handle it quite well. This fascinating, disturbing portrait of shifting power via the strange games this couple plays is definitely worth a look. ♫♫♫

1977 90m/C *FR* Victor Lanoux, Andrea Ferreol, David Pontremoli, Jean Rougerie; *W:* Dominique Fabre. *NYR*

Set It Off

Stony (Jada Pinkett), Cleo (Queen Latifah), single mom Tisean (newcomer Kimberly Elise), and bank teller Frankie (Vivica Fox) have shared similar miserable experiences with bosses, boyfriends, and the police. They decide to team up and pursue a life of crime by robbing banks. Their internal friction is complicated by the constant threat of the police, as well as banker Keith's (Blair Underwood) attraction to one of the women. Well acted by the four leads, but reviewers have learned to watch out for movies about robbing banks where the director says stuff in the press kits like, "'This movie is not about robbing banks, it's about personal sacrifice and commitment to friendship...robbing banks is a means to an end." As opposed to all those other movies where robbing banks is what? NOT a means to end? ♫♫

1996 (R) 121m/C Jada Pinkett, Queen Latifah, Vivica A. Fox, Kimberly Elise, Blair Underwood, John C. McGinley, Anna Maria Horsford, Ella Joyce, Charles Robinson, Chaz Lamas Shepard, Vincent Baum, Van Baum, Tom Byrd, Samantha MacLachlan; *D:* F. Gary Gray; *W:* Kate Lanier, Takashi Bufford; *C:* Marc Reshovsky; *M:* Christopher Young. Nominations: Independent Spirit Awards '97: Best Supporting Actress (Queen Latifah). **VHS** *NLC*

Seven Beauties

A single act of violence executed on a grand scale: how does it fit into the fabric

INDEPENDENT FILM GUIDE

Opposite page: **Kathleen Turner is *Serial Mom.***

of people's lives? Why does it happen? What manner of person commits the act? Lina Wertmuller demonstrates the foolishness of such a killing in *Seven Beauties.* Her protagonist (Giancarlo Giannini) kills his sister's pimp to avenge his honor, but makes the mistake of improperly setting the death scene. He is too impatient to wait for the pimp to defend himself. Consequently, he must serve time in an insane asylum and later in World War II. Then he is faced with different sorts of life choices: with so many killings in the concentration camps, does it matter who does the killing? Isn't he guilty everytime he looks the other way? Finally he is faced with his life and his life only, for he has nothing else. *Seven Beauties,* already hailed as Wertmuller's masterpiece, is a sizzling account of the solutions one man accepts for himself as a reaction to the

senseless patterns of life. Considering its content, it's amazing that Wertmuller is so successful at injecting a quality of comic zaniness into the grim proceedings. She moves swiftly from one insanity to the other with dizzying speed, yet she skillfully blends all the imagery so that the point of this cutting edge satire is strong and clear. NOTE: At press time, Lina Wertmuller and Jane Campion remain the only women in the entire history of the Academy Awards to receive Oscar nominations as Best Director. *AKA:* Pasqualino Settebellezze; Pasqualino: Seven Beauties. 🎵🎵🎵🎵

1976 116m/C *IT* Giancarlo Giannini, Fernando Rey, Shirley Stoler, Elena Fiore, Enzo Vitale; **D:** Lina Wertmuller; **W:** Lina Wertmuller; **C:** Tonino Delli Colli. Nominations: Academy Awards '76: Best Actor (Giannini), Best Director (Wertmuller), Best Foreign Language Film, Best Original Screenplay. **VHS, Beta, LV** *COL, APD*

sex, lies and videotape

No question about it, *sex, lies and videotape* is an impressive first feature for writer/director Steve Soderbergh, then 26. The movie was lionized at the 1989 Cannes Film Festival, where it won two major awards. We can't help feeling, though, that there was an "Oh, those funny Americans" factor about its lavish reception. Spike Lee's *Do the Right Thing*, a far more threatening view of American society, was virtually ignored by the same festival. James Spader as Graham illustrates what ruthless seducers have known forever: that if a man tells a potential conquest he's normally impotent around women and then shows her that he isn't around her, he's practically assured of another notch on his belt. And this is late-breaking news? Meanwhile across town, Peter Gallagher as John learns another astonishing lesson: that if a man fools around with his wife's sister, he's going to lose them both. Soderbergh is so wrapped up in these two urgent social statements that he ignores minor details. For example, Spader has a car and a place to live and an extensive video collection of assorted women discussing their sex lives on camera. At one point, he says that he supports himself with money under the mattress. One helpful sentence about where he gets his grocery money would have dissolved the notion that he might be a blackmailing slime instead of the film's only candidate for a romantic prince. The movie gets off to a slow start with an endless sequence between Andie MacDowell as Ann and her therapist. (Surprise: the therapist is a dope!) The rest of the film consists of sequences between Ann and husband John, Ann and sympathetic Graham, Ann and sister Cynthia, Cynthia and brother-in-law John, Cynthia and sympathetic Graham, and finally, dishonest John and honest Graham. The movie was made in Baton Rouge, Louisiana, on $1.2 million, which included the salary of our favorite actress in the film: Laura San Giacomo as Cynthia. When San Giacomo snarls "You are scum" to John and then hops into bed with him, she gives an understanding to these contradictory acts that isn't in the script. Despite his best actor award, Spader basically has three expressions: asleep, constipated, and adorable. *sex, lies and videotape* leaves unanswered the burning question of why it takes some men forever to realize what burns out many women long before they finish high school. 🦴🦴🦴

1989 (R) 101m/C James Spader, Andie MacDowell, Peter Gallagher, Laura San Giacomo, Ron Vawter, Steven Brill; **D:** Steven Soderbergh; **W:** Steven Soderbergh; **C:** Walt Lloyd; **M:** Cliff Martinez. Cannes Film Festival '89: Best Actor (Spader), Best Film; Independent Spirit Awards '90: Best Actress (MacDowell), Best Director (Soderbergh), Best Film, Best Supporting Actress (San Giacomo); Los Angeles Film Critics Association Awards '89: Best Actress (MacDowell); Sundance Film Festival '89: Audience Award; Nominations: Academy Awards '89: Best Original Screenplay. **VHS, Beta, LV, 8mm, Closed Caption** COL

Shades of Doubt

Deeply troubled teenagers were the focus of quite a number of the entries at 1995's Mill Valley Film Festival. Aline Issermann's *Shades of Doubt* accurately reflects the confusion a 12-year-old victim of incest experiences when she tries to bring the truth out into the open. Alexandrine's story begins in the most idyllic of settings: a family outing in beautiful surroundings. But the first of a series of brief encounters occurs with her father (off camera), and her life is forever changed. A sensitive teacher tries to help her come forward in order to stop the abuse, but Alexandrine buckles under family pressure, retracts her charges, and the abuse continues. When she runs away with her small brother, her family and the authorities finally listen to her. If *Shades of Doubt* had been a telefeature on American television, the issues would have been simplified with all

Andie MacDowell
and James Spader
in *sex, lies
and videotape.*

battle lines clearly drawn. But this French-made drama gains its strength from the subtlety of Issermann's script and direction as well as from the strikingly colorless camera work by Darius Khondji. And the acting, especially by the young protagonist, is frighteningly real. **AKA:** L'Ombre du Doute; Shadow of a Doubt. 𝄞𝄞𝄞

1993 105m/C FR Mireille Perrier, Alain Bashung, Sandrine Blancke, Emmanuelle Riva; **D:** Aline Issermann; **W:** Aline Issermann, Martine Fadier-Nisse, Frederique Gruyer; **C:** Darius Khondji; **M:** Reno Isaac. *NYR*

Shag: The Movie

Shag is a pleasant summer comedy about four teenage girls enjoying a fling in Myrtle Beach, South Carolina, circa 1963, a plot only its English producers would consider "a rarity." Phoebe Cates, a star of high school films since 1982, finally graduates in this one. She's clearly had some theatrical training: her performance as a future bride attracted to a one-night stand named "Buzz" is her most restrained to date. Daryl Hannah's sister Page, 25, plays the plain daughter of a Senator who has a crush on Cates' strict boyfriend, Tyrone Power, Jr., 30. Bridget Fonda, another 26-year-old teenager, gives her role of a preacher's wild daughter a poignant blend of self-mocking humor and desperation. Perhaps the only real teenager in the bunch is high school junior Annabeth Gish, who is charming as always. Carol Burnett's lookalike daughter Carrie Hamilton is also around to provide competition for Fonda in their star-struck pursuit of a teen idol who thinks Elvis Presley is pathetic. Beautiful British actress Shirley Anne Field, who once played a delinquent in 1960's *Beat Girl,* plays Page's Southern belle mama. Speaking of which, do all Southern beauty pageants require Scarlett's vomit scene at Tara plus American flag dance routines as part of their talent competitions? The film is your basic retread of the old "Beach Party" movies where the only black faces you'll see on the beach belong to "The Voltage Brothers" singing "Sixty Minute Man," where the emphasis on innocence evokes 1963 media caca rather than reality, and where a group of talented newcomers somehow manage to give the non-stop cliches a fresh twist. *Shag* is directed by Zelda (*Secret Places*) Barren. ♫♫♫

1989 (PG) 96m/C Phoebe Cates, Annabeth Gish, Bridget Fonda, Page Hannah, Scott Coffey, Robert Rusler, Tyrone Power Jr., Jeff Yagher, Carrie Hamilton, Shirley Anne Field, Leilani Sarelle Ferrer; **D:** Zelda Barron; **W:** Robin Swicord, Lanier Laney, Terry Sweeney. **VHS, Beta, LV** *HBO*

Shallow Grave

Shallow Grave is a nasty little tale about three flatmates looking for a fellow occupant to share their living space. As they grill prospective tenants, we learn that Juliet, David, and Alex have the sort of darkly humorous relationship that excludes nearly everyone else. Until Hugo arrives on the scene. He creates an interesting and rather charming first impression. And then they discover his body in his new room plus a million dollars in his suitcase. At this point, some logical viewers might have a best possible scenario all worked out for the three buddies. But anyone who's seen *The Treasure of Sierra Madre, Ocean's Eleven, Perfect Friday,* or countless other sure-fire heist movies knows that best possible scenarios never work out once greed kicks into gear. So we get to watch as Juliet turns crafty, David turns weird, and Alex turns, well, just a bit gallant. And screenwriter John Hodge plays fair with the outcome. Danny Boyle, too, directs the comedic moments with broad strokes and underplays the escalating violence with

fast cuts of real gore and artfully composed long shots that look far more grisly than they really are. *Shallow Grave* may not be the sort of movie police procedural buffs will care to examine too carefully, but as a psychological chiller, it supplies splendid value. Best of all, the expert ensemble work in *Shallow Grave* is a treat to watch: Kerry Fox, Christopher Eccleston, and Ewan McGregor are ideally cast as the best friends who know way too much and far too little about each other. (You may remember Fox from Jane Campion's *An Angel at My Table* and Eccleston from Peter Medak's *Let Him Have It.* McGregor would share the spotlight with the worst toilet in Scotland in another film by Boyle and Hodge, 1996's *Trainspotting.*) ♫♫♫

1994 (R) 91m/C *GB* Kerry Fox, Christopher Eccleston, Ewan McGregor, Keith Allen, Ken Stott, Colin McCredie, John Hodge; **D:** Danny Boyle; **W:** John Hodge; **C:** Brian Tufano; **M:** Simon Boswell. **VHS** *PGV*

Shelf Life

Shelf Life bears the surprising imprint of director Paul Bartel. Fans of Bartel's more outrageous works such as *Eating Raoul, Lust in the Dust,* and *Scenes from the Class Struggle in Beverly Hills,* may not know what to make of this modest stage-to-screen transfer of the play written by its three stars, the story of what would happen to the kids in a family that were whisked into a bomb shelter straight after the assassination of President Kennedy. Thirty years later, the parents are dead, but the grown-up children live on, entrenched in long-established rituals. It may not be life as you or I would know it, but it is life as they know it, take it or leave it. The idea of escape never seriously occurs to them, so the rituals are all they have, really. The three leads are excellent, especially O-lan Jones, who would make a terrific onscreen vampire. Along with co-stars Jim Turner and Andrea Stein, the three have the comedic timing of a highly polished vaudeville team. If you can accept the reality that, like the partici-

I was neither amused nor quite outraged by the Sundance Film Festival's assessment that *Shelf Life* was not a Paul Bartel movie, but I was certainly distressed by it. *Shelf Life* is a very offbeat, unusual, provocative little movie, and it needs the support of festivals, especially festivals which are dedicated to independent American film. *Shelf Life* was turned down by the San Francisco Film Festival, with the explanation that it was too odd. I thought that any festival that would reject a film on the basis of oddness needs to have the people who are selecting the films re-examined, so I was very upset when they declared *Shelf Life* not a real Paul Bartel film. What they meant was that it wasn't what they were expecting, which I suppose is something in the vein of *Eating Raoul* or *Scenes from the Class Struggle in Beverly Hills.* Next, I'm going to do an adaptation of *War and Peace* all set in Los Angeles and all performed by two actors...I'm kidding....

"These are difficult times in the movie business. I have several offbeat weird projects, but I have a feeling that now is not the moment for them. I have written with an old friend an erotic thriller... That's what I hope I'll be doing next, but I've been doing a lot of acting. I've appeared in about six films in the last two months, in one of which, a truly amazing movie, called *The Wacky Adventures of Dr. Boris and Nurse Shirley,* I play not a mad doctor, but a very sane doctor, who nevertheless murders beauty queens and sells their bodies to the richest man in the world, played by Clive Revill. He has all sorts of moral qualms about it, but goes on doing it anyway, because it pays so well.... Every so often I just have to make one of those movies. It's like the fluids have built up and I HAVE to do one....

"*Shelf Life* is entirely different. I think of it as my first underground family film.... We actually didn't film it in as tiny a space as it appears to be onscreen. When I first saw the material onstage in a version which only lasted about 50 minutes, it was in a very tiny space, but since part of what the movie is about is the way in which imagination can open up vistas no matter where or in what situation you're confined, we took great pains to make it feel like the set was quite large. We had a fairly large sound stage to shoot it on. We built a set which lent itself to re-lighting and re-arranging and re-dressing, so that when the various fantasy sequences began and the characters' imaginations took over, the space changed or enlarged or stretched to accommodate their fantasies. The story is almost a revue, set in the situation of three children who have been taken by their parents into a fall-out shelter under a house in Anaheim, California, in late 1963, right after

President Kennedy was assassinated. The parents thought that the country was about to be taken over by the Martians and the Communists. The parents died shortly thereafter from eating some bad tinned salmon, and the kids are in their early 40s as of 1994, but emotionally, they're still ten, eleven, and twelve years old. Just as the play did, the film represents a day in their lives underground. They've long since forgotten about the possibility of getting out. They've lived down there with their fantasies and their games and their little satires. They have a television set which only plays a few seconds of image and sound every half hour, and these set them off on new fantasies and new adventures. I thought it was very funny, and had a great deal to say about American culture and the relationship between siblings and men and women and children and adults, and I thought that a very large audience would appreciate it, much larger than would ever see it in a little theatre on Santa Monica Boulevard, so I decided to take the bit in my teeth and produce the movie myself without trying to raise money from other people or getting permission as one usually has to do to make a movie. The cast was very excited, the three actors who had written it were very eager to do it as a movie, and it was a wonderful collaboration. We found a great deal of support. All sorts of people gave us things, loaned us things, worked for nothing, worked for very little. I must say I am extremely pleased with the movie that came out of it. I think it's very original, very unique, not so much due to me, but due to the actors themselves, who are really actor-poets. When I saw the show onstage, I had a whole bunch of ideas for new scenes and new sequences to fill out the show, plus a new ending. They liked all my ideas, so we got along very well. I outlined the new scenes and they wrote them, then we refined them together. We built the set, we rehearsed for about a week because when they had done it as a play, it had been done very presentationally and very theatrically, and I wanted to make it a little more naturalistic. I can't say that the acting is naturalistic and I didn't want it to be. We had to re-scale it for the screen, bring it down a little bit, and also, since the set was going to be very three-dimensional and the camera was going to move all around and through it, we had to invent all new staging. I wanted the camera to be very mobile and to get into those little nooks and crannies and little houses that kids build with sheets and tables and what-not. That's one of the things I'm proudest of: the intimacy of the film."

PAUL BARTEL can be seen in *Hollywood Boulevard, Piranha, Rock 'n' Roll High School, Eating Raoul, Frankenweenie, Chopping Mall, Killer Party, Amazon Women on the Moon, Out of the Dark, Far Out Man, Pucker Up and Bark Like a Dog, Scenes from the Class Struggle in Beverly Hills, Mortuary Academy, The Pope Must Diet, Desire and Hell at Sunset Motel, Liquid Dreams, Number One Fan, The Jerky Boys,* and *The Usual Suspects.* Bartel also directed *Paul Bartel's Secret Cinema, Private Parts, Death Race 2000, Cannonball, Not for Publication, Lust in the Dust,* and *The Longshot.*

pants, you're stuck in a hermetically sealed environment for the duration, *Shelf Life* ain't a bad little way to spend 83 minutes. But then, at the very end, The Great Bartel makes a brief appearance. The larger-than-life Bartel, who can generate a laugh without even trying, had the effect of making me wish that the movie had started with his entrance. Such mutinous thoughts aside, *Shelf Life* is best watched on its own quirky terms and may be more widely enjoyed as a cult video item. ♫♫♪

1994 83m/C O-lan Jones, Jim Turner, Andrea Stein, Paul Bartel; **D:** Paul Bartel; **W:** O-lan Jones, Jim Turner, Andrea Stein. *NYR*

She's Gotta Have It

Nola Darling (Tracy Camilla Johns) is having an affair with Jamie Overstreet (Tommy Redmond Hicks), who thinks he can tell her what to do. Nola is also having an affair with Greer Childs (John Canada Terrell), a rich male model who's more in love with himself than with her. And finally, Nola is seeing Mars Blackmon (Spike Lee), a bit of a clown, who's young for his age. Jamie, Greer, and Mars are all jealous of each other and want Nola to settle down with one of them. Nola, a genuinely free spirit, resists the idea of being forced to make such a decision. *She's Gotta Have It* introduced the multi-talented Lee to the world. Within a decade, we would see ten of this fiercely free spirit's exciting, thoughtful films. His influence on the industry remains enormous, and he continues to create once-in-a-lifetime characters and to support the emergence of other new filmmakers. By 1992, cinematographer Ernest R. Dickerson was directing his own projects. Johns can be seen in Lee's *Mo' Better Blues* and in Mario Van Peebles' *New Jack City*. A milestone film in every respect, *She's Gotta Have It* is also fresh, beautifully shot and scored, and very, very funny. ♫♫♫

1986 (R) 84m/B Tracy C. Johns, Spike Lee, Tommy Redmond Hicks, Raye Dowell, John Canada Terrell, Joie Lee, Epatha Merkinson, Bill Lee, Cheryl Burr,

Aaron Dugger, Stephanie Covington, Renata Cobbs, Cheryl Singleton, Monty Ross, Lewis Jordan, Erik Dellums, Reginald Hudlin, Eric Payne, Marcus Turner, Gerard Brown, Ernest R. Dickerson; **D:** Spike Lee; **W:** Spike Lee; **C:** Ernest R. Dickerson; **M:** Bill Lee. Independent Spirit Awards '87: Best First Feature. **VHS, Beta, LV, Closed Caption** *FOX, FCT*

She's the One

Edward Burns, Mike McGlone, and newcomer Maxine Bahns return in the so-so follow-up to Burns' so-so breakthrough film, *The Brothers McMullen*. This time, they're surrounded by familiar television faces (John Mahoney from *Frasier,* whose career will neither be helped nor hindered by this picture, and Jennifer Aniston from *Friends,* who might do well to consider a new movie agent), PLUS clever Cameron Diaz, who runs away with the flick's only rave reviews. Expectations for *She's the One* were huge, never an auspicious climate for a second feature. Burns used to go with Diaz, who worked her way through college as a call girl, but now he's married to Bahns and driving a cab. McGlone (as his brother—yes, again) is fooling around with Diaz (now supporting herself as a broker), who doesn't think much of his technique. Meanwhile, wife Aniston tries her darndest to look sexy, but settles for a vibrator in the bathroom when McGlone ignores her. Mom Anita Gillette is supposed to be praying for her overgrown infants in Church, but she's actually...oh well, never mind.... Dad John Mahoney takes the brothers fishing and explains the facts of Catholic life to them, but he's actually...oh well, never mind.... Catholicism is (yes, again) a major motif. Diaz has an older lover (offscreen) whom she prefers to McGlone. Bahns has a lesbian admirer (onscreen) whom she doesn't prefer to Burns. I guess it would hurt worse to BE in this family than to watch them for 95 minutes. *She's the One* is no better and no worse than any average telefeature except that Robert Redford is one of the executive producers. ♫♫

1996 (R) 95m/C Edward Burns, Mike McGlone, Jennifer Aniston, Cameron Diaz, Maxine Bahns, John Mahoney, Leslie Mann, George McCowan, Leslie Mann, Amanda Peet, Anita Gillette, Frank Vincent; **D:** Edward Burns; **W:** Edward Burns; **C:** Frank Prinzi; **M:** Tom Petty. **VHS, LV, Closed Caption** *FXV*

Shine

Geoffrey Rush deservedly won a Golden Globe and an Academy Award for his full-throttle performance as David Helfgott, and Noah Taylor really deserved a nod, too, as adolescent David. Armin Mueller-Stahl was SO creepy as Helfgott's control freak father that he probably freaked out the Academy members who voted for Cuba Gooding, Jr., instead. *Shine* basked in a 90-something day glow until some nasty music critics said that Helfgott was no Van Cliburn. Man, they were mean! The credits clearly state that *Shine* was never meant to be a documentary and that many situations had been fictionalized, but the folks who bet on the Oscars actually said that there would be a backlash because Helfgott wasn't a better piano player. All of this had zip to do with Rush or *Shine,* but that didn't stop musical cognescenti from buzzing about both as if they were investigative reporters! Even after the Oscars, critics continued to gun for Helfgott as if it weren't enough that he'd conquered madness, he had to be a genius, too. (Oh, get a life/a heart/a grip...GRR!!!) Sir John Gielgud is so animated as one of young David's teachers, it's hard to believe that you're watching someone who made his movie debut at twenty in 1924's *Who Is the Man?* It's a treat to see Googie Withers again as another influential teacher and friend. And Lynn Redgrave is radiant as the delightful lady who sees past David's mumbling straight into his heart. That's sort of the point of the film, actually. ♪♪♪♪

1995 (PG-13) 105m/C *AU* Geoffrey Rush, Noah Taylor, Armin Mueller-Stahl, Lynn Redgrave, John Gielgud, Googie Withers, Chris Haywood, Sonia Todd, Alex Rafalowicz; **D:** Scott Hicks; **W:** Jan Sardi; **C:** Geoffrey Simpson; **M:** David Hirschfelder. Academy Awards '96: Best Actor (Rush); Australian Film Institute '95: Best Actor (Rush), Best Cinematography, Best Director (Hicks), Best Film, Best Film Editing, Best Screenplay, Best Sound, Best Supporting Actor (Mueller-Stahl), Best Score; Golden Globe Awards '97: Best Actor—Drama (Rush); Los Angeles Film Critics Association Awards '96: Best Actor (Rush); National Board of Review Awards '96: Best Film; New York Film Critics Awards '96: Best Actor (Rush); Screen Actors Guild Award '96: Best Actor (Rush); Broadcast Film Critics Association Awards '96: Best Actor (Rush); Nominations: Academy Awards '96: Best Director (Hicks), Best Film Editing, Best Picture, Best Supporting Actor (Mueller-Stahl), Best Writing, Original Dramatic/Comedy Score; Australian Film Institute '95: Best Actor (Taylor); British Academy Awards '96: Best Actor (Rush), Best Director (Hicks), Best Film, Best Original Screenplay, Best Supporting Actor (Gielgud), Best Supporting Actress (Redgrave); Directors Guild of America Awards '96: Best Director (Hicks); Golden Globe Awards '97: Best Director (Hicks), Best Film—Drama, Best Screenplay, Best Score; Screen Actors Guild Award '96: Best Supporting Actor (Taylor), Cast; Writers Guild of America '96: Best Original Screenplay. **VHS** *NLC*

The Shining

The 1997 miniseries may have had Stephen King's seal of approval, but nothing beats the eyes and ears of a world-class filmmaker. As I was nearly driven into a coma while Steven Weber and Rebecca DeMornay had a LOOONG chat about whether or not they should have sex, I knew that this would never happen in the original Stanley Kubrick movie starring Jack Nicholson and Shelley Duvall. They won't let us conk out on them. They grab our attention and they keep it for, okay, nearly two and a half hours. Yeah, that's a generous running time, but at least they have a legitimate claim on our interest the whole time (which is more than I can say for the remake). The quality that audiences have always responded to in Jack Nicholson is that he gives a role everything he has; that guy never reigns it in. When he loses his mind, he doesn't fool around. When he turns homicidal, he puts all those HOW TO BE SUBTLE instruction pamphlets in the shredder. And Shelley Duvall (although it is difficult imagining the two of them doing anything together that would result in the birth of Little Danny) is the ideal foil for Nicholson and

INDEPENDENT FILM GUIDE

his what-the-hell style. She lives in her own little world until her antibodies start warning her about life-threatening danger and then there's no stopping her; she knows how to fight! *The Shining* is not a movie about restraint or about an ordinary family battling the forces of darkness in the lonely Overlook Hotel. It's about three oddballs, one of whom was born to wind up in a haunted setting like this one, and the other two who will fight their apparent destiny to the death. The one flaw is Dick Halloran's (Scatman Crothers) exhaustively illustrated flight to save Danny. Crothers is excellent in the part, but we don't want to leave the hotel to watch a guy on a plane or a receptionist or a forest ranger. We want to see Jack and that weird bartender and those odd little twins in the hall and.... ♪♪♪♡

1980 (R) 143m/C Jack Nicholson, Shelley Duvall, Scatman Crothers, Danny Lloyd, Joe Turkel, Barry Nelson, Philip Stone, Lia Beldam, Billie Gibson, Barry Dennan, David Baxt, Lisa Burns, Alison Coleridge, Kate Phelps, Anne Jackson, Tony Burton; **D:** Stanley Kubrick; **W:** Stanley Kubrick, Diane Johnson; **C:** John Alcott. **VHS, Beta, LV, Closed Caption** *WAR*

Shirley Valentine

Surprise! Thanks to writer Willy Russell and actress Pauline Collins, *Shirley Valentine* emerges as one of the most charming mid-life crisis sagas ever. The plot revolves around a 42-year-old Liverpudlian housewife who's tired of talking to her kitchen wall. She leaves her husband with two weeks of frozen dinners and flies away to Greece with a friend. On the sunny island of Mykonos, Shirley confronts her fears of the unknown and successfully resists sliding back into her safe, predictable world. The best thing about Shirley's new adventures is the way the writer shows that she isn't running away from herself, only unpeeling the layers of muck which have separated her from her own bright, rebellious spirit. A delightful young actress named Gillian Kearney portrays Shirley as an impish schoolgirl alienated from the class kissy, Marjorie (also well played by Catherine Duncan). Years later, Shirley meets Marjorie, now a high-class call girl played by Joanna Lumley, and is surprised to note how well they get along. It's one of the film's best moments, perfectly capturing the pointless mutual envy that circumvents many friendships between women. Shirley has detached sympathy for the snobbish neighbor Julia McKenzie, for Greek native (Tom Conti?!) who always uses the same pick-up lines, and even for her husband Bernard Hill. In fact, the only person who seems to be under major attack in Willy Russell's script is the self-styled feminist portrayed by Alison Steadman. This "feminist" has her politically correct lingo down cold, but her rhetoric has nothing to do with what she feels or does. Shirley wisely recognizes a b.s. artist when she sees one and shoves her in the direction of the most boring tourists on the island. With "friends" like that, it's best to make friends with yourself, says Russell. In her first major feature, Pauline Collins fulfills the promise of her early performance as the feisty Sarah in the *Upstairs, Downstairs* television series. She has an honest face and an honest body (for once, no one asked the leading lady to go on a diet). Russell's sharp script is a blessing, but Pauline Collins is the main reason why this movie will remain a glowing memory long after you see *Shirley Valentine.* 🦴🦴🦴

1989 108m/C *GB* Pauline Collins, Tom Conti, Alison Steadman, Julia McKenzie, Joanna Lumley, Bernard Hill, Sylvia Syms, Gillian Kearney, Catherine Duncan; **D:** Lewis Gilbert; **W:** George Hadjinassios, Willy Russell; **M:** Willy Russell. British Academy Awards '89: Best Actress (Collins); Nominations: Academy Awards '89: Best Actress (Collins), Best Song ("The Girl Who Used to Be Me"). **VHS, LV, 8mm, Closed Caption** *PAR, TVC, HMV*

A Shock to the System

There are actors who reach the stage in their careers when they telephone in their performances. Then there is Michael Caine, who tackles each new role with the hunger of a beginner whose career depended on every movie he makes. Jan Egleson's *A Shock to the System* is vintage Caine. Surrounded by an excellent supporting cast, he outacts everyone on screen with fine character shadings and total attention to detail. He's the only actor we know who even seems to act with the nerve endings of his teeth! Andrew Klavan's clever screenplay is based on a novel by Simon Brett, the only flaw being its logical, but rather flat conclusion. This may be partly due to the competent but not especially sizzling performance of Will Patton as Caine's nemesis. The rest of the well-chosen cast includes Elizabeth McGovern, Peter Reigert, Swoosie Kurtz, Jenny Wright, John McMartin and the late, great Barbara Baxley. WITHOUT Michael Caine, this wicked tale of a frustrated businessman's cool plan to eliminate all the obstacles to his success might seem like a padded mystery of the week for television. But Michael Caine's hypnotic performance gives *A Shock to the System* its claustrophobic atmosphere and charges the narrative with its driving force. 🦴🦴🦴

1990 (R) 88m/C Michael Caine, Elizabeth McGovern, Peter Riegert, Swoosie Kurtz, Will Patton, Jenny Wright, John McMartin, Barbara Baxley; **D:** Jan Egleson; **W:** Andrew Klavan; **M:** Gary Chang. **VHS, Beta, LV, Closed Caption** *HBO*

Short Cuts

There is probably no filmmaker alive who is more expert at capturing the pulse of a community than Robert Altman. He examined the world of country music in *Nashville* with humor and affection, and the motion picture industry with savagery and wit in *The Player*. Now, in *Short Cuts*, he casts a dark gaze at the sunny world of

INDEPENDENT FILM GUIDE

Los Angeles where sex is plentiful and joy-less, where wrongful death is taken for granted, and where love never ever hits the right target. Despite the superficial milk-and-honey surroundings, the Los Angeles of *Short Cuts* is a bleak landscape, popu-lated by losers waiting for Armageddon. There is Jennifer Jason Leigh's wonderfully drawn white trash housewife who feeds her baby while paying the bills with phone sex. There is the idiotic mother, played with feeling by Andie MacDowell, who insists that her child not speak to strangers, but allows him to slip into a coma after a seri-ous head injury. There are three good old boys (Fred Ward, Buck Henry, and Huey Lewis) who continue to fish at their favorite watering hole after discovering the dead body of a young woman. There is the estranged grandfather, played to the hilt by Jack Lemmon, who tells wildly inappropri-ate stories of his past escapades in a hos-pital waiting room. There are the two jerks played by Robert Downey, Jr., and Chris Penn who look for women to ravish while on a picnic with their wives and kids. There is the doctor (Matthew Modine) and his wife (Julianne Moore) who make much ado about nothing (her long ago drunken indis-cretion), and then hiss at each other over a game of Jeopardy and a hot tub with anoth-er couple. And that's just for starters. For 189 minutes, Altman weaves his way through nine different plot threads, and through it all, nothing, nothing, nothing is anyone's fault. If someone dug up *Short Cuts* out of a time capsule in 500 years, it might be like watching the last days of Pompeii. Anne Archer as Fred Ward's wife goes through a temporary transformation where you think, "Oh, my God, is SOME-ONE in this movie actually going to give a damn about someone else?" But the trans-formation is over in a flash, and she duti-fully joins her husband for barbecued fish and that hot tub. Lily Tomlin's hit-and-run driver rationalizes her mistake. Annie Ross dismisses her suicidal daughter one too many times. Tim Robbins' character ditch-es the family dog, then tears it away from

the new owners. Lyle Lovett feeds muffins to Andie MacDowell after harassing her on the phone over an unpaid bill while her son is dying. In *Short Cuts,* the sun sparkles brightly on the dark ugliness of a world where a game show host like Alex Trebek is God and only an 8.6 earthquake can put everyone out of their misery. Until then, courtesy of Robert Altman, it's hard to tear our eyes away from the ants under the rock. ♫♫♫♫

1993 (R) 189m/C Annie Ross, Lori Singer, Jennifer Jason Leigh, Tim Robbins, Madeleine Stowe, Frances McDormand, Peter Gallagher, Lily Tomlin, Tom Waits, Bruce Davison, Andie MacDowell, Jack Lemmon, Lyle Lovett, Fred Ward, Buck Henry, Huey Lewis, Matthew Modine, Anne Archer, Julianne Moore, Lili Taylor, Christopher Penn, Robert Downey Jr., Jarrett Lennon, Zane Cassidy; **D:** Robert Altman; **W:** Frank Barhydt, Robert Altman; **C:** Walt Lloyd; **M:** Mark Isham. Independent Spirit Awards '94: Best Director (Altman), Best Film, Best Screenplay; National Society of Film Critics Awards '93: Best Supporting Actress (Stowe); Venice Film Festival '93: Best Film; Nominations: Academy Awards '93: Best Director (Altman); Golden Globe Awards '94: Best Screenplay; Independent Spirit Awards '94: Best Supporting Actress (Moore). **VHS, LV, Closed Caption** COL

Shy People

Andrei Konchalovsky strikes out with *Shy People,* a witless film about *Cosmopolitan* writer Jill Clayburgh, who drags teenage daughter Martha Plimpton off to the back-woods to visit their cousins for the pur-pose of a magazine article about families. The cousins are presided over by Barbara Hershey, whose husband is an omni-present ghost, whose sons are violent and strange, and whose pregnant daughter-in-law (Mare Winningham, wasted again) wants a battery-operated television set. There's a Biblical quote from Revelations to "explain" all the nonsense onscreen, only it doesn't. Before that, the married son nearly rapes Plimpton while Hershey is away shooting the hand of a man who hit her son in the head. She shoots him in the strip joint operated by yet another son who later chats with Clayburgh. Inexplicably, Clayburgh has left her daughter alone with the other three boys while she "helps" Hershey, and Winningham, too, of course. (Remember the television set?) Well, when Clayburgh finds out what happened to Plimpton, she goes looking for her with the help of the ghost and then Hershey explains that even though her dead husband pistol whipped her while she was pregnant, he still helped the family survive. Clayburgh learns the appropriate lesson and tells Plimpton that she's going to be a stricter mother to her in the future. The strip joint owner returns to the fold and breaks the television set right away, which must be yet another lesson on something or other. If *Shy People* represents the clash between urban and rural values in America to Soviet writer/director Konchalovsky, then perhaps some time away from the Cannon group might provide him with fresh understanding of the people about whom he will be making films in the future. His next three projects (*Homer and Eddie, Tango and Cash,* and *The Inner Circle*) were far from acclaimed for any startling insights into these films' characters. 🦴🦴

1987 (R) 119m/C Jill Clayburgh, Barbara Hershey, Martha Plimpton, Mare Winningham, Merritt Butrick, John Philbin, Don Swayze, Pruitt Taylor Vince; **D:** Andrei Konchalovsky; **W:** Gerard Brach, Marjorie David; **C:** Chris Menges; **M:** Tangerine Dream. Cannes Film Festival '87: Best Actress (Hershey). **VHS, Beta, LV, Closed Caption** *WAR*

Sidewalks of London

This tribute to the sidewalk entertainers who performed outside London theatres is a good early showcase for Vivien Leigh as Libby. The lion's share of the attention goes to Charles Laughton as a street performer who befriends Libby and makes her part of his act. Libby has greater ambitions for herself. She wants to be a star and, through her connection with the young songwriter played by Rex Harrison, she becomes one. She also insults Charles when he proposes to her, but then

thinks better of it and sets up an audition for him. Charles, needing the attention that he can only get by being a street performer, returns to his pals outside the theatre. Reportedly, Leigh didn't much enjoy the experience of making this picture. There is only one star in a Charles Laughton movie, and she wasn't it. After *Gone with the Wind* was released, British theatres, hungry for any Vivien Leigh vehicles, re-released this one in 1940. It wasn't up to the glossy MGM standards of 1940's *Waterloo Bridge,* but the feisty Libby was certainly a lot closer to Scarlett O'Hara than the doomed ballerina Leigh played opposite Robert Taylor. **AKA:** St. Martin's Lane. 🦴🦴🦴

1938 86m/B *GB* Charles Laughton, Vivien Leigh, Rex Harrison, Larry Adler, Tyrone Guthrie, Gus McNaughton, Bart Cormack, Edward Lexy, Maire O'Neill, Basil Gill, Claire Greet, David Burns, Cyril Smith, Ronald Ward, Romilly Lunge, Helen Haye, Jerry Verno; **D:** Tim Whelan; **W:** Clemence Dane; **C:** Jules Kruger; **M:** Arthur Johnson. **VHS, Beta** *KIV, HHT, CAB*

Silent Tongue

The conclusion of *Silent Tongue* is abrupt for a reason; reportedly, the original ending was scrapped because of the uneven quality of some of the performances. Watching the rest of the film, it isn't too difficult to identify the weakest cast members: Dermot Mulroney and River Phoenix, both of whom acquitted themselves with distinction in many other ensemble showcases. Mulroney is simply inept, but even Phoenix's most worshipful admirers will wince at his lack of focus here. He is supposed to be a grief-crazed widower, but in his eyes we see nothing but an artistic athlete dying young, and not appearing to care one way or another. But there are many other rewards to be found in Sam Shepard's western ghost story, namely the strong, deeply felt performances of Alan Bates, Richard Harris, Sheila Tousey, and Jeri Arrendondo. 🦴🦴

1992 (PG-13) 101m/C River Phoenix, Sheila Tousey, Richard Harris, Alan Bates, Jeri Arredondo, Der-

INDEPENDENT FILM GUIDE

mot Mulroney, Tantoo Cardinal; *Cameos:* Bill Irwin, David Shiner; *D:* Sam Shepard; *W:* Sam Shepard; *C:* Jack Conroy; *M:* Patrick O'Hearn. **VHS, LV, Closed Caption** *THV*

Silent Witness

Oral histories about the Holocaust are offered by Harriet Wichins' *Silent Witness,* a 1994 Canadian documentary. Wichins' study of the death camps at Dachau and Auschwitz is deliberately low-key. 🦴🦴🖤

1994 74m/C *CA D:* Harriet Wichins. *NYR*

Sirens

It's been so long since we've seen contemporary movies with sexual themes free of violence or devastating consequences that we were beginning to wonder if they were still being made. *Sirens* is certainly the most low-key sexual fantasy film that you're likely to see from the year 1994. It's partly based on the life of Australian artist Norman Lindsay, who died in 1968 at the age of 90. For most of Lindsay's career, his explicit works shocked the people of his own time. John Duigan's fictional film takes a look at a 1930s weekend in the life of the Lindsay family and three of their models. Anthony and Estella Campion, a fictitious twit of a minister and his repressed wife, come to pay a call in order to persuade the artist to withdraw his profane works from a major exhibition. The twit is played by the devilishly attractive Hugh Grant, with tongue firmly in cheek ("Call me Tony"), and his wife by the sultry Tara Fitzgerald, last seen in *Hear My Song.* True to the artist's code of never putting an amorous hand on a model, Sam Neill's Lindsay is far from the lecherous hedonist expected by the Campions. He is, rather, a devoted husband, kindly father, and disciplined worker. His feelings are expressed entirely in his art, whereas the women who pose for him express their sexuality in their own lives. (They're played by supermodels Elle MacPherson, Kate Fischer,

and Portia de Rossi, by far the best actress of the three.) The entire Lindsay clan are looked on with suspicion by the townspeople, but there is no predictable clash. Menacing snakes and spiders crawl through the film, but they do not destroy the Lindsays' Garden of Eden, either. Instead, we read about their mischief in the newspapers where they're presumably harming the good people who predict disaster for the Lindsays. *Sirens,* seen from Estella's perspective, reveals how she is seduced into having a rollicking good time, and, surprise, no one gets punished, goes mad, or brandishes a weapon. Beautifully photographed eroticism for its own sake, a few rattled conceptions about Bohemians, and the prevailing social order is all you will get from *Sirens,* and that's just fine, thank you. For doom and gloom, you will have to choose another movie from the umpteen thousands that occupy the SEX=TROUBLE file. 🦴🦴🦴

1994 (R) 96m/C *AU GB* Hugh Grant, Tara Fitzgerald, Sam Neill, Elle Macpherson, Kate Fischer, Portia de Rossi, Pamela Rabe, Ben Mendelsohn, John Polson, Mark Gerber, Julia Stone, Ellie MacCarthy, Vincent Ball; *Cameos:* John Duigan; *D:* John Duigan; *W:* John Duigan; *C:* Geoff Burton; *M:* Rachel Portman. Chicago Film Critics Awards '94: Most Promising Actor (Grant). **VHS, LV, Closed Caption** *MAX*

Sister My Sister

While it's by no means flawless, *Sister My Sister* has it all over *The Maids.* Based on a true French murder case, set in Le Mans, the story revolves around the Papin sisters, Christine, 28 (Joely Richardson), and Lea, 21 (Jodhi May). The two maids are treated like dirt by their employer Madame Lancelin, changed to Ranzard for the film (Julie Walters). With no other allies, they depend on each other for everything until the domestic situation reaches the boiling point, then it's Au Revoir, Madame, and Mademoiselle, too. Mademoiselle was Genevieve Lancelin, 27, changed to Isabelle Danzard for the film (Sophie Thursfield). Both were found brutally murdered on the evening of February 2. Their maids were found huddled together in bed, naked. The case fascinated intellectuals of 1933, who read Christine's confession in the newspapers: "I'd rather have had the skin of my mistresses than that they should have had mine or my sister's. I did not plan my crime and I didn't feel any hatred towards them." The sisters were both found to be sane and guilty. Christine was originally sentenced to death, then to a life of hard labor. Instead, she went mad and was dead within four years. Lea was sentenced to ten years of hard labor, was released, and then lived a life of quiet obscurity. Director Nancy Meckler and screenwriter Wendy Kellelman show how the nerves of all four women were at the breaking point. Madame was used to dominating her daughter, Christine was used to dominating her sister. Madame expected her orders to be obeyed, it did not occur to her that by only obsessing on the maids' faults and never on their accomplishments, she was contributing to a toxic atmosphere which, tragically, could only be relieved with violence. By focusing on the emotional landscape of Madame's house, we see the Maids of Le Mans as the sad, neglected, futureless creatures they really were. 🦴🦴🦴

1994 (R) 89m/C *GB* Julie Walters, Joely Richardson, Jodhi May, Sophie Thursfield; *D:* Nancy Meckler; *W:* Wendy Kellelman; *C:* Ashley Ropwe; *M:* Stephen Warbeck. **VHS** *APX*

Slacker

Slacker is the sort of movie that will either make you laugh hysterically or switch theatres when the manager isn't looking. It made me laugh hysterically. There is something about people talking to themselves (in a movie, NOT in real life) that gives me the giggles. I had to scrape myself off the floor after one windbag (Richard Linklater) droned on and on about alternate realities to a priceless taxi driver and another explained how the U.S. and Russia have already set up colonies on the moon. Even better, *Slacker* led directly to 1993's *Dazed and Confused,* one of my all-time favorite movies, and I've never quite been able to scrape myself off the floor after that one. 🦴🦴🦴

1991 (R) 97m/C Richard Linklater, Rudy Basquez, Jean Caffeine, Jan Hockey, Stephan Hockey, Mark James, Samuel Dietert; *D:* Richard Linklater; *W:* Richard Linklater; *C:* Lee Daniel. **VHS** *ORI*

The Sleazy Uncle

In 1963, Vittorio Gassman starred as Bruno Fortuna, a jerk who introduces a kid portrayed by Jean-Louis Trintingnant to *The Easy Life.* In spite of the fact that Bruno had virtually no redeeming qualities, he gave Roberto the kid the best time he ever had in his life, and with the charismatic Vittorio Gassman as his guide, the reasons why were abundantly clear. In 1989's *The Sleazy Uncle,* Gassman plays another lovable rogue, but Uncle Lucca, like all of Gassman's unique characters, is created out of whole cloth. Uncle Lucca, an obscure but genuine poet, is adored by a small group of devoted fans, but he drives his responsible nephew Ricardo crazy. Lucca lies, steals, and carries his medical history with him at all times to facilitate one-night stands. The exasperated Ricardo finally takes his old uncle to court, where Lucca wins everyone's sympathy by crying his eyes out. Since Lucca's history is truly reprehensible, no one but a great actor like Vittorio Gassman could carry off such a sequence, but get away with it, he does. He sits there and cries like a baby and it works. Giancarlo Giannini, an actor who usually steals every picture he's in, is a wonderful foil for his co-star, handing most of their moments together to Gassman on a platter. Franco Brusati's *The Sleazy Uncle* would make a memorable double bill on video along with Dino Risi's *The Easy Life.* An even more intriguing triple bill would include 1975's *Scent of a Woman* with Gassman originating the role that won Al Pacino the 1992 Oscar. This Italian clas-

**Karl and Frank
(Billy Bob Thornton
and Lucas Black)
enjoy each other's
company in
Sling Blade.**

sic, which won Gassman the Best Actor Award at the Cannes Film Festival, is, alas, not yet released on video, so in the meanwhile don't miss Vittorio Gassman's tour-de-force performance in 1989's *The Sleazy Uncle.* **AKA:** Lo Zio Indegno. 🎜🎜🎜

1989 104m/C *IT* Giancarlo Giannini, Vittorio Gassman, Andrea Ferreol, Stefania Sandrelli; **D:** Franco Brusati. **VHS, Beta** *TRI*

Sling Blade

It's been a while since Billy Bob Thornton wrote and starred in 1992's *One False Move.* At the time, his dialogue was better than his acting. But in *Sling Blade,* Thornton has written himself a role that any actor worth his salt would walk barefoot on ground glass to play, and son of a gun if he doesn't make the most of the chance. Thornton IS Karl Childers, a mentally disabled man with terrible posture who sounds like the late Edgar Buchanan and who's spent most of his life in a state hospital for killing his mother and a young man many years before. Now, Karl is well, and he can't stay in hospital anymore as much as he'd like to. The hospital administrator (James Hampton) helps him get a job as a repairman, and Karl befriends Frank Wheatley, a fatherless little boy who lives with his mother Linda, and, sometimes, her alcoholic and abusive boyfriend, Doyle Hargraves. Linda's best friend is Vaughan Cunningham, a gay co-worker. Vaughan is played by a nearly unrecognizable John Ritter, in a startling, fully shaded performance. Vaughan wants to leave town, but he has a boyfriend and he cares about Frank and Linda, particularly when Doyle starts drinking and hitting people. Frank attaches himself to Karl, even when he finds out why his new friend was in the state hospital, and Linda (Natalie Canerday) invites him to stay in their garage, even though she also knows he was in the state hospital. She doesn't ask Karl to leave when she finds about what he did to his mother and the young man or even when he comes into her bedroom in the night, holding a hammer and asking to be baptized. Doyle (played right on target by Dwight Yoakam) gets drunker and meaner and life in the Wheatley home gets more and more tense. Karl tries to confront his past, both by going to see his no-account Dad (Robert Duvall in a cameo) and by talking about his crummy childhood with Frank. The 134-minute film moves at a deliberate pace; we know where the plot is going, but we're in no real hurry to get there, with all those rich characters and quirky humor and the tremendous star turns by Thornton and by Lucas (*American Gothic*) Black as Frank. *Sling Blade* is a pure American original: filled with tenderness and understanding, but also with a sense of the harsh measures needed to fight evil when it's destroying the lives of the only folks you've ever loved. 🦴🦴🦴

1996 (R) 134m/C Billy Bob Thornton, Dwight Yoakam, John Ritter, Lucas Black, Natalie Canerday, James Hampton, Robert Duvall, J.T. Walsh, Rick Dial, Brent Briscoe, Christy Ward, Col. Bruce Hampton, Vic Chesnutt, Mickey Jones, Jim Jarmusch, Ian Moore; **D:** Billy Bob Thornton; **W:** Billy Bob Thornton; **C:** Barry Markowitz; **M:** Daniel Lanois. Academy Awards '96: Best Adapted Screenplay (Thornton); Independent Spirit Awards '97: Best First Feature (Thornton); Nominations: Academy Awards '96: Best Actor (Thornton); Screen Actors Guild Award '96: Best Actor (Thornton), Cast; Writers Guild of America '96: Best Adapted Screenplay. *TOU*

Small Change

Francois Truffaut's movies are filled with sweet observations, invariably from a detached viewpoint. *Small Change* is a delightful romp with a group of school children. At one point, a small child topples from a high building, lands on his fanny in some soft bushes, then laughs his head off. Kids bounce back from life at its hard-

est, Truffaut says. They live through experiences that would shatter adults, pick themselves up and go right on living, all the more resilient for their brushes with hardship. If only it really were that simple.... 🦴🦴🦴🦴

1976 (PG) 104m/C *FR* Geory Desmouceaux, Philippe Goldman, Jean-Francois Stevenin, Chantal Mercier, Claudio Deluca, Frank Deluca, Richard Golfier, Laurent Devlaeminck, Francis Devlaeminck, Sylvie Grezel, Pascale Bruchon, Nicole Felix; **D:** Francois Truffaut; **W:** Francois Truffaut, Suzanne Schiffman; **C:** Pierre William Glenn; **M:** Maurice Jaubert. National Board of Review Awards '76: 5 Best Foreign Films of the Year. **VHS, Beta, LV** *MGM, FCT, WAR*

The Smallest Show on Earth

This charming Basil Dearden comedy focuses entirely on the management of a dilapidated movie theatre. The elderly ticket taker (Dame Margaret Rutherford as Mrs. Fazackerlee) is used to accepting barter as the price of admission from many of the patrons, the elderly projectionist is an alcoholic named Percy Quill who occasionally muddles the reels (Peter Sellers was only 32 at the time), and the sweet young couple (Virginia McKenna and Bill Travers) who inherit this beat-up bijou haven't a clue about how to whip the place in shape. This affectionate look at the days before mall multiplexes is scripted with obvious affection by William Rose and John Eldridge, who really capture the essence of why the neighborhood theatre meant so much to those who still remember them. **AKA:** Big Time Operators. 🦴🦴🦴

1957 80m/B *GB* Bill Travers, Virginia McKenna, Margaret Rutherford, Peter Sellers, Bernard Miles, Leslie Phillips, Stringer Davis, Francis De Wolff, Sidney James, June Cunningham; **D:** Basil Dearden; **W:** William Rose, John Eldridge. **VHS** *NOS, FCT, VEC*

Smoke

Movies change our lives, for better and worse. *Smoke* is the movie that broke my heart after I saw it with a dear, much-respected male friend. The story takes

Sling Blade

I came up with this character [Karl Childers] when I was working on this little cable movie years ago, and I was kind of depressed and sometimes I asked people, 'You know when you're looking in the mirror at yourself and you're really depressed and you start making faces at yourself?' and they said 'No.' So I guess I'm the only one who does that. I was actually making faces at myself in the mirror and started talking in this weird voice to myself just because I felt bad. I was doing a little self-loathing in the mirror. That's kind of how the face came about. Then I did this monologue in the mirror the same day that's in the beginning of the movie now, and I wasn't sure where it came from, but I'm sure it came from somewhere in my subconscious. I think most things I write do come from there. From that monologue, I started doing a one man show with Karl as part of it and that's how it all came about.

"I got the voice [for Karl Childers], really, I know it's based on a lot of the old guys I used to know back in Arkansas. Rural, southern guys, mostly elderly men. I used to work in a nursing home. Those vocalizations that Karl does, that comes from a lot of the elderly men I worked around in the nursing home.

"I'm a psychiatrist's dream. I guess I have a bunch of stuff in my past that I try and work out. I don't know. I have three movies produced as a writer. Two along with Tom Epperson who co-wrote *One False Move* and *A Family Thing,* which we wrote for Robert Duvall. All three movies have to do with the past. I think, maybe I'm wrong about this, that

place in and around Auggie Wren's Brooklyn cigar shop. The stars are Harvey Keitel as Auggie, William Hurt as a sad writer whose wife was killed before the movie begins, Harold Perrineau, Jr., as a troubled kid whom Hurt tries to help, Forest Whitaker as the kid's father, and Victor Argo, Jared Harris, and Giancarlo Esposito as some other sketchy characters in the orbit of Auggie's shop. My friend was extremely moved by *Smoke,* I was entirely unmoved by 112 minutes well acted hot air. In a feature-length study of guys where the only women are (1) killed and not heard, (2) in a few sequences to flesh out a guy, namely Stockard Channing as Auggie's ex, and (3) strung out in one sequence only, namely Ashley Judd, I'd just as soon the screenwriter blue-penciled them from the flick. If they don't serve any real function in the story, they don't need to be there at all. I tried to explain this to my friend in the car on the way home and nearly derailed the friendship. It survives, but I still think he felt I was dissing guys for being alive, so now I vent my opinions more carefully in person.

most people want to hang onto their innocence somehow. I mean, I think nostalgia comes from that. I think there's something about the characters in *Sling Blade,* that they have some sort of purity, except maybe for Dwight Yoakam's character who I couldn't say has a lot of it, but Karl is sort of an anti-hero guy. He's really pure in his soul even though some of the things he does aren't exactly soulful things to do. I think that's it for me. I think I dig back into my past and write about it because I miss it. I think when you grow up and you realize that your mother's friend was sleeping with the postman, or whatever it is, it's like you don't want to know that stuff, and I think we're always wanting our past to come back to us in some way, that innocence of childhood, and that appeals to me.

"This movie, even though it's made as a realistic movie, it's very symbolic in a lot of ways. A lot of this stuff is symbolism and not so much what would really happen. Sometimes you have to exaggerate a little bit to make somebody truly feel what it is you are trying to get across. There was a 1987 movie called *Hope and Glory*...directed by John Boorman, who's a fine director and gentleman. A lot of my friends when they saw *Hope and Glory* they said 'You know what, that stuff looks all exaggerated to me. Would that really happen? Was that the way it was?' The point of that movie was that was a ten year-old boy looking at the world. It was what it was like to live in London during World War II through the eyes of a ten year-old boy. Well, that's very different than the way you see it when you grow up. Actually, when you grow up, you think about your grandmother's gingerbread, you think, boy, that was the best stuff there ever was, it was magic. Then you go back to your grandmother's house, you know, when you grow up, and you eat her gingerbread and it tastes like sand. So children see things in a sort of heightened reality and this movie's no exception to that. I was just trying to point out that the decent people gravitate towards the decent."

1995 (R) 112m/C Harvey Keitel, William Hurt, Stockard Channing, Forest Whitaker, Harold Perrineau Jr., Ashley Judd, Mary Ward, Victor Argo, Jared Harris, Giancarlo Esposito, Mel Gorham; *D:* Wayne Wang; *W:* Paul Auster; *C:* Adam Holender; *M:* Rachel Portman. Nominations: Independent Spirit Awards '96: Best Supporting Actor (Perrineau); Screen Actors Guild Award '95: Best Supporting Actress (Channing). **VHS, LV, Closed Caption** *TOU*

Smooth Talk

When *Smooth Talk* first played at Wheeler Auditorium at the University of California at Berkeley, the resounding hisses and boos were heard clear across campus; it was politically incorrect for a movie to show a teenage girl (Laura Dern) apparently asking to be raped by a stranger (Treat Williams). A closer look reveals that this is neither the point of Joyce Chopra's film, nor of the original story by Joyce Carol Oates. It's one thing to goof around in the safety of a shopping mall with girlfriends, quite another to be confronted with a psychotic adult male who threatens both his target and her family. There is nothing particularly seduc-

375

INDEPENDENT FILM GUIDE**INDEPENDENT FILM GUIDE**

So Long at
the Fair

You may have vague memories of *The Vanishing Lady,* a 1955 *Alfred Hitchcock Presents* episode starring his daughter Pat. Originally titled *Into Thin Air,* it was reportedly based on a true story of 1889's Paris World Exposition: a young woman checks into a hotel with a relative who immediately becomes quite ill. A doctor is called, he sends her to fetch the medication and when she comes back, the relative is gone, and absolutely no one recalls who they are. She thinks she's going mad, but there IS a rather horrible explanation. Well, there's only so much that can be done in 30 minutes and Hitchcock himself didn't direct, so try to find *So Long at the Fair,* an outstanding British drama co-directed by Anthony Darnborough and Terence Fisher. Jean Simmons and David Tomlinson are Victoria and John Barton, who check into the hotel run by Mme. Herve (Cathleen Nesbitt). Brother John gets sick, Victoria sends for Dr. Hart (Andre Morell, a future Professor Quatermass) and then the mystery begins. It's a beautifully done interpretation of Anthony Thorne's novel (Thorne co-scripted), and the acting throughout is first rate. And who could wish for a more attractive and kind ally than Dirk Bogarde's George Hathaway. Honor Blackman, then in her English rose period, is in it too, and so is another future Bond girl, Zena Marshall. 𝄞𝄞𝄞

1950 86m/B *GB* Jean Simmons, Dirk Bogarde, David Tomlinson, Honor Blackman, Cathleen Nesbitt, Felix Aylmer, Marcel Poncin, Austin Trevor, Andre Morell, Zena Marshall, Betty Warren; **D:** Terence Fisher, Anthony Darnborough; **W:** Hugh Mills, Anthony Thorne. *NYR*

tive about Williams' approach, and Dern does nothing to encourage him once she realizes the extreme danger of her situation. However, she IS playing a kid, and her perceptions and decisions are not as savvy as an adult's might be in the same predicament. The most memorable aspect of the film, which won the Grand Jury Prize at the Sundance Film Festival in 1986, is Dern's heartrending performance; the picture certainly did NADA for Williams' career! Chopra later made *The Lemon Sisters,* plus the telefeatures *Murder in New Hampshire: The Pamela Smart Story* and *Danger of Love.* Dern and Place worked together again in *Citizen Ruth.* 𝄞𝄞𝄞

1985 (PG-13) 92m/C Laura Dern, Treat Williams, Mary Kay Place, Levon Helm; **D:** Joyce Chopra; **W:** Tom Cole. Sundance Film Festival '86: Grand Jury Prize. **VHS, Beta, LV** *LIV, VES*

Song
of the Siren

My particular favorite at 1995's Jewish Film Festival was Eytan Fox's *Song of the Siren,* based on Irit Linur's best-selling novel. *Siren* takes place during the days of

Operation Desert Storm, but Talila Katz, its wry and funny protagonist, pretty much ignores the conflict, the news bulletins, and all the precautions she's supposed to be taking in order to outlive the war. Instead, she's concerned with finding a husband, and not just any husband. Her choice is Noah, a food engineer so cute that violins play when she first lays eyes on him. But things get in the way, as they often do during 91-minute love stories. The intense focus on the personal at a time when the media focused an nothing but the war seems very real. *AKA:* Shirat Ha'Sirena. 🦴🦴🦴

1994 91m/C *IS* Dalit Kahan, Boaz Gur-Lavi, Yair Lapid, Avital Dicker; *D:* Eytan Fox. *NYR*

Sorceress

Sorceress, directed by long-time Francois Truffaut-collaborator Suzanne Schiffman, is an immaculate film about a 13th century French village and the priest who confronts their "heretical" superstitions. Co-written by art history professor Pamela Berger, the story never lets you forget for an instant that it is told through 20th century eyes. For that reason, this rather remote film lacks one crucial ingredient: the element of surprise. Even so, *Sorceress* is well worth watching for the superb acting and fine period details. 🦴🦴🦴

1988 98m/C Tcheky Karyo, Christine Boisson, Jean Carmet; *D:* Suzanne Schiffman; *W:* Pamela Berger, Suzanne Schiffman. **VHS** *MFV*

S.O.S. Titanic

At press time, a Titanic musical and yet another Titanic movie (directed by James Cameron) were in the works and a sudsy, very boring miniseries had just aired on network television. So why include this ABC telefeature that aired in a 180-minute time slot in the fall of 1979 before it was released theatrically overseas in the spring of 1980? How many more movies do we need to see about this maritime cat-astrophe, anyway? Except for *A Night to Remember,* they all have the same plot: two-thirds fictional dramatizations of the lives of characters who may or may not have existed in real life, one-third rescue operations, with a moment or two at the end for someone to say something about The Folly of Man. As these make-believe yarns go, *S.O.S. Titanic* is pretty good. It's nearly the end of the line for David Janssen as the doomed John Jacob Astor. (Janssen's only 49 here, but looks much older and he died before an edited version played in theatres.) Susan St. James does a nice job in the role of a passenger whose name isn't on any of the Titanic lists. David Warner is quite effective in one of his more restrained roles as Laurence Beesley, a survivor who wrote an account of the disaster. Helen Mirren is on hand as May Sloan, another survivor, and Ian Holm is perfect as always as the self-important Bruce Ismay. James Costigan's script, while not in the same league as Eric Ambler's 1958 adaptation of Walter Lord's classic book, is intelligently low-key. But the question remains for filmmakers of the future: what else needs to be said about the Titanic? With all the time, energy, and money that have been spent since April 15, 1912, every microbe on the Titanic could have had a lifeboat of its very own. Historical Note: the very first movie about the Titanic starred actress Dorothy Gibson, a surviving first-class passenger who wears the same clothes in the 10-minute movie that she was wearing when she was rescued. Her co-stars include Alex Francis, Jack Adolfi, and Guy Oliver. *Saved from the Titanic* was released on May 14, 1912, and is considered a lost film so if anyone is hoarding it in an attic (and you know who you are), contact your nearest archive! 🦴🦴🦴

1979 102m/C *GB* David Janssen, Cloris Leachman, Susan St. James, David Warner, Ian Holm, Helen Mirren, Harry Andrews, David Battley, Ed Bishop, Peter Bourke, Shevaun Briars, Nick Brimble, Jacob Brooke, Catherine Byrne, Tony Caunter, Warren Clarke, Nicholas Davies, Deborah Fallender; *D:* Billy Hale; *W:* James Costigan; *C:* Christopher Challis; *M:* Howard

DAVID O. RUSSELL
Spanking the Monkey

I'd made two short films and I wanted to make a feature, and I had grants from the National Endowment for the Arts and the New York State Council for the Arts to make a feature, but I was not happy with the script that I had written. I felt it was merely glib and eccentric and ironic and inconsequential, the way a lot of independent cinema can be. I was inspired by early Mike Nichols with *The Graduate* and *Carnal Knowledge,* intense, unflinching emotionality and examination of sexual relations, tinged with dark humor. And that's what I decided to go with. I looked into my own past to find a personal story that was full of all those things and that's how I came up with *Spanking the Monkey*: the story of a family in a repressed suburban community. A lot of Ray [Jeremy Davies] came from my own life. I was always the one who was too serious and intense as a kid and you have a rough time if that's your case. I also think that when you're a ping pong ball for your parents' wishes, which was common in the 1970s, you're more the vehicle of your parents' unrealized ambitions. It's confusing. It makes you a bit unclear about what you want versus what is wanted from you.

"We were looking at a lot of actresses in their late 30s to play Ray's mother. She had to be very sexy, but not too sexy, she had to be capable of carrying a lot of intense inner life. She had to seem smart and sympathetic. This woman is by no means a shrew. Faye Dunaway was very interested at one point and I got to have cappuccino with her in her bungalow behind her pool, but ultimately she passed. She was concerned about the intensity of the film's content, she had a 12-year-old son, and she tried to do a situation comedy instead [1993's *It Had to Be You* for CBS]. I tried to tell her that the film would help her in her relationship with her son, make her more conscious, which I hope *Spanking the Monkey* does do for families, but at the end of the day, it was a blessing, because it would have become Faye Dunaway's movie, with me being a first-time director and I might have been fired. I would have been the nobody and she would have been the main reason it was being financed.... Alberta Watson is terrific; she carries the intelligence and frightening manipulativeness of Ray's mother very well, as well as a soft, loving quality. It's a tough act. I've been saying all along, 'This is not an incest movie. It touches on incest, but it's part of a broader canvas of Ray's sexual frustration and emotional journey.' *The New York Times* said in their great review, which, thankfully, helped us have a huge opening weekend in New York, 'Incest is almost incidental. It isn't the main thing in the film.' I quite agree. So it's great that they're discovering that now."

James Costigan; **C:** Christopher Challis; **M:** Howard Blake. **VHS, Beta** QHV

Spanking the Monkey

This is a good guy's movie, which is not damning it with feint praise. It's just that guys who dig this movie do so with such passion that it's clearly primal for them in a way that it isn't for me. *Spanking the Monkey* put David O. Russell on the map as an indie filmmaker and made it easier for him to assemble a big-name cast for his next project, *Flirting with Disaster.* I'd like to think that Russell simply has a vivid imagination than to guess about the inspiration for this one-of-a-kind flick. Features fine performances by a mostly unknown cast. 🦴🦴🦴

1994 (R) 99m/C Jeremy Davies, Alberta Watson, Benjamin Hendrickson, Carla Gallo, Matthew Puckett; **D:** David O. Russell; **W:** David O. Russell. Independent Spirit Awards '95: Best First Feature; Sundance Film Festival '94: Audience Award; Nominations: Independent Spirit Awards '95: Best Supporting Actress (Gallo), Debut Performance (Davies). **VHS, LV** NLC, IME

A Special Day

They can do anything to Sophia Loren: strip her of make-up, stuff her in dumpy dresses, rip her stockings, frazzle her hair, anything, and she'll still take your breath away. In *A Special Day,* she plays an unappreciated housewife who befriends a disgraced homosexual (played by the late Marcello Mastroianni in an imaginative casting coup that led straight to an Oscar nomination). Ettore Scola films Ruggero Maccari's script rather like a play, with the two characters providing a dash of reality against the unreal backdrop of an unseen Hitler/Mussolini parade. The stars, as usual, make 105 minutes seem like ten and a half. **AKA:** Una Giornata Speciale; The Great Day. 🦴🦴🦴

1977 105m/C IT Sophia Loren, Marcello Mastroianni, John Vernon, Francoise Berd; **D:** Ettore Scola; **W:** Ettore Scola, Ruggero Maccari, Maurizio Costanzo; **C:** Pasquale De Santos; **M:** Armando Travaioli. Golden Globe Awards '78: Best Foreign Film; National Board of Review Awards '77: 5 Best Foreign Films of the Year; Nominations: Academy Awards '77: Best Actor (Mastroianni), Best Foreign Language Film. **VHS, Beta, LV** COL, APD

Special Effects

We can never tell whether director Larry Cohen is putting everyone on or not. Just when we're convinced he's made one of the funniest FBI movies of all time (1977's *The Private Files of J. Edgar Hoover* starring the late Broderick Crawford), he'll come up with a genuinely scary film like 1982's *Q* starring Michael Moriarty. 1985's *Special Effects* falls somewhere between these two pictures in terms of quality. It's also filled with Cohen's weird sense of humor. Zoe Tamerlis plays a dual role as a doomed would-be actress and the Good Will employee who's hired to impersonate her. Tamerlis is no great shakes in either role, but maybe she isn't supposed to be. Eric Bogosian stars as a porno movie director who plans to make a film of the dead actress in order to trap the Killer. Yes, there is a catch. (Of course.) Cohen has a good time showing how the movie industry swallows everything it touches, including police detective Kevin J. O' Connor. Cohen also has fun with the victim's boring husband (and most likely suspect) who wants to drag back his first wife and later the Good Will employee to take care of him and the baby, a fate worse than anything anyone can imagine. Along with the *It's Alive* trilogy and most of Larry Cohen's other camp classics, *Special Effects* is great fun to watch. It is also interesting to observe Bogosian's emerging charisma, long before he made 1988's *Talk Radio.* 🦴🦴🦴

1985 (R) 103m/C Zoe Tamerlis, Eric Bogosian, Brad Rijn, Bill Oland, Richard Greene; **D:** Larry Cohen; **W:** Larry Cohen. **VHS, Beta** NLC

Spider Baby

Spider Baby is a movie to cure anyone's blues. For starters, Lon Chaney, Jr., stars as the butler and he also sings the title song. Other horror movie veterans like Mantan Moreland, Carol Ohmart (you loved her in *House on Haunted Hill*), and Beverly Washburn are also on hand in this weird little comedy about a family of cannibals which must be seen to be believed, and even then.... ***AKA:*** The Liver Eaters; Spider Baby, or the Maddest Story Ever Told; Cannibal Orgy, or the Maddest Story Ever Told. 🦴🦴🦴

1964 86m/B Lon Chaney Jr., Mantan Moreland, Carol Ohmart, Sid Haig, Beverly Washburn, Jill Banner; ***D:*** Jack Hill. **VHS, Beta** *SNC, AOV, MLB*

Spirit of the Beehive

Little Ana Torrent has a wistful, appealing quality, with sinister undertones. She and her sister are so enthralled by the *Frankenstein* movie that they begin to act it out in their own lives. Victor Erice directs in a tense, if leisurely style, and the cinematography, featuring extended dissolves, effectively captures Erice's haunting story of childhood. Torrent went on to star in 1976's *Cria!* for Carlos Saura, 1980's *The Nest* for Jaime De Arminian, and 1989's *Blood and Sand* for Javier Elorrieta. ***AKA:*** El Espiritu de la Colmena. 🦴🦴🦴

1973 95m/C *SP* Fernando Gomez, Teresa Gimpera, Ana Torrent, Isabel Telleria, Laly Soldevilla; ***D:*** Victor Erice; ***W:*** Victor Erice; ***C:*** Luis Cuadrado; ***M:*** Luis De Pablo. **VHS, Beta, LV** *HMV, CVC, TPV*

The Spitfire Grill

Alison Elliott may not be our first choice for Peter Gallagher's femme fatale in *The Underneath,* but she is THE best possible Percy Talbott in Lee David Zlotoff's *The Spitfire Grill.* Actually, there are three breathtaking performances here. Ellen Burstyn does a beautiful job as Hannah Ferguson, the owner of the Spitfire Grill, and Marcia Gay Harden turns the role of an unsophisticated small-town wife and mother inside out in her portrayal of Shelby Goddard. The weak link here is Will Patton as Shelby's mean husband Nathan. By playing the same cookie cutter villain in most of his films over the last 15 years, Patton has remained steadily employed. Except for the Maine "accent" he uses here, Nathan is basically the same bad guy you saw in *No Way Out,* without the subtle shading a John Mahoney or J.T. Walsh would give an ambiguous character. Fortunately, Patton's not in every other sequence here. Percy has just been released from prison on a manslaughter rap and Nathan has it in for her. She finds a home working at the Grill and soon becomes fast friends with Hannah and Shelby. She also wanders through the beautiful countryside that surrounds the town of Gilead and befriends a silent reclusive loner (John M. Jackson) she dubs Johnny B., after the song. Shelby then comes up with an idea to help Hannah, Shelby's for it, Nathan's against it, and a deliberately paced character study evolves into a full-fledged melodrama. The sterling work of Elliott, Burstyn, and Harding undoubtedly helped to make this one an Audience Award winner at 1996's Sundance Film Festival. ***AKA:*** Care of the Spitfire Grill. 🦴🦴🦴

1995 (PG-13) 117m/C Alison Elliott, Ellen Burstyn, Marcia Gay Harden, Will Patton, Kieran Mulroney, Gailard Sartain, Louise De Cormier, John M. Jackson; ***D:*** Lee David Zlotoff; ***W:*** Lee David Zlotoff; ***C:*** Rob Draper; ***M:*** James Horner. Sundance Film Festival '96: Audience Award. **VHS, LV, Closed Caption** *COL*

Stacking

In *Stacking,* Megan Follows, Christine Lahti, Frederic Forrest, Peter Coyote, and Jason Gedrick turn in remarkable performances, but this low-key film failed to find its proper audience. It's a shame because Victoria Jenkins' wise, cliche-free screenplay reveals that she knows her rural characters through and through. Sensitively directed by Martin Rosen and shot by Richard Bowen, the film takes a great many chances with its material and succeeds most of the time. A decade later, most of the cast were earning their bread and butter on television. The gifted Follows, after a strong, prolific start between 1984 and 1991, all but faded from view, except in a one-shot *Outer Limits* episode or in endless encore airings of *Anne of Green Gables/Anne of Avonlea*. **AKA:** Season of Dreams. 🦴🦴🦴

1987 (PG) 95m/C Christine Lahti, Megan Follows, Frederic Forrest, Peter Coyote, Jason Gedrick; **D:** Martin Rosen; **W:** Victoria Jenkins; **C:** Richard Bowen, Paul Elliott, Richard Bowen; **M:** Patrick Gleeson. **VHS, Beta, LV** *NLC*

Stand and Deliver

Stand and Deliver began life as *Walking on Water* when it was first shown at 1987's Mill Valley Film Festival. Jaime Escalante (Edward James Olmos) is a mathematics teacher at an East Los Angeles high school where half the students fail to graduate. Knowing that education is the only way that his students can escape a lifetime of low-paying jobs, Escalante is tough and demanding with his class as he inspires them to pass the California Advanced Placement Calculus Test with distinction. Olmos won an Oscar nomination for his impassioned performance and the kids (including Lou Diamond Phillips in the role of Angel) are totally believable as they prepare for the Olympic-style challenge of the test. 🦴🦴🦴

1988 (PG) 105m/C Edward James Olmos, Lou Diamond Phillips, Rosana De Soto, Andy Garcia, Will Gotay, Ingrid Oliu, Virginia Paris, Mark Eliot; **D:** Ramon Menendez; **W:** Ramon Menendez, Tom Musca; **C:** Tom Richmond; **M:** Craig Safan. Independent Spirit Awards '89: Best Actor (Olmos), Best Director (Menendez), Best Film, Best Screenplay, Best Supporting Actor (Phillips), Best Supporting Actress (De Soto); Nominations: Academy Awards '88: Best Actor (Olmos). **VHS, LV, 8mm, Closed Caption** *WAR, HMV*

Stardust

So you want to be a rock and roll star? Jim MacLaine (David Essex) starts out broke and happy and winds up rich and alienated. He doesn't want it that way, but isn't offered any other real alternatives. His pay-off in the back of an ambulance, being yelled at by his manager for his habitual selfishness, is wrenching to watch. *Stardust* could be the story of the Beatles and it resembles it in many ways, yet Ray Connolly's fascinating screenplay doesn't dwell on the obvious similarities. His attention to character detail is one of the best things about the film. Women, usually ignored or relegated to the roles of groupies in most scrutinies of rock stars, are intriguing in their own right here. Ines Des Longchamps is so affecting as MacLaine's girlfriend, Danielle, that her absence is keenly felt whenever she's off-screen. Rosalind Ayres as MacLaine's neglected wife, Jeanette, only has one sequence, but it's a gem. Larry Hagman is remarkable as Porter Lee Austin, the man who handles MacLaine's career and eventually dominates his life. Adam Faith as MacLaine's road manager, Mike Menary, starts out as a sweet, sincere hustler circa 1965, and winds up totally dependent on MacLaine to the extent that he must cut everyone out of his life. Even Edd "Kookie" Byrnes does well here as a television interviewer. Michael Apted directs a complex subject with sensitivity and originality. *Stardust* sustains its detached view without once losing its compassion. The music is produced by Dave Edmunds, who also appears as Alex and performs some of the songs, along with Essex and the Stray Cats. The excellent soundtrack is a fine time capsule of its era. (Essex, Ayres, and Moon played the same roles in 1973's *That'll Be the Day*, set in 1959 and also scripted by Connolly.) 🦴🦴🦴🦴

1974 111m/C *GB* David Essex, Adam Faith, Larry Hagman, Ines Des Longchamps, Rosalind Ayres, Marty Wilde, Edd Byrnes, Keith Moon, Dave Edmunds, Paul Nicholas, Karl Howman, Rick Lee Parmentier, Peter Duncan, John Normington, James

INDEPENDENT FILM GUIDE

Hazeldine, David Daker, Anthony Naylor, Charlotte Cornwell, Rose Marie Klespitz, David Jacobs; **D:** Michael Apted; **W:** Ray Connolly; **C:** Tony Richmond. **VHS** *NYR*

Steppenwolf

Steppenwolf is a visually striking and disturbing film, but admirers of Herman Hesse (1877-1962) will probably loathe it; it has a bubble gum quality that undercuts its impact. Film novice Fred Haines jazzes up his first movie with stylistic tricks, animation, and special effects, in an effort to come to terms with Hesse's 1927 novel. Haines runs the risk of becoming absurd, and he loses more often than not. Magnifique Dominique Sanda's work as Hermine here is both ethereal and complex, but Max von Sydow seems merely pathetic as Herr Haller. Occasionally amusing (especially in the 25-minute Magic Theatre sequence), the overall impact is unsatisfying. 🦴🦴

1974 (PG) 105m/C *SI* Max von Sydow, Dominique Sanda, Pierre Clementi, Carla Rominelli, Roy Bosier; **D:** Fred Haines; **W:** Fred Haines; **C:** Tomislav Pinter; **M:** George Gruntz. **VHS, Beta, LV** *THV, GLV*

Sticky Fingers

Sticky Fingers represents the directing debut of actress Catlin Adams, so perhaps Adams' intrusive "Look Ma, I'm directing" style will acquire more discipline on future projects. Adams wrote the script with actress Melanie Mayron, who co-stars in the movie with Helen Slater and a cast of mostly women: Shirley Stoler and the late Gwen Welles plus Oscar nominees Eileen Brennan and Carol Kane. The plot hinges around a bag which Mayron agrees to keep for Slater's drug connection. It turns out that the bag contains nearly a million dollars, which horrifies the roommates at first and later hypnotizes them into a $240,000 shopping binge. Along the way, we see a world frequently shot in extreme close-up through pale green or blue filters. We also hear self-conscious statements about relationships between women as well as some labored concessions to straight audiences who might be threatened by the suggestion that any of the major characters could be gay. Despite the obvious feminist sentiments of the filmmakers, it is irritating to observe how carelessly and how often the roommates lose money and how passive these two are about most of the circumstances in their lives. When the pair takes action, it is usually a dumb move. If a film history of female buddy movies is ever written, I predict that *Sticky Fingers* will warrant a small footnote as one of many attempts to repeat the success of 1987's *Outrageous Fortune*, a film which isn't worth imitating. It's a pity, because a lot of time and talent went into the film. (Mayron went on to direct 1995's *The Baby-Sitter's Club*.) 🦴

1988 (PG-13) 89m/C Melanie Mayron, Helen Slater, Eileen Brennan, Carol Kane, Christopher Guest, Danitra Vance, Gwen Welles, Stephen McHattie, Shirley Stoler; **D:** Catlin Adams; **W:** Catlin Adams, Melanie Mayron; **M:** Gary Chang. **VHS, Beta, LV** *MED*

The Story of Fausta

The Story of Fausta is a sexy, hilarious romp from Bruno Barreto and Betty Faria, his *Bye, Bye Brazil* star. Brandao Filho has a ball with one of the best senior citizen's parts ever; this Brazilian entry may well leave you breathless with laughter. **AKA:** Romance da Empregada. 🦴🦴🦴

1988 (R) 90m/C *BR* Betty Faria, Daniel Filho, Brandao Filho; **D:** Bruno Barreto; **M:** Ruben Blades. **VHS** *FXL, FCT*

The Story of Qui Ju

Peasant Qui Ju (Gong Li) is expecting a baby, but nonetheless fights for justice when her husband Liu (Liu Pei Qui) is kicked in the groin by their village head (Lei Lao Sheng). Arbitrators say the chief must compensate Qui Ju's husband, but she wants him to say he's sorry for what he's done, even when it appears that her relationship with her husband is being damaged by her tireless efforts on his behalf. This well directed look at Chinese village life benefits from powerful acting by Gong Li and from stunningly real cinematography, occasionally achieved with a concealed camera. *AKA:* Qui Ju Da Guansi. 𝄞𝄞𝄞

1991 (PG) 100m/C *CH* Gong Li, Lei Lao Sheng, Liu Pei Qu, Ge Zhi Jun, Ye Jun, Yang Liu Xia, Zhu Qanging, Cui Luowen, Yank Huiquin, Wang Jianfa, Lin Zi; *D:* Zhang Yimou; *W:* Liu Heng; *C:* Chi Xiaonin, Yu Xaioqun; *M:* Zhao Jiping. National Society of Film Critics Awards '93: Best Foreign Film; Venice Film Festival '92: Best Actress (Li), Best Film; Nominations: Independent Spirit Awards '94: Best Foreign Film. **VHS, LV** *COL*

Straight Out of Brooklyn

This would be a fair movie for an adult director, but Matty Rich was only 19 when he made *Straight Out of Brooklyn,* reportedly based on his own life. It's a depressing look at a Brooklyn family who live in the Red Hook Housing Project. Ray Brown (George T. Odom) beats his wife Frankie (Ann D. Sanders). Their kids Dennis (Laurence Gilliard) and Carolyn (Barbara Sanon) are desperate. Although girlfriend Shirley (Reana E. Drummond) tries to talk him out of it, Dennis and friends Larry (Rich) and Kevin (Mark Malone) plan a robbery to escape the poverty and the abuse. Generally shot with one camera and inadequate sound, *Straight Out of Brooklyn*'s painful narrative is often hard to watch. Still, for a teenager to raise the money, finish a whole movie, and get it released was such an accomplishment that Rich was overpraised (23-year-old John Singleton's Oscar-nominated *Boys N the Hood* was far superior). Rich's next film was 1994's *The Inkwell.* I give *Brooklyn* two bones for content and four bones for effort, for an average of 𝄞𝄞𝄞

1991 (R) 91m/C George T. Odom, Ann D. Sanders, Lawrence Gilliard, Mark Malone Jr., Reana E. Drum-

mond, Barbara Sanon, Matty Rich; *D:* Matty Rich; *W:* Matty Rich; *C:* John Rosnell; *M:* Harold Wheeler. Independent Spirit Awards '92: Best First Feature; Sundance Film Festival '91: Special Jury Prize. **VHS** *HBO, FCT, WAR*

The Stranger's Hand

Since Graham Greene wrote the stories for both *The Fallen Idol* and *The Stranger's Hand,* it might be interesting to see them both on a double bill for comparison purposes. Each involves a little boy lost (no parents in sight) who attaches himself to a guilty-looking couple who don't care half as much about him as he cares about them. Roger Court (Richard O'Sullivan, then 11) is in Venice to meet his father (Trevor Howard). But Dad is kidnapped and drugged by bad guy Dr. Vivaldi (Eduardo Ciannelli), who, coincidentally, also buys Roger some ice cream. Roger wanders around, waiting for Dad, and starts hanging out with Roberta (Alida Valli). Roberta's hung up on Joe Hamstringer (Richard Basehart), who has to make a fast getaway. Roger can't find Dad, he's scared of the authorities, and clings to Roberta and Joe because he doesn't know what else to do. O'Sullivan's large eyes and expressive face made him one of Great Britain's most sought-after juvenile actors, and he continued his career on television as an adult. Valli and Basehart are upstaged by their little co-star here, but the film's best performances are delivered by Howard and Ciannelli (did either of them ever do a less than sterling job EVER?). *AKA:* La Mano del Straniero. 𝄞𝄞𝄞

1954 85m/B *GB IT* Trevor Howard, Alida Valli, Richard Basehart, Eduardo Ciannelli, Richard O'Sullivan, Stephen Murray, Giorgio Constantini; *D:* Mario Soldati; *W:* Guy Elmes, Georgino Bassani. *NYR*

Strapless

A few minutes into David Hare's *Strapless,* we realized that we would be sitting

Bruno Ganz, who looks like he was scraped out of a gutter and sounds like Thug Number Three in an old gangster movie? Faster than you can say "plot device" or "deus ex machina" or whatever, Blair is obligingly writing checks for this slime, draining away her life savings and even marrying him. When Bruno arrives home one night with an expensive car as a gift for her, Blair tells him that she wants to be ordinary, so Bruno disappears into the night. Meanwhile, Bridget is pregnant by a drifter named Carlos and Blair yells at her because she's a slob. You can watch *The Hard Way* with Ida Lupino and Joan Leslie on the late movie or you can watch *Strapless* with Blair Brown and Bridget Fonda on video. *Strapless* will probably put you to sleep faster, especially David Hare's idea of a piece-de-resistance: Bridget Fonda designs a line of strapless gowns which are held in place with no visible means of support. And guess what? (nudge-nudge) Women hold their lives in place with no visible means of support EITHER. Give us a BREAK! 🎜🎜

1990 (R) 99m/C Blair Brown, Bridget Fonda, Bruno Ganz, Alan Howard, Michael Gough, Hugh Laurie, Suzanne Burden, Camille Coduri, Alexandra Pigg, Billy Roch, Gary O'Brien; ***D:*** David Hare; ***W:*** David Hare; ***M:*** Nick Bicat. **VHS, Beta, LV** *COL*

Streetwise.

through yet another long, pretentious movie in which a dense guy tries to explain how women feel (sigh). We suspect that some people think that Hare is cute when he tries to be clever, but he's not THAT cute, not with 99 minutes of our time. Blair Brown plays a 40-year-old doctor who goes on and on about how OLD she is. Although we see her in hospital wards, neither Hare's screenplay nor his direction give us an indication of any real emotional investment in her work. She lives with her flaky younger sister, Bridget Fonda. (We know that Bridget is a flake, because she enjoys fashion and parties and sex. Right.) According to the press kit, Blair "meets a mysterious, elegant stranger who is immediately taken with her." Who else but

Street Music

The elderly people living in an old hotel join forces with a young couple to organize a protest that may save their building. Well directed comedy drama; good location shooting in San Francisco's Tenderloin. 1982's Grand Jury Prize winner at the Sundance Film Festival. 🎜🎜🎝

1981 88m/C Larry Breeding, Elizabeth Daily, Ned Glass; ***D:*** Jenny Bowen; ***C:*** Richard Bowen. Sundance Film Festival '82: Grand Jury Prize. **VHS, Beta** *LIV, VES*

Street Smart

To be a great actor, you have to be able to project real emotion any which way you can. Morgan Freeman is a great actor.

Kathy Baker is a great actor. After a dozen movies in ten years, the empirical evidence that Christopher Reeve, then turning 35, was not a great actor was too compelling to be ignored. The same year that Robert Townsend was lampooning how black actors were invariably cast as pimps in *Hollywood Shuffle,* Morgan Freeman played the ultimate pimp in *Street Smart.* Like Bette Davis in 1935's *Dangerous,* Freeman defied you to ignore the alchemy in a no-holds-barred performance and made a stock part real. Baker took another favorite Hollywood stock part, that of a hooker, and turned it inside out. No matter what else was onscreen, Baker forced you to see what she saw, hear what she heard, feel what she felt. Needless to say, there were kudos galore for Freeman and Baker, and *Street Smart* is well worth watching for them alone, but *Street Smart* is not much of a movie. The story revolves around a fake scoop that ignites an authentic investigation. Reeve was unable to transform his essentially rigid role as a dishonest reporter, and the plot goes into slow motion whenever Freeman or Baker are offscreen. (The same thing occurred in 1995's *Above Suspicion* when Reeve was cast in an actor's dream role, brilliantly scripted by Jerry Lazarus, W.H. Macy, and director Steven Schachter. It's an eerily premonitory picture in light of actual events in Reeve's life, but he can't breathe life into his character as fellow cast members Joe Mantegna and William H. Macy can with their parts. Reeve's acclaimed debut as director of 1997's *In the Gloaming* suggests a career shift that might have been inevitable, anyway.) 🦴🦴🦴

1987 (R) 97m/C Christopher Reeve, Morgan Freeman, Kathy Baker, Mimi Rogers, Andre Gregory, Jay Patterson, Anna Maria Horsford; **D:** Jerry Schatzberg; **W:** David Freeman; **C:** Adam Holender; **M:** Miles Davis. Independent Spirit Awards '88: Best Supporting Actor (Freeman); Los Angeles Film Critics Association Awards '87: Best Supporting Actor (Freeman); New York Film Critics Awards '87: Best Supporting Actor (Freeman); National Society of Film Critics Awards '87: Best Supporting Actor (Freeman), Best Supporting Actress (Baker); Nominations: Academy Awards '87: Best Supporting Actor (Freeman). **VHS, Beta, LV, Closed Caption** *MED, IME*

Streetwise

Both 1981's *Pixote* by Hector Babenco and 1984's *Streetwise* by Martin Bell offer a harsh portrait of the lives led by street children. *Streetwise* has de-glamorized the runaway life for many young people who have seen Bell's movie, but for the Seattle children who appear in the film, life continues to run downhill. Erin, also known as Tiny, was one of the few participants who revealed genuine depth of feeling for the people in her life, but the pain reportedly led to more than one drug overdose. The others whistle in the dark by "pulling dates" between jail terms. We already know that Dewayne's imprisoned father loves him, but he can do nothing for his kid and Dewayne knows it. At another point, we see a mother excusing her husband's sexual abuse of her daughter ("Well, he isn't doing it anymore, is he?"). All the kids hear well meaning, BandAids-over-gangrene solutions to their problems. Bell and Babenco attracted considerable reputations for their honesty in showing the toll of street hustling on the very young. 🦴🦴🦴🦴

1984 92m/C D: Martin Bell; **M:** Tom Waits. **VHS, Beta, LV** *ORI, NWV*

Strictly Ballroom

Old-time film buffs describe their primal experiences at local Bijous of the '30s with such intense passion: "And I paid my dime every day and went to see *42nd Street* or *Golddiggers of 1933* or *Flying Down to Rio* over and over and over again; it was magic." Although movies with that sort of repeat value are indeed rare, we have found one, and so, apparently, have other romance-starved film buffs. *Strictly Ballroom* made its first U.S. appearance at the Mill Valley Film Festival in the fall of 1992. Not even a surfeit of critical euphoria prepared us for the night we first saw *Strictly Ballroom*, a classic example of the picture that F. Scott Fitzgerald once described as "the-little-girl-wanting-a-piece-of-candy original; our attention must be called with sharp novelty to the fact that she wants it." The girl in *Strictly Ballroom* is Fran, the inexpressibly plain dance student played by Tara Morice, and the candy is her big chance to turn into a swan and compete with a sexy open amateur at the Pan Pacific dance competition. The open amateur is Paul Mercurio as Scott Hastings, who is, quite literally, the most exciting dance personality to emerge onscreen since the Golden Age of the Hollywood musical. Unfortunately for film buffs, Mercurio headlines the Sydney Dance Company in Australia and is unlikely to leave it for a movie genre that has no real future. (He was wasted in *Exit to Eden*, and fared better in TNT's *Joseph*, but the Australian-made *Back of Beyond* is still waiting for a distributor.) It's a shame, because Mercurio is also a remarkable actor, ideally conveying his character's conflicting emotions. He wants to win, but he wants to dance his own steps, and he wants to win with flashy Tina Sparkle, but he wants to dance HIS way with the adoring Fran, and he doesn't want to wind up like his whipped father, but his father's approval is the only thing that can set him free. Who cares about the shenanigans that obsess all these ballroom fanatics? Thanks to director Baz Luhrmann and a superb cast (the late Pat Thomsen and Barry Otto are especially memorable as Scott's parents), WE care, even if we can't dance to save our lives. Luhrmann's wry understanding of the impact of every frame of his film is breathtaking. At one point, when Scott's shrill partner Liz screams that she wants Ken Railings to walk into the studio to say that HIS partner (Pam Short) has broken both her legs and he wants to dance with HER, Luhrmann with two quick, sure cuts, shows us both the stylized accident and Ken Railings' word-for-word delivery of Liz's implausible projection. That Luhrmann is able to

reinvent and revitalize this technique throughout the film, even in dance sequences that are already saturated with highly charged energy, is one of the reasons why *Strictly Ballroom* is as much of a delight to watch the twelfth time around as the first. ♫♫♫♫

1992 (PG) 94m/C *AU* Paul Mercurio, Tara Morice, Bill Hunter, Pat Thomsen, Barry Otto, Gia Carides, Peter Whitford, John Hannan, Sonia Kruger-Tayler, Kris McQuade, Pip Mushin, Leonie Page, Antonio Vargas, Armonia Benedito; *D:* Baz Luhrmann; *W:* Craig Pearce, Baz Luhrmann; *M:* David Hirshfelder. Australian Film Institute '92: Best Costume Design, Best Director (Luhrmann), Best Film, Best Film Editing, Best Supporting Actor (Otto), Best Supporting Actress (Thomsen), Best Writing; Nominations: Golden Globe Awards '94: Best Film—Musical/Comedy. **VHS, LV, Closed Caption** *MAX, TOU, BTV*

Strongman Ferdinand

One of the more amusing releases of 1976 failed to win much in the way of audience acceptance. It's a shame, really, because West Germany's *Strongman Ferdinand* had a great deal to say about the sort of mentality that may have made the Watergate break-in possible. Ferdinand (convincingly played by Heinz Schubert) is the security officer for a large corporation. He soon discovers that the continuation of his job is dependent on frequent states of emergency. When they fail to occur, he creates them, thus "proving" that his services are needed. Law and order carried to its logical end, director/screenwriter Alexander Kluge suggests, leads to probable sabotage and destruction. Ferdinand's rationale may be extreme, but it had its parallels in many political acts of the 1970s. *Ferdinand* is absorbing, yet so subtle that many audience members at 1976's San Francisco International Film Festival screening seemed to miss altogether the wry humor in the German voiceover statements. The inadequate subtitles did not quite provide the essential ironic counterpoint that Kluge clearly intended for them to have. **AKA:** Der Starke Ferdinand. ♫♫♫

1976 98m/C *GE* Heinz Schubert, Verena Rudolph, Gert Gunther Hoffman, Heinz Schimmelpfennig, Siegfried Wischnewski, Joachim Hackethal; **D:** Alexander Kluge; **W:** Alexander Kluge; **C:** Thomas Mauch. *NYR*

Struggle

Movie pioneer D.W. Griffith (1875-1948) couldn't get ARRESTED in 1931, so he financed his $300,000 swan song himself and released it through United Artists, the independent releasing corporation he founded with Charlie Chaplin (1889-1977), Douglas Fairbanks (1883-1939), and Mary Pickford (1892-1979). Even by 1931 standards, *The Struggle* is out of touch with its own era. King Vidor's version of Elmer Rice's *Street Scene*, starring Sylvia Sidney and William Collier, Jr., produced by Samuel Goldwyn and released by United Artists the same year, dealt with strong social issues in a harsh, realistic way, AND managed to achieve critical and audience acceptance. But Goldwyn did his job as producer, Vidor did his job as director, and both let Rice adapt his own screenplay. Griffith, by that time more than a little desperate, fiddled with Anita Loos' and John Emerson's screenplay until his whole reason for making this anti-Prohibition film was lost; *The Struggle* voices all the arguments for temperance that led to Prohibition in the first place. The first audience at New York's Rivoli Theatre (on December 10, 1931) giggled all through the picture, a painful reality for Griffith, who hoped that viewers would break into spontaneous applause as they had for his early silent masterpieces. Viewers of the 1990s may not feel that *The Struggle* is as bad as all that, but remember, this was Griffith, not some hack director churning out a Depression era quickie. The cast, except for Zita Johann (the future object of the *The Mummy*'s desire and then Mrs. John Houseman), is undistinguished, the grim visual realism is unmatched by the shrill aural melodramatics. *The Struggle* prompt-

ly went into exhibition limbo. Griffith lost two-thirds of his investment and, worse yet, wandered around Hollywood for the next 17 years, bitter and bewildered, until a cerebral hemorrhage killed him on July 23, 1948. ♫♫♪

1931 87m/B Hal Skelly, Zita Johann, Evelyn Baldwin, Charlotte Wynters, Helen Mack, Kate Bruce, Jackson Halliday, Edna Hagan, Claude Cooper, Arthur Lipson, Charles Richman, Dave Manley; **D:** D.W. Griffith; **W:** D.W. Griffith, Anita Loos, John Emerson; **C:** Joseph Ruttenberg; **M:** D.W. Griffith, Philip A. Scheib. **VHS** *KIV*

Stubby

Bo Widerberg's *Stubby* is such a dear, sweet movie. So how come we don't like it any better than 1967's *Elvira Madigan*, also by Widerberg? The title character is a precocious youngster, played by a cute kid named Johan Bergman, who plays for Sweden's national soccer team. Monica Zetterlund gives a nice, winning performance as his teacher and John Olsson tenderly photographs little kitties and pretty kiddies. Widerberg also edited and produced. Soccer fans may dig it, but cranky cynics, beware! ♫

1974 90m/C *SW* Johan Bergman, Monica Zetterlund, Magnus Harenstam, Ernst-Hugo Jaregard, Swedish National Soccer Team; **D:** Bo Widerberg; **W:** Bo Widerberg; **C:** John Olsson. *NYR*

Sudden Manhattan

A quirky entry at 1996's Mill Valley Film Festival, *Sudden Manhattan* is nicely written and directed by Adrienne Shelly, who also stars as Donna. This appealing black comedy is filled with goofy supporting characters (Roger Rees, Louise Lasser) and an oddball story line. Like Shelly herself, it all looks effortless and spontaneous, but clearly some very careful craftsmanship went into it. ♫♫♪

1996 80m/C Adrienne Shelly, Tim Guinee, Roger Rees, Louise Lasser, Hynden Walch; **D:** Adrienne Shelly; **W:** Adrienne Shelly; **C:** Jim Denault; **M:** Pat Irwin. *NYR*

Giancarlo Giannini
and Mariangela
Melato in
Swept Away....

A Summer Story

When young men play fast and loose with young women, they're only being human, according to the movies. This is the theme of *A Summer Story*. (When young women play fast and loose with young men, they're invariably monsters, but that's another story.) Upper-class English twit James Wilby shows his bad manners: (1) by falling in love with fetching country lass Imogen Stubbs, (2) by ditching her for aristocratic Sophie Ward, and (3) by later returning to the country with his childless wife to learn whatever became of his first love. His worst offense, according to another upper class twit, was in promising to marry the poor girl at all. This Piers Haggard film has nothing new to say about class differences, but the Somerset and Devon locations are pretty, and Imogen Stubbs makes a strong impression as the jilted farm girl. Susannah York, who specialized in playing bewitching heroines circa 1963, has a few brief scenes as a protective relation of Miss Stubbs. During the final credits, the period film breaks into a Moody Blues song for no apparent reason. It's the only unpredictable element in this a dusty romance based on John Galsworthy's *The Apple Tree*. *A Summer Story* focuses on a spineless and irritating character who doesn't deserve sympathy and who certainly doesn't rate an entire movie. 🦴🦴

1988 (PG-13) 97m/C *GB* James Wilby, Imogen Stubbs, Susannah York, Sophie Ward, Kenneth Colley, Jerome Flynn; *D:* Piers Haggard; *W:* Penelope Mortimer; *M:* Georges Delerue. **VHS, Beta, Closed Caption** *MED*

Suture

Suture is all about two guys who are almost identical twins, the "almost" being the centerpiece of another one-joke movie although it most certainly does not qualify as a deliberate comedy (at least I don't think so). In any event, I didn't get the joke. The film's conceit is that no one notices the extremely obvious difference between the two of them. I'd give *Suture* one bone for its concept and three bones for its look, which is impressive, thanks to superb black-and-white cinematography by Greg Gardiner. The presence of elegant Dina Merrill in the cast adds a touch of class to this very weird flick. 🦴🦴

1993 96m/B Dennis Haysbert, Sab Shimono, Mel Harris, Michael Harris, Dina Merrill, David Graf, Fran Ryan; *D:* Scott McGehee, David Siegel; *W:* Scott McGehee, David Siegel; *C:* Greg Gardiner; *M:* Cary Berger. Sundance Film Festival '94: Best Cinematography; Nominations: Independent Spirit Awards '95: Best Cinematography, Best First Feature. **VHS** *HMK*

Swastika

It is hard to imagine that anyone could recall the Third Reich with affection and nostalgia, but this 1973 British film by Philippe Mora did infuriate many who first saw it at the Cannes Film Festival that year. The most stunning portions of the film feature color home movies shot by Eva Braun at Berchtesgaden. Mora retained a lip reader to determine what Hitler and his friends were saying to each other and then found an actor who could mimic the Fuhrer's style of social chatter. The conversation is completely banal, and so are most of the activities on the terrace at Berchtesgaden. It was this very banality that disgusted the audiences who first saw the confiscated films, one referring to "the appalling normality of Hitler's home life." *Swastika* also includes propaganda movies extolling the virtues of National Socialism as well as segments of the infamous *Jud Suess,* a film which so horrified Ferdinand Marian, its guilt-ridden star, that he later committed suicide. Mora's objective in revealing Hitler and his cronies in all their boring blandness was to render them comprehensible as human beings rather than as monsters. But to watch Eva Braun preening in front of the camera to the tune of Helen Morgan's "What Wouldn't I Do for That Man" and to hear Hitler blather about how all the women present would prefer a screening of *Gone with the Wind* with Clark Gable is an absolutely surreal experience. How could Auschwitz and Bergen-Belsen and Dachau have existed with these numbskulls at the helm? *Swastika,* the sort of documentary that makes you want to crawl under your seat when you see it theatrically, is also available for private appraisal on home video. 🦴🦴🦴

1993 ?m/C *D:* Philippe Mora. **VHS**

Swept Away...

If anyone had told me what this movie was about before I saw it, I wouldn't have made it past the popcorn stand. Gorgeous Giancarlo Giannini and Mariangela Melato are stuck together on a Mediterranean island, he treats her terribly, even beats her up, and she loves it, and him, and doesn't want to leave. In anyone else hands but Lina Wertmuller's, it would have been unbearable for me to squirm through, much less sit through it. Yet Wertmuller's touch is deft and sure, savagely funny and deeply human, and the results are a sheer delight. Wertmuller's statements about sexual politics are well under her artistic control here, much as Pedro Almodovar's were at the time he made 1986's *Matador.* The acting by the two leads is wise and artful, and Julio Battiferri's cinematography is exquisite. *AKA:* Swept Away...By an Unusual Destiny in the Blue Sea of August. 🦴🦴🦴🦴

1975 (R) 116m/C *IT* Giancarlo Giannini, Mariangela Melato; *D:* Lina Wertmuller; *W:* Lina Wertmuller; *C:* Julio Battiferri; *M:* Piero Piccioni. National Board of Review Awards '75: 5 Best Foreign Films of the Year. **VHS** *FXL, APD*

S

INDEPENDENT FILM GUIDE

The Hound Salutes:
JACK HILL
Spider Baby,
Switchblade Sisters

Carol Ohmart was so excited about the *Spider Baby* script, she said, 'Do you think this movie might get an Academy Award?' I didn't know how to answer her. The only thing I can think of is that things change over time, and a movie that was just another movie in its day becomes an artifact after a certain passage of time. Four thousand years ago, some Egyptian had a plain, ordinary vase in his kitchen, and today it's in a museum. That's the only way I can figure it....

"It was a dream working with Lon Chaney, Jr. He was a doll. I had heard that he'd been very difficult, and had a way of throwing things away because he wasn't very interested in the job that he had. In fact, he liked the script so much because it gave him a chance to play a wide range of emotions and a chance to play a scene where he visibly cries, and particularly a chance to play comedy, and he really wanted to do a good job. He was an alcoholic, but he did us the courtesy of staying on the wagon up until the very last day. The last day, we ran overtime up until four o'clock in the morning, but other than that, he was perfect. I did very little direction. The cast played off each other so well and they were all so enthusiastic over it. The scene where Spider Baby ties up her uncle in the chair is quite good and the dinner scene was wonderful. All the actors had their own styles which seemed to be perfect for the roles (Jill Banner, Sid Haig, Mantan Moreland, Beverly Washburn). It was a miracle of good luck that we got that cast together and basically, I let them go with it. All I did was encourage them not to hold back. My first rule of directing is the same as the first rule of medicine: first, do no harm.

"[On *Switchblade Sisters*] I'd gotten the reputation of making pictures about active, aggressive, tough, sassy women, since I did like to work with that sort of material. The vision that I had there was that society seemed to be decaying and what we wanted to make was sort of a female *Clockwork Orange,* a picture that sort of projected things into the future."

The films of JACK HILL include *Portrait in Terror, Track of the Vampire, The Fear Chamber, The Big Doll House, The Big Bird Cage, Coffy, Foxy Brown,* and *The Swinging Cheerleaders.*

Swimming with Sharks

Once upon a time when a writer like William Somerset Maugham wanted to write about the games guys play with each other, he'd turn one of the guys, like Mildred Rogers in *Of Human Bondage,* into a girl. *Swimming with Sharks* explores the S&M relationship between a Hollywood executive named Buddy (Kevin Spacey), and Guy, his assistant (Frank Whaley). There's a girl in the picture, but Michelle (*Kalifornia*) Forbes plays her like an alley tomcat who's been in one fight too many. The previous assistant is so clearly gay and Guy and Buddy employ so many bitchy mannerisms and expressions that there's no real point addressing the issue of how deeply women are hated in this movie. Consider the source and all that. *Swimming with Sharks* admittedly owes a debt to *Sunset Boulevard* and *The Player,* and maybe writer/director George Huang will be in Billy Wilder's and/or Robert Altman's league someday. But not yet. He telegraphs the ending way too early with a sob story that doubles as character rationale and plot contrivance. All the admittedly clever observations about the master/servant relationship just hang in dead air when they're forced to support an artificially cynical climax that, frankly, belongs in the So What? Department. How wrapped up can we be in a situation that goes on for a year, and that two words would have ended at any time? (For contrast, think four words: "Death and the Maiden.") And then there's supposed to be a generational clash between Buddy and Guy that doesn't work because Kevin Spacey is a very healthy-looking 35 and Frank Whaley seems rather old and frail before his time at 32. Spacey is the film's producer and he's having such a rattling good time playing a creep that we can't help enjoying ourselves whenever he's onscreen. Whaley is a fine actor, but he's played an assassin one too many times and needs to develop a lighter touch for

satire (although the script's deck is clearly stacked in Spacey's favor). So, "A" for the director's efforts, his sharp ears, and for choosing a situation that virtually everyone can identify with, "C" for originality and for sexual circumspection, and "F" for spelling "accountant" in the credits with three Cs. ***AKA:*** The Buddy Factor. 🎬🎬

1994 (R) 93m/C Kevin Spacey, Frank Whaley, Michelle Forbes, Benicio Del Toro; *D:* George Huang; *W:* George Huang; *C:* Steven Firestone. New York Film Critics Awards '95: Best Supporting Actor (Spacey); Nominations: Independent Spirit Awards '96: Best Actor (Spacey). **VHS, LV, Closed Caption** *THV*

Switchblade Sisters

Quentin Tarantino dug this Jack Hill oldie a lot, so he re-released it for audiences of the 1990s to reappraise. The plot revolves around the lives of girl gang members. The leader of the Debs is Lace (Robbie Lee). Maggie (Joanne Nail) gets into the gang, but Patch (Monica Gayle) is jealous and tries to diss her to Lace. The Debs get into a rumble with the Silver Blades, who are all guys, and Lace winds up in hospital. (You ought to see the guys, though.) Maggie takes over the gang and calls them the Jezebels, and then there's a merging with an even tougher girl gang, and so forth and so on. It's way violent, obviously; the acting isn't bad; and Lenny Bruce's then-chubby daughter Kitty, then 21, plays a gang member aptly named Donut. Asher Brauner, who went on to make 1979's well received *The Boss' Son* with director Bobby Roth (Yves Montand dug THAT one a lot) plays Dominic, and Kate Murtagh IS Prison Warden Moms Smackley. Leonard Klady of *Variety* kvetched about why the "marginal" *Switchblade Sisters* was revived "while truly great films are neglected and decomposing." However, the Museum of Modern Arts' Eileen Bowser wisely observed that Charlie Chaplin was once widely regarded as "a low, vulgar comedian." Preserve and revive everything, if we can; what the heck does any one of us know about what's worth saving and see-ing? *Switchblade Sisters* is a genuine arti-fact! Thank you, Mr. Tarantino! *AKA:* The Jezebels; Playgirl Gang. 🦴🦴

1975 90m/C Robbie Lee, Joanne Nail, Monica Gayle, Kitty Bruce, Asher Brauner, Chase Newhart, Marlene Clark, Janice Karman, Don Stark, Kate Murtagh, Bill Adler; *D:* Jack Hill; *W:* F.X. Maier; *C:* Stephen M. Katz; *M:* Les Baxter, Medusa, Chuck Day, Richard Person. **VHS** *TOU, HHE*

Swoon

Swoon is an irritating intellectual exercise allowing filmmaker Tom Kalin to say in his movie what Richard Fleischer and Alfred Hitchcock didn't say in *Compulsion* and *Rope,* that Nathan Leopold and Richard Loeb were homosexuals. Fleischer and Hitchcock didn't have to SAY it, they SHOWED it. How can there be any doubt when you watch the interactions of the two fictional but clearly fact-based characters played by Farley Granger and John Dall in *Rope*? Any question in your mind as you check out the gnarled relationship of Dean Stockwell and Bradford Dillman in *Compul-sion*? It wasn't sexual politics that the real names and actual orientations of Leopold and Loeb couldn't be included onscreen; it was the fact that a reformed Leopold was very much alive and litigant right up to his death in 1971. *Swoon* is the cinematic equivalent of sitting through a dull lecture from a windbag, except for Ellen Kuras' black-and-white cinematography, which is outstanding. I give it three bones for the cognoscenti, but for me, just 🦴

1991 95m/B Daniel Schlachet, Craig Chester, Ron Vawter, Michael Kirby, Michael Stumm, Valda Z. Drabla, Natalie Stanford; *D:* Tom Kalin; *W:* Tom Kalin; *C:* Ellen Kuras; *M:* James Bennett. Sundance Film Festival '92: Best Cinematography. **VHS, LV, Closed Caption** *NLC, IME*

Teenage Gang Debs

Diane Conti, where are you? The guy I saw the movie with wants to know! Diane Conti IS Terry (she's from Manhattan) who moves to Brooklyn and quickly moves in on the leader of the pack. When he tells her he has to brand her (it's a rule), she decides to have him killed! So she moves in on the second-in-command and entices him to Take Over with herself as bait. She soon has him whipped into shape, but then, she starts picking on the Wrong People in the Gang: The Women. Hasn't this girl read ANY plays by Shakespeare? They're practi-cally a blueprint of what not to do when you Take Over a Gang. Terry looks so cool that first time she walked into the bar, I thought she was a detective working undercover. Sande N. Johnson does some interesting directorial-type stuff on a rock-bottom bud-get. There's a terrible group dance that was evidently meant to ignite a craze, so every-one at San Francisco's Roxie Cinema applauded charitably. All the rumbles are "choreographed" (someone gets a credit), which basically means that, while the cam-era's all over the place, you never get to see what's actually going on. I wonder if the cast members ever get together for reunions these days. 🦴🦴

1966 77m/B Diana Conti, Linda Gale, Eileen Scott, Sandra Kane, Robin Nolan, Linda Cambi, Sue McManus, Geri Tyler, Joey Naudic, John Batis, Tom Yourk, Thomas Andrisano, George Winship, Doug Mitchell, Tom Eldred, Frank Spinella, Alec Primrose, Gene Marrin, Lyn Kennedy, Janet Banzet; *D:* Sande N. Johnson; *W:* Hy Cahl. **VHS** *SMW, TPV*

Terminal Bliss

Another outstanding first feature at 1990's Mill Valley Film Festival was *Terminal Bliss,* scripted by its 22-year-old director Jordan Alan, when he was only 18 years old. Alan's drama of young friendships curdled by drugs and betrayal is not only keenly observed, it is also filled with a deep under-standing rare in this type of film. Alex the protagonist appears to be a flip, wisecrack-ing kid, but he is not so wrapped up in him-self that he is unaffected by other people's sorrows. Alex's best friend from childhood is John, who grows progressively weirder under the influence of drugs. John is used to having everything all his own way and in one miserable sequence he casually rapes a girl. Alan manages to convey the girl's intense pain and John's blurry detachment without a suggestion of the eroticism that far more experienced filmmakers often employ. The cast of unknowns (including Luke "Dylan McKay" Perry in his first starring role) is excellent, but it is Jordan Alan's steady control of his material that will linger in your memory. 🦴🦴🦴

1991 (R) 94m/C Luke Perry, Timothy Owen, Estee Chandler, Sonia Curtis, Micah Grant, Alexis Arquette; **D:** Jordan Alan; **W:** Jordan Alan; **C:** Greg Smith; **M:** Frank Becker. **VHS, LV, Closed Caption** WAR, CAN

That'll Be the Day

This is Part One of Jim MacLaine's (David Essex) meteoric rise and fall as a rock and roll star. As the story opens in 1959, Jim is dissatisfied with his drab existence and hopes that rock and roll will lead to a better life. The presence of Ringo Starr in a dramatic role adds to the film's authenticity. Neil Aspinall and Keith Moon supervise the music and David Essex and Billy Fury perform. The great soundtrack by early rock greats was clearly chosen with great care, not just slapped together. The sequel, *Stardust,* directed by Michael Apted, is even better (Essex, Ayres, and Moon played the same roles). 🦴🦴🦴

1973 (PG) 91m/C Ringo Starr, Keith Moon, David Essex, Rosemary Leach, James Booth, Billy Fury, Rosalind Ayres, Robert Lindsay, Brenda Bruce, Verna Harvey, James Ottoway, Deborah Watling, Beth Morris, Daphne Oxenford, Kim Braden, Ron Hackett, Johnny Shannon, Susan Holderness, The Debonairs; **D:** Claude Whatham; **W:** Ray Connolly; **C:** Peter Suschitzky. **VHS, Beta, LV** REP, TVC, CNG

They Drive by Night

In 1987, the late film historian William K. Everson contributed an important new article on British film noir to *Films in Review,* hoping that it might lead to a pioneering book on the subject. That it has not (so far) is every film noir fan's loss. In a later interview, Everson admitted that to most publishers, noir means American noir, period; ironic, considering that the roots of film noir are in France. Moreover, British noir directors were far more influenced by French films than were American directors (who often looked to German films for their inspiration). Leave it to Sinister Cinema to fill an important gap in film scholarship by releasing *They Drive by Night,* the film that Everson considers the first ever British noir. Released by Warner Bros. in December, 1938 for British home consumption only, *They Drive by Night* stars Emlyn Williams, then 35, as Shorty Matthews, an ex-convict wrongly accused of murdering a former lover upon his release from prison. With the help of Molly O'Neill, a friend of the deceased (played by the little-known Anna Konstam), Shorty tries to prove his innocence, an exercise in frustration until they bump into Mr. Walter Hoover, an erudite sex maniac played by that magnificent ham, Ernest Thesiger (loved by all as the immortal Dr. Pretorius in *The Bride of Frankenstein*). Directed in no-nonsense style by Arthur Woods from a script by Derek Twist, *They Drive by Night* scrupulously avoids what Sir Alfred Hitchcock was so fond of doing: depicting the lower social orders of Britain with sly and often patronizing humor. For there is no humor in the life of Shorty Matthews; his life is played out against a grimy background of pubs, back roads, and dance halls. *They Drive by Night* may not have the reputation of Renoir's *La Bete Humaine,* also made in 1938, but it is an altogether worthy addition to the noir canon. *They Drive by Night* may also have been an important influence on the future screenplays of Graham Greene; he praised the virtues of this realistic quota quickie as a young movie reviewer the same day that he panned the falseness of mighty MGM's overproduced version of *Idiot's Delight* by Pulitzer Prize winner Robert Sherwood. Sinister Cinema admits that their print of the extremely rare *They Drive by Night* is soft in comparison with their normally crisp video transfers, but we are lucky to have the film at all; many of the movies released by

INDEPENDENT FILM GUIDE

British Warner Bros. in the '30s and '40s no longer exist. 🦴🦴🦴🗨

1938 84m/B Emlyn Williams, Ernest Thesiger, Anna Konstam, Allan Jeayes, Antony Holles, Ronald Shiner, Yolande Terrell, Julie Barrie, Kitty De Legh; **D:** Arthur Woods; **W:** Derek Twist. **VHS** *SNC*

The Thin Blue Line

The Thin Blue Line was among the best entries at international film festivals in 1988. This Errol Morris movie is documentary filmmaking at its finest: it entertains and informs, magnetizes audiences, and stirs their emotions. It even helped to free a convicted man who was wrongly convicted for murder. How can a man be wrongly convicted for murder in this day and age? Morris shows us how in 101 absorbing minutes. It's frightening to watch how the man who is probably the real killer was able to fool so many people with his carefully cultivated attitude of innocence and respectfulness. Morris conducted the interviews of many subjects in shadows, evoking a film noir mood. A memorable score by Philip Glass enhances the suspense. Although Errol Morris admitted that much of the investigative work he had to do was boring, *The Thin Blue Line* is absolutely original, and with a pace and style like no other documentary ever made. 🦴🦴🦴🦴

1988 101m/C D: Errol Morris; **M:** Philip Glass. Edgar Allan Poe Awards '88: Best Screenplay. **VHS, Beta, LV, Closed Caption** *HBO, CCB*

The Thing Called Love

Let's try for just a moment to ignore some of the media ca-ca of the last few years. Before he died on Halloween morning 1993, River Phoenix made a couple of movies that failed to attract wide distribution: Sam Shepard's *Silent Tongue* and Peter Bogdanovich's *The Thing Called Love.* If Phoenix were still alive, one would be forced to confess that his acting was going through a bad patch. The way things

turned out, neither film offers much in the way of an enduring legacy. In *Silent Tongue,* Phoenix's performance is completely out of control; he mugs furiously, and, it must be said, artificially, in the role of a grief-stricken young widower. The same actor who acquitted himself with such distinction in many other ensemble showcases is entirely out-acted by Alan Bates, Richard Harris, Sheila Tousey, and Jeri Arrendondo. In *The Thing Called Love,* we see an ashen-faced Phoenix, old beyond his years, delivering a mannered performance by what appears to be rote. His expressions and gestures seem cluttered; he isn't feeling his way through the part, he's just passing through, with only the most perfunctory investment in the trip. Phoenix' artistic decline is all the more striking when contrasted with the glowing work of his co-star Samantha Mathis, who approaches her role with intelligent assurance. Even Dermot Mulroney, who was just as inept as Phoenix in *Silent Tongue,* does a pretty credible job under the guidance of Bogdanovich. The story of hopeful young singers looking for love with all the wrong partners is so slow and so slight that its eventual distributor deliberately kept the movie away from the claws of big city reviewers. Maybe they hoped *The Thing Called Love* would strike gold on video, but on its first day at our neighborhood outlet where ALL new releases are ripped off the shelves, every single copy was still in the store at five minutes to midnight. Overlooked at the time of release was Sandra Bullock, microseconds away from superstardom via *Speed.* 🦴🦴

1993 (PG-13) 116m/C River Phoenix, Samantha Mathis, Sandra Bullock, Dermot Mulroney, K.T. Oslin, Anthony Clark, Webb Wilder; **Cameos:** Trisha Yearwood; **D:** Peter Bogdanovich; **W:** Allan Moyle, Carol Heikkinen. **VHS, Beta, LV, Closed Caption** *PAR*

The Third Man

The Third Man is a vintage Graham Greene/Carol Reed collaboration about a

INDEPENDENT FILM GUIDE

Opposite page: The Thin Blue Line.

River Phoenix and
Samantha Mathis
in *The Thing
Called Love.*

some interesting directorial flourishes that Greene and Reed graciously kept in the finished film. Reportedly, most of the fighting on this movie was between producers Alexander Korda and David O. Selznick, who wound up in a lawsuit. Joseph Cotten made such a pleasant, self-deprecating impression as Holly that he extended his career for another 35 years playing mostly pleasant, self-deprecating characters, and Trevor Howard's immaculate performance as the wry Major was followed by nearly 40 more years of wonderfully shaded characters. Alida Valli didn't make nearly as nearly as many movies as her admirers would have liked, but *Senso, Eyes Without a Face, Oedipus Rex, The Spider's Strategem, 1900, Suspiria,* and *A Month by the Lake* are among her more memorable appearances after *The Third Man.* Anton Karas' zither became famous and Harry Lime was reincarnated as the hero (!) of Michael Rennie's 1960 television series. ♪♪♪♪

1949 104m/B Joseph Cotten, Orson Welles, Alida Valli, Trevor Howard, Bernard Lee, Wilfrid Hyde-White, Ernst Deutsch, Erich Ponto, Siegfried Breuer, Hedwig Bleibtreu, Paul Hoerbiger, Frederick Sehreicker, Herbert Halbik, Jenny Werner, Nelly Arno, Alexis Chesnakov, Leo Bieber, Paul Hardtmuth; **D:** Carol Reed; **W:** Graham Greene; **C:** Robert Krasker; **M:** Anton Karas. Academy Awards '50: Best Black and White Cinematography; British Academy Awards '49: Best Film; Cannes Film Festival '49: Best Film; Directors Guild of America Awards '49: Best Director (Reed); National Board of Review Awards '50: 5 Best Foreign Films of the Year; Nominations: Academy Awards '50: Best Director (Reed), Best Film Editing. **VHS, Beta, LV, 8mm** *SNC, REP, MED*

32 Short Films about Glenn Gould

32 Short Films about Glenn Gould was well received when it was first released, but for the uninitiated (yours truly), the structure of the film was too broken up for me to get a clear portrait of its subject. It's a decidedly different approach to film biography, but I left the film with the famed

serious subject. Harry Lime is no good (he distributes bad penicillin that results in brain-damaged children) and only Western hack writer Holly Martins can stop Harry IF he can find him. Actress Anna Schmidt (Alida Valli) is in love with Harry, but she isn't much interested in helping Holly find Harry, either. Mr. Crabbin (Wilfrid Hyde-White) is VERY interested in Holly; he wants him to speak for the Viennese literary society. After Holly flops there, he tells Major Calloway that he'll help him find Harry if the Major will let Anna get away. After hearing about Harry Lime for most of the movie, we can't wait to see him, and he turns out to be an even better bad guy than we could have imagined. Orson Welles wrote his own dialogue and added

piano player (1932-82) being as much of a mystery as ever. 🦴🦴🦴

1993 94m/C *CA* Colm Feore, Gale Garnett, David Hughes, Katya Ladan, Gerry Quigley, Carlo Rota, Peter Millard, Yehudi Menuhin, Bruno Monsaingeon; *D:* Francois Girard; *W:* Don McKellar, Francois Girard; *C:* Alan Dostie. Genie Awards '93: Best Cinematography, Best Director (Girard), Best Film, Best Film Editing; Nominations: Independent Spirit Awards '95: Best Foreign Film. **VHS, LV** *COL*

35 Up

We can think of few things we would LESS like to do than be interviewed every seven years for a movie between the ages of seven and thirty five. That said, there are few series that are more compelling to watch than Michael Apted's superb *7-14-21-28-35 Up* collection. It all began when the director spent a day with 14 English schoolchildren in 1963. There was pug-nosed Paul, and Tony who dreamed of being a disc jockey, and a bright-eyed little girl named Suzy, and a soft-spoken idealist named Bruce. Then there were two groups of three that he interviewed together: three insufferably stuck-up upper class twits (John, Andrew, and Charles), and three children of the working class (Jackie, Lynn, and Sue). Symon, the only black child on the program, was also interviewed, as well as Nick, and a cheerful, charismatic little boy named Neil. Like most children, the kids were blessed with elastic, expressive faces, and—except for the twits—with fresh, original views of the world and themselves. When Apted returned to talk with them in 1970, 1977, 1984, and 1991, he, and movie audiences, discovered how each child survived the process of growing up. The most riveting story, of course, is Neil. At the age of 14, his cheerful face seemed enormously sad. He no longer talked about being an astronaut, but still thought he would make a good coach driver. At 21, he looked even sadder, and by 28 he was not only sad, but downright unhealthy and homeless as well. His inexorable descent into mental illness is wrenching to watch, especially since, unlike the others, he believes that his condition is entirely due to something inside of him. He never discusses relatives or any other close relationships, and he fears that if he were ever to marry, his kids would wind up like him rather than his wife, however outgoing she might be. Nick, who lives in America, suggests that the process of making the series and accounting for one's life to an international audience every seven years can't help but change a person. His wife Jackie, who received tremendous criticism for the way she came off in *28 Up,* refuses to appear in the series anymore, and neither Nick nor Jackie will let their child participate. Nick, who now has an American accent, seems well, happy, and fairly philosophical about his many years under media scrutiny. He discusses the low-key British personality which may strike U.S. audiences as dull, and suggests that his and Jackie's frankness in *28 Up* was misinterpreted by many viewers as a sign that their marriage was on the rocks. As viewers who did feel that way, we might point out that things may not always be what they seem, even in a wonderfully revealing documentary like *35 Up.* 🦴🦴🦴🦴

1991 128m/C *GB* *D:* Michael Apted; *W:* Michael Apted. **VHS** *FXL, FCT*

The 39 Steps

Robert Donat, then 30, looks so hale and hearty in this key Alfred Hitchcock film, it's sad to realize that all his performances were a major triumph of mind over matter. A life-long sufferer of asthma, which finally killed him in 1958, the 1939 Oscar winner had to schedule movie roles around his delicate health. Donat is the quintessential Hitchcock hero: funny, charming, a bit of a flake, and completely unprepared for life as a fugitive. Splendid chemistry with beautiful Madeleine Carroll (1906-87) certainly helped, as did the exciting screenplay. Wylie Watson as Memory is to this one what Dame May Whitty as Miss Froy is to *The Lady Vanishes* (only SHE gets more to do). The McGuffin is basically twaddle, but NO

one is glued to a Hitchcock classic for the McGuffin; how he shows the way ordinary men and women behave in a crisis burns into our memory far longer than whatever set them spinning in the first place. Elizabeth Inglis (AKA Earl, Sigourney Weaver's mum) and Wilfrid Brambell (making his film debut at 23) are supposed to be in this one, but we've yet to do a frame-by-frame check to find them, or even to see Hitchcock himself in a street sequence. ♫♫♫♫

1935 81m/B *GB* Robert Donat, Madeleine Carroll, Godfrey Tearle, Lucie Mannheim, Peggy Ashcroft, John Laurie, Wylie Watson, Helen Haye, Frank Cellier, Gus McNaughton, Jerry Verno, Peggy Simpson, Hilda Trevelyan, John Turnbull, Elizabeth Inglis, Wilfred Brambell; *D:* Alfred Hitchcock; *W:* Charles Bennett, Alma Reville, Ian Hay; *M:* Louis Levy. **VHS, Beta, LV, 8mm** *CNG, NOS, VHE*

This Happy Breed

The name of director David Lean conjures up images of blistering heat, frozen tundra, sand dunes, and thousands of extras. From 1957-1984, with one exception, Lean was a director of lavish epics. But there was a time when Lean made small, intimate films like *This Happy Breed.* It's hard to imagine Robert Newton in an UNDER-the-top role, but that's who Frank Gibbons is and that's how he plays him. Dame Celia Johnson plays his no-nonsense wife, Ethel, their cat Percy plays himself (I guess), and Kay Walsh is their dissatisfied daughter, Queenie. She's meant to marry Billy Mitchell (Sir John Mills), the son of Frank's friend, Bob (Stanley Holloway). But Queenie wants more from life, and she leaves home and hearth to find it; Ethel is determined never to forgive her. In the meanwhile, Frank's sister (Alison Leggatt) and Ethel's mother (Amy Veness) bait each other day in and out, each to deflect their unhappiness with their lot in life. They feel lonely and unwanted and if they didn't needle each other, they wouldn't have much else. A milestone occurs when Reg Gibbons (John Blythe) marries a girl named Phyllis (Betty

Fleetwood), and another, sadder milestone occurs soon after, beautifully conveyed by Lean in a sequence without dialogue. Time passes, and people and their circumstances change. Noel Coward, who did not grow up like this, has a tendency to satirize the working classes. Lean, who might have grown up on the same block as the Gibbons and Mitchell families, paid his dues going for the director's tea. His interpretation here is filled with empathy, insight, and generosity of spirit. ♫♫♫♫

1947 114m/C *GB* Robert Newton, Celia Johnson, John Mills, Kay Walsh, Stanley Holloway, Amy Veness, Alison Leggatt, Eileen Erskine, John Blythe, Guy Verney, Betty Fleetwood, Merle Tottenham; *D:* David Lean; *W:* David Lean, Noel Coward, Ronald Neame; *C:* Ronald Neame; *M:* Noel Coward, Muir Mathieson. **VHS** *HMV, FCT*

Thomas Jefferson: A View from the Mountain

When President Kennedy honored a group of Nobel Prize winners at a White House dinner, he quipped, "I think this is the most extraordinary collection of talent and human knowledge that has ever been gathered together at the White House, with the possible exception of when Thomas Jefferson dined alone." Jefferson's memory has been burnished brightly into our national consciousness; any discussion of our greatest presidents (Lincoln, Washington, FDR, Wilson) always embraces the Virginia-born genius who drafted the Declaration of Independence at age 33 and won the presidency 25 years later. But according to *Thomas Jefferson: A View from the Mountain,* both Jefferson's life and his philosophy reveal a long series of contradictions that historians have been arguing about for over 170 years. Why, for example, if he believed that "all men are created equal," did he free only three of his own slaves during his lifetime? And why, if he truly believed in an agrarian democracy, did he maintain the paternalistic view that slaves were better off under his care and protection than they would be if he paid them a living wage and then threw in the care and protection as a bonus? The huge plantations of the South would not have survived intact if ALL the slaves were paid a living wage, and Jefferson and his fellow agrarian Democrats knew it. The same man who fought successfully to abolish the paternalistic system of primogeniture that still exists in Great Britain today, the same man who fought tirelessly for religious freedom, maintained the status quo of the slave-run plantation system during his own lifetime. There were deeply personal factors at work here, too, although genealogists are still wrangling about them as well. Did Jefferson father children by the mulatto daughter of his own father-in-law? Was Sally Hemings really his late wife's half-sister, and was his fear of disclosing their true origins the reason why he was so reluctant to free his own children? Well spoken historians of every persuasion thrash it out and the answers may continue to be elusive for many viewers. The documentary is taped in many historical locations and a wide-ranging selection of primary source materials from the era is also shown. Tackling yet another president among his gallery of statesman is Edward Herrmann as the voice of Jefferson, Sissy Spacek is daughter Martha, and Danny Glover reads the words of Jefferson's slave, Isaac. *Thomas Jefferson: A View from the Mountain* is a thoughtful point of departure for further research and is well worth seeing for its rigorous questioning and fresh perspectives on the Jefferson legend. ♫♫♫

1995 114m/C V: Edward Herrmann, Sissy Spacek, Danny Glover, Robert Prosky. **VHS** *MPI*

A Thousand Clowns

One of the best movies of 1965 is Fred Coe's *A Thousand Clowns,* written by Herb Gardner. Jason Robards plays Murray Burns, the sort of parent every kid would love to have: funny, flexible, free, and fearless. The only problem is, he isn't the sort of parent who receives grownup approval. In fact, he isn't even a parent, although you wouldn't know it from the warm relationship he has built with his nephew Nick, precociously played by Barry Gordon. Social worker Barbara Harris enters their lives with antiseptic William Daniels in tow. Daniels is a grownup with a capital "G," but Harris recognizes fellow free spirits when she sees them. Unfortunately, concessions to reality must be made and they drain a bit of the fearlessness from both Murray and his nephew. For his performance as Murray's brother, a New York businessman with "a gift for surrender," Martin Balsam (1914-96) won an Oscar, and future director Gene Saks set the standard for nauseating kiddie show hosts with his lacerating performance as Chuckles the Chipmunk. A thoughtful and hilarious film, *A Thousand Clowns.* ♫♫♫♫

1965 118m/B Jason Robards Jr., Barry Gordon, William Daniels, Barbara Harris, Gene Saks, Martin Balsam; **D:** Fred Coe; **W:** Herb Gardner. Academy Awards '65: Best Supporting Actor (Balsam); National Board of Review Awards '65: 10 Best Films of the Year; Nominations: Academy Awards '65: Best Adapted Screenplay, Best Picture, Best Original Score. **VHS, Beta** *MGM, FOX, BTV*

Thousand Pieces of Gold

Among the impressive domestic entries at 1990's Mill Valley Film Festival was Nancy Kelly's *Thousand Pieces of Gold,* starring Rosalind Chao as Lalu, a reluctant immigrant to America during the 1880s. Even though her father sells her to a marriage broker, she is filled with nostalgia for her family and her homeland. Her first stop on the West Coast is San Francisco's Chinatown, where she is bought and paid for by a Chinese agent named Jin, who delivers her to Oregon saloon keeper Hong King. To avoid the life of a whore, Lalu works hard around the saloon, still dreaming that she

NANCY KELLY AND KENJI YAMAMOTO

Director and producer/editor,
Thousand Pieces of Gold

Nancy Kelly: "The film is based on a novel by Ruthanne Lum McCann. There were quite a number of women who came here from China to the U.S. during the 1880s. What's unique about Lalu's [Rosalind Chao] experience is she came here and she survived."

Kenji Yamamoto: "Once upon a time...Nancy first found the novel in 1983. She was traveling in Idaho and she knew that she would be staying in an airport for a couple of hours, so she saw this novel in a book store and picked it up, brought it to the airport and read it. She called me and said, 'This would make an exciting movie,' and proceeded to read the entire novel to me as we drove from San Francisco to Lake Tahoe to a writers workshop in the Sierras. It seemed like quite an interesting premise."

Nancy Kelly: "I was working at the Squaw Valley Community of Writers and I was walking around with this novel in my hands saying, 'This is a great novel. I think it would make a wonderful film.' And I showed it to an agent who was there and she looked at it. Those people see so much material that they can look at the cover and one page of the inside and tell you yes or no. She said, 'A period piece? A Chinese woman in the lead? Are you crazy?' That just gives you an idea what they think is commercial: something with a white man in the lead, preferably Arnold Schwarzenegger, and set in modern day so you can have a car chase.... A writer who knew the author was at the conference and he introduced me to her. The rights weren't available then, but a couple of years later when they became available, she called a number of people and I was one of the people that she called to say that the rights were becoming available and if I'd like to put in a bid, she'd be receptive to it. We scrambled really fast and put an offer together and made it, and got the contracts signed and there were people right behind us."

Kenji Yamamoto: "In 1987, we were one of 700 projects that applied to the Sundance Institute for assistance in the development of the screenplay, and finally we were one of ten projects that were chosen. It was a wonderful experience. It's like going to summer camp in a ski resort. What you have there are Hollywood screenwriters that will help you and everyone of them were Academy Award winners that had read our script and gave us valuable advice on the characters and the story structure. Inevitably, we were able to come up with a very good and interesting draft after we spent some time up there with our screenwriter, Anne Makepeace.... In the beginning when we made it, we were trying to look for a town that would work for us and, because we were working with a very low budget, we weren't interested in raising money to build a town from the ground up. It would have been very expensive. So I contacted between 40 and 45 film commissioners throughout the gold country in California, the Yukon, as far south as Arizona, all the way up to British Columbia, everywhere. What we found when they reported back, in the way of photographs, were a lot of gold rush towns that, in fact, had been very lively many years ago, but today they're just sticks on the ground or they've been restored to such a point that you see Kodak signs and painted buildings, that aren't really true to the period of the 1880s. One afternoon, two and a half years after I'd started the research, I was entertaining my mother-in-law in Carmel—she wanted to see Mayor Clint Eastwood and I didn't want to go—so I stayed in the hotel and I was reading a magazine, and here was this small article all about this museum town, Nevada City, Montana. I took the article and wrote to these people, and they sent a videotape and it was truly wonderful. There were these authentic 100-year-old hand-hewn log cabins. We went up there and decided to shoot there. Many of the props that we used in our film were inside the buildings."

Nancy Kelly: "It looked good in photographs, and when we finally got to that location, we met the man who had actually assembled those buildings from places in the West. It was actually a town, but most of those buildings were gone and he restored it. When we walked down the street, it really felt, not like a Western movie set, but like a real town from those days. It's on the road that goes from West Yellowstone to Glacier National Park. A lot of people who are making that trip stop there. It's a little town of two people. When you're making a movie, you're totally in another reality, anyway, but it was wonderful what the production designer was able to do with that town as a basis; it makes it look that we built that town specifically for our purposes.... We knew that assimilation was important in both the novel and in the screenplay; the pain of leaving your home and being stuck in a new place that you had no choice about going to. That was one of the strong themes in both. I remember, in addition to the novel, reading about the immigration experience and how common it is for people who move from one place to another, from one country to another, from one town to another, to be looking over their shoulders all the time at the past and

can return home one day. She becomes infatuated with the agent who promises that he will earn the money to rescue her from Hong King. Instead, Hong King loses Lalu in a card game and she moves in with the winner, Charlie. Although she insists that their relationship remain platonic, she loses the respect of the agent who assumes the worst and rejects her. Lalu, with her new American name of Polly, is forced to fend for herself. Filmed entirely in Nevada City, Montana, *Thousand Pieces of Gold* accomplishes wonders with its small budget and straightforward narrative. Rosalind Chao gives such a remarkable performance as Lalu that you'll wish that she were offered more such roles instead of the supporting roles she normally plays in films like *Chinese Web, The Big Brawl, Twirl, Slamdance, White Ghost,* and *Memoirs of an Invisible Man.* (She got her chance in *The Joy Luck Club,* featuring Michael Paul Chan.) Equally good is John Sayles regular Chris Cooper (*Matewan, City of Hope, Lone Star*) in the beautifully written role of Charlie. Dennis (*The Last Emperor*) Dun and Michael Paul Chan do a good job revealing the negative aspects of Chinese assimilation into the get-rich-quick society of the Victorian era. Anne Makepeace's well-shaded screenplay for *Thousand Pieces of Gold* is based on Ruthanne Lum McCann's biographical novel. 🦴🦴🦴

1991 (PG-13) 105m/C Rosalind Chao, Dennis Dun, Michael Paul Chan, Chris Cooper, Jimmie F. Skaggs, William Oldham, David Hayward, Beth Broderick; **D:** Nancy Kelly; **W:** Anne Makepeace; **C:** Bobby Bukowski; **M:** Gary Remal Malkin. **VHS, LV, Closed Caption** *HMD*

Three Lives and Only One Death

Raul Ruiz is much loved by devotees of international film festivals and not particularly well known outside the festival circuit. The presence of the late Marcello Mastroianni in this 1996 movie may attract a few more viewers, but it's still a typical film festival entry, the details of which tend to blur, not over time, but the instant the closing credits start to roll. It is Mastroianni's ever wise, always humble face that gives the three tales their momentum. International audiences have trusted the naked honesty of that face since 1947, and wherever Marcello Mastroianni wants to take us, we will go, at least for the length of a movie. **AKA:** Trois Vies et Une Seule Mort. 🦴🦴

1996 124m/C *FR* Marcello Mastroianni, Anna Galiena, Marisa Paredes, Melvil Poupaud, Chiara Mastroianni, Arielle Dombasle, Feodor Atkine, Jean-Yves Gautier, Pierre Bellemare, Lou Castel; **D:** Raul Ruiz; **W:** Raul Ruiz. *NYR*

Three Sisters

The best of 1974's American Film Theatre productions had actually been waiting for U.S. release since 1970. Joan Plowright and Lord Laurence Olivier starred as Masha Prosorov and Dr. Chebutikin, Derek Jacobi and Alan Bates were Andrei Prosorov and Col. Vershinin, and Ronald Pickup and Daphne Heard were Baron Tusenbach and Anfissa. Most of the rest of the cast were unknown to American audiences. *Three Sisters* had received several notable Broadway stagings over the years: Eva Le Gallienne, Josephine Hutchinson, and Beatrice Terry starred in a 1927 production; 15 years later, Katherine Cornell, Gertrude Musgrove, and Dame Judith Anderson were the *Three Sisters*; and Geraldine Page, Kim Stanley, and Shirley Knight revived the play for 1964 audiences. As much as I wish that fragments of moving pictures of these revivals still existed, it's hard to imagine how anyone could have made a better film version of Anton Chekhov's play then Olivier. He sees straight into the heart of each character and brings every story to life in a fresh and startling way. The look of the film may have been accomplished more by accident than design, but the delicate color cinematography makes it appear that we are watching the lives of the Prosorov sisters through a mist. Plowright gives a wonderfully real performance as Masha. This one may be hard to find, but it's well worth the search. 🦴🦴🦴🦴

1970 (PG) 165m/C *GB* Jeanne Watts, Joan Plowright, Louise Purnell, Derek Jacobi, Alan Bates, Laurence Olivier, Kenneth Mackintosh, Sheila Reid, Ronald Pickup, Frank Wylie, Daphne Heard; *D:* Laurence Olivier; *W:* Moura Budberg; *C:* Geoffrey Unsworth. *NO*

Through the Olive Trees

Mohamad Ali Keshavarz tells us that he is really an actor playing a movie director and everyone else in the picture is an amateur. Mrs. Shivah is his assistant director and she wants everything to be just right. Taherek the star (Taherek Ladanian) won't address lines to Hossein (Hossein Rezai) because she turned down his marriage proposal. He confides in the director who changes the script. Taherek still won't talk to Hossein. Obligingly, the director changes the script again. This is part of a trilogy, but you don't need to see *Where Is My Friend's Home?* or *And Life Goes On* to appreciate Abbas Kiarostami's ingenious concept here and its thoughtful execution. *AKA:* Under the Olive Trees; Zire Darakhtan Zeyton. 🦴🦴🦴🦴

1994 (G) 104m/C Zarifeh Shivah, Hossein Rezai, Mohamad Ali Keshavarz, Taherek Ladania; *D:* Abbas Kiarostami; *W:* Abbas Kiarostami; *C:* Hossein Jafarian, Farhad Saba. Nominations: Independent Spirit Awards '96: Best Foreign Film. **VHS** *NYR*

Thursday's Child

Sally Ann Howes made a dozen films in the 1940s and 1950s, long before director Ken Hughes tried to turn her into another Julie Andrews opposite Dick Van Dyke in the 1968 musical dud, *Chitty Chitty Bang Bang*. She was, in fact, an enormously appealing juvenile actress, as evidenced by her debut in *Thursday's Child*.

Howes, then 12, plays Fennis Wilson, who has a scholarly life in mind for her future. Circumstances bring her into a film studio, where she is cast in a movie. Her new career leads to all sorts of family problems, a reality rarely addressed in Hollywood flicks where supposedly well adjusted kiddie stars then reigned supreme. Howes steadily improved as an actress, but as Nova Pilbeam discovered before her, great teen roles weren't consistently there in Great Britain between 1934-59. (Hayley Mills was England's first really big teen star and even she had to go to Hollywood to sustain her career.) Stewart Granger, then 29, appears as David Penley, a grownup sensitive to Fennis' true interests and ambitions. 🦴🦴🦴

1943 95m/B *GB* Stewart Granger, Sally Ann Howes, Wilfred Lawson, Kathleen O'Regan, Eileen Bennett, Marianne Davis, Gerhard Kempinski, Felix Aylmer, Margaret Yarde, Vera Bogetti, Percy Walsh, Ronald Shiner; *D:* Rodney Ackland; *W:* Rodney Ackland, Donald Macardle. **VHS, Beta** *NOS, DVT, HEG*

Thy Kingdom Come, Thy Will Be Done

Among the more intriguing entries at 1987's Mill Valley Film Festival was Antony Thomas' excellent documentary, *Thy Kingdom Come, Thy Will Be Done*. Originally intended as a *Frontline* special, but canceled prior to its May 1987 telecast, the film focuses on the significant relationship between Christian fundamentalists and right-wing politicians. Thomas' film provides a rich, detailed investigation of his controversial subjects, and his soft-spoken, veddy British interviewing style clearly soothes the fundamentalists into revealing themselves in ways they never would if his approach were more combative. (Antony Thomas is also credited as director on 1990's *Code Name: Chaos*.) 🦴🦴🦴

1987 107m/C *D:* Antony Thomas; *W:* Antony Thomas; *C:* Curtis Clark. *NYR*

Ticket to Heaven

Most movies about cults fall into the realm of propaganda, as in, hey kids, don't try this at home with your friends. *Ticket to Heaven* digs deeper than that, and because it does, it's an intensely frightening film to watch. Nick Mancuso plays a young man who's at a turning point in his life. He's just broken up with someone, he's miserable, he could go one way or the other. At the exact moment of his greatest vulnerability, he becomes attracted to some women in a cult who make it seem as if it's perfectly safe and cozy to be with them. Initially hoping to get laid, he sticks around the cult long enough to get sucked in and then he can't leave. Saul Rubinek (as the best friend in the whole world) takes a leave from his job to get his buddy back. The cult members try to suck him in, too, and he escapes, determined to try another (illegal) strategy: hiring a deprogrammer and kidnapping Mancuso's character from the cult. Director Ralph L. Thomas wisely focuses on the central character's emotional landscape, which is so isolated that the claustrophobic togetherness of cult life seems appealing in comparison. Anne Cameron's perceptive script, too, reveals that cult members are made, not born; severe sleep deprivation, non-stop programming, and constant supervision might turn any strong personality into a compliant recruit under the wrong circumstances. Mancuso and Rubinek deservedly won Genie awards for their sensitive, driven performances, and the film itself won a Genie as well. The two leads went on to make dozens of films in the 1980s and 1990s, while Thomas' next projects were 1983's Genie-winning *The Terry Fox Story* and 1988's *Apprentice to Murder.* ♫♫♫

1981 (PG) 109m/C *CA* Nick Mancuso, Meg Foster, Kim Cattrall, Saul Rubinek, R.H. Thomson, Jennifer Dale, Guy Boyd; **D:** Ralph L. Thomas; **W:** Anne Cameron. Genie Awards '82: Best Actor (Mancuso), Best Film, Best Supporting Actor (Rubinek). **VHS, Beta** *MGM*

Tie Me Up! Tie Me Down!

When Sigmund Freud asked "What do women want?," he, like many men, probably wasn't listening to the answer. We watched most of *Tie Me Up! Tie Me Down!* with clenched teeth. Pedro Almodovar's eighth movie deserves its "NC-17" rating and we dread its effects on grown-up weirdos who might be inspired by it. Ricky is an escaped mental patient who falls in love with a drug-addicted prostitute named Marina and vows to return as her husband. When Ricky is finally released from the institution, his true love has abandoned her former wild ways and is working hard to improve her life as an actress. Ricky kidnaps Marina, punches her in the face, gags her, ties her up, and keeps her a prisoner until she falls in love with him. Even though Marina swears this will NEVER, NEVER happen, Ricky the psycho obviously knows his willing female better than she knows herself. The gay version of this story, 1987's *Law of Desire,* made Almodovar a household name in America. Why did that film work while *Tie Me Up! Tie Me Down!* emerges as the uninspired retread that it is? Well, for one thing, Carmen Maura isn't around to distract us from the lameness of the central plot. Also, we suspect that Marina is really supposed to be a gay male who's into bondage, but Almodovar turned the character into a defenseless woman so it would look like he'd dreamed up a brand new plot. Without the wonderful Maura as his hilarious interpreter, Almodovar's humor seemed forced, corny, and misogynistic. Almodovar even throws away a promising subplot involving some amusing shenanigans on a movie set. Victoria Abril is lovely and poignant as Marina, but Antonio Banderas, once again, is completely unbearable as an obsessive lover. Almodovar has complained about the American ratings system, comparing it to France's repressive regime. But restricting access to adult patrons of *Tie! Me Up! Tie Me*

Down! in the U.S. is hardly the same as the internal censorship Almodovar would have faced if he were making films in Franco's Spain. If Almodovar's latest is not the huge international hit that *Women on the Verge of a Nervous Breakdown* was, his shaky sense of proportion and faltering artistic balance is largely to blame this time around. *AKA:* Atame. 𝆑𝆑

1990 (NC-17) 105m/C *SP* Victoria Abril, Antonio Banderas, Loles Leon, Francesco Rabal, Julieta Serrano, Maria Barranco, Rossy de Palma; *D:* Pedro Almodovar; *W:* Pedro Almodovar; *C:* Jose Luis Alcaine; *M:* Ennio Morricone. **VHS, LV** *COL*

The Tie that Binds

It's always a treat when an underhyped thriller that slips into theatres without the benefit of a press screening turns out to be better than expected. *The Tie that Binds,* dumped on unsuspecting audiences with the threadbare tagline that it's from the producers of *The Hand that Rocks the Cradle,* is actually pretty good. It boasts terrific performances by Keith Carradine as a psycho, Vincent Spano and Moira Kelly as the well rounded heroes, and remarkable acting by a little girl named Julia Devin. Wesley Strick's direction pushes all the right suspense buttons and only Daryl Hannah is a wash-out as Carradine's zombie-like partner in psychosis. Carradine and Hannah are irredeemable bad guys, dragging their small daughter along as they engage in sadistic crimes. When they're nearly busted, they manage to slip away from the cops who take their troubled child into custody. She winds up being adopted by Spano and Kelly, a nice, interesting couple who are hep enough to recognize her underlying sadness. Devlin captures all the nuances of a deeply frightened child so well that it's tough to believe she's only acting. She's a little young yet to compare to Lillian Gish, but her terror of violence does evoke memories of *Broken Blossoms,* not that the film as a whole is anywhere near

that league. The script slides in and out of focus (as does Hannah's character), which doubtless explains the skittishness of its eventual distributor. But *The Tie that Binds* earns most of its chills fairly and is worth a look on the small screen. 𝆑𝆑𝅘

1995 (R) 98m/C Daryl Hannah, Keith Carradine, Moira Kelly, Vincent Spano, Julia Devin, Ray Reinhardt, Cynda Williams; *D:* Wesley Strick; *W:* Michael Auerbach; *C:* Bobby Bukowski; *M:* Graeme Revell. **VHS, LV, Closed Caption** *MAX*

Tiger Bay

At the end of the '50s, director J. Lee Thompson wanted to make an offbeat crime film showing the tender relationship between a young killer and a little boy who witnesses his crime. He found himself in the garden of John and Mary Mills one day and watched their 12-year-old daughter at play. Thompson observed what international audiences would soon discover to their delight: that young Hayley Mills had a riveting, elastic face and that you never wanted to take your eyes off her for fear that you'd miss what she might do next. Thompson assembled the usual sterling British cast along with a young German discovery, Horst Buchholz. The resulting film, *Tiger Bay,* was well scripted and briskly paced, but as anticipated, Hayley Mills as the mischievous Gillie stole every scene she was in, even the ones she played with the police inspector portrayed by her father John. Watching *Tiger Bay* many years later, it is easy to see why Hayley Mills became a major star with this film. To be sure, the plot revolves around her, and later when she found herself upstaged by special effects, animals, and nuns, her popularity plummeted. As Hayley Mills became more of an actress, she tailored her work to meet the demands of each part and her strong personality became less evident. Parts like Gillie clearly come along once in a lifetime and Hayley Mills, soon to inherit the Little Miss Fixit roles that were once de rigueur for child stars, clearly made the most of her appealing role. 𝆑𝆑𝆑𝆑

group's leader, Zoran's personality asserts itself again and again and his worship of uniformed authority gradually dissolves. *Tito and Me* is a delight to watch from start to finish and child actor Dimitrie Vojnov is excellent as ten-year-old Zoran. 🦴🦴🦴

1992 104m/C *YU* Dimitrie Vojnov, Lazar Ristovski, Anica Dobra, Predrag Manojlovic, Olivera Markovic; *D:* Goran Markovic; *W:* Goran Markovic. **VHS** *FXL, FCT*

To Cross the Rubicon

Our favorite of all the films we had a chance to see at 1991's On Screen: A Celebration of Women in Film Festival was *To Cross the Rubicon.* Shot on a very low budget, it is not a perfect film and there are no name stars in it, but it does such a superb job revealing the best friendship of two very different women that I wish it had been chosen for the opening night film (instead of Mary Lambert's *Grand Isle*)! Lorraine Devon and Patricia Royce co-wrote their starring roles for the film and Royce co-produced *Rubicon* with director Barry Caillier. The dialogue between the two women is very real, fresh, and funny. *Rubicon* shows how women have the power to make each other feel better and worse than anyone else, and often both in the blink of an eye. Devon and Royce are an extremely appealing team and J.D. Souther and Billy Burke are excellent as two of the men in their lives. The Seattle-based *To Cross the Rubicon* also benefits from judicious editing. When the film was first screened six months before the festival, it was an unwieldy 2 1/2 hours in length; it was later trimmed to a far more manageable 120 minutes. 🦴🦴🦴

1991 120m/C Patricia Royce, J.D. Souther, Lorraine Devon, Billy Burke; *D:* Barry Caillier; *W:* Patricia Royce, Lorraine Devon. **VHS** *MTH*

Matt Dillon and Nicole Kidman in *To Die For.*

1959 107m/B *GB* John Mills, Horst Buchholz, Hayley Mills, Yvonne Mitchell, Megs Jenkins, Anthony Dawson, Kenneth Griffith, Michael Anderson Jr.; *D:* J. Lee Thompson; *W:* John Hawkesworth; *C:* John Hawkesworth; *M:* Laurie Johnson. **VHS, Beta** *PAR*

Tito and Me

Yugoslavia's *Tito and Me* has a great deal of the charm of the early Our Gang comedies, showing childhood on its own unique terms. Its protagonist is a little boy named Zoran who idolizes Marshall Tito. He wins a school essay competition in which he explains why he loves Tito so much and then finds himself in the midst of a group pilgrimage to visit the dictator's place. Confronted with the authoritarian nature of the

To Die For

Gus Van Sant's *To Die For* is indeed a movie to die for. With a fine-tuned screenplay by the great Buck Henry (who appears in a side-splitting cameo as a high school teacher), *To Die For* takes an up close and personal look at a cable TV weather girl who will do anything (well, almost anything) to be a network anchorwoman with a household name. Just one thing; she is initially attracted to the good-looking Italian lug played by Matt Dillon. But when Matt becomes her husband, he wants her to help out with the family restaurant and intends to fill her up with little bambinos. What's a future national celebrity to do? That's right, go to the local high school and enlist the three most dazed and confused kids there to rub out Dillon. How? Well, one chunky kid (Alison Folland) absolutely idolizes her and does anything her heroine asks her to do. And Joaquin Phoenix is so sexually obsessed with her that he lets himself be dragged into murder just to keep her in bed with him. Only the audience and the wonderfully snide Illeana Douglas as Dillon's sister see through this self-absorbed temptress played to the hilt by Nicole Kidman. The last time they filmed this variation on the Pamela Smart story, adorable Helen Hunt played it straight in 1991's *Murder in New Hampshire,* the obligatory "fact-based" television movie. But novelist Joyce Maynard, Buck Henry, and Gus Van Sant took the bare bones of the case and ran with it in a bold effort to shred our tattered visions of the media to a pulp. It won't, of course; this is Kidman's breakthrough movie, the one that she will always be identified with, even when she is wheeled out for cameo roles in the 21st century. We do worry about Joaquin Phoenix, though. River's kid brother looks so strung out in every single sequence that his presence feels like a cruelly evocative in-joke. Matt Dillon sheds his sexual charisma to play Kidman's worshipful schnook. And newcomer Folland is impressive as the clunky fan who, like the ill-fated Barbara Bates in *All About Eve,* fragments into many images of herself, even more than her role model. Slap this movie and the Simpson trial in a time capsule for centuries, and wonder what the future will think about our time. 🦴🦴🦴🦴

1995 (R) 103m/C Nicole Kidman, Matt Dillon, Joaquin Rafael (Leaf) Phoenix, Casey Affleck, Alison Folland, Illeana Douglas, Dan Hedaya, Wayne Knight, Kurtwood Smith, Holland Taylor, Maria Tucci, Susan Traylor; *Cameos:* George Segal, Buck Henry; *D:* Gus Van Sant; *W:* Buck Henry, Johnny Burne; *C:* Eric Alan Edwards; *M:* Danny Elfman. Golden Globe Awards '96: Best Actress—Musical/Comedy (Kidman); Broadcast Film Critics Association Awards '95: Best Actress (Kidman); Nominations: British Academy Awards '95: Best Actress (Kidman); MTV Movie Awards '96: Most Desirable Female (Kidman). **VHS, LV, 8mm, Closed Caption** *COL*

To Have and to Hold

We had been looking forward to another Rachel Griffiths movie ever since her award-winning performance as Rhonda in 1994's *Muriel's Wedding. To Have and to Hold,* sadly, is a depressing bore. Tcheky Karyo used to be married to Anni Finsterer, and is now trying to turn Griffiths into a facsimile of his first wife. If we gave a damn about any of the characters, this might make an intriguing minor noir entry, but we don't. Griffiths is a jewel, but *To Have and to Hold* isn't, and her innate intelligence is in conflict with the incomprehensible choices of her character. Watching this flick is like walking into the screwed-up household of a stranger where all you can do is fidget and wonder, "Why do we have to be here? May we go now, please?" **WOOF!**

1996 98m/C *AU* Tcheky Karyo, Rachel Griffiths, Steve Jacobs, Anni Finsterer, David Field, Robert Kunsa; *D:* John Hillcoat. *NYR*

To See Paris and Die

Award-winning actress Tatyana Vasilyeva stars in Alexander Proshkin's *To See Paris and Die.* Orekhova (Vasilyeva) and her adult son, Yuri, live together in a room in an apartment shared with many neighbors who are incapable of minding their own business. Orekheva hopes that Yuri will receive a prize in an upcoming music contest, so she tells him that he cannot marry Katya, his Jewish fiancee. A fierce anti-Semite, Orekhova firmly believes that Katya will destroy any chance Yuri may have to achieve success. This Russian entry suggests that talent only appears to transcend the perennial challenge of a Jewish identity, and its downbeat conclusions indicate that, drawn to its most illogical extremes, belief in such an apparition leads to tragic consequences. By some startling coincidence, Leonid Gorovets' *Coffee with Lemon,* made in Israel in 1994 and also starring Vasilyeva, had pretty much the same theme. 🦴🦴

1993 100m/C *RU* Tatyana Vasilyeva; **D:** Alexander Proshkin. *NYR*

To Sleep with Anger

One of the many exceptional entries at 1990's Mill Valley Film Festival was *To Sleep with Anger.* It is a wonderfully layered tale of family tensions, magic, and mystery set in a deceptively down-to-earth black neighborhood in Los Angeles. Refreshingly free of stereotypes, the film focuses on the disturbing effect of an intruder named Harry on the basically healthy family who offer him their hospitality. Who is Harry? No one seems to know, although they shared some stormy experiences together in their younger days. But Harry has changed over the years and so have they. Gradually he begins to chip away at their collective strengths, creating disharmony wherever he goes. Harry has cultivated a fairly delightful shell, however, so it takes a while before his friends realize why their lives have become so chaotic in his crafty presence. Although it is difficult to tear your eyes away from the spellbinding Danny Glover as Harry, the supporting cast is outstanding. Paul Butler and Mary Alice deliver warm, rich performances as Gideon and Suzie, the kindly couple who agree to take Harry on as a guest. Carl Lumbly and Vonetta McGee have such charisma in supporting roles that you wish you could see more of them. Ethel Ayler is also excellent in a scene-stealing role as a tough cookie who sees all the way through Harry's shenanigans and Davis Roberts is a treasure as one of Suzie's old but still hopeful suitors. Writer/director Charles Burnett has exceptional skill at sustaining suspense and then almost, but not quite, relieving it with humor, so even as you laugh, you're waiting for the tension to start building again. Gideon's family is an imperfect group who seemed to have made peace with an imperfect world until Harry arrived on their doorstep. Producer Glover, Charles Burnett, and company deserve credit for sustaining their unique vision throughout *To Sleep with Anger* and for bringing such a rare gem to the attention of movie audiences everywhere. 🦴🦴🦴🦴

1990 (PG) 105m/C Danny Glover, Mary Alice, Paul Butler, Richard Brooks, Carl Lumbly, Vonetta McGee, Sheryl Lee Ralph, Ethel Ayler, Davis Roberts; **D:** Charles Burnett; **W:** Charles Burnett; **C:** Walt Lloyd. Independent Spirit Awards '91: Best Actor (Glover), Best Director (Burnett), Best Screenplay, Best Supporting Actress (Ralph); National Society of Film Critics Awards '90: Best Screenplay; Sundance Film Festival '90: Special Jury Prize. **VHS, Beta, Closed Caption** *COL, FCT, IME*

Tommy

Tommy boasts a number of fine rock stars, as well as Oliver Reed (Frank Hobbs) and (Doctor) Jack Nicholson, who don't let their lack of vocal talent bother them too much. And (Preacher) Eric Clapton is outstanding as always. You'll either love *Tommy* or hate it, depending on how you feel about Ken Russell as a movie director. Russell's style is uniquely his own: wild, excessive, and gooey. He gets extravagant performances out of Ann-Margret as Nora Walker and Tina Turner as the Acid Queen, makes Roger Daltrey look good as Tommy Walker, and blasts everyone within six blocks of the movie theatre with Quinaphonic Sound, a system he reportedly dored in the 1970s. *Tommy*'s themes are harged with energy and pizzazz. They are lso, as interpreted by Russell, bigger-han-life, predictable, and completely obvi-us. Russell overindulges audiences, tuffs them to the gills, in fact. So how ome so many viewers tend to feel so empty afterwards? ♫♫♪

L975 **(PG) 108m/C** Ann-Margret, Elton John, Oliver Reed, Tina Turner, Roger Daltrey, Eric Clapton, Keith Moon, Pete Townshend, Jack Nicholson, Robert Pow-ell, Paul Nicholas, Barry Winch, Victoria Russell, Ben Aris, Mary Holland, Jennifer Baker, Susan Baker, Arthur Brown, John Entwhistle; *D:* Ken Russell; *W:* Ken Russell, Keith Moon, John Entwhistle; *C:* Dick Bush; *M:* The Who, Pete Townshend. Golden Globe Awards '76: Best Actress—Musical/Comedy (Ann-Margret); Nominations: Academy Awards '75: Best Actress (Ann-Margret), Best Original Score. **VHS, Beta, LV** *COL, MVD, WME*

Tommy Tricker & the Stamp Traveller

The owner of a stamp store gives Ralph a 60-year-old stamp album that happens to include a letter and an enchanted rhyme that will send him (in stamp form) to Aus-tralia, China—you name it! Ralph and mis-chievous 12-year-old Tommy (Anthony Rogers) then begin an international trea-sure hunt to find a fabulous stamp collec-tion in a mystery location. This wonderfully imaginative kid's flick was followed in 1994 by an equally good sequel, *The Return of Tommy Tricker* with Michael Stevens as Tommy. ♫♫♫

1987 **101m/C** Lucas Evans, Anthony Rogers, Jill Stanley, Andrew Whitehead; *D:* Michael Rubbo; *C:* Andreas Poulsson; *M:* Kate & Anna McGarrigle. **VHS, Beta** *FHE*

Tomorrow the World

kippy Homeier was all of 13 years when e stunned Broadway audiences with his electrifying performance as Emil Bruckner, a Hitler youth transplanted into the mid-western American home of his uncle, Pro-fessor Michael Frame (Ralph Bellamy), where he soon launches a verbal assault on his Jewish aunt-to-be, Leona Richards (Shirley Booth). Independent producer Lester Cowan rushed *Tomorrow the World* into production the following year with Homeier re-creating his original role, but Bellamy and Booth were replaced by Fredric March and Betty Field for the movie. As the screenplay makes clear, the little Nazi has been conditioned by the cir-cumstances of his life into rejecting the values of his late parents, including his American mother Mary. His German father Karl, a Nobel prize-winning opponent of National Socialism, died in a concentration camp, and the child was then raised to believe he was the son of a traitor. Uncle Michael believes that love and kindness will work wonders on the little Nazi in his home, but quickly learns that the damage done to his nephew may be irreparable. A series of incidents with the neighborhood children and Emil's potentially fatal fight with his cousin Patricia (Joan Carroll, replacing nine-year-old Joyce Van Patten) almost make Michael and Leona give up on the boy, just as he is beginning to learn how to feel. The theme of *Tomorrow the World* was both provocative and tricky. How do you persuasively show this kid's transformation into a human being capa-ble of living peacefully with other human beings? Fine acting by the three leads and by Agnes Moorehead (replacing Dorothy Sands as Aunt Jessie, Michael's unmar-ried sister) certainly helped. One-time actor Leslie Fenton, whose forte as a director lay in action pictures (mysteries, westerns) ventilated the script's philo-sophical concerns with a sharp sense of what it feels like to be a kid in an unfamil-iar environment. And, despite his age, Homeier had already had plenty of prac-tice; he began his acting career at age six in live radio dramas. As veteran radio actress Moorehead once said, "You had to

work to make the audience visualize you and that isn't easy to do. Many stage actors fall by the wayside because of their inability to make an audience 'see.'" Homeier made audiences see, alright, and luckily his early work has been preserved in this rarely revived (and therefore ideal!) candidate for home video release. Based on the play by James Gow and Armand D'Usseau. 🦴🦴🦴🦴

1944 86m/B Fredric March, Betty Field, Agnes Moorehead, Skip Homeier, Joan Carroll, Boots Brown, Edit Angold, Rudy Wiesler, Marvin Davis, Patsy Ann Thompson, Mary Newton, Tom Fadden; **D:** Leslie Fenton; **W:** Ring Lardner Jr., Leopold Atlas. *NYR*

Too Beautiful for You

Long before the 1996 divorce of T.R.H. Charles and Diana, The Prince and Princess of Wales (with frumpy Camilla Parker-Bowles unnamed, but widely believed to be THE contributing factor), Bertrand Blier explored a similar mystery in this 1988 French film. Why does Gerard Depardieu (hey—has anyone said anything mean about HIS stomach lately?) prefer his frumpy secretary to his meltingly lovely wife, Carole Bouquet? The line that the late Richard Jordan (courtesy of Woody Allen) springs on Mary Beth Hurt in 1978's *Interiors* comes to mind: "It's been so long since I've made love to a woman that I didn't feel inferior to." Is that it? Depardieu clearly doesn't feel worthy of his wife who suffers agonies while he trots off to share a bed with Balasko. (Fact of life: even some of the most beautiful women in the world NEVER really believe it and being strung along by just one underwhelmed guy can make them feel hideous.) Well, the premise IS primal and writer/director Blier develops it in a promising way...at first. But

then, he diddles it. Where do you take a situation like this? The three characters don't know because Blier doesn't, either. Maybe he feels that identifying the issue is enough. The truth may be larger and more ugly than one romantic melodrama can contain. Anyway, it's very well acted by the three principals and it won four Cesar awards in France, before U.S. viewers like yours truly started kvetching about trivialities like the denouement. *AKA:* Trop Belle Pour Toi. ♫♫

1988 (R) 91m/C *FR* Gerard Depardieu, Josiane Balasko, Carole Bouquet, Roland Blanche; *D:* Bertrand Blier; *W:* Bertrand Blier. Cannes Film Festival '89: Grand Jury Prize; Cesar Awards '90: Best Actress (Bouquet), Best Director (Blier), Best Film, Best Writing. **VHS** *ORI, FXL, FCT*

Too Late for Tears

The next time you get in a fight with your spouse and drive your convertible off the road, whatever you do, DON'T BLINK THE LIGHTS. Not only is your marriage probably doomed anyway, but some guys in another car might think it's a signal and throw $60 grand (the root of all evil) in your car. This is the lesson NOT learned by Jane and Alan Palmer (Lizabeth Scott and Arthur Kennedy). Jane wants to keep it, but Alan wants to turn it in, so Jane keeps it. Then, Danny Fuller (Dan Duryea) shows up at Jane's door, saying it's HIS money, but it's okay with him if she wants to share it. (Did I forget to mention that Jane is beautiful?) Jane temporizes, then puts an idea of her own in motion. (Did I forget to mention that Jane is greedy?) Lizabeth Scott was one of the great femme fatales of the silver screen between 1946 and 1951, starting with *The Strange Love of Martha Ivers* opposite Van Heflin, moving up in the world to *Dead Reckoning* opposite Humphrey Bogart, then came *Pitfall* with Dick Powell AND Raymond Burr and then came *I Walk Alone* with Burt Lancaster AND Kirk Douglas. *Too Late for Tears* was followed by *Two of a Kind,* in which she

crushed Edmond O'Brien's finger in a car door, and *The Racket,* in which she is a nightclub singer and a police informer, with Robert Mitchum as a police captain. But in none of these bad girl roles was she as vicious as Jane Palmer. Scott's really something to see as she sweet talks and murders her way to the bottom. *Too Late for Tears* was among Dan Duryea's many noir films. He specialized in playing tough guys (good, bad, and in-between) with mushy centers. For such a low-budget indie, the location sequences are impressive. *AKA:* Killer Bait. ♫♫♫

1949 99m/B Lizabeth Scott, Don DeFore, Dan Duryea, Arthur Kennedy, Kristine Miller, Barry Kelley, Denver Pyle, Jimmy Ames, Billy Halop, Jimmie Dodd; *D:* Byron Haskin; *W:* Roy Huggins; *C:* William Mellor; *M:* Dale Butts. **VHS, Beta** *SNC, VDM, NOS*

Tough Guys Don't Dance

Watching Norman Mailer's *Tough Guys Don't Dance* is like being chained to a blind date with a 14-year-old motor mouth. You know his batteries will run down eventually, but in the meanwhile you find yourself entertaining the stray fantasy that Godzilla will turn up and flatten the kid. Mailer wanted his film noir to be "a murder mystery, a suspense tale, a film of horror—and a comedy of manners." That's nice. Lots of little boys want to do five different things when they grow up. By the time they hit their 60s, they might wish for their film to be in a better league than *Tough Guys Don't Dance*. Mailer writes as if he spent most of his life running away from women whose sole aim is to chop off his "pride and joy" with a machete. Mailer thinks that life is like this film. He seems obsessed with the suspicion that any man anywhere might be abusing more women than he is. And if the man is black, or gay, or a preacher, or a policeman, the script takes especially vindictive turns. Much of the plot runs like something like this: A woman shoots a man. A woman shoots a woman. A man shoots a woman. A man

shoots himself. Another woman shoots another man for calling her "small potatoes." And so on. In a contrapuntal casting decision, Ryan O'Neal, arguably the most constipated actor in Hollywood, mouths Mailer's dialogue. Isabella Rossellini is around, presumably to lend an international panache to the proceedings, but she seems to be slumming. Clarence Williams III, who's done good work in bad films, has one entrance, which is also his exit from the plot. Veteran film heavy Lawrence Tierney is the only cast member who seems at ease in his tough guy role. The rest of the players do the best they can with what they have been given to do. The most revealing line in the film is, "I'm not a good enough writer to delineate how I really feel." *Tough Guys* is crammed with Mailer dialogue so excruciatingly bad that the best possible marketing ploy for this mess would have been to slap it on a Golden Turkeys triple bill so its filmmakers could nurse their hurt feelings all the way to the bank. **WOOF!**

1987 (R) 110m/C Ryan O'Neal, Isabella Rossellini, Wings Hauser, Debra Sandlund, John Bedford Lloyd, Lawrence Tierney, Clarence Williams III, Penn Jillette, Frances Fisher; *D:* Norman Mailer; *W:* Norman Mailer; *C:* John Bailey; *M:* Angelo Badalamenti. Golden Raspberry Awards '87: Worst Director (Mailer). **VHS, Beta, LV, Closed Caption** *MED, CDV, VTR*

Traces of Red

Jim Belushi is a good actor, but we've never really thought of him as Mr. Sex. Nevertheless, he has two sex scenes in the first 18 minutes of *Traces of Red,* a so-called thriller with a great beginning, a great ending, and an absolute mess of a middle. The movie looks like it was shot one way and then re-edited and re-mixed in a patch job. (For starters, most of the film is a flashback, but the flashback doesn't go back far enough, so we hear about characters dealing with stuff that we NEVER get to see. That's cheating!) This is one of those movies where we can tell instantly what all the relationships are from the way that everyone glances at each other, and we're talking about from scene one. Moreover, from scene two it's easy to spot who's going to get it next and when, another sure sign of an inexperienced director, which Andy Wolk definitely is; this is his first movie. The worst thing that Wolk achieves is something that we didn't think was possible: a mediocre performance from Lorraine Bracco as a high society tramp. Since Wolk had Bracco's great husky voice and strong personality to work with, why would he, or anyone, want to encourage her to adopt Melanie Griffith's voice and mannerisms? There's a poorly developed subplot involving Belushi's police partner; in fact, there are long stretches when we don't know which partner is the actual focus of the movie. Since the partner is played by Tony Goldwyn, grandson of Samuel Goldwyn, and *Traces of Red* IS a Goldwyn release, it might make career-track sense, but it sure makes the plot hard to follow. Some viewers may just want to give up on this one and laugh at the mind-boggling ineptness of it all; it's a textbook! 🎬🎬

1992 (R) 105m/C James Belushi, Lorraine Bracco, Tony Goldwyn, William Russ, Michelle Joyner, Joe Lisi, Jim Piddock; *D:* Andy Wolk; *M:* Graeme Revell. **VHS, LV, Closed Caption** *HBO*

Tracks

Tracks, seen from the perspective of a Viet Nam veteran, took the Cannes Film Festival by storm, and it certainly offers some fine ensemble acting. The movie was filmed on a train without permission, and it's more than obvious. Paul Glickman tries hard with the camera work, but the overall picture has a hurried, jerky quality. Maybe Henry Jaglom was trying to emphasize how honest his screenplay was by interspersing overlong sequences with swiftly edited shots. But as a dramatic device, it's way too transparent to be successful. There is an internal integrity to *Tracks* which is not altogether diminished by its inadequate attempts at technical flash. Jaglom should have had enough faith in his material and his cast to let the veteran's story emerge without artificial emphasis. 🎬🎬

1976 (R) 90m/C Dennis Hopper, Dean Stockwell, Taryn Power, Zack Norman, Michael Emil, Barbara Flood; *D:* Henry Jaglom; *W:* Henry Jaglom; *C:* Paul Glickman. **VHS, Beta, Closed Caption** *PAR*

Trainspotting

If we were to list even a fraction of the grim things that occur during the course of *Trainspotting,* it wouldn't sound anything like much of a laugh. But neither did the bald plot of John Osborne's *Look Back in Anger,* or its protagonist Jimmy Porter. The spiritual descendant of 1956's Angry Young Man may well be Mark Renton, who lives, in 1996 fashion, by slipping in and out of Edinburgh's shooting galleries. "Who needs reasons when you've got heroin?" Renton asks no one in particular. Maybe US, sitting in a movie trance, watching him dive into the worst toilet in Scotland in search of opium suppositories. The sequence, like many others in Danny Boyle's hypnotic film, drags us into squalor, and gives us a glimpse of the euphoria on the other side. But *Trainspotting* is more than a full-color drugalogue for naive and foolish neophytes. It captures the flip side, too; the horrors of cold turkey, the self-deception of hanging out with your old mates while trying to kick the habit, the screwed-up drug deals that seem like such a great idea after you've had a free sample. The lethargy that has always been so intrinsic to every drug movie ever made (with the exception of 1916's *The Mystery of the Leaping Fish*) has been replaced here by John Hodge's hyperkinetic screenplay and by the fluidity of Boyle's direction. If you try reading the original novel by Irvine Welsh, you're going

to need more than a glossary, even if you see the far more lucid film adaptation first. If ever a yarn with thick Scottish dialects and obscure drug references screamed out for graphic visual context, it's this one. Acting by skinny Ewan McGregor (he's more chubby in *Emma,* also released in 1996) is excellent and *Hackers'* Jonny Lee Miller is also first-rate as his larcenous crony, Sick Boy. Robert Carlyle is everybody's nightmare as the terrifying Bregbie and more benign, if misguided, spirits are played by Ewan Bremner as Spud and Kevin McKidd as Tommy. The undercurrents here are both wise and amoral, a heady mix for the Iggy Pop-heads who will flock to see *Trainspotting.* Add the fact that Irvine Welsh only dabbled with heroin before writing his account in the early 1980s, and you have a tale that reveals the best and the worst of drug times, told by a tourist, and interpreted by the manic

Scottish talent who reinvented the concept of a *Shallow Grave.* ♪♪♪♪

1995 (R) 94m/C *GB* Ewan McGregor, Ewen Bremmer, Jonny Lee Miller, Robert Carlyle, Kevin McKidd, Kelly Macdonald, Shirley Henderson, Pauline Lynch; **D:** Danny Boyle; **W:** John Hodge; **C:** Brian Tufano. British Academy Awards '95: Best Adapted Screenplay; Nominations: Academy Awards '96: Best Adapted Screenplay; Australian Film Institute '96: Best Foreign Film; British Academy Awards '95: Best Film; Independent Spirit Awards '97: Best Foreign Film; Writers Guild of America '96: Best Adapted Screenplay. **VHS, LV, Closed Caption** *TOU*

Trees Lounge

Trees Lounge marks Steve Buscemi's debut as an indie filmmaker after making dozens of films for other indie filmmakers. He wrote the main part of Tommy Basilio for himself, of course. Tommy is a 31-year-old screw-up, only he looks several years older than that. It's an important distinction, because he makes out with 17-year-old Debbie (Chloe Sevigny), the daughter of his former sister- and brother-in-law (Mimi Rogers and Daniel Baldwin). Debbie's dad is none too pleased about that, but...ah, well...only in the movies. But wait, there's more. Tommy had a girlfriend (Elizabeth Bracco), but then he took $1500 from his boss' till (Tommy MEANT to return it, of course), so now he isn't best friends with his former boss (Anthony LaPaglia) anymore, and, even worse, his girlfriend's having a baby with the guy! But there's hope: Tommy's Uncle Al, the Good Humor Man (Seymour Cassel), died at the wheel of his ice cream truck and Tommy can take his place! Debbie can be his little helper (and future make-out partner). When it all gets to be too much, Tommy can always go over to his favorite watering hole, Trees Lounge, to drink and pick up women and drink and pass out on women and wake up and drink some more. Connie (Carol Kane) serves the drinks. Sound like fun? The press kit included the following: one Trees Lounge mini poster, one Trees Lounge coaster, one Trees Lounge shot glass, one 50 ml. sample bottle of 80 proof Austin Nichols Wild Turkey Kentucky Straight Bourbon Whiskey, one set of lyrics for the Trees Lounge theme song, plus one audio cassette of Hayden singing same. There was also a Trees Lounge comedy web site at www.treeslounge.com. Talk about good, old fashioned promotional ballyhoo. *Trees Lounge* isn't exactly a fidget-proof experience, but, as *Movie Magazine* staffer Mary Weems puts it, "I guess a drunken mechanic is less tragic than a drunken writer." Well, maybe, but that doesn't mean I want to watch him drink for 94 minutes while listening to deathless lyrics like, "I need something to forget what got me in this mess...." 🦴🦴🐾

1996 (R) 94m/C Steve Buscemi, Chloe Sevigny, Daniel Baldwin, Elizabeth Bracco, Anthony LaPaglia, Debi Mazar, Carol Kane, Seymour Cassel, Mark Boone, Eszter Balint, Mimi Rogers, Kevin Corrigan, Samuel L. Jackson; *D:* Steve Buscemi; *W:* Steve Buscemi; *C:* Lisa Rinzler; *M:* Evan Lurie. Nominations: Independent Spirit Awards '97: Best First Feature. **VHS** *LIV*

The Trip to Bountiful

Unhappy living with her whipped son (John Heard) and nagging daughter-in-law (Carlin Glynn), an elderly woman (Geraldine Page) makes the trip to Bountiful, Texas, which no longer exists except in her happy memories. Her traveling companion is Rebecca DeMornay, who responds to her in an empathetic way that her family does not. The much-honored Geraldine Page (1924-87) won her only Oscar for her beautiful performance here. When first telecast in 1953, Lillian Gish, Eva Marie Saint, John Beal, and Eileen Heckart had the roles later played by Page, DeMornay, Heard, and Glynn. Based on the play by Horton Foote. 🦴🦴🦴

1985 (PG) 102m/C Geraldine Page, Rebecca DeMornay, John Heard, Carlin Glynn, Richard Bradford; *D:* Peter Masterson; *W:* Horton Foote; *C:* Fred Murphy. Academy Awards '85: Best Actress (Page); Independent Spirit Awards '86: Best Actress (Page), Best Screenplay; National Media Owl Awards '87: First Prize; Nominations: Academy Awards '85: Best Adapted Screenplay. **VHS, Beta, LV, 8mm, Closed Caption** *COL, BTV, NLC*

Trois Couleurs: Blanc

Although *White* is highly regarded by admirers of Krzysztof Kieslowski's trilogy, for me, it was the least involving segment of the three. The story revolves around Karol, a Polish hairdresser (Zbigniew Zamachowski) whose marriage to gorgeous French wife Dominique (Julie Delpy) is dissolving. Dominique wants Karol out of her life, out of their Paris hairdressing salon (she sets it on fire), and out of France. Isn't it always the way?—Karol still wants Dominique back after all that! After a brief period of insolvency, he goes to Warsaw, restores his lost fortune, and then comes up with a sure-fire scheme. *White* was the favorite installment of many followers of the series. *AKA:* White; Three Colors: White. 🦴🦴🦴

1994 (R) 92m/C *FR SI PL* Zbigniew Zamachowski, Julie Delpy, Janusz Gajos, Jerzy Stuhr, Aleksander Bardini, Grzegorz Warchol, Cezary Harasimowicz, Jerzy Nowak, Jerzy Trela, Cezary Pazura, Michel Lisowski, Philippe Morier-Genoud; *Cameos:* Juliette Binoche, Florence Pernel; *D:* Krzysztof Kieslowski; *W:* Krzysztof Kieslowski, Krzysztof Piesiewicz; *C:* Edward Klosinski; *M:* Zbigniew Preisner. Berlin International Film Festival '94: Best Director (Kieslowski). **VHS** *MAX*

Trois Couleurs: Bleu

The life of Julie de Caurcey (Juliette Binoche) is shattered. Her composer husband Patrice (Hugues Quester) and five-year-old child Anna have been killed in a car accident. She decides to withdraw from life and all her former associations and possessions (except for a blue crystal lamp) and live alone. Needless to say, her friends have things to say and do about the decision she made in a moment of deep depression and gradually, Julie works through her grief. A tour de force for Binoche, who won a Cesar for her performance. *AKA:* Three Colors: Blue; Blue. 🦴🦴🦴🦴

1993 (R) 98m/C *FR* Juliette Binoche, Benoit Regent, Florence Pernel, Charlotte Very, Helene Vincent, Phillipe Volter, Claude Duneton, Hugues Quester, Florence Vignon, Isabelle Sadoyan, Yann Tregouet, Jacek Ostaszewski; *Cameos:* Emmanuelle Riva; *D:* Krzysztof Kieslowski; *W:* Krzysztof Kieslowski, Krzysztof Piesiewicz, Slawomir Idziak, Agnieszka Holland, Edward Zebrowski; *C:* Slawomir Idziak. Cesar Awards '94: Best Actress (Binoche), Best Film Editing, Best Sound; Los Angeles Film Critics Association Awards '93: Best Score; Venice Film Festival '93: Best Actress (Binoche), Best Film; Nominations: Golden Globe Awards '94: Best Actress—Drama (Binoche), Best Foreign Film, Best Original Score. **VHS, LV** *TOU*

Trois Couleurs: Rouge

Valentine (Irene Jacob) hits a dog with her car. When she returns the injured animal to its owner, she meets a retired judge (Jean-Louis Trintignant, who has a ball with the role). The judge enjoys listening in while his neighbors whisper sweet nothings to their lovers on the telephone. Valentine isn't exactly crazy about the hobby of her new acquaintance, but she does like HIM. (And the judge's dog doesn't die.) Krzysztof Kieslowski wraps up the trilogy in this absorbing installment, which won a Cesar for best score. *AKA:* Three Colors: Red; Red. 🦴🦴🦴🦴

1994 (R) 99m/C *FR PL SI* Irene Jacob, Jean-Louis Trintignant, Frederique Feder, Jean-Pierre Lorit, Samuel Lebihan, Marion Stalens, Teco Celio, Bernard Escalon, Jean Schlegel, Elzbieta Jasinska; *Cameos:* Juliette Binoche, Julie Delpy, Benoit Regent, Zbigniew Zamachowski; *D:* Krzysztof Kieslowski; *W:* Krzysztof Kieslowski, Krzysztof Piesiewicz; *C:* Piotr Sobocinski; *M:* Zbigniew Preisner. Cesar Awards '94: Best Score; Independent Spirit Awards '95: Best Foreign Film; Los Angeles Film Critics Association Awards '94: Best Foreign Film; New York Film Critics Awards '94: Best Foreign Film; National Society of Film Critics Awards '94: Best Foreign Film; Nominations: Academy Awards '94: Best Cinematography, Best Director (Kieslowski), Best Original Screenplay; Cesar Awards '94: Best Actor (Trintignant), Best Actress (Jacob), Best Director (Kieslowski), Best Film; Golden Globe Awards '95: Best Foreign Film. **VHS, LV** *MAX*

Trouble in Mind

Trouble in Mind has one of the lushest, most evocative scores ever, with a fine rendering of the title song by Marianne Faithfull. The cinematography and the soundtrack give the film what Alan Rudolph fails to supply as writer/director: a mood straight out of 1940s film noir. Rudolph, always an intellectual tease, uses the aura of other times and places to play Games with Time and Place. You either worship the guy (I don't) or you just sit there wondering what in tarnation is going on. *Trouble in Mind* is set in "The Near Future," which helps to explain Coop the Thief's (Keith Carradine) weird curly hairstyle and loud yucky clothes. Kris Kristofferson is Hawk, a one-time cop just released from prison for killing a Bad Dude—a Mobster. Wanda (Genevieve

Bujold), who used to be his lover, runs the Rain City Diner. Hawk, about 50, gets hung up on Coop's wife Georgia (Lori Singer), about 24. Coop, already bizarre, gets MORE bizarre. Divine as (male) gangster Hilly Blue is almost worth the rental fee. Almost, because Rudolph seems determined to do everything but tell the story. A very frustrating movie, filmed in Seattle. P.S. If I ever see *Vortex* (with another one of my all-time favorite scores) and it turns out to be anything like *Trouble in Mind,* I will be SO disillusioned! It could be even worse, I suppose. I could be looking at Carradine in THIS movie and LISTENING to the music Richard Baskin wrote for *Welcome to L.A.* 🎧🎧

1986 (R) 111m/C Kris Kristofferson, Keith Carradine, Genevieve Bujold, Lori Singer, Divine, Joe Morton, George Kirby, John Considine, Dirk Blocker, Gailard Sartain, Tracy Kristofferson; *D:* Alan Rudolph; *W:* Alan Rudolph; *C:* Toyomichi Kurita; *M:* Mark Isham. Independent Spirit Awards '86: Best Cinematography. **VHS, Beta, LV, 8mm, Closed Caption** *COL, NLC*

The Trouble with Dick

There's plenty of trouble with this adolescent would-be comedy. An ambitious young science-fiction writer's personal troubles (which include being involved with several over-sexed women) begin to appear in his writing. This 1987 Grand Jury Prize Winner at Sundance is basically a genre-movie reworking of *The Secret Life of Walter Mitty,* but nowhere near as charming as that description might suggest. The story (what there is of it) gets very tedious after the first five minutes. 🎧

1988 (R) 86m/C Tom Villard, Susan Dey; *D:* Gary Walkow; *M:* Roger Bourland. Sundance Film Festival '87: Grand Jury Prize. **VHS, Beta** *ACA*

True Confessions

True Confessions, a United Artists release with Robert De Niro and Robert Duvall giving two of the best performances you'll ever see, was barely noticed when it first hit theatres, for reasons which escape me—it's a great movie! Like *Cutter's Way,* another 1981 United Artists release, it is quintessential neo noir, a re-invention of the genre for the '80s. Loosely based on the unsolved Black Dahlia murder of Elizabeth Ann Short in 1947, the film targets the corruption that would allow such a murder to occur. De Niro is ambitious Father Des Spellacy; Duvall is his brother Tom, a tough police detective. The killer is due to be named "Catholic layman of the year" at a lavish banquet and Tom's investigation eventually leads him to Father Des, who knows the killer but hasn't yet connected the dots (watch the movie!). The murder (and subsequent cover-up) changes both the brother's lives forever. Joan Didion and John Gregory Dunne's screenplay is sharp and incisive, and Owen Roizman's camera work is a classic evocation of the era. Director Ulu Grosbard, who made his film debut with *The Subject Was Roses,* is enormously skillful at conveying the complex, tangled relationship of siblings; he would make *Georgia* with Jennifer Jason Leigh and Mare Winningham in 1995. 🎧🎧🎧🎧

1981 (R) 110m/C Robert De Niro, Robert Duvall, Kenneth McMillan, Charles Durning, Cyril Cusack, Ed Flanders, Burgess Meredith, Louisa Moritz, Rose Gregorio, Dan Hedaya, Jeanette Nolan, Pat Corley, Matthew Faison, Richard Foronjy, James Hong; *D:* Ulu Grosbard; *W:* John Gregory Dunne, Joan Didion; *C:* Owen Roizman; *M:* Georges Delerue. **VHS, Beta, LV** *MGM*

True Love

Donna (Annabella Sciorra) and Michael (Ron Eldard) are getting married. She's down-to-earth, he's kind of a baby, and writer/director Nancy Savoca follows them all the way from their engagement to the wedding. The two leads are absolutely convincing, and the details of this Italian wedding in the Bronx are shown with plenty of humor and razor-sharp insight. 🎧🎧🎧

1989 (R) 104m/C Annabella Sciorra, Ron Eldard, Aida Turturro, Roger Rignack, Michael J. Wolfe, Star Jasper, Kelly Cinnante, Rick Shapiro, Suzanne Costallos, Vinny Pastore; **D:** Nancy Savoca; **W:** Nancy Savoca, Richard Guay; **C:** Lisa Rinzler. Sundance Film Festival '89: Grand Jury Prize. **VHS, Beta, LV, Closed Caption** *MGM*

Trust

If you liked Adrienne Shelly in *The Unbelievable Truth,* you'll enjoy seeing her as Maria Coughlin in *Trust.* Both Maria and her new-found friend (Martin Donovan as Matthew Slaughter) supply *Trust* with a quirky view of the roots of all evil, Suburbia and Families. Maria's father John (Marko Hunt) dies of a heart attack when she tells the folks she's having a baby, courtesy of her ex-boyfriend, the high school quarterback. On the other hand, Matthew's mother died in the delivery room. PLUS: Both Maria's mother Jean (Merritt Nelson) and Matthew's father Jim (John MacKay) are MEAN. Only in Hal Hartleyland! ♫♫♫

1991 (R) 107m/C Adrienne Shelly, Martin Donovan, Merritt Nelson, Edie Falco, John MacKay, Marko Hunt; **D:** Hal Hartley; **W:** Hal Hartley; **C:** Mark Spiller; **M:** Phil Reed. Sundance Film Festival '91: Best Screenplay. **VHS, LV, Closed Caption** *REP*

Try and Get Me

It was the last Saturday night in November, 1933, exactly one month before Christmas. The body of one of the best and brightest young men in San Jose had just been found, and his two confessed killers were in jail, awaiting trial. Only there was no trial. The town's angry citizens tried and executed the defendants that night, and California governor Sunny Jim Rolph praised their actions as he justified his own decision not to send in additional protection for the prisoners. This may sound like the plot for more than one movie, and it has, in fact, been filmed at least twice. (German emigre director Fritz Lang first chose the story for his 1936 American film debut, *Fury.*) The San Jose lynching of 1933 was never interpreted better than by the soon-to-be-blacklisted director Cy Endfield in 1950. *Try and Get Me* is a little-known film noir classic, focusing on Frank Lovejoy as an ordinary man with no money and no prospects. His wife and child don't mind, they love him anyway, but he turns out to be an absolutely vulnerable target for Lloyd Bridges' smooth-talking con man. Before long, they have pulled several small town robberies, but their big score arrives in the form of a rich young man whom they kidnap and rob. On a casual, but deliberate, impulse, Bridges kills his victim, sickening Lovejoy, whose conscience, too late, kicks into gear. The two men 'celebrate' their new-found riches by taking in a nightclub with two goodtime girls, but the fundamental decency of Lovejoy's character won't permit him to deny his horror and nausea over the killing. He pours out a confession to his pickup and then staggers home while she summons the police. Richard Carlson plays a newsman whose articles on the killing stir up the emotions of the townspeople to the point where he feels guilty for his part in the ultimate fate of the prisoners. However, director Endfield reinforces this point far more effectively by sticking with Frank Lovejoy, who conveys anguish with such conviction that he forces audiences to identify with his feelings, if not his actions. Lloyd Bridges never got a part that demanded more of him than he did as Lovejoy's amoral partner in crime. It was a real loss for American audiences that Endfield, who got his start making *Our Gang* comedies, was forced to leave the country as a result of the Hollywood red scare of that era. There are some movies that almost defy the term, they seem so real that you'd swear you were tailing real people and eavesdropping on them. (And the superb, offbeat, black-and-white camera work by Guy Roe certainly contributes to that illusion.) Endfield would later make some excellent British adventure films like *Mysterious*

Island, but *Try and Get Me* forces viewers to confront their feelings about retribution in a way that no other film, then or now, has quite been able to match. **AKA:** Sound of Fury. 🦴🦴🦴🦴

1950 91m/B Lloyd Bridges, Kathleen Ryan, Richard Carlson, Frank Lovejoy, Katherine Locke; **D:** Cy Endfield. **VHS** *REP*

Tune in Tomorrow

Writers are seldom captured well on the silver screen. Either we get Gregory Peck slumming his way through F. Scott Fitzgerald's drunken escapades in *Beloved Infidel* or we get the agonies but not the ecstasies of *The Bronte Sisters.* Leave it to Peter Falk to deliver a full-blooded interpretation of a radio writer in *Tune in Tomorrow,* a delightful homage to the soap operas that dominated the radio air waves in 1951. This is just about the first movie we've seen that captures how much fun the interior world of a writer really is, in and of itself. Falk portrays Pedro, an insatiable eavesdropper who uses anything and everything he sees and hears as material for a wildly convoluted soap opera serial. Two of Pedro's favorite subjects are his colleague Martin and his Aunt Julia, who fall head over heels in love with each other, despite unbelievable obstacles. Pedro plays games with their lives in order to flesh out his fictional creations, but no movie with this much fondness for its characters is going to betray their aspirations by passing judgment on their weaknesses. Keanu Reeves does a credible job as Martin and his performance picks up steam as he gets more and more caught up in Pedro's tangled web and his complicated affair with his aunt by marriage. Barbara Hershey is irresistible as Aunt Julia, and her nicely textured performance does much to lend density to her young co-star's performance as well. The sequences that recreate the charm and excitement of radio drama are beautifully edited, contrasting Pedro's lavish fan-tasies with the ordinary men and women who help to make those fantasies real for their captive audiences. William Boyd's *Tune in Tomorrow* script is based on Mario Vargas Llosa's novel *Aunt Julia and the Scriptwriter,* which was in turn based on Llosa's own early marriage to his Aunt Julia. We've seen so many contemporary movies that dance skittishly around the possibilities of authentic involvement that it's a pleasure to see a film in which the characters plunge wholeheartedly into life. It's good, too, to see a mercurial love affair in which the participants are crazy out of their minds in love with each other, consequences be hanged. As directed by Jon Amiel, *Tune in Tomorrow* approaches nostalgia for the 1950s at a devilishly skewed angle and the results are pretty exhilarating for audiences of the 1990s, too. 🦴🦴🦴

1990 (PG-13) 90m/C Barbara Hershey, Keanu Reeves, Peter Falk, Bill McCutcheon, Patricia Clarkson, Peter Gallagher, Dan Hedaya, Buck Henry, Hope Lange, John Larroquette, Elizabeth McGovern, Robert Sedgwick, Henry Gibson; **D:** Jon Amiel; **W:** William Boyd; **M:** Wynton Marsalis. **VHS, LV, Closed Caption** *HBO*

Turnabout

Carole Landis (1919-48) was one of the loveliest starlets who ever tried to make a splash in Hollywood. She deserved a better legacy than to be chiefly remembered for her morgue photograph in *Hollywood Babylon* (a persuasive argument AGAINST suicide if you've even achieved a flashlight beam's worth of fame!). *Turnabout* is brought to us through the courtesy of the vivid imagination of humorist Thorne (*Topper*) Smith, who, along with James Thurber and Robert Benchley, is on my "A" list for a heavenly cocktail party in the year 2050. *Turnabout* may not be the greatest sexual farce ever made, but it's pretty funny if you're in the right mood. Sally (Landis) and Tim Willows (John Hubbard, 1914-88) are discontented with their respective lots in life. She thinks that she'd make a better advertising executive and he thinks he'd

420

somehow, everyone muddles through the day. Unsurprisingly, Sally does a terrific job as the "new" Tim, but Tim bungles things at home as Sally. This screwball comedy gets wilder and nuttier until...but that would be telling. *Turnabout* was and still is considered tasteless, and the presence of the unfunny Hubbard (always best when he was being upstaged by Abbott and Costello or Roy Rogers and Dale Evans or Adolph Menjou or the Mummy!) is a severe blow, since audiences don't worry about taste when they're laughing hysterically. But it has a great supporting cast (Mary Astor, Adolphe Menjou, Verree Teasdale, William Gargan, Joyce Compton, Berton Churchill, Inez Courtney, Yolande Donlan) AND, lest we forget, Franklin Pangborn (1893-1958) as Mr. Pingboom! They might be able to re-make this with better writers and a much more appealing Tim, and I hope they go back to Thorne Smith's novel for inspiration; it's a gem. Other Landis movies on video: *One Million B.C., Dance Hall, I Wake Up Screaming, Moon over Miami, Road Show, Topper Returns, Orchestra Wives, Wintertime, Having Wonderful Crime,* and *Out of the Blue.* 🦴🦴▽

1940 83m/B Carole Landis, John Hubbard, Mary Astor, Adolphe Menjou, Verree Teasdale, William Gargan, Joyce Compton, Donald Meek, Inez Courtney, Polly Ann Young, Berton Churchill, Franklin Pangborn, Marjorie Main, Yolande Donlan, Miki Morita, Georges Renavent, Norman Budd, Ray Turner, Murray Alper, Eleanor Riley, Margaret Roach; **D:** Hal Roach; **W:** Rian James, John McClain, Berne Giler, Mickell Novack; **C:** Norbert Brodine. *NYR*

Twenty Bucks

A concept-driven movie about a twenty dollar bill and the people who hold it, however briefly. Nothing special, but it gives us a chance to see some of our favorite actors at work, like Elisabeth Shue as waitress Emily Adams, who aspires to be a writer. Steve Buscemi and the award-winning Christopher Lloyd have fun as Frank and Jimmy, a couple of hold-up men. Made in Minneapolis. 🦴🦴

have a swell time doing HER job at home. Mr. Ram, the genie in their bedroom (Georges Renavent, 1894-1969) is tired of hearing their brawls and changes Sally into Tim and Tim into Sally overnight. She wakes up butch, sort of, and he wakes up VERY effeminate (which Landis never was—real women don't need to be effeminate!) Sally has Tim's voice and mannerisms, and Tim has Sally's voice. Landis is really better at this sort of thing, but Hal Roach (1892-1992) probably couldn't afford someone like Cary Grant as Tim. The household help (wonderful character actors Donald Meek as Henry, 1880-1946, and Marjorie Main as Nora, 1890-1975) know there's definitely been a change in their eccentric employers, but

1993 (R) 91m/C Linda Hunt, David Rasche, George Morfogen, Brendan Fraser, Gladys Knight, Elisabeth Shue, Steve Buscemi, Christopher Lloyd, Sam Jenkins, Kamal Holloway, Melora Walters, William H. Macy, Diane Baker, Spalding Gray, Matt Frewer, Concetta Tomei, Nina Siemaszko; **D:** Keva Rosenfeld; **W:** Leslie Bohem, Endre Bohem; **C:** Emmanuel Lubezki; **M:** David Robbins. Independent Spirit Awards '94: Best Supporting Actor (Lloyd). **VHS, Closed Caption** COL

Twenty-One

Patsy Kensit wants to be a movie star in the worst way. *Twenty-One* is a skin-deep study of a skin-deep character involved in skin-deep relationships. Kensit is in virtually every scene, unlike *Lethal Weapon 2* or the ill-fated *Chicago Joe and the Showgirl* or *Absolute Beginners* where she drifted in and out of the protagonists' lives. Kensit's character Katie has sex with a married man she doesn't love because she doesn't have sex with the single junkie she does love. Got that? Later on Katie marries her best friend (appealingly played by Maynard Eziashi), then leaves him so that she can play the field with American men. In between men, Katie is nice to her Dad, mean to her Mum, and has dreary luncheon discussions with her girl friend Sophie. All this is shown without a shred of insight by *Twenty-One's* 'color-by-numbers' writer/director Don Boyd. You can always tell when Boyd knows that the action is leading nowhere; the direction gets very arty and tense. Key plot shifts occur offscreen as if it would be uncool to reveal Katie's life for the melodramatic mess it is. But at least showing the melodrama would be a choice, and *Twenty-One* avoids making choices for most of its 90-odd minute running time. The ambitious Ms. Kensit is not without talent, but she is definitely without a decent showcase here. She would fare a bit better in 1995's *Angels and Insects.* 🎞🎞

1991 (R) 92m/C Patsy Kensit, Jack Shepherd, Patrick Ryecart, Maynard Eziashi, Rufus Sewell, Sophie Thompson, Susan Wooldridge, Julia Goodman; **D:** Don Boyd; **W:** Don Boyd; **M:** Michael Berkeley. **VHS, LV** NO

25 Fireman's Street

Hungary's official entry in 1974's San Francisco International Film Festival was *25 Fireman's Street,* a puzzling, disturbing movie directed by Istvan Szabo. This beautifully photographed movie focuses on the residents of a soon-to-be-demolished building. Their memories, dreams, and fears are shown in unsparing detail, as well as their uncertain daily lives: a young girl jumps off the building to her death, a woman swims in the air of her room, an old man chews thoughtfully on broken glass. Piles of junk, old photographs, and used furniture are regretfully abandoned in the streets. The actors are all blessed with fascinating, well lined faces that any good cinematographer would sell his or her shirt to shoot, and every line tells a different story. Rita Bekes as the landlady and Lucyna Winnicka as a resident are especially memorable. Szabo successfully exposes the terror and vulnerability of the inhabitants of *25 Fireman's Street* and both his surrealistic style and his unconventional approach italicize the brutality repeated relocations inflict on the human spirit. **AKA:** Almok a hazrol. 🎞🎞🎞

1973 97m/C HU Rita Bekes, Peter Muller, Lucyna Winnicka; **D:** Istvan Szabo; **C:** Sandor Sara. **VHS, Beta** KIV

Twilight of the Cockroaches

Twilight of the Cockroaches/Gokiburi is anthropomorphism at its most extreme. Japanese animator Hiroaki Yoshida creates plenty of sweet little creatures with highly appealing faces in the hope that we will identify with a kingdom of humanized cockroaches. If you can accept that premise, you may not have any problem with the rest of the film, including the following line from a "roachette" named Naomi, torn between her poetic boyfriend

Ichiro and Hens the warrior: "I'm pregnant. I don't think the litter is Ichiro's." According to the press kit, the director "fear(s) that Japan will be treated like loathsome cockroaches by the rest of the world if it continues to aggravate other countries with unfair trade practices.... (He) hopes everyone will see a little of himself or herself in the cockroaches who thought the high life would go on forever." Small children may not understand the sophistication of Yoshida's theme and they may overidentify with real-life roaches when their parents try to protect their food supply from invasion. Yoshida's concept may be a bit far-fetched for adult audiences, too. You may not be crazy about the idea of peaceful coexistence with cockroaches, or feel guilty about evicting them from your living space. If there is one type of movie that demands dubbing, rather than subtitles, it is the animated film. Many of the backgrounds are too light to read the English subtitles, and the synopsis for *Twilight of the Cockroaches* (with Yoshida's comments) didn't even help the press all that much. It's hard for us to imagine an American filmmaker getting away with a film that depicts Japanese industrialists as greedy cockroaches. Yoshida's cautionary tale strains to fit his good intentions, and the results, even for die-hard animation fans, may be bewildering. *AKA:* Gokiburi. **WOOF!**

1990 105m/C *JP* **D:** Hiroaki Yoshida; **V:** Kaoru Kobayashi, Setsuko Karamsumarau. **VHS, LV** *FCT, STP, LUM*

Twisted Nerve

Hayley Mills was Walt Disney's top teen star in six films made between 1960 and 1965, but by 1968, she was scrambling to create a new cinematic identity for herself. It didn't help the fans who wanted her to stay a child forever that she was madly in love with 54-year-old director Roy Boulting.

Her career choices from 1966-69 compounded the difficulty. Although Mills' talents as an actress had not diminished, her roles during this crucial period were unshowy parts that were unlikely either to reveal range or to please the admirers who'd followed her career since she was 12. (Actually, Mills made her 1947 film debut as a BABY in her father's *So Well Remembered,* which also featured her sister Juliet, then five.) Boulting's *Twisted Nerve* is the best of this sorry bunch of career-scuttling flicks, but co-stars Hywel Bennett and Billie Whitelaw have the showy parts, not Mills. Moreover, the film is rarely shown, either in England or in the U.S., because of its "X" certificate, its flash of Bennett's bare butt, and its tricky subject matter. Before the opening credits, we see a blank screen for 20 seconds while a plummy male voice intones on the soundtrack: "Ladies and gentleman, because of the controversy already aroused, the producers of this film wish to re-emphasize what is already stated in the film, that there is no established scientific connection between Mongolism and psychotic or criminal behavior." Okay...so then we see Bennett acting like a psycho for the next couple of hours. The top-billed Mills tries hard, but she doesn't get the lines or the sequences to compete with Bennett. Anyone could have played her part and it would have made no difference to the finished film. In spite of the extraneous nature of her character and *Twisted Nerve*'s muddled psychological insights, it's still an intriguing film to watch today, with flashes of the controlled mania that Bennett would later convey so brilliantly in 1981's *Malice Aforethought.* By the time Mills and Bennet made their third picture together, in 1972's *Endless Night* by Agatha Christie, she had played just one small supporting role in three years (in the John Hurt film, *Cry of the Penguins*), and the Hayley Mills phenomenon was long over. At press time, Mills (the proud mother of 24-year-old Crispian MILLS, not Boulting, leader of the hot Brit rock band, Kula Shaker) was entering her 50s and planning to tour the U.S. as Anna in *The King and I,* so don't write her out of the game yet! 🦴🦴🦴

1968 118m/C *GB* Hayley Mills, Hywel Bennett, Billie Whitelaw, Phyllis Calvert, Frank Finlay, Barry Foster, Salmaan Peer, Gretchen Franklin, Christian Roberts, Thorley Walters, Timothy West, Russell Napier, Robin Parkinson, Timothy Bateson, Brian Peck, Richard Davies, Basil Dignam, Mollie Maureen; **D:** Roy Boulting; **W:** Roy Boulting, Roger Marshall, Jeremy Scott, Leo Marks; **C:** Harry Waxman; **M:** Bernard Herrmann. *NYR*

Twister

Twister is THE movie to watch the night that the cable system blitzes out and you're NOT in the mood to watch *A Man for All Seasons.* Writer/director Michael Almereyda keeps a cool grip on the antics of an oddball family headed by Harry Dean Stanton. Crispin Glover is part of the clan, so that should tell you something. At the time of its San Francisco engagement, we kept asking if Glover could make a personal appearance with the film, but more than one theatre manager patiently explained that anyone who made that many strange flicks just had to be strange himself. And then there was that one night with David Letterman...well, BIG deal and so WHAT, dudes?! This very enjoyable weirdomesticomedy ought to send anyone with a pulse straight to the floor, doubled up with laughter. 🦴🦴🦴

1989 (PG-13) 93m/C Dylan McDermott, Crispin Glover, Harry Dean Stanton, Suzy Amis, Jenny Wright, Lindsay Christman, Lois Chiles; **D:** Michael Almereyda; **W:** Michael Almereyda; **C:** Renato Berta; **M:** Hans Zimmer. **VHS, Beta, LV** *LIV, VES*

Two for the Road

True confession: I was no great admirer of Audrey Hepburn's unreal screen image throughout the '50s and most of the '60s. Born into quasi-royalty, she was, for a time, everyone's idea of a fairy princess, forever teaming up with male stars who were old enough to be her dad or even granddad, admittedly starving herself to remain 35 pounds underweight as a Givenchy mannequin her entire adult life, and always, always, in need of physical and emotional protection from a guy, any guy. And then, Hepburn got a chance to play women who could eat food and take care of themselves, in *Wait Until Dark* and *Two for the Road.* She won her fifth Oscar nomination for *Dark,* and she got to call her husband a bastard in *Road.* Stranger things were happening in 1967, but for Hepburn, who even gave up her Givenchy wardrobe to make the film, there was really nothing a 38-year-old symbol of frailty could do after two such ground-breaking performances but retire and so she did. Stanley Donen's *Two for the Road* is the story of a marriage, seen in a series of brilliantly edited flashbacks. The flashbacks are not seen in a linear fashion, but here, there, and everywhere, as a real married couple would review their life together. Mark Wallace is played by the wonderfully appealing Albert Finney, then 31, just seven years younger than Hepburn, a minor age gap dissolved by their great chemistry together. For once, Hepburn is in a relationship that has, thanks to Frederic Raphael's superb screenplay, some basis in reality. In the present, they bicker, but then we return to their far from romantic meeting and they bicker then, too. Mark doesn't want her at first, anyway—he wants Jacqueline Bisset, then 23, but Jackie gets the measles, so he's stuck with Joanna (Hepburn). Somehow, they manage to have an idyllic day on the beach, with passion-killing sunburn as the capper. Flash forward, flash back; we see problems at every stage of their marriage: to marry or not to marry, other women, other men, money, no money, another couple's child, their own child, and on and on. Underneath the waves of hostility are wit, humor, and a strong sense that these two belong together, and that no one else in their lives creates the sort of sparks that they do together. The romance in *Two for the Road* is intensified by the fact that the couple's feelings for each other are often rough and tangled, and always visceral. *Two for the Road,* featuring the once-in-a-lifetime magic created by Audrey Hepburn and Albert Finney, also stars the very funny Eleanor Bron, 33, and William Daniels, 40, as Cathy and Howard Manchester, the parents of an obnoxious brat named Ruthie, the most persuasive argument ever for adult holidays in France without the kiddies! 🦴🦴🦴🦴

1967 112m/C *GB* Audrey Hepburn, Albert Finney, Eleanor Bron, William Daniels, Claude Dauphin, Nadia Gray, Jacqueline Bisset, Georges Descrieres, Gabrielle Middleton, Judy Cornwell, Irene Hilda, Roger Dann, Libby Morris, Yves Barsac; **D:** Stanley Donen; **W:** Frederic Raphael; **C:** Christopher Challis; **M:** Henry Mancini. Nominations: Academy Awards '67: Best Story & Screenplay. **VHS, LV** *FXV, BTV, FUS*

Two Small Bodies

Fred Ward and Suzy Amis do their best to bring Neal Bell's ultra-contrived play to life onscreen. It's a gallant effort, but the 85-minute running time feels MUCH longer. Beth B had previously co-scripted and co-directed (with Scott B) the 1981 Lydia Lunch vehicle *Vortex,* and made her solo writing and directing debut with 1987's *Salvation!* starring Stephen McHattie. 🦴🦴

1993 85m/C Fred Ward, Suzy Amis; **D:** Beth B; **W:** Beth B, Neal Bell. **VHS** *ORI*

Ugly, Dirty and Bad

In *A Special Day,* Ettore Scola already demonstrated his unique gift for tackling a difficult subject with sensitivity, and then shaping a lovely and graceful film. The hilarious *Ugly, Dirty and Bad* is about a large Italian family who live in a hovel and who spend most of their time trying to kill each other. The humor here isn't the least bit polite, with Scola (who collaborated on the script with his *Special Day* co-writer, Ruggero Maccari) aiming for the broadest possible laughter. The impact of *Ugly, Dirty and Bad* is even more amazing because its entire cast looks, acts, and IS non-professional, with

the exception of Nino Manfredi, the leader of this lavishly gross clan. **AKA:** Dirty, Mean and Nasty; Brutti sporchi e cattivi. 🦴🦴🦴

1978 115m/C *IT* Nino Manfredi; **D:** Ettore Scola; **W:** Ettore Scola, Ruggero Maccari. *NYR*

The Unbearable Lightness of Being

Daniel Day-Lewis plays Czech surgeon Tomas, who makes love with Sabina (Lena Olin) and falls in love with Tereza (Juliette Binoche). The backdrop is Prague, 1968. Just before Russia invades Czechoslovakia, Tomas and Tereza escape to Switzerland. Tomas has spent his entire adult life avoiding politics and serious involvements; now events beyond his control require him to confront both. *Being* launched Binoche, then 24, as a very romantic international star, culminating in the Academy Award she received for 1996's *The English Patient. Being* also added to the universal perception that there was NO part that was beyond the range of Day-Lewis, as he demonstrated in his Oscar-winning interpretation of Christy Brown in 1989's *My Left Foot.* Philip Kaufman's previous films (*The Great Northfield Minnesota Raid, The White Dawn, Invasion of the Body Snatchers, Wanderers, The Right Stuff*) gave little indication of the masterpiece that he would make by the time he was 52. Many seemed shocked that an American director (oh, come now!) could make such a sensitive, sensual picture. His follow-up movie, 1990's *Henry and June,* virtually invented the NC-17 rating, but 1993's *Rising Son* was more like the popular entertainment Kaufman had made earlier in his career. Unlike *What Happened Was, The Unbearable Lightness of Being* is ideal for a romantic video date. Hmmm...maybe not on the very FIRST date.... Based on the novel by Milan Kundera. 🦴🦴🦴🦴

1988 (R) 172m/C Daniel Day-Lewis, Juliette Binoche, Lena Olin, Derek De Lint, Erland Josephson, Pavel Landovsky, Donald Moffat, Daniel Olbrychski, Stellan Skarsgard, Tormek Bork, Bruce Myers, Pavel Slaby, Pascale Kalensky, Jacques Ciron, Anne Lonnberg, Laszlo Szabo, Vladimir Valenta, Clovis Cornillac, Leon Lissek, Consuelo de Haviland; **D:** Philip Kaufman; **W:** Jean-Claude Carriere, Philip Kaufman; **C:** Sven Nykvist; **M:** Mark Adler, Ernie Fosselius, Leos Janacek. British Academy Awards '88: Best Adapted Screenplay; Independent Spirit Awards '89: Best Cinematography; National Society of Film Critics Awards '88: Best Director (Kaufman), Best Film; Nominations: Academy Awards '88: Best Adapted Screenplay, Best Cinematography. **VHS, Beta, LV, Closed Caption** *ORI*

The Unbelievable Truth

This may be one of the best movies ever made on an 11-day shooting schedule; I rarely stopped laughing at the onscreen antics which is not to say that it will have that effect on everyone. What is Robert (*Robocop 3*) Burke doing back in town after serving hard time? Everyone wants to solve this strange enigma, but the wonderfully appealing Adrienne Shelly finds out. (Her dad thinks she should go to school, even though she really doesn't see the point since the world is going to end, after all.) After enlivening several other indies, Shelly later wrote, directed, and starred in her own indie, 1996's *Sudden Manhattan*. Julia McNeal later battled *The Refrigerator*, an underrated 1993 chiller. Hal Hartley went on to make *Surviving Desire, Trust* (with Shelly), *Simple Men* (with Mark Bailey), *Amateur,* and *Flirt.* 🎵🎵🎵

1990 (R) 100m/C Adrienne Shelly, Robert John Burke, Christopher Cooke, Julia Mueller, Julia McNeal, Mark Bailey, Gary Sauer, Kathrine Mayfield; **D:** Hal Hartley; **W:** Hal Hartley; **M:** Jim Coleman. **VHS, LV** *THV*

Under Suspicion

Under Suspicion may look pretty good on cable television at one o'clock in the morning. But on the huge screen, well, there's nothing wrong with *Under Suspicion* that a good script doctor and/or a decent director couldn't have fixed. Simon Moore is the director of this British made-for-television "thriller" starring Liam Neeson and Laura San Giacomo. Neeson is cast as the traditional "wrong man" and plays the entire role that way. But there is one sequence when he whispers in San Giacomo's ear and another when he ignites a cigarette lighter that look just like the director told him, "Just do these shots and I'll explain why later." As any good thriller writer will tell you, you can use sleight of hand all you want, but the clues have got to be there or the audience will feel cheated. We wonder if Liam Neeson will feel cheated if he ever gets around to seeing *Under Suspicion.* We were eager to see Laura San Giacomo in a lead, since she's done some wonderful work in supporting roles, but alas, she'll have to wait for another lead to do her career some good. San Giacomo CAN play a femme fatale—we've seen her do it—but Simon Moore is no Steven Soderbergh or Lasse Hallstrom; San Giacomo looks and sounds like a little kid playing dress-up. This is the sort of movie that tries to evoke silent serials, film noir, kitchen sink dramas, and even the suspense-building style of Alfred Hitchcock, but fails on every count. Why is there a 1957 flashback? (It's a red herring.) Why is a stuck-up barrister in bed with a young boy? (That's a double red herring.) Why does most of the story take place on the eve of the '60s? (Well, partly to explain '50s British attitudes towards divorce and homosexuality, but mostly because Moore has a neat line about the passing of the decade. He seems to think it's neat, anyway.) This movie is so out of touch that a character has to say out loud twice "I'll never make it in time" when he's racing to save a man from the gallows. And GUESS what happens after that? One saving grace: Kenneth Cranham does a fine job in an incomprehensible character role. 🎵🎵

1992 (R) 99m/C *GB* Liam Neeson, Laura San Giacomo, Alphonsia Emmanuel, Kenneth Cranham, Maggie O'Neill, Martin Grace, Stephen Moore; *D:* Simon Moore; *W:* Simon Moore; *M:* Christopher Gunning. **VHS, LV, Closed Caption** *COL*

The Underneath

Recovering gambling addict Michael Chambers (Peter Gallagher) returns home after skipping out on his debts and his wife Rachel (sultry newcomer Elliot) several years before. Old passions ignite in more ways than one, and Michael's lust for his ex, now married to a hot-tempered hoodlum, leads him to risk it all for a final big score. Moody and tense study of the complexities of emotion is capped by smart lead performances but style wins out over substance and the finale definitely leaves more questions than answers. Remake of the 1949 film noir classic *Criss Cross*, based on Don Tracy's novel of the same name. 🦴🦴⚀

1995 (R) 99m/C Shelley Duvall, Richard Linklater, Dennis Hill, Peter Gallagher, Alison Elliott, William Fichtner, Elisabeth Shue, Adam Trese, Paul Dooley, Joe Don Baker, Anjanette Comer, Harry Goaz, Vincent Gaskins, Tony Perenski, Helen Cates, John Martin, David Jensen, Joseph Chrest; *D:* Steven Soderbergh; *W:* Daniel Fuchs, Sam Lowry; *C:* Elliot Davis; *M:* Cliff Martinez. Nominations: Independent Spirit Awards '96: Best Cinematography. **VHS** *USH*

Uneasy Terms

Two Slim Callaghan movies were made between 1948 and 1954, this one and *Meet Mr. Callaghan,* based on *The Urgent Hangman* starring Derrick de Marney as Slim, Delphi Lawrence as Effie, and Trevor Reid as Inspector Gringall. The first film starred Michael Rennie as Slim, Joy Shelton as Effie, and Barry Jones as Inspector Gringall. Peter Cheyney's original novels attempt to transplant most of the characteristics of the hard-boiled American detective into a smooth-talking British equivalent. Rennie's Slim is disrespectful, shifty, and a bit of a skirt chaser, but he does get results. Moira Lister gives another trade-marked acid performance as Corinne, one of three sisters who hire Slim and his side-kick Windy (Paul Carpenter) to figure out who killed their stepfather; Faith Brook and Patricia Goddard are Viola and Patricia, the other sisters. Effie does research from the office and fends off Windy's advances, Gringall issues daily bulletins about how many laws Slim and Windy are breaking, and Nigel Patrick does an intriguingly twisted job as one of the murder suspects. A dozen years later, Rennie played Harry Lime on *The Third Man* television series, but he still seemed a lot like Slim Callaghan. He's not a serious threat to Sam Spade or Philip Marlowe, but if you can't find *The Day the Earth Stood Still* on the video shelf, Rennie's cool, dapper approach to *Uneasy Terms* makes this entry a fairly easy way to spend 91 minutes. 🦴🦴⚀

1948 91m/B *GB* Michael Rennie, Moira Lister, Faith Brook, Joy Shelton, Patricia Goddard, Barry Jones, Nigel Patrick, Paul Carpenter, Marie Ney, Sydney Tafler, J.H. Roberts, John Robinson; *D:* Vernon Sewell; *W:* Peter Cheyney. **VHS, Beta** *SNC*

The Unfinished Sentence in 141 Minutes

An Unfinished Sentence is a long, complicated study about the efforts of an industrialist's son to better understand the workers' world, despite his own privileged position. Based on a long, complicated novel by Tibor Dery. **AKA:** 141 Perc a Befejezetlen Mondatbal; 141 Minutes from the Unfinished Sentence. 🦴

1975 141m/C *HU* Andras Balint, Zoltan Latonovits, Mari Csomos, Aniko Safar, Laszlo Mansaros, Maria Bisztray, Lujza Orosz; *D:* Zoltan Fabri; *W:* Zoltan Fabri; *C:* Gyorgy Iles; *M:* Gyorgy Vukan. *NYR*

Unzipped

Fashion designer Isaac Mizrahi is the whole show in this crowd-pleasing documentary that won the 1995 Audience Award at the Sundance Film Festival. The film focuses on Mizrahi's preparations for the showing of his 1994 collection. It also touches on how he reads fashion in classic Hollywood movies, like 1935's *Call of the Wild* starring a dressed-to-the-nines Loretta Young: "If you're going to freeze to death in the Yukon, this is the way to do it." Perhaps because of the surprise success of this movie, another film about fashion—*Catwalk*—was rushed into 1996 release, also featuring Mizrahi but to a lesser extent. If you can only see one movie about the trials and tribulations of assembling a fashion show, *Unzipped* is the one to see. It's unpretentious, it's stylish, and it's FUN! 🎞🎞🎞

1994 (R) 76m/C D: Douglas Keeve. Sundance Film Festival '95: Audience Award. **VHS, LV, Closed Caption** *WAR*

The Usual Suspects

The Usual Suspects was one of the best movies of 1995, featuring a dazzling, tautly constructed screenplay by Oscar winner Christopher McQuarrie and a star-making performance by Kevin Spacey. The less you know about the film in advance, the better, because the story will put you through more twists and turns than a roller coaster ride, and half the fun is the sheer unexpected inventiveness of it all. McQuarrie and director Bryan Singer had previously worked together on *Public Access,* 1993's Grand Jury Prize winner at the Sundance Film Festival. Spacey had been toiling in Hollywood since 1987 and steadily attracting a legion of admirers who believe there's nothing this brilliant actor can't play. 🎞🎞🎞🎞

1995 (R) 105m/C Kevin Spacey, Gabriel Byrne, Chazz Palminteri, Kevin Pollak, Stephen Baldwin, Benicio Del Toro, Giancarlo Esposito, Pete Postlethwaite, Dan Hedaya, Suzy Amis, Paul Bartel, Peter Greene; **D:** Bryan Singer; **W:** Christopher McQuarrie; **C:** Newton Thomas Sigel; **M:** John Ottman. Academy Awards '95: Best Original Screenplay, Best Supporting Actor (Spacey); British Academy Awards '95: Best

Original Screenplay; Independent Spirit Awards '96: Best Screenplay, Best Supporting Actor (Del Toro); National Board of Review Awards '95: Best Supporting Actor (Spacey); New York Film Critics Awards '95: Best Supporting Actor (Spacey); Broadcast Film Critics Association Awards '95: Best Supporting Actor (Spacey); Nominations: Academy Awards '95: Best Screenplay; British Academy Awards '95: Best Film; Golden Globe Awards '96: Best Supporting Actor (Spacey); Independent Spirit Awards '96: Best Cinematography; Screen Actors Guild Award '95: Best Supporting Actor (Spacey). **VHS, LV, Closed Caption, DVD** *PGV*

Vampyr

The films of Danish director Carl Theodor Dreyer require considerable patience from audiences, even horror film devotees. To a certain extent, Dreyer anticipates the viewers' perceptions and plays with them. (In a slow way.) (Very slow.) *Vampyr,* AKA *The Strange Adventure of David Gray,* stars the film's backer, Baron Nicholas de Gunzberg, AKA Julien West. The vampire in this film is an old woman in a village, a fact the hero may not comprehend but is forced to accept when he sees what happens to her fellow villagers. Dreyer shows that ordinary surroundings take on a different atmosphere when we know that vampires are in the vicinity. Many Dreyer aficionados consider this to be his masterpiece. Our rating reflects the boredom/fidget factor. Note: the sad real-life story of leading lady Sybille Schmitz inspired Rainer Werner Fassbinder to make 1982's *Veronika Voss.* **AKA:** Vampyr, Ou L'Etrang e Aventure De David Gray; Vampyr, Der Traum Des David Gray; Not Against the Flesh; Castle of Doom; The Strange Adventure of David Gray; The Vampire. 🎞🎞

1931 75m/B GE Julien West, Sybille Schmitz, Harriet Gerard, Maurice Schutz; **D:** Carl Theodor Dreyer; **W:** Carl Theodor Dreyer; **M:** Wolfgang Zeller. **VHS, Beta** *VYY, NOS, SNC*

The Vanishing

The Vanishing is one of the saddest, most chilling movies ever made. The first part of

playful, endearing kitten, and we begin to wish that the mystery of the film would fully engage them both, that maybe they would discover buried treasure together. Instead, the mystery haunts and torments Rex, and stakes a terrifying claim on our imaginations. We haven't been this spooked by a film with such understated visual information since we first caught up with the films of Val Lewton on the late, late show. *The Vanishing* shows us things that we don't fully understand until several reels later. They work extremely well as individual sequences, but when we finally realize what we've actually seen long after the fact, the initial panic and underlying sadness are incredibly powerful. Screenwriter Tim Krabbe and director George Sluizer obviously knew exactly what they were doing. Like the protagonist, you may find yourself replaying similar episodes in your own life, and you may also overidentify with Rex's obsession for real answers as he pursues Saskia. In any event, it'll be impossible to predict your exact response to the film's startling conclusion or to its final visual tag. After making *Utz* in Great Britain, Sluizer was lured by Fox to America to duplicate his indie success in 1993, but the studio insisted on a happy ending, infuriating admirers of the classic original. Sluizer then began the ill-fated *Dark Blood* with Jonathan Pryce and River Phoenix, a film left unfinished when Phoenix died on Halloween, 1993. **AKA:** Spoorloos. ♫♫♫♫

1988 107m/C *NL FR* Barnard Pierre Donnadieu, Johanna Ter Steege, Gene Bervoets; **D:** George Sluizer. **VHS** *FXL*

Vanya on 42nd Street

If you wanted to send away for *My Dinner with Andre* action figures when you saw *Waiting for Guffman*, you'll probably find *Vanya on 42nd Street* an equally rewarding experience. Louis Malle's swan song shows a 1993 rehearsal at New York's New Amsterdam theatre of Anton Chekhov's *Uncle Vanya*, adapted by David

the plot focuses on a young Dutch couple embarking on a holiday. Their relationship has slid into one of easy intimacy. They talk of inconsequentials, they bicker, they get separated for part of an evening because of car trouble. We learn that Saskia (charmingly portrayed by Johanna Ter Steege) is frightened of the dark and that Rex (played with intensity by Gene Bervoetes) tends to be dogged once he's started on a course of action. When they are reunited, they snap at each other, make up quickly, and resume their holiday with fresh enthusiasm. They stop at an all-purpose rest station and she runs an errand. They play on the lawn. These unstressed details will haunt both the audience and Rex the protagonist when he later searches for Saskia. She is like a

Mamet. Wallace Shawn acquits himself admirably in the title role, Julianne Moore is Yelena, Brooke Smith is Sonya, Larry Pine is Dr. Astrov, George Gaynes is Serybryakov, Lynn Cohen is Maman, Phoebe Brand is Nanny, Jerry Mayer is Waffles, Madhur Jaffrey is Mrs. Chao, and Andre Gregory appears as himself. (Phoebe Brand was a member of the influential Group Theatre, appearing in 1933's *Men in White* with Margaret Barker, Elia Kazan, Alexander Kirkland, and Sanford Meisner; 1935's *Awake and Sing* with Luther and Stella Adler, Roman Bohnen, J. Edward Bromberg, Morris Carnovsky, Art Smith, John Garfield, and Meisner; in *Weep for the Virgins* with Marie Hunt, Tony Kraber, Paula Miller, Ruth Nelson, William Nicholas, Dorothy Patten, Hilda Reis, Virginia Stevens, Eunice Stoddard, Mildred Van Dorn, Evelyn Varden, Barker, Bromberg, Kirkland, Smith, and Garfield; in 1936's *The Case of Clyde Griffiths* with Barker and Kirkland; and in 1937's *Golden Boy* with Luther Adler, Harry Bratsburg, Lee J. Cobb, Bert Conway, Charles Crisp, Howard da Silva, Frances Farmer, Michael Gordon, Robert Lewis, Karl Malden, Charles Niemeyer, John O'Malley, Martin Ritt, Bohnen, Carnovsky, Kazan, and Garfield. If the list sounds like a Who's Who of 1930s stage legends, it IS; what a wealth of theatrical lore this durable stage actress must have!) ♫♫♫

1994 (PG) 119m/C Wallace Shawn, Julianne Moore, Brooke Smith, Larry Pine, George Gaynes, Lynn Cohen, Madhur Jaffrey, Phoebe Brand, Jerry Mayer, Andre Gregory; *D:* Louis Malle; *W:* Andre Gregory, David Mamet; *C:* Declan Quinn; *M:* Joshua Redman. Nominations: Independent Spirit Awards '95: Best Supporting Actor (Pine), Best Supporting Actress (Smith). **VHS, LV** *COL*

Variety Lights

1950's *Variety Lights* is often overlooked and underrated by Federico Fellini buffs, partly because he shared directing credit on this maiden effort with Alberto Lattuada. But it is a jewel of a film to discover on a video shelf. Carla Del Poggio is its beautiful, but not particularly talented protagonist. She wants to be a star and the terribly smitten Peppino de Felippo wants her. Giulietta Masina is his long-suffering love, ready to scrape him out of the gutter after the inevitable moment when Carla breaks his heart. Besides this oh-so-familiar triangle, we have the joy and vitality of small-time show business, best appreciated on its own ephemeral terms. One of the best sequences involves a rich guy who wines and dines the entire theatrical troupe just so he can have his way with Carla. Everyone knows the game but him: eat first, then protect your virtue. Masina was to become Fellini's eternal gamine, but in this film she is well able to take care of herself. *Variety Lights* is Fellini's early tribute to Masina's unique ability to project a love that helps her to survive life's painful realities, and make her partner's grandiose visions possible. *AKA:* Luci Del Varieta; Lights of Variety. ♫♫♫♫

1951 93m/B *IT* Giulietta Masina, Peppino de Filippo, Carla Del Poggio, Folco Lulli; *D:* Federico Fellini, Alberto Lattuada; *W:* Federico Fellini, Tullio Pinelli, Ennio Flaiano, Alberto Lattuada. **VHS, Beta** *HMV, APD, CVC*

Vegas in Space

The making of *Vegas in Space* reveals how difficult assembling a truly independent film really is. The enormously talented, much-missed Doris Fish (1952-91) spent the last nine years of his life helping writer/director Philip R. Ford complete the project, three years before its premiere. It may have seemed like a fun thing to do after a successful party given by future cast member Ginger Quest, but raising even a tiny budget like $60,000 meant that Fish/Ford films had to shoot film, stop, make money, edit film, stop, make money, mix film, stop, make money...for many years. Under these trying circumstances, Ford was able to accomplish wonders and he assembled a lively cast of San Francisco drag queens who paid

that its filmmakers hoped it would be, it is, sadly, NOT the camp classic it might have been. The rollicking, unforced humor of the live stage appearances of drag queens Fish, "Tippi," and Miss X has not been effectively captured on film. *Vegas in Space* is a time capsule of the year 1982 in the same way that a daguerreotype preserves people's images from the year 1842. We can see what everyone looked like, but not the unique undercurrents that made them precious beyond their own era. Note: *Vegas in Space* received some technical support from San Francisco's Film Arts Foundation and was virtually complete when Troma Films picked it up for "distribution." Aside from its premiere at San Francisco's Castro Theatre, this seems to have consisted mainly of late night USA telecasts and its Troma Team Video release. Composer Timmy Spence sings the title song with Katie Guthorn. 🦴

1994 85m/C Doris Fish, Miss X, Ginger Quest, Ramona Fischer, Lori Naslund, Timmy Spence, Silvana Nova, Sandelle Kincaid, Tommy Pace, Arturo Galster, Jennifer Blowdryer, Freida Lay, Tippi; **D:** Phillip R. Ford; **W:** Phillip R. Ford, Doris Fish, Miss X; **C:** Robin Clark; **M:** Ramona Fischer, Timmy Spence. **VHS** *TTV*

The Very Edge

Among our favorite not-so-guilty pleasures is watching the early films of television's most iconographic heroes. Before his image congealed into sterling saintliness on the small screen, Raymond Burr was one of the toughest thugs you could ever find on the late, late, late show. And you haven't lived until you've seen William Talman play a vicious killer or a religious maniac. Although it sickened him to play the role, Basil Rathbone was chillingly effective as mean Mr. Murdstone, brutalizing little Freddie Bartholomew and delicate Elizabeth Allan in *David Copperfield*. Rathbone's successor as Sherlock Holmes, Jeremy Brett (1935-95), was the most monastic of Victorian sleuths. Not even a marginal hint

Federico Fellini's *Variety Lights.*

affectionate homage to the colorful science-fiction epics of the early '60s. Fish and Miss X, who also wrote the screenplay with Ford, have the film's most prominent roles as Captain Dan Tracey/Tracey Daniels and Vel Croford, Empress of Earth/Veneer, Queen of Police. Also worth noting are the late "Tippi" as the petulant Princess Angel and Lori Naslund in a brisk performance as Lieutenant Steve/Debbie Dane. Executive producer/production designer Fish worked hard on the film's make-up and wigs, costumes, and miniatures; not bad for the extremely skilled, very funny Fish, who could work droll wonders with the simplest dialogue. Although *Vegas in Space* IS the "easy-to-understand-no-hidden-meaning-entertainment"

of attraction to the opposite sex crept into his interpretation. Like a chess master at the top of his form, he was rather dry, brittle, precise, and obsessed. What a surprise, then, to discover *The Very Edge,* a dark little British film from the year 1963 in which Brett, then 27, played a full-fledged sexual psychopath, terrorizing gorgeous Anne Heywood. She is "happily" married to Richard Todd until Brett, who has been stalking her for some time, attacks her in her home while her husband fiddles helplessly with the latch key. She loses the baby she is expecting, and tries hard both to cooperate with the police and to rebuild her shattered marriage. Her wonderful husband, it seems, expects her to instantly recover from the incident without a mark. If she can't, well, there's always Nicole Maurey, his stunning French secretary, lurking in the wings. The intriguing element about *The Very Edge,* under Cyril Frankel's assured direction, is that Heywood has more of a psychic bond with her attacker than she does with her own husband. It isn't that she wants him or anything like that, but she has compassion for his illness, and she is, ironically, less of a victim around Brett than she is around Todd. Both men desire her for their own reasons, but in a life-and-death situation, her fighting spirit emerges with her obsessed stalker in a way that it never does within her marriage. Brett is riveting as the tortured psycho, and your real hisses will be reserved for Todd and the so-called normal life to which Heywood must return again and again; it is a tribute to her expert performance that you can appreciate why her struggle with Brett gives her such an authentic grip on life. The ending, in which the police ignore the poor tied-up handyman played by Patrick Magee, and focus their energies on the folks from a higher social order, is VEDDY, VEDDY British. ♫♫♫

1963 90m/B *GB* Anne Heywood, Richard Todd, Jeremy Brett, Jack Hedley, Barbara Mullen, Maurice Denham, William Lucas, Gwen Watford, Patrick Magee; *D:* Cyril Frankel; *W:* Elizabeth Jane Howard. **VHS, Beta** *NO*

Victim

Victim was an important film in 1961 when homosexuality was still illegal in Great Britain. Actor Dirk Bogarde was then famous as everybody's favorite Dr. Simon Sparrow in a series of four medical comedy films he made between 1954 and 1963. At the time, his decision to play a gay barrister might have called a halt to his thriving career. It didn't, but it certainly marked a professional turning point for him. In order to increase *Victim*'s impact, director Basil Dearden made the decision to show most of the gay characters not as drag queens but as dedicated professionals, vulnerable to violence and blackmail. *Victim* rates high marks for its pioneering efforts to confront previously unexplored issues with honesty and compassion. The title, which locks the film in an early '60s time capsule, says it all, though: for all his hard work, intelligence, and stature, Bogarde's character faces a sad and lonely life, isolated from frightened gays and cautious heterosexuals alike. ♫♫♫

1961 100m/C *GB* Dirk Bogarde, Sylvia Syms, Dennis Price, Peter McEnery, Nigel Stock, Donald Churchill, Anthony Nicholls, Hilton Edwards, Norman Bird, Derren Nesbitt, Alan McNaughton, Noel Howlett, Charles Lloyd Pack, John Barrie, John Bennett; *D:* Basil Dearden; *W:* John McCormick, Janet Green. **VHS, Beta**

Victory March

Victory March, filmed in Italy, is a savage examination of military life. Although there are no deaths until the final moment, it drew extended hissing at 1976's San Francisco International Film Festival, largely because director/screenwriter Marco Bellocchio also dabbles with another theme: the greatest enforcers of violence may be its greatest victims. He draws back from exploring this theme on any real depth, but one of the film's most revealing sequences occurs when a captain, played with feeling by Franco Nero, realizes that the tyranny he inflicted on his wife is exactly what drove her away. No one else in the movie emphasizes this as well, and 118 moments of brutality are in no way dismissed with this brief insight. This may be what Bellocchio intended, but by then he has spent a great deal of screen time preparing us for emotional connections between people that never pay off. Bellocchio later made *The Eyes, The Mouth, Henry IV,* and *Devil in the Flesh.* **AKA:** Marcia Trionfale. 🦴🦴♡

1976 118m/C *IT FR GE* Franco Nero, Miou-Miou, Michele Placido, Patrick Dewaere; **D:** Marco Bellocchio; **W:** Marco Bellocchio, Sergio Bazzini; **C:** Franco Di Giacomo; **M:** Nicola Piovani. *NYR*

Village of the Damned

Wolf Rilla's vintage 1960 chiller, *Village of the Damned,* based on John Wyndham's novel, *The Midwich Cuckoos,* was shot in creepy black and white and focused on the efforts of an unlikely married couple to humanize their weird offspring. (Well, if you were 27 years old, gorgeous, brilliant, and sensitive like Barbara Shelley, would 54-year-old GEORGE SANDERS be on YOUR short list of husbands?) The opening shots are beautifully done; the inhabitants of the quiet village of Midwich simply fall asleep mid-activity. The military gets wind of the unexpected afternoon siesta and, predictably, botch the investigation. Nine months later, any woman who's capable of bearing an infant delivers a precocious baby who quickly evolves into a genius demon child with straight blonde hair and spooky eyes. Spookiest of the bunch is Martin Stephens as David, Shelley's son. Stephens made a dozen films in his 12-year-career, becoming progressively less frightening as he entered his teens, but luckily for horror fans, *Village of The Damned* and 1961's *The Innocents* were filmed when Stephens was still at his blood-curdling best. You didn't need to have a bunch of great child actors with Stephens as the ringleader. In the film's finest moments, the grown-ups fight a los-

ing war of nerves with their cool, well spoken, would-be conquerors. The smash status of Rilla's film is partly due to the universal mutual distrust between adults and kids, but mostly because he stuck to basics and kept things simple. *Village of the Damned* is well worth a look on video, especially for 10- or 11-year-old fantasists who'd love to terrify their caretakers into doing everything they say with the help of one cold lethal stare. 🦴🦴🦴♡

1960 78m/B *GB* George Sanders, Barbara Shelley, Martin Stephens, Laurence Naismith, Michael C. Goetz, Michael Gwynn, John Phillips, Richard Vernon, Jenny Laird, Richard Warner, Thomas Heathcote, Charlotte Mitchell, John Stuart, Bernard Archard; **D:** Wolf Rilla; **W:** Wolf Rilla, Stirling Silliphant, George Harley. **VHS, Beta, LV** *MGM, MLB*

A Virgin Named Mary

A Virgin Named Mary is an effective and amusing religious satire by Sergio Nasca, who also made 1974's *The Profiteer.* The title says it all, with the contemporary twist that those who believe in the Virgin Birth the most are the village atheists. **AKA:** Virgine, E Di Nome Maria. 🦴🦴♡

1975 102m/C *IT* Turi Ferro, Andrea Ferreol, Cinzia de Carolis, Renato Pinciroli, Clelia Matania, Leopoldo Trieste, Tino Carraro, Marino Mase, Jean Louis, Sandra Dori; **D:** Sergio Nasca; **W:** Sergio Nasca; **C:** Giuseppe Acquari; **M:** Santa Maria Romitelli. *NYR*

Vortex

Punk/film noir style in which a female private eye becomes immersed in corporate paranoia and political corruption. Its soundtrack, by cast members Lydia Lunch and Adele Bertei, is one of our all-time favorites. Co-scripter and co-director Beth B later scripted and directed 1993's *Two Small Bodies* starring Fred Ward and Suzy Amis, which was just fair, in spite of that cast. 🦴♡

1981 87m/C Lydia Lunch, James Russo, Bill Rice, Richard France, Ann Magnuson, Haoui Montaug, Adele Bertei, Bill Landis; **D:** Scott B, Beth B; **W:** Scott B, Beth B; **M:** Lydia Lunch, Adele Bertei. **VHS** *ICA*

Waiting for the Moon

Were Linda Hunt and Andrew Lloyd Webber separated at birth? Just curious. Hunt is Alice B. Toklas and Linda Bassett is writer Gertrude Stein (1874-1946) in this dreary American Playhouse telecast about their lives which inexplicably won the Grand Jury Prize at 1987's Sundance Film Festival. Try watching it on PBS sometime: zzzzzz.... **WOOF!**

1987 (PG) 88m/C Linda Hunt, Linda Bassett, Andrew McCarthy, Bruce McGill, Jacques Boudet, Bernadette LaFont; **D:** Jill Godmilow. Sundance Film Festival '87: Grand Jury Prize. **VHS, Beta, Closed Caption** *FOX*

Walk on the Wild Side

The BBC has always been fascinated by American pop iconography, and *Walk on the Wild Side* might easily qualify to be a segment on A&E's *Biography* series. This portrait of the drag queens in Andy Warhol's factory is chockful of clips about what went wrong and when and why. Many of Warhol's superstars are no longer around; did his films provide valuable documentation for losers who would have died anyway, without leaving a trace, or was there something about the starmaking process itself that sped up their destruction? Don't look for the answers here, although Joe Dallesandro's appearance at 45 lends validity to Howard Hawks' assertion that real stars walk on the set thinking that everyone wants to lay them. Time has definitely been unkind to *Trash*'s once baby-faced star. 🦴🦴🦴

1993 40m/C *GB* **D:** James Marsh. *NYR*

Walking and Talking

One provincial critic recently expressed enormous concern for the career of Anne Heche, now that everyone knows that she and Ellen DeGeneres are an item; will audiences be able to accept a gay woman in a straight role? Well, why not? We've been accepting gay actors and actresses in straight roles since the movies began, the only difference is that the gossip and whispers have been replaced with dialogue and information. Anyway, the answer is, yeah, sure. If you caught *Walking and Talking* in theatres and saw Heche doing an absolutely credible job as a young woman in love, her performance hasn't changed since the video release. *Walking and Talking* is a sharp and funny look at the friendship of two women as they adjust to new men and new interests in their lives. It also shows what ought to be the very first etiquette guideline about what NOT to leave on a best friend's answering machine! And then there is a well observed vignette on the pointless nature of obsession: Amelia (Catherine Keener) finds herself following a guy around when she'd felt nothing for him prior to their one-night stand. She needs to know why she was frozen out more than she needs him, although the distinction escapes her during her dogged pursuit of this virtual stranger. Laura (Heche) has her share of self doubts masquerading as crises; she focuses on her boyfriend Frank's (Todd Field) mole until it takes on gigantic dimensions and she wakes up screaming bloody murder in the middle of the night. She gets a mild crush on another guy after a casual meeting. Nicole Holofcener's quirky study of how friendships evolve over time feels authentic; contrast the one-dimensional role Liev Schreiber has in Greg Mottola's *Daytrippers* with the fleshed-out character he has as Andrew here. *Walking and Talking* is a small yet altogether sparkling jewel of a movie. 🦴🦴🦴

1996 (R) 86m/C Anne Heche, Catherine Keener, Liev Schreiber, Todd Field, Kevin Corrigan, Randall Batinkoff, Joseph Siravo, Vinny Pastore, Lynn Cohen, Andrew Holofcener; **D:** Nicole Holofcener; **W:** Nicole Holofcener; **C:** Michael Spiller; **M:** Billy Bragg. Nominations: Independent Spirit Awards '97: Best Actress (Keener), Best Supporting Actor (Corrigan). **VHS, LV, Closed Caption** *MAX*

NICOLE HOLOFCENER
Walking and Talking

The title refers to something that WAS in the movie, but was cut out. There were a lot of flashbacks of Amelia and Andrew's old relationship, the relationship they had, and in one of them, they'd just spent the night together and they're walking down the street, and they're having an intimate moment and Amelia takes Andrew's hand on the street and he runs into someone he knows and immediately takes his hand back, because he doesn't want to be seen holding hands with Amelia. And she loses it and she says, 'What are we doing? What is this? What are we doing?' And he says, 'What do you mean? We're walking down the street and talking,' making it nothing."

The War Room

The Clinton team had been in the White House for less than a year when *The War Room* was released, but in many ways, the campaign and election of 1992 seemed incredibly far away, even then. P. F. Bentley's striking photographs for his book on the campaign, *Portrait of Victory,* were shot entirely in black and white, and these timeless yet pleasantly dated images are the ones we remember best. *The War Room,* the 1993 documentary by D.A. Pennebaker and Chris Hegedus, is further dated since Clinton's campaign team gave the press such generous access to behind-the-scenes strategy-making that we somehow took for granted how unique that was. In this film, the Clintons and Gores are seen largely through news footage, and Pennebaker and Hegedus focus instead on the efforts of James Carville and George Stephanopoulos to orchestrate the attack on George Bush. There are the inevitable segues: a *Star Magazine* representative stands between the now-famous splashy tabloid cover and Gennifer Flowers, trying vainly to pretend that the circus is a dignified press conference. In fact, hardly anything is an accident in a political campaign; the press reports every "disclosure" in the form of late-breaking news, as if all the campaign teams didn't repeatedly feed these so-called leaks until they catch fire. Sometimes, they never do. Carville tried to make something out of a report on Portuguese television that Bush-Quayle campaign materials were printed south of the border with cheap labor. But the story couldn't be nailed down with enough corroborative detail, and eventually it fizzled. Carville was luckier with his efforts to add key phrases to a major campaign speech. Meanwhile, Mary Matalin defended her candidate, George Bush, and 21st century audiences might wish that the personal relationship between Carville and Matalin had been made a little more clear. (How many details do we remember about individual members of past campaign teams, anyway?) As election day approached, both Carville and Stephanopoulos resorted to eerie gallows humor, presumably to stave off last-minute doubts and superstitions. The July, 1993 suicide of longtime

Clinton associate Vince Foster revealed a dark side to the political landscape that we didn't see in the glory days of November, 1992. *The War Room* supplies counterpoint to the old myth of smoke-filled rooms behind closed doors, while fueling a new myth about the folksy value of apparent candor; clearly, all the candor in the world won't blunt the brutality of contemporary politics. 🎞🎞🎞

1993 (PG) 93m/C D: Chris Hegedus, D.A. Pennebaker. National Board of Review Awards '93: Best Feature Documentary; Nominations: Academy Awards '93: Best Feature Documentary. **VHS, LV, Closed Caption** *THV*

Warm Nights on a Slow-Moving Train

Wendy Hughes is among the most gifted actresses in the world today yet her last two Australian films, *Shadows of the Peacock* and *Warm Nights on a Slow-Moving Train* are romantic fluff pieces in which travel represents sexual fulfillment. I can actually see very little difference between *Warm Nights* and the Sigourney Weaver flop *Half Moon Street.* In both films, we are asked to believe that intelligent, well educated women can only achieve a fair rate of exchange for their work if they moonlight as hookers. For all their independent chatter, they make stupid mistakes, act against their stated principles in pursuit of sexual highs, and live out every male fantasy in the book. Two questions: Do you have any trouble with the idea that a woman would willingly become a political assassin at the request of a man with terrific staying power she's bedded only twice? Would this concept seem even more ridiculous if a man agreed to kill a stranger just because a great two-night stand asked him to do it? In a popular film like *Body Heat,* William Hurt is seen as a sexually obsessed schmuck for doing everything femme fatale Kathleen Turner

commands. In *Warm Nights,* Wendy Hughes is just another woman in love. 🎞🎞

1987 (R) 90m/C *AU* Wendy Hughes, Colin Friels, Norman Kaye, John Clayton, Peter Whitford; **D:** Bob Ellis; **W:** Bob Ellis, Denny Lawrence. **VHS, Beta, LV** *PSM, PAR*

The Wash

The Wash is a wise, gentle film about the death of love and its rebirth. Nobu McCarthy portrays a woman who is leaving her husband after 40 years, yet who continues to care about him even though she is no longer in love with him. After watching film after film in which the Japanese male is portrayed as cold and unfeeling and wondering how he could stand such loneliness, viewers finally have an opportunity to see and hear Asian-American writer Philip Kan Kotanda expose the truth about such characters: maybe they cannot stand it any more than the women who love them. The Oscar-nominated actor Mako does a masterful job of revealing all the underlying cracks in the armor. Sab Shimono plays a very different type of man, the one Nobu's character has been yearning for all her life. When she is finally confronted with his kindness and sensitivity, all the old habits that bind her to her husband no longer mean anything. It is rare for a film to wring such extraordinary mileage out of very simple truths about relationships, but Philip Kan Kotanda is a writer with a unique ability to dig beneath rituals and structures. Deeply enhanced by Michael Toshiyuki Uno's intimate direction, *The Wash* provides a memorable and unusual film experience. 🎞🎞🎞

1988 94m/C Mako, Nobu McCarthy, Sab Shimono; **D:** Michael Toshiyuki Uno; **W:** Philip Kan Kotanda; **C:** Walt Lloyd. **VHS, Beta, LV** *ACA*

The Waterdance

Neal Jimenez, who was paralyzed in a 1984 accident, wrote and co-directed *The Waterdance,* an exceptional film about

the trials and tribulations of adjusting to paralysis. Eric Stoltz is wisely cast as Joel, the central character, and Helen Hunt delivers her usual beautifully understated performance as his girlfriend Anna. Wesley Snipes is a flamboyant scene stealer as Ray, who becomes the unlikely friend of Bloss, the bitter white hiker played by William Forsythe. Realistic and funny details make *The Waterdance* a fine video pick. Unaccountably, there were no long lines at the box office for this winning film, co-directed by Michael Steinberg. 🦴🦴🦴

1991 (R) 106m/C Eric Stoltz, Wesley Snipes, William Forsythe, Helen Hunt, Elizabeth Pena, Grace Zabriskie; **D:** Neal Jimenez, Michael Steinberg; **W:** Neal Jimenez; **C:** Mark Plummer; **M:** Michael Convertino. Independent Spirit Awards '93: Best First Feature, Best Screenplay; Sundance Film Festival '92: Best Screenplay, Audience Award. **VHS, LV, Closed Caption** COL, PMS, BTV

Way Down East

Way Down East was severely dated when D.W. Griffith spent the extravagant sum of $175,000 for the rights to turn it into a movie in 1920. Its star, Lillian Gish, was not the only one who wondered about the wisdom of acquiring a creaky piece of Americana which had been familiar to audiences since 1898. Clearly, Griffith realized that the tale of a country girl led astray by a rich adventurer had visceral appeal, and indeed it had and still does, even today. Viewers from other cultures wondered why the fragile Miss Lillian (or even a less virtuous heroine) had to be cast out into the snow by so-called good Christians. And contemporary viewers, realizing the physical dangers Griffith demanded from his cast and crew during a painfully realistic blizzard sequence, still wonder why anyone would put up with such sacrifices for the sake of a movie. But *Way Down East,* with all its flaws, is absolutely spellbinding, especially when Lillian Gish is onscreen. In the course of the story, she is transformed from a gauche poor relation, to an eager young bride, to a grief-stricken mother, to a hard-working family retainer. Like Hester Prynne (a role Miss Gish would later play), this discarded woman grows in strength and character by dealing directly with her limited lot in life, which is far more than can be said for those who ill-treat her. There is nice work by the ensemble players, too, notably the impossibly beautiful Richard Barthelmess as a farm boy who worships Miss Lillian from afar, but it is Gish's and Griffith's triumph all the way. An added bonus on some video transfers is a glistening toned and tinted 35 mm. print, plus a lovely score, personally approved by Griffith. ♫♫♫♫

1920 107m/B Lillian Gish, Richard Barthelmess, Lowell Sherman, Creighton Hale; **D:** D.W. Griffith. **VHS, Beta, LV** *NOS, BAR, VYY*

The Wedding Banquet

The Wedding Banquet is a charade for the benefit of Wai-Tung's parents. He's really gay and living happily with Simon. When tenant Wei-wei (May Chin) suggests marriage to Wai-Tung (Winston Chao) so she can get a green card, he says sure and so does Simon (Mitchell Lichtenstein). And then Wai-Tung's parents (Sihung Lung and Ah-Leh Gua as Mr. and Mrs. Gao) insist on attending the wedding. Ang Lee (*Pushing Hands, Eat Drink Man Woman*) works miracles with a tiny budget; *The Wedding Banquet* is a warm, funny flick, made two years before Lee's Oscar nomination as Best Director for *Sense and Sensibility.* **AKA:** Xiyan; Hsi Yen. ♫♫♫

1993 (R) 111m/C *TW* Winston Chao, May Chin, Mitchell Lichtenstein, Sihung Lung, Ah-Leh Gua; **D:** Ang Lee; **W:** Ang Lee, Neil Peng, James Schamus. Nominations: Academy Awards '93: Best Foreign

Language Film; Golden Globe Awards '94: Best Foreign Film; Independent Spirit Awards '94: Best Actor (Lichtenstein), Best Actress (Chin), Best Director (Lee), Best Film, Best Screenplay, Best Supporting Actress (Gua). **VHS, LV, Closed Caption** *FXV*

Welcome to the Dollhouse

This hilarious view of junior high as seen by 11-year-old Dawn Wiener is Todd Solondz' second film. (His first, 1989's *Fear, Anxiety and Depression* starring himself and Stanley Tucci, was generally panned for being unduly influenced by Woody Allen.) So we don't need to concern ourselves here with the Second Film Syndrome experienced by hot (overpraised) newcomers. Solondz' identification with the plight of his young heroine is total and so is ours. Dawn wears glasses and hair balls and is outshone in every way by her nauseatingly precious little sister, who whirls around in a ballerina costume. When Dawn refuses to apologize to the sister for something or other, her parents order her to remain at the table until she does. The soundtrack goes into a rebellious riff; hours later, Dawn is still sitting there. Then Dawn gets a crush on one of her older brother's no-good study partners (we know he's no good, because we catch him stealing when he comes to the house), and her life is transformed. She grills a former girlfriend of this guy, and when she discovers that they only did things to each other with their fingers, Dawn stares at her own fingers in wonder. It's an 11-year-old moment, something an older, superficially stunning adolescent would never be able to carry off. Dawn's world is dark, miserable, and seemingly endless. We know it isn't, but she doesn't, and Todd Solondz keeps the focus on Dawn's perceptions of events, where it belongs. It is this innocence of the vast future beyond junior high school that distinguishes *Welcome to the Dollhouse* from other coming-of-age stories about children. What 11-year old girl is blessed with ironic detachment, anyway? ♫♫♫♫

W

"High school's better than junior high. They'll call you names, but not as much to your face."

—Dawn's big brother Mark (Matthew Faber) dispenses wisdom in *Welcome to the Dollhouse.*

437

INDEPENDENT FILM GUIDE

TODD SOLONDZ
Welcome to the Dollhouse

Whatever character you're writing about, if you're going to try and make it authentic, it's always difficult. I don't think it makes it particularly more difficult that's it's a little girl then it would be if it were an older man. People often do ask me why a little girl instead of a little boy? Years ago I had made a short film about a little boy, a different kind of character and a different kind of story. I just didn't want to get even close to retreading the same ground. But, more importantly, it's true that little girls do mature somewhat more quickly in certain key ways, and I felt that a little girl might be taken more seriously with regard to her romantic yearnings, and there would be more room for emotional, complex depth and richness, etc. Finally, movies with little girl protagonists never seem to succeed at the box office, so the perversity in my nature, I suppose, rose to the challenge.

"The actress, Heather Matarazzo, is in fact a very well adjusted, gregarious, vivacious little girl who was very capable of drawing that distinction between herself and the character. Had she not been cast in the movie, she would have gone to basketball summer camp and been very happy. She has a certain tomboyish personality, or at least back then when she was eleven and a half, she did.

1995 (R) 87m/C Heather Matarazzo, Brendan Sexton III, Daria Kalinina, Matthew Faber, Angela Pietropinto, Eric Mabius; **D:** Todd Solondz; **W:** Todd Solondz; **C:** Randy Drummond; **M:** Jill Wisoff. Independent Spirit Awards '97: Debut Performance (Matarazzo); Sundance Film Festival '96: Grand Jury Prize; Nominations: Independent Spirit Awards '97: Best Director (Solondz), Best Film, Best Supporting Actor (Faber), Debut Performance (Sexton). **VHS, LV, Closed Caption** *COL*

Wes Craven's New Nightmare

Wes Craven's New Nightmare is a work of imagination and wit from the man who's been scaring us for over 25 years. In this film, he's written nice roles for himself and three participants in 1984's *The Nightmare on Elm Street*: Heather Langencamp, Robert Englund, and John Saxon, plus producers Marianne Maddalena, Robert Shaye, and Sara Risher. They all play themselves, caught up in a new nightmare that's much worse than Freddy Krueger circa 1984. Heather, now a wife and mom, doesn't want to make another horror movie, but bad things start happening, and she's dragged into another bout with Freddy to save her son Dylan (Miko Hughes) and herself. Hughes is a good little actor, and Tracy Middendorf is wonderfully effective as Julie the babysitter. But it's Langencamp's show and she holds our interest and attention for all 112 minutes of this

"I don't think she is an ugly little girl nor do I think the character is an ugly little girl. It's really about all the other children who call her ugly. In fact, I was afraid she was going to be too beautiful for the role. I had to provide certain flourishes that would make it believable that she would have a hard time, and yet not make her so pathetic that the audience would be so alienated from identifying, connecting with her on her journey through this childhood.

"It's true that when I was auditioning kids in the first place that while the kids were very unfazed by the material and recognized its authenticity, the parents were somewhat unsettled. But I'm not a child psychologist or a family therapist. My aim is really just to explore this time of life and to engage an audience, at the same time to recognize with a certain humor what's its about, and also there's a certain poignancy and pain attached to it at the same time.

"It's not comedy with a 'K'. It's funny, audiences seem to respond in two ways in general. Some people walk out and say, 'That's hilarious, it was so funny,' and the other half seem to walk out not laughing and saying 'Oh, my god, that was so sad. I feel that was so painful.' But I think the sources for both responses are present in the movie. That was my goal, I mean as a filmmaker because that is what draws me in: what is both simultaneously very funny and very sad at the same time."

TODD SOLONDZ also wrote and directed 1989's *Fear, Anxiety and Depression*.

enthralling yarn. In addition to the horrific aspects of the plot, Craven does a clever job scraping past our jaded response to cinematic terrors and jabbing at a much more basic source of fear. 🦴🦴🦴

1994 (R) 112m/C Heather Langenkamp, Robert Englund, Miko Hughes, David Newsom, Tracy Middendorf, Fran Bennett, John Saxon, Wes Craven, Robert Shaye, Sara Risher, Marianne Maddalena; **D:** Wes Craven; **W:** Wes Craven; **C:** Mark Irwin; **M:** J. Peter Robinson. Nominations: Independent Spirit Awards '95: Best Film. **VHS, LV, Closed Caption** *NLC*

The Whales of August

Lindsay Anderson's *The Whales of August*

features one luminous piece of work by Miss Lillian Gish, then in her 95th year, and four excellent performances by Bette Davis, then 79, Harry Carey, Jr., then 66, and Vincent Price and Ann Sothern, both then 78. The script by playwright David Berry is not so hot, with a confusing time-line and a fuzzy psychological grasp of its elderly characters. Berry offers a younger person's view of how older people see life. As two sisters bound by blood, finances, and circumstances, Davis' blind character might well wind up a crabby whiner, but Miss Lillian would not be blamed for giving Sis a good shaking instead of serenely waiting on her hand and foot. Price is so irresistible as a charming scrounge who tries to horn in on this pair that when he

VINCENT PRICE

On Bette Davis and Lillian Gish in the film *The Whales of August*

They're a whale of a pair of actresses, for sure. They're extraordinary ladies. I've known them both all my theatrical life. It was a joy to work with them, to see these people of extraordinary age—and I'm no chicken, so I can tell you—to see them work and go through really a very unpleasant and difficult location and come out with such performances. They really are extraordinary.

"Bette and I are friends, and have been for a long time. I did a film [1939's *Elizabeth and Essex*] with her a long time ago with Errol Flynn. We're not intimate friends. I don't know an awful lot of people in this business that well, but we got along marvelously well and enjoyed each other's company. She's a marvelous actress, I think probably the number one actress of the screen in the variety of roles she's played and the intensity in the comedy and the tragedy. A really extraordinary lady.

"Lillian is one of those miracles. She can only be referred to as a miracle, because I think the first movie I ever saw in my life was with Lillian Gish. To work with her is a fresh experience which doesn't happen that often."

makes his graceful exit from the plot with resignation, he takes much of the film's lightness of tone with him. Ann Sothern, too, is seen to good effect as a well meaning Maine friend. But Miss Lillian, defying every assumption about what a woman in her tenth decade should be, acts rings around all these outstanding pros, drawing every bit of emotion from each line, gesture, and expression, in a subtle yet richly textured portrayal that's as powerful as anything she did on film since her 1912 debut. ♫♫♫

1987 91m/C Lillian Gish, Bette Davis, Vincent Price, Ann Sothern, Mary Steenburgen, Harry Carey Jr., Tisha Sterling, Margaret Ladd; **D:** Lindsay Anderson; **W:** David Berry. National Board of Review Awards '87: Best Actress (Gish); National Media Owl Awards '88: First Prize; Nominations: Academy Awards '87: Best Supporting Actress (Sothern). **VHS, Beta, LV, 8mm** *NLC*

What Happened Was...

Co-workers Jackie and Michael discover that neither is what s/he appears to be on the first date from Hell. Well acted and well observed, but EXCRUCIATINGLY detailed. Not a good video bet on anyone's first date. ♫♫

1994 (R) 92m/C Tom Noonan, Karen Sillas; **D:** Tom Noonan; **W:** Tom Noonan; **C:** Joe DeSalvo; **M:** Lodovico Sorret. Sundance Film Festival '94: Best Screenplay, Grand Jury Prize; Nominations: Independent Spirit Awards '95: Best Actress (Sillas), First Screenplay. **VHS** *HMK*

Where Angels Fear to Tread

Where Angels Fear to Tread was E. M. Forster's first novel and it is filled with all the ambitious flaws of a 26-year-old writer who wants to say something important but doesn't quite know how to say it yet. His subsequent novels, *A Room with a View, Maurice,* and *A Passage to India,* reflected Forster's greater understanding of human nature, but when he wrote *Angels,* he was still struggling to understand people. Charles Sturridge's movie, sticking reverently to the text as it does, is therefore just as flawed as its original source material. *Angels* attempts to show how silly the British are to pre-judge the Italian culture, so we get 112 minutes of assorted twits thinking like fools and behaving like beasts. The wonderful Helen Mirren appears, all too briefly, as a rich widow who marries a broke Italian (Giovanni Guidelli). Judy Davis and Rupert Graves play Mirren's in-laws, who dash off to Italy to bring Mirren's Italian baby back to England, whether the father likes it or not. Helena Bonham Carter is on hand as a much-interested bystander and is the voice of reason in the film. A lot of melodramatic stuff happens in the film and there are plenty of discussions where people explain themselves and the world around them. 1905 readers probably read *Where Angels Fear to Tread* and hoped for better things from its talented young author. But today's Forster buffs and filmmakers seem to regard every Forster work, even this uneven effort, as a masterpiece. *Where Angels Fear to Tread* will not play well on video, as many of the sequences are darkly lit and hard to see. The soundtrack is also muddy, and some of Forster's elegant language is difficult to hear. That said, the cast, especially Davis and Mirren, is splendid, and you're unlikely to see a more sympathetic portrait of a twit than the one played by Rupert Graves. 🦴🦴

1991 (PG) 112m/C *GB* Rupert Graves, Helena Bonham Carter, Judy Davis, Helen Mirren, Giovanni Guidelli, Barbara Jefford, Thomas Wheatley, Sophie Kullman; *D:* Charles Sturridge; *M:* Rachel Portman. **VHS, LV, Closed Caption** *NLC*

The Whistle Blower

The British are fascinated with members of its upper classes who continue to enjoy their positions of privilege while betraying Queen and country as Soviet spies. This obsession has evolved into plays and films like *Another Country* and *Blunt,* and many books, one of which, by John Hale, was released as *The Whistle Blower,* starring Michael Caine in the title role. The most intriguing question, why does a pampered aristocrat turn traitor?, is one that screenwriter Julian Bond does not really try to answer in depth. There is still plenty of meat, however, in this gripping story of an agonized father's attempts to uncover the mystery behind the death of his much-loved son. Espionage is shown as a venomous game, mostly populated by players who neither know nor understand its true rules. As always, Michael Caine is excellent as Frank Jones, the businessman whose unquestioning faith in England is shattered by what he learns about her intelligence agencies. He is surrounded by an outstanding cast. James Fox portrays a chilling agent who euphemizes his deadliest work as "assessing the damage." Nigel Havers, in a slender but memorable role, turns in an appealing performance. Barry Foster's over-the-top style is well suited to his portrait of a man way out of his league. Sir John Gielgud, in a part clearly fashioned after Sir Anthony Blunt, remains a charming puzzle. Intelligence agent Gordon Jackson shares a brief, classy sequence with David Langton. It is stylishly directed, as is the entire movie, by David's son, Simon Langton, in his feature film debut after a long apprenticeship on British television, including *Upstairs, Downstairs.* One character observes that "the secret world" of British

I did it [*What Happened Was...*] as a play first, which I'm not supposed to say. I had been writing film scripts for a really long time, and I actually didn't show them to anyone. Then I showed a couple of scripts to some people at an agency in L.A. and they said I could write, but I had to write things more commercially oriented. So I started writing murder mysteries because I thought that's what would sell, and the first script that I wrote sold like immediately. I immediately got into the same kind of movies, writing them, the kind that I usually acted in. That was OK, but it wasn't really the kind of things I wanted to be writing, so about two and a half years ago I decided just to not do anything for about a year, just to see what would happen. After about six months this story came out of me kind of as a play. I have my own theatre in New York and I wanted to just do it as a play and see what would happen. In the course of doing it as a play, I really liked doing it; I didn't want

intelligence is "beyond the law." It is revealing that the Royal Family serves as the film's framing device; royalty has always been an attractive smokescreen for political shenanigans. As Frank Jones, Michael Caine lends an individual's conscience to the cold-blooded spying activities of today. If innocents are murdered when they stumble onto the truth and their bereaved families are neutralized with charges of insanity when they question the wisdom of such policies, if treacherous courtiers have tea with the Queen while intelligence agencies "assess the damage" they have done, the division between good and evil blurs. *The Whistle Blower* makes a penetrating stab at showing who the enemy might really be. 🦴🦴🦴

1987 98m/C *GB* Michael Caine, Nigel Havers, John Gielgud, James Fox, Felicity Dean, Gordon Jackson, Barry Foster, David Langton; **D:** Simon Langton; **W:** Julian Bond; **M:** John Scott. **VHS, Beta, LV, Closed Caption** *NLC*

White Mischief

White Mischief is a tale of lust and violence in the Happy Valley region of Kenya. It is based on a true story, and what a story it is: in 1940, Sir Henry Delves Broughton, known as Jock, arrived in Kenya with his beautiful wife Diana. At 27, Diana was 30 years younger than her rich new husband, and it took her all of one day in Nairobi to become attracted to jock's friend Lord Erroll, a dashing 39-year-old peer. The meeting led to an affair, a murder, and a mystery, which writer James Fox claims to solve in his book about the seamy side of Kenya's aristocratic night life. The couple who stir up all the fuss are portrayed by Greta Scacchi and Charles Dance, two physically perfect specimens who, oddly enough, have no sexual chemistry between them at all. Their characters

to stop, so I thought maybe this could make a movie. I had money around from having done these other big-budget movies, and also some other money I got through Sundance and it kind of turned into a movie.

"I did a script at Sundance Film Institute. I went there as a director and they have a summer program. I went there like in 1991 or 1992 with the movie I'd written to see what it would be like to act in something I directed. I'd never tried it. I find it a whole lot easier to direct when I'm acting, and also find it a whole lot easier to act when I am directing. When I'm on the set of movies where I am just acting I tend to get way too involved in the part for one. I also get way too involved in things I have no control over because I am very technically oriented. On movies where I'm acting I spend a lot of time with the sound people usually or the cinematographer to find out what they're doing and I've learned a lot that way. When I act and direct, it becomes very simple for me. It's actually easier than doing either."

TOM NOONAN can be seen as an actor in *Wolfen*, *The Man with One Red Shoe*, *Manhunter*, *The Monster Squad*, *Mystery Train*, *RoboCop 2*, and *Last Action Hero*.

share decidedly earthbound passions: she wants sex and money, he wants money and sex. Michael Radford's script also defines them as a deeply stupid pair, completely lacking in imagination or depth. Our interest shifts, therefore, to the lady's aristocratic husband played with understanding and irony by Joss Ackland, a fine character actor. He is the sort of chap who has been denying reality for nearly 60 years and would probably continue to lead a boring, uneventful life were he not forced to confront his true feelings about his young wife's affair with a cad. Facing himself proves catastrophic for all three, although the film's final blood-letting is a melodramatic shuck. In real life, Sir Jock ended his days alone in a Liverpool hotel room with an overdose of medinal. Well, the director obviously wanted to say some something about the self-indulgent and self destructive aspects of the idle class-

es. Imagine them lolling around on polo grounds and in orgies and on the beaches while Britishers at home were squaring their shoulders against the blitz! John Hurt, Geraldine Chaplin, and Trevor Howard (1916-88) are in it, too. And yet, except for Sarah Miles' sly performance as perhaps the worst woman in Kenya, Radford's concept of decadence is rather too carefully staged, and his understanding of his female characters is nil. If Radford had told the story with simple economy and psychological precision, his moral concerns would still be apparent and have a far greater impact than they do now. In 1994, Radford directed his finest work to date, *The Postman*. 🎬🎬🎬

1988 (R) 108m/C Greta Scacchi, Charles Dance, Joss Ackland, Sarah Miles, John Hurt, Hugh Grant, Geraldine Chaplin, Trevor Howard, Murray Head, Susan Fleetwood, Alan Dobie, Jacqueline Pearce; *D:* Michael Radford; *W:* Michael Radford; *C:* Roger Deakins; *M:* George Fenton. **VHS, Beta, LV, 8mm** *NLC*

INDEPENDENT FILM GUIDE

White Nights

When Maria Schell, then 31, and Marcello Mastroianni, then 34, played Natalia and Mario in *White Nights* in 1957, they were both too mature and worldly to play a pair of innocents. Feodor Dostoevsky's 1848 story, published when he was 27, makes sense for a girl of 17 and a lonely dreamer of 26 in cold St. Petersburg in the midst of the 30-year-reign of Tsar Nicholas I. For all the visual loveliness of the film, there is no getting around the fact that a beautiful, strong-willed woman of Venice in the reign of Elvis Presley is not going to be intimidated by her blind old grandmother who pins their skirts together to protect her. Nor would she wait an entire year for a man (icily played by Jean Marais) who embraced her once and never once wrote to her after he went away. Visconti tries to tackle the implausibility of his updated script by focusing on Mario's incredulous reaction. But if Natalia is in love with a fantasy, Mario's obsession with her fantasy is an absolute fetish. In her 1986 study of *Fascism in Film,* Marcia Landy suggests that in *Ossessione,* Visconti shows that "romantic aspirations are a source of repression, not liberation," and certainly this is true of *White Nights.* Locked into their romantic dreams, Natalia's and Mario's characters remain childlike and powerless in their efforts to control their destinies. Unfortunately, the results seem forced, contrived, and empty. *White Nights* is enhanced by Giuseppe Rotunno's beautiful camerawork, and by the sincerity of its cast, yet ultimately Visconti's emotional distance from the material limits our participation in his self-conscious fairy tale. ✂✂

1957 107m/C *IT* Maria Schell, Jean Marais, Marcello Mastroianni; **D:** Luchino Visconti; **C:** Giuseppe Rotunno; **M:** Nino Rota. **VHS** *FCT*

Who Are the DeBolts and Where Did They Get 19 Kids?

I wonder what's happened to Dorothy and Bob DeBolt and their large and enchanting family in the 20-something years since filmmaker John Korty won both an Oscar and an Emmy for making a documentary about their lives in Piedmont, California. Until it won the Oscar and ABC picked it up, television networks shied away from the project. They claimed it was depressing because many of the DeBolt kids are physically disabled war orphans, and Korty made no attempt to conceal how they adjust to the serious problems they face getting around the world. Two of the littlest girls sat next to me at the San Francisco International Film Festival screening, clearly UNdepressed, and giggling in delight at their movie antics. Korty, who won his first Oscar at 23 in 1964 for *Breaking the Habit,* has made some of television's best movies over the years: *The People, Go Ask Alice, Class of '63, The Autobiography of Miss Jane Pittman* (winner of nine Emmies), *Farewell to Manzanar* (an Emmy nominee), *Forever, The Haunting Passion, Second Sight, The Ewok Adventure, A Deadly Business, Resting Place* (another Emmy nominee), *Baby Girl Scott, They Watch,* and *Redwood Curtain.* 🦴🦴🦴

1978 72m/C D: John Korty; **W:** John Korty; **C:** John Else; **M:** Ed Bogas. Academy Awards '77: Best Feature Documentary. **VHS, Beta** *PYR*

Who Killed Teddy Bear?

Surviving pre-code film festivals provide a forcible reminder of just how much we missed onscreen between 1934 and 1969 when the Production Code had a stranglehold on major studio releases. But occasionally, independent filmmakers of "B" movies were able to slip a little something extra into their pictures that sailed clean past the censors. While moral guardians remained fixated on Anita Ekberg's neckline in 1958's *Screaming Mimi,* director Gerd Oswald revealed a straightforward lesbian relationship in an entirely unstressed manner; it was just there. Seven years later, Phoebe Cates' father Joseph turned out an arty, low-budget study of a Peeping Tom called *Who Killed Teddy Bear?* The star was 26-year-old Sal Mineo, on the verge of a ten-year career slide, despite winning two Oscar nominations by the time he was 21. This grim little story is crammed with homoerotic and autoerotic references throughout, but they're grafted onto a traditional boy-stalks-girl plotline. THAT the censors got, and since the outcome satisfied all the Code requirements, they let everything else go. Contemporary viewers should have a field day with this one; most of Mineo's wardrobe consists of snug underwear, skimpy swim briefs or form-fitting tee shirts and skin-tight jeans. He's a shirtless body builder and porno book browser, too. In contrast, the object of his attentions is almost demure. Athletic Juliet Prowse, long past her glory days in Frank Sinatra and Elvis Presley musicals, only gets one dance number with Mineo, but most of the time she's bundled up in nightgowns, bathrobes, godawful coats, and other terrible fashions and hairstyles of the mid-'60s. (Except she has a full-length mirror in her bedroom reflecting onto the street and she doesn't hang up when she hears heavy breathing on her telephone line.) Cates occasionally strays from the seamy side of obsession with lyrical visual interludes, suggesting the child-like innocence that is destroyed by twisted fantasies. Maybe these are efforts to distract us from the cheaper-than-cheap nightclub where Mineo and Prowse work, as well as from the wretched soundtrack. (They couldn't afford real 1965 chart-toppers, so they hired a couple of guys to write some inadequate approximations.) But for blatant marginal subversions of the dying

Code, you can't beat *Teddy Bear*: detective Jan Murray listens to recorded confessions of perverts while his real-life daughter Diane Moore tries to sleep in the next room; nightclub owner Elaine Stritch protests too much when Prowse accuses her of a lesbian advance; and then there's the definitely weird relationship Mineo has with his sister. For a catalog of sexual paranoia circa 1965, *Who Killed Teddy Bear?* has it all. Don't miss it if you get the chance! 🦴🦴🦴

1965 91m/B Juliet Prowse, Sal Mineo, Jan Murray, Elaine Stritch, Daniel J. Travanti, Diane Moore; *D:* Joseph Cates. *NYR*

The Whole Wide World

Renee Zellweger and Ann Wedgeworth last worked together in *Love and a .45,* not exactly my favorite movie of 1994. This time, they have a better vehicle for their talents, and the Oscar-worthy Vincent D'Onofrio, one of the outstanding character stars of his generation, gets a rare chance to be front and center for the length of a movie. Fans of Conan the Barbarian, Red Sonja, Solomon Kane, King Kull, and Black Turlough aren't going to rush out to rent *The Whole Wide World* simply because it describes a little-known incident in the life of their creator, pulp fiction writer Robert E. Howard. But *The Whole Wide World* will appeal to audiences looking for a thoughtful study of quiet passion, tentatively offered and desperately received. As usual there is a major obstacle: Howard is deeply dependent on his frail mother who, in turn, is frighteningly dependent on him. Their arrangement has worked out just fine for a long time and, as Wedgeworth makes threateningly clear to Zellweger's Novalyne Price, she will brook no interference from outsiders. But the force of Price's feelings for Howard has given her great reserves of courage. She fights for her happiness, and his, all the while knowing it's an uphill battle. Although Howard, who had lived in his own interior world most of his life, wants to

love Price, he can only open his heart to her so far. *The Whole Wide World* will give you a lump in your throat the next time you open your beat-up collector's edition of *Weird Tales.* Based on the book *One Who Walked Alone* by Novalyne Price Ellis. 🦴🦴🦴

1996 (PG) 120m/C Renee Zellweger, Vincent D'Onofrio, Ann Wedgeworth, Harve Presnell, Helen Cates, Benjamin Mouton, Michael Corbett, Marion Eaten, Leslie Berger, Chris Shearer, Sandy Walper, Dell Aldrich, Libby Villari, Antonia Bogdanovich, Elizabeth D'Onofrio, Stephen Marshall; *D:* Dan Ireland; *W:* Michael Scott Myers, Novalyne Price Ellis; *C:* Claudio Rocha; *M:* Hans Zimmer, Harry Gregson-Williams. Nominations: Independent Spirit Awards '97: Best Actress (Zellweger). **VHS** *NYR*

Why Not!

Coline Serreau made her vivid directorial debut with *Why Not!* The former actress explores the relationships of two men and a woman who live happily together in a house in the suburbs. This idyllic menage-a-trois is disrupted by the presence of a young girl who falls in love with one of the inhabitants, but doesn't know how to accept the living arrangements he obviously has no desire to change. In less capable directorial hands, *Why Not!* might be heavy going indeed, but Serreau's picture is blessed with delightful humor and a wonderfully daffy cast. Serreau also LIKES most of her characters, and this lends greatly to her film's overall appeal. In the 1980s, Serreau ignited a cottage industry on both sides of the Atlantic with the domestic comedy, *Three Men and a Cradle.* (An American re-make and a sequel followed.) Her next project was *Mama, There's a Man in Your Bed.* **AKA:** Pourquoi Pas! 🦴🦴🦴

1978 93m/C *FR* Sami Frey, Christine Murillo, Mario Gonzales, Michel Aumont, Nicole Jamet, Mathe Souverbie; *D:* Coline Serreau; *W:* Coline Serreau. *NYR*

Wicked Woman

Wicked Woman is a grade-Z movie with a vengeance, starting with the grungy title

447

INDEPENDENT FILM GUIDE

Opposite page: **Lula (Laura Dern) and Sailor (Nicolas Cage) in *Wild at Heart.***

song, belted with conviction by some cheesy male vocalist, circa 1954. Beverly Michaels IS the Wicked Woman, a gigantic blonde who destroys every life she touches, sort of. Her grubby neighbor down the hall is Percy Helton who'll do ANYTHING for the promise of a cheap thrill with her. Of course, NO ONE in this wonderfully sleazy movie really gets a cheap thrill, but happily, *Wicked Woman* escaped the attention of vigilant Hollywood censors: no one is punished for the film's many violations of the then-strict production code, not even Richard Egan as the bartender who is tempted to bump off his wife after ONE glance at Beverly! The sequence where the beefy Richard Egan is actually jealous of poor little Percy Helton is priceless!!! 🎵🎵🎵

1954 77m/B Beverly Michaels, Richard Egan, Evelyn Scott, Percy Helton, Robert Osterloh; **D:** Russel Rouse. *NYR*

Wild at Heart

At the start of 1947's *The Hucksters,* one of Sidney Greenstreet's sharply etched villains spits on a table. As he was quick to admit, it was a disgusting gesture, but he wanted to make sure that people would remember him. In the opening sequence of David Lynch's *Wild at Heart,* Nicolas Cage's character commits an act so violent and so grisly that you're unlikely ever to forget it. The act also has much the same effect as a shot of Novocaine. If you don't bag the movie at that point, you've already been anesthetized for everything that follows and everything certainly does. *Wild at Heart,* believe it or don't, is a comedy about Sailor Ripley and Lula Pace Fortune, two mixed-up kids who want to be wild at heart together, only her mean old mama Marietta won't leave them alone. Marietta hires killer Marcello Santos to kill Sailor, but he arranges to kill her boyfriend Johnnie Farragut instead. Sailor and Lula have a good time being wild at heart on the road together until they stumble across a fatal accident, which Lula interprets as a bad omen. They move into a crummy motel where she promptly gets sick and doesn't clean up after herself the whole time they are there. At the motel, they meet up with Bobby Peru, a born trouble maker. (You can tell by just by looking at his teeth.) After the trouble, Mariette takes Lula home with her until the climax of the movie when the Good Fairy brings Sailor and Bobby back together again—just like in the movies! (Or maybe just like in David Lynch movies.) Only in *Wild at Heart* will you see Nicolas Cage do a movie-long Elvis Presley impersonation in his very best Rattlesnake skin jacket. (Yes, he sings "Love Me Tender," too.) Only in *Wild at Heart* will you see the most amazing collection of bric-a-brac from hell. (Where DOES Lynch find all these radios with big bronze horses on top?) Only in *Wild at Heart* will you see a vision of an absolutely insane world accompanied by Lynch's crushing self-confidence and his equally crushing Sunday school morality. But *Wild at Heart* MOVES, it's funny, it's never boring, and it won't remind you of anyone else in the universe, except of course, David Lynch, trying to top himself in true Busby Berkeley fashion: tossing everything into this movie except for phallic bananas. And who NEEDS phallic bananas when you have Nicolas Cage, Laura Dern, Diane Ladd, Willem Dafoe, Isabella Rossellini (in a bad wig), Harry Dean Stanton, Crispin Glover, Grace Zabriskie, J.E. Freeman, Freddie Jones, Sherilyn Fenn, PLUS Sheryl Lee chewing up the scenery? 🎵🎵🎵🎵

1990 (R) 125m/C Nicolas Cage, Laura Dern, Diane Ladd, Willem Dafoe, Isabella Rossellini, Harry Dean Stanton, Crispin Glover, Grace Zabriskie, J.E. Freeman, Freddie Jones, Sherilyn Fenn, Sheryl Lee; **D:** David Lynch; **W:** David Lynch; **C:** Frederick Elmes; **M:** Angelo Badalamenti. Cannes Film Festival '90: Best Film; Independent Spirit Awards '91: Best Cinematography; Nominations: Academy Awards '90: Best Supporting Actress (Ladd). **VHS, Beta, LV, Closed Caption** *CCB, MED, IME*

The Wild Party

Immediately after delivering his second Oscar-winning performance in *Lust for*

Life, Anthony Quinn made two independent films for Oscar-winning art director Harry Horner. *The Wild Party,* made for Security Pictures, was the second. Horner directed several films between 1952 and 1956 before returning to art direction. (He would be nominated again in 1969 for *They Shoot Horses, Don't They?*) Imagine, if you can, Quinn, Jay Robinson, Kathryn Grant, and Nehemiah Persoff as...Beatniks. Quinn, then 41, is an over-the-hill football hero (uh-oh) named Big Tom Kupfen. Robinson, then 26, plays Gage Freeposter as a coded, but unmistakably gay hotel hustler. The future Mrs. Bing Crosby, then 23, plays Honey in some sort of a drug haze, although chemicals other than alcohol are nowhere in sight. And Persoff, then 36, is Kicks Johnson, the piano playing narrator, who's strung on Honey, who's strung on Tom, who's strung on rich Erica London (Carol Ohmart, then 28) who ISN'T strung on her rich fiancee Lt. Mitchell (Arthur Franz, then 36) but on Tom, although she doesn't want to be. Sounds sudsy, and the script IS, but Horner's interpretation isn't, and Quinn and Ohmart (who are both excellent) DEFINITELY aren't. Their characters strike genuine sexual sparks together in spite of themselves. (Tom's lamenting his long-lost past and the Lady Erica just wants to be turned ON for a change.) Paul Stewart and Barbara Nichols appear in, alas, just one sequence. Nestor Paiva is his usual colorful self as a club owner named Branson, and even the expository role of an articulate wino is deftly played by William Phipps. The brooding cinematography is by the great Sam Leavitt (Oscar winner for *The Defiant Ones* and nominee for *Anatomy of a Murder* and *Exodus*). The critics blasted *The Wild Party* and it went absolutely nowhere, but at least it isn't smug and complacent as so many 1956 flicks are. Moreover, it contains enough fascinating elements to warrant a video release. The television prints appear to have been shorn by at least ten minutes, and considering the direction of Quinn's

and Ohmart's psychosexual tango, we're more than a little curious about what's missing. 🦴🦴🦴

1956 91m/B Anthony Quinn, Carol Ohmart, Arthur Franz, Jay Robinson, Kathryn Grant, Nehemiah Persoff, Paul Stewart, Barbara Nichols, Jana Mason, William Phipps, Maureen Stephenson, Nestor Paiva; **D:** Harry Horner; **W:** John McPartland; **C:** Sam Leavitt; **M:** Ruddy Bregman. *NYR*

Wild West

Wild West: Cute idea, dumb execution. Not everything that comes out of the hallowed halls of London's Channel Four is an instant classic on the level of *My Beautiful Laundrette.* Three Pakistani brothers form a Country Western band called the Honky Tonky Cowboys. Their ultimate destination is Nashville, but on the road to fame and fortune, the oldest brother Zaf (Naveen Andrews) falls for Rifat (Sarita Choudhury), a beautiful woman married to a real churl. Strictly on the basis of his strong attraction to her, Zaf decides, without ever hearing her sing a note, that Rifat is the ideal leader for the band. She is. But the money men only want her, not the brothers. In a staggeringly cliched sequence that's right in keeping with everything else in *Wild West,* Rifat, Zaf, and the brothers all do the right thing, the credits roll, and that's that. *Wild West* is a cute movie to watch at home on a foggy London night, but it's pretty thin stuff on the big screen. *Mississippi Masala* fans may want to catch it for the always watchable Sarita Choudhury. 🦴🦴

1993 83m/C *GB* Naveen Andrews, Sarita Choudhury, Ronny Jhutti, Ravi Kapoor; **D:** David Attwood; **W:** Harwant Bains. **VHS** *THV*

The Windsors: A Royal Family

Four more hours on *The Windsors?* What is there left to be said about what may be the most chronicled family of all time? A great deal, actually, as can be seen in a 1994 documentary available through MPI

Home Video. What distinguishes this historical overview of Britain's royal family is an impending sense of closure. The choice of the narrator, Janet Suzman, is revealing. Suzman won an Oscar nomination for playing the doomed Czarina in *Nicholas and Alexandra,* and her sober voice is a steady reminder that the Windsors are a dying breed, one of the few dynasties permitted to retain their privileges and titles in a century when many other monarchies were swept away by wars and revolutions. Ruthlessness and shrewdness were essential at the outset. King George V refused to help his Russian cousins, fearing that their presence in his country might hasten the end of his newly retitled family's reign. His epileptic youngest son was hidden from public view until his early death. Strong ties to Germany were severed. Even George V's own premature death was orchestrated by his doctor so that it could be announced in the morning edition of the *London Times*. But nothing could be done to ease the Edward VII situation, which continued with his grandson Edward VIII and with the current Prince of Wales. The British monarchy requires that its heirs have virtually nothing to do for most of their adult lives. With no real role to play, these Prince Charmings can and do get into inevitable mischief while waiting for the King or Queen to die. It took a brush with death to restore the future Edward VII to the affections of the British people. The future Edward VIII was quoted in *Time* magazine making dark predictions about his future many years before his actual abdication. And Charles, well into middle age, continues to twiddle his thumbs and whine about Daddy. Andrew Morton observed that "When historians review the reign of Queen Elizabeth II they will point to a weakness and an overindulgence at the top that allowed an unnecessary degree of drift and damage within the family to occur." The most intriguing element of this 1994 documentary is that the Queen's friends and family candidly discuss the Windsors on camera, in addition to the usual assortment of biographers, journalists, and gadflies. Many of the carefully chosen and well researched film clips are unfamiliar to contemporary audiences. Clearly, the producers have done their homework and do in fact develop fresh insights about their increasingly vulnerable subjects. Who are the Windsors and why are they necessary? The British people are suckers for violent threats to the Establishment, and historically, the monarchy has often been revitalized as a result of such tragedies, so who knows? 𝄞𝄞𝄞

1994 228m/C *GB* **D:** Kathy O'Neill, Stephen White, Annie Fienburgh; **M:** Michael Bacon. **VHS** *MPI*

Wings of Desire

Did you ever see a movie that everyone in the world was raving about, that won a fistful of awards, that was considered the director's masterpiece, and that did absolutely nothing for you, so you shut up about it in mixed company? And then the director made a sequel five years later, so you disqualified yourself from reviewing it, but the sequel did not become the subject of mixed company, so at least you didn't have to go into seclusion. If you deify the projector that unleashes *Wings of Desire,* you are probably right. *It's a Wonderful Life* and *2001: A Space Odyssey* are also considered by many to be the masterpieces of Frank Capra and Stanley Kubrick, directors who mean much more to me than Wim Wenders does, so I've listened to skillions of explanations about why I should love those flicks, too, and I don't. Damiel (Bruno Ganz) and Cassiel (Otto Sander) are Der Himmel uber Berlin (Angels over Berlin). Ganz' angel falls in love with Marion, a circus acrobat (Solveig Dommartin), and decides to be mortal again. Curt Bois (1900-91), who played the pickpocket in *Casablanca,* is in it, too, as Homer, and Peter Falk is sublime as himself. Combined running time of *Wings of Desire* and the sequel *Angel in the Pizza Parlor*—scratch that—*Faraway, So Close*: four and a half hours. Why do angels see the world in black and white? I give it four bones for the cognoscenti, but for myself, no comment. **AKA:** Der Himmel Uber Berlin.

1988 (PG-13) 130m/C *GE* Bruno Ganz, Peter Falk, Solveig Dommartin, Otto Sander, Curt Bois; **D:** Wim Wenders; **W:** Wim Wenders, Peter Handke; **C:** Henri Alekan; **M:** Jurgen Knieper. Independent Spirit Awards '89: Best Foreign Film; Los Angeles Film Critics Association Awards '88: Best Cinematography, Best Foreign Film; New York Film Critics Awards '88: Best Cinematography; National Society of Film Critics Awards '88: Best Cinematography. **VHS, Beta, LV** *ORI, GLV, MOV*

Wired

There are lousy movies and then there is *Wired,* the film that will set the standard for bad screen biographies for years to come. Remember *Reefer Madness*? *Cocaine Fiends*? *Maniac*? *Wired* may be even more laughable than watching all three of those turkeys on a triple bill at the grungiest flea pit you can imagine. It's hard to believe that, in 1964, Larry Peerce directed *One Potato, Two Potato,* one of the best movies about an interracial marriage ever made. And he was attracted by the Earl MacRauch SCRIPT for *Wired*? Here's the premise: Michael Chiklis as John Belushi comes back to Earth as a ghost with guardian angel Ray Sharkey. He revisits all his old haunts (yes, producer Ed *The Royal Love Story of Charles and Diana* Feldman compares *Wired* to a Frank Capra comedy so maybe the screenwriter is a public domain channel junkie hooked on *It's a Wonderful Life*). Belushi watches himself with Dan Ayckroyd, with hip wife Judy, and with Billy Preston who plays himself. Meanwhile, *Washington Post* reporter Bob Woodward is doing some SERIOUS journalism. How serious? "Well, John, I think I'll play an after-the-fact voyeur while Cathy Smith gives you the fatal injection, how about THAT?" This, and I am not kidding, is the climax of the picture. Watch Belushi plead for a hit. Watch Cathy Smith try to find a vein on her own discolored arm before she shares her stash with her groveling victim. Watch Belushi shiver, listen to his death rattle, and then, as an extra special added attraction, see and hear him scream, "How about you, Woody? Want a hit?" UNBELIEVABLE. Even if you get off on crawling into the grave with dead movie stars via the constantly updated classic *Too Stupid to Live*—sorry!—*Too Young to Die, Wired* isn't worth 112 minutes of your time. Mis-cast Michael Chiklis, who is not without talent, went on to star in the title role of ABC's *The Commish* (1991-95) opposite Theresa Saldana. Mary Lambert's *Siesta,* Alan J. Pakula's *See You in the Morning,* plus *Wired* win our nomination for a triple bill in hell. **WOOF!**

1989 (R) 112m/C Michael Chiklis, Ray Sharkey, Patti D'Arbanville, J.T. Walsh, Gary Groomes, Lucinda Jenney, Alex Rocco, Jere Burns, Billy Preston; **D:** Larry Peerce; **W:** Earl MacRauch; **M:** Basil Poledouris. **VHS, Beta, LV** *LIV*

Wish You Were Here

Considerable controversy surrounded the making of *Wish You Were Here* because of its sexual candor and because its star was then just 16 years old. Yet Emily Lloyd's performance as the emotionally battered Linda is one of the most heartfelt and authentic portraits of a teen ever seen on film. You can always tell when Linda's guts have been ripped out—her sarcasm goes into high gear. Equally good is Tom Bell's seedy portrayal of a grungy older projectionist in dark glasses who stalks her in shadowy alleys and plays busy mitts with her when Daddy's out of the room. There is no nudity and there is nothing—repeat—nothing erotic about their scenes together. What is explicit is the enormous resilience of Linda's character as she survives repeated rejections by her father and the subsequent men in her life. 🦴🦴🦴

1987 92m/C *GB* Emily Lloyd, Tom Bell, Clare Clifford, Barbara Durkin, Geoffrey Hutchings, Charlotte Barker, Chloe Leland, Trudy Cavanagh, Jesse Birdsall, Geoffrey Durham, Pat Heywood; **D:** David Leland; **W:** David Leland; **M:** Stanley Myers. British

Anjelica Huston in
The Witches.

Academy Awards '87: Best Original Screenplay; National Society of Film Critics Awards '87: Best Actress (Lloyd). **VHS, Beta, LV** _FRH, TVC_

The Witches

We never could understand why so-called Mai Zetterling fans were always sighing about her looks because she couldn't stay 16 years old forever. To us, Mai Zetterling (1925-94), was beautiful and brilliant and never more so than in her lovely swan song as the 65-year-old grandmother in Nicolas Roeg's charming film adaptation of Roald Dahl's prize-winning fantasy, _The Witches_. As Helga, Zetterling perfectly captures the essence of everyone's favorite grandmother: she is completely tuned into her young grandson Luke, she doesn't dismiss his dreams or his nightmares, she helps him out of every imaginable scrape, and gives him a big kiss to encourage him to fight his own battles. Newcomer Jasen Fisher is equally endearing as Luke, not only as a vulnerable little seven-year-old boy but also in his transformation as a resourceful mouse, determined to protect other kids from the same fate. Anjelica Huston is appropriately flamboyant as the Grand High Witch who issues the order to her followers that all the children of England are to be changed into mice. By the time the Grand High Witch arrives on the scene, we've already been alerted to the tell-tale signs of every true witch: their purple eyes, their lack of toes and, most important of all, their deep aversion to children. _The Witches_ was among the late Jim Henson's last projects and his influence is clear as executive producer, not only in the striking make-up for the witches, but also in the appealing transformations that occur when Luke and other little boys are changed into mice. Director Roeg retains an atmosphere of wonder throughout the film's 92-minute running time and the color work on this picture is especially lovely. Worth noting among the supporting cast are Brenda (_Secrets and Lies_) Blethyn and the very funny Rowan Atkinson (hilarious as the minister in 1994's _Four Weddings and a Funeral_). Atkinson, a great comedy favorite in Great Britain, is a genuine side-splitter, etching his portrayal of the world's slimiest hotel manager in acid. _The Witches_ works effectively both as a satire and as a tale of terror and is highly recommended for free spirits of all ages. 🎬🎬🎬🎬

1990 (PG) 92m/C Anjelica Huston, Mai Zetterling, Jasen Fisher, Rowan Atkinson, Charlie Potter, Bill Paterson, Brenda Blethyn, Jane Horrocks; **D:** Nicolas Roeg; **W:** Allan Scott; **M:** Stanley Myers. Los Angeles Film Critics Association Awards '90: Best Actress (Huston); National Society of Film Critics Awards '90: Best Actress (Huston). **VHS, Beta, LV, 8mm, Closed Caption** _WAR, FCT, ORI_

With You and Without You

This exceptional, lovely Russian film begins with abduction, then evolves into a story of love and survival. Its then-youthful director gives his characters resourcefulness, strength, and courage and sets them against a difficult background. The two leads infuse their roles with a gutsy tenderness that is extremely effective. Based on M. Shetov's story, "Stepanida Basyrina." 🎵🎵🎵

1974 86m/C *RU* Marina Nejelova, Juosas Budraitis, Stanislaw Borodkin; **D:** Rodion Nakhapetov; **W:** Alexander Popov; **C:** Sergei Saizev; **M:** Rigdan Trozjuk. *NYR*

Withnail and I

There's nostalgic drek about the 1960s and then there's the bracing dark comedy *Withnail and I.* Who better to separate fantasy from reality about that era than George Harrison and Richard Starkey (AKA Ringo Starr)? As a spur to struggling creative geniuses, The Beatles' Apple was worm-ridden from Day One, but Handmade Films, Harrison's independent film company, did ensure that intriguing small films like this one saw the light of day. (The roster of Handmade Films also includes *Life of Brian, Time Bandits, Privates on Parade, Water, Track 29, Powwow Highway, How to Get Ahead in Advertising, Cold Dog Soup, Nuns on the Run,* and *The Raggedy Rawney,* demonstrating that there WAS an audience for well made indies. In the process, Handmade Films enjoyed great success for well over a decade.) The out-of-work title characters, Richard E. Grant and Mark McGann, escape their drug-and-cockroach-ridden London apartment to spend the weekend from hell in the rainy countryside where Withnail's chubby gay uncle Monty (Richard Griffiths) soliloquizes about vegetables and makes a pass at the totally freaked-out "I." Writer/director Bruce Robinson does a brilliant job translating his

vividly detailed novel to the screen, fully aware of the significance of the last few weeks of 1969, yet skillfully avoiding the trap of syrup-laden myopia 6,570 mornings after the fact. 🎵🎵🎵

1987 (R) 108m/C *GB* Richard E. Grant, Paul McGann, Richard Griffiths, Ralph Brown, Michael Elphick; **D:** Bruce Robinson; **W:** Bruce Robinson; **M:** David Dundas. **VHS, Beta, LV** *FCT*

The Wizard of Loneliness

The Wizard of Loneliness, a pile of nostalgic goo (although another word also comes to mind) from American Playhouse will eventually wind up on public television, interrupted by excruciating pledge breaks which will run a tight race to rival this film's boredom level. Lukas Haas, whose large brown eyes and riveting presence stole *Witness* and *The Lady in White* from award-winning adult actors, delivers a credible performance in an impossible, unsympathetic role. Lea Thompson and John Randolph, two fine and much underrated actors, also give their roles far more texture than is provided by John Nichols' novel. There was a sharply observed immediacy about 1987's British wartime valentine, *Hope and Glory,* which *Wizard of Loneliness* lacks. Set in a Vermont small town, *Wizard* seizes on obvious and not always accurate symbols of 1944: the Prince of Wales, when none existed between 1936 and 1958, *Life* magazines, 1988-style frankness about 1944-style sexual frustrations, yellow filters over the camera lenses, and trend-setting 1934 fashions. (Even in Vermont, they received mail-order clothing catalogues.) There is the obligatory goofball escapee from the trenches whom everyone protects (for reasons best known to the screenwriter) even after he punches Lea in the stomach and smashes a glass against his little son's forehead. Hey, without this wretchedly acted character, there would be no anti-war statement. Just in case we don't get the point, there is a parallel sequence

W

"How do we make it die?"

——A live chicken presents a problem for a very hungry Richard E. Grant in *Withnail and I.*

involving a large white male rabbit and his newly born offspring. (And everyone knows what fascists rabbits ran be.) Even if you ignore the sluggish pacing, the obnoxious dialogue, and the thematic falseness, you are still stuck with Jenny Bowen's leaden direction. Or then again, maybe not. **WOOF!**

1988 (PG-13) 110m/C Lukas Haas, Lea Thompson, John Randolph, Lance Guest, Anne Pitoniak, Jeremiah Warner, Dylan Baker; **D:** Jenny Bowen; **W:** Nancy Larson, Jenny Bowen; **C:** Richard Bowen; **M:** Michel Colombier. **VHS, Beta, LV, Closed Caption** *NO*

The Woman in Question

I've never understood why talented Jean Kent didn't become a bigger star than she did. She was attractive in an evil, insolent, menacing sort of way that was just right for noir films like this one. For that matter,

I've never understood why this fine Anthony Asquith film isn't better known than it is, either. Jean Kent is a fortune teller named Astra, who is already dead when the story begins. Who done it? Was it her sister, Catherine, and her fiancee, Bob Baker (Susan Shaw and Dirk Bogarde)? Was it the charlady (Hermione Baddeley)? How about a shopkeeper named Pollard (Charles Victor) or Murray the sailor (John McCallum)? Each has a different story to tell and Astra seems to be a different person to every one of them. It's a terrific part for any actress and Kent makes the most of it. She's so good that it's stunning to realize that Kent, only 29, had just one more success with Asquith (1951's *The Browning Version*) before her career sunk into a downward slide from which it never recovered. By 1957 and 1958, she was way down on the cast list in *The Prince and the Showgirl* and *Bonjour*

Tristesse. Kent kept working (she can be seen in a bit in 1976's *Shout at the Devil*) and I even saw an actress billed as Jean Kent in a *Lovejoy* episode, but she looked nothing at all like an aging fortune teller once known as Astra. Other Kent titles on video: *Man of Evil, Madonna of the Seven Moons, The Wicked Lady, The Magic Bow, Sleeping Car to Trieste, The Gay Lady,* and *The Haunted Strangler.* **AKA:** Five Angles on Murder. 𝄞𝄞𝄞

1950 82m/B *GB* Jean Kent, Dirk Bogarde, Susan Shaw, Duncan MacRae, John McCallum, Hermione Baddeley, Charles Victor, Lana Morris, Vida Hope, Joe Linnane, Duncan Lament, Bobbie Scroggins, Anthony Dawson, John Boxer, Julian D'Albie, Josephine Middleton, Everley Gregg, Albert Chevalier, Richard Pearson; **D:** Anthony Asquith; **W:** John Cresswell; **C:** Desmond Dickinson; **M:** John Wooldridge. **VHS** *HMV*

Women on the Verge of a Nervous Breakdown

How often have you seen an absolutely magnificent woman trash herself relentlessly over a jerk? Then you see HIM and wonder what all the fuss was about. Hollywood has supplied us with stunning examples of this phenomenon: observe Bette Davis or Joan Crawford work themselves into suicidal despair over assorted male contract players. Or watch Italy's Anna Magnani pine away because Ben Gazzara or Aldo Fabrizi doesn't care about her. Into this distinguished gallery of noble sufferers, please add Carmen Maura, the star of Pedro Almodovar's *Women on the Verge of a Nervous Breakdown.* Our favorite scene in the movie is when Carmen slugs the "feminist" attorney with whom her faithless lover is running away. With his merciless eye for the truth, Almodovar has correctly identified the "oh-so-politically correct-and-oh-so-full-of crap" self-styled representative of women. She may be representing herself, but she certainly isn't speaking for women like Carmen who have to fight their battles alone with no help from phony "advocates." In spite of his feminist critique, Almodovar's love and concern for women is evident in every frame of his film. Carmen achieves strength and understanding not by analyzing the politics of her pain but by working through it. The same woman who sets her bed on fire and then resignedly hoses it down can and does save lives, including her own. Almodovar's acceptance of human problems sets him apart from filmmakers who manipulate characters to illustrate their philosophies. Take a look at people as they are, good and bad, Almodovar's films tell us. Universal statements will emerge from such honest examination, not the other way around. "Women cry better," says Almodovar. *Women on the Verge of a Nervous Breakdown* is such a terrific comedy showcase for the great Carmen Maura, it's sad that it represents her last teaming with Almodovar to date. **AKA:** Mujeres al Borde de un Ataque de Nervios. 𝄞𝄞𝄞𝄞

1988 (R) 88m/C *SP* Carmen Maura, Fernando Guillen, Julieta Serrano, Maria Barranco, Rossy de Palma, Antonio Banderas; **D:** Pedro Almodovar; **W:** Pedro Almodovar; **C:** Jose Luis Alcaine; **M:** Bernardo Bonazzi. National Board of Review Awards '88: 5 Best Foreign Films of the Year; New York Film Critics Awards '88: Best Foreign Film; Nominations: Academy Awards '88: Best Foreign Language Film. **VHS, Beta, LV** *ORI*

The Wonderful Crook

This quiet little film is about a factory owner who steals to pay his worker's wages. The acting by Marlene Jobert and Gerard Depardieu is delightful, and Claude Goretta's direction brings out the elements of charm in his script. **AKA:** Pas Si Mechant que Ca. 𝄞𝄞𝄞

1975 115m/C *SI FR* Marlene Jobert, Gerard Depardieu, Dominique Labourier, Philippe Leotard, Jacques Debary, Michel Robin, Paul Crauchet; **D:** Claude Goretta; **W:** Claude Goretta; **C:** Renato Berta; **M:** Arie Dzierlatka. *NYR*

The Wonderful, Horrible Life of Leni Riefenstahl

At the age of 95, Leni Riefenstahl remains a vital, seductive ball of energy. Ray Muller's three-hour documentary about her life and career doesn't even begin to scratch the surface of this frustrating enigma. *The Wonderful, Horrible Life of Leni Riefenstahl* was somewhat hindered at the start by a major restriction; Riefenstahl would only cooperate with the filmmaker if no opposing viewpoints were presented on camera. Muller agreed, but that didn't stop him from incorporating these viewpoints into his questioning of Riefenstahl. And whenever he tried to do just that, Riefenstahl made her displeasure clear in no uncertain terms. Muller's far-from-frail subject would push him, shove him, yell at him, and, luckily for us, all these moments remain in the movie. The clips from Riefenstahl's early films, both as an actress and as a director, are crisp and clear and her filmmaking entries are razor-sharp. But when it comes to larger issues, namely her precise relationship with the leaders of National Socialism, Riefenstahl's recall softens, blurs, and becomes maddeningly selective. "I NEVER socialized with the Nazis," she insists right after Muller shows us a still of her dressed to the nines and doing just that. "I never used gypsies from concentration camps for my films," she cries, a few moments after we've seen the actual bill of lading. And what about the gushing fan letter she sent to Adolf Hitler after one of his many invasions? "Well, of course I was ecstatic, we all were, because we thought that the war was over." We know, because her surviving colleagues tell us so, that Riefenstahl would do anything, ANYTHING to make *Triumph of the Will* and *Olympia* exactly the way she wanted to make them. We've seen both her combative style with Muller as well as her skill as an actress, so we ought to be irritated when she tells us that she was an apolitical artist and that she didn't mean to glorify National Socialism with her powerful propaganda films. Empirical evidence and the weight of history contradict much of what she says. But Riefenstahl has the quality of Phyllis Dietrichson in *Double Indemnity* right after she's shot Walter Neff and tells him that she didn't mean it. There's always an element of doubt with a charming seductress. *The Wonderful, Horrible Life of Leni Riefenstahl* shows how one of the 20th century's most fascinating woman was able to play both ends against the middle in the 1930s, and was still able to do so well into the 1990s. ♪♪♪♪

1993 180m/C *GE D:* Ray Muller. **VHS** *KIV*

Wonderland

Wonderland was a curious choice for 1989's closing night at San Francisco's Lesbian and Gay Film Festival, an event which professes to celebrate positive gay images on film. Philip Saville's film is saturated with so many homophobic messages: If you're young, nice, and gay, prepare to die. If you're a thief, a liar, and a gay basher, you deserve to survive. Moreover, *Wonderland* exploits overly obvious gay symbols for ruthless plot advances which don't always make sense. The appealing Emile Charles plays Eddie, the film's most innocent character. Kind to his mother, who cherishes her blurry 1960s fantasy of ALMOST being cast in a bit role in *Saturday Night and Sunday Morning,* Eddie is addicted to Marilyn Monroe movies and is thrilled when he meets the famous opera star Vincent at a private buffet he crashes with his best friend Michael (played by Tony Forsyth). Earlier in the evening Eddie and Michael were the reluctant witnesses to a gangland slaying in a gay bar and their encounter with Vincent provides a temporary escape from the mob's hitman, Echo (Bruce Payne.) Eddie and Michael quickly accept an invitation to join Vincent and his manager Eve for a holiday in Brighton. Up to this point, the movie has been a colorful, mostly inoffensive series of character vignettes. The rest of the movie is a mess. It's hard to decide who gets trashed more in *Wonderland*'s final reels, gays or dolphins. Even a scienceless louse like Michael would not take all night to notice a major detail like a knife wound sustained by his best friend. And, not that it would matter to screenwriter Frank Clarke, but dolphins do not attack people, therefore the melodramatic ending is a complete shuck. "What a piece of crap," I overheard the man in back of me mutter as he left the theatre before the closing credits rolled onscreen. Even a ticket taker was knocking the film to the some of the sell-out festival crowd as they entered the theatre. There might be worse movies to see on your hard-earned entertainment budget, but there are plenty of better ones. *AKA:* The Fruit Machine. 🎜🎜

1988 103m/C *GB* Emile Charles, Tony Forsyth, Robert Stephens, Clare Higgins, Bruce Payne, Robbie Coltrane; *D:* Philip Saville; *W:* Frank Clarke; *M:* Hans Zimmer. **VHS, LV** *LIV, VES*

A World Apart

One of the major frustrations about being a child is that grownups often fail to explain matters in which kids have a very real stake. Sometimes, as in *A World Apart,* a mother can't explain what's going on to her 13-year-old daughter, even when it seems as if their entire world is caving in. These are the rough lessons screenwriter Shawn Slovo learned at a young age in South Africa. When her political activist mother was assassinated in 1982, Slovo developed a fictional screenplay about their early relationship. The social ostracism and psychological harassment of this white anti-apartheid family are carefully shown from a child's perspective. While her mother copes with her private nightmares in prison, young Molly suddenly finds herself without friends or guidance. The statements in *A World Apart* are not as threatening as the messages in the seldom-shown *A Place for Weeping,* which examines the black South African experience. Still, Chris Menges' film examines the unfairness of life in an observant, thoughtful way, and it is extremely well acted by Barbara Hershey as Diana and Jodhi May as her daughter, Molly. 🎜🎜🎜

1988 (PG) 114m/C *GB* Barbara Hershey, Jodhi May, Linda Mvusi, David Suchet, Jeroen Krabbe, Paul Freeman, Tim Roth; *D:* Chris Menges; *W:* Shawn Slovo; *C:* Peter Biziou; *M:* Hans Zimmer. British Academy Awards '88: Best Original Screenplay; Cannes Film Festival '88: Best Actress (Hershey), Best Actress (May, Mvusi), Grand Jury Prize; New York Film Critics Awards '88: Best Director (Menges). **VHS, Beta, LV, Closed Caption** *MED*

The World of Henry Orient

The World of Henry Orient was considerably overshadowed by another Peter Sellers release in 1964, *The Pink Panther,* but it remains one of the best films about teenagers ever made, and among the few to give anything like an accurate reading of the many crossed signals between kids and adults. Sellers portrays Henry Orient, a concert piano player of limited ability who becomes the reluctant idol of 14-year-old Elizabeth (Tippy) Walker. Sellers, who perfectly captures the personality of a not-terribly-bright, middle-aged slime, is incapable of coping with much more than one night stands with married women like Paula Prentiss. Unfortunately, although the talented Walker has a good mental grasp of his failings, she is unable to free herself from this pointless obsession. Walker involves her best friend Merrie Spaeth in a dogged pursuit of the dreary activities of Henry Orient, which takes the girls all over New York City. Walker collects his discarded cigarettes and other junk as if they were priceless relics and Spaeth is unable to resist the romantic compulsion of the chase. Both girls come from unconventional homes. The affluent, musical

Walker is the daughter of kind pushover Tom Bosley, who has resigned himself to life with the hard-as-nails Angela Lansbury. The decidedly middle-class Spaeth lives with her mother and a woman friend, sympathetically played by Phyllis Thaxter and Bibi Osterwald. Left to their own devices, Walker would probably drift into drugs or an early marriage while the more level-headed Spaeth would lend equally loyal support to any other best friend. Despite the difference in their fortunes, it is clear that Walker has a far more poverty-stricken life and that she needs Henry Orient to distract her from the sadness and emptiness she would otherwise feel. Walker's recognition that she must learn to grow up by seeing Henry Orient exactly as he is comprises the most painful fact of her life, circa 1964. The adults in this one, despite some fine acting, are rather shadowy figures, which is probably the way most kids see them. For a man who didn't begin directing movies until he was 40, George Roy Hill is clearly captivated by the girls' story and his enthusiasm for their adventures is contagious. Note the similarities in mood and tone between 1964's *The World of Henry Orient* and the first half of 1994's *Heavenly Creatures.* 🐾🐾🐾🐾

1964 106m/C Peter Sellers, Tippy Walker, Merrie Spaeth, Tom Bosley, Angela Lansbury, Paula Prentiss, Phyllis Thaxter, Bibi Osterwald; **D:** George Roy Hill; **W:** Nunnally Johnson, Nora Johnson; **C:** Boris Kaufman; **M:** Elmer Bernstein. National Board of Review Awards '64: 10 Best Films of the Year. **VHS, Beta, LV, Closed Caption** MGM, FCT

The World of Jacques Demy

The late Jacques Demy (1931-90) was a darling of the festival circuit for over 20 years. He was in love with Hollywood musicals and fairy tales that ended happily ever after. In *The World of Jacques Demy,* his widow Agnes Varda pays tribute to the unique filmmaker who thrived during the French New Wave without ever really being part of it. Demy's uneven career consisted of huge international successes (*Lola, The Umbrellas of Cherbourg*) and neglected follow-ups (*Model Shop, The Young Girls of Rochefort*). He left a vivid impression on the actors who worked with him and the many loyal admirers of his work, as Varda's loving homage makes crystal clear. **AKA:** The Universe of Jacques Demy; L'Universe de Jacques Demy. 🐾🐾🐾

1995 91m/C *FR* Anouk Aimee, Michel Legrand, Claude Berri, Richard Berry, Danielle Darrieux, Catherine Deneuve, Jean Marais, Harrison Ford, Jeanne Moreau, Michel Piccoli, Dominique Sanda, Bertrand Tavernier; **D:** Agnes Varda; **W:** Agnes Varda; **C:** Stephane Krausz, Georges Strouve, Peter Pilafian. *NYR*

The Yellow Ticket

Many of the films at 1995's 15th annual Jewish Film Festival reflected on the pioneering spirit necessary for survival over the long haul. The selections dated back as far as 1918 when a 24-year-old Polish actress named Pola Negri made Victor Janson's *The Yellow Ticket* in Warsaw. Her character wants to make medicine her life, but the only way the fledgling actress can afford to do that is through prostitution in a St. Petersburg brothel. Her brilliant medical future is threatened when another student (with whom she is romantically involved) discovers her source of financial aid. Negri had a long career in films: she made *Gypsy Blood, Passion,* and *One Arabian Night* for Ernst Lubitsch between 1918 and 1921; she starred in Mauritz Stiller's *Hotel Imperial* in 1927; she made the screwball comedy *Hi Diddle Diddle* for Andrew L. Stone in 1943; and she even appeared opposite Hayley Mills in the 1964 Disney film *The Moon-Spinners.* When Negri died in 1987, she had outlived most of the other stars of the silent era. 🐾🐾🐾

1918 68m/B *GE* Pola Negri; **D:** Victor Janson. *NYR*

y

Opposite page: Sylvia Sidney and **Henry Fonda** in **You Only Live Once.**

You Only Live Once

Director Fritz Lang escaped Nazi Germany in the nick of time, leaving behind his considerable fortune. Upon his arrival in America, he immediately addressed OUR social problems on film, starting with *Fury's* exploration of public lynchings. A lesser-known film, but in many ways, far more uncompromising, is 1937's *You Only Live Once,* made for independent producer Walter Wanger. Both *Fury* and *You Only Live Once* star Sylvia Sidney, the quintessential Depression-era actress whose dahlia-like appearance belied her deep emotional strength. Henry Fonda, with his gaunt, lean features, was her male equivalent, far more successful at conveying '30s angst than *Fury's* well fed Spencer Tracy. The perspective in *You Only Live Once* is in direct opposition to the one in *Fury,* which went out of its way to show that the system would eventually address social evils. In *You Only Live Once,* all good-intentioned liberalism is ineffectual. Fonda plays Eddie Taylor, a loser trying to buck his fate with the love and support of Jo Graham, played by Sidney. But he can NOT buck it, the couple can't even have a proper wedding night together; they are tossed out after their motel manager discovers Eddie's identity. Eddie tries to get and keep a job, but his past catches up with him and he is fired. He is unjustly accused of a crime he did not commit and cooperates with authorities upon Jo's recommendation. The attorney who is Jo's employer tries to help him, a priest tries to help him, and when Eddie rejects them, it is clear that he is rejecting a society that has always rejected him. Even as the real criminals are caught, Eddie is already in existential flight along with Jo, who abandons her well ordered life to join him. Lang treats the couple and everyone else in his sightline with understanding and sympathy. There are no real saints or sinners in *You Only Live Once,* only an overall atmosphere of despair. In the war that was to come, Lang would show other seemingly doomed couples in *Manhunt* and *Ministry of Fear,* as they struggled, not always in vain, against their destinies. But in *You Only Live Once* we see a rare time capsule that makes it clear the New Deal will not supply Eddie and Jo's salvation, only a grim acceptance of their fate. 🦴🦴🦴🦴

1937 86m/B Henry Fonda, Sylvia Sidney, Ward Bond, William Gargan, Barton MacLane, Margaret Hamilton, Jean Dixon, Warren Hymer, Chic Sale, Guinn "Big Boy" Williams, Jerome Cowan, John Wray, Jonathan Hale, Ben Hall, Jean Stoddard, Wade Boteler, Henry Taylor, Walter DePalma; **D:** Fritz Lang. **VHS, Beta** *NO*

Young and Innocent

Young and Innocent turns up so often in scratched and dupey prints on public domain channels that it's easy to under-appreciate what a gem it is. For starters, there's Erica, a wonderful teen heroine (Nova Pilbeam), who trusts her own instincts and relies on her resources to save Robert, a suspected killer (handsome Derrick DeMarney). Then there's the tramp (Edward Rigby) who's vital to her search for the real killer. The wonderful Basil Radford (a year before *The Lady Vanishes*) has a delightful cameo as a sympathetic ally. And there's that dazzling camera work at a tea dance where we RE-discover the killer we met in the first reel. A children's party game of Blind Man's Bluff mid-way through the film reinforces the light-hearted, intense quality of Erica and Robert's situation. It's very British, with few concessions to an international audience, but great fun. Based on Josephine Tey's *A Shilling for Candles.*

Hitchcock's cameo is as a court photographer. **AKA:** The Girl Was Young. 🦴🦴🦴

1937 80m/B *GB* Derrick DeMarney, Nova Pilbeam, Percy Marmont, Edward Rigby, Mary Clare, John Longden, George Curzon, Basil Radford, Pamela Carme, George Merritt, J.H. Roberts, Jerry Verno, H.F. Maltby, John Miller, Beatrice Varley, Syd Crossley, Frank Atkinson, Torin Thatcher; **D:** Alfred Hitchcock; **W:** Charles Bennett, Alma Reville, Gerald Savory, Antony Armstrong, Edwin Greenwood. **VHS, Beta, LV** *SNC, NOS, VDM*

Zebrahead

Zebrahead was first shown less than 18 months before Ray Sharkey died of AIDS in a Brooklyn Hospital, so Richard Glass, an agressively promiscuous character that seemed funny while Sharkey was still alive, is significantly less amusing now, especially since he wants his adolescent son to follow his example. Otherwise, *Zebrahead* is an enjoyable teen indie about a star-crossed romance between white kid/black wannabe Zack Glass (Michael Rapaport) and his best friend's cousin Nikki (N'Bushe Wright), who's black. Needless to say, Nikki's mother and everyone in school has an opinion on this couple. Similar in theme, although definitely not in approach to a better Australian teen flick, 1989's *Flirting,* directed by John Duigan and starring Noah Taylor and Thandie Newton. *Zebrahead* was filmed on location in Detroit, Michigan. 🦴🦴🦴

1992 (R) 102m/C Michael Rapaport, N'Bushe Wright, Ray Sharkey, DeShonn Castle, Ron Johnson, Marsha Florence, Paul Butler, Abdul Hassan Sharif, Dan Ziskie, Candy Ann Brown, Helen Shaver, Luke Reilly, Martin Priest, Kevin Corrigan; **D:** Tony Drazan; **W:** Tony Drazan; **C:** Maryse Alberti; **M:** Taj Mahal. Sundance Film Festival '92: Filmmakers Trophy. **VHS, LV, 8mm, Closed Caption** *COL*

Zohar: Mediterranean Blues

Zohar: Mediterranean Blues is the sad story of Zohar Arkov, who achieved musical stardom in Israel before his death in

"Go ahead, take a good look, you monkeys! Have a good time! Get a big kick out of it! It's fun to see an innocent man die, isn't it?"

—Eddie Taylor (Henry Fonda), indeed an innocent man, defies his accusers after being sentenced to death in *You Only Live Once*

1987 at the age of 32. Its content and structure are similar to 1985's *Shout,* about Australian rock legend Johnny O'Keefe (who was 43 when he died in 1978), and to *Stardust,* Michael Apted's fictional recreation of the quintessential pop star, circa 1974. Since most filmed biographies of rock stars end with them getting torn up in a wreck or done in by drugs (in this case, it's the latter), the significance of Arkov's pioneering musical contributions is that they laid the groundwork for other Yemenite artists to achieve success on a large scale. ♫♫♪

1993 116m/C *IS* Gabi Amrani, Dafna Dekel, Menahem Einy, Cochava Harari, Shaul Mizrahi; *D:* Eran Riklis; *W:* Amir Ben-David, Moshe Zonder; *C:* Amnon Alait; *M:* Avihu Medina. *NYR*

"Indie Connections" provides both the independent film devotee and the independent filmmaker (aspiring newcomers and old pros) with ways to keep on top of current happenings in the industry, news and opinions from other like-minded individuals, and behind-the-scenes stories from those behind the scenes. We tracked down web pages, magazines, books, and organizations all for and about independent film, many of them by independent filmmakers themselves. Go to it!

WEB PAGES

Association of Independent Video and Filmmakers

http://www.virtualfilm.com/AIVF/

Cashiers du Cinemart

http://www.gatecom.com/~cashiers/

Delta 9 Independent Film Resource

http://www.eden.com/WebOS/omf/neweden/indyfilms

Film Culture: America's Independent Motion Picture Magazine

http://www.arthouseinc.com/filmculture/

Film Threat Online

http://www.filmthreat.com

Film Vision

http://www.filmvision.com/

FilmDependent Cyberspot

http://www.filmdependent.com

Filmmaker: The Magazine of Independent Film

http://www.filmmag.com/

Flicker

http://www.sirius.com/~sstark/

iLINE Ltd: Indie Film Cyber Network

http://www.ilineltd.com/

The Independent Feature Project

http://www.ifp.org

The Independent Film and Video Alliance

http://www.culturenet.ca/ifva

The Independent Film and Video Makers Internet Resource Guide

http://www.echonyc.com/~mvidal/Indi-Film+Video.html

The Independent Film Channel

http://www.ifctv.com/

IndieFilms

http://www.indiefilms.com/

IndieZine

http://telluridemm.com/indizine.html

Kulture Void Pictures: Independent Film Web Journal

http://www.kulture-void.com

Movie Magazine International

http://www.shoestring.org

M.O.V.I.E.: Makers of Visual Independent Entertainment

http://www.moviefund.com/

MovieMaker Magazine Online

http://www.moviemaker.com

Reel Independence: Useful Stuff for Indie Filmmakers

http://www.globalserve.net/~reelind/

The Sundance Channel
http://www.sundancechannel.com/

Surfview Entertainment
http://www.surfview.com/

Zenomorph Filmworks
http://www.henninger.com/staff/jodoin/home.html

BOOKS

Almodovar on Almodovar
Pedro Almodovar. 1995. Faber & Faber.

The Cinema of Martin Scorsese
Lawrence S. Friedman. 1997. Continuum.

Clearance & Copyright: Everything the Independent Filmmaker Needs to Know
Michael C. Donaldson. 1997. Silman-James Press.

A Critical Cinema: Interviews with Independent Filmmakers
Scott MacDonald. 1988. University of California Press.

A Critical Cinema 2: Interviews with Independent Filmmakers
Scott MacDonald. 1992. University of California Press.

A Critical Cinema 3: Interviews with Independent Filmmakers
Scott MacDonald. 1997. University of California Press.

David Lynch
Michel Chion. 1995. British Film Institute.

Fellini's Films: From Postwar to Postmodern
Frank Burrke. 1996. Twayne.

Film Fatales: Independent Women Directors
Judith Redding. 1997. Seal Press Feminist Publishing.

43 Ways to Finance Your Feature Film: A Comprehensive Analysis of Film Finance
John W. Cones. 1995. Southern Illinois University Press.

Hitchcock on Hitchcock
Alfred Hitchcock. 1995. University of California Press.

I Wake Up Screening! Everything You Need to Know about Making Independent Films including a Thousand Reasons Not To
Frank D. Gilroy. 1993. Southern Illinois University Press.

Independent Feature Film Production: A Complete Guide from Concept through Distribution
Gregory Goodell. Revised ed., 1995. St. Martin's Press.

Independent Visions: A Critical Introduction to Recent Independent American Films
Donald Lyons. 1994. Ballantine Books.

Ingmar Bergman: Film and Stage
Robert Emmet Long. 1994. Harry Abrams.

Making Movies: The Inside Guide to Independent Movie Production
John A. Russo. 1989. Bantam/Doubleday/Dell.

Merchant Ivory's English Landscape: Rooms, Views, and Anglo-Saxon Attitudes
John Pym. 1995. Harry Abrams.

Orson Welles: A Biography
Barbara Leaming. 1995. Limelight.

Poverty Row Studios, 1929-1940: An Illustrated History of 53 Independent Film Companies, with a Filmography for Each
Michael R. Pitts. 1997. McFarland & Co.

Quentin Tarantino: The Man and His Movies
Jami Bernard. 1996. Harper Perennial.

Rebel without a Crew: Or How a 23-Year-Old Filmmaker with $7,000 Became a Hollywood Player
Robert Rodriguez. 1995. E P Hutton.

Robert Altman: Hollywood Survivor
Daniel O'Brien. 1995. Continuum.

Screen Writings: Scripts and Texts by Independent Filmmakers
Scott MacDonald, editor. 1995. University of California Press.

So You Want to Make Movies: My Life As an Independent Film Producer
Sidney Pink. 1989. Pineapple Press.

Spike, Mike, Slackers & Dykes: A Guided Tour across a Decade of American Independent Cinema
John Pierson and David Cashion. 1996. Hyperion.

Thinking in Pictures: The Making of the Movie Matewan
John Sayles. 1987. Houghton Mifflin Co.

MAGAZINES

Cashiers du Cinemart
Mike White
PO Box 2401
Riverview, MI 48192
$2.00/issue.

Film Culture Magazine: America's Independent Motion Picture Magazine
32 2nd Ave.
New York, NY 10003
(212)979-5663
Quarterly. $20.00/year.

Filmmaker Magazine
5858 Wilshire Blvd.
Los Angeles, CA 90036-0926
1-800-FILMMAG
Quarterly. $14.00/year ($17.00 in Canada).

The Independent Film and Video Monthly
AIVF
304 Hudson St., 6th Fl.
New York, NY 10013
(212)807-1400
independent@aivf.org
$45.00/10 issues. Includes membership in Association of Independent Video and Filmmakers.

Independent Spirit
Susan Leonard
South Carolina Arts Commision Media Arts Center
1800 Gervais St.
Columbia, SC 29201
(803)734-8696
Free. Publishes three times a year.

MovieMaker Magazine
1016 NW 65th St.
Seattle, WA 98117
888-MAKE MOVIES
movies@seanet.com
$30.00/12 issues.

Reel Independence
360A Bloor St. W.
PO Box 19030
Toronto, ON, Canada M5S 1X0
$15.00/6 issues ($18.00 in Canada).

ORGANIZATIONS/ ASSOCIATIONS

American Film Institute (AFI)
John F. Kennedy Center for the Performing Arts
Washington, DC 20566
800-774-4234
Jean Firstenberg, Director
A non-profit corporation dedicated to developing the nation's artistic and cultural resources in film and video.

American Film Marketing Association
10850 Wilshire Blvd., 9th Fl.
Los Angeles, CA 90024-4305
(310)447-1555
Jonas Rosenfield, President
Independent producers and distributors of feature-length theatrical films.

Association of Independent Video and Filmmakers
625 Broadway, 9th Fl.
New York, NY 10012
(212)473-3400
Ruby Lerner, Executive Director
Independent film and video makers, producers, writers, and others. Assists in financing and exhibiting independent work.

Black American Cinema Society
3617 Monclair St.
Los Angeles, CA 90018
(213)737-3292
Mayme Agnew Clayton, Founder and Director
Provides financial support to independent black filmmakers. Works to create awareness of black contributions to the motion picture industry.

Council of Film Organizations
334 W. 54th St.
Los Angeles, CA 90037
(213)752-5811
Dr. Donald A. Reed, President
Provides a forum for film organizations and individuals interested in filmmaking.

Film Arts Foundation
346 9th St., 2nd Fl.
San Francisco, CA 94103
(415)552-8760
Gail Silva, Director
Supports and encourages independent film and video makers through educational and information sevices.

Independent Feature Project
104 W. 29th St., 12th Fl.
New York, NY 10001-5301
(212)465-8200
Catherine Tait, Executive Director
Promotes the production and distribution of independent feature films.

Independent Film and Video Alliance
4550 Garnier
Montreal, PQ, Canada H2J 3S7

(514)522-8240

A national network linking independent film, video, and electronic media producers, distributors, and exhibitors. Works to promote the improvement of means and access for independents.

Independent Film Distributors' Association

c/o Connoisseur Video Ltd.
10A Stephen Mews
London W1A 0AX, England
(44-171)957-8957
Association of independent film distributors.

International Federation of Independent Film Producers

33 rue Washington
F-75008 Paris, France
(33-1)537-52700
Represents independent film producers; facilitates communication and cooperation among members.

International Film Seminars

305 21st St.
New York, NY 10011
(212)727-7262
Michelle A. Materrre, Executive Director
Sponsors the annual Robert Flaherty Seminar, an international convocation of those active in independent film and video production, distribution, and exhibition.

National Asian American Telecommunications Association

346 9th St., 2nd Fl.
San Francisco, CA 94103
(415)863-0814
Deann Borshay, Executive Director
Promotes the interests of Asian Americans in the media. Offers financial consultation sevices for independent film and video productions.

Out on the Screen

8455 Beverly Blvd., Ste. 309
Los Angeles, CA 90048
(213)951-1247
Morgan Rumpf, Director
Individuals and organizations serving as a programming group focusing on independent film and video projects dealing with gay and lesbian situations.

Satellite Video Exchange Society

1695 Marine St.
Vancouver, BC, Canada VAT 1Z2
(604)872-8337
Joe Sarahan, President
Seeks to promote independently produced film and video projects and provide access to production equipment.

Sundance Institute

RR 3, Box 624B
Sundance, UT 84604
(801)328-3456
Gary Beer, Executive VP
Resource center for independent filmmakers and other artists.

University Film and Video Foundation

c/o Dr. John Kuiper
University of North Texas
Dept. of Radio-T.V.-Film
PO Box 13138
Denton, TX 76203-3138
(817)565-2537
Supports university film and video production. Coordinates international screenings, film festivals, and education. Assists in distribution of independent films.

Women in Film

6464 Sunset Blvd., Suite 530
Hollywood, CA 90028
(213)463-6040
Harriet Silverman, Director
Supports women in the film and television industries.

Frankenstein Unbound or *Roger Corman's Frankenstein Unbound*? *L'Affiche Rouge* or *The Red Poster*? *Over Her Dead Body* or *Enid Is Sleeping*? These and other alternate title quandries are addressed here in the aptly named "Alternate Titles Index." Variant and foreign titles for the movies reviewed in this book are provided in alphabetical order (and please remember that foreign articles are NOT ignored in the alpha sort), followed by a cross-reference to the appropriate entry in the main review section.

A Bout de Souffle *See* Breathless (1959)

The Actress *See* Center Stage (1991)

Adele Hasn't Had Her Supper Yet *See* Dinner for Adele (1978)

Aelita: The Revolt of the Robots *See* Aelita: Queen of Mars (1924)

Almok a hazrol *See* 25 Fireman's Street (1973)

Amerikaner Shadkhn *See* American Matchmaker (1940)

Angel Street *See* Gaslight (1940)

Ansikte mot Ansikte *See* Face to Face (1976)

Atame *See* Tie Me Up! Tie Me Down! (1990)

The Beans of Egypt, Maine *See* Forbidden Choices (1994)

The Best Way to Walk *See* The Best Way (1976)

Big Time Operators *See* The Smallest Show on Earth (1957)

Bilans Kwartalny *See* The Balance (1975)

Blue *See* Trois Couleurs: Bleu (1993)

The Boat *See* Das Boot (1981)

Brian Wilson: I Just Wasn't Made for These Times *See* I Wasn't Made for These Times

Brutti Sporchi e Cattivi *See* Ugly, Dirty and Bad (1978)

Budding Love *See* L'Amour en Herbe (1977)

The Buddy Factor *See* Swimming with Sharks (1994)

Build a Fort Set It on Fire *See* Basquiat (1996)

Bye Bye Victor *See* Salut Victor! (1989)

Camada Negra *See* Black Litter (1977)

Cannibal Orgy, or the Maddest Story Ever Told *See* Spider Baby (1964)

Care of the Spitfire Grill *See* The Spitfire Grill (1995)

Caro Michele *See* Dear Michael (1976)

Castle of Doom *See* Vampyr (1931)

Ce Cher Victor *See* Dear Victor (1975)

Chelovek S. Kinooapparatom *See* The Man with the Movie Camera (1923)

Clean Slate *See* Coup de Torchon (1981)

Como Agua para Chocolate *See* Like Water for Chocolate (1993)

Cutter and Bone *See* Cutter's Way (1981)

Dal Polo all'Equatore *See* From the Pole to the Equator (1987)

Dangerous Love Affairs *See* Dangerous Liaisons (1960)

Das Falsche Gewicht *See* False Weights

Das Zweite Erwachen der Christa Klages *See* The Second Awakening of Christa Klages (1978)

Deadly Is the Female *See* Gun Crazy (1949)

Dellamorte Delamore *See* Cemetery Man (1995)

Der Himmel Uber Berlin *See* Wings of Desire (1988)

Der Starke Ferdinand *See* Strongman Ferdinand (1976)

Die Buechse Der Pandora *See* Pandora's Box (1928)

Die Freudlosse Gasse *See* Joyless Street (1925)

Dirty, Mean and Nasty *See* Ugly, Dirty and Bad (1978)

East of Shanghai *See* Rich and Strange (1932)

El Espiritu de la Colmena *See* Spirit of the Beehive (1973)

The Enigma of Kaspar Hauser *See* Every Man for Himself & God Against All (1975)

Entre Tinieblas *See* Dark Habits (1984)

Fabula de la Bella Palomera *See* The Fable of the Beautiful Pigeon Fancier (1988)

Father Master *See* Padre Padrone (1977)

Federico Fellini's 8 1/2 *See* 8 1/2 (1963)

Five Angles on Murder *See* The Woman in Question (1950)

Forvandlingen *See* Metamorphosis (1975)

The Fruit Machine *See* Wonderland (1988)

Gestapo *See* Night Train to Munich (1940)

The Girl Was Young *See* Young and Innocent (1937)

Gokiburi *See* Twilight of the Cockroaches (1990)

The Grail *See* Lancelot of the Lake (1974)

Gran Bollito *See* An Average Little Man (1977)

The Grand Highway *See* Le Grand Chemin (1987)

Grave Robbers from Outer Space *See* Plan 9 from Outer Space (1956)

The Great Day *See* A Special Day (1977)

Hagan *See* The Garden (1977)

Hsi Yen *See* The Wedding Banquet (1993)

Il Conformist *See* The Conformist (1971)

Il Etait une Fois dans l'Est *See* Once Upon a Time in the East (1974)

Il Postino *See* The Postman (1994)

Il Sorriso del Grande Tentatore *See* The Devil Is a Woman (1975)

Ivnana *See* Lullaby (1994)

Jeder fur Sich und Gott Gegen Alle *See* Every Man for Himself & God Against All (1975)

The Jezebels *See* Switchblade Sisters (1975)

Jonas—Qui Aura 25 Ans en l'An 2000 *See* Jonah Who Will Be 25 in the Year 2000 (1976)

Joyous Laughter *See* Passionate Thief (1960)

Kafe im Limon *See* Coffee with Lemon (1994)

The Kidnappers *See* The Little Kidnappers (1953)

Killer Bait *See* Too Late for Tears (1949)

La Belle et le Bete *See* Beauty and the Beast (1946)@ati:**La Cite des Enfants Perdus** *See* The City of Lost Children (1995)

La Communion Solonnelle *See* First Communion (1977)

La Ley del Deseo *See* Law of Desire (1986)

La Mano del Straniero *See* The Stranger's Hand (1954)

La Meilleure Facon de Marcher *See* The Best Way (1976)

Lady Jane Grey *See* Nine Days a Queen (1936)

The Lady Killers *See* The Ladykillers (1955)

L'Affiche Rouge *See* The Red Poster (1976)

Lancelot du Lac *See* Lancelot of the Lake (1974)

The Late Edwina Black *See* The Obsessed (1951)

Le Fantome de la Liberte *See* Phantom of Liberty (1974)

Le Graal *See* Lancelot of the Lake (1974)

Le Pays Bleu *See* Blue Country (1977)

Les Cent et Une Nuits *See* 101 Nights (1995)

Les Cent et Une Nuits de Simon Cinema *See* 101 Nights (1995)

Les Enfants du Paradise *See* Children of Paradise (1945)

Les Jeux Interdits *See* Forbidden Games (1952)

Les Liaisons Dangereuses *See* Dangerous Liaisons (1960)

Les Ordres *See* The Orders (1975)

Les Quartre Cents Coups *See* The 400 Blows (1959)

L'Homme Qui Aimait les Femmes *See* The Man Who Loved Women (1977)

Lian'ai Yu Yiwu *See* Love and Duty (1931)

Lights of Variety *See* Variety Lights (1951)

The Liver Eaters *See* Spider Baby (1964)

Lo Zio Indegno *See* The Sleazy Uncle (1989)

L'Ombre du Doute *See* Shades of Doubt (1993)

The Lost Illusion *See* The Fallen Idol (1949)

Luci Del Varieta *See* Variety Lights (1951)

L'Une Chante, L'Autre Pas *See* One Sings, the Other Doesn't (1977)

L'Universe de Jacques Demy *See* The World of Jacques Demy (1995)

Marcia Trionfale *See* Victory March (1976)

Meet Ruth Stoops *See* Citizen Ruth (1996)

Meet the Applegates *See* The Applegates (1989)

Mi Familia *See* My Family (1994)

Mike Leigh's Naked *See* Naked (1993)

Miracle of Life *See* Our Daily Bread (1934)

Mrs. Parker and the Round Table *See* Mrs. Parker and the Vicious Circle (1994)

Mr. 247 *See* A Modern Affair (1994)

Mitt Liv Som Hund *See* My Life As a Dog (1985)

Morgan: A Suitable Case for Treatment *See* Morgan! (1966)

Mujeres al Borde de un Ataque de Nervios *See* Women on the Verge of a Nervous Breakdown (1988)

Mutter Kusters Fahrt Zum Himmel *See* Mother Kusters Goes to Heaven (1976)

My Father, My Master *See* Padre Padrone (1977)

The Mystery of Kaspar Hauser *See* Every Man for Himself & God Against All (1975)

Na Samote u Lesa *See* Seclusion Near a Forest (1976)

The New China Woman *See* Center Stage (1991)

Night Legs *See* Fright (1971)

Night Train *See* Night Train to Munich (1940)

Nosferatu, A Symphony of Horror *See* Nosferatu (1922)

Nosferatu, A Symphony of Terror *See* Nosferatu (1922)

Nosferatu, Eine Symphonie des Grauens *See* Nosferatu (1922)

Nosferatu, The Vampire *See* Nosferatu (1922)

Not Against the Flesh *See* Vampyr (1931)

Nuovo Cinema Paradiso *See* Cinema Paradiso (1988)

O Casamento *See* The Marriage (1976)

Obsession *See* The Hidden Room (1949)

Of Death, Of Love *See* Cemetery Man (1995)

One Cup of Coffee *See* Pastime (1991)

101 Nights of Simon Cinema *See* 101 Nights (1995)

141 Minutes from the Unfinished Sentence *See* The Unfinished Sentence in 141 Minutes (1975)

141 Perc a Befejezetlen Mondatbal *See* The Unfinished Sentence in 141 Minutes (1975)

Orkobefogadas *See* Adoption (1975)

Otto E Mezzo *See* 8 1/2 (1963)

Outomlionnye Solntsem *See* Burnt by the Sun (1994)

Over Her Dead Body *See* Enid Is Sleeping (1990)

Paradistorg *See* Paradise Place (1977)

Pas Si Mechant que Ca *See* The Wonderful Crook (1975)

Pasqualino Settebellezze *See* Seven Beauties (1976)

Pasqualino: Seven Beauties *See* Seven Beauties (1976)

Pepita Jiminez *See* Bride to Be (1975)

Phenomena *See* Creepers (1985)

Playgirl Gang *See* Switchblade Sisters (1975)

Po Dezju *See* Before the Rain (1994)

Popiol i Diament *See* Ashes and Diamonds (1958)

Pourquoi Pas! *See* Why Not! (1978)

Precious *See* Citizen Ruth (1996)

Przesluchanie *See* The Interrogation (1982)

Q Planes *See* Clouds over Europe (1939)

The Quarterly Balance *See* The Balance (1975)

Qui Ju Da Guansi *See* The Story of Qui Ju (1991)

Red *See* Trois Couleurs: Rouge (1994)

Risate de Gioia *See* Passionate Thief (1960)

Roger Corman's Frankenstein Unbound *See* Frankenstein Unbound (1990)

Romance da Empregada *See* The Story of Fausta (1988)

Ruan Ling-Yu *See* Center Stage (1991)

St. Martin's Lane *See* Sidewalks of London (1938)

Season of Dreams *See* Stacking (1987)

Second Chance *See* If I Had It to Do Over Again (1976)

Servante et Maitresse *See* Servant and Mistress (1977)

Seven Waves Away *See* Abandon Ship (1957)

The Sex of the Stars *See* Le Sexe des Etoiles (1993)

Shadow of a Doubt *See* Shades of Doubt (1993)

Shadows of the Peacock *See* Echoes of Paradise (1986)

Shirat Ha'Sirena *See* Song of the Siren (1994)

Shtei Etzbaot Mi'Tzidon *See* Ricochets (1987)

Si C'Etait a Refaire *See* If I Had It to Do Over Again (1976)

Skyggen af Emma *See* Emma's Shadow (1988)

Something Fishy *See* Pas Tres Catholique (1993)

Sound of Fury *See* Try and Get Me (1950)

Souvenirs d'en France *See* French Provincial (1975)

The Specter of Freedom *See* Phantom of Liberty (1974)

Spider Baby, or the Maddest Story Ever Told *See* Spider Baby (1964)

The Spiritualist *See* The Amazing Mr. X (1948)

Spoorloos *See* The Vanishing (1988)

Sto Dnei rossle Detstwa *See* 100 Days after Childhood (1975)

Strah *See* Fear (1975)

The Strange Adventure of David Gray *See* Vampyr (1931)

The Strange Case of Madeleine *See* Madeleine (1950)

Street of Sorrow *See* Joyless Street (1925)

A Suitable Case for Treatment *See* Morgan! (1966)

Summer Place *See* Paradise Place (1977)

Swept Away...By an Unusual Destiny in the Blue Sea of August *See* Swept Away... (1975)

Tacones Lejanos *See* High Heels (1991)

Tell Her I Love Her *See* Dites-Lui Que Je L'Aime (1977)

Tender Love *See* L'Amour en Herbe (1977)

These Foolish Things *See* Daddy Nostalgia (1990)

This Sweet Sickness *See* Dites-Lui Que Je L'Aime (1977)

Three Colors: Blue *See* Trois Couleurs: Bleu (1993)

Three Colors: Red *See* Trois Couleurs: Rouge (1994)

Three Colors: White *See* Trois Couleurs: Blanc (1994)

Trois Vies et Une Seule Mort *See* Three Lives and Only One Death (1996)

Trop Belle Pour Toi *See* Too Beautiful for You (1988)

Tudor Rose *See* Nine Days a Queen (1936)@ati:**The Umbrella Woman** *See* The Good Wife (1986)

Un Borghese Piccolo Piccolo *See* An Average Little Man (1977)

Una Giornata Speciale *See* A Special Day (1977)

Under the Olive Trees *See* Through the Olive Trees (1994)

The Universe of Jacques Demy *See* The World of Jacques Demy (1995)

The Vampire *See* Vampyr (1931)

Vampyr, der Traum des David Gray *See* Vampyr (1931)

Vampyr, Ou L'Etrange Aventure de David Gray *See* Vampyr (1931)

A Very Little Man *See* An Average Little Man (1977)

Virgine, e Di Nome Maria *See* A Virgin Named Mary (1975)

The Wanting Weight *See* False Weights (1974)

Ways of Love *See* The Miracle (1948)

White *See* Trois Couleurs: Blanc (1994)

Woman Alone *See* Sabotage (1936)

A Woman's Decision *See* The Balance (1975)

Xiyan *See* The Wedding Banquet (1993)

Yanzhi Kou *See* Rouge (1987)

Zire Darakhtan Zeyton *See* Through the Olive Trees (1994)

The "Cast Index" provides a complete listing of—you guessed it—cast members cited within the reviews. The actors' names are alphabetical by last name, and the films they appeared in are listed chronologically, from most recent film to the oldest (note that only the films reviewed in this book are cited). Directors get the same treatment in the "Directors Index." How about that?

Frankie Allarcon
Chan Is Missing '82

Keith Allen
Shallow Grave '94
Kafka '91

Nancy Allen
Acting on Impulse '93

Patrick Allen
Never Take Candy from a
Stranger '60

Ronald Allen
Eat the Rich '87

Sheila Allen
Children of the Damned
'63

Sara Allgood
Blackmail '29

Claud Allister
The Private Life of Henry
VIII '33

Roy Alon
The Long Good Friday '80

Jose Alonso
Black Litter '77

**Maria Conchita
Alonso**
Caught '96
The House of the Spirits
'93

Murray Alper
Turnabout '40

Bruce Altman
The Favor, the Watch,
and the Very Big Fish
'92

Anicee Alvina
The Red Poster '76

Camila Amado
The Marriage '76

Betty Amann
Rich and Strange '32

Domingo Ambriz
Alambrista! '77

Amedee
Forbidden Games '52

Jimmy Ames
He Ran All the Way '51
Too Late for Tears '49

Suzy Amis
Nadja '95
The Usual Suspects '95
The Ballad of Little Jo '93
Two Small Bodies '93
Twister '89

John Amos
Mac '93

Gabi Amrani
Zohar: Mediterranean
Blues '93

Luana Anders
Easy Rider '69
Night Tide '63

Rudolph Anders
Actors and Sin '52

Tiffany Anders
Gas Food Lodging '92

Bibi Andersen
High Heels '91

Adisa Anderson
Daughters of the Dust
'91

Jean Anderson
Lucky Jim '58
The Little Kidnappers '53

Jeff Anderson
Clerks '94

John Anderson
Eight Men Out '88

Judith Anderson
The Red House '47

Laurie Anderson
Heavy Petting '89

**Michael Anderson,
Jr.**
Tiger Bay '59

Bibi Andersson
Law of Desire '86
Scenes from a Marriage
'73

**Christina
Andersson**
Mushrooms '95

Marcel Andre
Beauty and the Beast '46

**Natasha
Andreichenko**
Little Odessa '94

Carol Andrews
The Lady Confesses '45

Harry Andrews
S.O.S. Titanic '79

Jason Andrews
Federal Hill '94
Rhythm Thief '94
Last Exit to Brooklyn '90

Naveen Andrews
The English Patient '96
Kama Sutra: A Tale of
Love '96
Wild West '93

Thomas Andrisano
Teenage Gang Debs '66

Anemone
Pas Tres Catholique '93
Le Grand Chemin '87

**Jean-Hugues
Anglade**
La Femme Nikita '91

Edit Angold
Tomorrow the World '44

David Angus
The Hours and Times '92

Jennifer Aniston
She's the One '96

Ann-Margret
Tommy '75

Adam Ant
Acting on Impulse '93

Carl Anthony
Plan 9 from Outer Space
'56

Mark Anthony
Big Night '95

Paul Anthony
House Party '90

Steve Antin
Inside Monkey Zetterland
'93

**Vladimir Antolek-
Oresek**
Lancelot of the Lake '74

Omero Antonutti
Padre Padrone '77

**Michael "Tunes"
Antunes**
Eddie and the Cruisers
'83

Robert Apel
Red Rock West '93

Tina Apicella
Bellissima '51

Pilar Aranda
Like Water for Chocolate
'93

Ray Aranha
City of Hope '91

Jean Archambault
Once Upon a Time in the
East '74

Bernard Archard
Village of the Damned
'60

Anne Archer
Short Cuts '93

Robert Arden
Never Take Candy from a
Stranger '60

Niels Arestrup
Lumiere '76

Fiore Argento
Creepers '85

Victor Argo
Smoke '95
Household Saints '93
Bad Lieutenant '92

Ben Aris
Tommy '75
If... '69

Yareli Arizmendi
Like Water for Chocolate
'93

Arletty
Children of Paradise '45

**Angelina
Armeiskaya**
The Children of Theatre
Street '77

Alun Armstrong
Black Beauty '94

Nelly Arno
The Third Man '49

Joanne Arnold
Girl Gang '54

Richard Arnold
The Method '87

Victor Arnold
The Incident '67

Alexis Arquette
Grief '94
Terminal Bliss '91
Last Exit to Brooklyn '90

Lewis Arquette
The Linguini Incident '92
Nobody's Fool '86

Patricia Arquette
Lost Highway '96
Flirting with Disaster '95
Inside Monkey Zetterland
'93

Rosanna Arquette
Crash '95
Pulp Fiction '94
Search and Destroy '94
The Linguini Incident '92
Nobody's Fool '86
After Hours '85

Jeri Arredondo
Color of a Brisk and
Leaping Day '95
Silent Tongue '92

Timothy Arrington
Open Season '95

Bill Ash
Plan 9 from Outer Space
'56

Peggy Ashcroft
The 39 Steps '35

Jane Asher
Closing Numbers '93
Dreamchild '85
Deep End '70

Luke Askew
Easy Rider '69

Robin Askwith
Confessions of a Window
Cleaner '74

Adrianna Asti
Phantom of Liberty '74

Mary Astor
Turnabout '40

William Atherton
Grim Prairie Tales '89

Feodor Atkine
Three Lives and Only One
Death '96
High Heels '91

Christopher Atkins
It's My Party '95

Eileen Atkins
Let Him Have It '91

Frank Atkinson
Pygmalion '38
Young and Innocent '37

Rowan Atkinson
Four Weddings and a
Funeral '94
The Witches '90

Malcolm Atterbury
Crime of Passion '57

Rene Auberjonois
The Ballad of Little Jo '93

Michel Auclair
French Provincial '75

Beauty and the Beast '46

Maxine Audley
Peeping Tom '60

Stephane Audran
Coup de Torchon '81

Patrick Auffay
The 400 Blows '59

Jean-Pierre Aumont
Cat and Mouse '78

Michel Aumont
Why Not! '78

Georges Auric
Beauty and the Beast '46

William Austin
The Private Life of Henry VIII '33

Angel Aviles
Chain of Desire '93

Mili Avital
Dead Man '95

Dan Aykroyd
Chaplin '92

Ethel Ayler
To Sleep with Anger '90

Felix Aylmer
Never Take Candy from a Stranger '60
Separate Tables '58
So Long at the Fair '50
Thursday's Child '43
Night Train to Munich '40
Nine Days a Queen '36

Rosalind Ayres
Stardust '74
That'll Be the Day '73

Obba Babatunde
Miami Blues '90

Baby Peggy
Helen's Babies '25

Lauren Bacall
Mr. North '88
Murder on the Orient Express '74

Patrick Bachau
Acting on Impulse '93

Kevin Bacon
Queens Logic '91
Criminal Law '89

Michael Badalucco
Mac '93

Hermione Baddeley
Room at the Top '59
The Belles of St. Trinian's '53
The Woman in Question '50

Alan Badel
Luther '74
Children of the Damned '63

William Badget
Just Another Girl on the I.R.T. '93

Nuria Badia
Barcelona '94

Laurence Badie
Forbidden Games '52

Annette Badland
Angels and Insects '95

Lynne Baggett
D.O.A. '49

Maya Bagrationi
Lullaby '94

Maxine Bahns
She's the One '96
The Brothers McMullen '94

Bill Bailey
Heat and Sunlight '87

Mark Bailey
The Unbelievable Truth '90

Dave Bair
Gun Crazy '49

Antony Baird
Dead of Night '45

Don Bajema
Heat and Sunlight '87

Art Baker
Impact '49

Chet Baker
Let's Get Lost '88

Diane Baker
Twenty Bucks '93

Don Baker
In the Name of the Father '93

Dylan Baker
The Wizard of Loneliness '88

George Baker
For Queen and Country '88

Jennifer Baker
Tommy '75

Joe Don Baker
The Underneath '95
Criminal Law '89

Kathy Baker
Permanent Record '88
Street Smart '87

Stanley Baker
Bride to Be '75
The Hidden Room '49

Susan Baker
Tommy '75

Gary Bakewell
Backbeat '94

Shango Baku
Black Joy '77

Scott Bakula
My Family '94

Bob Balaban
Girlfriends '78

Josiane Balasko
Too Beautiful for You '88
Dites-Lui Que Je L'Aime '77

Balbina
The Belles of St. Trinian's '53

Adam Baldwin
The Chocolate War '88

Alec Baldwin
Miami Blues '90

Daniel Baldwin
Trees Lounge '96

Evelyn Baldwin
Struggle '31

Stephen Baldwin
The Usual Suspects '95
Last Exit to Brooklyn '90

Betty Balfour
Evergreen '34

Michael Balfour
The Private Life of Sherlock Holmes '70
Genevieve '53
Moulin Rouge '52

Andras Balint
The Unfinished Sentence in 141 Minutes '75

Eszter Balint
Trees Lounge '96
The Linguini Incident '92

Fairuza Balk
The Island of Dr. Moreau '96
Gas Food Lodging '92

Vincent Ball
Sirens '94
John and Julie '55

Edoardo Ballerini
I Shot Andy Warhol '96

Darmora Ballet
Gaslight '40

Martin Balsam
Murder on the Orient Express '74
A Thousand Clowns '65

Humbert Balsan
Lancelot of the Lake '74

Kirk Baltz
Reservoir Dogs '92

Cameron Bancroft
Love and Human Remains '93

Antonio Banderas
The House of the Spirits '93
Tie Me Up! Tie Me Down! '90
Women on the Verge of a Nervous Breakdown '88
Law of Desire '86
Matador '86

Leslie Banks
Madeleine '50
The Man Who Knew Too Much '34

Bob Bannard
The Incident '67

Ian Bannen
Eye of the Needle '81
Fright '71

Jill Banner
Spider Baby '64

Janet Banzet
Teenage Gang Debs '66

Li Bao-Tian
Ju Dou '90

Christine Baranski
New Jersey Drive '95

Adrienne Barbeau
Cannibal Women in the Avocado Jungle of Death '89

Frances Barber
Sammy & Rosie Get Laid '87

Paul Barber
The Long Good Friday '80

Joyce Barbour
Sabotage '36

Joel Barcellos
France, Incorporated '74

Trevor Bardette
Gun Crazy '49

Aleksander Bardini
Trois Couleurs: Blanc '94

Lynn Bari
The Amazing Mr. X '48

Charlotte Barker
Wish You Were Here '87

Ellen Barkin
Mac '93
The Big Easy '87
Eddie and the Cruisers '83

Ivor Barnard
Beat the Devil '53
Madeleine '50

Binnie Barnes
The Private Life of Henry VIII '33

Priscilla Barnes
Mallrats '95
The Crossing Guard '94

Susan Barnes
The Applegates '89

Charlie Barnett
Nobody's Fool '86

Lynda Baron
Hot Millions '68

Sandy Baron
Motorama '91

Byron Barr
Pitfall '48

Douglas Barr
Madeleine '50

Jean-Marc Barr
Breaking the Waves '95

Ramon Barragan
Cabeza de Vaca '90

Maria Barranco
Tie Me Up! Tie Me Down! '90
Women on the Verge of a Nervous Breakdown '88

Jean-Louis Barrault
Children of Paradise '45

Marie-Christine Barrault
Cousin, Cousine '76

Keith Barren
The Land That Time Forgot '75

Majel Barrett
Mommy '95

Ray Barrett
Brilliant Lies '96
Don's Party '76

Tony Barrett
Impact '49

John Barrie
Victim '61

Julie Barrie
They Drive by Night '38

Wendy Barrie
The Private Life of Henry VIII '33

Bruce Barry
The Good Wife '86

Gene Barry
Second Coming of Suzanne '80

Joan Barry
Rich and Strange '32

Neill Barry
Old Enough '84

Raymond J. Barry
Dead Man Walking '95

Toni Barry
A House in the Hills '93

Drew Barrymore
Guncrazy '92
Motorama '91

Yves Barsac
Two for the Road '67

Paul Bartel
Basquiat '96
The Usual Suspects '95
Shelf Life '94
Acting on Impulse '93
Scenes from the Class Struggle in Beverly Hills '89
Eating Raoul '82

Richard Barthelmess
Way Down East '20

Margaret Barton
Brief Encounter '46

Jack Barty
Gaslight '40

Richard Basehart
The Stranger's Hand '54

Alain Bashung
Shades of Doubt '93

Toni Basil
Easy Rider '69

Rudy Basquez
Slacker '91

Angela Bassett
Passion Fish '92
City of Hope '91

Linda Bassett
Waiting for the Moon '87

Michal Bat-Adam
Daughters, Daughters '74

Nikolai Batalov
Aelita: Queen of Mars '24

Geoffrey Bateman
Another Country '84

Alan Bates
Silent Tongue '92
In Celebration '75
Butley '74
Three Sisters '70
The Entertainer '60

Kathy Bates
Curse of the Starving Class '94

Michael Bates
Bedazzled '68

R.C. Bates
...And God Spoke '94

Timothy Bateson
Twisted Nerve '68

Randall Batinkoff
Walking and Talking '96
The Player '92

John Batis
Teenage Gang Debs '66

David Battley
S.O.S. Titanic '79

Patrick Bauchau
And the Band Played On '93
Chain of Desire '93
Creepers '85

Belinda Bauer
The Rosary Murders '87

Andrew Bauer-Gador
The Return of Tommy Tricker '94

Van Baum
Set It Off '96

Vincent Baum
Set It Off '96

Monika Baumgartner
The Nasty Girl '90

Barbara Baxley
A Shock to the System '90

David Baxt
The Shining '80

Francis Bay
Inside Monkey Zetterland '93

Nathalie Baye
And the Band Played On '93
The Man Who Loved Women '77

Eduardo Bea
Bride to Be '75

Michael Beach
One False Move '91

Simon Russell Beale
Persuasion '95

Jennifer Beals
Mrs. Parker and the Vicious Circle '94
In the Soup '92

Sean Bean
Black Beauty '94

Allyce Beasley
Motorama '91

Jackie Beat
Grief '94

Norman Beaten
Black Joy '77

The Beatles
The Making of a Hard Day's Night '94

Ned Beatty
Hear My Song '91
The Big Easy '87
Alambrista! '77

Hugh Beaumont
Money Madness '47
The Lady Confesses '45

Robert Beauvais
The 400 Blows '59

Konrad Becker
Das Boot '81

Kate Beckinsale
Much Ado about Nothing '93

Reginald Beckwith
Lucky Jim '58
Genevieve '53

Rod Bedall
Mona Lisa '86

Don Beddoe
Gun Crazy '49

John Bedford-Lloyd
Diary of a Hitman '91

Ed Begley, Jr.
The Applegates '89
Scenes from the Class Struggle in Beverly Hills '89
Eating Raoul '82

Rita Bekes
25 Fireman's Street '73

Doris Belack
The Luckiest Man in the World '89

Harry Belafonte
Kansas City '95

Lia Beldam
The Shining '80

Eileen Beldon
Pygmalion '38

Robert Anthony Bell
One False Move '91

Tom Bell
Let Him Have It '91
The Krays '90
Wish You Were Here '87

Rachael Bella
Household Saints '93

Bill Bellamy
Love Jones '96

Pierre Bellemare
Three Lives and Only One Death '96

Gil Bellows
Love and a .45 '94

Jean-Paul Belmondo
Breathless '59

Robert Beltran
Scenes from the Class Struggle in Beverly Hills '89
Eating Raoul '82

James Belushi
Destiny Turns on the Radio '95
Traces of Red '92
Diary of a Hitman '91
Salvador '86

Dudu Ben-Ze'ev
Ricochets '87

Robert Benchley
I Married a Witch '42

Armonia Benedito
Strictly Ballroom '92

John Benfield
In the Name of the Father '93

Hubertus Bengsch
Das Boot '81

Roberto Benigni
Night on Earth '91

Annette Bening
The Grifters '90

Floella Benjamin
Black Joy '77

Eileen Bennett
Thursday's Child '43

Fran Bennett
Wes Craven's New Nightmare '94

Hywel Bennett
Twisted Nerve '68

Jill Bennett
Hawks '89
Moulin Rouge '52

John Bennett
Priest '94
Eye of the Needle '81

The Woman in Question '50

Humphrey Bogart
Beat the Devil '53
The African Queen '51

Antonia Bogdanovich
The Whole Wide World '96

Vera Bogetti
Thursday's Child '43

Eric Bogosian
Special Effects '85

Richard Bohringer
Le Grand Chemin '87

Romane Bohringer
Mina Tannenbaum '93

Curt Bois
Wings of Desire '88

Christine Boisson
Pas Tres Catholique '93
Sorceress '88

Svetlana Bojakvic
The Dog Who Loved Trains '78

James Bolam
In Celebration '75

Eamon Boland
Business as Usual '88

J. Bolotova
Orphans '77

Catharine Bolt
The Brothers McMullen '94

Paolo Bonacelli
Night on Earth '91

Ward Bond
You Only Live Once '37

Ken Bones
Bellman and True '88

Helena Bonham Carter
Where Angels Fear to Tread '91
Maurice '87
A Room with a View '86

Priscilla Bonner
Charley's Aunt '25

Sorrell Booke
The Iceman Cometh '73

Mark Boone
Trees Lounge '96

Katrine Boorman
Camille Claudel '89

Anthony Booth
Confessions of a Window Cleaner '74

Connie Booth
Hawks '89

James Booth
That'll Be the Day '73

Caterina Boratto
8 1/2 '63

Nelly Borgeaud
The Man Who Loved Women '77

Tormek Bork
The Unbearable Lightness of Being '88

Gene Borkan
Bound '96

Stanislaw Borodkin
With You and Without You '74

Katherine Borowitz
Mac '93
Just Like in the Movies '90

Jesse Borrego
I Like It Like That '94

Philip Bosco
The Luckiest Man in the World '89

Lucia Bose
Lumiere '76

Miguel Bose
High Heels '91

Roy Bosier
Steppenwolf '74

Tom Bosley
The World of Henry Orient '64

Caitlin Bossley
Crush '93

Wade Boteler
You Only Live Once '37

Costa Botes
Forgotten Silver '96

Savannah Smith Boucher
The Applegates '89

Claude Bouchery
First Communion '77

Chili Bouchier
The Ghost Goes West '36

Patrick Bouchitey
The Best Way '76

Rene Boucicault
His Picture in the Papers '16

Jacques Boudet
Waiting for the Moon '87

Y. Boudraitis
Orphans '77

Jean Bouise
La Femme Nikita '91
I Am Cuba '64

Daniel Boulanger
Breathless '59

Gideon Boulting
Another Country '84

Matthew Boulton
Sabotage '36

Carole Bouquet
Too Beautiful for You '88

Michel Bouquet
France, Incorporated '74

Peter Bourke
S.O.S. Titanic '79

E. Bourkov
Orphans '77

Clara Bow
Helen's Babies '25

David Bower
Four Weddings and a Funeral '94

Tom Bower
River's Edge '87

Angie Bowie
Eat the Rich '87

David Bowie
Basquiat '96
The Linguini Incident '92
Absolute Beginners '86

Aldrich Bowker
I Married a Witch '42

Ryna Bowker
Living in Oblivion '94

Lisa Bowman
River of Grass '94

John Boxer
The Woman in Question '50

Sully Boyar
In the Soup '92

Alan Boyce
Permanent Record '88

Brandon Boyce
Public Access '93

Cameron Boyd
Manny & Lo '96

Guy Boyd
Ticket to Heaven '81

Sarah Boyd
Old Enough '84

Stephen Boyd
Abandon Ship '57

Miriam Boyer
Jonah Who Will Be 25 in the Year 2000 '76

Lara Flynn Boyle
Equinox '93
Red Rock West '93

Lisa Boyle
Lost Highway '96

Harvey Braban
Blackmail '29

Elizabeth Bracco
Trees Lounge '96
In the Soup '92

Lorraine Bracco
Hackers '95
Traces of Red '92

Kim Braden
That'll Be the Day '73

Jesse Bradford
Hackers '95

Richard Bradford
The Crossing Guard '94
Permanent Record '88
The Trip to Bountiful '85

Eric (Hans Gudegast) Braeden
The Ambulance '90

Sonia Braga
Kiss of the Spider Woman '85

Jill Braidwood
The Belles of St. Trinian's '53

Babs Bram
Red Rock West '93

Wilfrid Brambell
A Hard Day's Night '64
The 39 Steps '35

Kenneth Branagh
Much Ado about Nothing '93
High Season '88

Derrick Branche
My Beautiful Laundrette '85

Neville Brand
D.O.A. '49

Phoebe Brand
Vanya on 42nd Street '94

Marlon Brando
The Island of Dr. Moreau '96

Betsy Brantley
Another Country '84

Pierre Brasseur
Children of Paradise '45

Asher Brauner
Boss' Son '78
Switchblade Sisters '75

Mano Breckenridge
Chameleon Street '89

Bunny Breckinridge
Plan 9 from Outer Space '56

Larry Breeding
Street Music '81

Jacques Brel
Jacques Brel Is Alive and Well and Living in Paris '75

Ewen Bremmer
Trainspotting '95
Naked '93

Eileen Brennan
Reckless '95
Sticky Fingers '88

Michael Brennan
Fright '71

Edmund Breon
The Scarlet Pimpernel '34

Bernard Bresslaw
Morgan! '66

Jeremy Brett
The Good Soldier '81
The Very Edge '63

Cast Index

Sudha Chopra
Heat and Dust '82

Sarita Choudhury
Kama Sutra: A Tale of
Love '96
The House of the Spirits
'93
Wild West '93

Valerie Chow
Chungking Express '95

Joseph Chrest
The Underneath '95

Marilyn Chris
Rhinoceros '74

Julie Christie
Heat and Dust '82

Lindsay Christman
Twister '89

**Dennis
  Christopher**
It's My Party '95

Emily Chu
Rouge '87

Cheung Chung
Center Stage '91

David Chung
Color of a Brisk and
Leaping Day '95
The Ballad of Little Jo '93
Combination Platter '93

Berton Churchill
Turnabout '40

Donald Churchill
Victim '61

Iris Churn
An Angel at My Table '89

Eduardo Ciannelli
The Stranger's Hand '54

Kelly Cinnante
True Love '89

Bruno Cirino
Allonsanfan '73

Jacques Ciron
The Unbearable
Lightness of Being '88

Anthony Cistaro
The Method '87

Jennifer Claire
The Good Wife '86

Gordon Clapp
Eight Men Out '88
Matewan '87

Eric Clapton
Tommy '75
The Rolling Stones Rock
and Roll Circus '68

Christine Claravall
Hangin' with the
Homeboys '91

Mary Clare
Moulin Rouge '52
Young and Innocent '37

O.B. Clarence
Great Expectations '46
On Approval '44
Pygmalion '38

The Scarlet Pimpernel
'34

Anthony Clark
The Thing Called Love
'93

Ernest Clark
1984 '56

Fred Clark
Passionate Thief '60

Jameson Clark
The Battle of the Sexes
'60
The Little Kidnappers '53

Marlene Clark
Switchblade Sisters '75

Roger Clark
Girls in Chains '43

**Bernardette L.
  Clarke**
Love Jones '96

Jacqueline Clarke
Blithe Spirit '45

Richard Clarke
A Night to Remember '58

Warren Clarke
S.O.S. Titanic '79

D. A. Clarke-Smith
The Man Who Knew Too
Much '34

Patricia Clarkson
Tune in Tomorrow '90

John Claudio
Morgan's Cake '88

Christian Clavier
Dites-Lui Que Je L'Aime
'77

Jill Clayburgh
Shy People '87

John Clayton
Warm Nights on a Slow-
Moving Train '87

John Cleese
Interlude '67

**Christian
  Clemenson**
And the Band Played On
'93

Aurore Clement
Dear Michael '76
Lacombe, Lucien '74

Sophie Clement
Once Upon a Time in the
East '74

Pierre Clementi
The Red Poster '76
Steppenwolf '74
The Conformist '71

Edward Clements
Metropolitan '90

Edith Clever
The Marquise of O '76

Clare Clifford
Wish You Were Here '87

Richard Clifford
Carrington '95

Much Ado about Nothing
'93

Al Cliver
The Profiteer '74

Glenn Close
The House of the Spirits
'93

Julian Clover
Luther '74

Julie Cobb
Lisa '90

Renata Cobbs
She's Gotta Have It '86

Eva Cobo
Matador '86

Roberto Cobo
Cabeza de Vaca '90

Charles Coburn
Impact '49

Rory Cochrane
Love and a .45 '94

Gary Cockrell
Lolita '62

Camille Coduri
Nuns on the Run '90
Strapless '90
Hawks '89

Scott Coffey
Lost Highway '96
Shag: The Movie '89

Lynn Cohen
I Shot Andy Warhol '96
Walking and Talking '96
Vanya on 42nd Street '94

George Cole
Fright '71
The Belles of St. Trinian's
'53

Lester Cole
Hollywood on Trial '76

Charlotte Coleman
Different for Girls '96
Four Weddings and a
Funeral '94

Dabney Coleman
The Applegates '89

Jimmy Coleman
Priest '94

Alison Coleridge
The Shining '80

Sylvia Coleridge
I Met a Murderer '39

**Charles "Honi"
  Coles**
Dirty Dancing '87

Eileen Colgan
The Secret of Roan Inish
'94

Frederique Colin
Once Upon a Time in the
East '74

Gregoire Colin
Before the Rain '94
Pas Tres Catholique '93

Luz Maria Collazo
I Am Cuba '64

Toni Collette
Muriel's Wedding '94

Kenneth Colley
A Summer Story '88
Lisztomania '75

Peter Collingwood
Morgan! '66

Joanne Collins
Eddie and the Cruisers
'83

Pauline Collins
Shirley Valentine '89

Phil Collins
The Making of a Hard
Day's Night '94

Robert Collins
Anne of Green Gables
'85

Tara Collinson
Fright '71

Miriam Colon
Lone Star '95
The House of the Spirits
'93

Robbie Coltrane
Nuns on the Run '90
Wonderland '88
Mona Lisa '86

**Holly Marie
  Combs**
Chain of Desire '93

Jeffrey Combs
Love and a .45 '94

Anjanette Comer
The Underneath '95

Joyce Compton
Turnabout '40

Cristi Conaway
Nina Takes a Lover '94

**Laura Duke
  Condominas**
Lancelot of the Lake '74

Joe Conley
Crime of Passion '57

Howard Connell
The Little Kidnappers '53

Maureen Connell
Lucky Jim '58

Jennifer Connelly
Creepers '85

Sean Connery
A Good Man in Africa '94
Murder on the Orient
Express '74

Kenneth Connor
The Ladykillers '55

Chuck Connors
Salmonberries '91

Kevin Conroy
Chain of Desire '93

John Considine
Trouble in Mind '86

Eddie Constantine
The Long Good Friday '80

Neil Cunningham
My Beautiful Laundrette
'85

Alain Cuny
Camille Claudel '89
Emmanuelle '74

Lynette Curran
Mushrooms '95

Finlay Currie
Hand in Hand '60
Abandon Ship '57
Great Expectations '46

Tim Curry
Pass the Ammo '88

Bill Curtis
Eating Raoul '82

Donald Curtis
The Amazing Mr. X '48

Vondie Curtis-Hall
Passion Fish '92

Jamie Lee Curtis
Mother's Boys '94
Queens Logic '91
Road Games '81

Sonia Curtis
Terminal Bliss '91

Jacqueline Curtiss
Fire Maidens from Outer
Space '56

George Curzon
Clouds over Europe '39
Young and Innocent '37
The Man Who Knew Too
Much '34

Cyril Cusack
My Left Foot '89
Little Dorrit, Film 1:
Nobody's Fault '88
Little Dorrit, Film 2: Little
Dorrit's Story '88
True Confessions '81
The Homecoming '73

John Cusack
Bullets Over Broadway
'94
The Grifters '90
Eight Men Out '88

Peter Cushing
Moulin Rouge '52

Allan Cuthbertson
Room at the Top '59

Iain Cuthbertson
The Railway Children '70

Kate Cutler
Pygmalion '38

Zbigniew Cybulski
Ashes and Diamonds '58

Miriam Cyr
I Shot Andy Warhol '96

Henry Czerny
The Boys of St. Vincent
'93

**Fernando Ramos
Da Silva**
Pixote '81

Howard da Silva
Hollywood on Trial '76

Robert Dadies
One Sings, the Other
Doesn't '77

Marie Daems
One Night Stand '76

Willem Dafoe
Basquiat '96
The English Patient '96
Wild at Heart '90
Platoon '86

Elizabeth Daily
Street Music '81

David Daker
Stardust '74

Julian D'Albie
The Woman in Question
'50

Jennifer Dale
Ticket to Heaven '81

Marcel Dalio
First Communion '77

John Dall
Gun Crazy '49

Beatrice Dalle
Night on Earth '91

Joe Dallesandro
Guncrazy '92
Black Moon '75

Audrey Dalton
Separate Tables '58

Timothy Dalton
Hawks '89

Pierre Daltour
I Have Killed '24

Roger Daltrey
Lightning Jack '94
Lisztomania '75
Tommy '75

Mark Daly
The Ghost Goes West
'36

Seadia Damar
The Garden '77

Malcolm Danare
Popcorn '89

Charles Dance
Michael Collins '96
Century '94
White Mischief '88

Evan Dando
Heavy '94

John Danelle
The Rosary Murders '87

Beverly D'Angelo
Lightning Jack '94

Isa Danieli
Everything Ready,
Nothing Works '74

Eddie Daniels
Rhythm Thief '94

Jeff Daniels
The House on Carroll
Street '88

William Daniels
Two for the Road '67
A Thousand Clowns '65

Roger Dann
Two for the Road '67

Blythe Danner
Homage '95

Royal Dano
Killer Inside Me '76
Crime of Passion '57

Nelson Dantas
The Marriage '76

Maia Danzinger
Last Exit to Brooklyn '90

**Ingeborga
Dapkounaite**
Burnt by the Sun '94

Patti D'Arbanville
Wired '89

Mason Daring
Matewan '87

James Darren
Boss' Son '78

Danielle Darrieux
The World of Jacques
Demy '95

Claude Dauphin
Two for the Road '67

Elyssa Davalos
A House in the Hills '93

Nigel Davenport
Peeping Tom '60

Keith David
Platoon '86

Jaye Davidson
The Crying Game '92

Betty Ann Davies
The Belles of St. Trinian's
'53

Freddie Davies
Funny Bones '94

Jeremy Davies
Spanking the Monkey '94

Nicholas Davies
S.O.S. Titanic '79

Ray Davies
Absolute Beginners '86

Richard Davies
Twisted Nerve '68

Rudi Davies
Frankie Starlight '95
The Lonely Passion of
Judith Hearne '87

Stephen Davies
The Long Good Friday '80

Bette Davis
The Whales of August
'87

Clifton Davis
Lost in the Stars '74

Hope Davis
The Daytrippers '96

Judy Davis
Where Angels Fear to
Tread '91

Impromptu '90

Marianne Davis
Thursday's Child '43

Marvin Davis
Tomorrow the World '44

Sammi Davis
The Lair of the White
Worm '88
Mona Lisa '86

Stringer Davis
The Smallest Show on
Earth '57

Bruce Davison
Grace of My Heart '96
Homage '95
It's My Party '95
Short Cuts '93
Longtime Companion '90

Peter Davison
Black Beauty '94

Anthony Dawson
Tiger Bay '59
The Woman in Question
'50

Kamala Dawson
Lightning Jack '94

Rosario Dawson
Kids '95

Cora Lee Day
Daughters of the Dust
'91

Diana Day
The Belles of St. Trinian's
'53

Josette Day
Beauty and the Beast '46

Matt Day
Muriel's Wedding '94

Peter Day
Bride to Be '75

Daniel Day-Lewis
In the Name of the Father
'93
My Left Foot '89
The Unbearable
Lightness of Being '88
A Room with a View '86
My Beautiful Laundrette
'85

Gabrielle Daye
In Celebration '75

Isaach de Bankole
Night on Earth '91

Brenda de Banzie
The Mark '61
The Entertainer '60

**Renato de
Carmine**
Allonsanfan '73

Cinzia de Carolis
A Virgin Named Mary '75

Louise De Cormier
The Spitfire Grill '95

Peppino de Filippo
Variety Lights '51

Marina De Graaf
Antonia's Line '95

Consuelo de Haviland
The Unbearable Lightness of Being '88

Jaime de Hoyos
El Mariachi '93

Danny De La Paz
Miracle Mile '89

Kitty De Legh
They Drive by Night '38

Derek De Lint
The Unbearable Lightness of Being '88

Michael De Lorenzo
My Family '94

Maria De Medeiros
Pulp Fiction '94

Arthur De Montalembert
Lancelot of the Lake '74

Robert De Niro
True Confessions '81

Rossy de Palma
Kika '94
Tie Me Up! Tie Me Down! '90
Women on the Verge of a Nervous Breakdown '88

Miranda de Pencier
Anne of Green Gables '85

Portia de Rossi
Sirens '94

Anthony De Sando
Federal Hill '94
Party Girl '94
Grand Isle '91

Joe De Santis
A Cold Wind in August '61

Rosana De Soto
Stand and Deliver '88

Jules de Spoly
I Have Killed '24

Elsje de Wijn
For a Lost Soldier '93

Francis De Wolff
The Smallest Show on Earth '57
The Little Kidnappers '53

Allison Dean
Ruby in Paradise '93

Felicity Dean
Persuasion '95
The Whistle Blower '87

Jacques Debary
The Wonderful Crook '75

The Debonairs
That'll Be the Day '73

Diana Decker
Lolita '62

Eugene Deckers
Madeleine '50

Jan Decleir
Antonia's Line '95

Guy Decomble
The 400 Blows '59

Michelle DeCosta
The Refrigerator '91

Kutira Decosterd
Men in Love '90

Ruby Dee
The Incident '67
The Balcony '63

Don DeFore
Too Late for Tears '49

John Dehner
Killer Inside Me '76

Khigh Deigh
The Manchurian Candidate '62

Christine Dejoux
In a Wild Moment '78

Dafna Dekel
Zohar: Mediterranean Blues '93

Albert Dekker
Kiss Me Deadly '55

Carla Del Poggio
Variety Lights '51

Dulio Del Prete
The Devil Is a Woman '75

Benicio Del Toro
Basquiat '96
The Funeral '96
The Usual Suspects '95
Swimming with Sharks '94

Juan deLanda
Ossessione '42

Erik Dellums
She's Gotta Have It '86

Heather DeLoach
A Little Princess '95

Julie Delpy
Trois Couleurs: Blanc '94

Gerald Delsol
Children of the Damned '63

Claudio Deluca
Small Change '76

Frank Deluca
Small Change '76

Derrick DeMarney
Young and Innocent '37

Orane Demazis
French Provincial '75

David DeMering
Plan 9 from Outer Space '56

Kristine Demers
The Boys of St. Vincent '93

Rebecca DeMornay
Dealers '89
The Trip to Bountiful '85

Jeffrey DeMunn
Betrayed '88

Jacques Demy
The 400 Blows '59

Mathieu Demy
101 Nights '95

Judi Dench
A Handful of Dust '88
A Room with a View '86
Luther '74

Catherine Deneuve
The World of Jacques Demy '95
If I Had It to Do Over Again '76
Repulsion '65

Maurice Denham
Luther '74
The Very Edge '63
The Mark '61

Jacques Denis
Dites-Lui Que Je L'Aime '77
Jonah Who Will Be 25 in the Year 2000 '76

Anthony John Denison
City of Hope '91

Barry Dennan
The Shining '80

Brian Dennehy
The Belly of an Architect '91

Charles Denner
Robert et Robert '78
The Man Who Loved Women '77
If I Had It to Do Over Again '76

Nick Dennis
Kiss Me Deadly '55

Walter DePalma
You Only Live Once '37

Gerard Depardieu
Camille Claudel '89
Too Beautiful for You '88
Dites-Lui Que Je L'Aime '77
The Wonderful Crook '75

Johnny Depp
Dead Man '95
Platoon '86

Bruce Dern
After Dark, My Sweet '90

Laura Dern
Citizen Ruth '96
Rambling Rose '91
Wild at Heart '90
Blue Velvet '86
Smooth Talk '85

Ines Des Longchamps
Stardust '74

Gerard Desarthe
France, Incorporated '74

Georges Descrieres
Two for the Road '67

Geory Desmouceaux
Small Change '76

Ivan Desny
Madeleine '50

Louis D'Esposito
Eddie and the Cruisers '83

Ernst Deutsch
The Third Man '49

Marie Devereux
The Mark '61

Julia Devin
The Tie that Binds '95

Francis Devlaeminck
Small Change '76

Laurent Devlaeminck
Small Change '76

Alan Devlin
The Lonely Passion of Judith Hearne '87

William Devlin
I Met a Murderer '39

Lorraine Devon
To Cross the Rubicon '91

Felicity Devonshire
Lisztomania '75

Jon DeVries
Grand Isle '91

Patrick Dewaere
The Best Way '76
Victory March '76

Colleen Dewhurst
Anne of Green Gables '85

William Dewhurst
Non-Stop New York '37
Sabotage '36

Anthony Dexter
Fire Maidens from Outer Space '56

Susan Dey
The Trouble with Dick '88

Dalia di Lazzaro
Creepers '85

Carmelo Di Mazzarelli
Lamerica '95

Rodney Diak
Fire Maidens from Outer Space '56

Rick Dial
Sling Blade '96

Otto Diamont
Lisztomania '75

Cameron Diaz
She's the One '96

Chico Diaz
The Fable of the Beautiful
Pigeon Fancier '88

Edith Diaz
Scenes from the Class
Struggle in Beverly Hills
'89

Guillermo Diaz
Girls Town '95
Party Girl '94

Luigi Diberti
Everything Ready,
Nothing Works '74

Andy Dick
...And God Spoke '94

Avital Dicker
Song of the Siren '94

**Ernest R.
Dickerson**
She's Gotta Have It '86

George Dickerson
After Dark, My Sweet '90
Blue Velvet '86
Cutter's Way '81

Michel Didym
Pas Tres Catholique '93

Juan Diego
Cabeza de Vaca '90

John Diehl
Color of a Brisk and
Leaping Day '95
Motorama '91

Gustav Diesl
Pandora's Box '28

Samuel Dietert
Slacker '91

Basil Dignam
Twisted Nerve '68

Bradford Dillman
The Iceman Cometh '73

Kevin Dillon
Platoon '86

Matt Dillon
Grace of My Heart '96
Frankie Starlight '95
To Die For '95
Golden Gate '93
Drugstore Cowboy '89

Tom Dillon
Night Tide '63

**Francesca
DiMauro**
Living in Oblivion '94

Richard Dimbleby
John and Julie '55

Ayub Khan Din
Sammy & Rosie Get Laid
'87

Peter Dinklage
Living in Oblivion '94

Phillip Dinn
The Boys of St. Vincent
'93

Divine
Trouble in Mind '86
Female Trouble '74

Beth Dixon
The Ballad of the Sad
Cafe '91

Jean Dixon
You Only Live Once '37

Jill Dixon
A Night to Remember '58

Edward Dmytryk
Hollywood on Trial '76

Alan Dobie
White Mischief '88

Anica Dobra
Tito and Me '92

**Gosia
Dobrowolska**
Careful '94
Phobia '88

Peter Dobson
Last Exit to Brooklyn '90

Vernon Dobtcheff
Murder on the Orient
Express '74

**Michal
Docolomansky**
Dinner for Adele '78

Brian Dodd
The Boys of St. Vincent
'93

Jimmie Dodd
Too Late for Tears '49

John Doe
Georgia '95

Shannen Doherty
Mallrats '95
Heathers '89

Arielle Dombasle
Three Lives and Only One
Death '96

**Solveig
Dommartin**
Wings of Desire '88

Robert Donat
The Ghost Goes West
'36
The 39 Steps '35
The Private Life of Henry
VIII '33

Yolande Donlan
Turnabout '40

Brian Donlevy
Impact '49

**Barnard Pierre
Donnadieu**
The Vanishing '88

Donal Donnelly
The Dead '87

**Elizabeth
D'Onofrio**
The Whole Wide World
'96

Vincent D'Onofrio
The Whole Wide World
'96

Household Saints '93
The Player '92
Mystic Pizza '88

Amanda Donohoe
The Madness of King
George '94
The Lair of the White
Worm '88

Walter Donohue
My Beautiful Laundrette
'85

Martin Donovan
Nadja '95
Trust '91

Tate Donovan
Equinox '93
Inside Monkey Zetterland
'93

Brian Dooley
The Boys of St. Vincent
'93

Paul Dooley
The Underneath '95

Patric Doonan
John and Julie '55

Robert DoQui
Miracle Mile '89

Ann Doran
Pitfall '48

Stephen Dorff
I Shot Andy Warhol '96
Reckless '95
Backbeat '94

Cliff Dorfman
Acting on Impulse '93

Sandra Dori
A Virgin Named Mary '75

Sandra Dorne
Eat the Rich '87

Diana Dors
Deep End '70

John Dossett
Longtime Companion '90

Julian Roy Doster
Menace II Society '93

Els Dottermans
Antonia's Line '95

Doug E. Doug
Hangin' with the
Homeboys '91

Illeana Douglas
Grace of My Heart '96
To Die For '95
Grief '94
Search and Destroy '94
Household Saints '93

Kirk Douglas
Champion '49

Shirley Douglas
Lolita '62

Suzanne Douglas
Chain of Desire '93

Brad Dourif
London Kills Me '91
Grim Prairie Tales '89
Blue Velvet '86

Betsy Dowds
Ruby in Paradise '93

Raye Dowell
She's Gotta Have It '86

Alan Downer
The Good Soldier '81

Robert Downey, Jr.
Short Cuts '93
Chaplin '92

Jacqueline Doyen
Dear Victor '75

Jack Doyle
The Belles of St. Trinian's
'53

Valda Z. Drabla
Swoon '91

Billy Drago
Guncrazy '92

Claudia Drake
Detour '46
The Lady Confesses '45

Sylvie Drapeau
Le Sexe des Etoiles '93

Milena Dravic
Fear '75

Melanie Dreisbach
The Method '87

Sonia Dresdel
The Fallen Idol '49

Ruth Drexel
The Marquise of O '76

**Jean Claude
Dreyfus**
The City of Lost Children
'95

Richard Dreyfuss
Second Coming of
Suzanne '80

Minnie Driver
Big Night '95

Denis Drouin
Once Upon a Time in the
East '74

Tatiana Drubich
100 Days after Childhood
'75

**Reana E.
Drummond**
Straight Out of Brooklyn
'91

Jeanie Drynan
Muriel's Wedding '94
Don's Party '76

Roland Dubillard
France, Incorporated '74

Yudel Dubinsky
American Matchmaker
'40

Guilhaine Dubos
L'Amour en Herbe '77

David Duchovny
Kalifornia '93
Chaplin '92

Neil Dudgeon
Different for Girls '96**

Lesley Dudley
John and Julie '55

Shoshanah Duer
The Garden '77

Jacques Dufilho
Dear Victor '75

Huguette Duflos
I Have Killed '24

Aaron Dugger
She's Gotta Have It '86

Olympia Dukakis
In the Spirit '90

Bill Duke
Menace II Society '93

Robin Duke
Motorama '91

Denise Dumont
Kiss of the Spider
Woman '85

James DuMont
Combination Platter '93

Dennis Dun
Thousand Pieces of Gold
'91

Adrian Dunbar
The Crying Game '92
Hear My Song '91
My Left Foot '89

Catherine Duncan
Shirley Valentine '89

Peter Duncan
Stardust '74

Claude Duneton
Trois Couleurs: Bleu '93

Emma Dunn
I Married a Witch '42

Geoffrey Dunn
Leather Boys '63

Kevin Dunn
Chaplin '92

Nora Dunn
Passion Fish '92
Miami Blues '90

Griffin Dunne
I Like It Like That '94
Search and Destroy '94
After Hours '85

Philip Dupuy
Another Country '84

**Christopher
Durang**
In the Spirit '90
Mr. North '88

Geoffrey Durham
Wish You Were Here '87

Barbara Durkin
Wish You Were Here '87

Charles Durning
The Rosary Murders '87
True Confessions '81

Dan Duryea
Too Late for Tears '49

Ann Dusenberry
Cutter's Way '81

Charles S. Dutton
Menace II Society '93

James Duval
The Doom Generation
'95

Robert Duvall
Sling Blade '96
Rambling Rose '91
True Confessions '81

Shelley Duvall
The Underneath '95
The Shining '80

Franklin Dyall
The Private Life of Henry
VIII '33

Valentine Dyall
Brief Encounter '46
Pink String and Sealing
Wax '45

James Dyrenforth
Lolita '62
Never Take Candy from a
Stranger '60

Anulka Dziubinska
Lisztomania '75

Nicholas Eadie
Celia: Child of Terror '90

Marion Eaten
The Whole Wide World
'96

Marjorie Eaton
Night Tide '63

**Christopher
Eccleston**
Shallow Grave '94
Let Him Have It '91

**Jean-Philippe
Ecoffey**
Mina Tannenbaum '93

Dave Edmunds
Stardust '74

Beatie Edney
In the Name of the Father
'93

Richard Edson
Eight Men Out '88
Platoon '86

Annie-Joe Edwards
Bullets Over Broadway
'94

Anthony Edwards
Hawks '89
Miracle Mile '89
Mr. North '88

Henry Edwards
Madeleine '50

Hilton Edwards
Victim '61

Luke Edwards
Mother's Boys '94

Vince Edwards
Motorama '91

Richard Egan
Wicked Woman '54

Konstantin Eggert
Aelita: Queen of Mars
'24

Deven Eggleston
New Jersey Drive '95

Stan Egi
Golden Gate '93

Jennifer Ehle
Backbeat '94

Lisa Eichhorn
A Modern Affair '94
Grim Prairie Tales '89
Cutter's Way '81

**Christopher
Eigeman**
Barcelona '94
Metropolitan '90

Menahem Einy
Zohar: Mediterranean
Blues '93

Debra Eisenstadt
Oleanna '94

Britt Ekland
Scandal '89

Agneta Ekmanner
Paradise Place '77

Jack Elam
Kiss Me Deadly '55

Ron Eldard
Bastard out of Carolina
'96
True Love '89

Tom Eldred
Teenage Gang Debs '66

Michael Elgart
Permanent Record '88

Mark Eliot
Stand and Deliver '88

Kimberly Elise
Set It Off '96

Shawn Elliot
Caught '96

Alison Elliott
The Spitfire Grill '95
The Underneath '95

Denholm Elliott
Maurice '87
A Room with a View '86

Stephen Elliott
Cutter's Way '81

Aunjanue Ellis
Girls Town '95

James Ellis
Priest '94

Robin Ellis
The Good Soldier '81

Art Ellison
Carnival of Souls '62

Michael Elphick
Let Him Have It '91
Little Dorrit, Film 1:
Nobody's Fault '88
Little Dorrit, Film 2: Little
Dorrit's Story '88
Withnail and I '87

Robert Elross
The Method '87

Ben Elton
Much Ado about Nothing
'93

Cary Elwes
Another Country '84

Roy Emerton
Nine Days a Queen '36

Michael Emil
In the Spirit '90
Tracks '76

Daniel Emilfork
The City of Lost Children
'95

**Alphonsia
Emmanuel**
Under Suspicion '92

Takis Emmanuel
Caddie '76

Susan Engel
Butley '74

Tina Engel
The Second Awakening of
Christa Klages '78

Nadja Engelbrecht
Meier '87

Robert Englund
Wes Craven's New
Nightmare '94

Anthony Ennis
Chameleon Street '89

John Entwhistle
Tommy '75

Kathryn Erbe
The Addiction '95

R. Lee Ermey
Dead Man Walking '95

Eileen Erskine
This Happy Breed '47
Great Expectations '46

Victor Ertmanis
Paris, France '94

Bernard Escalon
Trois Couleurs: Rouge
'94

Giancarlo Esposito
Reckless '95
Smoke '95
The Usual Suspects '95
Fresh '94
Night on Earth '91

David Essex
Stardust '74
That'll Be the Day '73

Agnes Esterhazy
Joyless Street '25

Karl Ettlinger
Joyless Street '25

Douglas Evans
Actors and Sin '52

Evans Evans
The Iceman Cometh '73

Lee Evans
Funny Bones '94

Lucas Evans
Tommy Tricker & the
Stamp Traveller '87

Barbara Everest
Madeleine '50

Rupert Everett
Cemetery Man '95
The Madness of King
George '94
Inside Monkey Zetterland
'93
The Comfort of Strangers
'91
Dance with a Stranger
'85
Another Country '84

E. Evstigneev
Orphans '77

Dwight Ewell
Chasing Amy '97

Peter Eyre
Orlando '92

Maynard Eziashi
Twenty-One '91

Matthew Faber
Welcome to the
Dollhouse '95

Adriana Fachetti
Enchanted April '92

Tom Fadden
Tomorrow the World '44

Mary-Anne Fahey
Celia: Child of Terror '90

**Douglas
Fairbanks, Sr.**
His Picture in the Papers
'16

Donald A. Faison
New Jersey Drive '95

Frankie Faison
City of Hope '91

Matthew Faison
True Confessions '81

Adam Faith
Stardust '74

Marianne Faithfull
The Rolling Stones Rock
and Roll Circus '68

Amina Fakir
Chameleon Street '89

Anna Falchi
Cemetery Man '95

Edie Falco
The Addiction '95
Trust '91

Lisanne Falk
Night on Earth '91
Heathers '89

Peter Falk
In the Spirit '90
Tune in Tomorrow '90
Wings of Desire '88
The Balcony '63

Rossella Falk
8 1/2 '63

Deborah Fallender
S.O.S. Titanic '79

Mei Fang
One Night Stand '76

Rio Fanning
Priest '94

Souad Faress
My Beautiful Laundrette
'85

Betty Faria
The Story of Fausta '88

Carolyn Farina
Metropolitan '90

Dennis Farina
Mac '93

Gary Farmer
Dead Man '95
Powwow Highway '89

Mimsy Farmer
Allonsanfan '73

Virginia Farmer
Gun Crazy '49

**Richard
Farnsworth**
Anne of Green Gables
'85

Eric Farr
Rock Hudson's Home
Movies '92

Malik Farrakhan
Daughters of the Dust
'91

David Farrar
The Obsessed '51
Black Narcissus '47

Colin Farrell
The Land That Time
Forgot '75

Lily Farrell
Ladybird, Ladybird '93

Timothy Farrell
Girl Gang '54

Mia Farrow
Reckless '95

Andrew Faulds
Lisztomania '75

Lisa Faulkner
A Feast at Midnight '95

Consuelo Faust
Heat and Sunlight '87

Janina Faye
Never Take Candy from a
Stranger '60

Jan Fedder
Das Boot '81

Frederique Feder
Trois Couleurs: Rouge
'94

Frances Feist
Carnival of Souls '62

Nicole Felix
Small Change '76

Federico Fellini
The Miracle '48

Tanya Fenmore
Lisa '90

Sherilyn Fenn
Diary of a Hitman '91
Wild at Heart '90

Lance Fenton
Heathers '89

Colm Feore
32 Short Films about
Glenn Gould '93

Adam Ferency
The Interrogation '82

Rene Feret
First Communion '77
Lumiere '76

**Matthew
Ferguson**
Love and Human
Remains '93

Karen Fergusson
An Angel at My Table '89

Juan Fernandez
Salvador '86

Conchata Ferrell
Mystic Pizza '88
Heartland '81

Tyra Ferrell
Equinox '93

Andrea Ferreol
The Sleazy Uncle '89
Servant and Mistress '77
A Virgin Named Mary '75

Jose Ferrer
Moulin Rouge '52

**Leilani Sarelle
Ferrer**
Shag: The Movie '89

Benoit Ferreux
Murmur of the Heart '71

Lou Ferrigno
...And God Spoke '94

Barbara Ferris
The Krays '90
A Chorus of Disapproval
'89
Interlude '67
Children of the Damned
'63

Turi Ferro
A Virgin Named Mary '75

Gabriele Ferzetti
Julia and Julia '87

Larry Fessenden
River of Grass '94

William Fichtner
The Underneath '95

Betty Field
Tomorrow the World '44

David Field
To Have and to Hold '96

Mary Field
I Married a Witch '42

Sallie-Anne Field
Dance with a Stranger
'85

Shirley Anne Field
Hear My Song '91
Shag: The Movie '89
My Beautiful Laundrette
'85
The Entertainer '60
Peeping Tom '60

Todd Field
Walking and Talking '96
Ruby in Paradise '93

Robert Fields
Anna '87
The Incident '67

Ralph Fiennes
The English Patient '96

Patrick Fierry
First Communion '77

Harvey Fierstein
Bullets Over Broadway
'94

Denise Filatrault
Once Upon a Time in the
East '74

Audrey Fildes
Kind Hearts and
Coronets '49

Brandao Filho
The Story of Fausta '88

Daniel Filho
The Story of Fausta '88

Freddie Findlay
A Feast at Midnight '95

Agnes Fink
False Weights '74

Frank Finlay
Twisted Nerve '68

Siobhan Finneran
Rita, Sue & Bob Too '87

Warren Finnerty
Easy Rider '69

Albert Finney
Murder on the Orient
Express '74
Two for the Road '67
The Entertainer '60

Anni Finsterer
To Have and to Hold '96

Elena Fiore
Seven Beauties '76

Kristin Fiorella
Curse of the Starving
Class '94

Linda Fiorentino
The Last Seduction '94
Acting on Impulse '93
Chain of Desire '93
Queens Logic '91
After Hours '85

Colin Firth
The English Patient '96
Another Country '84

Kate Fischer
Sirens '94

Ramona Fischer
Vegas in Space '94

Cast Index

Warm Nights on a Slow-
Moving Train '87
Paul Frison
Gun Crazy '49
Gustav Froehlich
Metropolis '26
Piotr Fronczewski
The Balance '75
Sadie Frost
The Krays '90
Taylor Fry
A Little Princess '95
Leo Fuchs
American Matchmaker
'40
Kurt Fuller
Miracle Mile '89
Edward Furlong
Little Odessa '94
American Heart '92
Yvonne Furneaux
Repulsion '65
Judith Furse
Black Narcissus '47
Jaro Furth
Joyless Street '25
Billy Fury
That'll Be the Day '73
Christopher Gable
The Lair of the White
Worm '88
Zsa Zsa Gabor
Moulin Rouge '52
Renee Gadd
Dead of Night '45
Marjorie Gaffney
Evergreen '34
Jenny Gago
My Family '94
Michael Gahr
The Nasty Girl '90
Claude Gai
Once Upon a Time in the
East '74
M.C. Gainey
Citizen Ruth '96
**Charlotte
Gainsbourg**
Jane Eyre '96
Janusz Gajos
Trois Couleurs: Blanc '94
The Interrogation '82
Michel Galabru
L'Amour en Herbe '77
Eddra Gale
8 1/2 '63
Linda Gale
Teenage Gang Debs '66
Anna Galiena
Three Lives and Only One
Death '96
Megan Gallagher
The Ambulance '90
Peter Gallagher
The Underneath '95

Mrs. Parker and the
Vicious Circle '94
Mother's Boys '94
Short Cuts '93
The Player '92
Tune in Tomorrow '90
sex, lies and videotape
'89
Dreamchild '85
Carlos Gallardo
El Mariachi '93
Jose Gallardo
I Am Cuba '64
Carla Gallo
Spanking the Monkey '94
Vincent Gallo
The Funeral '96
Angela '94
The House of the Spirits
'93
Arturo Galster
Vegas in Space '94
James Gammon
Hard Traveling '85
Bruno Ganz
Strapless '90
Wings of Desire '88
Lumiere '76
The Marquise of O '76
Victor Garber
Exotica '94
Greta Garbo
Joyless Street '25
Andy Garcia
Stand and Deliver '88
Isaiah Garcia
I Like It Like That '94
Raul Garcia
I Am Cuba '64
Ginette Garcin
Blue Country '77
Cousin, Cousine '76
Henri Garcin
101 Nights '95
Joan Gardner
The Scarlet Pimpernel
'34
Katya Gardner
Careful '94
**Allen (Goorwitz)
Garfield**
Destiny Turns on the
Radio '95
Number One '76
John Garfield
He Ran All the Way '51
William Gargan
Turnabout '40
You Only Live Once '37
Beverly Garland
D.O.A. '49
Amulette Garneau
Once Upon a Time in the
East '74

Gale Garnett
32 Short Films about
Glenn Gould '93
Janeane Garofalo
Coldblooded '94
Teri Garr
After Hours '85
Bob Garrett
Eddie and the Cruisers
'83
Elizabeth Garvie
The Good Soldier '81
Vincent Gaskins
The Underneath '95
Vittorio Gassman
The Sleazy Uncle '89
Jany Gastaldi
First Communion '77
Jill Gatsby
The Ambulance '90
Mikkel Gaup
Breaking the Waves '95
Claude Gauthier
The Orders '75
Jean-Yves Gautier
Three Lives and Only One
Death '96
Julie Gayet
101 Nights '95
Monica Gayle
Switchblade Sisters '75
George Gaynes
Vanya on 42nd Street '94
Wendy Gazelle
Sammy & Rosie Get Laid
'87
Ben Gazzara
The Killing of a Chinese
Bookie '76
Passionate Thief '60
Anthony Geary
It Takes Two '88
Pass the Ammo '88
Karl Geary
Nadja '95
Jason Gedrick
Stacking '87
Ellen Geer
Hard Traveling '85
Daniel Gelin
Murmur of the Heart '71
Gladys George
He Ran All the Way '51
Heinrich George
Metropolis '26
Susan George
Fright '71
Jim Gerald
Moulin Rouge '52
Harriet Gerard
Vampyr '31
Mark Gerber
Sirens '94
Nane Germon
Beauty and the Beast '46

**Christopher-
Michael Gerrard**
Fly by Night '93
Gina Gershon
Bound '96
The Player '92
City of Hope '91
Valeska Gert
Joyless Street '25
Balthazar Getty
Lost Highway '96
John Getz
Blood Simple '85
**Mohammed
Ghaffari**
Little Odessa '94
Marilyn Ghigliotti
Clerks '94
Kulvinder Ghir
Rita, Sue & Bob Too '87
Giancarlo Giannini
The Sleazy Uncle '89
Seven Beauties '76
Swept Away... '75
Cynthia Gibb
Jack's Back '87
Salvador '86
Billie Gibson
The Shining '80
Colin Gibson
John and Julie '55
Dale Gibson
Red Rock West '93
Henry Gibson
Color of a Brisk and
Leaping Day '95
Tune in Tomorrow '90
Thomas Gibson
Barcelona '94
Love and Human
Remains '93
Pamela Gidley
Permanent Record '88
Therese Giehse
Black Moon '75
Lacombe, Lucien '74
John Gielgud
Shine '95
The Whistle Blower '87
Murder on the Orient
Express '74
Galileo '73
Roland Gift
Scandal '89
Sammy & Rosie Get Laid
'87
Jody Gilbert
Actors and Sin '52
Taylor Gilbert
The Method '87
Hilary Gilford
Living in Oblivion '94
Jack Gilford
The Incident '67
Basil Gill
Sidewalks of London '38

Jane Gray
The House of the Spirits
'93

Nadia Gray
Two for the Road '67

Sally Gray
The Hidden Room '49

Spalding Gray
Twenty Bucks '93
Heavy Petting '89

Vivean Gray
Picnic at Hanging Rock
'75

Calvin Green
Exotica '94

Danny Green
The Ladykillers '55
Non-Stop New York '37

Rev. Ervin Green
Daughters of the Dust
'91

Frances Green
Never Take Candy from a
Stranger '60

Marika Green
Emmanuelle '74

Martyn Green
The Iceman Cometh '73

Pamela Green
Peeping Tom '60

Bill Greene
Lolita '62

Graham Greene
Powwow Highway '89

Peter Greene
The Usual Suspects '95
Clean, Shaven '93

Richard Greene
Special Effects '85

Tom Greenway
Impact '49

Bruce Greenwood
Exotica '94

Joan Greenwood
Little Dorrit, Film 1:
Nobody's Fault '88
Little Dorrit, Film 2: Little
Dorrit's Story '88
Kind Hearts and
Coronets '49
Saraband for Dead
Lovers '48

Claire Greet
Sidewalks of London '38

Everley Gregg
The Woman in Question
'50
Brief Encounter '46
Great Expectations '46
Pygmalion '38
The Ghost Goes West
'36
The Private Life of Henry
VIII '33

Virginia Gregg
The Amazing Mr. X '48

Rose Gregorio
City of Hope '91
Five Corners '88
True Confessions '81

Andre Gregory
Vanya on 42nd Street '94
The Linguini Incident '92
Street Smart '87

James Gregory
The Manchurian
Candidate '62

John Gregson
Fright '71
Hand in Hand '60
Genevieve '53

Joyce Grenfell
The Belles of St. Trinian's
'53
Genevieve '53

Rainer Grenkowitz
Meier '87

Aidan Grennell
In the Name of the Father
'93

Laurent Grevill
Camille Claudel '89

Jennifer Grey
Dirty Dancing '87

Joel Grey
Kafka '91

Virginia Grey
Crime of Passion '57

Sylvie Grezel
Small Change '76

Jonathan Gries
Kill Me Again '89

Joe Grifasi
Heavy '94
Household Saints '93
City of Hope '91
Matewan '87

Robert Griffin
Crime of Passion '57

Guy Griffis
Blessing '94

Melora Griffis
Blessing '94

Hugh Griffith
Luther '74
Lucky Jim '58
Kind Hearts and
Coronets '49

Kenneth Griffith
The Englishman Who
Went Up a Hill But
Came Down a
Mountain '95
Four Weddings and a
Funeral '94
Tiger Bay '59
Lucky Jim '58
A Night to Remember '58
1984 '56

Melanie Griffith
In the Spirit '90
The Garden '77

Richard Griffith
Funny Bones '94

Michael Griffiths
Living in Oblivion '94

Rachel Griffiths
To Have and to Hold '96
Muriel's Wedding '94

Richard Griffiths
Withnail and I '87

John Grillo
The Good Soldier '81

Tammy Grimes
A Modern Affair '94
Mr. North '88

Unity Grimwood
The Hours and Times '92

**Herbert
Gronemeyer**
Das Boot '81

Gary Groomes
Wired '89

Gustav Grundgens
M '31

Ilka Gruning
Joyless Street '25

Ah-Leh Gua
Eat Drink Man Woman
'94
The Wedding Banquet
'93

Robert Guajardo
Red Rock West '93

Dominic Guard
Picnic at Hanging Rock
'75

Nikolai Gubenko
Orphans '77

Vanessa Guedj
Le Grand Chemin '87

Christopher Guest
Sticky Fingers '88
Girlfriends '78

Lance Guest
The Wizard of Loneliness
'88

Giovanni Guidelli
Where Angels Fear to
Tread '91

Paul Guilfoyle
Manny & Lo '96
Little Odessa '94
Mother's Boys '94
Actors and Sin '52

Fernando Guillen
Women on the Verge of a
Nervous Breakdown
'88

Tim Guinee
Sudden Manhattan '96
Chain of Desire '93

Alec Guinness
Kafka '91
A Handful of Dust '88
Little Dorrit, Film 1:
Nobody's Fault '88

Little Dorrit, Film 2: Little
Dorrit's Story '88
The Ladykillers '55
Kind Hearts and
Coronets '49
Great Expectations '46

Julien Guiomar
French Provincial '75

Devon Gummersall
It's My Party '95

Moses Gunn
The Iceman Cometh '73

Ernst Gunther
Metamorphosis '75

Bob Gunton
Matewan '87

Boaz Gur-Lavi
Song of the Siren '94

Tyrone Guthrie
Sidewalks of London '38

Lucy Gutteridge
Grief '94

Deryck Guyler
A Hard Day's Night '64

Michael Gwynn
Never Take Candy from a
Stranger '60
Village of the Damned
'60

Lukas Haas
Rambling Rose '91
The Lady in White '88
The Wizard of Loneliness
'88

**Joachim
Hackethal**
Strongman Ferdinand '76

Ron Hackett
That'll Be the Day '73

**Francois Hadji-
Lazaro**
Cemetery Man '95

Edna Hagan
Struggle '31

Sean Haggerty
Rhythm Thief '94

Larry Hagman
Stardust '74

Sid Haig
Spider Baby '64

Herbert Halbik
The Third Man '49

Creighton Hale
Way Down East '20

Georgina Hale
Butley '74

Jonathan Hale
You Only Live Once '37

Sonnie Hale
Evergreen '34

Albert Hall
Betrayed '88

Ben Hall
You Only Live Once '37

Brian Hall
The Long Good Friday '80

Lois Hall
Kalifornia '93

May Hallatt
Separate Tables '58

Jackson Halliday
Struggle '31

May Hallitt
Black Narcissus '47

Billy Halop
Too Late for Tears '49

Carrie Hamilton
Shag: The Movie '89

Margaret Hamilton
You Only Live Once '37

Patricia Hamilton
Anne of Green Gables '85

Victoria Hamilton
Persuasion '95

Kay Hammond
Blithe Spirit '45

Roger Hammond
The Good Soldier '81

Col. Bruce Hampton
Sling Blade '96

James Hampton
Sling Blade '96

Maggie Han
Open Season '95

Lou Hancock
Miracle Mile '89

Sheila Hancock
Hawks '89

Irene Handl
Secrets and Lies '95
The Private Life of Sherlock Holmes '70
Morgan! '66
The Belles of St. Trinian's '53
Brief Encounter '46
Night Train to Munich '40

Rene Handren-Seals
Powwow Highway '89

Clarence Handysides
His Picture in the Papers '16

Jimmy Hanley
Gaslight '40

Daryl Hannah
The Tie that Binds '95

Duncan Hannah
Art for Teachers of Children '95

John Hannah
Four Weddings and a Funeral '94

Page Hannah
Shag: The Movie '89

John Hannan
Strictly Ballroom '92

Lawrence Hanray
On Approval '44
The Private Life of Henry VIII '33

Joachim Hansen
Anne of Green Gables '85

Vlastimil Harapes
Day for My Love '77

Cochava Harari
Zohar: Mediterranean Blues '93

Cezary Harasimowicz
Trois Couleurs: Blanc '94

Sebastian Harcombe
Carrington '95

James Harcourt
The Hidden Room '49
Night Train to Munich '40
I Met a Murderer '39

Marcia Gay Harden
The Daytrippers '96
The Spitfire Grill '95
Crush '93

Kate Hardie
The Krays '90
Mona Lisa '86

Paul Hardtmuth
The Third Man '49

Cedric Hardwicke
Beware of Pity '46
Nine Days a Queen '36

Robert Hardy
A Feast at Midnight '95

Doris Hare
Nuns on the Run '90

Magnus Harenstam
Stubby '74

John Hargreaves
Don's Party '76

Zaharira Harifai
Daughters, Daughters '74

Dennis Harkin
Brief Encounter '46

Rufus Harley
Eddie and the Cruisers '83

Jamie Harold
Chain of Desire '93

Andrew Harpending
Poison '91

Frank Harper
In the Name of the Father '93

Jessica Harper
Safe '95
Eat a Bowl of Tea '89

Tess Harper
Criminal Law '89

Barbara Harris
A Thousand Clowns '65

Bruklin Harris
Girls Town '95

Jared Harris
I Shot Andy Warhol '96
Dead Man '95
Nadja '95
Smoke '95

Julius W. Harris
Alambrista! '77

Mel Harris
Suture '93

Michael Harris
Suture '93

Richard Harris
Silent Tongue '92

Robin Harris
House Party '90

Wendell B. Harris, Jr.
Chameleon Street '89

Cathryn Harrison
A Handful of Dust '88
Black Moon '75

George Harrison
A Hard Day's Night '64

Gregory Harrison
It's My Party '95

Jimmy Harrison
Charley's Aunt '25

John Harrison
Lolita '62

Rex Harrison
Blithe Spirit '45
Night Train to Munich '40
Sidewalks of London '38

Jamie Harrold
I Shot Andy Warhol '96

Lisa Harrow
The Devil Is a Woman '75

Deborah Harry
Heavy '94

John Hart-Dyke
The Missing Reel '90

Henry Hart
D.O.A. '49

Ian Hart
Michael Collins '96
The Englishman Who Went Up a Hill But Came Down a Mountain '95
Backbeat '94
The Hours and Times '92

Roxanne Hart
Old Enough '84

Rainbow Harvest
Old Enough '84

Don Harvey
American Heart '92
Eight Men Out '88

Harold (Herk) Harvey
Carnival of Souls '62

Laurence Harvey
The Manchurian Candidate '62
Room at the Top '59

Rodney Harvey
Guncrazy '92
My Own Private Idaho '91
Five Corners '88

Verna Harvey
That'll Be the Day '73

Mert Hatfield
The Ballad of the Sad Cafe '91

Rutger Hauer
Forbidden Choices '94

Alexander Hauff
Meier '87

Wings Hauser
Tough Guys Don't Dance '87

Willo Hausman
House of Games '87

Richie Havens
Boss' Son '78

Nigel Havers
The Whistle Blower '87

Robin Hawdon
Bedazzled '68

Jeremy Hawk
Lucky Jim '58

Ethan Hawke
Search and Destroy '94

Stephen Hawking
A Brief History of Time '92

Jack Hawkins
The Fallen Idol '49

Nigel Hawthorne
The Madness of King George '94

Charles Hawtrey
Sabotage '36

Sessue Hayakawa
I Have Killed '24

Marc Hayashi
Chan Is Missing '82

Harry Hayden
Gun Crazy '49

Sterling Hayden
Crime of Passion '57

Helen Haye
Sidewalks of London '38
The 39 Steps '35

Isaac Hayes
Acting on Impulse '93

Patricia Hayes
Little Dorrit, Film 1: Nobody's Fault '88
Little Dorrit, Film 2: Little Dorrit's Story '88

Jim Haynie
From Hollywood to Deadwood '89
Jack's Back '87
Hard Traveling '85

Cast Index

491

INDEPENDENT FILM GUIDE

Dennis Haysbert
Suture '93

James Hayter
Abandon Ship '57
The Fallen Idol '49

David Hayward
Thousand Pieces of Gold '91

Susan Hayward
I Married a Witch '42

Chris Haywood
Shine '95

Rita Hayworth
Separate Tables '58

James Hazeldine
Stardust '74

Murray Head
White Mischief '88

Ruby Head
The Long Good Friday '80

Lena Headey
Century '94

Glenne Headly
Bastard out of Carolina '96
And the Band Played On '93
Grand Isle '91

Anthony Heald
The Ballad of Little Jo '93

Dorian Healy
For Queen and Country '88

Daphne Heard
Three Sisters '70

John Heard
Rambling Rose '91
Betrayed '88
After Hours '85
The Trip to Bountiful '85
Cutter's Way '81

Thomas Heathcote
Luther '74
Village of the Damned '60

Anne Heche
Walking and Talking '96

Jenny Hecht
Actors and Sin '52

Dan Hedaya
Freeway '95
To Die For '95
The Usual Suspects '95
Tune in Tomorrow '90
Blood Simple '85
True Confessions '81

Jack Hedley
The Very Edge '63

Tippi Hedren
Citizen Ruth '96

Gerard Heinz
The Fallen Idol '49

Brigitte Helm
Metropolis '26

Levon Helm
Smooth Talk '85

Charlotte J. Helmkamp
Frankenhooker '90

Katherine Helmond
Inside Monkey Zetterland '93
The Lady in White '88

Percy Helton
Kiss Me Deadly '55
Wicked Woman '54

David Hemblen
Exotica '94

Martin Hemme
Das Boot '81

Jo Henderson
Matewan '87

Sarah Henderson
Kids '95

Shirley Henderson
Trainspotting '95

Benjamin Hendrickson
Spanking the Monkey '94

Ian Hendry
Repulsion '65
Children of the Damned '63
Room at the Top '59

Jill Hennessey
I Shot Andy Warhol '96

Paul Henreid
Night Train to Munich '40

Bobby Henrey
The Fallen Idol '49

Lance Henriksen
Dead Man '95

Buck Henry
Short Cuts '93
The Linguini Incident '92
Tune in Tomorrow '90
Eating Raoul '82

John Henry
Passion Fish '92

Douglas Henshall
Angels and Insects '95

Gladys Henson
Leather Boys '63

Audrey Hepburn
Two for the Road '67

Katharine Hepburn
A Delicate Balance '73
The African Queen '51

Hans Herbert
Impact '49

Louis Herbert
Forbidden Games '52

Irm Hermann
Mother Kusters Goes to Heaven '76

Jonathan Hernandez
My Family '94

Marcel Herrand
Children of Paradise '45

Mark Herron
8 1/2 '63

Barbara Hershey
Tune in Tomorrow '90
A World Apart '88
Shy People '87

Charles Heslop
The Obsessed '51

David Hewlett
The Boys of St. Vincent '93

Barton Heyman
Dead Man Walking '95

Anne Heywood
The Very Edge '63

Pat Heywood
Wish You Were Here '87

James Hickey
The Boy from Mercury '96

Tom Hickey
Nuns on the Run '90

Tommy Hicks
Daughters of the Dust '91

Tommy Redmond Hicks
She's Gotta Have It '86

Joan Hickson
Century '94

David Anthony Higgens
Coldblooded '94

Clare Higgins
Wonderland '88

Irene Hilda
Two for the Road '67

Bernard Hill
Mountains of the Moon '90
Shirley Valentine '89
Bellman and True '88

Dennis Hill
The Underneath '95

Wendy Hiller
The Lonely Passion of Judith Hearne '87
Murder on the Orient Express '74
Separate Tables '58
Pygmalion '38

Patricia Hilliard
The Ghost Goes West '36

Candace Hilligoss
Carnival of Souls '62

Pippa Hinchley
London Kills Me '91

Earl Hindman
The Ballad of the Sad Cafe '91

Ciaran Hinds
Persuasion '95

Pat Hingle
Lightning Jack '94
The Grifters '90

Joaquin Hinojosa
Black Litter '77

Mary Hinton
Gaslight '40

Paul Hipp
The Funeral '96

Thora Hird
The Entertainer '60

Judith Hoag
Acting on Impulse '93

Valerie Hobson
Kind Hearts and Coronets '49
Great Expectations '46
Clouds over Europe '39

Jan Hockey
Slacker '91

Stephan Hockey
Slacker '91

John Hodge
Shallow Grave '94

Paul Hoerbiger
The Third Man '49

Iris Hoey
Pygmalion '38

Abbie Hoffman
Heavy Petting '89

Gert Gunther Hoffman
Strongman Ferdinand '76

Thom Hoffman
Orlando '92

Thurn Hoffman
In the Spirit '90

Marco Hofschneider
The Island of Dr. Moreau '96

Bosco Hogan
In the Name of the Father '93

Paul Hogan
Lightning Jack '94

Jan Holden
Fire Maidens from Outer Space '56

Roy Holder
The Land That Time Forgot '75

Susan Holderness
That'll Be the Day '73

Agnieszka Holland
The Interrogation '82

Mary Holland
Tommy '75

Antony Holles
They Drive by Night '38

Kamal Holloway
Twenty Bucks '93

Stanley Holloway
The Private Life of Sherlock Holmes '70

**Cast
Index**

493

**INDEPENDENT
FILM GUIDE**

Wilfrid Hyde-White
John and Julie '55
The Third Man '49
The Man Who Knew Too
Much '34

Warren Hymer
You Only Live Once '37

Roger Ibanez
The Red Poster '76

Eric Idle
Nuns on the Run '90

Istvan Iglody
False Weights '74

Dimiter Ikonomov
Last Summer '74

Igor Illinski
Aelita: Queen of Mars
'24

Vladimir Ilyine
Burnt by the Sun '94

Michael Imperioli
I Shot Andy Warhol '96
The Addiction '95
Household Saints '93

Jennifer Inch
Anne of Green Gables
'85

Miguel Incian
Aventurera '49

Elizabeth Inglis
The 39 Steps '35

Jeremy Irons
The House of the Spirits
'93
Kafka '91
A Chorus of Disapproval
'89

Michael Ironside
Guncrazy '92

Bill Irwin
Eight Men Out '88

Frances Irwin
Gun Crazy '49

Chris Isaak
Grace of My Heart '96

Ryo Ishibashi
The Crossing Guard '94

Anne Jackson
The Shining '80

Chequita Jackson
Just Another Girl on the
I.R.T. '93

Freda Jackson
Beware of Pity '46
Great Expectations '46

Glenda Jackson
Business as Usual '88
The Devil Is a Woman '75
The Maids '75

Gordon Jackson
The Whistle Blower '87
The Prime of Miss Jean
Brodie '69
Abandon Ship '57
Pink String and Sealing
Wax '45

John M. Jackson
The Spitfire Grill '95

**Robert Jason
Jackson**
New Jersey Drive '95

**Rosemark
Jackson**
Hangin' with the
Homeboys '91

Samuel L. Jackson
Trees Lounge '96
Fresh '94
Pulp Fiction '94
Menace II Society '93

Selmer Jackson
Pitfall '48

Sherry Jackson
Daughters of the Dust
'91

Irene Jacob
Trois Couleurs: Rouge
'94

Joelle Jacob
The Lady in White '88

Derek Jacobi
Little Dorrit, Film 1:
Nobody's Fault '88
Little Dorrit, Film 2: Little
Dorrit's Story '88
The Odessa File '74
Three Sisters '70

David Jacobs
Stardust '74

Steve Jacobs
To Have and to Hold '96
Echoes of Paradise '86

Bobby Jacoby
The Applegates '89

Madhur Jaffrey
Vanya on 42nd Street '94
Heat and Dust '82

Saeed Jaffrey
The Deceivers '88
My Beautiful Laundrette
'85

Lisa Jakub
Rambling Rose '91

Brion James
American Strays '96
The Player '92

Clifton James
Lone Star '95
Eight Men Out '88

David James
Charley's Aunt '25

Godfrey James
The Land That Time
Forgot '75

Mark James
Slacker '91

Oscar James
Black Joy '77

Sidney James
The Smallest Show on
Earth '57
John and Julie '55

The Belles of St. Trinian's
'53

Steve James
The Land That Time
Forgot '75

Joyce Jameson
The Balcony '63

Nicole Jamet
Why Not! '78

Krystyna Janda
The Interrogation '82

Allison Janney
Big Night '95

David Janssen
S.O.S. Titanic '79

**Ernst-Hugo
Jaregard**
Stubby '74

Jim Jarmusch
Sling Blade '96

Elzbieta Jasinska
Trois Couleurs: Rouge
'94

Star Jasper
True Love '89

Ricky Jay
House of Games '87

Michael Jayston
The Homecoming '73

**Marianne Jean-
Baptiste**
Secrets and Lies '95

Jacqueline Jeanne
Dites-Lui Que Je L'Aime
'77

Allan Jeayes
The Hidden Room '49
Saraband for Dead
Lovers '48
They Drive by Night '38
The Scarlet Pimpernel
'34

Soulfood Jed
Fly by Night '93

Barbara Jefford
Where Angels Fear to
Tread '91

Peter Jeffrey
The Odessa File '74
If... '69

Lionel Jeffries
A Chorus of Disapproval
'89

Roger Jendly
Jonah Who Will Be 25 in
the Year 2000 '76

Jason Jenkins
Matewan '87

Ken Jenkins
Matewan '87

Megs Jenkins
The Innocents '61
Tiger Bay '59
John and Julie '55
Saraband for Dead
Lovers '48

Richard Jenkins
Flirting with Disaster '95

Sam Jenkins
Twenty Bucks '93

Michael Jenn
Dance with a Stranger
'85
Another Country '84

Lucinda Jenney
American Heart '92
Wired '89

David Jensen
The Underneath '95

Eulalie Jensen
Charley's Aunt '25

Ebony Jerido
Just Another Girl on the
I.R.T. '93

Clytie Jessop
The Innocents '61

Michael Jeter
Just Like in the Movies
'90

Jimmy Jewel
The Krays '90

Ronny Jhutti
Wild West '93

Zheng Jian
Ju Dou '90

Wang Jianfa
The Story of Qui Ju '91

Penn Jillette
Hackers '95
Tough Guys Don't Dance
'87

Elaine Jin
Love Unto Waste '86

Ebony Jo-Ann
Fly by Night '93

Marlene Jobert
The Wonderful Crook '75

Cameron Johann
Last Exit to Brooklyn '90

Zita Johann
Struggle '31

Peter Johansen
The Brothers McMullen
'94

**Scarlett
Johansson**
Manny & Lo '96

Zizi Johari
The Killing of a Chinese
Bookie '76

Elton John
Tommy '75

Georg John
M '31

Gottfried John
Mother Kusters Goes to
Heaven '76

Mervyn Johns
1984 '56
Dead of Night '45
Pink String and Sealing
Wax '45

Cecil Kellaway
I Married a Witch '42
Andrew Kelley
For a Lost Soldier '93
Barry Kelley
Too Late for Tears '49
Sheila Kelley
Passion Fish '92
Mike Kellin
Girlfriends '78
The Incident '67
Pamela Kellino
I Met a Murderer '39
David Patrick Kelly
Flirting with Disaster '95
Judy Kelly
Dead of Night '45
The Private Life of Henry VIII '33
Moira Kelly
The Tie that Binds '95
Little Odessa '94
Chaplin '92
Paula Kelly
Lost in the Stars '74
Moultrie Kelsall
The Battle of the Sexes '60
Abandon Ship '57
Gary Kemp
The Krays '90
Jeremy Kemp
Angels and Insects '95
Four Weddings and a Funeral '94
Martin Kemp
The Krays '90
Paul Kemp
M '31
Will Kempe
Metropolitan '90
Gerhard Kempinski
Beware of Pity '46
Thursday's Child '43
Jennifer Kendal
Heat and Dust '82
Henry Kendall
Rich and Strange '32
Kay Kendall
Genevieve '53
Aaron Leon Kenin
Morgan's Cake '88
Eliot Kenin
Morgan's Cake '88
Arthur Kennedy
Champion '49
Too Late for Tears '49
Gordon Kennedy
Just Like a Woman '95
Graham Kennedy
Don's Party '76
Lyn Kennedy
Teenage Gang Debs '66

Patsy Kensit
Grace of My Heart '96
Angels and Insects '95
Twenty-One '91
A Chorus of Disapproval '89
Absolute Beginners '86
Diana Kent
Heavenly Creatures '94
Jace Kent
Little Odessa '94
Jean Kent
The Woman in Question '50
Keneth Kent
Night Train to Munich '40
Alexia Keogh
An Angel at My Table '89
Deborah Kerr
The Innocents '61
Separate Tables '58
Black Narcissus '47
Corinne Kersten
Murmur of the Heart '71
Mohamad Ali Keshavarz
Through the Olive Trees '94
Sara Kestelman
Lisztomania '75
Alice Key
Actors and Sin '52
Sajid Khan
Heat and Dust '82
Arsinee Khanjian
Exotica '94
Eleonara Khilberg
Combination Platter '93
Michael Khumrov
Little Odessa '94
Nicole Kidman
To Die For '95
Dead Calm '89
Udo Kier
Breaking the Waves '95
My Own Private Idaho '91
Terence Kilburn
Lolita '62
David Kiley
Chameleon Street '89
Richard Kiley
The Little Prince '74
Val Kilmer
The Island of Dr. Moreau '96
Kill Me Again '89
Sandelle Kincaid
Vegas in Space '94
Andrea King
The Linguini Incident '92
Charmion King
Anne of Green Gables '85
Dave King
The Long Good Friday '80

Ben Kingsley
Death and the Maiden '94
Maurice '87
Danitza Kingsley
Jack's Back '87
Susan Kingsley
Old Enough '84
Alex Kingston
Carrington '95
Maeve Kinkead
City of Hope '91
Melinda Kinnaman
My Life As a Dog '85
Bruno Kirby
Golden Gate '93
George Kirby
Trouble in Mind '86
Michael Kirby
Swoon '91
Joe Kirk
Impact '49
Jess Kirkland
D.O.A. '49
Sally Kirkland
Cold Feet '89
Anna '87
Gene Kirkwood
The Crossing Guard '94
Mia Kirshner
Exotica '94
Love and Human Remains '93
Michael Kitchen
Enchanted April '92
Barry Kivel
Bound '96
Rudolf Klein-Rogge
Metropolis '26
Towje Kleiner
The Odessa File '74
Rose Marie Klespitz
Stardust '74
Kevin Kline
Chaplin '92
Joseph Knafelmacher
Kids '95
Bud Knapp
Never Take Candy from a Stranger '60
Rob Knepper
Gas Food Lodging '92
Esmond Knight
Peeping Tom '60
Black Narcissus '47
Gladys Knight
Twenty Bucks '93
Wayne Knight
To Die For '95
Andrew Knott
Black Beauty '94

Kathryn Knotts
The Method '87
Mickey Knox
Frankenstein Unbound '90
Bogumil Kobiela
Ashes and Diamonds '58
Y. Kochurov
Professor Mamlock '38
Max Kohlhase
Joyless Street '25
Kristina Kohoutova
Alice '88
Clarence Kolb
Impact '49
Maja Komorowska
The Balance '75
Tsang Kong
One Night Stand '76
Anna Konstam
They Drive by Night '38
Nada Konvalinkova
Dinner for Adele '78
Milos Kopecky
Dinner for Adele '78
Fritz Kortner
Pandora's Box '28
The Hands of Orlac '25
David Kossoff
1984 '56
Elias Koteas
Crash '95
Exotica '94
Chain of Desire '93
Maya Koumani
Fire Maidens from Outer Space '56
Linda Kozlowski
Pass the Ammo '88
Jeroen Krabbe
For a Lost Soldier '93
Kafka '91
Scandal '89
A World Apart '88
Werner Krauss
Joyless Street '25
Svetlana Krioutchkova
Burnt by the Sun '94
Sylvia Kristel
Emmanuelle '74
Jason Kristofer
The Crossing Guard '94
Kris Kristofferson
Lone Star '95
Trouble in Mind '86
Tracy Kristofferson
Trouble in Mind '86
Michael Kroecher
Every Man for Himself & God Against All '75
Berry Kroeger
Gun Crazy '49

Christine Laurent
Cat and Mouse '78
Hugh Laurie
Strapless '90
John Laurie
Madeleine '50
Clouds over Europe '39
Nine Days a Queen '36
The 39 Steps '35
Piper Laurie
The Crossing Guard '94
Boss' Son '78
Sandie Lavelle
Ladybird, Ladybird '93
Gabriele Lavia
The Devil Is a Woman '75
Phyllida Law
Much Ado about Nothing '93
Christopher Lawford
Mr. North '88
Josie Lawrence
Enchanted April '92
Marc Lawrence
The Big Easy '87
Martin Lawrence
House Party '90
Wilfred Lawson
Room at the Top '59
Thursday's Child '43
Pygmalion '38
Frank Lawton
A Night to Remember '58
Abe Lax
American Matchmaker '40
Freida Lay
Vegas in Space '94
Rosemary Leach
A Room with a View '86
That'll Be the Day '73
Cloris Leachman
S.O.S. Titanic '79
Kiss Me Deadly '55
Marianna Lead
Little Odessa '94
Jean-Pierre Leaud
The 400 Blows '59
Madeleine LeBeau
8 1/2 '63
Samuel Lebihan
Trois Couleurs: Rouge '94
Bryan Leder
Metropolitan '90
Erwin Leder
Das Boot '81
Francis Lederer
Pandora's Box '28
Anna Lee
Non-Stop New York '37
Belinda Lee
The Belles of St. Trinian's '53

Bernard Lee
Beat the Devil '53
The Fallen Idol '49
The Third Man '49
Bill Lee
She's Gotta Have It '86
Christopher Lee
A Feast at Midnight '95
The Private Life of Sherlock Holmes '70
Moulin Rouge '52
Dixie Lee
Legacy '75
Franchesca Lee
Children of the Damned '63
Jason Lee
Chasing Amy '97
Mallrats '95
Joanna Lee
Plan 9 from Outer Space '56
Joie Lee
She's Gotta Have It '86
Robbie Lee
Switchblade Sisters '75
Ruta Lee
Funny Bones '94
Sheryl Lee
Homage '95
Backbeat '94
Wild at Heart '90
Spike Lee
She's Gotta Have It '86
Virginia Lee
D.O.A. '49
Waise Lee
Center Stage '91
Denise Legeay
I Have Killed '24
Alison Leggatt
Never Take Candy from a Stranger '60
This Happy Breed '47
Michel Legrand
The World of Jacques Demy '95
James LeGros
Destiny Turns on the Radio '95
Safe '95
Living in Oblivion '94
Guncrazy '92
Drugstore Cowboy '89
John Leguizamo
Hangin' with the Homeboys '91
Janet Leigh
The Manchurian Candidate '62
Jennifer Jason Leigh
Bastard out of Carolina '96
Georgia '95
Kansas City '95

Mrs. Parker and the Vicious Circle '94
Short Cuts '93
Last Exit to Brooklyn '90
Miami Blues '90
Vivien Leigh
Sidewalks of London '38
Margaret Leighton
Galileo '73
Donovan Leitch
I Shot Andy Warhol '96
Gas Food Lodging '92
Chloe Leland
Wish You Were Here '87
Rachel Lemieux
Mommy '95
Tutte Lemkow
Moulin Rouge '52
Jack Lemmon
Short Cuts '93
Genevieve Lemon
The Piano '93
Jarrett Lennon
Short Cuts '93
John Lennon
The Rolling Stones Rock and Roll Circus '68
A Hard Day's Night '64
Loles Leon
Tie Me Up! Tie Me Down! '90
Robert Sean Leonard
Much Ado about Nothing '93
Marco Leonardi
Like Water for Chocolate '93
Cinema Paradiso '88
Tea Leoni
Flirting with Disaster '95
Philippe Leotard
Cat and Mouse '78
First Communion '77
The Wonderful Crook '75
Paul Leperson
Phantom of Liberty '74
Ken Lerner
Mother's Boys '94
Michael Lerner
Eight Men Out '88
Angela Leslie
Chameleon Street '89
Dan Lett
Paris, France '94
Tony Leung
Chungking Express '95
Center Stage '91
Love Unto Waste '86
Ted Levine
Georgia '95
Stan Levitt
Carnival of Souls '62
Jose Lewgoy
Kiss of the Spider Woman '85

Fiona Lewis
Lisztomania '75
Harry Lewis
Gun Crazy '49
Huey Lewis
Short Cuts '93
Jerry Lewis
Funny Bones '94
Jonathan Lewis
The Boys of St. Vincent '93
Juliette Lewis
Kalifornia '93
Richard Lewis
Leaving Las Vegas '95
Edward Lexy
Sidewalks of London '38
Gong Li
The Story of Qui Ju '91
Ju Dou '90
Mitchell Lichtenstein
The Wedding Banquet '93
Anki Liden
My Life As a Dog '85
Albert Lieven
Beware of Pity '46
Night Train to Munich '40
Marilyn Lightstone
Anne of Green Gables '85
Matthew Lillard
Hackers '95
Serial Mom '94
Beatrice Lillie
On Approval '44
Bridget Lin
Chungking Express '95
Dagny Lind
Paradise Place '77
Sven Lindberg
Face to Face '76
Cec Linder
Lolita '62
Viveca Lindfors
The Linguini Incident '92
Girlfriends '78
Delroy Lindo
Mountains of the Moon '90
Olga Lindo
The Hidden Room '49
Robert Lindsay
That'll Be the Day '73
Ruan Ling-Yu
Love and Duty '31
Theo Lingen
M '31
Richard Linklater
The Underneath '95
Slacker '91
Joe Linnane
The Woman in Question '50

Cast Index

Jennifer MacDonald
Clean, Shaven '93

Kelly Macdonald
Trainspotting '95

Andie MacDowell
Four Weddings and a
  Funeral '94
Short Cuts '93
sex, lies and videotape
  '89

Moyna MacGill
Gaslight '40

Niall MacGinnis
Never Take Candy from a
  Stranger '60

Helen Mack
Struggle '31

Barry Mackay
Evergreen '34

John MacKay
Trust '91

Stephen MacKenna
Eye of the Needle '81

Alex Mackenzie
The Battle of the Sexes
  '60

Kenneth Mackintosh
Three Sisters '70

Steven Mackintosh
Different for Girls '96
London Kills Me '91

Kyle MacLachlan
Blue Velvet '86

Samantha MacLachlan
Set It Off '96

Barton MacLane
You Only Live Once '37

Deborah MacLaren
Naked '93

Mary MacLeod
If... '69

Will MacMillan
Salvador '86

Peter MacNeill
Crash '95

Norman MacOwen
The Battle of the Sexes
  '60

Elle Macpherson
Jane Eyre '96
Sirens '94

Duncan MacRae
The Little Kidnappers '53
The Woman in Question
  '50

William H. Macy
Fargo '96
Oleanna '94
Twenty Bucks '93

Marianne Maddalena
Wes Craven's New
  Nightmare '94

Victor Maddern
Abandon Ship '57

Michael Madsen
A House in the Hills '93
Reservoir Dogs '92
Kill Me Again '89

Virginia Madsen
Mr. North '88

Patrick Magee
Luther '74
Galileo '73
The Very Edge '63

Anna Magnani
Passionate Thief '60
Bellissima '51
The Miracle '48

Ann Magnuson
Heavy Petting '89
Vortex '81

Oliver Maguire
Butley '74

Bill Maher
Cannibal Women in the
  Avocado Jungle of
  Death '89

Alix Mahieux
L'Amour en Herbe '77

John Mahoney
She's the One '96
Betrayed '88
Eight Men Out '88

Nuno Leal Maia
Kiss of the Spider
  Woman '85

Caludette Maille
Like Water for Chocolate
  '93

Marjorie Main
Turnabout '40

Valerie Mairesse
One Sings, the Other
  Doesn't '77

Mako
The Wash '88

Karl Malden
Hot Millions '68

Ruth Maleczech
The Ballad of Little Jo '93
In the Soup '92
Anna '87

Arthur Malet
A Little Princess '95

Laurent Malet
Roads to the South '78

Eddie Malin
A Hard Day's Night '64

Judith Malina
Household Saints '93

John Malkovich
Queens Logic '91

Miles Malleson
Kind Hearts and
  Coronets '49
Saraband for Dead
  Lovers '48
Dead of Night '45
Nine Days a Queen '36

Odile Mallet
The City of Lost Children
  '95

Jan Malmsjo
Scenes from a Marriage
  '73

Jena Malone
Bastard out of Carolina
  '96

Mark Malone, Jr.
Straight Out of Brooklyn
  '91

George Malpas
The Missing Reel '90

H.F. Maltby
Pygmalion '38
Young and Innocent '37

Leonard Maltin
Forgotten Silver '96

Albert Maltz
Hollywood on Trial '76

Eily Malyon
I Married a Witch '42

Irina Malysheva
100 Days after Childhood
  '75

Alex Man
Rouge '87

Nick Mancuso
Ticket to Heaven '81

Miles Mander
The Private Life of Henry
  VIII '33

Nino Manfredi
Ugly, Dirty and Bad '78

Dave Manley
Struggle '31

Dudley Manlove
Plan 9 from Outer Space
  '56

Claude Mann
French Provincial '75

Leslie Mann
She's the One '96

Lucie Mannheim
The 39 Steps '35

Predrag Manojlovic
Tito and Me '92

Laszlo Mansaros
The Unfinished Sentence
  in 141 Minutes '75

Joe Mantegna
Queens Logic '91
House of Games '87

Michael Mantell
City of Hope '91

Leslie Manville
Secrets and Lies '95

High Season '88
Dance with a Stranger
  '85

Mary Mara
Bound '96

Jean Marais
The World of Jacques
  Demy '95
White Nights '57
Beauty and the Beast '46

Fredric March
The Iceman Cometh '73
Tomorrow the World '44
I Married a Witch '42

Colette Marchand
Moulin Rouge '52

Guy Marchand
Coup de Torchon '81
Cousin, Cousine '76

Paul Marco
Plan 9 from Outer Space
  '56

Saverio Marconi
Padre Padrone '77

Stephen Marcus
My Beautiful Laundrette
  '85

Elio Marcuzzo
Ossessione '42

Miriam Margolyes
Different for Girls '96
Little Dorrit, Film 1:
  Nobody's Fault '88
Little Dorrit, Film 2: Little
  Dorrit's Story '88

Constance Marie
My Family '94

Jean-Pierre Marielle
Coup de Torchon '81
In a Wild Moment '78

Jacques Marin
Forbidden Games '52

Ed Marinaro
Queens Logic '91

Jeanne Marken
Children of Paradise '45

Olivera Markovic
Tito and Me '92

Scott Marlowe
A Cold Wind in August
  '61

Percy Marmont
Young and Innocent '37
Rich and Strange '32

Richard Marner
The African Queen '51

Peter Marquardt
El Mariachi '93

Ron Marquette
Public Access '93

Gene Marrin
Teenage Gang Debs '66

Kenneth Mars
Citizen Ruth '96

Cast
Index

Edie McClurg
Eating Raoul '82

Matthew McConaughey
Lone Star '95

Patty McCormack
Mommy '95

Emer McCourt
London Kills Me '91

George McCowan
She's the One '96

Alec McCowen
A Night to Remember '58

Colin McCredie
Shallow Grave '94

Alex McCrindle
Eye of the Needle '81

Andrew McCulloch
The Land That Time Forgot '75

Kyle McCulloch
Careful '94

Bill McCutcheon
Tune in Tomorrow '90

George McDaniel
Legacy '75

Dylan McDermott
Destiny Turns on the Radio '95
Twister '89

Robin McDonald
The Hours and Times '92

Caitlin Grace McDonnell
Art for Teachers of Children '95

Mary McDonnell
Passion Fish '92
Matewan '87

Frances McDormand
Fargo '96
Lone Star '95
Short Cuts '93
Blood Simple '85

Roddy McDowall
It's My Party '95

Malcolm McDowell
Chain of Desire '93
If... '69

Brian McElroy
Bad Lieutenant '92

John McEnery
Black Beauty '94
The Krays '90
The Land That Time Forgot '75
Galileo '73

Peter McEnery
Victim '61

Bobby Joe McFadden
Red Rock West '93

Monica McFarland
Back Street Jane '89

Mark McGann
Let Him Have It '91

Paul McGann
Dealers '89
Withnail and I '87

Parnell McGarry
Bedazzled '68

Patrick McGaw
Forbidden Choices '94

Gwen McGee
New Jersey Drive '95

Paula McGee
Chameleon Street '89

Vonetta McGee
To Sleep with Anger '90

Bruce McGill
Waiting for the Moon '87

Kelly McGillis
Grand Isle '91
The House on Carroll Street '88

John C. McGinley
Set It Off '96
Mother's Boys '94
Platoon '86

Sean McGinley
Michael Collins '96

Boris McGiver
Little Odessa '94

John McGiver
The Manchurian Candidate '62

Mike McGlone
She's the One '96
The Brothers McMullen '94

Elizabeth McGovern
A Shock to the System '90
Tune in Tomorrow '90

Rose McGowan
The Doom Generation '95

Tom McGowan
Mrs. Parker and the Vicious Circle '94

Leueen McGrath
Pygmalion '38

Charles McGraw
Killer Inside Me '76
A Boy and His Dog '75

Ewan McGregor
Trainspotting '95
Shallow Grave '94

Kim McGuire
Acting on Impulse '93

Stephen McHattie
Sticky Fingers '88

Elizabeth P. McKay
The Brothers McMullen '94

Donna McKechnie
The Little Prince '74

Gina McKee
Naked '93

Don McKellar
Exotica '94

Ian McKellen
And the Band Played On '93
The Ballad of Little Jo '93
Scandal '89

Breffini McKenna
The Crying Game '92

Virginia McKenna
The Smallest Show on Earth '57

Hannah McKenzie
Forgotten Silver '96

Julia McKenzie
Shirley Valentine '89

Kevin McKidd
Trainspotting '95

Mona McKinnon
Plan 9 from Outer Space '56

Ivor McLaren
Evergreen '34

Gibb McLaughlin
The Scarlet Pimpernel '34
The Private Life of Henry VIII '33

Gordon McLeod
Clouds over Europe '39

Allyn Ann McLerie
France, Incorporated '74

John McLiam
The Iceman Cometh '73

Ed McMahon
The Incident '67

Sue McManus
Teenage Gang Debs '66

John McMartin
A Shock to the System '90

Kenneth McMillan
True Confessions '81
Girlfriends '78

Roddy McMillan
The Battle of the Sexes '60

T. Wendy McMillan
Go Fish '94

Skipper McNally
Crime of Passion '57

Pat McNamara
The Daytrippers '96

Alan McNaughton
Victim '61

Gus McNaughton
Clouds over Europe '39
Sidewalks of London '38
The 39 Steps '35

Julia McNeal
The Refrigerator '91

The Unbelievable Truth '90

Ian McNeice
The Englishman Who Went Up a Hill But Came Down a Mountain '95
Funny Bones '94
The Lonely Passion of Judith Hearne '87

Kris McQuade
Strictly Ballroom '92

Frank McRae
Lightning Jack '94

Gerard McSorley
Michael Collins '96
In the Name of the Father '93

Janet McTeer
Carrington '95
Hawks '89

Colm Meaney
The Englishman Who Went Up a Hill But Came Down a Mountain '95

Anne Meara
The Daytrippers '96

Meat Loaf
Motorama '91

Paul Medford
Black Joy '77

Dana Medricka
Day for My Love '77

Michael Medwin
Genevieve '53

Donald Meek
Turnabout '40

Ralph Meeker
Kiss Me Deadly '55

Edith Meeks
Poison '91

Conrad Meertin Jr.
New Jersey Drive '95

Hannes Meesember
The Odessa File '74

Armand Meffre
Blue Country '77

Armin Meier
Mother Kusters Goes to Heaven '76

Kurt Meisel
The Odessa File '74

Mariangela Melato
Dear Michael '76
Swept Away... '75

Migdalia Melendez
Go Fish '94

Jack Melford
The Ladykillers '55

Jill Melford
Abandon Ship '57

**INDEPENDENT
FILM GUIDE**

505

Jan Niklas
The House of the Spirits
'93

**Jose Nilson dos
Santos**
Pixote '81

Rob Nilsson
Heat and Sunlight '87

Leonard Nimoy
The Balcony '63

Willi Ninja
Paris Is Burning '91

David Niven
Separate Tables '58

Paul Nocholls
The Return of Tommy
Tricker '94

Daniele Noel
Bedazzled '68

Tsachi Noi
The Garden '77

Philippe Noiret
The Postman '94
Cinema Paradiso '88
Coup de Torchon '81

Jeanette Nolan
True Confessions '81

Lloyd Nolan
Abandon Ship '57

Robin Nolan
Teenage Gang Debs '66

Claude Nollier
Moulin Rouge '52

Christine Noonan
If... '69

John Ford Noonan
Flirting with Disaster '95

Tom Noonan
What Happened Was...
'94

Kathleen Noone
Citizen Ruth '96

Susan Norman
Safe '95
Poison '91

Zack Norman
Tracks '76

John Normington
Stardust '74

Jeremy Northam
Carrington '95

Silvana Nova
Vegas in Space '94

Jerzy Nowak
Trois Couleurs: Blanc '94

Jan Nowicki
Nine Months '77

Danny Nucci
Homage '95

Bill Nunn
The Last Seduction '94

Mike Nussbaum
House of Games '87

Pascal Nzonzi
Night on Earth '91

Barbara O
Daughters of the Dust
'91

Cicely Oates
The Man Who Knew Too
Much '34

John Oates
Heavy Petting '89

Charles Oberly
Flirting with Disaster '95

Merle Oberon
The Scarlet Pimpernel
'34
The Private Life of Henry
VIII '33

Colleen O'Brien
Combination Platter '93

Edmond O'Brien
1984 '56
D.O.A. '49

Gary O'Brien
Strapless '90

Kieran O'Brien
Bellman and True '88

Tom O'Brien
The Big Easy '87

**Richard
O'Callaghan**
Butley '74
Galileo '73

Ronan O'Casey
1984 '56

Jacki Ochs
Heavy Petting '89

U. A. Ochsen
Das Boot '81

Deirdre O'Connell
Pastime '91

Eddie O'Connell
Absolute Beginners '86

Hugh O'Conner
The Boy from Mercury
'96

Derrick O'Connor
Dealers '89

Kevin J. O'Connor
Equinox '93

Simon O'Connor
Heavenly Creatures '94

Hugh O'Conor
My Left Foot '89

Denis O'Dea
The Fallen Idol '49

Fritz Odemar
M '31

George T. Odom
Straight Out of Brooklyn
'91

Cathy O'Donnell
The Amazing Mr. X '48

Brian O'Halloran
Mallrats '95
Clerks '94

Claudia Ohana
The Fable of the Beautiful
Pigeon Fancier '88

Brad O'Hara
Longtime Companion '90

Catherine O'Hara
After Hours '85

Dan O'Herlihy
The Dead '87
Actors and Sin '52

Carol Ohmart
Spider Baby '64
The Wild Party '56

Michael O'Keefe
Nina Takes a Lover '94

Miles O'Keeffe
Acting on Impulse '93

Bill Oland
Special Effects '85

Daniel Olbrychski
The Unbearable
Lightness of Being '88

William Oldham
Thousand Pieces of Gold
'91
Matewan '87

Gary Oldman
Basquiat '96
Criminal Law '89

Ken Olin
Queens Logic '91

Lena Olin
The Unbearable
Lightness of Being '88

Ingrid Oliu
Stand and Deliver '88

Tristan Oliver
Another Country '84

Laurence Olivier
Three Sisters '70
The Entertainer '60
Clouds over Europe '39

**Edward James
Olmos**
Caught '96
My Family '94
Stand and Deliver '88
Alambrista! '77

Anny Ondra
Blackmail '29

Anne O'Neal
Gun Crazy '49

Ryan O'Neal
Tough Guys Don't Dance
'87

Tatum O'Neal
Basquiat '96

Chris O'Neill
Backbeat '94

Maggie O'Neill
Under Suspicion '92

Maire O'Neill
Sidewalks of London '38

Yoko Ono
The Rolling Stones Rock
and Roll Circus '68

Lupe Ontiveros
My Family '94

Evelyne Opela
False Weights '74

Shai K. Ophir
The Garden '77
Daughters, Daughters
'74

Jerry Orbach
Delusion '91
Last Exit to Brooklyn '90
Dirty Dancing '87

Kathleen O'Regan
Thursday's Child '43

Vera Orlova
Aelita: Queen of Mars
'24

Roscoe Orman
New Jersey Drive '95

Lujza Orosz
The Unfinished Sentence
in 141 Minutes '75

Marina Orsini
Eddie and the Cruisers 2:
Eddie Lives! '89

Henry Oscar
The Man Who Knew Too
Much '34

Per Oscarsson
Metamorphosis '75

John O'Shea
Forgotten Silver '96

Kevin O'Shea
Black Joy '77

K.T. Oslin
The Thing Called Love
'93

**Jacek
Ostaszewski**
Trois Couleurs: Bleu '93

Robert Osterloh
Wicked Woman '54
Gun Crazy '49

Bibi Osterwald
The World of Henry Orient
'64

Beth Ostrosky
Flirting with Disaster '95

Michael O'Sullivan
Careful '94

Richard O'Sullivan
The Stranger's Hand '54

Hideji Otaki
A-Ge-Man: Tales of a
Golden Geisha '91

Barry Otto
Strictly Ballroom '92

James Ottoway
That'll Be the Day '73

Andre Oumansky
Burnt by the Sun '94

**Sverre Anker
Ousdal**
The Feldmann Case '87

Peter Outerbridge
Paris, France '94

Ron Pember
The Land That Time
    Forgot '75
**Charles
    Pemberton**
Black Joy '77
Tony Pemberton
Poison '91
Elizabeth Pena
Lone Star '95
The Waterdance '91
Freddie Pendavis
Paris Is Burning '91
Austin Pendleton
The Ballad of the Sad
    Cafe '91
Susan Penhaligon
The Land That Time
    Forgot '75
Christopher Penn
The Funeral '96
Short Cuts '93
Reservoir Dogs '92
Sean Penn
Dead Man Walking '95
John Penrose
Kind Hearts and
    Coronets '49
Alan Pentony
Frankie Starlight '95
Barbara Pepper
Girls in Chains '43
Our Daily Bread '34
Marilia Pera
Pixote '81
Esme Percy
Dead of Night '45
Pygmalion '38
Michel Perelon
Cat and Mouse '78
Tony Perenski
The Underneath '95
Jose Perez
Miami Blues '90
Rosie Perez
Night on Earth '91
Anthony Perkins
Murder on the Orient
    Express '74
Clare Perkins
Ladybird, Ladybird '93
Elizabeth Perkins
Enid Is Sleeping '90
Dr. Arpad Perlaky
Adoption '75
Rebecca Perle
Not of this Earth '88
Max Perlich
Georgia '95
Drugstore Cowboy '89
Rhea Perlman
Enid Is Sleeping '90
Ron Perlman
The Island of Dr. Moreau
    '96

The City of Lost Children
    '95
Florence Pernel
Trois Couleurs: Bleu '93
Mireille Perrier
Shades of Doubt '93
Jacques Perrin
Cinema Paradiso '88
**Harold Perrineau,
    Jr.**
Smoke '95
Leslie Perrins
Nine Days a Queen '36
Luke Perry
American Strays '96
Terminal Bliss '91
Lisa Jane Persky
The Big Easy '87
Nehemiah Persoff
The Wild Party '56
Sean Pertwee
London Kills Me '91
Ladislav Pesek
Dinner for Adele '78
Bernadette Peters
Impromptu '90
Brock Peters
Lost in the Stars '74
The Incident '67
Clarke Peters
Mona Lisa '86
Mattie Peters
Helen's Babies '25
Ralph Peters
I Married a Witch '42
**Cassandra
    Peterson**
Acting on Impulse '93
Anton Petje
Fear '75
Hay Petrie
Great Expectations '46
On Approval '44
Clouds over Europe '39
The Ghost Goes West
    '36
The Private Life of Henry
    VIII '33
Brian Pettifer
If... '69
Frank Pettingell
Gaslight '40
Chuck Pfeiffer
Basquiat '96
Kate Phelps
The Shining '80
John Philbin
Shy People '87
Gerard Philipe
Dangerous Liaisons '60
Angie Phillips
Manny & Lo '96
John Phillips
Village of the Damned
    '60

Leslie Phillips
Scandal '89
The Smallest Show on
    Earth '57
**Lou Diamond
    Phillips**
Stand and Deliver '88
Robert Phillips
The Killing of a Chinese
    Bookie '76
William Phipps
The Wild Party '56
**Joaquin Rafael
    (Leaf) Phoenix**
To Die For '95
River Phoenix
The Thing Called Love
    '93
Silent Tongue '92
My Own Private Idaho '91
Beatrice Picard
Once Upon a Time in the
    East '74
Robert Picardo
Motorama '91
Jack's Back '87
Michel Piccoli
101 Nights '95
The World of Jacques
    Demy '95
Martha and I '91
Phantom of Liberty '74
Sarah Pickering
Little Dorrit, Film 1:
    Nobody's Fault '88
Little Dorrit, Film 2: Little
    Dorrit's Story '88
Ronald Pickup
Three Sisters '70
Molly Picon
East and West '24
Jim Piddock
Traces of Red '92
Claude Pieplu
Dites-Lui Que Je L'Aime
    '77
The Best Way '76
Phantom of Liberty '74
Justin Pierce
Kids '95
Wendell Pierce
Hackers '95
Sarah Pierse
Heavenly Creatures '94
Angela Pietropinto
Welcome to the
    Dollhouse '95
Alexandra Pigg
Strapless '90
A Chorus of Disapproval
    '89
Tim Pigott-Smith
The Remains of the Day
    '93
Nova Pilbeam
Young and Innocent '37

Nine Days a Queen '36
The Man Who Knew Too
    Much '34
Bronson Pinchot
It's My Party '95
After Hours '85
Renato Pinciroli
A Virgin Named Mary '75
Larry Pine
Dead Man Walking '95
Vanya on 42nd Street '94
Anna '87
Vincent Pinel
First Communion '77
Jada Pinkett
Set It Off '96
Menace II Society '93
Dominique Pinon
The City of Lost Children
    '95
Roni Pinovich
Ricochets '87
Frederick Piper
Pink String and Sealing
    Wax '45
Sabotage '36
James Pirrie
Non-Stop New York '37
Joe Piscopo
Open Season '95
**Marie-France
    Pisier**
Cousin, Cousine '76
French Provincial '75
Anne Pitoniak
House of Cards '92
The Ballad of the Sad
    Cafe '91
The Wizard of Loneliness
    '88
Old Enough '84
Brad Pitt
Kalifornia '93
Marek Piwowski
The Balance '75
Mary Kay Place
Citizen Ruth '96
Manny & Lo '96
Smooth Talk '85
Michele Placido
Lamerica '95
Victory March '76
Tony Plana
Salvador '86
Scott Plank
Pastime '91
Karl Platen
M '31
Oliver Platt
Funny Bones '94
Angela Pleasence
The Favor, the Watch,
    and the Very Big Fish
    '92
Donald Pleasence
Creepers '85

Rosemary Radcliffe
Anne of Green Gables '85

Ronald Radd
Galileo '73

Basil Radford
Dead of Night '45
Night Train to Munich '40
The Lady Vanishes '38
Young and Innocent '37

John Rae
Morgan! '66
The Little Kidnappers '53

Alex Rafalowicz
Shine '95

Frances Rafferty
Money Madness '47

Patricia Raine
Madeleine '50

Ella Raines
Impact '49

Sheryl Lee Ralph
To Sleep with Anger '90

Esther Ralston
Oliver Twist '22

Cecil Ramage
Kind Hearts and Coronets '49

Steven Randazzo
Mac '93
In the Soup '92

Elsie Randolph
Rich and Strange '32

John Randolph
The Wizard of Loneliness '88

Michael Rapaport
Zebrahead '92

Sara Rapisarda
Everything Ready, Nothing Works '74

Stephen Rappaport
...And God Spoke '94

David Rasche
Twenty Bucks '93

Richard Rasof
The Man in the Glass Booth '75

Fritz Rasp
Metropolis '26

John Ratzenberger
The Good Soldier '81

Thyrza Ravesteijn
Antonia's Line '95

Adrian Rawlins
Breaking the Waves '95
Mountains of the Moon '90

Robin Ray
A Hard Day's Night '64

Bill Raymond
City of Hope '91

Candy Raymond
Don's Party '76

Cyril Raymond
Brief Encounter '46

Robin Raymond
Girls in Chains '43

Minnie Rayner
Gaslight '40

Michael Raynor
Federal Hill '94

Stephen Rea
Michael Collins '96
The Crying Game '92

Ronald Reagan
Hollywood on Trial '76

Craig Reay
Red Rock West '93

Ian Redford
Just Like a Woman '95

Rockets Redglare
In the Soup '92
After Hours '85

Corin Redgrave
Persuasion '95
Four Weddings and a Funeral '94
In the Name of the Father '93

Lynn Redgrave
Shine '95

Michael Redgrave
The Innocents '61
1984 '56
Dead of Night '45
The Lady Vanishes '38

Vanessa Redgrave
Little Odessa '94
Mother's Boys '94
The House of the Spirits '93
The Ballad of the Sad Cafe '91
Murder on the Orient Express '74
Morgan! '66

Amanda Redman
For Queen and Country '88

Rob Reece
The Method '87

Alan Reed
Actors and Sin '52

George Reed
Helen's Babies '25

James Reed
Eight Men Out '88

Oliver Reed
Funny Bones '94
Lisztomania '75
Tommy '75

Donough Rees
Crush '93

Roger Rees
Sudden Manhattan '96

Christopher Reeve
The Remains of the Day '93
Street Smart '87

Keanu Reeves
Much Ado about Nothing '93
My Own Private Idaho '91
Tune in Tomorrow '90
Permanent Record '88
River's Edge '87

Kynaston Reeves
Hot Millions '68

Saskia Reeves
Different for Girls '96
Butterfly Kiss '94

Steve Reevis
Fargo '96

Benoit Regent
Trois Couleurs: Bleu '93

Serge Reggiani
Cat and Mouse '78

Paul Regina
It's My Party '95

Regine
Robert et Robert '78

Hans Leo Reich
Metropolis '26

Alice Reichen
Dear Victor '75

Beryl Reid
The Belles of St. Trinian's '53

Christopher Reid
House Party '90

Kate Reid
A Delicate Balance '73

Sheila Reid
Three Sisters '70

Andrew Reilly
Lisztomania '75

John C. Reilly
Georgia '95

Luke Reilly
Zebrahead '92

Rob Reiner
Bullets Over Broadway '94

Ray Reinhardt
The Tie that Binds '95

Judge Reinhold
Enid Is Sleeping '90

Devi Rekha
Kama Sutra: A Tale of Love '96

James Remar
Drugstore Cowboy '89

Lee Remick
A Delicate Balance '73

Albert Remy
The 400 Blows '59
Children of Paradise '45

Simone Renant
Dangerous Liaisons '60

Gilles Renaud
Once Upon a Time in the East '74

Georges Renavent
Turnabout '40

Scott Renderer
Poison '91

Michael Rennie
Uneasy Terms '48

Jean Reno
La Femme Nikita '91

Pierre Renoir
Children of Paradise '45

Gastone Renzelli
Bellissima '51

Maggie Renzi
Passion Fish '92
City of Hope '91
Eight Men Out '88
Matewan '87

Clive Revill
Let Him Have It '91
The Little Prince '74
Galileo '73
The Private Life of Sherlock Holmes '70

Roberta Rex
Children of the Damned '63

Fernando Rey
Seven Beauties '76

Burt Reynolds
Citizen Ruth '96

Nancy Reynolds
Crime of Passion '57

Paul Reynolds
Let Him Have It '91

Hossein Rezai
Through the Olive Trees '94

Ving Rhames
Pulp Fiction '94

Julian Rhind-Tutt
The Madness of King George '94

Cynthia Rhodes
Dirty Dancing '87

Miranda Stuart Rhyne
Angela '94

Paul Rhys
Nina Takes a Lover '94
Chaplin '92

Jonathan Rhys Myers
Michael Collins '96

Christina Ricci
Bastard out of Carolina '96

Bill Rice
Vortex '81

Mandy Rice-Davies
Absolute Beginners '86

Matty Rich
Straight Out of Brooklyn '91

Addison Richards
Our Daily Bread '34

Beah Richards
Drugstore Cowboy '89

Cast Index

INDEPENDENT FILM GUIDE

Annie Ross
Short Cuts '93
David Ross
Little Odessa '94
Gene Ross
Lost Highway '96
Lee Ross
Secrets and Lies '95
Michael Ross
D.O.A. '49
Monty Ross
She's Gotta Have It '86
Willie Ross
Rita, Sue & Bob Too '87
Adrian Ross-Magenty
Another Country '84
Isabella Rossellini
The Funeral '96
Big Night '95
Wild at Heart '90
Tough Guys Don't Dance '87
Blue Velvet '86
Leo Rossi
River's Edge '87
Michele Rossignol
Once Upon a Time in the East '74
Norman Rossington
Let Him Have It '91
The Krays '90
A Hard Day's Night '64
Leonard Rossiter
Luther '74
Dzsoko Roszics
Nine Months '77
Carlo Rota
32 Short Films about Glenn Gould '93
Tim Roth
Little Odessa '94
Pulp Fiction '94
Bodies, Rest & Motion '93
Reservoir Dogs '92
A World Apart '88
Jean Rougerie
Servant and Mistress '77
Simon Rouse
Butley '74
Jean-Louis Roux
Salut Victor! '89
Michel Roux
Pas Tres Catholique '93
Gena Rowlands
Night on Earth '91
Lise Roy
The Boys of St. Vincent '93
Cornell (Kofi) Royal
Daughters of the Dust '91

Patricia Royce
To Cross the Rubicon '91
Selena Royle
He Ran All the Way '51
Gregory Rozakis
Five Corners '88
Maria Rubia
The Marriage '76
Jennifer Rubin
Delusion '91
Permanent Record '88
Saul Rubinek
Open Season '95
And the Band Played On '93
Ticket to Heaven '81
Zelda Rubinstein
Acting on Impulse '93
Alan Ruck
Just Like in the Movies '90
John Ruddock
The Fallen Idol '49
Claude-Oliver Rudolph
Das Boot '81
Verena Rudolph
Strongman Ferdinand '76
Kristin Rudrud
Fargo '96
Gene Ruffini
Little Odessa '94
Rufus
Jonah Who Will Be 25 in the Year 2000 '76
Waldemar Ruhl
The Good Soldier '81
Jose Carlos Ruiz
Salvador '86
Kicki Rundgren
My Life As a Dog '85
Helena Rupport
His Picture in the Papers '16
Deborah Rush
Reckless '95
Geoffrey Rush
Shine '95
Claire Rushbrook
Secrets and Lies '95
Jared Rushton
The Lady in White '88
Shimen Ruskin
Gun Crazy '49
Robert Rusler
Shag: The Movie '89
William Russ
Traces of Red '92
Pastime '91
Dick Russell
River of Grass '94
Kimberly Russell
Hangin' with the Homeboys '91

Robert Russell
Bedazzled '68
Theresa Russell
Kafka '91
Victoria Russell
Tommy '75
James Russo
American Strays '96
My Own Private Idaho '91
Vortex '81
Margaret Rutherford
The Smallest Show on Earth '57
Blithe Spirit '45
Allison Rutledge-Parisi
Metropolitan '90
Sif Ruud
Paradise Place '77
Face to Face '76
Eileen Ryan
The Crossing Guard '94
Fran Ryan
Suture '93
John P. Ryan
Bound '96
Kathleen Ryan
Try and Get Me '50
Michael Ryan
The Crossing Guard '94
Robert Ryan
The Iceman Cometh '73
Tim Ryan
Detour '46
Derek Rydell
Popcorn '89
Winona Ryder
The House of the Spirits '93
Night on Earth '91
Heathers '89
Patrick Ryecart
Twenty-One '91
Mark Rylance
Angels and Insects '95
Rex Ryon
Jack's Back '87
Bruno S
Every Man for Himself & God Against All '75
Sabu
Black Narcissus '47
Nicholas Sadler
Acting on Impulse '93
Isabelle Sadoyan
Trois Couleurs: Bleu '93
Marianne Saegebrecht
Martha and I '91
Aniko Safar
The Unfinished Sentence in 141 Minutes '75
Susan Saiger
Eating Raoul '82

Raymond St. Jacques
Lost in the Stars '74
Susan St. James
S.O.S. Titanic '79
Octavia St. Laurant
Paris Is Burning '91
Helen St. Rayer
I Married a Witch '42
Louis Sainteve
Forbidden Games '52
Gene Saks
A Thousand Clowns '65
Chic Sale
You Only Live Once '37
Mary Jo Salerno
A Modern Affair '94
Soupy Sales
...And God Spoke '94
John Salew
Kind Hearts and Coronets '49
Beware of Pity '46
Emmanuel Salinger
101 Nights '95
Tomi Salmela
Night on Earth '91
Jeffrey D. Sams
Fly by Night '93
Laura San Giacomo
Nina Takes a Lover '94
Under Suspicion '92
sex, lies and videotape '89
Barry Sand
Eddie and the Cruisers '83
Paul Sand
Second Coming of Suzanne '80
Dominique Sanda
The World of Jacques Demy '95
Steppenwolf '74
The Conformist '71
Walter Sande
The Red House '47
Otto Sander
Wings of Desire '88
The Marquise of O '76
Ann D. Sanders
Straight Out of Brooklyn '91
George Sanders
Village of the Damned '60
Henry Sanders
Boss' Son '78
Jay O. Sanders
Just Like in the Movies '90
Richard Sanders
Forbidden Choices '94

Martyn Sanderson
An Angel at My Table '89
Debra Sandlund
Tough Guys Don't Dance '87
Christopher Sandord
Deep End '70
Stefania Sandrelli
The Sleazy Uncle '89
The Conformist '71
Julian Sands
Leaving Las Vegas '95
Grand Isle '91
Impromptu '90
A Room with a View '86
Yip Sang
Center Stage '91
Barbara Sanon
Straight Out of Brooklyn '91
Renoly Santiago
Hackers '95
Richard Sarafian
Bound '96
The Crossing Guard '94
Susan Sarandon
Dead Man Walking '95
Martine Sarcey
In a Wild Moment '78
Dick Sargent
Acting on Impulse '93
Daniel Sarky
Emmanuelle '74
Gailard Sartain
Open Season '95
The Spitfire Grill '95
Equinox '93
The Grifters '90
Trouble in Mind '86
Gary Sauer
The Unbelievable Truth '90
Ann Savage
Detour '46
John Savage
American Strays '96
The Crossing Guard '94
Salvador '86
John Savident
Impromptu '90
Mountains of the Moon '90
Butley '74
Joe Savino
The Crying Game '92
Camille Saviola
Last Exit to Brooklyn '90
David Saxon
A Hard Day's Night '64
John Saxon
Wes Craven's New Nightmare '94
John Sayles
City of Hope '91
Eight Men Out '88

Greta Scacchi
The Player '92
White Mischief '88
Heat and Dust '82
Prunella Scales
A Chorus of Disapproval '89
The Lonely Passion of Judith Hearne '87
Room at the Top '59
Renato Scarpa
The Postman '94
Diana Scarwid
Bastard out of Carolina '96
Johnathon Schaech
The Doom Generation '95
Rebecca Schaeffer
Scenes from the Class Struggle in Beverly Hills '89
Sabrina Scharf
Easy Rider '69
Maria Schell
The Odessa File '74
The Mark '61
White Nights '57
Maximilian Schell
Little Odessa '94
The Man in the Glass Booth '75
The Odessa File '74
Vincent Schiavelli
Cold Feet '89
Peter Schildt
Metamorphosis '75
Heinz Schimmelpfennig
Strongman Ferdinand '76
Daniel Schlachet
Swoon '91
Jean Schlegel
Trois Couleurs: Rouge '94
Morgan Schmidt-Feng
Morgan's Cake '88
Hellena Schmied
Barcelona '94
Sybille Schmitz
Vampyr '31
Stefan Schnabel
Anna '87
Helen Schneider
Eddie and the Cruisers '83
Maria Schneider
Jane Eyre '96
Peter Schneider
The Second Awakening of Christa Klages '78
Lutz Schnell
Das Boot '81

Barbara Schock
From Hollywood to Deadwood '89
Michael Schoeffling
Longtime Companion '90
Jill Schoelen
Popcorn '89
Bitty Schram
Caught '96
Max Schreck
Nosferatu '22
Liev Schreiber
The Daytrippers '96
Walking and Talking '96
Party Girl '94
Ernst Schroder
The Odessa File '74
Greta Schroeder
Nosferatu '22
Steven Schub
Caught '96
Heinz Schubert
Strongman Ferdinand '76
Maurice Schutz
Vampyr '31
Rusty Schwimmer
A Little Princess '95
Annabella Sciorra
The Funeral '96
The Addiction '95
True Love '89
Paul Scofield
A Delicate Balance '73
Alan Randolph Scott
Night on Earth '91
Campbell Scott
The Daytrippers '96
Big Night '95
Mrs. Parker and the Vicious Circle '94
Longtime Companion '90
Eileen Scott
Teenage Gang Debs '66
Evelyn Scott
Wicked Woman '54
Lizabeth Scott
Too Late for Tears '49
Pitfall '48
Kristin Scott Thomas
The English Patient '96
Angels and Insects '95
Four Weddings and a Funeral '94
A Handful of Dust '88
Bobbie Scroggins
The Woman in Question '50
Sean Scully
Phobia '88
Jenny Seagrove
A Chorus of Disapproval '89

Heather Sears
Room at the Top '59
Jean Seberg
Breathless '59
Kyle Secor
Delusion '91
Jon Seda
I Like It Like That '94
Robert Sedgwick
Tune in Tomorrow '90
Alison Seebohm
A Hard Day's Night '64
George Segal
Flirting with Disaster '95
It's My Party '95
Nena Segal
The Refrigerator '91
Mil Seghers
Antonia's Line '95
Frederick Sehreicker
The Third Man '49
Edda Seipel
The Marquise of O '76
John Seitz
Five Corners '88
Jirinaova Sejbalova
Day for My Love '77
Doug Self
Men in Love '90
Elizabeth Sellars
Madeleine '50
Tom Selleck
Open Season '95
Peter Sellers
The World of Henry Orient '64
Lolita '62
The Battle of the Sexes '60
The Smallest Show on Earth '57
John and Julie '55
The Ladykillers '55
Mortan Selten
The Ghost Goes West '36
Martin Semmelrogge
Das Boot '81
Willy Semmelrogge
Every Man for Himself & God Against All '75
Rade Serbedzija
Before the Rain '94
Assumpta Serna
Chain of Desire '93
Matador '86
Julieta Serrano
Tie Me Up! Tie Me Down! '90
Women on the Verge of a Nervous Breakdown '88

Cast Index

513

Matador '86
Dark Habits '84

Nestor Serrano
Hangin' with the
Homeboys '91

Josephine Serre
Jane Eyre '96

Jacques Serres
Blue Country '77

Roshan Seth
London Kills Me '91
Little Dorrit, Film 1:
Nobody's Fault '88
Little Dorrit, Film 2: Little
Dorrit's Story '88
My Beautiful Laundrette
'85

Chloe Sevigny
Trees Lounge '96
Kids '95

Ninon Sevilla
Aventurera '49

Rufus Sewell
Carrington '95
Twenty-One '91

Brendan Sexton, III
Welcome to the
Dollhouse '95

Athene Seyler
Non-Stop New York '37

Delphine Seyrig
Dear Michael '76

Glenn Shadix
The Applegates '89
Heathers '89

Serge Shakurov
100 Days after Childhood
'75

Tony Shalhoub
Big Night '95

Amelia Shankley
Dreamchild '85

Ethel Shannon
Charley's Aunt '25

Harry Shannon
The Red House '47

Johnny Shannon
That'll Be the Day '73

Marlene Shapiro
Back Street Jane '89

Rick Shapiro
True Love '89

Abdul Hassan Sharif
Zebrahead '92

Ray Sharkey
Zebrahead '92
Scenes from the Class
Struggle in Beverly Hills
'89
Wired '89

Anastasia Sharp
Go Fish '94

Lesley Sharp
Priest '94

Naked '93
Rita, Sue & Bob Too '87

N. Shaternikova
Professor Mamlock '38

Helen Shaver
Open Season '95
Zebrahead '92

Anabel Shaw
Gun Crazy '49

Fiona Shaw
Jane Eyre '96
Persuasion '95
London Kills Me '91
Mountains of the Moon
'90
My Left Foot '89

Sandie Shaw
Eat the Rich '87
Absolute Beginners '86

Sebastian Shaw
High Season '88

Susan Shaw
Fire Maidens from Outer
Space '56
The Woman in Question
'50

Wallace Shawn
Mrs. Parker and the
Vicious Circle '94
Vanya on 42nd Street '94
Scenes from the Class
Struggle in Beverly Hills
'89

Robert Shaye
Wes Craven's New
Nightmare '94

Chris Shearer
The Whole Wide World
'96

Jack Shearer
Golden Gate '93

Moira Shearer
Peeping Tom '60

Charlie Sheen
Eight Men Out '88
Platoon '86

Martin Sheen
The Incident '67

Barbara Shelley
Village of the Damned
'60

Adrienne Shelly
Sudden Manhattan '96
Trust '91
The Unbelievable Truth
'90

Jean Shelton
The Method '87

Joy Shelton
Uneasy Terms '48

Lindsay Shelton
Forgotten Silver '96

Lei Lao Sheng
The Story of Qui Ju '91

Chaz Lamas Shepard
Set It Off '96

Jack Shepherd
Twenty-One '91

Mark Sheppard
In the Name of the Father
'93

Dinah Sheridan
The Railway Children '70
Genevieve '53

Richard Sheridan
The Secret of Roan Inish
'94

Geraldine Sherman
Interlude '67

Lowell Sherman
Way Down East '20

Anthony Sherwood
Eddie and the Cruisers 2:
Eddie Lives! '89

Siu Sheung
Center Stage '91

Brooke Shields
Freeway '95

Steve Shill
The Missing Reel '90

Yoseph Shiloah
Daughters, Daughters
'74

Shogo Shimada
A-Ge-Man: Tales of a
Golden Geisha '91

Sab Shimono
Suture '93
The Wash '88

Ronald Shiner
Thursday's Child '43
They Drive by Night '38

Zarifeh Shivah
Through the Olive Trees
'94

Craig Shoemaker
Acting on Impulse '93

Dan Shor
Red Rock West '93

Winifred Shotter
John and Julie '55

John Shrapnel
How to Get Ahead in
Advertising '89

Elisabeth Shue
Leaving Las Vegas '95
The Underneath '95
Twenty Bucks '93

Mort Shuman
Jacques Brel Is Alive and
Well and Living in Paris
'75

Harold Siddons
Genevieve '53

Sylvia Sidney
You Only Live Once '37
Sabotage '36

George Siegmann
Oliver Twist '22

Nina Siemaszko
Twenty Bucks '93

Clovis Siemon
Blessing '94

Simone Signoret
Room at the Top '59

Maurice Sigrist
I Have Killed '24

Karen Sillas
What Happened Was...
'94

Henry Silva
The Manchurian
Candidate '62

Trinidad Silva
Alambrista! '77

Joe Silver
Rhinoceros '74

Veronique Silver
Dites-Lui Que Je L'Aime
'77

Alastair Sim
The Belles of St. Trinian's
'53

Jean Simmons
So Long at the Fair '50
Black Narcissus '47
Great Expectations '46

Francois Simon
Lumiere '76

Luc Simon
Lancelot of the Lake '74

David Simonds
The Refrigerator '91

Peggy Simpson
The 39 Steps '35

Joan Sims
The Belles of St. Trinian's
'53

Frank Sinatra
The Manchurian
Candidate '62

Leon Singer
My Family '94

Lori Singer
Equinox '93
Short Cuts '93
Trouble in Mind '86

Cheryl Singleton
She's Gotta Have It '86

Joseph Siravo
Walking and Talking '96

Errol Sitahal
A Little Princess '95

Jimmie F. Skaggs
Thousand Pieces of Gold
'91

Lilia Skala
House of Games '87
Heartland '81

Stellan Skarsgard
Breaking the Waves '95
The Unbearable
Lightness of Being '88

**Cast
Index**

The Prime of Miss Jean
    Brodie '69
Morgan! '66
**Maureen
    Stephenson**
The Wild Party '56
Jan Sterling
The Incident '67
1984 '56
Tisha Sterling
The Whales of August
    '87
Killer Inside Me '76
Agnes Stevenin
Hu-Man '76
**Jean-Francois
    Stevenin**
Small Change '76
Brinke Stevens
Mommy '95
Acting on Impulse '93
Fisher Stevens
Hackers '95
Nina Takes a Lover '94
Michael Stevens
The Return of Tommy
    Tricker '94
**Scott Thompson
    Stevens**
Acting on Impulse '93
Cynthia Stevenson
The Player '92
Alexandra Stewart
Black Moon '75
Jack Stewart
The Little Kidnappers '53
**Kate McGregor
    Stewart**
Safe '95
Paul Stewart
The Wild Party '56
Kiss Me Deadly '55
Champion '49
Peggy Stewart
Girls in Chains '43
Ben Stiller
Flirting with Disaster '95
Sting
Julia and Julia '87
Michael Stipe
Color of a Brisk and
    Leaping Day '95
Nigel Stock
Victim '61
Dean Stockwell
The Player '92
Blue Velvet '86
Tracks '76
John Stockwell
Eddie and the Cruisers
    '83
Jean Stoddard
You Only Live Once '37
Malcolm Stoddard
Luther '74

Mink Stole
Serial Mom '94
Female Trouble '74
Shirley Stoler
Frankenhooker '90
Miami Blues '90
Sticky Fingers '88
Seven Beauties '76
Eric Stoltz
Grace of My Heart '96
Pulp Fiction '94
Bodies, Rest & Motion
    '93
The Waterdance '91
Lena Stolze
The Nasty Girl '90
Elly Stone
Jacques Brel Is Alive and
    Well and Living in Paris
    '75
Julia Stone
Sirens '94
Marianne Stone
Lolita '62
Philip Stone
The Shining '80
Sharon Stone
Diary of a Hitman '91
Adam Storke
Mystic Pizza '88
Olaf Storm
Metropolis '26
Peter Stormare
Fargo '96
Sandra Storme
Clouds over Europe '39
Ken Stott
Shallow Grave '94
Jerry Stovin
Lolita '62
Madeleine Stowe
Short Cuts '93
Closet Land '90
Jason Stracey
Ladybird, Ladybird '93
Susan Stranks
Madeleine '50
David Strathairn
Passion Fish '92
City of Hope '91
Eight Men Out '88
Matewan '87
John Stratton
Abandon Ship '57
Meryl Streep
The House of the Spirits
    '93
Stephen Strimpell
Hester Street '75
Elaine Stritch
Who Killed Teddy Bear?
    '65
Oliver Stritzel
Das Boot '81
Shiloh Strong
House of Cards '92

Don Stroud
Killer Inside Me '76
John Stuart
Village of the Damned
    '60
John and Julie '55
Imogen Stubbs
A Summer Story '88
Jerzy Stuhr
Trois Couleurs: Blanc '94
Neil Stuke
Century '94
Michael Stumm
Swoon '91
Michel Such
Dites-Lui Que Je L'Aime
    '77
David Suchet
A World Apart '88
Yoko Sugi
Picture Bride '94
Ania Suli
Fun '94
Francis L. Sullivan
Great Expectations '46
Non-Stop New York '37
Michelle Sullivan
Poison '91
Sarah Sullivan
Red Rock West '93
**Frank
    Summerscales**
Children of the Damned
    '63
Scott Sunderland
Pygmalion '38
Bjorn Sundquist
The Feldmann Case '87
Donald Sutherland
The Rosary Murders '87
Eye of the Needle '81
Interlude '67
James Sutherland
The Little Kidnappers '53
Kiefer Sutherland
Freeway '95
Dudley Sutton
Orlando '92
Leather Boys '63
Janet Suzman
Nuns on the Run '90
Zdenek Sverak
Seclusion Near a Forest
    '76
B. Svetlov
Professor Mamlock '38
Robert Swann
If... '69
Gloria Swanson
Queen Kelly '29
Maureen Swanson
Moulin Rouge '52
Peter Swanwick
The African Queen '51

Don Swayze
Shy People '87
Patrick Swayze
Dirty Dancing '87
**Swedish National
    Soccer Team**
Stubby '74
Birdie Sweeney
The Crying Game '92
D.B. Sweeney
Eight Men Out '88
Vonte Sweet
American Strays '96
Menace II Society '93
Nora Swinburne
Interlude '67
Tilda Swinton
Orlando '92
Deborah Swisher
The Method '87
Meera Syal
Sammy & Rosie Get Laid
    '87
Derek Sydney
Hand in Hand '60
Kary Sylway
Face to Face '76
Sylvia Syms
A Chorus of Disapproval
    '89
Shirley Valentine '89
Victim '61
Laszlo Szabo
The Unbearable
    Lightness of Being '88
The Red Poster '76
Adoption '75
Presco Tabios
Chan Is Missing '82
Kristopher Tabori
Girlfriends '78
Ljuba Tadic
Fear '75
Sydney Tafler
Fire Maidens from Outer
    Space '56
Uneasy Terms '48
**Cary-Hiroyuki
    Tagawa**
Picture Bride '94
Taj Mahal
The Rolling Stones Rock
    and Roll Circus '68
Akira Takayama
Picture Bride '94
Lyle Talbot
Plan 9 from Outer Space
    '56
Michael Talbot
Acting on Impulse '93
Russ Tamblyn
Gun Crazy '49
Jeffrey Tambor
A House in the Hills '93
Pastime '91
Lisa '90

519

Arnetia Walker
Scenes from the Class
    Struggle in Beverly Hills
    '89
Corban Walker
Frankie Starlight '95
Helen Walker
Impact '49
Jimmie Walker
Open Season '95
Kathryn Walker
Girlfriends '78
Kerry Walker
The Piano '93
Kim Walker
Heathers '89
Polly Walker
Enchanted April '92
Robert Walker, Jr.
Easy Rider '69
Stephen Walker
Alambrista! '77
Tippy Walker
The World of Henry Orient
    '64
Willie Boy Walker
Morgan's Cake '88
Anita Wall
Scenes from a Marriage
    '73
Max Wall
Little Dorrit, Film 1:
    Nobody's Fault '88
Little Dorrit, Film 2: Little
    Dorrit's Story '88
**Dee Wallace
Stone**
Popcorn '89
Eli Wallach
Girlfriends '78
Gunn Wallgren
Metamorphosis '75
Sandy Walper
The Whole Wide World
    '96
J.T. Walsh
Sling Blade '96
The Last Seduction '94
Red Rock West '93
The Grifters '90
Wired '89
House of Games '87
Kay Walsh
This Happy Breed '47
M. Emmet Walsh
Equinox '93
Blood Simple '85
Percy Walsh
Thursday's Child '43
Susan Walsh
Female Trouble '74
Ray Walston
Popcorn '89
Tracey Walter
Destiny Turns on the
    Radio '95

Delusion '91
Hal Walters
Sabotage '36
Julie Walters
Just Like a Woman '95
Sister My Sister '94
Melora Walters
American Strays '96
Twenty Bucks '93
Thorley Walters
Twisted Nerve '68
Irene Wan
Love Unto Waste '86
**Madame Sul Te
Wan**
Queen Kelly '29
Faye Wang
Chungking Express '95
Peter Wang
Chan Is Missing '82
Yu-Wen Wang
Eat Drink Man Woman
    '94
Grzegorz Warchol
Trois Couleurs: Blanc '94
Christy Ward
Sling Blade '96
Colin Ward
Mother's Boys '94
Fred Ward
Equinox '93
Short Cuts '93
Two Small Bodies '93
The Player '92
Miami Blues '90
Mary Ward
Smoke '95
Mary B. Ward
Hangin' with the
    Homeboys '91
Rachel Ward
After Dark, My Sweet '90
How to Get Ahead in
    Advertising '89
The Good Wife '86
Ronald Ward
Sidewalks of London '38
Sophie Ward
Little Dorrit, Film 1:
    Nobody's Fault '88
Little Dorrit, Film 2: Little
    Dorrit's Story '88
A Summer Story '88
Wally Ward
The Chocolate War '88
Harlan Warde
Money Madness '47
Jack Warden
Bullets Over Broadway
    '94
S. J. Warmington
Sabotage '36
Gordon Warnecke
London Kills Me '91
My Beautiful Laundrette
    '85

David Warner
Mr. North '88
S.O.S. Titanic '79
Morgan! '66
Jack Warner
The Ladykillers '55
Jeremiah Warner
The Wizard of Loneliness
    '88
Richard Warner
Village of the Damned
    '60
Steven Warner
The Little Prince '74
Betty Warren
So Long at the Fair '50
C. Denier Warren
Lolita '62
Gary Warren
The Railway Children '70
**Jennifer Leigh
Warren**
Grace of My Heart '96
The Crossing Guard '94
**Kenneth
Warrington**
Beware of Pity '46
Richard Warwick
If... '69
Robert Warwick
I Married a Witch '42
Mona Washbourne
If... '69
Beverly Washburn
Spider Baby '64
**Denzel
Washington**
Much Ado about Nothing
    '93
For Queen and Country
    '88
Isaiah Washington
Love Jones '96
Jerard Washington
Just Another Girl on the
    I.R.T. '93
Andre Wasley
Forbidden Games '52
Dick Wassel
Pitfall '48
Dennis Waterman
Fright '71
Russell Waters
The Hidden Room '49
Sam Waterston
Serial Mom '94
Gwen Watford
The Very Edge '63
Never Take Candy from a
    Stranger '60
Deborah Watling
That'll Be the Day '73
Jack Watling
A Night to Remember '58
Alberta Watson
Hackers '95

Spanking the Monkey '94
Emily Watson
Breaking the Waves '95
Jack Watson
Peeping Tom '60
Wylie Watson
The 39 Steps '35
Richard Wattis
The Belles of St. Trinian's
    '53
Jeanne Watts
Three Sisters '70
Ken Wayne
One Night Stand '76
Naunton Wayne
The Hidden Room '49
Dead of Night '45
Night Train to Munich '40
The Lady Vanishes '38
Jacki Weaver
Caddie '76
Picnic at Hanging Rock
    '75
Sigourney Weaver
Death and the Maiden
    '94
Hugo Weaving
The Adventures of
    Priscilla, Queen of the
    Desert '94
Alan Webb
Interlude '67
Chloe Webb
The Belly of an Architect
    '91
Queens Logic '91
Timothy Webber
The Boys of St. Vincent
    '93
Dewey Weber
Chain of Desire '93
Steven Weber
Leaving Las Vegas '95
Rupert Webster
If... '69
Ann Wedgeworth
The Whole Wide World
    '96
Love and a .45 '94
**Jimmie Ray
Weeks**
Dead Man '95
Li Wei
Ju Dou '90
Robert Weil
Rhinoceros '74
Harvey Weinstein
Forgotten Silver '96
Elizabeth Welch
Dead of Night '45
Raquel Welch
Bedazzled '68
Tahnee Welch
I Shot Andy Warhol '96
Gwen Welles
Sticky Fingers '88

Nobody's Fool '86
Orson Welles
The Third Man '49
Margaret Wells
Pitfall '48
John Welsh
Lucky Jim '58
Margaret Welsh
American Heart '92
Klaus Wennemann
Das Boot '81
Zhang Wenyao
The Blue Kite '93
Jenny Werner
The Third Man '49
Oskar Werner
Interlude '67
Otto Wernicke
M '31
Francois Wertheimer
One Sings, the Other Doesn't '77
Julien West
Vampyr '31
Lockwood West
Bedazzled '68
Leather Boys '63
Sam West
Carrington '95
A Feast at Midnight '95
Persuasion '95
Timothy West
Twisted Nerve '68
John Westbrook
Room at the Top '59
Cecil Weston
Money Madness '47
Celia Weston
Dead Man Walking '95
Flirting with Disaster '95
Jack Weston
Dirty Dancing '87
Frank Whaley
Homage '95
Pulp Fiction '94
Swimming with Sharks '94
Joanne Whalley
A Good Man in Africa '94
Mother's Boys '94
Kill Me Again '89
Scandal '89
Dance with a Stranger '85
Kevin Whately
The English Patient '96
Thomas Wheatley
Where Angels Fear to Tread '91
Rich Wheeler
Bodies, Rest & Motion '93
Alison Whelan
My Left Foot '89

Forest Whitaker
Smoke '95
The Crying Game '92
Diary of a Hitman '91
Platoon '86
Millie White
Poison '91
Sheila White
Confessions of a Window Cleaner '74
Steven C. White
Open Season '95
Andrew Whitehead
Tommy Tricker & the Stamp Traveller '87
Billie Whitelaw
Jane Eyre '96
The Krays '90
Maurice '87
Twisted Nerve '68
Jon Whiteley
The Little Kidnappers '53
Peter Whitford
Strictly Ballroom '92
Warm Nights on a Slow-Moving Train '87
Gordon Whiting
The Railway Children '70
Stuart Whitman
The Mark '61
Crime of Passion '57
May Whitty
The Lady Vanishes '38
William Whymper
The Missing Reel '90
Jeffrey Wickham
Another Country '84
Saskia Wickham
Angels and Insects '95
Ellen Widmann
M '31
Richard Widmark
Murder on the Orient Express '74
Kai Wiesinger
Backbeat '94
Rudy Wiesler
Tomorrow the World '44
Dianne Wiest
Bullets Over Broadway '94
Peter Wight
Naked '93
Robert Wightman
Living in Oblivion '94
Carlton Wilborn
Grief '94
James Wilby
A Handful of Dust '88
A Summer Story '88
Maurice '87
Dreamchild '85
Marty Wilde
Stardust '74

Gene Wilder
The Little Prince '74
Rhinoceros '74
Webb Wilder
The Thing Called Love '93
John Wildman
American Boyfriends '89
Valerie Wildman
Salvador '86
Catherine Wilkin
Brilliant Lies '96
Tom Wilkinson
Priest '94
Barbara Williams
City of Hope '91
Burt Williams
Public Access '93
Clarence Williams, III
Tough Guys Don't Dance '87
Cynda Williams
The Tie that Binds '95
One False Move '91
Emlyn Williams
They Drive by Night '38
Gareth Williams
Blessing '94
Guinn "Big Boy" Williams
You Only Live Once '37
Harcourt Williams
The Obsessed '51
Heathcote Williams
Orlando '92
Kimberly Williams
Coldblooded '94
Ryan Williams
Menace II Society '93
Samm-Art Williams
Blood Simple '85
Scot Williams
Backbeat '94
Treat Williams
Smooth Talk '85
Mykel T. Williamson
Miracle Mile '89
Noble Willingham
Pastime '91
Bruce Willis
Pulp Fiction '94
Shauntisa Willis
Passion Fish '92
Noel Willman
The Odessa File '74
Abandon Ship '57
Drusilla Wills
Non-Stop New York '37
Brian Wilson
I Wasn't Made for These Times '94

Carnie Wilson
I Wasn't Made for These Times '94
David Wilson
Eddie and the Cruisers '83
K.J. Wilson
An Angel at My Table '89
Lambert Wilson
The Belly of an Architect '91
Richard Wilson
How to Get Ahead in Advertising '89
Scott Wilson
Dead Man Walking '95
Stuart Wilson
Death and the Maiden '94
Wendy Wilson
I Wasn't Made for These Times '94
Penelope Wilton
Carrington '95
Barry Winch
Tommy '75
Michael Wincott
Basquiat '96
Dead Man '95
Marc Wincourt
Murmur of the Heart '71
Debra Winger
Betrayed '88
Lucyna Winnicka
25 Fireman's Street '73
Mare Winningham
Georgia '95
Miracle Mile '89
Shy People '87
Nobody's Fool '86
George Winship
Teenage Gang Debs '66
Kate Winslet
Heavenly Creatures '94
Ray Winstone
Ladybird, Ladybird '93
Vincent Winter
The Little Kidnappers '53
Shelley Winters
Heavy '94
An Average Little Man '77
The Balcony '63
Lolita '62
He Ran All the Way '51
Siegfried Wischnewski
Strongman Ferdinand '76
Googie Withers
Shine '95
Dead of Night '45
Pink String and Sealing Wax '45
On Approval '44
The Lady Vanishes '38

The "Director Index" provides a complete listing of directors cited within the reviews. The directors' names are listed alphabetically by last name, and the films they directed that are reviewed in this book are listed chronologically, from most recent to the oldest film. Take a peek back at the "Cast Index" to see if your favorite director also had a walk-on in his/her own or his/her best friend's film. Could happen.

Joe Berlinger
Paradise Lost: The Child Murders at Robin Hood Hills '95
Brother's Keeper '92

Claude Berri
In a Wild Moment '78

John Berry
He Ran All the Way '51

Bernardo Bertolucci
The Conformist '71

Dan Bessie
Hard Traveling '85

Luc Besson
La Femme Nikita '91

Radha Bharadwaj
Closet Land '90

Tony Bill
Five Corners '88

Kevin Billington
The Good Soldier '81
Interlude '67

Mira Reym Binford
Diamonds in the Snow '94

Antonia Bird
Priest '94

Whitney Blake
Reno's Kids: 87 Days Plus 11 '87

Bertrand Blier
Too Beautiful for You '88

Yurek Bogayevicz
Anna '87

Peter Bogdanovich
The Thing Called Love '93

Arthur Borman
...And God Spoke '94

John Boulting
Lucky Jim '58

Roy Boulting
Twisted Nerve '68

Jenny Bowen
The Wizard of Loneliness '88
Street Music '81

Don Boyd
Twenty-One '91

Danny Boyle
Trainspotting '95
Shallow Grave '94

Kenneth Branagh
Much Ado about Nothing '93

Andre Brassard
Once Upon a Time in the East '74

Michel Brault
The Orders '75

Robert Bresson
Lancelot of the Lake '74

Matthew Bright
Freeway '95

Clive Brook
On Approval '44

Kevin Brownlow
Cinema Europe '96

Franco Brusati
The Sleazy Uncle '89

Colin Bucksey
Dealers '89

Richard Bugajski
The Interrogation '82

Luis Bunuel
Phantom of Liberty '74

Charles Burnett
To Sleep with Anger '90

Edward Burns
She's the One '96
The Brothers McMullen '94

Steve Buscemi
Trees Lounge '96

Michael Cacoyannis
Iphigenia '77

Barry Caillier
To Cross the Rubicon '91

Simon Callow
The Ballad of the Sad Cafe '91

Ken Cameron
The Good Wife '86

Martin Campbell
Criminal Law '89

Jane Campion
The Piano '93
An Angel at My Table '89

Dyan Cannon
Number One '76

Marcel Carne
Children of Paradise '45

Marc Caro
The City of Lost Children '95

Denise Casano
Girls Town '95

John Cassavetes
The Killing of a Chinese Bookie '76

Frank Cassenti
The Red Poster '76

Joseph Cates
Who Killed Teddy Bear? '65

Michael Caton-Jones
Scandal '89

Alberto Cavalcanti
Dead of Night '45

Judy Chaikin
Legacy of the Hollywood Blacklist '87

Jackie Chan
Project A: Part 2 '87

Tony Chan
Combination Platter '93

Peter Chelsom
Funny Bones '94
Hear My Song '91

Joyce Chopra
Smooth Talk '85

Christo Christov
Last Summer '74

Gerard Ciccoritti
Paris, France '94

Rene Clair
I Married a Witch '42
The Ghost Goes West '36

Larry Clark
Kids '95

Alan Clarke
Rita, Sue & Bob Too '87

Jack Clayton
The Lonely Passion of Judith Hearne '87
The Innocents '61
Room at the Top '59

Rene Clement
Forbidden Games '52

Jean Cocteau
Beauty and the Beast '46

Fred Coe
A Thousand Clowns '65

Wayne Coe
Grim Prairie Tales '89

Joel Coen
Fargo '96
Blood Simple '85

Eli Cohen
Ricochets '87

Larry Cohen
The Ambulance '90
Special Effects '85

Max Allan Collins
Mommy '95

Peter Collinson
Fright '71

Carl Colpaert
Delusion '91

Kevin Connor
The Land That Time Forgot '75

Martha Coolidge
Rambling Rose '91

Roger Corman
Frankenstein Unbound '90

Alain Corneau
France, Incorporated '74

Henry Cornelius
Genevieve '53

Michael Corrente
Federal Hill '94

Constantin Costa-Gavras
Betrayed '88

Michael Covert
American Strays '96

Wes Craven
Wes Craven's New Nightmare '94

Charles Crichton
The Battle of the Sexes '60
Dead of Night '45

Donald Crombie
Caddie '76

David Cronenberg
Crash '95

Alfonso Cuaron
A Little Princess '95

John Dahl
The Last Seduction '94
Red Rock West '93
Kill Me Again '89

Damiano Damiani
The Devil Is a Woman '75

Anthony Darnborough
So Long at the Fair '50

Julie Dash
Daughters of the Dust '91

Jules Dassin
A Dream of Passion '78

Delmer Daves
The Red House '47

Martin Davidson
Eddie and the Cruisers '83

Robin Davis
Dear Victor '75

Tamra Davis
Guncrazy '92

Andre de Toth
Pitfall '48

Basil Dearden
Victim '61
The Smallest Show on Earth '57
Saraband for Dead Lovers '48
Dead of Night '45

Steve DeJarnatt
Miracle Mile '89

Peter Del Monte
Julia and Julia '87

Robert Derteno
Girl Gang '54

Joseph Destein
The Method '87

Tom DiCillo
Living in Oblivion '94

Thorold Dickinson
Gaslight '40

John Dingwall
Phobia '88

Edward Dmytryk
The Hidden Room '49

Stanley Donen
The Little Prince '74
Bedazzled '68
Two for the Road '67

Director Index

INDEPENDENT
FILM GUIDE

George Roy Hill
The World of Henry Orient
'64
Jack Hill
Switchblade Sisters '75
Spider Baby '64
John Hillcoat
To Have and to Hold '96
Arthur Hiller
The Man in the Glass
Booth '75
Alfred Hitchcock
The Lady Vanishes '38
Young and Innocent '37
Sabotage '36
The 39 Steps '35
The Man Who Knew Too
Much '34
Rich and Strange '32
Blackmail '29
P.J. Hogan
Muriel's Wedding '94
Nicole Holofcener
Walking and Talking '96
Dennis Hopper
Easy Rider '69
Harry Horner
The Wild Party '56
Leslie Howard
Pygmalion '38
George Huang
Swimming with Sharks
'94
Jean-Loup Hubert
Le Grand Chemin '87
Reginald Hudlin
House Party '90
Marc Huestis
Men in Love '90
Albert Hughes
Menace II Society '93
Allen Hughes
Menace II Society '93
Tim Hunter
River's Edge '87
William T. Hurtz
Little Nemo: Adventures
in Slumberland '92
Anjelica Huston
Bastard out of Carolina
'96
Danny Huston
Mr. North '88
John Huston
The Dead '87
Beat the Devil '53
Moulin Rouge '52
The African Queen '51
Nicholas Hytner
The Madness of King
George '94
Dan Ireland
The Whole Wide World
'96
Sam Irvin
Acting on Impulse '93

Aline Issermann
Shades of Doubt '93
Juzo Itami
A-Ge-Man: Tales of a
Golden Geisha '91
Anatoli Ivanov
The Last Days of the Last
Tsar '92
James Ivory
The Remains of the Day
'93
Maurice '87
A Room with a View '86
Heat and Dust '82
Arnaldo Jabor
The Marriage '76
Peter Jackson
Forgotten Silver '96
Heavenly Creatures '94
Alan Jacobs
Nina Takes a Lover '94
**Nicholas A.E.
Jacobs**
The Refrigerator '91
Just Jaeckin
Emmanuelle '74
Henry Jaglom
Tracks '76
Steve James
Hoop Dreams '94
Nan Janelidze
Lullaby '94
Victor Janson
The Yellow Ticket '18
Jim Jarmusch
Dead Man '95
Night on Earth '91
Lionel Jeffries
The Railway Children '70
Jean-Marie Jeunet
The City of Lost Children
'95
Neal Jimenez
The Waterdance '91
Sande N. Johnson
Teenage Gang Debs '66
L.Q. Jones
A Boy and His Dog '75
Neil Jordan
Michael Collins '96
The Crying Game '92
Mona Lisa '86
Mikhail Kalatozov
I Am Cuba '64
Tom Kalin
Swoon '91
Marek Kanievska
Another Country '84
Wong Kar-Wai
Chungking Express '95
Philip Kaufman
The Unbearable
Lightness of Being '88
Douglas Keeve
Unzipped '94

Roy Kellino
I Met a Murderer '39
Nancy Kelly
Thousand Pieces of Gold
'91
Burt Kennedy
Killer Inside Me '76
Roeland Kerbosch
For a Lost Soldier '93
Lodge Kerrigan
Clean, Shaven '93
Abbas Kiarostami
Through the Olive Trees
'94
Mark Kidel
Boy Next Door '93
**Krzysztof
Kieslowski**
Trois Couleurs: Blanc '94
Trois Couleurs: Rouge
'94
Trois Couleurs: Bleu '93
Randal Kleiser
It's My Party '95
Matjaz Klopcic
Fear '75
Alexander Kluge
Strongman Ferdinand '76
John Knoop
Cafe Nica: Portraits from
Nicaragua '87
**Andrei
Konchalovsky**
Shy People '87
Alexander Korda
The Private Life of Henry
VIII '33
John Korty
Who Are the DeBolts and
Where Did They Get 19
Kids? '78
**Soeren Kragh-
Jacobsen**
Emma's Shadow '88
Bill Krohn
It's All True '93
Lisa Krueger
Manny & Lo '96
Stanley Kubrick
The Shining '80
Lolita '62
Hanif Kureishi
London Kills Me '91
Stanley Kwan
Center Stage '91
Rouge '87
Love Unto Waste '86
Frank Laloggia
The Lady in White '88
Mary Lambert
Grand Isle '91
Fritz Lang
You Only Live Once '37
M '31
Metropolis '26

Simon Langton
The Whistle Blower '87
James Lapine
Impromptu '90
**Jerome
Lapperrousaz**
Hu-Man '76
Alberto Lattuada
Variety Lights '51
Frank Launder
The Belles of St. Trinian's
'53
J.F. Lawton
Cannibal Women in the
Avocado Jungle of
Death '89
Philip Leacock
Hand in Hand '60
The Little Kidnappers '53
Anton Leader
Children of the Damned
'63
David Lean
Madeleine '50
This Happy Breed '47
Brief Encounter '46
Great Expectations '46
Blithe Spirit '45
Ang Lee
Eat Drink Man Woman
'94
The Wedding Banquet
'93
Spike Lee
She's Gotta Have It '86
Michael Lehmann
The Applegates '89
Heathers '89
Mike Leigh
Secrets and Lies '95
Naked '93
David Leland
Wish You Were Here '87
Claude Lelouch
Cat and Mouse '78
Robert et Robert '78
If I Had It to Do Over
Again '76
Michael Lessac
House of Cards '92
Richard Lester
The Making of a Hard
Day's Night '94
A Hard Day's Night '64
Jefery Levy
Inside Monkey Zetterland
'93
Ben Lewin
The Favor, the Watch,
and the Very Big Fish
'92
Joseph H. Lewis
Gun Crazy '49
Victoria Lewis
Mystery of the Last Tsar
'97

Director Index

INDEPENDENT FILM GUIDE

Sean Penn
The Crossing Guard '94

D.A. Pennebaker
The War Room '93

Clare Peploe
High Season '88

Wolfgang Petersen
Das Boot '81

Donald Petrie
Mystic Pizza '88

Maurice Phillips
Enid Is Sleeping '90

Rex Pickett
From Hollywood to Deadwood '89

Harold Pinter
Butley '74

Anne Claire Poirier
Salut Victor! '89

Roman Polanski
Death and the Maiden '94
Repulsion '65

Stephen Poliakoff
Century '94

Sally Potter
Orlando '92

Michael Powell
Peeping Tom '60
Black Narcissus '47

Emeric Pressburger
Black Narcissus '47

Alexander Proshkin
To See Paris and Die '93

Yakov Protazanov
Aelita: Queen of Mars '24

Evelyn Purcell
Nobody's Fool '86

Michael Radford
The Postman '94
White Mischief '88

Bob Rafelson
Mountains of the Moon '90

Kevin Rafferty
Feed '92

Herbert Rappaport
Professor Mamlock '38

Mark Rappaport
From the Journals of Jean Seberg '95
Rock Hudson's Home Movies '92

Steve Rash
Queens Logic '91

Christopher Rawlence
The Missing Reel '90

Carol Reed
The Fallen Idol '49
The Third Man '49
Night Train to Munich '40

Kelly Reichardt
River of Grass '94

Karel Reisz
Morgan! '66

Norman Rene
Reckless '95
Longtime Companion '90

Matty Rich
Straight Out of Brooklyn '91

Peter Richardson
Eat the Rich '87

Tony Richardson
A Delicate Balance '73
The Entertainer '60

James Ridgeway
Feed '92

Marlon Riggs
Color Adjustment '91

Eran Riklis
Zohar: Mediterranean Blues '93

Wolf Rilla
Village of the Damned '60

Pierre Rissient
One Night Stand '76

Hal Roach
Turnabout '40

Tim Robbins
Dead Man Walking '95

Bruce Robinson
How to Get Ahead in Advertising '89
Withnail and I '87

Mark Robson
Champion '49

Alexandre Rockwell
In the Soup '92

Robert Rodriguez
El Mariachi '93

Nicolas Roeg
The Witches '90

Eric Rohmer
The Marquise of O '76

Joanelle Romero
Powwow Highway '89

Martin Rosen
Stacking '87

Keva Rosenfeld
Twenty Bucks '93

Roberto Rossellini
The Miracle '48

Bobby Roth
Boss' Son '78

Cy Roth
Fire Maidens from Outer Space '56

Russel Rouse
Wicked Woman '54

Michael Rubbo
The Return of Tommy Tricker '94

Tommy Tricker & the Stamp Traveller '87

Alan Rudolph
Mrs. Parker and the Vicious Circle '94
Equinox '93
Trouble in Mind '86

Raul Ruiz
Three Lives and Only One Death '96

David O. Russell
Flirting with Disaster '95
Spanking the Monkey '94

Ken Russell
The Lair of the White Worm '88
Lisztomania '75
Tommy '75

Richard Sale
Abandon Ship '57

David Salle
Search and Destroy '94

Philip Saville
Wonderland '88

Victor Saville
Evergreen '34

Nancy Savoca
Household Saints '93
True Love '89

John Sayles
Lone Star '95
The Secret of Roan Inish '94
Passion Fish '92
City of Hope '91
Eight Men Out '88
Matewan '87

Jerry Schatzberg
Street Smart '87

Suzanne Schiffman
Sorceress '88

Rick Schmidt
Morgan's Cake '88

Julian Schnabel
Basquiat '96

Paul Schrader
The Comfort of Strangers '91

Ettore Scola
Ugly, Dirty and Bad '78
A Special Day '77

Martin Scorsese
After Hours '85

Campbell Scott
Big Night '95

Sandra Seacat
In the Spirit '90

William A. Seiter
Helen's Babies '25

Dominic Sena
Kalifornia '93

Coline Serreau
Why Not! '78

Vernon Sewell
Uneasy Terms '48

Adrienne Shelly
Sudden Manhattan '96

Richard Shepard
The Linguini Incident '92

Sam Shepard
Silent Tongue '92

Jim Sheridan
In the Name of the Father '93
My Left Foot '89

Gary Sherman
Lisa '90

Barry Shils
Motorama '91

Mamoru Shinzaki
Barefoot Gen '83

Scott Sidney
Charley's Aunt '25

David Siegel
Suture '93

Joan Micklin Silver
Hester Street '75

Marisa Silver
Permanent Record '88
Old Enough '84

Anthony Simmons
Black Joy '77

Yves Simoneau
Mother's Boys '94

Alexander Singer
A Cold Wind in August '61

Bryan Singer
The Usual Suspects '95
Public Access '93

Bruce Sinofsky
Paradise Lost: The Child Murders at Robin Hood Hills '95
Brother's Keeper '92

Jerzy Skolimowski
Deep End '70

George Sluizer
The Vanishing '88

John N. Smith
The Boys of St. Vincent '93

Kevin Smith
Chasing Amy '97
Mallrats '95
Clerks '94

Michele (Michael) Soavi
Cemetery Man '95

Steven Soderbergh
The Underneath '95
Kafka '91
sex, lies and videotape '89

Iain Softley
Hackers '95
Backbeat '94

**Director
Index**

529

Jim Wynorski
Not of this Earth *'88*

Boaz Yakin
Fresh *'94*

Peter Yates
The House on Carroll
  Street *'88*

Zhang Yimou
The Story of Qui Ju *'91*

Ju Dou *'90*

Hiroaki Yoshida
Twilight of the
  Cockroaches *'90*

Harold Young
The Scarlet Pimpernel
  '34

Robert M. Young
Caught *'96*

Alambrista! *'77*

Krzysztof Zanussi
The Balance *'75*

Franco Zeffirelli
Jane Eyre *'96*

Paul Zehrer
Blessing *'94*

Rafael Zelinski
Fun *'94*

**Tian
  Zhuangzhuang**
The Blue Kite *'93*

Lee David Zlotoff
The Spitfire Grill *'95*

Terry Zwigoff
Crumb *'94*

So look up "Comedy" or "Drama" if you must. But you could be more specific and look up "Black Comedy" or "Tearjerkers." And the truly inspired among you will look up "Disorganized Crime," or "Edibles," or "Dates from Hell," or one of the many creative and slightly off-the-wall categories we categorize by. The "Category Index" includes subject terms ranging from straight genre descriptions (Westerns, Documentaries) to more unique categories (Flashback, Gender Bending). These terms can help you identify unifying themes (Late Bloomin' Love, Mad Scientists), settings (Nifty '50s, France), events (World War II, the Great Depression), occupations (Shrinks, Struggling Musicians), or foreign films by country of origin. Also included are a list of four-bone movies, as well as the woofs. Category terms are listed alphabetically. Have fun.

A Shock to the
System
Smooth Talk
Steppenwolf
The Story of Qui Ju
The Third Man
To Die For
Tough Guys Don't
Dance
Trainspotting
True Confessions
Tune in Tomorrow
Turnabout
The Unbearable
Lightness of Being
Uneasy Terms
Vampyr
Village of the
Damned
Where Angels Fear to
Tread
White Nights
The Witches
The Wizard of
Loneliness
The World of Henry
Orient

Adapted from a
Cartoon
The Belles of St.
Trinian's
Little Nemo:
Adventures in
Slumberland

Adapted from a
Fairy Tale
Beauty and the Beast
Freeway
The Witches

Adapted from a
Play or Musical
Aelita: Queen of Mars
Another Country
The Balcony
The Ballad of the Sad
Cafe
Black Joy
Blithe Spirit
Bodies, Rest &
Motion
Brilliant Lies
A Chorus of
Disapproval
Curse of the Starving
Class
Death and the Maiden
A Delicate Balance
Diary of a Hitman
The Entertainer
Fun
Gaslight
Homage
The Homecoming
In Celebration
Iphigenia
Love and Human
Remains

The Maids
The Man in the Glass
Booth
Much Ado about
Nothing
Never Take Candy
from a Stranger
Nobody's Fool
The Obsessed
Oleanna
On Approval
The Prime of Miss
Jean Brodie
Pygmalion
Reckless
Search and Destroy
Separate Tables
Shelf Life
Shirley Valentine
This Happy Breed
A Thousand Clowns
Three Sisters
Tomorrow the World
The Trip to Bountiful
Two Small Bodies
Vanya on 42nd Street
The Whales of
August

Adapted from a
Story
The Ballad of the Sad
Cafe
A Boy and His Dog
Brief Encounter
The Dead
Eat a Bowl of Tea
The Little Prince
Menace II Society
Metamorphosis
Sabotage
Salut Victor!
Short Cuts
Smooth Talk
A Summer Story

Adapted from
Memoirs or
Diaries
Heartland
In the Name of the
Father
Just Like a Woman
The Whole Wide
World
Wish You Were Here

Adolescence
See Coming of
Age; Hell High
School; Summer
Camp; Teen Angst

Adoption &
Orphans
See also Hard
Knock Life; Only
the Lonely

Adoption
Anne of Green
Gables
The Boys of St.
Vincent
Flirting with Disaster
Great Expectations
Jane Eyre
Oliver Twist
The Orphans
Pixote
Queen Kelly
Secrets and Lies
Sidewalks of London
Streetwise
The Tie that Binds
Who Are the DeBolts
and Where Did They
Get 19 Kids?

Adventure Drama
See also Action
Adventure; Drama
Abandon Ship
The Deceivers
Hackers
Mountains of the
Moon
Platoon

Africa
The African Queen
A Good Man in Africa
White Mischief
A World Apart

African America
See also New
Black Cinema
Black Joy
Daughters of the
Dust
Fly by Night
Fresh
Hangin' with the
Homeboys
Hoop Dreams
House Party
Just Another Girl on
the I.R.T.
Kansas City
Lone Star
Love Jones
Menace II Society
New Jersey Drive
One False Move
Paris Is Burning
Pastime
Pulp Fiction
Secrets and Lies
Set It Off
She's Gotta Have It
Straight Out of
Brooklyn
To Sleep with Anger
Zebrahead

AIDS
And the Band Played
On
Closing Numbers
It's My Party
Longtime Companion
Men in Love

Alcoholism
See On the Rocks

Alien Beings
Not of this Earth
Plan 9 from Outer
Space
Vegas in Space
Village of the
Damned

American Film
Theatre (AFT)
Production
Butley
A Delicate Balance
Homecoming
The Iceman Cometh
Jacques Brel Is Alive
and Well and Living
in Paris
Lost in the Stars
Luther
The Maids
The Man in the Glass
Booth
Rhinoceros
Three Sisters

American Indians
See Native
America

American South
The Ballad of the Sad
Cafe
Bastard out of
Carolina
The Big Easy
One False Move
Passion Fish
Rambling Rose
River of Grass
Shag: The Movie
Shy People
Sling Blade
The Trip to Bountiful
Tune in Tomorrow

Animation
Barefoot Gen
Little Nemo:
Adventures in
Slumberland
Princess and the
Goblin
Twilight of the
Cockroaches

Anthology
Actors and Sin
Dead of Night

Cate
gory
Index

Cate
gory
Index

INDEPENDENT
FILM GUIDE

**Cate
gory
Index**

539

**INDEPENDENT
FILM GUIDE**

The Boy from
Mercury
Breaking the Waves
Breathless
Burnt by the Sun
Camille Claudel
Carrington
Cat and Mouse
Children of Paradise
The City of Lost
Children
The Conformist
Coup de Torchon
Cousin, Cousine
Daddy Nostalgia
Dangerous Liaisons
Dear Victor
Dites-Lui Que Je
L'Aime
Emmanuelle
The Favor, the Watch,
and the Very Big
Fish
First Communion
Forbidden Games
The 400 Blows
France, Incorporated
French Provincial
Fresh
Hu-Man
I Have Killed
If I Had It to Do Over
Again
In a Wild Moment
Jacques Brel Is Alive
and Well and Living
in Paris
La Femme Nikita
Lacombe, Lucien
L'Amour en Herbe
Lancelot of the Lake
Le Grand Chemin
Lumiere
The Man Who Loved
Women
The Marquise of O
Mina Tannenbaum
Murmur of the Heart
101 Nights
One Night Stand
One Sings, the Other
Doesn't
Orlando
Pas Tres Catholique
Phantom of Liberty
Reasons of State
The Red Poster
Roads to the South
Robert et Robert
Servant and Mistress
Shades of Doubt
Small Change
Three Lives and Only
One Death
Too Beautiful for You
Trois Couleurs: Blanc
Trois Couleurs: Bleu
Trois Couleurs:
Rouge

The Vanishing
Victory March
Why Not!
The Wonderful Crook
The World of Jacques
Demy

Foreign: German
The Conformist
Das Boot
Deep End
Every Man for
Himself & God
Against All
False Weights
From the Pole to the
Equator
Joyless Street
M
The Marquise of O
Martha and I
Meier
Metropolis
Mother Kusters Goes
to Heaven
The Nasty Girl
Nico Icon
Nosferatu
The Odessa File
Pandora's Box
Salmonberries
The Second
Awakening of
Christa Klages
Strongman Ferdinand
Vampyr
Victory March
Wings of Desire
The Wonderful,
Horrible Life of Leni
Riefenstahl
The Yellow Ticket

Foreign: Greek
A Dream of Passion
Iphigenia

**Foreign: Hong
Kong**
Center Stage
Chungking Express
Love Unto Waste
One Night Stand
Rouge

**Foreign:
Hungarian**
Adoption
The Hungarians
Nine Months
25 Fireman's Street
The Unfinished
Sentence in 141
Minutes

Foreign: Indian
The Deceivers
Kama Sutra: A Tale
of Love

Foreign: Iranian
Through the Olive
Trees

Foreign: Irish
The Boy from
Mercury
The Crying Game
Frankie Starlight
In the Name of the
Father
My Left Foot

Foreign: Israeli
Coffee with Lemon
Daughters,
Daughters
The Garden
Ricochets
Song of the Siren
Zohar: Mediterranean
Blues

Foreign: Italian
Allonsanfan
An Average Little
Man
Bellissima
The Belly of an
Architect
Cemetery Man
Cinema Paradiso
The Conformist
Creepers
Dangerous Liaisons
Dear Michael
The Devil Is a Woman
8 1/2
Everything Ready,
Nothing Works
From the Pole to the
Equator
Lamerica
The Miracle
Ossessione
Padre Padrone
Passionate Thief
The Postman
The Profiteer
Seven Beauties
The Sleazy Uncle
A Special Day
The Stranger's Hand
Swept Away...
Ugly, Dirty and Bad
Variety Lights
Victory March
A Virgin Named Mary
White Nights

**Foreign:
Jamaican**
Rockers

**Foreign:
Japanese**
A-Ge-Man: Tales of a
Golden Geisha
Barefoot Gen
Picture Bride

Twilight of the
Cockroaches

**Foreign:
Macedonian**
Before the Rain

Foreign: Mexican
Aventurera
Cabeza de Vaca
El Mariachi
A Kiss to this Land
Like Water for
Chocolate
Reasons of State

**Foreign: New
Zealand**
An Angel at My Table
Crush
Forgotten Silver
Heavenly Creatures

**Foreign:
Norwegian**
The Feldmann Case

Foreign: Polish
Ashes and Diamonds
The Balance
The Interrogation
Trois Couleurs: Blanc
Trois Couleurs:
Rouge

Foreign: Russian
Aelita: Queen of
Mars
Burnt by the Sun
The Children of
Theatre Street
I Am Cuba
The Man with the
Movie Camera
100 Days after
Childhood
The Only One
Orlando
Orphans
Professor Mamlock
To See Paris and Die
With You and Without
You

Foreign: Spanish
Black Litter
Bride to Be
Cabeza de Vaca
Dark Habits
The Fable of the
Beautiful Pigeon
Fancier
High Heels
Kika
Law of Desire
Matador
Spirit of the Beehive
Tie Me Up! Tie Me
Down!

Cate
gory
Index

INDEPENDENT
FILM GUIDE

Mrs. Parker and the
Vicious Circle
Nina Takes a Lover
The Odessa File
Salvador
Shy People
Street Smart
A World Apart

Gambling
Eight Men Out
House of Games
Household Saints
The Underneath

Gangs
See also Crime &
Criminals;
Organized Crime
Menace II Society
Sticky Fingers
Teenage Gang Debs
Too Late for Tears
Wonderland

Gays
See also
Bisexuality; Gender
Bending; Lesbians
And the Band Played
On
Another Country
The Best Way
Carrington
Closing Numbers
The Conformist
The Crying Game
For a Lost Soldier
Four Weddings and a
Funeral
Go Fish
Grief
The Hours and Times
It's My Party
Kiss of the Spider
Woman
Longtime Companion
Love and Human
Remains
Maurice
Men in Love
My Beautiful
Laundrette
My Own Private Idaho
Once Upon a Time in
the East
Paris Is Burning
Priest
Rock Hudson's Home
Movies
Salut Victor!
Swoon
Victim
The Wedding
Banquet
Withnail and I
Wonderland

Gender Bending
See also Gays;
Lesbians; Role
Reversal
The Adventures of
Priscilla, Queen of
the Desert
The Crying Game
Different for Girls
I Like It Like That
I Shot Andy Warhol
Just Like a Woman
Law of Desire
Le Sexe des Etoiles
Nuns on the Run
Orlando
Paris Is Burning
Vegas in Space

Generation X
Bodies, Rest &
Motion
Chasing Amy
Clerks
Mallrats
Party Girl
Slacker

Germany
See also Foreign:
German
Backbeat
Nico Icon
The Odessa File
Salmonberries
Wings of Desire

Ghosts, Ghouls,
& Goblins
See also Death &
the Afterlife
The Ghost Goes
West
The Innocents
Rouge
Silent Tongue

Grand Hotel
Dirty Dancing
Separate Tables
The Shining

Great Britain
See also Ireland;
Scotland; Foreign:
British
Angels and Insects
Carrington
The Englishman Who
Went Up a Hill But
Came Down a
Mountain
For Queen and
Country
Four Weddings and a
Funeral
Funny Bones
The Innocents

The Krays
The Long Good Friday
The Madness of King
George
Naked
Nine Days a Queen
Persuasion
Pink String and
Sealing Wax
Scandal
35 Up
The Whistle Blower
White Mischief
The Windsors: A
Royal Family

Great Depression
See also Hard
Knock Life;
Homeless
The Ballad of the Sad
Cafe
The Funeral
Hard Traveling
Our Daily Bread
Rambling Rose
The Whole Wide
World
You Only Live Once

Growing Older
See also Death &
the Afterlife; Late
Bloomin' Love
Anna
Daddy Nostalgia
Lamerica
Lightning Jack
101 Nights
Pastime
The Private Life of
Henry VIII
Queens Logic
Salut Victor!
Shirley Valentine
A Shock to the
System
Street Music
Two for the Road
The Whales of
August

Hard Knock Life
See also Great
Depression;
Homeless
Blessing
Forbidden Choices
Lamerica
Set It Off
The Story of Fausta

Heists
See also Scams,
Stings & Cons
Bellman and True
Bound

Destiny Turns on the
Radio
Gun Crazy
Lightning Jack
Motorama
Passionate Thief
Reservoir Dogs
Set It Off
The Underneath
The Usual Suspects

Hell High School
See also School
Daze; Teen Angst
Creepers
Girls in Chains
Girls Town
Heathers
If...

Hispanic
America
I Like It Like That
Lone Star
My Family

Historical Drama
Cabeza de Vaca
Children of Paradise
I Shot Andy Warhol
Kama Sutra: A Tale
of Love
Luther
The Marquise of O
Nine Days a Queen
The Orders
The Private Life of
Henry VIII
Saraband for Dead
Lovers
The Scarlet
Pimpernel
White Mischief

Hit Men
See also
Assassinations
Diary of a Hitman
El Mariachi
The Funeral
La Femme Nikita
Little Odessa
Pulp Fiction
Red Rock West

The Holocaust
See also Germany;
Judaism; Nazis &
Other Paramilitary
Slugs; World War II
Diamonds in the
Snow
Hidden Children
Silent Witness

Homeless

See also Great
Depression; Hard
Knock Life; Yuppie
Nightmares
Caught
Oliver Twist
Streetwise

Homosexuality

See Bisexuality;
Gays; Lesbians

Horror

See also Bloody
Mayhem;
Cannibalism;
Classic Horror;
Horror Comedy;
Killer Bugs; Mad
Scientists;
Vampires; Zombies
The Addiction
The Ambulance
Cemetery Man
Creepers
Dead of Night
Grim Prairie Tales
The Hands of Orlac
The Innocents
The Island of Dr.
Moreau
Mommy
Popcorn
Teenage Gang Debs
Wes Craven's New
Nightmare

Horror Comedy

See also Horror
Frankenhooker
The Refrigerator
Spider Baby
The Witches

Identity

See also Role
Reversal
Orlando
Ruby in Paradise
Secrets and Lies
The Woman in
Question

Immigration
Combination Platter
Hester Street
A Kiss to this Land

Incest

See also Family
Ties
Angels and Insects
The Grifters
Spanking the Monkey

India

See also Foreign:
Indian
Black Narcissus
The Deceivers
Heat and Dust
Kama Sutra: A Tale
of Love

Ireland

See also Great
Britain; Foreign:
Irish
The Crying Game
The Dead
Frankie Starlight
Hear My Song
In the Name of the
Father
The Lonely Passion
of Judith Hearne
Michael Collins
My Left Foot
The Secret of Roan
Inish

Island Fare
Echoes of Paradise
The Island of Dr.
Moreau
The Postman
Swept Away…

Italy

See also Foreign:
Italian
Cemetery Man
Cinema Paradiso
The Conformist
Enchanted April
Ossessione
The Postman
A Special Day
Where Angels Fear to
Tread

Jail

See Men in Prison;
Women in Prison

Japanimation
Barefoot Gen
Twilight of the
Cockroaches

Journalism

See Front Page

Judaism

See also The
Holocaust
American
Matchmaker
Coffee with Lemon
East and West
Hester Street
Hidden Children
A Kiss to this Land

Martha and I

**Justice
Prevails…?**

See also Order in
the Court
In the Name of the
Father
Let Him Have It
The Story of Qui Ju

Kidnapped!

See also Missing
Persons
The City of Lost
Children
The Crying Game
Fargo
Kansas City
Lullaby
Manny & Lo
Tie Me Up! Tie Me
Down!
Try and Get Me

Killer Bugs
The Applegates
Creepers
The Lair of the White
Worm

Killer Dreams
Dead of Night
Wes Craven's New
Nightmare

Kings

See Royalty

Korean War
The Manchurian
Candidate

Labor & Unions
Last Exit to Brooklyn
Mac
Matewan

**Late Bloomin'
Love**

See also Growing
Older
The African Queen
Brief Encounter
Gal Young 'Un
The Lonely Passion
of Judith Hearne
Shirley Valentine

Law & Lawyers

See also Order in
the Court
Brother's Keeper
Criminal Law
Death and the
Maiden
In the Name of the
Father

The Island of Dr.
Moreau
Swoon
Trois Couleurs:
Rouge
Victim

Lesbians

See also
Bisexuality; Gays;
Gender Bending
Bound
Butterfly Kiss
Chasing Amy
Law of Desire
Nadja
Set It Off

Loneliness

See Only the
Lonely

**Lovers on the
Lam**
Gun Crazy
Guncrazy
Kalifornia
Love and a .45
Wild at Heart

Mad Scientists
The City of Lost
Children
Frankenhooker
Frankenstein
Unbound
The Island of Dr.
Moreau

**Made for
Television**

See TV Movies

Mafia

See Organized
Crime

Marriage

See also Divorce;
War Between the
Sexes; Wedding
Bells; Wedding Hell
American
Matchmaker
Breaking the Waves
Caught
Crash
Dangerous Liaisons
The Dead
Eat a Bowl of Tea
Eating Raoul
Emmanuelle
The Entertainer
Gaslight
The Good Wife
Grace of My Heart
Grand Isle
A Handful of Dust

Prison

See Men in Prison; Women in Prison

Prostitutes

See Oldest Profession

Psychiatry

See Shrinks

Psycho-Thriller

See also Mystery & Suspense

Bound
The Comfort of Strangers
Dead Calm
Freeway
House of Games
The Incident
Julia and Julia
Killer Inside Me
The Last Seduction
M
The Mark
Peeping Tom
Repulsion
Shallow Grave
The Shining
Suture
The Tie that Binds
To Have and to Hold
The Vanishing
Who Killed Teddy Bear?

Psychotics/ Sociopaths

Homage
Kalifornia
Killer Inside Me
Mother's Boys
Repulsion
Reservoir Dogs
The Shining
To Die For

Queens

See Royalty

Rape

See also Sexual Abuse

Bad Lieutenant
Bastard out of Carolina
Dead Man Walking
Death and the Maiden
Girls Town
Guncrazy
Kika

Rebel With a Cause

See also Rebel Without a Cause

The Applegates
Basquiat
In the Name of the Father
Luther
The Scarlet Pimpernel

Rebel Without a Cause

See also Rebel With a Cause

A Boy and His Dog
Breathless
Easy Rider
Guncrazy
If...
sex, lies and videotape

Red Scare

See also Russia

Golden Gate
The Interrogation
Mother Kusters Goes to Heaven
Tito and Me

Religion

See also Judaism; Nuns & Priests

The Addiction
...And God Spoke
Angela
Before the Rain
Breaking the Waves
Citizen Ruth
Dead Man Walking
The Favor, the Watch, and the Very Big Fish
Hand in Hand
Household Saints
Luther
The Miracle
Pass the Ammo
Priest
A Virgin Named Mary

Revenge

Aventurera
The Ballad of the Sad Cafe
Chan Is Missing
Creepers
The Crossing Guard
Death and the Maiden
The Funeral
The Hidden Room
A House in the Hills
I Married a Witch
I Met a Murderer
The Lady in White

Reservoir Dogs
Trois Couleurs: Blanc

Road Trip

See also Chases; Motor Vehicle Dept.

The Adventures of Priscilla, Queen of the Desert
Butterfly Kiss
Delusion
Detour
The Doom Generation
Easy Rider
Flirting with Disaster
It Takes Two
Kalifornia
Lamerica
Love and a .45
My Own Private Idaho
Night on Earth
Powwow Highway
Reckless
Road Games
Two for the Road
Wild at Heart

Roaring '20s

Bullets Over Broadway
Eight Men Out
Mrs. Parker and the Vicious Circle

Rock Stars on Film

Absolute Beginners
Backbeat
Boy Next Door
The Crossing Guard
A Hard Day's Night
Lisztomania
That'll Be the Day
Tommy

Role Reversal

See also Gender Bending; Identity

A Dream of Passion
La Femme Nikita
The Lady Vanishes
The Scarlet Pimpernel
Turnabout

Romance

See Late Bloomin' Love; Lovers on the Lam; Romantic Adventures; Romantic Comedy; Romantic Drama; Romantic Triangles

Romantic Adventures

The African Queen
Destiny Turns on the Radio
Gun Crazy
Guncrazy

Romantic Comedy

American Matchmaker
Blue Country
Charley's Aunt
Chasing Amy
East and West
The Englishman Who Went Up a Hill But Came Down a Mountain
Four Weddings and a Funeral
Go Fish
Hear My Song
I Married a Witch
Impromptu
It Takes Two
Just Like a Woman
The Linguini Incident
Love Jones
The Man Who Loved Women
A Modern Affair
Morgan!
Much Ado about Nothing
Nina Takes a Lover
Nobody's Fool
On Approval
Queens Logic
Roads to the South
She's Gotta Have It
She's the One
Song of the Siren
Strictly Ballroom
The Thing Called Love
To Cross the Rubicon
Too Beautiful for You
Tune in Tomorrow
The Wedding Banquet

Romantic Drama

The African Queen
Angels and Insects
The Ballad of the Sad Cafe
Beauty and the Beast
Before the Rain
Beware of Pity
Breathless
Brief Encounter
Caddie
Camille Claudel
Carrington
Enchanted April
The English Patient

The Fable of the
  Beautiful Pigeon
  Fancier
Gal Young 'Un
Golden Gate
Grand Isle
Heat and Dust
It's My Party
Jane Eyre
L'Amour en Herbe
Letters from the Park
Martha and I
Persuasion
The Piano
Room at the Top
A Room with a View
Rouge
A Special Day
Strapless
A Summer Story
Through the Olive
  Trees
Trouble in Mind
The Unbearable
  Lightness of Being
White Nights
Wild at Heart
Wings of Desire

Romantic Triangles
Carrington
Caught
The Doom
  Generation
The English Patient
Homage
A Room with a View
She's Gotta Have It
The Unbearable
  Lightness of Being
The Underneath
The Wedding
  Banquet

Royalty
See also Historical
  Drama
Kama Sutra: A Tale
  of Love
Kind Hearts and
  Coronets
Lancelot of the Lake
The Last Days of the
  Last Tsar
The Madness of King
  George
Mystery of the Last
  Tsar
Nine Days a Queen
Orlando
The Private Life of
  Henry VIII
Queen Kelly
Saraband for Dead
  Lovers
The Windsors: A
  Royal Family

Russia
See also Foreign:
  Russian; Red
  Scare
Burnt by the Sun
The Children of
  Theatre Street
The Last Days of the
  Last Tsar
Mystery of the Last
  Tsar
Orphans

Sail Away
See also
  Shipwrecked
Abandon Ship
The African Queen
Beat the Devil
Das Boot
Dead Calm
A Night to Remember
Rich and Strange

Sanity Check
See also Doctors
  & Nurses; Shrinks
An Angel at My Table
Camille Claudel
Dead of Night
Easy Rider
Fright
Heat and Sunlight
Heavenly Creatures
How to Get Ahead in
  Advertising
The Last Seduction
Morgan!
Mother Kusters Goes
  to Heaven
Peeping Tom
Poison
The Shining
Tracks
Twister

Satire & Parody
See also Black
  Comedy; Comedy
A-Ge-Man: Tales of a
  Golden Geisha
Abel
...And God Spoke
The Applegates
Citizen Ruth
Dark Habits
Forgotten Silver
Genevieve
High Season
Love and a .45
The Luckiest Man in
  the World
Open Season
Pass the Ammo
Phantom of Liberty
The Player
The Profiteer

Sammy & Rosie Get
  Laid
Scenes from the
  Class Struggle in
  Beverly Hills
Search and Destroy
Serial Mom
Seven Beauties
A Shock to the
  System
Swimming with
  Sharks
A Virgin Named Mary
White Mischief

Scams, Stings & Cons
See also Heists
The Amazing Mr. X
Chameleon Street
Destiny Turns on the
  Radio
Fargo
The Grifters
House of Games
In the Soup
Kind Hearts and
  Coronets
Lamerica
Ossessione
Pass the Ammo

School Daze
See also Hell High
  School
The Belles of St.
  Trinian's
Black Narcissus
The Chocolate War
Heavenly Creatures
A Little Princess
Oleanna
The Prime of Miss
  Jean Brodie
Stand and Deliver
Zebrahead

Sci Fi
See also Fantasy
Aelita: Queen of
  Mars
A Boy and His Dog
Children of the
  Damned
Fire Maidens from
  Outer Space
France, Incorporated
Hu-Man
The Land That Time
  Forgot
Metropolis
1984
Not of this Earth
Plan 9 from Outer
  Space
The Trouble with Dick
Vegas in Space

Village of the
  Damned

Scotland
See also Great
  Britain
Breaking the Waves
Madeleine
The Prime of Miss
  Jean Brodie
Trainspotting

Screwball Comedy
See also Comedy;
  Romantic Comedy
Bedazzled
The Favor, the Watch,
  and the Very Big
  Fish
A Hard Day's Night
The Smallest Show
  on Earth
Turnabout

Sea Disasters
See Titanic

Serial Killers
See also Crime &
  Criminals; Crime
  Sprees
American Strays
Butterfly Kiss
Freeway
Kalifornia
Lisa
Love and Human
  Remains
M
The Rosary Murders
Serial Mom

Sex & Sexuality
Acting on Impulse
Angels and Insects
Art for Teachers of
  Children
Bad Lieutenant
Blue Velvet
A Boy and His Dog
Breaking the Waves
Business as Usual
Chain of Desire
Chasing Amy
The Comfort of
  Strangers
Crash
Crush
Dites-Lui Que Je
  L'Aime
Don's Party
Eating Raoul
Echoes of Paradise
Emmanuelle
Exotica
Female Trouble

INDEPENDENT
FILM GUIDE

Frankenstein
  Unbound
Heavy Petting
Kama Sutra: A Tale
  of Love
Kids
Kika
Like Water for
  Chocolate
Lolita
Love and Human
  Remains
Love Unto Waste
The Man Who Loved
  Women
Paris, France
Peeping Tom
Rambling Rose
Repulsion
Rita, Sue & Bob Too
Salmonberries
Salut Victor!
Sammy & Rosie Get
  Laid
Scenes from the
  Class Struggle in
  Beverly Hills
sex, lies and
  videotape
She's Gotta Have It
Sirens
Tie Me Up! Tie Me
  Down!
Twenty-One
The Unbearable
  Lightness of Being
Under Suspicion
Wild at Heart
Wish You Were Here
Women on the Verge
  of a Nervous
  Breakdown

Sexual Abuse

See also Rape

The Boys of St.
  Vincent
Priest

Sexual
Harrassment

Brilliant Lies
Oleanna

Ships

See Sail Away;
  Shipwrecked

Shipwrecked

Cabeza de Vaca
Eye of the Needle
Rich and Strange
Swept Away...

Showbiz
Comedies

Bullets Over
  Broadway
Funny Bones
Hear My Song

Tune in Tomorrow

Showbiz Dramas

Actors and Sin
Anna
From the Journals of
  Jean Seberg
Grace of My Heart
The Player
Second Coming of
  Suzanne
Sidewalks of London
Wired

Shrinks

See also Doctors
  & Nurses

Face to Face
House of Cards
House of Games

Shutterbugs

See also Front
  Page

Art for Teachers of
  Children
Backbeat
The Favor, the Watch,
  and the Very Big
  Fish
Girlfriends
Heat and Sunlight
High Season
Kalifornia
Love Jones
Peeping Tom
The Unbearable
  Lightness of Being

Silent Films

Aelita: Queen of
  Mars
Charley's Aunt
East and West
The Hands of Orlac
His Picture in the
  Papers
Joyless Street
The Man with the
  Movie Camera
Metropolis
Nosferatu
Oliver Twist
Pandora's Box
Queen Kelly
Vampyr
Way Down East

South America

See also Central
  America

Death and the
  Maiden
The House of the
  Spirits
It's All True
The Story of Fausta

Spies &
Espionage

See also Foreign
  Intrigue; Terrorism

The English Patient
Eye of the Needle
The House on Carroll
  Street
Night Train to Munich
The Odessa File
Sabotage
The Third Man
The 39 Steps
The Whistle Blower

Sports

See Baseball;
  Basketball; Sports
  Dramas

Sports Dramas

Champion
Eight Men Out
Pastime

Strained
Suburbia

See also Yuppie
  Nightmares

Blue Velvet
Serial Mom
Short Cuts

Struggling
Musicians

See also Music

Backbeat
Eddie and the
  Cruisers
Eddie and the
  Cruisers 2: Eddie
  Lives!
Stardust

Suicide

See also Death &
  the Afterlife

American Strays
Bedazzled
Crumb
Golden Gate
Heathers
It's My Party
Leaving Las Vegas
Mother Kusters Goes
  to Heaven
Nobody's Fool
Peeping Tom
Permanent Record
Short Cuts

Survival

Abandon Ship
Das Boot
Dead Calm
Delusion
The Interrogation

The Land That Time
  Forgot
Last Exit to Brooklyn
Little Dorrit, Film 1:
  Nobody's Fault
Little Dorrit, Film 2:
  Little Dorrit's Story

Suspense

See Mystery &
  Suspense

Teachers

See Dedicated
  Teachers

Tearjerkers

A Little Princess
Struggle
Thursday's Child
Way Down East

Teen Angst

See also Coming
  of Age; Hell High
  School

Art for Teachers of
  Children
The Doom
  Generation
Freeway
Fun
Gas Food Lodging
Girls Town
Hackers
Heathers
Heavenly Creatures
Hoop Dreams
If...
Just Another Girl on
  the I.R.T.
Kids
L'Amour en Herbe
Lisa
Manny & Lo
Metropolitan
My Own Private Idaho
Mystic Pizza
New Jersey Drive
Paradise Lost: The
  Child Murders at
  Robin Hood Hills
The Prime of Miss
  Jean Brodie
Rambling Rose
River's Edge
Shag: The Movie
Shine
Stand and Deliver
Sticky Fingers
Straight Out of
  Brooklyn
Terminal Bliss
To Die For
Trust
Welcome to the
  Dollhouse
Wish You Were Here

Zebrahead

Television

See TV Movies

Terrorism

See also Crime & Criminals; Foreign Intrigue; Spies & Espionage

The Applegates
Barcelona
The Crying Game
In the Name of the Father
Women on the Verge of a Nervous Breakdown

This Is Your Life

See also Musician Biopics

An Angel at My Table
Backbeat
Basquiat
Boy Next Door
Cabeza de Vaca
Caddie
Camille Claudel
Carmen Miranda: Bananas Is My Business
Carrington
Center Stage
Chaplin
Crumb
Dance with a Stranger
Dreamchild
From the Journals of Jean Seberg
The Hours and Times
I Shot Andy Warhol
I Wasn't Made for These Times
Let's Get Lost
Lisztomania
Michael Collins
Mrs. Parker and the Vicious Circle
Moulin Rouge
My Left Foot
Nico Icon
Padre Padrone
Saraband for Dead Lovers
Shine
32 Short Films about Glenn Gould
Thomas Jefferson: A View from the Mountain
Waiting for the Moon
Wired
The Wonderful, Horrible Life of Leni Riefenstahl

Thrillers

See Mystery & Suspense; Psycho-Thriller

Titanic

A Night to Remember
S.O.S. Titanic

Torrid Love Scenes

See also Sex & Sexuality

The Big Easy
Blue Velvet
Law of Desire
Men in Love
Swept Away…
The Unbearable Lightness of Being
Wild at Heart

Tragedy

See also Drama; Tearjerkers

Deep End
Forbidden Choices
From the Journals of Jean Seberg
House of Cards
Law of Desire
Martha and I
Silent Tongue
Trois Couleurs: Bleu
Where Angels Fear to Tread

Trains

Color of a Brisk and Leaping Day
The Lady Vanishes
Murder on the Orient Express
Night Train to Munich
Tracks
Warm Nights on a Slow-Moving Train

Transvestites & Transsexuals

See Gender Bending

Trapped with a Killer!

See also Psychotics/Sociopaths

Dead Calm
Eye of the Needle
Kalifornia
The Shining
The Tie that Binds

True Crime

See also Crime & Criminals; This Is Your Life; True Stories

Paradise Lost: The Child Murders at Robin Hood Hills
Sister My Sister
Swoon

True Stories

See also This Is Your Life; True Crime

And the Band Played On
Art for Teachers of Children
Backbeat
The Ballad of Little Jo
The Boys of St. Vincent
Cabeza de Vaca
Chameleon Street
Dance with a Stranger
Drugstore Cowboy
Eight Men Out
Every Man for Himself & God Against All
Heartland
Heavenly Creatures
I Shot Andy Warhol
In the Name of the Father
It's My Party
The Krays
Ladybird, Ladybird
Let Him Have It
Madeleine
Matewan
Michael Collins
Mountains of the Moon
My Left Foot
The Nasty Girl
A Night to Remember
River's Edge
Scandal
Shine
Stand and Deliver
Street Smart
The Thin Blue Line
Thousand Pieces of Gold
True Confessions
White Mischief
The Whole Wide World
A World Apart

TV Movies

Acting on Impulse
And the Band Played On
An Angel at My Table

Anne of Green Gables
Bastard out of Carolina
The Boys of St. Vincent
Eat a Bowl of Tea
Face to Face
The Good Soldier
Grand Isle
Letters from the Park
Longtime Companion
Persuasion
Priest
Smooth Talk
S.O.S. Titanic
Under Suspicion
Waiting for the Moon

Twins

See also Family Ties

Equinox
Jack's Back
The Krays
Suture

Urban Drama

American Heart
Bad Lieutenant
Fly by Night
Fresh
Just Another Girl on the I.R.T.
Menace II Society
Naked
New Jersey Drive
Straight Out of Brooklyn
Zebrahead

Vampires

The Addiction
Nadja
Nosferatu
Not of this Earth
Vampyr

Vietnam War

See also Postwar

Platoon

War Between the Sexes

See also Divorce; Marriage

The African Queen
The Ballad of the Sad Cafe
Beware of Pity
Cannibal Women in the Avocado Jungle of Death
Dangerous Liaisons
Much Ado about Nothing
Song of the Siren
The Story of Fausta
True Love

The following list explains the three-letter distributor codes found at the end of each review. If the movie is available on video, you can look up the code here, and flip the page to the "Distributor Guide" to get the address, phone, fax, toll-free, and email addresses, when available, for the distributor. Puh-lease note that studio distributors do not sell to the general public; they act as wholesalers, selling only to retail outlets. Many video stores provide an ordering service; see p. xix for a list of establishments they may be able to track down your movie for you.

ACA—Academy Entertainment
AHV—Active Home Video
AOV—Admit One Video
APD—Applause Productions, Inc.
APX—A-PIX Entertainment Inc.
AUD—Audio-Forum
AVI—Arrow Video, Inc.
BAR—Barr Films
BMG—BMG
BTV—Baker & Taylor Video
CAB—Cable Films & Video
CAF—Cabin Fever Entertainment
CAL—California Newsreel
CAN—Cannon Video
CCB—Critics' Choice Video, Inc.
CCN—Cinevista
CCP—Cambridge Educational
CDV—Television International
CIG—The Cinema Guild

CNG—Congress Entertainment, Inc.
CNM—Cinemacabre Video
COL—Columbia Tristar Home Video
CRC—Criterion Collection
CVC—Connoisseur Video Collection
CYR—Cyrillic Films
DCL—Direct Cinema Ltd.
DIS—Walt Disney Home Video
DOV—Dove Kids
DVT—Discount Video Tapes, Inc./Hollywood's Attic
EPC—Epic Records
ERG—Ergo Media Inc.
EVE—Evergreen Entertainment
FAF—Fast Forward
FCT—Facets Multimedia, Inc.
FHE—Family Home Entertainment

FHS—Films for the Humanities & Sciences
FOX—CBS/Fox Video
FRA—Frameline
FRF—First Run Features
FRG—Fright Video
FRH—Fries Home Video
FST—Festival Films
FUS—Fusion Video
FXL—Fox/Lorber Home Video
FXV—FoxVideo
GEM—Video Gems
GKK—Goodtimes Entertainment
GLV—German Language Video Center
GPV—Grapevine Video
GRE—Greycat Films
GVV—Glenn Video Vistas, Ltd.
HBO—HBO Home Video
HEG—Horizon Entertainment
HHE—Hollywood Home Entertainment

HHT—Hollywood Home Theatre

HMD—Hemdale Home Video

HMK—Hallmark Home Entertainment

HMV—Home Vision Cinema

ICA—First Run/Icarus Films

IGP—Ignatius Press

IHF—International Historic Films, Inc. (IHF)

IME—Image Entertainment

ING—Ingram Entertainment Inc.

INT—Interama, Inc.

JEF—JEF Films, Inc.

KAR—Karol Video

KIV—Kino on Video

KUI—Knowledge Unlimited, Inc.

KUL—Kultur Video

LCA—Modern Curriculum Press - MCP

LEO—Leo Films

LIV—Live Entertainment

LSV—LSVideo, Inc.

LUM—Lumivision Corporation

MAX—Miramax Pictures Home Video

MCG—Management Company Entertainment Group (MCEG), Inc.

MED—Media Home Entertainment

MFV—Mystic Fire Video

MGM—MGM Home Entertainment

MIL—Milestone Film & Video

MLB—Mike LeBell's Video

MNC—Monarch Home Video

MON—Monterey Home Video

MOV—Movies Unlimited

MPI—MPI Home Video

MRV—Moore Video

MTH—MTI Home Video

MVD—Music Video Distributors

NCJ—National Center for Jewish Film

NFB—National Film Board of Canada

NHO—New Horizons Home Video

NLC—New Line Home Video

NOS—Nostalgia Family Video

NWV—New World Entertainment

NYF—New Yorker Video

NYR—*Not Yet Released*

OM—*On Moratorium*

ORI—Orion Home Video

PAR—Paramount Home Video

PBC—Princeton Book Co. Publishers

PBS—PBS Home Video

PGV—Polygram Video (PV)

PME—Public Media Video

PMS—Professional Media Service Corp.

PPI—Planet Pictures, Inc.

PSM—Prism Entertainment

PYR—Pyramid Film & Video

QHV—Questar Video, Inc.

RDG—Reader's Digest Home Video

REP—Republic Pictures Home Video

RXM—Rex Miller

SGE—Amsell Entertainment

SHV—Strand Home Video

SIG—Signals

SMW—Something Weird Video

SNC—Sinister Cinema

STP—Streamline Pictures

STS—Stagestep

TAI—Tai Seng Video Marketing

TCF—20th Century Fox Film Corporation

THV—Trimark Home Video

TIM—Timeless Video Inc.

TLF—Time-Life Video and Television

TOU—Buena Vista Home Video

TPV—Tapeworm Video Distributors

TRI—Triboro Entertainment Group

TTC—Turner Home Entertainment Company

TTV—Troma Team Video

TVC—The Video Catalog

USH—Universal Studios Home Video

VCI—VCI Home Video

VCN—Video Connection

VDM—Video Dimensions

VEC—Valencia Entertainment Corp.

VES—Vestron Video

VHE—VCII Home Entertainment, Inc.

VTR—Anchor Bay

VYY—Video Yesteryear

WAC—World Artists Home Video

WAR—Warner Home Video, Inc.

WBF—Water Bearer Films

WEA—Warner/Elektra/Atlantic (WEA) Corporation

WFV—Western Media Systems

WME—Warren Miller Entertainment

WSH—Wishing Well Distributing

XVC—Xenon

ZGI—Zeitgeist Films Ltd.

The Distributor Guide provides contact information, including address, phone, toll-free, and fax numbers, and even email addresses, for the distributors indicated within the reviews. Each movie in the main section has at least one code located at the end of the entry. The key to these codes, preceding this guide, will lead you to the appropriate distributor (if the movie is available on video). Those titles with the code **OM** are on moratorium, meaning that they were distributed at one time, but aren't currently (since they were once available, these movies may show up at your local video store). If the distributor for a movie is not known, the code **NO** will follow the review. Films that have not yet made it to video (including older titles) have the designation **NYR** (not yet released). Three warnings: 1) Not all movies are available on video; 2) From year to year, a small minority of distributors move without telling anyone, or just plain go out of business; and 3) Studio distributors do not sell to the general public—they generally act as wholesalers, selling only to retail outlets. Many video stores provide an ordering service; check out the "Video Sources" section on p. xix for a few suggested outlets to help you track down a title.

A-PIX ENTERTAINMENT INC. (APX)
500 5th Ave., 46th Fl.
New York, NY 10110
212-764-7171

ACADEMY ENTERTAINMENT (ACA)
9250 Wilshire Blvd., Ste. 400
Beverly Hills, CA 90212
fax: 310-275-2195

ACTIVE HOME VIDEO (AHV)
12121 Wilshire Blvd., No. 401
Los Angeles, CA 90025
310-447-6131
800-824-6109
fax: 310-207-0411

ADMIT ONE VIDEO (AOV)
PO Box 66, Sta. O
Toronto, ON, Canada M4A 2M8
416-463-5714
fax: 416-463-5714

AMSELL ENTERTAINMENT (SGE)
12001 Ventura Pl., 4th Fl., Ste. 404
Studio City, CA 91604
818-766-8500
fax: 818-766-7873

ANCHOR BAY (VTR)
500 Kirts Blvd.
Troy, MI 48084
810-362-9660
800-786-8777
fax: 810-362-4454

APPLAUSE PRODUCTIONS, INC. (APD)
85 Longview Rd.
Port Washington, NY 11050
516-883-2825
800-278-7326
fax: 516-883-7460
email: apptora@aol.com

ARROW VIDEO, INC. (AVI)
135 W. 50th St., Ste. 1925
New York, NY 10020
212-258-2200
fax: 212-245-1252

AUDIO-FORUM (AUD)
96 Broad St.
Guilford, CT 06437
203-453-9794
800-243-1234
fax: 203-453-9774
email:
  74537.550@compuserve.com

BAKER & TAYLOR VIDEO (BTV)
501 S. Gladiolus
Momence, IL 60954
815-472-2444
800-775-2300
fax: 800-775-3500

BARR FILMS (BAR)
12801 Schabarum
Irwindale, CA 91706
818-338-7878
800-234-7878
fax: 818-814-2672

BMG (BMG)
6363 Sunset Blvd., 6th Fl.
Hollywood, CA 90028-7318

BUENA VISTA HOME VIDEO (TOU)
350 S. Buena Vista St.
Burbank, CA 91521-7145
818-562-3568

CABIN FEVER ENTERTAINMENT (CAF)
100 W. Putnam Ave.
Greenwich, CT 06830
203-661-1100
fax: 203-863-5258

CABLE FILMS & VIDEO (CAB)
PO Box 7171, Country Club Sta.
Kansas City, MO 64113
816-362-2804
800-514-2804
fax: 816-341-7365

CALIFORNIA NEWSREEL (CAL)
149 9th St., Ste. 420
San Francisco, CA 94103
415-621-6196
fax: 415-621-6522
email: newsreel@ix.netcom.com

CAMBRIDGE EDUCATIONAL (CCP)
PO Box 2153
Charleston, WV 25328-2153
304-744-9323
800-468-4227
fax: 304-744-9351

CANNON VIDEO (CAN)
PO Box 17198
Beverly Hills, CA 90290
310-772-7765

CBS/FOX VIDEO *(FOX)*
PO Box 900
Beverly Hills, CA 90213
562-373-4800
800-800-2369
fax: 562-373-4803

THE CINEMA GUILD
   (CIG)
1697 Broadway, Ste. 506
New York, NY 10019
212-246-5522
800-723-5522
fax: 212-246-5525
email: thecinema@aol.com

CINEMACABRE VIDEO
   (CNM)
PO Box 10005-D
Baltimore, MD 21285-0005

CINEVISTA *(CCN)*
560 W. 43rd, No. 8J
New York, NY 10036
212-947-4373
800-341-CINE
fax: 212-947-0644

COLUMBIA TRISTAR
   HOME VIDEO *(COL)*
Sony Pictures Plz.
10202 W. Washington Blvd.
Culver City, CA 90232
310-280-5418
fax: 310-280-2485

CONGRESS
   ENTERTAINMENT,
   INC. *(CNG)*
PO Box 845
Tannersville, PA 18372-0845
717-420-8551
800-847-8273
fax: 717-420-8554
email: karolyn28@acx.com

CONNOISSEUR VIDEO
   COLLECTION *(CVC)*
1575 Westwood Blvd., Ste. 305
Los Angeles, CA 90024
310-231-1350
800-529-2300
fax: 310-231-1359
email: Eurocine@aol.com
email:
   76460.1327@compuserve.com

CRITERION
   COLLECTION *(CRC)*
c/o The Voyager Company
1 Bridge St.
Irvington, NY 10533-1543

CRITICS' CHOICE
   VIDEO, INC. *(CCB)*
900 N. Rohlwing Rd.
Itasca, IL 60143
708-775-3300
800-367-7765
fax: 708-775-3340

CYRILLIC FILMS *(CYR)*
Box 441
San Francisco, CA 94118

DIRECT CINEMA LTD.
   (DCL)
PO Box 10003
Santa Monica, CA 90410
310-636-8200
800-525-0000
fax: 310-636-8228
email: directcinema@attmail.com

DISCOUNT VIDEO
   TAPES,
   INC./HOLLYWOOD'S
   ATTIC *(DVT)*
PO Box 7122
Burbank, CA 91510
818-843-3366
fax: 818-843-3821

DOVE KIDS *(DOV)*
301 N. Canon Dr., Ste. 203
Beverly Hills, CA 90210

EPIC RECORDS *(EPC)*
550 Madison Ave.
New York, NY 10022-3297
212-833-7442
fax: 212-833-5719

ERGO MEDIA INC.
   (ERG)
668 American Legion Dr.
PO Box 2037
Teaneck, NJ 07666
201-692-0404
800-695-3746
fax: 201-692-0663
email: ergo@intec.com

EVERGREEN
   ENTERTAINMENT
   (EVE)
6100 Wilshire Blvd., Ste. 1400
Los Angeles, CA 90048

FACETS MULTIMEDIA,
   INC. *(FCT)*
1517 W. Fullerton Ave.
Chicago, IL 60614
312-281-9075
800-331-6197
fax: 312-929-5437

FAMILY HOME
   ENTERTAINMENT
   (FHE)
c/o Live Home Video
15400 Sherman Way
PO Box 10124
Van Nuys, CA 91410-0124
818-908-0303
800-677-0789
fax: 818-778-3259

FAST FORWARD *(FAF)*
3420 Ocean Park Blvd., Ste. 3075
Santa Monica, CA 90405
310-396-4434
fax: 310-396-2292

FESTIVAL FILMS *(FST)*
6115 Chestnut Terr.
Excelsior, MN 55331-8107
612-470-2172
800-798-6083
fax: 612-470-2172
email: fesfilms@aol.com

FILMS FOR THE
   HUMANITIES &
   SCIENCES *(FHS)*
PO Box 2053
Princeton, NJ 08543-2053
609-275-1400
800-257-5126
fax: 609-275-3767

FIRST RUN FEATURES
   (FRF)
153 Waverly Pl.
New York, NY 10014
212-243-0600
fax: 212-989-7649

FIRST RUN/ICARUS
   FILMS *(ICA)*
153 Waverly Pl.
New York, NY 10014
212-727-1711
800-876-1710
fax: 212-989-7649
email: frif@echonyc.com

FOX/LORBER HOME
   VIDEO *(FXL)*
419 Park Ave., S., 20th Fl.
New York, NY 10016
212-532-3392
fax: 212-685-2625

FOXVIDEO *(FXV)*
2121 Avenue of the Stars, 25th Fl.
Los Angeles, CA 90067
310-369-3900
800-800-2FOX
fax: 310-369-5811

FRAMELINE *(FRA)*
346 9th St.
San Francisco, CA 94103
415-703-8650
fax: 415-861-1404
email: frameline@aol.com

FRIES HOME VIDEO
   (FRH)
6922 Hollywood Blvd., 12th Fl.
Hollywood, CA 90028
213-466-2266
fax: 213-466-2126

FRIGHT VIDEO *(FRG)*
PO Box 277
North Billerica, MA 01862

FUSION VIDEO *(FUS)*
100 Fusion Way
Country Club Hills, IL 60478
708-799-2073
fax: 708-799-8375

GERMAN LANGUAGE
   VIDEO CENTER *(GLV)*
7625 Pendleton Pike
Indianapolis, IN 46226-5298
317-547-1257
800-252-1957
fax: 317-547-1263

GLENN VIDEO VISTAS,
   LTD. *(GVV)*
6924 Canby Ave., Ste. 103
Reseda, CA 91335
818-881-8110
fax: 818-981-5506
email: mglass@worldnet.att.net

GOODTIMES ENTERTAINMENT (GKK)
16 E. 40th St., 8th Fl.
New York, NY 10016-0113
212-951-3000
fax: 212-213-9319

GRAPEVINE VIDEO (GPV)
PO Box 46161
Phoenix, AZ 85063
602-973-3661
fax: 602-973-0060

GREYCAT FILMS (GRE)
3829 Delaware Ln.
Las Vegas, NV 89109
702-737-0670
fax: 702-734-3628
email: greycat@aol.com

HALLMARK HOME ENTERTAINMENT (HMK)
6100 Wilshire Blvd., Ste. 1400
Los Angeles, CA 90048
213-634-3000
fax: 213-549-3760

HBO HOME VIDEO (HBO)
1100 6th Ave.
New York, NY 10036
212-512-7400
fax: 212-512-7498

HEMDALE HOME VIDEO (HMD)
7966 Beverly Blvd.
Los Angeles, CA 90048
213-966-3700
fax: 213-653-5452

HOLLYWOOD HOME ENTERTAINMENT (HHE)
6165 Crooked Creek Rd., Ste. B
Norcross, GA 30092-3105

HOLLYWOOD HOME THEATRE (HHT)
9830 Charlieville Blvd.
Beverly Hills, CA 90212
310-203-9868

HOME VISION CINEMA (HMV)
5547 N. Ravenswood Ave.
Chicago, IL 60640-1199
312-878-2600
800-826-3456

HORIZON ENTERTAINMENT (HEG)
45030 Trevor Ave.
Lancaster, CA 93534
805-940-1040
800-323-2061
fax: 805-940-8511

IGNATIUS PRESS (IGP)
33 Oakland Ave.
Harrison, NY 10528-9974
914-835-4216
fax: 914-835-8406

IMAGE ENTERTAINMENT (IME)
9333 Oso Ave.
Chatsworth, CA 91311
818-407-9100
800-473-3475
fax: 818-407-9111

INGRAM ENTERTAINMENT INC. (ING)
2 Ingram Blvd.
La Vergne, TN 37086-7006
615-287-4000
800-759-5000
fax: 615-287-4992

INTERAMA, INC. (INT)
301 W. 53rd St., Ste. 19E
New York, NY 10019
212-977-4830
fax: 212-581-6582

INTERNATIONAL HISTORIC FILMS, INC. (IHF) (IHF)
PO Box 29035
Chicago, IL 60629
773-927-2900
fax: 773-927-9211

JEF FILMS, INC. (JEF)
Film House
143 Hickory Hill Circle
Osterville, MA 02655-1322
508-428-7198
fax: 508-428-7198
email: finchleyrd@aol.com

KAROL VIDEO (KAR)
PO Box 7600
350 N. Pennsylvania Ave.
Wilkes Barre, PA 18773
717-822-8899
fax: 717-822-8226
email: karolm@epix.net

KINO ON VIDEO (KIV)
333 W. 39th St., Ste. 503
New York, NY 10018
212-629-6880
800-562-3330
fax: 212-714-0871
email: kinoint@infunnse.com

KNOWLEDGE UNLIMITED, INC. (KUI)
Box 52
Madison, WI 53701-0052
608-836-6660
800-356-2303
fax: 608-831-1570

KULTUR VIDEO (KUL)
195 Hwy. No. 36
West Long Branch, NJ 07764
908-229-2343
800-458-5887
fax: 908-229-0066
email: kultur@monmouth.com

LEO FILMS (LEO)
1509 N. Hoover, Ste. 1/2
Los Angeles, CA 90027
213-666-7140
fax: 213-666-7414
email: LUSTGAR@IDT.NET

LIVE ENTERTAINMENT (LIV)
15400 Sherman Way
PO Box 10124
Van Nuys, CA 91410-0124
818-988-5060

LSVIDEO, INC. (LSV)
PO Box 415
Carmel, IN 46032

LUMIVISION CORP. (LUM)
877 Federal Blvd.
Denver, CO 80204-3212
303-446-0400
800-776-LUMI
fax: 303-446-0101

MANAGEMENT CO. ENTERTAINMENT GROUP (MCEG), INC. (MCG)
1888 Century Park, E., Ste. 1777
Los Angeles, CA 90067-1721
310-282-0871
fax: 310-282-8303

MEDIA HOME ENTERTAINMENT (MED)
510 W. 6th St., Ste. 1032
Los Angeles, CA 90014
213-236-1336
fax: 213-236-1346

MGM HOME ENTERTAINMENT (MGM)
2500 Broadway
Santa Monica, CA 90404-6061
310-449-3000
fax: 310-449-3100

MIKE LEBELL'S VIDEO (MLB)
75 Freemont Pl.
Los Angeles, CA 90005
213-938-3333
fax: 213-938-3334
email: mlvideo@aol.com

MILESTONE FILM & VIDEO (MIL)
275 W. 96th St., Ste 28C
New York, NY 10025
212-865-7449
fax: 212-222-8952
email: milesfilm@aol.com

REX MILLER (RXM)
Rte. 1, Box 457-D
East Prairie, MO 63845
314-649-5048

MIRAMAX PICTURES HOME VIDEO (MAX)
500 S. Buena Vista St.
Burbank, CA 91521

MODERN CURRICULUM PRESS - MCP (LCA)
PO Box 70935
108 Wilmot Rd.
Chicago, IL 60673-0933
800-777-8100

MONARCH HOME VIDEO (MNC)
2 Ingram Blvd.
La Vergne, TN 37086-7006
615-287-4632
fax: 615-287-4992

MONTEREY HOME VIDEO (MON)
28038 Dorothy Dr., Ste. 1
Agoura Hills, CA 91301
818-597-0047
800-424-2593
fax: 818-597-0105

MOORE VIDEO (MRV)
PO Box 5703
Richmond, VA 23220-0703
804-745-9785
fax: 804-745-9785

MOVIES UNLIMITED (MOV)
3015 Darnell Rd.
Philadelphia, PA 19154
215-637-4444
800-466-8437
fax: 215-637-2350
email:
movies@moviesunlimited.com

MPI HOME VIDEO (MPI)
16101 S. 108th Ave.
Orland Park, IL 60462
708-460-0555
fax: 708-873-3177

MTI HOME VIDEO (MTH)
14216 SW 136th St.
Miami, FL 33186
305-255-8684
800-821-7461
fax: 305-233-6943
email: mti@mtivideo.com

MUSIC VIDEO DISTRIBUTORS (MVD)
O'Neill Industrial Center
1210 Standbridge St.
Norristown, PA 19401
610-272-7771
800-888-0486
fax: 610-272-6074

MYSTIC FIRE VIDEO (MFV)
524 Broadway, Ste. 604
New York, NY 10012
212-941-0999
800-292-9001
fax: 212-941-1443

NATIONAL CENTER FOR JEWISH FILM (NCJ)
Brandeis University
Lown Bldg. 102
Waltham, MA 02254-9110
617-899-7044
fax: 617-736-2070
email: ncjf@logos.cc.branders.eu

NATIONAL FILM BOARD OF CANADA (NFB)
1251 Avenue of the Americas,
16th Fl.

New York, NY 10020-1173
212-596-1770
800-542-2164
fax: 212-596-1779

NEW HORIZONS HOME VIDEO (NHO)
2951 Flowers Rd., S., Ste. 237
Atlanta, GA 30341
404-458-3488
800-854-3323
fax: 404-458-2679

NEW LINE HOME VIDEO (NLC)
116 N. Robertson Blvd.
Los Angeles, CA 90048
310-967-6670
fax: 310-854-0602

NEW WORLD ENTERTAINMENT (NWV)
1440 S. Sepulveda Blvd.
Los Angeles, CA 90025
310-444-8100
fax: 310-444-8101

NEW YORKER VIDEO (NYF)
16 W. 61st St., 11th Fl.
New York, NY 10023
212-247-6110
800-447-0196
fax: 212-307-7855

NOSTALGIA FAMILY VIDEO (NOS)
PO Box 606
Baker City, OR 97814
503-523-9034
800-784-8362
fax: 503-523-7115

ORION HOME VIDEO (ORI)
1888 Century Park E.
Los Angeles, CA 90067
310-282-0550
fax: 310-282-9902

PARAMOUNT HOME VIDEO (PAR)
Bluhdorn Bldg.
5555 Melrose Ave.
Los Angeles, CA 90038
213-956-3952

PBS HOME VIDEO (PBS)
Catalog Fulfillment Center
PO Box 4030
Santa Monica, CA 90411
800-531-4727
800-645-4PBS

PLANET PICTURES, INC. (PPI)
PO Box 1151, Old Chelsea Sta.
New York, NY 10011
212-779-0660
fax: 212-779-9129

POLYGRAM VIDEO (PV) (PGV)
825 8th Ave.
New York, NY 10019

212-333-8000
800-825-7781
fax: 212-603-7960

PRINCETON BOOK CO. PUBLISHERS (PBC)
PO Box 57
Pennington, NJ 08534
609-737-8177
800-220-7149
fax: 609-737-1869

PRISM ENTERTAINMENT (PSM)
1888 Century Park, E., Ste. 350
Los Angeles, CA 90067
310-277-3270
fax: 310-203-8036

PROFESSIONAL MEDIA SERVICE CORP. (PMS)
19122 S. Vermont Ave.
Gardena, CA 90248
310-532-9024
800-223-7672
fax: 800-253-8853
email: promedia@class.org

PUBLIC MEDIA VIDEO (PME)
5547 N. Ravenswood Ave.
Chicago, IL 60640-1199
312-878-2600
800-826-3456
fax: 312-878-8406

PYRAMID FILM & VIDEO (PYR)
PO Box 1048
Santa Monica, CA 90406-1048
310-828-7577
800-421-2304
fax: 310-453-9083
email: info@pyramedia.com

QUESTAR VIDEO, INC. (QHV)
PO Box 11345
Chicago, IL 60611
312-266-9400
800-544-8422
fax: 312-266-9523

READER'S DIGEST HOME VIDEO (RDG)
Reader's Digest Rd.
Pleasantville, NY 10570

REPUBLIC PICTURES HOME VIDEO (REP)
5700 Wilshire Blvd., Ste. 525
North
Los Angeles, CA 90036-3659
213-965-6900
fax: 213-965-6963

SIGNALS (SIG)
7000 Westgate Dr.
St. Paul, MN 55114
612-659-3700
800-669-5225
fax: 612-659-0083
email: kyle@rivertrade.com

**SINISTER CINEMA
(SNC)**
PO Box 4369
Medford, OR 97501-0168
503-773-6860
fax: 503-779-8650

**SOMETHING WEIRD
VIDEO (SMW)**
c/o Mike Vraney
PO Box 33664
Seattle, WA 98133
206-361-3759
fax: 206-364-7526

STAGESTEP (STS)
2000 Hamilton St., Ste. C200
Philadelphia, PA 19130
215-636-9000
800-877-3342
fax: 215-829-0508
email: stagestep@juno.com

**STRAND HOME VIDEO
(SHV)**
225 Santa Monica Blvd., Ste. 810
Santa Monica, CA 90401
310-395-5002

**STREAMLINE PICTURES
(STP)**
2908 Nebraska Ave.
Santa Monica, CA 90404-4109
310-998-0070
800-846-1453
fax: 310-998-1145

**TAI SENG VIDEO
MARKETING (TAI)**
170 S. Spruce Ave., Ste. 200
San Francisco, CA 94080
415-871-8118
800-888-3836
fax: 415-871-2392
email: webstaff@taiseng.com

**TAPEWORM VIDEO
DISTRIBUTORS
(TPV)**
27833 Hopkins Ave., Unit 6
Valencia, CA 91355
805-257-4904
fax: 805-257-4820

**TELEVISION
INTERNATIONAL
(CDV)**
c/o Jason Films
2825 Wilcrest, Ste. 407
Houston, TX 77042
713-266-3097
fax: 713-266-3148

**TIME-LIFE VIDEO AND
TELEVISION (TLF)**
1450 E. Parham Rd.
Richmond, VA 23280
804-266-6330
800-621-7026

**TIMELESS VIDEO INC.
(TIM)**
9943 Canoga Ave., Ste. B2
Chatsworth, CA 91311
818-773-0284
800-478-6734
fax: 818-773-0176

**TRIBORO
ENTERTAINMENT
GROUP (TRI)**
12 W. 27th St., 15th Fl.
New York, NY 10001
212-686-6116
fax: 212-686-6178

**TRIMARK HOME VIDEO
(THV)**
2644 30th St.
Santa Monica, CA 90405-3009
310-314-2000
fax: 310-392-0252

**TROMA TEAM VIDEO
(TTV)**
1501 Broadway, Ste. 2605
New York, NY 10036
212-997-0595
fax: 212-997-0968

**TURNER HOME
ENTERTAINMENT
CO. (TTC)**
Box 105366
Atlanta, GA 35366
404-827-3066
800-523-0823
fax: 404-827-3266

**20TH CENTURY FOX
FILM CORP. (TCF)**
PO Box 900
Beverly Hills, CA 90213
310-369-1000
fax: 310-369-3318

**UNIVERSAL STUDIOS
HOME VIDEO (USH)**
100 Universal City Plz.
Universal City, CA 91608-9955
818-777-1000
fax: 818-866-1483

**VALENCIA
ENTERTAINMENT
CORP. (VEC)**
45030 Trevor Ave.
Lancaster, CA 93534-2648
805-940-1040
800-323-2061
fax: 805-940-8511

VCI HOME VIDEO (VCI)
11333 E. 60th Pl.
Tulsa, OK 74146
918-254-6337
800-331-4077
fax: 918-254-6117
email:
    vcihomevideo@mail.webter.com

**VCII HOME
ENTERTAINMENT,
INC. (VHE)**
13418 Wyandotte St.
North Hollywood, CA 91605
818-764-1777
800-350-1931
fax: 818-764-0231

VESTRON VIDEO (VES)
c/o Live Home Video
15400 Sherman Way
PO Box 10124
Van Nuys, CA 91410-0124

818-988-0303
800-367-7765
fax: 818-778-3194
email: cust_serv@live-
    entertainment.com

**THE VIDEO CATALOG
(TVC)**
7000 Westgate Dr.
Saint Paul, MN 55114
612-659-3700
800-733-6656
fax: 612-659-0083
email: kyle@rivertrade.com

**VIDEO CONNECTION
(VCN)**
3123 W. Sylvania Ave.
Toledo, OH 43613
419-472-7727
800-365-0449
fax: 419-472-2655

**VIDEO DIMENSIONS
(VDM)**
322 8th Ave., 1701
New York, NY 10001
212-929-6135
fax: 212-929-6135
email: video@cultvideo.com

VIDEO GEMS (GEM)
12228 Venice Blvd., No. 504
Los Angeles, CA 90066

**VIDEO YESTERYEAR
(VYY)**
Box C
Sandy Hook, CT 06482
800-243-0987
fax: 203-797-0819
email: video@yesteryear.com

**WALT DISNEY HOME
VIDEO (DIS)**
500 S. Buena Vista St.
Burbank, CA 91521
818-562-3560

**WARNER/ELEKTRA/AT
LANTIC (WEA)
CORP. (WEA)**
9451 LBJ Fwy., Ste. 107
Dallas, TX 75243
214-234-6200
fax: 214-699-9343

**WARNER HOME VIDEO,
INC. (WAR)**
4000 Warner Blvd.
Burbank, CA 91522
818-954-6000

**WARREN MILLER
ENTERTAINMENT
(WME)**
2540 Frontier Ave., Ste. 104
Boulder, CO 80301
303-442-3430
800-523-7117
fax: 303-442-3402
email: robd@wmfilms.com

**WATER BEARER FILMS
(WBF)**
48 W. 21st St., No. 301
New York, NY 10010

Distri-
butor
Guide

**INDEPENDENT
FILM GUIDE**

212-242-8686
800-551-8304
fax: 212-242-4560

WESTERN MEDIA SYSTEMS *(WFV)*

30941 W. Agoura Rd., Ste. 302
Westlake Village, CA 91361
818-889-7350
fax: 818-889-7350

WISHING WELL DISTRIBUTING *(WSH)*

PO Box 1008
Silver Lake, WI 53170
414-889-8501
800-888-9355
fax: 414-889-8591

WORLD ARTISTS HOME VIDEO *(WAC)*

5150 Wilshire Blvd., Ste. 506
Los Angeles, CA 90036
213-933-7057
800-821-1205
fax: 213-933-2356
email: world@worldarfists.com

XENON *(XVC)*

211 Arizona Ave.
Santa Monica, CA 90401

ZEITGEIST FILMS LTD. *(ZGI)*

247 Centre St., 2nd Fl.
New York, NY 10013
212-274-1989
fax: 212-274-1644
email: mail@zeitgeistfilm.com